ROGET'S
THESAURUS

OF
SYNONYMS
AND
ANTONYMS

1980 Edition

BY

PETER MARK ROGET, M.D., F.R.S.

ENLARGED BY

JOHN LEWIS ROGET, M.A.

NEW EDITION REVISED AND ENLARGED BY

SAMUEL ROMILLY ROGET, M.A.

MODERN PROMOTIONS
A Division of Unisystems Inc., New York, New York 10022

PLAN OF CLASSIFICATION

TABULAR SYNOPSIS OF CATEGORIES

Class I. ABSTRACT RELATIONS

I. EXISTENCE

1°. ABSTRACT...........	1. Existence.	2. Inexistence.
2°. CONCRETE.........	3. Substantiality.	4. Unsubstantiality.
3°. FORMAL...........	*Internal.*	*External.*
	5. Intrinsicality.	6. Extrinsicality.
4°. MODAL...........	*Absolute.*	*Relative.*
	7. State.	8. Circumstance.

II. RELATION

	9. Relation.	10. Irrelation.
	11. Consanguinity.	
1°. ABSOLUTE.........	12. Correlation.	
	13. Identity.	14. Contrariety.
	15. Difference.	
2°. CONTINUOUS........	16. Uniformity.	16a. Non-uniformity.
	17. Similarity.	18. Dissimilarity.
3°. PARTIAL...........	19. Imitation.	20. Non-imitation.
	20a. Variation.	
	21. Copy.	22. Prototype.
4°. GENERAL..........	23. Agreement.	24. Disagreement.

III. QUANTITY

	Absolute.	*Relative.*
1°. SIMPLE.............	25. Quantity.	26. Degree.
	27. Equality.	28. Inequality.
	29. Mean.	
	30. Compensation.	
	By Comparison with a Standard.	
2°. COMPARATIVE.......	31. Greatness.	32. Smallness.
	By Comparison with a similar Object.	
	33. Superiority.	34. Inferiority.
	Changes in Quantity.	
	35. Increase.	36. Decrease.
	37. Addition.	38. {Non-addition. / Subduction.
	39. Adjunct.	40. Remainder.
		40a. Decrement.
3°. CONJUNCTIVE.......	41. Mixture.	42. Simpleness.
	43. Junction.	44. Disjunction.
	45. Vinculum.	
	46. Coherence.	47. Incoherence.
	48. Combination.	49. Decomposition.

SYNOPSIS OF CATEGORIES

VII. CHANGE

1°. SIMPLE

140. Change.	141. Permanence.
142. Cessation.	143. Continuance.
144. Conversion.	
	145. Reversion.
146. Revolution.	
147. Substitution.	148. Interchange.

2°. COMPLEX

149. Changeableness.	150. Stability.
Present.	*Future.*
151. Eventuality.	152. Destiny.

VIII. CAUSATION

1°. CONSTANCY OF SEQUENCE

153.	{ *Constant Antecedent.* Cause.	154.	{ *Constant Sequent.* Effect.
155.	{ *Assignment of Cause.* Attribution.	156.	{ *Absence of Assignment.* Chance.

2°. CONNECTION BETWEEN CAUSE AND EFFECT

157. Power.	158. Impotence.

Degrees of Power.

159. Strength.	160. Weakness.

3°. POWER IN OPERATION

161. Production.	162. Destruction.
163. Reproduction.	
164. Producer.	165. Destroyer.
166. Paternity.	167. Posterity.
168. Productiveness.	169. Unproductiveness.
170. Agency.	
171. Energy.	172. Inertness.
173. Violence.	174. Moderation.

4°. INDIRECT POWER

175. Influence.	175a. Absence of Influence.
176. Tendency.	
177. Liability.	

5°. COMBINATIONS OF CAUSES

178. Concurrence.	179. Counteraction.

CLASS II. SPACE

I. SPACE IN GENERAL

1°. ABSTRACT SPACE

180.	{ *Indefinite.* Space.	180a.	Inextension.
		181.	{ *Definite.* Region.
		182.	{ *Limited.* Place.

2°. RELATIVE SPACE

183. Situation.	
184. Location.	185. Displacement.

3°. EXISTENCE IN SPACE

186. Presence.	187. Absence.
188. Inhabitant.	189. Abode.
190. Contents.	191. Receptacle.

II. DIMENSIONS

1°. GENERAL

192. Size.	193. Littleness.
194. Expansion.	195. Contraction.
196. Distance.	197. Nearness.
198. Interval.	199. Contiguity.

2°. LINEAR

200. Length.	201. Shortness.
202. { Breadth. Thickness.	203. { Narrowness. Thinness.
204. Layer.	205. Filament.
206. Height.	207. Lowness.
208. Depth.	209. Shallowness.

4°. WITH REFERENCE TO DIRECTION—*cont...*	305. Ascent.	306. Descent.
	307. Elevation.	308. Depression.
	309. Leap.	310. Plunge.
	311. Circuition.	
	312. Rotation.	313. Evolution.
	314. Oscillation.	
	315. Agitation.	

CLASS III. MATTER

I. MATTER IN GENERAL

	316. Materiality.	317. Immateriality.
	318. World.	
	319. Gravity.	320. Levity.

II. INORGANIC MATTER

1°. SOLIDS	321. Density.	322. Rarity.
	323. Hardness.	324. Softness.
	325. Elasticity.	326. Inelasticity.
	327. Tenacity.	328. Brittleness.
	329. Texture.	
	330. Pulverulence.	
	331. Friction.	332. Lubrication.

2°. FLUIDS	1. *In General*	333. Fluidity.	334. Gaseity.
		335. Liquefaction.	336. Vaporization.
		337. Water.	338. Air.
		339. Moisture.	340. Dryness.
	2. *Specific*	341. Ocean.	342. Land.
		343. { Gulf. Lake. }	
			344. Plain.
		345. Marsh.	346. Island.
		347. Stream.	
	3. *In motion*	348. River.	349. Wind.
		350. Conduit.	351. Air-pipe.

3°. IMPERFECT FLUIDS	352. Semiliquidity.	353. Bubble.
	354. Pulpiness.	355. Unctuousness.
		356. Oil.
		356a. Resin.

III. ORGANIC MATTER

1°. VITALITY	1. *In General*	357. Organization.	358. Inorganization.
		359. Life.	360. Death.
			361. Killing.
			362. Corpse.
			363. Interment.
	2. *Special*	364. Animality.	365. Vegetability.
		366. Animal.	367. Vegetable.
		368. Zoology.	369. Botany.
		370. Cicuration.	371. Agriculture.
		372. Mankind.	
		373. Man.	374. Woman.

SYNOPSIS OF CATEGORIES

Class IV. INTELLECT

Division (I.). Formation of Ideas

I. Operations of Intellect in General.....

450. Intellect.	450a. Absence of Intellect.
451. Thought.	452. Incogitancy.
453. Idea.	454. Topic.
455. Curiosity.	456. Incuriosity.
457. Attention.	458. Inattention.
459. Care.	460. Neglect.

II. Precursory Conditions and Operations......

461. Inquiry.	462. Answer.
463. Experiment.	
464. Comparison.	
465. Discrimination.	465a. Indiscrimination.
466. Measurement.	
467. Evidence.	468. Counter-evidence.

469. Qualification.

III. Materials for Reasoning..........

Degrees of Evidence.

470. Possibility.	471. Impossibility.
472. Probability.	473. Improbability.
474. Certainty.	475. Uncertainty.

IV. Reasoning Processes.

476. Reasoning.	477. { Intuition. Sophistry.
478. Demonstration.	479. Confutation.
480. Judgement.	481. Misjudgement.
480a. Discovery.	
482. Over-estimation.	483. Under-estimation.

V. Results of Reasoning.

484. Belief.	485. { Unbelief. Doubt.
486. Credulity.	487. Incredulity.
488. Assent.	489. Dissent.
490. Knowledge.	491. Ignorance.
492. Scholar.	493. Ignoramus.
494. Truth.	495. Error.
496. Maxim.	497. Absurdity.

Faculties.

498. { Intelligence. Wisdom.	499. { Imbecility. Folly.
500. Sage.	501. Fool.
502. Sanity.	503. Insanity.
	504. Madman.

VI. Extension of Thought

1°. *To the Past...*

505. Memory.	506. Oblivion.
507. Expectation.	508. Inexpectation.
	509. Disappointment.

2°. *To the Future.*

510. Foresight.
511. Prediction.
512. Omen.
513. Oracle.

VII. Creative Thought...

514. Supposition.
515. Imagination.

Class V. VOLITION

Division (I.). Individual Volition

I. Volition in General

1°. Acts....

600. Will.	601. Necessity.
602. Willingness.	603. Unwillingness.
604. Resolution.	605. Irresolution.
604a. Perseverance.	607. Tergiversation.
606. Obstinacy.	
	608. Caprice.
609. Choice.	609a. Absence of Choice.
	610. Rejection.

2°. Causes..

611. Predetermination.	612. Impulse.
613. Habit.	614. Desuetude.
615. Motive.	615a. Absence of Motive.
	616. Dissuasion.
617. Plea.	

3°. Objects..

618. Good.	619. Evil.
620. Intention.	621. Chance.
622. Pursuit.	623. Avoidance.
	624. Relinquishment.

II. Prospective Volition.......

1°. Conceptional..

625. Business.
626. Plan.
627. Method.
628. Mid-Course. 629. Circuit.
630. Requirement.

2°. Subservience to Ends...

1. *Actual Subservience.*

631. Instrumentality.
632. Means.
633. Instrument.
634. Substitute.
635. Materials.
636. Store.
637. Provision. 638. Waste.
639. Sufficiency.
641. Redundance. 640. Insufficiency.

2. *Degree of Subservience.*

642. Importance.	643. Unimportance.
644. Utility.	645. Inutility.
646. Expedience.	647. Inexpedience.
648. Goodness.	649. Badness.
650. Perfection.	651. Imperfection.
652. Cleanness.	653. Uncleanness.
654. Health.	655. Disease.
656. Salubrity.	657. Insalubrity.
658. Improvement.	659. Deterioration.
660. Restoration.	661. Relapse.
662. Remedy.	663. Bane.

3. *Contingent Subservience.*

664. Safety.	665. Danger.
666. Refuge.	667. Pitfall.
668. Warning.	
669. Alarm.	
670. Preservation.	
671. Escape.	
672. Deliverance.	

SYNOPSIS OF CATEGORIES

2°. Diffusive	906. Benevolence.	907. Malevolence.
		908. Malediction.
		909. Threat.
	910. Philanthropy.	911. Misanthropy.
	912. Benefactor.	913. Evil doer.
3°. Special	914. Pity.	914a. Pitilessness.
	915. Condolence.	
	916. Gratitude.	917. Ingratitude.
4°. Retrospective	918. Forgiveness.	919. Revenge.
		920. Jealousy.
		921. Envy.

IV. MORAL

1°. Obligations	922. Right.	923. Wrong.
	924. Dueness.	925. Undueness.
	926. Duty.	927. Dereliction.
		927a. Exemption.
	928. Respect.	929. Disrespect.
		930. Contempt.
2°. Sentiments	931. Approbation.	932. Disapprobation.
	933. Flattery.	934. Detraction.
	935. Flatterer.	936. Detractor.
	937. Vindication.	938. Accusation.
	939. Probity.	940. Improbity.
		941. Knave.
3°. Conditions	942. Disinterestedness.	943. Selfishness.
	944. Virtue.	945. Vice.
	946. Innocence.	947. Guilt.
	948. Good Man.	949. Bad Man.
	950. Penitence.	951. Impenitence.
	952. Atonement.	
4°. Practice	953. Temperance.	954. Intemperance.
		954a. Sensualist.
	955. Asceticism.	
	956. Fasting.	957. Gluttony.
	958. Sobriety.	959. Drunkenness.
	960. Purity.	961. Impurity.
		962. Libertine.
5°. Institutions	963. Legality.	964. Illegality.
	965. Jurisprudence.	
	966. Tribunal.	
	967. Judge.	
	968. Lawyer.	
	969. Lawsuit.	
	970. Acquittal.	971. Condemnation.
	973. Reward.	972. Punishment.
		974. Penalty.
		975. Scourge.

V. RELIGIOUS

1°. Superhuman Beings and Regions	976. Deity.	
	977. Angel.	978. Satan.
	979. Jupiter.	980. Demon.
	981. Heaven.	982. Hell.
2°. Doctrines	983. Theology.	
	983a. Orthodoxy.	984. Heterodoxy.
	985. Revelation.	986. Pseudo-revelation.
3°. Sentiments	987. Piety.	988. Impiety.
		989. Irreligion.

ABBREVIATIONS, &c.

Adj.	*adj.*	Adjectives, Participles, and Words having the power of Adjectives.
Adv.	*adv.*	Adverbs and Adverbial Expressions.
Int.	*int.*	Interjections.
Phr.	*phr.*	Phrases.
V.	*v.*	Verbs.

The numbers are those of the headings, or Categories.

Words in italics within parentheses are not intended to explain the meanings of the words which precede them, but to indicate the nature of allied group of words under the numbers which follow them.

THESAURUS

OF

ENGLISH WORDS AND PHRASES

1. Existence.—N. existence, being, entity, *ens, esse,* subsistence, quiddity.

reality, realness, actuality; positiveness etc. *adj.*; fact, matter of fact, sober reality; truth etc. 494; actual existence.

presence etc. (*existence in space*) 186; coexistence etc. 120.

stubborn fact; not a -dream etc. 515; no joke.

substance, essence, prime constituent, hypostatis. [Science of existence], ontology.

V. exist, be; have -being etc. *n.*; subsist, live, breathe, stand, obtain, be the case; occur etc. (*event*) 151; have place, rank, prevail; find oneself, pass the time, vegetate.

consist in, lie in, reside in, inhere in.

come into -existence etc. *n.*; arise etc. (*begin*) 66; come forth etc. (*appear*) 446.

become etc. (*be converted*) 144; bring into existence etc. 161; coexist, preexist, endure etc. 141.

Adj. existing etc. *v.*; existent, subsistent, under the sun; in -existence etc, *n.*; extant; afloat, on foot, current, prevalent, rife, in force, -vogue; undestroyed.

real, actual, positive, absolute; true etc. 494; substan-tial, -tive; self-existing, -ent.

well-founded, -grounded; un-ideal, -imagined; not -potential etc. 2.

Adv. actually etc. *adj.*; in -fact, – point of fact, – reality; indeed; *de* –, *ipso-facto.*

2. Nonexistence.—N. nonexistence; inexistence, -subsistence; nonentity, *nil*; negativeness etc. *adj.*; nullity; nihil-ity, -ism; *tabula rasa,* blank; abeyance; absence etc. 187; no such thing etc. 4; nothingness, oblivion, *non esse.*

annihilation; extinction etc. (*destruction*) 162.

V. not -exist etc. 1; have no -existence etc. 1; be null and void; cease to -exist etc. 1; pass away, perish; be –, become-extinct etc. *adj.*; die out; disappear etc. 449; melt away, dissolve, leave not a rack behind, leave no trace; go, be no more; die etc. 360.

annihilate, render null, nullify; abrogate etc. 756; destroy etc. 162; take away; remove etc. (*displace*) 185.

Adj. inexistent, non-existent etc. 1; negative, blank, null and void; missing, omitted; absent etc. 187; visionary etc. 515.

unreal, potential, virtual; baseless, *in nubibus*; unsubstantial etc. 4; vain.

un-born, -created, -begotten, -conceived, produced, -made.

perished, annihilated etc. *v.*; extinct, exhausted, gone, lost, departed; defunct etc. (*dead*) 360;

fabulous, ideal etc. (*imaginary*) 515; suppositititous etc. 514.

Adv. negatively, virtually, etc. *adj.*

3. Substantiality.—N. substantiality, *hypostasis*; person, thing, object, article; something, a being, an existence; creature, body, substance, flesh and blood, stuff, *substratum*; matter etc. 316; physical nature.

[Totality of existences], world etc. 318; *plenum.*

Adj. substan-tive, -tial, concrete; hypostatic; personal, bodily; tangible etc. (*material*) 316; real, corporeal, evident.

Adv. substantially etc. *adj.*; bodily, essentially.

4. Unsubstantiality.—N. un-, in-substantiality; nothingness, nihility.

nothing, naught, *nil*, nullity, zero, cipher, no one, nobody; never – , ne'er -a one; no such thing, none in the world; nothing -whatever, – at all, – on earth; not a -particle etc. (*smallness*) 32; all - talk, – moonshine, – stuff and nonsense, matter of no import.

thing of naught, man of straw, John Doe and Richard Roe; *nominis umbra*, nonentity, figurehead, lay figure; flash in the pan, *vox et praeterea nihil.*

shadow; phantasm, phantom etc. (*fallacy of vision*) 443; dream etc. (*imagination*) 515; *ignis fatuus* etc. (*luminary*) 423; 'such stuff as dreams are made of;' air, thin air; bubble etc. 353; 'baseless fabric of a vision;' mockery.

hollowness, blank; vacuity, void etc. (*absence*) 187.

inanity, fool's paradise, fatuity, stupidity, emptiness of mind.

V. vanish, evaporate, fade, sink, fly – , die –, melt- away, dissolve, disappear etc. 449; become extinct, become invisible.

Adj. unsubstantial; fleeting; base-, ground-less; ungrounded; without – , having no- foundation.

visionary etc. (*imaginary*) 515; immaterial etc. 317; spectral etc. 980; dreamy; shadowy; ethereal, airy, imponderable, tenuous, vague.

vacant, vacuous; empty etc. 187; eviscerated; blank, hollow; nominal; null; inane.

Phr. there's nothing in it.

1

5. Intrinsicality.—N. intrinsicality, inbeing, inherence, inhesion, immanence; subjectiveness; *ego*; essence; essentialness etc. *adj.*; essential part, essential stuff, substance, quintessence, incarnation, quiddity, gist, pith, core, kernel, marrow, sap, life-blood, backbone, heart, soul, life, flower; important part etc. (*importance*) 642.

principle, nature, constitution, character, ethos, type, quality, crasis, *diathesis*.

habit; temper, -ament; spirit, humor, grain, disposition, streak, tendency etc. 176.

endowment, capacity; capability etc. (*power*) 157; moods, declensions, features, aspects; peculiarities etc. (*specialty*) 79; idiosyncrasy; idiocrasy; diagnostics.

V. be −, run- in the blood; be born so; be -intrinsic etc. *adj.*

Adj. derived from within, subjective; idiocratic, idiosyncratic, intrin-sic, -sical; fundamental, cardinal, normal, inherent, essential, natural; in-nate, -born, -bred, -dwelling, -grained; -wrought; radical, incarnate, thoroughbred, hereditary, inherited, im-manent; congen-ital, -ite; connate, running in the blood; coeval with birth, genetic, ingenerate, -genite; indigenous; in the -grain etc. *n.*; bred in the bone, instinctive; inward, internal etc. 221; to the manner born; virtual.

characteristic etc. (*special*) 79, (*indicative*) 550; invariable, incurable, ineradicable, fixed, settled, constant, unchanging.

Adv. intrinsically etc. *adj.*; at bottom, in the main, in effect, essentially, practically, virtually, substantially, *au fond;* fairly.

6. Extrinsicality.—N. extrinsicality, objectiveness, *non ego;* extraneousness etc. 57; accident; letter of the law.

Adj. derived from without; objective; extrinsic, -sical; extraneous etc. (*foreign*) 57; modal, adventitious, additional, supervenient, fortuitous; a-, ad-scititious; incidental, casual, accidental, unessential, non-essential, accessory.

implanted, ingrafted; instilled, inculcated.

outward etc. (*external*) 220.

Adv. extrinsically etc. *adj.*

7. State.—N. state, condition, category, estate, lot, case, trim, mood, pickle, plight etc. 704; temper; aspect etc. (*appearance*) 448.

constitution, habitude, *diathesis;* frame, fabric etc. 329; stamp, set, fit, mold.

mode, modality, schesis; fettle; form etc. (*shape*) 240.

tone, tenor, turn; trim, guise, fashion, light, complexion, style, character.

V. be in −, possess −, enjoy −, labor under- a -state etc. *n.;* be on a footing, do, fare; come to pass.

Adj. conditional, modal, formal; structural, organic.

Adv. conditionally etc. *adj.;* as -the matter stands, − things are; such being the case etc. 8.

8. Circumstance.—N. circumstance, situation, phase, position, posture, attitude, place, point; terms; *régime;* footing, standing, status.

occasion, juncture, conjuncture; contingency etc. (*event*) 151.

predicament; emergen-ce, -cy; exigency, crisis, pinch, pass, push; turning point; crossroads.

bearings, how the land lies.

Adj. circumstantial; given, conditional, provisional; critical; modal; contingent, incidental; adventitious etc. (*extrinsic*) 6.

Adv. in the circumstances etc. *n.,* under the conditions etc. 7; thus, in such wise.

accordingly; that −, such- being the case; that being so, since, seeing that.

as matters stand; as -things, − times- go.

conditionally, provided, if, in case; if -so, − so be, − it be so; if it so -happen, − turn out; in the event of; in such a -contingency, − case, − event; provisionally, unless, without.

according to -circumstances, − the occasion; as it may -happen, − turn out, − be; as the -case may be, − wind blows; *pro re natâ.*

9. Relation.—N. relation, bearing, reference, connection, apposition, interconnection, concern, cognation; applicability, appositeness; correlation etc. 12; analogy; similarity etc. 17; affinity, intimacy, friendship; homology, alliance, homogeneity, association, rapport; approximation etc. (*nearness*) 197; filiation etc. (*consanguinity*) 11; interest; relevancy etc. 23; relationship, relative position; relativity; interrelation etc. 12.

comparison etc. 464; ratio, proportion.

link, tie, bond, bond of union.

V. be-related etc. *adj.;* have a relation etc. *n.;* relate −, refer- to; bear upon, regard, concern, touch, affect, have to do with; pertain −, belong −, appertain- to; have respect to; answer to; interest.

bring -into relation with, − to bear upon; connect, associate, draw a parallel; link etc. 43.

Adj. relative; correlative etc. 12; cognate; relating to etc. *v.;* relative to, in relation with, referable *or* referrible to; belonging to etc. *v.;* appurtenant to, in common with.

related, connected; implicated, associated, affiliated, akin, allied to; collateral, cognate, congenial, kindred, affinitive, *en rapport,* in touch with.

approxima-tive, -ting; approaching; proportion-al, -ate, -able; allusive, comparable.

in the same -category etc. 75; like etc. 17; relevant etc. (*apt*) 23.

Adv. relatively etc. *adj.;* pertinently etc. 23.

thereof; as -to, − for, − respects, − re-gards; about; concerning etc. *v.;* anent; relating −, as relates- to; with -relation, − reference, − respect, − regard-to; in respect of; while speaking −, *à propos* -of; in connection with; by the -way, − by; whereas; for −, in -as much as; in point of, as far as; on the -part, − score- of; *quoad hoc; pro re natâ;* under the -head etc. (*class*) 75- of; in the matter of, *in re.*

Phr. 'thereby hangs a tale.'

10. Irrelation. [Want, or absence of relation.]—N. irrelation, dissociation; inapplicability; inconnection; multifariousness; disconnection etc. (*disjunction*) 44; inconsequence, independence; incommensurability; irreconcilableness etc. (*disagreement*) 24; heterogeneity;

unconformity etc. 83; irrelevancy, impertinence, *nihil ad rem;* intrusion etc. 24.

V. have no -relation etc. 9 to, − bearing upon, − concern etc. 9 with, − business with; not -concern etc. 9; have -nothing to do with, − no business there; intrude, etc. 24.

bring −, drag −, haul −, lug- in head and shoulders.

Adj. irrelative, irrespective, unrelated, irrelated; arbitrary; independent, unallied; un-, dis-connected; adrift, isolated, insular; extraneous, strange, alien, foreign, outlandish, exotic.

not comparable, incommensurable, heterogeneous; unconformable etc. 83.

irrelevant; rambling etc. 279; inapplicable; not -pertinent, − to the purpose; impertinent, inapposite, beside the mark, *à propos de bottes;* away from −, foreign to −, beside- the -purpose, − question, − transaction, − point; misplaced etc. (*intrusive*) 24.

remote, far fetched, out of the way, forced, neither here nor there, quite another thing; detached, segregated, segregate:

multifarious; discordant etc. 24.

incidental, parenthetical, *obiter dictum,* episodic.

Adv. parenthetically etc. *adj.;* by the -way, − by; *en passant,* incidentally; irrespecitively etc. *adj.;* without reference, − regard- to; in the abstract etc. 87; *a se.*

11. Consanguinity. [Relations of kindred.]—N. consanguinity, relationship, kindred, blood; parentage etc. (*paternity*) 166; filiation, affiliation; lineage, agnation, connection, cognation, alliance; family -connection, − tie; ties of blood; blood relationship; nepotism.

kins-man, -folk; people; kith and kin; relation, -tive; connection; sib; next of kin; uncle, aunt, nephew, niece; cousin, -german; first −, second- cousin; cousin -once, − twice etc.- removed; near −, distant-relation; brother, sister, one's own flesh and blood.

family, patriarch, matriarch; fraternity; brother-, sister-, cousin-hood.

race, stock, generation; sept etc. 166 ; stirps, side; strain; breed, clan, tribe.

V. be -related etc. *adj.* − to; claim -relationship etc. *n.*- with.

Adj. related, akin, consanguineous, matrilinear, patrilineal, of the blood, family, allied, collateral; cog-, ag-, con-nate; kindred; affiliated, affine; fraternal, avuncular.

intimately −, nearly −, closely −, remotely −, distantly- related, − allied; german.

12. Correlation. [Double or reciprocal relation.]—N. reciprocalness etc. *adj.;* recipro-city, -cality, -cation; mutuality, correlation, correspondence, interdependence; interchange etc. 148; exchange, barter; interrelation, interconnection; alternation, see-saw.

V. reciprocate, alternate; interchange etc. 148; exchange; counterchange; interact, correspond, mutualize, give and take.

Adj. reciprocal, mutual, commutual, correlative; alternate; interchangeable; international; correspondent, complementary, analogous.

Adv. *mutatis mutandis; vice versâ;* each other; by turns etc. 148; reciprocally etc. *adj.;* to and fro etc. 314.

13. Identity.—N. identity, sameness, oneness, ditto, homogeneity; unity, coincidence, coalescence; convertibility; equality etc. 27; selfness, self, oneself; identification.

monotony, tautology etc. (*repetition*) 104.

synonym.

fac-simile etc. (*copy*) 21; *alter ego* etc. (*similar*) 17; *ipsissima verba* etc. (*exactness*) 494; same; self − , very −, one and the same; very −, actual-thing, no other.

V. be -identical etc. *adj.;* match, coincide, coalesce.

treat as −, render--the same , −identical; identify; recognize the identity of.

Adj. identical; self, ilk; the -same etc. *n.;* self same; synonymous; one and the same.

coincid-, coalesc-ent, -ing; indistinguishable; one; equivalent etc. (*equal*) 27; much -the same, − of a muchness; unaltered.

Adv. identically etc. *adj.;* on all fours; ibid-, -em.

14. Contrariety. [Non-coincidence.]—N. contrariety, contrast, foil, antithesis, oppositeness; counterpole; contradiction; antagonism etc. (*opposition*) 708; counteraction etc. 179.

inversion etc. 218; the -opposite, − reverse, − inverse, − converse, − antipodes, − other extreme etc. 237.

antonym.

V. be -contrary etc. *adj.;* contrast with, oppose; differ *toto coelo.*

invert, reverse, turn the tables etc. 218.

contra-dict, -vene; antagonize etc. 708.

Adj. contrar-y, -ious, -iant; opposite, counter, dead against; ad-, con-, reverse; opposed, antithetical, contrasted, antipodean, antagonistic, opposing; conflicting, inconsistent, contradictory, at cross purposes; negative; hostile etc. 708.

differing *toto coelo;* diametrically opposite; as opposite as -black and white, − light and darkness, − fire and water, − the poles, as different as chalk from cheese; 'Hyperion to a satyr;' quite the -contrary, − reverse; no such thing, just the other way, *tout au contraire.*

Adv. contrarily etc. *adj.; contra,* contrariwise; *per contra,* on the contrary, nay rather; topsyturvy; *vice versâ;* on the other hand etc. (*in compensation*) 30.

15. Difference.—N. difference, unlikeness; heterogeneity; vari-ance, -ation, -ety; diversity, dissimilarity etc. 18; disagreement etc. 24; disparity etc. (*inequality*) 28; distinction, contra-distinction; distinctness; discrepancy, divergence, contrast etc. 18; nonconformity, incompatibility, antithesis.

discord etc. 713.

modification, moods and tenses.

nice −, fine −, delicate −, subtle- distinction; shade of difference, nuance; discrimination etc. 465; *differentia.*

different thing, something else, variant, apple

off another tree, horse of another color, another pair of shoes; this that or the other.

V. be -different etc. adj.; differ, vary, ablude, mismatch, contrast; diverge −, depart −, deviate- -from; divaricate; differ -toto coelo, − longo intervallo.

disagree etc. 713.

vary, modify etc. (change) 140.

discriminate etc. 465.

Adj. differing etc. v.; different, diverse, divided, heterogeneous; distinguishable; varied, modified; divergent, incongruous, diversified, various; discrepant, dissentient, differential; divers, all manner of; variform etc. 81; discordant etc. 713.

other, another, not the same; unequal etc. 28; unmatched; widely apart.

distinctive, characteristic; discriminative; distinghishing.

Adv. differently etc. adj.

Phr. il y a fagots et fagots; tot nomines tot sententiae; one man's meat is another man's poison.

16. Uniformity.—N. uniformity; homogeneity, -ousness; continuity, stability, consistency; connatural-ity, -ness; homology; accordance; conformity etc. 82; agreement etc. 23.

regularity, constancy, even tenor, routine; monotony, evenness, sameness, dead level; steadiness, equability, unity.

V. be -uniform etc. adj.; accord with etc. 23; run through.

become -uniform etc. adj.; conform to etc. 82.

render uniform etc. adj.; assimilate, level, smooth, dress.

Adj. uniform; homo-geneous, -logous; of a piece, consistent, steady; connatural; monotonous, changeless, dreary, even, invariable, equable, level, regular, stereotyped, unchanged, unvarying; methodical etc. 60; habitual etc. 613.

Adv. uniformly etc. adj.; uniformly with etc. (conformably) 82; in harmony with etc. (agreeing) 23; in a -rut, − groove.

always, ever etc. 112; invariably; without exception, never otherwise; by clock-work; endlessly etc. 112.

Phr. ab uno disce omnes.

16a. Non-uniformity. [Absence or want of uniformity.]—N. diversity, irregularity, unevenness; multiformity etc. 81; unconformity etc. 83; roughness etc. 256; heterogeneity, heteromorphism.

Adj. diversified, varied, irregular, uneven, rough etc. 256; multifarious; multiform etc. 81; of various kinds; all -manner, − sorts, − kinds- of.

Adv. in all manner of ways, here there and everywhere.

17. Similarity.—N. similarity, resemblance, likeness, similitude, semblance; affinity, approximation, parallelism; parity; agreement etc. 23; ana-logy, -logicalness; correspondence, equality etc.

connatural-ness, -ity; brotherhood, family likeness.

alliteration, rhyme, pun.

repetition etc. 104; sameness etc. (identity) 13; uniformity etc. 16.

analogue; the like; match, pendant, fellow, companion, pair, mate, twin, double, counterpart, brother, sister; one's second self, alter ego, chip of the old block, par nobile fratrum, Arcades ambo, birds of a feather, et hoc genus omne.

parallel; simile; type etc. (metaphor) 521; image etc. (representation) 554; photograph; close −, striking −, speaking −, faithful etc adj. − likeness, − resemblance.

V. be -similar etc. adj.; look like, resemble, bear resemblance, favor; savor −, smack- of; approximate; parallel, match, rhyme with; take after; imitate etc. 19; run in pairs.

Adj. similar; resembling etc. v.; like, alike, twin.

analog-ous, -ical; parallel, of a piece; such as, so.

connatural, congeneric, allied to; corresponding, cognate; akin to etc. (consanguineous) 11.

approximate, much the same, near, close, something like, such like; a show of; mock, pseudo, simulating, representing.

exact etc. (true) 494; lifelike, faithful, realistic; true to -nature, − the life; the -very image − pic·ure- of; for all the world like, comme deux gouttes d'eau; as like as -two peas, − it can stare; instar omnium, case in the same mold, ridiculously like.

Adv. as if, so to speak; as −, as if- it were; quasi, just as, veluti in speculum.

18. Dissimilarity.—N. dissimil-arity, -itude; unlikeness, diversity, disparity, dissemblance; divergence, inequality, difference etc. 15; novelty; variation, variety, originality, disguise.

V. be -unlike etc. adj.; vary etc. (differ) 15; bear no resemblance to, differ toto coelo.

render -unlike etc. adj.; vary etc. (diversify) 140.

Adj. dissimilar, unlike, disparate; of a different kind etc. (class) 75; unmatched, unique; new, novel; unprecedented etc. 83; original.

nothing of the kind; no such −, quite another-thing; far from it, other than, cast in a different mold, tertium quid, as like a dock as a daisy, 'very like a whale;' as different as -chalk from cheese, − Macedon and Monmouth; lucus a non lucendo.

diversified etc. 16a.

Adv. otherwise, alias.

19. Imitation.—N. imitation; copying etc. v.; transcription; repetition, mimeograph, mimeotype, duplication, reduplication; quotation; reproduction.

mockery, mimicry, mime, simulation, personation; representation etc. 554; semblance, pretence; copy etc. 21; assimilation.

paraphrase, parody etc. 21.

plagiarism; forgery etc. (falsehood) 544.

imitator; echo, cuckoo, parrot, ape, monkey, mocking-bird, mimic, impersonator, copyist.

V. imitate, copy, mirror, reflect, reproduce, repeat, borrow; do like, echo, re-echo, catch; transcribe; match, parallel.

mock, take off, mimic, ape, simulate, personate, impersonate; forge; act etc. (*drama*) 599; represent etc. 554; counterfeit, duplicate; portray, parody, travesty, caricature, burlesque.

follow −, tread- in the- -steps, − footsteps, − wake- of; pattern after, take pattern by; follow - suit, − the example of; walk in the shoes of, take a leaf out of another's book, strike in with; take −, model -after; emulate.

Adj. imitated etc. *v.;* mock, mimic; counterfeit, false, pseudo; modelled after, molded on, paraphrastic; literal; imitative, apish; secondhand; imitable; sham etc. 545.

Adv. literally, to the letter, strictly, precisely, *verbatim, literatim, sic, totidem verbis,* word for word, *mot à mot.*

Phr. like master like man.

20. Non-Imitation.—N. no imitation, genuineness, originality; creativeness.

Adj. unimitated, uncopied; unmatched, unparalleled; inimitable etc. 33; *unique,* original, primordial, primary, pristine, underived, firsthand, archetypal, prototypal.

20a. Variation.—N. variation; alteration etc. (*change*) 140. modification, moods and tenses; modulation.

divergency etc. 291; deviation etc. 279; aberration; innovation.

V. vary etc. (*change*) 140; deviate etc. 279; diverge etc. 291.

Adj. varied etc. *v.;* modified; dissimilar etc. 18; diversified etc. 16*a.*

21. Copy. [Result of imitation.]—N. copy, facsimile, counterpart, *effigies,* effigy, symbol, image, form, likeness, similitude, semblance, resemblance, cast, electrotype, stereotype, tracing, ectype; imitation etc. 19; model, representation, adumbration, study; counterfeit presentment, portrait etc. (*representment*) 554.

duplicate; transcript, -ion; reflex, -ion; shadow, echo; chip of the old block; reprint, reproduction, casting, engraving, replica; transfer; second edition etc. (*repetition*) 104; *réchauffé* apograph, fair copy; revise.

parody, caricature, cartoon, burlesque, travesty, paraphrase.

servile -copy, − imitation; counterfeit etc. (*deception*) 545; *pasticcio.*

Adj. faithful; lifelike etc. (*similar*) 17.

22. Prototype. [Thing copied.]—N. prototype, original, model, pattern, founding, precedent, standard, scantling, type, arche-, anti-type: protoplast, copy-book, module, exemplar, example, ensample, specimen; paradigm; guide; templet; lay-figure.

text, copy, manuscript, MS., design; fugleman, keynote.

die, mold; matrix, engraving, last, plasm; pro-, proto-plasm; mint; seal, punch, *intaglio,* negative, stamp.

V. be −, set- an example; set a copy; standardize.

23. Agreement.—N. agreement; ac-cord, -cordance; unison, harmony, concord etc. 714; concordance, concert, understanding, convention, *entente -cordiale, consortium,* consensus of opinion, pact, mutual understanding, unanimity.

conformity etc. 82; conformance; uniformity etc. 16; consonance, consentaneousness, consistency; congruity, -ence; keeping; congeniality; correspondence, concinnity, parallelism, apposition, union.

fitness, aptness etc. *adj.;* relevancy; pertinence, -cy; sortance; case in point; aptitude, propriety, applicability, admissibility, commensurability, compatibility, suitability; cognation etc (*relation*) 9.

adaptation, adjustment, arrangement, graduation, accommodation; reconcil-iation - ement; assimilation; attunement.

consent etc. (*assent*) 448; concurrence etc. 178; co-operation etc. 709.

right man in the right place, very thing; quite −, just- the thing.

V. be -accordant etc. *adj.;* agree, accord, harmonize; correspond, tally, respond; meet, suit, fit, befit, do, adapt itself to; fall in −, chime in −, square −, quadrate −, consort −, comport- with; dovetail, assimilate; fit like a glove; fit to a -tittle, − T; match etc. 17; become one.

consent etc. (*assent*) 488.

render -accordant etc. *adj.;* fit, suit, adapt, accommodate; graduate; adjust etc. (*render equal*) 27; dress, regulate, readjust; accord, harmonize, reconcile; fadge, dovetail, square.

Adj. agreeing, suiting etc. *v.;* in accord, accordant, concordant, consonant, congruous, consentaneous, correspondent, corresponding, homologous, congenial; becoming; harmonious, reconcilable, conformable; in -accordance, − harminy, − keeping, − unison, etc. *n.;*-with; at one with, of one mind, of a piece; consistent, compatible, proportionate, answerable; commensurate; on all fours.

apt, apposite, pertinent, pat; to the -point, −- purpose; happy, felicitous, germane, *ad rem.* in point, bearing upon, applicable, relevant, admissible.

fit, adapted, *in loco, à propos,* appropriate, seasonable, sortable, suitable, idoneous, deft; meet etc. (*expedient*) 646.

at home, in one's proper element.

Adv. *à propos of;* pertinently etc. *adj.; pro rata.*

Phr. *rem acu tetigisti,* the cap fits.

24. Disagreement.—N. disagreement, discord, -cordance; disunion, dissonance, dissidence, discrepancy; unconformity - etc. 83; incongru-ity, -ence; discongruity, *mésalliance, oxymoron;* jarring etc. *v.;* clash, collision, dissension etc. 713; conflict etc. (*opposition*) 708; controversy etc. 720; falling out, wrangle, argument.

disparity, mismatch, misfit, disproportion; disproportionateness etc. *adj.;* variance, divergence, repugnance.

unfitness etc. *adj.;* inaptitude, impropriety; inapplicability etc. *adj.;* inconsistency, inconcinnity; irrelevancy etc. (*irrelation*) 10.

misjoin-ing, -der; syncretism, intrusion, interference; *concordia discors.*

fish out of water.

V. disagree; clash, quarrel, jar etc. (*discord*) 713; interfere, intrude, come amiss; not concern etc. 10; mismatch; *hymano capiti cervicem jungere equinam.*

Adj. disagreeing etc. *v.;* discordant, discrepant; at -variance, — war; hostile, antagonistic, repugnant, factious, contradictory, dissentious, incompatible, irreconcilable, inconsistent with; unconformable, exceptional etc. 83; intrusive, incongruous; disproportionate, -ed; unharmonious; unconsonant; divergent, repugnant to.

inapt, unapt, inappropriate, inept, infelicitous, improper; unsuit-ed, -able; inapplicable; un-fit, -fitting, -befitting; unbecoming; ill-timed, ill-adapted, unseasonable, *mal â propos,* inadmissible; inapposite etc. (*irrelevant*) 10.

uncongenial; ill-assorted, -sorted, -matched; mis-matched, -mated, -joined, -placed; unaccommodating, irreducible, uncommensurable, unsympathetic.

out of -character, — keeping, — proportion, — joint, — tune, — place, — season, — its element; at -odds, — variance with.

Adv. in -defiance, — contempt, — spite-of; discordantly etc. *adj.; à tort et à travers.*

25. Quantity. [Absolute quantity.]—**N.** quantity, magnitude; size etc. ((*dimensions*) 192; amplitude, mass, amount, *quantum,* measure, measurement, substance, strength.

[Science of quantity.] Mathematics, Mathesis.

[Definite or finite quantity] arm-, hand-, mouth-, spoon-, thimble-, capful; stock, batch, lot, dose, ration, quotum, quota, pittance, driblet, part, portion etc. 51.

Adj. quantitative, some, any, more or less.

Adv. to the tune of.

26. Degree. [Relative quantity.]—**N.** degree, grade, extent, measure, proportion, amount, ratio, stint, standard, height, pitch; reach, amplitude, range, scope, size, caliber; gradation, shade; tenor, compass; sphere, station, rank, standing; way, sort.

point, mark, step, stage etc. (*term*) 71; intensity, strength etc. (*greatness*) 31.

V. compare, graduate, calibrate, measure.

Adj. comparative; gradual, shading off, gradational; within the bounds etc. (*limit*), 233.

Adv. by degrees, gradually, inasmuch, *pro tanto;* how-ever, -soever; step by step, bit by bit, little by little, inch by inch, drop by drop, gradatim; by -inches, — slow degrees, — little and little; in some -degree, — measure; to some extent; just a bit.

27. Equality. [Sameness of quantity or degree.]—**N.** equality, parity, co-extension, symmetry, balance, poise; evenness, monotony, level.

equivalence; equi-pollence, -poise, -librium, -ponderance; par, quits; not a pin to choose; distinction without a difference, six of one and half a dozen of the other; identity etc. 13; similarity etc. 17; isotropism; coequality.

equalization, equation, equilibration, co-ordination, adjustment, readjustment.

drawn -game, -battle, draw, stalemate; neck and neck race; tie, dead heat.

match, peer, compeer, equal, mate, fellow, brother; equivalent.

V. be -equal etc. *adj.;* equal, match, reach, keep pace with, run abreast; come —, amount —, come upto; be —, lie- on a level with; balance; cope with; come to the same thing; level off.

render -equal etc. *adj.;* equalize, level, dress, balance, equate, handicap, give points, trim, adjust, poise; fit, accommodate; adapt etc. (*render accordant*) 23; strike a balance; establish —, restore- equality, — equilibrium; readjust; stretch on the bed of Procrustes.

Adj. equal, even, level, monotonous, coequal, symmetrical, coordinate; on a -par, — level, — footing- with; up to the mark; equiparent.

equivalent, tantamount; quits; homologous; synonymous etc. 522; resolvable into, convertible, much at one, as broad as long, neither more nor less; much the same —, the same thing —, as good- as; all -one, — the same; equi-pollent, -ponderant, -ponderous, -balanced; equalized etc. *v.;* drawn; half and half; isochronous; isoperimetrical.

Adv. equally etc. *adj.; pari passu, ad eundem, caeteris paribus; in equilibrio;* to all intents and purposes.

Phr. it -comes, -adds up, — amounts- to the same thing.

28. Inequality. [Difference of quantity or degree.]—**N.** inequality; dis-, im-parity; odds; difference etc. 15; ill-balanced; unevenness; inclination of the balance, partiality; shortcoming; casting —make- weight; superiority etc. 33; inferiority etc. 34.

V. be -unequal etc. *adj.;* countervail; have —, give- the advantage; turn the scale; kick the beam; topple, -over; over-match etc. 33; not come up to etc. 34.

Adj. unequal, uneven, disparate, partial; un-, over-balanced; top-heavy, lop-sided.

Adv. *haud passibus aequis.*

29. Mean.—**N.** mean, medium, intermedium, average, run of the mill, normal, balance; mediocrity, generality, rule, ordinary -run, -ruck; golden mean etc. (*mid-course*) 628; middle etc. 68; compromise etc. 774; neutrality; middle point, middle course.

V. split the difference; take the -average etc. *n.;* reduce to a -mean etc. *n.;* strike a balance, pair off.

Adj. mean, intermediate; medial; middle etc. 68; average, normal, standard, neutral; middling, moderate.

médiocre, middle-class; *bourgeois,* commonplace etc. (*unimportant*) 643.

Adv. on an average, in the long run; taking one with another, — all things together, — it for all in all; *communibus annis,* in round numbers.

30. Compensation.—**N.** compensation, equation; commutation; indemnification; compromise etc. 774; neutralization, nullification; counteraction etc. 179; reaction; measure for measure; retaliation etc. 718; equalization etc. 27; redemption, recoupment, recompense.

set-off, offset; make- casting-weight; counterpoise, equipoise, ballast; indemnity, reparation etc. 790; equivalent, *quid pro quo;* bribe, hush-money, tribute etc. 784; amends etc. (*atonement*) 952; counterclaim, counterbalance, equiponderance, countervail, cross demand.

V. make -amends, – compensation; compensate, -pense; indemnify; counter-act, -vail, -poise; equiponderate; balance; out-, over-, counterbalance; set off, offset, cancel; hedge, square, give and take; make up -for, – lee way; cover, fill up, neutralize, nullify; equalize etc. 27; make good; redeem etc. (*atone*) 952; recoup, pay etc. 973.

Adj. compensat-ing, -ory; amendatory, reparative, countervailing etc. *v.;* in the opposite scale; equivalent etc. (*equal*) 27.

Adv. in -return, – consideration; but, however, yet, still, notwithstanding; neverthe-, nathless; although, though; al-, how-beit; in spite of, despite; mauger; at -all events, – any rate; be that as it may, for all that, even so, on the other hand, at the same time, *quoad minus, quand même,* however that may be; after all, – is said and done; taking one thing with another etc. (*average*) 29.

31. Greatness.— N. greatness etc. *adj.;* magnitude; size etc. (*dimensions*) 192; multitude etc. (*number*) 102; immensity, enormity, infinity etc. 105; might, strength, intensity, fulness; importance etc. 642; fame etc. 873.

great quantity, quantity, deal, power, sight, pot, volume, world; mass, heap etc. (*assemblage*) 72; stock etc. (*store*) 636; peck, bushel, load, cargo; cart –, wagon –, car –, truck –, shipload; flood, spring tide; abundance etc. (*sufficiency*) 639.

principal –, chief –, main –, greater –, major –, best –, essential- part; bulk, mass etc. (*whole*) 50.

V. be -great etc. *adj.;* run high, soar, loom up, tower, bulk large, transcend; rise –, carry- to a great height; know no bounds; scale, overtop, ascend.

enlarge etc. (*increase*) 35, (*expand*) 194.

Adj. great; greater etc. 33; large, considerable, fair, above par; big, massive, huge etc. (*large in size*) 192; ample; abundant etc. (*enough*) 639; Herculean etc. 159; full, intense, strong, sound, passing, heavy, plenary, deep, high; signal, at its height, in the zenith.

world-wide, wide-spread, extensive; wholesale; many etc. 102.

goodly, noble, precious, mighty; sad, grave, serious; far gone, arrant, downright; utter, -most; crass, gross, arch, profound, intense, consummate; rank, unmitigated, red-hot, desperate; glaring, flagrant, stark staring; thorough-paced, -going; roaring, thumping, thundering, strapping, whacking; extraordinary; important etc. 642; unsurpassed etc. (*supreme*) 33; complete etc. 52.

vast, immense, enormous, extreme; inordinate, excessive, extravagant, exorbitant, outrageous, preposterous, unconscionable, swinging, monstrous, over-grown; towering, stupendous, prodigious, astonishing, incredible; terrific, frightful; marvelous etc. (*wonder*) 870; grand.

unlimited etc. (*infinite*) 105; unapproachable, unutterable, indescribable, ineffable, unspeakable, inexpressible, beyond expression, fabulous.

un-diminished, -abated, -reduced, -restricted.

absolute, positive, stark, decided, unequivocal, essential, perfect, finished.

remarkable, of mark, marked, pointed, veriest; noticeable, uncommon, noteworthy, eminent etc. 873.

Adv. [in a positive degree] truly etc. (*truth*) 494; decidedly, unequivocally, purely, absolutely, seriously, essentially, fundamentally, radically, downright, in all conscience; for the most part, in the main.

[in a complete degree] entirely etc. (*completely*) 52; abundantly, etc. (*sufficiently*) 639; widely, far and wide.

[in a great or high degree] greatly etc. *adj.;* much, muckle, well, indeed, very, very much, a deal, no end of, most not a little; pretty, – well; enough, in a great measure, passing richly; to a -large, – great, – gigantic- extent; on a large scale; so; never –, ever- so; ever so much; by wholesale; mightily, mighty, powerfully; with a witness, *ultra,* in the extreme, extremely, exceedingly, intensely, exquisitely, acutely, indefinitely, immeasurably; beyond -compare, – comparison, – measure, – all bounds; incalculably, infinitely.

[in a supreme degree] pre-eminently, superlatively etc. (*superiority*) 33.

[in a too great degree] immoderately, unduly, monstrously, grossly, preposterously, inordinately, exorbitantly, excessively, enormously, out of all proportion, with a vengeance.

[in a marked degree] particularly, remarkably, singularly, curiously, uncommonly, unusually, peculiarly, notably, signally, strikingly, pointedly, mainly, chiefly; famously, egregiously, prominently, glaringly, emphatically, strangely, wonderfully, amazingly, surprisingly, astonishingly, incredibly, marvelously, awfully, stupendously.

[in an exceptional degree] peculiarly etc. (*unconformity*) 83.

[in a violent degree] furiously etc. (*violence*) 173; severely, desperately, tremendously, extravagantly, confoundedly, deucedly, devilishly, with a vengeance; *à –, à toute- outrance.*

[in a painful degree] painfully, sadly, grossly, sorely, bitterly, piteously, grievously, miserably, cruelly, woefully, lamentably, shockingly, frightfully, dreadfully, fearfully, terribly, horribly, distressingly, balefully.

32. Smallness.—N. smallness etc. *adj.;* littleness etc. (*small size*) 193; tenuity; paucity; fewness etc. (*small number*) 103; meanness, insignificance etc. (*unimportance*) 643; mediocrity, moderation.

small quantity, *modicum, minimum;* vanishing point; material point, electron, atom, particle, molecule, corpuscle, point, dab, fleck, speck, dot, mote, jot, iota, ace; *minutiae,* details; look, thought, idea, *soupçon, scintilla,* whit, tittle, shade, shadow; spark, gleam; touch, cast; grain, scruple, granule, globule, minim, sup, sip, sop, spice, drop, droplet, sprinkling, dash, smack, tinge, tincture; inch, patch, scantling, dole; scrap, shred, tag, splinter, rag, tatter, cantlet, flitter, gobbet, mite, bit, morsel, crumb, seed, fritter, shive; snip, -pet; snick, snack, snatch, slip, scrag; chip, -ping; shiver, sliver, driblet, clipping, paring, shaving, hair.

nutshell; thimble-, spoon-, hand-, cap-, mouthful; fragment; fraction etc. (*part*)51; drop in the ocean, drop in the bucket.

animalcule etc. 193.

trifle etc. (*unimportant thing*) 643; mere −, next to- nothing; hardly anything; just enough to swear by; the shadow of a shade.

finiteness, finite quantity.

V. be -shall etc. *adj.;* lie in a nutshell.

diminish etc. (*decrease*) 36, (*contract*) 195.

Adj. small, little, tiny, weeny; diminutive etc. (*small in size*) 193; minute; minikin, fine, inconsiderable, dribbling, paltry etc. (*unimportant*) 643; faint etc. (*weak*) 160; slender, light, slight, scanty, scant, limited; meager etc. (*insufficient*) 640; sparing; few etc. 103; low, so-so, middling, tolerable, no great shakes; below −, under-par, − the mark; at a low ebb; halfway; moderate, modest; tender, subtle; petty, shallow, skin-deep.

inappreciable, evanescent, infinite-simal, homeopathic, very small, atomic, molecular, ultra-, -microscopic.

petty, shallow etc. 499.

mere, simple, sheer, stark, bare; near run.

Adv. [in a small degree] to a small extent, on a small scale; a -little, − wee, − tiny bit; slightly etc. *adj.;* imperceptibly miserably, wretchedly; insufficiently etc. 640; imperfectly; faintly etc. 160; passably, pretty well, well enough.

[in a certain or limited degree] partially, in part; in −, to a certain degree; to a certain extent; comparatively; some, rather; in some -degree, -measure; some-thing, -what; simply, only, purely, merely; at −, at the- -least, − most; ever so little, as little as may be, *tant soit peu,* in ever so small a degree; thus far, *pro tanto;* within bounds, in a manner, after a fashion.

almost, nearly, well nigh, short of, not quite, all but; near −, close- upon; *peu s'en faut,* near the mark; within an -ace, − inch- of; on the brink of; scarcely, hardly, barely, only just, no more than.

[in an uncertain degree] about, therabouts, somewhere about, nearly, say; be the same - more, − little more- or less.

[in no degree] no- ways, − wise; not -at all, − in the least, − a bit, − a bit of it, − a whit, − a jot, − a shadow; in no -wise, − respect; by no -means, − manner of means; on no account, at no hand.

33. Superiority.—N. superiority, supremacy, majority; greatness etc. 31; advantage, odds, pull; preponderance, -ation; predominance, vantage ground, coign of vantage, prevalence, partiality; personal superiority; sovereignty etc. 737; nobility etc. (*rank*) 875; Triton among the minnows, *primus inter pares, nulli secundus,* superman; captain etc. 475.

supremacy, pre-eminence; primacy, lead, *maximum;* record; climax, crest, top; culmination etc. (*summit*) 210; transcendence; *ne plus ultra;* lion's share, Benjamin's mess; excess; bisque, surplus etc. (*remainder*) 40, (*redundance*) 641.

V. be -superior etc. *adj.;* exceed, excel, transcend; out-do, -balance, -weigh, -rival, -Herod, outrank, pass, surpass, surmount, get ahead of; over-top, -ride, -pass, -balance, -weigh, -match; top, o'er-top, cap, beat, win out, cut out; beat hollow; outstrip etc. 303; eclipse, throw into the shade, take the shine out of, put one's nose out of joint; have the -upper hand, − whip hand of, − advantage; turn the scale, play first fiddle etc. (*importance*) 642; preponderate, predominate, prevail; precede, take .precedence, come first; come to a head, culminate; beat etc. all others, bear the palm; break the record, take the cake.

become −, render- -larger, etc. (*increase*) 35, (*expand*) 194.

Adj. superior, greater, major, higher; exceeding etc. *v.;* great etc. 31; distinguished, *ultra;* vaulting; more than a match for.

supreme, greatest, maximal, maximum, utmost, paramount, pre-eminent, foremost, crowning; first-rate etc. (important) 642, (*excellent*) 648; unrivalled; peer-, match-less; none such, second to none, *sans pareil;* un-paragoned, -paralleled, -equalled, -approached, -surpassed; superlative, inimitable, *facile princeps,* incomparable, sovereign, without parallel, *nulli secundus, ne plus ultra;* beyond -compare, − comparison; culminating etc. (*topmost*) 210; transcendent, -ental; *plus royaliste que le Roi.*

increased etc. (*added to*) 35; enlarged etc. (*expanded*) 194.

Adv. beyond, more, over; over −, above- the mark; above par; upwards −, in advance- of; over and above; at the top of the scale, on the crest, at it height.

[in a superior or supreme degree] eminently, egregiously, pre-eminently, surpassing, prominently, superlatively, supremely, above all, of all things, the most, to crown all, *par excellence,* principally, especially, particularly, peculiarly, *a fortiori,* even, yea, still more.

Phr. 'we shall not look upon his like again.'

34. Inferiority.—N. inferiority, minority, subordinancy; shortcoming, deficiency; handicap; *minimum;* smallness etc. 32; imperfection, shabbiness.

[personal inferiority] commonalty etc. 876; subordinate, substitute, sub.

V. be -inferior etc. *adj.;* fall −, come- short of; not -pass, − come up to; want.

become −, render- smaller etc. (decrease) 36, (*contract*) 195; hide its diminished head, retire into the shade, yield the palm, play second fiddle, take a back seat; bow.

Adj. inferior, smaller; small etc. 32; minor, less, lesser, deficient, minus, lower, subordinate, secondary; second-rate etc. (*imperfect*) 651; sub, subaltern; thrown into the shade; weighed in the balance and found wanting; not fit to hold a candle to.

least, smallest etc. (*see* little, small etc. 193); lowest.

diminished etc. (*decreased*) 36; reduced etc. (*contracted*) 195; unimportant etc. 643.

Adv. less; under −, below- -the mark, − par; at -the bottom of the scale, − a low ebb, − a disadvantage; short of, under.

35. Increase.—N. increase; augmentation, addition, enlargement, extension; dilatation etc. (*expansion*) 194; multiplication; increment, accretion; accession etc. 37; production etc. 161; development, growth; aggrandizement, aggravation, intensification; rise; ascent etc. 305; anabasis; ex-aggeration; -acerbation; spread etc. (*dispersion*) 73; flood-, spring-, -tide; gain, produce, profit etc. 618; booty, plunder etc. 793.

V. increase, augment, add to, enlarge; dilate etc. (*expand*) 194; grow, wax, mount, swell, get ahead, gain strength; advance; run —, shoot- up; rise; ascend etc. 305; sprout etc. 194.

aggrandize; raise; exalt; deepen, heighten; lengthen; thicken; strengthen; intensify, enhance, inflate, magnify, double, redouble; multiply; aggravate, exaggerate; ex-asperate, -acerbate; add fuel to the flame, *oleum addere camino*, superadd etc. (*add*) 37; spread etc. (*disperse*) 73.

Adj. increased etc. *v.;* on the increase, undiminished, additional etc. (*added*) 37; increasing etc. *v.;* growing, crescent, intensive, cumulative.

Adv. *crescendo,* increasingly.

Phr. *vires acquirit eundo.*

36. Non-Increase, Decrease.—N. decrease, diminution, lessening etc. *v.;* subtraction etc. 38; reduction, abatement, declension; shrinkage etc. (*contraction*) 195; coarctation; abridgment etc. (*shortening*) 201; extenuation.

subsidence, catabasis, wane, ebb-, neap-tide, decline; descent etc. 306; decrement, reflux, depreciation; erosion, wear and tear, deterioration etc. 659; anticlimax; mitigation etc. (*moderation*) 174.

V. decrease, diminish, lessen; abridge etc. (*shorten*) 201; shrink etc. (*contract*) 195; drop —, fall —, tail- off; fall away, waste, wear, erode; wane, ebb, decline; descent etc. 306; subside; deliquesce, melt —, die -away; retire into the shade, hide its diminished head, fall to a low ebb, run low, languish, decay, crumble, consume away.

bate, abate, dequantitate; discount; depreciate; extenuate, lower, weaken, attenuate, fritter away; mitigate etc.(*moderate*) 174; belittle, minimize; dwarf, throw into the shade; keep down, reduce etc. 195; shorten etc. 201; subtract etc. 38.

Adj. unincreased etc. (*see* increase etc. 35); decreased etc. *v.;* decreasing etc. *v.;* on the -wane etc. *n.;* deliquescent.

Adv. *diminuendo, decrescendo,* decreasingly.

37. Addition.—N. addition, annexation, adjection; junction etc. 43; super-position, -addition, -junction, -fetation; accession, reinforcement; increase etc. 35; increment, supplement; accompaniment etc. 88; interposition etc. 228; insertion etc. 300; summation etc. 85; adjunct etc. 39.

V. add, annex, adject, affix, attach, superadd, subjoin, superpose; clap —, saddle- on; tack to, postfix, append, tag; ingraft; saddle with; sprinkle; introduce etc. (*interpose*) 228; insert etc. 300.

become added, accrue; ad-, supervene; add up etc. 85.

reinforce, strengthen, swell the ranks of; augment etc. 35.

Adj. added etc. *v.;* additional; supplement, -al, -ary; suppletory, subjunctive; adjec-, adsci-, ascititious; additive, extra, spare, further, fresh, more, new, ulterior, other, auxiliary, supernumerary, accessory.

Adv. in addition, more, plus, extra; and, also, likewise, too, furthermore, further, item; and - also, — eke; else, besides, to boot, *et cetera;* etc.; and so -on, — forth; into the bargain, *cum multis aliis,* over and above, moreover.

with, withal; including, inclusive, as well as, not to mention, let alone; together —, along —, coupled —, in conjunction- with; conjointly; jointly etc. 43.

38. Non-Addition. Subduction.—N. sub-traction, -duction; deduction, retrenchment; removal; ab-, sub-lation; abstraction etc. (*taking*) 789; garbling etc. *v.;* mutilation, detruncation; amputation, severance; abs-, ex-, re-cision; curtailment etc. 201; minuend, subtrahend; decrease etc. 36; abrasion.

V. sub-tract, -duct; rebate, de-duct, — duce; bate, retrench; remove, withdraw; take — from, — away; detract.

garble, mutilate, amputate, sever, detruncate; cut -off, — away, — out; expurgate; abscind, excise; pare, thin, prune, decimate; abrade, scrape, file; geld, castrate, emasculate, unman, spay, caponize; eliminate.

diminish etc. 36; curtail etc. (*shorten*) 201; deprive of etc. (*take*) 789; weaken.

Adj. subtracted etc. *v.;* subtractive.

tailless, acaudal.

Adv. in -deduction etc. *n.;* less; short of; minus, without, except, excepting, with the exception of, barring, bar, save, exclusive of, save and except, with a reservation.

39. Adjunct. [Thing added.]—N. adjunct, addit-ion, -ament; *additum,* affix, appendage, annex; augment, -ation; increment, reinforcement, supernumerary, accessory, item; garnish, sauce; accompaniment etc. 88; adjective, *addendum,* accession, complement, supplement; continuation; extension, subscript, tag, appendix, postscript, interlineation, interpolation, insertion.

rider, codicil, off-shoot, episode, side issue, corollary; piece; flap, lapel, label, tab, strip, fold, lappet, apron, skirt, embroidery, trappings, *cortège;* tail, suffix etc. (*sequel*) 65; wing.

Adj. additional etc. 37.

Adv. in addition etc. 37.

40. Remainder. [Thing remaining.]—N. remainder, residue; remains, *remanet,* remnant, rest, relic, relict; leavings, heel-tap, odds and ends, cheese-parings, candle ends, orts; *residuum;* dottle, dregs, etc. (*dirt*) 653; refuse etc. (*useless*) 645; stubble, result, educt; fag-end, stub; ruins, wreck, skeleton, stump; *alluvium.*

surplus, overplus, excess; balance, complement; superfluity etc. (*redundance*) 641; survival, -ance; afterglow.

V. remain; be -left etc. *adj.*; exceed, survive; leave.

Adj. remaining, left; left -behind, — over;

residu-al, -ary; over, odd; unconsumed, sedimentary; surviving; net; exceeding, over and above; outlying, -standing; cast off etc. 782; superfluous etc. (*redundant*) 641.

V. remain; be -left; left -behind, − over; redidual, -ary; over, odd; unconsumed, sedimentary; surviving; net; exceeding, over and above; outlying, -standing; cast off etc. 782; superfluous etc. (*redundant*) 641.

40a. Decrement. [Thing deducted.]—N. decrement, discount, rebate, defect, loss, deduction, eduction, tare; drawback; waste, wastage; reprise.

41. Mixture. [Forming a whole without coherence.]—N. mix-, admix-, commix-ture, -tion, mingling; commixion, immixture, interfusion, intermixture, alloyage, matrimony; junction etc. 43; combination etc. 48; entanglement, interlacing; miscegenation, interbreeding.

impregnation; in-, dif-, suf-, transfusion; infiltration; seasoning, sprinkling, interlarding; interpolation etc. 228; adulteration, sophistication.

[Thing mixed] tinge, tincture, touch, dash, smack, sprinkling, spice, seasoning, infusion, *soupçon*.

[Compound resulting from mixture] alloy, brass, bronze, pewter etc.; amalgam, *magma*, blend, half-and-half, *mélange, tertium, quid*, miscellany, *ambigu*, medley, mess, hash, hotchpotch, hodgepodge, *pasticcio*, patchwork, odds and ends, all sorts; jumble etc. (*disorder*) 59; salad, sauce, mash, *omnium gatherum*, gallimaufry, ragout, *olla podrida, olio*, salmagundi, *potpourri*, Noah's ark; texture, mingled yarn; mosaic etc. (*variegation*) 440.

half-blood, -caste, -breed, Eurasian; mulatto; terc-, quart-, quinteron etc.; quad-, octo-roon; *griffo, zambo*; cross, hybrid, mongrel etc. 83.

V. mix; join etc. 43; combine etc. 48; com-, im-, inter-mix; mix up with, mingle; com-, inter-, bemingle; shuffle etc. (*derange*) 61; pound together; hash −, stir- up; knead, brew; impregnate with; interlard etc. (*interpolate*) 228; intertwine, -weave etc. 219; associate with, miscegenate, interbreed.

be mixed etc.; get among, be entangled with.

instil, imbue; in-, suf-, trans-fuse; infiltrate, dash, tinge, tincture, season, sprinkle, besprinkle, attemper, medicate, blend, cross; alloy, amalgamate, compound, adulterate, sophisticate, infect.

Adj. mixed etc. *v.;* implex, composite, half-and-half; linsey-wolsey, hybrid, mongrel, heterogeneous; motley etc. (*variegated*) 440; miscellaneous, promiscuous, indiscriminate; miscible.

Adv. among, amongst, amid, amidst, with; in the midst of, in the crowd.

42. Simpleness [Freedom from mixture.]—N. simpleness etc. *adj.;* purity, homogeneity.

elimination; sifting etc. *v.;* purification etc. (*cleanness*) 652.

V. render -simple etc. *adj.;* simplify.

sift, winnow, bolt, eliminate; narrow down; get rid of, exclude etc. 55; clear; purify etc. (*clean*) 652; disentangle etc. (*disjoin*) 44.

Adj. simple, uniform, of a piece, homogeneous, single, pure, clear, sheer, neat; Attic.

un-mixed, -mingled, -blended, -combined, -compounded; elementary, undecomposed; un-adulterated, -sophisticated, -alloyed, -tinged, -fortified; pure and simple.

free −, exempt- from; exclusive.

Adv. simply etc. *adj.;* only.

43. Junction.—N. junction; joining etc. *v.;* joinder, union; con-nection, -junction, -jugation, compendency, annex-ion, -ation, -ment; coalition; astriction, attachment, compagination, vincture, ligation, alligation; accouplement; marriage etc. (*wedlock*) 903; infibulation, inosculation, symphysis, anastomosis, confluence, communication, concatenation; concurrence, meeting, reunion; assemblage etc. 72.

copulation, coition, intercourse.

joint, joining, juncture, chiasma, pivot, hinge, articulation, commissure, seam, suture, gusset, stitch, splice; link etc. 45; miter, mortise.

closeness, tightness etc. *adj.;* coherence etc. 46; combination etc. 48.

V. join, unite; con-join, -nect; associate; put −, lay −, clap −, hang −, lump −, hold −, piece −, tack −, fix −, bind up- together; embody, re-embody; roll into one.

attach, fix, affix, saddle on, fasten, bind, secure, clinch, twist, make -fast etc. *adj.;* tie, pinion, string, strap, sew, lace, stitch, tack, paste, knit, button, buckle, hitch, lash, truss, bandage; braid, splice, swathe, gird, tether, moor, picket, harness, chain; fetter etc. (*restrain*) 751; lock, latch, belay, brace, hook, grapple, leash, couple, accouple, link, yoke, bracket; marry etc. (*wed*) 903; bridge over, span.

pin, nail, bolt, hasp, clasp, clamp, screw, rivet; impact, solder, braze, cement, set; weld −, fuse-together; wedge, rabbet, mortise, miter, jam, dovetail, enchase; graft, ingraft, inosculate; en-, in-twine; inter-link, -lace, -twine, -twist, -weave; entangle; twine round, belay; tighten; trice −, screw-up.

be -joined etc.; hang −, hold- together; cohere etc. 46.

Adj. joined etc. *v.;* joint; con-joint, -junct; corporate, compact; hand in hand.

firm, fast, close, tight, taut, taught, tense, secure, set, intervolved; in-separable, -dissoluble, -secable, -severable.

Adv. jointly etc. *adj.;* in conjunction with etc. (*in addition to*) 37; fast, firmly etc. *adj.;* intimately.

44. Disjunction.—N. dis-junction, -connection, -unity, -union, -association, -engagement, -sociation; discontinuity etc. 70; inconnection; abstraction, -edness; isolation; insul-arity, -ation; oasis; separateness etc. *adj.;* severalty; *disjecta membra;* dispersion etc. 73; apportionment etc. 786.

separation; parting etc. *v.;* detachment, segregation; divorce, sejunction, seposition, diduction, diremption, discerption; elision; *caesura*, division, subdivision, break, fracture, rupture; compartition; dis-memberment, -integration, -location; luxation; sever-, dis-severance; scission; re-, ab-scission; circumcision;

lacer-, dilacer-ation; dis-, ab-ruption; avulsion; divulsion; section, resection, cleavage; fission; separability; separatism.

fissure, breach, rent, split, rift, crack, slit, slot, incision.

dissection, anatomy; decomposition etc. 49; cutting instrument etc. (*sharpness*) 253; saw.

V. be -disjoined etc.; come −, fall- -off, − to pieces; peel off; get loose.

dis-join, -connect, -engage, -unite, -sociate, -pair; divorce, part, dispart, detach, uncouple, separate, cut off, rescind, segregate; set −, keep-apart; insulate, isolate; throw out of gear; cut adrift; loose; un-loose, -do, -bind, -tie, -hitch, -chain, -lock etc. (*fix*) 43, -pack, -ravel; disentangle; set free etc. (*liberate*) 750.

sunder, divide, subdivide, sectionalize, sever, dissever, abscind; cut; segment; in-cide, -cise; circumcise; saw, snip, nib, nip, cleave, rive, rend, slit, split, splinter, chip, crack, snap, break, tear, burst; rend etc. -asunder, − in twain; wrench, rupture, shatter, shiver, cranch, crunch, craunch, chop; rip up; hack, hew, slash; whittle; haggle, hackle, discind, lacerate, scamble, mangle, gash, hash, slice.

cut up, carve, quarter, dissect, anatomize; take −, pull −, pick −, tear- to pieces; tear to tatters, − piecemeal; divellicate; skin etc. 226; dis-integrate, -member, -branch, -band; disperse etc. 73; dis-locate, -joint; break up; mince; comminute etc. (*pulverize*) 330; distribute, apportion etc. 786.

part, − company; separate, leave; alienate, estrange.

Adj. disjoined etc. *v.;* discontinuous etc. 70; bipartite, multipartite, abstract; digitate; disjunctive; isolated etc. *v.;* insular, separate, disparate, discrete, apart, asunder, far between, loose, free; unattached, -annexed, -associated, -connected; distinct; adrift; straggling; rift, reft, cleft, split.

[capable of being divided] scissile, partible, divisible, separable, severable, detachable.

Adv. separately etc. *adj.;* one by one, severally, apart; adrift, asunder, in twain; in the abstract, abstractedly.

45. Vinculum. [Connecting medium.]—N. vinculum, link, *nexus;* connec-tive, -tion; junction etc. 43; bond of union, copula, intermedium, hyphen; bracket; bridge, stepping-stone, isthmus.

bond, tendon, tendril; fiber; cord, -age; riband, ribbon, rope, guy, cable, line, halser, hawser, painter, moorings, wire, chain; string etc. (*filament*) 205.

fastening, tie; liga-ment, -ture; strap; bowline, halliard, tackle, lanyard, rigging, shrouds; standing −, running- rigging; traces, harness; yoke; band, -age; brace, roller, fillet; inkle; with, withe, withy; thong, braid; girder, tie-beam; girt, cinch, girth, girdle, cestus, garter, braces, suspenders, halter, noose, lasso, lariat, surcingle, knot, hitch, running knot, frog.

pin, corking pin, nail, brad, tack, skewer, staple, cleat, clamp; cramp, screw, button, buckle, clasp, hasp, hinge; hank, catch, latch, bolt, ring, latchet, pawl, tag; tooth; stud; hook, − and eye; morse, lock, holdfast, padlock, rivet; anchor, grappling-iron, drawbar, coupler, draw-

head, coupling, treenail, trennel, stake, pale, pile, post, bollard.

cement, glue, gum, paste, size, wafer, solder, lute, putty, bird-lime, mortar, stucco, plaster, grout.

shackle, rein etc. (*means of restraint*) 752; suspender etc. 214; prop etc. (*support*) 215.

V. bridge over, span; connect etc. 43; hang etc. 214.

46. Coherence.—N. co-, ad-herence, -hesion, -hesiveness; concretion, accretion; con-, agglutination, -glomeration; aggregation; consolidation, set, cementation; sticking, soldering etc. *v.;* connection.

tenacity, toughness; stickiness etc. 352; insepara-bility, -bleness; bur, remora.

conglomerate, concrete etc. (*density*) 321.

V. cohere, adhere, stick, cling, cleave, hold, take hold of, hold fast, close with, embrace, clasp, hug; grow −, hang-together; twine round etc. (*join*) 43.

stick like -a leech, − wax; stick close; cling like -ivy, − a bur; adhere like -a remora, − Dejanira's shirt.

glue; ag-, con-glutinate; cement, lute, paste, gum; solder, weld; cake, coagulate, consolidate etc. (*solidify*) 321; agglomerate.

Adj. co-, ad-hesive, -hering etc. *v.;* tenacious, tough; sticky etc. 352.

united, unseparated, sessile, inseparable, inextricable, infrangible; compact etc. (*dense*) 321.

47. Incoherence. [Want of adhesion, non-adhesion, immiscibility.]—N. non-adhesion; immiscibility; incoherence; looseness etc. *adj.;* laxity; relaxation; loosening etc. *v.;* freedom; disjunction etc. 44; rope of sand.

V. make -loose etc. *adj.;* loosen, slacken, relax; un-glue etc. 46; detach etc. (*disjoin*) 44.

Adj. non-adhesive, immiscible; incoherent, detached, loose, slack, baggy, lax, relaxed, flapping, streaming; dishevelled; segregated, like grains of sand; un-consolidated etc. 321; -combined etc. 48; non-cohesive.

48. Combination.—N. combination; mixture etc. 41; alloy; junction etc. 43; union, unification, synthesis, incorporation, amalgamation, embodiment, coalescence, crasis, fusion, blend, blending, absorption, centralization, federation. compound, amalgam, composition, *tertium quid;* resultant, impregnation.

V. combine, unite, incorporate, alloy, intertwine etc. 41; amalgamate, embody, absorb, re-embody, blend, merge, fuse, melt into one, consolidate, coalesce, centralize, impregnate; put −, lump- together; federate, associate; fraternize; cement a union, marry, wed, couple, pair, ally.

Adj. combined etc. *v.;* conjunctive, conjugate, conjoint, allied, confederate; impregnated with, ingrained, inoculated.

49. Decomposition.—N. decomposition, analysis, diaeresis dissection, resolution, catalysis, electrolysis, hydrolysis, photolysis, dissolution; dispersion etc. 73; disjunction etc. 44;

putrescence, caries, necrosis, corruption etc. (*uncleanness*) 653.

V. decom-pose, -pound; analyze, disembody, dissolve; resolve –, separate- into its elements; electrolyze; dissect, decentralize, break up; disintegrate; disperse etc. 73; unravel etc. (*unroll*) 313; crumble into dust; decay etc. *n.;* deteriorate etc. 659.

Adj. decomposed etc. *v.;* catalytic, analytical.

50. Whole. [Principal part.]—**N.** whole, totality, integrity; totalness etc. *adj.;* entirety, *ensemble,* collectiveness; unity etc. 87; completeness etc. 52; indivisibility, indiscerptibility; integration, embodiment; integer, integral.

all, the whole, total, aggregate, one and all, gross amount, sum, sum-total, *tout ensemble,* length and breadth of, Alpha and Omega, 'be all and end all,' lock, stock and barrel.

bulk, mass, lump, tissue, staple, body, torso, *compages;* truck, bole, hull, hulk, skeleton; greater –, major –, best –, principal –, mainpart; essential part etc. (*importance*) 642; lion's share, Benjamin's mess; the long and the short; nearly –, almost- all.

V. form –, constitute- a whole; integrate, embody, amass; aggregate etc. (*assemble*) 72; amount to, come to.

Adj. whole, total, integral, entire; complete etc. 52; one, individual.

un-broken, -cut, -divided, -severed, -clipped, -cropped, -shorn; seamless; undiminished; undemolished, -dissolved, -destroyed, -bruised.

in-divisible, -dissoluble, -dissolvable, -discerptible.

wholesale, sweeping, comprehensive.

Adv. wholly, altogether; totally etc. (*completely*) 52; entirely, all, all in all, considering all things, in a body, collectively, all put together; in the -aggregate, – lump; – mass, – gross, – main, – long run; *en masse,* on the whole, as a whole, bodily, *en bloc, in extenso,* throughout, every inch; substantially.

51. Part.—**N.** part, portion; dose; item, particular; aught, any; division, ward; subdivision, section; chapter, verse; article, clause, count, paragraph, passage; phrase; number, volume, book, fascicule; sector, segment; fraction, fragment; cantle, -t; frustum; detachment, parcel, unit, class etc. 75.

piece, lump, bit; cut, -ting; chip, chunk, collop, slice, scale, shard; lamina etc. 204; moiety; small part; morsel, scrap, crumb; particle etc. (*smallness*) 32; instalment, dividend; share etc. (*allotment*) 786.

débris, odds and ends, oddments, *detritus; excerpta;* member, limb, lobe, lobule, arm, wing, scion, branch, bough, joint, link, offshoot, ramification, twig, stipule, tendril, bush, spray, sprig; runner; leaf, -let; stump; constituent, ingredient, component part etc. 56.

compartment; department etc. (*class*) 75; county etc. (*region*) 181.

V. part, divide, break etc. (*disjoin*) 44; partition etc. (*apportion*) 786.

Adj. fractional, fragmentary; sectional, aliquot; divided etc. *v.;* in compartments, multifid, incomplete, partial, divided etc. 44.

Adv. partly, in part, partially; piecemeal, part by part; by -instalments, – snatches, – inches, – driblets; bit by bit, inch by inch, foot by foot, drop by drop; in -detail, – lots.

52. Completeness.—**N.** completeness etc. *adj.;* completion etc. 729; integration; integrality.

entirety; universality; totality; perfection etc. 650; solid-ity, -arity; unity; all; *ne plus ultra,* ideal, limit.

complement, supplement, make-weight; filling up etc. *v.*

impletion; satur-ation, -ity; high water; high –, flood –, spring- tide; fill, load, bumper, bellyful; brimmer; sufficiency etc. 639.

V. be -complete etc. *adj.;* come to a head.

render -complete etc. *adj.;* complete etc. (*accomplish*) 729; fill, charge, load, replenish; make-up, – good; piece –, eke- out; supply deficiencies; fill -up, – in, – to the brim, – the measure of; saturate etc. 869.

go the whole -hog, – length, go all lengths.

Adj. complete, entire; whole etc.50; perfect etc. 650; full, good, absolute, thorough, plenary; solid, undivided; with all its parts.

exhaustive, radical, sweeping, thorough-going; dead.

regular, consummate, unmitigated, sheer, unqualified, unconditional, free; abundant etc. (*sufficient*) 639.

brimming; brim-, top-ful; chock –, chokefull; as full as- an egg is of meat, – a vetch, – a tick; saturated, crammed; replete etc. (*redundant*) 641; fraught, laden; full-laden, -fraught, -charged; heavy laden.

completing etc. *v.;* supplement-al, -ary; ascititious.

Adv. completely etc. *adj.;* altogether, outright, wholly, totally, *in toto,* quite; over head and ears; effectually, for good and all, nicely, fully, through thick and thin, head and shoulders; neck and -heel, – crop; all out; in -all respects, – every respect; at all points, out and out, to all intents and purposes; *toto coelo;* utterly, clean, – as a whistle; to the -full, – utmost, – backbone; hollow, stark; heart and soul, root and branch; down to the ground.

to the top of one's bent, as far as possible, *à outrance.*

throughout; from -first to last, – beginning to end, – end to end, – one end to the other, – Dan to Beersheba, – head to foot, – head to heels, – top to toe, – top to bottom; *de fond en comble; à fond, a capite ad calcem, ab ovo usque ad mala,* fore and aft; every -whit, – inch; *cap-à-pie,* to the end of the chapter; up to the -brim, – ears, – eyes; as ... as can be.

on all accounts; *sous tous les rapports;* with a -vengeance, – witness.

53. Incompleteness.—**N.** incompleteness etc. *adj.;* deficiency, short -measure, – weight; shortcoming etc. 304; insufficiency etc. 640; imperfection etc. 651; immaturity etc. (*nonpreparation*) 674; half measures.

[part wanting] defect, deficit, shortage, ullage, defalcation, omission, *caret;* interval etc. 198; break etc. (*discontinuity*) 70; non-completion etc. 730; missing link.

V. be -incomplete etc. *adj.;* fall short of etc. 304; lack etc. (*be insufficient*) 640; neglect etc. 460.

Adj. incomplete; imperfect etc. 651; unfinished; uncompleted etc. (*see* complete etc. 729); defective, deficient, wanting; failing; in -default, − arrear; short, − of; hollow, meagre, lame, half-and-half, perfunctory, sketchy; crude etc. (*unprepared*) 674.

mutilated, garbled, mangled, docked, lopped, truncated; bobtailed, cropped, bobbed, shingled.

in -progress, − hand; going on, proceeding.

Adv. incompletely etc. *adj.;* by halves.

Phr. *caetera desunt; caret.*

54. Composition.—N. composition, constitution, crasis, synthesis; make-up; combination etc. 48; inclusion, admission, comprehension, reception; embodiment, formation, conformation, production.

compilation etc. 72. (*musical*) composition etc. 415; painting etc. 556; writing etc. 590; typography etc. 591.

V. be -composed, − made, − formed, − made up- of; consist of, be resolved into.

include etc. (*in a class*) 76; subsume; synthesize; contain, hold, comprehend, take in, admit, embrace, embody; involve; implicate, drag into.

compose, constitute, form, make; make −, fill −, build- up; weave, construct, fabricate; compile; write, draw; set up (*printing*); enter into the composition of etc. (*be a component*) 56.

Adj. containing, constituting etc. *v.*

55. Exclusion.—N. exclusion, non-admission, omission, exception, rejection, repudiation; exile etc. (*seclusion*) 893; preclusion, lock out, ostracism, prohibition; disbarment, expulsion, ban.

separation, segregation, seposition, elimination, coffer-dam.

V. be excluded from etc.

exclude, bar, ban; leave −, shut −, thrust −, bar- out; reject, repudiate, spurn, blackball; ostracize, boycott; lay −, put −, set-apart, − aside; relegate, segregate; throw overboard; strike -off, − out; neglect etc. 460; banish etc. (*seclude*) 893; separate etc. (*disjoin*) 44.

pass over, omit; garble; eliminate, weed, winnow.

Adj. excluding etc. *v.;* exclusive.

excluded etc. *v.;* unrecounted, not included in; inadmissible; preventive, interdictive.

Adv. exclusive of, barring, except; with the exception of; save, bating.

56. Component.—N. component; component −, integral −, integrant-part; element, constituent, ingredient, leaven; part and parcel; contents; appurtenance; feature; member etc. (*part*) 51; personnel.

V. enter into, − the composition of; be a -component etc. *n.;* be −, form- part of; merge −, be merged- in; be implicated in; share in etc. (*participate*) 778; belong −, appertain- to.

form, make, constitute, compose.

Adj. forming etc. *v.;* inclusive; inherent etc. 5.

57. Extraneousness.—N. extraneousness etc. *adj.;* extrinsicality etc. 6; exteriority etc. 220; alienism.

foreign -body, − substance, − element; alien, stranger, intruder, interloper, foreigner, tramontane, *novus homo,* new comer, immi-, emi-grant; creole, Afrikander; outsider, outlander, tenderfoot.

Adj. extraneous, foreign, alien, ulterior; exterior, external, outside, outlandish; oversea; tra-, ultra-montane.

excluded etc. 55; inadmissible; exceptional.

Adv. in foreign -parts, − lands; abroad, beyond seas, overseas.

58. Order.—N. order, regularity etc. 80; uniformity, symmetry, *lucidus ordo;* harmony, music of the spheres.

gradation, progression; series etc. (*continuity*) 69.

subordination; course, even tenor; routine; method, disposition; arrangement, array, system, economy, discipline; orderliness etc. *adj.*

rank, place etc. (*term*) 71.

V. be −, become- in order etc. *adj.;* form, fall in, draw up; arrange −, range −, place- itself; adjust; fall into −, take- -one's place, − rank; rally round; arrange etc. 60.

Adj. orderly, regular; in -order, − trim, − apple-pie order, according to Cocker, − its proper place, neat, neat as a pin, tidy, *en règle,* well regulated, correct, methodical, uniform, symmetrical, ship-shape, business-like, systematic; habitual; unconfused etc. (*see* confuse etc. 61) arranged etc. 60.

Adv. in order; methodically etc. *adj.;* in -turn, − its turn; step by step; by regular -steps, − gradations, − stages, − intervals; *seriatim,* systematically, by clockwork, *gradatim;* at stated periods etc. (*periodically*)138.

59. Disorder. [Absence, or want of Order, etc.]—N. disorder; derangement etc. 61; irregularity; anomaly etc. (*unconformity*) 83; anar-chy, -chism; want of method; dishevelment, untidiness etc. *adj.;* disunion; discord etc. 24.

confusion; confusedness etc. *adj.;* disarray, jumble, mix-up, huddle, litter, lumber; *cahotage;* farrago; mess, muss, mash, muddle, hash; hotchpotch; *imbroglio,* chaos, *omnium gatherum,* medley; mere -mixture etc. 41; fortuitous concourse of atoms, *disjecta membra, rudis indigestaque moles.*

complexity; complexness etc. *adj.;* com-, implication; intri-cacy, -cation; perplexity; network, maze, labyrinth, wilderness, jungle; involution, ravelling, entanglement; coil etc. (*convolution*) 248; sleave, tangled skein, knot, Gordian know, kink, web; wheels within wheels.

turmoil; ferment, etc. (*agitation*) 315; to do, trouble, pudder, pother, row, disturbance, convulsion, tumult, pandemonium, uproar, riot, rumpus, stour, scramble, *fracas,* embroilment, *mêlée,* spill and pelt, rough and tumble; whirlwind etc. 349; bear garden, Babel, Saturnalia, Donnybrook Fair, confusion worse confounded, most admired disorder, *concordia discors;* Bedlam −, hell- broke loose; bull in a china shop;

all the fat in the fire, *diable à quatre,* Devil to pay; pretty kettle of fish; pretty piece of -work, — business.

slattern, slut, sloven; draggle-tail.

V. be -disorderly etc. *adj.;* ferment, play at cross purposes.

put out of order; derange etc. 61; ravel etc. 219; ruffle, rumple; bungle, botch.

Adj. disorderly, orderless; out of -order; — place, — gear, — whack; irregular, desultory; anomalous etc. (*unconformable*) 83; aceph-alous, disorganized, straggling; un-, im-methodical; unsymmetric; unsystematic; untidy, slovenly, bedraggled, messy; dislocated; out of sorts; promiscuous, indiscriminate; chaotic, anarchical, lawless; unarranged etc. 60; confused, tumultuous, turbulent, tempestuous; deranged etc. 61; topsy turvy etc. (*inverted*) 218; shapeless etc. 241; disjointed, out of joint.

com-plex, -plexed; intricate, complicated, perplexed, involved, ravelled, entangled, knotted, tangled, inextricable; irreducible.

troublous; riotous etc. (*violent*) 173.

Adv. irregularly etc. *adj.;* by fits and -snatches, — starts; pell-mell; higgledy-piggledy; helter-skelter; harum-scarum; in a ferment; at -sixes and sevens, — cross purposes; upside down etc. 218.

Phr. the cart before the horse, chaos is come again.

60. Arrangement. [Reduction to Order.]—**N.** arrangement; plan etc. 626; preparation etc. 673; dispos-al, -ition; col-, al-location; distribution; sorting etc. *v.;* assortment, allotment; grouping; apportionment, *taxis,* taxonomy, *syn-taxis,* graduation, organization, grading; re-organization, rationalization.

analysis, classification, division, digestion; systematism.

[Result of arrangement] order, orderliness, form, array; digest, synopsis etc. (compendi -um) 596; *syntagma,* table, atlas; register etc. (*record*) 551; score etc. 415; cosmos, organism, architecture.

[Instrument for sorting] sieve etc. 260; file, card index.

V. reduce to - , bring into- order; introduce order into; rally.

arrange, dispose, place, form; put —, set —, place- in order; straighten up, tidy up; set out, collocate, allocate, pack, marshal, range, size, rank, array, group, parcel out, allot, space, distribute, deal; cast —, assign- the parts; dispose of, assign places to; assort, sort; sift, riddle; put —, set- -to rights, — into shape, — in trim, — in array.

class, -ify; divide; file, string together; thread; register etc. (*record*) 551; list, catalogue, tabulate, index, alphabeticize, graduate, digest, grade, codify; orchestrate, score.

methodize, regulate, systematize, standard-ize, co-ordinate, organize, settle, fix.

unravel, disentangle, ravel, card; disembroil.

Adj. arranged etc. *v.;* embattled, in battle array; cut and dried; methodical, orderly, regular, systematic, tabular.

61. Derangement. [Subversion of Order; bringing into disorder.]—**N.** derangement etc. *v.;* dis-

order etc. 59; evection, discomposure, disturbance; dis-, de-organization; involvement; dislocation; perturbation, interruption; shuffling etc. *v.;* inversion etc. 218; corrugation etc. (*fold*) 258; insanity etc. 503.

V. derange; dis-, mis-arrange; dis-, mis-place; mislay, discompose, disorder, de-, dis-organize; embroil, unsettle, disturb, confuse, trouble, perturb, jumble, tumble; huddle, shuffle, muddle, toss, hustle, fumble, riot; bring —, put —, throw-into -disorder etc. 59; break the ranks, disconcert, convulse; break in upon.

unhinge, dislocate, put out of joint, throw out of gear.

turn topsy-turvy etc. (*invert*) 218; bedevil; complicate, involve, perplex, confound; im-, em-brangle; tangle, en-tangle, ravel, tousle, dishevel, ruffle, rumple etc. (*fold*) 258; dement.

litter, scatter; mix etc. 41.

Adj. deranged etc. *v.;* syncre-tic, -tistic.

62. Precedence.—**N.** precedence; coming before etc. *v.;* the lead, *le pas;* superiority etc. 33; importance etc. 642; anteced-ence, -ency; anteriority etc. (*front*) 234; precursor etc. 64; priority etc. 116; precession etc. 280; anteposition, preference.

V. precede; come -before, — first; forerun, head, lead, take the lead; lead the -way, — dance; introduce, usher in; have the *pas;* set the fashion etc. (*influence*) 175; lead off, kick off, open the ball; take —, have- precedence; outrank; have the start etc. (*get before*) 280.

place before; prefix; premise, prelude, preface.

Adj. preceding etc. *v.;* pre-, antecedent; anterior, prior etc. 116; before; former, foregoing; before-, above-mentioned; aforesaid, said; precurs-ory, -ive; prevenient, preliminary, prefatory, introductory; prelus-ive, -ory; proemial, preparatory.

Adv. before; in advance etc. (*precession*) 280.

Phr. *seniores priores.*

63. Sequence.—**N.** sequence, coming after; going after etc. (*following*) 281; consecution, succession; posteriority etc. 117.

continuation; prolongation, order of succussion; successiveness; Elijah's mantle.

secondariness; subordinancy etc. (*inferiority*) 34.

V. succeed; come -after, — on, — next; follow, ensue, step into the shoes of; alternate.

place after, suffix, append.

Adj. succeeding etc. *v.;* sequent; sub-, consequent; sequacious, proximate, next; consecutive etc. (*continuity*) 69; alternate, amoebaean.

latter; posterior etc. 117.

Adv. after, subsequently; behind etc. (*rear*) 235.

64. Precursor.—**N.** precursor, antecedent, precedent, predecessor; forerunner, van-courier, *avant-coureur,* pioneer, prodrome, *prodromos,* outrider; leader, bell-wether; herald, harbinger; dawn.

prelude, preamble, preface, prologue, foreword, *avant-propos, protasis,* prolusion, proem, *prolepsis, prolegomena,* prefix, introduction;

lead, heading, frontispiece, groundwork; preparation etc. 673; overture, voluntary, *exordium*, symphony, *ritornello;* premises.

prefigurement etc. 511; omen etc. 512.

Adj. precursory; prelu-sive, -sory, -dious; pro-emial, introductory, prefatory, prodromous, inaugural, preliminary; precedent etc. (*prior*) 116.

65. Sequel.—N. sequel, suffix, successor; tail; *queue,* train, wake, trail, rear; retinue, suite; appendix, postscript, subscript; epilogue; conclusion; peroration; codicil; continuation, *sequela;* appendage etc. 39; tail —, heel-piece; tag, more last words; *colophon.*

follower, after-glow, -growth, -crop, -taste, -math.

after-part, -piece, -course, -thought, -game; *arrière pensée,* second thoughts.

66. Beginning.—N. beginning, commencement, opening, outset, incipience, inception, inchoation; introduction etc. (*precursor*) 64; *alpha;* initial; foundation; inauguration, *début, le premier pas,* embarcation, rising of the curtain; zero hour; exordium, curtain raiser; maiden speech; prelude; outbreak, onset, brunt; initiative, move, first move; gambit, narrow —, thin- end of the wedge; fresh start, new departure; forefront.

origin etc. (*cause*) 153; source, rise; bud, germ etc. 153; egg, rudiment; genesis, birth, nativity, cradle, infancy, incunabula; start, starting-point etc. 293; dawn etc. (*morning*) 125.

title-page; head, -ing, caption; van etc. (*front*) 234.

en-trance, -try; inlet, orifice, mouth, chops, lips, porch, portal, portico, *propylon,* door; gate, -way; postern, wicket, threshold, vestibule; skirts, border etc. (*edge*) 231; tee.

first -stage, — blush, — glance, — impression, — sight.

rudiments, elements, outlines, *principia,* grammar, *protasis;* alphabet, ABC.

V. begin, commence, inchoate, rise, arise, originate, institute, conceive, initiate, open, dawn, set in, take its rise, enter upon, start; enter; set out etc. (*depart*) 293; embark in.

usher in; lead -off, — the way; take the -lead, — initiative; inaugurate, head; stand -at the head, — first, — for; lay the foundations etc. (*prepare*) 673; found etc. (*cause*) 153; set -up, — on foot, — agoing, — abroach, — the ball in motion; apply the match to a train; launch, broach; open -up, — the door to; set -about, — to work; make a -beginning, — start; handsel; take the first step, lay the first stone, cut the first turf; break -ground, — the ice, — cover; pass —, cross- the Rubicon; open -fire, — the ball; ventilate, air; undertake etc. 676.

come into -existence, — the world; make one's *début,* take birth; burst forth, break out; spring —, crop- up.

begin -at the beginning, — *ab ovo,* — again, — *de novo;* start afresh, make a fresh start, shuffle the cards, resume, recommence.

Adj. beginning etc. *v.;* initi-al, -atory, -ative; inceptive, introductory, incipient, proemial, inaugural; incho-ate, -ative; embryonic, rudimental; primogenial; primeval etc. (*old*) 124; rudimentary, aboriginal; natal, nascent.

first, foremost, front, leading, head; maiden.

begun etc. *v.;* just -begun etc. *v.*

Adv. at —, in- the beginning etc. *n.;* first, in the first place, *imprimis,* first and foremost; *in limine;* in -the bud, — embryo, — its infancy; from -the beginning, — its birth; *ab -initio,* — *ovo,* — *incunabilis,* primarily, originally.

67. End.—N. end, close, termination; desinence, conclusion, *finis, finale,* period, term, *terminus,* last, *omega;* extreme, -tremity; gable —, butt —, fagend; tip, nib, point; tail etc. (*rear*) 235; verge etc. (*edge*) 231; tag, epilogue, peroration; *bonne bouche,* bitter end, tail end; terminal; *apodosis;* appendix.

consummation, *dénouement;* finish etc. (*completion*) 729; fate;-doom, -sday; crack of doom, day of Judgment, fall of the curtain, wind-up; goal, destination; limit, stoppage, end all, determination; expiration, expiry; death etc. 360; end of all things; finality; eschatology.

break up, *commencement de la fin,* last stage, turning point; *coup de grâce,* death-blow; knock-out.

V. end, close, finish, terminate, conclude, be all over; expire; die etc. 360; come —, draw- to a -close etc. *n.;* have run its course; run out, pass away.

bring to an -end etc. *n.;* put an end to, make an end of; determine; get through; achieve etc. (*complete*) 729; stop etc. (*make to cease*) 142; shut up shop.

Adj. ending etc. *v.;* final, terminal, definitive, conclusive; crowning etc. (*completing*) 729; last, ultimate; hindermost; rear etc. 235; caudal.

contermin-ate, -ous, -able.

ended etc. *v.;* at an end; settled, decided, over, played out, set at rest.

penultimate; last but -one, — two, etc.

unbegun, uncommenced; fresh.

Adv. finally etc. *adj.;* in fine; at the last; once for all.

68. Middle.—N. middle, midst, mediety; mean etc. 29; medium, middle term; center etc. 222; mid-course etc. 628; *mezzo termine; juste milieu* etc. 628; half-way house, nave, navel, omphalos; nucle-us, -olus.

equidistance, bisection, half-distance; equator, diaphragm, midriff; interjacence etc. 228.

Adj. middle, medial, mesial, mean, mid; middle-, mid-most; middling; mediate; intermediate etc. (*interjacent*) 228; equidistant; central etc. 222; mediterranean, equatorial.

Adv. in the middle; in the thick; mid-, half-way; midships, *in medias res.*

69. Continuity. [Uninterrupted sequence.]—N. continuity; consecu-tion, -tiveness etc. *adj.;* succession, round, suite, progression, series, train, chain; cat-, concatenation; catena; scale; gradation, course, constant flow, perpetuity.

procession, column; retinue, *cortège,* cavalcade, rank and file, line of battle, array.

pedigree, genealogy, lineage, race etc. 166.

rank, file, line, row, range, tier, string, thread; team; suit; colonnade.

V. follow in —, form- a series etc. *n.;* fall in.

arrange in a -series etc. *n.;* string together, catenate, file, thread, graduate, tabulate.

Adj. continu-ous. -ed; consecutive; pro-gressive, gradual; serial, successive; immediate, unbroken, entire; linear; in a -line, − row etc. *n.;* uninter-rupted, -mitting; unremitting; perennial, evergreen; constant.

Adv. continuously etc. *adj.; seriatim;* in a -line etc. *n.;* in -succession, − turn; running, gradual-ly, step by step, *gradatim,* at a stretch; in -file, − column, −single file, − Indian file.

70. Discontinuity. [Interrupted se-quence.]—**N.** discontinuity; disjunction etc. 44; anacoluthon; interruption, break, fracture, flaw, fault, split, crack, cut; gap etc. *(interval)* 198; solution of continuity, *caesura;* broken thread; parenthesis, episode; rhapsody, patchwork; intermission; alternation etc. *(periodicity)* 138; dropping fire.

V. be -discontinuous etc. *adj.;* alternate, intermit.

discontinue, pause, interrupt; intervene; break, − in upon; interpose etc. 228; break −, snap- the thread; disconnect etc. *(disjoin)* 44.

Adj. discontinuous, unsuccessive, broken, in-terrupted, *décousu;* dis-, un-connected, discrete, disjunctive; fitful etc. *(irregular)* 139; spas-modic, desultory, intermit-ting etc. *v.;* -tent; alternate; recurrent etc. *(periodic)* 138; few and far between.

Adv. at intervals; by -snatches, − jerks, − skips, − catches, − fits and starts; skippingly, *per saltum; longo intervallo.*

71. Term.—**N.** term, rank, station, stage; step; degree etc. 26; scale, remove, grade, link, peg, round −, rung- of the ladder, *status,* position, place, point, mark, *pas,* period, pitch; stand, -ing; footing, range.

V. hold −, occupy −, fall into- a place etc. *n.*

72. Assemblage.—**N.** assemblage; col-lection, location, -ligation; compilation, levy, gathering, ingathering, mobilization, meet, foregathering, muster, *attroupement;* con-course, -flux, - gregation, -tesseration, -vergence etc. 290; meeting, *levée, réunion,* drawing room, at home; con-versazione etc. *(social gathering)* 892; assembly, congress, eisteddfod; conven-tion, -ticle; gemote; conclave, etc. *(council)* 696; posse, *posse com-itatus;* Noah's ark.

miscellany, *collectanea,* symposium; muse-um, menagerie, etc. *(store)* 636.

crowd, throng, multitude; flood, rush, deluge; rout, rabble, mob, press, crush, *cohue,* jam, horde, body, tribe; crew, gang, knot, squad, band, party; swarm, shoal, school, covey, flock, herd, drove, kennel; array, bevy, galaxy; *corps,* company, troop, *troupe;* army, force, regiment, etc. *(combatants)* 726; host etc. *(multitude)* 102; populousness.

clan, brotherhood, association etc. *(party)* 712.

volley, shower, storm, cloud.

group, cluster, Pleiades, clump, pencil; set, batch, lot, pack; budget, *dossier,* assortment, bunch; parcel; pack-et, -age; bundle, *fasciculus,* fascine, bale; ser-on, oon; faggot, wisp, truss,

tuft; shock, rick, fardel, stack, sheaf, swath, gavel, haycock, stook.

accumulation etc. *(store)* 636; congeries, heap, lump, pile, *rouleau,* tissue, mass, pyramid; drift; snow-ball, -drift; acervation, cumulation; amass-ment, glom-, agglom-eration; conglobation; con-glomeration, -ate; còacervation, coagmentation, aggregation, concentration, congestion, *omnium gatherum, spicilegium,* black hole of Calcutta; quantity etc. *(greatness)* 31.

collector, gatherer; whip, -per in.

V. [be or come together] assemble, collect, muster; meet, unite, join, rejoin; cluster, flock, swarm, surge, stream, herd, crowd, throng, associate; con-gregate, -glomerate, -centrate; center round, *rendezvous,* resort; come −, flock −, get −, pig- together; forgather; huddle; reassemble.

[get or bring together] assemble, muster, mobilize; bring −, get −, put −, draw −, scrape −, lump- together; col-lect, -locate, -ligate; get −, whip- in; gather; hold a meeting; con-vene, -voke, -vocate; rake up, dredge; heap, mass, pile; pack, put up, truss, cram; acervate; ag-glomerate, -gregate; compile; group, aggroup, concentrate, unite; collect −, bring- into a focus; amass, ac-cumulate etc. *(store)* 636; collect in a drag-net; heap Ossa upon Pelion.

Adj. assembled etc. *v.;* closely packed, dense, serried, crowded to suffocation, teeming, swarm-ing, populous; as thick as hops; all of a heap, fas-ciculated; cumulative.

Phr. the plot thickens.

73. Non-assemblage. Dispersion.—**N.** disper-sion; disjunction etc. 44; divergence etc. 291; scat-tering etc. *v.;* dissemination, broadcasting, dif-fusion, dissipation, distribution; apportionment etc. 786; spread, respersion, circumfusion, in-terspersion, spargefaction.

waifs and estrays, flotsam and jetsam, *disjecta membra.*

V. disperse, scatter, sow, disseminate, radiate, diffuse, shed, spread, ted, bestrew, overspread, dispense, disband, disembody, demobilize, dis-member, distribute; apportion etc. 786; blow off, let out, dispel, cast forth, draught off; strew, straw, strow; spirtle, cast, sprinkle, shatter; issue, deal out, retail, utter; re-, inter-sperse; set abroach, circumfuse.

turn −, cast- adrift; scatter to the winds; sow broadcast.

spread like wildfire, disperse themselves.

Adj. unassembled etc. *(see* assemble etc. 72); dispersed etc. *v.;* sparse, dispread, broadcast, sporadic, widespread; far-flung; epidemic etc. *(general)* 78; adrift, stray; dishevelled, streaming.

Adv. *sparsim,* here and there, *passim.*

74. Focus. [Place of meeting.]—**N.** focus; point of- convergence etc. 290; corradiation; center etc. 222; gathering-place, resort; haunt; retreat; *venue, rendezvous;* rallying ʼ point, head-quarters, home, club; *dépôt* etc. *(store)* 636; tryst, trysting-place; place of -meeting, − resort, − assignation; *point de −, lieu de- réunion;* issue.

V. bring to- a point, − a focus, − an issue; focus.

75. Class.—N. class, category, *categorema*, head, order, section; division, subdivision; department, province, domain, sphere.

kind, sort, genus, species, variety, branch, family, race, tribe, caste, sept, clan, breed; *clique, coterie;* type, kit, sect, set; assortment; feather, kidney; suit; range; gender, sex, kin.

manner, description, denomination, persuasion, connection, designation, character, stamp; predicament; conviction etc. 484.

similarity etc. 17.

76. Inclusion. [Comprehension under, or reference to a class.]—N. inclusion, admission, incorporation, comprehension, reception.

composition etc. (*inclusion in a compound*) 54.

V. be -included in etc.; come −, fall −, range-under; belong −, pertain- to; range with; merge in.

include, compromise, comprehend, contain, admit, embrace, receive; enclose etc. (*circumscribe*) 229; incorporate, cover, embody, encircle.

reckon −, enumerate −, number- among; refer to; place −, arrange-under, − with; take into account.

Adj. includ-ed; -ing etc. *v.;* inclusive; comprehensive, all-embracing; congen-er, -erous; of the same -class etc. 75.

Phr. *et hoc genus omne,* etc.; *et caetera.*

77. Exclusion.*—N. exclusion etc. 55.

* The same set of words is used to express *Exclusion from a class* and *Exclusion from a compound*. Reference is therefore made to the former at 55. This identity does not occur with regard to *Inclusion,* which therefore constitutes a separate category.

78. Generality.—N. general-ity, -ization; universality; catholic-ity, -ism; miscel-lany, -laneousness; drag-net.

every-one, -body; all hands, all the world and his wife; any body, N or M, all sorts; *tout le monde.*

prevalence, run.

V. be -general etc. *adj.;* prevail, obtain, be going about, stalk abroad.

render -general etc. *adj.;* generalize; spread, broadcast.

Adj. general, usual, current, generic, collective; broad, comprehensive, sweeping; encyclopedical, panoramic, widespread etc. (*dispersed*) 73.

universal; catho-lic, -lical; common, world-wide; e-cumenical; transcendental; prevalent, prevailing, rife, epidemic, besetting; all over, covered with.

every, all; indeterminate, indefinite, unspecified, impersonal.

customary etc. (*habitual*) 613.

Adv. what-ever, -soever; to a man, one and all, without exception.

generally etc. *adj.;* always, for better for worse; in general, generally speaking; speaking generally; for the most part; in the long run etc. (*on an average*) 29.

79. Speciality.—N. speciality, *spécialité;* individ-uality, -uity; particularity, pecuiairity;

idiocrasy etc. (*tendency*) 176; personality, characteristic, mannerism, idiosyncrasy, attribute specificness etc. *adj.;* singularity etc. (*unconformity*) 83; reading, version, lection; state; *trait;* distinctive feature; technicality; *differentia.*

particulars, details, minutiae, items, counts.

I, self, I myself, *ego;* my-, him-, her-, it-self.

V. specify, particularize, individualize, realize, specialize, designate, differentiate, determine, define, denote, indicate, itemize, detail.

descend to particulars, enter into detail, come to the point.

Adj. special, particular, individual, specific, proper, personal, intimate, original, private, respective, definite, concrete, determinate, especial, certain, esoteric, endemic, partial, party, peculiar, marked, appropriate, several, characteristic, diagnistic, exact, exclusive; singular etc. (*exceptional*) 83; idiomatic; typical, representative, distinctive.

this, that; yon, -der.

Adv. specially etc. *adj.;* in particular, *in propriâ personâ; ad hominem;* for my part.

each, apiece, one by one; severally, respectively, each to each; *seriatim,* in detail, bit by bit; *pro hac vice,* − *re natâ.*

namely, that is to say, *videlicet,* viz.; to wit.

80. Rule.—N. regularity, uniformity etc. 16; clock-work precision; punctuality etc. (*exactness*) 494; routine etc. (*custom*) 613; formula; system; rut; canon, convention, maxim; rule etc. (*form, regulation*) 697; key-note, standard, model; precedent etc. (*prototype*) 22; conformity etc. 82.

nature, principle; law; order of things; normal −, natural −, ordinary −, model- -state, − condition; standing -dish, − order; normality; Procrustean law; law of the Medes and Persians; hard and fast rule.

Adj. regular, uniform, symmetrical, constant, steady; according to rule etc. (*conformable*) 82; customary etc. 613; orderly etc. 58.

81. Multiformity.—N. multi-, omniformity; variety, diversity; multifariousness etc. *adj.*

Adj. multi-form, -fold, -farious, -generous; multiplex, variform, manifold, many-sided, multiplicate; omni-form, -genous, -farious; polymorphic; protean; heterogeneous, motley, mosaic; epicene, indiscriminate, desultory, irregular, diversified, different, divers; all manner of; of -every description, − all sorts and kinds; *et hoc genus omne;* and what not? *de omnibus rebus et quibusdam aliis.*

82. Conformity.—N. conform-ity, -ance; observance.

naturalization; conventionality etc. (*custom*) 613; agreement etc. 23.

example, instance, specimen, sample, quotation; exemplification, illustration, case in point; object lesson.

conventionalist, formalist, Philistine.

pattern etc. (*prototype*) 22.

V. conform to, − rule; accommodate −, adapt- oneself to; rub off corners.

be -regular etc. *adj.;* move in a groove; follow −, observe −, go by −, bend to −, obey- -rules, − precedents; comply −, tally −, chime in −, fall in-with; be -guided, − regulated- by; fall into a -custom, − usage; follow the -fashion, − multitude; pass muster, do as others do, *hurler aves les loups;* do at Rome as the Romans do; go −, swim- with the -stream, − current, − tide; tread the beaten track etc. (*habit*) 613; rubber-stamp; keep one in countenance.

exemplify, illustrate, cite, quote, put a case; produce an- instance etc. *n.*

Adj. conformable to rule, adaptable, compliant, consistent, agreeable; regular etc. 80; according to -regulation, − rule, − Cocker; *en règle, selon les règles,* well regulated, orderly; symmetric etc. 242.

conventional commonplace etc. (*customary*) 613; of -daily, − every day- occurrence; in the natural order of things; ordinary, common, − or garden, prosaic, habitual, usual.

in the order of the day; naturalized.

typical, normal, formal; canonical, orthodox, sound, strict, rigid, positive, uncompromising, Procrustean; point device.

secundum artem, ship-shape, technical.

exemplary, illustrative, in point.

Adv. conformably etc. *adj.;* by rule; agreeably to; in -conformity, − accordance, − keeping-with; according to; consistently with; as usual, *ad instar, instar omnium; more -solito, − majorum.*

for the sake of conformity; of −, as a matter of- course; *pro formâ,* for form's sake, by the card; according to plan.

invariably etc. (*uniformly*) 16.

for -example, − instance; *exempli gratiâ; e.g.; inter alia.*

Phr. *cela va sans dire, ex pede Herculem, noscitur a sociis.*

83. Unconformity.—**N.** non-conformity etc. 82; un-, dis-conformity; unconventionality, informality, abnormity, anomaly; anomalousness etc. *adj.;* exception, peculiarity, etc. 79; infraction −, breach −, violation −, infringement- of -law, − custom, − usage; eccentricity, *bizarrerie,* oddity, *je ne sais quoi,* monstrosity, rarity; freak of Nature.

individuality, idiosyncrasy, singularity, oritinality, mannerism.

aberration; irregularity; variety; singularity; exemption; salvo etc. (*qualification*) 469.

nonconformist; nondescript, character, original, nonsuch, monster, prodigy, wonder, miracle, curiosity, missing link, flying fish, black swan, *lusus naturae, rara avis,* queer fish; mongrel; half-caste, -blood, -breed; *métis,* cross breed, hybrid, mule, mulatto, sacatra, marabou; *tertium quid,* hermaphrodite, gynander, androgyn.

phoenix, chimera, hydra, sphinx, minotaur; griff-in, -on; centaur; hippogriff, -centaur; sagit-tary; kraken; cockatrice, wyvern, roc, liver, dragon, sea-serpent; mermaid; unicorn; Cyclops, 'men whose heads do grown beneath their shoulders;. Teratolgy.

fish out of water; neither -one thing nor another, − fish flesh nor fowl nor good red her-ring; one in a -way, − thousand; out-cast, -law; Ishmael, pariah; oasis.

V. be -unconformable etc. *adj.;* leave the beaten -track, − path; infringe −, break −, violate- a -law, − habit, − usage, − custom; drive a coach and six through; stretch a point; have no business there; baffle −, beggar- all description.

Adj. unconformable, exceptional; abnorm-al, -ous; anomal-ous, -istic; out of -order, − place, − keeping, − tune, − one's element; irregular, arbitrary; lawless, informal, aberrant, stray, wandering, wanton; peculiar, exclusive, un-natural, eccentric, crotchety, egregious; out of the -beaten track, − common, − common run, − pale of; misplaced; funny.

un-usual, -accustomed, -customary, -wonted, -common; rare, singular, *unique,* curious, odd, extraordinary, strange, monstrous; wonderful etc. 870; unexpected, unaccountable; *outré,* out of the way, remarkable, noteworthy; queer, quaint, nondescript, none such, *sui generis;* original, unconventional, Bohemian, unfashion-able; un-described, -precedented, -paralleled, -exampled, -heard of, -familiar; fantastic, new-fangled, grotesque, *bizarre;* outlandish, exotic, *tombé de nues,* preternatural; denaturalized.

heterogeneious, heteroclite, amorphous, mongrel, amphibious, epicene, half-blood, hybrid; androgyn-ous, -al; unsymmetric etc. 243.

qualified etc. 469.

Adv. unconformably etc. *adj.;* except, unless, save, barring, beside, without, save and except, let alone.

however, yet, but.

Int.-what -on earth! − in the world!

Phr. never was -seen, − heard, − known- the like.

84. Number.—**N.** number, symbol, numeral, figure, cipher, digit, integer; counter; round number; formula; function; series.

sum, total, aggregate, difference, complement, subtrahend; product; multipli-cand, -er, -cator; coefficient, multiple; dividend, divisor, factor, quotient, sub-multiple, fraction; mixed number; numerator, denominator; decimal, circulating decimal, repetend; common measure, aliquot part; reciprocal; prime number; totitive, totient.

permutation, combination, variation; election. ratio, proportion; progression; arithmetical −, geometrical −, harmonical- progression; per-centage.

figurate −, pyramidal −, polygonal- num-bers.

power, root, exponent, index, logarithm, anti-logarithm; modulus.

differential, integral, fluxion, fluent.

Adj. numeral, complementary, divisible, ali-quot, reciprocal, prime, fractional, decimal, figurate, incommensurable.

proportional, exponential, logarithmic, logo-metric, differential, fluxional, integral.

positive, negative; rational, irrational; surd, radical, real, imaginary, impossible.

85. Numeration.—**N.** numeration, numbering etc. *v.;* pagination; tale, tally, recension, enumer-

tion, summation, reckoning, computation, sup-
putation; calcu-lation, -lus; algorithm, rhabdology,
dactylonomy; measurement etc. 466; statistics.

arithmetic, analysis, algebra, fluxions;
differential −, integral −, infinitesimal-calculus;
calculus of differences.

[Statistics] dead reckoning, muster, poll, census, capitation, roll-call, recapitulation; account
etc. (list) 86.

[Operations] notation, addition, subtraction,
multiplication, division, proportion, rule of
three, practice, equations, extraction of roots,
reduction, involution, evolution, approximation,
interpolation, differentiation, integration.

[Instruments] abacus, swan-pan, logometer,
sliding −, slide- rule, tallies, Napier's bones, calculating −, adding- machine, difference engine;
cash register.

arithmetician, calculator, abacist; math-
ematician, actuary, statistician, surveyor,
geodesist.

V. number, count, tell; call −, run- over, take
an account of, enumerate, call the roll, muster,
poll, recite, recapitulate; sum; sum −, cast- up;
tell off, score, cipher, compute, calculate, set a
price, reckon, − up, estimate; suppute, add, sub-
tract, multiply, divide, extract roots.

check, prove, demonstrate, balance, audit,
overhaul, take stock; affix numbers to, page,
foliate, paginate.

amount −, come- to.

Adj. numer-al, -ical; arithmetical, analytic,
algebraic, statistical, numerable, computable,
calculable; commensur-able, -ate; incommen-
sur-able, -ate.

86. List.—N. list, catalogue, enumeration,
inventory, schedule; register etc. (record) 551;
account; bill, − of costs, syllabus; terrier, tally,
file; almanac, calendar, index, table, atlas, contents, card index; rota, ticket; book, ledger;
synopsis, catalogue raisonné; tableau, scroll,
manifest, invoice, bill of lading; prospectus,
programme; bill of fare, menu, carte; score,
census, statistics, returns; Red −, Blue −,
Domesday- book; cadaster; directory, gazetteer,
dictionary, glossary, lexicon, thesaurus, gradus.

roll; check −, chequer −, bead- roll, − of
honor; muster -roll, − book; roster, panel; cartulary, diptych.

V. list, enrol, schedule, register etc. n.; indent,
post, docket; matriculate.

Adj. cadastral, listed etc. v.

87. Unity.—N. unity; oneness etc. adj.; individuality; solitude etc. (seclusion) 893; isolation
etc. (disjunction) 44; unification etc. 48.

one, unit, ace; item; individual; solo, none else,
no other, naught beside.

V. be -one, − alone etc. adj.; dine with Duke
Humphrey.

isolate etc. (disjoin) 44.

render one; unite etc. (join) 43, (combine) 48.

Adj. one, sole, single, solitary, only- begotten;
individual, apart, alone; kithless.

un-accompanied, -attended; solus, single-
handed; singular, odd, unique, unrepeated,
azygous, first and last; isolated etc. (disjoined)
44; insular; unitary.

lone; lone-ly, -some; desolate, dreary.

in-secable, -severable, -discerptible; compact,
irresolvable.

Adv. singly etc. adj.; alone, by itself, per se,
only, apart, in the singular number, in the
abstract; one -by one, − at a time; simply; one
and a half, sesqui-.

Phr. natura il fece, e poi roppe la stampa.

88. Accompaniment.—N. accompaniment; appurtenance, adjunct etc. 39; context.

coexistence, concomitance, company,
association, companionship; part-, copart-ner-
ship; coefficiency.

concomitant, accessory, coefficient; companion, attendant, fellow, associate, consort,
spouse, colleague, fidus Achates; part-, co-partner; satellite, hanger on, shadow; escort, entourage, suite, cortège; convoy, follower etc. 65;
attribute.

V. accompany, coexist, attend, convoy,
chaperon; hang −, wait- on; go hand in hand
with; synchronize etc. 120; bear −, keep- company; row in the same boat; bring in its train,
associate −, couple- with.

Adj. accompanying etc. v.; concomitant,
fellow, twin, joint; associated −, coupled- with;
accessory, attendant, obbligato.

Adv. with, withal; together −, along −, in
company- with; hand in hand, side by side; cheek
by -jowl, − jole; arm in arm; there-, here-with;
and etc. (addition) 37.

together, in a body, collectively.

89. Duality.—N. dual-ity, -ism; duplicity; biplicity, -formity; span, polarity.

two, deuce, couple, couplet, doublet, brace,
pair, cheeks, twins, Castor and Pollus, gemini,
Siamese twins; fellows; yoke, conjugation, dyad,
distich.

V. [unite in pairs] pair, couple, bracket, yoke;
conduplicate, mate.

Adj. two, twain; dual, -istic; binary, binomial;
twin, biparous; dyadic; conduplicate; duplex etc.
90; tête-à-tête; paired; dihedral.

coupled etc. v.; conjugate.

both, − the one and the other.

90. Duplication.—N. duplication, doubling
etc. v.; gemi-, ingemi-nation; reduplication;
iteration etc. (repetition) 104; renewal.

V. double; re-double, -duplicate; geminate;
repeat etc. 104; renew etc. 660; duplicate, copy
etc. 21.

Adj. double; doubled etc. v.; bicameral,
bicapital, bi-fold, -form, -lateral, -farious, -
facial; two-fold, -sided, -headed, -edged etc.;
duplex; double-faced; twin, duplicate, ingem-
inate; second; dual etc. 29.

Adv. twice, once more; over again etc.
(repeatedly) 104; as much again; twofold.

secondly, in the second place, again.

91. Bisection. [Division into two parts.]—N.
bi-section, -partition; di-, subdi-chotomy; halv-
ing etc. v.; dimidiation; hendiadis.

bifurcation, forking, branching, furcation,
ramification, divarication; fork, prong; fold.

half, moiety.

V. bisect, halve, divide, split, cut in two, cleave, dimidiate, dichotomize, divaricate.

go halves, divide with.

separate, fork, bifurcate; branch -off, — out; ramify.

Adj. bisected etc. v.; cloven, cleft; bipartite, biconjugate, bicuspid, bifid; bifur-cous, -cate, -cated; semi-, demi- hemi-.

92. Triality.—N. triality, trinity,* triplicity.

three, triad, triplet, trey, trio, ternion, trinomial, leash; tierce; triennium; trefoil, triangle, trident, tripod, triumvirate, *troika*.

third power, cube.

Adj. three; tri-form, -nal, -nomial; tertiary; triune.

*Trinity is hardly ever used except in a theological sense; see Deity 976.

93. Triplication.—N. tripli-cation, -city; trebleness, trine, trilogy.

V. treble, triple, triplicate, cube.

Adj. treble, triple; tern, -ary; triplex, triplicate, threefold, trilogistic; third; trinal; trihedral.

Adv. three -times, — fold; thrice, in the third place, thirdly; trebly etc. *adj.*

94. Trisection. [Division into three parts.]—N. tri-section, -partition, -chotomy; third, — part.

V. trisect, divide into three parts, trifurcate.

Adj. trifid; trisected etc. v.; tripartite, -chotomous, -sulcate.

95. Quaternity.—N. quaternity, four, tetrad, quartet, quaternion, square, quadrature, quarter, quadruplet; quadrilateral, quadrangle, quatrefoil; *quadriga*.

V. reduce to a square, square.

Adj. four; quat-ernary, -ernal; quadratic; quartile, quartic, tetractic, tetrad, tetrahedral; quadrennial; quadrivalent.

96. Quadruplication.—N. quadruplication.

V. multiply by four, quadruplicate, biquadrate.

Adj. fourfold; quad-ruple, -ruplicate, -rible; quadruplex; fourth.

Adv. four times; in the fourth place, fourthly.

97. Quadrisection. [Division into four parts.]—N. quadri-section, -partition; quartering etc. v.; fourth; quart, -er, -ern; farthing (*i.e.* fourthing); quarto.

V. quarter, divide into four parts, quadrisect.

Adj. quartered etc. v.; quadri-fid, -partite.

98. Five, etc.—N. five, cinque, quint, quincunx, quintuplet, quintet, pentagon, pentameter, Pentateuch; six, half-a-dozen; sextet, hexagon, hexameter; seven, Heptarchy; eight, octet, octagon, octave; nine, three times three; ten, decade; eleven; twelve, dozen; thirteen; long —, baker's-dozen.

twenty, score; twenty-four, four and twenty, two dozen; twenty-five, five and twenty, quarter

of a hundred; forty, two score; fifty, half hundred: sixty, three score, sexagenarian; seventy, three score and ten, septuagenarian; eighty, four score, octogenarian; ninety, four score an ten, nonagenarian.

hundred, centenary, hecatomb, century hundredweight, cwt.; one hundred and forty four, gross; bicentenary, tercentenary etc.

thousand, chiliad; myriad, millennium, te thousand; lac, lakh, one hundred thousand plum; million; thousand million, *milliard*.

billion, trillion etc.

V. centuriate.

Adj. five, quinary, quintuple; fifth; senary sextuple; sixth; seventh; octuple; eighth; nine fold, ninth; tenfold, decimal, denary, decuple tenth; eleventh; duo-denary, -denal; twelfth; i one's 'teens, thirteenth.

vices-, viges-imal; twentieth; twenty-fourt etc. *n*.

cent-uple, -uplicate, -ennial, -enary, -uria secular, hundredth; thousandth; millenary etc.

99. Quinquesection, etc.—N. division by -fiv etc. 98; quinquesection etc.; fifth etc.; decima tion.

V. decimate, quinquesect.

Adj. quinque-fid, -partite; quinquarticula octifid; decimal, tenth, tithe, teind; duodecima twelfth; sexagesimal, -genary; hundredth centesimal; millesimal etc.

100. Plurality. [More than one.]—N. plurality a -number; — certain number; one or two, two o three etc.; a few, several; multitude etc. 102.

Adj. plural, more than one, upwards of, some certain; not -alone etc. 87.

Adv. *et cetera, etc.*, etc.

Phr. *non deficit alter.*

100a. Fraction [Less than one.]—N. fraction fractional part, fragment; part etc. 51.

Adj. fractional, fragmentary, partial.

101. Zero.—N. zero, nothing, naught, nought duck's egg, goose egg; cipher, none, nobody not a soul; *âme qui vive*; absence etc. 187 unsubstantiality etc. 4.

Adj. not -one, — any.

102. Multitude.—N. multitude; numerousnes etc. *adj.*; numer-osity, -ality; multiplicity; profu sion etc. (*plenty*) 639; legion, host; great —, large —, round —, enormous- number; a quantity numbers, array, sight, army, sea, galaxy; scores peck, bushel, school, shoal, swarm, draft, bevy cloud, flock, herd, drove, flight, covey, hive brood, litter, farrow, fry, nest; mob, crowd etc (*assemblage*) 72; lots, loads, heaps; all the worl and his wife.

[Increase of number] greater number, ma jority; multiplicity, multiple.

V. be -numerous etc. *adj.*; swarm —, teem — crawl —, creep -with; crowd, swarm, come thic upon; outnumber, multiply; people; swarm like locusts, — bees.

Adj. many, several, sundry, divers, various

not a few; a -hundred, − thousand, − myriad, − million, − thousand and one; some -ten or a dozen, − forty or fifty etc.; half a -dozen, − hundred etc.; very −, full −, ever so- many; numer-ous, -ose; profuse, in profusion; manifold, multiplied, multitudinous, multiferous, multiple, multinomial, teeming, crawling, populous, peopled, crowded, thick, studded; galore.

thick coming, many more, more than one can tell, a world of; no end -of, − to; *cum multis aliis*; thick as -hops, − hail; plenty as blackberries; numerous as the -stars in the firmament, − sands on the sea-shore, − hairs on the head; and -what not, − heaven knows what; endless etc. (*infinite*) 105.

Phr. their name is 'Legion.'

103. Fewness.—N. fewness etc. *adj.*; paucity, small number; small quantity etc. 32; scarcity, sparsity; rarity; infrequency etc. 137; handfull; maniple; minority, exiguity.
[Diminution of number] reduction; weeding etc. *v.*; elimination, sarculation, decimation.

V. be -few etc. *adj.*
render -few etc. *adj.*; reduce, diminish the number, weed; eliminate, thin, decimate.

Adj. few; scarce; scant, -y; thin, rare, thinly scattered, few and far between; exiguous; infrequent etc. 137; *rari nantes*; hardly −, scarcely- any; to be counted on one's fingers; reduced etc. *v.*; unrepeated.

Adv. here and there.

104. Repetition.—N. repetition, iteration, reiteration, duplication, ding-dong, alliteration; *epistrophe;* harping, recurrence, succession, run; batto-, tauto-logy; monotony, tautophony; rhythm etc. 138; pleonasm, redundancy, diffuseness.

chimes, repetend, echo, *ritornello*, burden of a song, *refrain;* rehearsal; encore; *réchauffé, rifacimento,* recapitulation.

cuckoo etc. (*imitation*) 19; reverberation etc. 408; drumming etc. (*roll*) 407; renewal etc. (*restoration*) 660.

twice-told tale; old -story, − song, chestnut; second −, new- edition; reprint, new impression; return game, return match, reappearance, reproduction; periodicity etc. 138.

V. repeat, iterate, reiterate, reproduce, parrot, echo, re-echo, drum, harp upon, battologize, hammer, redouble.

recur, revert, return, reappear; renew etc. (*restore*) 660.

rehearse; do −, say- over again; ring the changes on; harp on the same string; din −, drum- in the ear; conjugate in all its moods, tenses and inflexions, begin again, go over the same ground, go the same round, never hear the last of; resume, return to, recapitulate, reword.

Adj. repeated etc. *v.*; repetition-al, -ary; recurrent, -ring; ever recurring, thick coming, frequent, incessant, redundant, pleonastic, tautological.

monotonous, harping, iterative; mocking, chiming; retold; aforesaid, -named; above-mentioned, said; habitual etc. 613; another.

Adv. repeatedly, often, again, afresh, anew, over again, once more; ditto, *encore, de novo, bis, da capo.*

again and again; over and over, − again; many times over; time- and again, − after time; year after year; day by day etc.; many −, several −, a number of- times; many −, full many- a time; times out of number, year in and year out, morning, noon and night; frequently etc. 136.

Phr. *ecce iterum Crispinus, toujours perdrix,* cut and come again; 'tomorrow and tomorrow.'

105. Infinity.—N. infini-ty, -tude, -teness etc. *adj.;* perpetuity etc. 112.

V. be -infinite etc. *adj.;* know −, have- no -limits, − bounds; go on for ever.

Adj. infinite, immense; number-, count-, sum-, measure-less; innumer-, immeasur-, incalcul-, illimit-, intermin-, unfathom-, unapproach-able; exhaustless, inexhaustible, indefinite; without -number, − measure, − limit, − end; incomprehensible; limit-, end-, bound-, termless; un-told, -numbered, -measured, -bounded, -limited; il-limited; perpetual etc. 112.

Adv. infinitely etc. *adj.; ad infinitum.*

106. Time.—N. time, duration; period, term, stage, space, span, spell, season; the whole -time, − period; course etc. 109.

intermediate, time, while, *interim,* interval, bit, pendency; inter-vention, -mission, -mittence, -regnum, -lude; respite.

era, epoch, eon, cycle; time of life, age, year, date; decade etc. (*period*) 108; moment, etc. (*instant*) 113; reign etc. 737.

glass −, ravages −, whirligig −, noiseless foot- of time; scythe.

V. continue, last, endure, go on, hold out, remain, stay, persist, abide, run; intervene; elapse etc. 109.

take −, take up −, fill −, occupy- time.

pass −, pass away −, spend −, while away −, consume −, talk against −, kill- time; tide over; use −, employ- time; tarry etc. 110; seize an opportunity etc. 134; waste time etc. (*be inactive*) 683.

Adj. continuing etc. *v.;* on foot; permanent etc. (*durable*) 110.

Adv. while, whilst, during, pending; during the -time, − interval; in the course of; for the time being, day by day; in the time of, when; meantime, -while; in the -meantime, − *interim; ad interim, pendente lite; de die in diem;* from -day to day, − hour to hour etc.; hourly, always; for a -time, − season; till, until, up to, yet; the whole −, all the- time; all along; throughout etc. (*completely*) 52, for good etc. (*diuturnity*) 110.

here-, there-, where-upon; then; *anno, − Domini;* A.D.; *ante Christum;* A.C.; before Christ; B.C.; *anno urbis conditae;* A.U.C.; *anno regni,* A.R.; once upon a time, one fine morning.

Phr. time -runs, − runs against; *tempus fugit.*

107. Neverness.—N. 'neverness;' absence of time, no time; *dies non;* Tib's eve; Greek Kal-ends.

Adv. never; at no -time, − period; on no occasion, never in all one's born days, nevermore, *sine die.*

108. Period. [Definite duration, or portion of time.]—N. period; second, minute, hour, day, week, sennight, octave, month, moon, quarter, semester, year, *lustrum, quinquennium*, decade, *decennium*, indiction, lifetime, generation, epoch, era, cycle.

century, age, *millennium; annus magnus.*

Adj. horary; hourly, annual etc. (*periodical*) 138.

108a. Contingent Duration.—**Adv.** during - pleasure, — good behavior; *quamdiu se bene gesserit.*

109. Course. [Indefinite duration.]—N. course —, progress —, process —, succession —, lapse —, flow —, flux —, effluxion, stream —, tract —, current —, sweep —, tide —, march —, step —, flight- of time; duration etc. 106.

[Indefinite time] aorist.

V. elapse, lapse, flow, run, proceed, advance, pass; roll —, wear —, press —, drag- on; flit, fly, slip, slide, glide, crawl; run -its course.

out; expire; go —, pass- by; be -past etc. 122.

Adj. elapsing etc. *v.;* aoristic; progressive, transient etc. 111.

Adv. in due -time, — season; in -course, — process, — the fulness- of time; in time.

Phr. *labitur et labetur; truditur dies die; fugaces labuntur anni;* 'tomorrow and tomorrow and tomorrow creeps in this petty pace from day to day.'

110. Diuturnity. [Long duration.]—N. diuturnity; a -long —, length of -time; an age, a century, an eternity, aeons; slowness etc. 275; perpetuity etc. 112; blue moon.

dura-bleness, -bility; persistence, lastingness etc. *adj.;* continuance, assiduity, endurance, standing; permanence etc. (*stability*) 150; survival, -vance; longevity etc. (*age*) 128; distance of time.

protraction —, prolongation —, extension- of time; delay etc. (*lateness*) 133.

V. last, endure, stand, remain, abide, continue, brave a thousand years.

tarry etc. (*be late*) 133; drag -on, — its slow length along, — a lengthening chain; protract, prolong; spin —, eke —, draw —, lengthen- out; temporize; gain —, make —, talk against- time.

out-last, -live; survive; live to fight again.

Adj. durable; perdurable; lasting etc. *v.;* of long -duration, — standing; permanent, chronic, long-standing; intransi-ent, -tive; intransmutable, persistent; life-, live-long; longeval, long-lived, macrobiotic, diuturnal, sempervirent, evergreen, perennial; unin-, ter-, unremitting; perpetual etc. 112.

lingering, protracted, prolonged, spun out etc. *v.;* long-pending, -winded; slow etc. 275.

Adv. long; for -a long time, — an age, — ages, — ever so long, — many a long day; long ago etc. (*in a past time*) 122; *longo intervallo.*

all the -day long, — year round; the livelong day, as the day is long, morning, noon and night; hour after hour, day after day, etc.; for good; permanently etc. *adj.*

111. Transientness. [Short duration.]—N. transientness etc. *adj.;* evanescence, impermanence, fugacity, transitoriness, volatility, caducity, mortality, span; flash in the pan, nine days' wonder, bubble, May-fly; spurt; temporary arrangement, interregnum.

velocity etc. 274; suddenness etc. 113; changeableness etc. 149.

V. be -transient etc. *adj.;* flit, pass away, fly, gallop, vanish, fade, fleet, melt away, evaporate; pass away like a -cloud, — summer cloud, — shadow, — dream.

Adj. transi-ent, -tory; passing, evanescent, fleeting; flying etc. *v.;* fug-acious, -itive; shifting, slippery; spasmodic.

tempor-al, -ary; provis-ional, -ory; cursory, short-lived, ephemeral, deciduous; perishable, mortal, precarious; impermanent.

brief, quick, brisk; cometary, meteoric, extemporaneous, summary; pressed for time etc. (*haste*) 684; sudden, momentary etc. (*instantaneous*) 113.

Adv. temporarily etc. *adj.; pro tempore;* for - the moment, — a time; awhile, *en passant, in transitu;* in a short time; soon etc. (*early*) 132; briefly etc. *adj.;* at short notice; on the -point, — eve -of; *in articulo;* between cup and lip.

Phr. one's days are numbered; the time is up; her to-day and gone tomorrow; *non semper erit aestas; eheu! fugaces labuntur anni; sic transit gloria mundi.*

112. Perpetuity. [Endless duration.]—N. perpetuity, eternity, timelessness; everness, aye, sempiternity, immortality, athanasia; everlastingness etc. *adj.;* perpetuation; infinite duration.

V. last —, endure —, go on- for ever; have no end.

eternize, eternify, perpetuate, immortalize.

Adj. perpetual, eternal, eterne; everlasting, - living, -flowing; continual, constant, sempiternal; co-eternal; endless, unending; ceaseless, incessant, uninterrupted, indesinent, unceasing; interminable, having no end; unfading, evergreen, amaranthine; neverending, -dying, -fading; deathless, immortal, undying, imperishable.

Adv. perpetually etc. *adj.;* always, ever, evermore, aye; for -ever, — aye, — evermore, — ever and a day, —, ever and ever; in all ages, from age to age; without end; world —, time- without end; *in saecula saeculorum;* to the -end of time, — crack of doom, — 'last syllable of recorded time;' till doomsday; constantly etc. (*very frequently*) 136.

Phr. *esto perpetuum; labitur et labetur in omne volubilis aevum.*

113. Instantaneity. [Point of time.]—N. instantane-ity, -ousness; sudden-, abrupt-ness.

moment, instant, second, minute; twinkling, trice, flash, breath, crack, jiffy, *coup*, burst, flash of lightning, stroke of time.

epoch, time; time of -day, — night; hour, minute; very -minute etc., — time, — hours; present —, right —, true —, exact —, correct-time.

V. be -instantaneous etc. *adj.;* twinkle, flash.

Adj. instantaneous, momentary, extempore, sudden, instant, abrupt; subitaneous, hasty; quick as- thought,* — lightning, — a flash; rapid as electricity.

Adv. instantaneously etc. *adj.*; in — in less than-no time; *presto, subito, instanter,* suddenly, at a stroke, like- a shot, — greased lightning; in a trice, in a moment etc. *n.*; eftsoons, in the twinkling of - an eye, — a bed post; at one jump, in the same breath, *per saltum, uno saltu*; at —, all at- once; in one's tracks; plump, slap; 'at one fell swoop;' at the same -instant etc. *n.*; immediately etc. (*early*) 132; *ex tempore*, on the -spot, — spur of the moment, — dot; just then; slap- dash etc. (*haste*) 684; before you could -turn round, — say -knife, — Jack Robinson.

Phr. touch and go; no sooner said than done.

*See note on 264.

114. Chronometry. [Estimation, measurement, and record of time.]—**N.** chrono-, horo-metry, -logy; date, epoch; style, era.

almanac, calendar, ephemeris; register, -try; chronicle, annals, journal, diary, chronogram.

[Instruments for the measurement of time] clock, watch; chrono-meter, -scope, -graph; repeater, alarum; time-keeper, -piece; dial, sundial, *gnomon, pendule,* horologe, pendulum, hourglass, water clock, clepsydra.

mean —, Greenwich —, solar —, sidereal —, local —, summer- time; daylight saving.

chrono-grapher, -loger, -logist; annalist.

V. fix —, mark- the time; date, register, chronicle; measure —, beat —, mark- time; bear date.

Adj. chrono-logical, -metrical, -grammatical; isochronal.

Adv. o'clock; *a.m., p.m.*

115. Anachronism. [False estimate of time.]—**N.** ana-, meta-, para-, prochronism; *prolepsis,* misdate; anticipation, antichronism.

disregard —, neglect —, oblivion- of time.

intempestivity etc. 135.

V. mis-, ante-, post-, over-date; anticipate; take no note of time.

Adj. misdated etc. *v.;* undated; overdue; out of date; anachronous etc. *n.*

116. Priority.—**N.** priority, antecedence, anteriority, pre-existence, precedence etc. 62; precession etc. 280; precursor etc. 64; the past etc. 122; premises.

V. precede, come before; forerun; antecede, go before etc. (*lead*) 280; pre-exist; dawn; premise, presage etc. 511.

be -beforehand etc. (*be early*) 132; steal a march upon, anticipate, forestall; have —, gain-the start.

Adj. prior, previous; preced-ing, -ent; anterior, antecedent; pre-existing, -existent; foresighted; former, foregoing; afore —, before-, above-mentioned; aforesaid, said; introductory etc. (*precursory*) 64; pre-war.

Adv. before, prior to; earlier; previously etc. *adj.;* afore, ere, theretofore, erewhile, ere —, before- -then, — now; erewhile, already, yet, beforehand; aforetime; on the eve of, in anticipation.

117. Posteriority.—**N.** posteriority; succession, sequence; following etc. 281; subsequence,

supervention; futurity etc. 121; successor; sequel etc. 65; remainder, reversion.

V. follow etc. 281 —, come —, go- after; ensue, result; succeed, supervene; step into the shoes of.

Adj. subsequent, posterior, following, after, later, succeeding, postliminious, postnate; successive etc. 63; postdiluvial, -an; *puisné;* posthumous; post-war, future etc. 121.

Adv. subsequently, after, afterwards, since, later; at a -subsequent, — later- period; next, in the sequel, close upon, thereafter; thereupon, upon which, eftsoons; from that -time, — moment; after a -while, — time; in process of time.

postcenal, postcibal, postprandial, afterdinner.

118. The Present Time.—**N.** the present -time, — day, — moment, — juncture, — occasion; the times, existing time, time being; twentieth century; nonce, crisis, epoch, day, hour.

age, time of life.

Adj. present, actual, instant, current, latest, existing, that is.

Adv. at this -time, — moment etc. 113; at the -present time etc. *n.;* now, at present.

at this time of day, to-day, now-adays; already; even —, but —, just-now; on the present occasion; for the -time being, — nonce; *pro hâc vice;* on the -nail, — spot; on the spur of the -moment, — occasion.

until now; to -this, — the present day.

119. Different Time. [Time different from the present.]—**N.** different —, other- time.

[Indefinite time] aorist.

Adj. aoristic.

Adv. at that —, at which- -time, — moment, — instant; then, on that occasion, upon.

when; when-ever, -soever; upon which, on which occasion; at -another, — a different, — some other, — any - time; at various times; some —, one- -of these days, — fine morning, — day; sooner or later; some time or other; once upon a time, once.

120. Synchronism.—**N.** synchronism; coexistence, coincidence; simultaneousness etc. *adj.;* concurrence, concomitance, unity of time, interim.

[Having equal times] isochronism, syntony.

contemporary, coetanian.

V. coexist, concur, accompany, go hand in hand, keep pace with; synchronize, isochronize.

Adj. synchron-ous, -al, -ical, -istical; simultaneous, coexisting, coincident, concomitant, concurrent; coev-al, -ous; contempora-ry, -neous; coetaneous; coterminous, coeternal; isochronous.

Adv. at the same time; simultaneously etc. *adj.;* together, in concert, during the same time; in the same breath; *pari passu;* in the interim.

at the -very moment etc. 113; just as, as soon as; meanwhile etc. (*while*) 106.

121. Futurity. [Prospective time.]—**N.** futurity, -ition; future, hereafter, time to come; approaching —, coming —, after- -time, — age, — days, — hours, — years, — ages, — life;

morrow, to-morrow, by and by: millennium, doomsday, day of judgment, crack of doom, remote future.

approach of time, advent, time drawing on, womb of time; destiny etc. 152; eventuality.*

heritage, heirs, posterity, descendants.

prospect etc. (*expectation*) 507; foresight etc. 510.

V. look forwards; anticipate etc. (*expect*) 507, (*foresee*) 510; forestall etc. (*be early*) 132.

come −, draw- on; draw near; approach, await, threaten; impend etc. (*be destined*) 152.

Adj. future, to come; coming etc. (*impending*) 152; next, near; near −, close- at hand; eventual, ulterior; expectant, prospective, in prospect etc. (*expectation*) 507.

Adv. prospectively, hereafter, on the knees of the gods, in future; to-morrow, the day after to-morrow; in -course, − process, − the fulness- of time; eventually, ultimately, sooner or later; *proximo; paulo post futurum;* in after time; one of these days; after a -time, − while.

from this time; hence-forth, -forwards; thence; thence-forth, -forward; whereupon, upon which.

soon etc. (*early*) 132; on the -eve, − point, − brink- of; about to; close upon.

122. Preterition. [Retrospective time.]—**N.** preterition, priority etc. 116; the past, past time; days −, times- -of yore, − of old, − past, − gone by; bygone days, good old days; old −, ancient −, former -times; fore time; yesterdays; the olden −, good old- time; auld lang syne; eld.

antiquity, antiqueness, *status quo;* time im-memorial; distance of time; remote -age, − time; ancient history; remote past; rust of antiquity; ancientness.

pale-ontology, -ography, -ology; palaetiol-ogy,* archaeology; archaism, antiquarianism, mediaevalism, pre- Raphaelitism; retrospection, looking back, memory etc. 505.

laudator temporis acti; mediaevalist, pre-Raphaelite; antiqu-ary, -arian; archaeologist etc.; Oldbuck, Dryasdust.

ancestry etc. (*paternity*) 166.

V. be -past etc. *adj.;* have -expired etc. *adj.;* − run its course, − had its day; pass; pass −, go- - by, − away, − off; lapse, blow over.

look −, trace −, cast the eyes- back; exhume.

Adj. past, gone, gone by, over, passed away, bygone, foregone; elapsed, lapsed, preterlapsed, expired, no more, run out, blown over, that has been, whilom, extinct, never to return, exploded, forgotten, irrecoverable; obsolete etc. (*old*) 124; extinct as the dodo.

former, pristine, *quondam, ci-devant,* late; ancestral.

foregoing; last, latter; recent, overnight; past, preterite, preter-perfect, -pluperfect, past perfect.

looking back etc. *v.;* retro-spective, -active; archaelogical etc. *n.*

Adv. formerly; of -old, −yore; erst, whilom, erewhile, time was, ago, over; in -the olden time etc. *n.;* anciently, long -ago, − since; a long - while, − time- ago; years −, ages-ago; some time -ago, − since, − back.

yesterday, the day before yesterday; last -year, − season, − month etc.; *ultimo,* lately etc. (*newly*) 123.

retrospectively; ere −, before −, till- now; hitherto, heretofore; no longer; once, − upon a time; from time immemorial; in the memory of man; time out of mind; already, yet, up to this time; *ex post facto.*

Phr. time was; the time -has, − hath- been.
Whewell.

123. Newness.—N. newness etc. *adj.;* neologism, neoterism; novelty, recency; im-maturity; youth etc. 127; gloss of novelty.

innovation; renovation etc. (*restoration*) 660.

modernist, neologist, neoteric.

modernism, modernity; mushroom; latest fashion, *dernier cri.*

upstart, *parvenu, nouveau riche.*

V. renew etc. (*restore*) 660; modernize.

Adj. new, novel, recent, fresh, green; young etc. 127; evergreen; raw, immature; virgin; un-tried, -handseled, -used, -trodden, -beaten; fledgling.

late, modern, neoteric; new-born, -fashioned, -fangled, -fledged; of yesterday; just out, brand −, span-new, up to date, topical; vernal, renovated; innovatory.

fresh as -a rose, − a daisy, − paint; spick and span.

Adv. newly etc. *adj.;* afresh, anew, lately, just now, only yesterday, the other day; latterly, of late.

not long −, a short time- ago.

124. Oldness.—N. oldness etc. *adj.;* age, antiq-uity; cobwebs of antiquity.

maturity, ripeness; decline, decay; senility etc. 128.

seniority, eldership, primogeniture.

archaism etc. (*the past*) 122; thing −, relic- of the past; megatherium.

tradition, prescription, custom, folklore, im-memorial usage, common law.

V. be -old etc. *adj.;* have -had, − seen- its day; become -old etc. *adj.;* age, fade.

Adj. old, olden, ancient, antique; of long standing, time-honored, venerable; eld-er, -est; first-born.

prime; prim-itive, -eval, -igenous; primordi-al, -nate; aboriginal etc. (*beginning*) 66; diluvian, antediluvian; pre-historic; patriarchal; preadamite; paleocrystic; fossil, paleozoic, pre-glacial, ante-mundane; archaic, classic, mediaeval, pre-Raphaelite, ancestral, black-letter.

immemorial, traditional, prescriptive, customary, whereof the memory of man runneth not to the contrary; inveterate, rooted.

antiquated, of other times, rococo, of the old school, after-age, obsolete; fusty, moth-eaten; out of -date, − fashion; stale, old-fashioned, behind the -age, − times; exploded; gone out, − by; *passé,* outworn, run out; disused; senile etc. 128; time-worn; crumbling etc. (*deteriorated*) 659; second-hand.

old as -the hills, − Methuselah, − Adam, − history.

Adv. since the -world was made, − year one, − days of Methuselah.

125. Morning. [Noon.]—**N.** morning, morn, matins, forenoon, *a.m.,* prime, dawn, daybreak, daylight, sun-up, peep −, break- of day; aurora,

Eos; first blush —, prime- of the morning;
twilight, crepuscule, sunrise, cockcrow.

spring; vernal equinox.

noon; mid-, noon-day; noontide, meridian,
prime.

summer, midsummer; summer solstice.

Adj. matin, matutinal; vernal, aestival.

Adv. at -sunrise etc. *n.*; with the lark, when the
morning dawns.

126. Evening. [Midnight.]—N. evening, eve;
decline —, fall —, close- of day; eventide,
evensong, vespers; candlelight; nightfall, curfew,
dusk, twilight, blind man's holiday; eleventh
hour; sun-set, -down; going down of the sun,
cock-shut, dewy eve, gloaming, bed-time.

afternoon, *post meridiem, p.m.*

autumn; fall, — of the leaf; autumnal equinox,
Indian summer, harvest-time.

midnight; dead —, witching time- of night;
winter, — solstice.

Adj. vespertine, autumnal, nocturnal, wintry,
brumal, hiemal.

127. Youth.—N. youth; juven- -ility, -escence;
juniority; infancy; baby-, child-, boy-, girl-,
youth-hood; *incunabula;* minority, immaturity,
nonage, teens, tender age, bloom.

cradle, nursery, leading-strings, pupilage,
puberty, *pucelage.*

prime —, flower —, spring-tide —, seedtime —,
golden season - of life; heyday of youth, school
days; rising generation, younger generation.

Adj. young, youthful, juvenile, green, callow,
budding, sappy, *puisné,* beardless, unfledged,
unripe, under age, in one's teens; *in statu
pupillari;* younger, junior.

128. Age.—N. age; oldness etc. *adj.;* old —,
advanced- age; sen-ility, -escence; years, anility,
grey hairs, climacteric, grand climacteric, declining years, decrepitude, hoary age, caducity,
superannuation; second childhood, -ishness;
dotage; vale of years, decline of life, 'sear and
yellow leaf;' three-score years and ten; green old
age, ripe old age; longevity; time of life.

seniority, eldership; elders etc. (*veteran*) 130;
firstling; *doyen,* dean, father; primogeniture;
nostology.

V. be -aged etc. *adj.;* grow —, get- old etc. *adj.;*
age; decline, wane.

Adj. aged; old etc. 124; elderly, senile;
matronly, anile; in years; ripe, mellow, run to
seed, declining, waning, past one's prime; grey, -
headed; hoar, -y; venerable, time-worn, antiquated, *passé,* effete, doddering, decrepit, super-
annuated; advanced in -life, — years; stricken in
years; wrinkled, marked with the crow's foot;
having one foot in the grave; doting etc.
(*imbecile*) 499.

old-, eld-er, -est; senior; first-born.

turned of, years old; of a certain age, no
chicken, old as Methuselah; gerontic; ancestral,
patriarchal etc. (*ancient*) 124.

129. Infant.—N. infant, babe, baby; nurse-,
suck-, year-, wean-ling; *papoose, bambino.*

child, bairn, little- one, — tot, — mite, chick,
brat, chit, pickaninny, kid, urchin; bant-, brat-
ling; elf.

youth, boy, lad, slip, sprig, stripling,
youngster, cub, unlicked cub, younker, callant,
whipster, whipper-snapper, schoolboy,
hobbledehoy, hopeful, cadet, minor, master.

scion; sap-, seed-ling; tendril, olive branch,
nestling, chicken, duckling; larva, caterpillar,
chrysalis, cocoon; tadpole, whelp, cub, pullet,
fry, callow; codlin, -g; *foetus,* calf, colt, pup, foal,
kitten; lamb, -kin.

girl; lass, -ie; wench, miss, damsel, *demoiselle,*
damozel; maid, -en; virgin; nymph; colleen;
minx, baggage, school-girl; tomboy, flapper,
hoyden.

Adj. infant-ine, -ile; puerile; boy-, girl-, child-,
baby-, kitten-ish; baby; new-born, unfledged,
new-fledged, callow.

in -the cradle, — swaddling clothes, — long
clothes, — arms, — leading strings; at the breast;
in one's teens; young etc. 127.

130. Veteran.—N. veteran, old man, seer,
patriarch, greybeard, dugout, grand-father, -sire;
grandam, beldam; gaffer, gammer; hag, crone;
pantaloon; sexage-, octoge-, nonage-, cente-nar-
ian; old stager; dotard etc. 501.

preadamite, Methuselah, Nestor, Rip van
Winkle, old Parr; elders; forefathers etc. (*paternity*) 166.

131. Adolescence.—N. adolescence, pubes-
cence, majority; adultness etc. *adj.;* manhood,
virility, maturity; flower of age; prime —,
meridian- of life.

man etc. 373; woman etc. 374; adult, no
chicken.

V. come -of age, — to man's estate, — to years
of discretion; attain majority, assume the *toga
virilis;* have -cut one's eye-teeth, — sown one's
wild oats, settle down.

Adj. adolescent, pubescent, of age; of -full, —
ripe- age; out of one's teens, grown up, mature,
full- blown, — grown, in one's prime, in full
bloom, manly, virile, adult; womanly, matronly;
marriageable, nubile.

132. Earliness.—N. earliness etc. *adj.;* morning etc. 125.

punctuality; promptitude etc. (*activity*) 682;
haste etc. (*velocity*) 274; suddenness etc. (*instantaneity*) 113.

prematurity, precocity, precipitation, anticipation; prevenience, a stitch in time.

V. be -early etc. *adj.;* — beforehand etc. *adv.;*
keep time, take time by the forelock, anticipate,
forestall; have —, gain- the start; steal a march
upon; gain time, draw on futurity; bespeak,
secure, engage, pre-engage.

accelerate; expedite etc. (*quicken*) 274; make
haste etc. (*hurry*) 684.

Adj. early, prime, timely, in time, punctual,
forward; prompt etc. (*active*) 682; summary.

premature, precipitate, precocious; prevenient, anticipatory; rathe.

sudden etc. (*instantaneous*) 113; unexpected
etc. 508; impending, imminent; near, — at hand;
immediate.

Adv. early, soon, anon, betimes, rathe; eft, - soons; ere −, before- long; punctually etc. *adj.;* to the minute; in time; in -good, − military, − pudding, − due- time; time enough.

beforehand; prematurely etc. *adj.;* precipitately etc. *(hastily)* 684; too soon; before -its, − one's- time; in anticipation; unexpectedly etc. 508.

suddenly etc. *(instantaneously)* 113; before one can say 'Jack Robinson,' at short notice, extempore; on the spur of the -moment, − occasion; at once; on the -spot, − instant; at sight; off −, out of- hand; *à vue d'oeil;* straight, - way, -forth; forthwith, incontinently, summarily, instanter, immediately, briefly, shortly, quickly, speedily, apace, before the ink is dry, almost immediately, presently, at the first opportunity, in no long time, by and by, in a while, directly.

Phr. touch and go, no sooner said than done.

133. Lateness.—N. lateness etc. *adj.;* tardiness etc. *(slowness)* 275.

de-lay, -lation; cunctation, procrastination; detention; deferring etc. *v.;* filibuster, postponement, adjournment, prorogation, retardation, respite, reprieve, stay; protraction, prolongation, moratorium; contango; demurrage; remand; Fabian policy, *médecine expectante,* chancery suit; leeway; high time.

V. be -late etc. *adj.;* tarry, wait, stay, bide, take time; dawdle etc. *(be inactive)* 683; linger, loiter, saunter, lag behind; bide −, take- one's time; hang -about, − around, − back, − in the balance; gain time; hang fire; stand −, lie-over.

put off, defer, delay, lay over, suspend; shift −, stave- off; waive, retard, remand, postpone, adjourn; procrastinate; dally; prolong, protract; spin −, draw −, lengthen- out; prorogue; keep back; tide over; push −, drive- to the last; let the matter stand over; reserve etc. *(store)* 636; temporize; consult one's pillow, sleep upon it.

shelve, table, lay on the table.

lose an opportunity etc. 135; be kept waiting, dance attendance; kick −, cool- one's heels; *faire antichambre;* wait impatiently; await etc. *(expect)* 507; sit up, − at night.

Adj. late, tardy, slow, behindhand, belated, postliminious, posthumous, backward, unpunctual; dilatory etc. *(slow),* overdue 275; delayed etc. *v.;* in abeyance.

Adv. late; late-, back-ward; late in the day; at - sunset, − the eleventh hour, − length, − last, − long; ultimately; after −, behind- time; too late; too late for etc. 135.

slowly, leisurely, deliberately, at one's leisure; *ex post facto; sine die.*

Phr. *nonum prematur in annum.*

134. Occasion.—N. occasion, opportunity, opening, room, scope, field; suitable −, proper- time, − season; high time; opportuneness etc. *adj.;* tempestivity.

crisis, turn, juncture, emergency, conjuncture; turning point; given time.

nick of time; golden −, well-timed −, fine −, favorable- opportunity; clear stage, fair field; *mollia tempora; fata Morgana;* spare time etc. *(leisure)* 685.

V. seize etc. *(take)* 789 −, use etc. 677 −, give etc. 784- an -opportunity, − occasion; improve the occasion.

suit the occasion etc. *(be expedient)* 646.

strike the iron while it is hot, *battre le fer sur l'enclume,* make hay while the sun shines, take time by the forelock, *prendre la balle au bond.*

Adj. opportune, timely, well-timed, timeous, timeful, seasonable.

providential, lucky, fortunate, happy, favorable, propitious, auspicious, critical; suitable etc. 23; *obiter dicta.*

Adv. opportunely etc. *adj. ;* in -proper, − due- -time, − course, − season; for the nonce; in the - nick, − fulness- of time; all in good time; just in time, at the eleventh hour, now or never.

by the -way, − by; *en passant, à propos; pro re natâ, − hac vice; par parenthèse,* parenthetically, by way of parenthesis; while -speaking of, − on this subject; *ex tempore;* on the spur of the -moment, − occasion; on the spot etc. *(early)* 132.

Phr. *carpe diem; occasionem cognosce;* one's hour is come, the time is up; that reminds me.

135. Intempestivity.—N. intempestivity; unseasonableness; unsuitable −, improper-time; unreasonableness etc. *adj.;* evil hour; *contretemps;* intrusion; anachronism etc. 115.

V. be -ill timed etc. *adj.;* mistime, intrude, come amiss, break in upon; have other fish to fry; be -busy, − engaged, − tied up, − occupied.

lose −, throw away −, waste −, neglect etc. 460- an opportunity; allow −, suffer- the - opportunity, − occasion- to -pass, − slip, − go by, − escape, − lapse; waste time etc. *(be inactive)* 683; let slip through the fingers, lock the stable door when the steed is stolen.

Adj. ill-, mis-timed; untimely, intrusive, unseasonable; out of -date, − season; inopportune, timeless, untoward, *mal à propos,* unlucky, inauspicious, unpropitious, unfortunate, unfavorable; unsuited etc. 24; inexpedient etc. 647.

unpunctual etc. *(late)* 133; too late for; premature etc. *(early)* 132; too soon for; wise after the event.

Adv. inopportunely etc. *adj.;* as ill luck would have it, in an evil hour, the time having gone by, a day after the fair.

Phr. after meat mustard, after death the doctor.

136. Frequency.—N. frequency, oftness; repetition, etc. 104.

V. recur etc. 104; do nothing but; keep, − on.

Adj. frequent, many times, not rare, thickcoming, incessant, perpetual, continual, constant, recurrent, repeated etc. 104; habitual etc. 613; hourly, etc. 138.

Adv. often, often to be met with, oft; oft-, often-times; frequently; repeatedly etc. 104; un-seldom, not unfrequently; in -quick, − rapid- succession; many a time and oft; daily, hourly etc.; every -day, − hour, − moment etc.

perpetually, continually, constantly, incessantly, without ceasing, at all times, daily and hourly, night and day, day and night, day after day, morning, noon and night, ever and anon.

most often; commonly etc. *(habitually)* 613.

sometimes, occasionally, at times, now and then, from time to time, there being times when, *toties quoties*, often enough, again and again etc. 104.

137. Infrequency.—N. infrequency, infrequence, rareness, rarity; fewness etc. 103; seldomness, uncommonness.

V. be -rare etc. *adj.*

Adj. un-, in-frequent; uncommon, sporadic, rare, — as a blue diamond; few etc. 103; scarce; almost unheard of, unprecedented, which has not occurred within the memory of the oldest inhabitant, not within one's previous experience.

Adv. seldom, rarely, scarcely, hardly; not often, unfrequently, infrequently, unoften; scarcely —, hardly- ever; once in a blue moon.

once; once -for all, — in a way; *pro hac vice;* like angels' visits, few and far between.

138. Regularity of recurrence. **Periodicity.—N.** periodicity, intermittence; beat; oscillation etc. 314; pulse, pulsation; rhythm; alternation, -nateness, -nativeness, -nity.

bout, round, revolution, rotation, turn.

anniversary, birthday, jubilee, centenary, bi-, ter-centenary.

[Regularity of return] rota, cycle, period, stated time, routine; days of the week; Sunday, Monday etc.; months of the year; January etc.; feast, fast, saint's day etc.; Christmas, Easter, New Year's Day etc. 998; quarter-, Lady-, Midsummer-, Michaelmas-day; May Day, the King's Birthday; leap year, seasons.

punctuality, regularity, steadiness.

V. recur in regular -order, — succession; return, revolve, rotate; come -again, — in its turn; come round, — again; beat, pulsate; alternate; intermit.

Adj. periodic, -al; serial, recurrent, cyclic-, -al, rhythmic-, -al, even; recurring etc. *V.;* inter-, remittent; alternate, every other.

hourly; diurnal, daily; quotidian, tertian, weekly; hebdomad-al, -ary; bi-weekly, fortnightly; monthly, menstrual, catamenial; yearly, annual; biennial, triennial, etc.; bissextile; centennial, secular; paschal, lenten, etc.

regular, steady, punctual, constant, methodical, regular as clockwork.

Adv. periodically etc. *adj.;* at -regular intervals, — stated times; at -fixed, — established-periods; punctually etc. *adj.; de die in diem;* from day to day, day by day.

by turns, in -turn, — rotation; alternately, every other day, off and on, ride and tie, round and round.

139. Irregularity of recurrence.—**N.** irregularity, uncertainty, unpunctuality; fitfulness etc. *adj.*

Adj. irregular, uneven, uncertain, unpunctual, capricious, erratic, desultory, fitful, flickering; rambling, rhapsodical; spasmodic, unsystematic, unequal, variable, halting.

Adv. irregularly etc. *adj.;* by fits and starts etc. (*discontinuously*) 70.

140. Change. [Difference at different times.]—N. change, alteration, mutation, permutation, variation, modification, modulation, inflexion, mood, qualification, innovation, *metastasis,* deviation, shift, turn; diversion; break.

transformation, transfiguration; metamorphosis; metabolism; transmutation; transsubstantiation; metagenesis, transanimation, transmigration, metempsychosis; version, metathesis, transmogrification; catalysis; *avatar;* alterative.

conversion etc. (*gradual change*) 144; revolution etc. (*sudden or radical change*) 146; inversion etc. (*reversal*) 218; displacement etc. 185; transference etc. 270.

changeableness etc. 149; tergiversation etc. (*change of mind*) 607.

V. change, alter, vary, wax and wane; modulate, diversify, qualify, tamper with; turn, shift, veer, jibe, tack, chop, shuffle, swerve, dodge, warp, deviate, turn aside, evert, intervert; pass to, take a turn, turn the corner, resume.

work a change, modify, vamp, revamp, superinduce; trans-form, —mute, -ume, -figure etc. *n.;* metamorphose, ring the changes; convert, resolve; revolutionize; chop and change; patch, re-shape.

innovate, introduce new blood, shuffle the cards, spin the wheel; give a -turn, — color- to; influence, turn the scale; shift the scene, turn over a new leaf.

recast etc. 146; reverse etc. 218; disturb etc. 61; convert into etc. 144.

Adj. changed etc. *v.;* new-fangled; changeable etc. 149; transitional; modifiable; alterative.

Adv. *mutatis mutandis.*

Int. *quantum mutatus!*

Phr. 'a change came o'er the spirit of my dream;' *nous avons changé tout cela; tempora mutantur et nos mutamur in illis; non sum qualis eram.*

141. Permanence. [Absence of change.]—**N.** stability etc. 150; quiescence etc. 265; obstinacy etc. 606.

permanence, -cy, persistence, fixity, fixity of purpose, endurance, durability; standing, *status quo;* maintenance, preservation, conservation; conservatism; *laissez-faire;* law of the Medes and Persians; standing dish.

V. let -alone, — be; persist, remain, stay, tarry, rest; hold, — on; last, endure, bide, abide, aby, dwell, maintain, keep; stand, — still, — fast; subsist, live, outlive, survive; hold —, keep- one's ground, — footing; hold good.

Adj. stable etc. 150; persisting etc. *v.;* permanent; established, fixed; durable; unchanged etc. (change etc. 140); unrenewed; intact, inviolate; persistent; monotonous, uncheckered; unfailing.

un-destroyed, -repealed, -suppressed; conservative, *qualis ab incepto;* prescriptive etc. (*old*) 124; stationary etc. 265.

Adv. *in statu quo;* for good, finally; at a stand, -still; *uti possidetis;* without a shadow of turning.

Phr. as you were!; *j'y suis j'y reste; esto perpetua; nolumus leges Angliae mutari;* let sleeping dogs lie.

142. Cessation. [Change from action to

rest.]—N. cessation, discontinuance, desistance, desinence.

inter-, re-mission; sus-pense, -pension, interruption, hitch; hartal; stop; stopping etc. *v.;* closure, stoppage, halt; arrival etc. 292.

pause, rest, lull, respite, truce, armistice, drop; interregnum, abeyance.

closure etc. 261.

dead -stop, — stand, — lock; checkmate; comma, colon, semicolon, period, full stop; end etc. 67; death etc. 360; *caesura.*

V. cease, discontinue, desist, stay; break —, leave- off; hold, stop, pull up, stall, stop short, check; stick, deadlock, hand fire; halt; pause, rest.

have done -with, give over, surcease, shut up shop; give up etc. (*relinquish*) 624.

hold —, stay- one's hand; rest on one's oars, repose on one's laurels.

come to a -stand, — standstill, — dead lock, — full stop; arrive etc. 292; go out, die away, peter out; wear -away, — off; pass away etc. (*be past*) 122; be at an end.

intromit, interrupt, suspend, interpel; inter-, re-mit; put -an end, — a stop, — a period- to; bring to a stand, -still; stop, cut out, cut short, arrest, avast; stem the -tide, — torrent; pull the check string; switch off.

Int. halt! hold! stop! enough! avast! have done! a truce to! soft! leave off! shut up! give over! chuck it!

143. Continuance in action.—**N.** continu-ance, -ation; run; extension, prolongation; maintenance, perpetuation; persistence etc. (*perseverance*) 604a; repetition etc. 104.

V. continue, persist; go —, jog —, keep —, carry —, run — hold- on; abide, keep, pursue, stick to; endure; take —, maintain- its course; keep up.

sustain, uphold, hold up, keep on foot; follow up, perpetuate. prolong; maintain; preserve etc. 604a; harp upon etc. (*repeat*)104.

keep -going, — alive, — at it, — the pot boiling, — the ball rolling, — up the ball; plod-, plug- along; slog on; die in harness; hold on —, pursue- the even tenor of one's way.

let be; *stare super antiquas vias; quieta non movere;* let things take their course.

Adj. continuing etc. *v.;* uninterrupted, unintermitting, unremitting, unvarying, unshifting; unreversed, unstopped, unrevoked, unvaried; sustained; undying etc. (*perpetual*) 112; inconvertible.

follow-up.

Int. carry on! right away!

Phr. *vestigia nulla retrorsum, labitur et labetur.*

144. Conversion. [Gradual change to something different.]—**N.** conversion, reduction, transmutation, transformation, development, resolution, assimilation; assumption; naturalization.

chemistry, alchemy; progress, growth, lapse, flux.

passage; transit, -ion; transmigration, shifting etc. *v.;* conjugation; convertibility.

crucible, alembic, caldron, retort, test tube etc.

convert, neophyte, proselyte, pervert, renegade, deserter, apostate, turncoat.

V. be converted into; become, get, wax; come —, turn- -to, — into; turn out, lapse, shift; run —, fall —, pass —, slide —, glide —, grow —, ripen -, open —, resolve itself —, settle —, merge- into; melt, grow, come round to, mature, mellow; assume the -form, — shape, — state, — nature, — character- of; illapse; assume a new phase, undergo a change.

convert —, resolve- into; make, render; mold, form etc. 240; remodel, new model, refound, reform, reorganize; assimilate —, bring —, reduce- to; transform.

Adj. converted into etc. *v.;* convertible, resolvable into; transitional; naturalized.

Adv. gradually etc. (*slowly*) 275; *in transitu* etc. (*transference*) 270.

145. Reversion.—**N.** reversion, return; revulsion; reaction.

turning point, turn of the tide; *status quo ante bellum;* calm before a storm.

alternation etc. (*periodicity*) 138; inversion etc. 219; recoil etc. 277; regression etc. 283; restoration etc. 660; relapse etc. 661; vicinism, atavism, throwback.

V. revert, turn back, return; relapse etc. 661; recoil etc. 277; retreat etc. 283; restore etc. 660; undo, unmake; turn the -tide, — scale; escheat.

Adj. reverting etc. *v.;* revulsive, reactionary.

Adv. *à rebours,* wrong side out.

146. Revolution. [Sudden or violent change.]—**N.** revolution, *bouleversement,* subversion. break up; destruction etc. 162; sudden —, radical —, sweeping —, organic- change; clean sweep, *coup d'état,* overthrow, *débâcle;* counter-revolution, rebellion etc. 742.

transilience, jump, leap, plunge, jerk, start; explosion; spasm, convulsion, throe, revulsion; storm, earthquake, eruption, upheaval, cataclysm.

legerdemain etc. (*trick*) 545.

V. revolutionize; new model, remodel, recast; strike out something new, break with the past; change the face of, unsex; revert etc. 742.

Adj. unrecognizable.

Revolutionary, Bolshevik etc. 742.

147. Substitution. [Change of one thing for another.]—**N.** substitution, subrogation, commutation; supplanting etc. *v.;* supersession, metonymy etc. (*figure of speech*) 521.

[Thing substituted.] substitute, *succedaneum,* make-shift, temporary expedient, shift, *pis aller,* stop-gap, jury-mast, *locum tenens,* warming-pan, dummy, goat, scape-goat; double; change-ling; *quid pro quo,* alternative; remount; representative etc. (*deputy*) 759; palimpsest.

price, purchase-money, consideration, equivalent.

V. substitute, put in the place of, change for; make way for, give place to; supply —, take- the place of; supplant, supersede, replace, cut out, serve as a substitute; step into —, stand in- the shoes of; make a shift —, put up- with; borrow of Peter to pay Paul; commute, redeem, compound for.

Adj. substituted etc. *v.;* vicarious, subdititious; substitutional.

Adv. instead; in -place, — lieu, — the stead, — the room- of; *faute de mieux.*

---

148. Interchange. [Double or mutual change.]—N. inter-, ex-change; com-, per-, intermutation; reciprocation, transposal, transposition, shuffling; reciprocity, castling [at chess]; hocus-pocus.

interchange-ableness, -ability.

barter etc. 794; tit for tat etc. (*retaliation*) 718; cross fire, battledore and shuttlecock; *quid pro quo.*

V. inter-, ex-, counter-change; bandy, transpose, shuffle, change hands, swap, trade, permute, reciprocate, commute; give and take, return the compliment; play at -puss in the corner, — battledore and shuttlecock; retaliate etc. 718; barter etc. 794.

Adj. interchanged etc. *v.;* reciprocal, mutual, commutative, interchanged etc. *v.;* interchangeable, intercurrent.

Adv. in exchange, *vice versâ, mutatis mutandis,* backwards and forwards, by turns, turn and turn about, turn about; each —, every one- in his turn.

---

149. Changeableness.—N. changeableness etc. *adj.;* mutability, inconstancy; versatility, mobility; instability, unstable equilibrium; vacillation etc. (*irresolution*) 605; fluctuation, vicissitude; alternation etc. (*oscillation*) 314.

restlessness etc. *adj.;* fidgets, disquiet; dis-, inquietude; unrest; agitation etc. 315.

moon, Proteus, chameleon, kaleidoscope, quicksilver, shifting sands, weathercock, harlequin, Cynthia of the minute, April showers; wheel of Fortune; transientness etc. 111.

V. fluctuate, vary, waver, flounder, flicker, flitter, flit, flutter, shift, shuffle, shake, totter, tremble, vacillate, wamble, turn and turn about, ring the changes; sway —, shift- to and fro; change and change about; oscillate etc. 314; vibrate —, oscillate- between two extremes; alternate; have as many phases as the moon.

Adj. change-able, -ful; changing etc. 140; mutable, variable, checkered, ever changing, kaleidoscopic, prote-an, -iform; versatile.

unstaid, inconstant; un-steady, -stable, -fixed, -settled; fluctuating etc. *v.;* restless; mercurial; agitated etc. 315; erratic, fickle; irresolute etc. 605; capricious etc. 608; touch-and-go; inconsonant, fitful, spasmodic; vibratory; afloat; alternating; alterable, plastic, mobile; fleeting, transient etc. 111.

Adv. see-saw etc. (*oscillation*) 314; off and on.

---

150. Stability.—N. stability; immutability etc. *adj.;* unchangeableness etc. *adj.;* constancy; stable equilibrium, immobility, soundness, vitality, stabiliment, stabilization, stiffness, ankylosis, solidity, *aplomb.*

establishment, fixture; rock, pillar, tower, foundation, leopard's spots, Ethiopian's skin, law of the Medes and Persians.

stabilimeter, stabilizator.

permanence etc. 141; obstinacy etc. 606.

V. be -firm etc. *adj.;* stick fast; stand —, keep —, remain- firm; weather the storm.

settle, establish, stablish, ascertain, fix, set, stabilitate, stabilize; retain, stet, keep hold; make -good, — sure; fasten etc. (*join*) 43; set on its legs, float; perpetuate.

settle down; strike —, take- root; take up one's abode etc. 184; build one's house on a rock.

Adj. unchangeable, immutable; unalter-ed, -able; not to be changed, constant; permanent etc. 141; invariable, undeviating; stable, durable; perennial etc. (*diuturnal*) 110.

fixed, steadfast, firm, fast, steady, balanced; confirmed, valid, fiducial, immovable, irremovable, riveted, rooted; settled, established etc. *v.;* vested; incontrovertible, stereotyped, indeclinable.

tethered, anchored, moored, at anchor, on a rock, firm as a rock; firmly -seated, — established etc. *v.;* deep-rooted, ineradicable; inveterate; obstinate etc. 606.

transfixed, stuck fast, aground, high and dry, stranded.

indefeasible, irretrievable, intransmutable, incommutable, irresoluble, irrevocable, irreversible, reverseless, inextinguishable, irreducible; indissol-uble, -vable; indestructible, undying, imperishable, indelible, indeciduous; insusceptible, — of change.

Int. *stet.*

---

151. Eventuality.—N. eventuality, event, occurrence, incident, affair, transaction, proceeding, fact; matter of —, naked- fact; phenomenon; advent.

business, concern; circumstance, particular, casualty, happening, accident, adventure, passage, crisis, pass, emergency, contingency, consequence etc. 154.

the world, life, things, doings, affairs, matters; things —, affairs- in general; the times, state of affairs, order of the day; course —, tide —, stream —, current —, run —, march- of -things, — events; ups and downs of life; chapter of accidents etc. (*chance*) 156; situation etc. (*circumstances*) 8.

V. happen, occur; take -place, — effect; come, become of; come -off, — about, — round, — into existence, — forth, — to pass, — on; pass, present itself; fall; fall —, turn- out; run, be on foot, fall in; be-fall, -tide, -chance; prove, eventuate, draw on; turn —, crop —, spring —, cast- up; super-, sur-vene; issue, emanate, arrive, ensue, arise, start, hold, take its course; pass off etc. (*be past*) 122.

meet with; experience; fall to the lot of; be one's -chance, — fortune, — lot; find; encounter, undergo; pass —, go- through; endure etc. (*feel*) 821.

Adj. happening etc. *v.;* going on, doing, current; in the wind, afloat; on -foot, — the *tapis;* at issue, in question; incidental.

eventful, momentous, signal; stirring, bustling, full of incident.

Adv. eventually, ultimately, in -the event of, — case; in the course of things; in the -natural, — ordinary- course of things; as -things, — times- go; as the world -goes, — wags; as the -tree falls, — cat jumps; as it may -turn out, — happen.

Phr. the plot thickens.

152. Destiny.—N. destiny etc. (*necessity*) 601;
hereafter, future −, post- existence; future state,
next world, world to come, after life; futurity etc.
121; everlasting -life, − death; prospect etc. (*expectation*) 507.

V. impend; hang −, lie −, hover- over;
threaten, loom, await, come on, approach, stare
one in the face; fore-, pre-ordain; predestine,
doom, foredoom, foreshadow, have in store for.

Adj. impending etc. *v.;* destined; about to -be,
− happen; coming, in store, to come, going to
happen, instant, at hand, near; near −, close- at
hand; overhanging, hanging over one's head, imminent; brewing, preparing, forthcoming; in the
wind, on the cards, in reserve; that -will, − is to-
be; in prospect etc. (*expected*) 507; looming in
the -distance, − horizon, − future; unborn, in
embryo; in the womb of -time; − futurity; on the
knees of the gods; pregnant etc. (*producing*) 161.

Adv. in -time, − the long run; all in good time;
eventually etc. 151; whatever may happen etc.
(*certainly*) 474; as -chance etc. 156- would have
it.

153. Cause. [Constant antecedent.]—N. cause,
origin, source, principle, element; occasioner,
prime mover, engine, turbine, motor, *primum
mobile; vera causa;* author etc. (*producer*) 164;
main-spring, agent; dynamo, generator, battery
(electric); leaven; groundwork, foundation etc.
(*support*) 215.

spring, fountain, well, font; fountain −,
spring- head; *fons et origo,* genesis; descent etc.
(*paternity*) 166; remote cause; influence.

pivot, hinge, turning-point, lever; key; kernel,
core; proximate cause, *causa causans;* last straw
that breaks the camel's back.

ground; reason, − why; why and wherefore,
rationale, occasion, derivation; final cause etc.
(*intention*) 620; *le dessous des cartes;* undercur-
rents.

rudiment, egg, germ, embryo, fetus, bud, root,
radix, radical, etymon, nucleus, seed, stem, stalk,
stock, *stirps,* trunk, tap-root; latent organism.

nest, cradle, nursery, womb, *nidus,* birth-,
breeding-place, hot-bed.

caus-ality, -ation; origination; production etc.
161.

V. be the -cause etc. *n.-* of; originate; give −
origin, − rise, − occasion- to; cause, occasion,
sow the seeds of, kindle, suscitate; bring -on, −
to pass, − about; produce; create etc. 161; set -
up, − afloat, − on foot; found, broach, institute,
lay the foundation of, inaugurate; lie at the root
of.

procure, induce, draw down, open the door to,
superinduce, evoke, entail, operate; elicit, provoke.

conduce to etc. (*tend to*) 176; contribute; promote; have a -hand in, − finger in- the pie; determine, decide, turn the scale, give the casting vote;
have a common origin; derive its origin etc.
(*effect*) 154.

Adj. caused etc. *v.;* causal, original; prim-ary, -
itive, -ordial; aboriginal; radical; inceptive,
embry-onic, -otic; *in -embryo,* − *ovo;* seminal,
germinal; formative, productive etc. 168; at the
bottom of; connate, having a common origin.

Adv. because etc. 155; behind the scenes.

154. Effect. [Constant sequent.]—N. effect,

consequence, sequela; derivative, -tion; result;
result-ant, -ance; upshot, issue, *dénouement;* out-
come; termination, end etc. 67; development,
outgrowth, fruit, crop, harvest, product, bud,
blossom, florescence, ear.

production, produce, product, finished product, work, handiwork, fabric, performance;
creature, creation; offspring, -shoot; first-fruits, -
lings; *prémices.*

V. be the -effect etc. *n.-* of; be -due, − owing-
to; originate -in, − from; rise −, arise −, take its
rise −, spring −, proceed −, emanate −, come
−, grow −, bud −, sprout −, germinate −, issue
−, flow −, result −, follow −, derive its origin
−, accrue- from; come -to, − of, − out of;
depend −, hand −, hinge −, turn- upon.

take the consequences, sow the wind and reap
the whirlwind.

Adj. owing to; resulting from etc. *v.;* resultant;
derivable from; due to; caused etc. by, 153;
dependent upon; derived −, evolved- from;
derivative; hereditary.

Adv. of course, it follows that, naturally, consequently; as a −, in- consequence; through all,
all along of, necessarily, eventually.

Phr. *cela va sans dire,* thereby hangs a tale.

155. Attribution. [Assignment of cause.]—N.
attribution, theory, etiology, ascription, reference to, rationale; accounting for etc. *v.;* imputation, derivation from.

fil-, affil-iation; pedigree etc. (*paternity*) 166.
explanation etc. (*interpretation*) 522; reason
why etc. (*cause*) 153.

V. attribute −, ascribe −, impute −, refer −,
lay −, point −, trace −, bring home- to; put −,
set- down- to; charge −, ground- on; invest with,
assign as cause, charge with, blame, lay at the
door of, father upon; saddle with; affiliate; account for, derive from, point out the -reason etc.
153; theorize; tell how it comes; put the saddle on
the right horse.

Adj. attributed etc. *v.;* attributable etc. *v.;*
refer-able, -rible; due to, derivable from; owing
to etc. (*effect*) 154; putative.

Adv. hence, thence, therefore, for, since, on
account of, because, owing to; on that account;
from -this, − that- cause; thanks to, forasmuch
as; whence, *propter hoc.*

why? wherefore? whence? how -comes, − is, −
happens- it? how does it happen?

in -some, − some such- way; somehow, − or
other.

Phr. that is why; *hinc illae lachrymae; cher-
chez la femme.*

156. Chance.† [Absence of assignable
cause.]—N. chance, indetermination, accident,
fortune, hazard, hap, haphazard, chance-med-
ley, random, luck, *raccroc,* casualty, fortuity, con-
tingence, coincidence, adventure, hit; fate etc.
(*necessity*) 601; equal chance; lottery, raffle, tom-
bola, sweepstake; toss up etc. 621; turn of the -
table, − cards; hazard of the die, chapter of accidents; cast −, throw- of the dice; heads or tails,
wheel of Fortune, whirligig of chance; *sortes; −
Virgilianae.*

probability, possibility, contingency, odds,
long odds, run of luck; main- chance.

theory of -probabilities, − chances; book-making; assurance; speculation, gamble, gaming etc. 621.

V. chance, hap, turn up; fall to one's lot; be one's -fate etc. 601; stumble on, light −, blunder −, hit- upon; take one's chance etc. 621.

Adj. casual, fortuitous, accidental, haphazard, random, stray, adventitious, adventive, causeless, incidental. contingent, uncaused, undetermined, indeterminate; possible etc. 470; unintentional etc. 621.

Adv. by -chance, − accident; casually; perchance etc. (possibly) 470; for aught one knows; as -good, − bad, − ill-luck etc. n.- would have it; as it may -be, − chance, − turn up, − happen; as the case may be.

†The word Chance has two distinct meanings: the first, the absence of assignable cause, as above; and the second, the absence of design—for the latter see 621.

157. Power.

—N. power; poten-cy, -tiality; puissance, might, force; energy etc. 171; dint; right -hand, − arm; ascendency, sway, control; pre-potency, -pollence; almightiness, omnipotence; authority etc. 737; strength etc. 159.

ability; ableness etc. adj.; competency; efficiency, -cacy; validity, cogency; enablement; vantage ground; influence etc. 175; horse power; dynamometer.

pressure; elasticity; gravity; attraction, repulsion; vis -inertiae, − mortua, − viva; friction, suction.

electricity, magnetism, galvanism, voltaic electricity, voltaism, electro-magnetism, electro-statics, electrification; electric − current, − power; potential −, dynamic −, kinetic −, electrical −, chemical −, atomic- energc; electric field, circuit, charge, discharge, shock, polarity, pole; amperage, voltage, wattage, resistance, conduction, induction, electrification, electrolysis.

electronics, radionics, electron physics, electrophysics, avionics, radiometry, photoelectronics; electron, negatron, positron, photoelectron, thermion, barytron; electronic effect; electron emission; electron −, cathode −, anode −, positive − ray; electron − current, − flow − stream, − beam, − volt; electronic circuit; conductance; electron tube, tube, vacuum tube, photoelectric tube, call; transistor.

capability, capacity; quid valeant humeri quid ferre recusent; faculty, quality, attribute, endowment, virtue, gift, property, qualification, susceptibility.

V. be -powerful etc. adj.; gain -power etc. n. belong −, pertain- to; lie −, be- in one's power; can.

electrify, generate, magnetize.

give −, confer −, exercise- power etc. n.; empower, enable, invest; in-, en-due; endow, arm; strengthen etc. 159; compel etc. 744.

Adj. powerful, puissant; potent, -ial; capable, able; equal −, up- to; cogent, valid; effect-ive, -ual; efficient, efficacious, adequate, competent; multi-, pleni-, omni-, armi- potent; mighty, ascendent; almighty.

electric, electrical, electronic etc.

forcible etc. adj. (energetic) 171; influential etc. 175; productive etc. 168.

Adv. powerfully etc. adj.; by -virtue, − dint-of.

158. Impotence.

—N. impotence; in-, dis-ability; disablement, impuissance, imbecility, caducity; incapa-city, -bility; inapt-, inept-itude; indocility; invalidity, inefficiency, incompetence, disqualification.

telum imbelle, brutum fulmen, blank cartridge, flash in the pan, vox et praeterea nihil, dead letter, bit of waste paper, dummy; scrap of paper.

inefficacy etc. (inutility) 645; failure etc. 732.

helplessness etc. adj.; prostration, paralysis, palsy, ataxia, apoplexy, syncope, sideration, deliquium, collapse, exhaustion, softening of the brain, e nasculation, inanition, senility etc. 128; castrato, eunuch.

cripple, old woman, muff, molly-coddle, milk-sop.

V. be -impotent etc. adj.; not have a leg to stand on.

vouloir -rompre l'anguille au genou, − prendre la lune avec les dents.

collapse, faint, swoon, fall into a swoon, drop; go by the board; end in smoke etc. (fail) 732.

render -powerless etc. adj.; deprive of power; decontrol; dis-able, -enable; disarm, incapacitate, disqualify, unfit, invalidate, undermine, deaden, cramp, tie the hands; double up, prostrate, paralyze, muzzle, cripple, be-cripple, maim, lame, hamstring, draw the teeth of; throttle, strangle, garrotte; ratten, silence, sprain, clip the wings of, render hors de combat, spike the guns; take the wind out of one's sails, scotch the snake, put a spoke in one's wheel; break the -neck, − back; un-hinge, -fit; put out of gear.

unman, unnerve, devitalize, attenuate, enervate; emasculate, spay, caponize, castrate, geld; effeminize.

shatter, exhaust; weaken etc. 160.

Adj. powerless, impotent, unable, incapable, incompetent; ineff-icient, -ective; inept; un-fit, -fitted; uñ-, dis-qualified; unendowed; in-, un-apt; crippled, decrepit; disabled etc. v.; armless.

harmless, unarmed, weaponless, defenceless, sine ictu, unfortified, indefensible, vincible, pregnable, untenable.

para-lytic, -lyzed; palsied, imbecile; nerve-, sinew-, marrow-, pith-, lust-less; emasculate, disjointed, out of -joint, − gear; un-nerved, -hinged; water-logged, on one's beam ends, rudderless; laid on one's back; done up, dead beat, exhausted, shattered, demoralized; gravelled etc. (in difficulty) 704; helpless, unfriended, fatherless; without a leg to stand on, hors de combat, laid on the shelf.

null and void, nugatory, imoperative, good for nothing; dud; invertebrate; ineffectual etc. (failing) 732; inadequate etc. 640; inefficacious etc. (useless) 645.

159. Strength. (Degree of power.]

—N. strength; power etc. 157; energy etc. 171; vigor, force; main −, physical −, brute- force; spring, elasticity, tone, tension, tonicity.

stoutness etc. adj.; lustihood, stamina, nerve,

muscle, sinew, thews and sinews, *physique;* pith, - iness; virility, vitality.

athlet-ics, -icism; gymnastics, feats of strength.

adamant, steel, iron, oak, heart of oak; iron grip; grit, bone.

athlete, gymnast, tumbler, acrobat; Atlas, Hercules, Antaeus, Samson, Cyclops, Goliath, Titan; tower of strength; giant refreshed.

strengthening etc. *v.;* invigoration, refreshment, refocillation.

[Science of forces] dynamics, statics.

V. be -strong etc. *adj.*, − stronger; overmatch.

render -strong etc. *adj.;* give -strength etc. *n.;* strengthen, invigorate, brace, nerve, fortify, buttress, sustain, harden, case-harden, steel; gird; screw −, wind −, set- up; gird −, brace- up one's loins; recruit, set on one's legs; vivify; refresh etc. 689; refect; reinforce etc. (*restore*) 660.

Adj. strong, mighty, vigorous, forcible, hard, adamantine, stout, robust, sturdy, hardy, powerful, potent, puissant, valid.

resistless, irresistible, invincible, proof against, impregnable, unconquerable, indomitable, inextinguishable, unquenchable; incontestable; more than a match for; over-powering, -whelming; all-powerful; sovereign.

able-bodied; athletic, gymnastic; Herculean, Cyclopean, Atlantean; muscular, husky, brawny, wiry, well-knit, broad-shouldered, sinewy, strapping, stalwart, gigantic.

man-ly, -like, -ful; masculine, male, virile, in the prime of manhood.

un-weakened, -allayed, -withered, -shaken, - worn, -exhausted; in full -force, − swing; in the plenitude of power.

stubborn, thick-ribbed, made of iron, deep-rooted; strong as -a lion, − a horse, − brandy; sound as a roach; in -fine, − high- feather; in fine fettle; like a giant refreshed.

Adv. strongly etc. *adj.*; by -force etc. *n.*; by main force etc. (*by compulsion*) 744.

Phr. 'our withers are unwrung.'

160. Weakness.—**N.** weakness etc. *adj.;* debility, atony, relaxation, languor, enervation; impotence etc. 158; infirmity; effeminacy, feminality; fragility, flaccidity; inactivity etc. 683.

declension −, loss −, failure- of strength; delicacy, invalidation, decrepitude, asthenia, adynamy, cachexy, *cachexia*, anemia, bloodlessness, sprain, strain.

reed, thread, rope of sand, broken reed, house -of cards, − built on sand.

soft-, weak-ling; infant etc. 129; youth etc. 127.

V. be -weak etc. *adj.;* drop, crumble, give way, totter, tremble, shake, halt, limp, fade, languish, decline, flag, fail, have one foot in the grave.

render -weak etc. *adj.;* weaken, enfeeble, debilitate, shake, deprive of strength, relax, enervate; un-brace, -nerve; cripple, unman, etc. (*render powerless*) 158; cramp, reduce, sprain, strain, blunt the edge of; dilute, impoverish; decimate; extenuate; reduce -in strength, − the strength of; invalidate; *mettre de l'eau dans son vin.*

Adj. weak, feeble, debile; impotent etc. 158; relaxed, unnerved etc. *v.*; sap-, strength-, powerless; weakly, unstrung, flaccid, adynamic, asthenic; nervous.

soft, effeminate, feminate, womanish.

frail, fragile, shattery, frangible, brittle etc. 328; flimsy, unsubstantial, gimcrack, gingerbread; rickety, cranky; creachy; drooping, tottering etc. *v.*; broken, lame, halt, game, withered, shattered, shaken, crazy, shaky, tumble-down; palsied etc. 158; decrepit; C3.

lanquid, poor, poorly, infirm; faint, -ish; sickly etc. (*disease*) 655; dull, slack, evanid, spent, short-winded, effete; weatherbeaten; decayed, rotten, worn, seedy, languishing, wasted, washy, wishy-washy, laid low, pulled down, the worse for wear.

un-strengthened etc. 159, -supported, -aided, -assisted; aidless, defenceless etc. 158.

on its last legs; weak as a -child, − baby, − chicken, − cat, − rat; weak as -water, − water gruel, − gingerbread, − milk and water; colorless etc. 429.

Phr. *non sum qualis eram.*

161. Production.—**N.** production, creation, construction, formation, fabrication, manufacture; building, architecture, erection, edification; coinage; organization; *nisus formativus;* putting together etc. *v.;* establishment; workmanship, performance; achievement etc. (*completion*) 729; effect etc. 154.

flowering, fructification fruition.

bringing forth etc. *v.;* parturition, birth, birth-throe, child-birth, delivery, confinement, *accouchement*, travail, labour, midwifery, obstetrics; geniture; gestation etc. (*maturation*) 673; evolution, development, growth; genesis, fertilization, breeding, conception, germination, generation, *epigenesis*, pro-creation, -generation, -pagation; fecundation, impregnation; spontaneous generation; *arche-genesis*, *-biosis; bio-, abio-, homo-, xeno-genesis.*

authorship, publication; works, *oeuvre, opus.*

edifice, building, structure, fabric, erection, pile, tower, flower, fruit.

V. produce, perform, operate, do, make, gar, form, construct, fabricate, frame, contrive, manufacture; weave, forge, coin, carve, chisel; build, raise, edify, rear, erect, put together; set −, run- up; establish, constitute, compose, organize, institute, get up; achieve, accomplish etc. (*complete*) 729.

flower, sprout, blossom, burgeon, bear fruit, fructify, spawn, teem, ean, yean, farrow, drop, calf, pup, whelp, kitten, kindle; bear, lay, bring forth, give birth to, lie in, be brought to bed of, evolve, pullulate, usher into the world.

make productive etc. 168; create, beget, conceive, get, generate, fecundate, impregnate; pro-create, -generate, -pagate; engender; bring −, call- into -being, − existence; breed, hatch, develop, bring up.

induce, superinduce; suscitate; cause etc. 153; acquire etc. 775.

Adj. produc-ed, -ing etc. *v.;* productive of; prolific etc. 168; creative; formative; gen-etic, -ial, -ital; fertile, pregnant; *enceinte*, big −, fraught-with; with child, in the family way, teeming, parturient, in the straw, brought to bed of; puerper-al, -ous.

architectonic; constructive.

162. Destruction. [Non-production.]—N. destruction; waste, dissolution, breaking up; di-, dis-ruption; consumption; disorganization.

fall, downfall, ruin, perdition, crash, smash, havoc, *délabrement, débâcle;* break -down, — up; prostration; desolation, *bouleversement,* wreck, crack-up, crash, wrack, shipwreck, cataclysm; Caudine Forks, Sedan.

extinction, annihilation; destruction of life etc. 361; knock-out, knock-down blow; doom, crack of doom.

destroying etc. *v.;* demo-lition, -lishment; biblioclasm; overthrow, subversion, suppression; abolition etc. (*abrogation*) 756; sacrifice; ravage, devastation, *sabotage, razzia;* incendiarism; revolution etc. 146; extirpation etc. (*extraction*) 301; *commencement de la fin,* road to ruin; dilapidation etc. (*deterioration*) 659.

V. be -destroyed etc.; perish; fall, — to the ground; tumble, topple; go —, fall- to pieces; break up; crumble, — to dust; go to -the dogs, — the wall, — smash, — shivers, — wreck, — pot, — wrack and ruin; go -by the board, — all to smash, — to pieces, — under; be all -over, — up- with; totter to its fall.

destroy; do —, make- away with; nullify; annul etc. 756; sacrifice, demolish; tear up; over-turn, -throw, -whelm; upset, subvert, put an end to; seal the doom of, do for, dish, undo; break -, cut- up; break —, cut —, pull —, mow —, blow —, beat-down; suppress, quash, put down; cut short, take off, blot out; dispel, dissipate, dissolve; consume.

smash, — to smithereens, quell, squash, squelch, crumple up, shatter, shiver; batter; tear —, crush —, cut —, shake —, pull —, pick- to pieces; nip; tear to -rags, — tatters; crush —, knock- to atoms; pulverize; ruin; strike out; throw —, knock- -down, — over; lay by the heels; fell, sink, swamp, scuttle, wreck, crash, shipwreck, engulf, submerge; lay in -ashes, — ruins; sweep away, erase, expunge, strike out, delete, efface, raze; level, — with the -ground, — dust.

deal destruction, lay waste, ravage, gut; disorganize; dismantle etc. (*render useless*) 645; devour, swallow up, desolate, devastate, sap, mine, blast, confound; exterminate, extinguish, quench, annihilate; snuff —, put —, stamp —, trample- out; lay —, trample- in the dust; prostrate; tread —, crush —, trample- under foot; lay the axe to the root of; make -short work, — a clean sweep, — mincemeat- of; cut up root and branch; fling —, scatter- to the winds; throw overboard; strike at the root of, sap the foundations of, spring a mine, blow up; ravage with fire and sword; cast to the dogs; eradicate etc. 301.

Adj. destroyed etc. *v.;* perishing etc. *v.;* trembling —, nodding —, tottering- to its fall; in course of destruction etc. *n.;* extinct.

destructive, subversive, ruinous, incendiary, deletory; destroying etc. *v.;* suicidal; deadly etc. (*killing*) 361.

Adv. with -crushing effect, — a sledge-hammer.

Phr. *delenda est Carthago.*

163. Reproduction.—N. reproduction, renovation; restoration etc. 660; renewal; new edition, reprint etc. 21; revival, regeneration, palingenesia, revivification; apotheosis; resuscitation, reanimation, resurrection, resurgence, reappearance, atavism; Phoenix; reincarnation.

generation etc. (*production*) 161; multiplication.

V. reproduce; restore etc. 660; revive, renovate, renew, regenerate, revivify, resuscitate, reanimate, refashion, stir the embers, put into the crucible; multiply, repeat, resurge.

crop up, spring up like mushrooms.

Adj. reproduced etc. *v.;* renascent, reappearing; reproductive; resurgent; progenitive; Hydra-headed.

164. Producer.—N. producer, creator, deviser, designer, originator, inventor, author, founder, generator, mover, architect; grower, constructor, maker etc. (*agent*) 690.

165. Destroyer.—N. destroyer etc. (destroy etc. 162); cankerworm etc. (*bane*) 663; iconoclast; assassin etc. (*killer*) 361; executioner etc. (*punish*) 975; Hun, Vandal, nihilist, anarchist.

166. Paternity.—N. paternity; parentage; fatherhood; consanguinity etc. 11.

parent, father, sire, dad, daddy, papa, governor, *pater, paterfamilias, abba;* genitor, progenitor, procreator, begetter; ancestor; grandsire, -father; great-grandfather.

house, stem, truck, tree, stock, *stirps,* pedigree, lineage, line, family, tribe, sept, race, clan; genealogy, descent, extraction, birth, ancestry; forefathers, forbears, patriarchs.

motherhood, maternity; mother, dam, mamma, *materfamilias;* grand-mother; matriarch.

Adj. paternal, parental; maternal; family, ancestral, linear, matrilinear, patrilineal, patriarchal.

167. Posterity.—N. posterity, progeny, breed, issue, offspring, brood, litter, seed, farrow, spawn, spat; family, children, grandchildren, heirs; great-grandchild.

child, son, daughter; kid; infant etc. 129; bantling, scion; shoot, sprout, olive branch, sprit, branch; off-shoot, -set; ramification; descendant; heir, -ess; heir -apparent, — presumptive; chip of the old block; heredity; rising generation.

straight descent, sonship, line, lineage, filiation, promogeniture.

Adj. filial.

168. Productiveness.—N. productiveness etc. *adj.;* fecundity, fertility, luxuriance, uberty.

pregnancy, pullulation, fructification, multiplication, propagation, procreation; superfetation.

milch cow, rabbit, hydra, warren, seed-plot, land flowing with milk and honey; second crop, after-crop, -growth, -math; fertilization.

V. make -productive etc. *adj.;* fructify; pro-create, generate, fertilize, spermatize, impregnate; fecund-ate, -ify; teem, pullulate, multiply; produce etc. 161; conceive.

Adj. productive, prolific; teem-ing, -ful; fertile, fruitful, frugiferous, fruit-bearing; fructiferous; fecund, luxuriant; pregnant, uberous.

procre-ant, -ative; generative, life-giving, spermatic; originative; multiparous; omnific; propagable.

parturient etc. (*producing*) 161; profitable etc. (*useful*) 644.

169. Unproductiveness.—N. unproductiveness etc. *adj.;* infertility, steril; ity, infecundity; impotence etc. 158- unprofitableness etc. (*inutility*) 645.

waste, desert, Sahara, wild, wilderness, howling wilderness.

V. be -unproductive etc. *adj.;* hang fire, flash in the pan, come to nothing.

Adj. unproductive, inoperative, barren, addle, unfertile, unprolific, arid, sterile, unfruitful, acarpous, infecund; *sine prole;* fallow; teem-, issue-, fruitless; unprofitable etc. (*useless*) 645; null and void, of no effect.

170. Agency.—N. agency, operation, force, working, strain, function, office, maintenance, exercise, work, swing, play; inter-working, -action, procuration, procurement.

causation etc. 153; instrumentality etc. 631; influence etc. 175; action etc. (*voluntary*) 680; *modus operandi* etc. 627.

quickening –, maintaining- power; home stroke.

V. be -in action etc. *adj.;* operate, work; act, – upon; perform, play, support, sustain, strain, maintain, take effect, quicken, strike.

come –, bring- into -operation, – play; have -play, – free play; bring to bear upon.

Adj. operative, efficient, efficacious, practical, effectual.

at work, on foot; acting etc. (*doing*) 680; in -operation, – force, – action, – play, – exercise; acted –, wrought- upon.

Adv. by the -agency etc. *n.-* of; through etc. (*instrumentality*) 631; by means of etc. 632.

171. Physical Energy.—N. energy, physical energy, force; keenness etc. *adj.;* intensity, vigor, strength, elasticity; go; pep, live wire, high pressure; backbone, mettle, fire, vim.

acri-mony, -tude, -dity; causticity, virulence, poignancy; harshness etc. *adj.;* severity, edge, point; pungency etc. 392.

cantharides; Spanish fly; seasoning etc. (*condiment*) 393, stimulant, excitant.

activity, agitation, effervescence; ferment, -ation; ebullition, splutter, perturbation, stir, bustle; voluntary energy etc. 682; quicksilver.

resolution etc. (*mental energy*) 604; exertion etc. (*effort*) 686; excitation etc. (*mental*) 824.

V. give -energy etc. *n.;* energize, stimulate, kindle, excite, activate, exert; sharpen, pep up, intensify; inflame etc. (*render violent*) 173; wind up etc. (*strengthen*) 159.

strike, – into, – hard, – home; make an impression.

Adj. strong, energetic, forcible, active; strenuous, forceful, mettlesome, enterprising, go ahead; intense, deep-dyed, severe, keen, vivid, sharp, acute, incisive, trenchant, brisk, vigorous, live.

rousing, irritating; poignant; virulent, caustic, corrosive, mordant, harsh, stringent; double-edged, – shotted, – distilled; drastic, escharotic; racy etc. (*pungent*) 392; sarcastic etc. 932.

potent etc. (*powerful*) 157; radio-active.

Adv. strongly etc. *adj.; fortiter in re;* with telling effect.

Phr. the steam is up; *vires acquirit eundo.*

172. Physical Inertness.—N. inertness, dulness etc. *adj.;* inertia, *vis inertiae,* inertion, inactivity, torpor, languor; dormancy, quiescence etc. 265; latency, inaction, passivity.

mental inertness; sloth etc. (*inactivity*) 683; inexcitability etc. 826; irresolution etc. 605; obstinacy etc. 606; permanence etc. 141.

V. be -inert etc. *adj.;* hang fire, smoulder.

Adj. inert, inactive, passive, pacific; torpid etc. 683; sluggish, stagnant, dull, heavy, flat, slack, tame, slow, blunt; lifeless, dead, uninfluential.

latent, dormant, smouldering, unexerted.

Adv. inactively etc. *adj.;* in -suspense, -abeyance.

173. Violence.—N. violence, inclemency, vehemence, might, impetuosity; boisterousness etc.; *adj.;* effervescence, ebullition; turbulence, bluster; uproar, riot, row, rumpus, *le diable à quatre,* devil to pay, all the fat in the fire.

severity etc. 739; ferocity, rage, berserk, fury; exacerbation, exasperation, malignity; fit, paroxysm, orgasm; force, brute force; outrage; *coup de main;* strain, shock, shog; spasm, convulsion, throe; hysterics, passion etc. (*state of excitability*) 825.

out-break, -burst; burst, bounce, dissilience, discharge, volley, explosion, blow up, blast, detonation, rush, eruption, displosion, torrent.

turmoil etc. (*disorder*) 59; ferment etc. (*agitation*) 315; storm, tempest, rough weather; squall etc. (*wind*) 349; earthquake, volcano, thunderstorm.

fury, dragon, demon, tiger, beldame, Tisiphone, Megaera, Alecto, madcap, wild beast; fire-eater etc. (*blusterer*) 887.

V. be -violent etc. *adj.;* run high; ferment, effervesce; romp, rampage; run -wild, – riot; break the peace; rush, tear; rush head-long, -foremost; run amuck, raise a storm, make a riot; make –, kick up- a row, – a fuss; bluster, rage, roar, riot, storm; boil, – over; fume, foam, come in like a lion, wreak, bear down, ride roughshod, out-Herod Herod; spread like wildfire.

break –, fly –, burst- out; bounce, shock, strain; break-, pry-, force-, prize- open.

render -violent etc. *adj.;* sharpen, stir up, quicken, excite, incite, urge, lash, stimulate; irritate, inflame, exacerbate, kindle, suscitate, foment; accelerate, aggravate, exasperate, convulse, infuriate, madden, lash into fury; fan –, add fuel to- the flame; *oleum addere camino.*

explode, go off, displode, fly, detonate, thunder, blow up, flash, flare, erupt, burst; let-off, − fly; discharge, detonize, fulminate.

Adj. violent, vehement, forcible; warm; acute, sharp; rough, rude, ungentle, bluff, boisterous, wild, vicious; brusque, abrupt, waspish; impetuous; rampant.

turbulent; disorderly; blustering, raging etc. v.; troublous, riotous; tumultu-ary, -ous; obstreperous, uproarious; extravagant; unmitigated; ravening, tameless; frenzied etc. (insane) 503; desperate etc. (rash) 863; infuriate, towering, furious, outrageous, frantic, hysteric, in hysterics.

fiery, flaming, scorching, hot, red-hot, ebullient.

savage, fierce, ferocious, fierce as a tiger.

excited etc. v.; un-quelled, -quenched, -extinguished, -repressed, -bridled, -ruly; headstrong; un-governable, -appeasable, -mitigable; un-, in-controllable; insup-, irre-pressible.

spasmodic, convulsive, explosive; detonating etc. v.; volcanic, meteoric; stormy etc. (wind) 349.

Adv. violently etc. adj.; amain; by -storm, − force, − main force; with might and main; tooth and nail, vi et armis, at the point of the -sword, − bayonet; at one fell swoop; with a high hand, through thick and thin; in desperation, with a vengeance; à −, à touteoutrance; head-long, -foremost, -first; like a bull at a gate.

174. Moderation.—N. moderation; lenity etc. 740; temperance, temperateness, gentleness etc. adj.; sobriety; quiet; mental calmness etc. (inexcitability) 826.

moderating etc. v.; relaxation, remission, mitigation etc. 834; tranquilization, alleviation, assuagement, appeasement, contemporation, pacification.

measure, juste milieu, golden mean etc. 29.

moderator; lullaby, sedative, lenitive, demulcent, rose-water, balm, soothing syrup, poppy, opiate, anodyne, milk, opium, laudanum, 'poppy or mandragora;' wet blanket; palliative, calmative.

V. be -moderate etc. adj.; keep within -bounds, − compass; sober −, settle- down; keep the pease, remit, relent; take in sail.

moderate, soften, mitigate, temper, accoy; at-, con-temper; mollify, lenify, dull, take off the edge, blunt, obtund, sheathe, subdue, chasten; sober −, tone −, smooth- down; censor, blue-pencil, weaken etc. 160; lessen etc. (decrease) 36; check; palliate.

tranquilize, assuage, appease, dulcify, swage, lull, soothe, compose, still, calm, cool, quiet, hush, quell, sober, pacify, tame, damp, lay, allay, rebate, slacken, smooth, alleviate, rock to sleep, deaden, smother; throw -cold water on, − a wet blanket over; slake; curb etc. (restrain) 751; tame etc. (subjugate) 749; smooth over; pour oil on the -waves, − troubled waters; pour balm into, mettre de l'eau dans son vin.

go out like a lamb, 'roar you as gently as any sucking dove.'

Adj. moderate; lenient etc. 740; gentle, mild; cool, sober, temperate, reasonable, measured; tempered etc. v.; calm, unruffled, quiet, tranquil, still; slow, smooth, untroubled; tame; peaceful, -able; pacific, halcyon.

un-exciting, -irritating; soft, bland, oily, demulcent, lenitive, anodyne; hypnotic etc. 683; sedative; assuaging.

mild as mother's milk; milk and water; gentle as a lamb.

Adv. moderately etc. adj.; gingerly; piano; under easy sail, at half speed; within -bounds, − compass; in reason.

Phr. est modus in rebus.

175. Influence.—N. influence; importance etc. 642; weight, pressure, preponderance, prevalence, sway, pull; predomi-nance, -nancy; ascendency; control, dominance, reign; authority etc. 737; capability etc. (power) 157; interest; spell, magic, magnetism.

footing; purchase etc. (support) 215; play, leverage, vantage ground.

tower of strength, host in himself; protection, patronage, auspices.

V. have -influence etc. n.; be -influential etc. adj.; carry weight, actuate, sway, bias, weigh, tell; have a hold upon, magnetize, bear upon, gain a footing, work upon; take -root, − hold; strike root in.

run through, pervade, prevail, dominate, predominate, subject; out-, over-weigh; over-ride, -bear, − come; gain head; rage; be -rife etc. adj.; spread like wildfire; have −, get −, gain- -the upper hand, − full play.

be -recognized, − listened to; make one's voice heard, gain a hearing; play a -part, − leading part- in; lead, control, rule, master; get the mastery over; make one's influence felt, cut ice with; take the lead, pull the strings; turn −, throw one's weight into- the scale; set the fashion, lead the dance.

Adj. influential; important etc. 642; weighty; prevailing etc. v.; prevalent, rife, rampant; dominant, regnant, predominant, in the ascendant, hegemonical; authoritative, recognized, telling, with authority.

Adv. with telling effect.

175a. Absence of Influence.—N. impotence etc. 158; inertness etc. 172; irrelevancy etc. 10.

V. have no -influence etc. 175.

Adj. uninfluential; unconduc-ing, -ive, -ting to; powerless etc. 158; irrelevant etc. 10.

176. Tendency.—N. tendency; apt-ness, -itude; proneness, proclivity, bent, turn, tone, bias, set, warp, leaning to, predisposition, inclination, conatus, propensity, susceptibility; liability etc. 177; quality, nature, temperament; character-istic, idio-crasy, -syncrasy; cast, vein, grain; humor, mood; drift etc. (direction) 278; conduciveness, -ducement; applicability etc. (utility) 644; subservience etc. (instrumentality) 631.

V. tend, contribute, conduce, lead, dispose, incline, verge, bend to, warp, turn, trend, affect, carry, redound to, bid fair to, gravitate towards; promote etc. (aid) 707.

Adj. tending etc. v.; conducive, working to-

wards, in a fair way to, calculated to; liable etc.
177; subservient etc. (*instrumental*) 631; useful
etc. 644; subsidiary etc. (*helping*) 707.

Adv. for, whither.

177. Liability.—N. lia-bility, -bleness; possibility, contingency; suscepti-vity, -bility.

V. be -liable etc. *adj.*; incur, lay oneself open
to; run the −, stand a- chance; lie under, expose
oneself to, open a door to.

Adj. liable, subject; in danger etc. 665; open −,
exposed −, obnoxious- to; answerable, responsible, accountable, amenable; unexempt from; apt
to; dependent on; incident to.

contingent, incidental, possible, on the cards,
within range of, at the mercy of.

178. Concurrence.—N. concurrence, co-
operation, coagency; coincidence, consilience;
union; agreement etc. 23; consent etc. (*assent*)
488; alliance; concert etc. 709; partnership etc.
712; collaboration, conformity.

V. con-cur, -duce, -spire, -tribute; agree, unite,
harmonize; hang −, pull- together etc. (*co-
operate*) 709; help to etc. (*aid*) 707.

keep pace with, run parallel to; go −, go along
−, go hand in hand- with.

Adj. concurring etc. *v.*; concurrent, conformable, joint, co-operative, concordant, coincident, concomitant, harmonious; in alliance with,
banded together, of one mind, at one with;
parallel.

Adv. with one consent.

179. Counteraction.—N. counteraction, opposition; contrariety etc. 14; antagonism, polarity; clashing etc. *v.*; collision, interference,
resistance, renitency, friction; reaction; retro-
action; repercussion etc. (*recoil*) 277; counterblast; neutralization etc. (*compensation*) 30; *vis
inertiae;* check etc. (*hindrance*) 706.

voluntary -opposition etc. 708, − resistance
etc. 719; repression etc. (*restraint*) 751.

V. counteract; run counter, clash, cross; interfere −, conflict- with; jostle; go −, run −, beat
−, militate- against; stultify; antagonize, frustrate, oppose etc. 708; withstand etc. (*resist*) 719;
hinder etc. 706; repress etc. (*restrain*) 751; react
etc. (*recoil*) 277.

undo, neutralize, cancel; counterpoise etc.
(*compensate*) 30; overpoise.

Adj. counteracting etc. *v.*; antagonistic, conflicting, retroactive, renitent, reactionary; contrary etc. 14.

Adv. although etc. 30; in spite of etc. 708;
malgré; against.

180. Space. [Indefinite space.]—N. space,
extension, extent, superficial extent, expanse,
stretch; capacity, volume, room, accommodation,
scope, range, latitude, field, way, expansion, compass, sweep, play, swing, spread.

dimension, fourth dimension; relativity, geo-
metry.

spare −, elbow −, house- room; stowage,
roomage, margin; opening, sphere, arena; lee-,
sea-, head-way.

open −, free- space; wide open spaces, void etc.
(*absence*) 187; waste; wild-, wilder-ness; up-, bot-
tom-, moor -land; *campagna, veldt,* prairie,
steppe.

abyss etc. (*interval*) 198; unlimited space;
infinity etc. 105; world, wide world; ubiquity etc.
(*presence*) 186; length and breadth of the land.

proportions, acreage; acres, − roods and
perches; square -inches, − yards etc.

V. reach, extend, stretch, sweep, spread,
range, cover, thrust out, reach forth.

Adj. spacious, roomy, extensive, expansive,
capacious, ample; wide-spread, vast, world-wide,
uncircumscribed; boundless etc. (*infinite*) 105;
shore-, track-, path-less; large etc. 192.

spatial, dimensional, proportional; two-,
three-, four-dimensional; stereoscopic.

Adv. extensively etc. *adj.*; wherever; everywhere; far and -near, − wide; right and left, all
over, all the world over; throughout the -world,
− length and breadth of the land; under the sun,
in every quarter; in all -quarters, − lands; here,
there and everywhere; from -pole to pole, −
China to Peru, − Indus to the pole, − Dan to
Beersheba, − end to end; on the face of the earth,
in the wide world, from all points of the compass; to the -four winds, − uttermost parts of the
earth.

180a. Inextension.—N. in-, non-extension;
point; atom etc. (*smallness*) 32; pinprick; limitation etc. 229.

181. Region. [Definite space.]—N. region,
sphere, sphere of influence, corridor, ground,
soil, area, realm, hemisphere, quarter district,
beat, orb, orbit, zone, belt, circuit, circle; pale etc.
(*limit*) 233; com-, department; domain, tract,
territory, terrain, country, canton, county, shire,
province, *arrondissement,* diocese, parish, town-
ship, borough, constituency, *commune,* ward,
wapentake, hundred, riding, lathe, garth, soke,
tithing, bailiwick; empire, kingdom, principality,
duchy, grand −, arch- duchy, palatinate, republic,
commonwealth, dominion, colony, state, island.

arena, precincts, *enceinte,* walk, march; patch,
plot, enclosure, etc. 232; close, *enclave,* field,
court; street etc. (*abode*) 189.

clime, climate, zone, meridian, latitude.

Adj. territorial, local, parochial, provincial,
insular.

182. Place. [Limited space.]—N. place, lieu,
spot, point, dot; niche, nook, etc. (*corner*) 244;
hole; pigeonhole etc. (*receptacle*) 191; compartment; premises, precinct, station, confine; area,
court, yard, quadrangle, square, compound;
abode etc. 189; locality etc. (*situation*) 183.

ins and outs; every hole and corner.

Adv. somewhere, in some place, wherever it
may be, here and there, in various places,
passim.

183. Situation.—N. situation, position, local-ity, *locale, status,* latitude and longitude; foot-ing, standing, standpoint, post; stage, aspect, attitude, posture, *pose.*

place, site, base, station, seat, *venue,* where-abouts, environment, neighborhood; bearings etc. (*direction*) 278; spot etc. (*limited space*) 182.

top-, ge-, chor-ography; map etc. 554.

V. be -situated, − situate; lie; have its seat in.

Adj. situ-ate, -ated; local, topical, topograph-ical etc. *n.*

Adv. *in -situ, − loco;* here and there, *passim;* here-, there-, whereabouts; in place, here, there.

in −, amidst- such and such- -surroundings, − *environs, − entourage.*

184. Location.—N. loca-tion, -lization; lodge-ment; de-, re-position; stow-, pack-age; colloca-tion; packing, lading; establishment, settlement, installation; fixation; insertion etc. 300.

anchorage, roadstead, mooring, mooring mast, encampment, camp, bivouac.

-plantation, colony, settlement, cantonment, encampment, reservation; colonization, domestication, situation; habitation etc. (*abode*) 189; cohabitation; 'a local habitation and a name;' indenization, naturalization.

V. place, situate, locate, localize, make a place for, put, lay, set, scat, station, lodge, quarter, post, install; storehouse, stow; extablish, fix, pin, root; graft; plant etc. (*insert*) 300; shelve, pitch, camp, lay down, deposit, reposit; cradle; moor, tether, picket; pack, tuck in; embed; vest, invest in.

billet on, quarter upon, saddle with; load, lade, freight; pocket, put up, bag.

inhabit etc. (*be present*) 186; domesticate, colonize, populate, people; take −, strike-root; anchor; cast −, come to an- anchor; sit −, settle-down; settle; take up one's -abode, − quarters; plant −, establish −, locate- oneself; squat, perch, hive, *se nicher,* bivouac, burrow, get a footing; encamp, pitch one's tent; put up -at, − one's horses at; keep house.

indenizen, naturalize, adopt.

put back, replace etc. (*restore*) 660.

Adj. placed etc. *v.;* situate, posited, ensconc-ed, embedded, embosomed, rooted; · domestica-ted; vested in. unremoved; settled, stationed, established.

moored etc. *v.;* at anchor.

185. Displacement.—N. displacement, eloca-tion, transposition.

ejectment etc. 297; exile etc. (*banishment*) 893; removal etc. (*transference*) 270; unshipment.

misplacement, dislocation etc. 61; fish out of water.

V. dis-place, -plant, -lodge, -nest, -establish; misplace, unseat, disturb; exile etc. (*seclude*) 893; ablegate, set aside, remove; take −, cart- away; take −, draft- off; lade etc. 184, unship.

unload, empty etc. (*eject*) 297; transfer etc. 270; dispel.

vacate; depart etc. 293.

Adj. displaced etc. *v.;* un-placed, -housed, -harbored, -established, -settled; house-, home-less; out of -place, − a situation.

misplaced, out of its element.

186. Presence.—N. presence; occupancy, -ation; attendance; whereness.

permeation, pervasion; diffusion etc. (*dis-persion*) 73.

ubi-ety, -quity, -quitariness; omnipresence.

bystander etc. (*spectator*) 444.

V. exist in space, be -present etc. *adj.;* assist at; make one -of, − at; look on, attend, remain; find −, present- oneself; show one's face; fall in the way of, occur in a place; lie, stand; occupy.

people; inhabit, dwell, reside, stay, sojourn, live, room, abide, bunk, lodge, nestle, roost, perch; take up one's abode etc. (*be located*) 184; tenant, occupy.

resort to, frequent, haunt; revisit.

fill, pervade, permeate; be -diffused, − dis-seminated- through; over-spread, -run; run through; meet one at every turn.

Adj. present; occupying, inhabiting etc. *v.;* moored etc. 184; residential, resi-ant, -dent, -dentiary; domiciled.

ubiquit-ous, -ary; omnipresent.

peopled, populous, full of people, inhabited.

Adv. here; there, where, everywhere, aboard, on board, at home, afield; on the spot; here, there and everywhere etc. (*space*) 180; in presence of, before; under the -eyes, −nose- of; in the face of; *in propriâ personâ.*

187. Absence. [Nullibiety.]—N. absence; inexistence etc. 2; non-residence, absenteeism; non-attendance, *alibi.*

emptiness etc. *adj.;* void, *vacuum;* vac-uity, -ancy; *tabula rasa;* exemption; *hiatus* etc. (*inter-val*) 198; no man's land.

truant, absentee.

nobody; nobody -present, − on earth; no one; not a soul; *âme qui vive.*

V. be -absent etc. *adj.;* keep -away, − out of the way; play truant, absent oneself, stay away.

withdraw, make oneself scarce, vacate; go away, slip out, slip away, retreat etc. 293.

Adj. absent, not present, away, nonresident, gone, from home; missing; lost; wanted, wanting; omitted; nowhere to be found; inexistent etc. 2.

empty, void; blank, vac-ant, -uous; unten-anted, -occupied, -inhabited; tenantless; desert, -ed; devoid; un-, uninhabitable.

exempt from, not having.

Adv. without, *minus,* nowhere; elsewhere; neither here nor there; in default of; *sans;* behind one's back.

Phr. the bird has flown, *non est inventus.*

188. Inhabitant.—N. inhabitant; habitant, resident, -iary; dweller, in-dweller; occup-ier, -ant, farmer, planter; householder, lodger, boarder, paying guest; inmate, tenant, renter, incumbent, sojourner, *locum tenens,* commor-ant; settler, squatter, backwoodsman, colonist; islander; denizen, citizen; burgher, oppidan, cockney, cit, townsman, burgess; villager; cot-tager, -tier, -ter; compatriot.

native, indigene, aboriginal, aborigines, auto-chthones; Briton, Englishman, John Bull; new comer etc. (*stranger*) 57.

garrison, crew; population; people etc. (*man-kind*) 372; colony, settlement; household.

V. inhabit etc. (*be present*) 186; indenizen etc. (*locate oneself*) 184.

Adj. indigenous; enchorial; national, nat-ive, -al; autochthonous; British, English; colonial; domestic, domiciliated, -ed; naturalized, vernacular, domesticated; domiciliary.

in the occupation of; garrisoned −, occupied-by.

189. Abode. [Place of habitation, or resort.]—**N.** abode, dwelling, lodging, -s; diggings, domicile, residence, address, habitation, where one's lot is cast, local habitation, berth, seat, lap, sojourn, housing, quarters, headquarters, resiance, tabernacle, throne, ark.

home, fatherland, mother country, country etc. 181; home-stead, -stall; fireside, chimney corner; hearth, − stone; household gods, *lares et penates,* roof, household, housing, *dulce domum,* paternal domicile; native -soil, − land, blighty.

nest, *nidus,* snuggery; arbor, bower etc. 191; lair, den, cave, hole, hidingplace, cell, *sanctum sanctorum,* aerie, eyry, rookery, hive; *habitat,* haunt, covert, resort, retreat, perch, roost; nidification.

bivouac, camp, encampment, cantonment, castrametation; barrack, casemate, casern.

tent etc. (*covering*) 223; building etc. (*construction*) 161; chamber etc. (*receptacle*) 191.

tenement, messuage, farm, farmhouse, grange, *hacienda.*

cot, cabin, log cabin, shack, hut, *châlet,* croft, shed, booth, stall, hovel, bothy, shanty, igloo, tepee, wigwam; pen etc. (*inclosure*) 232; barn, bawn; kennel, sty, dog-hole, cote, coop, hutch, byre; cowhouse, -shed; stable, dove-cote, shippen.

house, mansion, place, villa, cottage, box, lodge, hermitage, *rus in urbe,* folly, rotunda, tower, *château,* castle, pavilion, hotel, court, manor-house, capital messuage, hall, palace, alcazar; country seat; kiosk, bungalow; temple etc. 1000; home of rest, alms-, poor-, work-house, asylum; boarding-, lodging-house; flat, maisonette, duplex, penthouse, suite of rooms, apartments, rooms, room building etc. 161; Mansion House, town hall, Capitol.

assembly-room, auditorium, coliseum, meeting-house, pump-room, spa, health resort, watering-place; club; theatre etc. 840; drill hall, gymnasium, church etc. 1000; Houses of Parliament etc. 696; school etc. 542; inn; hostel, -ry; hotel, tavern, caravansary, khan, hospice; public-, ale-, pot-, mug-house; gin-palace, gin mill; coffee-, eating-house; canteen, *restaurant, rotisserie,* cafeteria, grill-room, *buffet, café, estaminet, posada, bodega;* bar; saloon, speakeasy, shebeen.

hamlet, village, thorp, dorp, ham, kraal; borough, burgh, town, county-seat, − town, city, capital, metropolis; suburb, quarter, parish etc. 181; ghetto; province, country.

street, place, terrace, parade, esplanade, promenade, pier, embankment, road, villas, row, walk, lane, alley, court, quadrangle, quad, wynd, close, yard, passage, rents, mansions, buildings, mews.

square, polygon, circus, crescent, mall, *piazza,* arcade, colonnade, peristyle, cloister; gardens, grove, residences; block of buildings, marketplace, *place.*

anchorage, roadstead, roads; dock, basin, wharf, quay, port, harbor; dry-, graving-, floating-dock.

garden, park, pleasure-ground, pleasance, demesne.

V. take up one's abode etc. (*locate oneself*) 184; inhabit etc. (*be present*) 186.

Adj. urban, oppidan, metropolitan; suburban; provincial, rural, rustic; countrified; regional, parochial, domestic; cosmopolitan; palatial.

190. Contents. [Things contained.]—**N.** contents; cargo, lading, freight, shipment, load, bale, burden; cart-, ship-load; cup −, basket −, etc. (*receptacle*) 191 - of; inside etc. 221; stuffing, ullage.

V. load, lade, ship, charge, fill, stuff.

191. Receptacle.—N. receptacle, container; inclosure etc. 232; recipient, receiver, reservatory.

compartment; cell, -ule; follicle; hole, corner, niche, recess, nook; crypt, stall, pigeon-hole, cove, oriel; cave etc. (*concavity*) 252.

capsule, vesicle, cyst, pod, calyx, *cancelli,* utricle, bladder, udder.

stomach, paunch, *venter,* abdomen, ventricle, crop, craw, ingluvies, maw, gizzard, bread-basket, belly, little Mary; mouth.

pocket, pouch, fob, sheath, scabbard, socket, bag, vanity bag, compact, sac, sack, saccule, despatch −, attaché-, tachy- case, wallet, scrip, card-, note-, case, billfold, poke, knit, knap-, haver-, ruck-sack, sachel, satchel, reticule, budget, net; ditty-, -box, -bag, kitbag; portfolio; saddlebags, holster; quiver etc. (*magazine*) 636.

chest, box, coffer, caddy, case, casket, pyx, pix, *caisson,* desk, *bureau,* reliquary, shrine; trunk, portmanteau, band-box, *valise,* suitcase, hand-, traveling-, overnight-, Gladstone-, carpet-bag, brief case; boot, imperial; *vache;* cage, manger, rack.

vessel, vase, bushel, barrel; canister, jar; pottle, basket, punnet, pannier, buck-basket, hopper, maund, creel, cran, crate, cradle, bassinet, wisket, whisket, *jardinière, corbeille,* hamper, wastepaper basket, dosser, dorser, tray, hod, scuttle, utensil, spittoon, cuspidor.

[For liquids] cistern etc. (*store*) 636; vat, caldron, barrel, cask, puncheon, keg, rundlet, tun, butt, firkin, hogshead, kilderkin, carboy, amphora, ampulla, bottle, jar, leather bottle, decanter, ewer, cruse, carafe, crock, kit, canteen, flagon; demijohn; flask, -et; stoup, noggin, vial, phial, ampoulé, cruet, caster; gourd; urn, *épergne,* salver, *patella, tazza, patera;* pig-, big-gin; tea-, coffee-pot, percolator, *samovar;* tyg, nipperkin, pocket-pistol; tub, bucket, pail, skeel, pot, tankard, jug, pitcher, toby, mug, pipkin; gal-, gall-ipot, pannikin; matrass, receiver, retort, alembic, bolthead, can, kettle; bowl, basin, jorum, punch-bowl, cup, goblet, chalice, tumbler, glass, wineglass, rummer, beaker, tass, horn, saucepan, skillet, posnet, tureen, terrine, *casserole,* sauce-, gravy-boat.

plate, platter, paten, dish, vegetable −, *entrée*-dish, trencher, calabash, porringer, potager, saucer, pan, crucible.

shovel, trowel, spoon; table-, dessert-, tea-, egg-salt-spoon; spatula, ladle; dipper; baler; watch-glass, thimble.

closet, commode, cupboard, cellaret, *chiffonnière*, locker, bin, bunker, *buffet*, press, safe, sideboard, drawer, chest of drawers, till, *scrutoire*, *secrétaire*, *éscritoire*, davenport, book-case, cabinet, canterbury; corner cupboard, wardrobe.

chamber, apartment, room, cabin; office, court, hall, atrium; suite of rooms, flat, story; saloon, *salon*, parlor; presence-chamber; sitting-, drawing-, reception-, state-, living-, work-room; gallery, cabinet, closet, cubicle; pew, box; *boudoir*; *adytum, sanctum*; bed-room, dormitory, dressing-room; refectory, dining-room, *salle-à-manger*; nursery, schoolroom; library, study; *studio*; billiard-, bath-, smoking-room; den, canteen, mess, officers' mess; gun-, ward-, mess-room.

attic, loft, garret, cockloft, clerestory; cellar, vault, hold, cockpit; *entre-sol*; mezzanine floor; ground-floor, *rez-de-chaussée*; basement, kitchen, cook-house, galley, pantry, scullery, offices; store-room etc. (*depository*) 636; lumber-room; dust-hole, -bin; dairy, laundry, coachhouse; *garage*; *hangar*; out-, pent-house; lean-to.

portico, porch, piazza, verandah, lobby, court, hall, vestibule, corridor, passage; ante-room, chamber; lounge; *foyer, loggia*.

conservatory, green-house, glass-house, vinery, bower, arbor, summer-house, alcove, grotto, hermitage, pergola.

lodging etc. (*abode*) 189; bed etc. (*support*) 215; carriage etc. (*vehicle*) 272.

Adj. capsular; saccu-lar, -lated; recipient; ventricular, cystic, vascular, vesicular, cellular, camerated, locular, multilocular, poly-gastric; marsupial; siliqu-ose, -ous.

192. Size.—N. size, magnitude, dimension, bulk, volume; largeness etc. *adj.*; greatness etc. (*of quantity*) 31; expanse etc. (*space*) 180; amplitude, mass; proportions.

capacity; ton-, tun-nage; caliber, scantling.

turgidity etc. (*expansion*) 194; corpulence, obesity; plumpness, etc. *adj.*; *embonpoint*, corporation, flesh and blood, lustihood.

hugeness etc. *adj.*; enormity, immensity, monstrosity.

giant, Brobdingnagian, Antaeus, Goliath, Gog and Magog, Gargantua, monster, mammoth, Cyclops; whale, porpoise, behemoth, leviathan, elephant, hippopotamus; colossus; tun, lump, bulk, block, loaf, mass, clod, nugget, bushel, thumper, whopper, spanker, strapper; Triton among the minnows.

mountain, mound; heap etc. (*assemblage*) 72.

largest portion etc. 50; full-, life-size.

V. ve- large etc. *adj.*; become -large etc. (*expand*) 194.

Adj. large, big; great etc. (*in quantity*) 31; considerable, bulky, voluminous, ample, massive, massy; capacious, comprehensive; spacious etc. 180; mighty, towering, fine, magnificent.

corpulent, stout, fat, plump, squab, full, lusty, strapping, bouncing; portly, burly, well-fed, full-grown; stalwart, brawny, fleshy; goodly; in good -case, − condition; in condition; chopping, jolly; chub-, chubby-faced.

lubberly, hulky, unwieldy, lumpish, gaunt, spanking, whacking, whopping, thumping, thundering, hulking; overgrown; puffy etc. (*swollen*) 194.

huge, immense, enormous, mighty; vast, -y; amplitudinous, stupendous; monst-er, -rous; gigantic, elephantine; giant, -like; colossal, Cyclopean, Brobdingnagian, Garguantuan, Titanic; infinite etc. 105.

large as life; plump as a dumpling, − partridge; fat as -a pig, − a quail, − butter, − brawn, − bacon.

193. Littleness.—N. littleness etc. *adj.*; smallness etc. (*of quantity*) 32; exiguity, inextension; parvi-tude, -ty; duodecimo; Elzevir edition, epitome, microcosm; rudiment; vanishing point; thinness etc. 203.

dwarf, pigmy, atomy, Liliputian, midget, chit, pigwidgeon, urchin, elf; doll, puppet; Tom Thumb, Hop-o'-my thumb, Humpty-dumpty; man-, mannikin; *homunculus*, dapperling, fingerling, dandiprat, cock-sparrow, scalawag.

animalcule, monad, mite, insect, emmet, fly, midge, gnat, shrimp, minnow, worm, maggot, entozoon; *bacillus*, microbe, micro-organism, *bacteria; infusoria*; microbe; grub; tit, tomtit, runt, mouse, small fry; millet-, mustard-seed; barleycorn; pebble, grain of sand; mole-hill, button, bubble.

point; atom etc. (*small quantity*) 32; fragment etc. (*small part*) 51; powder etc. 330; point of a pin, mathematical point; *minutiae* etc. (*unimportance*) 643.

micro-graphy, -meter, -scope; vernier; scale.

V. be -little etc. *adj.*; lie in a nutshell; become small etc. (*decrease*) 36, (*contract*) 195.

Adj. little; small etc. (*in quantity*) 32; minute, diminutive, microscopic; inconsiderable etc. (*unimportant*) 643; exiguous, puny, tiny, wee, petty, minikin, miniature, pigmy, elfin; under sized; dwarf, -ed, -ish; spare, stunted, limited; cramp, -ed; pollard, Liliputian, dapper, pocket; port-ative, -able; duodecimo; dumpy, squat; compact, handy; short etc. 201.

impalpable, intangible, evanescent, imperceptible, invisible, inappreciable, infinitesimal, homeopathic; atomic, corpuscular, molecular; rudiment-ary, -al; embryonic.

weazen, scant, scraggy, scrubby; thin etc. (*narrow*) 203; granular etc. (*powdery*) 330; shrunk etc. 195.

Adv. in a -small compass, − nutshell; on a small scale.

194. Expansion.—N. expansion; increase etc. 35 -of size; enlargement, extension, augmentation; ampli-fication, -ation; aggrandizement, spread, increment, growth, development, pullulation, swell, dilation, dilatation, rarefaction; turg-escence, -idness, -idity; obesity etc. (*size*) 192; dropsy, tumefaction, intumescence, swelling, tumor, *diastole*, distension; puff-ing, -iness; inflation; pandiculation.

dilatability, expansibility.

germination, growth, upgrowth; accretion etc. 35.

over-growth, -distension; hypertrophy, tympany.

bulb etc. (*convexity*) 250; plumper; superiority of size.

V. become -larger etc. (large etc. 192); expand, widen, enlarge, extend, grow, increase, incrassate, swell, gather; fill out; deploy, take open order, dilate, stretch, spread; mantle, was; grow –, spring- up; bud, bourgeon, shoot, sprout, germinate, put forth, vegetate, pullulate, open, burst forth, flower, blow etc. 734; gain –, gather- flesh; outgrow; spread like wildfire, overrun.

be larger than; surpass etc. (*be superior*) 33.

render -larger etc. (large etc. 192); expand, spread, extend, aggrandize, distend, develop, amplify, spread out, widen, magnify, rarefy, inflate, puff, puff out, blow up, stuff, pad, cram; exaggerate; fatten.

Adj. expanded etc. *v.*; larger etc. (large etc. 192); swollen; expansive; wide-open, -spread; fan-shaped; flabelliform; overgrown, exaggerated, bloated, fat, turgid, tumid, hypertrophied, dropsical; pot-, swag-bellied; edematous, obese, puffy, pursy, blowzy, distended; patulous; bulbous etc. (*convex*) 250; full-blown, -grown, -formed; big etc. 192.

195. Contraction.—**N.** contraction, reduction, diminution; decrease etc. 36- of size; defalcation, decrement; lessening, shrinkage; collapse, emaciation, attenuation, tabefaction, comsumption, marasmus, atrophy; systole, neck, hourglass.

condensation, compression, constraint, compactness; compendium etc. 596; squeezing etc. *v.* ; strangulation; corrugation; astringency, constringency; astringents, sclerotics; contractility, compressibility; coarctation.

inferiority in size.

V. become -small, – smaller; lessen, decrease etc. 36; grow less, dwindle, shrink, contract, narrow, shrivel, collapse, wither, lose flesh, wizen, fall away, waste, wane, ebb; decat etc. (*deteriorate*) 659.

be smaller than; fall short of; not come up to etc. (*be inferior*) 34.

render smaller, lessen, diminish, contract, draw in, shrink, shrivel, narrow, coarctate; constrict, constringe; condense, compress, boil down, deflate, exhaust, empty; squeeze, corrugate, crush, crumple up, warp, purse up, pack, stow; pinch, tighten, strangle; cramp; dwarf, bedwarf; shorten etc. 201; circumscribe etc. 229; restrain etc. 751; fold etc. 258.

pare, reduce, attenuate, rub down, scrape, file, grind, chip, shave, shear.

Adj. contracting etc. *v.*; astringent; shrunk, contracted etc. *v.*; strangulated, tabid, wizened, stunted, tabescent; marasmic; waning etc. *v.*; neap; compact; shriveled, preshrunk.

unexpanded etc. (expand etc. 194); inswept; contractile; compressible; smaller etc. small etc. 193).

196. Distance.—**N.** distance; space etc. 180; remoteness, farness; far- cry to; longinquity, elongation; offing, background; removedness; parallax; reach, span, stride; drift.

out-post, -skirt; horizon, sky-line; aphelion; foreign parts, *ultima Thule*, *ne plus ultra*, antipodes; long range, giant's stride.

dispersion etc. 73.

V. be -distant etc. *adj.*; extend –, stretch –, reach –, spread –, go –, get –, stretch away- to; range, outrange, outreach.

remain at a distance; keep –, stand- -away, – off, – aloof, – clear of.

Adj. distant; far -off, away; remote, telescopic, distal, wide of; stretching to etc. *v.*; yon, -der; ulterior; trans-marine, -pontine, -atlantic, -pacific, - continental, -polar, -equatorial, -alpine; tramontane; ultra-montane, -mundane; hyperborean, antihodean; inaccessible, out of the way; unapproached, -able; incontiguous.

Adv. far -off, – away; afar, -off; off; away; a -long, – great, – good- way off; wide away, aloof; wide –, clear- of; out of -the way, – reach; abroad, ' yonder, farther, further, beyond; *outre mer*, over the border, far and wide, over the hills and far away; from pole to pole etc. (*over great space*) 180; to the -uttermost parts, – ends- of the earth; out of -hearing, – range, nobody knows where, *à perte de vue*, out of the sphere of, wide of the mark; a far cry to.

apart, asunder; wide -apart, – asunder; *longo intervallo*; at arm's length.

197. Nearness.—**N.** nearness etc. *adj.*; proximity, propinquity; vicinity, -age; neighborhood, adjacency; contiguity etc. 199.

short -distance, – step, – cut; earshot, close quarters, brief span; stone's throw; bow –, gun –, pistol- shot; hair's breadth; span; close-up.

purlieus, neighborhood, vicinage, *environs*, *alentours*, suburbs, confines, *banlieue*, borderland; whereabouts.

bystander; neighbor, borderer.

approach etc. 286; convergence etc. 290; perihelion.

V. be -near etc. *adj.*; adjoin, hang about, trench on; border-, verge upon; stand by, approximate, tread on the heels of; cling to, clasp, hug; cuddle, huddle; hang about the skirts of, hover over; burn; abut.

bring –, draw- -near etc. 286; converge etc. 290; crowd etc. 72; place -side by side etc. *adv.*

Adj. near, nigh; close-, near- at hand; close, neighboring, propinquent, bordering upon; adjacent, adjoining, limitrophe; proxim-ate, ~al; at hand, handy; near the mark, near run; home, intimate.

Adv. near, ' nigh; hard –, 'fast- by; close -to. upon, – up; at the point of; next door to; within - reach, – call, – hearing, – earshot, – range; within an ace of; but a step, not far from, at no great distance; on the -verge, – brink, – skirts- of; in the -environs etc. *n.*; at one's -door, – feet, – elbow, – finger's end, – side; on the tip of one's tongue; under one's nose; within a -stone's throw etc. *n.*; in -sight, – presence- of; at close quarters; cheek by -jole, – jowl; beside, alongside, side by side, *tête-à-tête*; in juxtaposition etc. (*touching*) 199; yard-arm to yard-arm; at the heels of; on the confines of, at the threshold, bordering upon, verging to; in the way.

about; here-, there-abouts; roughly, in round

numbers; approxim- -ately, – atively; as good as, well nigh.

198. Interval.—N. interval, interspace; separation etc. 44; break gap, opening; hole etc. 260; chasm, *hiatus,* caesura; inter-ruption,-regnum; interstice, *lacuna,* cleft, mesh, crevice, chink, rime, creek, cranny, crack, chap, slit, slot, fissure, scissure, rift, flaw, breach, fracture, rent, gash, cut, leak, dike, ha-ha.

gorge, defile, ravine, canon, *crevasse,* abyss, abysm; gulf; inlet, frith, strait, gully, gulch, nullah; pass; notch; furrow etc. 259; yawning gulf; *hiatus - maxime, – valde- deflendus*; parenthesis etc. (*interjacence*) 228; void etc. (*absence*) 187; incompleteness etc. 530.

V. gape etc. (*open*) 260; part, remove.

Adj. with an interval, far between; separated, spaced, split.

Adv. at intervals etc. (*discontinuously*) 70; *longo intervallo.*

199. Contiguity.—N. contiguity, contact, proximity, apposition, juxtaposition, touching etc. *v.*; abutment, osculation; meeting, appulse, appulsion, *rencontre,* rencounter, syzygy, coincidence, conjunction, coexistence; adhesion etc. 46.

border-land; frontier etc. (*limit*) 233; tangent.

V. be -contiguous etc. *adj.*; join, adjoin, abut on, march with, border; tick, graze, touch, meet, osculate, kiss, come in contact; coincide; coexist; adhere etc. 46.

Adj. contiguous; touching etc. *v.*; in -contact etc, *n.*, conterminous, end to end, osculatory; pertingent; tangential.

hand to hand; close to etc. (*near*) 197; with no - interval etc. 198.

200. Length.—N. length, longitude, span, .extent, mileage.

line, bar, rule, stripe, streak, spoke, radius.

lengthening etc. *v.*; pro-longation, -duction, -traction; ten-sion, -sure; extension.

[Measures of length] line, nail, inch, hand, palm, foot, cubit, yard, ell, fathom, rod, pole, perch, furlong, mile, league; chain, meter, kilo-, centi-, milli- etc meter.

pedometer, perambulator, odometer, odograph, speedometer, cyclometer, log, telemeter, range finder; scale etc. (*measurement*) 466.

V. be -long etc. *adj.*; stretch out, sprawl; extend –, reach –, stretch -to; make a long arm, 'drag its slow length along.'

render -long etc. *adj.*; lengthen, extend, elongate; stretch; pro-long, -duce, -tract; let –, pay –, draw –, spin- out; drawl.

enfilade, look along, view in perspective.

Adj. long, -some; lengthy, lank, wiredrawn, outstretched; stretched, drawn out, lengthened etc. *v.*; sesquipedalian etc. (*words*) 577; interminable, no end of.

line-ar, -al; longitudinal, oblong.

as long as -my arm, –to-day and to-morrow; unshortened etc. (shorten etc. 201).

Adv. lengthwise, at length, longitudinally, endlong, along; *tandem*; in a line etc. (*continuously*) 69; in perspective.

from -end to end; –stern to stern, –head to foot, –the crown of the head to the sole of the foot, – top to toe, –head to heels; fore and aft.

201. Shortness.—N. shortness etc. *adj.*; brevity; littleness etc. 193; a span.

shortening etc. *v.*; abbrevia-tion, -ture; abridgment, concision, retrenchment, curtailment, decurtation; reduction etc. (*contraction*) 195; epitome etc. (*compendium*) 596.

abridger, abstractor, epitomiser.

elision, ellipsis; conciseness etc. (*in style*) 572.

V. be -short etc. *adj.*; render -short etc. *adj.*; shorten, curtail, abridge, abbreviate, take in, reduce; compress etc. (*contract*) 195; epitomize etc. 596.

retrench, cut short, obtruncate; scrimp, cut, chop up, hack, hew; cut –, pare- down; clip, snip, dock, lop, prune; shear, shave, mow, reap, crop; snub; truncate, pollard, stunt, nip, nip in the bud, check the growth of; [in drawing] foreshorten.

Adj. short, brief, curt; compendious, compact; stubby, scrimp, shorn, stubbed; stumpy, thickset, podgy, stocky, pug; squab, -by; squat, dumpy; little etc. 193; curtailed of its fair proportions; short by; oblate; concise etc. 572; summary.

Adv. shortly etc. *adj.*; in short etc. (*concisely*) 572.

202. Breadth. Thickness.—N. breadth, width, latitude, amplitude; diameter, bore, calibre, radius; superficial extent etc. (*space*) 180.

thickness, crassitude; corpulence etc. (*size*) 192; dilatation etc. (*expansion*) 194.

V. be -broad etc. *adj.*; become – , render- -broad etc. *adj.*; expand etc. 194; thicken, widen.

Adj. broad, wide, ample, extended; discous; fanlike; out-spread, -stretched; wide as a church-door. thick, dumpy, squab, squat, thickset, tubby; thick as a rope, stubby etc. 201.

203. Narrowness. Thinness.—N. narrowness etc. *adj.*; closeness, exility; exiguity etc. (*little*) 193.

line; hair's –, finger's -breadth; strip, streak, vein.

thinness etc. *adj.*; tenuity; emaciation, slenderness, macilency, *marcor.*

shaving, slip etc. (*filament*) 205; threadpaper; skeleton, shadow, scrag, anatomy, spindle-shanks, barebones, lantern jaws, mere skin and bone.

middle construction, stricture, neck, waist, isthmus, wasp, hour-glass; ridge, *ghaut,* pass; ravine etc. 198.

narrowing, coarctation, angustation, tapering; contraction etc. 195.

V. be-narrow etc. *adj.*; narrow, taper, diminish, contract etc. 195; render -narrow etc. *adj.*

Adj. narrow, close; slender, thin, fine; *svelte;* thread-like etc. (*filament*) 205; finespun, taper, slim, gracile, slight, slight-made; scant, -y; spare, delicate, incapacious; contracted etc. 195; unexpanded etc. (expand etc. 194); slender as a thread, capillary.

emaciated, lean, meager, gaunt, macilent; lank, -y; weedy, skinny, scrawny, scraggy; starv-ed, -eling; attenuated, shrivelled; wizened, pinched, peaky, skeletal, spindling, spindle- -legged, -shanked; extenuated, tabid, marcid, bare-bone, raw-boned; herring-gutted; worn to a shadow, lean as a rake; thin as a -lath,—whipping post,—wafer; hatchet-faced; lantern-jawed.

204. Layer.—N. layer, stratum, course, bed, zone, *substratum,* floor, flag, stage, story, tier, slab, escarpment, table, tablet, panel, plaque; board, plank; trencher, platter.

plate; lam-ina, -ella; sheet, flake, foil, wafer, scale, coat, peel, pellicle, ply, thickness, membrane, film, leaf, slice, shive, cut, rasher, shaving, integument etc. (*covering*) 223.

V. slice, shave, pare, peel; plate, coat, veneer; cover etc. 223.

Adj. lamell-ar, -ated, -iform; laminated, -iferous; micaceous; schist-ose, -ous; scaly; filmy, membranous, flaky, squamous; folia-ted, -ceous; stratified, -form; tabular, discoid, spathic.

205. Filament.—N. filament, line; fiber, fibril; funicle, vein, hair, capillament, *cilium,* tendril, gossamer; hair-stroke; harl.

wire, string, thread, packthread, cotton, sewing-silk, twine, twist, whip-cord, cord, rope, cable, yarn, hemp, oakum, jute, wool, worsted.

strip, shred, slip, spill, list, band, fillet, *fascia,* ribbon, riband, tape, roll, lath, slat, strake, splinter, shiver, shaving.

beard etc. (*roughness*) 256; ramification; strand.

Adj. fil-amentous, -aceous, -iform; fibr-ous, -illous; thread-like, wiry, stringy, ropy; capill-ary, -iform; funicular, wire-drawn; anguilliform; flagelliform; hairy etc. (*rough*) 256; ligulate.

206. Height.—N. height, altitude, elevation, ceiling; eminence. pitch; loftiness etc. *adj.*; sublimity.

tallness etc. *adj.*; stature, procerity; prominence etc. 250.

colossus etc. (*size*) 192; giant, grenadier, giraffe.

mount, -ain; hill, butte, monticle, fell, knap; cape; head-, fore-land; promontory; ridge, hog's back, dune; rising –, vantage- ground; down; moor, -land; Alp; up-, table-, high-lands; heights etc. (*summit*) 210; knoll, hummock, hillock, barrow, mound, mole, *kopje*; steeps, bluff, cliff, craig, tor, peak, pike, clough; escarpment, edge, ledge, brae; dizzy height.

tower, pillar, column, pylon, obelisk, monument, steeple, spire, minaret, *campanile*, belfry, turret, roof, dome, cupola, pagoda, pyramid; sky scraper; Eiffel tower.

pole, pikestaff, maypole, flagstaff; mast, top—, topgallant- mast.

ceiling etc. (*covering*) 223.

high water; high—, flood—, spring-tide.

altimetry etc. (*angle*) 244; altimeter, height-finder, hypsometer, barograph.

V. be -high etc. *adj.*; tower, soar, command;

hover; cap, culminate; overhang, hang over, impend, beetle; bestride, ride, mount; perch, surmount; cover etc. 233; overtop etc. (*be superior*) 33; stand on tiptoe.

become -high etc. *adj.*; grow, – higher, – taller; upgrow; rise etc. (*ascend*) 305.

render -high etc. *adj.*; heighten etc. (*elevate*) 307.

Adj. high, elevated, eminent, exalted, lofty, supernal; tall; gigantic etc. (*big*) 192; Patagonian; towering, beetling, soaring, hanging [gardens] ; elevated etc. 307; upper; highest etc. (*topmost*) 210; monticulous, perching, hill-dwelling.

up-, moor-land; hilly, mountainous, alpine, subalpine, heaven-kissing; cloud-topt, -capt, -touching; aerial.

overhanging etc. *v.*; incumbent, overlying; super-incumbent, -natant, -imposed; prominent etc. 250.

tall as a -maypole, —poplar,—steeple; lanky etc. (*thin*) 203.

Adv. on high, high up, aloft, up, above, aloof, overhead; up—, above- stairs; in the clouds; on -tiptoe, —stilts,—the shoulders of; over head and ears; breast high.

over, upwards; from top to bottom etc. (*completely*) 52.

207. Lowness.—N. lowness etc. *adj.*; debasement, depression; prostration etc. (*horizontal*) 213; depression etc. (*concave*) 252.

molehill; lowlands; bottomlands; basement-ground-floor; *rez de chaussée* etc. 211; hold; feet, heels.

low water; low—, ebb—, neap—, spring- tide.

V. be -low etc. *adj.*; lie -low, —flat; underlie; crouch, slouch, wallow, grovel; lower etc. (*depress*) 308.

Adj. low, neap, debased; nether, -most; flat, level with the ground; lying low etc. *v.*; crouched, subjacent, squat, prostrate etc. (*horizontal*) 213.

Adv. under; be-, under-neath; below; down, -wards; adown, at the foot of; under-foot, -ground; down—, below-stairs; at a low ebb; below par.

208. Depth.—N. depth; deepness etc. *adj.*; profundity, depression etc. (*concavity*) 252.

hollow, pit, shaft, well, crater, abyss; gulf etc. 198; bowels of the earth, bottomless pit, hell.

soundings, sonar, depth of water, water, draught, submersion; plummet, sound, probe; sounding -rod, – line, – machine; lead; submarine, diving bell, bathysphere; diver.

V. be -deep etc. *adj.*; render -deep etc. *adj.*; deepen.

plunge etc. 310; sound, heave the lead, take soundings; dig etc. (*excavate*) 252.

Adj. deep, -seated; profound, sunk, buried; submerged etc. 310; sub-aqueous, -marine, -terranean, -terrene; underground.

bottom-, sound-, fathom-less; unfathom-ed, -able; abysmal; deep as a well, deep-sea.

knee-, ankle-deep.

Adv. beyond—, out of- one's depth; over head and ears; over one's head.

209. Shallowness.—N. shallowness etc. *adj.*; shoals; mere scratch; veneer, gloss, pinprick.

Adj. shallow, superficial; skin–, ankle–, knee-deep; just enough to wet one's feet; shoal, -y.

V. shallow, shoal, skim– over, –the surface, touch on.

210. Summit.—N. summit, -y; top, vertex, apex, zenith, pinnacle, acme, acropolis, culmination, meridian, utmost height, *ne plus ultra*, height, pitch, maximum, climax, apogee; culminating –, crowning –, turning- point; turn of the tide, fountain head; water-shed, -parting; sky, pole.

tip, -top; crest, crow's nest, cap, truck, peak, nib; end etc. 67; crown, brow; head, nob, noddle, pate, skull, cranium.

high places, heights.

top-, top-gallant mast, sky scraper; quarter –, hurricane- deck.

architrave, frieze, cornice, coping, coping-stone, zoophorus, capital, headpiece, capstone, epistyle, sconce, pediment, entablature; tympanum; ceiling etc. (*covering*) 223.

attic, loft, garret, house-top, upper story, roof. topping, icing, frosting.

V. culminate, cap, crown, top; overtop etc. (*be superior to*) 33.

Adj. highest etc. (high etc. 206); top; top-, upper-most; tip-top; culminating etc. *v.*; meridi-an, -onal; capital, head, polar, supreme, supernal, top-gallant.

Adv. a-top, at the top of – the tree, – the heap.

211. Base.—N. base, -ment; plinth, dado, wainscot, baseboard; foundation etc. (*support*) 215; substructure, sub · *stratum*, sump, ground, earth, pavement, floor, paving, flag, carpet, ground-floor, deck; footing, groundwork, basis; hold, bilge, orlop deck.

bottom, nadir, foot, sole, toe, hoof, keel, kelson, root.

Adj. bottom; under-, nether-most; fundamental; founded –, based –, grounded –, built- on.

212. Verticality.—N. verticality; erectness etc. *adj.*; perpendicularity; right angle, normal; azimuth circle.

wall, palisade, precipice, cliff, steep, bluff.

elevation, erection; square, plumb-line, plummet.

V. be -vertical etc. *adj.*; stand -up, – on end, – erect, – upright; stick –, cock-up.

render -vertical etc. *adj.*; set –, stick –, raise –, cock- up; erect, rear, raise, pitch, raise on its legs.

Adj. vertical, upright, erect, perpendicular, normal, plumb, straight, bolt upright; rampant; straight –, standing- up etc. *v.*; rectangular, orthogonal.

Adv. vertically etc. *adj.*; up, on end; up –, right- on end; *à plomb*, endwise; on one's legs; at right angles.

213. Horizontality.—N. horizontality; flatness; level, plane; stratum etc. 204; dead -level, – flat; level plane.

recumbency; lying down etc. *v.*; reclination, decumbence; de-, discumbency; proneness etc. *adj.*; accubation, supination, resupination, prostration; azimuth.

plain, floor, platform, bowling-green; cricket--ground; court; gridiron; base-ball diamond; hockey rink; tennis-, croquet-ground, – lawn; billiard table; terrace, estrade, esplanade, *parterre*, table-land, *plateau,* ledge.

spirit-, level; T-square.

V. be -horizontal etc. *adj.*; lie, recline, couch; lie -down, – flat, – prostrate; sprawl, loll; sit down.

render -horizontal etc. *adj.*; lay, – down, – out; level, flatten, even, raze, equalize, smooth, align; prostrate, knock down, floor, fell, ground.

Adj. horizontal, level, even, plane; flat etc. 251; flat as a -billiard table, – bowling green; alluvial; calm, – as a mill-pond; smooth, –as glass.

re-, de-, pro-, ac-cumbent; lying etc. *v.*; prone, supine, couchant, jacent, prostrate.

Adv. horizontally etc. *adj.*; on -one's back. –all fours, – its beam ends.

214. Pendency.—N. pend-, dependency; suspension, hanging etc. *v.*

pendant, drop, tippet, tassel, lobe, tail, train, flap, lappet, skirt, pig-tail, queue, pendulum, hanger, suspender, supporter.

peg, knob, button, hook, nail, stud, ring, staple, tenterhook; davit; fastening etc. 45; spar, horse. chande-, gase-, electro-lier.

V. be -pendent etc. *adj.*; hang, depend, swing, dangle, droop, sag; swag; daggle, flap, trail, flow. suspend, hang, sling, hook up, hitch, fasten to, append.

Adj. pend-ent, -ulous; pensile; hanging etc. *v.*; dependent; suspended etc. *v.*; lowering, overhanging, beetling, decumbent; loose, flowing.

having a -peduncle etc. *n.*; pedunculate, tailed, caudate.

215. Support.—N. support, backing, ground, foundation, base, basis; *terra firma*, bearing. fulcrum, *point d'appui*, caudex, purchase, footing, hold, -*locus standi*; landing, – stage, – place; stage, platform; block; rest, resting-place; ground--work, *substratum*, sustentation, subvention; floor etc. (*basement*) 211.

supporter; aid etc. 707; prop, stand, anvil, fulciment; hod, stay, shore, skid, rib, sprag, truss, bandage; sleeper; stirrup, stilts, shoe, sole, heel, splint, lap; bar, rod, boom, sprit, outrigger.

staff, stick, crutch, alpenstock, bourdon; *bâton*, maulstick, colstaff, cowlstaff, staddle; stalk, ped-icel, -icle, – uncle.

post, pillar, shaft, column, pilaster; pediment, pedestal; plinth, shank, leg, socle, zocle; buttress, jamb, mullion, abutment; pile, baluster, banister, stanchion, king post; balustrade.

frame, -work, body, *chassis*, *fuselage*; scaffold, skeleton, beam, rafter, girder, lintel, joist, cantilever, travis, trave, corner-stone, summer, transom; rung, round, step, sill.

columella, back-bone; key-stone; axle, -tree; axis; arch, ogive, mainstay.

trunnion, pivot, rowlock; peg etc. (*pendency*)

214; tie-beam etc. (*fastening*) 45; thole pin.

board, ledge, shelf, hob, bracket, trevet, trivet, arbor, rack, hatrack; mantel, -piece. -shelf; slab, console; counter, dresser; flange, corbel; table, trestle, teapoy; shoulder; perch; horse; easel, desk; retable, predella.

seat, throne, dais; divan, musnud; chair, bench, form, stool, camp-stool, sofa, settee, davenport, stall, miserere, arm —, easy —, elbow —, rocking-chair; couch, day bed, *fauteuil*, woolsack, ottoman, settle, squab, bench, box, dicky; saddle, pannel, pillion; side —, pack- saddle; pommel.

bed, berth, pallet, tester, crib, cot, bassinet, hammock, shakedown, camp bed, bunk, truckle-bed, cradle, litter, stretcher, bedstead; four-poster, French bed; bedding, mattress, *paillasse*; pillow, bolster; mat, rug, cushion.

stool, footstool, hassock, faldstool, *prie-dieu*; tabouret; tripod.

Atlas, Persides, Atlantes, Caryatides, Hercules.

V. be -supported etc.; lie —, sit —, recline —, lean —, loll —, rest —, stand —, step —, repose —, abut —, beat —, be based etc.- on; have at one's back; be-stride, -straddle.

support, bear, carry, hold, sustain, shoulder; hold —, back —, bolster —, shore- up; up-hold, -bear; prop; under-prop, -pin, -set; bandage, etc. 43; brace, truss; cradle, pillow.

give —, furnish —, afford —, supply —, lend- -support, — foundations; bottom, found, base, ground, embed.

maintain, keep on foot; aid etc. 707.

Adj. support-ing, -ed, etc.*v.*; atlantean, columellar; sustentative, fundamental, basal.

Adv. astride on, astraddle; pick-a-back.

216. Parallelism.—N. parallelism; coextension, concentricity, collimation.

V. be —, lie- parallel to; collimate; equate, match.

Adj. parallel; coextensive, collateral, concentric, concurrent, abreast, aligned.

Adv. alongside, abreast etc. (*laterally*) 236.

217. Obliquity.—N. obliquity, inclination, skew, slope, slant; crookedness etc. *adj.*; slopeness; leaning etc. *v.*; bevel, bezel, ramp, tilt; bias, list, twist, warp, swag, cant, lurch; distortion etc. 243; bend etc. (*curve*) 245; tower of Pisa.

acclivity, rise, ascent, grade, gradient, *glacis*, rising ground, hill, bank, declivity, downhill, dip, fall, devexity; gentle —, rapid- slope; easy -ascent, — descent; shelving beach; *talus; montagne Russe; facilis descensus Averni.*

steepness etc. *adj.*; cliff, precipice etc. (*vertical*) 212; escarpment, scarp.

[Measure of inclination]clinometer, theodolite, level, sextant, quadrant, protractor; angle, sine, cosine, tangent etc. hypothenuse.

diagonal; zigzag, chevron.

V. be -oblique etc. *adj.*; slope, slant, lean, incline, shelve, stoop, decline, descent, bend, heel, careen, sag, swag, seel, slouch, cant, sidle.

render -oblique etc. *adj.*; sway, bias; slope, slant; incline, bend, crook; cant, tilt; distort etc. 243.

Adj. oblique, inclined; sloping etc. *v.*; tilted etc.

v.; recumbent, clinal, skew, askew, slant, aslant, bias, plagiedral, indirect, wry, awry, ajee, crooked; knock-kneed etc. (*distorted*) 243; bevel, out of the perpendicular.

uphill, rising, ascending, acclivous; downhill, falling, descending; declining, declivous, devex, anticlinal; steep, abrupt, precipitous, breakneck.

diagonal; trans-verse, -versal; athwart, antiparallel; curved etc. 245.

Adv. obliquely etc. *adj.*; on —, all on- one side; askew, askant, askance, aslope, asquint, edgewise, at an angle; side-long, -ways; slope-, slant-wise; by a side wind.

218. Inversion.—N. in-, e-, sub-, re-, retro-, intro-version; contraposition etc. 237; contrariety etc. 14; reversal; turn of the tide.

overturn, upset, capsize; somer-sault, -set; summerset; *culbute*; revulsion; *pirouette*.

transposition, transposal, anastrophy, metastasis, hyperbaton, anastrophe, hysteron--proteron, hypallage, synchysis, tmesis, parenthesis; *metathesis*; palindrome; Spoonerism.

pronation and supination.

V. be -inverted etc.; turn —, go —, wheel- -round, — about, — to the right about; turn —, go —, tilt —, topple-over; capsize, turn turtle.

in-, sub-, retro-, intro-vert; reverse; up-, overturn, -set; turn -topsy turvy etc. *adj.*; *culbuter*; transpose, put the cart before the horse, turn the tables.

Adj. inverted etc. *v.*; wrong side -out, — up; inside out, upside down; bottom —, keel- upwards; supine, on one's head, topsy turvy, *sens dessus sens dessous*.

inverse; reverse etc. (*contrary*) 14; opposite etc. 237.

topheavy, unstable.

Adv. inversely etc.*adj.*; hirdie-girdie; heels over head, head over heels.

219. Crossing.—N. crossing etc. *v.*; intersection, — lacement, — twinement, -digitation; decussation, transversion; convolution etc. 248.

reticulation, meshwork, network; inosculation, anastomosis, inter-texture, mortise.

net, *plexus*, web, mesh, twill, skein, sleeve, felt, lace; wicker; mat, -ting; plait, trellis, wattle, lattice, grating, *grille*, gridiron, tracery, fretwork, filigree, reticle; tissue, netting, mokes.

cross, crucifix, rood, crisscross, crux; chain, wreath, braid, cat's cradle,knot; entanglement etc. (*disorder*) 59.

[woven fabrics] cloth, linen, muslin, cambric, drill, homespun, tweed, broadcloth etc.

V. cross, decussate; inter-sect, -lace, -twine, -twist, -weave, -digitate, -link.

twine, entwine, weave, inweave, twist, wreathe; anastomose, inosculate, dovetail, splice, link.

mat, plait, plat, braid, felt, twill; tangle, entangle, ravel; net, knot; dishevel, raddle.

Adj. crossing etc.*v.*; crossed, matted etc. *v.*; transverse.

cross, cruciform, crucial; reti-form, -cular, -culated; arcolar, cancellated, mullioned, latticed, grated, barred, streaked; textile, secant, plexal; interfretted.

Adv. across, thwart, athwart, transversely, crosswise.

220. Exteriority.—N. exteriority; outside, exterior; surface, superficies; skin etc. (*covering*) 223; *superstratum*; disk, disc; face, facet, external, the open.

excentricity; circumjacence etc. 227.

V. be -exterior etc. *adj.*; lie around etc. 227.

place -exteriorly, — outwardly, — outside; put —, turn- out.

Adj. exter-ior, -nal; extraneous, outer, -most; out-ward, -lying, -side, -door; round about etc. 227; extramural.

superficial, skin-deep; frontal, discoid.

extraregarding; eccentric; outstanding; extrinsic etc. 6.

Adv. externally etc. *adj.*; out, without, over, outwards, *ab extra*, out of doors; *extra muros.*

in the open air; *sub -Jovè, — dio; à la belle étoile, al fresco.*

221. Interiority.—N. interiority; inside, -land, interior, endocrine; interspace, subsoil, *substratum.*

contents etc. 190; substance, pith, marrow; backbone etc. (*center*) 222; heart, bosom, breast, abdomen; vitals, viscera, entrails, bowels, belly, intestines, guts, chitterlings, womb, lap; gland, cell; internal organs, *penetralia*, recesses, innermost recesses; cave etc. (*concavity*) 252.

inhabitant etc. 188.

V. be -inside etc. *adj.*, — within etc. *adv.*

place —, keep- within; enclose etc. (*circumscribe*) 229; intern; embed etc. (*insert*) 300.

Adj. inter-ior, -nal; inner, inside, intimate, inward, intraregarding; in-, inner-most; deep-seated; visceral, intestine, -tinal; inland; subcutaneous; interstitial etc. (*interjacent*) 228; inwrought etc. (*intrinsic*) 5; enclosed etc. *v.*

home, domestic, indoor, intramural, vernacular; endemic.

Adv. internally etc. *adj.*; inwards, within, in, inly; here-, there-, where-in; *ab intra*, withinside; in —, within- doors; at home, in the bosom of one's family.

222. Centrality.—N. centrality, centricalness, center; middle etc. 68; focus etc. 74.

core, kernel; nucleus, nucleolus; heart, pole, axis, pivot, fulcrum, bull's eye; hub, nave, navel; *umbilicus*, spine, backbone, marrow, pith; hot-bed; concentration etc. (*convergence*) 290; centralization; symmetry.

center of -gravity, — pressure, — percussion, — oscillation, — buoyancy etc. metacenter.

V. be -central etc. *adj.*; converge etc. 290.

render central, centralize, concentrate; bring to a focus.

Adj. centr-al, -ical; middle etc. 68; axial, pivotal, focal, umbilical, concentric; middlemost, nuclear, centric, centroidal; spinal, vertebral.

Adv. middle; midst; centrally etc. *adj.*

223. Covering.—N. covering, cover; canopy, tilt, awning, baldachin, tent, marquee, *tente d'abri*, umbrella, parasol, sunshade; veil (*shade*) 424; shield etc. (*defense*) 717; hall.

roof, dome, cupola, mansard roof; ceiling; thatch, tile; pan-, pen-tile; tiling, shingles, slates, slating, leads; shed etc. (*abode*) 189.

top, lid, coverde, door, *operculum*, eyelid, blind, curtain.

bandage, plaster, lint, wrapping, dossil, finger stall.

coverlet, counterpane, sheet, quilt, comforter, eiderdown; tarpaulin, blanket, rug, drugget, linoleum, oilcloth; housing.

in-, tegument; skin, pellicle, fleece, fell, fur, ermine, miniver, sable, sealskin etc.; fabrikoid; leather, morocco, calf, pigskin, elk, kid, cowhide etc.; shagreen, hide; pelt, -ry; cuticle, *dermis*, scarf-skin, *epidermis.*

clothing etc. 225; mask etc. (*concealment*) 530.

peel, crust, bark, rind, *cortex*, husk, shell, coat.

capsule; ferrule; sheath, -ing; pod, cod; casing, case, theca; *elytron; involucrum*; wrapp-ing, -er, cellophane; envelope, vesicle; dermatology, conchology.

armor, -plate, armoring; veneer, facing; pavement; scale etc. (*layer*) 204; coating, paint, stain; varnish etc. (*resin*) 356*a*; anointing etc. *v.*; inunction; incrustation, superposition, obduction, ground, enamel, whitewash, plaster, stucco, rough cast, pebble dash, compo; rendering; cerement; ointment etc. (*grease*) 356.

V. cover; super-pose, -impose; over-lay, -spread; wrap etc. 225; incase; face, case, veneer, pave, paper; tip, cap, bind, revet.

coat, paint, varnish, pay, incrust, stucco, cement, dab, plaster, tar; wash; be-, smear; be-, daub; anoint, do over; gild, plate, electroplate, japan, laquer, lacker, enamel, whitewash; lay it on thick.

over-lie, -arch; conceal etc. 528.

Adj. covering etc. *v.*; cutaneous, dermal, cortical, cuticular, tegumentary, skinny, scaly, squamous; covered etc. *v.*; imbricated, loricated, armor-plated, iron-clad; under cover, hooded, cloaked, cowled.

224. Lining.—N. lining, inner coating; coating etc. (*covering*) 223; stalactite, -agmite.

filling, stuffing, wadding, padding, bushing, wainscot, *parietes*, wall brattice.

V. line, stuff, incrust, wad, pad, fill.

Adj. lined etc. *v.*

225. Investment.—N. investment; covering etc. 223; dress, clothing, raiment, drapery, costume, attire, guise, toilet, *toilette*, trim; habiliment; vesture, -ment; garment, garb, palliament, apparel, wardrobe, wearing apparel, clothes, things.

array; tailoring, millinery; best bib and tucker; finery etc. (*ornament*) 847; full dress etc. (*show*) 882; garniture; theatrical properties.

outfit, equipment, *trousseau*; uniform, khaki, regimentals; academicals, canonicals etc. 999; livery, gear, harness, turn out, accoutrement, caparison, suit, rigging, trappings, traps, slops, togs, toggery; masquerade.

dishabille, morning dress, lounge suit, tea-gown, *kimono, néglige*, dressing-gown, *peignoir*, wrapper, undress; shooting-coat; smoking jacket, mufti; rags, tatters, old clothes; mourning, weeds; duds; slippers.

robe, tunic, dolman, *paletot*, habit, gown, coat, coatee, frock, blouse, *pelisse*, middy, sagum, *toga*, smock-frock; frock-, dress-, morning-, tail- coat; dress-suit, − clothes, swallow-tail coat, dinner-, Eton-jacket.

cloak, pall; mantle, mantlet, mantua, shawl, *pelisse*, veil, yashmak; cape, tippet, kirtle, plaid, muffler, comforter, Balaclava helmet, haik, huke, chlamys, mantilla, tabard, housing, horse-cloth, burnous, *roquelaure*, *houppelande*; sur-, top-, over-, great-coat; *surtout*, spencer, cardigan, sweater, blazer; mackintosh, waterproof, slicker, raincoat, oilskin, trench coat, ulster, monkey-, pea-, pilot-jacket, redingote; wraprascal, poncho, cardinal, pelerine, talma.

jacket, jumper, vest, jerkin, waistcoat, doublet, *camisole*, gabardine; stays, *corsage*, corset, corselet, bodice; stomacher; skirt, petticoat, slip, farthingale, kilt, jupe, crinoline, bustle, hobble skirt, *panier*, apron, pinafore; loin cloth.

trousers; breeches, trews, pantaloons, unmentionables, inexpressibles, overalls, pajamas, smalls, small-clothes; tights, pants, shorts, drawers; knickerbockers, knickers, plus fours, bloomers, divided skirt; phil-, fill-ibeg.

head-dress, -gear; cap, *béret*, tam o' shanter, glengarry, topee, sombrero; hat; cocked −, high −, tall −, top −, silk −, opera −, crush - hat, *gibus*, beaver, castor, bonnet, tile, wideawake, billy-cock; bowler; soft felt −, straw −, leghorn- hat, panama; toque; wimple; night-, mob-, skull-cap, biretta; hood, cowl, coif; capote, calach; scull-cap; kerchief, snood; head, *coiffure*; crown etc. *(circle)* 247; *chignon*, pelt, wig, front, peruke, periwig; caftan, turban, fez, *tarboosh*, taj, shako, csako, busby; *képi*, forage cap, bearskin; helmet etc. 717; mask, domino.

body clothes; linen; shirt, sark, smock, shift, *chemise*, *lingerie*; night-gown, -shirt; bed-gown, *sac de nuit*; jersey, guernsey; underclothing, - waistcoat.

neck-erchief, -cloth; tie, ruff, collar, cravat, stock, handkerchief, bandana, scarf; bib, tucker; dicky; boa; girdle etc. *(circle)* 247; cummerbund.

shoe, pump, brogue, boot, slipper, sandal, galoche, galoshes, arctics, rubber boots, overshoes, patten, clog, sabot; high-low; Blucher −, Wellington −, Hessian −, jack −, top- boot; Balmoral; legging, puttee, buskin, greave, galligaskin, moccasin, *gamache*, gambado, gaiter, spatter-dash, spat, antigropeles; stocking, hose, gaskins, trunk-hose, sock, hosiery.

glove, gauntlet, mitten, cuff, muffettee, wristband, sleeve.

swaddling cloth, baby-linen, *layette*; pocket-handkerchief.

shroud, etc. 363.

clothier, tailor, milliner, *costumier*, sempstress, seamstress, snip; dress-, habit-, breeches-, shoemaker; cordwainer, cobbler, Crispin, hosier, hatter; draper, linendraper, haberdasher, mercer.

V.invest; cover etc. 223; envelop, lap, involve; in-, en-wrap; wrap; fold −, wrap −, lap −, muffleup; overlap; sheathe, swathe, swaddle, roll up in, shroud, circumvest.

vest, clothe, array, dress, dight, drape, robe, enrobe, attire, tire, garb, habilitate, apparel, accouter, rig, fit out; bedizen, deck etc. *(ornament)* 847; perk; equip, harness, caparison; dress up.

wear; don; put −, huddle −, slip- on; mantle.

Adj. invested etc. *v.*; habited; dight, -ed; clad, *costumé*, shod, *chaussé*; *en grande tenue* etc. *(show)* 882.

sartorial.

---

226. Divestment.—N. divestment; taking off, stripping, removal etc. *v.*

nudity; bareness etc. *adj.*; undress; dishabille etc. 225, altogether; nu-, denu-dation; decortication, depilation, excoriation, desquamation; molting; exfoliation.

baldness, alopecia, acomia.

V. divest; uncover etc. *(cover* etc. 223); denude, bare, strip; undress, unclothe, disrobe etc. *(dress, enrobe, etc.* 225); uncoif; dismantle; uncase; put −, take −, cast- off; shed, doff; husk, peel, pare, decorticate, desquamate; excoriate, skin, scalp, flay, bark, expose, lay open; exfoliate, molt, mew; cast the skin.

Adj. divested etc. *v.*; bare, naked, nude; undressed, -draped, -clad, -clothed, -appareled; exposed; in dishabille; *décolleté*; bald, threadbare, ragged, callow, roofless.

in -a state of nature, − nature's garb, − buff, − native buff, − birthday suit; *in puris naturalibus*; with nothing on, stark naked; bald as a coot, bare as the back of one's hand; out at elbows; barefoot; bareback; leaf-, nap-, hairless, shaved, clean shaven, tonsured, beardless, bald-headed, acomous.

---

227. Circumjacence.—N. circumjacence, - ambience; environment, encompassment; atmosphere, medium; surroundings, *entourage*.

outpost; border etc. *(edge)* 231; girdle etc. *(circumference)* 230; outskirts, *boulevards*, suburbs, purlieus, precincts, *faubourgs*, environs, *banlieue*; neighborhood, vicinity.

V.lie -around etc. *adv.*; surround, beset, compass, encompass, environ, inclose, enclose, encircle, circle, embrace, circumvent, lap, gird; begird, girdle, engird; skirt, twine round; hem in etc. *(circumscribe)* 229; besiege, invest, blockade.

Adj. circum-jacent, -ambient, -fluent; ambient; surrounding etc. *v.*; circumferential, suburban.

Adv. around, about; without; on -every side, − all sides; right and left, all round, round about; in the neighborhood.

---

228. Interjacence.—N. inter-jacence, - currence, -venience, -location, -digitation, - penetration; permeation.

inter-jection, -polation, -lineation, -spersion, - calation; embolism.

inter-vention, -ference, -position; in-, ob-trusion; insinuation; insertion etc. 300; dovetailing; infiltration; intromission.

intermedi-um, -ary; go-between, agent, middleman, medium, bodkin, intruder, interloper; parenthesis, episode; fly-leaf.

partition, *septum*, diaphragm, mid-riff; party-wall, panel, vail, bulkhead, brattice, *cloison*; halfway house.

V.lie −, come −, get- between; intervene, slide in, interpenetrate, permeate.

put between, introduce, intromit, import; throw –, wedge –, edge –, jam –, worm –, foist –, run –, plough –, work- in; interpose, -ject, -calate, -polate, -line, -leave, -sperse, -weave, -lard, -digitate; let in, dovetail, splice, mortise; insinuate, smuggle; infiltrate, ingrain.

interfere, put in an oar, thrust one's nose in; intrude, obtrude; have a finger in the pie; introduce the thin end of the wedge; thrust in etc. (*insert*) 300.

Adj. inter-jacent, -current, -venient, -vening etc. *v.*, -mediate, -mediary, -calary, -sitital, -costal, -mural, -planetary, -stellar; embolismal.

parenthetical, episodic; mediterranean; intrusive; embosomed; merged, mean, middle, medium, median.

Adv. between, betwixt; 'twixt; among, -st; amid, st; 'mid, -st; in the thick of; betwixt and between; sandwich-wise; parenthetically, *obiter dictum*.

229. Circumscription.—N. circumscription, limitation, inclosure; confinement etc. (*restraint*) 751; circumvallation, encincture; envelope etc. 232.

V. circumscribe, limit, bound, confine, restrict, enclose; surround etc. 227; compass about; imprision etc. (*restrain*) 751; hedge –, wall –, rail- in; fence –, hedge- round; embar; picket, corral.

enfold, bury, incase, pack up, enshrine, inclasp; wrap up etc. (*invest*) 225; embosom.

Adj. circumscribed etc. *v.*; begirt, lapt; circumambient; buried –, immersed- in; embosomed, in the bosom of, imbedded, encysted, mewed up; imprisoned etc. 751; land-locked, in a ring fence.

230. Outline.—N. outline, circumference; perimeter, -phery; ambit, circuit, lines, *tournure, contour*, profile, *silhouette*, lineaments; bounds, coastline.

zone, belt, girth, band, baldric, zodiac, girdle, tire, cingle, clasp, girt; *cordon* etc. (*inclosure*) 232; circlet etc. 247.

V. outline, delineate, *silhouette*, circumscribe etc. 229; profile, block out.

Adj. outlined etc. *v.*; circumferential, perimetric, peripheral.

231. Edge.—N. edge, verge, brink, brow, brim, margin, border, confines, skirt, rim, felloe, felly, flange, side, mouth; jaws, chops, chaps, *fauces*; lip, muzzle.

threshold, door, porch; portal etc. (*opening*) 260; coast, shore, strand, beach, bank, wharf, quay, dock.

frame, fringe, flounce, frill, list, trimming, edging, skirting, hem, selvedge, welt; furbelow, valance, exergue.

Adj. border, marginal, skirting; labial; labiated, marginated.

232. Inclosure.—N. inclosure, enclosure, envelope; package, box, crate, case etc. (*receptacle*) 191; wrapper; girdle etc. 230.

pen, fold, croft, sty; pen-, in-, sheep--fold; paddock, pound, corral, kraal; yard, compound; net, seine net.

wall; hedge, -row; *espalier*; fence etc. (*defence*) 717; pale, paling, balustrade, rail, railing, gunwale; quickset hedge, park paling, circumvallation, *enciente*, ring fence.

barrier, barricade; gate; -way; door, hatch, *cordon*; prison etc. 752.

dike, dyke, ditch, fosse, moat, trench.

V. inclose; circumscribe etc. 229.

233. Limit.—N. limit, boundary, bounds, confine, *enclave*, term, bourn, verge, kerb-stone, curbstone, but, pale; termin-ation, -us; stint, frontier, precinct, marches.

boundary line, landmark; line of -demarcation, – circumvallation; pillars of Hercules; Rubicon, turning-point; *ne plus ultra*; sluice, flood-gate.

V. limit, bound, confine, define, circumscribe, demarcate, delimit, encompass.

Adj. definite; contermin-ate, -able, terminable, limitable; terminal, frontier, border, bordering, boundary.

Adv. thus far, – and no further.

234. Front.—N. front; fore, – part; foreground; forefront, face, disk, disc, frontage, *façade, proscenium*, facia, frontispiece; priority, anteriority; obverse [of a medal].

fore –, front- rank, first line; van, -guard; advanced guard; outpost, scout.

brow, forehead, visage, physiognomy, phiz, features, countenance, map, mug; rostrum, beak, bow, stem, prow, prore, jib, bowsprit; forecastle. pioneer etc. (*precursor*) 64; metoposcopy.

V. be –, stand- in front etc. *adj.*; front, face, confront, breast, brave; bend forwards; come to the -front, – fore.

Adj. fore, forward, anterior, front, frontal, head-on, leading, first, primary.

Adv. before; in -front, – the van, – advance; ahead, right ahead; fore-, head-most; in the foreground; before one's -face, – eyes; face to face, *vis-à-vis*.

235. Rear.—N. rear, back, posterior-ity; rear- rank, – guard; background, *hinterland*.

occiput, nape, scruff, chine; heels; tail, rump, croup, buttock, posteriors, bottom, seat, backside, scut, breech, *dorsum*, loin; dorsal –, lumbar-region; hind quarters.

stern poop, after-part, counter; postern, heel-, tail-piece, crupper.

wake; train etc. (*sequence*) 281.

reverse; other side of the shield.

V. be -behind etc. *adv.*; fall astern; bend backwards; bring up the rear; follow etc. 622; tail, shadow.

Adj. back, rear; hind, -er, -most, -ermost; postern, -erior; dorsal, after; caudal, lumbar; mizzen.

Adv. behind; in the -rear, – ruck, – background; behind one's back; at the -heels, — tail, — back- of; back to back.

after, -most, aft, abaft, astern, stern- most, aback, rear-, hind-, back-ward.

236. Laterality.—N. laterality; side, flank, beam, quarter, lee; hand; cheek, jowl, jole, wing; profile; temple, *parietes*, loin, haunch, hip.

gable, -end; broadside; lee side.

points of the compass; East, Orient, Levant; West, occident; orientation.

V. be -on one side etc. *adv.*; flank, outflank; sidle; skirt, border.

Adj. lateral, sidelong; collateral; parietal, flanking, skirting; flanked; sideling.

many-sided; multi-, bi-, tri-, quadri- lateral.

East-ern, -ward, -erly; orient, -al, auroral, Levantine; West-ern, -ward, -erly; occidental, Hesperian; equatorial.

Adv. side-ways, -long; broadside on; on one side, abreast, abeam, alongside, beside, aside; by, — the side of; side by side; cheek by jowl etc. (*near*) 197; to -windward, — leeward; laterally etc. *adj.*; right and left; on her beam ends.

237. Contraposition.—N. contraposition, opposition; polarity; inversion etc. 218; opposite side; antithesis; reverse, inverse; counterpart; antipodes; opposite poles, North and South.

V. be -opposite etc. *adj.*; subtend.

Adj. opposite; reverse, inverse; antipodal, subcontrary; fronting, facing, diametrically opposite.

Northern, Septentrional, Boreal, arctic; Southern, Austral, antarctic, polar.

Adv. over, — the way, — against; against; face to face, vis-à-vis; as poles asunder.

238. Dextrality.—N. dextrality; right, — hand; dexter, offside, starboard.

Adj. dextral, right-handed; ambidextral; dexterous, dextrorsal etc.

239. Sinistrality.—N. sinistrality; left, — hand; *sinister*, nearside, larboard, port.

Adj. sinistral, sinister, sinistrorsal etc., left-handed, sinistromanual, sinistrous.

240. Form.—N. form, figure, shape, physique; con-formation, -figuration; make, formation, frame, construction, design, cut, set, build, trim, cut of one's jib; stamp, type, cast, mold; fashion; contour etc. (*outline*) 230; structure etc. 329.

feature, lineament, outline, turn; phase etc. (*aspect*) 448; posture, attitude, *pose*.

[Science of form] morphology.

[Similarity of form] isomorphism.

forming etc. *v.*; form-, figur-, efform- ation; sculpture.

V. form, shape, figure, fashion, efform, carve, cut, chisel, hew, cast; rough-hew, -cast; sketch; block —, hammer- out; trim; lick —, put- into

shape; model, knead, work up into, set, mold, sculpture; cast, stamp; built etc. (*construct*) 161.

Adj. formed etc. *v.*

[Receiving form] plastic, fictile, full- fashioned etc.

[Giving form] plasmic, etc.

[Similar in form] isomorphous etc.

241. Amorphism. [Absence of form.]—N. amorphism, informity, uncouthness; unlicked cub, rough diamond; *rudis indigestaque moles*; disorder etc. 59; deformity etc. 243.

disfigure-, deface-ment, deformation; mutilation.

V. [Destroy form] deface, disfigure, deform, mutilate, truncate; derange etc. 61.

Adj. shapeless, amorphous, malformed, formless; un-formed, -hewn, -fashioned, -shapen; rough, rude, Gothic, barbarous, rugged, in the rough; misshapen etc. 243.

242. Symmetry. [Regularity of form.]—N. symmetry, shapeliness, finish; beauty etc. 845; proportion, eurythmy, eurythmic, uniformity, parallelism; bi-, tri-, multi-lateral symmetry; centrality etc. 222.

arborescence, branching, ramification.

Adj. symmetrical, shapely, well set, finished; beautiful etc. 845; classic, chaste, severe.

regular, uniform, balanced; equal etc. 27; parallel, coextensive.

arbor-escent, -iform; dendr-iform, -oid; branching; ramous, ramose.

243. Distortion. [Irregularity of form.]—N. dis-, de-, con-tortion; knot, mop, warp, buckle, screw, twist; crookedness etc. (*obliquity*) 217; grimmace; deformity; mal-, malcon-formation; monstrosity, misproportion, want of symmetry, *anamorphosis*; ugliness etc. 846; teratology.

V. distort, contort, twist, warp etc. *n.*; wrest, writhe, make faces, deform, misshape.

Adj. distorted etc. *v.*; out of shape, irregular, unsymmetric, awry, wry, askew, crooked, sinuous; anamorphous; not -true, — straight; on one side, crump, deformed; mis-shapen, -begotten; mis-, ill-proportioned; ill-made; grotesque, crooked as a ram's horn; hump-, hunch-, bunch-, crook-backed; bandy; bandy-, bow-legged; bow-, knock-kneed; splay-, club-footed; taliped; round-shouldered; snub-nosed; curtailed of one's fair proportions; scalene, stumpy etc. (*short*) 201; gaunt etc. (*thin*) 203; bloated etc. 194.

Adv. all manner of ways.

244. Angularity.—N. angular-ity, -ness; aduncity; angle, cusp, bend; fold etc. 258; notch etc. 257; fork, bifurcation.

elbow, knee, knuckle, ankle, groin, crotch, crane, fluke, scythe, sickle, zigzag, kimbo.

corner, nook, recess, niche, oriel.

right angle etc. (*perpendicular*) 212; obliquity etc. 217; angle of 45 degrees, miter; acute —, obtuse —, salient —, re-entrant —, spherical —, solid —, dihedral- angle.

angular -measurement, – elevation, – distance, – velocity; trigon-, goni-ometry; altimetry; clin-, graph-, goni-ometer; theodolite; transit circle; sextant, quadrant; dichotomy.

triangle, trigon, wedge; rectangle, square, lozenge, diamond; rhomb, -us; quadr-angle, -ilateral; parallelogram; quadrature; poly-, penta-, hexa-, hepta-, octa-, deca-gon.

Platonic bodies; cube, rhomboid; tetra-, penta-, hexa-, octa-, dodeca-, icosa-hedron; prism, pyramid; parallelopiped.

V. bend, fork, bifurcate, crinkle, divaricate, branch, ramify.

Adj. angular, bent, crooked, aduncous, uncinated, aquiline, jagged, serrated; falc-iform, -ated; furcular, furcated, forked, bifurcate, crotched; zigzag; dovetailed; knock-kneed, crinkled, akimbo, kimbo, geniculated; oblique etc. 217.

fusiform, wedge-shaped, cuneiform; tri-angular, -gonal, -lateral; quadr-angular, -ilateral; rectangular, square, foursquare, multilateral; polygonal etc. *n.*; cubical, rhomboidal, pyramidal.

245. Curvature.—N. curv-ature, -ity, -ation; incurv-ity, -ation; bend; flex- ure, -ion; conflexure; crook, hook, bought, bending; de-, inflexion; arcuation, devexity, turn; deviation, *détour*, sweep; curl, -ing; bough; recurv-ity, -ation; sinuosity etc. 248; aduncity.

curve, arc, arch, arcade, vault, dome, bow, crescent, *meniscus*, half-moon, lunule, horse-shoe, loop, crane-neck; para-, hyper-bola; catenary; festoon; conch-, cardi-oid; caustic, instep; tracery.

V. be -curved etc. *adj.*; sweep, swag, sag; deviate etc. 279; turn; re-enter.

render -curved etc. *adj.*; bend, curve, incurvate; de-, in-flect; crook; turn, round, arch, arcuate, arch over, loop the loop, concamerate; bow, coil, curl, recurve, frizzle.

Adj. curved etc. *v.*; curvi-form, -lineal, -linear, devex, devious; recurv-ed, -ous; *retroussé*; crump; bowed etc. *v.*; vaulted; hooked; falc-iform, -ated; semicircular, crescentic; lun-iform, -ular; semilunar, meniscal; conchoidal; cord-iform, -ated; cardioid; heart-, bell-, pear-, fig-shaped; reniform; lenti-form, -cular; bow-legged etc. (*distorted*) 243; oblique etc. 217; circular etc. 247.

246. Straightness.—N. straightness, rectilinearity, directness; inflexibility etc. (*stiffness*) 323; straight –, right –, direct-, bee- line; short cut.

V. be -straight etc. *adj*; have no turning; not -incline, – bend, – turn, – deviate- to either side; go straight; steer for etc. (*direction*) 278.

render straight, straighten, rectify; set –, put-straight; un-bend, -fold, -curl etc. 248, -ravel etc. 219, -wrap.

Adj. straight; rectiline-ar, -al; direct, even, right, true, in a line; unbent etc. *v.*; un-deviating, -turned, -distorted, -swerving; straight as an arrow etc. (*direct*) 278; inflexible etc. 323.

247. Circularity. [Simple circularity.]—N. circularity, roundness; rotundity etc. 249.

circle, circlet, ring, washer, areola, hoop, round-let, *annulus*, annulet, bracelet, armlet, armilla; ringlet; eye, loop, wheel; cycle, orb, orbit, rundle, zone, belt, *cordon*, band; sash, girdle, cestus, cincture, baldric, fillet, *fascia*, wreath, garland; crown, corona, coronet, chaplet, snood, necklace, collar; noose, lasso, lariat.

ellipse, oval, ovule; ellipsoid, cycloid; epi-cycloid, -cycle; semi-circle; quadrant, sextant, sector.

V. make -round etc. *adj.*; round.

go round; encircle etc. 227; describe -a circle etc. 311.

Adj. round, rounded, circular, annular, or-bicular; oval, ovate; elliptic, -al; ovoid, egg-shaped; pear-shaped etc. 245; cycloidal etc. *n.*; spherical etc. 249.

248. Convolution. [Complex circularity.]—N. winding etc. *v.*; con-, in-, circum-volution; wave, undulation, tortuosity, anfractuosity; sinu-osity, -ation, sinuousness; meandering, circuit, circumbendibus, twist, twirl, windings and turnings, *ambages*; torsion; inosculation; reticulation etc. (*crossing*) 219.

coil, roll, curl, buckle, spire, spiral, helix, corkscrew, worm, volute, whorl, rundle; tendril; scollop, scallop, escalop; kink.

serpent, snake, eel, maze, labyrinth.

V. be -convoluted etc. *adj.*; wind, twine, turn and twist, twirl; wave, undulate, meander; inosculate; entwine, intwine; twist, coil, roll; wrinkle, curl, crisp, twill; frizz, -le; crimp, crape, indent, scollop, scallop; wring, intort; contort; wreathe etc. (*cross*) 219.

Adj. convoluted; winding, twisted etc. *v.*; tortile, tortive; wavy; und-ated, -ulatory; circling, snaky, snake-like, serpentine; serpent-, anguill-, verm-iform; vermicular; mazy, tortuous, anfractuous, sinuous, flexuous, wavy, sigmoidal.

involved, intricate, complicated, perplexed; labyrinth-ic, -ian, -ine; circuitous; peristaltic; daedalian, curly.

wreathy, frizzly, *crêpé*, buckled; ravelled etc. (*in disorder*) 59.

spiral, coiled, helical, turbinated.

Adv. in and out, round and round.

249. Rotundity.—N. rotundity; roundness etc. *adj.*; cyclindricity; spher-icity, -oidity; globosity.

cylin-der, -droid; barrel, drum; roll, -er; *rouleau*, column, rolling-pin, rundle; chimney-pot, drain-pipe.

cone, conoid; pear-, egg-, bell-shape.

sphere, globe, orb, orbit, ball, boulder, bowlder; spher-, ellips-, ge-, glob-oid, oblong –, oblate-spheroid; drop, spherule, globule, vesicle, bulb, bullet, pellet, *pelote*, clew, pill, marble, pea, knob, pommel, knot.

V. render -spherical etc. *adj.*; form into a sphere, sphere, roll into a ball; give -rotundity etc. *n.*; round.

Adj. rotund; round etc. (*circular*) 247; cylindr-ic, -ical, -oid; columnar, lumbriciform; conic, -al; spher-ical, -oidal; glob-ular, -ated, -ous, -ose; egg-, bell-, pear-shaped; ov-oid, -iform; gibbous; cam-paniform, -ulate, -iliform; fungiform, bead-like, moniliform, pyriform, bulbous; *teres atque rotundus*; round as -an orange, – an apple, – a ball, – a billiard ball, – a cannon ball.

250. Convexity.—N. convexity, prominence, projection, swelling, gibbosity, bilge, bulge, protuberance, protrusion; excrescency, camber.

intumescence; tumor; tubercle, -osity; excrescence; hump, hunch, bunch, gnarl.

tooth, knob, elbow, process, *apophysis*, condyle, bulb, node, nodule, nodosity, tongue, *dorsum*, boss, embossment, bump, clump; sugar-loaf etc. (*sharpness*) 253; bow; mamelon.

pimple, wen, wheal, *papula*, postule, pock, proud flesh, growth, goiter, *sarcoma*, caruncle, corn, bunion, wart, furnuncle, polypus, adenoid, fungus, fungosity, *exostosis*, bleb, blister, blain; boil etc. (*disease*) 655; bubble, blob.

papilla, nipple, teat, pap, breast, dug, mammilla; proboscis, .ose, neb, beak, snout, nozzle, snozzle; Adam's apple; belly, paunch, corporation; withers, back, shoulder, lip, flange.

peg, button, stud, ridge, rib, jutty, trunnion, snag.

cupola, dome, bee-hive; arch, balcony, eaves; pilaster.

relief, relievo, *cameo*; *basso-*, *mezzo-*, *alto-rilievo*; low-, bas-, high-relief.

hill etc. (*height*) 206; cape, promontory, mull; fore-, head-land; point of land, naze, ness, mole, jetty, hummock, ledge, spur.

V. be -prominent etc. *adj.*; project, bulge, protrude, bag, belly, pout, bouge, bunch; jut –, stand –, stick –, poke- out; stick –, bristle –, start –, cock –, shoot- up; swell –, hang –, bend-over; beetle.

render -prominent etc. *adj.*; raise 307; emboss, chase.

Adj. convex, prominent, protuberant, underhung, undershot; projecting etc. *v.*; bossed, bossy, nodular, bunchy; clav-ate, -ated; hummocky, *moutonné*, mammiform; papul-ous, -ose; hemispheric, bulbous; bowed, arched; bold; bellied; tuber-ous, -culous; tumorous; cornute, knobby, odontoid; lenti-form, -cular; gibbous.

salient, in relief, raised, *repoussé*; bloated etc. (*expanded*) 194.

251. Flatness.—N. flatness etc. *adj.*; smoothness etc. 255.

plane; level etc. 213; plate, platter, table, tablet, slab.

V. render flat, flatten, squash; level etc. 213.

Adj. flat, plane, even, flush, scutiform, discoid; level etc. (*horizontal*) 213; smooth; flat as -a pancake, – a fluke, – a flounder, – a board, – my hand.

252. Concavity.—N. concavity, depression, dip; hollow, -ness; indentation, *intaglio*, cavity, antrum, dent, dint, dimple, follicle, pit, *sinus*, *alveolus*, *lacuna*; excavation, trench, shaft, sap, mine, tunnel, burrow; trough etc. (*furrow*) 259; honeycomb.

cup, basin, crater, punch-bowl; cell etc. (*receptacle*) 191; socket, faucet.

valley, vale, dale, dell, gap, dingle, combe, bottom, slade, strath, glade, grove, glen, cave, cavern, cove; grot, -to; alcove, *cul-de-sac*, blind alley; gully etc. 198; arch etc. (*curve*) 245; bay etc. (*of the sea*) 343.

excavator, sapper, miner.

V.be -concave etc. *adj.*; retire, cave in.

render -concave etc. *adj.*; depress, hollow; scoop, – out; gouge, dig, delve, excavate, dent, dint, mine, sap, undermine, burrow, tunnel, stave in.

Adj. depressed etc. *v.*; concave, hollow, stove in; dished; spoon-like; retiring; retreating; cavernous; porous etc. (*with holes*) 260; cellular, spongy, spongious; honeycombed, alveolar; infundibul-ar, -iform; funnel-, bell-shaped; campaniform, capsular; vaulted, arched.

253. Sharpness.—N. sharpness etc. *adj.*; acuity, acumination; spinosity.

point, spike, spine, *spiculum*, tine; needle, pin; tack, nail; prick, -le; spur, rowel, barb; spit, cusp; horn, antler; snag; tag; thorn, bristle.

nib, tooth, incisor, tusk; spoke, cog, ratchet.

crag, crest *arête*, cone, peak, sugar-loaf, pike, *aiguille*; spire, pyramid, steeple.

beard, *chevaux de frise*, porcupine, hedgehog, brier, bramble, thistle; comb, awn, bur.

wedge; knife-, cutting- edge; blade, edge-tool, cutlery, knife, penknife, whittle, razor; scalpel, bistoury, lancet; chisel; ploughshare, coulter; hatchet, axe, pick-axe, mattock, pick, adze, bill; billhook, cleaver, cutter; skiver; scythe, sickle, scissors, shears; sword etc. (*arms*) 727; bodkin etc. (*perforator*) 262.

sharpener, hone, strop; grind-, whet-stone; steel, emery.

V. be -sharp etc. *adj.*; taper to a point; bristle with.

render -sharp etc. *adj.*; sharpen, point, aculeate, acuminate, whet, barb, spiculate, set, strop, grind.

cut etc. (*sunder*) 44.

Adj. sharp, keen; acute; aci-cular, -form; aculeated, -minated; pointed; tapering; conical, pyramidal; mucron-ate, -ated; spindle-, needle-shaped; spiked, spiky, ensiform, peaked, salient, cusp-ed; -idate, -idated; corn-ute, -uted, -iculate; prickly; spiny, spinous; thorny, bristling, muricated, pectinated, studded, thistly, briery; craggy etc. (*rough*) 256; snaggy; digitated, two-edged, fusiform; denti-form, -culated; toothed; odontoid; star-like; stell-ated, -iform; arrow-headed; arrowy, barbed, spurred, sagittal; spear-shaped, hastate; horned; conical.

cutting; sharp-, knife-edged; sharp –, keen-as a razor; sharp as a needle; sharpened etc. *v.*; set.

254. Bluntness.—N. bluntness etc. *adj.*; abruptness, dullness.

V. be –, render- blunt etc. *adj.*; obtund, dull; take off the -point, – edge; turn.

Adj. blunt, obtuse, dull, bluff.

255. Smoothness.—N. smoothness etc. *adj.*; polish, gloss; lubric-ity, -ation.

down, velvet, silk, satin; slide; bowling green etc. (*level*) 213; glass, ice; asphalt, pavement, flags.

roller, steam-roller; iron, flat-iron, tailor's goose; sand-, emery-paper; burnisher, turpentine and bees-wax.

V. smooth, -en; plane; file; mow, shave; level, roll; macadamize; polish, burnish, planish, levigate, calender, glaze; iron, hot-press, mangle; lubricate etc. (*oil*) 332.

Adj. smooth; polished etc. *v.*; even; level etc. 213; plane etc. (*flat*) 251; sleek, glossy; silken, silky; lanate, downy, velvety; glabrous, slippery, glassy, lubricous, oily, soft; unwrinkled; smooth as -glass, − ice, − velvet; − oil; slippery as an eel; wooly etc. (*feathery*) 256.

256. Roughness.—N. roughness etc. *adj.*;
tooth, grain, texture, ripple; asperity, rugosity, salebrosity, corrugation, nodosity; arborescence etc. 242.

brush, hair, beard, shag, mane, whisker, mutton-chops, *moustache*, *mustachio*, imperial, Van Dyke, tress, lock, curl, ringlet, *fimbriae, cilia, villi*; eye-lashes, eye-brows, love-lock.

plum-age, -osity; plume, *panache*, crest; feather, tuft, tussock, fringe, toupee.

wool, velvet, plush, nap, pile, floss, fluff, fur, down; byssus, moss, bur.

V. be -rough etc. *adj.*; go against the grain.

render -rough etc. *adj.*; roughen, rough cast, knurl; ruffle, crisp, crumple, crinkle, corrugate, engrail; set on edge, stroke − , rub- the wrong way, rumple.

Adj. rough, uneven; scabrous, knotted; nodular, rug-ged, -ose, -ous; asperous, crisp, salebrous, gnarled, unpolished, unsmooth, rough-hewn; knurled, cross-grained, crag-gy, -ged; crankling, scraggy, jagged, unkempt, prickly etc. (*sharp*) 253; arborescent etc. 242; leafy, well-wooded; feathery; plum-ose, -igerous; tufted, fimbriated, hairy, bristly, ciliated, filamentous, hirsute; crin-ose, -ite; bushy, hispid, villous, pappous, bearded, pilous, shaggy, shagged; fringed, befringed; set-ous, -ose, - aceous; 'like quills upon the fretful porcupine;' rough as a -nutmeg grater, − bear.

downy, velvety, flocculent, wolly; lan-ate, -ated; lanugin-ous, ose; tomentous.

Adv. against the grain, in the rough, on edge.

257. Notch.—N. notch, dent, nick, cut; indent,
-ation; serration; dimple.

embrasure, battlement, machicolation; saw, tooth, crenelle, scallop, scollop, vandyke.

V. notch, nick, cut, pink, mill, score, dent, in-dent, jag, scarify, scotch, crimp, scollop, crenulate, vandyke.

Adj. notched etc. *v.*; crenate, -d; dentate, -d; denticulate, -d; toothed, palmated, serrated.

258. Fold.—N. fold, plicature, pleat, plait, ply,
crease; tuck, gather; flexion, flexure, joint, elbow, doubling, duplicature, wrinkle, rimple, crinkle, crankle, crumple, rumple, rivel, ruck, ruffle, dog's ear, corrugation, frounce, flounce, lapel; pucker, crow's feet.

V. fold, double, plicate, pleat, plait, crease, wrinkle, crinkle, crankle, curl, smock, cockle up, crocker, rimple, rumple, frizzle, frounce, rivel, twill, corrugate, ruffle, crimple, crumple, pucker; turn −, double- -down, − under; tuck, ruck, hem, gather.

Adj. folded etc. *v.*

259. Furrow.—N. furrow, groove, rut, *sulcus*,
scratch, streak, *striae*, crack, score, incision, slit; chamfer, fluting.

channel, gutter, trench, ditch, dike, dyke, moat, fosse, trough, kennel; ravine etc. (*interval*) 198.

V. furrow etc. *n.*; flute, groove, carve, corrugate, plough; incise, chase, enchase, grave, engrave, etch, bite in, cross-hatch.

Adj. furrowed etc. *v.*; ribbed, straited, sulcated, fluted, canaliculated; bisulc-ous, -ate; trisulcate; corduroy.

260. Opening.—N. hole, foramen; puncture,
blow-out, perforation; pin-, key-, loop-, port-, peep-, mouse-, pigeon-hole; eye, − of a needle; eyelet; slot.

opening; apert-ure, -ness; hiation, yawning, oscitancy, dehiscence, patefaction, pandiculation; gap, chasm etc. (*interval*) 198.

embrasure, window, casement, light; sky-, fan-light; lattice; bay-, bow-window; oriel; dormer, lantern.

out-, in-let; vent, vomitory; *embouchure*; orifice, mouth, sucker, muzzle, throat, gullet, placket, weasand, wizen, nozzle, *esophagus*.

portal, porch, gate, ostiary, postern, wicket, trap-door, hatch, door; arcade; gate-, door-, hatch-, gang-way; lych-gate.

way, path etc. 627; thoroughfare; channel, passage, tube, pipe; waterpipe etc. 350; air-pipe etc. 351; vessel, tubule, canal, gut, fistula; adjutage, ajutage; chimney, smoke stack, flue, tap, funnel, gully, tunnel, main; mine, pit, adit, shaft; gallery.

alley, aisle, glade, lane, vista.

bore, caliber; pore; blind orifice.

por-ousness, -osity; sieve, cullender, colander; grater, shredder; cribble, riddle, screen; honeycomb.

apertion, perforation; piercing etc. *v.*; terebration, empalement, pertusion, puncture, acupuncture, penetration.

opener, corkscrew, can opener, key, master-key, *passe-partout*.

V. open, ope, gape, dehisce, yawn, bilge; fly open.

perforate, pierce, empierce, tap, bore, drill; mine etc. (*scoop out*) 252; tunnel; trans-pierce, -fix; en-filade, impale, spike, spear, gore, spit, stab, pink, puncture, lance, trepan, trephine, stick, prick, rid-dle, punch; stave in.

cut a passage through; make -way, − room- for. un-cover, -close, -rip;.lay −, cut −, rip −, throw-open.

Adj. open; perforated etc. *v.*; perforate; wide open, agape, ajar; un-closed, -stopped; oscitant, gaping, yawning; patent.

tubular, cannular, fistulous; per-vious, -meable; foraminous; vesi-, vas-cular; porous, follicular.

cribriform, honeycombed, infundibular, riddled; tubul-ous, -ated, piped.

opening etc. *v.*; aperient.

Int. *open sesame!*

261. Closure.—N. closure, occlusion, blockade; shutting up etc. *v.*; obstruction etc. (*hindrance*) 706; gag; embolism; contraction etc. 195; infarction; con-, ob-stipation; blind -alley, — corner; *cul-de-sac, caecum*; imperforation, -viousness etc. *adj.*; -meability; stopper etc. 263; *operculum.*

V. close, occlude, plug; block —, stop —, fill —, bung —, cork —, button —, stuff —, shut —, dam-up, obturate; blockade; obstruct etc. (*hinder*) 706; bar, bolt, stop, seal, plumb; choke, throttle; ram down, tamp, dam, cram; trap, clinch; put to —, shut- the door; batten down the hatches.

Adj. closed etc. *v.*; shut, operculated; unopened.

unpierced, imporous, caecal; imperforate, - vious, -meable; impenetrable; un-, im-passable; invious; path-, way-less; untrodden.

unventilated; air-, water-tight; hermetically sealed; tight, snug.

262. Perforator.—N. perforator, piercer, borer, auger, gimlet, stylet, drill, wimble, awl, bradawl, scoop, terrier, corkscrew, dibble, trocar, trepan, trephine, probe, bodkin, needle, stiletto, broach, reamer, rimer, warder, lancet; punch, - eon; spikebit, gouge; spear etc. (*weapon*) 727.

263. Stopper.—N. stopper, stopple; plug, cork, bung, spike, spill, stop-cock, tap; rammer; ram, -rod; piston; stopgap; wadding, stuffing, padding, stopping, dossil, pledget, tompion, tourniquet, obturator; wad.

cover etc. 223; valve, slide valve; vent-peg, spigot.

janitor, door —, gate- keeper, porter, commissionaire, *concierge*, warder, beadle, Cerberus, usher, guard, sentry, sentinel; ostiary.

264. Motion. [Successive change of place. *] —N.** motion, movement, move; motivity, motility, going etc. *v.*; unrest.

stream, current, flow, flux, run, course, stir; conduction, evolution; kinematics.

step, rate, pace, tread, stride, gait, clip, port, footfall, cadence, carriage, velocity, angular velocity; progress, locomotion; journey etc. 266; voyage etc. 267; transit etc. 270.

restlessness etc. (*changeableness*) 149; mobility; movableness, motive power; laws of motion; mobilization.

V. be -in motion etc. *adj.*; move, go, hie, gang, budge, stir, pass, flit; hover -round, — about; shift, slide, slither, glide; roll, — on; flow, stream, run, drift, sweep along; wander etc. (*deviate*) 279; walk etc. 266; change —, shift- one's -place, — quarters; dodge; keep -going, — moving.

put —, set- in motion; move; impel etc. 276; propel etc. 284; render movable, mobilize.

Adj. moving etc. *v.*; in motion; motile, transitional; motory, motive; shifting, movable, mobile, mercurial, unquiet; restless etc. (*changeable*) 149; nomadic etc. 266; erratic etc. 279.

Adv. under way; on the -move, — wing, — tramp, — march.

*A thing cannot be said to *move* from one place to another, unless it passes in succession through every intermediate place; hence motion is only such a change of place as is *successive*. 'Rapid, swift, etc., as thought' are therefore incorrect expressions.

265. Quiescence.—N. rest; stillness etc. *adj.*; quiescence; stag-nation, -nancy; fixity, immobility, catalepsy; indisturbance; quietism.

quiet, tranquillity, calm; repose etc. 687; peace; dead calm, anticyclone; statue-like repose; silence etc. 403; not a -breath of air, — mouse stirring; sleep etc. (*inactivity*) 683.

pause, lull etc. (*cessation*) 142; stand, — still; standing still etc. *v.*; lock; dead -lock, — stop, — stand; full stop; fix; embargo.

resting-place; bivouac; home etc. (*abode*) 189; pillow etc. (*support*) 215; haven etc. (*refuge*) 666; goal etc. (*arrival*) 292.

V. be -quiescent etc. *adj.*; stand —, lie- still; keep quiet, repose, hold the breath.

remain, stay; stand, lie to, ride at anchor, remain *in situ*, mark time, tarry; bring —, heave —, lay- to; pull —, draw- up; hold, halt; stop, — short; rest, pause, anchor; cast —, come to an- anchor; rest on one's oars; repose on one's laurels, take breath; stop etc. (*discontinue*) 142.

stagnate, vegetate; *quieta non movere*; let - alone, — well alone; abide, rest and be thankful; keep within doors, stay at home, go to bed.

dwell etc. (*be present*) 186; settle etc. (*be located*) 184; alight etc. (*arrive*) 292.

stick, — fast; stand, — like a post; not stir a -peg, — step; be at a -stand etc. *n.*

quell, becalm, hush, stay, lull to sleep, lay an embargo on; put the brake on.

Adj. quiescent, still; motion-, move-less; fixed; stationary; at -rest, — a stand, — a stand-still, — anchor; stock-still; immotile; standing still etc. *v.*; sedentary, untravelled, stay-at-home; becalmed, stagnant, quiet; un-moved, -disturbed, -ruffled; calm, restful; cataleptic; immovable etc. (*stable*) 150; sleeping etc. (*inactive*) 683; silent etc. 403; still as -a statue; — a post, — a mouse, — death.

Adv. at a stand etc. *adj.*; *tout court*; at the halt.

Int. stop! stay! avast! halt! hold, — hard! whoa!

Phr. *requiescat in pace.*

266. Journey. [Locomotion by land.]—N. travel; traveling etc. *v.*; wayfaring, campaigning.

journey, excursion, expedition, tour, trip, grand tour, circuit, peregrination, discursion, ramble, pilgrimage, *trek*, course, ambulation, march, walk, hike, promenade, constitutional, stroll, saunter, tramp, jog-trot, turn, stalk, perambulation; noctambulation; somnambulism, sleep walking; outing, ride, drive, airing, jaunt.

equitation, horsemanship, riding, *manège*, ride and tie.

roving, vagrancy, pererration; marching and countermarching; nomadism; vagabond-ism, -age; gadding; flit, -ting; migration; e-, im-, de-, inter-migration.

plan, itinerary, guide; hand-, road- book; Baedeker, Murray, Bradshaw, time table.

, procession, parade, cavalcade, caravan, file, *cortège*, column.

[Organs and instruments of locomotion] vehicle etc. 272; locomotive etc. 271; legs, feet, pegs, pins, trotters.

traveler etc. 268.

V. travel, journey, course; tour; take —, go- a journey, take —, go out for- -a walk etc. *n.*; have a run; take the air.

flit, take wing; migrate, emigrate, *trek*; rove, prowl, roam, range, patrol, pace up and down, traverse; scour —, traverse- the country; peragrate; per-, circum-ambulate; nomadize, wander, ramble, stroll, saunter, hover, go one's rounds, straggle; gad; — about; expatiate.

walk, march, step, tread, pace, plod, wend; promenade; trudge, tramp; stalk, stride, straddle, strut, foot it, stump; bundle, bowl along, toddle; paddle; tread —, follow —, pursue- a path.

take horse. ride, drive, trot, amble, canter, prance, fisk, frisk, *caracoler*; gallop etc. (*move quickly*) 274; motor, cycle, taxi; go by -car, — train, — tram, — bus, — plane.

peg -, jog -, wag -, shuffle- on; stir one's stumps; bend one's -steps, — course; make -, find -, wend -, pick -, thread -, plough-one's way; coast, slide, glide, skim, skate, ski; march in procession, file off, defile.

go —, repair —, resort —, hie —, betake oneself-to.

Adj. traveling etc. *v.*; ambulatory, itinerant, peripatetic, perambulatory, roving, rambling, gadding, discursive, vagrant, migratory, nomadic; circumforane-an, -ous; somnambular, nocti-, mundivagant; locomotive, automotive, self-moving.

way-faring, -worn; travel-stained.

Adv. on -foot, — horseback, — Shanks's mare; by the Marrowbone stage; *in transitu* etc. 270; *en route* etc. 282.

Int. come along!

267. Navigation. [Locomotion by water, or air.]—**N.** navigation; aquatics; boating, cruising, yachting; ship etc. 273; oar, scull, sweep, punt pole, paddle, — wheel, screw, propeller, stern wheel, sail, canvas.

natation, swimming; fin, flipper, fish's tail.

aeronautics, aviation, flying, winging, cruising, gliding, ballooning; blind —, instrument — flying; avigation, take-off.

flight, trip, run; solo —, nolo (pilotless) —, supersonic —, test — flight; air -lift, -drop; shuttle, reconnaisence, mission, dry run (coll.), search mission, combat flight, sortie, air raid, bombing mission; air — support, — cover, — umbrella; formation flying, maneuvers, aerobatics, stunt flying (coll.), diving, rolling, barrel roll, spin, tail spin, loop, buzzing, landing, instrument —, crash — landing.

angle, center, axis, stability, load, pressure, torsion, torque, thrust, propulsion, jet propulsion, pitch, lift, dray, yaw; resistance, drift, flow, wash.

course, heading, altitude; air -route, -lane.

voyage, sail, cruise, passage, circumnavigation, *periplus*; head-, stern-, lee-way.

astro-, cosmo- nautics; space —, interplanetary — travel; space — exploration, — flight.

mariner, aeronaut etc. 269.

V. sail; put to sea etc. (*depart*) 293; take ship, get under way; spread -sail, — canvas; gather way, have way on; make —, carry- sail; plough the -waves, — deep, — main, — ocean; walk the waters.

navigate, warp, luff, scud, boom, kedge; drift, course, cruise, coast; hug the -shore, — land; circumnavigate.

ply the oar, row, paddle, pull, scull, punt, steam, swim, float; buffet the waves, ride the storm, skim, *effleurer*, dive, wade.

fly, pilot, copilot, astronavigate, solo, take off, taxi, ascend, climb, stunt, spin, loop, roll, dive, buzz, land, descend, level off, bail out, parachute.

Adj. sailing etc. *v.*; seafaring, nautical, maritime, naval; sea-going, coasting; afloat; navigable, aquatic, natatory.

volitant, volant, aerostatic, aerial, aeronautic; alar, alate, pennate.

Adv. under -way, — sail, — canvas, — steam; on the wing.

268. Traveler.—N. traveler, wayfarer, voyager, itinerant, passenger.

tourist, excursionist, globe-trotter; explorer, adventurer, mountaineer, Alpine Club; peregrinator, wanderer, rover, straggler, rambler; bird of passage; gad-about, -ling; vagrant, scattering, land-loper, waifs and estrays, wastrel, stray; loafer; tramp, -er, hobo, beachcomber, vagabond, nomad, Bohemian, gipsy, Arab, Wandering Jew, Hadji, pilgrim, palmer; peripatetic; somnambulist; sleep walker, noctambulist; emigrant, fugitive, refugee, *émigré*.

runner, courier, King's messenger; Mercury, Iris, Ariel, comet.

pedestrian, walker, foot-passenger; cyclist; wheelman.

rider, horseman, equestrian, cavalier, jockey, rough rider, trainer, breaker, huntsman.

driver, coachman, whip, Jehu, charioteer, postilion, post-boy, carter, wagoner, drayman, truckman; cab-man, -driver; *voiturier, vetturino, condottiere*; engine-driver; stoker, fireman, guard, brakeman, conductor; chauffeur, automobilist, motorist, motor —, truck —, taxi- driver.

269. Mariner.—N. sailor, mariner, navigator, argonaut; sea-man, -farer, -faring man; yachtsman; tar, jack tar, salt, gob, sea-dog, shellback, able seaman, A.B.; man-of-war's man, bluejacket, marine, jolly; midshipman, middy, reefer; captain, commander, master mariner, skipper, mate; ship-, boat-, ferry-, water-, lighter-, barge-, longshore-man, hoveller; bargee, gondolier; oar-, -sman; rower; boat-, cock-swain; coxswain; steersman, helmsman, pilot; crew; lascar.

aerial navigator, navigator; aero-, astro-, cosmo-naut; balloonist, Icarus, aviator, pilot, flyer, copilot, spaceman; fighter —, bomber — pilot; bombardier, gunner; meteorologist; stewardess, aviatrix, aviatress; ground crew, aeromechanic, aeronautical engineer; parachutist, paratrooper.

270. Transference.—N. transfer, -ence; trans-, e-location; displacement; *meta-stasis*, -*thesis*; removal; re-, a-motion; relegation; de-, asportation; extradition, conveyance, draft; carrying, carriage; convection, -duction, -tagion, infection; transfusion; transfer etc. (*of property*) 783.

transit, transition; passage, ferry, gestation; portage, porterage, carting, cartage; shoveling etc. *v.*; vect-ion, -ure, -itation; shipment, freight, wafture; trans-mission, -port, -portation, -umption, -plantation, -lation; shift-, dodg-ing; dispersion etc. 73; transposition etc. (*interchange*) 148; traction etc. 285.

[Thing transferred] drift, alluvium, detritus, *moraine*; gift, legacy, bequest, lease; freight, mails, cargo, luggage, baggage, goods.

V. trans-fer, -mit, -port, -place, -plant; convey, assign, carry, bear, fetch and carry; carry —, ferryover; hand, pass, forward; shift; conduct, convoy, bring, fetch, reach.

send, delegate, consign, mail post, relegate, turn over to, pass the buck, deliver; ship, embark; waft; switch, shunt; transpose etc. (*interchange*) 148; displace etc. 185; throw etc. 284; drag etc. 285.

shovel, lade, dip, ladle, bale, decant, draft off, transfuse.

Adj. transferred etc. *v.*; drifted; movable, portable, -ative; conductive; contagious, infectious.

transferable, assignable, conveyable, devisable, negotiable, transmissible.

Adv. from -hand to hand, — pillar to post.

on —, by- the way; on the -road, — wing; as one goes; *in transitu*, *en route*, *chemin faisant*, *en passant*, in mid-progress.

271. Carrier.—N. carrier, porter, red cap, bearer, messenger, postman, tranter, conveyer; stevedore; coolie; conductor, locomotive, tractor, caterpillar tractor, motor.

beast of burden, cattle, horse steed, nag, palfrey, Arab, blood horse, -thorough-bred, galloway, charger, courser, racer, hunter, jument, pony, filly, colt, foal, barb, roan, jade, hack, *bidet*, pad, cob, tit, punch, roadster, goer; race-, pack-, draft-, cart-, dray-, post-horse, mount; Shetland pony, sheltie; garran; jennet, genet, bayard, mare, stallion, gelding; stud.

Pegasus, Bucephalus, Rozinante.

ass, donkey, jackass, mule, hinny; sumpter - horse, — mule; reindeer; camel, dromedary, mehari, llama, elephant; carrier pigeon.

carriage etc. (*vehicle*) 272; ship etc. 273.

Adj. equine, asinine.

272. Vehicle.—N. vehicle, conveyance, carriage, car, caravan, van, furniture van, pantechnicon; wagon, wain, dray, cart, lorry.

carriole; sledge, sled, sleigh, bob-sleigh, toboggan, *luge*, truck, tram; limber, tumbrel, pontoon; barrow; wheel-, hand- -barrow, — cart, trolley; perambulator; Bath —, wheel —, sedanchair, jinriksha, rickshaw; ekka; chaise; palankeen, -quin; litter, horse-litter, brancard, crate, hurdle, stretcher, ambulance; velocipede, hobbyhorse, coaster, scooter, go-cart; cycle; bi-, tri-, quadri-cycle; tandem, safety; skate, roller —, ice — skate; sled, sleigh; ski, snow-shoe.

equipage, turn-out; coach, chariot; *quadriga*, chaise, phaëton, break, brake, mail-phaëton, wagonette, drag, curricle, tilbury, whisky, landau, *barouche*, victoria, brougham, clarence, calash, *calèche*, britzska, *araba*, kibitka; berlin; sulky, *désobligeant*, sociable, *vis-à-vis*, *dormeuse*; jaunting —, outside- car; *tarantass*; runabout; shay.

post-chaise; diligence, stage; stage —, mail —, hackney —, glass- coach; stage-wagon; car, omnibus, bus, fly, *cabriolet*, cab, hansom, shofle, fourwheeler, growler, *droshki*, drosky.

dog-cart, trap, gig, whitechapel, buggy, four-in-hand, unicorn, random, tandem; shandredhan, *char-à-banc*.

automobile, motor-, auto-, touring-, racing-, cycle-, side-, steam-, electric- car; motor — cycle, — bike; motorized vehicle; bus, mini-bus; buggy, crate, tub, flivver, jalopy, wreck, clunker, dog, heap (all. slang); coupe, coup, sedan, convertible, hard-top; camper, trailer, mobile home; limosine, landaulette, cabriolet, *coupé*, *voiturette*, runabout, electromobile, taxi, -cab.

train; passenger —, express —, freight —, subway —, special —, corridor —, parliamentary —, luggage —, goods- train, *train de luxe*; 1st-, 2nd-, 3rd- class- -train, — carriage, — compartment; Pullman —, sleeping-, club-, observation-, dining-, restaurant-car; mail-, luggage-, brake-van, coach, car, carriage; rolling stock; horse-box, cattle- truck.

273. Ship.—N. ship, vessel, sail; craft, bottom, navy, marine, fleet, flotilla, squadron; shipping.

man of war etc. (*combatant*) 726; transport, tender, store-ship; merchant ship, merchantman; packet, liner; whaler, slaver, collier, coaster, tanker, freighter, freight steamer, cargo boat, lighter; fishing-, pilot- boat; trawler, drifter; cable ship; hulk; yacht; floating palace, ocean greyhound.

ship, bark, barque, brig, snow, hermaphrodite brig; brigantine, barquentine; schooner; topsail —, fore and aft —, three masted- schooner; *chassemarée*; sloop, cutter, corvette, clipper, foist, yawl, dandy, ketch, smack, lugger, barge, hoy, cat-, -boat, buss; sail-er, -ing vessel, wind jammer; steamer, -boat -ship; mail—, paddle —, screw —, sternwheel- steamer; tug; train-ferry; line of steamers etc.

boat, pinnace, launch, motor-boat, picket-boat; hydroplane; life-, long-, jolly-, bum-, fly-, cock-, ferry-, canal- boat, dory, dugout, galliot; shallop, gig, funny, skiff, dingy, scow, cockleshell, wherry, coble, punt, cog, lerret; eight-, four-, pair- oar; randan; out- rigger; float, raft, pontoon; prame, iceyacht.

state barge, bucentaur.

catamaran, coracle, gondola, carvel, caravel; felucca, caique, canoe, trireme; galley, — foist; bilander, dogger, hooker, howker, argosy, carack; galliass, galleon; galliot, polacca, polacre, corsair, tartane, junk, lorcha, praam, proa, prahu, saick, sampan, xebec, dhow; dahabeah; nuggar, cayak, piroque; trireme.

submarine, submersible.

aircraft (*combatant*) etc. 726; flying machine, air mail, aero-, air-, mono-, bi-, tri-, hydro aeroplane, plane, cabin —, transport —, propeller — plane; *avion*, flying boat, glider; helicopter, rotor —, gyro-plane, whirlybird, autogyro, gyrodine; sea-, hydro-plane; amphibian; jet. — plane; turbo-, ram-, pulse-, subsonic —, supersonic —, strato- jet; rocket — plane, — ship,; space ship; war-, combat — plane; kamikaze, fleet, armada; trainer, fliight simulator; aerostat, dirigible, blimp (coll.), zeppelin; parachute, chute (coll.); kite.

rocket, flying —, ballistic —, guided — missile; projectile; rocket —, robot —, buzz-bomb; multistage —, step —, test — rocket; booster; satellite; flying saucer, unidentified flying object. (UFO).

nacelle, car, gondola, aileron; hangar, airport, landing field, airdrome; catwalk, controls, rudder, tail.

Adj. marine, maritime, naval, nautical, seafaring, sea-, ocean-going, sea-worthy.

aerial, aeronautical, air-worthy, flying etc. *n.*

Adv. afloat, aboard; on -board, — ship board, — board ship.

274. Velocity.—N. velocity, speed, celerity; swiftness etc. *adj.*; rapidity, eagle speed; expedition etc. (*activity*) 682; pernicity; acceleration; haste etc. 684.

spurt, rush, dash, race, steeplechase; smart —, lively —, swift etc. *adj.* —, rattling —, spanking —, strapping- -rate, — pace; round pace; flying, flight.

gallop, canter, trot, round trot, run, scamper; hand —, full- gallop; swoop.

lightning, light, electricity, wind; cannon-ball, rocket, arrow, dart, quicksilver; telegraph, express train; torrent; swallow flight.

eagle, antelope, courser, race-horse, gazelle, greyhound, hare, doe, squirrel.

Mercury, Ariel, Camilla, Harlequin.

[Measurement of velocity.] speedometer, log, - line, tachometer.

air speed, speed of sound, sonic —, subsonic —, supersonic —, ultrasonic —, hypersonic —, transonic — speed.

V. move quickly, trip, fisk; speed, hie, hasten, sprint, spurt, post, spank, scuttle; scud, -dle, scurry; scour, — the plain; scamper, sprint, dash, run, — like mad; fly, race, run a race, cut away, cut and run, shoot, tear, whisk, whiz, sweep, skim, brush; cut —, bowl- along; rush etc. (*be violent*) 173; dash -on, — off, — forward; bolt; trot, gallop, bound, flit, spring, dart, boom; march in -quick, — double-time; ride hard; et over the ground, scorch.

hurry etc. (*hasten*) 684; accelerate, put on; quicken; quicken —, mend- one's pace; clap spurs to one's horse; make-haste, — rapid strides, — forced marches, — the best of one's way; put one's best leg foremost, stir one's stumps, wing one's way, set off at a score; carry —, crowd- sail; go off like a shot, go ahead, gain ground; outstrip the wind, fly on the wings of the wind.

keep -up, — pace- with; outstrip etc. 303.

Adj. fast, speedy, swift, rapid, quick, fleet; nimble, agile, expeditious; express; active etc. 682; flying, galloping etc. *v.*; light- nimble-footed; winged; eagle-winged, mercurial, electric telegraphic; light-legged; light of heel; swift as -an arrow etc. *n.*; quick as -lightning etc. *n.*, — thought. *

Adv. swiftly etc. *adj.*; with -speed etc. *n.*; apace; at -a great rate, — full speed, — railway speed; full - drive, — gallop; post-haste, in full sail, tantivy; trippingly; instantaneously etc. 113; like a shot.

under press of -sale, — canvas, — sail and steam; *velis et remis*, on eagle's wing, in double quick time; with -rapid, — giant- strides; *à pas de géant*; in seven league boots; whip and spur; *ventre à terre*; as fast as one's -legs, — heels- will carry one; as fast on one can lay feet to the ground, at the top of one's speed; by leaps and bounds; with haste etc. 684; in- high — gear. — speed.

Phr. *vires acquirit eundo.*

*See note on 274.

275. Slowness.—N. slowness etc. *adj.*; languor etc. (*inactivity*) 683; drawl; creeping etc. *v.*, lentor.

retardation; slackening etc. *v.*; delay etc. (*lateness*) 133; claudication.

jog-, dog-trot, walk; mincing steps; slow -march, — time.

slow -goer, — coach, — back; lingerer, loiterer, sluggard, tortoise, snail; dawdle etc. (*inactive*) 683.

V. move -slowly, etc. *adv.*; creep, crawl, lag, slug, walk, drawl, linger, loiter, saunter, plod, trudge, stump along, lumber; trail; drag; dawdle etc. (*be inactive*) 683; grovel, worm one's way, steal along; jog —, rub —, bundle- on; toddle, waddle, wabble, slug; traipse, slouch, shuffle, halt, hobble, limp, claudicate, shamble; flag, falter, totter, stagger; mince, step short; march in -slow time, — funeral procession; take one's time; hang fire etc. (*be late*) 133.

retard, relax; slacken, check, moderate, rein in, curb; reef; strike —, shorten —, take in- sail; put on the drag, apply the brake; clip the wings; reduce the speed, decelerate; slacken -speed, — one's pace, lose ground; back -water, — pedal, put the engines astern, throttle down.

Adj. slow, slack, tardy, dilatory etc. (*inactive*) 683; gentle, easy; leisurely; deliberate, gradual; insensible, imperceptible; languid, sluggish, apathetic, phlegmatic, slow-paced, tardigrade, snail-like; creeping etc. *v.*

Adv. slowly etc. *adj.*; leisurely; *piano, adagio; largo, larghetto*; at half speed, under easy sail; at a -foot's, — snail's, — funeral- pace; slower than molasses in January; in slow time; with -mincing steps, — clipped wings; *haud passibus aequis*; in-low —, gear, — speed.

gradually etc. *adj.*; *gradatim*; by -degrees, — slow degrees, — inches, — little and little; step by step; inch by inch, bit by bit, little by little, *seriatim*; consecutively.

276. Impulse.—N. impulse, impulsion, impetus; momentum; push, pulsion, thrust, shove, jog, jolt, boom, booming, boost, throw; explosion etc. (*violence*) 173; propulsion etc. 284, jet propulsion; firing, launching, projection, trajection.

percussion, concussion, collision, occursion, clash, encounter, cannon, *carambole*, appulse, shock, crash, bump; impact; *élan*; charge etc. (*attack*) 716; beating etc. (*punishment*) 972.

blow, dint, stroke, knock, tap, rap, slap, smack, pat, dab; fillip; slam, bang; hit, whack, thwack, clout; cuff etc. 972; squash, dowse, whap, swap, punch, thump, swipe, jab, pelt, kick, punce, calcitration; *ruade*; arietation; cut, thrust, lunge, yerk.

hammer, sledge-hammer, mall, maul, mallet, flail; ram, -mer; battering-ram, monkey, pile-driver, punch, bat, tamper, tamping iron; cudgel etc. (*weapon*) 727; axe etc. (*sharp*) 253.

[Science of mechanical forces] mechanics, dynamics etc.

V. give an -impetus etc. *n.*; impel, push; start, give a start to, set going; drive, urge, boom; thrust, prod, foin; cant; elbow, shoulder, jostle, justle, hustle, hurtle, shove, jog, jolt, bean, encounter; run –, bump –, butt- against; knock –, run- one's head against; impinge.

fire, launch, project, traject, propel, 284.

strike, knock, hit, bash, tap, rap, bat, slap, flap, dab, pat, thump, beat, bang, slam, dash; punch, thwack, whack; hit –, strike- hard; swap, batter, dowse, baste; pelt, patter, skelter, buffet, belabor, tamp; fetch one a blow, swat; poke at, pink, lunge, yerk; kick, calcitrate; butt; strike at etc. (*attack*) 716; whip etc. (*punish*) 972; propel etc. 284.

come –, enter- into collision; collide; foul; fall –, run- foul of.

throw etc.

Adj. impelling etc. *v.*; im-pulsive, -pellent; booming; dynamic, -al; impelled etc. *v.*

277. Recoil.—N. recoil; re-, retro-action; revulsion; rebound, *ricochet*; re-percussion, -calcitration; kick, *contre-coup*; springing back etc. *v.*; elasticity etc. 325; reflexion, reflex, reflux; reverberation etc. (*resonance*) 408; rebuff, repulse; return.

ducks and drakes; boomerang; spring; reactionist, -reactionary.

V. recoil, resile, react; spring –, fly –, bound-back; rebound, reverberate, repercuss, recalcitrate, echo, *ricochet*.

Adj. recoiling etc. *v.*; re-fluent, -percussive, -calcitrant, -actionary; retroactive.

Adv. on the -recoil etc. *n.*

278. Direction.—N. direction, bearing, course, set, drift, tenor; tendency etc. 176; incidence; bending, trending etc *v.*; dip, tack, aim, collimation; steer-ing, -age.

point of the compass, cardinal –, half –, quarter- points; North, East, South, West; N by E, ENE, NE by N, NE etc; rhumb, azimuth, line of collimation.

line, path, road, range, quarter, line of march; alignment; straight shot, bee-line.

course, bearing, heading, altitude, air -route, -lane, angle, center, axis, torsion, torque, pitch, lift, drift, flow, wash.

V. tend –, bend –, point- towards; conduct –, go- to; point -to, – at; bend, trend, verge, incline, dip, determine.

steer –, make- -for, – towards; aim –, level- at; take aim; keep –, hold- a course; be bound for; bend one's steps towards; direct –, steer –, bend –, shape- one's course; align –, align- one's march; go straight, – to the point; march -on, – on a point.

ascertain one's -direction etc. *n.*; *s'orienter*, see which way the wind blows; box the compass.

Adj. directed etc. *v.*, – towards; pointing towards etc. *v.*; bound for; aligned –, with; direct, straight; un-deviating, -swerving; straightforward; North, -ern, -erly, etc. *n.*

directable etc. *v.*

Adv. towards; on the -road, – high road- to; versus, to; hither, thither, whither; directly; straight, – forwards, – as an arrow; point blank; in a -direct, – straight- line -to, – for, – with; in a line with; full tilt at, as the crow flies.

before –, near –, close to –, against- the wind; windwards, in the wind's eye.

through, *via*, by way of; in all -directions, – manner of ways; *quaqua-versum*, from the four winds.

279. Deviation.—N. deviation; swerving etc. *v.*; obliquation, warp, refraction; flection, flexion; sweep; de-flection, -flexure; declination.

diversion, digression, departure from, aberration, drift, sheer; divergence etc. 291; zigzag; *détour* etc. (*circuit*) 629.

[Desultory motion] wandering etc. *v.*; vagrancy, evagation; by-paths and crooked ways.

[Motion sideways, oblique motion] sidling etc. *v.*; *échelon*, leeway; knight's move (at chess).

V. alter one's course, deviate, depart from, turn, trend; bend, curve, etc. 245; swerve, heel, bear off.

intervert; deflect; divert, – from its course; put on a new scent, shift, shunt, switch, wear, draw aside, crook, warp, short circuit.

stray, straggle; sidle, edge; diverge etc. 291; tralineate, digress, divagate, wander; wind, twist, meander, meander around Robin Hood's barn; veer, tack, sheer; turn -aside, – a corner, – away from; wheel, steer clear of; ramble, rove, drift; go -astray, – adrift; yaw, dodge; step aside, ease off, make way for, shy.

fly off at a tangent; glance off; turn, wheel –, face- about; turn –, face- to the right about; wabble etc. (*oscillate*) 314; go out of one's way etc. (*perform a circuit*) 629; lose one's way.

Adj. deviating etc. *v.*; aberrant, errant; ex-, dis-cursive; devious, desultory, loose; rambling; stray, erratic, vagrant, undirected; circuitous, indirect, zigzag; crab-like.

Adv. astray from, round about, wide of the mark; to the right about; all manner of ways; circuitously etc. 629.

obliquely, sideling, like the move of the knight on a chessboard.

280. Precession. [Going before.]—**N.** precession, leading, heading; precedence etc. 62; priority etc. 116; the lead, *le pas*; van etc. (*front*) 234; precursor etc. 64.

V. go -before, – ahead, – in the van, – in advance; precede, forerun; usher in, introduce, herald, head, take the lead; lead, – the way, – the dance; get –, have- the start; steal a march; get -before, – ahead, – in front of; outstrip etc. 303; take precedence etc. (*first in order*) 62.

Adj. foremost, first, leading etc. *v.*

Adv. in advance, before, ahead, in the van; fore-head-most; in front.

Phr. *seniores priores.*

281. Sequence. [Going after.]—**N.** sequence, run; coming after etc. (*order*) 63; (*time*) 117; following; pursuit etc. 622.

follower, attendant, satellite, shadow, dangler, train.

V. follow; pursue etc. 622; go −, fly- after.

attend, beset, dance attendance on, dog, be-dog; tread -in the steps of, − close upon; be −, go −, follow- in the -wake, − trail, − rear- of; trail, follow as a shadow, hang on the skirts of; tread −, follow- on the heels of, tag after.

lag, get behind.

Adj. following etc. v.

Adv. behind; in the -rear etc. 235, − train of, wake of; after etc. (*order*) 63, (*time*) 117.

282. Progression. [Motion forwards; progressive motion.]—**N.** progress, -ion, -iveness; advancing etc. v.; advance, -ment; ongoing; flood-tide, headway; march etc. 266; rise; improvement etc. 658.

V. advance; proceed, progress; get -on, − along, − over the ground; gain ground; jog −, rub −, wag- on; go with the stream; keep −, hold on-one's course; go −, move −, come −, get −, pass −, push −, press- -on, − forward, − forwards, − ahead; press onwards, step forward; make −, work −, carve −, push −, force −, edge −, elbow-one's way; make -progress, − head, − way, − headway, − advances, − strides, − rapid strides etc. (*velocity*) 274; go −, shoot- ahead; distance; make up leeway.

Adj. advancing etc. v.; pro-gressive, -fluent; advanced.

Adv. forward, onward; forth, on ahead, under way, *en route* for, on -one's way, − the way, − the road, − the high road- to; in -progress, − mid progress; *in transitu* etc. 270.

Phr. *vestigia nulla retrorsum.*

283. Regression. [Motion backwards.]—**N.** regress, -ion; retro-cession, -gression, -gradation, -action; *reculade*; retreat, withdrawal, retirement, remigration; recession etc. (*motion from*) 287; recess; crab-like motion.

re-fluence, -flux; backwater, regurgitation, ebb, return; resilience; reflexion (*recoil*) 277; *volte-face.*

counter -motion, − movement, − march; veering, tergiversation, recidivation, backsliding, fall, relapse; deterioration etc. 659.

turning point etc. (*reversion*) 145.

V. re-cede. -grade, -turn, -vert, -treat, -tire; retro-grade, -cede; back, − down, − out, crawl; withdraw; rebound etc. 277; go −, come −, turn −, hark −, draw −, fall −, get −, put −, run-back; lose ground; fall −, drop- astern; back water, put about; veer, − round; double, wheel, counter-march; ebb, regurgitate; jib, shrink, shy.

turn -tail, − round, − upon one's heel, − one's back upon; retrace one's steps, dance the back step; sound −, beat- a retreat; go home.

Adj. receding etc. v.; retro-grade, -gressive; re-gressive, -fluent, -flex, -cidivous, -silient; crab-like; reactionary etc. 277; counter-clockwise.

Adv. back, -wards; reflexively, to the right about; *à reculons, à rebours.*

Phr. *revenons à nos moutons,* as you were.

284. Propulsion. [Motion given to an object situated in front.]—**N.** pro-pulsion, -jection; *vis a tergo*; push etc. (*impulse*) 276; e-, jaculation; ejection etc. 297; throw, fling, toss, shot, discharge, shy.

[Science of propulsion] steam −, gas −, diesel −, jet −, rocket − propulsion, gunnery, ballistics, archery.

missile, projectile, ball, *discus*, javelin, hammer, quoit, brickbat, shot, bullet; arrow, shaft, gun etc. (*arms*) 727.

shooter, shot; gunner, gun-layer; archer, toxophilite; bow-, rifle-, marks- man; good −, crack- shot; sharpshooter etc. (*combatant*) 726.

V. propel, project, throw, fling, cast, pitch, chuck, toss, jerk, heave, shy, hurl; flirt, fillip.

dart, lance, tilt; e-, jaculate; fulminate, bolt, drive, sling, pitchfork.

send; send −, let −, fire- off; discharge, shoot; launch, send forth, let fly; dash.

put −, set- in motion; set agoing, start; give -a start, − an impulse- to; push, impel etc. 276; trun-dle etc. (*set in rotation*) 312; expel etc. 297.

carry one off one's legs; put to flight.

Adj. propelled etc. v.; propelling etc. v.; pro-pulsive, -jectile.

285. Traction. [Motion given to an object situated behind.]—**N.** traction; drawing etc. v.; draft, pull, tug, haul; rake; 'a long pull, a strong pull and a pull all together;' towage, haulage.

V. draw, pull, haul, lug, rake, drag, draggle, tug, tow, trail, trawl, train; take in tow.

wrench, jerk, twitch.

Adj. drawing etc. v.; tractive, tractile; ductile, pulling, hauling, tugging, towing.

286. Approach. Motion towards.]—**N.** ap-proach, approximation, appropinquation; access; appulse; afflux, -ion; advent etc. (*approach of time*) 121; pursuit etc. 622; convergence etc. 290.

V. approach, approximate; near; get −, draw- near; come, − near, − to close quarters; move −, set in- towards; drift; make up to; gain upon; pursue etc. 622; tread on the heels of; bear up; make the land; hug the -shore, − land.

Adj. approaching etc. v.; approximative; con-vergent; affluent; impending, imminent etc. (*destined*) 152.

Adv. on the road.

Int. come hither! approach! here! come! come near!

287. Recession. [Motion from.]—**N.** recession, retirement, withdrawal; retreat; retrocession etc. 283; departure etc. 293; recoil etc. 277; flight etc. (*avoidance*) 623.

V. recede, go, move from, retire, ebb, withdraw, shrink; come −, move −, go −, get −, drift-away; depart etc. 293; retreat etc. 283; move −, stand −, sheer- off; swerve from; fall back, stand aside; run away etc. (*avoid*) 623.

remove, shunt, side track, switch off.

Adj. receding etc. v.

288. Attraction. [Motion towards, ac-tively.]—**N.** attract-ion, -iveness; pull; drawing to, pulling towards, adduction, magnetism, gravity, attraction of gravitation; lure, bait, decoy.

lode-stone, -star; magnet, siderite, magnetite.

V. attract; draw –, pull –, drag- towards; adduce.

lure, bait, decoy.

Adj. attracting etc. *v.*; attrahent, attractive, adducent, adductive, alluring.

289. Repulsion. [Motion from, actively.]—**N.** repulsion; driving from etc. *v.*; repulse; abduction.

V. repel; push –, drive – etc. 276; from; chase, dispel; retrude; abduce, abduct; send away, repulse, dismiss.

keep at arm's length, turn one's back upon, give the cold shoulder; send packing; send -off, – away- with a flea in one's ear, – about one's business.

Adj. repelling etc. *v.*; repellant, repulsive; abducent, abductive.

290. Convergence. [Motion nearer to.]—**N.** con-vergence, -fluence, -course, -flux, -gress, -currence, -centration; appulse, meeting; corradiation.

assemblage etc. 72; resort etc. (*focus*) 74; asymptote.

V. converge, concur; come together, unite, meet, fall in with; close -with, – in upon; center -round, – in; enter in; pour in.

gather together, unite, concentrate, bring into a focus.

Adj. converging etc. *v.*; con-vergent, -fluent, -current; centripetal; asymptotical.

291. Divergence. [Motion further off.]—**N.** diverg-ence, -ency; divarication, ramification, radiation; separation etc. (*disjunction*) 44; dispersion etc. 73; deviation etc. 279; aberration, declination.

V. diverge, divaricate, radiate; ramify; branch –, glance –, file- off; fly off, – at a tangent; spread, scatter, disperse etc. 73; deviate etc. 279; part etc. (*separate*) 44; splay apart.

Adj. diverging etc. *v.*; divergent, radiant, centrifugal; aberrant.

292. Arrival. [Terminal motion at.]—**N.** arrival, advent; landing; de-, disem-barkation; reception, welcome, *vin d'honneur.*

home, goal, bourn; landing-place, -stage; resting –, stopping -place; destination, harbor, haven, port; terminal, terminus, railway station, depot, airport; halt, halting -place, – ground; anchorage etc. (*refuge*) 666.

return, recursion, remigration; meeting; ren-, encounter.

completion etc. 729.

V. arrive; get to, come to; come; reach, attain; come up, – with, – to; overtake; make, fetch; complete etc. 729; join, rejoin.

light, alight, dismount; land, go ashore; debark, disembark; put -in, – into; visit, cast anchor, pitch

one's tent; sit down etc. (*be located*) 184; get to one's journey's end; make the land; be in at the death; come –, get- -back, – home; return; come in etc. (*ingress*) 294; make one's appearance etc. (*appear*) 446; drop in; detrain; outspan.

come to hand; come -at, – across; hit; come –, light –, pop –, bounce –, plump –, burst –, pitch- upon; meet; en- ren-counter; come in contact.

Adj. arriving etc. *v.*; homewardbound; terminal.

Adv. here, hither.

Int. welcome! hail! all hail! good- day, – morrow; greetings! hullo! well!

293. Departure. [Initial motion from.]—**N.** departure, decession, decampment; embarkation; take-off; outset, start; removal; exit etc. (*egress*) 295; exodus, Hejira, flight.

leave-taking, *congé*, valediction, valedictory, adieu, farewell, good-bye, stirrup-cup.

starting -point, – post; point –, place- of -departure, – embarkation; port of embarkation.

V. depart; go, – away; take one's departure, set out; set –, march –, put –, start –, be –, move –, get –, whip –, pack –, go –, take oneself-off; start, issue, march out, debouch; go –, sally-forth; sally, set forward; be gone.

leave a place, quit, vacate, evacuate, abandon; go off the stage, make ones' exit; retire, withdraw, remove; go -one's way, – along, – from home; take -flight, – wing; spring, fly, flit, wing one's flight; fly –, whip- away; take off, hop off; embark; go -on board, – aboard; set sail; put –, go- to sea; sail, take ship; hoist blue Peter; get under way, weigh anchor; strike tents, break camp, decamp; walk one's chalks, make tracks, cut one's stick; cut and run; take leave; say –, bid- -good-bye etc. *n.*; disappear etc. 449; abscond etc. (*avoid*) 623; entrain, embus, emplane; saddle –, harness –, hitch- up; inspan.

Adj. departing etc. *v.*; valedictory; outward bound.

Adv. whence, hence, thence; with a foot in the stirrup; on the -wing, – move.

Int. begone! etc. (*ejection*) 297; to horse! all aboard! farewell! adieu! good-bye, – day! *au revoir! auf wiedersehen!* fare you well! so long! God -bless you, – speed! *bon voyage!*

294. Ingress. [Motion into.]—**N.** ingress; entrance, entry; introgression; influx; intrusion, inroad, incursion, invasion, irruption; pene-, interpene- tration; illapse, import, importation, infiltration; immigration; admission etc. (*reception*) 296; insinuation etc. (*interjacence*) 228; insertion etc. 300.

inlet; way in; mouth, door etc. (*opening*) 260; path etc. (*way*) 627; conduit etc. 350; immigrant, visitor, incomer, newcomer, colonist.

V. have the *entrée*; enter; go –, come –, pour –, flow –, creep –, slip –, pop –, break –, burst- -into, – in; set foot on; burst –, break-in upon; invade, intrude, butt in, horn in, crash; insinuate itself; inter-, penetrate; infiltrate; find one's way –, wriggle –, worm oneself- into.

give entrance to etc. (*receive*) 296; insert etc. 300.

Adj. incoming, ingressive etc. *n.*; inward bound.

Adv. inward.

295. Egress. [Motion out of.]—**N.** egress, exit, issue; emer-sion, -gence; disemboguement; out-break, -burst; e-, pro-ruption; emanation; evacuation; ex, trans-udation; extravasation, per-spiration, sweating, leakage, percolation, distillation, oozing; gush etc. (*water in motion*) 348; outpour, -ing; effluence, effusion; efflux, -ion; drain; dribbling etc. *v.*; defluxion; drainage; out-come, -put; discharge etc. (*excretion*) 299.

export; expatriation; e-, re-migration; *débouche*; exodus etc. (*departure*) 293; emigrant, migrant, *émigré*, colonist.

outlet, vent, spout, tap, sluice, floodgate; pore; vomitory, out-gate, sally-port; way out; mouth, door etc. (*opening*) 260; path etc. (*way*) 627; conduit etc. 350; air-pipe etc. 351.

V. emerge, emanate, issue; go –, come –, move –, pass –, pour –, flow- out of; pass off, evacuate; migrate.

ex-, trans-ude; leak; run, – out, – through; per-, trans-colate; seep; strain, distil; perspire, sweat, drain, ooze; filter, filtrate; dribble, gush, spout, flow out; well, – out; pour, trickle etc. (*water in motion*) 348; effuse, extravasate, disembogue, discharge itself, debouch; come –, break-forth; burst- out, – through; find vent, escape etc. 671.

Adj. effused etc. *v.*; outgoing, outward bound.

Adv. outward.

296. Reception. [Motion into, actively.]—**N.** reception; admission, admittance, *entrée*, im-portation; initiation; intro-duction, -mission, -ception; immission, ingestion, imbibition, ab-sorption, ingurgitation, inhalation; suction, sucking; eating, drinking etc. (*food*) 298; insertion etc. 300; interjection etc. 228.

V. give -entrance to, – admittance to, – the *entrée*; intro-duce, -mit; usher, admit, receive, im-port, initiate, bring in, open the door to, throw open, ingest, absorb, imbibe, inhale, infiltrate; let –, take –, suck- in; re-admit, -sorb, -absorb; snuff up; swallow, ingurgitate; enfulf, engorge; gulp; eat, drink etc. (*food*) 298.

Adj. admit-ting etc. *v.*, -ted etc. *v.*; admissible; absorbent; introductory, introceptive, intromittent, initiatory.

297. Ejection. [Motion out of, actively.]—**N.** ejection, emission, effusion, rejection, expulsion, eviction, extrusion, trajection; discharge.

egestion, evacuation, vomition, disgorgement, voidance, eruption, eruptiveness; ruc-, eruc-tation; blood-letting, venesection, phlebotomy, paracen-tesis; tapping, drainage; clear-ance, -age, voidance; vomiting, excretion etc. 299.

deportation; banishment etc. (*punishment*) 972; rogue's march; relegation, extradition; dislodgment.

V. give -exit, – vent- to; let –, give –, pour –, send- out; des-, dis-patch; exhale, excern, ex-crete, disembogue, secrete, secern; extravasate,

shed, void, evacuate, egest, emit; open the -sluices, – floodgates; turn on the tap; extrude, detrude; ef-fuse, spend, expend; pour forth; squirt, spirt, spill, slop; perspire etc. (*exude*) 295; breathe, blow etc. (*wind*) 349.

tap, draw off; bale –, lade- out; let blood, broach.

eject, reject; expel, discard; cut, send to Coven-try, boycott, ostracize; *chasser*; banish etc. (*punish*) 972; throw etc. 284 -out, – up, – off, – away, – aside; push etc. 276 -out, – off, – away, – aside; shovel –, sweep- out, – away; brush –, whisk –, turn –, send- -off, – away; discharge; send –, turn –, cast- adrift; turn –, bundle- out; throw overboard; give the sack to; send -packing, – about one's business, – to the right about; strike off the roll etc. (*abrogate*) 756; turn out-neck and heels, – head and shoulders, – neck and crop; pack off; send away with a flea in the ear; send to Jericho; bow out, show the door to, dismiss, fire, sack.

turn out of -doors, – house and home; evict, oust; exorcise, un-house, -kennel; dislodge; un-, dis-people; depopulate; relegate, deport.

empty; drain, – to the dregs; sweep off; clear, – off, – out, – away; such, draw off, extract; clean out, make a clean sweep of, clear decks, purge.

em-, dis-, disem-bowel; eviscerate, gut; unearth, root -out, – up; averruncate; weed –, get out; eliminate, get rid of, do away with, shake off; exen-terate.

vomit, spew, puke, keck, retch; belch, – out, eruct, eructate; cast –, bring- up; disgorge; ex-pectorate, salivate, clear the throat, hawk, spit, sputter, splutter, slobber, drool, drivel, slaver, slab-ber.

unpack, unlade, unload, unship; break bulk.

be let out; ooze etc. (*emerge*) 295.

Adj. emitt-ing, -ed etc. *v.*

begone! get you gone! get –, go- away, – along, – along with you! go your way! away, – with! off with you! go, – about your business! be off! avaunt! aroynt! get out!

298. Food. [Eating.]—**N.** eating etc. *v.*; deglutition, gulp, epulation, mastication, man-ducation, rumination, gastronomy, gastrology; panto-, hippo-, ichthyo-phagy etc.; gluttony etc. 957; carnivorousness, vegetarianism.

mouth, jaws, mandible, mazard, chops.

drinking etc. *v.*; potation, draught, libation; carousal etc. (*amusement*) 840; drunkenness etc. 959.

food, *pabulum*; aliment, nourishment, nutriment; susten-ance, -tation; nurture, sub-sistence, provender, feed, fodder, provision, ration, keep, commons, board; commissariat etc. (*provision*) 637; prey, forage, pasture, pasturage; fare, cheer; diet, -ary; regimen; belly timber, staff of life; bread, -and cheese; proteins, carbohydrates, vitamines.

comestibles, eatables, victuals, edibles, *ingesta*; grub, prog, tack, hard tack, meat; bread, -stuffs; cereals; viands, cates, delicacy, dainty, creature comforts, contents of the larder, flesh-pots; festal board; ambrosia; good -cheer, – living.

hors-d'oeuvre; soup, pottage, *potage*, broth,

bouillon, consommé, purée, borsch, stock, skilly, gumbo; fish, – cakes, – pie; joint, *rôti, pièce de résistance,* hash, *réchauffé,* stew, *ragoût,* fricassee, mince, *salim, goulash, bouillabaisse, remove, entrée, croquette, rissole,* sausage, curry, bubble and squeak; haggis, collops, giblets; poultry, game etc.; biscuit, bun, scone, rusk, pancake, pie, pastry, pasty, patty, *patisseria,* tart, turnover, *vol-au-vent, soufflé,* dumpling, pudding, duff, *compote,* fritters, cake, napoleon, *blancmange,* custard, jelly, jam, sweets etc. 396; *entremet;* oatmeal, porridge, hasty pudding, gruel; eggs, omelet, cheese, matzoon, savory; vegetable, salad, *mayonnaise,* fruit; sauce, condiment etc. 393; kickshaws.

table, *cuisine,* bill of fare, *menu, table d'hôte,* ordinary, *à la carte;* cover.

meal, repast, feed, spread; mess; dish, plate, course, side dish; regale; regale-, refresh-, entertain-ment; refection, collation, picnic, feast, banquet, junket; breakfast; lunch, -eon, *déjeuner;* bever, tiffin, tea, dinner, supper, snack, whet, bait, dessert; pot-luck, *table d'hôte, déjeuner à la fourchette;* hearty – square –, substantial –, full--meal; blow out; light refreshment; pemmican.

mouthful, bolus, gobbet, tit-bit, morsel, sop, sippet.

drink, beverage, liquor, broth, soup; potion, dram, draft, drench, swill; nip, peg, sip, sup, gulp.

wine, champagne, spirits, *liqueur* beer, porter, stout, ale, malt liquor, julep, Sir John Barleycorn, stingo, heavy wet, bitter, lager- beer, cider; grog, toddy, flip, purl, punch, negus, cup, bishop, posset, wassail; bitters, *apéritif,* high-ball, cocktail; whisky, rum, absinthe; gin etc. (*intoxicating liquor*) 959; coffee, chocolate, cocoa, tea, *maté,* the cup that cheers but not inebriates.

eating-house etc. 189.

V. eat, feed, fare, devour, swallow, take; gulp, bolt, snap; fall to; despatch, dispatch; discuss; take –, get –, gulp-down; lay –, tuck- in; lick, pick, peck; gormandize etc. 957; bite, champ, munch, cranch, craunch, crunch, chew, masticate, nibble, gnaw, mumble.

live on; feed –, batten –, fatten –, feast- upon; browse, graze, crop, regale; carouse etc. (*make merry*) 840; eat heartily, do justice to, play a good knife and fork, banquet.

break -bread, – one's fast; breakfast; lunch, dine, take tea, sup.

drink, – in, – up, – one's fill; quaff, sip, sup; suck, – up; lap; swig, swill, tipple etc. (*be drunken*) 959; empty one's glass, drain the cup; toss -off, – one's glass; wash down, crack a bottle, wet one's whistle.

cater, purvey etc. 637.

Adj. eatable, edible, esculent, comestible, alimentary; cereal, cibarious; dietetic; culinary; nutri-tive, -tious; succulent; drinkable, pot-able, -ulent; bibulous.

omn-, carn-, herb-, frug-, gran-, gramin-, phytivorous; ichthyophagous.

prandial.

299. Excretion.—N. excretion, discharge, emanation; ejection etc. 297; exhalation, exudation, extrusion, secretion, effusion, extravasation, *ecchymosis,* evacuation, cacation, defecation, dysentery, dejection, *feces,* excrement;

perspiration, sweat; sub-, exud-ation; *diaphoresis;* sewage.

saliva, spittle, rheum; ptyalism, salivation, catarrh, distemper; diarrhea; *ejecta, egesta, sputum, sputa; excreta;* lava; *exuviae* etc. (*uncleanness*) 653.

hemorrhage, bleeding; catamenia, menses; outpouring etc. (*egress*) 295; leucorrhea.

V. excrete etc. (*eject*) 297; emanate etc. (*come out*) 295.

Adj. excretory, fecal, secretory; ejective, eliminant.

300. Insertion. [Forcible ingress.]—**N.** insertion, implantation, intercalation, embolism, introduction; interpolation, insinuation etc. (*intervention*) 228; planting etc. *v.*; injection, inoculation, importation, infusion; forcible -ingress etc. 294; immersion; submersion, -gence; dip, plunge; bath etc. (*water*) 337; interment etc. 363.

V. insert; intro-duce, -mit; put –, run- into; import; inject; interject etc. 228; infuse, instil, inoculate, impregnate, imbue, imbrue.

graft, ingraft, bud, plant, implant; dovetail.

obtrude; thrust –, stick –, ram –, stuff –, tuck –, press –, drive –, pop –, whip –, drop –, put- in; impact; empierce etc. (*make a hole*) 260.

embed; immerse, immerge, merge; bathe, soak etc. (*water*) 337; dip, plunge etc. 310.

bury etc. (*inter*) 363.

insert etc. -itself; plunge *in medias res.*

Adj. inserted etc. *v.*

301. Extraction. [Forcible egress.]—**N.** extraction; extracting etc. *v.*; removal, elimination, extrication, eradication, evolution.

evulsion, avulsion; wrench; expression, squeezing; extirpation, extermination; ejection etc. 297; export etc. (*egress*) 295; distillation.

extractor, corkscrew, forceps, pliers.

V. extract, draw, pit; take –, draw –, pull –, tear –, pluck –, pick –, get- out; wring from, wrench; extort; root –, weed –, grub –, rake-up, – out; eradicate; pull –, pluck- up by the roots; averruncate; unroot; uproot, pull up, extirpate, dredge.

remove; educe, elicit; evolve, extricate; eliminate etc. (*eject*) 297; eviscerate etc. 297.

express, squeeze –, press- out; distil.

Adj. extracted etc. *v.*

302. Passage. [Motion through.]—**N.** passage, transmission; permeation; pene-, interpene-tration; transudation, infiltration; *osmosis,* osmose, endos-, exos-mose; intercurrence; ingress etc. 294; egress etc. 295; path etc. 627; conduit etc. 350; opening etc. 260; journey etc. 266; voyage etc. 267.

V. pass, – through; perforate etc. (*hole*) 260; penetrate, permeate, thread, thrid, enfilade; go through, – across; go –, pass- over; cut across; ford, cross; pass and repass, work; make –, thread –, worm –, force- one's way; make –, force- a passage; cut one's way through; find its -way, –

vent; transmit, make way, clear the course;
traverse, go over the ground.

Adj. passing etc. *v.*; intercurrent; osmotic etc. *n.*
Adv. *en passant* etc. (*transit*) 270.

303. Overstep. [Motion beyond.]—**N.** transcursion, -ilience, -gression; infraction, intrusion;
trespass; encroach-, infringe-ment; extravagation,
transcendence; redundance etc. 641; ingress etc.
294.

V. transgress, surpass, pass; go- beyond, – by;
show in –, come to the- front; shoot ahead of;
steal a march –, gain- upon.

over-step, -pass, -reach, -go, -ride- -leap, -jump, -
skip, -lap, -shoot the mark; out-strip, -leap, -jump,
-go, -step, -run, -ride, -rival, -do; beat, – hollow;
distance; leave in the -lurch, – rear; go one better,
throw into the shade; exceed, transcend, surmount;
soar etc. (*rise*) 305.

encroach, intrude, trespass, infringe, invade,
trench upon, intrench on; strain; stretch – , strain-
a point; pass the Rubicon.

Adj. surpassing etc. *v.*
Adv. beyond the mark, ahead.

304. Shortcoming. [Motion short of.]—**N.**
-shortcoming, failure; delinquency; falling short etc.
v.; de-fault, -falcation; leeway; labor in vain, no
go.

incompleteness etc. 53; imperfection etc. 651;
insufficiency etc. 640; noncompletion etc. 730;
failure etc. 732.

V. come – , fall – , stop- -short, – short of; not
reach; want; keep within -bounds, – the mark, –
compass.

break down, stick in the mud, collapse, come to
nothing; fall -through, – to the ground, –. down;
cave in, end in smoke, fizzle out, miss the mark,
fail; lose ground; miss stays, slump.

Adj. unreached; deficient; short, – of; *minus*;
out of depth; perfunctory etc. (*neglect*) 460.

Adv. within -the mark, – compass, – bounds;
behindhand; *re infectâ*; to no purpose; far from it.
Phr. the bubble burst.

305. Ascent. [Motion upwards.]—**N.** ascent,
ascension; rising etc. *v.*; rise, upgrowth; leap etc.
309; acclivity, hill etc. 217; stair, stairs, stair-case, -
way, flight of -steps, – stairs; ladder, companion,
– way; lift, elevator etc. 307.

rocket, lark; sky-rocket, -lark; Alpine Club.

V. ascend, rise, mount, arise, uprise; go – , get
– , work one's way – , start – , spring – , shoot-
up; zoom; aspire.

climb, clamber, ramp, scramble, swarm,
escalade, surmount; scale, – the heights.

tower, soar, hover, spire, plane, swim, float,
surge; leap etc. 309.

Adj. rising etc. *v.*; scandent, buoyant; super-
natant, -fluitant; excelsior.

Adv. uphill.

306. Descent. [Motion downwards.]—**N.**
descent, descension, declension, declination; fall;
falling etc. *v.*; drop, cadence; subsidence, lapse;
come-down, downfall, tumble, slip, tilt, trip, lurch;
cropper, *culbute*; titubation, stumble; fate of
Icarus; dive, nose-dive, *volpané*.

avalanche, *débâcle*, landslip, slide.

V. descend; go – , drop – , come-down; fall,
gravitate, drop, slip, slide, glissade, dive, plunge,
settle; decline, slump, set, sink, droop, come down
a peg.

dismount, alight, light, get down; swoop; stoop
etc. 308; fall prostrate, precipitate oneself; let fall
etc. 308.

tumble, trip, stumble, titubate, lurch, pitch,
swag, topple; topple – , tumble- -down, – over;
tilt, sprawl, plump down, come a cropper.

Adj. descending etc. *v.*; descendent, declivitous;
downcast; decur-rent, sive; labent, deciduous;
nodding to its fall.

Adv. down, -hill, -wards.

307. Elevation.—**N.** elevation; raising etc. *v.*;
erection, lift; sublevation, upheaval; sublimation,
exaltation; prominence etc. (*convexity*) 250.

lever etc. 633; crane, derrick, windlass, capstan,
winch, dredger, lift, elevator, escalator, dumb
waiter.

V. heighten, elevate, raise, lift, erect; set –,
stick – , perch – , perk – , tilt- up; rear, hoist,
heave; up-lift, -raise, -rear, -bear, -cast, -hoist, -
heave; buoy, weigh, mount, give a lift; exalt,
sublimate; place – , set- on a pedestal.

take – , drag – , fish- up; dredge.

stand – , rise – , get – , jump- up; spring to
one's feet; hold -oneself, – one's head- up; draw
oneself up to his full height.

Adj. elevated etc. *v.*; standing up; stilted, attollent, rampant.

Adv.on -stilts, – the shoulders of, – one's legs,
– one's hind legs.

308. Depression.—**N.** lowering etc. *v.*;
depression; dip etc. (*concavity*) 252; abasement;
detrusion; reduction.

over-throw, -set, -turn; upset; prostration, subversion, precipitation.

bow; courtesy, curtsy; genuflexion, *kowtow*,
obeisance, *salaam*.

V. depress, lower; let – , take- -down, – down
a peg; cast; let -drop, – fall; sink, debase, bring
low, abase, slash, reduce, detrude, pitch,
precipitate.

over-throw, -turn, -set; upset, subvert, prostrate,
level, fell; cast – , take – , throw – , fling – , dash
– , pull – , cut – , knock – , hew- down; raze –,
to the ground; humiliate, trample in the dust, pull
about one's ears.

sit, – down; couch, squat, crouch, stoop, bend,
bow, courtsey, curtsy; bob, duck, dip, genuflect,
kneel; *kowtow*, *salaam*, make obeisance, prostrate
oneself; bend, bow- the -head, – knee; incline the
head; bow down; cower; recline etc. (*be horizontal*) 213.

Adj. depressed etc. *v.*; at a low ebb; prostrate
etc. (*horizontal*) 213; detrusive.

309. Leap.—**N.** leap, jump, hop, spring,
bound, vault, saltation.

dance, caper, gambol; curvet, caracole; *gam-bade*, *-bado*; capriole, demivolt; buck, – jump; hop, skip and jump.

kangaroo, jerboa, chamois, goat, frog, grasshopper, flea.

V. leap; jump -up, – over the moon; hop, spring, bound, vault, ramp, cut capers, gambol, trip, skip, dance, caper, curvet, *caracole*; foot it, bob, bounce, flounce, start, frisk etc. (*amusement*) 840; jump about etc. (*agitation*) 315; trip it on the light fantastic toe, dance oneself off one's legs.

Adj. leaping etc. *v.*; saltatory, frisky.

Adv. on the light fantastic toe.

310. Plunge.—N. plunge, dip, dive, header; ducking etc. *v.*; submergence, immersion, diver.

V. plunge, dip, souse, duck; dive, plump; take a -plunge, – header, make a plunge; bathe etc. (*water*) 337.

sub-merge, -merse; immerse, douse, sink, engulf, send to -the bottom, – Davy Jones' locker.

get out of one's depth; go -to the bottom, – down like a stone; founder, welter, wallow.

311. Circuition. [Curvilinear motion.]**—N.** circuition, circulation; turn, curvet; excursion; cir-cum-vention, -navigation, -ambulation; north-west passage; ambit, gyre, lap, circuit etc. 629.

turning etc. *v.*; wrench; evolution; coil, helix, spiral; corkscrew.

V. turn, bend, wheel; go – , put- about; heel; go –, turn -round, – to the right about; turn on one's heel; make – , describe- a -circle, – complete circle; encircle; go – , pass- through -180°, – 360°.

circum-navigate, -aviate, -ambulate, -vent; put a girdle round the earth, go the round, make the round of.

turn – , round- a corner; double a point.

wind, circulate, meander; whisk, twirl; twist etc. (*convolution*) 248; make a *détour* etc. (*circuit*) 629.

Adj. turning etc. *v.*; circuitous; circum-foraneous, -fluent; devious, roundabout, circum-ambient, -flex, -navigable.

Adv. round about.

312. Rotation. [Motion in a continued circle.]**—N.** rotation, revolution, gyration, cir-culation, roll; circum-rotation, -volution, -gyration; volutation, circination, turbination, *pirouette*, convolution.

verticity; whir, whirl, swirl, eddy, vortex, whirlpool, gurge; cyclone, tornado; surge; *vertigo*, dizzy round; Maelstrom, Charybdis; Ixion; wheel of Fortune.

wheel, screw, propeller, whirligig, rolling stone, windmill; top, teetotum, merry-go-round; roller; cog-, fly-wheel, spit; jack; caster.

axis, axle, spindle, spool, pivot, pin, hinge, pole, swivel, gimbals, arbor, bobbin, mandrel, shaft.

[Science of rotatory motion] trochilics, gyrostatics.

V. rotate; roll, – along; revolve, spin; turn, – round; circumvolve; circulate; gyre, gyrate, wheel,

whirl, swirl, twirl, trundle, troll, bowl; slew round.

roll up, furl; wallow, welter; box the compass; spin like a -top, – teetotum.

Adj. rotating etc. *v.*; rota-tory, -ry; cir-cumrotatory, trochilic, vertiginous, gyratory; vor-tic-al, -ose.

Adv. head over heels, round and round, like a horse in a mill.

313. Evolution. [Motion in a reverse circle.]**—N.** evolution, unfolding, development; eversion etc. (*inversion*) 218.

V. evolve; un-fold, -roll, -wind, -coil, -twist, -furl, -twine, -ravel; disentangle; develop.

Adj. evolving etc. *v.*; evolved etc. *v.*

314. Oscillation. [Reciprocating motion, motion to and fro.]**—N.** oscillation; vibration, libration; motion of a pendulum; nutation; un-dulation; pulsation; pulse; throb; seismic disturb-ance.

alternation; coming and going etc. *v.*; ebb and flow, flux and reflux, ups and downs; wave, vibratiuncle; swing, beat, shake, wag, see-saw, dance, lurch, dodge; fluctuation; vacillation etc. (*irresolution*) 605.

seismometer, vibroscope, seismograph.

V. oscillate; vi-, li-brate; alternate, undulate, wave; sway, rock, swing; pulsate, beat; wag, -gle; nod, bob, courtesy, curtsy; tick; play; chatter, wam-ble, wabble; teeter, dangle, swag.

fluctuate, dance, curvet, reel, quake; quiver, quaver, shake, flicker; wriggle; roll, toss, pitch; flounder, stagger, totter, waddle; move – , bob- up and down etc. *adv.*; pass and repass, ebb and flow, come and go, shuttle; vacillate etc. 605.

brandish, shake, flourish.

Adj. oscillating etc. *v.*; oscill-, undul-, puls-, libr-atory; vibrat-ory, -ile; pendulous, shutterwise; seismic.

Adv. to and fro, up and down, backwards and forwards, see-saw, zigzag, wibble-wabble, in and out, from side to side, like buckets in a well.

315. Agitation. [Irregular motion.]**—N.** agitation, stir, tremor, shake, ripple, jog, jolt, jerk, shock, succession, trepidation, quiver, quaver, dance; jactit-ation, -ance; shuffling etc. *v.*; twitter, flicker, flutter.

disquiet, perturbation, commotion, turmoil, tur-bulence; tumult, -uation; hubbub, rout, bustle, fuss, racket, *subsultus*, staggers, megrims, epilepsy, fits, twitching, vellication, St. Vitus' dance.

spasm, throe, throb, palpitation, convulsion, paroxysm; tetanus.

disturbance etc. (*disorder*) 59; restlessness etc. (*changeableness*) 149.

ferment, -ation; ebullition, effervescence, hurly burly, *cahotage*; tempest, storm, ground swell, heavy sea, whirlpool, vortex etc. 312; whirlwind etc. (*wind*) 349.

V. be -agitated etc.; shake; tremble, – like an aspen leaf; quiver, quaver, quake, shiver, twitter, twire, dither, dodder; twitch, writhe, toss, shuffle, tumble, stagger, bob, reel, sway; wag, -gle, wiggle; wriggle, – like an eel; squirm; dance, stumble, shamble. flounder, totter, flounce, flop, curvet, prance.

throb, pulsate, beat, palpitate, go pit-a-pat; flut-ter, flitter, flicker, bicker; bustle.

ferment, effervesce, foam; boil, – over; bubble, – up; simmer.

toss –, jump- about; jump like a parched pea; shake like an aspen leaf; shake to its -center, – foundations; be the sport of the winds and waves; reel to and fro like a drunken man; move – , drive-from post to pillar and from pillar to post; keep between hawk and buzzard.

agitate, shake, convulse, toss, tumble, bandy, wield, brandish, flap, flourish, whisk, jerk, hitch, jolt; jog, -gle; hostle, buffet, hustle, disturb, stir, shake up, churn, jounce, wallop, whip, vellicate.

Adj. shaking etc. *v.*; agitated, tremulous; de-, sub-sultory; shambling; giddy-paced, saltatory, convulsive, jerky, unquiet, restless, all of a twitter.

Adv. by fits and starts; subsultorily etc. *adj.*; *per saltum*; hop, skip and jump; in -convulsions, – fits, pit-a-pat.

316. Materiality.—N. material-ity, -ness; materialization; corpor-eity, -ality; substantiality, material existence, incarnation, flesh and blood, *plenum*; physical condition.

matter, body, substance, brute matter, stuff, element, principle, protoplasm, plasma, *paren-chyma*, material, *substratum*, hyle, *corpus*, *pabulum*; frame.

object, article, thing, something; still life; stocks and stones; materials etc. 635.

[Science of matter] physics; somatology, -ics; natural –, experimental- philosophy; physical science, *philosophie positive*, materialism, hylism; applied –, micro-, molecular –, nuclear – physics.

atomics, atomic science, nucleonics, quantum mechanics, radiology.

atom, radical, tracer, isotope, pleiad; atomic – nucleus, – cluster; nuclear particle, neutron, protron, shell, valence electron.

materialist, physicist, atomic scientist, radiologist.

V. materialize, incorporate, incarnate, sub-stantiate, embody.

atomize, split –, smash – the atom; radio-activate.

Adj. material, bodily; corpor-eal, -al; physical; somat-ic, -oscopic; sensible, tangible, ponderable, palpable, substantial; fleshly, incarnate.

physical, bio-, electro-, geo-physical; atomic, nuclear, thermonuclear, radio-active.

objective, impersonal, neuter, unspiritual, materialistic.

317. Immateriality.—N. immaterial-ity, -ness; incorporeity, dematerialization, unsubstantiality, spirituality; inextension; astral plane.

personality; I, myself, me; *ego*, spirit etc. (*soul*) 450; astral body; immaterialism; spiritual-ism, -ist; subliminal –, subconscious- self.

V. disembody, spiritualize, dematerialize.

Adj. immateri-al, -ate; incorpor-eal, -al; asomatous, unextended; un-, dis-embodied; ex-tramundane, supersensible, unearthly;

pneumatoscopic; spiritual etc. (*psychical*) 450; aery.

personal, subjective.

318. World.—N. world, creation, nature, universe; earth, globe, wide world; *cosmos*; terraqueous globe, sphere; macro-, mega-cosm; music of the spheres; strato-, tropo-sphere.

heavens, sky, welkin, empyrean; starry -heaven, – host; firmament; vault –, canopy- of heaven; celestial spaces.

heavenly bodies, stars, luminaries, nebulae; galaxy, milky way, galactic circle, *via lactea.*

sun, orb of day, Apollo, Phoebus; photo-, chromo-sphere; solar system; planet, -oid, asteroid; comet; satellite; moon, orb of night, Diana, Luna; aerolite, meteor; falling – , shooting-star; meteorite.

constellation, zodiac, signs of the zodiac, Charles's wain, Great Bear, Southern Cross, Orion's belt, Cassiopeia's chair, Pleiades etc.

colures, equator, ecliptic, orbit.

[Science of heavenly bodies] astronomy; urano-graphy, -logy; cosmo-logy, -graphy, -gony; *eidouranion*, orrery; geography; geodesy etc. (*measurement*) 466; star-gazing, -gazer; astronomer; cosmogonist, geodesist, geographer; observatory.

Adj. cosmic, cosmical, mundane; terr-estrial, -estrious, -aqueous, -ene, -eous; telluric, earthly, geotic, geodetic, cosmogonal, under the sun; sub-lunary, -astral.

solar, heliacal; lunar; celestial, heavenly, em-pyreal, sphery; starry, stellar; sider-eal, -al; astral; nebular.

Adv. in all creation, on the face of the globe, here below, under the sun.

319. Gravity.—N. gravi-ty, -tation; weight; heaviness etc. *adj.*; specific gravity; ponderosity, pressure, load; bur-den, -then; ballast, coun-terpoise; lump –, mass –, weight- of.

lead, millstone, mountain, Ossa on Pelion.

weighing, ponderation, trutination; weights; avoirdupois –, troy –, apothecaries'- weight; grain, scruple, drachm, ounce, pound, lb., load, stone, hundredweight, cwt., ton, quintal, carat, pen-nyweight, tod, gram, kilogram etc.

[Weighing instrument] balance, scales, steelyard, beam, weighbridge, spring balance, weighing machine.

[Science of gravity] statics.

V. be -heavy etc. *adj.*; gravitate, weigh, press, cumber, load.

[Measure the weight of] weigh, poise.

Adj. weighty; weighing etc. *v.*; heavy, – as lead; ponder-ous, -able; lump-ish, -y; cumber-, burden-some; cumbrous, unwieldy, massive.

in-, superin-cumbent.

320. Levity.—N. levity; lightness etc. *adj.*; im-ponderability, imponderables, buoyancy, volatility.

feather, dust, mote, down, thistledown, flue, cob-web, gossamer, straw, cork, bubble; float, bouy; ether, air.

leaven, ferment, barm, yeast, enzyme.

V. be -light etc. *adj.*; float, swim, be buoyed up.
render -light etc. *adj.*; lighten, levitate; leaven.

Adj. light, subtile, subtle, airy; imponder-ous, -able; astatic, weightless, ethereal, sublimated; un-compressed, volatile; buoyant, floating etc. *v.*; barmy, frothy; portable.

light as -a feather, − thistle down, − air.
fermenting etc. *n.*

321. Density.—N. density, solidity; solidness etc. *adj.*; impenetra-, impermea-bility; in-compressibility; imporosity; cohesion etc. 46; constipation, consistence, spissitude.

specific gravity; hydro-, areo-meter.

condensation; solid-ation, -ification; consolidation; concretion, caseation, coagulation; petrifaction etc. (*hardening*) 323; crystallization, precipitation; deposit, precipitate, silt; inspissation; thickening etc. *v.*

indivisibility, indiscerptibility, indissolvableness.
solid body, mass, block, knot, lump; con-cretion, -crete, -glomerate; cake, clot, stone, curd, coagulum, grume; bone, gristle, cartilage.

V. be -dense etc. *adj.*; become −, render- solid etc. *adj.*; solid-ify, -ate; concrete, set, take a set, consolidate, congeal, coagulate; curd, -le; fix, clot, cake, candy, precipitate, deposit, cohere, crystallize; petrify etc. (*harden*) 323.

condense, thicken, inspissate, incrassate; compress, squeeze, ram down, constipate.

Adj. dense, solid, solidified etc. *v.*; cohe-rent, -sive etc. 46; compact, close, serried, thickset; substantial, massive, lumpish; impenetrable, impermeable, imporous; incompressible; constipated; concrete etc. (*hard*) 323; knot-ted, -ty; gnarled; crystal-line, -lizable; thick, grumous, stuffy.

un-dissolved, -melted, -liquified, -thawed.
in-divisible, -discerptible, -frangible, -dissolvable, -dissoluble, -soluble, -fusible.

322. Rarity.—N. rarity; tenuity; absence of -solidity etc. 321; subtility; sponginess, compressibility.

rarefaction, expansion, dilatation, inflation, subtilization.

ether etc. (*gas*) 334.

V. rarefy, expand, dilate, subtilize, attenuate, thin.

Adj. rare, subtile, thin, fine, tenuous, compressible, flimsy, slight; light etc. 320; cavernous, spongy etc. (*hollow*) 252.

rarefied etc. *v.*; unsubstantial; uncom-pact, -pressed.

323. Hardness.—N. hardness etc. *adj.*; rigidity, renitence, inflexibility, temper, callosity, durity.

induration, petrifaction; lapid-ification, -escence; vitri-, ossi-, corni-fication; crystallization.

stone, pebble, flint, marble, rock, fossil, crag, crystal, quartz, granite, adamant; bone, cartilage; heart of oak, block, board, deal board; iron, steel; cast −, wrought- iron; nail; brick, concrete; cement.

V. render -hard etc. *adj.*; harden, stiffen, indurate, petrify, temper, ossify, vitrify.

Adj. hard, rigid, stubborn, stiff, firm; starch, -ed; stark, unbending, unlimber, unyielding; inflexible, tense; indurate, -d; gritty, proof.

adamant-ine, -ean; concrete, stony, rocky, lithic, granitic, vitreous; crystalline; horny, corneous; bony; oss-eous, -ific; cartilaginous; hard as a -stone etc. *n.*; stiff as -buckram, − a poker.

324. Softness.—N. softness, pliableness etc. *adj.*; flexibility; pli-ancy, -ability; sequacity, malleability; flabbiness; duct-, tract-ility; extend-, extensibility; plasticity; inelasticity; flaccidity, laxity.

clay, wax, butter, dough, pudding; cushion, pillow, feather-bed, pad, down, padding, wadding.
mollification; softening etc. *v.*

V. render -soft etc. *adj.*; soften, mollify, mellow, relax, temper; mash, knead, squash, *massage*.

bend, yield, relent, relax, give.

Adj. soft, tender, supple; pli-ant, -able; flex-ible, -ile; lithe, -some; lissom, limber, plastic; duc-tile; tract-ile, -able; malleable, extensile, sequacious, inelastic, mollient.

yielding etc. *v.*; flabby, limp, flimsy.
flaccid, flocculent, downy, spongy, edematous, medullary, doughy, argillaceous, mellow.

soft as -butter, − down, − silk; yielding as wax; tender as a chicken.

325. Elasticity.—N. elasticity, springiness, spring, resilience, renitency, buoyancy.

india-rubber, caoutchouc, gutta-percha, whale-bone, gum elastic.

V. be -elastic etc. *adj.*; spring back etc. (*recoil*) 227.

Adj. elastic, tensile, springy, ductile, resilient, renitent, buoyant.

326. Inelasticity.—N. want of −, absence of-elasticity etc. 325; inelasticity etc. (*softness*) 324.

Adj. inelastic etc. (*soft*) 324.

327. Tenacity.—N. tenacity, toughness, strength; cohesion etc. 46; sequacity; stubbornness etc. (*obstinacy*) 606; viscidity etc. 352.

leather; gristle, cartilage.

V. be -tenacious etc. *adj.*; resist fracture.

Adj. tenacious, tough, cohesive, adhesive, strong, resisting, sequacious, stringy, gristly, cartilaginous, leathery, coriaceous, tough as whit-leather; stubborn etc. (*obstinate*) 606.

328. Brittleness.—N. brittleness etc. *adj.*; frag-, friab-, frangib-, fiss-ility; frailty; house of -cards, − glass.

V. be -brittle etc. *adj.*; live in a glass house.
break, crack, snap, split, shiver, splinter, crumble, break short, burst, fly, give way; fall to pieces; crumble -to, − into- dust.

Adj. breakable, brittle, frangible, fragile, frail, friable, delicate, gimcrack, shivery, fissile; splitting etc. *v.*; lacerable, splintery, crisp, crimp, short, brittle as glass.

329. Texture. [Structure.]—N. structure, organization, anatomy, frame, mold, fabric, construction; frame-work, carcass, architecture; stratification, cleavage.

substance, stuff, *compages, parenchyma*; constitution, staple, organism.

[Science of structures]organ-, oste-, my- splanchn-, neur-, angi-, aden-ology; angi-, aden-ography.

texture; inter-, con-texture; tissue, grain, web, surface; warp and -woof, – -weft; tooth, nap etc. (*roughness*) 256; fineness –, coarseness- of grain.

[Science of textures] histology.

Adj. structural, organic; anatomic, -al.

text-ural, -ile; fine-, coarse-grained; fine, delicate, subtile, gossamery, filmy; coarse; homespun; linsey-woolsey.

330. Pulverulence. [State of powder.]—N. pulverulence; sandiness etc. *adj.*; efflorescence; friability.

powder, dust, sand, shingle; sawdust; grit; attrition; meal, bran, flour, *farina*, spore, sporule; crumb, seed, grain; particle etc. (*smallness*) 32; thermion; limature, filings, *débris, detritus*, scobs, magistery, fine powder; *flocculi*.

smoke; cloud of -dust, – sand, – smoke; puff –, volume -of smoke; sand –, dust- storm.

[Reduction to powder] pulverization, comminution, attenuation, granulation, disintegration, subaction, contusion, trituration, levigation, abrasion, detrition, multure; limation; filing etc. *v.*

[Instruments for pulverization] mill, millstone, grater, rasp, file, pestle and mortar, nutmeg grater, teeth, molar, grinder, chopper, grindstone, kern, quern, muller.

V. come to dust; be -disintegrated, – reduced to powder etc.

reduce –, grind- to powder; pulverize, comminute, granulate, triturate, levigate; scrape, file, abrade, rub down, grind, grate, rasp, pound, bray, bruise; con-tuse, -tund; beat, crush, cranch, craunch, crunch, muller, scranch, crumble, disintegrate; attenuate etc. 195.

Adj. powdery, pulverulent, granular, mealy, floury, farinaceous, branny, furfuraceous, flocculent, dusty, sandy, sabulous; aren-ose, -arious, -aceous; gritty; efflorescent, impalpable.

pulverizable; friable, crumbly, shivery; pulverized etc. *v.*; attrite; in pieces.

331. Friction.—N. friction, attrition; rubbing etc. *v.*; erasure; con-frication, -trition; affriction, abrasion, arrosion, limature, frication, rub; elbowgrease; rosin; *massage*.

V. rub, scratch, abrade, scrape, scrub, fray, rasp, graze, curry, scour, polish, rub out, erase, gnaw; file, grind etc. (*reduce to powder*) 330; *massage*. set one's teeth on edge; rosin.

Adj. anatriptic, abrasive.

332. Lubrication. [Absence of friction. Prevention of friction.]—N. smoothness etc. 255; unctuousness etc. 355.

lubri-cation, -fication; anointment; oiling etc. *v.* synovia; lubricant, graphite, glycerine, oil etc. 356; saliva; lather.

V. lubri-cate, -citate; oil, grease, lather, soap; wax.

Adj. lubricated etc. *v.*

333. Fluidity.—N. fluidity, liquidity; liquidness etc. *adj.*; gaseity etc. 334; liquefaction etc. 334.

fluid, inelastic fluid; liquid, liquor; lymph, humor, juice, sap, serum, blood, serosity, gravy, rheum, ichor, sanies.

solu-bility, -bleness.

[Science of liquids] hydro-logy, -statics, -dynamics, hydraulics. etc.

V. be -fluid etc. *adj.*; flow etc. (*water in motion*) 348; liquefy etc. 335.

Adj. liquid, fluid, serous, juicy, succulent, sappy; fluent etc. (*flowing*) 348.

liquefied etc. 335; uncongealed; soluble, hydrostatic etc. *n.*

334. Gaseity.—N. gaseity, gaseousness, vapourousness etc. *adj.*; flatulence, -lency; volatility, aeration, gasification.

elastic fluid, gas, air, vapor, ether, steam, fume, reek, *effluvium, flatus*; cloud etc. 353.

[Science of elastic fluids] pneumat-ics, -ostatics; aero-statics, -dynamics etc.

gas-, gaso-meter.

V. gassify, aerate, aerify; emit vapor etc. 336.

Adj. gaseous, aeriform, ethereal, aerial, airy, vaporous, volatile, evaporable; flatulent; aerostatic etc. *n.*

335. Liquefaction.—N. liquefaction; liquescen-ce, -cy, deliquescence; melting etc. (*heat*) 384; colliqu-ation, -efaction; thaw; de-, liquation; lixiviation, dissolution.

solution, apozem, lixivium, infusion, decoction, flux.

solvent, diluent, menstruum, alkahest, *aqua fortis*.

V. render -liquid etc 333; liquefy, run, deliquesce; melt etc. (*heat*) 384; solve; dissolve, resolve; liquate; hold in solution; leach, lixiviate.

Adj. lique-fied etc. *v.*, -scent, -fiable; deliquescent, soluble, colliquative; solvent.

336. Vaporization.—N. vapor-, volatilization; gasification; e-, vaporation; distillation, cohobation, sublimation, exhalation; volatility.

vaporizer, still, retort, spray, atomizer; fumigation, steaming.

V. render -gaseous etc. 334; vaporize, volatilize; distil, sublime; evaporate, exhale, smoke, transpire, emit vapor, fume, reek, steam, fumigate.

Adj. volatilized etc. *v.*; reeking etc. *v.*; volatile; evaporable, vaporizable.

337. Water.—N. water; serum, serosity; lymph; rheum; diluent.

dilution, maceration, lotion; washing etc. *v.*; immersion; humectation, infiltration, spargefaction, affusion, irrigation, *douche*, balneation, bath.

deluge etc. (*water in motion*) 348; high water, flood-, spring-tide.

V. be -watery etc. *adj.*; reek.

add water, water, wet; moisten etc. 339; dilute, dip, immerse; merge; im-, sub-merge; plunge, souse, duck, drown; soak, steep, macerate, pickle, wash, sprinkle, sparge, lave, bathe, affuse, splash, swash, douse, slosh, drench; dabble, slop, slobber, irrigate, inundate, deluge; syringe, inject, gargle; infiltrate, percolate.

Adj. watery, aqueous, aquatic, lymphatic; balneal, diluent; drenching etc. *v.*; diluted etc. *v.*; weak; wet etc. (*moist*) 339.

Phr. the waters are out.

338. Air.—N. air etc. (*gas*) 334; common —, atmospheric- air; atmosphere, stratosphere, isothermal layer, troposphere, Heaviside layer.

open; – air; sky, welkin; blue, – sky; cloud etc. 353.

weather, climate, rise and fall of the barometer, isobar.

[Science of air] pneumatics, aero-logy, -scopy, -graphy; meteorology, climatology; eudio-, baro-, aero-meter; aneroid, baro-graph, -scope; weather-gauge, -glass, -cock.

exposure to the -air, – weather; ventilation; aero-station; -nautics; -naut etc. 265 and 269.

V. air, ventilate; fan etc. (*wind*) 349.

Adj. containing air, flatulent, effervescent; windy etc. 349.

atmospheric, airy; aeri-al, -form; pneumatic; meteorological; weather-wise.

Adv. in the open air, out of doors, *à la belle étoile, al fresco; sub -Jove, – dio.*

339. Moisture.—N. moisture; moistness etc. *adj.*; hum-idity, -ectation; madefaction, dew; *serein*; marsh etc. 345; Hygromet-ry, -er.

V. moisten, wet; humect, -ate; sponge, damp, dampen, bedew; imbue, imbrue, infiltrate, saturate; seethe, sop; soak, drench etc. (*water*) 337.

be -moist etc. *adj.*; not have a dry thread; perspire etc. (*exude*) 295.

Adj. moist, damp; watery etc. 337; undried, humid, wet, dank, muggy, dewy; roric; roscid; juicy.

wringing wet; wet -through, – to the skin; saturated etc. *v.*

swashy, soggy, dabbled; reeking, seething, dripping, soaking, soft, sodden, sloppy, muddy; swampy etc. (*marshy*) 345; irriguous.

340. Dryness.—N. dryness etc. *adj.*; siccity, aridity, drought, ebb-, neap-tide, low water.

drying, – ex-, de-siccation; · evaporation; dehydration; arefaction, dephlegmation, drainage.

drier, desiccator.

V. be -dry etc. *adj.*; render -dry etc. *adj.*; dry; dry –, soak- up; sponge, swab, wipe; ex-, desiccate, dehydrate, anhydrate; drain, parch.

be fine, hold up.

Adj. dry, anhydrous, arid, waterless; dried etc. *v.*; undamped; juice-, sap- less; sear; husky; rainless, without rain, fine; dry as -a bone, – dust, – a stick, – a mummy, – a biscuit; disiccated; dehydrated; water-proof, -tight.

341. Ocean.—N. sea, ocean, main, deep, brine, salt water, waters, waves, billows, high seas, offing, great waters, watery waste, 'vasty deep,' briny ocean, herring pond, steamer track, the seven seas; wave, tide, etc. (*water in motion*) 348.

hydrograph-y, -er, oceanography; Neptune, Thetis, Triton, Naiad, Nereid; sea-nymph, Siren, mer-maid, -man; trident, dolphin.

Adj. oceanic; mar-ine, -itime; pleagic, -ian; sea-going, -worthy; hydrographic.

Adv. at –, on- sea; afloat, on the high seas.

342. Land.—N. land, earth, ground, dry land, *terra firma.*

continent, mainland, peninsula, delta; tongue –, neck- of land; isthmus; oasis; promontory etc. (*projection*) 250; highland etc. (*height*) 206.

coast, shore, scar, strand, beach; bank, lea; sea-board, -side, -shore, -bank, -coast, -beach; rock-, iron- bound coast; loom of the land; derelict; innings; *alluvium*, alluvion.

soil, glebe, clay, loam, marl, clodge, chalk, gravel, mold, subsoil, clod, clot; rock, crag, cliff.

acres; real estate etc. (*property*) 780; landsman, land-lubber, farmer.

geography etc. 318; agriculture etc. 371.

V. land, come to land; set foot on -the soil, – dry land; come –, go- ashore.

Adj. earthy; continental, midland; littoral, riparian, ripuarian; alluvial; terrene etc. (*world*) 318; landed, predial, territorial.

Adv. ashore; on -shore, – land.

343. Gulf. Lake.—N. land covered with water, gulf, gulph, bay, inlet, bight, estuary, arm of the sea, fiord, armlet; frith, firth, ostiary, mouth; lagune, lagoon; indraught; cove, creek; natural harbor; roads; strait, narrows; Euripus; sound, belt, gut, kyles.

lake, loch, lough, mere, tarn, plash, broad, pond, pool, lin, puddle, well, artesian well, tank, sump; standing –, dead –, sheet of- water; fish –; mill-pond; race; ditch, dike, dyke, dam; reservoir etc. (*store*) 636.

Adj. lacustrine; land locked.

344. Plain.—N. plain, table land, mesa, face of the country; open –, champaign-country; basin, downs, waste, weary waste, desert, tundra, wild, steppe, pampas, savanna, prairie, champaign, heath, common, wold, veld; moor, -land, uplands, fell; bush; *plateau* etc. (*level*) 213; *campagna.*

meadow, mead, haugh, pasturage, park, field,

lawn, green, plat, plot, grass-plat, greensward, sward, grass, turf, sod, heather; lea, ley, lay; grounds.

Adj. campestrian, champaign, alluvial.

345. Marsh.—N. marsh, swamp, morass, marish, moss, fen, bog, quagmire, slough, sump, wash; mud, squash, slush.

Adj. marsh, -y; swampy, boggy, plashy, poachy, quaggy, soft; muddy, sloppy, squashy, spongy; paludal; moor-ish, -y; fenny.

346. Island.—N. island, isle, islet, eyot, ait, holm, reef, atoll, breaker; archipelago; islander.

Adj. insular, sea-girt.

347. Stream. [Fluid in motion.]**—N.** stream etc. (*of water*) 348, (*of air*) 349.

V. flow etc. 348; blow etc. 349.

348. River. [Water in motion.]**—N.** running water.

jet, spirt, squirt, spout, splash, swash, rush, gush, *jet d'eau*; sluice, chute.

water-spout, -fall; fall, cascade, force, foss; lin, -n, ghyll, Niagara; cata-ract, -dupe, -clysm; *débâcle*, inundation, deluge.

rain, -fall; *serein*; shower, scud; downpour, cloud burst; driving −, pouring −, drenching-rain; hyeto-logy, -graphy; rainy season, monsoon; predominance of Aquarius, reigh of St. Swithin; mizzle, drizzle, *stillicidium*, plash; dropping etc. *v.*

stream, course, flux, flow, profluence; effluence etc. (*egress*) 295; defluxion; flowing etc. *v.*; current, tide, race.

spring; fount, -ain; rill, rivulet, gill, gullet, rillet; stream-, brook-let; runnel, sike, burn, beck, brook, stream, river; reach; tributary.

body of water, torrent, rapids, flush, flood, swash, spate; spring −, high −, full-tide; bore; eagre, *hugre*; fresh, -et; undertow, indraught, reflux, undercurrent, eddy, vortex, gurge, whirlpool, Maelstrom, regurgitation, overflow; confluence, corrivation.

wave, billow, surge, swell, ripple; roller, ground swell, surf, breaker, white horses; comber, beach-comber; rough −, heavy −, cross −, long −, short −, chopping −, choppy- sea, choppiness; tidal wave.

[Science of fluids in motion] Hydrodynamics; Hydraul-ics etc.; raingauge etc.

water-bearer, − carrier, Aquarius.

irrigation etc. (*water*) 337; pump; watering-pot, − cart; hydrant, standpipe, hose, sprinkler, drencher; fire engine, squirt, syringe.

V. flow, run; meander; gush, pour, spout, roll, jet, well, issue; drop, drip, dribble, plash, squirt, spurt, spirtle, trill, trickle, distil, percolate; stream; overflow, inundate, deluge, flow over, splash, swash, guggle, murmur, babble, bubble, purl, gurgle, sputter, regurgitate; ooze, flow out etc. (*egress*) 295.

rain, − hard, − in torrents, − cats and dogs, − pitchforks; come down in sheets; pour with rain, drizzle, mizzle, spit, sprinkle, set in.

flow −, fall −, open −, drain- into; discharge itself, desembogue.

[Cause a flow] pour; pour out etc. (*discharge*) 297; shower down; irrigate, drench etc. (*wet*) 337; spill, splash.

[Stop a flow] stanch; dam, -up etc. (*close*) 261; obstruct etc. 706.

Adj. fluent; dif-, pro-, af-fluent; tidal; flowing etc. *v.*; meand-ering, -ry, -rous; fluvi-al, -atile; streamy, showery, rainy, drizzly, drizzling, pluvial, pluviose, stillicidous.

349. Wind. [Air in motion.]**—N.** wind, draught, *flatus, afflatus,* air; breath, − of air; puff, whiff, zephyr; blow, drift; *aura*; stream, current; under-current.

gust, blast, breeze, squall, gale, half a gale, storm, tempest, hurricane, whirlwind, tornado, samiel, cyclone, typhoon; simoon; harmattan, monsoon, trade wind, sirocco, *mistral, bise, föhn,* tramontane, levanter; capful of wind; fresh −, stiff- breeze; keen blast; blizzard.

windiness etc. *adj.*; ventosity; rough −, dirty −, ugly −, stress of- weather; dirty-, windy-, mackerel- sky; mare's tail; thick −, black −, white- squall.

anemography, aerodynamics; windgauge; anemometer, weather-cock, vane.

suf-, insuf-, per-, in-, af-flation; blowing, fanning etc. *v.*; ventilation.

sneezing etc. *v.*; sternutation; hic-cup, -cough; catching of the breath; breathing etc.

Eolus, Eurus, Boreas, Zephyr, cave of Eolus.

air-pump, lungs, bellows, blow-pipe, fan, blower; pulmotor, ventilator, punkah, aspirator, exhauster, ejector.

V. blow, waft; blow -hard, − great guns, − a hurricane etc. *n.*; whistle, roar, howl, ring in the shrouds; stream, issue.

respire, breathe, in-, ex-hale, puff; whif, -fle; gasp, wheeze; snuff, -le; sniff, -le; sneeze, cough, belch.

fan, ventilate; in-, per-flate; blow −, pump- up.

Adj. blowing etc. *v.*; windy, airy, aeolian, flatulent; breezy, gusty, squally; stormy, tempestuous, blustering; boisterous etc. (*violent*) 173.

pulmon-ic, -ary.

350. Conduit. [Channel for the passage of water.]**—N.** conduit, channel, duct, watercourse, race; head −, tail- race; adit, aqueduct, canal, trough, flume, gutter, pantile; dike, canyon, ravine, gorge, hollow, main, gully, moat, ditch, drain, sewer, culvert, *cloaca,* sough, kennel, siphon, *piscina*; pipe etc. (*tube*) 260; funnel; tunnel etc. (*passage*) 627; water −, waste- pipe; emunctory, gully-hole, artery, aorta, vein, blood vessel; lymphatic; throat, alimentary canal, intestine; pore, spout, scupper; ad-, a-jutage; hose; gar-, gur-goyle; penstock, weir; flood-, water-gate; sluice, lock, valve; rose; waterworks.

Adj. vascular etc. (*with holes*) 260.

351. Air-pipe. [Channel for the passage of air.]**—N.** air-pipe, − shaft, − way, − passage, −

tube; shaft, flue, chimney, funnel, vent, blow-hole, nostril, nozzle, throat, weasand, *trachea*; *bronch-us,*-*ia*; larynx, tonsils, wind-pipe, spiracle; venti-duct, -lator; louvre, Venetian blinds; blow-pipe etc. (*wind*) 349; pipe etc. (*tube*) 260.

352. Semiliquidity.—N. semiliquidity; stickiness etc. *adj.*; visc-idity, -osity; gumm-, glûtin-, muc-osity; spiss-, crass-itude; lentor; adhesiveness etc. (*cohesion*) 46.

inspiss-, incrass-ation; thickening, coagulation.

jelly, aspic, mucilage, gelatin, isinglass; colloid, mucus, phlegm; pituite, lava; glair, starch, gluten, albumen, milk, cream, protein; syrup, treacle; gum, size, glue, paste; wax, bee's-wax; emulsoid, emulsion, soup; squash, mud, slush, slime, ooze; moisture etc. 339; marsh etc. 345.

V. inspiss-, incrass-ate; coagulate, gelatinize, gelatinify, gel, jell, emulsify, thicken; mash, squash, churn, beat up.

Adj. semi-fluid, -liquid; half-melted, -frozen; milky, muddy etc. *n.*; lact-eal, -ean, -eous, -escent, -iferous; emulsive, curdled, thick, succulent, uliginous.

gelat-, album-, mucilag-, glut-inous; gelatine, mastic, amylaceous, ropy, clammy, clotted; vis-cid, -cous; sticky, tacky; slab, -by; lentous, pituitous; mu-cid, -culent, -cous.

353. Bubble. [Mixture of air and water.] [Cloud.]—**N.** bubble; foam, froth, head, fume, spume, lather, suds, spray, surf, yeast, barm, spin-drift.

cloud, vapor, fog, mist, haze, steam; scud, rack, *nimbus*; *cumulus*, woolpack, *cirrus*, *stratus*; *cirro-*, *cumulo-stratus*; *cirro-cumulus*; mackerel sky, mare's tail, dirty sky.

[Science of clouds] nephelognosy, nephology.

effervescence, fermentation; bubbling etc. *v.*

nebula; cloudiness etc. (*opacity*) 426; nebulosity etc. (*dimness*) 422.

V. bubble, boil, foam, froth, spume, mantle, sparkle, guggle, gurgle; effervesce, ferment, fizzle; aerate; cloud, overcast, befog.

Adj. bubbling etc. *v.*; frothy, nappy, ef-fervescent, sparkling, *mousseux*, up, fizzy, with a head on.

cloudy etc. *n.*; vaporous, nebulous, overcast; nubiferous, nephological; foggy, brumous.

354. Pulpiness.—N. pulpiness etc. *adj.*; pulp, paste, dough, sponge, curd, pap, rob, jam, pudding, mush, fool, poultice, grume.

Adj. pulpy etc. *n.*; pultaceous, grumous.

V. pulp, pulpify, mash.

355. Unctuousness.—N. unctuousness etc. *adj.*; unctuosity, lubricity; ointment etc. (*oil*) 356; anointment; lubrication etc. 332.

V. oil etc. (*lubricate*) 332.

Adj. unctuous, oily, oleaginous, adipose, sebaceous, fat, -ty; greasy, waxy, butyraceous, soapy, saponaceous, pinguid, lardaceous; slippery.

356. Oil.—N. oil, fat, butter, cream, grease, tallow, suet, lard, dripping, margarine, oleomargarine, exunge, blubber; glycerine, stearine, elaine, oleagine; soap; soft soap, wax, cerement; paraffin, spermaceti, adipocere; petroleum, mineral −, rock −, crystal- oil, kerosene, vegetable −, colza −, olive −, linseed −, cotton seed −, rape −, nut −, fusel- oil; animal −, neat's foot −, signal −, train- oil; oint-ment, unguent, liniment, salve, pomade, pomatum, brilliantine, spike −, nard.

356a. Resin.—N. resin, rosin, colophony; gum; lac, shellac, sealing-wax; amber, -gris; bitumen, pitch, tar, asphalt, -e, -um; varnish, copal, mastic, magilp, lacquer, japan.

V. varnish etc. (*overlay*) 223.

Adj. resinous, bituminous, pitchy, tarry.

357. Organization.—N. organized -world, − nature; living −, animated- nature; living beings; organic remains, organism; fossils; animal and vegetable kingdom, *fauna* and *flora*, biota.

prot-oplasm, -ein; albumen; structure etc. 329; organ-ization, -ism.

[Science of living beings] biology; natural history,* organic −, bio-chemistry; anatomy, physiology, embryology, morphology, evolution, Darwinism, Lamarkism, zoology etc. 368; botany etc. 369; naturalist, biologist etc.

Adj. organ-ic, -ized.

*The term *Natural History* is also used as relating to all the objects in Nature whether organic or inorganic, and in-cluding therefore *Mineralogy, Geology, Meteorology*, etc.

358. Inorganization.—N. mineral -world, − kingdom; unorganized −, inorganic −, brute −, inanimate- matter.

[Science of the mineral kingdom] mineralogy; geo-logy, -gnosy, -scopy; metall-urgy, -ography; lithology; orycto-logy, -graphy.

V. turn to dust, pulverize.

Adj. in-organic, -animate; unorganized; azoic; mineral.

359. Life.—N. life; vi-tality, -ability; animation; vital -spark, − flame, − force.

respiration, wind; breath -of life, − of one's nostrils; life-blood; Archeus; existence etc. 1.

vivification, vitalization; revivification etc. 163; Prometheus; life to come etc. (*destiny*) 152.

[Science of life] physiology, etiology, em-bryology, biology; animal economy.

nourishment, staff of life etc. (*food*) 298.

V. be -alive etc. *adj.*; live, breathe, respire; sub-sist etc. (*exist*) 1; walk the earth; strut and fret one's hour upon a stage; be spared.

see the light, be born, come into the world; fetch −, draw- -breath, − the breath of life; quicken; revive; come to, − life.

give birth to etc. (*produce*) 161; bring to life, put into life, vitalize; vivi-fy, -ficate; reanimate etc. (*restore*) 660; keep -alive, − body and soul together, − the wolf from the door; support life.

have nine lives like a cat.

Adj. living, alive; in -life, − the flesh, − the land of the living; on this side of the grave, above ground, breathing, quick, animated, viable; lively etc. (*active*) 682; alive and kicking; tenacious of life.

vital; vivi-fying; -fied etc. *v.*; Promethean.

Adv. *vivendi causâ.*

360. Death.—**N.** death, dying etc. *v.*; de-cease, -mise; dissolution, departure, *obit*, release, rest, *quietus*, fall; loss, bereavement.

end etc. 67 −, cessation etc. 142 −, loss −, extinction −, ebb- of -life etc. 359.

death-warrant, -watch, -rattle, -bed; stroke −, agonies −, shades −, valley of the shadow −, jaws −, hand- of death; last -breath, − gasp, − agonies; dying -day, − breath, − agonies; swan song, *chant du cygne*; *rigor mortis*; Stygian shore; crossing the bar, the great adventure.

King -of terrors, − Death; Death, Angel of Death; mortality; doom etc. (*necessity*) 601.

euthanasia; happy release; break up of the system; natural -death, − decay; sudden −, violent- death; untimely end, watery grave; suffocation, *asphyxia*; heart failure; fatal disease etc. (*disease*) 655; death-blow etc. (*killing*) 361.

necrology, bills of mortality, obituary; death-song etc. (*lamentation*) 839.

V. die, expire, perish; meet one's -death, − end; pass away, be taken; yield −, resign- one's breath; resign one's -being, − life; end one's -days, − life, − earthly career; breathe one's last; cease to -live, − breathe; depart this life; be -no more etc. *adj.*; go −, drop −, pop -off; lose −, lay down −, relinquish −, surrender- one's life; drop −, sink- into the grave; close one's eyes; fall −, drop- dead, − down dead; break one's neck; give −, yield- up the ghost; be all over with one.

pay the debt to nature, shuffle off this mortal coil, take one's last sleep; go the way of all flesh; join the -greater number, − majority, − choir invisible; to life immortal awake; come −, turn- to dust; cross the Stygian ferry; go to -one's long account, − one's last home, − Davy Jones's locker, − the wall; receive one's death warrant, make one's will, die a natural death, go out like the snuff of a candle; come to an untimely end; catch one's death; go off the hooks, kick the bucket, pet out; go West; hop the twig, turn up one's toes; die a violent death etc. (*be killed*) 361; make the supreme sacrifice.

Adj. dead, lifeless; deceased, demised, departed, defunct; late, gone, no more; ex-, in-animate; out of the world, taken off, released; departed this life etc. *v.*; dead and gone; bereft of life, stone dead, dead as -a door nail, − a door post, − mutton, − a herring, − nits; launched into eternity, gathered to one's fathers, numbered with the dead, gone to a better land, behind the veil, beyond the grave, − mortal ken.

dying etc. *v.*; mori-bund, -ent, Acherontic; hippocratic; *in -articulo, − extremis*; in the -jaws, − agony- of death; going, − off; *aux abois*; on one's -last legs, − death bed; at -the point of death, − death's door, − the last gasp; near one's end, given over, booked, fey; with one foot in −, tottering on the brink of- the grave.

still-born; mortuary; deadly etc. (*killing*) 361.

Adv. *post -obit, − mortem.*

Phr. life -ebbs, − fails, − hangs by a thread; one's -days are numbered, − hour is come, − race is run, − doom is sealed; Death -knocks at the door, − stares one in the face; the breath is out of the body; the grave closes over one; *sic itur ad astra*.

361. Killing. [Destruction of life; violent death.]—**N.** killing etc. *v.*; homicide, man-slaughter, murder, assassination, trucidation, occision; lynching, effusion of blood; blood, -shed; gore, slaughter, carnage, butchery; *battue*, gladiatorial . combat.

massacre; *fussillade, noyade, pogrom*; thuggism; racketeering.

death blow, finishing stroke, *coup de grâce, quietus*; execution etc. (*capital punishment*) 972; judicial murder; martyrdom.

butcher, slayer, murderer, Cain, assassin, cut-throat, garrotter, *bravo*, thug, racketeer, gunman, mobster, gangster, Moloch, *matador, sabreur; guet-à-pens*; gallows, executioner etc. (*punishment*) 975; man-eater.

regicide, parricide, fratricide, infanticide, aborticide etc.

suicide, *felo de se, suttee, hara kiri*, Juggernaut; immolation, holocaust.

suffocation, strangulation, *garrotte*; hanging etc. *v.*

deadly weapon etc. (*arms*) 727; Aceldama; the potter's field, the field of blood.

fatal accident, violent death, casualty.

[Destruction of animals] slaughtering; phthiozoics;* sport, -ting; the chase, venery; hunting, coursing, shooting, fishing; pig-sticking; sports-, hunts-, fisher-man; hunter, Nimrod; slaughterer, knacker, slaughter-house, shambles, *abattoir*.

V. kill, put to death, slay, shed blood; murder, assassinate, butcher, slaughter; victimize, immolate; massacre; take away −, deprive of- life; make away with, put an end to; despatch, dispatch; burke settle, do, − to death, − for.

strangle, garrotte, hang, lynch, throttle, choke, stifle, suffocate, stop the breath, smother, asphyxiate, drown.

saber; cut -down, − to pieces, − the throat; jugulate; stab, run through the body, bayonet; put to the -sword, − edge of the sword.

shoot, − dead; blow one's brains out; brain, knock on the head; stone, lapidate; give −, deal- a death blow; give a -quietus, − coup de grâce.

behead, bowstring etc. (*execute*) 972.

hunt, shoot etc. *n.*

cut off, nip in the bud, launch into eternity, send to one's last account, bump off, rub out, sign one's death warrant, strike the death knell of.

give no quarter, pour out blood like water; decimate; run amuck, wade knee-deep −, imbrue one's hands- in blood.

die a violent death, welter in one's blood; dash −, blow- out one's brains; commit suicide; kill − -make away with −, put an end to- oneself.

Adj. killing etc. *v.*; murd-, slaught-erous; sanguin-ary, -olent; blood-stained, -thirsty;

homicidal, red-handed; bloody, -minded; ensanguined, gory, sanguineous.

mortal fatal, lethal; dead-, death-ly; mort-, lethiferous; unhealthy etc. 657; internecine; suicidal.

sporting; piscator-ial, -y.

Adv. in at the death.

*Bentham, 'Chrestomathia.'

362. Corpse.—**N.** corpse, corse, carcass, bones, skeleton, dry-bones; defunct, relics, *relinquiae*, remains, mortal remains, dust, ashes, earth, clay; mummy; carrion; food for- worms, — fishes; tenement of clay, this mortal coil.

shade, ghost, *manes*, apparition etc. 980.

organic remains, fossils.

Adj. cadaverous, corpse-like; unburied etc. 363.

363. Interment.—**N.** interment, burial, inhumation, sepulture, entombment; in-, humation; obs-, ex-equies; funeral, wake, pyre, funeral pile; cremation.

funeral -rite, — solemnity; knell, passing bell, tolling; dirge etc. (*lamentation*) 839; cypress; *obit*, dead march, muffled drum; coroner, mortician, undertaker, mute, mourner, professional mourner, pallbearer; elegy; funeral -oration, — sermon; epitaph.

grave clothes, shroud; winding-sheet, cere-cloth; cerement.

coffin, shell, sarcophagus, urn, pall, bier, hearse, catafalque, cinerary urn.

grave, pit, sepulcher, tomb, vault, crypt, catacomb, mausoleum, *Golgotha*, house of death, narrow house, long home; cemetery, necropolis, boneyard; burial-place, -ground; grave-, churchyard; God's acre; mortuary, tope, cromlech, dolmen, menhir, barrow, tumulus, cairn; ossuary; bone-, charnel-, dead-house; *Morgue*; lich-gate; crematorium.

sexton, grave-digger.

monument, memorial, cenotaph, shrine; grave-, head-, tomb-stone; *memento mori*; hatchment, stone, cross.

exhumation, disinterment; necropsy, autopsy, *post mortem* examination.

V. inter, bury, lay in —, consign to- the -grave, — tomb; en-, in-tomb; inhume; lay out, prepare for burial, embalm, mummify; conduct a funeral, hold services; toll the knell; put to bed with a shovel.

exhume, disinter, unearth.

Adj. buried etc. *v.*; burial; fune-real, -brial; mortuary, sepulchral, cinerary; elegiac; necroscopic.

Adv. *in memoriam*; *post-obit*, -mortem; beneath —, under- -the sod.

Phr. *hic jacet, ci-git, requiescat in pace.*

364. Animality.—**N.** animal life; anima-tion, -lity, -lization; breath.

flesh, — and blood; corporeal nature; *physique*; strength etc. 159.

V. animalize, incorporate.

Adj. fleshly, incarnate, carnal, corporeal, human.

365. Vegetability.—**N.** vegetable life; vegetation, -bility; herbage.

V. vegetate, germinate, sprout, shoot; cultivate.

Adj. vegetable etc. 367; rank, lush.

366. Animal.*—**N.** animal, — kingdom; *fauna*; brute creation.

beast, brute, creature, created being; creeping —, living- thing; dumb -animal, — creature.

flocks and herds, live stock; domestic —, wild-animals; game, *ferae naturae*; beasts of the fields, fowls of the air, denizens of the day.

vertebrate, bi-, quadru-ped, mammal, marsupial, bird, reptile, batrachian, amphibian, fish, crustacean, shell fish, articulate, mollusc, worm, insect, zoophyte; protozoon, animalcule etc. 193.

horse etc. (*beast of burden*) 271; cattle, kine, ox; bull, -ock; steer, stot; cow, milch-cow, calf, heifer, shorthorn; sheep; lamb, -kin; ewe —, pet-lamb; ewe, ram, tup; pig, swine, boar, hog, shoat, sow; tag, teg, wether.

dog, bitch, hound; pup, -py; whelp, cur, mutt, mongrel; house-, watch-, sheep-, shepherd's, sporting-, fancy-, lap-, toy-, bull-, badger-dog; mastiff; blood-, grey-, stag-, deer-, fox-, otter-, hound; harrier, beagle, spaniel, pointer, setter, retriever; Newfoundland; water -dog, — spaniel; pug, poodle; dachshund; Pinscher; turnspit; terrier; fox —, Skye- terrier; Dandie Dinmont; colley.

cat; puss,-y; kitten; grimalkin; gib-, tom-cat; mouser; fox, Reynard, vixen, stag, deer, hart, buck, doe, roe, antelope.

bird; poultry, fowl, cock, hen, chicken, chanticleer, partlet, rooster, dunghill cock, barn-door fowl; feathered -tribes, — songster; singing —, dicky- bird; canary; finch; auk, dodo, moa, roc, phoenix.

snake, serpent, viper, adder; newt, eft; asp, vermin.

Adj. animal, zoological.

equine, bovine, vaccine, canine, feline; fishy; piscator-y, -ial; molluscous, vermicular.

*Extended lists of names of specific varieties of animals, vegetables, etc., are beyond the scope of this work.

367. Vegetable.*—**N.** vegetable, — kingdom; *flora*, verdure.

plant; tree, shrub, bush; creeper; vine; herb, -age; grass.

annual; per-, bi-, tri-ennial; exotic.

timber; primeval —, virgin- forest; wood, -lands; hurst; frith, holt, weald, park, chase, greenwood, brake, grove, copse, coppice, *bocage, tope*, clump of trees, thicket, spinet, spinney; under-, brushwood; boscage, scrub; the oak and the ash and the bonny ivy tree.

bush, jungle, prairie; heath, -er; fern, bracken, furze, gorse, whin, broom; grass, turf, grassland, greensward, green, lawn, meadow; pas-ture, -turage; turbary; sedge, rush, weed; fungus, mushroom, toadstool; lichen, moss, conferva, mold; seaweed etc.; growth, crop.

foliage, leafage, branch, bough, ramage; spray etc. 51; leaf, frond, flag, petal, shoot, tendril.

flower, blossom, bud, bloom, bine; flowering plant; tree, sapling, pollard; timber-, fruit-tree; palm-, gum-tree; pulse, legume.

Adj. veget-able, -ous; herb-aceous, -al; botanic; sylvan, silvan; arbor- ary, -eous, -escent, -ical; dendritic, dendriform; woody, grassy; ver-dant, - durous; floral, mossy; lign-ous, -eous; wooden, leguminous; end-, ex-ogenous.

*Extended lists of names of specific varieties of animals, vegetables, etc., are beyond the scope of this work.

368. Zoology. [The science of animals.]—**N.** zoo-logy, -nomy, -graphy, -tomy; anatomy; comparative anatomy; animal —, comparative-physiology; morphology.

anthrop-, ornith-, ichthy-, herpet-, ophi-, malac-, helminth-, entom-, oryct-, paleont-ology; ichthy- etc. -otomy; taxidermy.

zo- etc. -ologist.

Adj. zoological etc. *n.*

369. Botany. [The science of plants.]—**N.** botany; phyto-graphy, -logy, -tomy; vegetable physiology, herborization, dendr-, myc-, fung-, alg-ology; flora, pomona; botanist etc.; botanic garden etc. (*garden*) 371; *hortus siccus, herbarium,* her-bal.

herb-ist, -arist, -alist, -orist, -arian etc.

V. botanize, herborize.

Adj. botanical etc. *n.*

370. Cicuration. [The economy or management of animals.]—**N.** taming etc. *v.;* cicuration, zoohygiantics; domestication, -ity; *manège*; veterinary art; breeding, pisciculture, apiculture etc.

menagery, vivarium, zoological garden, zoo; bear-pit; aviary, apiary, hive; aquarium, fishery, fish hatchery; duck-; fish-pond; stud-farm; stock farm, dairy.

[Destruction of animals] phthisozoics etc. (*killing*) 361.

neat-, cow-, shep-herd, shepherdess; grazier, drover, cowboy, cowkeeper; trainer, breeder, groom, ostler etc. 746; veterinary surgeon, vet, horse doctor; farrier; keeper; game keeper.

cage etc. (*prison*) 752; hen-coop, bird-cage, cauf; sheep-fold etc. (*inclosure*) 232.

V. tame, domesticate, acclimatize, breed, tend, break in, train, corral, round up; cage, bridle etc. (*restrain*) 751; ride etc. 266.

drive, yoke, harness, hitch; groom, curry-comb; milk; shear; hatch; incubate.

Adj. pastoral, bucolic; tame, domestic, domesticated, broken in, gentle, docile.

371. Agriculture. [The economy or management of plants.]—**N.** agriculture, cultivation, husbandry, farming; georgics, geoponics; tillage, tilth, agronomy, gardening, spade husbandry, vintage; hort-, arbor-, silv-, citr-, vit-, flor-iculture; intensive culture; landscape gardening; forestry, afforestation.

husbandman, horticulturist, citriculturist, gardener, florist; agricult-or, -urist; yeoman, farmer, cultivator, tiller of the soil, ploughman, sower, reaper; woodcutter, backwoodsman, forester; vine grower, vintager; Boer; Triptolemus.

field, meadow, garden; botanic —, winter —, or-

namental —, flower —, kitchen —, truck —, market —, hop- garden; nursery; green-, hot-, glass-house; conservatory, cucumber frame, *cloche,* bed, border, seed-plot; grass-plat, lawn; park etc. (*pleasure ground*) 840; *partere,* shrubbery, plantation, avenue, *arboretum,* pinery, *pinetum,* orchard, vineyard, vinery; orangery; farm etc. (*abode*) 189.

V. cultivate; till, — the soil; farm, garden; sow, plant; reap, mow, cut; manure, dress the ground, dig, delve, dibble, hoe, plough, plow, harrow, rake, weed, lop and top, force, transplant, thin out, bed out, prune, graft.

Adj. agr-icultural, -airan, -estic.

arable; predial, rural, rustic, country, bucolic, Boeotian; horticultural.

372. Mankind.—N. man, -kind; human -race, — species, — nature; humanity, mortality, flesh, generation.

[Science of man] anthropo-logy, -graphy, -sophy; ethno-logy, -graphy; humanitarianism.

human being: person, -age; individual, creature, fellow creature, mortal, body, somebody, one; such a —, someone; soul, living soul; earthling; party, head, hand; *dramatis personae.*

people, persons, folk, public, society, world; community, — at large; general public; nation, -ality; state, realm; common-weal, -wealth; republic, body politic; million etc. (*commonalty*) 876; population etc. (*inhabitant*) 188.

cosmopolite; lords of the creation; ourselves.

Adj. human, mortal, personal, individual, national, civic, public, cosmopolitan; anthropoid.

373. Man.—N. man, male, he; manhood etc. (*adolescence*) 131; gentleman, sir, master; yeoman, wight, swain, fellow, guy, blade, *beau,* chap, gaffer, good man; husband etc. (*married man*) 903; Mr., mister, *monsieur, sahib, Herr, señor, signor;* boy etc. (*youth*) 129; Adonis.

[Male animal] cock, drake, gander, dog, boar, stag, hart, buck, horse, entire horse, stallion; gib-, tom-cat; he-, Billy-goat; ram, tup; bull, -ock; capon, ox, gelding; steer, stot.

Adj. male, he, masculine; manly, virile; un-womanly, -feminine.

374. Woman.—N. woman, she, female, pet-ticoat, skirt, moll, broad.

feminality, feminity, muliebrity; womanhood etc. (*adolescence*) 131; feminism; gynecology, gyniatrics, gynics.

womankind; the -sex, — fair; fair —, softer- sex; weaker vessel; the distaff side.

dame, madam, *madame,* mistress, Mrs., lady, *mem-sahib, Frau, señora, signora, donna, belle,* matron, dowager, goody, gammer; good -woman, — wife; squaw; wife etc. (*marriage*) 903; matron-age, -hood.

Venus, nymph, wench, *grisette;* little bit of fluff; girl etc. (*youth*) 129.

inamorata (love) etc. 897; courtesan etc. 962.

spinster, old maid, virgin, bachelor girl, new woman, amazon.

[Female animal] hen, slut, bitch, sow, doe, roe, mare; she-, Nanny-goat; ewe, cow; lioness, tigress; vixen.

gynecaeum, harem, *seraglio*, *zenana*, *purdah*.

Adj. female, she; feminine, womanly, ladylike, matronly, maidenly; womanish, effeminate, unmanly, gynecic.

---

375. Physical Sensibility.—N. sensibility; sensitiveness etc. *adj.*; physical sensibility, feeling, perceptivity, anaphylaxis, susceptibility, esthetics; moral sensibility etc. 882.

sensation, impression, effect; consciousness etc. (*knowledge*) 490.

external senses.

V. be -sensible etc. *adj.* -of; feel, perceive.

render, -sensible etc. *adj.*; excite, stir, sharpen, cultivate, tutor.

cause sensation, impress; excite -, produce- an impression.

Adj. sens-ible, -itive, -uous; esthetic, perceptive, sentient; conscious etc. (*aware*) 490; impressionable, responsive, alive to.

acute, sharp, keen, vivid, lively, impressive, thinskinned.

Adv. to the quick.

---

376. Physical Insensibility.—N. insensibility, physical insensibility; obtuseness etc. *adj.*; palsy, paralysis, *anesthesia*, *analgesia*, *narcosis*, *hypnosis*, twilight sleep, stupor, coma, trance, catalepsy; sleep etc. (*inactivity*) 683; moral insensibility etc. 823; numbness etc. 381.

anesthetic agent, general -, local- anesthetic, opium, ether, chloroform, cocaine, novocaine, chloral; nitrous oxide, laughing gas; refrigeration.

V. be -insensible etc. *adj.*; have a -thick skin, - rhinoceros hide.

render -insensible etc. *adj.*; blunt, pall, obtund, benumb, deaden, paralyze; anesthetize, drug, dope; put under the influence of -chloroform etc. *n.*; hypnotize; stupefy, stun, narcotize.

Adj. insensible, unfeeling, senseless, comatose, dazed, impercipient, callous, thick-skinned, pachydermatous; hard, -ened; case-hardened; proof; obtuse, dull; anesthetic; paralytic, palsied, numb, dead.

---

377. Physical Pleasure.—N. pleasure; physical -, sensual -, sensuous- pleasure; bodily enjoyment, animal gratification, sensuality; hedonism, luxuriousness etc. *adj.*; dissipation, round of pleasure; titillation, *gusto*, creature comforts, comfort, ease; pillow etc. (*support*) 215; luxury, lap of luxury; purple and fine linen; bed of -down, - roses; velvet, clover; cup of Circe etc. (*intemperance*) 954.

treat; diversion, divertisement, entertainment; refreshment, regale; feast; *délice*; dainty etc. 394; *bonne bouche*.

source of pleasure etc. 829; happiness etc. (*mental enjoyment*) 827.

V. feel -, experience -, receive- pleasure; enjoy, relish; luxuriate -, revel -, riot -, bask -, swim -, wallow- in; feast on; gloat -over, - on; smack the lips.

live -on the fat of the land, - in comfort etc. *adv.*; bask in the sunshine, *faire ses choux gras*.

give pleasure etc. 829.

Adj. enjoying etc. *v.*; luxurious, voluptuous, sensual, hedonistic, comfortable, cosy, snug, in comfort, at ease.

agreeable etc. 829; grateful, refreshing, comforting, cordial, genial; sensuous; palatable etc. 394; sweet etc. (*sugar*) 396; fragrant etc. 400; melodious etc. 413; lovely etc. (*beautiful*) 845.

Adv. in -comfort etc. *n.*; on -a bed of roses etc. *n.*; at one's ease.

---

378. Physical Pain.—N. pain; suffering, -ance; bodily - physical -pain, - suffering; mental suffering etc. 828; dolor, ache, aching etc. *v.*; smart, shoot, -ing; twinge, twitch, gripe, head-, ear-, toothache; *migraine*, neuralgia, neuritis, lumbago, gout, sciatica; hurt, cut; sore, -ness; discomfort, *malaise*; *tic douloureux*.

spasm, cramp; nightmare, *ephialtes*; crick, stitch, kink; thrill, convulsion, throe; throb etc. (*agitation*) 315; pang.

sharp -, piercing -, throbbing -, shooting -, gnawing -, burning- pain; anguish, agony.

torment, torture; rack; cruci-ation, -fixion; martyrdom; martyr, toad under a harrow, vivisection.

V. feel -, experience -, suffer -, undergo- pain etc. *n.*; suffer, ache, smart, bleed; tingle, shoot; twinge, twitch, lancinate; writhe, wince, make a wry face; sit on -thorns, - pins and needles.

give -, inflict- pain; pain, hurt, chafe, sting, bite, gnaw, gripe, stab, grind; pinch, tweak; grate, gall, fret, prick, pierce, wring, convulse; torment, torture; rack, agonize; crucify; excruciate; break on the wheel, put to the rack; flag etc. (*punish*) 972; grate on the ear etc. (*harsh sound*) 410.

Adj. in -pain etc. *n.*; - a state of pain; pained etc. *v.*

painful; aching etc. *v.*; biting, poignant; sore, raw, tender, with exposed nerve.

---

379. Touch. [Sensation of pressure.] **—N.** touch; tact, -ion, -ility; feeling; palp-ation, -ability; manipulation; brush, tick, graze, contact etc. 199.

[Organ of touch] hand, finger, fore-finger, thumb, paw, feeler, *antenna*.

V. touch, feel, handle, finger, thumb, paw, fumble, grope, grabble; twiddle, tweedle; pass -, run-the fingers over, massage, rub, knead; palpate, stroke, manipulate, wield; throw out a feeler.

Adj. tact-ual, -ile; tangible, palpable; lambent.

---

380. Sensations of Touch.—N. itching etc. *v.*; titillation, formication, *aura*.

V. itch, tingle, creep, thrill, sting; prick, -le; tickle, titillate.

Adj. itching etc. *v.*

---

381. Numbness. [Insensibility to touch.] **—N.**

numbness etc. (*physical insensibility*) 376; pins and needles.
local anesthetic, cocaine novocaine etc.; morphia.
V. benumb etc. 376; freeze, dull, deaden.
Adj. numb; benumbed etc. *v.*; intangible, impalpable.

382. Heat.—N. heat, caloric; temperature, warmth, fervor, calidity; incal-, incand-, recal-, decal-escence; glow, flush, blush; fever, hectic.

phlogiston; fire, spark, scintillation, flash, flame, blaze; arc; bonfire; firework, pyrotechny; wild-fire; sheet of fire; lambent flame; devouring element; conflagration.

summer, dog-days, canicule; baking etc. 384 —, white —, tropical —, Afric —, Bengal —, summer —, blood- heat; heat wave, sirocco, simoon; broiling sun; isolation; warming etc. 384.

sun etc. (*luminary*) 423; fire worshipper etc. 991; furnace etc. 386.

geyser, hot spring, volcano.

; Science of heat. pyrology; thermology, -otics; thermometer etc. 389.

V. be -hot etc. *adj.*; glow, incandesce, flush, sweat, swelter, bask, smoke, reek, stew, simmer, seethe, boil, burn, singe, scorch, scald, grill, broil, blaze, flame; smoulder; parch, fume, pant.

heat etc. (*make hot*) 384; thaw, fuse, melt, give.

Adj. hot, heated, warm, mild, genial, tepid, lukewarm, unfrozen; therm-al, -ic; calorific; fervent, -id; ardent; aglow.

sunny, torrid, tropical, estival, canicular; close, sultry, stifling, stuffy, suffocating, oppressive; reeking etc. *v.*; baking etc. 384.

red —, white —, smoking —, bruning etc. *v.* —, piping- hot; like -a furnace, — an oven; hot as -fire, — pepper; hot enough to roast an ox.

fiery; incand-, incal-escent; candent, ebullient, glowing, smoking; on fire; blazing etc. *v.*; in -flames, — a blaze; alight, afire, ablaze; unquenched, -extinguished; smouldering; in a -heat, — glow, — fever, — perspiration, — sweat; sudorific; swelter-ing, -ed; blood-hot, -warm; warm as -a toast, — wool; recalescent, thermogenic, pyrotechnic, feverish, febrile, inflamed.

volcanic, plutonic, igneous; isother-mal, -mic, -al.

Phr. Not a breath of air.

383. Cold.—N. cold, -ness etc. *adj.*; frigidity, gelidity, algidity, inclemency, *fresco*.

winter; depth of —, hard- winter; Siberia, Nova Zembla; Ant-, arctic, North —, South- Pole.

ice; snow, — flake, —-crystal — drift; sleet; hail, -stone; rime, frost; hoar —, white —, hard —, sharp- frost; icicle, thick-ribbed ice; fall of snow, snow storm, heavy fall, *avalanche*; ice-berg, -floe; floe, berg; *glacier*; *nevée, serac*.

[Sensation of cold] chilliness etc. *adj.*; chill shivering etc. *v.*; goose- skin, -flesh; *rigor*, horripilation, chattering of teeth; frostbite, chilblain.

V. be -cold etc. *adj.*; shiver, starve, quake, shake, tremble, shudder, didder, quiver; perish with cold; chill etc. (*render cold*) 385.

Adj. cold, cool; chill, -y; gelid, frigid, algid; fresh, keen, bleak, raw, inclement, bitter, biting,

niveous, cutting, nipping, piercing, pinching; clay-cold; starved etc. (*made cold*) 385; shivering etc. *v.*; aguish, *transi de froid*; frost- bitten, -bound, -nipped.

cold as -a stone, — marble, — lead, — iron, — a frog, — charity, — Christmas; cool as -a cucumber, — custard.

icy, glacial, frosty, freezing, wintry, brumal, hibernal, boreal, arctic, antarctic, polar, Siberian, hyemal; hyperbore-an, -al; ice-bound; frozen out.

un-warmed, -thawed, -heated; isocheimal, -chimenal.

Adv. coldly, bitterly etc. *adj.*; *à pierre fendre*.

384. Calefaction.—N. increase of temperature; heating etc. *v.*; calc-, tepe-, torre-faction; melting, fusion; liquefaction etc. 335; burning etc. *v.*; kindling, combustion; in-, ac-cension; con-, cremation; scorification; cauter-y, -ization; ustulation, calcination; in-, cineration; cupellation; carbonization.

ignition, inflammation, adustion, flagration; de-, con-flagration; empyrosis, incendiarism; arson; *auto da fé*; suttee.

boiling etc. *v.*; coction, ebullition, estuation, elixation, decoction.

furnace etc. 386; blanket, flannel, fur, muffler, wrap; wadding etc. (*lining*) 224; clothing etc. 225.

match etc. (*fuel*) 388; incendiary, pyromaniac; *pétroleur, pétroleuse*; cauterant; caustic, lunar caustic, apozem, moxa.

sunstroke, *coup de soleil*; insolation, sunburn.

pottery, ceramics, crockery, porcelain, china; earthen-, stone-ware; pot, mug, *terra-cotta*, brick, clinker; cinder, ash, *scoriae*; embers, dress, slag, products of combustion, coke, carbon, charcoal.

inflamma-, combusti-bility.

[Transmission of heat] diathermancy, trans-calency, diathermy.

V. heat, warm, chafe, stive, foment; make -hot etc. 382; sun oneself, bask in the sun.

fire; set -fire to, — on fire; kindle, enkindle, light, ignite, strike a light; apply the -match, — torch- to; re-kindle, -lume; fan —, add fuel to- the flame; poke —, stir —, blow- the fire; make a bonfire of; burn at the stake.

melt, thaw, fuse; liquefy etc. 335.

burn, inflame, roast, toast, fry, grill, singe, parch, bake, torrefy, scorch; brand, cauterize, sear, burn in; corrode, char, carbonize, calcine, incinerate; smelt, cupel, scorify; reduce to ashes; burn to a cinder; commit —, consign- to the flames.

boil, digest, stew, cook, seethe, scald, parboil, simmer; do to rags.

take —, catch- fire; blaze etc. (*flame*) 382.

Adj. heated etc. *v.*; molten, sodden; réchauffe; heating etc. *v.*

inflammable, burnable, inflammatory, combustible; diatherm-al, -anous; burnt etc. *v.*; volcanic.

386. Refrigeration.—N. refrigeration, infrigidation, reduction of temperature; cooling etc. *v.*; con-gelation, -glaciation; ice etc. 383; solidification etc. (*density*) 321; refrigerator etc. 387.

extincteur; fire, – engine, – extinguisher, –
annihilator, – brigade, – man; sprinkler, hose,
hydrant, standpipe.

incombusti-bility, -bleness etc. *adj.*

V. cool, fan, refrigerate, refresh, ice; congeal,
freeze, glaciate; benumb, starve, pinch, chill,
petrify, chill to the marrow, nip, cut, pierce, bite,
make one's teeth chatter; damp, slack; quench; put
–, stamp- out; extinguish.

go –, burn- out.

Adj. cooled etc. *v.*; frozen out; cooling etc. *v.*;
.frigorific.

incombustible; un-, unin-flammable; fire-proof.

386. Furnace.—N. furnace, blast furnace, fire-
box, stove, incinerator, destructor, crematorium,
crematory, kiln, oven, oast-house; hot-, bake-,
wash-house; laundry; conservatory; hearth, focus;
athanor, hypocaust, reverberatory; volcano; forge,
fiery furnace; *tuyère*, brasier, salamander, heater,
warming-pan, foot-warmer, hot-water bottle;
radiator; boiler, geyser, caldron, seething caldron,
pot; urn, kettle; chafing-dish; retort, crucible, alembic, still; saggar.

fire-place, -dog, -irons; hearth, ingle, grate,
range, kitchener; kitchen range; oil-, gas-, electric,
-cooker, -stove; fireless cooker; fire; galley; ca-
cam-boose; poker, tongs, shovel, hob, trivet; and-,
grid-iron; frying-, stew-pan etc.

hot –, Turkish –, Russian –, vapor –, shower
–, warm- bath; *calidarium*, *tepidarium*,
sudatorium, sudatory; *hammam*.

387. Refrigerator.—N. refrigerator, -y;
frigidarium; cold storage; refrigerating-plant, –
machine; ice-house, -pail, -bag, -chest, -pack;
cooler, damper; wine-cooler, freezing mixture.

388. Fuel.—N. fuel, firing, combustible, coal,
wallsend, anthracite, bituminous coal, slack, culm,
cannel coal, lignite, briquette, coke, carbon, charcoal; turf, peat, fire-wood, bobbing, faggot, log,
yule log, ember, cinder etc. (*products of combustion*) 384; kindling wood, tinder, touch-wood;
fumigator, sulphur, brimstone; incense; port-fire;
fire-barrel, -ball, -brand.

fuel oil, gas, gasoline, electricity.

brand, torch, fuse; wick; spill, match, safety
match, light, lucifer, congreve, vesuvian, vesta,
fusee, locofoco; linstock; illuminant.

candle etc. (*luminary*) 423; oil etc. (*grease*) 356;
petrol, gasoline, methylated –, spirit; gas,
acetylene.

Adj. carbonaceous; combustible, inflammable.

V. stoke, fire, feed, add fuel to the flames.

389. Thermometer.—N. thermo-meter, -scope,
-stat, -pile, differential thermometer; pyro-, calori-
meter; radio micrometer etc.

390. Taste.—N. taste, flavor, gust, *gusto*, relish,
savor; sapor, sapidity; twang, smack, smatch; after-
taste, tang.

tasting; de-, gustation.

palate, tongue, tooth, stomach.

V. taste, savor, smatch, smack, flavor, twang;
tickle the palate etc. (*savory*) 394; smack the lips.

Adj. sapid, saporific; gusta-ble, -tory; strong;
flavored, spiced, savory; palatable etc. 394.

391. Insipidity.—N. insipidity; tastlessness etc.
adj.

V. be -tasteless etc. *adj.*

Adj.void of -taste etc. 390; insipid; jejune; taste-,
gust-, savor-less; ingustible, mawkish, milk and
water, weak, stale, flat, vapid, *fade*, wishy-washy,
mild; untasted.

392. Pungency.—N. pungency, piquancy,
poignancy, *haut-goût*, strong taste, twang, race,
tang.

sharpness etc. *adj.*; acrimony, acridity; roughness
etc. (*sour*) 397; unsavoriness etc. 395.

niter, saltpeter; mustard, cayenne, caviar;
seasoning etc. (*condiment*) 393; brine.

dram, cordial, nip, pick-me-up, bracer, potion.

nicotine, tobacco, snuff, quid; segar; cigar, -ette,
gasper, fag; cheroot; weed; fragrant –, Indian-
weed; pipe, clay pipe, churchwarden, brier, meerschaum, hookah, hubble-bubble.

V. be -pungent etc. *adj.*; bite the tongue.

render -pungent etc. *adj.*; season, spice, salt,
pepper, pickle, brine, devil, curry.

smoke, chew, take snuff.

Adj. pungent, strong; high-, full-flavored; high-
tasted, -seasoned; gamy; sharp, stinging, rough,
piquant, racy; biting, mordant; spicy; seasoned etc.
v.; hot, – as pepper; peppery, vellicating,
escharotic, meracious; acrid, acrimonious, bitter;
rough etc. (*sour*) 397; unsavory etc. 395.

salt, saline, brackish, briny; salt as -brine, – a
herring, – Lot's wife.

393. Condiment.—N. condiment, flavoring,
salt, mustard, pepper, cayenne, curry, seasoning,
sauce, spice, cinnamon, chillies, relish, *sauce
piquante*, caviare, pot-herbs, onion, garlic, pickle,
chutney, nutmeg etc.

V. season etc. (*render pungent*) 392.

394. Savoriness.—N. savoriness etc. *adj.*;
relish, zest.

tit-bit, dainty, delicacy, ambrosia, nectar, *bonne
bouche*; game, turtle, venison.

V. taste good, be -savory etc. *adj.*; tickle the -
palate, – appetite; flatter the palate.

render -palatable etc. *adj.*

relish, like, smack the lips.

Adj. savory, well-tasted, to one's taste, tasty,
good, palatable, nice, dainty, delectable; tooth-ful,
-some; gustful, appetizing, lickerish, delicate,
delicious, exquisite, rich, luscious, ambrosial.

Adv. *per amusare la bocca.*

Phr. *cela se laisse manger.*

395. Unsavoriness.—N. unsavoriness etc. *adj.*; amaritude; acri-mony, -tude; roughness etc. (*sour*) 397; acerbity, austerity; gall and worm-wood, rue, quassia, aloes; sickener.

V. be -unpalatable etc. *adj.*; sicken, disgust, nauseate, pall, turn the stomach.

Adj. un-savory, -palatable, -sweet; ill-flavored, un-appetizing, -eatable, inedible; bitter, — as gall; acrid, acrimonious; rough.

offensive, repulsive, nasty; sickening etc. *v.*; nauseous; loath-, ful-some; unpleasant etc. 830.

396. Sweetness.—N. sweetness, dulcitude, saccharinity.

sugar, cane-, beet-sugar; saccharine, glucose, syrup, treacle, molasses, honey, manna; confection, -ary; sweets, grocery, conserve, preserve, *confiture*, jam, marmalade, julep; sugar-candy, -plum; licorice, liquorice, plum, lollipop, *bon bon*, *jujube*, comfit, sweetmeat, caramel, toffee, butterscotch.

nectar; hydromel, mead, metheglin, honeysuckle, *liqueur*, sweet wine.

pastry, pie, tart, puff, pudding, cake.

dulc-ification, -oration.

V. be sweet etc. *adj.*

render -sweet etc. *adj.*; sugar, saccharize, sweeten; edulcorate; dulc-orate, -ify; candy; mull.

Adj. sweet, sugary; sacchar-ine, -iferous; dulcet, honied, candied, luscious, nectarious, melliferous; sweetened etc. *v.*

sweet as -a nut, — sugar, — honey.

397. Sourness.—N. sourness etc. *adj.*; acid, -ity; acetous fermentation; acerbity.

vinegar, verjuice, crab, alum.

V. be —, turn- -sour etc. *adj.*; set the teeth on edge.

render -sour etc. *adj.*; acid-ify, -ulate.

Adj. sour; acid, -ulous, -ulated; acerb; tart, crabbed; acet-ous, -ose; sour as vinegar, sourish, acescent, sub-acid; styptic, hard, rough; unripe, green.

398. Odor.—N. odor, smell, odorament, scent, effluvium; eman-, exhal-ation; fume, essence, trail, nidor, redolence.

sense of smell; scent; act of -smelling etc. *v.*

V. have an -odor etc. *n.*; smell, — of, — strong of; exhale; give out a -smell etc. *n.*; scent.

smell, scent; snuff, — up; sniff, nose, inhale.

Adj. odor-ous, -iferous; smelling, strong-scented; redolent, graveolent, nidorous, pungent.

[Relating to the sense of smell] olfactory, quick-scented..

399. Inodorousness.—N. inodorousness; absence —, want- of smell.

V. be -inodorous etc. *adj.*; not smell.

deodorize.

Adj. inodor-ous, -ate; scentless; without —, wanting- smell etc. 398.

deodoriz-ed, -ing.

400. Fragrance.—N. fragrance, aroma, redolence, perfume, *bouquet*; sweet smell, aromatic perfume.

perfumery; incense; musk, frankincense; pastil, -le; myrrh, perfumes of Arabia, chypre; otto, ottar, attar; bergamot, balm, civet, *pot-pourri*, pulvil; nosegay, *boutonnière*; scent, -bag; *sachet*, scent-bottle, smelling bottle, *vinaigrette*; toilet water, *eau de Cologne*; thurible, censer, thurification.

perfumer; incense bearer.

V. be -fragrant etc. *adj.*; have a -perfume etc. *n.*; smell sweet, scent, perfume, thurify, embalm.

Adj. fragrant, aromatic, redolent, spicy, balmy, scented; sweet-smelling, -scented; perfum-ed, -atory; thuriferous; fragrant as a rose, muscadine, ambrosial.

401. Fetor.—N. fetor, fetidness; bad etc. *adj.*; -smell, — odor; stench, stink, mephitis, foul —, mal- odor; *empyreuma*; mustiness etc. *adj.*; rancidity; foulness etc. (*uncleanness*) 653.

stoat, polecat, skunk; asafetida; fungus, garlic; stink-pot, -bomb.

V. have a -bad smell etc. *n.*; smell; stink, — in the nostrils, — like a polecat; smell -strong etc. *adj.*; — offensively.

Adj. fetid; strong-smelling; high, bad, strong, fulsome, offensive, noisome, rank, rancid, reasty, tainted, musty, fusty, frouzy; olid, -ous; nidorous; smelling, stinking; putrid etc. 653; suffocating, mephitic; empyreumatic.

402. Sound.—N. sound, noise, strain; accent, twang, intonation, tone, tune; cadence; sonority, sonorousness etc. *adj.*; audibility; resonance etc. 408; voice etc. 580.

[Science of sound] acou-, acu-stics; catacoustics; cataphonics; phon-ics, -etics, -ology, -ography; diacoustics, -phonics.

telephone, phonograph etc. 418.

V. produce sound; sound, make a noise; give out —, emit- sound; phonetize, phonate; resound etc. 408.

Adj. sounding; soniferous; sonorific; resonant, audible, acoustic, auditory, distinct; stertorous; phonic, sonant; phonetic.

403. Silence.—N. silence; stillness etc. (*quiet*) 265; peace, hush, lull, rest; muteness etc. 581; solemn —, awful —, dead —, deathlike- silence.

V. be -silent etc. *adj.*; hold one's tongue etc. (*not speak*) 585.

render -silent etc. *adj.*; silence, still, hush; stifle, muffle, gag, stop; muzzle, put to silence etc. (*render mute*) 581.

Adj. silent; still, -y; calm, quiet; noise-, sound-, speech-less; hushed etc. *v.*; mute etc. 581; aphonic.

soft, solemn, awful, deathlike, silent as the grave; inaudible etc. (*faint*) 405.

Adv. silently etc. *adj.*; *sub silentio*; in perfect silence.

Int. hush! 'sh! silence! soft! whist! tush! chut! tut! *pax!* mum's the word! hold your tongue! shut up! be silent! be quiet! stop that noise! hold your row! dry up! peace, be still!

Phr. one might hear a -feather, − pin- drop.

404. Loudness.—N. loudness, power; loud noise, din; clang, -or; clatter, noise, bombilation, roar, uproar, racket, static, grinders, hubbub, *fracas, charivari*, trumpet blast, blare, flourish of trumpets, fanfare, *tintamarre*, peal, swell, blast, alarum, boom; resonance etc. 408.

vociferation; pandemonium, hullaballoo etc. 411; lungs; Stentor; megaphone; siren.

artillery, cannon, gunfire, shellburst, bomb; thunder.

V. be -loud etc. *adj.*; peal, swell, clang, boom, thunder, fulminate, roar; resound etc. 408; speak up, shout etc. (*vociferate*) 411; bellow etc. (*cry as an animal*) 412; give tongue.

rend the -air, − skies; fill the air; din −, ring −, thunder- in the ear; pierce −, split −, rend-the-ears, − head; deafen, stun; *faire le diable a quatre*; make one's windows shake; awaken −, startle- the echoes; make the welkin ring.

Adj. loud, sonorous; high-, big- sounding; blatant; deep, full, powerful, noisy, clangorous, multisonous, *fortisimo*; thundering, deafening etc. *v.*; trumpet-tongued; ear-splitting, -rending, -deafening; piercing; obstreperous, rackety, uproarious; enough to wake the -dead, − seven sleepers.

shrill etc. 410; clamorous etc. (*vociferous*) 411; stentor-ian, -ophonic.

Adv. loudly etc. *adj.*; aloud; at the top of one's voice, lustily, in full cry.

Phr. the air rings with.

405. Faintness.—N. faintness etc. *adj.*; faint sound, whisper, breath; under-tone, -breath; murmur, hum, rustle, buzz, purr; plash; sough, moan, sigh, susurration; tinkle; 'still small voice.'

hoarseness etc. *adj.*; raucity.

silencer, soft pedal, damper, mute, *sourdine*.

V. whisper, breathe, murmur, purl, hum, gurgle, ripple, babble, flow; tinkle; mutter etc. (*speak imperfectly*) 583.

steal on the ear; melt in −, float on- the air. muffle, mute, deaden, damp, stifle.

Adj. inaudible; scarcely −, just- audible; low, dull; stifled, muffled; hoarse, husky; gentle, soft, faint; floating; purling, flowing etc. *v.*; whispered etc. *v.*; liquid; soothing; dulcet etc. (*melodious*) 413.

Adv. in a whisper, with bated breath, *sotto voce*, between the teeth, aside; *pian-o, -issimo; à la sourdine; con sourdine*; out of earshot, inaudibly etc. *adj.*

406. Snap. [Sudden and violent sounds.]—**N.** snap etc. *v.*; rapping etc. *v.*; de-, crepitation; smack, clap, report; thud; burst, explosion, discharge, detonation, blow-out, back-fire, firing, salvo, volley, pistol-shot.

squib, cracker, gun, rifle, pop-gun.

V. rap, snap, tap, knock; click; clash; crack, -le; crash; pop; slam, bang, clap, thump, plump; toot; back-fire, explode, burst on the ear.

Adj. rapping etc. *v.*

Int. crash! bang!

407. Roll. [Repeated and protracted sounds.]—**N.** roll etc. *v.*; drumming etc. *v.*; tattoo; ding-dong; tantara; rataplan; whirr; rat-a-tat; rub-a-dub; pit-a-pat; quaver, clutter, *charivari*, racket; cuckoo; repetition etc. 104; peal of bells, devil's tattoo; reverberation etc. 408.

drumfire, barrage.

machine gun.

V. roll, drum, rumble, rattle, clatter, rustle, roar, drone, patter, clack.

hum, trill, shake; chime, peal, toll; tick, beat. drum −, din- in the ear.

Adj. rolling etc. *v.*; monotonous etc. (*repeated*), 104; like a bee in a bottle.

408. Resonance.—N. resonance; ring etc. *v.*; ringing etc. *v.*; tintinnabulation; reflection, reverberation, clangor.

low −, base −, bass −, flat −, grave −, deep −, pedal- note; bass; *basso, − profondo*; bari-, bary-tone; *contralto*.

V. re-sound, -verberate, -echo; ring. ding. sing. jingle, gingle, chink, clink; tink. -le; chime; gurgle etc. 405; plash, guggle, echo, ring in the ear.

Adj. resounding etc. *v.*; resonant, tinnient; tintinnabulary; deep-toned, -sounding, -mouthed; hollow, sepulchral; gruff etc. (*harsh*) 410.

408a. Non-resonance.—N. thud, thump, dead sound; non-resonance; muffled drums, cracked bell; silencer, damper; mute, *sourdine*.

V. sound dead; stop −, damp- the -sound, − reverberations; deaden, muffle.

Adj. non-resonant, dead, muted, muffled.

409. Sibilation. [Hissing sounds.]—**N.** sibilation; hiss etc. *v.*; sternutation; high note etc. 410.

goose, serpent, snake.

V. hiss, buzz, whiz, rustle; fizz, -le, sizzle, swish; wheeze, whistle, snuffle; squash; sneeze.

Adj. sibilant; hissing etc. *v.*; wheezy.

410. Stridor. [Harsh sounds.]—**N.** creak etc. *v.*; creaking etc. *v.*; discord etc. 414; stridor; harshness, roughness, sharpness etc. *adj.*; cacophony.

acute −, high- note; *soprano*, treble, tenor, *alto*, falsetto, *voce di testa*; shriek, cry etc. 411.

piccolo, fife, penny -whistle, − trumpet.

V. creak, grate, jar, burr, pipe, twang, jangle, clank, clink; scream etc. (*cry*) 411; yelp etc. (*animal sound*) 412; buzz etc. (*hiss*) 409.

set the teeth on edge, écorcher les orielles; pierce −, split- the -ears, − head; offend −, grate upon −, jar upon- the ear.

Adj. creaking etc. *v.*; strident, stridulous, harsh,

coarse, hoarse, horrisonous, raucous, metallic, rough, gruff, grum, sepulchral.

sharp, high, acute, shrill, high-pitched; trumpet-toned; piercing, ear-piercing; cracked; discordant etc. 414; cacophonous.

411. Cry.—N. cry etc. *v.*; voice etc. (*human*) 580; bark etc. (*animal*) 412.

vociferation, outcry, hullaballoo, chorus, clamor, hue and cry, plaint; lungs; stentor.

V. cry, roar, shout, bawl, brawl, halloo, halloa, hail, hoop, whoop, yell, bellow, howl, scream, screech, screak, shriek, shrill, squeak, squeal, squall, whine, whinny, pule, pipe, yaup.

cheer, hurrah; hoot; grumble, maon, groan.

snore, snort; grunt etc. (*animal sounds*) 412.

vociferate; raise −, lift up- the voice; call −, sing −, cry- out; exclaim; rend the air; thunder −, shout- at the -top of one's voice, − pitch of one's breath; s'égosiller; strain the -throat, − voice, − lungs; give a -cry etc.

Adj. crying etc. *v.*; clam-ant, -orous; vociferous; stentorian etc. (*loud*) 404; open-mouthed.

412. Ululation. [Animal sounds.]—**N.** cry etc. *v.*; crying etc. *v.*; ululation, latration, belling; reboation; call, note; bark, howl, yelp; twittering, woodnote; insect cry, fritinancy, drone; screech; cuckoo.

V. cry, ululate, howl, roar, bellow, blare, rebellow, bark, yelp; bay, − the moon; yap, growl, yarr, yawl, snarl, howl; grunt, -le; snort, squeak; neigh, bray; mew, mewl; purr, caterwaul, pule; bleat, low, moo; troat, croak, crow, screech, caw, coo, gobble, quack, cackle, gaggle, guggle; chuck, -le; cluck; clack; cheep, chirp, chirrup, twitter, sing, cuckoo; pout, wail, hum, buzz; hiss, blatter; hoot.

Adj. crying etc. *v.*; blatant, latrant; re-, mugient; deep-, full-mouthed.

Adv. in full cry.

413. Melody. Concord.—N. melody, rhythm, measure; rhyme etc. (*poetry*) 597.

pitch, *timbre*, intonation, tone, overtone.

scale, gamut; diapason; diatonic −, chromatic −, enharmonic- scale; key, clef, chords.

modulation, temperament, syncope, syncopation, preparation, suspension, resolution.

staff, stave, line, space, brace; bar, rest; *appogiato*, *-tura*; *acciaccatura*, shake, *arpeggio*.

note, musical note, notes of a sclae; sharp, flat, natural; high note etc. (*shrillness*) 410; low note etc. 408; interval; semitone; second, third, fourth etc.; diatessaron.

breve, semibreve, minim, crotchet, quaver; semi-, demisemi- quaver; sustained note, drone, burden.

tonic; key-, leading-, fundamental-, note; supertonic, mediant, dominant; sub-mediant, -dominant, organ-, pedal-point; octave, tetrachord; major −, minor- -mode, − scale, − key; Doric mode, passage, phrase.

concord, harmony; unison, -ance; chime, homophony; euphon-y, -ism; tonality; consonance; concent; part.

orchestration; harmonization, − phrasing.

[Science of harmony] harmon-y, -ics; thorough-, fundamental- bass; counterpoint; faburden.

piece of music etc. 415; composer, harmonist, contrapuntist.

V. be -harmonious etc. *adj.*; harmonize, chime, symphonize, transpose; put in tune, tune, accord, string; score, arrange, orchestrate.

Adj. harmoni-ous, -cal; in -concord etc. *n.*, − tune, − concert; unisonant, concentual, symphonizing, isotonic, homophonous, assonant, consonant.

measured, rhythmical, diatonic, chromatic, enharmonic.

melodious, musical; tuneful, tunable; sweet, dulcet, canorous; mell-ow, -ifluous; soft; clear, − as a bell; silvery; euphon-ious, -ic, -ical; symphonious; enchanting etc. (*pleasure-giving*) 829; fine-, full-, silver-toned.

Adv. harmoniously etc. *adj.*

414. Discord.—N. discord, -ance; dissonance, cacophony, caterwauling; harshness etc. 410; consecutive fifths.

[Confused sounds] Babel, pandemonium; Dutch −, cat's- concert; marrow-bones and cleavers.

V. be -discordant etc. *adj.* ; jar- etc. (*sound harshly*) 410.

Adj. discordant; dis-, ab-sonant; out of tune, tuneless; un-musical, -tunable; un-, im-melodious; un-, in-harmonious; sing-song; cacophonous; jarring, harsh etc. 410.

415. Music.—N. music, classical −, modern −, descriptive- music; concert, recital; strain, tune, air, *motif*; melody etc. 413; *aria, arietta*; piece of music, *sonata; rond-o, -eau; pastorale, cavatina*, roulade, *fantasia, toccata, concerto*, overture, symphony, symphonic poem, tone poem, prelude, voluntary, *intermezzo*, variations, *cadenza*; cadence; fugue, canon, serenade, *nocturne, notturno*, rhapsody, romance, *aubade*, dithyramb; opera, operetta; oratorio; composition, movement, stave.

instrumental music; full-, orchestral- score; minstrelsy, tweedledum and tweedledee, band, orchestra etc. 416; concerted piece, *potpourri*, medley, *capriccio*, incidental music; improvisation; peal.

vocal music, vocalism; chaunt, chant; psalm, -ody; hymn; song etc. (*poem*) 597; canticle, canzonet, *cantata, bravura, coloratura*; lay, ballad, ditty, carol, barcarolle, pastoral, recitative, *recitativo, solfeggio*, tonic sol-fa.

Lydian measures; slow -music, − movement; *adagio* etc. *adv.*; minuet; siren strains, soft music, lullaby; *berceuse*, cradle song, dump; dirge etc. (*lament*) 839; pibroch; martial music, march, funeral-, dead- march; dance music; waltz etc. (*dance*) 840; rag-time, syncopation, jazz.

solo, duet, *duo, trio*; quartet; quintet, sextet, septet; part song, descant, glee, madrigal, catch, round, chorus, *chorale*; antiphon, -y; accompaniment, second −, alto −, tenor −, bass-part; score, thorough bass; counterpoint.

composer etc. 413; musician etc. 416.

V. compose, perform etc. 416; attune.

Adj. musical; instrumental, orchestral, vocal, choral, lyric, operatic; harmonious etc. 413.

Adv. *adagio*; *largo, larghetto, andan-te, -tino*; *alla capella*; *maestoso, moderato*; *allegr-o, -etto*; *spiritoso, vivace, veloce*; *prest-o, -issimo*; *pian-o, -issimo, fort-e, -issimo, sforzando*; *con brio*; *capriccioso*; *scherz-o, -ando*; *legato, sostenuto, staccato, crescendo*, diminuendo, *rallentando, affettuoso, arioso*; *parlante, cantabile*; *obbligato*; *pizzacato, tremolo, vibrato*.

416. Musician. [Performance of Music.]—**N.** musician, *artiste, virtuoso*, performer, player, minstrel; bard etc. (*poet*) 597; instrumental-, organ-, accompan-, pian-, violin-, flaut-, harp-ist; harper, fiddler, fifer, trumpeter, piper, drummer; catgut scraper.

band, orchestra, waits.

vocal-, melod-ist; singer, warbler; songst-, chaunt-er, -ress; *diva, cantatrice*, coloratura, soprano, mezzo-soprano, alto, contralto, tenor, baritone, bass, *basso, -profundo*.

choir, quire, chorister; chorus, - singer; choral society, festival, *eisteddfod*.

nightingale, philomel, thrush; siren; Orpheus, Apollo, the Muses, Erato, Euterpe, Terpsichore; tuneful -nine, - quire.

composer etc. 413.

performance, virtuosity, execution, touch, expression, solmization.

V. play, pipe, strike -, tune-up, sweep the chords, tickle -, paw- the ivories, vamp, tweedle, fiddle; strike the lyre, beat the drum; blow -, sound -, wind- the horn; grind the organ; touch the -guitar etc. (*instruments*) 417; thrum, strum, twang, drum, beat -, keep- time, conduct.

execute, perform; accompany; sing -, play- a second; compose, write music, set to music, arrange, harmonize, orchestrate.

sing, chaunt, chant, hum, warble, carol, chirp, chirrup, lilt, purl, quaver, trill, shake, twitter, whistle; sol-fa; intone.

have -an ear for music, - a musical ear, - a correct ear, - absolute pitch.

Adj. playing etc. *v.*; musical, lyric.

Adv. *adagio, andante* etc. (*music*) 415.

417. Musical Instruments.—N. musical instruments; band; string-, brass-, drum and fife-, military-, bugle-, German-, dance-, jazz-band; orchestra, string quartet; orchestration, orchestrelle.

[Stringed instruments] mono-, poly-chord; harp, lyre, lute, archlute, thearbo; mandol-a, -in, -ine; guitar; *ukulele*; psaltery, zither; bandore, cither, -n; gittern, rebeck, *bandurria*, banjo, zither banjo, *balalaika, samisen*; plectrum.

viol, -in, Cremona, Stradivarius; fiddle; kit; *vielle, viola, - d'amore, - di gamba*; tenor, *violoncello*, cello; bass, bass-, bass-viol; double-bass, *contrabasso, violone*, hurdy-gurdy; strings, catgut; bow, fiddlestick.

piano, -forte; grand -, concert grand -, baby -, upright -, cottage- piano; pianino, pianette; harpsi-, clavi-, clari-, mani-chord; *clavier*, spinet, virginals; dulcimer, *cymbalo*; Eolian harp; piano-

organ, -player, electric piano, player-piano, pianola.

[Wind instruments] organ, church -, pipe -, American- organ; harmoni-um, -phon; accordion, seraphina, concertina; melodeon; barrel- organ; humming top.

flute, fife, piccolo, flageolet, penny-whistle, reed instrument; clari-net, -onet; bass clarionet; saxophone; basset horn, *corno di bassetto*; musette, shawm, oboe, hautboy, *cor Anglais, corno Inglese*, bassoon, double bassoon, *contrafagotto*; bag-, union-pipes; ocarina, Pandean pipes; calliope; sirene, pipe, pitch-pipe; sourdet; whistle, catcall.

horn, bugle, key bugle, cornet, *cornet-à-pistons*, cornopean, clarion, trumpet, trombone, ophicleide, serpent; English-, French-, bugle-, sax-, flugel-, alt-, helicon-, post-horn; sackbut, euphonium, bombardon, tuba, bass tuba.

[Vibrating surfaces] cymbal, bell, gong, peal of bells, *carillon*; tambour, -ine; drum, tom-tom, tabor, -ret, -ourine, -orin; *sistrum, grand caisse*, bass-, big-, side-, kettle-drum; *tympani*; war drums; tymbal, timbrel, castanet, bones; musical-glasses, - stones; harmonica, sounding— board, rattle; gramophone, phonograph.

[Vibrating bars] reed, tuning-fork, triangle, Jew's harp, musical box, harmonicon, xylophone, marimba, *celeste*.

sord-ine, -et; *sourd-ine, -et;* mute.

418. Hearing. [Sense of sound.]—**N.** hearing etc. *v.*; audition, auscultation; eavesdropping; audibility; acoustics etc. 402.

acute -, nice -, delicate -, quick -, sharp -, correct -, musical -ear; ear for music.

ear, auricle, lug, acoustic organs, auditory apparatus, ear-drum, tympanum; ear-, speaking-trumpet, megaphone; telephone, radiophone, stethoscope, phonograph, gramophone, microphone.

hearer, auditor, listener, eavesdropper; audi-tory, -ence.

V. hear, overhear; hark, -en; list, -en; give -, lend -, bend- an ear; give attention; catch a sound, prick up one's ears; give -a hearing, - audience -to.

hang upon the lips of, be all ear, listen with both ears, monitor.

become audible; meet -, fall upon -, catch -, reach- the ear; be heard; ring in the ear etc. (*resound*) 408.

Adj. hearing etc. *v.*; auditory, auricular, aural, auditive, acoustic.

Adv. *arrectis auribus.*

Int. hark, - ye! hear! list, -en! *Oyez!* attention! lend me your ears!

419. Deafness.—N. deafness, hardness of hearing, surdity; inaudibility.

V. be -deaf etc. *adj.*; have no ear; shut -, stop -, close- one's ears; turn a deaf ear to.

render deaf, stun, deafen.

Adj. deaf, earless, surd; hard -, dull- of hearing; deaf-mute, stunned, deafened; stone deaf; deaf as a post, - an adder, - a beetle, - a trunk-maker.

inaudible etc. 405; out of hearing.

420. Light.—N. light, ray, beam, stream, gleam, streak, pencil; sun-, moon-beam; dawn, aurora.

day; sunshine; light of -day, − heaven; sun etc. (*luminary*) 432, day-, broad day-, noontide- light; noon-tide, -day; glare.

glow etc. *v.*; afterglow, sunset; glimmering etc. *v.*; glint; play −, flood- of light; phosphorescence, flush, halo, glory, nimbus, aureole, *aureola.*

spark, *scintilla*; *facula*; sparkling etc. *v.*; emication, scintillation, flash, blaze, coruscation, fulguration; flame etc. (*fire*) 382; lightning, *ignis fatuus*, etc. (*luminary*) 423, radio-activity.

luster, sheen, shimmer, reflection; gloss, tinsel, spangle, brightness, brilliancy, splendor; ef-, re-fulgence; ful-gor, -gidity; dazzlement, resplendence, transplendency; luminousness etc. *adj.*; luminosity; lucidity; renitency; radi-ance, -ation; irradiation, illumination, phosphorescence, luminescence.

radiation, radiant heat, infra-red rays, visible radiation, ultra-violet −, actinic- rays, actinism; X −, Roentgen- rays; phot-, heli-ography; optical instruments etc. 445.

[Science of light] optics; photo-logy, -metry; di-, cat-optrics.

[Distribution of light] chiaroscuro, *clair-obscur*, clear obscure, breadth, light and shade, black and white, tonality, half-tone, mezzotint.

reflection, refraction, dispersion, double refraction, polarization, diffraction, interference.

illuminant etc. 423.

V. shine, glow, glitter, phosphoresce; glis-ter, -ten; twinkle, gleam; flare, − up; glare, beam, shimmer, glimmer, flicker, sparkle, scintillate, coruscate, flash, fulgurate, blaze; be -bright etc. *adj.*; reflect light, daze, dazzle, bedazzle, radiate, shoot out beams.

clear up, brighten.

lighten, enlighten; light, − up; irradiate, shine upon; relume −, hang out- a light; cast −, throw −, shed- -luster, − light- upon; illum-e, -ine, -inate; relume, strike a light; kindle etc. (*set fire to*) 384.

Adj. shining etc. *v.*; lumin-ous, -iferous; luc-id, -ent, -ulent, -ific, -iferous; illuminating, light, -some; bright, vivid, splendent, nitid, lustrous, shiny, brilliant, beamy, scintillant, radiant, lambent; sheen, -y; glossy, burnished, glassy, sunny, orient, meridian; noon-day, -tide; cloudless, clear; unclouded, -obscured.

garish; re-, tran-splendent; re-, effulgent; ful-gid, -gent; relucent, splendid, blazing, in a blaze, ablaze, rutilant, meteoric, phosphorescent; aglow.

bright as silver; light −, bright- as -day, − noonday, − the sun at noonday.

optical, actinic; photo-genic, -graphic; heliographic, radioactive.

421. Darkness.—N. darkness etc. *adj.*; blackness etc. (*dark color*) 431; obscurity, gloom, murk; dusk etc. (*dimness*) 422; tenebrosity, umbrageousness.

Cimmerian −, Stygian −, Egyptian- darkness; night; midnight; dead of −, witching time of-night; blind man's holiday; darkness -visible; − that can be felt; palpable, obscure; Erebus.

shade, shadow, umbra, penumbra; sciagraphy; *silhouette*; radiograph, skiagraph.

obscuration; ad-, ob-umbration; obtenebration, offuscation, caligation; extinction; eclipse, total eclipse; gathering of the clouds.

shading; distribution of shade; *chiaroscuro* etc. (*light*) 420.

noctivagation, noctograph, noctuary.

obscurantist.

V. be -dark etc. *adj.*

darken, obscure, shade; dim; tone down, lower; over-cast, -shadow; cloud, eclipse; ob-, of-fuscate; ob-, ad-umbrate, cast into the shade; be-cloud, -dim, -darken; cast −, throw −, spread- a -shade, − shadow, − gloom.

extinguish; put −, blow −, snuff- out; doubt.

Adj. dark, -some, -ling; obscure, tenebrous, tenebrious, sombrous, pitch dark, pitchy, caliginous; black etc. (*in color*) 431.

sunless, lightless etc. (*see* sun, light etc. 423); somber, dusky; unilluminated etc. (*see* illuminate etc. 420); nocturnal; dingy, lurid, gloomy; murk-y, -some; shady, umbrageous; overcast etc. (*dim*) 422; cloudy etc. (*opaque*) 426; darkened etc. *v.*

dark as -pitch, − a pit, − Erebus.

benighted; noctivag-ant, -ous.

Adv. in the -dark, − shade; at night.

422. Dimness.—N. dimness etc. *adj.*; darkness etc. 421; paleness etc. (*light color*) 429.

half-light, *demi-jour*; partial -shadow, − eclipse; shadow of a shade; glimmer, -ing; nebulosity; cloud etc. 353; eclipse.

aurora, dusk, twilight, gloaming, blind man's holiday, shades of evening, crepuscule, cockshut time; break of day, daybreak, dawn.

moon-light, -beam, -shine; star- owl's-, candle-rush-, fire-light; farthing candle.

V. be −, grow- -dim etc. *adj.*; flicker, twinkle, glimmer; loom, lower; fade, darken; pale, − its ineffectual fire.

render -dim etc. *adj.*; dim, bedim, obscure.

Adj. dim, dull, lack-luster, dingy, darkish, shorn of its beams; dark 421.

faint, shadowed forth; glassy; bleary; cloudy; misty etc. (*opaque*) 426; muggy, fuliginous; nebulous, -ar; obnubilated, overcast, crepuscular, twilight, muddy, lurid, leaden, dun, dirty; looming etc. *v.*

pale etc. (*colorless*) 429; confused etc. (*invisible*) 447.

423. Luminary. [Source of light.]—**N.** luminary; light etc. 420; flame etc. (*fire*) 382.

spark, *scintilla*; phosphorescence.

sun, orb of day, day star, Phoebus, Apollo, Helios, Phaethon, Hyperion, Ra, Aurora; star, orb, meteor; falling −, shooting- star; blazing −, dog-star; Sirius, canicula, Aldebaran; morning star, Lucifer, Phosphor, evening star; Hesperus, Venus, planet, moon etc. 318; constellation, galaxy; northern light, *aurora -borealis*, − *australis*, zodiacal light; mock sun, parhelion.

lightning; fork −, sheet −, summer- lightning, St. Elmo's fire; phosphorus; *ignis fatuus*; Jack o' − Friar's- lantern; Will o' the wisp, fire-drake, *Fata Morgana.*

glow-worm, fire-fly.

radium, luminous paint.

[Artificial light] gas; gas –, lime –, electric –, head –, search –, spot –, flash –, flood –, footlight; lamp, oil –, gas –, arc –, incandescent-lamp; flare; lant-ern, -horn; dark lantern, bull's eye, projector; candle, *bougie*, tallow –, wax- candle; dip, farthing dip; taper, rush-light; oil etc. (*grease*) 356; wick, burner; Argand, moderator, duplex; torch, *flambeau*, link, brand; cresset; gase-, chande-, electro-lier; candelabrum, *girandole*, sconce, luster, candle-stick.

firework, fizgig; pyrotechnics; Roman candle, Very light, star shell, parachute light; rocket, lighthouse etc. (*signal*) 550.

V. illuminate etc. (*light*) 420.

Adj. self-luminous, incandescent; phosphor-ic, -escent; luminescent, fluorescent, radiant etc. (*light*) 420.

424. Shade.—N. shade; awning etc. (*cover*) 223; parasol, sunshade, umbrella; screen, curtain, shutter, blind, gauze, veil, mantle, mask; cloud, mist, gathering of clouds; smoke screen; smoked glasses, colored spectacles; blinkers, blinders.

umbrage, glade; shadow etc. 421.

V. draw a curtain; put up –, close- a shutter; veil etc. *v.*; cast a shadow etc. (*darken*) 421; screen, obstruct the view.

Adj. shady, umbrageous, bowery.

425. Transparency.—N. transparen-ce, -cy; translucen-ce, -cy; diaphaneity; luc-, pelluc-, limpidity.

transparent medium, glass, crystal, mica; lymph, water.

v. be -transparent etc. *adj.*; transmit light.

Adj. transparent, pellucid, lucid, diaphanous; trans-, tra-lucent; limpid, clear, serene, crystalline, clear as crystal, vitreous, transpicuous, glassy, hyaline.

426. Opacity.—N. opacity; opaqueness etc. *adj.*

film; cloud etc. 353.

V. be -opaque etc. *adj.*; obstruct the passage of light; ob-, of-fuscate.

Adj. opaque, impervious to light.

dim etc. 422; turbid, thick, muddy, opacous, obfuscated, fuliginous, cloudy, hazy, foggy, vaporous, nubiferous, muggy.

smoky, fumid, murky, dirty.

427. Semitransparency.—N. semitransparency, opalescence, milkiness, pearliness; gauze, muslin; film; mist etc. (*cloud*) 353; frosted glass.

Adj. semi-transparent, -pellucid, -diaphanous, -opacous, -opaque; opal-escent, -ine; pearly, milky, frosted, mat; misty.

428. Color.—N. color, hue, tint, tinge, dye, complexion, shade, tincture, cast, livery, coloration, chromatism, glow, flush; tone, key.

pure –, positive –, primary –, primitive –, complementary- color; three primaries; spectrum, chromatic dispersion; broken –, secondary –, tertiary- color.

local color, coloring, keeping, tone, value, aerial perspective.

[Science of color] chromatics, spectrum analysis; prism, spectroscope.

pigment, coloring matter, paint, dye, wash, distemper, stain; medium; mordant; oil-paint etc. (*painting*) 556.

V. color, dye, tinge, stain, tint, tinct, tone, paint, wash, ingrain, grain, illuminate, emblazon, imbue; paint etc. (*fine art*) •556; daub.

Adj. colored etc. *v.*; colorific, tingent, tinctorial; chromatic, prismatic; full-, high-, deep-colored; doubly-dyed; polychromatic.

bright, vivid, intense, deep; fresh, unfaded; rich, gorgeous; highly colored; gay; variegated etc. 440.

gaudy, florid; garish; showy, flaunting, flashy; raw, crude; glaring, flaring; discordant, inharmonious.

mellow, harmonious, pearly, sweet, delicate, tender, refined.

429. Achromatism. [Absence of color.]—**N.** achromatism; de-, dis-coloration; pall-or, -idity; paleness etc. *adj.*; etoilation; neutral tint, monochrome, black-and-white.

V. lose -color etc. 428; fade, fly, go; become -colorless etc. *adj.*; turn pale, pale, whiten.

deprive of color, decolorize, bleach, tarnish, achromatize, blanch, etiolate, wash out, tone down.

Adj. uncolored etc. (*see* color etc. 428); colorless, achromatic, hueless, pale, pallid; pale-, tallow-faced; faint, dull, cold, muddy, leaden, dun, wan, sallow, dead, dingy, ashy, ashen, ghastly, cadaverous, glassy, lack-luster; discolored etc. *v.*

light-colored, fair, *blond*; white etc. 430.

pale as -death, – ashes, – a witch, – a ghost, – a corpse.

430. Whiteness.—N. whiteness etc. *adj.*; argent.

albification, albescence, albinism, etiolation.

snow, paper, chalk, milk, lily, ivory, silver, alabaster; white lead, chinese –, flake –, ivory –, zinc- white, white-wash, -ning, whiting.

V. be -white etc. *adj.*

render -white etc. *adj.*; whiten- bleach, blanch, etiolate, whitewash, silver, frost.

Adj. white; milky, milk-, snow-white; snowy, niveous, candid, chalky; hoar, -y; frosted, silvery; argent, -ine; canescent.

whitish, creamy, pearly, ivory, fair, *blond*, ash-blond, platinum blond; blanched etc. *v.*; high in tone, light.

white as -a sheet, – driven snow, – a lily, – silver; like -ivory etc. *n.*

431. Blackness.—N. blackness etc. *adj.*; darkness etc. (*want of light*) 421; swarthness, lividity, dark color, tone, color; *chiaroscuro* etc. 420.

nigrification, infuscation, denigration.

jet, ink, ebony, coal, pitch, soot, smudge, charcoal, sloe, raven, crow; black.

[Pigments] lamp –, ivory –, blue-black; writing –, printing –, printer's –, Indian- ink.

V. be -black etc. *adj.*

render -black etc. *adj.*; blacken, infuscate, denigrate; blot, -ch; smutch; smirch; darken etc. 421.

Adj. black, sable, swarthy, somber, dark, inky, ebon, atramentous, jetty; coal-, jet-black; fuliginous, pitchy, sooty, swart, dusky, dingy, murky, low-toned, low in tone; of the deepest dye.

black as -jet etc. *n.*, – my hat, – a shoe, – a tinker's pot, – November, – thunder, – midnight; nocturnal etc. (*dark*) 421; nigrescent; gray etc. 432; obscure etc. 421.

Adv. in mourning.

432. Gray.—N. gray etc. *adj.*; neutral tint, silver, pepper and salt, *chiaroscuro*, *grisaille*, grayness.

[Pigments] Payne's gray; black etc. 431.

Adj. gray, grey; steel –, iron- gray, dun, drab, dingy, leaden, livid, somber, sad, pearly; silver, -y, -ed; ash-en, -y; ciner-eous, -itious; grizzl-y, -ed; dove-, slate-, stone-, mouse-, ash-colored; mole; cool.

433. Brown.—N. brown etc. *adj.*

[Pigments] bister, ocher, sepia, Vandyke brown.

Adj. brown, adust, bay, dapple, auburn, chestnut, nutbrown, cinnamon, hazel, fawn, puce, *écru*, russet, tawny, fuscous, chocolate, maroon, foxy, tan, brunette, whitey-brown; snuff-, liver-colored; brown as -a berry, – mahogany; reddish brown; copper-, rust- colored; henna, bronze, khaki; russet, roan, sorrel.

sub-burnt; tanned etc. *v.*

V. render -brown etc. *adj.*; tan, embrown, bronze.

434. Redness.—N. red, scarlet, vermilion, cardinal, Post Office, red, carmine, crimson, pink, lake, *cerise*, cherry red, maroon, carnation, *couleur de rose*, *rose du Barry*; magenta, damask; flesh -color, – tint; color; fresh –, high- color; warmth; gules.

ruby, garnet, carbuncle; rose; rust, iron-mold.

[Dyes and pigments] cinnabar, cochineal; fuchsine; ruddle, madder, redlead; light –, Venetian- red; red ink, annotto.

redness etc. *adj.*; rub-escence, -icundity, -ification; erubescence, blush.

V. be –, become- red etc. *adj.*; blush, flush, color up, mantle, redden.

render- red etc. *adj.*; redden, rouge; rub-ify, -ricate; incarnadine; ruddle.

Adj. red etc. *n.*; -dish; rufous, ruddy, florid, incarnadine, sanguine, bloody, gory; ros-y, -eate; blowz-y, -ed; brunt; rubi-cund, -form; lurid, stammel, blood-red; russet, murrey, carroty, sorrel, lateritious.

rose-, ruby-, cherry-, claret-, wine-, plum-,

flame-, flesh-, peach-, salmon-, brick-, brickdust-colored, reddish brown etc. 433.

red as -fire, – blood, – scarlet, – a turkeycock, – a lobster; warm, hot; foxy.

435. Greenness.—N. green etc. *adj.*; blue and yellow; vert.

emerald, verd antique, verdigris, malachite, beryl, aquamarine, reseda.

[Pigments] *terre verte*, verditer, bice, chlorophyl.

greenness, verdure, verdancy; viridity, -escence.

Adj. green, verdant; glaucous, olive; porraceous; green as grass.

emerald –, pea –, grass –, apple –, sea – olive –, bottle –, leaf- green.

greenish; vir-ent, -escent.

436. Yellowness.—N. yellow etc. *adj.*; or.

[Pigments] gamboge; cadmium –, chrome –, Indian –, lemon- yellow; orpiment, yellow ocher, Claude tint, aureolin.

crocus, saffron, topaz, gold.

jaundice; London fog; yellowness etc. *adj.*

Adj. yellow, aureate, gold, golden, gilt, gilded, flavous, citrine, fallow; fulv-ous, -id; sallow, luteous, fawny, creamy, sandy; xanth-ic, -ous; jaundiced.

gold-, citrón-, saffron-, lemon-, sulphur-, amber-, straw-, primrose-, cream-colored; flazen, yellowish, buff.

yellow as a -quince, – guinea, – crow's foot.

437. Purple.—N. purple etc. *adj.*; blue and red, bishop's purple; aniline dyes, gridelin, amethyst; purpure.

livid-ness, -ity.

V. empurple.

Adj. purple, violet, plum-colored, lavender, lilac, puce, *mauve*; livid.

438. Blueness.—N. blue etc. *adj.*; garter-blue; watchet.

[Pigments] ultramarine, smalt, cobalt, cyanogen; Prussian –, syenite- blue; bice, indigo, woad.

lapis lazuli, sapphire, turquoise.

blue-, bluish-ness; bloom

Adj. blue, azure, cerulean; sky-blue, -colored, -dyed; navy-blue, aquamarine, electric blue, royal blue, cyanic; bluish; atmospheric, retiring; cold.

439. Orange.—N. orange, red and yellow; gold; or; flame etc. color, *adj.*

[Pigments] ochre, Mars orange, cadmium.

V. gild, warm.

Adj. orange; ocherous; orange-, gold-, flame-, copper-, brass-, apricot-colored; warm, hot, glowing.

440. Variegation.—N. variegation; di-, trichromism; iridescence, irisation, play of colors, polychrome, maculation, spottiness, striae.

spectrum, rainbow, iris, tulip, peacock, chameleon, butterfly, tortoiseshell; mackerel, − sky; zebra, leopard, mother-of-pearl, nacre, opal, marble, batik.

check, plaid, tartan, patchwork; mar-, parquetry; mosiac, *tesserae*, tesselation, chess-board, checkers, chequers; harlequin; Joseph's coat; tricolor; patches, bands, stripes, spots etc of color.

V. be -variegated etc. *adj.*; variegate, stripe, streak, checker, chequer; be-, speckle, fleck; be-, sprinkle; stipple, maculate, dot, bespot; tattoo, inlay, tesselate, damascene; embroider, braid, quilt.

Adj. variegated etc. *v.*; many-colored, -hued; divers-, parti-colored; di-, poly-chromatic; bi-, tri-, versi-color; of all -the colors of the rainbow, − manner of colors; kaleidoscopic.

iridescent; opal-ine, -escent; prismatic, nacreous, pearly, shot, *gorge de pigeon*, *chatoyant*, irisated.

pied, piebald, skewbald; motley; mottled, marbled; pepper and salt, paned, dappled, clouded, cymophanous.

mosiac, tesselated, chequered; plaid; tortoiseshell etc. *n.*

spott-ed, -y; punctuated, powdered; speckled etc. *v.*; freckled, fleabitten, studded; fleck-ed, -ered; striated, barred, veined; brind-ed, -led; tabby; watered; grizzled; listed; embroidered etc. *v.*; daedal.

441. Vision.—N. vision, sight, optics, eye-sight.

view, look, espial, glance, ken, *coup d'oeil*; glimpse, peep, glint; gaze, stare, leer; perlustration; contemplation; conspect-ion, -uity; regard, survey; in-, intro-spection; *reconnaissance*, speculation, watch, espionage, *espionnage*, autopsy; ocular - inspection; − demonstration; sight-seeing.

macrography, micrography.

point of view; view-, stand- point; gazebo, loophole, *belvedere*, watchtower.

field of view; theater, amphitheater, arena, vista, horizon; commanding −, bird's eye −, panoramic- view; periscope.

visual organ, organ of vision; eye; naked −, unassisted- eye; eye-ball, retina, pupil, iris, cornea, white; optics, orbs; saucer −, goggle −, gooseberry-eyes.

short sight etc. 443; clear −, sharp −, quick −, eagle −, piercing-, −, penetrating- -sight, − glance, − eye; perspicacity, discernment; catopsis.

eagle, hawk; cat, lynx; Argus.

evil eye; basilisk, cockatrice.

spectacles, telescope etc. 445.

V. see, behold, discern, perceive, have in sight, descry, sight, make out, discover, distinguish, recognize, spy, espy, ken; get −, have −, catch- a - sight, − glimpse- of; command of view of; witness, contemplate, speculate; cast − . set- the eyes on; be a -spectator etc. 444- of; look on etc. (*be present*) 186; see sights etc. (*curiosity*) 445; see at a glance etc. (*intelligence*) 498.

look, view, eye; lift up the eyes, open one's eye; look -at, − on, − upon, − over, − about one, − round; survey, scan, inspect; run the eye -over, − through; reconnoiter, glance -round, − on, − over; turn −, bend- one's looks upon; direct the eyes to, turn the eyes on, cast a glance, make eyes at.

observe etc. (*attend to*) 457; watch etc. (*care*) 459; see with one's own eyes; watch for etc. (*expect*) 507; peek, peep, peer, pry, take a peep; play at bo-peep.

look -full in the face, − hard at, − intently; strain one's eyes; fix − , rivet- the eyes upon; stare, gaze; pore over, gloat -over, − on; leer, ogle, glare; goggle; cock the eye, squint, gloat, look askance; give the glad eye.

Adj. seeing etc. *v.*; visual, ocular, -al; ophthalmic.

far-, clear-sighted etc. *h.*; eagle-, hawk-, lynx-, keen-, Argus-eyed.

visible etc. 446.

Adv. visibly etc. 446; in sight of, with one's eyes open.

at -sight, − first sight, − a glance, − the first blush; *primâ facie.*

Int. look! etc. (*attention*) 457.

Phr. the scales falling from one's eyes.

442. Blindness.—N. blindness, anopsia, cecity, execcation, *amaurosis*, cataract, ablepsy, prestriction; dim-sightedness etc. 443.

V. be -blind etc. *adj.*; not see; lose sight of; have the eyes bandaged; grope in the dark.

not look; close −, shut −, turn away −, avert-the eyes; look another way; wink etc. (*limited vision*) 443; shut the eyes −, be blind- to; wink −, blink- at.

render -blind etc. *adj.*; blind, -fold; hoodwink, dazzle; put one's eyes out; throw dust into one's eyes; *jeter de la poudre aux yeux;* screen from sight etc. (*hide*) 528.

Adj. blind; eye-, sight-, vision-less; dark; stone-, sand-, stark-blind; undiscerning; dim-sighted etc. 443.

blind as -a bat, − a buzzard, − a beetle, − a mole, − an owl; wall-eyed.

blinded etc. *v.*

Adv. blind-ly, -fold; darkly.

443. Dim-sightedness. [Imperfect vision.] [Fallacies of vision.]**—N.** dim −, dull −, half −, short −, near −, long −, double −, astigmatic−, failing- sight; dim etc -sightedness; snow blindness; purblindness, lippitude; my-, presby-opia; confusion of vision; astigmatism; nystagmus; color-blindness, dichromism, chromato-pseudo-blepsis, Daltonism; nyctalopy; *strabismus*, strabism, squint, cast in the eye, swivel eye, goggle eyes; obliquity of vision.

winking etc. *v.*; nictitation; blinkard, albino.

dizziness, swimming, scotomy; cataract; ophthalmia.

[Limitation of vision] eye shade, blinker, blinder; screen etc. (*hider*) 530.

[Fallacies of vision] *deceptio visûs;* refraction, distortion, illusion, false light, *anamorphosis*, virtual image, *spectrum*, *mirage*, looming, phasma; phant-asm, -asma, -om; vision; specter, apparition; ghost; *ignis fatuus* etc. (*luminary*) 423; specter of the Brocken; magic mirror; magic lantern etc. (*show*) 448; mirror, lens etc. (*instrument*) 445.

V. be -dim-sighted etc. *n.*; see double; have a - mote in the eye, — mist before the eyes, — film over the eyes; see through a -prism, — glass darkly; wink, blink, nictitate; squint; look ask-ant, -ance; screw up the eyes, glare, glower.

dazzle, glare, blur, swim, loom.

Adj. dim-sighted etc. *n.*; my-, presby-opic; astigmatic; moon-, mope-, blear-, goggle-, gooseberry-, one-eyed; blind of one eye, monoculous; half-, pur-, color-blind; dichromatic.

blind as a bat etc. (*blind*) 442; winking etc. *v.*

---

444. Spectator.—N. spectator, beholder, observer, inspector, viewer, looker-on, onlooker, witness, eye-witness, bystander, passer by; sight-seer.

spy, scout; sentinel etc. (*warning*) 668.

v. witness, behold etc. (*see*) 441; look on etc. (*be present*) 186.

---

445. Optical Instruments.—N. optical instruments; lens, meniscus, magnifier, reading –, burning- glass; micro-, mega-, teino-scope; spectacles,. glasses, barnacles, goggles, giglamps, eyeglass, *pince-nez*, monocle; periscopic lens; telescope, glass, lorgnette, binocular; spy-, opera-, field-glass, periscope, range finder.

mirror, reflector, speculum; looking-, pier-, cheval-, hand-glass.

prism; camera, *camera-lucida*, *-obscura*; projector, stereopticon, magic lantern etc. (*show*) 448; chro-, thau-matrope; stereo-, pseudo-, poly-, kaleido-scope.

photo-, opto-, erio-, actino-, luci-, radio-, spectro-meter; polari-, polemo-, spectro-scope, diffraction grating.

optics, optician, optometry, optometrist; microscop-y, -ist; photometry, photography; photographer.

---

446. Visibility.—N. visibility, perceptibility; conspicuousness, distinctness etc. *adj.*; conspicuity; appearance etc. 448; exposure; manifestation etc. 525; ocular -proof, — evidence, — demonstration; field of view etc. (*vision*) 441.

V. be –, become- -visible etc. *adj.*; appear, emerge, open to the view; meet –, catch- the eye; present –, show –, manifest –, produce –, discover –, reveal –, expose –, betray- itself; stand -forth, — out; show; arise; peep –, peer –, crop- out; start –, spring –, show –, turn –, crop- up; glimmer, glitter, glow, loom; glare; burst forth, scintillate; burst upon the -view, — sight; heave in sight; come -in sight, — into view, — out, — forth, — forward; see the light of day; break through the clouds; make its appearance, show its face, materialize, appear to one's eyes, come upon the stage, enter; float before the eyes, speak for itself. etc. (*manifest*) 525; attract the attention etc. 457; reappear; live in a glass house.

expose to view etc. 525.

Adj. visible, perceptible, perceivable, discernible, apparent; in -view, — full view, — sight; exposed to view, *en evidence*; unclouded.

obvious etc. (*manifest*) 525; plain, clear,

---

distinct, definite; well-defined, -marked; in focus; recognizable, palpable, autoptical; glaring, staring, conspicuous; stereoscopic; in -bold, — strong, — high- relief.

periscopic, panoramic.

before –, under- one's eyes; before one, *à vue d'oeil*, in one's eye, *oculis subjecta fidelibus*.

Adv. visibly etc. *adj.*; in sight of; before one's eyes etc. *adj.*; *veluti in speculum*.

---

447. Invisibility.—N. invisibility, nonappearance, imperceptibility; indistinctness etc. *adj.*; mystery, delitescence.

concealment etc. 528; latency etc. 526.

V. be -invisible etc. *adj.*; be hidden etc. (*hide*) 528; lurk etc. (*lie hidden*) 526; escape notice.

render -invisible etc. *adj.*; conceal etc. 528; put out of sight.

not see etc. (*be blind*) 442; lose sight of.

Adj. invisible, imperceptible; un-, in-discernible; un-, non-apparent; out of –, not in- sight; *à perte de vue*; behind the -scenes, – curtain; view-, sightless; in-, un-conspicuous; unseen etc. (*see* see etc. 441); covert etc. (*latent*) 526; eclipsed, under an eclipse.

dim etc. (*faint*) 422; mysterious, dark, obscure, confused; indistin-ct, -guishable; shadowy, indefinite, undefined; ill-defined, -marked; blurred, fuzzy, out of focus; misty etc. (*opaque*) 426; veiled etc. (*concealed*) 528; delitescent.

---

448. Appearance.—N. appearance, phenomenon, sight, spectacle, show, premonstration, scene, species, view, *coup d'oeil*; look-out, out-look, prospect, vista, perspective, bird's-eye view, scenery, landscape, picture, *tableau*; display, exposure, *mise en scène*; scenery, *décor*; rising of the curtain.

phant-asm, -om etc. (*fallacy of vision*) 443.

pageant, *spectacle*; peep-, raree-, gallanty-show; *ombres chinoises*; projector, optical –, magic-lantern, phantasmagoria, dissolving views; cinema, -tograph; bio-scope, -graph; moving pictures, movies, film, screen etc.; pan-, di-, cosm-, georama; *coup* –, *jeu- de théâtre*; pageantry etc. (*ostentation*) 882; insignia etc. (*indication*) 550.

aspect, phase, *phasis*, seeming; shape etc. (*form*) 240; guise, look, complexion, color, image, mien, air, cast, carriage, port, demeanor; presence, expression, first blush, face of the thing; point of view, light.

lineament, feature, trait, lines; out-line, -side; contour, *silhouette*, face, countenance, physiognomy, visage, phiz, mug, cast of countenance, profile, *tournure*, cut of one's jib, metoposcopy; outside etc. 220.

V. appear; be –, become- visible etc. 446; seem, look, show; present –, wear –, carry –, have –, bear –, exhibit –, take –, take on –, assume- the -appearance, — semblance- of; look like; cut a figure, figure; present to the view; show etc. (*make manifest*) 525.

Adj. apparent, seeming, ostensible; on view.

Adv. apparently; to all -seeming, — appearance; ostensibly, seemingly, as it seems, on the face of it, *primâ facie*; at the first blush, at first sight; in the eyes of; to the eye.

449. Disappearance.—N. disappearance, evanescence, eclipse, occultation.

departure etc. 293; exit, vanishing point; dissolving views.

V. disappear, vanish, dissolve, fade, melt away, pass, go, avaunt; be -gone etc. *adj.*; leave -no trace, - 'not a rack behind;' go off the stage etc. (*depart*) 293; suffer -, undergo- an eclipse; be lost to -, retire from- -sight, - view.

- lose sight of.

efface etc. 552.

Adj. disappearing etc. *v.*; evanescent; missing, lost; lost to -sight, - view; gone; *spurlos versenki.*

Int. vanish! disappear! avaunt! etc. (*ejection*) 297.

450. Intellect.—N. intellect, mind, understanding, reason, thinking principle; rationality; cogitative -, cognitive -, intellectual- faculties; faculties, senses, consciousness, observation, percipience, apperception, mentality, intelligence, intellection, intuition, association of ideas, instinct, flair, conception, judgment, wits, parts, capacity, intellectuality, reasoning power, brains, genius; wit etc. 498; ability etc. (*skill*) 698; wisdom etc. 498.

soul, spirit, ghost, inner man, heart, breast, bosom, *penetralia mentis, divina particula aurae*, heart's core; ego, psyche, pneuma, subconsciousness, subconscious, subliminal self; dual personality.

organ -, seat- of thought; *sensorium*, sensory, brain, gray matter; head, -piece; pate, noddle, skull, scull, *pericranium, cerebrum, cranium*, brain-pan, -box; sconce, upper story.

[Science of mind] metaphysics; psychics, psycho-logy, -metry, -genesis, -analysis, -physics, psychi-atry, -cal research, thought reading etc. 992; ideology; mental - , moral- philosophy; philosophy of the mind; pneumat-, phren-ology; no - , cranio-logy, -scopy.

ideal-ity, -ism; transcendental-, spiritual-ism; immateriality etc. 317.

metaphysician, psychologist etc.

V. note, notice, mark; take -notice, - cognizance- of; be ' -aware, - conscious- of; realize; appreciate; ruminate etc. (*think*) 451; fancy etc. (*imagine*) 515; conceive, reason, understand.

Adj. [Relating to intellect] intellectual, mental, rational, subjective, metaphysical, noöscopic, spiritual; ghostly; psych-ical, -ological; cerebral.

immaterial etc. 317; endowed with reason.

Adv. *in petto.*

450a. Absence or want **of Intellect.—N.** absence -, want- of -intellect etc. 450; imbecility etc. 499; brutality; brute -instinct, - force.

Adj. unendowed with reason.

451. Thought.—N. thought; exercitation - , exercise- of the intellect; reflection, cogitation, consideration, meditation, study, lucubration, speculation, deliberation, pondering; head-, brain-work; cerebration; mentation, deep reflection; close study, application etc. (*attention*) 457.

abstract thought, abstraction, contemplation, musing; brown study etc. (*inattention*) 458; reverie, Platonism; depth of thought, workings of the mind, thoughts, inmost thoughts; self-counsel, communing, -consultation.

association -, succession -, flow -, train -, current- of -thought, - ideas.

after -, mature- thought; reconsideration, second thoughts; retrospection etc. (*memory*) 505; excogitation; examination etc. (*inquiry*) 461; invention etc. (*imagination*) 515.

thoughtfulness etc. *adj.*

V. think, reflect, reason, cogitate, excogitate, consider, deliberate; bestow -thought, - consideration- upon; speculate, contemplate, meditate, ponder, muse, dream, ruminate; brood -, con-over; animadvert, study; bend-, apply- the mind etc. (*attend*) 457; digest, discuss, hammer at, weigh, perpend; realize, appreciate, fancy etc. (*imagine*) 515; trow.

take into consideration; take counsel etc. (*be advised*) 695; commune with -, bethink- oneself; collect one's thoughts; revolve -, turn over -, run over- in the mind; chew the cud -, sleep- upon; take counsel of -, advise with- one's pillow.

rack -, ransack -, crack -, beat -, cudgel-one's brains; set one's -brain, - wits- to work.

harbor -, entertain -, cherish -, nurture- an idea etc. 453; take into one's head; bear in mind; reconsider.

occur; present -, suggest- itself; come -, get-into one's head; strike one, flit across the view, come uppermost, run in one's head; enter -, pass in -, cross -, flash on -, flash across -, float in -, fasten itself on -, be uppermost in -, occupy- the mind; have in one's mind.

make an impression; sink -, penetrate- into the mind; engross the thoughts.

Adj. thinking etc. *v.*; thoughtful, pensive, meditative, reflective, cogitative, museful, wistful, contemplative, speculative, deliberative, studious, sedate, introspective, Platonic, philosophical.

lost -, engrossed -, rapt -, absorbed- in thought etc. (*inattentive*) 458; deep musing etc. (*intent*) 457.

in the mind, under consideration, in contemplation.

Adv. all things considered; taking everything into account.

Phr. the mind being on the stretch; the -mind, - head- -turning, - running- upon.

452. Incogitancy. [Absence or want of thought.]—**N.** incogitancy, vacancy, inun-derstanding, inanity, fatuity etc. 499; thoughtlessness etc. (*inattention*) 458.

V. not -think etc. 451; not think of; dismiss from the -mind, - thoughts etc. 451.

indulge in reverie etc. (*be inattentive*) 458.

put away thought; unbend -, relax -, divert- the mind.

Adj. vacant, unintellectual, unideal, unoccupied, unthinking, inconsiderate, thoughtless; absent etc. (*inattentive*) 458; diverted; irrational etc. 499; narrow-minded etc. 481.

un-thought of, -dreamt of, -considered; off one's mind; incogitable, not to be thought of, inconceivable.

453. Idea. [Object of thought.]—**N.** idea, notion, conception, thought, apprehension, impression, perception, image, sentiment, reflection, observation, consideration; abstract idea, principle; archetype.

view etc. (*opinion*) 484; theory etc. 514; conceit, fancy; phantasy etc. (*imagination*) 515.

point of view etc. (*aspect*) 448; field of view.

454. Topic. [Subject of thought.]—**N.** subject of —, material for- thought; food for the mind, mental *pabulum*.

subject, -matter; matter, theme, topic, what it is about, *thesis*, text, business, affair, matter in hand, argument; motion, resolution; head, chapter; case, point; proposition, theorem; field of inquiry; moot point, problem, etc. (*question*) 461.

V. float —, pass- in the mind etc. 451.

Adj. thought of; uppermost in the mind; *in petto*.

Adv. under -discussion, — consideration, — advisement; in -question, — the mind; on -foot, — the carpet, — the *tapis*; before the house, relative to etc. 9.

455. Curiosity. [The desire of knowledge.]—**N.** interest, thirst for knowledge; curi-osity, -ousness; inquiring mind; inquisitiveness.

sight-seer, quidnunc, newsmonger, Paul Pry, peeping Tom, eavesdropper; gossip etc. (*news*) 532; questioner, *enfant terrible*.

V. be -curious etc. *adj.*; take an interest in, stare, gape; prick up the ears, see sights, lionize; pry, speer; dig up.

Adj. curious, inquisitive, burning with curiosity, overcurious, nosey; inquiring etc. 461; prying; inquisitorial; agape etc. (*expectant*) 507; attentive etc. 457.

Phr. what's the matter? what next?

456. Incuriosity. [Absence of curiosity.]—**N.** incuriosity; incuriousness etc. *adj.*; *insouciance* etc. 866; indifference, apathy.

V. be -incurious etc. *adj.*; have no -curiosity etc. 455; take no interest in etc. 823; mind one's own business.

Adj. incurious, uninquisitive, uninterested, indifferent, bored; impassive etc. 823.

457. Attention.—**N.** attention; mindfulness etc. *adj.*; intent-ness, -iveness; thought etc. 451; adverten-ce, -cy; observ-ance, -ation; consideration, reflection, perpension; heed; particularity; notice, regard etc. *v.*; circumspection etc. (*care*) 459; study, scrutiny, once-over; in-, intro-spection; revision, -al.

active —, diligent —, exclusive —, minute —, close —, intense —, deep —, profound —, abstract —, labored —, deliberate- -thought, — attention, — application, — study.

minuteness, attention to detail etc. 459.
absorption of mind etc. (*abstraction*) 458.
indication, calling attention to etc. *v.*

V. be -attentive etc. *adj.*; attend, advert to, observe, look, see, view, remark, notice, regard, take notice, mark; give —, pay- -attention, — heedto; listen in, incline —, lend- an ear to; trouble one's head about; give a thought —, animadvert- to; occupy oneself with; contemplate etc (*think of*) 451; look -at, — to, — after, — into, — over; see to; turn —, bend —, apply —, direct —, give- the -mind, — eye, — attention- to; have -an eye to, — in one's eye; bear in mind; take into -account, — consideration; keep in -sight, — view; have regard to, heed, mind, take cognizance of, be engaged in, entertain, recognize; make —, take- note of; note.

examine cursorily; glance -at, — upon, — over; cast —, pass- the eyes over; run over, turn over the leaves, dip into, perstringe; skim etc. (*neglect*) 460; take a cursory view of.

examine, — closely, — intently; scan, scrutinize, consider; give —, bend- one's mind to; overhaul, revise, pore over; inspect, review, pass under review; take stock of; fix —, rivet —, focus —, devote- the - eye, — mind, — thoughts. — attention-on *or* to; hear —, think- out; mind one's business.

revert —, hark back- to; watch etc. (*expect*) 507, (*take care of*) 459; hearken —, listen- to; prick up the ears; have —, keep- the eyes open; come to the point.

meet with attention; fall under one's -notice, — observation; be -under consideration etc. (*topic*) 454.

catch —, strike- the eye; attract notice; catch —, awaken —, wake —, invite —, solicit —, attract —, claim —, excite —, engage —, occupy —, strike —, arrest —, fix —, engross —, absorb —, rivet-the-attention, — mind, — thoughts; be -present to, — uppermost in- the mind.

bring under one's notice; point -out, — to, — at, — the finger at; lay the finger on, indigitate, indicate; direct —, call- attention to; show; put a -mark upon, (*sign*) 550- upon; call soldiers to 'attention;' bring forward etc. (*make manifest*) 525.

Adj. attentive, mindful, heedful, observant, regardful; alive —, awake- to, alert; observing etc. *v.*; taken up —, occupied- with; engaged —, engrossed —, interested —, wrapped- in; absorbed, rapt; breathless; pre-occupied etc. (*inattentive*) 458; watchful etc. (*careful*) 459; intent on, open-eyed, breathless, undistracted, upon the stretch; on the watch etc. (*expectant*) 507.

steadfast.

Int. see! look, — here, — out, — alive, — you, — to it! mark! lo! behold! soho! hark, — ye! mind ! halloo! observe! lo and behold! attention! *nota bene*;N.B.; *, †; I'd have you to know; notice! take notice! O yes! *Oyez!*

Phr. this is —, these are- to give notice.

458. Inattention.—**N.** in-attention; — consideration; inconsiderateness etc. *adj.*; oversight; inadverten-ce, -cy; non-observance, disregard.

supineness etc. (*inactivity*) 683; *étourderie*; want of thought; heedlessness etc. (*neglect*) 460; *insouciance* etc. (*indifference*) 866.

abstraction; absence –, absorption- of mind; preoccupation, distraction, reverie, brown study, deep musing, fit of abstraction, woolgathering.

V. be -inattentive etc. *adj.*; overlook, disregard; pass by etc. (*neglect*) 460; not -observe etc. 457; think little of.

close –, shut- one's eyes to; wink at; pay no attention to; dismiss –, discard –, discharge- from one's -thoughts, – mind; drop the subject, think no more of; set –, turn –, put- aside; turn -away from, – one's attention from, – a deaf ear to, – one's back upon.

abstract oneself, dream, indulge in reverie.

escape -notice, – attention; come in at one ear and go out at the other; forget etc. (*have no remembrance*) 506.

call off –, draw off –, call away –, divert –, distract- the -attention, – thoughts, – mind; put out of one's head; dis-concert, -compose; put out, confuse, perplex, bewilder, fluster, muddle, dazzle; throw a sop to Cerberus.

Adj. inattentive; un-observant, -mindful, -heeding, -discerning; inadvertent; mind-, regard-, respect-less; listless etc. (*indifferent*) 866; blind, deaf; flighty, hand over head; cur-, percur-sory; giddy-, scatter-, hare-brained; unreflecting, *écervelé*, inconsiderate, off-hand, thoughtless, dizzy, muzzy, brainsick; giddy, – as a goose; wild, harum-scarum, ranipole, high-flying; heed-, care-less etc. (*neglectful*) 460.

absent, absent-minded, abstracted, *distrait*; lost; lost –, wrapped- in thought, woolgathering; rapt, in the clouds, bemused; dreaming –, musing- on other things; pre-occupied; engrossed etc. (*attentive*) 457; in a -reverie etc. *n.*; off one's guard etc. (*inexpectant*) 508; napping; dreamy.

disconcerted, put out etc. *v.*; rattled.

Adv. inattentively, inadvertently etc. *adj.*; *per incuriam, sub silentio.*

Int. stand -at ease, – easy!

Phr. the attention wanders; one's wits gone a -woolgathering, – bird's nesting; it never entered into one's head; the mind running on other things; one's thoughts being elsewhere; had it been a bear it would have bitten you.

---

459. Care. [Vigilance.]—**N.** care, solicitude, heed; heedfulness etc. *adj.*; scruple etc. (*conscientiousness*) 939.

watchfulness etc. *adj.*; vigilance, *surveillance*, eyes of Argus, watch, vigil, look out, watch and ward, *l'oeil du maître*.

alertness etc. (*activity*) 682; attention etc. 457; prudence etc., circumspection etc. (*caution*) 864; forethought etc. 510; precaution etc. (*preparation*) 673; tidiness etc. (*order*) 58, (*cleanliness*) 652; accuracy etc. (*exactness*) 494; minuteness, attention to detail; meticulousness, nicety, circumstantiality.

V. be -careful etc. *adj.*; reck; take care etc. (*be cautious*) 864; pay attention to etc. 457; take care of; look –, see- -to, – after; keep -an eye, – a sharp eye- upon; keep -watch, – watch and ward; mount guard, set watch, watch; keep in -sight, – view; chaperon, play gooseberry; mind, – one's business.

look -sharp, – about one; look with one's own eyes; keep a -good, – sharp- look-out; have all one's -wits, – eyes- about one; watch for etc. (*ex-*

pect) 507; stand to; keep one's eyes –, have the eyes –, sleep with one eye- open.

take precautions etc. 673; protect etc. (*render safe*) 664.

do one's best etc. 682; mind one's Ps and Qs, speak by the card, pick one's steps.

Adj. care-, regard-, heed-ful; taking care etc. *v.*; particular; prudent etc. (*cautious*) 864; considerate; thoughtful etc. (*deliberative*) 451; provident etc. (*prepared*) 673; alert etc. (*active*) 682; sure-footed.

guarded, on one's guard; on the *-qui vive*, – alert, – watch, – look-out; awake, broad awake, vigilant; watch-, wake-, wist-ful; Argus-, lynx-eyed; wide awake etc. (*intelligent*) 498; on the watch for etc. (*expectant*) 507.

tidy etc. (*orderly*) 58, (*clean*) 652; accurate etc. (*exact*) 494; scrupulous etc. (*conscientious*) 939; *cavendo tutus* etc. (*safe*) 664.

Adv. carefully etc. *adj.*; with care, gingerly.

Phr. *quis custodiet ipsos custodes?*

---

460. Neglect.—**N.** neglect; carelessness etc. *adj.*; trifling etc. *v.*; negligence; omission, laches, default; remissness, slackness, procrastination; supineness etc. (*inactivity*) 683; inattention etc. 458; *nonchalance* etc. (*insensibility*) 823; imprudence, recklessness etc. 863; slovenliness etc. (*disorder*) 59; (*dirt*) 653; improvidence etc. 674; non-completion etc. 730; inexactness etc. (*error*) 495.

paraleipsis [in rhetoric].

trifler, slacker, waster, waiter on Providence; Micawber.

V. be -negligent etc. *adj.*; take no care of etc. (take care of etc. 459); neglect; let -slip, – go; lay –, set –, cast –, put- aside; keep –, leave- out of sight; lose sight of.

overlook, disregard; pass -over, – by; let pass; blink, wink –, connive- at; gloss over; take no -note, – notice, – thought, – account- of; pay no regard to; *laisser aller*; allow to lie on the table.

scamp; trifle, fribble; do by halves; skimp; cut; slight etc. (*despise*) 930; play -, trifle- with; slur; skim, – the surface; *effleurer*; take a cursory view of etc. 457.

slur –, slip –, skip –, jump- over; pertermit, miss, skip, jump, omit, give the go-by to, push aside, throw into the background, shelve, sink; ignore, shut one's eyes to, refuse to hear, turn a deaf ear to; leave out of one's calculation; not -attend to etc. 457, – mind; not trouble -oneself, – one's head -with, – about; forget etc. 506; be caught napping etc. (*not expect*) 508; leave a loose thread; let the grass grow under one's feet.

render -neglectful etc. *adj.*; put -, throw- off one's guard.

Adj. neglecting etc. *v.*; unmindful, negligent, neglectful; heedless, careless, thoughtless; perfunctory, remiss, slack.

inconsiderate; un-, in-circumspect; off one's guard; un-wary, -watchful, -guarded; offhand.

supine etc. (*inactive*) 683; inattentive etc 458; *insouciant* etc. (*indifferent*) 823; imprudent, reckless etc. 863; slovenly etc. (*disorderly*) 59, (*dirty*) 653; inexact etc. (*erroneous*) 495; improvident etc. 674.

neglected etc. *v.*; un-heeded, -cared for, –

perceived, -seen, -observed, -noticed, -noted, -marked, -attended to, -thought of, -regarded, -remarked, -missed; shunted, shelved.

un-examined, -studied, -searched, -scanned, -weighed, -sifted, -explored.

Adv. negligently etc. *adj.*; hand over head, anyhow; in an unguarded moment etc. (*unexpectedly*) 508; *per incuriam*.

Int. never mind, no matter, let it pass; it will be all the same a hundred years hence.

461. Inquiry. [Subject of Inquiry. Question.]—**N.** inquiry; request etc. 765; search, research, quest; pursuit etc. 622.

examination, review, scrutiny, investigation, indagation; per-quisition, -scrutation, -vestigation; inqu-est, -isition; exploration; *exploitation*, ventilation.

sifting; calculation, analysis, dissection, resolution, induction; Baconian method.

strict —, close —, searching —, exhaustive-inquiry; narrow —, strict- search; study etc. (*consideration*) 451.

scire facias, ad referendum; trial.

questioning etc. *v.*; interroga-tion, -tory; third degree; interpellation; challenge, examination, cross-examination, catechism; feeler, Socratic method, zetetic philosophy; leading question; discussion etc. (*reasoning*) 476; questionnaire, questionary.

reconnoitering, *reconnaissance*; prying etc. *v.*; espionage, *espionnage*; domiciliary visit, peep behind the curtain; lantern of Diogenes.

question, query, problem, *desideratum*, point to be solved, porism; subject —, field- of -inquiry, — controversy; point —, matter- in dispute; moot-point; issue, question at issue; bone of contention etc. (*discord*) 713; plain —, fair —, open- question; enigma etc. (*secret*) 533; knotty point etc. (*difficulty*) 704; *quod-libet*; threshold of an inquiry.

inquirer, investigator, experimenter, inquisitor, inspector, querist, examiner, catechist; scrut-ator, -ineer; analyst; quidnunc etc. (*curiosity*) 455.

V. make -inquiry etc. *n.*; inquire, seek, search, frisk, speer, look -for, — about for, — out for; scan, reconnoiter, explore, sound, rummage, ransack, pry, peer, look round; look —, go- -over, — through; spy, over-haul.

scratch the head, slap the forehead.

look —, peer —, pry- into every hole and corner; look behind the scenes; trace up; hunt —, fish —, dig —, ferret- out; unearth; leave no stone unturned.

seek a -clue, — clew; hunt, track, trail, shadow, mouse, dodge, trace; follow the -trail, — scent; pursue etc. 622; beat up one's quarters; fish for; feel for etc. (*experiment*) 463.

investigate; take up —, institute —, pursue —, follow up —, conduct —, carry on —, prosecute- -an inquiry etc. *n.*; look -at, — into; pre-examine; discuss, canvass, agitate.

examine, study, consider, calculate; dip —, dive —, delve —, go deep- into; make sure of, probe, sound, fathom; probe to the -bottom, — quick; scrutinize, analyze, anatomize, dissect, parse, resolve, sift, winnow; view —, try- in all its phases; thresh out.

bring in question, subject to examination; put to

the proof etc. (*experiment*) 463; audit, tax, pass in review; take into consideration etc. (*think over*) 451; take counsel etc. 695.

ask, question, demand; put —, pop —, propose —, propound —, moot —, start —, raise —, stir —, suggest —, put forth —, ventilate —, grapple with —, go into- a question.

put to the question, interrogate, catechize, pump, grill; cross-question, -examine; dodge; require an answer; pick —, suck- the brains of; feel the pulse.

be -in question etc. *adj.*; undergo examination.

Adj. inquiry etc. *v.*; inquisitive etc. (*curious*) 455; requisit-ive, -ory; catechetical, inquisitorial, analytic; in -search, — quest- of; on the look-out for, interrogative, zetetic; all-searching.

un-determined, -tried, -decided; in -question, — dispute, — issue, — course of inquiry; under -discussion, — consideration, — investigation etc. *n.*, *sub judice*, moot, proposed; doubtful etc. (*uncertain*) 475.

Adv. what? why? wherefore? whence? whither? where? *quaere?* how -comes, — happens, — is- it? what is the reason? what's -the matter, — up, in the wind? what on earth? when? who?

462. Answer.—**N.** answer, response, reply, replication, *riposte*, rejoinder, surrejoinder, rebutter, surrebutter, counter-evidence etc. 468, counter-charge, defence, plea; retort, repartee; contradiction etc. 536; rescript, -ion; antiphon, -y; acknowledgment; password; echo.

discovery etc. 480*a*; solution etc. (*explanation*) 522; rationale etc. (*cause*) 153; clue etc. (*indication*) 550.

Oedipus; oracle, etc. 513; return etc. (*record*) 551.

V. answer, respond, reply, rebut, retort, rejoin; give —, return for- answer; acknowledge, echo.

explain etc. (*interpret*) 522; solve etc. (*unriddle*) 522; discover etc. 480*a*; fathom, hunt out etc. (*inquire*) 461; satisfy, set at rest, determine.

Adj. answering etc. *v.*; respon-sive, -dent; oracular; antiphonal; conclusive.

Adv. because etc. (*cause*) 153; on the -scent, — right scent.

Int. *eureka!*

463. Experiment.—**N.** experiment; essay etc. (*attempt*) 675; research etc. (*investigation*) 461; trial, tentative method, *tâtonnement*.

verification, probation, *experimentum crucis*, proof, criterion, diagnostic test, tryout, crucial test, acid test.

crucible, reagent, check, touchstone, pix; assay, ordeal; ring.

empiricism, rule of thumb.

feeler; pilot —, messenger- balloon, *ballon d'essai*; pilot engine; scout; straw to show the wind.

speculation; random shot, leap in the dark.

analy-zer, -st; adventurer, explorer, sourdough, prospector; experiment-er, -ist, -alist; assayer.

V. experiment; essay etc. (*endeavor*) 675; try, assay, sample; make -an experiment, — trial of; give a trial to; put upon —, subject to- trial; experiment upon; rehearse; put —, bring —, submit-to the -test, — proof; prove, verify, test, touch, practise upon, try one's strength.

grope; feel —, grope- -for, — one's way; fumble; *tâttonner, aller à tâtons*; put —, throw- out a feeler; send up a pilot balloon; see how the -land lies, — wind blows; consult the barometer; feel the pulse; fish —, bob- for; cast —, beat- about for; angle, trawl, cast one's net, beat the bushes.

venture, try one's fortune etc. (*adventure*) 675; explore etc. (*inquire*) 461.

Adj. experimental; probat-ive, ory, -ionary; analytic, docimastic; tentative; empirical; speculative, tentive.

under probation, on one's trial, on trial, on approval.

464. Comparison.—N. comparison, collation, contrast; identification.

sim-ile, -ilitude; allegory etc. (*metaphor*) 521.

V. compare -to, — with; collate, confront; place side by side etc. (*near*) 197; set —, pit- against one another; contrast balance.

identify, draw a parallel, parallel.

compare notes; institute a comparison; *parva componere magnis*.

Adj. comparative, relative; metaphorical etc. 521.

compared with etc. *v.*; comparable.

Adv. relatively etc. (*relation*) 9; as compared with etc. *v.*

465. Discrimination.—N. discrimination, distinction, differentiation, diagnosis, diorism; nice perception; perception —, appreciation- of difference; acuteness; estimation etc. 466; nicety, refinement; taste etc. 850; *critique*, judgement, tact; insight, discernment etc. (*intelligence*) 498; *nuances*.

V. discriminate, distinguish, differentiate, severalize; separate; draw the line, sift; separate —, winnow- the chaff from the wheat; split hairs.

estimate etc. (*measure*) 466; know -which is which, — one's stuff, — one's way about, — what is what, — 'a hawk from a handsaw.'

take- into -account, — consideration; give —, allow- due weight to; weigh carefully.

Adj. discriminating etc. *v.*; dioristic, discriminative, critical, distinctive; nice.

Phr. *il y a fagots et fagots*; *rem acu tetigisti.*

465a. Indiscrimination.—N. indiscrimination; promiscuity; indistinctness, -ion; uncertainty etc. (*doubt*) 475; obtuseness.

V. not -indiscriminate etc. 465; overlook etc. (*neglect*) 460- a distinction; con-found, -fuse, jumble; swallow whole.

Adj. indiscriminate, undiscriminating, promiscuous; undistinguish-ed, -able, -ing; unmeasured.

466. Measurement.—N. measurement, ad-measurement, mensuration, survey, valuation, ap-

praisment, assessment, assize; estim-ate, -ation; dead reckoning; reckoning etc. (*numeration*) 85; gauging etc. *v.*

metrology, weights and measures, compound arithmetic.

measure, yard measure, standard, rule, foot-rule, chain, tape, staff, compass, callipers; dividers; gage, gauge, planimeter; meter, line, rod, check.

volt, kilowatt, ampere, candle power; horse power; axle load; foot pound.

flood —, high water- mark; Plimsoll mark; index etc. 550.

scale; gradu-ation, -ated scale; nonius; vernier etc. (*minuteness*) 193; pedo (*length*)- 200, sounding line etc. (*depth*) 208, thermo (*heat* etc. 398)-, baro (*air* etc. 338)-, dynamo (*power*)- 276, anemo (*wind* 349)-, gonio (*angle* 244)- meter; landmark etc. (*limit*) 233; balance etc. (*weight*) 310; optical instruments etc. 445.

co-ordinates, ordinate and abscissa, polar co-ordinates, latitude and longitude, declination and right ascension, altitude and azimuth.

geo-, stereo-, hypso-metry, metage; surveying, land surveying; geo-desy, -detics, -desia; ortho-, alti-metry; *cadastre*.

astrolabe, armillary sphere.

land, -surveyor; geometer, topographer, cartographer, hydrographer.

V. measure, meter, mete; value, assess, rate, appraise, estimate, form as estimate, set a value on; appreciate; standardize.

span, pace, step; apply the -compass etc. *n.*; gauge, plumb, probe, calliper, sound, fathom etc. 208; heave the -log, — lead; weigh etc. 319; survey.

take an average etc. 29; graduate.

Adj. measuring etc. *v.*; metric, -al; measurable; geodetical, cadastral, topographical.

467. Evidence, [on one side]**—N.** evidence; facts, premises, *data, praecognita*, grounds.

indication etc. 550; criterion etc. (*test*) 463.

testi-mony, -fication; attestation; deposition etc. (*affirmation*) 535; examination.

admission etc. (*assent*) 488; authority, warrant, credential, diploma, voucher, certificate, docket; record etc. 551; document, muniments; *pièce justificative*; deed, warranty etc. (*security*) 771; signature, seal etc. (*identification*) 550; exhibit, citation, reference.

witness, indicator; eye-, ear-witness; deponent; sponsor.

oral —, documentary —, hearsay —, external —, extrinsic —, internal —, intrinsic —, circumstantial —, cumulative —, *ex parte* —, presumptive —, collateral —, constructive- evidence; proof etc. (*demonstration*) 478; evidence in chief; finger prints, dactylogram.

secondary evidence; confirmation, corroboration, adminicle, support; ratification etc. (*assent*) 488; authentication, verification; compurgation, wager of law, comprobation.

citation, reference.

V. be -evidence etc. *n.*; evince, show, betoken, tell of; indicate etc. (*denote*) 550; imply, involve, argue, bespeak, breathe.

have —, carry- weight; tell, speak volumes; speak for itself etc. (*manifest*) 525.

rest —, depend- upon; repose on.

bear -witness etc. *n.*; give -evidence etc. *n.*; testify, depose, witness, vouch for; sign, seal, undersign, set one's hand and seal, sign and seal, deliver as one's act and deed, certify, attest; acknowledge etc. (*assent*) 488.

make absolute, confirm, ratify, corroborate, endorse, countersign, support, bear out, vindicate, uphold, warrant.

adduce, attest, cite, quote; refer —, appeal- to; call, — to witness; bring -forward, — into court; allege, plead; produce —, confront- witnesses; collect —, bring together —, rake up- evidence.

have —, make out- a case; establish, circumstantiate, authenticate, substantiate, verify, make good, quote chapter and verse; bring -home to, — to book.

Adj. showing etc. *v.*; evidential, indica-tive, -tory; deducible etc. 478; grounded —, founded —, based- on; first hand, authentic, verifiable; corroborative, confirmatory; significant, conclusive.

Adv. by inference; according to, witness, *a fortiori*; still -more, — less; *raison de plus*; in corroboration etc. *n.* of; *valeat quantum*; under -seal, — one's hand and seal.

468. Counter-evidence. [Evidence on the other -side, on the other hand.]—**N.** counter-evidence; evidence on the other -side, — hand; disproof; refutation etc. 479; negation etc. 536; conflicting evidence.

plea etc. 617; vindication etc. 937; counter-protest; *tu quoque* argument; other side —, reverse-of the shield.

V. countervail, oppose; run counter; rebut etc. (*refute*) 479; subvert etc. (*destroy*) 162; check, weaken; contravene; contradict etc. (*deny*) 536; tell another story, turn the -tables, — scale; alter the case; cut both ways; prove a negative.

audire alteram partem.

Adj. countervailing etc. *v.*; contradictory, in rebuttal.

un-attested, -authenticated, -supported by evidence; suppositious, trumped up.

Adv. *per contra,* conversely, on the other hand.

469. Qualification.—N. qualification, limitation, modification, coloring.

allowance, grains of allowance, consideration, extenuating circumstances.

condition, proviso, exception; exemption; salvo, saving clause; discount etc. 813.

V. qualify, limit, modify, affect, temper, leaven, give a color to, introduce new conditions.

allow —, make allowance- for; admit exceptions, take into account.

take exception, object.

Adj. qualifying etc. *v.*; conditional; extenuatory; exceptional etc. (*unconformable*) 83.

hypothetical etc. (*supposed*) 514; contingent etc. (*uncertain*) 475.

Adv. provided, — always; if, unless, but, yet; according as; conditionally, admitting, supposing; on the supposition of etc. (*theoretically*) 514; with the understanding, even, although, though, for all that, after all, at all events.

with grains of allowance, *cum grano salis; exceptis excipiendis*; wind and weather permitting; if possible etc. 470.

subject to; with this -proviso etc. *n.*

470. Possibility.—N. possibility, potentiality; what -may be, — is possible etc. *adj.*; compatibility etc. (*agreement*) 23.

practicability, feasibility; practicableness etc. *adj.*

contingency, chance etc. 156.

V. be -possible etc. *adj.*; stand a chance, have a leg to stand on; admit of, bear.

render -possible etc. *adj.*; put in the way of.

Adj. possible; on the -cards, — dice; *in posse*, within the bounds of possibility, conceivable, credible, imaginable; compatible etc. 23.

practicable, feasible, workable, performable, achievable; within -reach, — measurable distance; accessible, superable, surmountable; at-, obtainable; contingent etc. (*doubtful*) 475.

Adv. possibly, by possibility; perhaps, -chance, -adventure; may be, haply, mayhap.

if possible, wind and weather permitting, God willing, *Deo volente,* D.V.

471. Impossibility.—N. impossibility etc. *adj.*; what -cannot, — can never- be; sour grapes; infeasibility, impracticability; hopelessness etc. 859.

V. be -impossible etc. *adj.*; have no chance whatever.

attempt impossibilities; square the circle; discover the -philosopher's stone — elixir of life, — secret of perpetual motion; wash a blackamoor white; skin a flint; make -a silk purse out of a sow's ear, — bricks without straw; have nothing to go upon; weave a rope of sand, build castles in the air, *prendre la lune avec les dents,* extract sunbeams from cucumbers, set the Thames on fire, milk a he-goat into a sieve, catch a weasel asleep, *rompre l'anguille au genou,* be in two places at once.

Adj. impossible; not -possible etc. 470; absurd, contrary to reason; unlikely, at variance with facts; unreasonable etc. 477; incredible etc. 485; beyond the bounds of -reason, — possibility; from which reason recoils; visionary; inconceivable etc. (*improbable*) 473; prodigious etc. (*wonderful*) 870; un-, in-imaginable, unthinkable, not a Chinaman's chance.

impracticable, unachievable; un-, in-feasible; insuperable; un-, in-surmountable; unat-, unobtainable; out of -reach, — the question; not to be -had, — thought of; beyond control; desperate etc. (*hopeless*) 859; incompatible etc. 24; inaccessible, uncomeatable, impassable, impervious, innavigable, inextricable.

out of —, beyond- one's -power, — depth, — reach, — grasp; too much for; *ultra crepidam.*

Phr. the grapes are sour; *non possumus; non nostrum tantas componere lites.*

472. Probability.—N. probability, likelihood; likeliness etc. *adj.*

vraisemblance, verisimilitude, plausibility;

color, semblance, show of; presumption; presumptive -, circumstantial- evidence; credibility.

reasonable -, fair -, good -, favorable- -chance, - prospect; prospect, well-grounded hope; chance etc. 156.

V. be -probable etc. *adj.*; give -, lend^d- color to; point to; imply etc. (*evidence*) 467; bid fair etc. (*promise*) 511; stand fair for; stand -, run- a good chance.

presume, infer, suppose, take for granted.

think likely, dare say, flatter oneself; expect etc. 507; count upon etc. (*believe*) 484.

Adj. probable, likely, hopeful, to be expected, in a fair way.

plausible, specious, ostensible, colorable, *ben trovato*, well-founded, reasonable, credible, easy of belief, presumable, presumptive, apparent.

Adv. probably etc. *adj.*; belike; in all -probability, - likelihood; very -, most- likely; as likely as not; like enough; ten etc. to one; apparently, seemingly, according to every reasonable expectation; *primâ facie*; to all appearance etc. (*to the eye*) 448.

Phr. the -chances, - odds- are; appearances -. chances- are in favor of; there is reason to -believe, - think, - expect; I dare say; all Lombard Street to a China orange.

473. Improbability.—N. improbability, unlikelihood; unfavorable -, bad -, little -, small -, poor -, scarcely any -, no -, not a ghost of a- chance; bare possibility; long odds; incredibility etc. 485.

V. be -improbable etc. *adj.*; have a -small chance etc. *n.*

Adj. improbable, unlikely, contrary to all reasonable expectation, implausible.

rare etc. (*infrequent*) 137; unheard of, inconceivable; un-, in-imaginable; incredible etc. 485; more than doubtful.

Int. not likely! no fear!

Phr. the chances are against.

474. Certainty.—N. certainty; necessity etc. 601; certitude, certainness, surety, assurance, sureness; dead -, moral- certainty; infallibleness etc. *adj.*; infallibility, reliability.

gospel, scripture, church, pope, court of final appeal; *res judicata*, *ultimatum*.

positiveness; dogmat-ism, -ist, -izer; *doctrinaire*, know-all, bigot, -ry; opinionist, Sir Oracle; *ipse dixit*; zealot.

fact; positive -, matter of- fact; *fait accompli*.

V. be -certain etc. *adj.*; stand to reason.

render -certain etc. *adj.*; in-, en-, as-sure; clinch, make sure; determine, decide, set at rest, 'make assurance double sure;' know etc. (*believe*) 484; dismiss all doubt.

dogmatize, lay down the law.

Adj. certain, sure; assured etc. *v.*; solid, well-founded.

unqualified, absolute, positive, determinate, definite, clear, unequivocal, categorical, unmistakable, decisive, decided, ascertained.

inevitable, unavoidable, ineluctable, avoidless.

unerring, infallible; unchangeable etc. 150; to be depended on, trustworthy, reliable, bound.

un-impeachable, -deniable, -questionable; indisputable, -contestable, -controvertible, -defeasible, -dubitable; irrefutable etc. (*proven*) 478; conclusive, without power of appeal, final.

indubious; without -, beyond a -, without a shade or shadow or- -doubt - question; past dispute; beyond all -question, - dispute; undoubted, -contested, -questioned, -disputed; question-, dount-less.

bigoted, fanatical, dogmatic, opinionat-ed, -ive, *doctrinaire*.

authoritative, authentic; official.

sure as -fate, - death and taxes, - a gun.

evident, self-evident, axiomatic; clear, - as day, - as the sun at noonday; obvious.

Adv. certainly etc. *adj.*; certes, sure, no doubt, doubtless, and no mistake, *flagrante delicto*, sure enough, to be sure, of course, as a matter of course, *à coup sur*, to a certainty, undoubtedly; in truth etc. (*truly*) 494; at -any rate, - all events; without fail; *coûte que coûte*; whatever may happen, if the worst come to the worst; come -, happen- what -may, - will; sink or swim; rain or shine.

Phr. *cela va sans dire*; there is -no question, - not a shadow of doubt; the die is cast etc. (*necessity*) 601.

475. Uncertainty.—N. uncertainty, incertitude, doubt; doubtfulness etc. *adj.*; dubi-ety, -tation, -tancy, -ousness.

hesitation, suspense; perplexity, embarrassment, dilemma, quandary, Morton's fork, bewilderment; timidity etc. (*fear*) 860; indecision, vacillation etc. 605; *diaporesis*, indetermination.

vagueness etc. *adj.*; haze, fog; obscurity etc. (*darkness*) 421; ambiguity etc. (*double meaning*) 520; contingency, double contingency, possibility upon a possibility; conjecture; open question etc. (*question*) 461; *onus probandi*; blind bargain, pig in a poke, leap in the dark, something or other; needle in a bottle of hay; roving commission.

fallibility, unreliability, untrustworthiness, precariousness.

V. be -uncertain etc. *adj.*; wonder whether.

lose the -clue, - clew, - scent; miss one's way.

not know -what to make of etc. (*unintelligibility*) 519, - which way to turn, - whether one stands on one's head or one's heels; float in a sea of doubt, hesitate, flounder; lose -oneself, - one's head, - one's way, wander aimlessly; muddle one's brains.

render -uncertain etc. *adj.*; put out, pose, puzzle, perplex, embarrass; confuse, -found; bewilder, mystify; bother, nonplus, addle the wits, throw off the scent; *ambiguas in vulgus spargere voces*; keep in suspense.

doubt etc. (*disbelieve*) 485; hang -, tremble- in the balance; depend.

Adj. uncertain; casual; random etc. (*aimless*) 621; changeable etc. 149.

doubtful, dubious; indecisive; unsettled, -decided, -determined; in suspense, open to discussion; controvertible; in question etc. (*inquiry*) 461; insecure, unstable.

vague; in-determinate, -definite; ambiguous, equivocal; undefin-ed, -able; confused etc. (*indistinct*) 447; mystic, mysterious, veiled, obscure, cryptic, oracular.

perplexing etc. *v.*; enigmatic, paradoxical; apocryphal, problematical, hypothetical; experimental etc. 463.

fallible, questionable, precarious, slippery, ticklish, debatable, disputable; un-reliable, -trustworthy.

contingent, — on, dependent on; subject to; dependent on circumstances; occasional; provisional.

unauth-entic, -enticated, -oritative; un-ascertained, -confirmed; undemonstrated; un-told, -counted.

in a -state of uncertainty, — cloud, — maze; ignorant etc. 491; on the horns of a dilemma; afraid to say; out of one's reckoning, astray, adrift; as -sea, — fault, — a loss, — one's wit's end, — a *nonplus*; puzzled etc. *v.*; lost abroad, *désorienté*; dis-tracted, -traught.

Adv. *pendente lite*; *sub spe rati.*

Phr. Heaven knows; who can tell? who shall decide when doctors disagree?

476. Reasoning.—N. reasoning; ratio-cination, -nalism; dialectics, induction, generalization.

discussion, comment; ventilation; inquiry etc. 461.

argumentation, controversy, debate; polemics, wrangling; contention etc. 720; logomachy; disputation, -ceptation; paper war.

art of reasoning, logic.

process —, train —, chain- of reasoning; de-, induction; synthesis, analysis.

argument; case, plea, *plaidoyer*, opening; *lemma*, proposition, terms, premises, postulate, data, starting point, principle; inference etc. (*judgment*) 480.

pro-, syllogism; enthymeme, sorites, dilemma, *perilepsis*, *a priori* reasoning, *reductio ad absurdum*, horns of a dilemma, *argumentum ad hominem*, comprehensive argument.

reasoner, logician, dialectician; disputant; controver-sialist, -tist; wrangler, arguer, debater, polemic, casuist, rationalist; scientist.

logical sequence; good case; correct —, just —, sound —, valid —, cogent —, logical —, forcible —, persuasive —, persuasory —, consectary —, conclusive etc. 478 —, subtle- reasoning; force of argument; strong -point, — argument.

arguments, reasons, pros and cons.

V. reason, argue, discuss, debate, dispute, wrangle, bandy -words, — arguments; chop logic; hold —, carry on- an argument; controvert etc. (*deny*) 536; canvass; comment —, moralize-upon; consider etc. (*examine*) 461.

open a -discussion, — case; join —, be at- issue; moot; come to the point; stir —, agitate —, ventilate —, torture- a question; try conclusions; take up a -side, — case.

contend, take one's stand upon, insist, lay stress on; infer etc. 480.

follow from etc. (*demonstration*) 478.

Adj. rational; reasoning etc. *v.*; rationalistic; argumentative, controversial, dialectic, polemical; discurs-ory, -ive; disputations.

debatable, controvertible.

logical; in-, de-ductive; synthetic, analytic; relevant etc. 23.,

Adv. for, because, hence, whence, seeing that, since, sith, then, thence, so; for -that, — this, — which- reason; for-, inasmuch as; whereas, *ex cessoo*, considering, in consideration of; there-, where-fore; consequently, *ergo*, thus, accordingly; *a fortiori*.

in -conclusion, — fine; finally, after all, *au bout du compte*, on the whole, taking one thing with another.

rationally etc. *adj.*

477. Sophistry. [The absence of reasoning.] **Intuition.** [False or vicious reasoning; show of reason.]—**N.** intuition, instinct, association; presentiment; rule of thumb.

sophistry, paralogy, perversion, casuistry, jesuitry, equivocation, evasion, mental reservation; chicane, -ry; quiddit, quiddity; mystification; special pleading; speciousness etc. *adj.*; nonsense etc. 497; word-, tongue-fence.

false —, vicious- reasoning; *petitio principii, ignoratio elenchi; post hoc ergo propter hoc; non sequitur, ignotum per ignotius.*

misjudgment etc. 481; false teaching etc. 538.

sophism, solecism, paralogism; quibble, quirk, *elenchus*, elench, fallacy, *quodlibet*, subterfuge, subtlety, quillet; inconsistency, antilogy; 'a mockery, a delusion and a snare;' claptrap, mere words; 'lame and impotent conclusion.'

meshes —, cobwebs- of sophistry; flaw in an argument; weak point, bad case.

over-refinement; hair-splitting etc. *v.*

sophist, casuist, paralogist.

V. judge -intuitively, — by intuition; hazard a proposition, talk at random.

reason -ill, — falsely etc. *adj.*; paralogize; misjudge etc. 481.

pervert, quibble; equivocate, mystify, evade, elude; gloss over, varnish; misteach etc. 538; mislead etc. (*error*) 495; cavil, refine, subtilize, split hairs; misrepresent etc. (*lie*) 544.

beg the question, reason in a circle, cut blocks with a razor, beat about the bush, play fast and loose, blow hot and cold, prove that black is white and white black, travel out of the record, *parler à tort et à travers*, put oneself out of court, not have a leg to stand on.

Adj. intuitive, instinctive, impulsive; independent of —, anterior to- reason; gratuitous; hazarded; unconnected.

unreasonable, illogical, false, unsound, invalid; unwarranted, not following; inconsequent, -ial; inconsistent, incongruous; abson-ous, -ant; unscientific; untenable, inconclusive, incorrect; fall-acious; -ible; groundless, unproved.

deceptive, sophistical, sophisticated, casuistical, jesuitical; illus-ive, -ory; specious, hollow, plausible, *ad captandum*, evasive; irrelevant etc. 10.

weak, feeble, poor, flimsy, loose, vague, irrational; nonsensical etc. (*absurd*) 497; foolish etc. (*imbecile*) 499; frivolous, pettifogging, quibbling; finespun, over-refined.

at the end of one's tether, *au bout de son latin.*

Adv. intuitively etc. *adj.*; by intuition; illogically etc. *adj.*

Phr. *non constat*; that goes for nothing.

478. Demonstration.—N. demonstration, proof; conclusiveness etc. *adj.*; *apodixis*, probation, comprobation.

logic of facts etc. (*evidence*) 467; *experimentum curcis* etc. (*test*) 463; argument etc. 476; irrefragability.

V. demonstrate, prove, establish, make good; show; evince etc. (*be evidence of*) 467; verify etc. 467; settle the question, reduce to demonstration, set the question at rest.

make out, — a case; prove one's point, have the best of the argument; draw a conclusion etc. (*judge*) 480.

follow, — of course; stand to reason; hold -good, — water.

Adj. demonstra-ting etc. *v.*, -tive, -ble; probative, unanswerable, conclusive; apodictic, -al; irre-sistible, -futable, -fragable, undeniable.

categorical, decisive, crucial.

demonstrated etc. *v.*; proven; unconfuted, -answered, -refuted; evident etc. 474.

deducible, consequential, consectary, inferential, following.

Adv. of course, in consequence, consequently, as a matter of course.

Phr. *probatum est*; there is nothing more to be said, Q.E.D., it must follow.

479. Confutation.—N. con-, re-futation; answer, complete answer; disproof, conviction, redargution, invalidation; expos-ure, -ition; clincher; retort; *reductio ad absurdum*; knock down — , *tu quoque*- argument.

V. con-, re-fute; parry, negative, disprove, redargue, expose, show the fallacy of, rebut, defeat; demolish etc. (*destroy*) 162; over-throw, -turn; scatter to the winds, explode, invalidate; silence; put▽, reduce- to silence; clinch -an argument, — a question; give one a set down, stop the mouth, shut up; have, — on the hip; get the better of; confound, convince.

not leave a leg to stand on, cut the ground from under one's feet.

be confuted etc.; fail; expose —, show- one's weak point.

Adj. confut-ing, -ed etc. *v.*; capable of refutation; re-, con-futable.

condemned -on one's own showing, — out of one's own mouth.

Phr. the argument falls to the ground, *cadit quaestio*, it does not hold water, `suo sibi gladio hunc jugulo.`

480. Judgment. [Conclusion.]—**N.** result, conclusion, upshot; deduction, inference, ergotism; illation; corollary, porism; moral.

estimation, valuation, appreciation, judication; di-, ad-judication; arbitr- ament, -ement, -ation; assessment, ponderation.

award, estimate; review, criticism, *critique*, notice, report.

decision, determination, judgment, finding, verdict, sentence, decree, — nisi, — absolute, — interlocutory; dictum; *res judicata*.

plébiscite, referendum, voice, casting vote; vote etc. (*choice*) 609; opinion etc. (*belief*) 484; good judgment etc. (*wisdom*) 498.

judge, jurist, umpire; arbi-ter, -trator; assessor, referee; censor, reviewer, critic; *connoisseur*; commentator etc. 524; inspector, inspecting officer.

V. judge, conclude; come to —, draw —, arrive at- a conclusion; ascertain, determine, make up one's mind.

deduce, derive, gather, collect, draw an inference, make a deduction, weet, ween.

form an estimate, estimate, size up, appreciate, value, count, assess, rate, rank, account; regard, consider, think of; look upon etc. (*believe*) 484.

settle; pass —, give- an opinion; decide, try, pronounce, rule; pass -judgment, — sentence; sentence, doom; find; give —, deliver- judgment; ad-jud-ge, -icate; arbitrate, award, report; bring in a verdict; make absolute, set a question at rest; confirm etc. (*assent*) 488.

comment, criticize; review, pass under review etc. (*examine*) 457; investigate etc. (*inquire*) 461.

hold the scales, sit in judgment; try —, hear- a cause.

Adj. judging etc. *v.*; judicious etc. (*wise*) 498; determinate, conclusive, censorious, critical etc. 932.

Adv. on the whole, all things considered.

480a. Discovery. [Result of search or inquiry.]—**N.** discovery, invention, detection, disenchantment, disclosure, find, ascertainment, revelation.

trover etc. 775.

V. discover, find, determine, evolve; fix upon; find —, trace —, make —, hunt —, fish —, worm —, ferret —, root-out; fathom; bring —, draw-out; educe, elicit, bring to light, invent; dig —, grub —, fish- up; unearth, disinter.

solve, resolve; un-riddle, -ravel, -lock; pick —, open- the lock; find a -clue, — clew- to; interpret etc. 522; disclose etc. 529.

trace, get at; hit it, have it; lay one's -finger, — hands- upon; spot; get —, arrive- at the -turth etc. 494; put the saddle on the right horse, hit the right nail on the head.

be near the truth, burn; smoke, scent, sniff, smell a rat.

open the eyes to; see -through, — daylight, — in its true colors, — the cloven foot; detect; catch, — tripping.

pitch —, fall —, light —, hit —, stumble —, pop- upon; come across; meet —, fall in- with.

recognize, realize, verify, make certain of, identify.

Int. *eureka!*

481. Misjudgment.—N. misjudgment, obliquity of —, warped- judgment; mis-calculation, -computation, -conception etc. (*error*) 495; hasty conclusion.

prejud-gment, -ication, -ice; foregone conclusion; pre-notion, -vention, -conception, -dilection, -possession, -apprehension, -sumption, -sentiment; fixed —, preconceived- idea; *idée fixe*; *mentis gratissimus error*; fool's paradise.

esprit de corps, party spirit, race —, class-prejudice, partisanship, clannishness, *prestige*.

bias, warp, twist; hobby, fad, whim, craze, quirk, crotchet, partiality, infatuation, blind side, mote in the eye.

one-sided —, partial —, narrow —, confined —, superficial- -views, — ideas,— conceptions, — notions; narrow mind; bigotry etc. (*obstinacy*) 606; *odium theologicum*; pedantry; hypercriticism.

doctrinaire etc. (*positive*) 474.

V. mis-judge, -estimate, -think, -conjecture, -conceive etc. (*error*) 495; fly in the face of facts; mis-calculate, -reckon, -compute.

overestimate etc. 482; underestimate etc. 483.

pre-, fore-judge; pre-suppose, -sume, -judicate; dogmatize; have a -bias etc. *n.*; have only one idea; *jurare in verba magistri*, run away with the notion; jump —, rush- to a conclusion; look only at one side of the shield; view -with jaundiced eye, — through distorting spectacles; not see beyond one's nose; *dare pondus fumo*; get the wrong sow by the ear etc. (*blunder*) 699.

give a -bias, — twist; bias, warp, twist; prejudice, -possess.

Adj. misjudging etc. *v.*; ill-judging, wrong-headed; prejudiced, prejudicial, etc. *v.*; jaundiced; short-sighted, pur-blind; partial, one-sided, superficial.

narrow-minded; confined, insular, provincial, parochial, illiberal, intolerant, narrow, besotted, infatuated, fanatical, cracked, warped, *entêté*, positive, dogmatic, dictatorial; conceited; opin-, opini-ative; opinion-ed, -ate, -ative, -ated; self-opinioned, wedded to an opinion, *opinâtre*; bigoted etc. (*obstinate*) 606; crotchety, fussy, impracticable; unreason-able, -ing; stupid etc. 499; credulous etc. 486.

misjudged etc. *v.*

Adv. *ex parte.*

Phr. nothing like leather; the wish the father to the thought.

482. Overestimation.—N. overestimation etc. *v.*; exaggeration etc. 549; vanity etc. 880; optim-, pessim-ism, -ist; megalomania.

much -cry and little wool, — ado about nothing; storm in a teacup; fine talking, rodomontade, gush, hot air, gas, bombast.

egotism etc. 880; boasting etc. 884.

V. over-estimate, -rate, -value, -prize, -weigh, -reckon, -strain, -praise; estimate too highly, attach too much importance to, make mountains of molehills, catch at straws; strain, magnify; exaggerate etc. 549; set too high a value upon; think —, make- -much, — too much- of; outreckon.

extol, — to the skies; make the -most, — best, — worst- of, eulogize, panegyrize, gush, puff, boost; make two bites of a cherry.

have too high an opinion of oneself etc. (*vanity*) 880.

Adj. overestimated etc. *v.*; oversensitive etc.

(*sensibility*) 822; inflated, puffed up, exaggerated etc. 549.

Phr. all his geese are swans; *parturiunt montes.*

483. Underestimation.—N. underestimation; depreciation etc. (*detraction*) 934; pessim-ism, -ist; undervaluing etc. *v.*; modesty etc. 881.

V. under-rate, -estimate, -value, -reckon; depreciate; disparage etc. (*detract*) 934; not do justice to; mis-, dis-prize; ridicule etc. 856; slight etc. (*despise*) 930; neglect etc. 460; slur over, under-state.

make -light, — little, — nothing, — no account- of; minimize, belittle, run down, think nothing of; set -no store by, — at naught; shake off as dewdrops from the lion's mane.

Adj. depreciat-ing, -ed, -ive, -ory, etc. *v.*; unappreciated, -valued, -prized; pejorative.

484. Belief.—N. belief; credence; credit; assurance; faith, trust, troth, confidence, presumption, sanguine expectation etc. (*hope*) 858; dependence on, reliance on.

persuasion, conviction, convincement, plerophory, self-conviction; certainty etc. 474; opinion, mind, view; conception, thinking; impression etc. (*idea*) 453; surmise etc. 514; conclusion etc. (*judgment*) 480.

tenet, dogma, principle, way of thinking; popular belief etc. (*assent*) 488.

firm — implicit —, settled —, fixed —, rooted —, deep-rooted —, staunch —, unshaken —, steadfast —, inveterate —, calm —, sober —, dispassionate —, impartial —, well-founded- -belief, — opinion etc.; *uberrima fides.*

system of opinions, school, doctrine, articles, canons; declaration —, profession- of faith; tenets, *credenda*, creed; thirty-nine articles etc. (*orthodoxy*) 983*a*; catechism; assent etc. 488; *propaganda* etc. (*teaching*) 537.

credibility etc. (*probability*) 472.

V. believe, credit; give -faith, — credit, — credence- to; see, realize; assume, receive; set down —, take- for; have —, take- it; consider, esteem, presume.

count —, depend —, calculate —, pin one's faith —, reckon —, lean —, build —, rely —, rest-upon; lay one's account for; make sure of.

make oneself easy -about, — on that score; take on -trust, — credit; take for -granted, —; gospel; allow —, attach- some weight to.

know, — for certain; have —, make- no doubt; doubt not; be — rest- assured etc. *adj.*; persuade —, assure —, satisfy- oneself; make up one's mind.

give one credit for; confide —, believe —, put one's trust- in; place —, repose- implicit confidence in; take -one's word for, — at one's word; place reliance on, rely upon, swear by, regard to.

think, hold; take, — it; opine, be of opinion, conceive, trow, ween, fancy, apprehend; have —, hold —, possess —, entertain —, adopt —, imbibe —, embrace —, get hold of —, hazard —, foster —, nurture —, cherish- -a belief, — an opinion etc. *n.*

view —, consider —, take —, hold —, conceive —, regard —, esteem —, deem —, look upon —, account —, set down- as; surmise etc. 514.

get –, take- it into one's head; come round to an opinion; swallow etc. (*credulity*) 486.

cause to -be believed etc. *v.*; satisfy, persuade, have the ear of, gain the confidence of, assure; convince, -vict, -vert; put across, sell; wean, bring round; bring –, put –, win- over; indoctrinate etc. (*teach*) 537; cram down the throat; produce –, carry- conviction; bring –, drive- home to.

go down, find credence, pass current; be - received etc. *v.*, – current etc. *adj.*; possess –, take hold of –, take possession of- the mind.

Adj. believing etc. *v.*; certain, sure, assured, positive, cocksure, satisfied, confident, unhesitating, convinced, secure.

under the impression; impressed –, imbued –, penetrated- with.

confiding, trustful, suspectless; unsusp-ecting, -icious; void of suspicion; credulous etc. 486; wedded to.

believed etc. *v.*; accredited, putative; un- suspected.

worthy of –, deserving of –, commanding- - belief, – confidence; credible, reliable, trusted, trustworthy, to be depended on, undoubted; satisfactory; probable etc. 472; fiduci-al, -ary; persuasive, impressive.

relating to belief, doctrinal.

Adv. in the -opinion, – eyes- of; *me judice*; me-seems, -thinks; to the best of one's belief; I - dare say, – doubt not, – have no doubt, – am sure; in my opinion; sure enough etc. (*certainty*) 474; depend –, rely- upon it; be –, rest- assured; I'll warrant you etc. (*affirmation*) 535.

485. Unbelief. Doubt.—N. un-, dis-, mis- belief; discredit, miscreance; infidelity etc. (*irreligion*) 989; dissent etc. 489; change of - opinion etc. 484; retraction etc. 607.

doubt etc. (*uncertainty*) 475; skepticism, misgiving, demur; dis-, mis-trust; misdoubt, suspicion, jealousy, scruple, qualm; *onus probandi*.

incredib-ility, -leness; incredulity; unbeliever etc. 487.

V. dis-believe, -credit; not -believe etc. 484; misbelieve; refuse to admit etc. (*dissent*) 489; refuse to believe etc. (*incredulity*) 487.

doubt; be -doubtful etc. (*uncertain*) 475; doubt the truth of; be -skeptical as to etc. *adj.*; diffide; dis-, mis-trust; suspect, smoke, scent, smell a rat; have –, harbor –, entertain- -doubts, – suspicions; have one's doubts.

demur, stick at, pause, hesitate, scruple, waver, stop and consider.

hang in -suspense, – doubt.

throw doubt upon, raise a question; bring –, call- in question; question, challenge, query; dispute; deny etc. 536; cavil; cause –, raise –, start –, suggest –, awake- a -doubt, – suspicion; ergotize.

startle, stagger; shake –, stagger- one's faith, – belief.

Adj. unbelieving; incredulous –, skeptical- as to; distrustful –, shy –, suspicious- of; doubting etc. *v.*

doubtful etc. (*uncertain*) 475; disputable; un- worthy –, undeserving- of -belief etc. 484; questionable; sus-pect, -picious; open to -suspicion,

– doubt; staggering, hard to believe, incredible, not to be believed, inconceivable.

fallible etc. (*uncertain*) 475; undemonstrable; controvertible etc. (*untrue*) 495.

Adv. *cum grano salis.*

Phr. *fronti nulla fides; nimium ne crede colori; 'timeo Danaos et dona ferentes;' credat Judaeus Apella;* let those believe who may.

486. Credulity.—N. credul-ity, -ousness etc. *adj.*; gull-, cull-ibility; gross credulity, infatuation; self-delusion, -deception; blind reasoning; superstition; one's blind side; bigotry etc. (*obstinacy*) 606; hyper-orthodoxy etc. 984; misjudgment etc. 481.

credulous person etc. (*dupe*) 547.

V. be -credulous etc. *adj.*; *jurare in verba magistri*; follow implicitly; swallow, – whole, gulp down; take on trust; take for -granted, – gospel; run away with -a notion, – an idea; jump –, rush- to a conclusion; think the moon is made of green cheese; take –, grasp- the shadow for the substance; catch at straws.

impose upon etc. (*deceive*) 545.

Adj. credulous, gullible; easily -deceived etc. 545; simple, green, soft, childish, silly, stupid; over-credulous, -confident; infatuated, superstitious; confiding etc. (*believing*) 484.

Phr. the wish the father to the thought; *credo quia impossibile.*

487. Incredulity.—N. incredul-ous-ness, -ity; skepticism, pyrrhonism; want of faith etc. (*irreligion*) 989.

suspiciousness etc. *adj.*; scrupulosity; suspicion etc. (*unbelief*) 485; dissent etc. 489.

unbeliever, skeptic, aporetic; atheist, agnostic, infidel, disbeliever, misbeliever, pyrrhonist etc. 989; heretic etc. (*heterodox*) 984.

v. be -incredulous etc. *adj.*; distrust etc. (*disbelieve*) 485; refuse to believe; shut one's -eyes, – ears- to; turn a deaf ear to; hold aloof; ignore; *nullis jurare in verba magistri*.

Adj. incredulous, skeptical, unbelieving, inconvincible; hard –, shy- of belief; suspicious, scrupulous, distrustful, heterodox etc. 984.

488. Assent.—N. assent, -ment; acquiescence, admission; nod; ac-, con-cord, -cordance; agreement etc. 23; affirm-ance, -ation; recognition, acknowledgment, avowal; confession, – of faith.

unanimity, common consent, *consensus*, acclamation, chorus, *vox populi*; popular –, current- -belief, – opinion; public opinion; concurrence etc. (*of causes*) 178; co-operation etc. (*voluntary*) 709.

ratification, confirmation, corroboration, approval, acceptance, *visa*; indorsement etc. (*record*) 551.

consent etc. (*compliance*) 762.

affirmant, consenter, covenantor, subscriber, endorser, upholder.

V. assent; give –, yield –, not- assent; acquiesce; agree etc. 23; receive, accept, accede, accord, concur, lend oneself to, consent, coincide, reciprocate, go with; be -at one with etc. *adj.*; go along −, chime in −, strike in −, close- with; echo, enter into one's views, agree in opinion; vote −, give one's voice- for; recognize; subscribe −, conform −, defer- to; say -yes, − ditto, − amen; − aye- to.

acknowledge, own, admit, allow, avow, confess; concede etc. (*yield*) 762; come round to; abide by; permit etc. 760.

come to −, arrive at- -an understanding, − terms, − an agreement.

con-, af-firm; ratify, approve, endorse, countersign; visa; corroborate etc. 467.

go −, swim- with the stream, float with the current; be in the fashion, join in the chorus; be in every mouth.

Adj. assenting etc. *v.*; of one -accord, − mind; of the same mind, at one with, agreed, acquiescent, content; willing etc. 602.

un-contradicted, -challenged, -questioned, - controverted.

carried −, agreed- -*nem. con.* etc. *adv.*; unanimous; agreed on all hands, carried by acclamation.

affirmative etc. 535.

Adv. yes, yea, ay, aye, true; good; well; very - well, − true; well and good; granted; *placet*; even −, just- so; to be sure, surely, 'thou hast said;' truly, exactly, precisely, that's just it, indeed, certainly, certes, *ex concesso*; of course, unquestionably, assuredly, no doubt, doubtless, undoubtedly.

be it so; so -be it, − let it be, so mote it be; amen; with all my heart; willingly etc. 602.

with one -consent, − voice, − accord; unanimously, *unâ voce*, by common consent, in chorus, to a man, *nem. con.*; *nemine - contradicente, − dissentiente*; without a dissentient voice; as one man, one and all, on all hands.

489. Dissent.—N. dissent; discordance etc. (*disagreement*) 24; difference −, diversity- of opinion.

non-conformity etc. (*heterodoxy*) 984; protestantism, recusancy, schism; disaffection; secession etc. 624; recantation etc. 607.

dissension etc. (*discord*) 713; discontent etc. 832; cavilling.

protest; contradiction etc. (*denial*) 536; noncompliance etc. (*rejection*) 764; disapprobation etc. 932; hartal.

dissent-ient, -er; non-juror, -content; recusant, sectary, schismatic, protestant, non-conformist, separatist, non-co-operator, conscientious objector, passive resister.

V. dissent, demur; call in question etc. (*doubt*) 485; differ in opinion, disagree; say -no etc. 536; refuse -assent, − to admit; cavil, protest, raise one's voice against, make bold to differ; repudiate; contradict etc. (*deny*) 536; agree to differ.

have no notion of, differ *toto caelo*; revolt -at, − from the idea.

shake the head, shrug the shoulders; look - askance, − askant.

secede; recant etc. 607.

Adj. dissenting etc. *v.*; negative etc. 536; dissident, -entient; unconsenting etc. (*refusing*) 764;

non-content, -juring; protestant, recusant; unconvinced, -verted.

unavowed, unacknowledged; out of the question.

discontented etc. 832; unwilling etc. 603; extorted.

sectarian, denominational, schismatic, heterodox, intolerant.

Adv. no etc. 536; at -variance, − issue- with; under protest; *non placet.*

Int. God forbid! not for the world; not on your life; I beg to differ; I'll be hanged if; never tell me; your humble servant, pardon me; tell that to the marines.

Phr. many men many minds; *quot homines tot sententiae; tant s'en faut; il s'en faut bien.*

490. Knowledge.—N. knowledge; cogn-izance, -ition, -oscence; acquaintance, experience, ken, privity, insight, familiarity; com-, ap-prehension; recognition; appreciation etc. (*judgment*) 480; intuition; consci-ence, -ousness; preception, precognition; acroamatics.

light, enlightenment; glimpse, inkling; side light; glimmer, -ing; dawn; scent, suspicion; impression etc. (*idea*) 453; discovery etc. 480*a.*

system −, body- of knowledge; science, philosophy, pansophy; theory, Etiology; circle of the sciences; pandect, doctrine, body of doctrine; cy-, ency-clopedia; school etc. (*system of opinions*) 484.

tree of knowledge; republic of letters etc. (*language*) 560.

erudition, learning, lore, scholarship, reading, letters; literature; booklearning, bookishness; biblio-mania, -latry; information, general information; store of -knowledge etc.; education etc. (*teaching*) 537; culture, attainments; acquirements, -sitions; accomplishments, proficiency; practical knowledge etc. (*skill*) 698; higher education, liberal education; dilettantism; rudiments etc. (*beginning*) 66.

deep −, profound −, solid −, accurate −, acroatic −, acroamatic −, vast −, extensive −, encyclopedical- -knowledge; − learning; omniscience, pantology.

march of intellect; progress −, advance- of -science, − learning; schoolmaster abroad.

V. know, ken, scan, wot; wot −, be aware etc. *adj.*- of; ween, weet, trow, have, possess.

conceive; ap-, com-prehend; take, realize, understand, appreciate; fathom, make out; recognize, discern, perceive, see, get a sight of, experience.

know full well; have −, possess- some knowledge of; be -*au courant* etc. *adj.*; have -in one's head, − at one's fingers' ends; know by -heart, − rote; be master of; *connaître le dessous des cartes*, know what's what etc. 698.

see one's way; learn, discover etc. 480*a.*

come to one's knowledge etc. (*information*) 527.

Adj. knowing etc. *v.*; cognitive; acroamatic.

aware −, cognizant −, conscious- of; acquainted −, made acquainted- with; privy −, no stranger- to; *au -fait, − courant*; in the secret; up −, alive- to; sensible of; behind the -scenes, − curtain; let into; apprized −, informed- of; undeceived.

proficient −, versed −, read −, forward −,

strong –, at home- in; conversant –, familiar-
with.

erudite, instructed, learned, lettered, educated;
high-brow; well-conned, -informed, -read, -
grounded, -educated; enlightened, shrewd, in-
sightful, *savant*, blue, bookish, scholastic, solid,
profound, deep-read, book-learned; accomplished
etc. (*skilful*) 698; omniscient; self-taught, -
educated.

known etc. *v.*; ascertained, well-known,
recognized, received, notorious, noted; proverbial;
familiar, – as household words, to every
schoolboy; hackneyed, trite, commonplace.

knowable, cogn-oscible, -izable.

Adv. to –, to the best of- one's knowledge.

Phr. one's eyes being opened etc. (*disclosure*)
529.

491. Ignorance.—N. ignorance, nescience,
tabula rasa, crass ignorance, *ignorance crasse*;
unacquaintance; unconsciousness etc. *adj.*; dark-,
blind-ness; incomprehension, inexperience, simplicity.

unknown quantities, *x, y, z.*

sealed book, *terra incognita*, virgin soil, unexplored ground; dark ages.

[Imperfect knowledge] smattering, super-
ficiality, half-learning, sciolism, glimmering;
bewilderment etc. (*uncertainty*) 475; incapacity.

[Affectation of knowledge] pedantry; charlatan-
ry, -ism.

V. be -ignorant etc. *adj.*; not -know etc. 490;
know -not, – not what, – nothing of; have no -
idea, – notion, – conception; not have the
remotest idea; not know chalk from cheese.

ignore, be blind to; keep in ignorance etc. (*conceal*) 528.

see through a glass darkly; have a -film over the
eyes, – glimmering etc. *n.*; wonder whether; not
know what to make of etc. (*unintelligibility*) 519;
not pretend –, not take upon oneself to say.

Adj. ignorant, nescient; un-knowing, -aware, -
acquainted, -apprized, -witting, -weeting, -
conscious; wit-, weet-less; a stranger to; unconversant.

un-informed, -cultivated, -versed, -instructed, -
taught, -initiated, -tutored, -schooled, -guided, -
enlightened; Philistine; behind the age.

shallow, superficial, green, rude, empty, half-
learned, illiterate; un-read, -informed, -educated, -
learned, -lettered, -bookish; empty-headed;
lowbrow; pedantic.

in the dark; be-nighted, -lated; blind-ed, -fold;
hoodwinked; misinformed; *au bout de son latin*, at
the end of his tether; at fault; at sea etc. (*uncertain*)
475; caught tripping.

un-known, -apprehended, -explained, -
ascertained, -investigated, -explored, -heard of, -
perceived; concealed etc. 528; novel.

Adv. ignorantly etc. *adj.*; unawares; for -
anything, – aught- one knows; not that one knows.

Int. God –, Heaven –, the Lord- –, nobody-
knows.

Phr. a little learning is a dangerous thing.

492. Scholar.—N. scholar, *connoisseur*,
savant, pundit, schoolman, professor, graduate,
wrangler, moonshee; academ-ician, -ist; fellow,
don, post graduate, advanced student; master –,
bachelor- of arts; doctor, licentiate, gownsman;
philo-sopher, -math; scientist, clerk; soph, -ist, -
ister; linguist, classicist; glosso-, etymo-, philologist;
philologer; lexico-, glosso-grapher; scholiast, commentator. annotator, grammarian; *littérateur,
literati, dilettanti, illuminati*; Mezzofanti, admirable Crichton, Maecenas.

book-worm, *helluo librorum*, biblio-phile, -
maniac; blue-stocking, *bas-bleu*; big-wig, learned
Theban.

learned –, literary- man; *homo multarum
literarum*; man of -learning, – letters, –
education; high-brow, intelligentsia.

antiquar-ian, -y; archeologist; sage etc. (*wise
man*) 500.

pendant, *doctrinaire*; pedagogue, Dr. Pangloss;
pantologist.

teacher etc. 540; schoolboy etc. (*learner*) 541.

Adj. learned etc. 490; brought up at the feet of
Gamaliel.

493. Ignoramus.—N. ignoramus, illiterate,
moron, dunce, numskull; wooden spoon; no
scholar.

sciolist, smatterer, dabbler, half-scholar;
charlatan; wiseacre.

novice, griffin; greenhorn etc. (*dupe*) 547; tyro
etc. (*learner*) 541.

lubber etc. (*bungler*) 701; fool etc. 501; pedant
etc. 492.

Adj. bookless, shallow, simple, dense, dumb,
thick, dull, ignorant etc. 491.

494. Truth. [Object of knowledge.]—**N.** fact,
reality etc. (*existence*) 1; plain matter of fact;
nature etc. (*principle*) 5; truth, verity; gospel; orthodoxy etc. 983a; authenticity; veracity etc. 543.

accuracy, exactitude; exact-, precise-ness etc.
adj.; precision, delicacy; rigor, mathematical
precision, punctuality; clockwork precision etc.
(*regularity*) 80.

orthology; *ipsissima verba*; letter of the law,
realism.

plain –, honest –, sober –, naked –,
unalloyed –, unqualified –, stern –, exact –, in-
trinsic- truth; *nuda veritas*; the very thing; not an -
illusion etc. 495; real Simon Pure; unvarnished
tale; the truth, the whole truth and nothing but the
truth; just the thing.

V. be -true etc. *adj.*, – the case; stand the test;
have the true ring; hold -good, – true, – water;
conform to rule.

render –, prove- -true etc. *adj.*; substantiate etc.
(*evidence*) 467.

get at the truth etc. (*discover*) 480a.

Adj. real, actual etc. (*existing*) 1; veritable, true;
certain etc. 474; substantially –, categorically-
true etc; true -to the letter; – to life, – to scale, –
the facts, – as gospel; unimpeachable; veracious
etc. 543; unre-, uncon-futed; un-ideal -imagined;
realistic.

exact, accurate, definite, precise, well defined,
just, right, correct, strict, severe; close etc. (*similar*)
17; literal; rigid, rigorous; scrupulous etc. (*con-*

scientious) 939; religiously exact, punctual, mathematical, scientific; faithful, constant, unerring; curious, particular, punctilious, meticulous, nice, delicate, fine.

genuine, authentic, legitimate, pukka; orthodox etc. 983*a*; official, *ex officio*.

pure, natural, sound, sterling; un-sophisticated, -adulterated, -varnished, -colored; in its true colors.

well-grounded, -founded; solid, substantial, tangible, valid; undis-torted, -guised; un-affected, -exaggerated, -romantic, -flattering.

Adv. truly etc.*adj.*; verily, indeed, in reality; as a matter of fact; beyond -doubt, – question; with truth etc. (*veracity*) 543; certainly etc. (*certain*) 474; actually etc. (*existence*) 1; in effect etc. (*intrinsically*) 5.

exactly etc. *adj.* ; *ad amussim*; *verbatim*, – *et literatim*; word for word, literally, *literatim*, *totidem verbis, sic*, to the letter, chapter and verse, *ipsissimis verbis; ad unguem*; to an inch; to a -nicety, – hair, – tittle, – turn, – T; *au pied de la lettre*; neither more nor less; in -every respect, – all respects; *sous tous les rapports*; at -any rate, – all events; strictly speaking.

Phr. the -truth, – fact- is; *rem acu tetigisti.*

495. Error.—**N.** error, fallacy; misconception, -apprehension, -understanding; inexactness etc. *adj.*; laxity; misconstruction etc. (*misinterpretation*) 523; miscomputation etc. (*misjudgment*) 481; *non-sequitur* etc. 477; misstatement, -report; anachronism; malapropism.

mistake; miss, fault, blunder, boner, bloomer, howler, *quid pro quo*, cross purposes, oversight, misprint, *erratum, corrigendum*, slip, blot, flaw, loose thread; trip, stumble etc. (*failure*) 732; botchery etc. (*want of skill*) 699; slip of the -tongue, – pen; *lapsus -linguae*, – *calami*, clerical error; bull etc. (*absurdity*) 497.

il-, de-lusion; false -impression, – idea; bubble; self-deceit, -deception; warped notion; mists of error; superstition, exploded notion.

heresy etc. (*heterodoxy*) 984; hallucination etc. (*insanity*) 503; false light etc. (*fallacy of vision*) 443; dream etc. (*fancy*) 515; fable etc. (*untruth*) 546; bias etc. (*misjudgment*) 481; misleading etc. *v.*

V. be -erroneous etc. *adj.*

cause error; mis-lead, -guide; lead -astray, – into error; beguile, misinform etc. (*misteach*) 538; delude; give a false -impression, – idea; falsify, garble, misstate; deceive etc. 545; lie etc. 544.

err; be -in error etc. *adj.*; – mistaken etc. *v.*; be deceived etc. (*duped*) 547; mistake, receive a false impression, deceive oneself; fall into –, lie under –, labor under- -an error etc. *n.*; be in the wrong, blunder; mis-apprehend, -conceive, -understand, -reckon, -count, -calculate etc. (*misjudge*) 481.

play –, be- at cross purposes etc. (*misinterpret*) 523.

trip, stumble; lose oneself etc. (*uncertainty*) 475; go astray; fail etc. 732; take the wrong sow by the ear etc. (*mismanage*) 699; put the saddle on the wrong horse; reckon without one's host; take the shadow for the substance etc. (*credulity*) 486; dream etc. (*imagine*) 515.

Adj. erroneous, untrue, false, devoid of truth, fallacious, faulty, apocryphal, unreal, ungrounded,

groundless; unsubstantial etc. 4; heretical etc. (*heterodox*) 984; unsound; illogical etc. 477; wrong.

in-, un-exact; in-accurate, -correct; indefinite etc. (*uncertain*) 475.

illus-ive, -ory; delusive; mock; ideal etc. (*imaginary*) 515; spurious etc. 545; deceitful etc. 544; perverted.

controvertible, unsustain-able, -ed; unauthenticated, untrustworthy.

exploded, refuted, discarded.

in –, under an- error etc. *n.*; mistaken etc. *v.*; tripping etc. *v.*; out, – in one's reckoning; aberrant; beside –, wide of the- -mark, – truth; astray etc. (*at fault*) 475; on -a false, – the wrongscent; in the wrong box; at cross purposes, all in the wrong, all abroad, at sea.

Adv. more or less.

496. Maxim.—**N.** maxim, aphorism; apo-, apoph-thegm; *dictum*, saying, gnome, adage, saw, proverb, epigram; sentence, *mot*, motto, word, byword, precept, moral, phylactery, *protasis*, brocard.

axiom, postulate, theorem, *scholium*, truism.

reflection etc. (*idea*) 453; conclusion etc. (*judgment*) 480; golden rule etc. (*precept*) 697; principle, *principia*; profession of faith etc. (*belief*) 484; formula.

wise –, sage –, received –, admitted –, recognized- maxim etc.; true –, common –, hackneyed –, trite –, commonplace- saying etc.

Adj. aphoristic, proverbial, phylacteric; axiomatic, gnomic.

Adv. as -the saying is, – they say.

497. Absurdity.—**N.** absurd-ity, -ness etc. *adj.*; imbecility etc. 499; alogy, nonsense, paradox, inconsistency; stultiloqu-y, -ence, futility.

blunder, muddle, bull; Irish-, Hibernic-ism; slip-slop; anti climax; bathos; sophism etc. 477.

farce, burlesque, *galimatias*, *amphigouri*, rhapsody; farrago etc. (*disorder*) 59; extravagance, romance; sciomachy.

joke, catch, sell, pun, verbal quibble, macaronic, jargon, fustian, twaddle etc. (*no meaning*) 517; exaggeration etc. 549; moonshine, stuff; mare's nest.

vagary, tomfoolery, mummery, monkey trick, practical joke, *boutade, escapade.*,

V. play the fool etc. 499; stultify, blunder, muddle; joke; talk nonsense, *parler à tort et à travers; battre la campagne*; be -absurd etc. *adj.*

Adj. absurd, nonsensical, preposterous, egregious, senseless, farcical, inconsistent, ridiculous, extravagant, quibbling, futile; macaronic, punning, paradoxical.

foolish etc. 499; sophistical etc. 477; unmeaning etc. 517; without rhyme or reason; fantastic.

Int. fiddle-de-dee! pish! pish and tush! pho! stuff and nonsense! rubbish! !rot! bosh! in the name of the Prophet—figs!

Phr. *credat Judaeus Apella*; tell it to the marines.

498. Intelligence. Wisdom.—**N.** intelligence, capacity, comprehension, understanding, intellect etc. 450; nous, parts, sagacity, mother wit, wit, *esprit*, gumption, quick parts, grasp of intellect; acuteness etc. *adj.*; acumen, subtlety, penetration; perspica-cy, -city; discernment; long-headedness, due sense of, good judgment; discrimination etc. 465; craftiness, cunning etc. 702; refinement etc. (*taste*) 850.

head, brains, gray matter, headpiece, upper story, long head; eagle -eye, — glance; eye of a -lynx, — hawk.

wisdom, sapience, sense; good —, common —, plain —, horse- sense; clear thinking; rationality, reason; reasonableness etc. *adj.*; judgment; solidity, depth, profundity, caliber; enlarged views; reach —, compass- of thought; enlargement of mind.

genius, inspiration, *geist*, fire of genius, heaven-born genius, soul; talent etc. (*aptitude*) 698.

[Wisdom in action] prudence etc. 864; vigilance etc. 459; tact etc. 698; foresight etc. 510; sobriety, self-possession, *aplomb*, ballast, mental -poise, — balance.

a bright thought, inspiration, brainwave, not a bad idea.

V. be -intelligent etc. *adj.*; have all one's wits about one; understand etc. (*intelligible*) 518; catch —, take in- an idea; take a -joke, — hint.

see -through, — at a glance, — with half an eye, — far into, — through a millstone; penetrate; discern etc. (*descry*) 441; foresee etc. 510.

discriminate etc. 465; know what's what etc. 698; listen to reason.

Adj. [Applied to persons] intelligent, quick of apprehension, keen, acute, alive, brainy, awake, bright, quick, sharp; quick-, keen-, clear-, sharp-eyed, -sighted, -witted; wide awake; canny, shrewd, astute; clear-headed; far-sighted etc. 510; discerning, perspicacious, penetrating, piercing; argute nimble-, needle-witted; sharp as a needle; alive to etc. (*cognizant*) 490; clever etc. (*apt*) 698; arch etc. (*cunning*) 702; *pas si bête*; acute etc. 682.

wise, sage, sapient, sagacious, reasonable, rational, sound, in one's right mind, sensible, *abnormis sapiens*, judicious, strong-minded.

un-prejudiced, -biassed, -bigoted, -prepossessed; un-dazzled, -perplexed; of unwarped judgment, impartial, equitable, fair, broad-minded.

cool; cool-, long-, hard-, strong-headed; long-sighted, calculating, thoughtful, reflecting; solid, deep, profound.

oracular; heaven-directed, -born.

prudent etc. (*cautious*) 864; sober, staid, solid; considerate, politic, wise in one's generation; watchful etc. 459; provident etc. (*prepared*) 673; in advance of one's age; wise as -a serpent, — Solomon, — Solon.

[Applied to actions] wise, sensible, reasonable, judicious; well-judged, -advised; prudent, politic; expedient etc. 646.

499. Imbecility. Folly.—N. want of -intelligence etc. 498, — intellect etc. 450; shallow-, silli-, foolish-ness etc. *adj.*; imbecility, incapacity, vacancy of mind, poverty of intellect, clouded perception, poor head, apartments to let; stup-, stolidity; hebetude, dull understanding, meanest capacity; short-sightedness; incompetence etc. (*unskilfulness*) 699.

one's weak side; bias etc. 481; infatuation etc. (*insanity*) 503.

simplicity, puerility, babyhood; dotage, anility, second childishness, senile dementia, fatuity; idiocy, -tism; driveling.

folly, frivolity, desipience, irrationality, trifling, ineptitude, nugacity, inconsistency, lip-wisdom, conceit; sophistry etc. 477; giddiness etc. (*inattention*) 458; eccentricity etc. 503; extravagance etc. (*absurdity*) 497; rashness etc. 863.

act of folly etc. 699.

V. be -imbecile etc. *adj.*; have no -brains, — sense etc. 498.

trifle, drivel, *radoter*, dote; ramble etc. (*madness*) 503; play the -fool, — monkey, — goat, take leave of one's senses; not see an inch beyond one's nose; stultify oneself etc. 699; talk nonsense etc. 497.

Adj. [Applied to persons] un-intelligent, -intellectual, -reasoning; mind-, wit-, reason-, brainless; having no -head etc. 498; not -bright etc. 498; inapprehensible.

weak-, addle-, puzzle-, blunder-, muddle-, muddy-, pig-, beetle-, maggotty-, gross-headed; beef-, fat- -witted, -headed.

weak, feeble-minded; dull-, shallow-, rattle-, lack-brained; half-, nit-, short-, dull-, blunt-witted; shallow-, clod-, addle-pated; dim-, short-sighted; thick-skulled; weak in the upper story.

shallow, *borné*, weak, wanting, soft, nutty, sappy, spoony; dull, — as a beetle; stupid, heavy, insulse, obtuse, blunt, stolid, doltish, asinine; inapt etc. 699; prosaic etc. 843.

child-ish, -like; infant-ine, -ile; baby-, bab-ish; puerile; anile; simple etc. (*credulous*) 486.

fatuous, idiotic, imbecile, moronic, driveling; blatant, babbling; vacant; sottish; bewildered etc. 475.

blockish, unteachable; Boeot-ian, -ic; bovine; un-gifted, -discerning, -enlightened, -wise, -philosophical; apish.

foolish, silly, senseless, irrational, insensate, nonsensical, inept; maudlin.

narrow-minded etc. 481; bigoted etc. (*obstinate*) 606; giddy etc. (*thoughtless*) 458; rash etc. 863; eccentric etc. (*crazed*) 503.

[Applied to actions] foolish, unwise, indiscreet, injudicious, improper, unreasonable, without reason, ridiculous, silly, stupid, asinine; ill-imagined, -advised, -judged, -devised; inconsistent, irrational, unphilosophical; extravagant etc. (*nonsensical*) 497; sleeveless, idle; useless etc. 645; inexpedient etc. 647; frivolous etc. (*trivial*) 643; absurd etc. 497.

Phr. *Davis sum non Oedipus.*

500. Sage.—N. sage, wise man; pundit; master-mind, — spirit of the age; longhead, thinker, philosopher.

authority, oracle, mentor, luminary, shining light, *esprit fort*, *magnus Apollo*, Solon, Solomon, Nestor, Magi, 'second Daniel.'

man of learning etc. 492; expert etc. 700; wizard etc. 994.

[Ironically] wiseacre, bigwig.

Adj. wise, learned; authoritative, oracular; erudite etc. 490; venerable, reverenced, revered, *emeritus*.

501. Fool.—N. fool, idiot, tomfool, wiseacre, simpleton, Simple Simon, nit-wit, witling, dizzard, donkey, ass; ninny, -hammer; moron, dolt, booby, Tom Noddy, looby, hoddy-doddy, noddy, nonny, noodle, nizy, owl; goose, -cap; *imbécile*; gaby, *radoteur*, nincompoop, *badaud*, zany; trifler, babbler; pretty fellow; natural, *niais*.

child, baby, infant, innocent, milksop, sop.

oaf, lout, loon, lown, dullard, doodle, calf, colt, buzzard, block, put, stick, stock, numps, tony.

bull-, dunder-, addle-, block-, dull-, logger-, dolt-, jolter-, beetle-, gross-, thick-, giddy-head; num-, thick- skull; lack-, shallow-brain; half-, lack-wit; dunder-pate; fat-head, poor stick.

sawney, gowk; clod, -hopper; clod-, clot-poll, · pate; bull-calf; men of Boeotia, wise men of Gotham.

un sot à triple étage, sot; jobbernowl, changeling, mooncalf, *gobemouche*.

dotard, driveller; old -fogey, – woman; crone, grandmother.

greenhorn etc. (*dupe*) 547; dunce etc. (*ignoramus*) 493; lubber etc. (*bungler*) 701; madman etc. 504.

one who -will not set the Thames on fire, – did not invent gunpowder; *qui n'a pas inventé la poudre*; no conjuror.

502. Sanity.—N. sanity; soundness etc. *adj.*; rationality, normality, sobriety, lucidity, lucid interval; senses, sober senses, sound mind, *mens sana*.

V. be -sane etc. *adj.*; retain one's senses, – reason.

become -sane etc. *adj.*; come to one's senses, sober down.

render -sane etc. *adj.*; bring to one's senses, sober.

Adj. sane, rational, reasonable, *compos mentis*, of sound mind; sound, -minded.

self-possessed; sober, -minded.

in one's -sober senses, – right mind; in possession of one's faculties.·

Adv. sanely etc. *adj.*

503. Insanity.—N. disordered -reason, – intellect; diseased –, unsound –, abnormal- mind; derangement, unsoundness.

insanity, lunacy; madness etc. *adj.*; mania, *rabies*, *furor*, mental alienation, paranoia, aberration; *amentia*, dementation, -tia, -cy; *dementia praecox*; *morosis*, idiocy, phrenitis, frenzy, raving, incoherence, wandering, delirium, calenture of the brain, delusion, hallucination; lycanthropy, brain storm, *delirium tremens*, D.T.'s.

vertigo, dizziness, swimming; sunstroke, *coup de soleil*, siriasis.

fanaticism, infatuation, craze; oddity, eccentricity, twist, monomania; klepto-, dipso-mania; hypochondriasis etc. (*low spirits*) 837; *melancholia*, hysteria.

screw –, tile –, slate- loose; bee in one's bonnet, rats in the upper story.

dotage etc. (*imbecility*) 499.

V. be –, become- -insane etc. *adj.*; lose one's senses, – reason, – faculties, – wits; go –, run-

mad, run amuck; rave, dote, ramble, wander; drivel etc. (*be imbecile*) 499; have a -screw loose etc. *n.*, – devil; *avoir le diable au corps*; lose one's head etc. (*be uncertain*) 475.

derange, render – , drive- -mad etc. *adj.*; madden, dementate, addle the wits, derange the head, infatuate, befool; turn -the brain, – one's head.

Adj. insane, mad, lunatic; crazy, crazed, *aliéné*, *non compos mentis*; not right, cracked, touched; bereft of reason; unhinged, deranged, unsettled in one's mind; insensate, reasonless, beside oneself, demented, daft; phren-, fren-zied, -etic; possessed, – with a devil; far gone, maddened, moonstruck; shatterpated; barmy; mad-, scatter-, shatter-, crackbrained, off one's head; bug-house, *loco*.

maniacal; manic, manic-depressive; delirious, light-headed, incoherent, rambling, doting, wandering; frantic, raving, stark staring mad, amok, amuck.

corybantic, dithyrambic; rabid, giddy, vertiginous, dizzy, wild, haggard, mazed; flighty; distracted, -aught; bewildered etc. (*uncertain*) 475.

mad as a -March hare, – hatter; of -unsound mind etc. *n.* touched –, wrong –, not right- in one's -head, – mind, – wits, – upper story; out of one's -mind, – senses, – wits; not in one's right mind.

fanatical, infatuated, odd, eccentric; hypp-ed, -ish.

imbecile, silly etc. 499.

Adv. like one possessed.

Phr. the mind having lost its balance; the reason under a cloud; *tête -exaltée, -montée*.

504. Madman—N. madman, lunatic, maniac, bedlamite, candidate for Bedlam, raver, madcap; energumen; paranoiac; auto-, mono-, pyro-, megalo-, dipso-, klepto-maniac; hypochondriac etc. (*low spirit*) 837.

dreamer etc. 515; rhapsodist, seer, high-flier, enthusiast, crank, eccentric, nut, fanatic, *fanatico*; *exalté*; knight errant, Don Quixote.

idiot etc. 501.

505. Memory.—N. memory, remembrance; reten-tion, -tiveness; tenacity; *veteris vestigia flammae*; tablets of the memory; readiness.

reminiscence, recognition, recurrence, recollection, rememoration; retrospect, -ion; after-thought.

suggestion etc. (*information*) 527; prompting etc. *v.*; hint, reminder, token of remembrance, *memento*, *souvenir*, keepsake, relic, *memorandum*; remembrancer, flapper; memorial etc. (*record*) 551; commemoration etc. (*celebration*) 883.

things to be remembered, *memorabilia*.

art of –, artificial- memory; *memoria technica*; mnemo-nics, -technics; phrenotypics; Mnemosyne; memorandum-, note-, engagement-, prompt-book.

retentive –, tenacious –, green –, trustworthy –, capacious –, faithful –, correct –, exact –, ready –, prompt- memory.

V. remember, mind; retain the -memory, – remembrance- of; keep in view.

have –, hold –, bear –, carry –, keep –, retain- in *or* in the -thoughts, – mind, – memory, – remembrance; be in –, live in –, remain in –, dwell in –, haunt –, impress- one's -memory, – thoughts, – mind.

sink in the mind; run in the head; not be able to get it out of one's head; be deeply impressed with; rankle etc. (*revenge*) 919.

recur to the mind; flash -on the mind, – across the memory.

recognize, recollect, bethink oneself, recall, call up, conjure up, retrace; look –, trace- -back, – backwards; think –, look back- upon; review; call –, recall –, bring- to mind; remembrance; carry one's thoughts back; rake up the past.

suggest etc. (*inform*) 527; prompt; put –, keep-in mind; remind; fan the embers; call –, summon –, rip- up; renew; *infandum renovare dolorem*; task –, tax –, jog –, flap –, refresh –, rub up –, awaken- the memory; pull by the sleeve; bring back the memory, put in remembrance, memorialize.

get –, have –, learn –, know –, say –, repeat- by -heart, – rote; drive –, get- into -one's head; say one's lesson; repeat, – as a parrot; have at one's finger's ends.

commit to memory; memorize; con, – over; fix –, rivet –, imprint –, impress –, stamp –, grave –, engrave –, store –, treasure up –, bottle up –, embalm –, enshrine- in the memory; load –, store –, stuff –, burden- the memory with.

redeem from oblivion; keep the memory -alive, – green; *tangere ulcus*; keep up the memory of;. commemorate etc. (*celebrate*) 883.

make a note of etc. (*record*) 551.

Adj. remember-ing, -ed etc. *v.*; mindful, reminiscential; retained in the memory etc. *v.*; pent up in one's memory; fresh; green, – in remembrance, still vivid; unforgotten, present to the mind; within one's -memory etc. *n.*; indelible; not to be forgotten, unforgettable, enduring; uppermost in one's thoughts; memorable etc. (*important*) 642.

Adv. by -heart, – rote; without book, *memoriter*.

in memory of; *in memoriam*; suggestive.

Phr. *manet altâ mente repostum*; *forsan et haec olim meminisse juvabit*.

506. Oblivion.—N. oblivion; forgetfulness etc. *adj.*; obliteration etc. 552, of –, insensibility etc. 823 to- the past.

short –, treacherous –, loose –, slippery –, failing- memory; decay –, failure –, lapse- of memory; memory like a sieve; waters of -Lethe, – oblivion, *amnesia*.

pardon, acquittal, amnesty, oblivion; absolution.

V. forget; be -forgetful etc. *adj.*; fall –, sink-into oblivion; have -a short memory etc. *n.* – no head.

forget one's own name, have on the tip of one's tongue, come in at one ear and go out at the other.

slip –, escape –, fade from –, die away from-the memory; lose, – sight of.

unlearn; efface etc. 552 –, discharge- from the memory; consign to -oblivion, – the tomb of the Capulets; think no more of etc. (*turn the attention from*) 458; cast behind one's back, wean one's thoughts from; let bygones be bygones etc. (*forgive*) 918.

Adj. forgotten etc. *v.*; unremembered, past recollection, bygone, out of mind; buried –, sunk-in oblivion; clean forgotten; gone out of one's - head, – recollection.

forgetful, oblivious, mindless, heedless, Lethean; insensible etc. 823- to the past.

Phr. *non mi ricordo*; the memory -failing. – deserting one, – being at (*or* in) fault.

507. Expectation.—N. expect-ation, -ance, - ancy; anticipation, reckoning, calculation; contingency; foresight etc. 510.

contemplation, prospection, look out; prospect, perspective, horizon, vista; destiny etc. 152.

suspense, waiting, abeyance; curiosity etc. 455; anxious –, ardent –, eager –, breathless –, sanguine- expectation; torment of Tantalus.

presumption, hope etc. 858; trust etc. (*belief*) 484; prognostication, auspices etc. (*prediction*) 511.

V. expect; look -for, – out for, – forward to; hope for, anticipate; have in -prospect, – contemplation; keep in view; contemplate, promise oneself; not -wonder etc. 870 -at, – if.

wait –. tarry –, lie in wait –, watch –, bargain- for; keep a good, – sharp- look-out for; await; stand at 'attention,' abide, bide one's –, mark- time, watch.

foresee etc. 510; prepare for etc. 673; forestall etc. (*be early*) 132; count upon etc. (*believe in*) 484; think likely etc. (*probability*) 472; make one's mouth water.

lead one to expect etc. (*predict*) 511; have in store for etc. (*destiny*) 152.

prick up one's ears, hold one's breath.

Adj. expectant; expecting etc. *v.*; in -expectation etc. *n.*; on the watch etc. (*vigilant*) 459; open - eyed, -mouthed; agape, gaping, all agog; on - tenterhooks, – tiptoe, – the tiptoe of expectation; *aux aguets*; ready; curious etc. 455; looking forward to; prepared for; on the rack.

expected etc. *v.*; long expected, foreseen; in prospect etc. *n.*; prospective; in -one's eye, – view, – the horizon; impending etc. (*destiny*) 152.

Adv. expectantly; in the event of; on the watch etc. *adj.*; with -breathless expectation etc. *n.*; – bated breath, – eyes, – ears strained; *arrectis auribus*; on edge.

Phr. we shall see; *nous verrons*.

508. Inexpectation.—N. in-, non-expectation; false expectation etc. (*disappointment*) 509; miscalculation etc. 481; unforeseen contingency, the unforeseen, the unexpected.

surprise, sudden burst, thunderclap, blow, shock; bolt out of the blue; eye-opener; wonder etc. 870.

V. not -expect etc. 507; be taken by surprise; start; miscalculate etc. 481; not bargain for; come –, fall- upon.

be -unexpected etc. *adj.*; come -unawares etc. *adv.*; turn up, pop, drop from the clouds; come –, burst –, flash –, bounce –, steal –, creep- upon one; come –, burst- like a thunder-clap; -bolt; take –, catch- -by surprise, – unawares, – napping.

pounce –, spring a mine- upon.

surprise, startle, take aback, electrify, stun, stagger, take away one's breath, throw off one's guard; astonish etc. (*strike with wonder*) 870.

Adj. non-expectant; surprised etc. *v.*; un-warned, -aware; off one's guard; inattentive etc. 458.

un-expected, -anticipated, -prepared for, -looked for, -foreseen, -hoped for; dropped from the clouds; beyond −, contrary to −, against- expectation; out of one's reckoning; unheard of etc. (*exceptional*) 83; startling; sudden etc. (*instantaneous*) 113.

Adv. abruptly, unexpectedly, plump, pop, *à l'improviste*, unawares; without -notice, − warning, − saying 'by your leave;' like a -thief in the night, − thunderbolt; in an unguarded moment; suddenly etc. (*instantaneously*) 113.

Int. heyday! etc. (*wonder*) 870.

Phr. little did one -think, − expect; nobody would ever -suppose, − think, − expect; who would have thought?'

509. Disappointment. [Failure of expectation.]—**N.** disappointment, disillusionment; blighted hope, balk; blow; slip 'twixt cup and lip; non-fulfilment of one's hopes; sad −, bitter- disappointment; trick of fortune; afterclap; false −, vain- expectation; miscalculation etc. 481; fool's paradise; much cry and little wool.

V. be disappointed; look -blank, − blue; look −, stand- -aghast etc. (*wonder*) 870; find to one's cost; laugh on the wrong side of one's mouth; find one a false prophet.

disappoint; crush −, dash −, balk −, disappoint −, blight −, falsify −, defeat −, not realize- one's -hope, − expectation; balk, jilt, bilk; play one -false, − a trick; dash the cup from the lips; tantalize; dumb-found, -founder; disillusion, -ize; dissatisfy, disgruntle.

Adj. disappointed etc. *v.*; disconcerted, aghast; out of one's reckoning; disgruntled.

Phr. the mountain brought forth a mouse; *nascitur ridiculus mus*; *parturiunt montes*; *diis aliter visum*, the bubble burst; one's countenance falling.

510. Foresight.—**N.** foresight, prospicience; prevision, longsightedness; anticipation; providence etc. (*preparation*) 673.

fore-thought, -cast; pre-deliberation, -surmise; foregone conclusion etc. (*prejudgment*) 481; prudence etc. (*caution*) 864.

foreknowledge; *prognosis*; pre-cognition, -science, -notion, -sentiment; second sight; sagacity etc. (*intelligence*) 498.

prospect etc. (*expectation*) 507; foretaste; prospectus etc. (*plan*) 626.

V. foresee; look -forwards to, − ahead, − beyond; scent from afar; feel in one's bones; look −, pry −, peep into the future.

see one's way; see how the -land !ies, − wind blows, − cat jumps.

anticipate; expect etc. 507; be beforehand etc. (*early*) 132; predict etc. 511; fore-know, -judge, -cast; surmise; have an eye to the -future, − main chance; *respicere finem*; keep a sharp look-out etc. (*vigilance*) 459; forewarn etc. 668.

Adj. foreseeing etc. *v.*; prescient; anticipatory; far-seeing, -sighted; sagacious etc. (*intelligent*) 498; weather-wise; provident etc. (*prepared*) 673; prospective etc. 507.

Adv. against the time when.

511. Prediction.—**N.** prediction, announcement; program, programme etc. (*plan*) 626; premonition etc. (*warning*) 668; *prognosis*, prophecy, vaticination, Mantology, prognostication, premonstration, augur-y, -ation; a-, ha-riolation; fore-, a-boding; bode-, abode-ment; omin-ation, -ousness; auspices, forecast; sign, presage, prognostic; omen etc. 512; horoscope, nativity; sooth, -saying; fortune-telling; divination; crystal gazing, necromancy etc. 992; prophet etc. 512.

[Divination by the stars] astrology, horoscopy, astromancy, judicial astrology.*

[Place of prediction] *adytum*.

prefigur-ation, -ement; prototype, type.

V. predict, prognosticate, prophesy, vaticinate, divine, foretell, soothsay, augurate, tell fortunes; cast a -horoscope, − nativity; advise; forewarn etc. 668.

presage, augur, bode; a-, fore-bode, -cast; fore-be-token; pre-figure, -show; portend; fore-show, -shadow, shadow forth, typify, ominate, signify, point to, precurse.

usher in, herald, premise, announce; lower.

hold out −, raise −, excite- -expectation, − hope; bid fair, promise, lead one to expect; be the -precursor etc. 64.

Adj. predicting etc. *v.*; predictive, prophetic, fatidical, vaticinal, oracular, Sibylline, haruspical, weatherwise.

ominous, presageful, portentous; augur-ous, -al, -ial; auspici-al, -ous; prescious, monitory, ex-tispicious, premonitory, precusory, significant of, pregnant with, big with the fate of.

Phr. 'coming events cast their shadows before.'

*The following terms, expressive of different forms of divination, have been collected from various sources, and are here given as a curious illustration of bygone superstitions:

Divination *by oracles*, Theomancy; *by the Bible*, Bibliomancy; *by ghosts*, Psychomancy; *by spirits seen in a magic lens*, Cristallomantia; *by shadows or manes*, Sciomancy; *by appearances in the air*, Aeromancy, Chaomancy, *by the stars at birth*, Genethliacs; *by meteors*, Meteoromancy; *by winds*, Austromancy; *by sacrificial appearances*, Aruspicy (*or Haruspicy*), Hieromancy, Hieroscopy; *by the entrails of animals sacrificed*, Hieromancy; *by the entrails of a human sacrifice*, Anthropomancy; *by the entrails of fishes*, Ichthyomancy; *by sacrificial fire*, Pyromancy; *by red-hot iron*, Sideromancy; *by smoke from the alter*, Capnomancy; *by mice*, Myomancy; *by birds*, Orniscopy, Ornithomancy; *by a cock picking up grains*, Alectryomancy (*or Alectoromancy*); *by fishes*, Ophiomancy; *by herbs*, Botanomancy; *by water*, Hydromancy; *by fountains*, Pegomancy; *by a wand*, Rhabdomancy; *by dough of cakes*, Crithomancy; *by meal*, Aleuromancy, Alphitomancy; *by salt*, Halomancy; *by dice*, Cleromancy; *by arrows*, Belomancy; *by a balanced hatchet*, Axinomancy; *by a balanced sieve*, Coscinomancy; *by a suspended ring*, Dactyliomancy; *by dots made at random on paper*, Geomancy; *by precious stones*, Lithomancy; *by pebbles*, Pessomancy; *by pebbles drawn from a heap*, Psephomancy; *by mirrors*, Catoptromancy; *by writings in ashes*, Tephramancy; *by dreams*, Oneiromancy; *by the hand*, Palmistry, Chiromancy; *by nails reflecting the sun's rays*, Onychomancy; *by finger rings*, Dactylomancy; *by numbers*, Arithmancy; *by drawing lots*, Sortilege; *by passages in books*, Stichomancy; *by the letters forming the name of the person*, Onomancy, Nomancy; *by the*

features. Anthroposcopy; *by the mode of laughing.*
Geloscopy; *by ventriloquism,* Gastromancy; *by walking in
a circle,* Gyromancy; *by dropping melted wax into water,*
Ceromancy; *by currents,* Bletonism.

512. Omen.—N. omen, portent, presage,
prognostic, augury, auspice; sigh etc. (*indication*)
550; herald, forerunner, harbinger etc. (*precursor*)
64.

bird of ill omen, signs of the times; gathering
clouds; warning etc. 668.

prefigurement etc. 511.

513. Oracle.—N. oracle; prophet, -ess; seer,
soothsayer, augur, fortune-teller, palmist, medium,
clairvoyant, crystal gazer, witch, geomancer,
aruspex; a-, ha-ruspice; Sibyl; Python, -ess; Pythia;
Pythian −, Delphian- oracle; Monitor, Sphinx,
Tiresias, Cassandra, Sibylline leaves; Zadkiel, Old
Moore; sorcerer etc. 994; interpreter etc. 524.

514. Supposition.—N. supposition, assumption, postulation, condition, pre-supposition,
hypothesis, postulate, *postulatum*, theory, *data*;
pro-, position; *thesis*, theorem; proposal etc. (*plan*)
626.

bare −, vague −, loose- -supposition, −
suggestion; conceit; conjecture; guess, − work;
rough guess, shot; conjecturality; surmise,
suspicion, inkling, suggestion, suggestiveness,
association of ideas, hint; presumption etc. (*belief*)
484; divination, speculation.

theorist, speculator, doctrinarian, hypothesist.

V. suppose, conjecture, surmise, suspect, guess,
divine; theorize; pre-sume, -surmise, -suppose;
assume, fancy, wis, take it; give a guess, speculate,
believe, dare say, take it into one's head, take for
granted.

put forth; pro-pound, -pose; moot; hypothesize;
start, put a case, submit, move, make a motion;
hazard −, throw out −, put forward- a -
suggestion; − conjecture.

allude to, suggest, hint, put it into one's head.

suggest itself etc. (*thought*) 451; run in the head
etc. (*memory*) 505; marvel −, wonder- -if, −
whether.

Adj. supposing etc. *v.*; given, mooted,
postulatory; assumed etc. *v.*; supposit-ive, -itious;
gratuitous, speculative, conjectural, hypothetical,
suppositional, theoretical, academic, supposable,
presumptive, putative.

suggestive, allusive, stimulating.

Adv. if, − so be; an; on the -supposition etc. *n.*;
ex hypothesi; in -case, − the event of; *quasi*, as if,
provided; perhaps etc. (*by possibility*) 470; for
aught one knows.

515. Imagination.—N. imagination;
originality; invention; fancy; inspiration; *verve*;
empathy.

warm −, heated −, excited −, sanguine −, ardent −, fiery −, boiling −, wild −, bold −,
daring −, playful −, lively −, fertile- -
imagination, − fancy.

'mind's eye;' 'such stuff as dreams are made of.'

ideal-ity, -ism; romanticism, utopianism, castle-
building; dreaming; frenzy; ecs-, ex-tasy; calenture
etc. (*delirium*) 503; reverie, brown study, trance;
somnambulism.

conception, *vorstellung*, ercogitation, 'a fine
frenzy,' poetic frenzy, divine afflatus; cloud-,
dream-land; flight −, fumes- of fancy; 'thickcoming fancies;' creation −, coinage- of the brain;
imagery, word painting.

conceit, maggot, figment, myth, dream, vision,
shadow, chimera; phan-tasm, -tasy; fantasy, fancy;
whim, -sey; vagary, rhapsody, romance, *extravaganza*; air-drawn dagger, bugbear, nightmare;
flying Dutchman, great sea-serpent, man in the
moon, castle in the air, *château en Espagne*;
Utopia, Atlantis, happy valley, millennium, fairy
land; land of Prester John, kingdom of Micomicon;
work of fiction etc. (*novel*) 594; poetry etc. 597;
drama etc. 599; Arabian nights; *le pot au lait*;
dream of Alnaschar etc. (*hope*) 858; day −,
golden- dream

illusion etc. (*error*) 495; phantom etc. (*fallacy
of vision*) 443; *Fata Morgana* etc. (*ignis fatuus*)
423; vapor etc. (*cloud*) 353; stretch of the
imagination etc. (*exaggeration*) 549.

idealist, romanticist, visionary; mopus; romancer, dreamer; somnambulist; rhapsodist etc.
(*fanatic*) 504.

V. imagine, fancy, conceive; ideal-, real-ize;
dream, − of; 'give to airy nothing a local
habitation and a name.'

create, originate, devise, invent, coin, fabricate;
improvise, strike out something new.

set one's wits to work; strain −, crack- one's invention; rack −, ransack −, cudgel- one's brains;
excogitate.

give -play, − the reins, − a loose- to the -
imagination, − fancy; empathize; indulge in
reverie.

conjure up a vision; fancy −, represent −, picture −, figure- to oneself; envisage.

float in the mind; suggest itself etc. (*thought*)
451.

Adj. imagined etc. *v.*; *ben trovato*; air-drawn, -
built.

imagin-ing etc. *v.*, -ative; original, inventive,
creative, fertile, productive; ingenious.

romantic, high-flown, flighty, extravagant,
fanatic, ' enthusiastic, Utopian, Quixotic;
preposterous, rhapsodical.

ideal, unreal; in the clouds, *in nubibus*; unsubstantial etc. 4; illusory etc. (*fallacious*) 495; fictitious, theoretical, hypothetical.

fabulous, legendary; myth-ic, -ological;
chimerical; imagin-, vision-ary; notional; fan-cy, -
ciful, -tastic, -tastical; whimsical; fairy, -like.

dreamy, entranced, vaporous.

516. Meaning. [Idea to be conveyed.] [Thing
signified.]—**N.** meaning; signific-ation, -ance;
sense, expression; im-, pur-port; drift, tenor, implication, connotation, essence, force, spirit
bearing, coloring; scope.

matter; subject, -matter; argument, text, sum and
substance; gist etc. 5.

general –, broad –, substantial – colloquial –, literal –, plain –, simple –, accepted –, natural –, unstrained –, true etc. (*exact*) 494 –, honest etc. 543 –, *primâ facie* etc. (*manifest*) 525- meaning.

literality; literal interpretation; after acceptation; allusion etc. (*latency*) 526; suggestion etc. (*information*) 527; synonym; figure of speech etc. 521; acceptation etc. (*interpretation*) 522.

V. mean, signify, express, connote, denote; im-, pur-port; convey, imply, breathe, indicate, bespeak, bear a sense; tell –, speak- of; touch on; point –, allude- to; drive at; involve etc. (*latency*) 526; delcare etc. (*affirm*) 535.

understand by etc. (*interpret*) 522.

Adj. meaning etc. *v.*; expressive, suggestive, meaningful, allusive; signific-ant, -ative, -atory; pithy; full of –, pregnant with- meaning.

declaratory etc. 535; intelligible etc. 518; literal, metaphrastic; synonymous; tantamount etc. (*equivalent*) 27; implied etc. (*latent*) 526; explicit etc. 525; literal etc. 562.

Adv. to that effect; that is to say etc. (*being interpreted*) 522.

literally; evidently, from the context.

517. Unmeaningness. [Absence of meaning.]—**N.** unmeaningness etc. *adj.*; scrabble, scribble, scrawl, daub, (*painting*), strumming (*music*).

empty sound, dead letter, *vox et praeterea nihil*; 'a tale told by an idiot, full of sound and fury, signifying nothing;' 'sounding brass and a tinkling cymbal.'

nonsense, jargon, gibberish, jabber, mere words, hocus-pocus, fustian, rant, bombast, balderdash, palaver, patter, flummery, *verbiage*, babble, *bavardage*, *baragouin*, platitude, *niaiserie*; inanity; rigmarole, rodomontade; truism; *nugae canorae*; twaddle, twattle, fudge, trash; stuff, – and nonsense; bosh, rubbish, rot, drivel, moonshine, wishwash, fiddle-faddle, flapdoodle; absurdity etc. 497; vagueness etc. (*unintelligibility*) 519.

V. mean nothing; be -unmeaning etc. *adj.*; twaddle, quibble, rant, gabble, scrabble etc. *n.*

Adj. unmeaning; meaning-, sense-less; nonsensical; void of -sense etc. 516.

in-, un-expressive; vacant, fatuous; not significant; insignificant,.

trashy, washy, inane, vague, trumpery, trivial, fiddle-faddle, twaddling, quibbling.

unmeant, not expressed; tacit etc. (*latent*) 526.

inexpressible, undefinable, incommunicable.

Int. rubbish! etc. 497.

518. Intelligibility.—N. intelligibility, clearness, clarity, explicitness etc. *adj.*; lucidity, perspicuity; legibility, plain speaking etc. (*manifestation*) 525; precision etc. 494; a word to the wise.

V. be -intelligible etc. *adj.*; speak -for itself, – volumes; tell its own tale, lie on the surface.

render -intelligible etc. *adj.*; popularize, simplify, clear up; elucidate etc. (*explain*) 522.

understand, comprehend; 'take, – in; catch, grasp, recognize, follow, collect, master, make out;

see -with half an eye, – daylight, – one's way; enter into the ideas of; come to an understanding.

Adj. intelligible; clear, – as -day, – crystal, – noonday; lucid; per-, tran-spicuous; luminous, transparent; comprehensible.

easily understood, easy to understand, for the million, intelligible to the meanest capacity, popularized.

plain, distinct, explicit, clear-cut; positive; definite etc. (*precise*) 494.

graphic, vivid, telling; expressive etc. (*meaning*) 516; illustrative etc. (*explanatory*) 522.

un-ambiguous, -equivocal, -mistakable etc. (*manifest*) 525, -confused; legible, recognizable; obvious etc. 525.

Adv. in plain -terms, – words, – English.

Phr. he that runs may read etc. (*manifest*) 525.

519. Unintelligibility.—N. unintelligibility, incomprehensibility, imperspicuity; inconceivableness, vagueness etc. *adj.*; obscurity; ambiguity etc. 520; doubtful meaning; uncertainty etc. 475; perplexity etc. (*confusion*) 59; spinosity; *obscurum per obscurius*; mystification etc. (*concealment*) 528; latency etc. 526; transcendentalism.

paradox; enigma, riddle etc. (*secret*) 533; *dignus vindice nodus*; sealed book; steganography, freemasonry.

pons asinorum, asses' bridge; double –, high-Dutch, Greek, Hebrew; jargon etc. (*unmeaning*). 517.

obscurantist.

V. be -unintelligible etc. *adj.*; require - explanation etc. 522; have a doubtful meaning, pass comprehension.

render -unintelligible etc. *adj.*; conceal etc. 528; darken etc. 421; confuse etc. (*derange*) 61; perplex etc. (*bewilder*) 475.

not -understand etc. 518; lose, – the clue; miss; not know what to make of, be able to make nothing of, give it up; not be able to -account for, – make either head or tail of; be at sea etc. (*uncertain*) 475; wonder etc. 870; see through a glass darkly etc. (*ignorance*) 491.

not understand one another; play at cross purposes etc. (*misinterpret*) 523.

Adj. un-intelligible, -accountable, -decipherable, -discoverable, -knowable, -fathomable; in-cognizable, -explicable, -scrutable; inap-, incomprehensible; insol-uable, -uble; impenetrable.

illegible, indecipherable, as Greek to one, unexplained, paradoxical; enigmatic, -al; puzzling, baffling.

obscure, dark, muddy, clear as mud, seen through a mist, dim, nebulous, shrouded in mystery; undiscernible etc. (*invisible*) 447; misty etc. (*opaque*) 426; hidden etc. 528; latent etc. 526.

indefinite etc. (*indistinct*) 447; perplexed etc. (*confused*) 59; undetermined, vague, loose, ambiguous; mysterious; mystic, -al; transcendental; occult, recondite, esoteric, abstruse, crabbed.

incon-ceivable, -ceptible; searchless; above –, beyond –, past- comprehension; beyond one's depth; unconceived.

inexpressible, undefinable, incommunicable, unutterable, ineffable, unpronounceable.

520. Equivocalness. [Having a double sense.]—**N.** equivocalness etc. *adj.*; double - meaning etc. 516; ambiguity, *double entendre*, pun, paragram, *calembour*, quibble, *équivoque*, anagram; conundrum etc. (*riddle*) 533; word-play etc. (*wit*) 842; homonym, -y; amphibo-ly, -logy; ambiloquy.

Sphinx, Delphic oracle.

equivocation etc. (*duplicity*) 544; white lie, mental reservation etc. (*concealment*) 528.

V. be -equivocal etc. *adj.*; have two -meanings etc. 516; equivocate etc. (*palter*) 544.

Adj. equivocal,- ambiguous, amphibolous, homonymous; double-tongued etc. (*lying*) 544.

521. Metaphor.—**N.** figure of speech; *façon de parler*, way of speaking, colloquialism.

phrase etc. 566; figure, trope, metaphor, tralatition, metonymy, enallage, *catachresis*, synecdoche, autonomasia; irony, satire, figurativeness etc. *adj.*; image, -ry; *metalepsis*, type, anagoge, simile, personification, *prosopopaeia*, allegory, apologue, parable, fable; allusion, adumbration; application; euphemism; euphuism.

V. employ -metaphor etc. *n.*; personify, allegorize, adumbrate, shadow forth, apply, allude -, refer- to.

Adj. metaphorical etc. *n.*; figurative, catachrestical, typical, tralatitious, parabolic, allegorical, allusive, anagogical; ironical; colloquial.

Adv. so to -speak, - say, - express oneself; as it were.

Phr. *mutato nomine de te fabula nattatur.*

522. Interpretation.—**N.** interpretation, definition; explan-, explic-ation; solution, answer; rationale; plain -, simple -, strict- interpretation; meaning etc. 516.

translation; rend-ering, -ition; reddition; literal -, free- translation; key, crib; secret; clew etc. (*indication*) 550; Rosetta stone.

exegesis; ex-pounding, -position; Hermeneutics; comment, -ary; inference etc. (*deduction*) 480; illustration, exemplification; gloss, annotation, *scholium*, note; e-, di-lucidation, enucleation; *éclaircissement, mot de l'énigme.*

symptomat-, semei-ology; metoposcopy, physiognomy; diagnosis, prognosis; paleography etc. (*philology*) 560.

accept-ion, -ation, -ance; light, reading, lection, construction, version.

equivalent, - meaning etc. 516; synonym; para-, meta-phrase; convertible terms, apposition; dictionary etc. 562; polyglot.

V. interpret, explain, define, construe, translate, render; do -, turn- into; transfuse the sense of. find out etc. 480*a*- -the meaning etc. 516- of; read; spell -, figure -, make- out; decipher, decode, unravel, disentangle, puzzle out; find the key of, enucleate, resolve, solve; read between the lines.

account for; find -, tell- the cause etc. 153- of; throw -, shed- -light, - new light, - a fresh light- upon; clear up, elucidate.

illustrate, exemplify; unfold, expound, comment upon, annotate; popularize etc. (*render intelligible*) 518.

take -, understand -, receive -, accept- in a particular sense; understand by, put a construction on, be given to understand.

Adj. explanatory, expository; explica-tive, -tory; exegetical; hermeneutic, interpretive, illustrative, elucidative, annotative, scholiastic.

polyglot; literal; para-, meta-phrastic; cosignificative, synonymous; equivalent etc. 27.

Adv. in -explanation etc. *n.*; that is to say, *id est, videlicet*, to wit, namely, in other words.

literally, strictly speaking; in -plain, - plainer- - terms, - words, - English; more simply.

523. Misinterpretation.—**N.** misinterpretation, -apprehension, -understanding, - acceptation, -construction, -application; *catachresis*; cross -reading, - purposes; mistake etc. 495.

misrepresentation, perversion, exaggeration etc. 549; false -coloring, - construction; abuse of terms; parody, travesty; falsification etc. (*lying*) 544.

V. mis-interpret, -apprehend, -understand, - conceive, -judge, -doubt, -spell, -translate, - construe, -apply; mistake etc. 495.

misrepresent, pervert; garble etc. (*falsify*) 544; distort; detort; travesty, play upon words; stretch -, strain -, wrest- the -sense, - meaning; explain away; put a -bad, - false- construction on; give a false coloring, look through -rose colored -, - dark - spectacles.

be -, play- at cross purposes.

Adj. misinterpreted etc. *v.*; untranslat-ed, -able.

Adv. at cross purposes.

524. Interpreter.—**N.** interpreter, translator, ex-positor, -pounder, -ponent, -plainer; demonstrator.

scholiast, commentator, annotator; meta-, para-phrast.

spokesman, speaker, mouthpiece, prolocutor; diplomat etc. 758.

guide, courier, dragoman, *valet de place, cicerone*, showman; oneirocritic; Oedipus; oracle etc. 513.

525. Manifestation.—**N.** manifestation; unfolding; plainness etc. *adj.*; plain speaking; expression; showing etc. *v.*; exposition, demonstration, *séance*; exhibition, production; display, showing off etc. 882; premonstration. [Thing shown] exhibit, show.

indication etc. (*calling attention to*) 457; publicity etc. 531; disclosure etc. 529; openness etc. (*honesty*) 543, (*artlessness*) 703; *épachement*, prominence.

V. make -, render- -manifest etc. *adj.*; bring - forth, - forward, - to the front, - into view; give notice, express; represent, set forth, exhibit; show,

– up; expose; produce; hold up –, expose- to view; set –, place –, lay- before -one, – one's eyes; tell to one's face; trot out, put through one's paces, unfold, show off, show forth, unveil, bring to light, display, demonstrate, unroll; lay open; draw –, bring- out; bring out in strong relief; call –, bring- into notice; hold up the mirror; wear one's heart upon his sleeve; show one's -face, – colors; manifest oneself; speak out; make no -mystery, – secret- of; unfurl the flag; proclaim etc. (*publish*) 531.

indicate etc. (*direct attention to*) 457; disclose etc. 529; elicit etc. 480*a*; interpret etc. 522.

be -manifest etc. *adj.*; appear etc. (*be visible*) 446; transpire etc. (*be disclosed*) 529; speak for itself, stand to reason; stare one in the face; loom large, appear on the horizon, rear its head; give - token, – sign, – indication of; tell its own tale etc. (*intelligible*) 518; go without saying.

Adj. manifest, apparent; salient, striking, demonstrative, prominent, in the foreground, notable, pronounced.

flagrant; notorious etc. (*public*) 531; arrant; stark staring; unshaded, glaring.

defin-ed, -ite; distinct, conspicuous etc. (*visible*) 446; obvious, evident, incontestable, unmistakable, not to be mistaken, plain, clear, palpable, self-evident, autoptical; intelligible etc. 518; clear as - day, – daylight, – noonday; plain as -a pikestaff, – the sun at noonday, – the nose on one's face, – the way to the parish church.

ostensible; open, – as day; overt, patent, express, explicit; naked, bare, literal, downright, undisguised, exoteric.

unreserved; frank, plain spoken etc. (*artless*) 703; barefaced, brazen, bold, shameless, daring, flaunting, loud.

manifested etc. *v.*; disclosed etc. 529; expressible, capable of being shown, producible; in-, un-concealable.

Adv. manifestly, openly etc. *adj.*; before one's eyes, under one's nose, to one's face, face to face, above board, *cartes sur table*, on the stage, in plain sight, in open court, in the open, – streets; at the cross roads; in market overt; in the face of -day, – heaven; in -broad –, open- daylight; without reserve; at first blush, *primâ facie*, on the face of; in set terms.

Phr. *cela saute aux yeux*; he that runs may read; you can see it with half an eye; it needs no ghost to tell us; the meaning lies on the surface; *cela va sans dire*; *res ipsa loquitur*.

526. Latency.—N. latency, inexpression; hid-den –, occult- meaning; occultness, occultism, mysticism, mystery, cabala, symbolism, anagoge; silence etc. (*taciturnity*) 585; concealment etc. 528; more than meets the -eye, – ear; Delphic oracle; *les dessous des cartes*, undercurrent.

allusion, insinuation, implication; innuendo etc. 527; adumbration; 'something rotten in the state of Denmark.'

snake in the grass etc. (*pitfall*) 667; secret etc. 533.

darkness, invisibility, imperceptibility.

latent influence, power behind the throne; friend at court, wire puller.

V. be -latent etc. *adj.*; lurk, smoulder, underlie,

make no sign; escape -observation, – detection, – recognition; lie hid etc. 528.

laugh in one's sleeve; keep back etc. (*conceal*) 528.

involve, imply, implicate, connote, import, understand, allude to, infer, leave an inference; symbolize; whisper etc. (*conceal*) 528.

Adj. latent; lurking etc. *v.*; secret etc. 528; occult, symbolic, mystic; implied etc. *v.*; dormant.

un-apparent, -known, -seen etc. 441; in the background; invisible etc. 447; indiscoverable, dark; impenetrable etc. (*unintelligible*) 519; un-spied, -suspected.

un-said, -written, -published, -breathed, -talked of, -told etc. 527, -sung, -exposed, -proclaimed, -disclosed etc. 529, -pronounced, -mentioned, -expressed; not expressed, tacit.

un-developed, -solved, -explained, -traced, -discovered etc. 480*a*, -tracked, -explored, -invented.

indirect, crooked, inferential; by -inference, – implication; implicit; constructive; allusive, covert, muffled; steganographic; under-stood, -hand, -ground; concealed etc. 528; delitescent.

Adv. by a side wind; *sub silentio*; in the background; behind -the scenes, – one's back, – the veil; below the surface; on the tip of one's tongue; secretly etc. 528; between the lines; by a mutual understanding.

Phr. 'thereby hangs a tale.' 'that is another story.'

527. Information.—N. information, enlightenment, acquaintance, knowledge etc. 490; publicity etc. 531.

communication, intimation; not-ice, -ification; e-an-nunciation; announcement; representation, round robin, presentment.

case, estimate, specification, report, advice, monition; news etc. 532; return etc. (*record*) 551; account etc. (*description*) 594; statement etc. (*affirmation*) 535.

mention; acquainting etc. *v.*; instruction etc. (*teaching*) 537; outpouring; intercommunication, communicativeness.

informant, authority, teller, announcer, an-nunciator, harbinger, herald, intelligencer, commentator, columnist, reporter, exponent, mouth-piece; informer, keek, cavesdropper, delator, detective, sleuth; *mouchard*, spy, stool pigeon, newsmonger; messenger etc. 534; *amicus curiae*.

valet de place, *cicerone*, pilot, guide; guide-, hand-book; *vade mecum*; manual; map, plan, chart, gazetteer; itinerary etc. (*journey*) 266.

hint, suggestion, wrinkle, innuendo, inkling, whisper, passing word, word in the ear, subaudition, cue, by-play; gesture etc. (*indication*) 550; gentle ± broad- hint; *verbum sapienti*; word to the wise; insinuation etc. (*latency*) 526.

V. tell; inform, – of; acquaint, – with; impart, – to; make acquainted with, bring to the ears of, apprise, advise, enlighten, awaken.

let fall, mention, express, intimate, represent, communicate, make known; publish etc 531; notify, signify, specify, convey the knowledge of.

let one – , have one to- know; serve notice, give one to understand; give notice; set –, lay –, put-before; point out, put into one's head; put one in possession of; instruct etc. (*teach*) 537; direct the attention to etc. 457.

an-nounce, -nunciate; report, — progress; bring —, send —, leave —, write- word; tele-graph, -phone; ring —, call- up; wire; retail, render an account; give an account etc. (*describe*) 594; state etc. (*affirm*) 535.

disclose etc. 529; show cause; explain etc. (*interpret*) 522.

hint; give an inkling of; give —, drop —, throw out- a hint; insinuate; allude —, make allusion- to; glance at; tip off, tip the wink etc. (*indicate*) 550; suggest, prompt, give the cue, breathe; whisper, — in the ear.

give a bit of one's mind; tell one plainly, — once for all; speak volumes.

un-deceive, -beguile; set right, correct, open the eyes of, disabuse.

be -informed of etc.; know etc. 490; learn etc. 539; get scent of, gather from; awaken —, open one's eyes- to; become -alive, — awake- to; keep posted; hear, overhear, understand.

come to one's -ears, — knowledge; reach one's ears.

Adj. informed etc. *v.*; *communiqué*; reported etc. *v.*; published etc. 531; advisory.

expressive etc. 516; explicit etc. (*open*) 525, (*clear*) 518; plain-spoken etc. (*artless*) 703.

declara-, nuncupa-, exposi-tory; declarative, enunciative, communicat-ive, -ory; oral.

Adv. from information received; according to - rumor, — report; in the air; from what one can gather.

Phr. a little bird told me.

528. Concealment.—N. concealment; hiding etc. *v.*; occultation, mystification.

seal of secrecy; screen etc. 530; disguise etc. 530; masquerade; masked battery; hiding place etc. 530; cipher, code, crypt-, stegan-ography; invisible —, sympathetic- ink; palimpsest; freemasonry.

stealth, -iness; obreption; slyness etc. (*cunning*) 702.

latit-ancy, -ation; seclusion etc. 893; privacy, secrecy, secretness; *incognita*.

reticence; reserve; mental —, reservation, aside; *arrière pensée*, suppression, evasion, white lie, misprision; silence etc. (*taciturnity*) 585; suppression of truth etc. 544; underhand dealing; close-, secretive-ness etc. *adj.*; mystery.

latency etc. 526; snake in the grass; secret etc. 533.

V. conceal, hide, secrete, stow away, put out of sight; lock —, seal —, bottle- up.

cover, screen, cloak, veil, shroud; screen from -sight, — observation; draw the veil; draw —, close- the curtain; curtain, shade, eclipse, throw a veil over; be-cloud, -fog, -mask; mask, disguise; ensconce, muffle, smother; whisper.

keep -from, — back, — to oneself; keep -snug, — close, — secret, — dark; bury; sink, suppress; keep -from, — out of- -view, — sight; keep in —, throw into- the -shade, — background; cover up one's tracks; stifle, hush up, withhold, reserve; fence with a question; ignore etc. 460.

code, codify, use a cipher.

keep -a secret, — one's own counsel; hold one's tongue etc. (*silence*) 585; make no sign, not let it go further; not breathe a -word, — syllable- about; not let the right hand know what the left is doing; hide one's light under a bushel, bury one's talent in a napkin.

keep —, leave- in -the dark, — ignorance; blind, — the eyes; blindfold, hoodwink, mystify; puzzle etc. (*render uncertain*) 475; bamboozle etc. (*deceive*) 545.

be -concealed etc. *v.*; suffer an eclipse; retire from sight, couch; hide oneself; lie -hid, — in ambush, — low, — *perdu*, — snug, — close; seclude oneself etc. 893; lurk, sneak, skulk, slink, pussyfoot, prowl; steal -into, — out of, — by, — along; play at -bopeep, — hind and seek; hide in holes and corners.

Adj. concealed etc. *v.*; hidden; veiled, secret, recondite, mystic, cabalistic, occult, dark; cryptic, -al, private, privy, *in petto*, auricular, clandestine, close, inviolate.

behind a -screen etc. 530; under -cover, — an eclipse; in -ambush, — hiding, — disguise; in a -cloud, — fog, — mist, — haze, — dark corner; in the -shade, — dark; clouded, wrapt in clouds; invisible etc. 447; buried, underground, *perdu*; incommunicado; secluded etc. 893.

un-disclosed etc. 529; -told etc. 527; covert etc. (*latent*) 526; mysterious etc. (*unintelligible*) 519.

irrevealable, inviolable; confidential; esoteric; not ot be spoken of.

obreptitious, furtive, stealthy, feline; skulking etc. *v.*; surreptitious, underhand, hole and corner; sly etc. (*cunning*) 702; secretive, evasive, non-committal, reserved, reticent, uncommunicative, buttoned up; close, — as wax; taciturn etc. 585.

Adv. secretly etc. *adj.*; in -secret, — private, — one's sleeve, — holes and corners; in the dark etc. *adj.*

januis clausis, with closed doors, *à huis clos*; hugger-mugger, *à la dérobée*; under the -cloak of, — rose, — table; *sub rosâ*, *en tapinois*, in the background, aside, on the sly, with bated breath, *sotto voce*, in a whisper, without beat of drum, *à la sourdine*.

in —, strict- confidence; confidentially etc. *adj.*; between -ourselves, — you and me; *entre nous*, *inter nos*, under the seal of secrecy; in -code, — cipher.

underhand, by stealth, like a thief in the night; stealthily etc. *adj.*; behind -the scenes, — the curtain, — one's back, — a screen etc. 530; *incognito*; *in camerâ*.

Phr. it -must, — will- go no further; 'tell it not in Gath,' nobody the wiser.

529. Disclosure.—N. disclosure; retection; unveiling etc. *v.*; deterration, revealment, revelation; divulgence, expos-ition, -ure; *exposé*; whole truth; tell-tale etc. (*news*) 532.

acknowledgment, avowal; confession, -al; shrift.

bursting of a bubble; *dénouement*.

V. dis-close, -cover, -mask; draw —, draw aside —, lift —, raise —, lift up —, remove —, tear- the -veil, — curtain; un-mask, -veil, -fold, -cover, -seal, -kennel; take off —, break- the seal; lay -open, — bare; expose; open, — up; bare, bring to light; evidence; make -clear, — evident, — manifest; evince.

divulge, reveal, break; let into the secret; reveal the secrets of the prison-house; tell etc. (*inform*) 527; breathe, utter, blab, peach; let -out, – fall, – drop, – the cat out of the bag; betray; tell tales, – out of school; come out with; give -vent, – utterance- to; open the lips, blurt out, vent, whisper about; speak out etc. (*make manifest*) 525; make public etc. 531; unriddle etc. (*find out*) 480*a*; split; blow the gaff; break the news.

acknowledge, allow, concede, grant, admit, own, confess, avow, throw off all disguise, turn inside out, make a clean breast; show one's -hand, – cards; unburden –, disburden- one's -mind, – conscience, – heart; open – , lay bare – , tell a piece of- one's mind; unbosom oneself, own to the soft impeachment; say – , speak- the truth; turn - King's, – Queen's, – States's- evidence.

raise – , drop – , lift – , remove – , throw off- the mask; expose; debunk; lay open; un-deceive, - beguile; disabuse, set right, correct, open the eyes of; *désillusionner*.

be -disclosed etc.; transpire, come to light; come in sight etc. (*be visible*) 446; become known, escape the lips; come – , ooze – , creep – , leak –, peep – , crop- out; show its -face, – colors; discover etc. itself; break through the clouds, flash on the mind.

Adj. disclosed etc. *v.*

Int. out with it!

Phr. the murder is out; a light breaks in upon one; the scales fall from one's eyes; the eyes are opened.

530. Ambush. [Means of concealment.]—**N.** hiding-place; secret -place,   drawer; recess, hole, funk hole, holes and corners; closet, crypt, *adytum*, abditory, *oubliette*, safe, – deposit.

am-bush, -buscade; stalking horse; lurking-hole, -place; secret path, backstairs; retreat etc. (*refuge*) 666.

screen, cover, shade, blinder; veil, curtain, blind,' *purdah*, cloak, cloud.

mask, vizor, visor, disguise, masquerade dress, domino; *camouflage*.

pitfall etc. (*source of danger*) 667; trap etc. (*snare*) 545.

v. ambush, ambuscade, lie in ambush etc. (*hide oneself*) 528; lie in wait for; set a trap for etc. (*deceive*) 545.

Adv. *aux aguets*.

531. Publication.—**N.** publication; public - announcement etc. 527; promulgation, propagation, proclamation, pronouncement, encyclical, *pronunciamento*; circulation, indiction, edition, imprint, impression, printing; hue and cry.

publicity, notoriety, currency, flagrancy, cry, *bruit*; *vox populi*; report etc. (*news*) 532.

the Press, fourth estate, public press, newspaper, periodical, journal, gazette; house organ, trade publication, tabloid, daily, weekly, monthly, quarterly, annual, magazine, monograph, book; review; news sheet, special edition, supplement, feature, rotogravure, comic strips; leaflet, pamphlet; telegraphy; publisher etc. *v.*

circular, – letter; manifesto, advertisement,

puff, placard, bill, *affiche*, broadside, poster; notice etc. 527; program.

V. publish; make -public, – known etc. (*information*) 527; speak –, talk- of; broach, utter; put forward; circulate, propagate, promulgate; spread – , abroad; rumor, diffuse, disseminate, evulgate; put – , give – , send- forth; emit, edit, get out; issue; cover, report; bring – , lay – , dragbefore the public; give -out, – to the world; put – , bandy – , hawk – , buzz – , whisper – , bruit – , blaze- about; drag into the -open day, – limelight; voice.

proclaim, herald, blazon; blaze –, noiseabroad; sound a trumpet; trumpet – , thunderforth; give tongue; announce with -beat of drum, – flourish of trumpets; proclaim -from the housetops, – at Charing Cross, at the cross roads; declare, declaim.

advertise, placard; post, – up; *afficher*, publish in the Gazette, send round the crier.

raise a -cry, – hue and cry, – report; set news afloat.

telegraph, cable, wireless, broadcast.

be -published etc; be – , become- public etc. *adj.*; come out; go – , fly – , buzz – , blow- about; get -about, – abroad, – afloat, – wind; find vent; see the light; go forth, take air, acquire currency, pass current; go -the rounds, – the round of the newspapers, – through the length and breadth of the land; *virum volitare per ora*; pass from mouth to mouth; spread; run – , spread- like wildfire.

Adj. published etc. *v.*; current etc. (*news*) 532; in circulation, public; notorious; flagrant, arrant; open etc. 525; trumpet-tongued; encyclical, promulgatory; exoteric.

Adv. publicly etc. *adj.*; in open court, with open doors; in the limelight.

Int. *Oyez!* O yes! notice!

Phr. notice is hereby given; this is – , these are- to give notice.

532. News.—**N.** news; information etc. 527; piece – , budget- of -news, – information; report, story, yarn, copy, filler, intelligence, tidings; stop press news.

word, advice, *aviso*, message; dis-, des-patch; telegram, cable, wireless telegram, radio-gram, marconi-gram, communication, errand, embassy; *bulletin*.

microphone; public address system, P.A.; walkie talkie, radio -telephone, -phone.

radio, wireless (Eng.), high fidelity, hi fi, radio set, transistor, receiver; speaker, loudspeaker, amplifier, tweeter, woofer; transmitter, broadcaster; AM –, FM –, short wave – transmitter; radio station, studio, control room, network, hookup, circuit;‘ frequency, kilocycles, megacycles; band, channel, modulation, amplification; broadcast, program, newscast; network show, commerical announcement, serial, sound effects; signature, station – identification, – break; radio listener, audiophile.

television, TV, video, color television; television –, live – broadcast, telecast, TV show; televising, telecasting, transmission, television channel, video, audio, beam, reception, image, test pattern; rain, snow, ghost; television –, TV – station, mobile unit, TVmobile, transmitter, televisor, boost, camera; set, monitor, tube, screen.

rumor, hearsay, on dit, flying rumor, news stirring, cry, buzz, bruit, fame; talk, ouï-dire, scandal, eavesdropping; town –, table- talk; tittle-tattle; canard, topic of the day, idea afloat.

fresh –, stirring –, old – stale- news; glad tidings; old –, stale- story.

narrator etc. (describe) 594; news-, scandalmonger; tale-bearer; tell-tale, gossip, tattler, busybody, chatterer; informer.

broad-, news-, sports-caster; commentator, announcer, master of ceremonies, M.C., programmer, sound man, radioman, ham, radioperator.

television technician, TV man, cameraman, soundman.

V. transpire etc. (be disclosed) 529; rumor etc. (publish) 531.

broadcast, radio, transmit, send, release, beam; sign – on, – off; go on –, go off – the air, monitor; listen –, tune – in.

tele-vise, -cast; color cast.

Adj. many-tongued; rumored; publicly –, currently- -rumored, – reported; rife, current, floating, afloat, going about, in circulation, in everyone's mouth, all over the town.

Adv. as the story -goes, – runs; as they say, it is said.

533. Secret.—N. secret; dead –, profound-secret; arcanum, mystery; latency etc. 526; Asian mystery; sealed book, secrets of the prison-house; le dessous des cartes.

enigma, riddle, puzzle, nut to crack, conundrum, charade, rebus, logogriph; mono-, ana-gram; acrostic, cross-word puzzle; Sphinx; crux criticorum.

maze, labyrinth, Hyrcynian wood.

problem etc. (question) 461; paradox etc. (difficulty) 704; unintelligibility etc. 519; terra incognita etc. (ignorance) 491.

Adj. secret etc. (concealed) 528.

534. Messenger.—N. messenger, envoy, emissary, legate; nuncio, internuncio; intermediary; ambassador etc. (diplomatist) 758.

marshal, flag-bearer, herald, crier, trumpeter, bellman, pursuivant, parlementaire, apparitor.

courier, runner, dawk, estafette; Hermes, Mercury, Iris, Ariel.

postman, letter carrier, telegraph boy, messenger boy, district messenger; despatch rider, commissionaire, erand-boy.

mail; post, -office; letter-bag; mail -boat, – train, – coach, – van, aerial mail; tele-graph, -phone; cable, wire; carrier-pigeon; wireless telegraph, -phone; radiotele-graph, -phone.

journalist, newspaperman, reporter; gentleman –, representative- of the press; sob sister; penny-a-liner; special –, war –, own- correspondent; spy, scout; informer etc. 527.

535. Affirmation.—N. affirm-ance, -ation; statement, allegation, assertion, predication, declaration, word, averment.

asseveration, adjuration, swearing, oath, af-fidavit; deposition etc. (record) 551; avouchment, assurance; protest, -ation; profession; acknowledgment etc. (assent) 488; pledge.

vote, voice, suffrage, ballot.

remark, observation; position etc. (proposition) 514; saying, dictum, sentence, ipse dixit.

emphasis, positiveness, peremptoriness; dogmatism etc. (certainty) 474; dogmatist etc. 887.

V. assert; make -an assertion etc. n.; have one's say; say, affirm, predicate, declare, state, represent; protest, profess.

put -forth, – forward; advance, allege, propose, propound, enunciate, enounce, broach, set forth, hold out, maintain, contend, pronounce, pretend.

depose, depone, aver, avow, avouch, asseverate, swear; make –, take one's- oath; make –, swear –, put in- an affidavit; take one's Bible oath, kiss the book, vow, vitam impendere vero; swear till - one is black in the face, – all's blue; be sworn, call Heaven to witness; vouch, warrant, certify, assure, swear by bell, book and candle.

swear by etc. (believe) 484; insist –, take one's stand- upon; emphasize, lay stress on; assert - roundly, – positively; lay down, – the law; raise one's voice, dogmatize, have the last word; rap out; repeat; re-assert, -affirm.

announce etc. (information) 527; acknowledge etc. (assent) 488; attest etc. (evidence) 467; adjure etc. (put to one's oath) 768.

Adj. asserting etc. v.; declaratory, predicatory, pronunciative, affirmative, soi-disant; positive; certain etc. 474; express, explicit etc. (patent) 525; absolute, emphatic, flat, broad, round, pointed, marked, distinct, decided, confident, assertive, insistent, trenchant, dogmatic, definitive, formal, solemn, categorical, peremptory; unretracted; predicable, affirmable.

Adv. affirmatively etc. adj.; in the affirmative. with emphasis, ex cathedrâ, without fear of contradiction.

I must say, indeed, i' faith, let me tell you, why, give me leave to say, marry, you may be sure, I'd have you to know; upon my -word, – honor; by my troth, egad, I assure you; by -jingo, – Jove, – George, – etc.; troth, seriously, sadly; in –, in sober- -sadness, – truth, – earnest; of a truth, truly, pardi, perdy; in all conscience, upon oath; be assured etc. (belief) 484; yes etc. (assent) 488; I'll - warrant, – warrant you, – engage, – answer for it, – be bound, – venture to say, – take my oath; in fact, as a matter of fact, forsooth, joking apart; so help me God; not to mince the matter.

Phr. quoth he; dixi.

536. Negation.—N. ne-, abne-gation; denial; dis-avowal, -claimer; abjuration; contra-diction, -vention; recusation, protest; rebuttal; recusancy etc. (dissent) 489; flat –, emphatic- -contradiction, – denial; démenti.

qualification etc. 469; repudiation etc. 610; retraction etc. 607; confutation etc. 479; refusal etc. 764; prohibition etc. 761.

V. deny; contra-dict, -vene; controvert, give denial to, gainsay, negative, shake the head.

dis-own, -affirm, -claim, -avow; recant etc. 607; revoke etc. (abrogate) 756.

dispute, impugn, traverse, rebut, join issue upon; bring —, call- in question etc. (*doubt*) 485.

deny -flatly, – peremptorily, – emphatically, – absolutely, – wholly, – entirely; give the lie to, belie.

repudiate etc. 610; set aside, ignore etc. 460; rebut etc. (*confute*) 479; qualify etc. 469; refuse etc. 764.

Adj. denying etc. *v.*; denied etc. *v.*; contradictory; negat-ive, -ory; revocatory; recusant etc. (*dissenting*) 489; at issue upon.

Adv. no, nay, not, nowise; not a -bit, – whit, – jot; not -at all, – in the least, – so; no such thing; nothing of the -kind, – sort; quite the contrary, *tout au contraire*, far from it; *tant s'en faut*; on no account, in no respect; by -no, – no manner of-means; negatively.

phr. there never was a greater mistake; I know better; *non haec in foedera*.

537. Teaching.—N.
teaching etc. *v.*; instruction; edification; education; pedagogy; tuition; tutor-, tutel-age; direction, guidance.

qualification, preparation; train-, school-ing etc. *v.*; discipline; exer-cise, -citation; drill, practice.

persuasion, proselytism, propagandism, *propaganda*; in-doctrination, -culcation, oculation.

explanation etc. (*interpretation*) 522; lesson, lecture, sermon, homily; apologue, parable; discourse, prelection, preachment, disquisition.

exercise, task; *curriculum*; course, – of study; grammar, three R's, initiation, A.B.C. etc. (*beginning*) 66.

elementary –, primary –, secondary –, grammar school –, high school –, college –, university –, technical –, liberal –, classical –, religious –, denominational –, moral –, secular-education; technical –, vocational- training; university extension lectures; propaedeutics, moral tuition; evening classes, correspondence course.

physical education, gymnastics, calisthenics, eurythmics; *sloyd*.

V. teach, instruct, edify, school, tutor; cram, prime, coach; enlighten etc. (*inform*) 527.

in-culcate, -doctrinate, -oculate, -fuse, -stil, -fix, -graft, -filtrate; im-bue, -pregnate, -plant; graft, sow the seeds of, disseminate, propagandize.

give an idea of; put -up to, – in the way of; set right.

sharpen the wits, enlarge the mind; give new ideas, open the eyes, bring forward, 'teach the young idea how to shoot;' improve etc. 658.

expound etc. (*interpret*) 522; lecture; prelect; read –, give- a -lesson, – lecture, – sermon, – discourse; hold forth, preach; sermon-, moral-ize; point a moral.

train, discipline; bring up, – to; educate, form, ground, prepare, qualify, drill, exercise, practice, habituate, familiarize with, nurture, dry-nurse; breed, rear, take in hand; break, – in; tame; pre-instruct; initiate; inure etc. (*habituate*) 613.

put to nurse, send to school.

direct, guide; direct attention to etc. (*attention*) 457; impress upon the -mind, – memory; beat into, – the head; convince etc. (*belief*) 484.

Adj. teaching etc. *v.*; taught etc. *v.*; educational; scholastic, academic, doctrinal; disciplinal; in-structive, didactic, hortative, pedagogic, tutorial.

Phr. the schoolmaster abroad.

538. Misteaching—N.
mis-teaching, -information, -intelligence, -guidance, -direction, -persuasion, -instruction, -leading etc. *v.*; per-version, false teaching; sophistry etc. 477; college of Laputa; the blind leading the blind.

V. mis-inform, -teach, -direct, -guide, -instruct, -correct; pervert; put on a false –, throw off the-scent; deceive etc. 545; mislead etc. (*error*) 495; misrepresent; lie etc. 544; *ambiguas in vulgum spargere voces*, preach to the wise, teach one's grandmother to suck eggs.

render unintelligible etc. 519; bewilder etc. (*uncertainty*) 475; mystify etc. (*conceal*) 528; un-teach.

Adj. misteaching etc. *v.*; unedifying.

Phr. *piscem natare doces*.

539. Learning.—N.
learning; acquisition of -knowledge etc. 490, – skill etc. 698; acquirement, attainment; edification, scholarship, erudition; lore; information; self-instruction; study, reading, perusal; inquiry etc. 461.

ap-, prenticeship; pupil-age, -arity; tutelage, novitiate; matriculation.

docility etc. (*willingness*) 602; aptitude etc. 698.

V. learn; acquire –, gain –, receive –, take in –, drink in –, imbibe –, pick up –, gather –, get –, obtain –, collect –, glean- -knowledge, – information, – learning.

acquaint oneself with, master; make oneself -master of, – acquainted with; grind, cram; get –, coach- up; learn by -heart, – rote.

read, spell, peruse; con –, pore –, thumb- over; wade through; dip into; run the eye -over, – through; turn over the leaves.

study; be -studious etc. *adj.*; consume the mid-night oil, mind one's book.

go to -school, – college, – the university; serve -an (*or* one's) apprenticeship, – one's time; learn one's trade; be -informed etc. 527; be -taught etc. 537.

Adj. studious; schol-astic, -arly; teachable; docile etc. (*willing*) 602; apt etc. 698; industrious etc. 682; learned erudite.

Adv. at one's books; *in statu pupillari* etc. (*learner*) 541.

540. Teacher.—N.
teacher, trainer, instructor, institutor, master, tutor, don, director, Corypheus, dry nurse, coach, grinder, crammer; governor, bear-leader; governess, duenna; disciplinarian.

professor, lecturer, reader, prelector, prolocutor, preacher; Boanerges; pastor etc. (*clergy*) 996; schoolmaster, dominie, usher, pedagogue, abecedarian; schoolmistress, dame, monitor, proctor, pupil-teacher.

expositor etc. 524; preceptor, guide; mentor etc. (*adviser*) 695; pioneer, apostle, missionary, propagandist, moonshee; example etc. (*model for imitation*) 22.

professorship etc. (*school*) 542.

tutelage etc. (*teaching*) 537.

Adj. professorial, tutorial etc. 537.

541. Learner.—N. learner, scholar, student, *alumnus*, *élève*, pupil; ap-, prentice; articled clerk; school-boy, -girl, beginner, tyro, abecedarian, alphabetarian.

recruit, novice, neophyte, tenderfoot, inceptor, *débutant*, catechumen, probationer; undergraduate; freshman, frosh; sophomore, junior, senior; junior –, senior-· soph; sophister, questionist, fellow-, commoner, pensioner, exhibitioner, sizar, scholar, fellow, advanced –, post graduate –, research- student.

class, form, grade, standard, remove; pupilage etc. (*learning*) 539.

disciple, follower, apostle, proselyte; fellow student, school-mate, -fellow, class mate, condisciple.

Adj. *in statu pupillari*, in leading strings, sophomoric.

542. School.—N. school, academy, university, *alma mater*, college, seminary, Lyceum; instit-ute, -ution, *conservatoire*; *palaestra*, *gymnasium*.

day –, boarding –, public –, preparatory –, elementary –, primary –, nursery –, dame's –, grammar –, Board –, County –, Council –, parochial –, denominational –, Sunday –, religious –, collegiate –, secondary –, continuation –, night –, correspondence –, secretarial –, military –, law –, medical –, business –, technical- · school; technical –, training- college; Polytechnic; training ship; *Kindergarten*, nursery, *crèche*, reformatory.

pulpit, desk, reading desk, ambo, class-, lecture-room, theater, amphitheater, forum, stage, rostrum, platform, hustings, tribune.

school –, horn –, text-book; grammar,'primer, abecedary, rudiments, manual, *vade mecum*, Lindley, Murray, Cocker.

professor-, lecture-, reader-ship; chair; schoolmaster etc. 540.

School Board, Council of Education; *propaganda*.

Adj. scholastic. academic, collegiate; educational.

Adv. *ex cathedrâ*.

543. Veracity.—N. veracity; truthfulness, frankness etc. *adj.*; truth, sooth, sincerity, candor, honesty, fidelity; plain dealing, *bona fides*; love of truth; probity etc. 939; ingenuousness etc. (*artlessness*) 703.

the truth the whole truth and nothing but the truth; honest –, sober- truth etc. (*fact*) 494; unvarnished tale; light of truth.

V. speak –, tell- the truth; speak by the card; paint in its –, show oneself in ones -true colors; make a clean breast etc. (*disclose*) 529; speak one's mind etc. (*be blunt*) 703; not -lie etc. 544, – deceive etc. 545.

Adj. truthful, true; ver-acious, -edical; scrupulous etc. (*honorable*) 939; sincere, candid, frank, open, straightforward, unreserved; open-, true-, simple- hearted; honest, trustworthy; undissembling etc. (dissemble etc. 544); guileless, pure; unperjured, ture blue, as good as one's word;

unaffected, unfeigned, *bonâ fide*; outspoken, ingenuous etc. (*artless*) 703; undisguised etc. (*real*) 494.

Adv. truly etc. (*really*) 494; on oath; in plain words etc. 703; in –, with –, of a –, in good –, very- truth; as the -dial to the sun, – needle to the pole; honor bright; troth; in good -sooth, – earnest; unfeignedly, with no nonsense, in sooth, sooth to say, *bonâ fide*, in foro conscientiae; without equivocation; *cartes sur table*, from the bottom of one's heart; by my troth etc. (*affirmation*) 535.

544. Falsehood.—N. false-hood, -ness; fals-ity, -ification; misrepresentation; deception etc. 545; untruth etc. 546; guile; bad faith; lying etc. *v.*; misrepresentation; mendacity, perjury, false swearing; forgery, invention, fabrication; subreption; covin.

perversion –, suppression- of truth; *suppressio veri*; perversion, distortion, false coloring; exaggeration etc. 549; prevarication, shuffling, fencing, evasion, fraud; *suggestio falsi* etc. (*lie*) 546; mystification etc. (*concealment*) 528; simulation etc. (*imitation*) 19; dis-simulation, -sembling; deceit.

sham; pretence, pretending, malingering.

lip-homage, – service; mouth honor; hollowness; mere -show, – outside, eye-wash, window dressing; duplicity, double dealing, insincerity, hypocrisy, cant, humbug, casuistry; jesuit-ism, -ry; pharisaism; Machiavelism, 'organized hypocrisy;' crocodile tears, mealy-mouthedness, quackery; charlatan-ism, -ry; gammon; bun-kum, -come; flam, ban, flim-flam, cajolery, flattery; Judas kiss; perfidy etc. (*bad faith*) 940; *il volto sciolto i pensieri stretti*.

unfairness etc. (*dishonesty*) 940; artfulness etc. (*cunning*) 702; misstatement etc. (*error*) 495.

V. be -false etc. *adj.*, – a liar etc. 548; speak -falsely etc. *adv.*; tell a -lie etc. 546; lie, fib; lie like a trooper; swear falsely, forswear, perjure oneself, bear false witness.

mis-state, -quote, -cite, -report, -represent; belie, falsify, pervert, distort; put a false construction upon etc. (*misinterpret*) 523.

prevaricate, equivocate. quibble; palter, – to the understanding; *répondre en Normand*; trim, shuffle, fence, mince the truth, beat about the bush, blow hot and cold, play fast and loose.

garble, gloss over, disguise, give a color to; give –, put- a -gloss, – false coloring- upon; color, varnish, cook, dress up, embroider; varnish right and puzzle wrong, exaggerate etc. 549.

invent, fabricate; trump –, get- up; forge, hatch, concoct; romance etc. (*imagine*) 515; cry 'wolf!'

dis-semble, -simulate; feign, assume, put on, pretend, make believe; play -false, – a double game; coquet; act –, play- a part; affect etc. 855; simulate, pass off for; counterfeit, fake, sham, make a show of; malinger; swing the lead; say the grapes are sour.

cant, play the hypocrite, sham Abraham, *faire pattes de velours*, put on the mask, clean the outside of the platter, lie like a conjuror; hang out –, hold out –, sail under- false colors; 'commend the poisoned chalice to the lips;' *ambiguas in vulgus spargere voces*; deceive etc. 545.

Adj. false, deceitful, mendacious, unveracious,

fraudulent, untruthful, dishonest; faith-, truth-, troth-less; un-fair, -candid; evasive; un-, dis-ingenuous; hollow, insincere, *Parthis mendacior*; forsworn.

canting; hypocrit-, jesuit-, pharisa-ical; tartuffish; Machiavelian; double-tongued, -faced, -handed, -minded, -hearted, -dealing; two-faced, bare-faced; Janus-faced; smooth-faced, -spoken, -tongued; plausible; mealy-mouthed; affected etc. 855.

collus-ive, -ory; artful etc. (*cunning*) 702; perfidious etc. 940, spurious etc. (*deceptive*) 545; untrue etc. 546; falsified etc. *v.*; covinous.

Adv. falsely etc. *adj.*; *à la Tartufe*, with a double tongue; out of whole cloth; slily etc. (*cunning*) 702.

545. Deception.—N. deception; falseness etc. 544; untruth etc. 546; impos-ition, -ture; fraud, deceit, guile; fraudulen-ce, -cy; covin; knavery etc. (*cunning*) 702; misrepresentation etc. (*falsehood*) 544.

delusion, gullery, bluff, spoof, *blague*; juggl-ing, -ery; sleight of hand, legerdemain; presti-giation, -digitation; magic etc. 992; conjur-ing, -ation; hocus pocus, jockeyship; trickery, coggery, hanky-panky, chicanery, pettifogging, sharp practice; *supercherie*, cozenage, circumvention, ingannation; collusion; treachery etc. 940; practical joke.

trick, cheat, wile, blind, feint, plant, bubble fetch, catch, chicane, juggle, reach, hocus, bite; thimble-rig, card-sharping, artful dodge, machination, swindle, hoax; tricks upon travellers; confidence trick; strategem etc. (*artifice*) 702; theft etc. 791.

snare, trap, pitfall, decoy, gin; sprin-ge, -gle; noose, hook; bait, decoy-duck, tub to the whale, baited trap, *guet-à-pens*; cobweb, net, meshes, toils, mouse-trap, bird-lime; ambush etc. 530; trap-door, sliding panel, false bottom; spring-net, -gun; mask, -ed battery; mine; booby trap.

Cornish hug; wolf in sheep's clothing etc. (*deceiver*) 548; disguise, -ment; false colors, masquerade, mummery, borrowed plumes; *pattes de velours*.

mockery etc. (*imitation*) 19; copy etc. 21; counterfeit, sham, brummagem, make-believe, forgery, fraud, fake; lie etc. 546; 'a mockery, a delusion, and a snare,' hollow mockery.

whited −, painted- sepulcher; tinsel, paste, false jewelry, scagliola, ormolu, German silver, Britannia metal, paint; jerry building; man of straw.

illusion etc. (*error*) 495; *ignis fatuus* etc. 423; *mirage* etc. 443.

V. deceive, take in; defraud, cheat, jockey, do, cozen, diddle, nab, gyp, chouse, double cross, play one false, bilk, cully, jilt, bite, pluck, swindle, victimize; abuse; mystify; blind one's eyes; blindfold, hoodwink, spoof, bluff; throw dust into the eyes, 'keep the word of promise to the ear and break it to the hope,' 'draw a herring across the trail.'

impose −, practice −, play −, put −, palm −, foist- upon; snatch a verdict.

circumvent, overreach; out-reach, -wit, maneuvre; steal a march upon, give the go-by to, leave in the lurch.

set −, lay- a -trap, − snare- for; bait the hook, forlay, spread the toils, lime; decoy, waylay, lure,

beguile, delude, inveigle; tra-, tre-pan; kidnap; let-, hook-in; trick; en-, in-trap, -snare, entoil, benet; nick, springe; catch, − in a trap; sniggle, entangle, illaqueate, hocus, practice on one's credulity, dupe, gull, hoax, fool, befool, bamboozle; hum, -bug; gammon, stuff up, dope, sell; play a -trick, − practical joke- upon one; balk, trip up, throw a tub to a whale; fool to the top of one's bent, send on -a wild goose chase, − a fool's errand; make -game, − a fool, − an April fool, − an ass- of; trifle with, cajole, flatter; come over etc. (*influence*) 615; gild the pill, make things pleasant, divert, put a good face upon; dissemble etc. 544.

cog, − the dice, play with marked cards; live by one's wits, play at hide and seek; obtain money under false pretences etc. (*steal*) 791; conjure, juggle, practice chicanery; gerrymander.

play −, palm −, foist −, fob- off.

lie etc. 544; misinform etc. 538; mislead etc. (*error*) 495; betray etc. 940; be -deceived etc. 547.

Adj. deceived etc. *v.*; deceiving etc. *v.*; cunning etc. 702; prestigi-ous, -atory; decept-ive, -ious; deceitful, covinous; delus-ive, -ory; illus-ive, -ory; elusive, insidious, *ad captandum vulgus*.

untrue etc. 546; mock, sham, make-believe, counterfeit, faked, pseudo, spurious, so-called, pretended, feigned, trumped up, bogus, scamped, fraudulent, tricky, factitious, artificial, bastard; surreptitious, illegitimate, contraband, adulterated, sophisticated; unsound, rotten at the core; colorable; disguised; meretricious; tinsel, pinchbeck, plated; catch-penny; Brummagem; simulated etc. 544.

Adv. under -false colors, − the garb of, − cover of; over the left.

Phr. *fronti nulla fides.*

546. Untruth.—N. untruth, falsehood, lie, story, thing that is not, fib, bounce, crammer, taradiddle, whopper.

forgery, fabrication, invention; mis-statement, -representation; perversion, falsification, gloss, *suggestio falsi*; exaggeration etc. 549.

fiction; fable, nursery tale; romance etc. (*imagination*) 515; untrue −, false −, trumped up- -story, − statement; thing devised by the enemy; *canard*; shave, sell, hum, yarn, traveler's tale, Canterbury tale, cock and bull story, fairy tale, clap-trap.

myth, moonshine, bosh, all my eye, -and Betty Martin, mare's nest, farce.

irony; half truth, white lie, pious fraud; mental reservation etc. (*concealment*) 528.

pretence, pretext; false -plea etc. 617; subterfuge, evasion, shift, shuffle, make-believe; sham etc. (*deception*) 545.

profession, empty words; Judas kiss etc. (*hypocrisy*) 544; disguise etc. (*mask*) 530.

V. have a false meaning; not ring true.

pretend, sham, feign, counterfeit, make believe.

Adj. untrue, false, trumped up; void of −, without- foundation; far from the truth, false as dicer's oaths; unfounded, *ben trovato*, invented, fabulous, fabricated, forged; fict-, fact-, supposit-, surrept-itious; e-, il-lusory; ironical; satirical; evasive; *soi-disant* etc. (*misnamed*) 565.

Phr. *se non e vero e ben trovato.*

547. Dupe.—N. dupe, gull, gudgeon, *gobemouche*, cull, cully, victim, sucker, pigeon, April fool; laughing stock etc. 857; Cyclops, simple Simon, flat, mug, greenhorn; fool etc. 501; puppet, cat's paw.

V. be -deceived etc. 545, – the dupe of; fall into a trap; swallow –, nibble at- the bait; bite; catch a Tartar.

Adj. credulous etc. 486; mistaken etc. (*error*) 495.

548. Deceiver.—N. deceiver etc. (deceive etc. 545); dissembler, hypocrite; sophist, Pharisee, Jesuit, Mawworm, Pecksniff, Joseph Surface, Tartufe, Janus; serpent, snake in the grass, cockatrice, Judas, wolf in sheep's clothing; Molly Maguire; jilt; shuffler.

liar etc. (lie etc. 544; story-teller, perjurer, false-witness, *mentuer à triple étage*, Scapin.

imposter, pretender, capper, decoy, fraud, *soi-disant*, humbug; adventurer; Cagliostro, Fernam Mendez Pinto; ass in lion's skin etc. (*bungler*) 701; actor etc. (*stage player*) 599.

quack, *charlatan*, mountebank, saltimbanco, *saltimbanque*, empiric, quacksalver, medicaster.

conjuror, juggler, magician, necromancer, trickster, prestidigitator, medium, jockey; crimp; decoy-duck, stool pigeon; rogue, knave, cheat; swindler etc. (*thief*) 792; jobber.

549. Exaggeration.—N. exaggeration; expansion etc. 194; hyperbole, stretch, strain, coloring; high coloring, caricature, *caricatura*; extravagance etc. (*nonsense*) 497; Baron Munchausen; men in buckram, yarn, fringe, embroidery, traveler's tale; Pelion upon Ossa.

storm in a teacup; much ado about nothing etc. (*over-estimation*) 482; puffery etc. (*boasting*) 884; rant etc. (*turgescence*) 577.

figure of speech, *façon de parler*; stretch of -fancy, – the imagination; flight of fancy etc. (*imagination*) 515.

false coloring etc. (*falsehood*) 544; aggravation etc. 835.

V. exaggerate, magnify, pile up, aggravate; amplify etc. (*expand*) 194; overestimate etc. 482; hyperbolize; over-charge, -state, -draw, -lay, -shoot the mark, -praise; make -much, – the most- of; strain, – a point; stretch, – a point; go great lengths; spin a long yarn; draw –, shoot with- a long-bow; deal in the marvelous.

out -Herod Herod, run riot, talk at random.

heighten, overcolor; color -highly, – too highly; embroider, *broder*; flourish; color etc. (*misrepresent*) 544; puff etc. (*boast*) 884.

Adj. exaggerated etc. *v.*; overwrought; bombastic etc. (*magniloquent*) 577; hyperbolical, on stilts; fabulous, extravagant, preposterous, egregious, *outré*, high-flying.

Adv. hyperbolically etc. *adj.*

550. Indication.—N. indication; symbol-ism, -ization; semeio-logy, -tics; sign of the times. .

lineament, feature, *trait*, characteristic, trick,

diagnostic; divining-rod; cloven hoof; footfall; means of recognition; earmark.

sign, symbol; ind-ex, -ice, -icator; point, -er; marker; exponent, note, token, symptom.

type, figure, emblem, cipher, device; representation etc. 554; epigraph, motto, posy.

gest-ure,. -iculation; pantomime; wink, glance, leer; nod, shrug, beck; touch, nudge; grip; dactylology, -nomy; freemasonry, telegraphy, chirology, by-play, dumb-show; cue; hint etc. 527; clue, clew, key, scent, tract etc. 551.

signal, -post; rocket, blue light; watch-fire, - tower; telegraph, semaphore, flag-staff; cresset, fiery cross; calumet; heliograph, signal-, flash-lamp; radar, radar signal, pulse –, microwave –, radar; tracing, blips, pips.

mark, line, stroke, dash, score, stripe, streak, scratch, tick, dot, point, notch, nick, blaze; asterisk, red letter, Italics, heavy type, inverted commas, quotation marks, sublineation, underlining, jotting; print; impr-int, -ess, ession; note, annotation, mark of exclamation.

[For identification] badge, criterion; counter-check, -mark, -sign, -foil, duplicate, tally; label, tab, ticket, stub, billet, letter, counter, *tessera*, card, bill, check; witness, voucher; stamp; *cachet*; trade –, Hall- mark; broad arrow; signature; address –, visiting- card; *carte de visite*; credentials etc. (*evidence*) 467; passport, identity book; attestation; hand, – writing, sign-manual; cipher; monogram, – mark, seal, sigil, signet; autograph, -y, paraph, brand; superscription; in-, en-dorsement; title, heading, rubric, docket; *mot -de passe*, – *du guet*; *passe-parole*; shibboleth; watch-, catch-, password; open *sesame*.

insignia, banner, -et, -ol; bandrol; flag, colors, streamer, standard, eagle, labarum, oriflamb, *oriflamme*; figure-head; ensign; pen-non, -nant, -dant; burgee, blue Peter, jack, ancient, gonfalon, union-jack; tricolor, stars and stripes; bunting.

hearldry, crest; coat of –, arms; armorial bearings, hatchment; e-, scutcheon; shield, supporters; livery, uniform; cockade, *epaulette*, brassard, chevron; garland, chaplet, love-knot, fillet, favor.

[Of locality] beacon, cairn, post, staff, flagstaff, hand, pointer, vane, cock, weathercock; guide-, hand-, finger-, directing-, sign-post; pillars of Hercules, pharos, signal fire; land-, sea-mark; lighthouse, balize; pole-, load-, lode-star; cynosure, guide; address, direction, name; sign, -board.

[Of the future] warning etc. 668; omen etc. 512; prefigurement etc. 511. [Of the past] trace record etc. 551. [Of danger] warning etc. 668; alarm etc. 669. [Of authority] scepter etc. 747. [Of triumph] trophy etc. 733. [Of quantity] gauge etc. 466. [Of distance] mile-stone, -post. [Of disgrace] brand, fool's cap, stigma, mark of Cain. [For detection] check, tell-tale; test etc. (*experiment*) 463.

notification etc. (*information*) 527; advertisement etc. (*publication*) 531.

word of command, call; bugle-, trumpet-call; reveille, taps; bell, alarum, cry; battle –, rallying-cry.

church, bell, angelus, sacring bell; muezzin.

exposition etc. (*explanation*) 522; proof etc. (*evidence*) 463; pattern etc. (*prototype*) 22.

V. indicate; be the -sign etc. *n.*- of; denote,

betoken; argue, testify etc. (*evidence*) 467; bear the
-impress etc. *n.*- of; con-note, -notate.

represent, stand for; typify etc. (*prefigure*) 511;
symbolize.

put -an indication, − a mark, − etc. *n.*; note,
mark, tick, blaze, stamp, earmark; set one's seal
upon; label, ticket, docket; dot, spot, score, dash,
trace, chalk; print; im-print, -press, surprint;
engrave, stereotype, electrotype.

signal, transmit, send, radiate, beam, deflect,
echo, bounce back, return.

make a -sign etc. *n.*; signalize; give −, hang out-
a signal; beck, -on; gesture; not; wink, glance, leer,
nudge, shrug, tip the wink; gesticulate; raise −,
hold up- the-finger, − hand; saw the air, suit the
action to the word.

wave −, unfurl −, hoist −, hang out- a banner
etc. *n.*; wave -the hand, − a kerchief; give the cue
etc. (*inform*) 527; show one's colors; give −,
sound- an alarm; beat the drum, sound the trumpets, raise a cry.

sign, seal, attest etc. (*evidence*) 467; underline
etc. (*give importance to*) 642; call attention to etc.
(*attention*) 457; give notice etc. (*inform*) 527.

Adj. indicat-ing etc. *v.*; -ive, -ory; de-, con-
notative; diacritical, representative, typical, symbolic, pantomimic, pathognomonic, symptomatic,
ominous, characteristic, demonstrative, diagnostic,
exponential, emblematic, armorial; individual etc.
(*special*) 79.

known −, recognizable- by; indicated etc. *v.*;
pointed, marked.

[Capable of being denoted] denotable; indelible.

Adv. in token of; symbolically etc. *adj.*; in
dumb show.

Phr. *ecce signum*; *ex ungue leonem, ex pede
Herculem.*

551. Record.—N. trace, vestige, relic, remains;
scar, *cicatrix*; foot-step, -mark, -print; track, mark,
wake, trail, spoor, scent, *piste.*

monument, hatchment, escutcheon, slab, tablet,
trophy, achievement; obelisk, pillar, column,
monolith, cromlech, dolmen; memorial; *memento*
etc. (*memory*) 505; testimonial, medal, ribbon, order; commemoration etc. (*celebration*) 883.

record, note, minute; *dossier*; register, -try; census, roll etc. (*list*) 86; cartulary, diptych,
Domesday book; entry, memorandum, indorsement, inscription, copy, duplicate, docket;
notch etc. (*mark*) 550; muniment, deed etc.
(*security*) 771; document, deposition, *procès-
verbal*; affidavit; certificate etc. (*evidence*) 467.

note-, memorandum-, pocket-, commonplace-
book; portfolio; scoring-board, -sheet; bulletin
board; card index, file; pigeon-holes, *excerpta, adversaria*, jottings, dottings.

gazette, -er; newspaper, magazine etc. 531;
alman-ac, -ack; calendar, ephemeris, noctuary,
diary, log, journal, account-, cash-, day-book,
ledger.

archive, scroll, state-paper, Congressional
Record, return, blue-book; statistics etc. 86;
compte rendu; Acts −, Transactions −,
Proceedings- of; Hansard's Debates; chronicle, annals; legend; history, biography etc. 594.

registration; en-, in-rolment; tabulation; entry,

booking; signature etc. (*identification*) 550; recorder etc. 553; journalism.

drawing, photograph etc. 554; phonograph −,
gramophone- record; music roll.

V. record; put −, place- upon record; go on
record; chronicle, calendar, hand down to
posterity; keep up the memory of etc. (*remember*)
505; commemorate etc. (*celebrate*) 883; report
etc. (*inform*) 527; commit to −, reduce to-
writing; put −, set down- -in writing, − in black
and white; put −, jot −, take −, write −, note
−, set-down; note, minute, put on paper; take −,
make- a -note, − minute, − memorandum; make
a return.

mark etc. (*indicate*) 550; sign etc. (*attest*) 467.

enter, book; post, − up; insert, make an entry
of; mark −, tick- off; register, list, docket, enroll,
inscroll; file etc. (*store*) 636.

Adv. on record.

552. Obliteration. [Suppression of sign.]—**N.**
obliteration; erasure, rasure; effacement; interference; cancel, -lation; cassation; cir-
cumduction; deletion, blot; *tabula rasa.*

V. efface, obliterate, erase, rase, expunge, cancel; blot −, take −, rub −, scratch −, strike −,
wipe −, wash −, sponge- out; wipe −, rub- off;
wipe away; deface, render illegible; draw the pen
through, apply the sponge.

interfere, jam, black-, block-out; clutter, screen.

be -effaced etc.; leave no -trace etc. 449; 'leave
not a rack behind.'

Adj. obliterated etc. *v.*; out of print; printless;
leaving no trace; intestate; un-recorded, -registered,
-written.

Int. *dele*; out with it!

553. Recorder.—N. recorder, notary, clerk;
regis-trar, -trary, -ter; prothonotary; amanuensis,
secretary, scribe, stenographer, remembrancer,
book-keeper, *custos rotulorum*, Master of the
Rolls.

annalist; histori-an, -ographer; chronicler, journalist, reporter, columnist; biographer etc.
(*narrator*) 594; antiquary etc. (*antiquity*) 122;
memorialist.

draughtsman etc. 559; engraver 558;
photographer, cinematographer, camera man.

Recording instrument, recorder, camera;
phonograph, gramophone, dictaphone,
telegraphone, telautograph, printing telegraph, tape
recorder, ticker, time recorder, cash register, turn-
stile, speedometer, voting machine, seismograph,
radar, oscilloscope, teletypewriter, pari-mutuel,
photostat.

554. Representation.—N. represent-ation, -
ment; imitation etc. 19; illustration, delineation,
depictment, portrayal; imagery, portraiture,
iconography; design, -ing; art, fine arts; painting
etc. 556; sculpture etc. 557; engraving etc. 558;
photography, radiography, skiagraphy.

person-ation, -ification; impersonation; drama
etc. 599.

picture, drawing, sketch, draught, draft; tracing; copy etc. 21; photo-, helio-graph; daguerreo-, talbo-, calo-, helio-type; cabinet, *carte-de-visite*, snapshot; X-ray photograph; radio-gram, -graph, skia-graph, -gram.

image, likeness, icon, portrait; striking –, speaking- likeness; very image; effigy, fac-simile.

figure, – head; puppet, doll, *figurine*, aglet, manikin, lay-figure, model, *marionnette*, *fantoccini*, bust; waxwork, statue, -tte, automaton, Robot.

hieroglyphic, anaglyph; dia-, mono-gram, graph.

map, plan, chart; ground plan, projection, elevation; ichno-, carto-graphy; atlas; outline, scheme; view etc. (*painting*) 556.

artist, draughtsman etc. 559.

V. represent, delineate; depict, -ure; portray; picture; take –, catch- a likeness etc. *n.*; hit off, photograph, daguerreotype; figure; shadow -forth, – out; adumbrate; body forth; describe etc. 594; trace, copy; mold.

dress up; illustrate, symbolize.

paint etc. 556; carve etc. 557; engrave etc. 558.

person-ate, -ify; impersonate; assume a character; pose as; act; play etc. (*drama*) 599; mimic etc. (*imitate*) 19; hold the mirror up to nature.

Adj. represent-ing etc. *v.*, -ative; illustrative; represented etc. *v.*; imitative, figurative.

like etc. 17; graphic etc. (*descriptive*) 594.

555. Misrepresentation.—N. misrepresentation, distortion, exaggeration; daubing etc. *v.*; bad likeness, daub, sign-painting; scratch, caricature; *anamorphosis*.

V. misrepresent, distort, overdraw, travesty, parody, burlesque, exaggerate, caricature, daub.

Adj. misrepresented etc. *v.*

556. Painting.—N. painting; depicting; drawing etc. *v.*; design; perspective, skiagraphy; *chiaroscuro* etc. (*light*) 420; composition; treatment, values, atmosphere, tone, technique.

historical –, portrait –, miniature –, land-scape –, marine –, flower –, scene- painting; scenography.

school, style; the grand style, high art, *genre*, portraiture; ornamental art etc. 847.

mono-, poly-chrome; *grisaille*.

pallet, palette; easel; brush, pencil, stump; blacklead, charcoal, crayons, chalk, pastel; paint etc. (*coloring matter*) 428; water-, body-, oil-color; oils, oil-paint; varnish etc. 356a; *gouache*, tempera, distemper, fresco, water-glass; enamel, encaustic painting; *graffito*, *gesso*; mosiac; tapestry.

picture, painting, piece, *tableau*, canvas; oil etc.- painting; fresco, cartoon; easel –, cabinet- picture; drawing, draught, draft; pencil etc. –, watercolor- drawing; sketch; outline; study.

portrait etc. (*representation*) 554; whole –, full –, half- length; kitcat, head; miniature; shade, *silhouette*; profile.

landscape, sea-piece, -scape; view, scene, prospect; interior; bird's- eye view; pan-, di-orama; still life.

picture –, art- gallery; *studio*, *atelier*.

V. paint, design, limn, draw, sketch, pencil, scratch, shade, stipple, hatch, dash off, chalk out, square up; color, dead-color, wash, varnish; draw in -pencil etc. *n.*; paint in -oils etc. *n.*; stencil; depict etc. (*represent*) 554.

Adj. painted etc. *v.*; pictorial, graphic, picturesque, decorative; classical, romantic, pre-Raphaelite, modern, cubist, futurist, vorticist.

pencil, oil etc. *n.*

Adv. in -pencil etc. *n.*

Phr. *fecit, delineavit.*

557. Sculpture.—N. sculpture, insculpture; carving etc. *v.*; statuary, ceramics, plastic arts.

high –, low –, bas- relief; relievo; *basso-*, *alto-*, *mezzo-relievo*; *intaglio*, anaglyph; medal, -lion; *cameo*.

marble, bronze, *terra cotta*; ceramic ware, pottery, porcelain, china, earthenware, faïence, enamel, *cloisonné*.

statue etc. (*image*) 554; cast etc. (*copy*) 21; glyptotheca.

V. sculpture, carve, cut, chisel, model, mold; cast.

Adj. sculptured etc. *v.*; in relief, anaglyptic, ceroplastic, ceramic; parian; marble etc. *n.*

558. Engraving.—N. engraving, chalcography; line –, mezzotint –, stipple –, chalk- engraving; dry-point, bur; etching, aquatinta; plate –, copper-plate –, steel –, wood-, process-, photo-engraving; xylo-, ligno-, glypto-, cero-, litho-, chromolitho-, photolitho-, zinco-, glypho- -graphy, -graph.

impression, print, engraving, plate; steel-, copper-plate; etching; mezzo-, aqua-, litho-tint; cut, woodcut, block; stereo-, grapho-, auto-, helio-type; half-tone; *photogravure, rotogravure.*

graver, *burin*, etching-point, style; plate, stone, wood-block, negative; die, punch, stamp.

printing; plate –, copper-plate –, intaglio –, anastatic –, lithographic –, color –, three color- printing; type-printing etc. 591.

illustr-, illumin-ation; *vignette*, initial letter, *cul de lampe*, tail-piece.

V. engrave, grave, stipple, scrape, etch; bite, – in; lithograph etc. *n.*; print.

Adj. insculptured; engraved etc. *v.*

Phr. *sculpsit, imprimit.*

559. Artist.—N. artist; painter, limner, drawer, sketcher, delineator; cartoon-, caricatur-ist, designer, engraver; draughtsman; copyist; enameller, -list.

historical –, landscape –, genre –, marine –, flower –, portrait –, miniature –, scene –, sign-painter; engraver; Apelles; sculptor, carver, chaser, modeller, lapidary, *figuriste*, statuary; Phidias, Praxiteles; Royal Academician.

photographer, retoucher.

560. Language.—N. language; phraseology etc.
59; speech etc. 582; tongue, lingo, vernacular,
ang; mother −, vulgar −, native- tongue;
ousehold words; King's *or* Queen's English;
liom; dialect etc. 563.

volapuk, esperanto, ido, occidental, Ro.

confusion of tongues, Babel, *pasigraphie*; pan-
mime etc. *(signs)* 550; *onomatopaeia*.

phil-, gloss-, glott-ology; linguistics,
hrestomathy; paleo-logy; -graphy; comparative
-ammar.

literature, letters, polite literature, *belles lettres*,
uses, humanities, *literae humaniores*, republic of
etters, dead languages, classics; genius of a
nguage; scholarship etc. *(knowledge)* 490.

linguist etc. *(scholar)* 492.

V. speak, say, express by words etc. 566.

Adj. lingu-al, -istic; dialectic; vernacular,
urrent, colloquial, slangy; bilingual, polyglot;
terary.

561. Letter.—N. letter; character; hieroglyphic
c. *(writing)* 590; type etc. *(printing)* 591;
apitals; majus-, minus-cule; alphabet, ABC,
becedary, christcross row, chrisscross row.

consonant, vowel, diphthong; mute, surd;
onant, liquid, labial, dental, palatal, gutteral.

syllable; mono-, dis-, poly-syllable; affix, prefix,
affix.

spelling, orthography; phon-ography, -etic
pelling; ana-, meta-grammatism.

cipher, monogram, anagram; double − acrostic.

V. spell.

Adj. literal; alphabetical, abecedarian; syllabic;
ncial etc. *(writing)* 590; phonetic, voiced, mute
tc. *n.*

562. Word.—N. word, term, vocable; name
tc. 564; phrase etc. 566; root, etymon; derivative;
art of speech etc. *(grammar)* 567.

dictionary, vocabulary, word book, lexicon, index, glossary, thesaurus, *gradus, delectus*, concordance.

etymology, lexicology, derivation; phonology,
orthoepy; gloss-; termin-, orism-ology; paleology
tc. *(philology)* 560; comparative philology.

lexicograph-er, -y; glossographer etc. *(scholar)*
92; etymologist; logolept.

verbosity, verbiage, loquacity etc. 584.

Adj. verbal, literal; titular, nominal. [Similarly
lerived] conjugate, paraonymous; derivative.

Adv. verbally etc. *adj.*; *verbatim* etc. *(exactly)*
494.

563. Neology.—N. neolo-gy; -gism; new-
angled expression; barbarism; caconym; archaism,
black letter, monkish Latin; corruption; missaying,
antiphrasis.

paronomasia, play upon words; wordplay etc.
wit) 842; *double-entente* etc. *(ambiguity)* 520;
palindrome, paragram, clinch; abuse of -language,
− terms.

dialect, brogue, *patois*, provincialism, broken
English, *lingua franca*; Brit-, Gall-, Scott-, Hibern-
icism; American-ism; Gipsy lingo, Romany, pidgin
English.

dog Latin, macaronics, gibberish, confusion of
tongues, Babel; jargon.

colloquialism etc. *(figure of speech)* 521; by-
word; technicality, lingo, slang, cant, *argot*, St.
Giles's Greek, thieves' Latin, peddler's French,
flash tongue, Billingsgate, Wall Street slang.

pseudonym etc. *(misnomer)* 565; Mr. So-and-so;
what d'ye call 'em, what's his name; thingum-my, -
bob; *je ne sais quoi*.

neologist, coiner of words.

V. coin words.

Adj. neologic, -al; rare; archaic; obsolete etc.
(old) 124; colloquial, dialectic, slang, cant.

564. Nomenclature.—N. nomenclature;
naming etc. *v.*; nuncupation, nomination, baptism;
orismology; *onomatopaeia*; antonomasia.

name; appella-tion, -tive; designation; title;
head, -ing, caption; denomination; by-name,
epithet.

style, proper name; prae-, ag-, cog-nomen;
patronymic, surname; cognomination; com-
pellation, description; empty -title, − name; handle to one's name; namesake, eponym.

synonym, antonym.

term, expression, noun; by-word; convertible
terms etc. 522; technical term; cant etc. 563.

V. name, call, term, denominate, designate,
style, entitle, intitule, clepe, dub, christen, baptize,
nickname, characterize, specify, define, distinguish
by the name of; label etc. *(mark)* 550.

be -called etc. *v.*; take −, bear −, go *(or* be
known) by −, go *(or* pass) under −, rejoice in- the
name of.

Adj. named etc. *v.*; hight, yclept, known as;
what one may -well, − fairly, − properly, − fitly-
call.

nuncupa-tory, -tive; cognominal, titular,
nominal; orismological.

565. Misnomer.—N. misnomer; *lucus a non
lucendo*; Mrs. Malaprop; what d'ye call 'em etc.
(neologism) 563.

nickname, *sobriquet*, by-name, handle,
moniker; assumed -name, − title; *alias*; *nom de -
guerre*, − *plume*, − *theâtre*; pseudonym, pen
name, stage name.

V. mis-name, -call, - term; nickname; assume -a
name, − an alias.

Adj. misnamed etc. *v.*; pseudonymous; *soi-
disant*; self-called, -styled, -christened; so-called.

nameless, anonymous; without a −, having no-
name; innominate, unnamed.

Adv. in no sense.

566. Phrase.—N. phrase, expression, set
phrase; sentence, paragraph; figure of speech etc.
521; idi-om, -otism; turn of expression.

paraphrase etc. (*synonym*) 522; periphrase etc. (*circumlocution*) 573; motto etc. (*proverb*) 496. phraseology etc. 569.

V. express, phrase; word, − it; give -words, − expression- to; voice; arrange in −, clothe in −, put into −, express by- words; couch in terms; find words to express; speak by the card.

Adj. expressed etc. *v.*; idiomatic.

Adv. in -round, − set, − good, set- terms; in set phrases.

567. Grammar.—N. grammar, accidence, syntax, *praxis*, analysis, paradigm, punctuation; parts of speech, inflexion, case, declension, conjugation; *jus et norma loquendi*; Lindley Murray etc. (*school-book*) 542; correct style; philology etc. (*language*) 560.

V. parse, analyze; decline, conjugate; punctuate.

Adj. grammatical; syntactic; inflexional.

568. Solecism.—N. solecism; bad −, false −, faulty- grammar; slip, error; slip of the -pen, − tongue; *lapsus calami-*, − *linguae*; *faux pas*; slip-slop; bull.

V. use -bad, − faulty- grammar; solecize, commit a solecism; murder the -King's, − Queen's-English; break Priscian's head.

Adj. ungrammatical; in-correct, -accurate; faulty, improper, incongruous, abnormal.

569. Style.—N. style, diction, phraseology, wording; manner, strain; composition; mode of expression, choice of words, literary power, ready pen, pen of a ready writer; command of language etc. (*eloquence*) 582; authorship; *la morgue littéraire*.

V. express by words etc. 566; write.

570. Perspicuity.—N. perspicuity etc. (*intelligibility*) 518; plain speaking etc. (*manifestation*) 525; defin-iteness, -ition; exactness etc. 494; perspicuousness, logical acuteness.

Adj. lucid etc. (*intelligible*) 518; explicit etc. (*manifest*) 525; exact etc. 494.

571. Obscurity.—N. obscurity etc. (*unintelligibility*) 519; involution; hard words; ambiguity etc. 520; vagueness etc. 475, inexactness etc. 495; what d'ye call 'em etc. (*neologism*) 563; cloudiness, confusion.

Adj. obscure etc. *n.*; crabbed, involved, confused.

572. Conciseness.—N. conciseness etc. *adj.*; brevity, 'the soul of wit,' laconism; Tacitus; ellipsis; syncope; abridgment etc. (*shortening*) 201; compression etc. 195; epitome etc. 596; monostitch; portmanteau word, telescope word, protogram.

V. be -concise etc. *adj.*; condense etc. 195; abridge etc. 201; abstract etc. 596; come to the point.

Adj. concise, brief, short, terse, close; to the point, exact; neat, compact, condensed, pointed laconic, curt, pithy, trenchant, summary; pregnant compendious etc. (*compendium*) 596; succinct elliptical, epigrammatic, crisp, sententious.

Adv. concisely etc. *adj.*; briefly, summarily; in brief, − short, − a word, − few words, − a nutshell; for shortness sake; to -come to the point, − make a long story short, − cut the matter short, − be brief; it comes to this, the long and short of it is.

573. Diffuseness.—N. diffuseness etc. *adj.* amplification etc. *v.*; dilating etc. *v.*; verbosity, *verbiage*, wordiness, cloud of words, *copia verborum* flow of words etc. (*loquacity*) 584.

poly-, tauto-, batto-, perisso-logy; pleonasm exuberance, redundance; thrice-told tale; prolixity circumlocution, *ambages*; periphra-se, -sis; round-about phrases; episode; expletive; penny-a-lining padding, drivel, twaddle, rigmarole; richness etc 577.

V. be -diffuse etc. *adj.*; run out on, descant, expatiate, enlarge, dilate, amplify, expand, inflate pad; launch −, branch- out; rant.

maunder, prose; harp upon etc. (*repeat*) 104 dwell on, insist upon.

digress, ramble, *battre la campagne*, beat about the bush, perorate, spin a long yarn, protract; spin −, swell −, draw- out, drivel.

Adj. dif-, pro-fuse; wordy, verbose, largiloquent, copious, exuberant, effusive, pleonastic, lengthy; long, -some, -winded, -spun, -drawn out; diffusive, spun out, protracted, prolix, prosing, maundering; circumlocutory, periphrastic, ambagious, round-about; digressive; dis-, ex-cursive; rambling, episodic; flatulent, frothy.

Adv. diffusely etc. *adj.*; at large, *in extenso*; about it and about it.

574. Vigor.—N. vigor, power, force; boldness, raciness etc. *adj.*; spirit, point, antithesis, piquancy; *verve*, glow, fire, warmth, ardor, enthusiasm; 'thoughts that breathe and words that burn;' strong language; punch; gravity, sententiousness; elevation, loftiness, sublimity.

eloquence; command of -words, − language.

Adj. vigorous, nervous, powerful, forcible, trenchant, mordant, biting, incisive, impressive; sensational.

spirited, lively, glowing, sparkling, racy, bold, slashing; pungent, *piquant*, full of point, pointed, pithy, antithetical; sententious.

lofty, elevated, sublime, grand, weighty, ponderous; eloquent, vehement, petulant, impassioned; poetic.

Adv. in -glowing, − good set, − no measured-terms.

575. Feebleness.—N. feebleness etc. *adj.*;

Adj. feeble, bald, tame, meager, insipid, nerve-les, jejune, vapid, trashy, cold, frigid, poor, dull, dry, languid; pros-ing, -y, -aic; unvaried, monotonous, weak, frail, washy, wishy-washy, sloppy; sketchy, slight; careless, slovenly, loose, lax; slip-shod, -slop; inexact; dis-jointed, -connected; puerile, childish; flatulent; rambling etc. (*diffuse*) 573.

576. Plainness.—N. plainness etc. *adj.*; simplicity, severity; plain -terms, – English; Saxon English; household words.

V. speak plainly; call a spade 'a spade;' plunge *in medias res*; come to the point.

Adj. plain, simple; un-ornamented, -adorned, -varnished; home-ly, -spun; neat; severe, chaste, pure, Saxon; commonplace, matter of fact, natural, prosaic, sober, unimaginative.

dry, unvaried, monotonous etc. 575.

Adv. in plain -terms, – words, – English, – common parlance; point blank.

577. Ornament.—N. ornament; floridness etc. *adj.*; turg-idity, -escence; altiloquence etc. *adj.*; orotundity; declamation; teratology; well-rounded periods; elegance etc. 578.

inversion, antithesis, alliteration, *paronomasia*; figurativeness etc. (*metaphor*) 521.

flourish; flowers of -speech, – rhetoric; euphuism, -emism.

big-, high-sounding words; macrology, *sesquipedalia verba*, sesquipedalianism; Alexandrine; inflation, pretension; rant, bombast, fustian, bunkum, balderdash, prose run mad; fine writing; Minerva press.

phrasemonger; euph-uist, -emist.

V. ornament, overlay with ornament, overcharge; smell of the lamp.

Adj. ornamented etc. *v.*; beautified etc. 847; ornate, florid, rich, flowery; euph-uistic, -emistic; sonorous; high-, big-sounding; inflated, swelling, tumid; turg-id, -escent; pedantic, pompous, stilted; high-flown, -flowing; sententious, rhetorical, declamatory; grandiose; grand-, magn-, alt-iloquent; sesquipedal, -ian; Johnsonian, mouthy; bombastic; fustian; frothy, flashy, flaming, flamboyant.

antithetical, alliterative; figurative etc. 521; artificial etc. (*inelegant*) 579.

Adv. *ore rotundo*; with rounded phrase.

578. Elegance.—N. elegance, purity, grace, ease, felicity, distinction, gracefulness, refinement, readiness etc. *adj.*; concinnity, euphony, numerosity, balance, rythm, symmetry, proportion; restraint; good taste, propriety.

well rounded –, well turned –, flowing-periods; the right word in the right place; antithesis etc. 577.

purist, stylist.

V. point an antithesis, round a period.

Adj. elegant, polished, classical, Attic, correct, Ciceronian, artistic; chaste, pure, Saxon, academical.

graceful, easy, readable, fluent, flowing, tripping; unaffected, natural, unlabored; mellifluous; euph-onious, -emistic; rhythmical, balanced, symmetrical.

felicitous, happy, neat; well –, neatly- -put, – expressed.

579. Inelegance.—N. inelegance; vulgarity, bad taste; stiffness etc. *adj.*; unlettered Muse; barbarism; slang etc. 563; solecism etc. 568; mannerism etc. (*affectation*) 855; euphuism; fustian etc. 577; cacophony; want of balance; words that break the teeth, – dislocate the jaw.

V. be -inelegant etc. *adj.*

Adj. inelegant, graceless, ungraceful, unpolished; harsh, abrupt; dry, stiff, cramped, formal, *guindé*; forced, labored, awkward; artificial, mannered, ponderous; turgid etc. 577; affected, euphuistic; barbarous, uncouth, grotesque, rude, crude, halting; vulgar, offensive to ears polite.

580. Voice.—N. voice; vocality; organ, lungs, bellows; good –, fine –, powerful etc. (*loud*) 404 –, musical etc. 413- voice; intonation; tone etc. (*sound*) 402- of voice.

vocalization; cry etc. 411; strain, utterance, prolation; exclam-, ejacul-, vocifer-ation; enunci-, articul-ation; articulate sound; distinctness; clearness, – of articulation; stage whisper; delivery; attack.

accent, -uation; emphasis, stress; broad –, strong –, pure –, native –, foreign- accent; pronunciation.

[Word similarly pronounced] homonym.

orthoepy; euphony etc. (*melody*) 413.

gastri-, ventri-loquism; ventriloquist; polyphonism, -ist.

[Science of voice] phonology etc. (*sound*) 402.

V. sing, speak, utter, breathe, voice; give -utterance, – tongue; cry etc. (*shout*) 411; ejaculate, rap out; vocalize, prolate, articulate, enunciate, enounce, pronounce, accentuate, aspirate, deliver, mouth; emit, murmur, whisper, – in the ear, croon, yodel.

Adj. vocal, phonetic, oral; ejaculatory, articulate, distinct, stertorous; enunciative; accentuated, aspirated; euphonious etc. (*melodious*) 413.

581. Aphony—N. aphony, *aphonia*; dumbness etc. *adj.*; obmutescence; absence –, want- of voice; dysphony; silence etc. (*taciturnity*) 585; raucity; harsh etc. 410 –, unmusical etc. 414- voice; *falsetto*, 'childish treble;' mute, dummy, deaf mute.

V. keep silence etc. 585; speak -low, – softly; whisper etc. (*faintness*) 405.

silence; render -mute, – silent etc. 403; muzzle, muffle, suppress, smother, gag, strike dumb, dumbfound, -founder; drown the voice, put to silence, stop one's mouth, cut one short.

stick in the throat.

Adj. aphon-ous, -ic, dumb, mute; deaf-mute, –

and dumb; mum; tongue-tied; breath-, tongue-, voice-, speech-, word-less; mute as a -fish, – stock-fish, – mackerel; silent etc. (*taciturn*) 585; muzzled; in-articulate, -audible.

croaking, raucous, hoarse, husky, dry, hollow, sepulchral, hoarse as a raven.

Adv. with -bated breath, – the finger on the lips; *sotto voce*; in a -low tone, – cracked voice, – broken voice; in an aside.

Phr. *vox faucibus haesit.*

582. Speech.—N. speech, faculty of speech; locution, talk, parlance, verbal intercourse, prolation, oral communication, word of mouth, *parole*, palaver, prattle; effusion.

oration, recitation, delivery, say, address, speech, lecture, harangue, sermon, *tirade*, screed, formal speech, salutatory, peroration; prelection; speechifying; soliloquy etc. 589; allocution etc. 586; interlocution etc. 588.

oratory; elo-cution, -quence; rhetoric, declamation; grandi-, multi-loquence; burst of eloquence; facundity; talkativeness; flow –, command- of -words, – language; *copia verborum*; power of speech, gift of the gab; *usus loquendi.*

speaker etc. *v.*; spokesman, pro-, inter-locutor; mouthpiece, Hermes; ora-tor, -trix, -tress; Demosthenes, Cicero; rhetorician; stump –, platform- orator, tub-thumper; elocutionist; speech-maker, patterer, *improvisatore.*

V. speak, – of; say, utter, pronounce, deliver, give utterance to; utter –, pour- forth; breathe, let fall, come out with; rap –, blurt- out; have on one's lips; have at the -end, – tip- of one's tongue.

break silence; open one's -lips, – mouth; lift –, raise- one's voice; give –, wag the- tongue; talk, outspeak; put in a word or two.

hold forth; make –, deliver- -a speech etc. *n.*; speechify, harangue, declaim, stump, flourish, spout, rant, recite, lecture, preach, sermonize, discourse, be on one's legs; have –, say- one's say; expatiate etc. (*speak at length*) 573; speak one's mind.

soliloquize etc. 589; tell etc. (*inform*) 527; speak to etc. 586; talk together etc. 588.

be -eloquent etc. *adj.*; have -a tongue in one's head, – the gift of the gab etc. *n.*

pass –, escape- one's lips; fall from the -lips, – mouth.

Adj. speaking etc., spoken etc. *v.*; oral, lingual, phonetic, not written, unwritten, outspoken; eloquent, -cutionary; orat-, rhetorical; declamatory; grandiloquent etc. 577; talkative etc. 584.

Adv. orally etc. *adj.*; by word of mouth, *vivâ voce*, from the lips of.

Phr. quoth –, said- -he etc.

583. Stammering. [Imperfect Speech.]—**N.** inarticulateness; stammering etc. *v.*; hesitation etc. *v.*; impediment in one's speech; aphasia, titubancy, traulism; whisper etc. (*faint sound*) 405; lisp, drawl, tardiloquence; nasal -tone, – accent; twang; *falsetto* etc. (*want of voice*) 581; broken -voice, – accents; – sentences.

brogue etc. 563; slip of the tongue, *lapsus linguae.*

V. stammer, stutter, hesitate, falter, hammer; balbu-tiâte, -cinate; haw, hum and haw, be unable to put two words together.

mumble, mutter; maund, -er; whisper etc. 405; mince, lisp; jabber, gabble, gibber; sp-, spl-utter; muffle, mump; drawl, mouth; croak; speak -thick, – through the nose; snuffle, clip one's words; murder the -language, – King's (*or* Queen's) English; mis-pronounce, -say.

Adj. stammering etc. *v.*; inarticulate, guttural, nasal; tremulous.

Adv. *sotto voce* etc. (*faintly*) 405.

584. Loquacity.—N. loquac-ity, -iousness; talkativeness etc. *adj.*; garrulity; multiloquence, much speaking, effusion, wordiness.

jaw; gab, -ble; jabber, chatter; prate, prattle, cackle, clack; twaddle, trattle, rattle; *caquet, -terie*; blabber, *bavardage*, bibble-babble, gibble-gabble; small talk etc. (*converse*) 588.

fluency, flippancy, volubility, flowing tongue; flow, – of words; *flux de -bouche, – mots, – paroles*; *copia verborum*, *cacoëthes loquendi*; verbosity etc. (*diffuseness*) 573; gift of the gab etc. (*eloquence*) 582.

talker; chatter-er, -box; babbler etc. *v.*; rattle; ranter; sermonizer, proser, driveller; wind bag; gossip etc. (*converse*) 588; magpie, jay, parrot, poll, Babel; *moulin à paroles.*

V. be -loquacious etc. *adj.*; talk glibly, pour forth; patter; prate, palaver, prose, chatter, prattle, clack, jabber, jaw; rattle, – on; twaddle, twattle; babble, gabble; out-talk; talk oneself -out of breath, – hoarse; maunder, gush, blatter; talk a donkey's hind leg off; expatiate etc. (*speak at length*) 573; gossip etc. (*converse*) 588; din in the ears etc. (*repeat*) 104; talk -at random, – nonsense etc. 497; be hoarse with talking.

Adj. loquacious, talkative, conversational, garrulous, linguacious, multiloquous; chattering etc. *v.*; chatty etc. (*sociable*) 892; declamatory etc. 582; open-mouthed.

fluent, voluble, glib, flippant; long-tongued, -winded etc. (*diffuse*) 573.

Adv. trippingly on the tongue; glibly etc. *adj.*

Phr. the tongue running -fast, – loose, – on wheels.

585. Taciturnity.—N. silence, muteness, obmutescence; taciturnity, pauciloquy, costiveness, curtness; reserve, reticence etc. (*concealment*) 528; *aposiopesis.*

man of few words.

V. be -silent etc. *adj.*; keep silence; hold one's -tongue, – peace, – jaw; not speak etc. 582; say nothing; seal –, close –, put a padlock on- the -lips, – mouth; put a bridle on one's tongue; keep one's tongue between one's teeth; make no sign, not let a word escape one; keep a secret etc. 528; not have a word to say; lay –, place- the finger on the lips; render mute etc. 581.

stick in one's throat.

Adj. silent, mute, mum; silent as -a post, – a stone, – the grave etc. (*still*) 403; dumb etc. 581.

taciturn, sparing of words; close, – mouthed, –

tongued; laconic, costive, inconversable, curt; reserved; reticent etc. (*concealing*) 528.
Int. tush! silence! mum! hush! *chut!* hist! tut! etc. 403.

586. Allocution.—N. allocution, alloquy, address; speech etc. 582; apostrophe, interpellation, appeal, invocation, salutation; word in the ear.

[Feigned dialogue] dialogism.
platform etc. 542; audience etc. (*interview*) 588.
V. speak to, address, accost, make up to, apostrophize, appeal to, invoke; hail, salute; call to, halloo.
take -aside, – by the button, button-hole; talk to in private.
lecture etc. (*make a speech*) 582.
Int. soho! halloo! hey! hist! hi!

587. Response etc.; *see* Answer 462.

588. Interlocution.—N. interlocution; collocution, colloquy, converse, conversation, confabulation, talk, discourse, verbal intercourse; communion, oral communication, commerce; dia-, duo-, tria-logue.

causerie, chat, chit-chat; small –, table –, teatable –, town –, village –, idle- talk; tattle, gossip, tittle-tattle; babble, -ment; *tripotage*, cackle, prittle-prattle, *on dit*; talk of the -town, – village.
conference, parley, interview, audience, *pourparler*; *tête-à-tête*; reception, *conversazione*; congress etc. (*council*) 696; pow-wow.
hall of audience, *durbar*, coliseum, assembly hall, auditorium.
palaver, debate, logomachy, war of words, controversy.
talker, gossip, tattler; Paul Pry; tabby; chatterer etc. (*loquacity*) 584; interlocutor etc. (*spokesman*) 582; conversation-ist, -alist; dialogist.
'the feast of reason and the flow of soul;' *mollia tempora fandi.*
V. talk together, converse, confabulate; hold –, carry on –, join in –, engage in- a conversation; put in a word; shine in conversation; bandy words; parley; palaver; chat, gossip, tattle; prate etc. (*loquacity*) 584.
discourse –, confer –, commune –, commerce- with; hold -converse, – conference, – intercourse; talk it over; be closeted with; talk with one -in private, – *tête-à-tête*.
Adj. conversing etc. *v.*; interlocutory; conversational, -able; discursive, -coursive; chatty etc. (*sociable*) 892; colloquial, *tête-à-tête*, confabulatory.

589. Soliloquy.—N. soliloquy, monologue, apostrophe.

solilo-quist, -quizer, monologist.

V. soliloquize; say –, talk- to oneself; say aside, think aloud, apostrophize.
Adj. soliloquizing etc. *v.*
Adv. aside.

590. Writing.—N. writing etc. *v.*; chiro-, stelo-, cero-graphy, graphology; stylography; pen-craft, - script, -manship; quill-driving; typewriting.

writing, manuscript, MS., *literae scriptae*; these presents.
stroke –, dash- of the pen; *coup de plume*; line; pen and ink.
letter etc. 561; uncial writing, cuneiform character, arrow-head, Ogham, Runes, futhorc; hieroglyphic, hieratic, demotic; script; contraction.
short-hand; steno-, brachy-, tachy-graphy; secret writing, writing in cipher; crypt-, stegan-ography; phono-, pasi-, poly-, logo-graphy.
copy; tran-, re-script; draft, rough –, fair- copy; handwriting; signature, sign-manual; auto-, mono-, holo-graph; hand, fist; mark.
calligraphy; good –, running –, flowing –, cursive –, legible –, copperplate –, round –, bold-hand.
cacography, *griffonage*, *barbouillage*; bad –, cramped –, crabbed –, illegible- hand; scribble etc. *v.*; *pattes de mouche*; ill-formed letters; pot-hooks and hangers.
stationery; pen, quill, goose-quill, reed; stylographic-, fountain-pen; pencil, style, stylus; paper, foolscap, parchment, vellum, papyrus, pad, tablet, block, note book, slate, marble, pillar, table, black board.
ink-bottle, -pot, -stand, -well, -horn; typewriter.
transcription etc. (*copy*) 21; inscription etc. (*record*) 551; superscription etc. (*indication*) 550.
composition, authorship; *cacoethes scribendi*.
writer, scribe, amanuensis, scrivener, secretary, clerk, penman, copyist, transcriber, quill-driver; writer for the press etc. (*author*) 593.
shorthand writer, stenographer; typewriter, typist.
V. write, pen; copy, engross; write out, – fair; transcribe; scribble, scrawl, scrabble, scratch; interline; stain paper; write down etc. (*record*) 551; sign etc. (*attest*) 467; take down, – in shorthand; typewrite, type.
compose, indite, draw up, redact, draft, formulate; dictate; inscribe, throw on paper, dash off; concoct.
take -up the pen, – pen in hand; shed –, spill –, dip one's pen in- ink.
Adj. writing etc. *v.*; written etc. *v.*; in -writing, – black and white; under one's hand.
uncial, Runic, cuneiform, hieroglyphical etc. *n.*
Adv. *currente calamo*; pen in hand.

591. Printing.—N. printing; block –, type-printing, lino-, mono-type; plate printing etc. (*engraving*) 558; the press etc. (*publication*) 531; composition.

print, letterpress, text, matter, standing type; context, note, page, column; over-running; head-, foot-line, title.
typography; stereo-, electro-, apro-type; type,

black letter, heavy type, font, fount; pi, pie; capitals etc. (*letters*) 561; diamond, pearl, nonpareil, minion, brevier, bourgeois, long primer, small pica, pica, english, great primer.

folio etc. (*book*) 593; copy, impression, pull, proof, galley –, author's –, page- proof, revise.

printer, compositor, reader; printer's devil.

V. print; compose; put –, go- to press; pass –, see- through the press; publish etc. 531; bring out; appear in –, rush into- print.

Adj. printed etc. *v.*; in type; typographical etc. *n.*

592. Correspondence.—N. correspondence, letter, epistle, note, *billet*, post-, letter-card, missive, circular, form letter; favor, *billet-doux*; des-, dis-patch; *bulletin*, communication etc. 532; these presents; rescript, -ion; post etc. (*messenger*) 534; letter writer, correspondent.

V. correspond, – with; write –, send a letter-to; keep up a correspondence; drop a line to; despatch; communicate with; circularize.

Adj. epistolary.

593. Book.—N. book, -let; writing, work, volume, tome, opuscule; tract, -ate; *livret*; *brochure, libretto*, handbook, treatise, text-book, codex, manual, pamphlet, monograph, en-chiridion, circular, publication; book of poems; novel; chap-book.

part, issue, number, *livraison*; album, portfolio; periodical, serial, magazine, *ephemeris*, annual, journal.

paper, bill, sheet, broadsheet, screed; leaf, -let; fly-leaf, page; quire, ream.

chapter, section, head, article, paragraph, passage, clause, supplement, appendix; *feuilleton*.

folio, quarto, octavo; duo-, sexto-, octo-decimo.

en-, cyclopedia, dictionary, lexicon, thesaurus, concordance, anthology, bibliography; com-pilation, compendium, catalogue etc. 86; library, bibliotheca; the press etc. (*publication*) 531.

writer, author, *littérateur*, essayist, journalist, publicist; scribe, penman, war –, special –, correspondent; pen, scribbler, the scribbling race; ghost, hack, literary hack, Grub-street writer; writer for –, gentlemen of –, representative of-the press; reporter, penny-a-liner; editor, sub-editor; playwright etc. 599; poet etc. 597.

bookseller, publisher; biblio-pole, -polist, - grapher; librarian; book -collector, – worm.

book -shop, – club, circulating –, lending –, public- library; publishing house.

knowledge of books, bibliography; book-learning etc. (*knowledge*) 490.

594. Description.—N. description, account, statement, report; *exposé* etc. (*disclosure*) 529; specification, particulars, scenario, plot; state –, summary- of facts; brief etc. (*abstract*) 596; return etc. (*record*) 551; *catalogue raisonné* etc. (*list*) 86; guide-book etc. (*information*) 527.

delineation etc. (*representation*) 554; sketch, vignette; monograph; minute –, detailed –, particular –, circumstantial –, graphic- account; narration, recital, rehearsal, relation.

histori-, chron-ography; historic Muse, Clio; history; bi-, autobi-ography; necrology, obituary.

narrative, history; memoir, memorials; annals etc. (*chronicle*) 551; tradition, legend, saga, epic, epos, story, tale, historiette; personal narrative, journal, letters, life, adventures, fortunes, ex-periences, confessions; anecdote, ana, *trait*.

work of fiction, short story, novelette, novel, romance, penny dreadful, shilling, shocker, Minerva press; fairy –, nursery- tale; fable, allegory, parable, apologue.

relator etc. *v.*; *raconteur*; historian etc. (*recorder*) 553; biographer, fabulist, novelist, story teller, romancer, teller of tales, spinner of yarns, anecdotist.

V. describe; set forth etc. (*state*) 535; draw a picture, picture; portray etc. (*represent*) 554; characterize, particularize; narrate, relate, recite, recount, sum up, run over, recapitulate, rehearse, fight one's battles over again.

unfold etc. (*disclose*) 529- a tale; tell; give –, render- an account of; report, make a report, draw up a statement.

detail; enter into –, descend to- -particulars, – details.

Adj. descriptive, graphic, narrative, epic, suggestive, well-drawn; historic; auto-, biographical, realistic, expository, tradition-al, -ary; legendary; fabulous, mythical; anecdotic, storied; described etc. *v.*

595. Dissertation.—N. dissertation, treatise, essay; *thesis*, theme; tract, -ate, -ation, excursus; discourse, memoir, disquisition, lecture, sermon, homily, pandect.

commentary, review, *critique*, criticism, article; lead-er, -ing article, editorial; argument, running commentary.

investigation etc. (*inquiry*) 461; study etc. (*consideration*) 451; discussion etc. (*reasoning*) 476; exposition etc. (*explanation*) 522.

commentator, critic, essayist, pamphleteer; publicist, reviewer, leader writer, editor, an-notator.

V. dissert –, descant –, write –, touch- upon a subject; dissertate; treat of –, take up –, ven-tilate –, discuss –, deal with –, go into –, can-vass –, handle –, do justice to- a subject; com-ment, criticize, interpret etc. 522.

Adj. dis-cursive, -coursive; disquisitional, disquisitionary; expository, critical.

596. Compendium.—N. compend, -ium; ab-stract, *précis*, epitome, *multum in parvo*, analysis, pandect, digest, sum and substance, brief, abridgment, summary, *aperçu*, draft, minute, note; synopsis, textbook, *conspectus*, outlines, syllabus, contents, heads, prospectus.

album; scrap –, note –, memorandum –; commonplace- book; extracts, *excerpta*, cuttings; fugitive -pieces, – writings; *spicilegium*, flowers, anthology, miscellany, *collectanea, analecta*; compilation.

recapitulation, *résumé*, review.

abbrevia-tion, -ture; contraction; shortening etc. 201; compression etc. 195.

V. abridge, abstract, epitomize, summarize; make −, prepare −, draw −, compile- an abstract etc. *n.*

recapitulate, review, skim, run over, sum up.

abbreviate etc. (*shorten*) 201; condense etc. (*compress*) 195; compile etc. (*collect*) 72; edit, blue pencil.

Adj. compendious, synoptic, analectic, analytical; abridged etc. *v.*

Adv. in -short, − epitome, − substance, − few words.

Phr. it lies in a nutshell.

597. Poetry.—**N.** poetry, poetics, poesy, Muse, Calliope, tuneful Nine, Parnassus, Helicon, Pierides, Pierian spring, afflatus, inspiration.

versification, rhyming, making verses; prosody, scansion, orthometry.

poem; epic, − poem; epopee, *epopaea*, ode, epode, idyl, lyric, eclogue, pastoral, bucolic, georgic, dithyramb, anacreontic, sonnet, roundelay, *rondel, rondoletto, rondeau, rondo*, triolet, madrigal, canzonet, *cento*, monody, elegy, palinode; rhapsody.

dramatic −, lyric- poetry; opera; posy, anthology.

song, ballad, lay; love −, drinking −, war −, folk −, sea- song; lullaby; music etc. 415; nursery rhymes.

[Bad poetry] doggerel, Hudibrastic verse, prose run mad; macaronics; macaronic −, leonine-verse; runes.

canto, stanza, distich, verse, line, couplet, triplet, quatrain, sestet; *strophe, antistrophe*, refrain, chorus, burden.

verse, rhyme, assonance, crambo, meter, measure, foot, numbers, strain, rhythm; accentuation etc. (*voice*) 580; iambus, dactyl, spondee, trochee, anapaest etc.; hex-, pent-ameter; Alexandrine; blank verse, alliteration.

elegiacs etc. *adj.*; elegiac etc. *adj.* -verse, − meter, − poetry.

poet, − laureate; laureate; minor poet, bard, lyrist, scald, troubadour, *trouvère*; mistrel; minne-, meister-singer; *improvisatore*; versifier, sonneteer; ballad monger; rhym-er, -ist, -ester; poetaster.

V. poetize, sing, versify, make verses, rhyme, scan.

Adj. poetic, -al; lyric, -al; tuneful; epic; dithyrambic etc. *n.*; metrical; a-, catalectic; elegiac, iambic, trochaic, spondaic, anapest; Ionic, Sapphic, Alcaic, Pindaric.

598. Prose.—**N.** prose, − writer, pros-aism, - aist, -er.

V. prose, write prose.

write -prose, − in prose.

Adj. pros-y, -aic; unpoetical.

rhymeless, unrhymed, in prose, not in verse.

599. Drama.—**N.** drama, the -drama, − stage,

− theater, − play; theatricals, dramaturgy, histrionic art, buskin, sock, *cothurnus*, Melpomene and Thalia, Thespis.

play, stage-play, piece, five-act play, tragedy, comedy, opera, comic opera, *vaudeville, comedietta, lever de rideau*, curtain raiser, interlude, afterpiece, exode, farce, *divertissement, extravaganza*, burletta, harlequinade, pantomime, mimodrama, burlesque, *opéra bouffe*, musical comedy, review, revue, intimate revue, variety, cabaret entertainment, *ballet, spectacle*, masque, *drame, comédie drame*; melo-drama, -drame; *comédie larmoyante*, emotional drama, sensation drama, tragi-, farcical-comedy; mono-drame, - logue; duologue; trilogy; charade, *proverbe*; mystery, miracle −, morality- play.

act, scene, *tableau*; in-, intro-duction; pro-, epilogue, curtain; *libretto*, book, script.

performance, representation, show, *mise en scène*, stagery, *jeu de théâtre*, stage-craft; acting; gesture etc. 550; impersonation etc. 554; stage business, gag, patter, buffoonery.

theater; play-, opera-house; house; music hall; *cabaret*; amphitheater, circus, hippodrome; puppet-show, *fantoccini*; *marionnettes*, Punch and Judy.

cinema, -tograph-, picture −, theater, the pictures, the movies, the talkies.

auditory, *auditorium*, front of the house, stalls, boxes, balcony, dress −, upper- -circle, − boxes, amphitheater, pit, gallery; *foyer*; greenroom; dressing rooms, *coulisses*.

flat; drop, − scene; wing, screen, side-scene; transformation scene, curtain, act-drop, safety −, fire- curtain; *proscenium*, forestage.

stage, revolving stage, scene, the boards; star −, grave −, trap, mezzanine floor; flies; gridiron, floats, battens, footlights; lime −, spot −, flood −, bunch-lights; scenery, set, *décor*; orchestra.

theatrical -costume, − properties, props.

part, *rôle*, character, cast, *dramatis personae*; *répertoire*.

actor, player; stage −, strolling- player; old −, stager, performer; mime, -r; *artiste*; com-, tragedian, straight man; *tragédienne*, Thespian, Roscius, star.

pantomimist, clown, harlequin, *buffo*, buffoon, *farceur, grimacier*, pantaloon, columbine; *Pierrot, Pierrette*; punch, -inello; *pulcinell-o, -a*; mute, *figurante*, general utility; super, -numerary, extra.

mummer, guiser, guisard, gysart, masque.

mountebank, Jack Pudding; tumbler, posture-master, acrobat, equilibrist, juggler, contortionist; *danseuse, ballerina*, ballet -dancer, − girl, *coryphée; bayadère, geisha*; chorus -singer, − girl.

company; first tragedian, *prima donna*, lead, leading lady, protagonist; *jeune premier*; juvenile lead, *débutant, -e*; light −, genteel −, low- comedy, − comedian; *soubrette*, walking gentleman, *amoroso*, heavy, heavy father, *ingénue, jeune veuve, commère, compère*.

property man, *costumier*, machinist, stage hand, electrician, prompter, call-boy; director, manager; stage −, acting −, business- manager; *entrepreneur, impresario*, producer, press agent.

dramatic -author, − writer; play-writer, -wright; dramatist, mimographer; dramatic critic.

V. act, play, perform; stage, produce, put on the stage; personate etc. 554; mimic etc. (*imitate*) 19; enact; play −, act −, go through −, perform- a part; rehearse, spout, gag, rant; 'strut and fret one's hour upon a stage;' tread the -stage, – boards; come out;, star.

Adj. dramatic; theatric, -al; scenic, histrionic, anctorial, comic, tragic, buskined, farcical, tragi-comic, melodramatic, operatic; stagey spectacular; stagestruck.

Adv. on the -stage, – boards; before -the floats, – an audience; in the limelight, behind the footlights; behind the scenes.

600. Will.—N. will, volition, conation, velleity; will and pleasure, free-will; freedom etc. 748; discretion; choice, inclination, intent, purpose, option etc. (*choice*) 609; voluntariness; spontane-ity, -ousness; originality.

pleasure, wish, desire, mind; frame of mind etc. (*inclination*) 602; intention etc. 620; predetermination etc. 611; self-control etc. determination etc. (*resolution*) 604; will-power.

V. will, list; see –, think- fit; determine etc. (*resolve*) 604; settle etc. (*choose*) 609; volunteer.

have a will of one's own; do what one chooses etc. (*freedom*) 748; have it all one's own way; have one's -will, – own way.

use –, exercise- one's discretion; take -upon oneself, – one's own course, – the law into one's own hands; do -of one's own accord, – upon one's own -responsibility, – authority; take the bit between one's teeth; take responsibility; originate etc. (*cause*) 153.

Adj. voluntary, volitive, volitional, wilful; free etc. 748; optional; discretion-al, -ary; volitient; dictatorial.

minded etc. (*willing*) 602; prepense etc. (*predetermined*) 611; intended etc. 620; autocratic; unbidden etc. (bid etc. 741); spontaneous; original etc. (*causal*) 153.

Adv. voluntarily etc. *adj.*; at -will, – pleasure; *à -volonté*, – *discrétion*; *al piacere*; *ad -libitum*, – *arbitrium*; as -one thinks proper, – it seems good to.

of one's own -accord, – free will; *proprio -*, *suo –*, *ex mero- motu*; out of one's own head; by choice etc. 609; purposely etc. (*intentionally*) 620; deliberately etc. 611.

Phr. *stet pro ratione voluntas*; *sic volo sic jubeo*.

601. Necessity.—N. involuntariness, instinct, blind –, natural- impulse; inborn –, innate-proclivity; the force of circumstances.

necessi-ty, -tation, necessarianism; obligation; compulsion etc. 744; subjection etc. 749; stern –, hard –, dire –, imperious –, inexorable –, iron –, adverse- -necessity, – fate; what must be.

desti-ny, -nation; fatality, fate, *kismet*, doom, foredoom, election, predestination; pre–, fore-ordination; lot, fortune; fatalism, determinism; inevitableness etc. *adj.*; spell etc. 993.

star, -s; planet, -s; astral influence; sky, Fates, Norns, *Parcae*, Sisters three, Clotho, Lachesis, Atropos; book of fate; God's will, will of Heaven; wheel of Fortune, Ides of March, Hobson's choice.

last -shift, – resort; *dernier ressort*; *pis aller* etc. (*substitute*) 147; necessaries etc. (*requirement*) 630.

necess-arian, -itarian; fatalist, determinist; automaton.

V. lie under a necessity; be -fated, – doomed, – destined etc., – in for, – under the necessity of; have no -choice, – alternative; be- obliged –, forced –, driven –, one's -fate etc. *n.*- to; be -pushed to the wall, – driven into a corner, – unable to help, – drawn irresistibly.

destine, doom, foredoom, devote; pre-destine, -ordain; cast a spell etc. 992; necessitate; compel etc. 744.

Adj. necessary; needful etc. (*requisite*) 630.

fated; destined etc. *v.*; fateful; elect; spell-bound. compulsory etc. (*compel*) 744; uncontrollable, inevitable, unavoidable, irrestible, irrevocable, inexorable, binding; avoid-, resist-less; written in the book of fate.

involuntary, instinctive, automatic, blind, mechanical; un-conscious, -witting, -thinking; unintentional etc. (*undesigned*) 621; impulsive etc. 612.

Adv. necessarily etc. *adv.*; of -necessity, – course; *ex necessitate rei*; needs must; perforce etc. 744; *nolens volens*; will he nil he, willy nilly, *bon gré mal gré*, willing or unwilling, *coûte que coûte*, forcefully.

faute de mieux; by stress of; if need be.

Phr. it cannot be helped; there is no- help for, – helping- it; it -will, – must, – must needs- be, – be so, – have its way; the die is cast; *jacta est alea*; *che sarà sarà*; 'it is written;' one's- days are numbered, – fate is sealed; *Fata obstant; diis aliter visum.*

602. Willingness.—N. willingness, voluntariness etc. *adj.*; willing mind, heart.

disposition, inclination, leaning, *animus*; frame of mind, humor, mood, vein; bent etc. (*turn of mind*) 820; *penchant* etc. (*desire*) 865; aptitude etc. 698.

doc-ility, -ibleness, tractability; persuasi-bleness, -bility; pliability etc. (*softness*) 324.

geniality, cordiality; goodwill; alacrity, readiness, earnestness, forwardness, enthusiasm; zeal, eagerness etc. (*desire*) 865.

assent etc. 488; compliance etc. 762; pleasure etc. (*will*) 600.

labor of love, self-appointed task; volunteer, -ing, gratuitous service; unpaid worker, amateur.

V. be -willing etc. *adj.*; incline, lean to, mind, propend; had as lief; lend –, give –, turn- a willing ear; have -a, – half a, – a great- mind to; hold –, cling- to; desire etc. 865.

see –, think- -good, – fit, – proper; acquiescent etc. (*assent*) 488; comply with etc. 762.

swallow –, nibble at- the bait; gorge the hook; swallow hook, line and sinker; have –, make- no scruple of; make no bones of; jump –, catch- at; meet half way; volunteer, offer oneself etc. 763.

Adj. willing, minded, fain, disposed, inclined, favorable, favorably- minded, -inclined, -disposed; nothing loth; in the -vein, – mood, – humor, – mind.

ready, forward, enthusiastic, earnest, eager; bent upon etc. (*desirous*) 865; predisposed, propense.

docile; persua-dable, -sible; suasible, easily persuaded, facile, easy-going; amenable; tractable etc.
(*pliant*) 324; genial, gracious, cordial, hearty; content etc. (*assenting*) 488.

voluntary, gratuitous, spontaneous; unasked etc.
(ask etc. 765); unforced etc. (*free*) 748.

Adv. willing etc. *adj.*; fain, freely, as lief, heart
and soul; with -pleasure, − all one's heart, − open
arms; with -good, − right good- will; *de bonne
volonté, ex animo; con amore*, heart in hand,
nothing loth, without reluctance, of one's own accord, graciously, with a good grace, without demur.

à la bonne heure; by all -means, − manner of
means; to one's heart's content; yes etc. (*assent*)
488.

Int. sure, -ly! of course!

603. Unwillingness.—**N.** unwillingness etc.
adj.; indispos-ition, -edness; disinclination, aver-
sation, aversion; nolleity, nolition; renitence; reluctance; indifference etc. 866; backwardness etc.
adj.; slowness etc. 275; want of -alacrity, −
readiness; indocility etc. (*obstinacy*) 606.

scrupul-ousness, -osity; qualms of conscience,
delicacy, demur, scruple, qualm, shrinking, recoil;
hesitation etc. (*irresolution*) 605; fastidiousness
etc. 868.

averseness etc. (*dislike*) 867; dissent etc. 489;
refusal etc. 764.

slacker, scrimshanker, *embusqué*, unwilling
worker, forced labor.

V. be -unwilling etc. *adj.*; nill; dislike etc. 867;
grudge, begrudge; not be able to find it in one's
heart to, not have the stomach to.

demur, stick at, scruple, stickle; hang fire, run
rusty, slack, shirk, scamp, give up, fight shy of, not
pull fair; recoil, shrink, swerve; hesitate etc. 605;
avoid etc. 623.

oppose etc. 708; dissent etc. 489; refuse etc.
764.

Adj. unwilling; not in the vein, loth, shy of,
disinclined, indisposed, averse, reluctant, not content; adverse etc. (*opposed*) 708; laggard, back-
ward, remiss, slack, slow to; renitent; indifferent
etc. 866; scrupulous; squeamish etc. (*fastidious*)
868; repugnant etc. (*dislike*) 867; rest-iff, -ive;
demurring etc. *v.*; unconsenting etc. (*refusing*)
764; involuntary etc. 601; grudging, irreconcilable.

Adv. unwilling etc. *adj.*; grudgingly, with a
heavy heart; with -a bad, − an ill- grace; against
−, sore against- -one's wishes, − one's will, − the
grain; *invitâ Minervâ; à contre coeur; malgré soi*;
in spite of -one's teeth, − oneself; *nolens volens*
etc. (*necessity*) 601; perforce etc. 744; under
protest; no etc. 536; not for the world, far be it
from me; not if I can help it; if I must I must.

604. Resolution.—**N.** determination, will; iron
−, unconquerable- will; will of one's own,
decision, resolution, backbone, grit; strength of -
mind, − will; resolve etc. (*intent*) 620; *intransigeance*; firmness etc. (*stability*) 150; energy,
manliness, vigor; game, pluck, resoluteness etc.
(*courage*) 861; zeal etc. 682; *aplomb*; desperation;
devot-ion, -edness.

mastery over self; self-control, -command, -

mastery, -possession, -reliance, -government, -
restraint, -conquest, -denial; moral -courage, -
strength, − fiber; perseverance etc. 604*a*; tenacity;
obstinacy etc. 606; bull-dog; British lion.

V. have -determination etc. *n.*; know one's own
mind; be -resolved etc. *adj.*; make up one's mind,
will resolve, determine; decide etc. (*judgment*)
480; form −, come to- a -determination, −
resolution, − resolve; conclude, fix, seal, determine once for all, bring to a crisis, drive matters to
an extremity; take a decisive step etc. (*choice*) 609;
take upon oneself etc. (*undertake*) 676.

devote oneself −, give oneself up- to; throw
away the scabbard, kick down the ladder, nail
one's colors to the mast, set one's back against the
wall, set one's teeth, put one's foot down, burn
one's bridges, take one's stand; stand firm etc.
(*stability*) 150; steel oneself; stand no nonsense,
not listen to the voice of the charmer.

buckle to; put −, lay −, set- one's shoulder to
the wheel; put one's heart into; run the gantlet,
make a dash at, take the bull by the horns; beard
the lion in his den; rush −, plunge- *in medias res*;
go in for; insist upon, make a point of; set one's
heart, − mind- upon.

stick at nothing; make short work of etc. (*activity*) 682; not stick at trifles; go -all lengths, −
the whole hog; persist etc. (*persevere*) 604*a*; go
down with colors flying, die game; go through fire
and water, ride in the whirlwind and direct the
storm.

Adj. resolved etc. *v.*determined; strong-willed, -
minded; resolute etc. (*brave*) 861; self-possessed,
plucky, tenacious; decided, definitive, peremptory;
un-hesitating, -flinching, -shrinking; firm, cast iron,
indomitable, game to the backbone; inexorable,
relentless, not to be -shaken, − put down; *tenax
propositi*; inflexible etc. (*hard*) 323; obstinate etc.
606; steady etc. (*persevering*) 604*a*; unbending,
unyielding, irrevocable; firm as a rock; grim.

earnest, serious; set −, bent −, intent- upon.
steeled −, proof- against; *in utrumque paratus*.

Adv. resolutely etc. *adj.*; in −, in good- earnest;
seriously, joking apart, earnestly, heart and soul; on
one's metal; manfully, like a man, with a high
hand; with a strong hand etc. (*exertion*) 686.

at any -rate, − risk, − hazard, − price, −
cost, − sacrifice; at all -hazards, − risks, −
events; cost what it may; *coûte que coûte; à tort et
à travers*; once for all; neck or nothing; rain or
shine; with colors nailed to the mast.

Phr. *spes sibi quisque*.

604a. Perseverance. —**N.** perseverance; continuance etc. (*inaction*) 143; permanence etc. (*absence of change*) 141; firmness etc. (*stability*) 150.

constancy, steadiness; singleness −, tenacity- of
purpose; persistence, plodding, patience; sedulity
etc. (*industry*) 682; pertina-cy, -city, -ciousness;
iteration etc. 104.

bottom, game, pluck, stamina, backbone, grit;
indefatiga-bility, -bleness; bulldog courage.

V. persevere, persist; hold -on, − out; die in the
last ditch, be in at the death; stick −, cling −,
adhere- to ; stick to one's text, keep on; keep to −,
maintain- one's -course, − ground; bear −, keep
−, hold-up; plod; stick to work etc. (*work*) 686;

continue etc. 143; follow up; die -in harness, – at one's post.

Adj. persevering, constant; stead-y, -fast; un-deviating, -wavering, -faltering, -swerving, -flinching, -sleeping, -flagging, -drooping; steady as time; uninter-, un-remitting; plodding; industrious etc. 682; strenuous etc. 686; pertinacious; persist-ing, -ent.

solid, sturdy, staunch, stanch, ture to oneself; un-changeable etc. 150; unconquerable etc. (*strong*) 159; indomitable, game to the last, indefatigable, untiring, unwearied, never tiring.

Adv. through -evil report and good report, – thick and thin, – fire and water; *per fas et nefas*; without fail, sink or swim, at any price, *vogue la galère*; in sickness and in health.

Phr. never say die; *vestigia nulla retrorsum.*

605. Irresolution.—N. irresolution, infirmity of purpose, indecision; in-, un-determination, loss of will power; unsettlement; uncertainty etc. 475; demur, suspense; hesi-tating etc. v., -tation, -tancy; vacillation; ambivalence; changeableness etc. 149; fluctuation; alternation etc. (*oscillation*) 314; caprice etc. 608; lukewarmness.

fickleness, levity, *légèreté*; pliancy etc. (*softness*) 324; weakness; timidity etc. 860; cowardice etc. 862; half measures.

waverer, ass between two bundles of hay; shut-tlecock, butterfly; timeserver, opportunist, turn coat.

V. be -irresolute etc. *adj.*; hang –, keep- in suspense; heave '*ad referendum*;' think twice about, pause; dawdle etc. (*inactivity*) 683; remain neuter; dilly dally. hesitate, boggle, hover, wobble, shilly-shally, hum and haw, demur, not know one's own mind; debate, balance; dally –, coquet- with; will and will not, *chasser-balancer*; go half-way, compromise, make a compromise; be thrown off one's balance, stagger like a drunken man; be afraid etc. 860; let 'I dare not' wait upon 'I would;' falter, waver.

vacillate etc. 149; change etc. 140; retract etc. 607; fluctuate; alternate etc. (*oscillate*) 314; keep off and on, play fast and loose; blow hot and cold etc. (*caprice*) 608.

shuffle, palter, blink; trim.

Adj. irresolute, infirm of purpose, double-minded, half-hearted; un-decided, -resolved, -determined; drifting; shilly-shally; fidgety, tremulous; wobbly; hesitating etc. v.; off one's balance; at a loss etc. (*uncertain*) 475.

vacillating etc. v.; unsteady etc. (*changeable*) 149; unsteadfast, fickle, unreliable, irresponsible, unstable, without ballast; capricious etc. 608; volatile, frothy; light, -some, -minded; giddy, fast and loose.

weak, feeble-minded, frail; timid etc. 860; cowardly etc. 862; facile; pliant etc. (*soft*) 324; unable to say 'no,' easy-going.

revocable, reversible.

Adv. irresolutely etc. *adj.*; irresolvedly; in faltering accents; off and on; from pillar to post; see-saw etc. 314.

Int. 'how happy could I be with either!'

606. Obstinacy.—N. obstinateness etc. *adj.*; obstinacy, tenacity; perseverance etc. 604a; im-

movability; old school; inflexibility etc. (*hardness*) 323; obdur-acy, -ation; dogged resolution; resolution etc. 604; ruling passion; blind side.

self-will, contumacy, perversity; pervica-cy, -city; indocility.

bigotry, intolerance, dogmatism; opinia-try, -tiveness; fixed idea etc.; intractibility, in-corrigibility; (*prejudgment*) 481; fanaticism, zealotry, infatuation, monomania, opinionativeness.

mule; opin-ionist, -ionatist, -iator, -ator; stickler, dogmatist, die-hard, bitter-ender; bigot; zealot, en-thusiast, fanatic.

V. be -obstinate etc. *adj.*; stickle, take no denial, fly in the face of facts; opinionate, be wedded to an opinion, hug a belief; have one's own way etc. (*will*) 600; persist etc. (*persevere*) 604a; have –, insist on having- the last word.

die -hard, – fighting, fight -against destiny, – to the last ditch; not yield an inch, stand out.

Adj. obstinate, tenacious, stubborn, obdurate, case-hardened; inflexible etc. (*hard*) 323; im-movable, not to be moved; inert etc. 172; un-changeable etc. 150; inexorable etc. (*determined*) 604; mulish, obstinate as a mule, pig-headed.

dogged; sullen, sulky; un-moved, -influenced, -affected.

wilful, self-willed, perverse; res-ty, -tive, -tiff; pervicacious, wayward, refractory, unruly; head-y, -strong; *entete*; contumacious; cross-grained.

arbitrary, dogmatic, opinionated, positive, bigoted; prejudiced etc. 481; prepossessed, in-fatuated; stiff-backed, -necked, -hearted; hard-mouthed, hidebound; unyielding; im-pervious, -practicable, -persuasible; unpersuasible; in-, un-tractable; incorrigible, deaf to advice, impervious to reason; crotchety etc. 608.

Adv. obstinately etc. *adj.*

Phr. *non possumus*; no surrender.

607. Tergiversation.—N. change of -mind, – intention, – purpose; afterthought.

tergiversation, recantation; palinode, -ody; renunciation; abjur-ation, -ement; defection etc. (*relinquishment*) 624; going over etc. v.; apostasy; retract-ion, -ation; withdrawal, disavowal etc. (*negation*) 536; revo-cation, -kement; reversal; repentance etc. 950; *redintegratio amoris.*

coquetry, flirtation; vacillation etc. 605; back-sliding, recidivation.

turn-coat, -tippet; rat, apostate, renegade, mugwump; con-, per-vert; proselyte, deserter; backslider, recidivist; black leg.

time-server, -pleaser; timist, Vicar of Bray, trim-mer, ambidexter; weathercock etc. (*changeable*) 149; Janus.

V. change one's -mind, – intention, – purpose, – note; abjure, renounce; withdraw from etc. (*relinquish*) 624; wheel –, turn –, veer- round; turn a *pirouette*; go over –, pass –, change –, skip- from one side to another; go to the right about; box the compass, shift one's ground, go upon another tack; back down, crawl, crawfish.

apostatize, change sides, go over, rat; recant, retract, revoke; rescind etc. (*abrogate*) 756; recall, forswear, abjure, unsay; come -over, – round- to an opinion.

draw in one's horns, eat one's words; eat –,

swallow- the leek; swerve, flinch, back out of, retrace one's steps, think better of it; come back –, return- to one's first love; turn over a new leaf etc. (*repent*) 950.

trim, shuffle, play fast and loose, blow hot and cold, coquet, flirt, hold with the hare but run with the hounds; straddle; *nager entre deux eaux*; wait to see how the -cat jumps, – wind blows.

Adj. changeful etc. 149; irresolute etc. 605; ductile, slippery as an eel, trimming, ambidextrous, timeserving; coquetting etc. *v.*

revocatory, reactionary.

Phr. 'a change came o'er the spirit of my dream.'

608. Caprice.—N. caprice, fancy, humor, whim, -sey, -wham; crotchet, *capriccio*, quirk, freak, maggot, fad, vagary, prank, fit, flim-flam, *escapade*, *boutade*, wild-goose chase; capriciousness etc. *adj.*; kink.

V. be -capricious etc. *adj.*; have a maggot in the brain; take it into one's head, strain at a gnat and swallow a camel; blow hot and cold; play -fast and loose, – fantastic tricks.

Adj. capricious; erratic, eccentric, fitful, hysterical; full of -whims etc. *n.*; maggoty; inconsistent, fanciful, fantastic, whimsical, crotchety, particular, humorsome, freakish, skittish, wanton, wayward; contrary; captious; arbitrary; unrestrained, undisciplined; not amenable to reason; uncomfortable etc. 83; penny wise and pound foolish; fickle etc. (*irresolute*) 605; frivolous, sleeveless, giddy, volatile.

Adv. by fits and starts, without rhyme or reason, at one's own sweet will.

Phr. *nil fuit unquam six impar sibi*; the deuce is in him.

609. Choice.—N. choice, option; discretion etc. (*volition*) 600; preoption; alternative; dilemma; *ambarras de choix*; adoption, co-optation; novation; decision etc. (*judgment*) 480.

election, poll, ballot, vote, voice, suffrage, plumper, cumulative vote; *plebiscitum, plébiscite, vox populi*; *referendum*, electioneering; voting etc. *v.*; franchise; ballot box; slate; ticket.

selection, excerption, gleaning, eclecticism; *excerpta*, gleanings, cuttings, scissors and paste; pick etc. (*best*) 650.

preference, prelation; predilection etc. (*desire*) 865.

V. offer for one's choice, set before; hold out –, present –, offer- the alternative; put to the vote.

use –, exercise –, one's- -discretion, – option; adopt, take up, embrace, espouse; choose, elect, co-opt; take –, make- one's choice; make choice of, fix upon.

vote, poll, hold up one's hand; divide.

settle; decide etc. (*adjudge*) 480; list etc. (*will*) 600; make up one's mind etc. (*resolve*) 604.

select; pick, – and choose; pick –, single- out, excerpt; cull, glean, winnow; sift –, separate –, winnow- the chaff from the wheat; pick up, pitch upon; pick one's way; indulge one's fancy.

set apart, reserve, mark out for; mark etc. 550.

prefer; have -rather, – as lief; fancy etc. (*desire*) 865; be persuaded etc. 615.

take a -decided, – decisive- step; commit oneself to a course; pass –, cross- the Rubicon; cast in one's lot with; take for better or for worse.

Adj. optional; co-optative; discretional etc. (*voluntary*) 600; on approval.

ecletic; choosing etc. *v.*; preferential; chosen etc. *v.*; choice etc. (*good*) 648.

Adv. optionally etc. *adj.*; at pleasure etc. (*will*) 600; either, – the one or the other; or; at the option of; whether or not; once for all; for one's money.

by -choice, – preference; in preference; rather, before.

609a. Absence of Choice.—N. no –, Hobson's- choice; first come, first served; necessity etc. 601; not a pin to choose etc. (*equality*) 27; any, the first that comes.

neutrality, indifference; indecision etc. (*irresolution*) 605.

V. be -neutral etc. *adj.*; have no choice; waive, not vote; abstain –, refrain- from voting; leave undecided; make a virtue of necessity.

Adj. neu-tral, -ter; indifferent; undecided etc. (*irresolute*) 605.

Adv. either etc. (*choice*) 609.

610. Rejection.—N. rejection, repudiation, exclusion; declination; refusal etc. 764.

V. reject; set –, lay- aside; give up; decline etc. (*refuse*) 764; exclude, except, eliminate; pluck, spin; cast.

repudiate, scout, set at naught; fling –, cast –, thrown –, toss- -to the winds, – to the dogs, – overboard, – away; send to the right about; disclaim etc. (*deny*) 536; discard etc. (*eject*) 297, (*have done with*) 678.

Adj. rejected etc. *v.*; reject-aneous, -itious; not chosen etc. 609, – to be thought of; out of the question.

Adv. neither, – the one nor the other; no etc. 536.

Phr. *non haec in foedera*.

611. Predetermination.—N. premeditation, -deliberation, -determination, -destination; foreordination; foregone conclusion; *parti pris*; resolve, propendency; intention etc. 620; project etc. 626.

V. pre-determine, -destine, -meditate, -resolve, -concert; foreordain; resolve beforehand.

Adj. pre-pense, -meditated etc. *v.*, -designed; advised, studied, designed, calculated; aforethought; intended etc. 620; foregone.

well-laid, -devised, -weighed; maturely considered; cut and dried; cunning.

Adv. advisedly etc. *adj.*; with premeditation, deliberately, all things considered, with eyes open, in cold blood; intentionally etc. 620.

612. Impulse.—N. impulse, sudden thought; *impromptu*, improvisation; inspiration, hunch, flash, spurt.

improvisatore, *improvisatrice*, improviser, extemporizer; creature of impulse.

V. flash on the mind.

say what comes uppermost; improvise, extemporize; rise to the occasion; spurt.

Adj. extemporaneous, impulsive, indeliberate; improvis-ed, -ate, -atory; un-, unpre-meditated; *improvisé*; unprompted, -guided; natural, unguarded; spontaneous etc. (*voluntary*) 600; instinctive etc. 601.

Adv. extem-pore, -poraneously; offhand, *impromptu, à l'improviste*; improviso; on the spur of the -moment, – occasion.

---

613. Habit.—N. habit, -ude; assuetude, -faction; wont; run, way.

common –, general –, natural –, ordinary –, habitual- -course, – run, – state- of things; matter of course; beaten -path, – track, – ground.

prescription, custom, use, usage, immemorial usage, practice; tradition; prevalence, observance; conventionalism, -ity; mode, fashion, vogue; *etiquette* etc. (*gentility*) 852; order of the day, cry; conformity etc. 82.

habitué, addict.

one's old way, old school, consuetude, *veteris vestigia flammae*; *laudator temporis acti*.

rule, standing order, precedent, routine; red-tape, -tapism; pipe-clay; rut, groove.

cacoëthes; bad –, confirmed –, inveterate –, intrinsic etc. 5- habit; addiction, trick.

training etc. (*education*) 537; seasoning, hardening, inurement; radication; second nature, acclimatization; knack etc. (*skill*) 698.

V. be -wont etc. *adj.*

fall into a custom etc. (*conform to*) 82; tread –, follow- the beaten -track, – path; *stare super antiquas vias*; move in a rut, run on in a groove, go round like a horse in a mill, go on in the old jobtrot way.

habituate, inure, harden, season, caseharden; accustom, familiarize; naturalize, acclimatize; keep one's hand in; train etc. (*educate*) 537.

get into the -way, – knack- of; learn etc. 539; cling –, adhere- to; repeat etc. 104; acquire –, contract –, fall into- a -habit, – trick; addict oneself –, take- to; accustom oneself to.

be -habitual etc. *adj.*; prevail; come into use, become a habit, take root; gain –, grow- upon one.

Adj. habitual; ac-, customary; prescriptive; accustomed etc. *v.*; traditional; of -daily, – everyday- occurrence; wonted, usual, general, ordinary, common, frequent, every-day, household, jog-trot; well-trodden, -known; familiar, vernacular, trite, commonplace, banal, bromidic, conventional, regular, set, stock, officinal, established, stereotyped; pre-vailing, -valent; current, received, acknowledged, recognized, accredited; of course, admitted, understood.

conformable etc. 82; according to -use, – custom, – routine; in -vogue, – fashion; fashionable etc. (*genteel*) 852.

wont; used – given – addicted –, attuned –, habituated etc. *v.*- to; in the habit of; *habitué*; at home in etc. (*skilful*) 698; seasoned; permeated –, imbued- with; devoted –, wedded- to; never free from.

hackneyed, fixed, rooted, deep-rooted, ingrafted, permanent, inveterate, besetting; naturalized; ingrained etc. (*intrinsic*) 5.

Adv. habitually etc. *adj.*; always etc. (*uniformly*) 16.

as -usual, – is one's wont, – things go, – the world goes, – the sparks fly upwards; *more -suo, – solito*.

as a rule, for the most part; generally etc. *adj.*; most often, – frequently.

Phr. *cela s'entend.*

---

614. Desuetude.—N. desuetude, disusage; disuse etc. 678; want of -habit, – practice; inusitation; newness to; new brooms.

infraction of usage etc. (*unconformity*) 83; non-prevalence; 'a custom more honored in the breach than the observance.'

V. be -unaccustomed etc. *adj.*; leave off –, cast off –, break off –, wean oneself of –, violate –, break through –, infringe- -a habit, – a custom, – a usage; break one's fetters; disuse etc. 678; wear off.

Adj. un-accustomed, -used, -wonted, -seasoned, -inured, -habituated, -trained; new; green etc. (*unskilled*) 699; fresh, original, unhackneyed.

unusual etc. (*unconformable*) 83; unconventional, non-observant; disused etc. 678.

Adv. just for once.

---

615. Motive.—N. motive, springs of action.

reason, ground, call, principle; mainspring, *primum mobile*, key-stone; the why and the wherefore; *pro* and *con*, reason why; secret –, ulterior- motive, *arrière-pensée*; intention etc. 620.

inducement, consideration; attraction etc. 288; loadstone; magnet, -ism, -ic force; allect-ation, -ive; temptation, enticement, *agacerie*, allurement, witchery; bewitch-ment, -ery; charm; spell etc. 993; fascination, blandishment, cajolery; seduc-tion, -ement; honeyed words, voice of the tempter, son of the Sirens; forbidden fruit, golden apple.

persuasi-bility, -bleness; attractability; impress-, suscept-ibility; softness; persuas-, attract-iveness; tantalization.

influence, prompting, dictate, instance; impuls-e, -ion; incit-ement, -ation; press, instigation; provocation etc. (*excitation of feeling*) 824; inspiration; per-, suasion; encouragement, advocacy; exhortation, advice etc. 695; solicitation etc. (*request*) 765; lobbying.

incentive, stimulus, spur, fillip, whip, goad, rowel, provocative, whet, dram.

bribe, lure, decoy, – duck; bait, trail of a red herring; bribery and corruption; sop, – for Cerberus.

prompter, tempter; seduc-er, -tor; suggester; coaxer, wheedler; instigator, firebrand, incendiary; Siren, Circe; *agent provocateur*; lobbyist.

V. induce, move; draw, – on; bring in its train, give an -impulse etc. *n.*- to; inspire; put up to, prompt, call up; attract, beckon.

stimulate etc. (*excite*) 824; spirit up, inspirit; a-, rouse; ecphorize; animate, incite, provoke, instigate, set on, actuate; act –, work –, operate-

upon; encourage; pat −, clap- on the -back, −
shoulder.

influence, weigh with, bias, sway, incline,
dispose, predispose, turn the scale, inoculate; lead,
− by the nose; have −, exercise- influence- -with,
− over, − upon; go −, come- round one; turn the
head, magnetize.

persuade; prevail -with, − upon; overcome,
carry; bring -round, − to one's senses; draw −,
win −, gain −, come −, talk- over; procure,
enlist, engage; invite, court.

tempt, seduce, overpersuade, entice, allure, captivate, fascinate, intrigue, bewitch, carry away,
charm, conciliate, wheedle, coax, lure, suggest; inveigle; tantalize; cajole etc. (*deceive*) 545.

tamper with, bribe, suborn, grease the palm, bait
with a silver hook, gild the pill, make things
pleasant, put a sop into the pan, throw a sop to,
bait the hook.

enforce, force; impel etc. (*push*) 276; propel etc.
284; whip, lash, goad, spur, prick, urge; egg −,
hound −, hurry- on; drag etc. 285; exhort; advise
etc. 695; call upon etc.; press etc. (*request*) 765;
advocate.

set -an example, − the fashion; keep in countenance; back up.

be -persuaded etc.; yield to temptation, come
round; concede etc. (*consent*) 762; obey a call;
follow -advice, − the bent, − the dictates of; act
on principle.

Adj. impulsive, motive; suas-, persuas-, hortative, -ory; protreptical; inviting, tempting etc. *v.*;
seductive, attractive, irresistible; fascinating etc.
(*pleasing*) 829; provocative etc. (*exciting*) 824.

induced etc. *v.*; disposed; persuadable etc.
(*docile*) 602; spellbound; instinct −, smitten- with;
inspired etc. *v.*- by.

Adv. because, therefore etc. (*cause*) 155; from -
this, − that- motive; for -this, − that- reason; for;
by reason −, for the sake −, on the score −, on
account- of; out of, from, as, forasmuch as.

for all the world; on principle.

615a. Absence of Motive.—**N.** absence of
motive; caprice etc. 608; chance etc. (*absence of
design*) 621.

V. have no motive; scruple etc. (*be unwilling*)
603.

Adj. without rhyme or reason; aimless etc.
(*chance*) 621.

Adv. capriciously; out of mere caprice.

616. Dissuasion.—**N.** dissuasion, dehortation,
expostulation, remonstrance; deprecation etc. 766.

discouragement, damper, wet blanket;
warning.

cohibition etc. (*restraint*) 751; curb etc. (*means
of restraint*) 752; check etc. (*hindrance*) 706.

reluctance etc. (*unwillingness*) 603; contraindication.

V. dissuade, dehort, cry out against, remonstrate, expostulate, warn, contraindicate.

disincline, indispose, shake, stagger; dispirit; discourage, -hearten, -enchant; deter; hold −, keepback etc. (*restrain*) 751; render -averse etc. 603;

repel; turn aside etc. (*deviation*) 279; wean from;
act as a drag etc. (*hinder*) 706; throw cold water
on, damp, cool, chill, blunt, calm, quiet, quench;
deprecate etc. 766.

Adj. dissuading etc. *v.*; dissuasive; dehortatory,
expostulatory; monit-ive, -ory.

dissuaded etc. *v.*; uninduced etc. (induce etc.
615); unpersuadable etc. (*obstinate*) 606; averse
etc. (*unwilling*) 603; repugnant etc. (*dislike*) 867.

617. Plea. [Ostensible motive, ground, or
reason assigned.]—**N.** plea, pretext; allegation,
advocation; ostensible -motive, − ground, −
reason; excuse etc. (*vindication*) 937; color; gloss,
guise.

loop-, starting-hole; how to creep out of, salvo,
come off.

handle, peg to hang on room, *locus standi*;
stalking horse, *cheval de bataille*, cue.

pretence etc. (*untruth*) 546; put off, subterfuge,
dust thrown in the eyes; blind; moonshine; mere
−, shallow- pretext; lame -excuse, − apology, tub
to a whale; flase plea, sour grapes; makeshift, shift,
white lie; special pleading etc. (*sophistry*) 477; soft
sawder etc. (*flattery*) 933.

V. plead, allege; shelter oneself under the plea
of; excuse etc. (*vindicate*) 937; gloss over; lend a
color to; furnish a -handle etc. *n.*; make a -pretext,
− handle- of; use as a plea etc. *n.*; take one's stand
upon, make capital out of; pretend etc. (*lie*) 544.

Adj. ostensible etc. (*manifest*) 525; excusing;
alleged, apologetic; pretended etc. 545.

Adv. ostensibly; under -color, − the plea, −
the pretence- of.

618. Good.—**N.** good, benefit, advantage; improvement etc. 658; interest, service, behoof,
behalf; weal; main chance, *summum bonum*, common weal; 'consummation devoutly to be wished;'
gain, boot; profit, harvest.

boon etc. (*gift*) 784; good turn; blessing,
benison; world of good; piece of good -luck, − fortune; nuts, prize, windfall, godsend, waif, treasure
trove.

good fortune etc. (*prosperity*) 734; happiness
etc. 827.

[Source of good] goodness etc. 648; utility etc.
644; remedy etc. 662; pleasure-giving etc. 829.

Adj. commendable etc. (*manifest*) 931; useful etc. 644;
good etc., beneficial etc. 648.

V. benefit, profit, advantage, serve, help, avail;
do good to, gain, prosper, flourish.

Adv. well, aright, satisfactorily, favorably, not
amiss; all for the best; to one's -advantage etc. *n.*;
in one's -favor, − interest etc. *n.*

Phr. so far so good.

619. Evil.—**N.** evil, ill, harm, hurt, mischief,
nuisance; machinations of the devil, Pandora's box,
ills that flesh is heir to.

blow, buffet, stroke, scratch, bruise, wound,
gash, mutilation; mortal -blow, − wound; *im-*

medicabile vulnus; damage, loss etc. (*deterioration*) 659.

disadvantage, prejudice, drawback.

disaster, accident, casualty; mishap etc. (*misfortune*) 735; bad job, devil to pay; calamity, bale, woe, catastrophe, tragedy; ruin etc. (*destruction*) 162; adversity etc. 735.

mental suffering etc. 828. [Evil spirit] demon etc. 980. [Cause of evil] bane etc. 663. [Production of evil] badness etc. 649; painfulness etc. 830; evil doer etc. 913.

outrage, wrong, injury, foul play; bad −, ill-turn; disservice; spoliation etc. 791; grievance, crying evil.

V. be in trouble etc. (*adversity*) 735; harm, injure, hurt, do disservice to.

Adj. disastrous, bad etc. 649; awry, out of joint; disadvantageous, injurious, harmful.

Adv. amiss, wrong, ill, to one's cost.

620. Intention.—**N.** intent, -ion, -ionality; purpose; *quo animo*; project etc. 626; undertaking etc. 676; predetermination etc. 611; design, ambition.

contemplation, mind, *animus*, view, purview, proposal; study; look out.

final cause; *raison d'être*; *cui bono*; object, aim, end; 'the be all and the end all;' drift etc. (*meaning*) 516; tendency etc. 176; destination, mark, point, butt, goal, target, bull's-eye, quintain; prey, quarry, game.

decision, determination, resolve; set −, settled-purpose; *ultimatum*; resolution etc. 604; wish etc. 865; *arrière-pensée*; motive etc. 615.

[Study of final causes] teleology.

V. intend, purpose, design, mean; have to; propose to oneself; harbor a design; have in -view, − contemplation, − one's eye, − *petto*; have an eye to.

bid −, labor- for; be −, aspire −, endeavour-after; be −, aim −, drive −, point −, level- at; take aim; set before oneself; study to.

take upon oneself etc. (*undertake*) 676; take into one's head; meditate, contemplate; think −, dream −, talk- of; premeditate etc. 611; compass, calculate; dest-ine, -inate, propose.

project etc. (*plan*) 626; have a mind to etc. (*be willing*) 602; desire etc. 865; pursue etc. 622.

Adj. intended etc. *v.*; intentional, advised, express, determinate; prepense etc. 611; bound for; intending etc. *v.*; minded, disposed, inclined; bent upon etc. (*earnest*) 604; at stake, on the -anvil, -*tapis*; in -view; − prospect, − the breast of; *in petto*; teleological.

Adv. intentionally etc. *adj.*; advisedly, wittingly, knowingly, designedly, purposely, on purpose, by design, studiously, pointedly; with -intent etc. *n.*; deliberately etc. (*with premeditation*) 611; with one's eyes open, in cold blood.

for; with -a view, − an eye- to; in order -to, − that; to the end −, with the intent- that; for the purpose −, with the view −, in contemplation −, on account- of.

in pursuance of, pursuant to; *quo animo*; to all intents and purposes.

621. Chance.†[Absence of purpose in the succession of events.]—**N.** chance etc. 156; lot, fate

etc. (*necessity*) 601; luck; good luck etc. (*good*) 618; bad luck etc. 735; wheel of fortune; mascot; swastika.

speculation, venture, stake, flutter, flier, gamble, game of chance; mere −, random- shot; blind bargain, leap in the dark; pig in a poke etc. (*uncertainty*) 475; fluke, pot-luck.

drawing lots; sorti-legy, -tion; *sortes*, − *Virgilianae*; *rouge et noir*, hazard, roulette, pitch and toss, chuck-farthing, cup-tossing, heads or tails, cross and pile, wager; bet, -ting; risk, stake, plunge; gambling; the turf.

stock exchange, bourse, board of trade, curb exchange.

gaming-, gambling-, betting-house; hell; betting ring, totalizator; dice, − box; dicer; gam-bler, -ester, plunger, stock operator, manipulator, punter; man of the turf; adventurer, speculator; bookmaker, layer, backer.

V. chance etc. (*hap*) 156; stand a chance etc. (*be possible*) 470.

toss up; cast −, draw- lots; leave −, trust- -to chance, − to the chapter of accidents; tempt fortune; chance it, take one's chance; run −, incur −, encounter- the -risk, − chance; stand the hazard of the die.

speculate, try one's luck, set on a cast, raffle, put into a lottery, buy a pig in a poke, shuffle the cards.

risk, venture, hazard, stake; lay, − a wager; make a bet, wager, bet, gamble, game, play for; play at chuck-farthing.

Adj. fortuitous etc. 156; unintentional, -ded; accidental; not meant; un-designed, -purposed; unpremeditated etc. 612; never thought of.

indiscrim-inate, promiscuous; undirected, random; aim-, drift-, design-, purpose-, cause-less; without purpose.

possible etc. 470.

Adv. casually etc. 156; unintentionally etc. *adj.*; unwittingly.

en passant, by the way, incidentally; as it may happen; at -random, − a venture, − haphazard; as luck would have it, by -chance, − good fortune; un-, -luckily.

† See note on 156.

622. Pursuit. [Purpose in action.]—**N.** pursuit; pursuing etc. *v.*; prosecution; pursuance; enterprise etc. (*undertaking*) 676; business etc. 625; adventure etc. (*essay*) 675; quest etc. (*search*) 461; scramble, hue and cry, game; hobby.

chase, hunt, *battue*, race, steeplechase, hunting, coursing; ven-ation, -ery; fox-chase; sport, -ing; shooting, angling, fishing, hawking.

pursuer; hunt-er, -sman; sportsman, Nimrod, the field; hound etc. 366.

V. pursue, prosecute, follow; run −, make −, be −, hunt −, prowl- after; shadow; carry on etc. (*do*) 680; engage in etc. (*undertake*) 676; set about etc. (*begin*) 66; endeavor etc. 675; court etc. (*request*) 765; seek etc. (*search*) 461; aim at etc. (*intention*) 620; follow the trail etc. (*trace*) 461; fish for etc. (*experiment*) 463; press on etc. (*haste*) 684; run a race etc. (*velocity*) 274.

chase, give chase, course, dog, hunt, hound, stalk; tread −, follow- on the heels of etc. (*sequence*) 281.

rush upon; rush headlong etc. (*violence*) 173;

ride −, run- full tilt at; make a leap −, jump −, snatch- at; run down; start game.

tread a path; take −, hold- a course; shape −, direct −, bend- one's -steps, − course; play a game; fight −, elbow- one's way; follow up; take - to, − up; go in for; ride one's hobby.

Adj. pursuing etc. *v.*; in quest of etc. (*inquiry*) 461; in -pursuit, − full cry, − hot pursuit; on the scent.

Adv. in pursuance of etc. (*intention*) 620; after.

Int. tally-ho! yoicks! so-ho!

623. Avoidance. [Absence of pursuit.]—**N.** abst-ention, -inence; forbearance; refraining etc. *v.*; inaction etc. 681; neutrality.

avoidance, evasion, elusion; seclusion etc. 893.

avolation, flight; escape etc. 671; retreat etc. 287; recoil etc. 277; departure etc. 293; rejection etc. 610.

shirker etc. *v.*; slacker; truant; fugitive, refugee; runa-way, -gate; renegade; deserter.

V. abstain, refrain, spare, not attempt; not do etc. 681; maintain the even tenor of one's way.

eschew, keep from, let alone, have nothing to do with; keep −, stand −, hold- -aloof, − off; take no part in, have no hand in.

avoid, shun; steer −, keep- clear of; fight shy of; keep -one's −, − at a respectful- distance; keep −, get- out of the way; evade, elude, turn away from; set one's face against etc. (*oppose*) 708; deny oneself.

shrink; hang −, hold −, draw- back; recoil etc. 277; retire etc. (*recede*) 287; flinch, blink, blench, shy, shirk, dodge, parry, make way for, give place to.

beat a retreat; turn -tail, − one's back; take to one's heels; run, -away, − for one's life; cut and run; be off, − like a shot; fly, flee; fly −, flee −, run away- from; take −, take to- flight; desert, elope; make −, scamper −, sneak −, shuffle −, sheer- off; break −, burst −, tear oneself −, slip −, slink −, steal- -away, − away from; slip cable, part company, turn on one's heel; sneak out of, play truant, give one the go by, give leg bail, take French leave, slope, decamp, flit, bolt, abscond, levant, skedaddle, absquatulate, cut one's stick, walk one's chalks, show a light pair of heels, make oneself scarce; escape etc. 671; go away etc. (*depart*) 293; abandon etc. 624; reject etc. 610.

lead one a -dance, − a merry chase, − pretty dance; throw off the scent, play at hide and seek.

Adj. unsought, unattempted; avoiding etc. *v.*; neutral; shy of etc. (*unwilling*) 603; elusive, evasive, distant; fugitive, runaway; shy, wild.

Adj. lest, in order to avoid.

Int. forebear! keep −, hands- off! *sauve qui peut!* devil take the hindmost.

624. Relinquishment.—**N.** relinquish-, abandon-ment; desertion, defection, secession, withdrawal; cave of Adullam; *nolle prosequi.*

discontinuance etc. (*cessation*) 142; renunciation etc. (*recantation*) 607; abrogation etc. 756; resignation etc. (*retirement*) 757; desuetude etc. 614; cession etc. (*of property*) 782.

V. relinquish, give up, abandon, desert, forsake, leave in the lurch; depart −, secede −, withdraw- from; back − out of, − down from, leave, go back on one's word, quit, take leave of, bid a long farewell; vacate etc. (*resign*) 757.

renounce etc. (*abjure*) 607; forego, have done with, drop; write off; disuse etc. 678; discard etc. 782; wash one's hands of; drop all idea of; *nolle-pros.*; lose interest in.

break −, leave- off; desist; stop etc. (*cease*) 142; hold −, stay- one's hand; quit one's hold; give over, shut up shop.

throw up the -game, − cards; give up the -point, − argument; pass to the order of the day, move the previous question, table the motion.

Adj. unpursued; relinquished etc. *v.*; relinquishing etc. *v.*

Int. avast etc.! (*stop*) 142.

625. Business.—**N.** business, occupation, employment; pursuit etc. 622; what one is doing-, − about; affair, concern, matter, case, undertaking.

matter in hand, irons in the fire; thing to do, *agendum*, task, work, job, chore, errand, transaction, commission, mission, charge, care; duty etc. 926.

part, *rôle*, cue; province, function, look-out, department, capacity, sphere, orb, field, line; walk, − of life; beat, round, routine; race, career.

office, place, post, incumbency, living situation, appointment, billet, berth, employ; service etc. (*servitude*) 749; engagement; undertaking etc. 676.

vocation, calling, profession, *métier*, cloth, faculty; industry, art; industrial arts; craft, mystery, handicraft; trade etc. (*commerce*) 794.

exercise; work etc. (*action*) 680; avocation; press of business etc. (*activity*) 682.

V. pass −, employ −, spend- one's time in; employ oneself -in, − upon; occupy −, concern- oneself with; make it one's -business etc. *n.*; undertake etc. 676; enter a profession; betake oneself to, turn one's hand to; have to do with etc. (*do*) 680.

drive a trade; carry on −, do −, transact- business, − a trade etc. *n.*; keep a shop; ply one's task, − trade; labor in one's vocation; pursue the even tenor of one's way; attend to -business, − one's work.

officiate, serve, act; act −, play- one's part; do duty; serve −, discharge −, perform- the -office, − duties, − functions- of; hold −, fill- -an office, − a place, − a situation; hold a portfolio.

be -about, − doing, − engaged in, − employed in, − occupied with, − at work on; have one's hands in, have in hand; have on one's -hands, − shoulders; bear the burden; have one's hands full etc. (*activity*) 682.

be -in the hands of, − on the stocks, − on the anvil; pass through one's hands.

Adj. business-like; work-a-day; professional; official, functional; busy etc. (*actively employed*) 682; on −, in- -hand, − one's hands; afoot; on - foot, − the anvil; going on; acting.

Adv. in the course of business, all in a day's work; professionally etc. *adj.*

626. Plan.—**N.** plan, scheme, design, project; propos-al, -ition; suggestion; resolution, motion;

precaution etc. (*provision*) 673; deep-laid etc. (*premeditated*) 611- plan etc.; racket.

system etc. (*order*) 58; organization etc. (*arrangement*) 60; germ etc. (*cause*) 153; Five Year Plan.

sketch, skeleton, outline, draught, draft, *ébauche, brouillon*; rough-cast, – draft, – draught, – copy; proof, revise.

forecast, *programme*, prospectus, scenario; *carte du pays*; card; bill, protocol; order of the day, list of agenda, *memorandum*; bill of fare etc. (*food*) 298; base of operations; platform, plank.

rôle; policy etc. (*line of conduct*) 692.

contrivance, invention, expedient, receipt, nostrum, artifice, device, gadget; stratagem etc. (*cunning*) 702; trick etc. (*deception*) 545; alternative, loophole, shift etc. (*substitute*) 147; last shift etc. (*necessity*) 601.

measure, step; stroke, – of policy; master stroke; trump-, court-card; *chaval de bataille*, great gun; *coup, – d'état*; clever –, bold –, good- -move, – hit, – stroke; bright -thought, – idea, great idea.

intrigue, cabal, plot, frame-up, conspiracy, complot, machination; under-, counter-plot.

schem-ist, -atist; strategist, machinator, schemer; projector, author, builder, artist, promoter, designer etc. *v.*; conspirator; *intrigant* etc. (*cunning*) 702.

V. plan, scheme, design, frame, contrive, project, forecast, sketch; conceive, devise, invent etc. (*imagine*) 515; set one's wits to work etc. 515; spring a project; fall –, hit- upon; strike –, chalk –, cut –, lay –, map-out; lay down a plan; shape –, mark- out a course; predetermine etc. 611; concert, preconcert, preestablish; prepare etc. 673; hatch – a plot; concoct; take -steps, – measures.

cast, recast, systematize, organize; arrange etc. 60; digest, mature.

plot; counter-plot, -mine; dig a mine; lay a train; intrigue etc. (*cunning*) 702.

Adj. planned etc. *v.*; strategic, -al; planning etc. *v.*; in course of preparation etc. 673; under consideration; on the *-tapis*, – carpet, – table.

627. Method. [Path.]—**N.** method, way, manner, wise, gait, form, mode, tone, guise; *modus operandi*; procedure etc. (*line of conduct*) 692.

path, road, route, course; line of -way, – road; trajectory, orbit, track, beat, tack.

steps; stair, -case; flight of stairs, ladder, stile. bridge, viaduct, gauntry, pontoon, stepping stone, plank, gangway, catwalk, drawbridge; pass, ford, ferry, tunnel, subway, elevated; pipe etc. 260.

door; gateway etc. (*opening*) 260; channel, passage, avenue, means of access, approach, perron, adit, entrance; artery, lane, alley, aisle, lobby, corridor, cloister; back- door, -stairs; secret passage; covert-way.

road-, path-, stair-way; thoroughfare; highway, pike, turnpike, trail, parkway, *boulevard*; turnpike –, royal –, coach- road; broad –, King's –, Queen's- highway; beaten -track, – path; horse –, bridle- road, – track, – path; pathway; walk, *trottoir*, foot-path, pavement, flags, side-walk; by –, cross- -road, – path, – way; cut; short -cut

etc. (*mid-course*) 628; *carrefour*; private –, occupation- road; highways and byways; rail-, tramroad, -way; funicular, ropeway, causeway; defile, cutting; canal etc. (*conduit*) 350; street etc. (*abode*) 189.

Adv. how; in what -way, – manner; by what mode; so, in this way, after this fashion, on these lines.

one way or another, anyhow; somehow or other etc. (*instrumentality*) 631; by way of; *viâ; in transitu* etc. 270; on the high road to.

Phr. hae tibi erunt artes.

628. Mid-course.—N. middle-, mid-course; moderation, mean etc. 29; middle etc. 68; *juste milieu, mezzo termine*, golden mean, *aurea mediocritas*.

straight etc. (*direct*) 278 -course, – path; short –, cross- cut; short- circuit; great circle sailing.

neutrality; half –, half and half- measures; compromise.

V. keep in –, steer –, preserve- -a middle, – an even- course; go straight etc. (*direct*) 278.

go half way, compromise, make a compromise.

Adj. neutral, average, even, impartial, moderate, straight etc. (*direct*) 278.

629. Circuit.—N. circuit, round-about way, digression, divagation, *détour*, circum-ambience, -ambulation, bendibus, *ambages*, loop; winding etc. (*circuition*) 311; zigzag etc. (*deviation*) 279.

V. perform –, make- a circuit; go -round about, – out of one's way; make a *détour*; meander etc. (*deviate*) 27; circumambulate.

lead a pretty dance; beat about, – the bush; make two bites of a cherry.

adj. circuitous, indirect, round-about; zig-zag etc. (*deviating*) 279; circum-ambient, -ambulatory.

Adv. by -a side wind, – an indirect course; in a roundabout way; from pillar to post.

630. Requirement.—N. requirement, need, wants, necessities; necessaries, – of life; stress, exigency, pinch, *sine quâ non*, matter of necessity; case of -need, – life or death.

needfulness, essentiality, necessity, indispensability, urgency, prerequisite.

requisition etc. (*request*) 765; (*exaction*) 741; run upon; demand –, call- for.

desideratum etc. (*desire*) 865; want etc. (*deficiency*) 640.

charge, claim, command, injunction, requisition, mandate, order, *ultimatum*.

V. require, need, want, have occasion for; entail; not be able to -do without, – dispense with; prerequire.

render necessary, necessitate, create a necessity for, call for, put in requisition; make a requisition etc. (*ask for*) 765; (*demand*) 741.

stand in need of; lack etc. 640; desiderate; desire etc. 865; be -necessary etc. *adj.*

Adj. required etc. *v.*; requisite, needful,

necessary, imperative, essential, indispensable, prerequisite; called for; in -demand, – request.

urgent, exigent, pressing, instant, crying, absorbing.

in want of; destitute of etc. 640.

Adv. *ex necessitate rei* etc. (*necessarily*) 601; of –, out of stern- necessity; at a pinch.

Phr. there is no time to lose; it cannot be - spared, – dispensed with.

631. Instrumentality.—N. instrumentality; aid etc. 707; subservien-ce, -cy; mediation, intervention, -mediacy, medium, inter-medium, -mediary, vehicle, hand; agency etc. 170.

minister, handmaid, servant, slave, maid, valet; midwife, *accoucheur*, obstetrician; go-between; cat's paw; stepping-stone.

key; master –, pass –, latch- key; 'open seseme,' passport, *passe partout*, safe-conduct; influence.

instrument etc. 633; expedient etc. (*plan*) 626; means etc. 632.

V. subserve, minister, tend, mediate, intervene; come –, go- between, interpose; pull the strings; be -instrumental etc. *adj.*; pander to.

Adj. instrumental; useful etc. 644; ministerial, subservient, mediatorial; inter-mediate, -vening; conducive.

Adv. through, by, *per*; where-, there-, here-by; by the -agency etc. 170- of; by dint of; by –, invirtue of; through the -medium etc. *n*.- of; along with; on the shoulders of; by means of etc. 632; by –, with- -the aid etc. (*assistance*) 707- of.

per fas et nefas, by fair means or foul; somehow, – or other; by hook or by crook.

632. Means.—N. means, resources, revenue, wherewithal, ways and means, income; capital etc. (*money*) 800; stock in trade etc. 636; provision etc. 637; a shot in the locker; appliances etc. (*machinery*) 633; means and appliances; conveniences; cards to play; expendients etc. (*measures*) 626; two strings to one's bow; sheet anchor etc. (*safety*) 666; aid etc. 707; medium etc. 631.

V. find –, have –, possess- means etc. *n.*; provide the wherewithal.

Adj. instrumental etc. 631; mechanical etc. 633.

Adv. by means of, with; by -what, – all, – any, – some- means; where-, here-, there-with; wherewithal.

how etc. (*in what manner*) 627; through etc. (*by the instrumentality of*) 631; with –, by- the aid etc. (*assistance*) 707- of; by the -agency etc. 170- of.

633. Instrument.—N. machinery, mechanism, engineering.

instrument, organ, tool, implement, utensil, contrivance, machine, motor, engine, lathe, gin, mill, pump.

gear; tack-le, -ling, trice, rigging, gear, apparatus, appliances; plant, *matériel*; harness, trap-pings, fittings, accouterments; equip-ment, -age; appointments, furniture, upholstery; chattels; paraphernalia etc. (*belongings*) 780; *impedimenta*.

mechanical powers; lever, -age; mechanical advantage; crow, -bar; handspike, gavelock, jemmy, arm, limb, wing; oar, paddle; pulley, sheave; parbuckle; wheel and axle; wheel-, clock-work; wheels within wheels; piñion, gear wheel, spur –, bevel-gearing, chains, belting, crank, winch, capstan, windlass, crane, derrick, hoist, lift etc. 307; cam; pedal; wheel etc. (*rotation*) 312; inclined plane; wedge; screw; jack; spring, mainspring.

handle, hilt, haft, shaft, heft, shank, blade, trigger, tiller, helm, treadle, key; turnscrew, screwdriver, spanner, wrench.

hammer etc. (*impulse*) 276; edge tool etc. (*cut*) 253; borer etc. 262; vice, teeth etc. (*hold*) 781; nail, rope etc. (*join*) 45; peg etc. (*hang*) 214; support etc. 215; spoon etc. (*vehicle*) 272; arms etc. 727; oar etc. (*navigation*) 267.

Adj. instrumental etc. 631; mechanical, machinal, automatic, self-acting; brachial.

634. Substitute.—N. substitute etc. 147; deputy etc. 759; proxy, alternative, understudy.

635. Materials.—N. material, raw material, stuff, stock, staple; building materials, bricks and mortar; metal; stone; clay, brick; crockery etc. 384; compo, -sition; reinforced –, ferro-, concrete; cement; wood, ore, timber; gravel, cobbles, macadam, asphalt, tarmac.

materials; supplies, munition, fuel, grist, household stuff; *pabulum* etc. (*food*) 298; ammunition etc. (*arms*) 727; contingents; relay, reinforcement; baggage etc. (*personal property*) 780; means etc. 632.

Adj. raw etc. (*unprepared*) 674; wooden etc. *n.*

636. Store.—N. stock, fund, mine, vein, lode, quarry; spring; fount, -ain; well, -spring; milch-cow.

stock in trade, supply; heap etc. (*collection*) 72; treasure; reserve, *corps de réserve*, reserve fund, nest-egg, savings, *bonne bouche*.

crop, harvest, mow, vintage; yield, product, gleanings.

store, accumulation, hoard, rick, stack; lumber; relay etc. (*provision*) 637.

store-house, -room, -closet; depository, *dépôt*, cache, safe deposit, vault, pantechnicon, repository, -servatory, -pertory; *repertorium*; promptuary, warehouse, *entrepôt*, magazine, dump, buttery, larder, pantry, panary, lanary, still-room, spence; crib, garner, granary, silo, barn; bunker; thesaurus; bank etc. (*treasury*) 802; armoury; arsenal; dock; gallery, museum, library, conservatory, hot-house; manag-ery, -erie, aquarium, zoological gardens.

reservoir, cistern, tank, sump, pond, mill-pond; gasometer.

budget, quiver, bandolier, portfolio; coffer etc. (*receptacle*) 191.

conservation; storing etc. v.; storage.

dictionary etc. 562; list etc. 86.

V. store; put –, lay –, set- by; stow away; set –, lay- apart; store –, hoard –, treasure –, lay –, heap –, put –, garner –, save- up; *cache*; accumulate, amass, hoard, fund, garner, save, bank.

conserve, reserve; keep –, hold- back; husband, – one's resources.

deposit; stow, stack, load, dump; harvest; heap, collect etc. 72; lay -in, – down, – by, store etc. *adj.*; keep, file [papers] lay in etc. (*provide*) 637; preserve etc. 670; put by for a rainy day.

Adj. stored etc. v.; in -store, – reserve, – ordinary; spare, supernumerary.

637. Provision.—N. provision, supply; grist, – to the mill; subvention etc. (*aid*) 707; resources etc. (*means*) 632.

provising etc. v.; purveyance; reinforcement; commissary, commissariat.

rations; iron –, emergency- rations; provender etc. (*food*) 298; *viaticum*; ensilage.

caterer, purveyor, commissary, quartermaster, steward, housekeeper, manciple, feeder, batman, victualler, storekeeper, grocer, provision merchant, green-, grocer, *comprador*, *restaurateur*; sutler etc. (*merchant*) 797; innkeeper, publican, confectioner, baker, butcher, wine merchant, vintner.

V. provide; make -provision, – due provision for; lay in, – a stock, – a store.

sup-ply, -peditate; furnish; find, – one in; arm.

cater, victual, provision, purvey, forage; beat up for; stock, – with; make good, replenish; fill, – up; recruit, feed, ration.

have in -store. – reserve; keep, – by one, – on foot; have to fall back upon; store etc. 636; provide against a rainy day etc. (*economy*) 817.

638. Waste.—N. consumption, expenditure, exhaustion; dispersion etc. 73; ebb; leakage etc. (*exudation*) 295; loss etc. 776; wear and tear; waste; prodigality etc. 818; misuse etc. 679; wasting etc. v.; rubbish etc. (*useless*) 645.

mountain in labor.

v. spend, expend, use, consume, swallow up, exhaust, deplete; impoverish; spill, drain, empty; disperse etc. 73.

cast –, throw –, fling –, fritter- away; burn the candle at both ends, waste; squander etc. 818.

'waste its sweetness on the desert air;' cast -one's bread upon the waters, – pearls before swine; employ a steam engine to crack a nut, waste powder and shot, break a butterfly on a wheel; labor in vain etc. (*useless*) 645; cut a whetstone with a razor, pour water into a sieve; tilt at windmills.

leak etc. (*run out*) 295; run to waste; ebb; melt away, run dry, dry up.

Adj. wasted etc. v.; at a low ebb.

wasteful etc. (*prodigal*) 818; penny wise and pound foolish.

Phr. *magno conatu magnas nugas; le jeu n'en vaut pas la chandelle.*

639. Sufficiency.—N. sufficiency, adequacy, enough, withal, *quantum sufficit*, satisfaction, competence; no less.

mediocrity etc. (*average*) 29.

fill; fullness etc (*completeness*) 52; plen-itude, -ty; abundance; copiousness etc. *adj.*; amplitude, galore, lots, profusion; full measure; 'good measure pressed down, shaken together and running over.'

luxuriance etc. (*fertility*) 168; affluence etc. (*wealth*) 803; fat of the land; 'a land flowing with milk and honey;' cornucopia; horn of -plenty, – Amalthaea; mine etc. (*stock*) 636.

outpouring; flood etc. (*great quantity*) 31; tide etc. (*river*) 348; repletion etc. (*reduncance*) 641; satiety etc. 869; rich man etc. 803.

V. be -sufficient etc. *adj.*; suffice, do, just do, satisfy, pass muster; have -enough etc. n.; eat –, drink –, have- one's fill; roll –, swim- in; wallow in etc. (*superabundance*) 641.

abound, exuberate, teem, flow, stream, rain, shower down; pour, – in; swarm; bristle with.

render -sufficient etc. *adj.*; replenish etc. (*fill*) 52.

Adj. sufficient, enough, adequate, up to the mark, commensurate, competent, satisfactory, valid, tangible.

measured; moderate etc. (*temperate*) 953.

full etc. (*complete*) 52; ample; plen-ty, -tiful, -teous; plenty as blackberries; copious, abundant; abounding etc. v.; replete, enough and to spare, flush; choke-full; well-stocked, -provided; liberal; unstint-ed, -ing; stintless; without stint; un-sparing, -measured; lavish etc. 641; wholesale.

rich, luxuriant etc. (*fertile*) 168; affluent etc. (*wealthy*) 803; wantless; big with etc. (*pregnant*) 161.

un-exhausted, -wasted; exhaustless, inexhaustible.

Adv. sufficiently, amply etc. *adj.*; full; in -abundance etc. n.; with no sparing hand; to one's heart's content, *ad libitum*, without stint.

Phr. cut and come again.

640. Insufficiency.—N. insufficiency; inadequa-cy, -teness; incompetence etc. (*impotence*) 158; deficiency etc. (*incompleteness*) 53; imperfection etc. 651; shortcoming etc. 304; paucity; stint; scantiness etc. (*smallness*) 32; none to spare; bare subsistence.

scarcity, dearth; want, need, lack, poverty, exigency; inanition, starvation, famine, drought.

dole, pittance, mite; short -allowance, – commons; half-rations; banyan –, fast- day, Lent.

emptiness, poorness etc. *adj.*; depletion, vacancy, flaccidity; ebb-tide; low water; 'a beggarly account of empty boxes;' indigence etc. (*poverty*) 804; insolvency etc. (*non-payment*) 808; poor man etc. 804; bankrupt etc. 808.

V. be -insufficient etc. *adj.*; not -suffice etc. 639; come short of etc. 304; run dry.

want, lack, need, require; *caret*; be in want etc. (*poor*) 804; live from hand to mouth.

render- insufficient etc. *adj.*; drain of resources; impoverish etc. (*waste*) 638; stint etc. (*begrudge*) 819; put on short -commons, – allowance.

do -insufficiently etc. *adv.*; scotch the snake.

Adj. insufficient, inadequate; too -little etc. 32; not -enough etc. 639; unequal to; incompetent etc. (*impotent*) 158; 'weighed in the balance and found wanting;' perfunctory etc. (*neglect*) 460; deficient etc. (*incomplete*) 53; wanting etc. *v.*; imperfect etc. 651; ill-furnished, -provided, -stored, -off.

slack, at a low ebb; empty, vacant, bare; short –, out –, destitute –, devoid –, bereft etc. 789 –, denuded- of; dry, drained.

un -provided, -supplied, -furnished; un-replenished, -fed; un-stored, -treasured; empty-handed.

meager, poor, thin, scrimp, sparing, spare, stint-ed, stunted; skimpy; starv-ed, -eling; half-starved, emaciated, famine-stricken, famished, underfed, undernourished; jejune.

scant etc. (*small*) 32; scarce; not to be had, – for love or money, – at any price; scurvy; stingy etc. 819; at the end of one's tether; without -resources etc. 632; in want etc. (*poor*) 804; in debt etc. 806.

Adv. insufficiently etc. *adj.*; in default –, for want- of; failing.

641. Redundance.—N. redundance; too -much, – many; superabundance, -fluity, -fluence, -saturation; nimiety, transcendency, exuberance, profuseness; profusion etc. (*plenty*) 639; repletion, enough in all conscience, *satis superque*, lion's share; more than -enough etc. 639; plethora, engorgement, congestion, load, surfeit, sickener; turgescence etc. (*expansion*) 194; over-dose, -measure, -supply, -flow; inundation etc. (*water*) 348; avalanche.

accumulation etc. (*store*) 636; heap etc. 72; drug, – in the market; glut; crowd; burden.

excess; sur-, over-plus, epact; margin; remainder etc. 40; duplicate; surplusage; expletive; work of –, supererogation; *bonus, bonanza.*

luxury; intemperance etc. 954; extravagance etc. (*prodigality*) 818; exorbitance, lavishment.

pleonasm etc. (*diffuseness*) 573; too many irons in the fire; embarassment of riches; money to burn.

V. super-, over-abound; know no bounds, swarm; meet one at every turn; creep –, bristle-with; overflow; run –, flow –, well –, brim-over; run riot; over-run, -stock, -lay, -charge, -dose, -feed, -burden, -load, -do, -whelm, -shoot the mark etc. (*go beyond*) 303; surcharge, supersaturate, gorge, glut, load, drench, whelm, inundate, deluge, flood; drug, – the market.

choke, cloy, accloy, suffocate; pile up, lay it on, – with a trowel, lay on thick; impregnate with; lavish etc. (*squander*) 818.

send –, carry- coals to Newcastle, – owls to Athens; teach one's grandmother to suck eggs; *pisces natare docere*; kill the slain, 'gild refined gold,' 'paint the lily;' butter one's bread on both sides, put butter upon bacon; employ a steam-engine to crack a nut etc. (*waste*) 638.

exaggerate etc. 549; wallow in; roll in etc. (*plenty*) 639; remain on one's hands, hang heavy on hand, go a begging.

Adj. redundant; too -much, – many; exuberant, inordinate, superabundant, excessive, overmuch, replete, profuse, lavish; prodigal etc. 818; exor-bitant; overweening; extravagant; overcharged etc. *v.*; supersaturated, drenched, overflowing; running -over, – to waste, – down.

crammed –, filled- to overflowing; gorged, stuff-ed, ready to burst; dropsical, turgid, plethoric, full-blooded; obese etc. 194; voluminous.

superfluous, unnecessary, needless, super-vacaneous, uncalled for, to spare, in excess; over and above etc. (*remainder*) 40; *de trop*; adscititious etc. (*additional*) 37; supernumerary etc. (*reserve*) 636; on one's hands, spare, duplicate, supererogatory, expletive; *un peu fort.*

Adj. over, too, over and above; over –, too-much; too far; without –, beyond – out of-measure; with … to spare; over head and ears; up to one's eyes, – ears; *extra*; beyond the mark etc. (*transcursion*) 303; over one's head.

Phr. It never rains but it pours.

642. Importance.—N. importance, consequence, moment, prominence, consideration, mark, materialness.

import, significance, concern; emphasis, interest.

greatness etc. 31; superiority etc. 33; notability etc. (*repute*) 873; weight etc. (*influence*) 175; value etc. (*goodness*) 648; usefulness etc. 644.

gravity, seriousness, solemnity; no -joke, – laughing matter; pressure, urgency, stress; matter of life and death.

memorabilia, notabilia, great doings; red-letter day.

great -thing, – point; main chance, 'the be all and end all,' cardinal point, outstanding feature; substance, gist etc. (*essence*) 5; sum and substance, *gravamen,* head and front; important –, principal –, prominent –, essential- part; half the battle; *sine quâ non*; breath of one's nostrils etc. (*life*) 359; cream, salt, core, kernel, heart, nucleus; key, -note, -stone; corner stone; trumpcard etc. (*device*) 626; salient points.

top-sawyer, first fiddle, *prima donna*, chief, big-wig; triton among the minnows.

V. be -important etc. *adj.*, – somebody, – something; import, signify, matter, be an object; carry weight etc. (*influence*) 175; make a figure etc. (*repute*) 873; be in the ascendant, come to the front, lead the way, take the lead, play first fiddle, throw all else into the shade; lie at the root of; deserve –, merit –, be worthy- -of notice, – regard, – consideration.

attach –, ascribe –, give- importance etc. *n.*- to; value, care for; set store -upon, – by; mark etc. 550; mark with a white stone, underline; write –, put –, print- in -italics, – capitals, – large letters, – large type, – letters of gold; accentuate, em-phasize, lay stress on.

make -a fuss, – a stir, – a piece of work, – much ado- about; make -of, – much of.

Adj. important; of -importance etc. *n.*; momen-tous, material; to the point; not to be -overlooked, – despised, – sneezed at; egregious; weighty etc. (*influential*) 175; of note etc. (*repute*) 873; notable, prominent, salient, signal; memorable, remarkable; worthy of -remark, – notice; never to be forgotten; stirring, eventful.

grave, serious, earnest, noble, grand, solemn, im-pressive, commanding, imposing.

urgent, pressing, critical, instant.

paramount, essential, vital, all-absorbing, radical, cardinal, chief, main, prime, primary, prin-cipal, leading, capital, foremost, overruling; of vital etc. importance.

in the front rank, first-rate, A1; superior etc. 33; considerable etc. (*great*) 31; marked etc. *v.*; rare etc. 137.

significant, telling, trenchant, emphatic, pregnant; *tanti*.

Adv. materially etc. *adj.*; in the main; above all, *par excellence*, to crown all.

643. Unimportance.—N. unimportance, insignificance, nothingness, immateriality.

triviality, trivia, fribble, levity, frivolity; paltriness etc. *adj.*; poverty; smallness etc. 32; vanity etc. (*uselessness*) 645; matter of - indifference etc. 866; no object; side issue.

nothing, – to signify, – worth speaking of, – particular, – to boast of, – to speak of; small –, no great –, trifling etc. *adj.*-matter; mere -joke, – nothing; hardly –, scarcely- anything; nonentity, cipher, figurehead; no great shakes, *peu de chose*; child's play; small beer.

toy, plaything, popgun, paper pellet, gimcrack, geegaw, bauble, trinket, *bagatelle*, kickshaw, knicknack, whim-wham, trifle, 'trifles light as air.'

trumpery, trash, rubbish, stuff, *fatras*, frippery; 'leather or prunello;' chaff, drug, froth, bubble, smoke, cobweb; weed; refuse etc. (*inutility*) 645; scum etc. (*dirt*) 653.

joke, jest, snap of the fingers; fudge etc. (*unmeaning*) 517; fiddlestick, – end; pack of nonsense, mere farce.

straw, pin, fig, continental, button, rush; bulrush, feather, halfpenny, farthing, brass farthing, doit, peppercorn, jot, rap, pinch of snuff, old song.

minutiae, details, minor details, small fry; dust in the balance, feather in the scale, drop in the ocean, flea-bite, molehill; fingle-fangle.

nine days' wonder, *ridiculus mus*; flash in the pan etc. (*impotence*) 158; much ado about nothing etc. (*overestimation*) 482; storm in a teacup.

V. be -unimportant etc. *adj.*; not -matter etc. 642; go for –, matter –, signify- -little, – nothing, – little or nothing; not matter a -straw etc. *n.*

make light of etc. (*underestimate*) 483; catch at straws etc. (*overestimate*) 482.

Adj. unimportant; of -little, – small, – no- -account, – importance etc. 642; immaterial; un-, non-essential; not vital; irrelevant, incidental, indifferent.

subordinate etc. (*inferior*) 34; *médiocre* etc. (*average*) 29; passable, fair, respectable, tolerable, commonplace; uneventful, mere, common; ordinary etc. (*habitual*) 613; inconsiderable, so-so, insignificant, inappreciable, nugatory.

trifling, trivial; slight, slender, light, flimsy, frothy, idle; puerile etc. (*foolish*) 499; airy, shallow; weak etc. 160; powerless etc. 158; frivolous, petty, niggling; pid-, ped-dling; fribble, inane, ridiculous, farcical; fini-cal, -kin; fiddle-faddle, namby-pamby, wishy-washy, milk and water.

poor, paltry, pitiful; contemptible etc. (*contempt*) 930; sorry, mean, meager, shabby, miserable, wretched, vile, scrubby, scrannel, weedy, niggardly, scurvy, putid, beggarly, worthless, twopenny-half penny, cheap, trashy, catchpenny, gimcrack, trumpery, one-horse; toy.

not worth -the pains, – while, – mentioning, – speaking of, – a thought, – a curse, – a straw, – rap etc. *n.*; beneath –, unworthy of- -notice, –

regard, – consideration, – contempt; *de lanâ caprinâ*; vain etc. (*useless*) 645.

Adv. slightly etc. *adj.*; rather, somewhat, pretty well, fairly well, tolerably.

for aught one cares.

Int. no matter! pish! tush! tut! pshaw! pugh! pooh, -pooh! fudge! bosh! humbug! fiddle-stick, – end! fiddlededee! never mind! *n'importe!* what - signifies, – matter, – boots it, – of that, – 's the odds! a fig for! stuff ! nonsense! stuff and nonsense!

Phr. *magno conatu magnas nugas*; *le jeu n'en vaut pas la chandelle*; it -matters not, – does not signify; it is of no -consequence, – importance.

644. Utility.—N. utility; usefulness etc. *adj.*; efficacy, efficiency, adequacy; service, use, stead, avail; help etc. (*aid*) 707; applicability etc. *adj.*; subservience etc. (*instrumentality*) 631; function etc. (*business*) 625; value; worth etc. (*goodness*) 648; money's worth; productiveness etc. 168; *cui bono* etc. (*intention*) 620; utilization etc. (*use*) 677; step in the right direction.

common weal, public good; utilitarianism etc. (*philanthropy*) 910.

V. be -useful etc. *adj.*; avail, serve; subserve etc. (*be instrumental to*) 631; conduce etc. (*tend*) 176; answer –, serve- -one's turn, – a purpose.

act a part etc. (*action*) 680; perform –, discharge- -a function etc. 625; do –, render- -a service, – good service, – yeoman's service; bestead, stand one in good stead; be the making of; help etc. 707.

bear fruit etc. (*produce*) 161; bring grist to the mill; profit, remunerate; benefit etc. (*do good*) 648.

find one's -account, – advantage- in; reap the benefit of etc. (*be better for*) 658.

render useful etc. (*use*) 677.

Adj. useful; of -use etc. *n.*; serviceable, usable, proficuous, good for; subservient etc. (*instrumental*) 631; conducive etc. (*tending*) 176; subsidiary etc. (*helping*) 707.

advantageous etc. (*beneficial*) 648; profitable, gainful, remunerative, worth one's salt; in-, valuable; prolific etc. (*productive*) 168.

adequate; ef-ficient, -ficacious; effect-ive, -ual; practicable, expedient etc. 646.

applicable, available, ready, handy, at hand, tangible; commodious, adaptable; of all work.

Adv. usefully etc. *adj.*; *pro bono publico*.

645. Inutility.—N. inutility; uselessness etc. *adj.*; inefficacy, futility; inep-, inap-titude; un-subservience; inadequacy etc. (*insufficiency*) 640; inefficiency etc. (*incompetence*) 158; unskilfulness etc. 699; disservice; unfruitfulness etc. (*un-productiveness*) 169; labor -in vain, – lost, – of Sisyphus; lost -trouble, – labor; work of Penelope; sleeveless errand, wild goose chase, mere farce.

tautology etc. (*repetition*) 104; supererogation etc. (*redundance*) 641.

vanitas vanitatum, vanity, inanity, worthlessness, nugacity; triviality etc. (*unimportance*) 643.

caput mortuum, waste paper, dead letter; blunt tool.

litter, rubbish, lumber, odds and ends, cast-off clothes; button-top; shoddy; rags, orts, trash, refuse, sweepings, scourings, off-scourings, dross, slag, waste, rubble, dottle, drast, *débris*; stubble, leavings; broken meat; dregs etc. (*dirt*) 653; weeds, tares; rubbish heap, dust hole; *rudera*, deads.

fruges consumere natus etc. (*drone*) 683.

V. be -useless etc. *adj.*; go a begging etc. (*redundant*) 641; fail etc. 732.

seek –, strive- after impossibilities; use vain efforts, labor in vain, roll the stone of Sisyphus, beat the air, lash the waves, *battre l'eau avec un bâton*, *donner un coup d'épée dans l'eau*, fish in the air, milk the ram, drop a bucket into an empty well, sow the sand; bay the moon; preach –, speak- to the winds; whistle jigs to a milestone; kick against the pricks, *se battre contre des moulins*; lock the stable door when the steed is stolen etc. (*too late*) 135; hold a farthing candle to the sun; cast pearls before swine etc. (*waste*) 638; carry coals to Newcastle etc. (*redundance*) 641; wash a blackamoor white etc. (*impossible*) 471.

render -useless etc. *adj.*; dis-mantle, -mast, -mount, -qualify, -able; unrig; cripple, lame etc. (*injure*) 659; spike guns, clip the wings; put out of gear.

Adj. useless, inutile, inefficacious, futile, unavailing, bootless, inoperative etc. 158; inadequate etc. (*insufficient*) 640; in-, un- subservient; inept, inefficient etc. (*impotent*) 158; of no -avail etc. (*use*) 644; ineffectual etc. (*failure*) 732; incompetent etc. (*unskilful*) 699; 'stale, flat and unprofitable;' superfluous etc. (*redundant*) 641; dispensable; thrown away etc. (*wasted*) 638; abortive etc. (*immature*) 674.

worth–, value-less; unsaleable; not worth a straw etc. (*trifling*) 643; dear at any price.

vain, empty, inane; gain-, profit-, fruit-less; unserviceable, -profitable; ill-spent; unproductive etc. 169; *hors de combat*; barren, sterile, impotent, unproductive; effete, past work etc. (*impaired*) 659; obsolete etc. (*old*) 124; fit for the -dust-hole, – wastepaper basket; good for nothing; of no earthly use; not worth -having, – powder and shot; leading to no end, uncalled for; un-necessary, -needed, superfluous.

Adv. uselessly etc. *adj.*; to -little, – no, – little or no- purpose.

Int. *cui bono?* what's the good!

646. Expedience. [Specific subservience.]—N. expedien-ce, -cy; desirableness, -bility etc. *adj.*; fitness etc. (*agreement*) 23; utility etc. 644; propriety; advantage; opportunism, pragmatism.

high time etc. (*occasion*) 134.

V. be -expedient etc. *adj.*; suit etc. (*agree*) 23; befit; suit –, befit- the -time, – season, – occasion.

conform etc. 82.

Adj. expedient; desir-, advis-, accept-able; convenient; worth while, meet; fit, -ting; due, proper, eligible, seemly, becoming; befitting etc. *v.*; opportune etc. (*in season*) 134; *in loco*; suitable etc. (*accordant*) 23; applicable etc. (*useful*) 644; practical, effective, pragmatical; suitable, handy.

Adv. in the right place; conveniently etc. *adj.*; in the nick of time.

Phr. *operae pretium est.*

647. Inexpedience.—N. enexpedien-ce, -cy; undesira-bleness, -bility etc. *adj.*; discommodity, impropriety; unfitness etc. (*disagreement*) 24; inutility etc. 645; inconvenience, inadvisability; disadvantage.

V. be -inexpedient etc. *adj.*; come amiss etc. (*disagree*) 24; embarrass etc. (*hinder*) 706; put to inconvenience; pay too dear for one's whistle.

Adj. inexpedient, undesirable; un-, in-advisable; objectionable; troublesome, in-apt, -eligible, -admissable, -convenient; in-, dis-commodious; disadvantageous; inappropriate, unsuitable, unfit etc. (*inconsonant*) 24.

ill-contrived, -advised; unsatsifactory; unprofitable etc., unsubservient etc. (*useless*) 645; inopportune etc. (*unseasonable*) 135; out of –, in the wrong- place; improper, unseemly.

clumsy, awkward; cum-brous, -bersome; lumbering, unwieldy, hulky; unmanageable etc. (*impracticable*) 704; impedient (*in the way*) 706.

unnecessary etc. (*redundant*) 641.

Phr. it will never do.

648. Goodness. [Capability of producing good. Good qualities.]—N. goodness etc. *adj.*; excellence, merit; virtue etc. 944; value, worth, price.

super-excellence, -eminence; superiority etc. 33; perfection etc. 650; *coup de maître*; master-piece, *chef d'oeuvre*, prime, flower, cream, *élite*, pick, A1, none such, *nonpareil*, *crême de la crême*, flower of the flock, cock of the roost, salt of the earth; champion.

tid-bit; gem, – of the first water; *bijou*, precious stone, jewel, pearl, diamond, ruby, brilliant, treasure; good thing; *rara avis*, one in a thousand.

beneficence etc. 906; good man etc. 948.

V. be -beneficial etc. *adj.*; produce –, do- good etc. 618; profit etc. (*be of use*) 644; benefit; confer a -benefit etc. 618.

be the making of, do a world of good, make a man of.

produce a good effect; do a good turn, confer an obligation; improve etc. 658.

do no harm, break no bones.

be -good etc. *adj.*; excel, transcend etc. (*be superior*) 33; bear away the bell.

stand the -proof, – test; pass -muster, – an examination.

challenge comparison, vie, emulate, rival.

Adj. harm-, hurt-less; unobnoxious; in-nocuous, -nocent, -offensive.

beneficial, valuable, of value; serviceable etc. (*useful*) 644; advantageous, profitable, edifying; salutary etc. (*healthful*) 656.

favorable; propitious etc. (*hopegiving*) 858; fair.

good, – as gold; excellent; better; superior etc. 33; above par; nice, fine; genuine etc. (*true*) 494.

best, choice, select, picked, elect, eximious, *recherché*, rare, priceless; unpara-goned, -lleled etc. (*supreme*) 33; superlatively etc. 33- good; super-fine, -excellent; bonzer; of the first water; first-rate, -class; high-wrought; exquisite, very best, crack, prime, tip-top, gilt-edged, capital, cardinal; standard etc. (*perfect*) 650; inimitable.

admirable, estimable; praiseworthy etc. (*approve*) 931; pleasing etc. 829; *couleur de rose*, precious, of great price; costly etc. (*dear*) 814; worth -its weight in gold, – a Jew's eye, – a king's ransom; matchless, peerless, invaluable, inestimable, precious as the apple of the eye.

tolerable etc. (*not very good*) 651; up to the mark, un-exceptionable, -objectionable; satisfactory, tidy.

in -good, – fair- condition; fresh; unspoiled; sound etc. (*perfect*) 650.

Adv. beneficially etc. *adj.*; well etc. 618.

649. Badness. [Capability of producing evil. Bad qualities.]**—N.** hurtfulness etc. *adj.*; virulence.

evil doer etc. 913; bane etc. 663; plague-spot etc. (*insalubrity*) 657; evil star, ill wind; snake in the grass, skeleton in the closet; *amari aliquid*, thorn in the side; Jonah, jinx, hoodoo.

malignity; malevolence etc. 907; tender mercies [ironically].

ill-treatment, annoyance, molestation, abuse, oppression, persecution, outrage; misusage etc. 679; injury etc. (*damage*) 659.

badness etc. *adj.*; peccancy, abomination; painfulness etc. 830; pestilence etc. (*disease*) 655; guilt etc. 947; depravity etc. 945.

V. be -hurtful etc. *adj.*; cause –, produce –, inflict –, work –, do- evil etc. 619; damnify, endamage, hurt, harm, scathe; injure etc. (*damage*) 659; pain etc. 830.

wrong, aggrieve, oppress, persecute; trample –, tread –, bear hard –, put-upon; overburden; weigh -down, – heavy on; victimize; run down; molest etc. 830.

maltreat, abuse; ill-use, -treat; thwart, buffet, bruise, scratch, maul; smite etc. (*scourge*) 972; do - violence, – harm, – a mischief; stab, pierce, outrage.

do –, make- mischief; bring –, get- into trouble.

destroy etc. 162.

Adj. hurt-, harm-, scath-, bane-, bale-ful; injurious, deleterious, detrimental, noxious, pernicious, mischievous, full of mischief, mischief-making, malefic, malignant, nocuous, noisome; prejudicial; dis-serviceable, advantageous; wide-wasting.

unlucky, sinister; obnoxious, untoward, disastrous.

oppressive, burdensome, onerous; malign etc. (*malevolent*) 907.

corrupting etc. (corrupt etc. 659) virulent, venomous, envenomed, corrosive; poisonous etc. (*morbific*) 657; deadly etc. (*killing*) 361; destructive etc. (*destroying*) 162; inauspicious etc. 859.

bad, ill, arrant, as bad bad can be, dreadful; horrid, -rible; dire, rank, peccant, foul, fulsome; rotten, – at the core.

vile, base, villainous; mean etc. (*paltry*) 643; injured etc., deteriorated etc. 659; unsatisfactory, exception, -able, indifferent; below par etc. (*imperfect*) 651; ill-contrived, -conditioned; wretched, sad, grievous, deplorable, lamentable; piti-ful, -able, woeful etc. (*painful*) 830.

evil, wrong; depraved etc. 945; shocking; reprehensible etc. (*disapprove*) 932.

hateful, – as a toad; abominable, detestable, execrable, cursed, accursed, confounded; damn-ed, -able; infernal; diabolic etc. (*malevolent*) 907.

inadvisable etc. (*inexpedient*) 647; unprofitable etc. (*useless*) 645; incompetent etc. (*unskilful*) 699; irremediable etc. (*hopeless*) 859.

Adv. badly etc. *adj.*; wrong, ill; to one's cost; where the shoe pinches.

Phr. bad is the best; the worst come to the worst.

650. Perfection.—N. perfection; perfectness etc. *adj.*; indefectibility; inpecc-ancy, -ability.

pink, *beau idéal*, phoenix, paragon; pink –, acme- of perfection; *ne plus ultra*; summit etc. 210.

cygne noir; philosopher's stone; chrysolite, Koh-i-noor, black tulip.

model, standard, pattern, mirror, admirable Crichton; trump; very prince of.

master-piece, -stroke, super-excellence etc. (*goodness*) 648; transcendence etc. (*superiority*) 33.

V. be -perfect etc. *adj.*; transcend etc. (*be supreme*) 33.

bring to perfection, perfect, ripen, mature; consummate, complete etc. 729; put in trim etc. (*prepare*) 673; put the finishing touch to.

Adj. perfect, faultless, ideal; indefective, -ficient, -fectible; immaculate, spotless, impeccable; free from -imperfection etc. 651; un-blemished, - injured etc. 659; sound, – as a roach; in perfect condition; scathless, intact, harmless; seaworthy etc. (*safe*) 644; right as a trivet; *in seipso totus teres atque rotundus*; consummate etc. (*complete*) 52; finished etc. 729; complete in itself.

best etc. (*good*) 648; model, standard; inimitable, unparagoned, unparalleled etc. (*supreme*) 33; superhuman, divine; beyond all praise etc. (*approbation*) 931; *sans peur et sans reproche*.

Adj. to perfection, to the limit; perfectly etc. *adj.*; *ad unguem*; clean, – as a whistle.

651. Imperfection.—N. imperfection; imperfectness etc. *adj.*; deficiency; inadequacy etc. (*insufficiency*) 640; peccancy etc. (*badness*) 649; immaturity etc. 674.

fault, defect, weak point; screw loose; rift within the lute; fly in the ointment; flaw etc. (*break*) 70; gap etc. 198; twist etc. 243; taint, attainder; bar sinister, hole in one's coat; blemish etc. 848; weakness etc. 160; half-blood, touch of the tar brush; shortcoming etc. 304; drawback; seamy side.

mediocrity; no great -shakes, – catch; not much to boast of.

V. be -imperfect etc. *adj.*; have a -defect etc. *n.*; lie under a disadvantage; spring a leak.

not –, barely- pass muster; fall short etc. 304.

Adj. imperfect; not -perfect etc. 650; de-ficient, -fective; faulty, unsound, mutilated, tainted; out of -order, – tune; cracked, leaky; sprung; warped etc. (*distort*) 243; lame; injured etc. (*deteriorated*) 659; peccant etc. (*bad*) 649; frail etc. (*weak*) 160; inadequate etc. (*insufficient*) 640; crude etc. (*unprepared*) 674; incomplete etc. 53; found wanting; below par; shorthanded; below –, under- its full -strength, – complement.

indifferent, middling, ordinary, mediocre; average etc. 29; so-so; *così-così*, milk and water; tolerable, fair, passable; pretty -well, – good; rather –, moderately- good; good –, well-enough; decent; not -bad, – amiss; inobjectionable, admissable, bearable, only better than nothing.

secondary, inferior; second-rate, -best, one-horse.

Adv. almost etc.; to a limited extent, rather etc. 32; pretty, moderately; only; considering, all things considered, enough.

Phr. *surgit amari aliquid.*

652. Cleanness.—N. cleanness etc. *adj.*; purity; cleaning etc. *v.*; purification, defecation etc. *v.*; purgation, lustration; de-, abs-tersion; epuration, mundation, ablution, lavation, colature; disinfection etc. *v.*; drain-, sewerage.

lavatory, bath, -room; swimming pool, natatorium; public baths; hot –, cold –, Turkish –, Swedish –, Russian – vapor- bath; *hammam*, laundry, washhouse; washerwoman, laundress, laundryman; scavenger, cleaner, sweeper, goodie; crossing sweeper, white wings, dustman, sweep.

brush; broom, besom, carpet-sweeper, vacuum-cleaner, mop, squilgee, rake, shovel, sieve, riddle, screen, filter; scraper, strigil.

napkin, *serviette*, cloth, table-, carving-cloth, table-linen, napery, maukin, handkerchief, towel, sudary; doyley, doily, duster, sponge, mop, swab.

cover, drugget, mat, doormat.

soap, wash, lotion, detergent, cathartic, purgative; purifier etc. *v.*; dentifrice, tooth-powder, -paste; mouth wash; disinfectant.

V. be –, render- clean etc. *adj.*

clean, -se; mundify, rinse, wring, flush, full, wipe, mop, sponge, scour, swab, scrub, holystone, brush up.

wash, shampoo, lave, launder, buck; abs-, deterge; clear, purify; de-purate, -spumate, -fecate; purge, expurgate; Bowdlerize; elutriate, lixiviate, edulcorate, clarify, refine, rack; fil-ter, -trate; drain, strain.

disinfect, sterilize, pasteurize, fumigate, ventilate, deodorize; whitewash.

sift, winnow, screen, riddle, pick, weed, comb, rake, brush, sweep.

rout –, clear –, sweep etc.- out; make a clean sweep of.

Adj. clean, -ly; pure; immaculate; spot-, stain-, taint-less; without a stain, un-stained, -spotted, -soiled, -sullied, -tainted, -infected, -adulterated; aseptic; sweet, – as a nut.

neat, spruce, tidy, trim, gimp, clean as a new penny, like a cat in pattens; cleaned etc. *v.*; kempt.

Adv. neatly etc. *adj.*; clean as a whistle.

653. Uncleanness.—N. uncleanness etc. *adj.*; impurity; immundi-ty, -city; impurity etc. [of mind] 961.

defilement, contamination etc. *v.*; defedation; soil-ure, -iness; abomination; leaven; taint, -ure; fetor etc. 401.

decay; putre-scence, -faction; corruption; mold, must, mildew, dry-rot, *mucor*, rubigo, caries.

slovenry; slovenliness etc. *adj.*; squalor.

dowdy, drab, slut, malkin, slattern, sloven, slammerkin, scrub, draggletail, mudlark, dustman, sweep; beast.

dirt, filth, soil, slop; dust, cobweb, flue; smoke, soot, smudge, smut, grime, raff.

sordes, dregs, grounds, lees; sedi-, settle-ment; heel-tap; dross, -iness; mother, precipitate, *scoria*; ashes, cinders, recrement, slag; scum, froth.

hog-wash, swill, ditch-, dish-, bilge-water; rinsings, cheese-parings; sweepings etc. (*useless refuse*) 645; off-, out-scourings; off-scum; *caput mortuum*, *residuum*, sprue, feculence, clinker, draff; scurf, -iness; *exuviae*, morphew; fur, -fur; dandruff; tartar.

riffraff; vermin, louse, cootie, flea, bug.

mud, mire, quagmire, *alluvium*, silt, sludge, slime, slush, slosh.

spawn, offal, garbage, carrion; *excreta* etc. 299; slough, peccant humor, pus, matter, suppuration, *lienteria*; *feces*, excrement, ordure, dung; sew-, sewer-age; muck, coprolite; guano, manure, compost.

dunghill, *coluvies*, mixen, midden, bog, laystall, sink, w.c., water-, earth-closet, latrine, privy, jakes, John's, cess, -pool; sump, sough, *cloaca*, drain, sewer, common sewer; Cloacina; dust-hole.

sty, pig-sty, lair, den, Augean stable, sink of corruption; slum, rookery.

V. be –, become- unclean etc. *adj.*; rot, putrefy, fester, rankle, reek; stink etc. 401; mold, -er; go - bad etc. *adj.*

render -unclean etc. *adj.*; dirt, -y; soil, smoke, tarnish, slaver, spot, smear, daub, blot, blur, smudge, smutch, smirch; d-, dr-abble, -aggle; spatter, slubber; be-smear etc.; -mire, -slime, -grime, - foul; splash, stain, distain, maculate, sully, pollute, defile, debase, contaminate, taint, leaven; corrupt etc. (*injure*) 659; cover with -dust etc. *n.*; drabble in the mud.

wallow in the mire; slob-, slab-ber.

Adj. unclean, dirty, filthy, grimy; soiled etc. *v.*; not to be handled with kid gloves; dusty, snuffy, smutty, sooty, smoky; thick, turbid, dreggy; slimy.

uncleanly, slovenly, untidy, sluttish, dowdy, slatternly, draggletailed; un-combed, -kempt, -scoured, -swept, -wiped, -washed, -strained, -purified; squalid.

nasty, coarse, foul, impure, offensive, abominable, beastly, reeky, reechy; fetid etc. 401.

moldy, lentiginous, musty, mildewed, rusty, moth-eaten, mucid, rancid, bad, gone bad, touched, fusty, reasty, rotten, corrupt, tainted, high, fly-blown, maggoty; putr-id, -escent, -efied; purulent, carious, peccant, fec-al, -ulent; stercoraceous, excrementitious; scurfy, impetiginous; gory, bloody; rotting etc. *v.*; rotten as -a pear, – cheese.

crapulous etc. (*intemperate*) 954; gross etc. (*impure in mind*) 961.

654. Health.—N. health, sanity; soundness etc. *adj.*; vigor; good –, perfect –, excellent –, rude –, robust- health; bloom, *mens sana in corpore sano*; Hygeia; incorrupti-on, -bility; good state –, clean bill- of health, eupepsia.

V. be in health etc. *adj.*; bloom, flourish.

keep -body and soul together, – on one's legs; enjoy -good, – a good state of - health; have a clean bill of health.

return to health; recover etc. 660; get better etc. (*improve*) 658; take a -new, – fresh- lease of life; convalesce, be convalescent, recruit; restore to health; cure etc. (*restore*) 660.

Adj. health-y, -ful; in -health etc. *n.*; well, sound, strong, fit, hearty, hale, fresh, blooming, green, whole; florid, flush, hardy, stanch, staunch, brave, robust, vigorous, weather-proof; convalescent.

un-scathed, -injured, -maimed, -marred, -tainted; sound of wind and limb, safe and sound; without a scratch.

on one's legs; sound as a -roach, – bell; fresh as -a daisy, – a rose, – April; picture of health; bursting with health; fit as a fiddle; hearty as a buck; in -fine, – high- feather; in -good case, – full bloom; in fine fettle; pretty bobbish, tolerably well, as well as can be expected.

sanitary etc. (*health-giving*) 656; sanatory etc. (*remedial*) 662.

655. Disease.*—N. disease, illness, sickness etc. *adj.*; ailing etc. *v.*; 'the ills that flesh is heir to;' morb-idity, -osity; infirmity, ailment, indisposition; complaint, disorder, malady; distemper, -ature.

visitation, attack, seizure, stroke, fit, epilepsy, apoplexy, shock, shell-shock.

delicacy, loss of health, valetudinarianism, invalidism, cachexy; *cachexia*, atrophy, *marasmus*; indigestion, *dyspepsia*; decay etc. (*deterioration*) 659; malnutrition, decline, consumption, palsy, paralysis, prostration; occupational diseases.

taint, pollution, infection, contagion, septicity, septicaemia, blood poisoning, pyaemia, epi-, endemic; murrain, plague, pestilence, virus, pox.

sore, ulcer, abscess, fester, boil; pimple etc. (*swelling*) 250; carbuncle, gathering, whitlow, imposthume, peccant humor, issue; rot, canker, cancer, *carcinoma*, *caries*, mortification, corruption, gangrene, *sphacelus*, leprosy, eruption, rash, breaking out, venereal disease.

fever, calenture; inflammation.

fatal etc. (*hopeless*) 859- -disease etc.; dangerous illness, galloping consumption, churchyard cough; general breaking up, break up of the system.

[Disease of the mind] neurasthenia; idiocy etc. 499; insanity etc. 503.

martyr to disease; cripple; 'the halt, the lame and the blind;' valetudinar-y, -ian; invalid, patient, case; sick-room, -chamber, hospital etc. 662.

[Science of disease] path-, eti-, nos-ology, therapeutics, diagnosis, prognosis.

V. be -ill etc. *adj.*; ail, suffer, labor under, be affected with, complain of; droop, flag, languish, halt; sicken, peak, pine, waste away, fail, lose strength; gasp.

keep one's bed; feign sickness etc. (*falsehood*) 544; malinger.

lay -by, – up; take – , catch- -a disease etc. *n.*, – an infection; be stricken by; break out.

Adj. diseased; ailing etc. *v.*; ill, – of; taken ill, seized with; indisposed, unwell, sick, squeamish, poorly, seedy; affected – , afflicted- with illness; laid up, confined, bed-ridden, invalided, in hospital, on the sick list; out of -health, – sorts; valetudinary.

un-sound, -healthy; sickly, morbose, healthless,

infirm, chlorotic, unbraced, drooping, flagging, lame, halt, crippled, halting.

morbid, tainted, vitiated, peccant, contaminated, poisoned, septic, tabid, mangy, leprous, cankered; rotten, – to, – at- the core; withered, palsied, paralytic, tuberculous; dyspeptic.

touched in the wind, broken-winded, spavined, gasping; *hors de combat* etc. (*useless*) 645.

weak-ly, -ened etc. (*weak*) 160; decrepit; decayed etc. (*deteriorated*) 659; incurable etc. (*hopeless*) 859; in declining health; cranky; in a bad way, in danger, prostrate; moribund etc. (*death*) 360.

morbific, epidemic etc. 657.

*Extended lists of different diseases are beyond the scope of this work.

656. Salubrity.—N. salubrity, salubriousness; healthiness etc. *adj.*

fine -air, – climate; eudiometer.

[Preservation of health] *hygiène*; valetudinarian, -ism, preventorium, sanitarian; *sanitarium*, *sanitorium*, immunity.

V. be -salubrious etc. *adj.*; agree with, be good for; assimilate etc. 23.

Adj. salu-brious, -tary, -tiferous, wholesome; health-y, -ful; sanitary, prophylactic, benign, bracing, tonic, invigorating, good for, nutritious, hyg-eian, -ienic.

in-noxious, -nocuous, -nocent; harmless, uninjurious, uninfectious; immune.

sanative etc. (*remedial*) 662; restorative etc. (*reinstate*) 660; useful etc. 644.

657. Insalubrity.—N. insalubrity, unhealthiness etc. *adj.*; non-naturals; plague spot; malaria etc. (*poison*) 663; death in the pot, contagion.

Adj. insalubrious; un-healthy, -wholesome; noxious, noisome, foul; morbi-fic, -ferous; mephitic, septic, azotic, deleterious; pesti-lent, -ferous, -lential; virulent, venomous, envenomed, poisonous, toxic, narcotic.

contagious, infectious, catching, taking, communicable, epidemic, zymotic, sporadic, endemic, pandemic, epizoötic.

innutritious, indigestible, ungenial, uncongenial etc. (*disagreeing*) 24.

deadly etc. (*killing*) 361.

658. Improvement.—N. improvement; a-, melioration; betterment; mend, amendment, emendation; mending etc. *v.*; advancement; advance etc. (*progress*) 282; ascent etc. 305; promotion, preferment; elevation etc. 307; increase etc. 35.

cultiv-, civiliz-ation; menticulture, culture, march of intellect; eugenics, euthenics, meliorism, telesis.

reform, -ation; revision, radical reform; second thoughts, correction, *limae labor*, refinement, elaboration; purification etc. 652; repair etc. (*restoration*) 660; recovery etc. 660.

revise; revised – , new- edition.

reformer, radical, progressive.

V. improve; be –, become –, get- better; mend, amend.

advance etc. (*progress*) 282; ascend etc. 305; increase etc. 35; fructify, ripen, mature; pick up, come about, rally, take a favorable turn; turn -over a new leaf, – the corner; raise one's head, sow one's wild oats; recover etc. 660.

be -better etc. *adj.*, – improved by; turn to - right, – good, – best- account; profit by, reap the benefit of; make -good use of, – capital out of; place to good account; take advantage of.

render better, improve, emend, make over, better; a-, meliorate; correct.

improve –, refine- upon; rectify; enrich, mellow, elaborate, fatten.

promote, cultivate, advance, forward, enhance; bring -forward, – on; foster etc. 707; invigorate etc. (*strengthen*) 159.

touch –, rub –, brush –, furbish –, bolster –, vamp –, brighten –, warm- up; polish, cook, make the most of, set off to advantage; prune; repair etc. (*restore*) 660; put in order etc. (*arrange*) 60.

review, revise, edit, redact; make -corrections, – improvements etc. *n.*; doctor etc. (*remedy*) 662; purify etc. 652.

relieve, refresh, revive, infuse new blood into, recruit, re-invigorate, renew, revivify, freshen, build -afresh, – anew; uplift, inspire.

re-form, -model, -organize; new model, civilize.

view in a new light, think better of, appeal from Philip drunk to Philip sober.

palliate, mitigate; lessen etc. 36- an evil.

Adj. improving etc. *v.*; progressive, improved etc. *v.*; better, – off, – for; all the better for; better advised.

reform-, emend -atory; reparatory etc. (*restorative*) 660; remedial etc. 662.

corrigible, improvable, curable, accultural.

Adv. on -consideration, – reconsideration, – second thoughts, – better advice; *ad melius inquirendum*; on the -mend, – up grade.

659. Deterioration.—N. deterioration, debasement; want, ebb; recession etc. 287; retrogradation etc. 283; decrease etc. 36.

degenera-cy, -tion, -teness; degradation; depravation, -ement; depravity etc. 945; demoralization, retrogression.

impairment, inquination, injury, damage, loss, detriment, delaceration, outrage, havoc, inroad, ravage, scath; perversion, prostitution, vitiation, discoloration, oxidation, pollution, defedation, poisoning, venenation, leaven, contamination, canker, corruption, adulteration, alloy.

decl-ine, -ension, -ination; decadence, -cy; falling off etc. *v.*; caducity, decreptitude, senility.

decay, dilapidation, ravages of time, wear and tear; cor-, e-rosion; mouldi-, rotten-ness; moth and rust, dry-rot, blight, marasmus, atrophy, collapse; disorganization; *délabrement* etc. (*destruction*) 162.

wreck, mere wreck, honeycomb, *magni nominis umbra*.

V. be –, become- -worse, – deteriorated etc. *adj.*; have seen better days, deteriorate, degenerate, fall off; wane etc. (*decrease*) 36; ebb; retrograde etc. 283; decline, droop; go down etc. (*sink*) 306; go -downhill, – on from bad to worse, – farther and fare worse; jump out of the frying pan into the fire.

run to -seed, – waste; swale, sweal; lapse, be the worse for; break, – down; spring a leak, crack, start; shrivel etc. (*contract*) 195; fade, go off, wither, molder, rot, rankle, decay, go bad; go to – fall into- decay; 'fall into the sear and yellow leaf,' rust, crumble, shake; totter, – to its fall; perish etc. 162; die etc. 360.

[Render less good] deteriorate; weaken etc. 160; put back; taint, infect, contaminate, poison, empoison, envenom, canker, corrupt, exulcerate, pollute, vitiate, inquinate; de-, em-base; denaturalize, leaven; de-flower, -bauch, -file, -prave, -grade; stain etc. (*dirt*) 653; discolor; alloy, adulterate, sophisticate, tamper with, prejudice.

pervert, prostitute, demoralize, brutalize; render vicious etc. 945; compromise.

embitter, ex-, acerbate, aggravate.

injure, impair, labefy, damage, harm, hurt, shend, scathe, spoil, mar, despoil, dilapidate, waste; overrun; ravage; pillage etc. 791.

wound, stab, pierce, maim, lame, surbate, cripple, hough, hamstring, hit between the wind and water, scotch, mangle, mutilate, disfigure, blemish, deface, warp.

blight, rot; cor-, e-rode, eat away; wear -away, – out; gnaw, – at the root of; sap, mine, undermine, shake, sap the foundations of, break up; dis-organize, -mantle, -mast; destroy etc. 162.

damnify etc. (*aggrieve*) 649; do one's worst; knock down; deal a blow to; play -havoc, – sad havoc, – the mischief, – the deuce, – the very devil- -with, – among; decimate.

Adj. unimproved etc. (improve etc. 658); deteriorated etc. *v.*; altered, – for the worse; injured etc. *v.*; sprung; withering, spoiling, etc. *v.*; on the -wane, – decline; tabid; degenerate; worse; the –, all the- worse for; out of -repair, – tune; imperfect etc. 651; the worse for wear; battered; weather-ed, -beaten; stale, *passé*, shaken, dilapidated, frayed, faded, wilted, shabby, second-hand, second-rate, threadbare; worn, – to- -a thread, – a shadow, – the stump, rags; reduced, – to a skeleton, skeletonized; far gone.

decayed etc. *v.*; moth-, worn-eaten; mildewed, rusty, moldy, spotted, seedy, time-worn, moss-grown; discolored; effete, wasted, crumbling, moldering, rotten, cankered, blighted, tainted; depraved etc. (*vicious*) 945; decrep-id, -it; broken down; done, – for, – up; worn out, used up; fit for the -dust-hole, – wastepaper basket; past work etc. (*useless*) 645.

at a low ebb, in a bad way, on one's last legs, washed -up; – out; undermined, deciduous; nodding to its fall etc. (*destruction*) 162; tottering etc. (*dangerous*) 665; past cure etc. (*hopeless*) 859; fatigued etc. 688; backward, retrograde etc. (*retrogressive*) 283; deleterious etc. 649; behind the times.

Adv. on the down grade; beyond hope.

Phr. out of the frying pan into the fire; *aegrescit medendo*.

660. Restoration.—N. restor-ation, -al; re-instatement, -placement, -habilitation, -

establishment, -construction; reporduction etc. 163; re-novation, -newal; reviv-al, -escence; refreshment etc. 689; re-suscitation, -animation, - vivification, -viction; Phoenix; reorganization.

renaissance, renascence, rebirth, second youth, rejuvenation, rejuvenescence, new birth; regeneration, -cy, -teness; palingenesis, reconversion, resurgence, resurrection.

redress, retrieval, reclamation, recovery; convalescence; resumption, *résumption*.

recurrence etc. (*repetition*) 104; *réchauffé*, *rifacimento*.

cure, recure, sanation; healing etc. *v.*; redintegration; rectification, instauration.

repair, reparation, mending; recruiting etc. *v.*; cicatrization; disinfection; tinkering.

reaction; redemption etc. (*deliverance*) 672; restitution 790; relief etc. 834.

mender, repairer, rénewer; tinker, cobbler; doctor etc. 662; *vis medicatrix* etc. (*remedy*) 662. curableness.

V. return to the original state; recover, rally, revive; come -to, – round, – to oneself; pull through, weather the storm, be oneself again; get - well, – round, – the better of, – over, – about; rise from -one's ashes, – the grave; resurge, resurrect; survive etc. (*outlive*) 110; resume, reappear; come to, – life again; live –, rise- again; relive.

heal, skin over, cicatrize; right itself.

restore, put back, place *in statu quo*; re-instate, - place, -seat, -habilitate, -establish, -estate, -install.

re-construct, -build, -organize, -constitute; reconvert; re-new, -novate; recondition; regenerate; rejuvenate.

re-deem, -claim, -cover, -trieve; rescue etc. (*deliver*) 672.

redress, recure; cure, heal, remedy, doctor, physic, medicate; break of; bring round, set on one's legs.

re-suscitate, -vive, -animate, -vivify, -call to life; reproduce etc. 163; warm up; reinvigorate, refresh etc. 689.

redintegrate, make whole; recoup etc. 790; make -good, – all square; rectify; put – , set- -right, – to rights, – straight; set up, correct; put in order etc. (*arrange*) 60; refit, recruit; fill up, – the ranks; reinforce.

repair, mend; put in -repair, – thorough repair, – complete repair; retouch, botch, vamp, tinker, doctor, cobble; do – , patch – , plaster – , vamp-up; darn, fine-draw, heel-piece; stop a gap, stanch, staunch, caulk, calk, careen, splice, bind up wounds.

Adj. restored etc. *v.*; *redivivus*, convalescent; in a fair way; none the worse; rejuvenated, renascent.

restoring etc. *v.*; restorative, recuperative; sana-, repara-tive, -tory; curative, remedial.

restor-, recover-, san-, remedi-, retriev-, cur-able.

Adv. *in statu qho*; as you were.

Phr. *revenons a nos moutons.*

661. Relapse.—N. relapse, lapse; falling back etc. *v.*; retrogradation etc. (*retrogression*) 283; deterioration etc. 659.

[Return to, or recurrence of a bad state] backsliding, recidivation, recrudescence.

V. relapse, lapse; fall –, slide –, sink- back; have a relapse; return; retrograde etc. 283; recidivate; fall off etc. 659- again.

662. Remedy.—N. remedy, help, redress; antidote, anti-toxin, -biotic; anti-, counter-poison, prophylactic, antiseptic, germicide, bactericide, corrective, restorative, stimulant, pick-me-up, tonic; sedative etc. 174; palliative; febrifuge; alterant, -ative; specific; emetic, carminative; narcotic etc. *adj.*; Nepenthe, Mithridate.

cure; radical – , perfect – , certain- cure; sovereign remedy.

physic, medicine, patent medicine, Galenicals, simples, drug, wonder – drugs; miracle – drugs; potion, draught, dose, pill, bolus, lozenge, tablet, tabloid, capsule; electuary; linct-us, -ure; medicament.

nostrum, receipt, recipe, prescription; catholicon, panacea, elixir, *elixir vitae*, philosopher's stone; balm, balsam, cordial, theriac, ptisan.

salve, ointment, cerate, oil, lenitive, lotion, cosmetic; plaster; epithem, embrocation, liniment, cataplasm, sinapism, arquebusade, traumatic, vulnerary, pepastic, poultice, collyrium, depilatory.

compress, pledget; bandage etc. (*support*) 215.

treatment, medical treatment, regimen; diet-ary, -etics; *vis medicatrix*, – *naturae*; *médicine expectante*; seton, blood-letting, bleeding, venesection, phlebotomy, cupping, leeches; operation, surgical operation; tonsillectomy, appendectomy; injection, electrolysis, massage.

pharma-cy, -cology, -ceutics; acology; materia medica, pharmacopoeia, therapeutics, therapy, posology, pathology etc. 655; home-, hetero-, all-, hydr-opathy; cold water – , open air- cure; dietetics; sur-, chirur-gery, osteopathy; healing art, leechcraft, practice of medicine; ortho-paedy, - praxy; dentistry, midwifery, obstetrics, gynecology.

faith -cure, – healing, Christian science; psychotherapy, -analysis, psychiatry.

hospital, infirmary, clinic; pest-, lazar-house; lazaretto, lazaret; lock hospital; *maison de santé; ambulance*; dispensary; *sanatorium, sanitarium,* spa, baths, pump-room, well; *hospice*; Red Cross; nursing home; asylum.

doctor, physician, surgeon; medical – , general-practitioner, consultant, specialist; medical attendant; medical student, medico; chemist, apothecary, pharmacopolist, druggist; leech; Aesculapius, Hippocrates, Galen; *accoucheur,* gynecologist, midwife, oculist, aurist, dentist; operator; osteopath, bonesetter; nurse, monthly nurse, sister; dresser; *masseur, masseuse.*

V. apply a -remedy etc. *n.*; doctor, dose, physic, nurse, minister to, attend, dress the wounds, plaster, bandage, poultice; heal, cure, work a cure, kill or cure, remedy, stay (disease), snatch from the jaws of death; prevent etc. 706; relieve etc. 834; palliate etc. 658; restore etc. 660; drench with physic; consult, operate, extract, deliver; bleed, cup, let blood, transfuse; electrolyse; psychoanalyse.

Adj. remedial; restorative etc. 660; corrective, palliative, healing; sana-tory, -tive; prophylactic; salutiferous etc. (*salutary*) 656; medic-al, -inal; therapeutic, surgical, chirurgical, orthopedic, epulotic, paregoric, tonic, corroborant, analeptic, balsamic, anodyne, hypnotic, neurotic; narcotic, sedative, lenitive, demulcent, emollient; depuratory; deter-sive, -gent; abstersive, disinfectant, febrifugal, alternative; traumatic, vulnerary.

dietetic, alimentary; nutrit-ious, -ive; peptic; alexi-pharmic, -teric; remedi-, cur-able.

663. Bane. —N. bane, curse, thorn in the -side, -flesh, bugbear, *bête noire*; evil etc. 619; hurtfulness etc. (*badness*) 649; painfulness etc. (*cause of pain*) 830; scourge etc. (*punishment*) 975; *damnosa hereditas*; white elephant.

sting, fang, thorn, tang, bramble, briar, nettle.

poison, leaven, virus, venom; intoxicant; arsenic, Prussic acid, antimony, tartar emetic, strychnine, nicotine, cyanide of potassium, corrosive sublimate; curare; hyoscine etc.; poison-, mustard-. tear-gas; carbon di-, mon-oxide; ptomaine poisoning, botulism; miasm, mephitis, malaria, azote, sewer gas; pest, stench etc. 401.

rust, worm, moth, moth and rust, fungus, mildew; dry-rot; canker, -worm; cancer; torpedo; viper etc. (*evil-doer*) 913; demon etc. 980.

hemlock, hellebore, nightshade, *belladonna*, henbane, aconite; Upas tree.

drugs, dope, opium, morphia, morphine, cocaine, heroin, hashish, bhang.

[*Science of poisons*] Toxicology.

Adj. baneful etc. (*bad*) 649; poisonous etc. (*unwholesome*) 657.

664. Safety. —N. safety, security, impregnability; invulnera-bility, -bleness etc. *adj.*; danger -past, — over; storm blown over; coast clear; escape etc. 671; means of escape, safety-valve; safeguard, palladium, sheet anchor, rock, tower of strength.

guardian-, ward-, warden-ship; tutelage, custody, safe keeping; preservation etc. 670; protection, auspices.

safe-conduct, escort, convoy; guard, sheild etc. (*defense*) 717; guardian angel, tutelary -god, — deity, — saint; *genius loci*.

protector, guardian; ward-en, -er; preserver, custodian, *duenna chaperon*, third person.

watch-, ban-dog; Cerberus; watch-, patrol-, police-man, constable, peeler, bobby, copper, cop, bull, flat-foot, detective, armed guard; sentinel, sentry, scout etc. (*warning*) 668; garrison; guardship.

[Means of safety] refuge etc., anchor etc. 666; precaution etc. (*preparation*) 673; quarantine, *cordon sanitaire*. [Sense of security] confidence etc. 858.

V. be -safe etc. *adj.*; keep one's head above water, tide over, save one's bacon; ride out —, weather- the storm; light upon one's feet; bear a charmed life; escape etc. 671; possess nine lives.

make —, render- -safe etc. *adj.*; protect, watch over; take care of etc. (*care*) 459; preserve etc. 670; cover, screen, shelter, shroud, flank, ward; guard etc. (*defend*) 717; secure etc. (*restrain*) 751; intrench, fence round etc. (*circumscribe*) 229; house, nestle, ensconce; take charge of.

escort, convoy; garrison; watch, mount guard, patrol, scout, spy.

make assurance double sure etc. (*caution*) 864; take up a loose thread; take precautions etc. (*prepare for*) 673; take in a reef; double reef top-sails.

seek safety; take — , find- shelter etc. 666; run into port.

Adj. safe, secure, sure; in -safety, — security; have an anchor to windward; on the safe side; under the -shield of, — shade of, — wing of, — shadow of one's wing; under -cover, — lock and key; out of -danger, — the meshes, — harm's way; in -harbor, — port; on sure ground, at anchor, high and dry, above water, on *terra firma*; unthreatened, -molested; protected etc. *v.*; cavendo tutus; panoplied etc. (*defended*) 717.

snug, sea-, air-worthy; weather-, water-, fire-, bomb-proof.

defensible, tenable, proof against, invulnerable; un-assailable, -attackable; im-pregnable, -perdible; founded on a rock; inexpugnable.

safe and sound etc. (*preserved*) 670; harmless; scathless etc. (*perfect*) 650; unhazarded; not -dangerous etc. 665.

protecting etc. *v.*; guardian, tutelary; per-servative etc. 670; trustworthy etc. 939.

Adv. *ex abundanti cautela*; with impunity.

Phr. all's well; all clear; *salva res est*; *suave mari magno*; safety first.

665. Danger. —N. danger, peril, insecurity, jeopardy, risk, hazard, venture, precariousness, slipperiness; instability etc. 149; defenselessness etc. *adj.*

exposure etc. (*liability*) 177; vulnerability; vulnerable point, heel of Achilles; forlorn hope etc. (*hopelessness*) 859.

[Dangerous course] leap in the dark etc. (*rashness*) 863; road to ruin, *facilis descensus Averni*, hair-breadth escape.

cause for alarm; source of danger etc. 667. [Approach of danger] rock —, breakers- ahead; storm brewing; clouds -in the horizon, — gathering; warning etc. 668; alarm etc. 669. [Sense of danger] apprehension etc. 860.

V. be -in danger etc. *adj.*; be exposed to — , run into — , incur — , encounter- -danger etc. *n.*; run a risk; lay oneself open to etc. (*liability*) 177; lean on — , trust to- a broken reed; feel the ground sliding from under one, have to run for it; have the -chances, — odds- against one.

hang by a thread, totter; tremble on the -verge, — brink; sleep — stand -on a volcano; sit on a barrel of gunpowder, live in a glass house.

bring — , place — , put- in -danger etc. *n.*; endanger, expose to danger, imperil; jeopard, -ize, compromise; sail too near the wind etc. (*rash*) 863; put one's head in the lion's mouth.

adventure, risk, hazard, venture, stake, set at hazard; run the gauntlet etc. (*dare*) 861; engage in a forlorn hope.

threaten etc. 909- danger; run one hard; lay a trap for etc. (*deceive*) 545.

Adj. in -danger etc. *n.*; endangered etc. *v.*; fraught with danger; danger-, hazard-, peril-, parl-, pericul-ous; unsafe, unprotected etc. (safe, protect etc. 664); insecure, untrustworthy, unreliable; built upon sand, on a sandy basis.

defence-, fence-, guard-, harbor-less; unshielded; vulnerable, expugnable, unsheltered, exposed; open to etc. (*liable*) 177.

aux abois, at bay; on -the wrong side of the wall, – a lee shore, – the rocks.

at stake, in question; precarious, aleatory, critical, ticklish; slip-pery, -py; hanging by a thread etc. *v.*; with a halter round one's neck; between - the hammer and the anvil, – Scylla and Charybdis, – two fires; on the -edge, – brink, – verge of a- -precipice, – volcano; in the lion's den, on slippery ground, under fire; not out of the wood.

un-warned, -admonished, -advised; unprepared etc. 674; off one's guard etc. (*inexpectant*) 508.

tottering; un-stable, -steady; shaky, top-heavy, tumble-down, ramshackle, crumbling, waterlogged; help-, guide-less; in a bad way; reduced to –, at- the last extremity; trembling in the balance; nodding to its fall etc. (*destruction*) 162.

threatening etc. 909; ominous, ill-omened; alarming etc. (*fear*) 860; explosive; poisonous etc.-657.

adventurous etc. (*rash*) 863, (*bold*) 861.

Int. stop! look out! beware! take care!

Phr. *incidit in Scyllam qui vult vitare Charybdim; nam tua res agitur paries dum proximus ardet.*

666. Refuge. [Means of safety.]—**N.** refuge, sanctuary, retreat, fastness; stronghold, keep, last resort; ward; prison etc. 752; asylum, ark, home, almshouse, refuge for the destitute; hiding-place etc. (*ambush*) 530; *sanctum sanctorum* etc. (*privacy*) 893.

roadstead, anchorage; breakwater, mole, port, haven; harbor, – of refuge; sea-port; pier, jetty, embankment, quay.

covert, shelter, abri, screen, lee-wall, wing, shield, umbrella; splash-, dash-board, mudguard.

wall etc. (*inclosure*) 232; fort etc. (*defence*) 717.

anchor, kedge; grap-nel, -pling iron; sheet-, mushroom-anchor, main-stay; support etc. 215; check etc. 706; ballast.

jury-mast; vent-peg; safety -valve, – lamp; lightning conductor.

means of escape etc. (*escape*) 671; life-boat, swimming belt, cork jacket; life preserver, breeches buoy; parachute, plank, stepping-stone.

safeguard etc. (*protection*) 664.

V. seek – , take – , find- refuge etc. *n.*; seek –, find- safety etc. 664; throw oneself into the arms of; claim sanctuary; take to the -hills, – woods; make port, reach shelter, bar –, bolt –, lock -the door, – gete; let the portcullis down; raise the drawbridge.

667. Pitfall. [Source of danger.]—**N.** rocks, reefs, coral reef, sunken rocks, snags; sands, quicksands, Goodwin sands, sandy foundation; slippery ground; breakers, shoals, shallows, bank, shelf, flat, lee shore, iron-bound coast; rock –, breakers- ahead; derelict.

precipice; abyss, chasm, pit, crevasse; maelstrom, whirlpool, eddy, vortex, rapids, current, bore, tidal wave; storm, squall, hurricane, whirlwind; volcano;

ambush etc. 530; pitfall, trap-door; trap etc. (*snare*) 545.

sword of Damocles; wolf at the door, snake in the grass, viper in one's bosom, death in the pot; latency etc. 526.

ugly customer, dangerous person, *le chat qui dort*; firebrand, hornet's nest.

Phr. *latet anguis in herbâ; proximus ardet Ucalegon.*

668. Warning.—**N.** warning, caution, *caveat*; notice etc. (*information*) 527; premoni-tion, -shment; prediction etc. 511; contraindication; symptom; lesson, dehortation; admonition, monition; alarm etc. 669.

handwriting on the wall, *tekel upharsin*, yellow flag; fog-signal, -horn; siren; monitor, warning voice, Cassandra, signs of the times, Mother Carey's chickens, stormy petrel, bird of ill omen, gathering clouds, clouds in the horizon, cloud no bigger than a man's hand, death-watch.

watch-tower, beacon, signal-post; light-house etc. (*indication of locality*) 550.

sent-inel, -ry; watch, -man; watch and ward; watch-, ban-, house-dog; patrol, vedette, picket, bivouac, scout, spy, spial; advanced –, rear-guard, lookout, flagman.

cautiousness etc. 864.

V. warn, caution; fore-, pre-warn; ad-, pre-monish; give -notice, – warning; menace etc. (*threaten*) 909; put on one's guard; sound the alarm etc. 669; croak.

beware, ware; take -warning, – heed at one's peril; watch out for; keep watch and ward etc. (*care*) 459.

Adj. warning etc. *v.*; premonitory, monitory, cautionary; admonitory, -tive; ominous, threatening, lowering, minatory, symptomatic.

warned etc. *v.*; on one's guard etc. (*careful*) 459; (*cautious*) 864.

Adv. *in terrorem* etc. (*threat*) 909.

Int. beware! ware! take care! mind –, take care-what you are about; mind! look out!

Phr. *ne reveillez pas le chat qui dort; foenum habet in cornu.*

669. Alarm. [Indication of danger.]—**N.** alarm; alarum, larum, alarm bell, tocsin, *alerte*; beat of drum, sound of trumpet, note of alarm, hue and cry, signal of distress, S.O.S.; blue-lights; war-cry, -whoop; warning etc. 668; fog-signal, -horn; siren; yellow flag; danger signal; red -light, – flag; fire -bell, – alarm; burglar alarm, police whistle, watchman's rattle.

false alarm, cry of wolf; bug-bear, -aboo.

V. give – , raise – , sound – , beat- the *or* an- alarm etc. *n.*; alarm; warn etc. 668; ring the tocsin; *battre la générale*; cry wolf.

Adj. alarming etc. *v.*

Int. *sauve qui peut! qui vive?* who goes there?

670. Preservation.—**N.** preservation; safe keeping; conservation etc. (*storage*) 636; maintenance, upkeep, support, sustentation, con-

servatism; *vis conservatrix*; salvation etc.
(*deliverance*) 672; drying etc. *v.*

[Means of preservation] prophylaxis; preserv-er,
-ative; canned goods; cold pack; hygi-astics, -antics;
cover, durgget; *cordon sanitaire.*

[Superstitious remedies] charm etc. 993.

V. preserve, maintain, keep, sustain, support;
keep -up, – alive; not willingly let die; shore –,
bank- up; nurse; save, rescue; be –, make- safe etc.
664; take care of etc. (*care*) 459; guard etc.
(*defend*) 717.

stare super antiquas vias; hold one's own; hold
–, stand- -one's ground etc. (*resist*) 719.

embalm, dry, cure, smoke, salt, pickle, season,
kyanize, bottle, pot, tin, can; husband etc. (*store*)
636.

Adj. preserving etc. *v.*; conservative;
prophylatic; preserva-tory, -tive; hygienic.

preserved etc. *v.*; un-impaired, -broken, -injured,
-hurt, -singed, -marred; safe, – and sound; intact,
with a whole skin, without a scratch.

Phr. *nolumus leges Angliae mutari.*

671. Escape.—N. escape, scape; avolation,
elopment, flight, get-away; evasion etc. (*avoidance*)
623; retreat; narrow –, hairbreadth- escape; close
–, near- shave; come off, impunity.

[Means of escape] loophole etc. (*opening*) 260;
path etc. 627; secret -door, – passage; refuge etc.
666; vent; – peg; safety-valve; drawbridge, fire-
escape.

reprieve etc. (*deliverance*) 672; liberation etc.
750.

refugee etc. (*fugitive*) 623.

V. escape, scape; make –, effect –, make
good- one's escape, make a get-away; get -off, –
clear off, – well out of; *échapper belle*, save one's
bacon; weather the storm etc. (*safe*) 664; escape
scot-free.

elude etc., make off etc. (*avoid*) 623; march off
etc. (*go away*) 293; give one the slip; slip through
the -hands, – fingers; slip the collar, wriggle out
of; break -loose, – from prison; break –, slip –,
get- away; find -vent, – a hole to creep out of.

Adj. escap-ing, -ed etc. *v.*; stolen away, fled.

Phr. the bird has flown.

672. Deliverance.—N. deliverance, extrication, rescue; repriev-e, -al; respite; ransom;
liberation etc. 750; truce, armistice; redemption,
salvation; riddance; gaol delivery; exemption, day
of grace; redeemableness.

V. deliver, extricate, rescue, save, redeem, ransom, free, liberate, release, set free, redeem, emancipate; bring -off, – through; *tirer d'affaire*, get
the wheel out of the rut; snatch from the jaws of
death, come to the rescue; rid; retrieve etc.
(*restore*) 660; be –, get- rid of.

Adj. saved etc. *v.*; extric-, redeem-, rescu-able.

Phr. to the rescue!

673. Preparation.—N. preparation; providing
etc. *v.*; provi-sion, -dence; anticipation etc.
(*foresight*) 510; precaution, -concertation,

disposition; forecast etc. (*plan*) 626; rehearsal, not
of preparation.

[Putting in order] arrangement etc. 60;
clearance; adjustment etc. 23; tuning; equipment,
outfit, accoutrement, armament, array.

ripening etc. *v.*; maturation, evolution;
elaboration, concoction, digestion; gestation, hatching, incubation, sitting.

groundwork, datum, first stone, cradle, stepping-
stone; foundation, scaffold etc. (*support*) 215; scaffolding, *échafaudage.*

[Preparation -of men] training etc. (*education*)
537; inurement etc. (*habit*) 613; novitiate; [– of
food] cook-ing, -ery; brewing, culinary art; [– of
the soil] till-, plough-, sow-ing; semination,
cultivation.

[State of being prepared] prepared-, readi-,ripe-,
mellow-ness; maturity; *un impromptu fait à loisir.*

[Preparer] preparer, teacher, coach, trainer,
pioneer; *avant-courrier, -coureur*; sappers and
miners, paver, navvy; packer, stevedore; warm-
ingpan; precursor etc. 64.

V. prepare; get –, make- ready; make
preparations, settle preliminaries, get up, sound the
note of preparation; address oneself to.

set –, put- in order etc. (*arrange*) 60; forecast
etc. (*plan*) 626; prepare –, plough –, dress- the
ground; till –, cultivate- the soil; predispose, sow
the seed, lay a train, dig a mine; lay –, fix- the -
foundations, – basis, -groundwork; dig the foundations, erect the scaffolding; lay the first stone etc.
(*begin*) 66.

rough-hew; cut out work; block –, hammer-
out; lick into shape etc. (*form*) 240.

elaborate, mature, ripen, mellow, season, bring
to maturity; nurture etc.

(*aid*) 707; hatch, cook, brew; temper; anneal,
smelt; dry, cure etc. 670.

equip, arm, man; fit-out, -up; furnish, rig, dress,
garnish, betrim, accouter, array, fettle, fledge; dress
–, furbish –, brush –, vamp- up; refurbish; sharp-
en one's tools, trim one's foils, set, prime, attune;
whet the -knife, – sword; wind –, screw- up; adjust etc. (*fit*) 27; put in- trim, – train, – gear, –
working order, – tune, – a groove for, – harness; pack, stow away, store.

train etc. (*teach*) 537; inure etc. (*habituate*) 613;
breed; prepare etc.- for; rehearse; make provision
for; take -steps, – measures, – precautions;
provide, – against; beat up for recruits; open the
door to etc. (*facilitate*) 705.

set one's house in order, make all snug; clear -
decks, – for action; close one's ranks; shuffle the
cards.

prepare oneself; serve an apprenticeship etc.
(*learn*) 539; lay oneself out for, get into harness,
gird up one's loins, buckle on one's armor, *reculer
pour mieux sauter*, prime and load, shoulder arms,
get the steam up, put the horses to.

guard –, make sure- against; forearm, make
sure, prepare for the evil day, have a rod in pickle,
provide against a rainy day, feather one's nest; lay
in provisions etc. 637; make investments; keep on
foot.

be -prepared, – ready etc. *adj.*; hold oneself in
readiness, watch and pray, keep one's powder dry;
lie in wait for etc. (*expect*) 507; anticipate etc.
(*foresee*) 510; *principiis obstare*; *veniente occurrere morbo.*

Adj. preparing etc. *v.*; in -preparation, – course

of preparation, – agitation, – embryo, – hand, – train; afoot, afloat; on -foot, – the stocks, – the anvil; under consideration etc. (*plan*) 626; brewing, hatching, forthcoming, brooding; in -store for, – reserve.

precautionary, provident; prepara-tive, -tory; provisional, inchoate, under revision; preliminary etc. (*precedent*) 62.

prepared etc. *v.*; in readiness; ready, – to one's hand, – made, cut and dried; ready for use, reach me down; made to one's hand, handy, on the table, made to order; in gear; in working -order, – gear; snug; in practice.

ripe, mature, mellow; practiced etc. (*skillet*) 698; labored, elaborate, highly-wrought, smelling of the lamp, worked up.

in -full feather, – best bib and tucker; in – , at-harness; in – the saddle, – arms, – battle array, – war paint; up in arms; armed -at all points, – to the teeth, – cap-à-pie; sword in hand; booted and spurred.

in utrumque – , semper- paratus; on the alert etc. (*vigilant*) 459; at one's post.

Adv. in -preparation, – anticipation of; afoot, astir, abroad; abroach.

674. Non-preparation.—N. non-, absence of – , want of- preparation; unpreparedness; in-culture, inconcoction, improvidence.

immaturity, crudity; rawness etc. *adj.*; abortion; disqualification.

[Absence of art] nature, state of nature; virgin soil, unweeded garden; rough diamond, neglect etc. 460.

rough copy etc. (*plan*) 626; germ etc. 153; raw material etc. 635.

improvisation etc. (*impulse*) 612.

V. be -unprepared etc. *adj.*; want – , lack-preparation; lie fallow; *s'embarquer sans biscuits*; live from hand to mouth.

[Render unprepared] dismantle etc. (*render useless*) 645; undress etc. 226.

extemporize, improvise.

surprise, pay a surprise visit, take by surprise, drop in upon, take unawares; take pot-luck.

Adv. un-prepared etc. prepare etc. 673] without -preparation etc. 673; incomplete etc. 53; rudimental, embryonic, abortive; immature, unripe, raw, green, crude; coarse; rough, -cast, -hewn; in the rough; un-hewn, -formed, -fashioned, -wrought, -labored, -blown, -cooked, -boiled, -concocted, -cut, -polished.

callow, un-hatched, -fledged, -nurtured, -licked, -taught, -educated, -cultivated, -trained, -tutored, -drilled, -exercised; precocious, premature; un-, indigested; un-mellowed, -seasoned, -leavened.

fallow; un-sown, -tilled; natural, in a state of nature; undressed; in dishabille, *en déshabille, en négligé*.

un-, dis-qualified; unfitted; ill-digested; un-begun, -ready, -arranged, -organized, -furnished, -provided, -equipped, -trimmed; out of -gear, – order; dismantled etc. *v.*

shiftless, improvident, unthrifty, thoughtless, unguarded; happy-go-lucky; caught napping etc. (*inexpectant*) 508; unpremeditated etc. 612.

Adv. extempore; etc. 612.

675. Essay.—N. essay, trial, endeavor, aim, at-tempt; venture, adventure, speculation, *coup d'essai, début*; probation etc. (*experiment*) 463.

V. try, essay; experiment etc. 463; endeavor, strive; tempt, tackle, take on, attempt, make an at-tempt; venture, adventure, speculate, take one's chance, tempt fortune, try one's -fortune, – luck, – hand; use one's endeavor; feel – , grope – , pick- one's way.

try hard, push, make a bold push, use one's best endeavor; do one's best etc. (*exertion*) 686.

Adj. essaying etc. *v.*; experimental etc. 463; tentative, empirical, probationary.

Adv. experimentally etc. *adj.*; on trial, at a venture; by rule of thumb.

if one may be so bold.

676. Undertaking.—N. undertaking, compact etc. 769; engagement etc. (*promise*) 768; enter-, em-prise; venture etc. 675; pilgrimage; matter in hand etc. (*business*) 625; move; first move etc. (*beginning*) 66.

V. undertake; engage – , embark- in; launch – , plunge- into; volunteer; apprentice oneself to; engage etc. (*promise*) 768; contract etc. 769; take upon -oneself, – one's shoulders; devote oneself to etc. (*determination*) 604.

take -up, – in hand; tackle; set – , go- about; set – , fall- -to, – to work; launch forth; set up shop; put in -hand, – execution; set forward; break the neck of a business, be in for; put one's hand to; betake oneself to, turn one's hand to, go to do; begin etc. 66; broach, institute, etc. (*originate*) 153; put – , lay- one's -hand to the plough, – shoulder to the wheel.

have in hand etc. (*business*) 625; have many irons in the fire etc. (*activity*) 682.

Adj. undertaking etc. *v.*; on the anvil etc. 625; adventurous, venturesome.

Int. here goes!

677. Use.—N. use; employ, -ment; exer-cise, -citation; appli-cation, -ance; adhibition, disposal; consumption; agency etc. (*physical*) 170; usufruct; usefulness etc. 644; recourse, resort, avail, pragmatism.

[Conversion to use] utilization, service, wear.

[Way of using] usage.

V. use, make use of, employ, put to use; apply, put in -action, – operation, – practice; set -in motion, – to work.

ply, work, wield, handle, manipulate; play, – off; exert, exercise, practice, avail oneself of, profit by; resort – , have recourse – , recur – , take – , betake oneself- to; take -up with, – advantage of; lay one's hands on, try.

render useful etc. 644; mold; turn to -account, – use; convert to use, utilize, administer; work up; call – , bring- into play; put into requisition; call – , draw- forth; press – , enlist- into the service; bring to bear upon, devote, dedicate, consecrate, apply, adhibit, dispose of; make a -handle, – cat's paw- of.

fall beak upon, make a shift with; make the -most, – best- of.

use – , swallow- up; consume, absorb, expend; tax, task, wear, put to task.

Adj. in use; used etc. *v.*; well-worn, -trodden. useful etc. 644; subservient etc. (*instrumental*) 631; utilitarian; pragmatical.

678. Disuse.—N. forbearance, abstinence; disuse; relinquishment etc. 782; desuetude etc. (*want of habit*) 614.

V. not use; do without, dispense with, let alone, not touch, forbear, abstain, spare, waive, neglect; keep back, reserve.

lay -up, – by, – on the shelf, – up in a napkin; shelve; set – , put – , lay- aside; disuse, leave off, have done with; supersede; discard etc. (*eject*) 297; dismiss, give warning.

throw aside etc. (*relinquish*) 782; make away with etc. (*destroy*) 162; cast – , heave – , throw-overboard; cast to the -dogs, – winds; dismantle etc. (*render useless*) 645.

lie – , remain- unemployed etc. *adj.*

Adj. not used etc. *v.*; un-employed, -applied, -disposed of, -spent, -exercised, -touched, -trodden, -essayed, -gathered, -culled; uncalled for, not required.

disused etc. *v.*; done with; run down, used up, cast off.

679. Misuse.—N. mis-use, -usage, -employment, -application, -appropriation.

abuse, profanation, prostitution, desecration; waste etc. 638.

V. mis-use, -employ, -apply, -appropriate.

desecrate, abuse, profane, prostitute; waste etc. 638; over-task, -tax, -work; squander etc. 818.

cut a whetstone with a razor, employ a steam-engine to crack a nut; catch at a straw.

Adj. misused etc. *v.*

680. Action.—N. action, performance; doing etc. *v.*; perpetration; exercise, -citation; movement, operation, evolution, work; labor etc. (*exertion*) 686; *praxis*, execution; procedure etc. (*conduct*) 692; handicraft; business etc. 625; agency etc. (*power at work*) 170.

deed, act, overt act, stitch, touch, gest; transaction, job, doings, dealings, proceeding, measure, step, maneuver, bout, passage, move, stroke, blow; *coup*, – *de main*, – *d'état*; *tour de force* etc. (*display*) 882; feat, exploit, stunt; achievement etc. (*completion*) 729; handiwork, workmanship, craftsmanship; manufacture; stroke of policy etc. (*plan*) 626.

actor etc. (*doer*) 690.

V. do, perform, execute; achieve etc. (*complete*) 729; transact, enact; commit, perpetrate, inflict; exercise, prosecute, carry on, work, practice, play.

employ oneself, ply one's task; officiate, have in hand etc. (*business*) 625; labor etc. 686; be at work; pursue a course; shape one's course etc. (*conduct*) 692.

act, operate; take -action, – steps; strike a blow, lift a finger, stretch forth one's hand; take in hand etc. (*undertake*) 676; put oneself in motion; put in practice; carry into execution etc. (*complete*) 729; act upon.

be -an actor etc. 690; take – , act – , play – , perform- a part in; participate in; have a -hand in, – finger in the pie; have to do with; be a -party to, – participator in; bear – , lend- a hand; pull an oar, run in a race; mix oneself up with etc. (*meddle*) 682.

be in action; come into operation etc. (*power at work*) 170.

Adj. doing etc. *v.*; acting; in action; in harness; on duty; at work; in operation etc. 170; up to one's ears in work, in the midst of things.

Adv. in the -act, – midst of, – thick of; redhanded, *in flagrante delicto*; while one's hand is in.

681. Inaction.—N. inaction, passiveness, abstinence from action; non-interference; Fabian – , conservative- policy; neglect etc. 460; stagnation, vegetation; loafing.

inactivity etc. 683; rest etc. (*repose*) 687; quiescence etc. 265; want of – , in- occupation; unemployment; idle hours, time hanging on one's hands; *dolce far niente*; sinecure.

V. not -do, – act, – attempt; be -inactive etc. 683; abstain from doing, do nothing, hold, spare; not -stir, – move, – lift- a -finger, – foot, – peg; fold one's -arms, – hands; leave – , let- alone; let -be, – pass, – things take their course, – it have its way, – well alone; *quieta non movere*; *stare super antiquas vias*; rest and be thankful, live and let live; lie – , rest- upon one's oars; *laisser -aller, – faire*; stand aloof; refrain etc. (*avoid*) 623; keep oneself from doing; remit – , relax- one's efforts; desist etc. (*relinquish*) 624; stop etc. (*cease*) 142; pause etc. (*be quiet*) 265.

wait, lie in wait, bide one's time, take time, tide it over.

cool – , kick- one's heels; loaf, while away the -time, – tedious hours; pass – , fill – , beguile- the time; talk against time; waste time etc. (*inactive*) 683.

lie -by, – on the shelf, – in ordinary, – idle, – to, – fallow; keep quiet, slug; have nothing to do, whistle for want of thought; twiddle one's thumbs.

undo, do away with; take -down, – to pieces; destroy etc. 162.

Adj. not doing etc. *v.*; not done etc. *v.*; undone; passive; un-occupied, -employed; out of -employ, – work, – a job; fallow; *désoeuvré*.

Adv. *re infectâ*, at a stand, *les bras croisés*, with folded arms; with the hands -in the pockets, – behind one's back; *pour passer le temps*.

Int. so let it be! stop! let. 142; hands off!

Phr. nothing doing; *cunctando restituit rem*.

682. Activity.—N. activity; briskness, liveliness etc. *adj.*; animation, life, vivacity, spirit, verve, dash, energy, go.

nimbleness, agility; smartness, quickness etc. *adj.*; velocity etc. 274; alacrity, promptitude; des-, dis-patch; expedition; haste etc. 684; punctuality etc. (*early*) 132.

eagerness, zeal, ardor, *perfervidum ingenium*, *empressement*, earnestness, intentness; *abandon*; vigor etc. (*physical energy*) 171; devotion etc. (*resolution*) 604; exertion etc. 686.

industry, assiduity; assiduousness etc. *adj.*; sedulity; laboriousness; drudgery etc. (*labor*) 686; painstaking, diligence; perseverance etc. 604*a*; indefatigation; habits of business.

vigilance etc. 459; wakefulness; sleep-, restlessness; *pervigilium, insomnia*; racketing.

movement, bustle, hustle, stir, fuss, ado, bother, pottering; fidget, -iness; flurry etc. (*haste*) 684.

officiousness; dabbling, meddling; inter-ference, -position, -meddling, butting in, intrusiveness; tampering with, intrigue.

press of business, no sinecure, plenty to do, many irons in the fire, great doings, busy hum of men, battle of life, thick of -things, – the action; the madding corwd.

housewife, busy bee; new brooms; sharp fellow, blade; hustler, devotee, enthusiast, fan, zealot, fanatic; meddler, intermeddler, intriguer, busybody, kibitzer, pickthank.

V. be -active etc. *adj.*; busy oneself in; stir, -about, – one's stumps; bestir –, rouse- oneself; speed, hasten, peg away, lay about one, bustle, fuss; raise –, kick up- a dust; push; make a -push, – fuss, – stir; go ahead, push forward; flight –, elbow- one's way; make progress etc. 282; toil etc. (*labor*) 686; drudge, plod, persist etc. (*persevere*) 604*a*; keep -up the ball, – the pot boiling.

look sharp; have all one's eyes about one etc. (*vigilance*) 459; rise, arouse oneself, get up early, hustle, push; be about, keep moving, steal a march, kill two birds with one stone; seize the opportunity etc. 134; lose no time, not lose a moment, make the most of one's time, not suffer the grass to grow under one's feet, improve the shining hour, make short work of; dash off; make haste etc. 684; do one's best, take pains etc. (*exert oneself*) 686; do –, work- wonders.

have -many irons in the fire, – one's hands full, – much on one's hands; have other -things to do, – fish to fry; be busy; not have a moment -to spare, – that one can call one's own.

have one's fling, run the round of; go all lengths, stick at nothing, run riot.

outdo; over-do, -act, -lay, -shoot the mark; make a toil of a pleasure.

have a hand in etc. (*act in*) 680; take an active part, put in one's oar, have a finger in the pie, mix oneself up with, trouble one's head about, intrigue; agitate.

tamper with, meddle, moil; inter-meddle, -fere, -pose; obtrude; poke –, thrust- one's nose in, butt in.

Adj. active; brisk, – as a lark, – as a bee; lively, animated, vivacious; alive, – and kicking; frisky, spirited, stirring.

nimble, – as a squirrel; agile; light-, nimblefooted; featly, tripping.

quick, prompt, yare, instant, ready, alert, spry, sharp, smart, slick, go-ahead; fast etc. (*swift*) 274; quick as a lamplighter, expeditious; awake, broad awake; wide awake etc. (*intelligent*) 498.

forward, eager, ardent, strenuous, zealous, enterprising, pushing, in earnest; resolute etc. 604.

industrious, assiduous, diligent, sedulous, notable, painstaking; intent etc. (*attention*) 457; indefatigable etc. (*persevering*) 604*a*; unwearied; unsleeping, sleepless, never tired; plodding, hardworking etc. 686; business-like, workaday.

bustling; restless, – as a hyena; fussy, fidgety, pottering; busy, – as a hen with one chicken.

working, laboring, at work, on duty, in harness; up in arms; on one's legs, at call; up and -doing, – stirring.

busy, occupied; hard at -work, – it; up to one's ears in, full of business, busy as a bee.

meddling etc. *v.*; meddlesome, pushing, officious, overofficious, *intrigant*.

astir, stirring; a-going, -foot; on foot; in full swing; eventful; on the alert etc. (*vigilant*) 459.

Adv. actively etc. *adj.*; with -life and spirit, – might and main etc. 686, – haste etc. 684, – wings; full tilt, *in mediis rebus*.

Int. be –, look- -alive, – sharp! move –, push-on! keep moving! go ahead! stir your stumps! *age quod agis!*

Phr. *carpe diem* etc. (*opportunity*) 134; *nulla dies sine lineâ*; *nec mora nec requies*; no sooner said than done etc. (*early*) 132; catch a weasel asleep.

683. Inactivity.—N. inactivity; inaction etc. 681; inertness etc. 172; obstinacy etc. 606.

lull etc. (*cessation*) 142; quiescence etc. 265; rust, -iness.

idle-, remiss-ness etc. *adj.*; sloth, indolence, indiligence; otiosity, dawdling etc. *v.*

dullness etc. *adj.*; languor; segni-ty, -tude; lentor; sluggishness etc. (*slowness*) 275; procrastination etc. (*delay*) 133; torp-or, -idity, -escence; stupor etc. (*insensibility*) 823; somnolence; drowsiness etc. *adj.*; nodding etc. *v.*; oscitation, -ancy; pandiculation, hypnotism, lethargy; heaviness, heavy eye-lids, sand in the eyes.

sleep, slumber; sound –, heavy –, balmy-sleep; Morpheus, dreamland; coma, trance, catalepsy, hypnosis, *ecstasis*, dream, hibernation, nap, doze, snooze, *siesta*, wink of sleep, forty winks, snore; Hypnology.

dull work; pottering; relaxation etc. (*loosening*) 47; Castle of Indolence.

[Castle of inactivity] lullaby, *berceuse*; anesthetic, sedative etc. 174; torpedo.

idler, drone, droil, dawdle, mopus; do-little, *fainéant*, dummy, sleeping partner; afternoon farmer; truant etc. (*runaway*) 623; lounger, *lazzarone*, floater, loafer, tramp, beggar, cadger; lubber, -bard; slow-coach etc. (*slow*) 275; opium –, lotus- eater; slug; lag-, slug-gard, lie-abed; slumberer, dormouse, marmot; waiter on Providence, *fruges consumere natus*.

V. be -inactive etc. *adj.*; do nothing etc. 681; move slowly etc. 275; let the grass grow under one's feet; take one's time, dawdle, poke, drawl, droil, lag, hang back, slouch; loll, -op; lounge, loaf, loiter; go to sleep over; sleep at one's post; *ne battre que d'une aile.*

take -it easy, – things as they come; lead an easy life, vegetate, swim with the stream, eat the bread of idleness; loll in the lap of -luxury, – indolence; waste –, consume –, kill –, lose time; burn daylight, waste the precious hours.

idle –, trifle –, fritter –, fool- away time; spend –, take- time in; ped-, pid-dle; potter, putter, dabble, faddle, fribble, fiddle-faddle; dally, dilly-dally.

sleep, slumber, be asleep; hibernate; oversleep; sleep like a -top, – log, – dormouse; sleep -soundly, – heavily; doze, drowze, snooze, nap; take a -nap etc. *n.*; dream; snore; settle –, go –, go off- to sleep; drop off; fall – , drop- asleep; close – , seal up- -the -eyes, – eyelids; weigh down the eyelids; get sleepy, nod, yawn; go to bed, turn in.

languish, expend itself, flag, hang fire; relax.

render -idle etc. *adj.*; sluggardize; mitigate etc. 174.

Adj. inactive; motionless etc. 265; unoccupied etc. (*doing nothing*) 681.

indolent, lazy, slothful, idle, otiose, lusk, remiss, slack, inert, torpid, sluggish, languid, supine, heavy, dull, leaden, lumpish; exanimate, soulless; listless; dron-y, -ish; lazy as Ludlam's dog.

dilatory, laggard; lagging etc. *v.*; slow etc. 275; rusty, flagging; lackadaisical, maudlin, fiddle-faddle; pottering etc. *v.*; shilly-shally etc. (*irresolute*) 605.

sleeping etc. *v.*; alseep; fast – , dead – , sound-alseep; in a sound sleep; sound as a top, dormant, comatose; in the -arms, – lap- of Morpheus.

sleep-y, -ful; dozy, drowsy, somnolent, tor-pescent; lethargic, -al; heavy, – with sleep; nap-ping; somni-fic, -ferous; sopor-ous, -ific, -iferous; hypnotic; balmy, dreamy; un-, una-wakened.

sedative etc. 174.

Adv. inactively etc. *adj.*; at leisure etc. 685.

Phr. the eyes begin to draw straws.

684. Haste.—N. haste, urgency; des-, dis-patch; acceleration, spurt, spirt, forced march, rush, dash; velocity etc. 274; precipit-ancy, -ation, -ousness etc. *adj.*; impetuosity; *brusquerie*; hurry, scurry, scuttle, drive, scramble, push, hustle, bustle, fuss, fidget, flurry, flutter, splutter.

V. haste, hasten; make -haste, – a dash etc. *n.*; hurry –, dash –, whip –, push –, press- -on, – forward; hurry, skurry, scuttle along, bundle on, dart to and fro, bustle, flutter, scramble; plunge, – headlong; run, race, speed; dash off; rush etc. (*violence*) 173.

bestir oneself etc. (*be active*) 682; lose -no time, – not a moment, – not an instant; make short work of; make the best of one's -time, – way.

be -precipitate etc. *adj.*; jump at; be in -haste, – a hurry etc. *n.*; have -no time, – not a moment- – to lose, – to spare; work -under pressure, – against time.

quicken etc. 274; accelerate, expedite, put on, precipitate, urge, whip, spur, flog, goad.

Adj. hasty, hurried, *brusque*; scrambling, cur-sory, precipitate, headlong, furious, boisterous, im-petuous, hot-headed; feverish, fussy; pushing.

in -haste, – a hurry etc. *n.*; in -hot, – all- haste; breathless, pressed for time, hard pressed, urgent.

Adv. with -haste, – all haste, – breathless speed; in haste etc. *adj.*; apace etc. (*swiftly*) 274; amain; all at once etc. (*instantaneously*) 113; at short notice etc., immediately etc. (*early*) 132; posthaste; by -express, – telegraph, – wire, – wireless, – air mail.

hastily, precipitately etc. *adj.*; helter-skelter, hurry-scurry, holusbolus; slap-dash, -bang; full-tilt, -drive; heels over head, head and shoulders, headlong, *à corps perdu*.

by -fits and starts, – spurts; hop, skip and jump.

Phr. *sauve qui peut*, devil take the hindmost, no time to be lost; no sooner said than done etc. (*early*) 132; a word and a blow.

Int. hurry up! look alive! get a move on! buck up! double march! rush! urgent!

685. Leisure.—N. leisure; spare -time, – hours, – moments; vacant hour; time, – to spare, – on one's hands; holiday etc. (*rest*) 687; *otium cum dignitate*, ease.

V. have -leisure etc. *n.*; take one's -time, – leisure, – ease; repose etc. 687; move slowly etc. 275; while away the time etc. (*inaction*) 681; be - master of one's time, – an idle man; *desipere in loco*.

Adj. leisurely; slow etc. 275; deliberate, quiet, calm, undisturbed; at -leisure, – one's ease, – a loose end.

Phr. time hanging heavy on one's hands.

686. Exertion.—N. exertion, effort, strain, tug, pull, stress, force, pressure, throw, stretch, struggle, spell, spurt, spirt; stroke – , stitch- of work.

'a stong pull, a long pull and a pull all together;' dead lift; heft; gymnastics, sports; exer-cise, - citation; wear and tear; ado; toil and trouble; uphill – , hard – , warm- work; harvest time.

labor, work, toil, travail, manual labor, sweat of one's brow, swink, operoseness, drudgery, slavery, fagging, hammering; *limae labor*.

trouble, pains, duty; resolution etc. 604; energy etc. (*physical*) 171.

V. exert oneself; exert – , tax- one's energies; use exertion.

labor, work, toil, moil, sweat, fag, drudge, slave, drag a lengthened chain, wade through, strive, strain; make – , stretch- a long arm; pull, tug, ply; ply – , tug at- the oar; do the work; take the laboring oar.

bestir oneself (*be active*) 682; take trouble, trouble oneself.

work hard; rough it; put forth -one's strength, – a strong arm; fall to work, bend the bow; buckle to, set one's shoulder to the wheel etc. (*resolution*) 604; work like a -Briton, – horse, – carthorse, – galley-slave, – coalheaver; labor –, work-day and night; redouble one's efforts; do double duty; work double -hours, – tides; sit up, burn the -midnight oil, – candle at both ends; stick to etc. (*persevere*) 604a; work – , fight- one's way; lay about one, hammer at.

take pains; do one's -best, – level best, – ut-most; do -the best one can, – all one can, – all in one's power, – as much as in one lies, – what lies in one's power; use one's -best, – utmost- en-deavor; try one's -best, – utmost; play one's best card; put one's -best, – right- leg foremost; have one's whole soul in one's work, put all one's strength into, strain every nerve; spare no -efforts, – pains; go all lengths; go through fire and water etc. (*resolution*) 604; move heaven and earth, leave no stone unturned.

Adj. laboring etc. *v.*

laborious, operose, elaborate; strained; toil-, trouble-, burden-, weari-some; uphill; herculean, gymnastic, athletic, palestric.

hardworking, painstaking, strenuous, energetic.

hard at work, on the stretch.

Adv. laboriously etc. *adj.*; lustily; with -might and main, – all one's might, – a strong hand, – sledge-hammer; – much ado; to the best of one's abilities, *totis viribus, vi et armis, manibus pedibusque*, tooth and nail, *unguibus et rostro,* hammer and tongs, heart and soul; through thick and thin etc. (*perseverance*) 604*a*.

by the sweat of one's brow, *suo Marte*.

687. Repose.—N. repose, rest, silken repose; sleep etc. 683.

relaxation, breathing time; halt, pause etc. (*cessation*) 142; respite.

day of rest, *dies non*, Sabbath, Lord's day, holiday, red-letter day, vacation, recess.

V. repose; rest, – and be thankful; take -rest, – one's ease.

relax, unbend, slacken; take breath etc. (*refresh*) 689; rest upon one's oars; pause etc. (*cease*) 142; stay one's hand.

lie down; recline, – on a bed of down, – on an easy chair; go to -rest, – bed, – sleep etc. 683.

take a holiday, shut up shop; lie fallow etc. (*inaction*) 681.

Adj. reposing etc. *v.*; unstrained.

Adv. at rest.

688. Fatigue.—N. fatigue; weariness etc. 841; yawning, drowsiness etc. 683; lassitude, tiredness, fatigation, exhaustion; sweat.

anhelation, shortness of breath, panting; faintness; collapse, prostration, swoon, fainting, *deliquium*, syncope, lipothymy.

V. be -fatigued etc. *adj.*; yawn etc. (*get sleepy*) 683; droop, sink, flag; lose -breath, – wind; gasp, pant, puff, blow, drop, swoon, faint, succumb.

fatigue, tire, weary, bore, irk, fag, jade, harass, exhaust, knock up, wear out, prostrate.

tax, task, strain; over-task, -work, -burden, -tax, -strain.

Adj. fatigued etc. *v.*; weary etc. 841; drowsy etc. 683; drooping etc. *v.*; haggard; toil-, way-worn; footsore, surbated, weatherbeaten; faint; done –, used –, knock- up; exhausted, prostrate, spent; over-tired, -spent, -fatigued; forspent; unre-freshed, -stored.

worn, – out; battered, shattered, pulled down, seedy, altered.

breath-, wind-less; short of –, out of -breath, – wind; blown, puffing and blowing; short-breathed; anhelous; broken-, short-winded.

ready to drop, more dead than alive, dog -tired, – weary, walked off one's legs, tired to death, on one's last legs, played out, *hors de combat*.

fatiguing etc. *v.*; tire-, irk-, weari-some; weary; trying.

689. Refreshment.—N. bracing etc. *v.*; recovery of -strength etc. 159; restoration, revival etc. 660; repair, refection, refocillation, refreshment, regalement, bait; relief etc. 834.

V. brace etc. (*strengthen*) 159; reinvigorate; air, freshen up, refresh, recruit; repair etc. (*restore*) 660; fan, revocillate.

breathe, respire; draw –, take –, gather –, take a long –, regain –, recover- breath; get better, raise one's head; recover –, regain –, renew- one's strength etc. 159; perk up.

come to oneself etc. (*revive*) 660; feel like a giant refreshed.

Adj. refreshing etc. *v.*; recuperative etc. 660. refreshed etc. *v.*; un-tired, -wearied.

690. Agent.—N. doer, actor, agent, performer, perpetrator, operator; execu-tor, -trix; practitioner, worker, stager.

bee, ant, working bee, laboring oar, shaft horse, servant –, maid- of all work, general servant, factotum.

workman, artisan; crafts-, handicrafts-man; mechanic, operative; working –, laboring- man; hewers of wood and drawers of water, laborer, navvy; hand, man, day laborer, journeyman, hack; mere -tool etc. 633; porter, docker, stevedore, beast of burden, drudge, fag.

maker, artificer, artist, wright, manufacturer, architect, contractor, builder, mason, bricklayer, smith, forger, Vulcan; black-, tin-smith; carpenter; ganger, platelayer.

machinist, mechanician, engineer, electrician, plumber, gasfitter etc.

semp-, sem-, seam-stress; needle-, char-, work-woman; tailor, cordwainer.

minister etc. (*instrument*) 631; servant etc. 746; representative etc. (*commissioner*) 758; (*deputy*) 759.

co-worker, fellow-worker, party to, participator in, co-operator, colleague, associate, collaborator, *particeps criminis, dramatis personae; personnel*.

Phrs. *'quorum pars magna fui.'*

691. Workshop.—N. work-shop, -house; laboratory; manufactory, mill, factory, armory, arsenal, mint, forge, loom; cabinet, *studio, bureau, atelier*; hive, – of industry; nursery; hot-house, -bed; kitchen, kitchenette; dock, -yard; slip, yard, wharf; found-ry, -ery; furnace; vineyard, orchard, farm, kitchen garden.

melting pot, crucible, alembic, caldron, mortar, *matrix*.

692. Conduct.—N. dealing, transaction etc. (*action*) 680; business etc. 625.

tactics, game, policy, polity; general-, statesman-, seaman-ship; strate-gy, -gics; plan etc. 626.

husbandry; house-keeping, -wifery; stewardship; *ménage*; regimen, *régime*; econom-y, -ics; political economy; management; government etc. (*direction*) 693.

execution, manipulation, treatment, campaign, career, life, course, walk, race.

conduct; behavior; de-, com-portment; carriage, *maintien*, demeanor, guise, bearing, manner, mien, air, observance.

course –, line- of -conduct, – action, – proceeding; *rôle*; process, ways, practice, procedure, *modus operandi*; method etc., path etc. 627.

V. transact, execute; des-, dis-patch; proceed with, discharge; carry -on, – through, – out, – into effect; work out; go –, get- through; enact; put into practice; officiate etc. 625.

behave −, comport −, demean −, carry −,
bear −, conduct −, acquit- oneself.

run a race, lead a life, play a game; take −,
adopt- a course; steer −, shape- one's course; play
one's- part, − cards; shift for oneself; paddle one's
own canoe.

conduct; manage etc. (*direct*) 693.

deal −, have to do- with; treat, handle a case;
take -steps, − measures.

Adj. conducting etc. *v.*; strategical, business-
like, practical, economic, executive.

693. Direction.—N. direction; manage-ment, -
ry; government, gubernation, conduct, legislation,
regulation, guidance; steer-, pilot-age; reins, − of
government; helm, rudder, controls, joy stick,
needle, compass, binnacle; guiding −, load −,
lode −, pole- star; cynosure.

super-vision, -intendence; *surveillance*, oversight;
eye of the master; control, charge, auspices; board
of control etc. (*council*) 696; command etc.
(*authority*) 737.

premier-, senator-ship; director etc. 694; chair,
seat, portfolio.

statesmanship; state-, king-craft.

minis-try, -tration; administration; steward-,
proctor-ship; agency.

V. direct, manage, govern, conduct; order,
prescribe, cut out work for; head, lead; lead −,
show- the way; take the lead, lead on; regulate,
guide, steer, pilot; take −, be at- the helm; have
−, handle −, hold −, take- the reins, handle the
ribbons; drive, tool; tackle.

super-intend, -vise; overlook, control, keep in
order, look after, see to, oversee, legislate for; administer, ministrate; patronize; have the -care, −
charge- of; have −, take- the direction; pull the -
strings, − wires; rule etc. (*command*) 737; have
−, hold- -office, − the portfolio; preside, − at the
board; take −, occupy −, be in- the chair; pull the
stroke oar.

Adj. directing etc. *v.*; executive, supervisory,
hegemonic.

Adv. at the -helm, − head of, in charge of; under the auspices of.

694. Director.—N. director, manager, governor, rector, comptroller; super-intendent, -visor;
intendant; over-seer, -looker; foreman, boss, straw
boss; supercargo, husband, inspector, visitor,
ranger, surveyor, aedile, moderator, monitor, task-
master; master etc. 745; leader, ringleader,
demagogue, corypheus, conductor, fugleman,
precentor, bellwether, agitator.

guiding star etc. (*guidance*) 693; adviser etc.
695; guide etc. (*information*) 527; pilot; helmsman; steers-man, -mate; man at the wheel; wire-
puller.

driver, whip, Jehu, charioteer; coach-, car-, cab-
man, jarvey; postilion, *vetturino*, muleteer, team-
ster; whipper in; engineer, engine driver, motor-
man, *chauffeur*.

head, − man; principal, president, speaker;
chair, -man; captain etc. (*master*) 745; superior;
dean; mayor etc. (*civil authority*) 745; vice-

president, prime minister, premier, vizier, grand
vizier; dictator.

officer, functionary, minister, official, red-tapist,
bureaucrat; man −, Jack- in office; office-bearer;
person in authority etc. 745.

statesman, strategist, legislator, lawgiver, politician, administrator, statist, statemonger; Minos,
Draco; arbiter etc. (*judge*) 967; king maker, power
behind the throne.

board etc. (*council*) 696.

secretary, − of state; Reis Effendi; vicar etc.
(*deputy*) 759; steward, factor; agent etc. 758;
bailiff, middleman; ganger, clerk of works; land-
reeve; factotum, major-domo, seneschal, housekeeper, shepherd, *croupier*; proctor, procurator,
curator, librarian.

Adv. *ex officio*.

695. Advice.—N. advice, counsel, adhortation;
word to the wise; suggestion, submonition, recom-
mendation, advocacy, consultation.

exhortation etc. (*persuasion*) 615; expostulation
etc. (*dissuasion*) 616; admonition etc. (*warning*)
668; guidance etc. (*direction*) 693.

instruction, charge, injunction.

adviser, prompter; counsel, -lor; monitor, mentor, Nestor, *magnus Apollo*, senator; teacher etc.
540.

guide, manual, chart etc. (*information*) 527.

physician, leech, archiater; arbiter etc. (*judge*)
967.

refer-ence, -ment; consultation, conference,
parley, *pourparler* etc. 696.

V. advise, counsel; give -advice, − counsel, − a
piece of advice; suggest, prompt, submonish,
recommend, prescribe, advocate; exhort etc. (*persuade*) 615.

enjoin, enforce, charge, instruct, call; call upon
etc. (*request*) 765; dictate.

expostulate etc. (*dissuade*) 616; admonish etc.
(*warn*) 668.

advise with; lay heads −, consult- together;
compare notes; hold a council, deliberate, be
closeted with.

confer, consult, refer to, call in; take −, follow-
advice; follow implicitly; be advised by, have at
one's elbow, take one's cue from.

Adj. recommendatory; hortative etc. (*persuasive*) 615; dehortatory etc. (*dissuasive*) 616; admonitory etc. (*warning*) 668; consultative.

Int. go to!

696. Council.—N. council, committee, subcommittee, *comitia*, court, chamber, cabinet,
board, bench, staff; consultation.

senate, *senatus*, parliament, house, − of Lords,
− Peers, − Commons, legislature, legislative
assembly, federal council, chamber of deputies,
directory, *reichsrath, rigsdag, cortes*, storthing,
witenagemote, *junta*, divan, *musnud, sanhedrim*,
Amphictyonic council; *duma, zemstvo, soviet,
cheka, ogpu; Dail Eireann*; caput, consistory,
chapter, syndicate; court of appeal etc. (*tribunal*)
966; board of -control, − works; vestry; county −,
borough −, district −, parish −, town- council,
local board.

cabinet –, privy- council, royal commission; cockpit, convocation, synod, congress, congregation, convention, diet, states-general, aulic council.

League of Nations, assembly, *caucus*, conclave, *clique*, conventicle; meeting, sitting, *séance*, conference, session, hearing, palaver, *pourparler*, *durbar*, pow-wow, house; *quorum*.

senator; member, – of parliament; councilor, M.P., representative of the people.

Adj. senatorial, curule, parliamentary.

697. Precept.—N. precept, direction, instruction, charge; prescript, -ion; *recipe*, receipt; golden rule; maxim etc. 496.

commandment, rule, ruling, canon, law, code, *corpus juris*, *lex scripta*, common –, unwritten –, canon- law; the Ten Commandments; act, statute, convention, rubric, stage direction, regulation; form, -ula, -ulary; technicality; nice point.

order etc. (*command*) 741.

698. Skill.—N. skill, skilfulness, address; dexter-ity, -ousness; adroitness, expertness etc. *adj.* ; proficiency, competence, craft, callidity, facility, knack, trick, sleight; master-y, -ship; excellence, panurgy; ambidext-erity, -rousness; sleight of hand etc. (*deception*) 545.

sea-, air-, marks-, horse-manship; tight-, rope-dancing.

accomplish-, acquire-, attain-ment; art, science; techn-icality, -ology, -ique; practical –, technical-knowledge; technocracy; finish, technic.

knowledge of the world, world wisdom, *savoir-faire*; tact; mother- wit etc. (*sagacity*) 498; discretion etc. (*caution*) 864; *finesse*; craftiness etc. (*cunning*) 702; management etc. (*conduct*) 692; *ars celare artem*; self-help.

cleverness, talent, ability, ingenuity, capacity, parts, talents, faculty, endowment, *forte*, turn, gift, genius, flair, feeling; intelligence etc. 498; sharpness, readiness etc. (*activity*) 682; invention etc. 515; turn –, -itude; turn –, capacity –, genius-for; felicity, capability, *curiosa felicitas*, qualification, habilitation.

proficient etc. 700.

masterpiece, *coup de maître*, *chef- d'oeuvre*, *tour de force*; good stroke etc. (*plan*) 626.

V. be -skilful etc. *adj.* ; excel in, be master of; have -a turn for etc. *n.*

know -what's what, – a hawk from a handsaw, – what one is about, – on which side one's bread is buttered, – what's o'clock, – a thing or two; have cut one's -eye, – wisdom- teeth.

see -one's way, – where the wind lies, – which way the wind blows; have -all one's wits about one, – one's hand in; *savoir vivre*; *scire quid valeant humeri quid ferre recusent*

look after the main chance; cut one's coat according to one's cloth; live by one's wits; exercise one's discretion, feather the oar, sail near the wind; stoop to conquer etc. (*cunning*) 702; play one's -cards well, – best card; hit the right nail on the head, put the saddle on the right horse.

take advantage of, make the most of; profit by etc. (*use*) 677; make a hit etc. (*succeed*) 731; make a virtue of necessity; make hay while the sun shines etc. (*occasion*) 134.

Adj. skilful, dexterous, adroit, expert, apt, slick, handy, quick, deft, ready, resourceful, gain; smart etc. (*active*) 682; proficient, good at, up to, at home in, master of, a good hand at, *au fait*, thoroughbred, masterly, crack, accomplished; conversant etc. (*knowing*) 490.

experienced, practiced, skilled; up –, well up-in; in -practice, – proper cue; competent, efficient, qualified, capable, fitted, fit for, up to the mark, trained, initiated, prepared, primed, finished.

clever, able, ingenious, felicitous, gifted, talented, endowed, cute, inventive etc. 515; shrewd, sharp etc. (*intelligent*) 498; cunning etc. 702; alive to, up to snuff, not to be caught with chaff; discreet.

neat-handed, fine-fingered, ambidextrous, sure-footed; cut out –, fitted- for.

technical, artistic, scientific, daedalian, ship-shape; workman-, business-, statesman-like.

Adv. skilfully etc. *adj.* ; well etc. 618; artistically; with -skill, – consummate skill; *secundum artem, suo Marte*; to the best of one's abilities etc. (*exertion*) 686; like a machine.

699. Unskillfulness.—N. unskillfulness etc. *adj.* ; want of -skill etc. 698; incompeten-ce, -cy; in-ability, -felicity, -dexterity, -experience; clumsiness; disqualification, unproficiency; quackery.

folly, stupidity etc. 499; indiscretion etc. (*rashness*) 863; thoughtlessness etc. (*inattention*) 458, (*neglect*) 460.

mis-management, -conduct; impolicy; malad-ministration; mis-rule, -government, -application, -direction, -feasance.

absence of rule, rule of thumb; bungling etc. *v.* ; failure etc. 732; screw loose; too many cooks.

blunder etc. (*mistake*) 495; *étourderie*, *gaucherie*, act of folly, *balourdise*; botch, -ery; bad job, sad work.

sprat sent out to catch a whale, much ado about nothing, wildgoose chase.

bungler etc. 701; fool etc. 501.

layman, amateur.

V. be -unskillful etc. *adj.*; not see an inch beyond one's nose; blunder, bungle, boggle, fumble, muff, botch, bitch, flounder, loppet, stumble, trip; hobble etc. 275; put one's foot in it; make a -mess, – hash, – sad work- of; overshoot the mark.

play -tricks with, – Puck; mismanage, -conduct, -direct, -apply, -send.

stultify –, make a fool of –, commit- oneself; act foolishly; play the fool; put oneself out of court; lose one's -head, – cunning.

begin at the wrong end; do things by halves etc. (*not complete*) 730; make two bites of a cherry; play at cross purposes; strain at a gnat and swallow a camel etc. (*caprice*) 608; put the cart before the horse; lock the stable door when the horse is stolen etc. (*too late*) 135.

not know -what one is about, – one's own interest, – on which side one's bread is buttered; stand in one's own light, quarrel with one's bread and butter, throw a stone in one's own garden, kill the goose which lays the golden eggs, pay dear for one's whistle, cut one's own throat, burn one's fingers; knock –, run- one's head against a stone wall; fall into a trap, catch a Tartar, bring the house about one's ears; have too many -eggs in one basket (*imprudent*) 863, – irons in the fire.

mistake etc. 495; take the shadow for the substance etc. (*credulity*) 486; be in the wrong box, aim at a pigeon and kill a crow; take –, get- the wrong sow by the ear, – the dirty end of the stick; put -the saddle on the wrong horse, – a square peg into a round hole, – new wine into old bottles.

cut a whetstone with a razor; hold a farthing candle to the sun etc. (*useless*) 645; fight with –, grasp at- a shadow; catch at straws, lean on a broken reed, reckon without one's host, pursue a wildgoose chase; go on a fool's –, sleeveless-errand; go further and fare worse; loose –, miss-one's way; fail etc. 732.

Adj. un-skillful etc. 698; unskilled, inexpert; bungling etc. ⱴ ; awkward, clumsy, unhandy, lubberly, *gauche*, *maladroit*; left-, heavy-handed; slovenly, slatternly; gawky.

adrift, at fault.

in-, un-apt; inhabile; un-tractable, -teachable; giddy etc. (*inattentive*) 458; inconsiderate etc. (*neglectful*) 460; stupid etc. 499; inactive etc. 683; incompetent; un-, dis-, ill-qualified; unfit; quackish; raw, green, inexperienced, rusty, out of practice.

un-accustomed, -used, -trained etc. 537; -initiated, -conversant etc. (*ignorant*) 491; shiftless; unbusinesslike, unpractical; unstatesmanlike.

un-, ill-, mis-advised; ill-devised, -imagined, -judged, -contrived, -conducted; un-, mis-guided; misconducted, foolish, wild; infelicitous; penny wise and pound foolish etc. (*inconsistent*) 608.

Phr. one's fingers being all thumbs; the right hand forgets its cunning.

il se noyerait dans une goutte d'eau.

incidit in Scyllam qui vult vitare Charybdim; out of the frying pan into the fire.

700. Proficient.—N. proficient, expert, adept, dab; *connoisseur* etc. (*scholar*) 492; master, -hand; top-sawyer, *prima donna*, first fiddle, *chef de cuisine*; protagonist; past master; profess-or, -ional, specialist.

picked man; medalist, prizeman.

veteran; old -stager, – campaigner, – soldier, – file, – hand; man of -business, – the world.

nice –, good –, clean- hand; practised –, ex-perienced- -eye, – hand; marksman; good –, dead –, crack- shot; rope-dancer, funambulist, acrobat, contortionist; cunning man; conjuror etc. (*deceiver*) 548; wizard etc. 994.

genius; master-mind, – head, – spirit.

cunning –, sharp -blade, – fellow; jobber; cracksman etc. (*thief*) 792; politician, tactician, diplomat, -ist, strategist.

pantologist, admirable Crichton, Jack of all trades; prodigy of learning; walking encyclopedia; mine of information.

701. Bungler.—N. bungler; blunderer, -head; marplot, fumbler, lubber, lout, oaf, duffer, stick, clown; bad –, poor- -hand, – shot; butter-fingers.

no conjuror, flat, muff, slow coach, looby, lub-

ber, swab; clod, yokel, hick, awkward squad, novice, greenhorn, jaywalker, *blanc-bec*.

land lubber; fresh water –, fair weather- sailor; horse-marine; fish out of water, ass in lion's skin, jackdaw in peacock's feathers; quack etc. (*deceiver*) 548; Lord of Misrule.

sloven, slattern, trapes.

Phr. *il n'a pas inventé la poudre*; he will never set the Thames on fire.

702. Cunning.—N. cunning, craft; cun-ningness, craftiness etc. *adj.*; subtlety, artificiality; maneuvring etc. *v.*; temporization; circumvention.

chicane, -ry; sharp practice, knavery, jugglery; concealment etc. 528; nigger in the woodpile; guile, duplicity etc. (*falsehood*) 544; foul play.

diplomacy, politics; Machiavellism; jobbery, back-stairs influence; gerrymandering.

art, -ifice; device, machination; plot etc. (*plan*) 626; maneuver, stratagem, dodge, artful dodge, wile; trick, -ery etc. (*deception*) 545; ruse, – de guerre; finesse, side-blow, thin end of the wedge, shift, go by, subterfuge, evasion; white lie etc. (*un-truth*) 546; juggle, *tour de force*; tricks -of the trade, – upon travelers; imposture, deception; *ex-pié-glerie*, net, trap etc. 545.

Ulysses, Machiavel, sly boots, fox, reynard; Scotch-, Yorkshire-man; Jew, Yankee; intriguer, *intrigant*, schemer, trickster.

V. be -cunning etc. *adj.*; have cut one's eye-teeth; contrive etc. (*plan*) 626; live by one's wits; maneuver; intrigue, gerrymander, *finesse*, double, temporize, stoop to conquer, *reculer pour mieux sauter*, circumvent, steal a march upon; overreach etc. 545; throw off one's guard; surprise etc. 508; outdo, get the better of, snatch from under one's nose; snatch a verdict; waylay, undermine, in-troduce the thin end of the wedge; play -a deep game, – tricks with; have an axe to grind; *am-biguas in vulgum ·spargere voces*; flatter, make things pleasant.

Adj. cunning, crafty, artful; skilful etc. 698; sub-tle, feline, vulpine; cunning as a -fox, – serpent; deep, – laid; profound; designing, contriving; in-triguing etc. *v.*; strategic, diplomatic, politic, Machiavellian, time-serving; artificial; trick-y, -sy; wily, sly, slim, insidious, stealthy, foxy; underhand etc. (*hidden*) 528; subdolous; deceitful etc. 545; double-tongued, -faced; shifty; crooked; arch, pawky, shrewd, acute; sharp, – as a needle; canny, astute, leery, knowing, up to snuff, too clever by half, not to be caught with chaff.

Adv. cunningly etc. *adj.*; slily, on the sly, by a side wind.

Phr. diamond cut diamond.

703. Artlessness.—N. artlessness etc. *adj.*; nature, simplicity; innocence etc. 946; *bonhomie*, *naïveté*, *abandon*, candor, sincerity; singleness of -purpose, – heart; honesty etc. 939; plain speaking; *épanchement*.

rough diamond, matter of fact man; *le palais de vérité*; *enfant terrible*.

V. be -artless etc. *adj.*; look one in the face; wear one's heart upon his sleeves for daws to peck

at; think aloud; speak -out, – one's mind; be free
with one, call a spade a spade.

Adj. artless, natural, pure, native, simple, plain,
inartificial, untutored, unsophisticated, *ingénu,*
unaffected, *naïve*; sincere, frank; open, – as day;
candid, ingenuous, guileless, unsuspicious,
childlike; honest etc. 939; innocent etc. 946; Arcadian; undesigning, straightforward; unreserved,
unvarnished, above-board; simple-, single-minded;
frank-, open-, single-, simple-hearted; open and
above-board.

free-, plain-, out-spoken; blunt, downright,
direct, matter of fact, unpoetical; unflattering.

Adv. in plain -words, – English; without mincing the matter; not to mince the matter etc. *(affirmation)* 535.

Phr. *Davus sum non Oedipus; liberavi animam
meam.*

704. Difficulty.—N. difficulty; hardness etc.
adj.; impracticability etc. *(impossibility)* 471;
tough –, hard –, uphill- work; hard –, Herculean –, Augean- task; task of Sisyphus,
Sisyphean labor, tough job, teaser, rasper, dead lift.

dilemma, embarrassment; perplexity etc. *(uncertainty)* 475; involvement; intricacy; entanglement etc. 59; cross fire; awkwardness,
delicacy, ticklish card to play, deadlock, knot,
Gordian knot, *dignus vindice nodus*, net, meshes,
maze; coil etc. *(convolution)* 248; crooked path.

nice –, delicate –, subtle –, knotty-point;
vexed question, *vexata quaestio*, poser; puzzle etc.
(riddle) 533; paradox; hard –, nut to crack; bone
to pick, *crux, pons asinorum*, where the shoe pinches.

nonplus, quandary, strait, pass, pinch, pretty
pass, stress, brunt; critical situation, crisis; trial,
rub, emergency, exigency, scramble.

scrape, hobble, slough, quagmire, hot water, hornet's nest; sea – , peck- of troubles; pretty kettle of
fish; pickle, stew, *imbroglio*, mess, muddle, botch,
fuss, bustle, ado; false position; set fast, stand; dead
-lock, – set; fix, horns of a dilemma, *cul de sac*;
hitch; stumbling block etc. *(hindrance)* 706.

V. be -difficult etc. *adj.*; run one hard, go
against the grain, try one's patience, put one out;
put to one's -shifts, – wit's end; go hard with – ,
try- one; pose, perplex etc. *(uncertain)* 475; bother,
nonplus, gravel, bring to a dead lock; be -
impossible etc. 471; be in the way of etc. *(hinder)*
706.

meet with –, labor under –, get into –, plunge
into –, struggle with –, contend with –, grapple
with- difficulties; labor under a disadvantage; be -in
difficulty etc. *adj.*

fish in troubled waters, buffet the waves, swim
against the stream, scud under bare poles.

have -much ado with, – a hard time of it; come
to the -push, – pinch; bear the brunt.

grope in the dark, lose one's way, weave a
tangled web, walk among eggs.

get into a -scrape etc. *n.*; bring a hornet's nest
about one's ears; be put to one's shifts; flounder,
boggle, struggle; not know which way to turn etc.
(uncertain) 475; get -tangled up, – wound up;
perdre son latin; stick - at, – in the mud, – fast;
come to a -stand, – dead lock; hold the wolf by
the ears.

render -difficult etc. *adj.*; encumber, embarrass,
ravel, entangle; put a spoke in the wheel etc. *(hinder)* 706; lead a pretty dance.

Adj. difficult, not easy, hard, tough; trouble-,
toil-, irk-some; operose, laborious, onerous, arduous, Herculean, formidable; sooner –, more
easily- said than done; difficult –, hard- to deal
with; ill-conditioned, crabbed; not -to be handled
with kid gloves, – made with rosewater.

awkward, unwieldy, unmanageable; intractable,
stubborn etc. *(obstinate)* 606; perverse, refractory,
plaguy, trying, thorny, rugged; knot-ted, -ty; invious; path-, track-less; labyrinthine etc. *(convoluted)* 59; impracticable etc. *(impossible)* 471; not -
feasible etc. 470; desperate etc. *(hopeless)* 859.

embarrassing, perplexing etc. *(uncertain)* 475;
delicate, ticklish, critical; beset with –, full of –,
surrounded by –, entangled by –, encompassed
with- difficulties.

under a difficulty; in -difficulty, – hot water, –
the suds, – a cleft stick, – a fix, – the wrong
box, – a scrape etc. *n.*; – deep water, – a fine
pickle; *in extremis*; between -two stools, – Scylla
and Charybdis; surronded by -shoals, – breakers,
– quicksands; at cross purposes; not out of the
wood.

reduced to straits; hard –, sorely- pressed; run
hard; pinched, put to it, straitened; hard -up, – put
to it, – set; put to one's shifts; puzzled, at a loss
etc. *(uncertain)* 475; at -the end of one's tether, –
one's wit's end, – a nonplus, – a standstill;
graveled, nonplussed, stranded, aground; stuck –,
set- fast; up a tree, at bay, *aux abois*, driven -into a
corner, – from post to pillar, – to extremity, –
to one's wit's end, – to the wall; *au bout de son
latin*; out of one's -depth, – reckoning; put –,
thrown -out.

accomplished with difficulty; hard-fought, -
earned.

Adv. with -difficulty, – much ado; hardly etc.
adj.; uphill; against the -stream, – grain; *à
rebours*; *invitâ Minervâ*; in the teeth of; at –,
upon- a pinch; at long odds.

Phr. ay there's the rub; *hic labor hoc opus*;
things are come to a pretty pass.

705. Facility.—N. facility, ease; easiness etc.
adj.; capability; feasibility etc. *(practicability)* 470;
flexibility, pliancy etc. 324; smoothness etc. 255;
convenience.

plain –, smooth –, straight- sailing; mere
child's play, holiday task.

smooth water, fair wind; smooth – royal- road;
clear -coast, – stage; *tabula rasa; full play* etc.
(freedom) 748.

disen-cumbrance, -tanglement; deoppilation;
permission etc. 760.

V. be -easy etc. *adj.*; go on –, run- smoothly;
have -full play etc. *n.*; go –, run- on all fours; obey
the helm, work well.

flow –, swim –, drift –, go- with the- -stream,
– tide; see one's way; have -it all one's own way,
– the game in one's own hands; walk over the
course, win -at a canter, – hands down; make -
light of, – nothing of; be at home in etc. *(skilful)*
698.

render -easy etc. *adj.*; facilitate, smooth, ease; popularize; lighten, – the labor; free, clear; dis-encumber, -embarrass, -entangle, -engage; deob-struct, unclog, extricate, unravel; untie –, cut- the knot; disburden, unload, exonerate, emancipate, free from, deoppilate; humor etc. (*aid*) 707; lubricate etc. 332; relieve etc. 834.

leave -a hole to creep out of, – a loophole, – the matter open; give -the reins to, – full play, – full swing; make way for; open the -door to, – way; prepare –, smooth –, clear- the -ground, – way, – path, – road; pave the way, bridge over; permit etc. 760.

Adj. easy, facile; feasible etc. (*practicable*) 470; easily -managed, – accomplished; within reach, accessible, easy of access, for the million, open to.

manageable,'" wieldy; towardly, tractable; sub-missive; yielding, ductile; pliant etc. (*soft*) 324; glib, slippery; smooth etc. 255; on -friction wheels, – velvet; convenient.

un-, dis-burdened, -encumbered, -embarrassed; exonerated; un-loaded, -obstructed, -trammeled, -impeded, -restrained etc. (*free*) 748; at ease, light.

at –, quite at- home; in -one's element, – smooth water.

Adv. easily etc. *adj.*; readily, smoothly, swim-mingly, *ad lib.*, on easy terms, single-handed.

Phr. touch and go.

Int. all clear!

706. Hindrance.—N. prevention, preclusion, obstruction, stoppage; prohibition; inter-ruption, -ception, -clusion; hindrance, impedition; retard-ment, -ation; constriction; embarrassment, op-pilation; coarctation, stricture, restriction; anchor etc. 666; restraint etc. 751 & 752; inhibition etc. 761; blockade etc. (*closure*) 261; picketing.

inter-ference, -position; obtrusion; dis-couragement, -countenance, -approval, -approbation; opposition etc. 708.

impedimen', let, obstacle, obstruction, knot, knag; check, hitch, *contretemps, impasse,* screw loose, grit in the oil.

bar, stile, barrier; turn-stile, -pike; gate, port-cullis; bulwark, parapet, barricade etc. (*defence*) 717; wall, dead wall, breakwater, groyne; bulkhead, block, buffer; stopper etc. 263; boom, dam, weir, burrock.

drawback, objection; stumbling-block, -stone; lion in the path; snag; snags and sawyers.

en-, in-cumbrance; clog, skid, shoe, spoke; brake, drag, – chain; – weight; stay, stop; preven-tive, prophylactic; contraception; load, burden, far-del, *onus,* millstone round one's neck, *im-pedimenta*; dead weight; lumber, pack; nightmare, Ephialtes, incubus, old man of the sea; remora.

difficulty etc. 704; insuperable etc. 471; ob-stacle; estoppel; ill wind; head wind etc. (*op-position*) 708; trammel, tether etc. (*means of restraint*) 752; hold back, counterpoise; damper, wet blanket, hinderer, marplot, kill-joy, dog in the manger, interloper; trail of a red herring; opponent etc. 710.

V. hinder, impede, impedite, embarrass.

keep –, stave –, ward- off; picket; obviate; a-, ante-vert; turn aside, draw off, prevent, forefend, nip in the bud; retard, slacken, check, let; counter-act, -check; preclude, debar, foreclose, estop; inhibit etc. 761; shackle etc. (*restrain*) 751; restrict, restrain, cohibit.

obstruct, filibuster, stop, stay, bar, bolt, lock; block, – up; belay, barricade; block –, stop- the way; dam up etc. (*close*) 261; put on the -brake etc. *n.*; scotch –, lock –, put a spoke in- the wheel; put a stop to etc. 142; traverse, contravene; inter-rupt, -cept; oppose etc. 708; hedge -in, – round; cut off; interclude.

inter-pose, -fere, -meddle etc. 682.

cramp, hamper; clog, – the wheels; cumber; en-, in-cumber; handicap; choke; saddle –, load-with; overload, lay; lumber, trammel, tie one's hands, put to inconvenience; in-, discommode; discompose; hustle, drive into a corner; choke off.

run –, fall- foul of; cross the path of, break in upon.

thwart, frustrate, disconcert, balk, foil, baffle, snub, override, circumvent; defeat etc. 731; spike guns etc. (*render useless*) 645; spoil, mar, clip the wings of; cripple etc. (*injure*) 659; put an ex-tinguisher on; damp; dishearten etc. (*dissuade*) 616; discountenance, throw cold water on, spoil sport; lay –, throw- a wet blanket on; cut the ground from under one, take the wind out of one's sails, undermine; be –, stand- in the way of; act as a drag; hang like a millstone round one's neck.

Adj. hindering etc. *v.*; obstr-uctive, -uent; im-pedi-tive, -ent; intercipient; prophylactic etc. (*remedial*) 662.

in the way of, unfavorable; onerous, bur-densome; cumb-rous, -ersome; obtrusive.

hindered etc. *v.*; wind-bound, water-logged, heavy laden; hard pressed.

unassisted etc. (*see* assist etc. 707); single-handed, alone; deserted etc. 624.

707. Aid.—N. aid, -ance; assistance, help, opitulation, succor; support, lift, advance, fur-therance, promotion; coadjuvancy etc. (*co-operation*) 709.

patronage, championship, countenance, favor, interest, advocacy, auspices.

sustentation, subvention, subsidy, bounty, alimentation, nutrition, nourishment, maintenance; manna in the wilderness; food etc. 298; means etc. 632.

ministr-y, -ation; subministration; accomodation.

relief, rescue; help at a dead lift; supernatural aid; *deus ex machinâ.*

supplies, reinforcements, succors, contingents, recruits; support etc. (*physical*) 215; adjunct, ally etc. (*helper*) 711.

V. aid, assist, help, succor, lend one's aid; come to the aid etc. *n.-* of; contribute, subscribe to; bring –, give –, furnish –, afford –, supply- -aid etc. *n.*; render assistance; give –, stretch –, lend –, bear –, hold out- a -hand, – helping hand; give one a -lift, – cast, – turn; take -by the hand, – in tow; help a lame dog over a stile, lend wings to.

relieve, rescue; set -up, – agoing, – on one's legs; bear –, pull- through; give new life to, be the making of; reinforce, recruit; set –, put' –, push-forward; give -a lift, – a shove, – an impulse- to; promote, further, forward, advance; speed, ex-pedite, quicken, hasten.

support, sustain, uphold, prop, hold up, bolster.

cradle, nourish; nurture, nurse, dry nurse, suckle, put out to nurse; manure, cultivate, force; foster; cherish, foment; feed –, fan- the flame.

serve; do service to, tender to, pander to; ad-, sub-, minister to; tend, attend, wait on; take care of etc. 459; entertain; smooth the bed of death.

oblige, accomodate, consult the wishes of; humor, cheer, encourage.

second, stand by; back, – up; pay the piper, abet; work –, make interest –, stick up –, take up the cudgels- for; take up –, espouse –, adopt- the cause of; advocate, beat up for recruits, press into the service; squire, give moral support to, keep in countenance, countenance, patronize; lend - oneself, – one's countenance- to; smile –, shine- upon; favor, befriend, take up, take in hand, enlist under the banners of; side with etc. (*co-operate*) 709.

be of use to; subserve etc. (*instrument*) 631; benefit etc. 648; render a service etc. (*utility*) 644; conduce etc. (*tend*) 176.

Adj. aiding etc. *v.*; auxiliary, adjuvant, helpful; coadjuvant etc. 709; subservient, ministrant, ancillary, accessory, subsidiary.

at one's beck; friendly, amicable, favorable, propitious, well-disposed; neighborly; obliging etc. (*benevolent*) 906.

Adv. with –, by- -the aid etc. *n.*- of; on –, in- behalf of; in -aid, – the service, – the name, – favor, – furtherance- of; on account of; for the sake of, on the part of; *non obstante*.

Int. help! save us! to the rescue! S.O.S.!

708. Opposition.—N. opposition, antagonism, oppug-nancy, -nation; impugnation; contravention; counteraction etc. 179; counterplot.

cross-fire, under-current, head-wind.

clashing, collision, conflict, lack of harmony, contest.

competition, two of a trade, rivalry, emulation, race; war to the knife.

absence of -aid etc. 707; resistance etc. 719; restraint etc. 751; hindrance etc. 706.

V. oppose, conteract, run counter to; withstand etc. (*resist*) 719; control etc. (*restrain*) 751; hinder etc. 706; antagonize, oppugn, fly in the face of, go dead against, kick against, fall foul of; set –, pit- against; face, confront, cope with; make a -stand, – dead set- against; set -oneself, one's face- against; protest –, vote –, raise one's voice- against; disfavor, turn one's back upon; set at naught, slap in the face, slam the door in one's face.

be –, play- at cross purposes; counter-work, -mine; thwart, overthwart.

stem, breast, encounter; stem –, breast- the - tide, – current, – flood; buffet the waves; beat up –, make head- against; grapple with; kick against the pricks etc. (*resist*) 719; contend etc. 720 –, do battle etc. (*warfare*) 722- with, – against.

contra-dict, -vene; belie; go –, run –, beat –, militate- against; come in conflict with.

emulate etc. (*compete*) 720; rival, spoil one's trade.

Adj. oppos-ing, -ed etc. *v.*; adverse, antagonistic; ambivalent; contrary etc. 14; at variance etc. 24; at issue, at war with; in opposition; 'agin the Government.'

un-favorable, -friendly; hostile, inimical, cross, unpropitious.

in hostile array, front to front, with crossed bayonets, at daggers drawn; up in arms; resistant etc. 791.

competitive, emulous.

Adv. against, *versus*, counter to, in conflict with, at cross purposes.

against the -grain, – current, – stream, – wind, – tide; with a headwind; with the wind - ahead, – in one's teeth.

in spite, in despite, in defiance; in the -way, – teeth, – face- of; across; a-, over-thwart; where the shoe pinches.

though etc. 30; even; *quand même*; *per contra*.

Phr. *nitor in adversum.*

709. Co-operation.—N. co-operation; coadjuvancy, -tancy; coagency, coefficiency; concert, concurrence, complicity, participation; union etc. 43; amalgamation, combination etc. 48; collusion.

association, alliance, colleagueship, jointstock, copartnership, trust, cartel, pool, ring, combine, interlocking directorate; confederation etc. (*party*) 712; federation, coalition, fusion; a long pull, a strong pull and a pull all together; log-rolling, freemasonry.

unanimity etc. (*assent*) 488; *esprit de corps*, party spirit; clan-, partisan-ship; reciprocity, concord etc. 714.

V. co-operate, co-adjute, concur; conduce etc. 178; combine, cartelize, unite one's efforts; keep –, draw –, pull –, club –, hang –, hold –, league –, band –, be banded- together; stand –, put- shoulder to shoulder; act in concert, join forces, fraternize, cling to one another, conspire, concert, lay one's heads together; confederate, be in league with; collude, understand one another, play into the hands of, hunt in couples.

side –, take side –, go along –, go hand in hand –, join hands –, make common cause –, strike in –, unite –, join –, mix oneself up –, take part –, play along –, cast in one's lot- with; join –, enter into- partnership with; rally round, follow the lead of; come to, pass over to, come into the views of; be –, row –, sail- in the same boat; sail on the same tack.

be a party to, lend oneself to; participate; have a -hand in, – finger in the pie; take –, bear- part in; second etc. (*aid*) 707; take the part of, play the game of; espouse a -cause, – quarrel.

Adj. co-operating etc. *v.*; in -co-operation etc. *n.*, – league etc. (*party*) 712; coadju-vant, -tant; hand and glove with.

favorable etc. 707- to; un-opposed etc. 708.

Adj. as one man etc. (*unanimously*) 488; shoulder to shoulder; in co-operation with.

710. Opponent.—N. opponent, antagonist, adversary; adverse party, opposition; enemy etc. 891; assailant.

oppositionist, obstructive; obscurantist; brawler, wrangler, brangler, disputant, extremist, irreconcilable, diehard, bitter-ender.

malcontent; Jacobin, Fenian etc. 742; demagogue, reactionist.

passive resister, conscientious objector.

rival, competitor, contestant.

711. Auxiliary.—N. auxiliary; recruit; assistant; adju-vant, -tant; adjunct; help, er, -mate, -ing hand; midwife; colleague, partner, mate, *confrère*, co-operator; coadju-tor, -trix; collaborator.

ally; friend etc. 890; confidant, *fidus Achates*, pal, chum, buddy, *alter ego*.

confederate; ac-, complice; accessory, − after the fact; *particeps criminis*.

aide-de-camp, secretary, clerk, associate, marshal; right-hand; candle-, bottle-holder; hand-maid; servant etc. 746; puppet, cat's-paw; stooge, dependent, creature, jackal; tool, *âme damnée*; satellite, adherent, parasite.

votary, disciple; secta-rian, -ry; seconder, backer, upholder, supporter, abettor, advocate, partisan, champion, patron, friend at court, mediator.

friend in need, Jack at a pinch, *deus ex machinâ*, guardian angel, fairy godmother; special providence, tutelary genius.

712. Party.—N. party, faction, side, denomination, class, communion, set, crowd, crew, band, horde, posse, phalanx; regiment etc. 726; family, clan etc. 166.

Tories, Conservatives, Unionists, Whigs, Liberals, Radicals, Labour party, Socialists, Communists etc.; Republicans, Democrats, Farmer-Labor; *Fascisti*, Revolutionaries etc. 742.

community, body, fellowship, sodality, solidarity; con-, fraternity; sorority; brother-, sister-hood.

Freemasons, Knights Templars, Odd Fellows, Ku Klux Klan etx.

knot, gang, *clique*, ring, circle; *coterie*, club, *casino*.

corporation, corporate body, guild; establishment, company, copartnership, firm, house, joint concern, joint-stock company, trust, investment trust, combine etc. 709.

society, association; instit-ute, -ution; union; trade-union; league, syndicate, alliance, *Verein*, *Bund*, *Zollverein*, combination; league −, alliance- offensive and defensive; coalition; federation; confedera -tion, -cy; junto, cabal, *camarilla*, *camorra*, *brigue*; freemasonry; party spirit etc. (*co-operation*) 709.

staff; 'cast, *dramatis personae*.

V. unite, join; club together etc. (*co-operate*) 709; cement −, form- a party etc. *n.*; associate etc. (*assemble*) 72.

Adj. in -league, − partnership, − alliance etc. *n.*

bonded −, banded −, linked etc. (*joined*) 43- together; embattled; confederated, federative, joint, corporate, leagued, fraternal, masonic, cliquish.

Adv. hand in hand, side by side, shoulder to shoulder, *en masse*, in the same boat.

713. Discord.—N. disagreement etc. 24; discord, -accord, -sidence, -sonance; jar, clash, shock; jarring, jostling etc. *v.*; screw loose.

variance, difference, dissension, misunderstanding, cross purposes, odds, *brouillerie*; division, split, rupture, disruption, division in the camp, house divided against itself, rift within the lute; disunion, breach; schism etc. (*dissent*) 489; feud, faction.

quarrel, dispute, rippet, spat, tiff, *tracasserie*, squabble, altercation, words, high words; wrangling etc. *v.* ; jangle, brabble cross questions and crooked answers, snip-snap; family jars.

polemics; litigation; strife etc. (*contention*) 720; warfare etc. 722; outbreak, open rupture; breaking off of negotiations, recall of ambassadors; declaration of war.

broil, brawl, row, racket, hubbub, rixation; embroilment, embranglement, *imbroglio*, *fracas*, breach of the peace, piece of work, scrimmage, rumpus; breeze, squall; riot, disturbance etc. (*disorder*) 59; commotion etc. (*agitation*) 315; bear garden, Donnybrook Fair.

subject of dispute, ground of quarrel, battle ground, disputed point; bone -of contention, − to pick; apple of discord, *casus belli*; question at issue etc. (*subject of inquiry*) 461; vexed question, *vexata quaestio*, brand of discord.

troublous times; cat-and-dog life; contentiousness etc. *adj.* ; enmity etc. 889; hate etc. 898; Kilkenny cats; disputant etc. 710; strange bedfellows.

V. be -discordant etc. *adj.* ; disagree, come amiss etc. 24; clash, jar, jostle, pull different ways, conflict, have no measures with, misunderstand one another; live like cat and dog; differ; dissent etc. 489; have a -bone to pick, − crow to pluck- with.

fall out, quarrel, dispute; litigate; controvert etc. (*deny*) 536; squabble, wrangle, jangle, brangle, bicker, nag; spar etc. (*contend*) 720; have -words etc. *n.* with; fall foul of.

split; break −, break squares −, part company-with; declare war, try conclusions; join −, put in-issue; pick a quarrel, fasten a quarrel on; sow −, stir up- -dissension etc. *n.*; embroil, estrange, entangle, disunite, widen the breach; set -at odds, − together by the ears; set −, pit- against; rub up the wrong way.

get into hot water, fish in troubled waters, brawl; kick up a -row, − dust; turn the house out of window.

Adj. discordant; disagreeing etc. *v.* ; out of tune, dissonant, inharmonious, harsh, grating, jangling, ajar, on -bad terms; dissentient etc. 489; inconsistent, contradictory, incongruous, discrepant; un- reconciled, -pacified.

quarrelsome, unpacific; gladiatorial, controversial, polemic, disputatious; factious; liti-gious, -gant; pettifogging.

at odds, at loggerheads, at daggers drawn, at variance, at issue, at cross purposes, at sixes and sevens, at feud, at high words; up in arms, together by the ears, in hot water, embroiled.

torn, disunited.

Phr. *quot homines tot sententiae*; no love lost between them, *non nostrum tantas componere lites.*

714. Concord.—N. concord, accord, harmony, symphony, homology; agreement etc. 23; sympathy etc. (*love*) 897; response; union, unison, unity; bonds of harmony; peace etc. 721; unanimity etc. (*assent*) 488; league etc. 712; happy family.

rapprochement; *réunion*; amity etc. (*friendship*) 888; reciprocity; alliance, *entente cordiale*, good understanding, conciliation, arbitration, peacemaker etc. 724.

V. agree etc. 23; accord, harmonize with; fraternize; be -concordant etc. *adj.* ; go hand in hand; blend −, tone in- with; run parallel etc. (*concur*) 178; understand one another; pull together etc. (*co-operate*) 709; put up one's horses together, sing in chorus.

side −, sympathize −, go −, chime in −, fall in- with; come round; be pacified etc. 723; assent etc. 488; enter into the -ideas, − feelings- of; reciprocate.

hurler avec les loups; go −, swim- with the stream.

pour oil on troubled waters, keep in good humor, render accordant, put in tune; come to an understanding, meet half-way; keep the −, remain at- peace.

Adj. concordant, congenial; agreeing etc. *v.*; in-accord etc. *n.*; harmonious, united, cemented; banded together etc. 712; allied; friendly etc. 888; fraternal; conciliatory; at one with; of one mind etc. (*assent*) 488.

at peace, in still water; tranquil etc. (*pacific*) 721.

Adv. with one voice etc. (*assent*) 488; in concert with, hand in hand; on one's side, unanimously.

715. Defiance.—N. defiance; daring etc. *v.*; dare, challenge, *cartel*; threat etc. 909; war-cry, -whoop.

V. defy, dare, beard; brave etc. (*courage*) 861; bid defiance to; set at -defiance, − naught; hurl defiance at; dance the war dance; snap the fingers at, laugh to scorn; disobey etc. 742.

show -fight, − one's teeth, − a bold front; bluster, look big, stand akimbo; double −, shake-the fist; threaten etc 909.

challenge, call out; throw −, fling- down the - gauntlet, − gage, − glove.

Adj. defiant; defying etc. *v.* ; with arms akimbo; rebellious, insolent; reckless, greatly daring.

Adv. in -defiance, − the teeth- of; under one's very nose.

Int. do your worst! come if you dare! come on! marry come up! hoity toity!

Phr. *noli me tangere*; *nemo me impune lacessit.*

716. Attack.—N. attack; assault, − and battery; onset, onslaught, charge.

aggression, drive, offence; incursion, inroad; invasion; irruption; outbreak; *estrapade*, *ruade*; *coup de main*, sally, *sortie*, *camisade*, raid, foray; run - at, − against; dead set at.

storm, -ing; boarding, *escalade*; siege, investment, obsession, bombardment, cannonade; air raid.

fire, volley; platoon −, file −, rapid-fire; *fusillade*; sharp-shooting, sniping; broadside; raking −, cross −, machine gun- fire; − volley of grapeshot, *feu d'enfer*; salvo.

cut, thrust, lunge, pass, *passado*, *carte* and

tierce, home thrust, *coup de pied*; kick, punch, etc. (*impulse*) 276.

battue, *razzia*, *Jacquerie*, *dragonnade*; devastation etc. 162.

assailant, aggressor, invader.

base of operations, point of attack.

V. attack, assault, assail; set −, fall- upon; charge, impugn, break a lance with, enter the lists.

assume −, take- the offensive; be −, become- the aggressor; strike the first blow, fire the first shot, throw the first stone at; lift a hand −, draw the sword- against; take up the cudgels; advance −, march- against; march upon, invade, harry; come on, show fight.

strike at, poke at, thrust at; aim −, deal- a blow at; give −, fetch- one a -blow, − kick; have a -cut, − shot, − fling, − shy- at; be down −, pounce-upon; fall foul of, pitch into, launch out against; bait, slap on the face; make a -thrust, − pass, − set, − dead set- at; dunt; bear down upon.

close with, come to close quarters, bring to bay.

ride full tilt against; let fly at, dash at, run a tilt at, rush at, tilt at, run at, fly at, hawk at, have at, let out at; make a -dash, − rush at; attack tooth and nail; strike home; drive −, press- one hard; be hard upon, run down, strike at the root of.

lay about one, run amuck.

fire -upon, − at, − a shot at; shoot at, pop at, level at, let off a gun at; open fire, pepper, bombard, shell, pour a broadside into; fire -a volley, − red-hot shot; spring a mine.

throw -a stone, − stones- at; stone, lapidate, pelt; hurl -at, − against, − at the head of.

beset, besiege, beleaguer; lay siege to, invest, open the trenches, plant a battery, sap, mine; storm, board, scale the walls.

cut and thrust, bayonet, butt; kick, strike etc. (*impulse*) 276; whip etc. (*punish*) 972.

Adj. attacking etc. *v.*; aggressive, offensive, obsidional.

up in arms; on the warpath; over the top.

Adv. on the offensive.

Int. 'up and at them!'

717. Defense.—N. defense, protection, guard, ward; shielding etc. *v.*; propugnation; preservation etc. 670; guardianship.

self-defense, -preservation; resistance etc. 719.

safeguard etc. (*safety*) 664; screen etc. (*shelter*) 666, (*concealment*) 530; barrage; fortification; muni-tion, -ment; bulwark, fosse, moat, ditch, intrenchment, trench, dugout, gas mask; dike, dyke; parapet, parados, sunk fence, embankment, mound, mole, bank; earth- field-work, gabions; fence, wall, dead wall, contravallation; paling etc. (*inclosure*) 232; palisade, haha, stockade, *stoccado*, *laager*, *sangar*; barri-er, -cade; boom; portcullis, *chevaux de frise*; aba-, abat-, abba-tis; *vallum*, circumvallation, battlement, rampart, scarp; e-, counter-scarp; glacis, casemate.

mine, countermine.

buttress, abutment; shore etc. (*support*) 215.

breastwork, *banquette*, curtain, mantlet, bastion, demilune, redan, ravelin; advanced −, horn −, out- work, lunette; barb-acan, -ican; redoubt; fort-elage, -alice; lines; coast defense.

loop-hole, machicolation; sally-port, postern gate.

hold, stronghold, fastness; asylum etc. (*refuge*) 666; keep, donjon, fortress, citadel; capitol, castle; tower, – of strength; fort, barracoon, pah, sconce, martello tower, peel-house, block-house, rath; wooden walls; turret, barbette.

buffer, corner-stone, fender, apron, mask, gauntlet, thimble, carapace, armor, shield, buckler; target, targe, aegis, breastplate, cuirass, plastron, habergeon, mail, coat of mail, brigandine, hauberk, lorication, helmet, helm, basinet, sallet, salade, heaume, morion, murrion, armet, cabaset, vizor, casquetel, siege-cap, head-piece, casque, steel helmet, tin hat; *pickelhaube*, csako; shako etc. (*dress*) 225; bearskin; panoply; truncheon etc. (*weapon*) 727.

garrison, picket, piquet; defender, protector; guardian etc. (*safety*) 664; trabant, body guard, champion; knight-errant, Paladin; propugner.

V. defend, forfend, fend; shield, screen, shroud; fence round etc. (*circumscribe*) 229; fence, intrench; guard etc. (*keep safe*) 664; guard against; take care of etc. (*vigilance*) 459; bear harmless; keep –, ward –, beat- off; hinder etc. 706.

parry, repel, propugn, put to flight; give a warm reception to [*ironical*]; hold –, keep- at -bay, – arm's length.

stand –, act- on the defensive; show fight; maintain –, stand- one's ground; stand by; hold one's own; bear –, stand- the brunt; fall back upon, hold, stand in the gap.

Adj. defending etc. *v.*; defensive; mural; armed, – at all points, – *cap-à-pie*, – to the teeth; panoplied; accoutred, harnessed; iron-plated, -clad; loop-holed, castellated, machicolated; casemated; defended etc. *v.*; proof against, bomb-, bullet-proof; protective.

Adv. defensively; on the -defense, – defensive; in defense; at bay, *pro aris et focis*.

Int. no surrender! *il ne passeront pas!*

Phr. defense not defiance.

718. Retaliation.—N. retaliation, reprisal, retort; counter-stroke, -blast, -plot, -project; retribution, *lex talionis*; reciprocation etc. (*reciprocity*) 12.

requital, desert, tit for tat, give and take, blow for blow, *quid pro quo,* a Roland for an Oliver, measure for measure, an eye for an eye, diamond cut diamond, the biter bit, a game at which two can play; boomerang.

recrimination etc. (*accusation*) 938; revenge etc. 919; compensation etc. 30; reaction etc. (*recoil*) 277.

V. retaliate, retort, turn upon; pay -off, – back; pay in -one's own, – the same- coin; cap; reciprocate etc. 148; turn the tables upon, return the compliment; give -a *quid pro quo* etc. n., – as much as one takes; give and take, exchange -blows, – fisticuffs; be -quits, – even- with; pay off old scores.

serve one right, be hoist on one's own petard, throw a stone in one's own garden, cathch a Tartar.

Adj. retaliating etc. *v.*; retalia-tory, -tive; retributive, recriminatory, reciprocal.

Adv.. in retaliation; *en revanche.*

Phr. *mutato nomine de te fabula narratur; par pari refero; tu quoque*; you're another; *suo sibi gladio hunc jugulo.*

719. Resistance.—N. resistance, stand, front, oppugnation; opposition etc. 708; renitence, reluctation, recalcitration, recalcitrance; repugnance; kicking etc. *v.*

repulse, rebuff.

insurrection etc. (*disobedience*) 742; strike; turn –, lock –, barring- out; *levée en masse, Jacquerie*; riot etc. (*disorder*) 59.

V. resist; not -submit etc. 725; repugn, reluctate, withstand; stand up –, strive –, bear up –, be proof –, make head- against; stand, – firm, – one's ground, – the brunt of, – out; hold -one's ground, – one's own, – out.

breast the -wave, – current; stem the -tide, – torrent; face, confront, grapple with; show a bold front etc. (*courage*) 861; present a front; make a –, take one's- stand.

kick, – against; recalcitrate, kick against the pricks; oppose etc. 708; fly in the face of; lift the hand against etc. (*attack*) 716; rise up in arms etc. (*war*) 722; strike, turn out; draw up a round robin etc. (*remonstrate*) 932; revolt etc. (*disobey*) 742; make a riot.

prendre le mors aux dents; take the bit between the teeth; sell one's life dearly, die hard, keep at bay; repel, repulse.

Adj. resisting etc. *v.*; resist-ive, -ant; refractory etc. (*disobedient*) 742; recalcitrant, re-nitent, -pulsive, -pellant; up in arms.

proof against; unconquerable etc. (*strong*) 159; stubborn, unconquered; indomitable etc. (*persevering*) 604a; unyielding etc. (*obstinate*) 606.

Int. hands off! keep off!

720. Contention.—N. contention, strife; contest, -ation; struggle; belligerency; opposition etc. 708.

controversy, polemics; debate etc. (*discussion*) 476; war of words, logomachy, litigation; paper war, ink slinging; high words etc. (*quarrel*) 713; sparring etc. *v.*

competition, rivalry; corrival-ry, -ship; agonism, *concours*, match, race, horse-racing, heat, steeple chase, point-to-point race, handicap; boat race, regatta; field-day; sham fight, Derby day; turf, sporting, bull-fight, tauromachy, *gymkhana*, rodeo, Olympiad.

wrestling, *ju-jitsu*, pugilism, boxing, fisticuffs, spar, mill, set-to, scrap, round, bout, event; prize-fighting; quarter-staff, single stick; gladiatorship, gymnastics; athletic-s, – sports; games of skill etc. 840.

shindy; *fracas* etc. (*discord*) 713; clash of arms; tussle, scuffle, broil, fray; affray, -ment; velitation; col-, luctation; brabble, *brique*, scramble, *mêlée*, scrimmage, stramash, bush-fighting.

free –, stand up –, hand to hand –, running-fight.

conflict, skirmish; ren-, en-counter; *rencontre*, collision, affair, brush, fight; battle, – royal; combat, action, engagement, joust, tournament; tilt, – ing; tourney, list; pitched battle, guerilla warfare.

death-struggle, struggle for life or death, Armageddon; hard knocks, sharp contest, tug of war.

naval -engagement, – battle; *naumachia*, sea-fight.

duel, -lo; single combat, monomachy, satisfaction, *passage d'armes*, passage of arms, affair of honor; triangular duel; hostile meeting, digladiation; appeal to arms etc. (*warfare*) 722.

deeds —, feats- of arms; pugnacity; combativeness etc. *adj.*; bone of contention etc. 713.

V. contend; contest, strive, struggle, scramble, wrestle; spar, square; exchange -blows, – fisticuffs; scrap, mix with, fib, justle, tussle, tilt, box, stave, fence; skirmish; fight etc. (*war*) 722; wrangle etc. (*quarrel*) 713.

contend etc. –, grapple –, engage –, close –, buckle –, bandy –, try conclusions –, have a brush etc. *n.* – tilt- with; encounter, fall foul of, pitch into, clapperclaw, run a tilt at; oppose etc. 708; reluct.

join issue, come to blows, be at loggerheads, set-to, come to the scratch, exchange shots, measure swords, meet hand to hand; take up the -cudgels, – glove, – gauntlet; enter the lists; couch one's lance; give satisfaction; appeal to arms etc. (*warfare*) 722.

lay about one; break the peace.

compete –, cope –, vie –, race- with; outvie, emulate, rival; run a race; contend etc. –, stipulate –, stickle- for; insist upon, make a point of.

Adj. contending etc. *v.*; together by the ears, at loggerheads, at war, at issue.

competitive, rival; belligerent; contentious, combative, bellicose, unpeaceful; warlike etc. 722; quarrelsome etc. 901; pugnacious; pugilistic, gladiatorial; palestric, -al.

Phr. *a verbis ad verbera*; a word and a blow.

721. Peace.—N. peace; amity etc. (*friendship*) 888; harmony etc. (*concord*) 714; tranquility etc. (*quiescence*) 265; truce etc. (*pacification*) 723; pacificism; pipe –, calumet- of peace.

piping time of peace, quiet life; neutrality.

V. be at peace; keep the peace etc. (*concord*) 714; make peace etc. 723.

Adj. pacific; peace-able, -ful; calm, tranquil, untroubled, halcyon; bloodless; neutral.

Phr. the storm blown over; the lion lies down with the lamb.

722. Warfare.—N. warfare; fighting etc. *v.*; hostilities; war, arms, the sword; Mars, Bellona, grim visaged war, *horrida bella*, Armageddon.

appeal to -arms, – the sword; ordeal –, wager- of battle; *ultima ratio regum*, arbitrament of the sword.

battle array, campaign, crusade, expedition; mobilization; state of siege; battle-field etc. (*arena*) 728; warpath.

art of war, tactics, strategy, castrametation; general-, soldier-ship; aerial –, submarine –, naval –, chemical-, atomic-, guerilla- warfare; military evolutions, ballistics, gunnery; chivalry; poison gas; gun-powder, shot, – and shell.

battle, tug of war etc. (*contention*) 720; service; campaigning, active service, tented field; fiery cross, trumpet, clarion, bugle, pibroch, slogan; war-cry, -whoop; battle cry, beat of drum, rappel, tom-tom; word of command; pass-, watch-word.

war to the -death, – knife; *guerre à -mort*, – *outrance*; open –, internecine –, civil- war.

V. arm; raise –, mobilize- troops; raise up in arms; take up the cudgels etc. 720; take up –, fly to –, appeal to- -arms, – the sword; draw –, unsheathe- the sword; dig up the hatchet; go to –, declare –, wage –, let slip the dogs of- war; cry havoc; kindle –, light- the torch of war; raise one's banner, send round the fiery cross; hoist the black flag; throw –, fling- away the scabbard; enrol, enlist, join up; take the field; take the law into one's own hands; do –, give –, join –, engage in –, go to- battle; flesh one's sword; set to, fall to, engage, measure swords with, draw the trigger, cross swords; come to -blows, – close quarters; fight; combat; contend etc. 720; battle –, break a lance- with.

serve –, be on- -service, – active service; campaign; wield the sword, shoulder a musket, smell powder, be under the fire; spill –, imbrue the hands in- blood; be on the warpath.

carry on -war, – hostilities; keep the field; fight the good fight; go over the top; cut one's way through; fight -it out, – like devils, – one's way, – hand to hand; sell one's life dearly.

Adj. conten-ding, -tious etc. 720; armed, – to the teeth, – cap-a-pie; sword in hand; in –, under –, up in- arms; at war with; bristling with arms; in -battle array, – open arms, – the field; embattled.

unpacific, unpeaceful; belligerent, combative, armigerous, bellicose, martial, warlike; mili-tary, – tant; soldier-like, -ly; chivalrous; strategical, internecine.

Adv. *flagrante bello*, in the -thick of the fray, – cannon's mouth; at the -swords's point, – point of the bayonet.

Int. *vae victis!* to arms! to your tents O Israel! **Phr.** the battle rages.

723. Pacification.—N. pacification, conciliation; reconcil-iation, -ement; shaking of hands, accomodation, arrangement, adjustment; terms, compromise; amnesty, deed of release.

peace-offering; olive-branch; overtures; pipe –, calumet –, preliminaries- of peace.

truce, armistice; suspension of -arms, – hostilities; breathing-time; convention; *modus vivendi*; flag of truce, white flag, *parlementaire*, cartel.

hollow truce, *pax in bello*; drawn battle.

V. pacify, tranquilize, compose; allay etc. (*moderate*) 174; reconcile, propitiate, placate, conciliate, meet half-way, hold out the olive-branch, heal the breach, make peace, restore harmony, bring to terms.

settle –, arrange –, accommodate- -matters, – differences; set straight; make up a quarrel, *tantas componere lites*; come to -an understanding, – terms; bridge over, hush up; make -it, – matters- up; shake hands.

raise a siege; put up –, sheathe- the sword; bury the hatchet, lay down one's arms, turn swords into ploughshares; smoke the calumet of peace, close the temple of Janus; keep the peace etc. (*concord*) 714; be -pacified etc.; come round.

Adj. conciliatory, pacificatory; composing etc *v.*; pacified etc. *v.*

Phr. *requiescat in pace*.

724. Mediation.—N. media-tion, -torship, -tization; inter-vention, -position, -ference, -meddling, -cession; parley, negotiation, arbitration; flag of truce etc. 723; good offices, peace -offering; diploma-tics, -cy; compromise etc. 774.

mediator, intercessor, peacemaker, make-peace, negotiator, go-between; diplomatist etc. (*consignee*) 758; moderator, propitiator, umpire, arbitrator.

V. media-te, -tize; inter-cede, -pose, -fere, -vene; step in, negotiate; meet half-way; arbitrate; *magnas componere lites.*

Adj. mediatory, propitiatory, diplomatic.

725. Submission.—N. submission, yielding, acquiescence, compliance; non-resistance; obedience etc. 743; submissiveness, deference.

surrender, cession, capitulation, resignation.

obeisance, homage, kneeling, genuflexion, courtesy, curtsy, *salaam, kowtow;* prostration.

V. succumb, submit, yield, bend, resign, defer to, accede.

lay down —, deliver up- one's arms; hand over one's sword; lower —, haul down —, strike- one's flag, — colors; deliver the keys of the city.

surrender, — at discretion; cede, capitulate, come to terms, retreat, beat a retreat; draw in one's horns etc. (*humility*) 879; give -way, — ground, — in, — up; cave in; suffer judgment by default; bend, — to one's yoke, — before the storm; reel back; bend —, knuckle- -down, — to, — under; knock under.

humble oneself; eat -dirt, — the leek, — humble pie; bite —, lick- the dust; be —, fall- at one's feet; craven; crouch before, throw oneself at the feet of; swallow the -leek, — pill; kiss the rod; turn the other cheek; *avaler des couleuvres,* gulp down.

obey etc. 743; kneel to, bow to, pay homage to, cringe to, truckle to; bend the -neck, — knee; kneel, fall on one's knees, bow submission, courtesy, curtsy, *kowtow;* make obeisance.

pocket the affront; make -the best of, — a virtue of necessity; grin and abide, shrug the shoulders, resign oneself; submit with a good grace etc. (*bear with*) 826.

Adj. surrendering etc. *v.*; submissive, resigned, crouching; down-trodden; down on one's marrow bones; on one's bended knee; weak-kneed, un-, non-resisting; pliant etc. (*soft*) 324; undefended.

untenable, indefensible; humble etc. 879.

Phr. have it your own way; it can't be helped; amen etc. (*assent*) 488.

726. Combatant.—N. combatant; disputant, controversialist, polemic, litigant, belligerent; competitor, rival, corrival; fighter, assailant, aggressor; champion, Paladin; moss-trooper, swashbuckler, fire-eater, duellist, bully, bludgeon-man, rough, fighter, fighting-man, prize-fighter, pugilist, pug, boxer, bruiser, the fancy, gladiator, athlete, wrestler; fighting-, game-cock; swordsman, *sabreur.*

warrior, soldier, Amazon, man-at-arms, armigerent; campaigner, veteran; red-coat, military man, *rajpoot,* brave.

armed force, troops, soldiery, military, forces, sabaoth, the army, standing army, regulars, the line, troops of the line, militia, territorials, yeomanry, volunteers, trainband, fencible; auxiliary —, reserve- forces; reserves, *posse comitatus,* national guard, *gendarme,* beefeater; guards, -man; yeoman of the guard, life guards, household troops.

janissary; myrmidon; Mama-, Mame-luke; spahee, *spahi,* Cossack, Croat, Pandour; irregular, free lance, *franc-tireur, bashi-bazouk,* guerilla, *condottiere;* mercenary.

levy, draught; commando; *Land-wehr, -sturm;* conscript, recruit, rookie, cadet, raw levies.

private, — soldier; Tommy Atkins, rank and file, peon, trooper, doughboy, sepoy, *askari, legionnaire,* legionary, food for powder, cannon fodder; officer etc. (*commander*) 745; subaltern, ensign, shave-tail, standard bearer, non-com; spear-pike-man; halberdier, lancer; musketeer, carabineer, rifleman, sharpshooter, yager, skirmisher; grenadier, fusileer; archer, bowman.

horse and foot; horse —, foot- soldier; cavalry, horse, artillery, horse —, field —, heavy —, mountain- artillery, infantry, light horse, *voltigeur, Uhlan,* mounted rifles, dragoon, hussar, trooper; light —, heavy- dragoon; heavy; *cuirassier;* gunner, cannoneer, bombardier, artillery-man, matross; sapper, — and miner; engineer; light infantry, rifles, *chasseur, zouave;* military train, supply and transport, coolie.

army, — corps, *corps d'armée,* host, division, column, wing, detachment, *escadrille,* garrison, flying column, brigade, regiment, *corps,* battalion, squadron, company, platoon, battery, subdivision, section, squad; piquet, picket, guard, rank, file; legion, phalanx, cohort; cloud of skirmishers; impi.

war-horse, charger, *destrier.*

armored -train, — car; tank.

marine, man of war's man etc. (*sailor*) 269; navy, first line of defense, wooden walls; naval forces, fleet, flotilla, armada, squadron.

man-of-war, warship; H.M.S., U.S.S.; capital ship; line-of-battle ship, battle ship; super-, dreadnought, battle —, armored —, protected — light-cruiser; scout, flotilla leader; destroyer, torpedo boat; submarine, submersible, U-boat; submarine chaser, eagle boat, mystery ship, Q-boat; mine-layer, -sweeper; ship of the line, iron-clad, turret-ship, ram, Monitor, floating battery; first-rate, frigate, sloop of war, corvette, gunboat, bomb-vessel, fire-boat; flag ship, guard ship, cruiser; airplane carrier; privateer; tender; depôt —, parent-ship; store —, troop- ship; transport, catamaran.

aircraft etc. 273; air force, scout, fighter, bomber, troop carrier, aerial patrol, seaplane, flying boat, torpedo plane; airship, Zeppelin; rigid —, semi-rigid —, non-rigid- airship; dirigible —, free —, captive —, kite —, observation- balloon.

anti-aircraft guns, searchlights, sound locators; catapult.

727. Arms.—N. arm, -s; weapon, deadly weapon; arma-ment, -ture; panoply, stand of arms; armor etc. (*defense*) 717; armory etc. (*store*) 636.

ammunition; powder, — and shot; explosive; propellant; gun-powder, -cotton; dynam-, melin-, cord-, lydd-ite; trinitrotoluene, T.N.T., ammonal; cartridge; ball cartridge, *cartouche,* fire-ball, dud, black Marie; 'villainous saltpeter;' poison –, mustard –, lachrymatory –; tear- gas.

sword, saber, broadsword, cutlass, falchion, scimitar, cimeter, brand, whinyard, bilbo, glaive, glave, rapier, skean, Toledo, Ferrara, tuck, claymore, creese, kris, *kukri*, dagger, dirk, hanger, poniard, stiletto, stylet, dudgeon, bayonet; sword-bayonet, -stick; side arms, foil, blade, steel; axe, bill; pole-, battle-axe; gisarm, halberd, partisan, tomahawk, bowie-knife; at-, att-, yat-aghan; yatachan; good –, trusty –, naked- sword; cold –, naked-steel.

club, mace, truncheon, staff, bludgeon, cudgel, life-preserver, shillelagh, sprig; hand-, quarter-staff; bat, cane, stick, knuckle-duster, sand bag.

gun, piece; fire-arms; artillery, ordnance; siege –, battering-train; park, battery; cannon, gun of position, heavy –, siege –, field –, mountain –, anti-aircraft –, breech loading –, quick firing-gun; field piece, mortar, trench mortar; mine –, flame- -thrower, napalm; howitzer, carronade, culverin, basilisk; falconet jingal, swivel, *pederero, bouche à feu*; smooth bore, rifled cannon; Armstrong –, Lancaster –, Paixhan –, Whitworth –, Parrott –, Krupp –, Gatling –, Maxim –, Vickers –, Hotchkiss –, Lewis –, machine- gun; tommy gun, Thompson's submachine gun; *mitrailleu-r, -se*; pompom; blow pipe.

small arms; musket, -ry, firelock, flintlock, fowling-piece, shot gun, rifle, *fusil*, caliver, carbine, blunderbuss, musketoon, Brown Bess, matchlock, harquebuss, *arquebuse*, haguebut; petronel; smallbore; breech-, muzzle-loader; Minie –, Enfield –, Westly Richards –, Snider –, Springfield –, Martini-Henry –, Lee-Metford –, Lee-Enfield –, Mauser –, Männlicher –, magazine –, repeating- rifle; needle-gun, *chassepot*; pis-tol, -et; revolver, automatic pistol, automatic; wind-, air-gun; flame –, gas- projector.

bow, cross-bow, arbalest, balister, catapult, sling; battering-ram etc. (*impulse*) 276; gunnery, ballistics etc. (*propulsion*) 284.

missile, bolt, projectile, shot, pellet, ball; grape; grape –, canister –, bar –, cannon –, langrel –, langrage –, round –, chain- shot; explosive; incendiary –, expanding –, soft-nosed –, dum-dum- bullet; slug, stone, brickbat; hand –, rifle-grenade; high explosive –, incendiary –, stink-, A-, H-, atomic –, hydrogen – bomb; petard, torpedo, carcass, rocket; congreve, – rocket; shrapnel, *mitraille*; thunderbolt; mine, land mine, infernal machine.

pike, lance, spear, spontoon, javelin, assagai, throwing stick, dart, djerrid, arrow, reed, shaft, bolt, boomerang, harpoon, gaff.

728. Arena.—N. arena, field, platform; scene of action, theater; walk, course; hustings; stage, boards etc. (*playhouse*) 599; amphitheater; Coli-, Colos-seum; Flavian amphitheater, hippodrome, circus, race-course, track, *stadium, corso*, turf, cockpit, bear-garden, play-ground, playing fields, *gymnasium, palaestra*, ring, lists; tilt-yard, -ing ground; *Campus Martius, Champ de Mars*; aerodrome, airport, air base, flying field.

theater –, seat- of war; battle-field, -ground; field of -battle, – slaughter; no man's land; Aceldama, camp; the enemy's camp; trysting- place etc. (*place of meeting*) 74.

729. Completion.—N. completion; ac-complish-, achieve-, fulfil-ment; performance, execution; des-, dis-patch; consummation, culmination, climax; finish, conclusion, ef-fectuation; close etc. (*end*) 67; terminus etc. (*arrival*) 292; winding up; *finale, dénouement,* catastrophe, issue, upshot, result; final –, last –, crowning –, finishing- -touch, – stroke; last finish, *coup de grâce*; crowning of the edifice; coping-, keystone; missing link etc. 53; super-structure, *ne plus ultra*, work done, *fait accompli.*

elaboration; finality; completeness etc. 52.

V. effect, -uate; accomplish, achieve, compass, consummate, hammer out; bring to -maturity, – perfection; perfect, complete; elaborate.

do, execute, make; go –, get- through; work out, enact; bring -about, – to bear, – to pass, – through, – to a head.

des-, dis-patch; knock –, finish –, polish- off; make short work of; dispose of, set at rest; perform, discharge, fulfil, realize; put in -practice, – force; carry -out, – into effect, – into execution; make good; be as good as one's word.

. do thoroughly, not do by halves, go the whole hog; drive home; be in at the death etc. (*persevere*) 604a; carry through, play out, exhaust, deliver the goods, fill the bill.

finish, bring to a close etc. (*end*) 67; wind up, stamp, clinch, seal, set the seal on, put the seal to; give the -final touch etc. *n.* to; put the -last, – finishing- hand to; crown, – all; cap.

ripen, culminate; come to a -head, – crisis; come to its end; die -a natural death, – of old age; run -its course, – one's race; touch –, reach –; attain- the goal; reach etc. (*arrive*) 292; get in the harvest.

Adj. completing, final; conclu-ding, -sive; crowning etc. *v.*; exhaustive, complete, mature, perfect, consummate.

done, completed 'etc. *v.*; done for, sped, wrought out; highly wrought etc. (*preparation*) 673; thorough etc. 52; ripe etc. (*ready*) 673.

Adv. completely etc. (*thoroughly*) 52; to crown all, out of hand.

Phr. the race is run; *actum est; finis coronat opus; consummatum est; c'en est fait*; it is all over; the game is played out, the bubble has burst.

730. Non-Completion.—N. non-completion, -fulfilment; shortcoming etc. 304; incompleteness etc. 53; drawn -battle, – game; work of Penelope, task of Sisyphus.

non-performance, inexecution; neglect etc. 460.

V. not -complete etc. 729; leave -unfinished etc. *adj.*, – undone; neglect etc. 460; let -alone, – slip; lose sight of.

fall short of etc. 304; do things by halves; scotch the snake, not kill it; hang fire; be slow to; collapse etc. 304.

Adj. not completed etc. *v.*; incomplete etc. 53; uncompleted, unfinished; unaccomplished; un-performed, unexecuted; sketchy, addle.

in progress, in hand; going on, proceeding; on one's hands; on the fire; on the stocks; in preparation; lacking the finishing touch.

Adv. *re infectâ.*

731. Success.—N. success, -fulness; speed; advance etc. (*progress*) 282.

trump card; hit, stroke; lucky −, fortunate −, good- -hit, − stroke; bold −, master- stroke; *coup de maître*, checkmate; half the battle, prize; profit etc. (*acquisition*) 775; best seller.

continued success; good fortune etc. (*prosperity*) 734; time well spent.

advantage over; edge; upper-, whiphand; ascendancy, mastery; expugnation, conquest, victory, subdual; subjugation etc. (*subjection*) 749.

triumph etc. (*exultation*) 884; proficiency etc. (*skill*) 698; conqueror, victor, winner, champion; master of the -situation, − position.

V. succeed; be -successful etc. *adj.*; gain one's - end, − ends; crown with success.

gain −, attain −, carry −, secure −, win- -a point, − an object; put over; make a go of; manage to, contrive to; accomplish etc. (*effect, complete*) 729; do −, work- wonders.

come off -well, − successfully, − with flying colors; make short work of; take −, carry- by storm; bear away the bell; win -one's spurs, − the battle; win −, carry −, gain- the -day, − prize, − palm; climb on the bandwagon; have -the best of it, − it all one's own way, − the game in one's own hands, − the ball at one's feet, − one on the hip; walk over the course; carry all before one, remain in possession of the field; score a success, win hands down.

speed; make progress etc. (*advance*) 282; win −, make −, work −, find- one's way; strive to some purpose, prosper etc. 734; drive a roaring trade; make profit etc. (*acquire*) 775; reap −, gather- the -fruits, − benefit of, − harvest; make one's fortune, get in the harvest, turn to good account; turn to account etc. (*use*) 677.

triumph, be triumphant; gain −, obtain- -a victory, − an advantage; chain victory to one's car.

surmount −, overcome −, get over- -a difficulty, − an obstacle etc. 706; *se tirer d'affaire*; make head against; stem the -torrent, − tide, − current; weather the storm, − a point; turn a corner, keep one's head above water, tide over; master; get −, have −, gain- the -better of, − best of, − upper hand, − ascendancy, − whip hand, − start of; distance; surpass etc. (*superiority*) 33.

defeat, conquer, vanquish, discomfit; over-come, throw, -power, -master, -match, -set, -ride, -reach; out-wit, -do, -flank, -maneuver, -general, -vote; take the wind out of one's adversary's sails; beat, − hollow; rout, lick, drub, floor, worst; put -down, − to flight, − to the rout, − *hors de combat*; − out of court.

silence, quell, nonsuit, checkmate, upset, confound, nonplus, trump; baffle etc. (*hinder*) 706; circumvent, elude; trip up − the heels of; drive - into a corner, − to the wall; run hard, put one's nose out of joint.*

settle, do for; break the -neck of, − back of; capsize, sink, shipwreck, drown, swamp; subdue; subjugate etc. (*subject*) 749; reduce; make the enemy bite the dust; victimize, roll in the dust, trample under foot, put an extinguisher upon.

answer, − the purpose; avail, prevail, take effect, do, turn out well, work well, take, tell, bear fruit; hit -it, − the mark, − the right nail on the head; nick it; turn up trumps, make a hit; find one's account in.

Adj. succeeding etc. *v.*; successful; prosperous

etc. 734; triumphant; flushed −, crowned- with success; victorious; set up; in the ascendant; unbeaten etc. (*see* beat etc. *v.*); well-spent; felicitous, effective, in full swing.

Adv. successfully etc. *adj.*; with flying colors, in triumph, swimmingly; *à merveille*, beyond all hope; to some −, good- purpose; to one's heart's content.

Phr. *veni vidi vici*, the day being one's own, one's star in the ascendant; *omne tulit punctum*.

732. Failure.—N. failure; non-success, -fulfilment; dead failure, successlessness; abortion, miscarriage; *brutum fulmen* etc. 158; labor in vain etc. (*inutility*) 645; no go; inefficacy; inefficaciousness etc. *adj.*; vain −, ineffectual −, abortive- -attempt, − efforts; flash in the pan, 'lame and impotent conclusion;' frustration; slip 'twixt cup and lip etc. (*disappointment*) 509.

blunder etc. (*mistake*) 495; fault, omission, miss, oversight, slip, trip, stumble, claudication, footfall; false −, wrong- step; *faux pas*, titubation, *bévue, faute*, lurch; botchery etc. (*want of skill*) 699; scrape, jam, mess, muddle, foozle, *fiasco*, breakdown.

mishap etc. (*misfortune*) 735; split, collapse, smash, blow, explosion.

repulse, rebuff, defeat, rout, overthrow, discomfiture; beating, drubbing; *quietus*, nonsuit, subjugation; check-, fool's-mate.

fall, downfall, ruin, perdition; wreck etc. (*destruction*) 162; death-blow; bankruptcy etc. (*non-payment*) 808.

losing game, *affaire flambée*.

victim, prey; bankrupt.

V. fail; be -unsuccessful etc. *adj.*; not -succeed etc. 731; make -vain efforts etc. *n.*; do −, labor −, toil- in vain; lose one's labor, take nothing by one's motion; bring to naught, make nothing of; wash a blackamoor white etc. (*impossible*) 471; roll the stone of Sisyphus etc. (*useless*) 645; do by halves etc. (*not complete*) 730; lose ground etc. (*recede*) 283; flunk; fall short of etc. 304.

miss, − one's aim, − the mark, − one's footing, − stays; slip, trip, stumble; make a -slip etc. *n.*, − blunder etc. 495, − mess of, − botch of; bitch it, miscarry, abort, go up like a rocket and come down like the stick, reckon without one's host; get the wrong sow by the ear etc. (*blunder, mismanage*) 699.

limp, halt, hobble, titubate; fall, tumble; lose one's balance; fall -to the ground, − between two stools; flounder, falter, stick in the mud, run aground, split upon a rock; run −, knock −, dash- one's head against a stone wall; break one's back; break down, sink, drown, founder, have the ground cut from under one; get into -trouble, − a mess, − a scrape; come to grief etc. (*adversity*) 735; go to - the wall, − the dogs, − pot; lick −, bite- the dust; be -defeated etc. 731; have the worst of it, lose the day, come off second best, lose; fall a prey to; succumb etc. (*submit*) 725; not have a leg to stand on.

come to nothing, end in smoke; fall -to the ground, − through, − dead, − still-born, − flat; slip through one's fingers; hang −, miss- fire; flash in the pan, collapse; topple down etc. (*descent*) 305; go to wrack and ruin etc. (*destruction*) 162.

go amiss, go wrong, go cross, go hard with, go on a wrong tack; go on −, come off −, turn out

– , work- ill; take -a wrong, – an ugly- turn; gang agley.

be all -over with, – up with; explode; dash one's hopes etc. (*disappoint*) 509; defeat the purpose; upset the apple cart; sow the wind and reap the whirlwind, jump out of the frying pan into the fire.

Adj. unsuccessful, successless; failing, tripping etc. *v.*; at fault; unfortunate etc. 735.

abortive, addle, still-born; fruitless, sterile, bootless; ineffect-ual, -ive; inefficient etc. (*impotent*) 158; inefficacious; lame, hobbling, *décousu*; insufficient etc. ˙640; unavailing etc. (*useless*) 645; of no effect.

aground, grounded, swamped, stranded, cast away, wrecked, foundered, capsized, shipwrecked, non-suited; foiled; defeated etc. 731; struck –, borne –, broken- down; down-trodden; over-borne, -whelmed; all up with; beaten to a frazzle.

lost, undone, ruined, broken; bankrupt etc. (*not paying*) 808; played out; done -up,˙ – for; dead beat, ruined root and branch, *flambé*, knocked on the head; destroyed etc. 162. ˙

frustrated, thwarted, crossed, unhinged, discon-certed, dashed; thrown -off one's balance, – on one's back, – on one's beam ends; unhorsed, in a sorry plight; hard hit.

stultified, befooled, dished, hoist on one's own petard, victimized, sacrificed.

wide of the mark etc. (*error*) 495; out of one's reckoning etc. (*inexpectation*) 508; left in the lurch; thrown away etc. (*wasted*) 638; unattained; uncompleted etc. 730.

Adv. unsuccessfully etc. *adj.*; to little or no pur-pose, in vain, *re infectâ*.

Phr. the bubble has burst, the game is up, all is lost; the devil to pay; *parturiunt montes* etc. (*disappointment*) 509.

733. Trophy.—**N.** trophy; medal, prize, palm; ribbon, blue ribbon, *cordon bleu*; citation; cup, laurel, -s; bays, crown, chaplet, wreath, civic crown; Victoria Cross, V.C., *Croix de Guerre*, Iron Cross; Distinguished Service Cross, Medal of Honor, Congressional Medal; insignia etc. ˙550; feather in one's cap etc. (*honor*) 873; decoration etc. 877; garland, triumphal arch.

triumph etc. (*celebration*) 883; flying colors etc. (*show*) 882.

monumentum aere perennius.

734. Prosperity.—**N.** prosperity, welfare, well-being; affluence etc. (*wealth*) 803; success etc. 731; thrift, roaring trade; chicken in every pot, the full dinner paid; good –, smiles of- fortune; blessings, godsend.

luck; good –, run of- luck; sunshine; fair -weather, – wind; palmy –, bright –, halcyon-days; piping times, tide, flood, high tide.

Saturnia regna, Saturnian age; golden -time, – age; bed of roses; fat of the land, milk and honey, loaves and fishes, fleshpots of Egypt.

made man, lucky dog, *enfant fâté*, spoiled child of fortune.

upstart, *parvenu*, *nouveau riche*, profiteer, skip-jack, mushroom.

V. prosper, thrive, flourish; be -prosperous etc. *adj.*; drive a roaring trade; go on -well, – smoothly, – swimmingly; sail before the wind, swim with the tide; run -smooth, – smoothly, – on all fours.

rise –, get on- in the world; work –, make-one's way; look up; lift –, raise- one's head, make one's -fortune, – pile, feather one's nest.

flower, blow, blossom, bloom, fructify, bear fruit, fatten, batten.

keep oneself afloat; keep –, hold- one's head above water; light –, fall- on one's -legs, – feet; drop into a good thing; bear a charmed life; bask in the sunshine; have a -good, – fine- time of it; have a run, – of luck; have the -good fortune etc. *n.* to; take a favorable turn; live -on the fat of the land, – in clover. ˙

Adj. prosperous; thriving etc. *v.*; in a fair way, buoyant; well -off, – to do, – to do in the world; set up, at one's ease; rich etc. 803; in good case; in -full, – high- feather; fortunate, lucky, in luck; born -with a silver spoon in one's mouth, – under a lucky star; on the sunny side of the hedge.

auspicious, propitious, providential.

palmy, halcyon; agreeable etc. 829; *couleur de rose.*

Adv. prosperously etc. *adj.*; swimmingly; as good luck would have it; beyond all -expectation, – hope, – one's wildest dreams.

Phr. one's star in the ascendant, all for the best, one's course runs smooth.

735. Adversity.—**N.** adversity, evil etc. 619; failure etc. 732; bad –, ill –, evil –, adverse –, hard- -fortune, – hap, – luck, – lot; frowns of fortune; evil -dispensation, – star, – genius; ups and downs of life, broken fortunes; hard -case, – lines, – life; sea –, peck- of troubles; hell upon earth; slough of despond; jinx.

trouble, humiliation, hardship, curse, blight, blast, load, pressure.

pressure of the times, iron age, evil day, time out of joint; hard –, bad –, sad- times; rainy day, cloud, dark cloud, gathering clouds, ill wind; visitation, infliction; affliction etc. (*painfulness*) 830; bitter -pill, – cup; care, trial; the sport of for-tune.

mis-hap, -chance, -adventure, -fortune; disaster, calamity, catastrophe; accident, casualty, cross, reverse, check, *contretemps*, rub, pinch, setback.

losing game; falling etc. *v.*; fall, down-fall, come-down; ruin-ation, -ousness; undoing; extremity; ruin etc. (*destruction*) 162.

V. be -ill off etc. *adj.*; go hard with; fall on evil, – days; go on ill; not -prosper etc. 734.

go -downhill, – to rack and ruin etc. (*destruc-tion*) 162, – to the dogs; fall, – from one's high estate; decay, sink, decline, go down in the world; have seen better days; bring down one's grey hairs with sorrow to the grave; come to grief; be all -over, – up- with; bring a -wasp's, – hornet's- nest about one's ears.

Adj. unfortunate, unblest, unhappy, unlucky; im-, un-prosperous; luck-, hap-less; out of luck; in trouble, in a bad way, in an evil plight; under a cloud; clouded; ill –, badly- off; in adverse cir-cumstances; poor etc. 804; behindhand, down in the world, decayed, undone; on the road to ruin, on its last legs, on the wane; in one's utmost need.

planet-struck, devoted; born -under an evil star, — with a wooden ladle in one's mouth; ill-fated, - starred, -omened; inconspicuous, ominous, doomed, unpropitious.

adverse, untoward; disastrous, calamitous, ruinous, dire, deplorable.

Adv. if the worst come to the worst, as ill luck would have it, from bad to worse, out of the frying pan into the fire.

Phr. one's star is on the wane; one's luck -turns, — fails; the game is up, one's doom is sealed, the ground crumbles under one's feet, *sic transit gloria mundi, tant va la cruche à l'eau qu'à la fin elle se casse.*

736. Mediocrity.—N. moderate —, average- circumstances; respectability; middle classes, *bourgeoisie*; mediocrity; golden mean etc. (*mid- course*) 628, (*moderation*) 174.

V. jog on; go —, get on- -fairly, — quietly, — peaceably, — tolerably, — respectably; steer a middle course etc. 628.

Adj. middling, so-so, fair, medium, moderate, mediocre, second-, third- etc. -rate.

737. Authority.—N. authority; influence, patronage, power, preponderance, credit, *prestige*, prerogative, jurisdiction; right etc. (*title*) 924.

divine right, dynastic rights, authoritativeness; absolut-eness, -ism; despotism, tyranny; *jus nocendi*.

command, empire, sway, rule; domin-ion, - ation; sovereignty, supremacy, suzerainty; lord-, head-ship; chiefdom; seignior-y, -ity, hegemony, patriarchate, patriarchy; master-y, -ship, -dom; government etc. (*direction*) 693; dictation, control.

hold, grasp, grip, -e; reach; iron sway etc. (*severity*) 739; fangs, clutches, talons; rod of em- pire etc. (*scepter*) 747.

reign, regnancy, *régime*, dynasty; director-, dic- tator-ship; protector-ate, -ship; caliphate, pashalic, electorate; presiden-cy, -tship; administration; pro-, consulship; prefecture; seneschalship; magistra-ture, -cy; raj.

empire; monarchy; king-hood, -ship; royalty, regality, autocracy, monocracy, arist-archy, - ocracy; oligarchy, democracy, demogogy; republic, -anism, federalism; socialism, collectivism; com- munism, bolshevism, syndicalism; mob law, mobocracy, ochlocracy, ergatocracy; *vox populi, imperium in imperio*; bureaucracy; beadle-, bum- ble-dom; stratocracy; martial law, military -power, — government; feodality, feudal system, feudalism.

Thearchy, diarchy; du-, tri-, heter-archy; du-, tri- umvirate; auto-cracy, -nomy; limited monarchy; constitutional -government, — monarchy; home rule, autonomy; self-government, -determination; representative government; Soviet government.

gyn-archy, -ocracy, -aeocracy; petticoat govern- ment, matriarchate, matriarchy.

[Vicarious authority] commission etc. 755; deputy etc. 759; permission etc. 760.

country, state, realm, commonwealth, canton, constituency, toparchy, municipality, polity, body politic, *posse comitatus.*

person in authority etc. (*master*) 745; judicature etc. 965; cabinet etc. (*council*) 696; usurper; seat of -government, — authority; head-quarters.

[Acquisition of authority] accession; installation etc. 755; usurpation.

V. authorize etc. (*permit*) 760; warrant etc. (*right*) 924; dictate etc. (*order*) 741; have —, hold —, possess —, exercise —, exert —, wield- - authority etc. *n.*

be -at the head of etc. *adj.*; hold —, be in —, fill an- office; hold —, occupy- a post; be -master etc. 745.

rule, sway, command, control, administer; govern etc. (*direct*) 693; lead, preside over, reign; possess —, be seated on —, occupy- the throne; sway —, wield- the scepter; wear the crown.

have —, get- the -upper, — whip- hand; gain a hold upon, preponderate, dominate, boss, rule the roost; over-ride, -rule, -awe; lord it over, hold in hand, keep under, make a puppet of, lead by the nose, hold in the hollow of one's hand, turn round one's little finger, bend to one's will, hold one's own, wear the breeches; have -the ball at one's feet, — it all one's own way, — the game in one's own hand, — on the hip, — under one's thumb; be master of the situation; take the lead, play first fid- dle, set the fashion; give the law to; carry with a high hand; lay down the law; ride in the whirlwind and direct the storm; rule with a rod of iron etc. (*severity*) 739.

ascend —, mount- the throne, take the reins, — into one's hand; assume -authority etc. *n.*, — the reins of government; take —, assume the- com- mand.

be -governed by, — in the power of; be under - the rule of, — the domination of.

Adj. ruling etc. *v.*; regnant, at the head, dominant, paramount, supreme, predominant, preponderant, in the ascendant, influential; guber- natorial; imperious; authoritative, executive, ad- ministrative, clothed with authority, official, *ex of- ficio*, ministerial, bureaucratic, departmental, im- perative, peremptory, overruling, absolute; hegemonic, -al; arbitrary; compulsory etc. 744; stringent.

regal, sovereign; royal, -ist; monarchical, kingly; imperial, -istic; princely; feudal; aristo-, auto-cratic; oligarchic etc. *n.*; democratic, republican, dynastic.

at one's command; in one's -power, — grasp; un- der control; authorized etc. (*due*) 924.

Adv. in the name of, by the authority of, *de par le Roi*, in virtue of; under the auspices of, in the hands of.

at one's pleasure; by a -dash, — stroke- of the pen; *ex mero motu; ex cathedrâ.*

Phr. the grey mare the better horse; 'every inch a king.'

738. Laxity. [Absence of authority.]—**N.** laxity; lax-, loose-, slack-ness; toleration etc. (*lenity*) 740; freedom etc. 748.

anarchy, interregnum; relaxation; loosening etc. *v.*; remission; dead letter, *brutum fulmen*, misrule; license, licentiousness; insubordination etc. (*disobedience*) 742; lynch law etc. (*illegality*) 964; nihilism.

[Deprivation of power.] dethronement, deposition, usurpation, abdication.

V. be -lax etc. *adj.*; *laisser -faire*, − *aller*; hold a loose rein; give -the reins to, − rope enough, − a loose to; tolerate; relax; misrule.

go beyond the length of one's tether; have one's -swing, − fling; act without -instructions, − authority; act on one's own responsibility, usurp authority.

dethrone, depose; abdicate.

Adj. lax, loose; slack; remiss etc. (*careless*) 460; weak.

relaxed; licensed; reinless, unbridled; anarchical; unauthorized etc. (*unwarranted*) 925.

739. Severity.—N. severity; strictness, formalism, harshness etc. *adj.*; rigor, stringency, austerity; inclemency etc. (*pitilessness*) 914*a*; arrogance etc. 885.

arbitrary power; absolut-, despot-ism; dictatorship, autocracy, tyranny, domineering, oppression; assumption, usurpation; inquisition, reign of terror, martial law; iron -heel, − rule, − hand, − sway; tight grasp; brute -force, − strength; coercion etc. 744; strong −, tight- hand.

hard -lines, − measure; tender mercies [ironical.]; sharp practice; bureaucracy, red tape; pipe-clay, officialism.

tyrant, disciplinarian, martinet, stickler, formalist, bashaw, despot, hard master, Draco, oppressor, inquisitor, extortioner, harpy, vulture, bird of prey.

V. be -severe etc. *adj.*

assume, usurp, arrogate, take liberties; domineer, bully etc. 885; tyrannize, inflict, wreak, stretch a point, put on the screw; be hard upon; bear −, lay- a heavy hand on; be −, come- down upon; illtreat; deal-hardly with, − hard measure to; rule with a rod of iron, chastise with scorpions; dye with blood; oppress, override; trample −, tread--down, − upon, − under foot; crush under an iron heel, ride roughshod over; rivet the yoke; hold −, keep- a tight hand; force down the throat; coerce etc. 744; give no quarter etc. (*pitiless*) 914*a*.

Adj. severe; strict, hard, harsh, dour, rigid, stiff, stern, rigorous, uncompromising, exacting, exigent, *exigeant*, inexorable, inflexible, obdurate, austere, relentless, Spartan, Draconian, stringent, strait-laced, puritanical, prudish, searching, unsparing, ironhanded, hard-headed, peremptory, absolute, positive, arbitrary, imperative; coercive etc. 744; tyrannical, despotic, masterful, extortionate, grinding, withering, oppressive, inquisitorial; inclement etc. (*ruthless*) 914*a*; cruel etc. (*malevolent*) 907; haughty, arrogant etc. 885.

Adv. severely etc. *adj.*; with a -high, − strong, − tight, − heavy-hand.

at the point of the -sword, − bayonet.

Phr. *Delirant reges plectuntur Achivi.*

740. Leniency.—N. leni-ency, -ence, -ty; moderation etc. 174; toler-ance, -ation; mildness, gentleness; favor; indulgen-ce, -cy; clemency, mercy, forbearance, quarter; compassion etc. 914.

V. be -lenient etc. *adj.*; tolerate, bear with; *parcere subjectis*, give quarter.

indulge, allow one to have his own way, spoil.

Adj. lenient; mild, − as milk; gentle, soft; tolerant, indulgent, easy-going; clement etc. (*compassionate*) 914; forbearing; complaisant, long-suffering.

741. Command.—N. command, order, ordinance, act, *fiat*, bidding, *dictum*, hest, behest, call, beck, nod.

des-, dis-patch; message, direction, injunction, charge, instructions; appointment, fixture.

demand, exaction, imposition, requisition, claim, reclamation, revendication; *ultimatum* etc. (*terms*) 770; request etc. 765; requirement.

dictation; dict-, mand-ate; *caveat*, decree, decree -nisi, − absolute, *senatus consultum*; precept; pre-, re-script; writ, ordination, bull, edict, decretal, dispensation, prescription, brevet, placet, ukase, *firman*, hatti-sheriff, warrant, passport, *mittimus, mandamus*, summons, subpoena, *nisi prius*, interpellation, citation; word, − of command; *mot d'ordre*; bugle −, trumpet- call; beat of drum, tattoo; order of the day; enactment etc. (*law*) 963; *plébiscite* etc. (*choice*) 609.

V. command, order, decree, enact, ordain, dictate, direct, give orders.

prescribe, set, appoint, mark out; set −, prescribe −, impose- a task; set to work, put in requisition etc. 926.

bid, enjoin, charge, call upon, instruct; require, − at the hands of; exact, impose, tax, task; demand; insist on etc. (*compel*) 744.

claim, lay claim to, revendicate, reclaim.

cite, summon; call −, send- for; subpoena; beckon.

issue a command; make −, issue −, promulgate- -a requisition, − a decree, − an order etc. *n.*; give the -word of command, − word, − signal; call to order; give −, lay down- the law; assume the command etc. (*authority*) 737; remand.

be -ordered etc.; receive an order etc. *n.*

Adj. commanding etc. *v.*; authoritative etc. 737; decret-ory, -ive, -al; imperative, jussive, decisive, final.

Adv. in a commanding tone; by a -stroke, − dash- of the pen; by order, at beat of drum, on the first summons; at the word of command.

Phr. the decree is gone forth; *sic volo sic jubeo*; *le Roi le veut.*

742. Disobedience.—N. disobedience, insubordination, contumacy; infraction, -fringement; violation, non-compliance; non-observance etc. 773.

revolt, rebellion, mutiny, outbreak, rising, uprising, putsch, insurrection, *émeute*; riot, tumult etc. (*disorder*) 59; strike etc. (*resistance*) 719; barring out; defiance etc. 715.

mutinousness etc. *adj.*; mutineering; sedition, treason; high −, petty −, misprison of- treason; *premunire*; *lèse- majesté*; violation of law etc. 964; defection, secession, revolution, *sabotage*, bolshevism, *Sinn Fein.*

insurgent, mutineer, rebel, revolter, rioter, traitor, *carbonaro*, *sansculottes*, red republican, communist, Fenian, chartist, *frondeur*; seceder, runagate, brawler, anarchist, demagogue; suffragette; Spartacus, Masaniello, Wat Tyler, Jack Cade; bolshevist, bolshevik, maximalist, ringleader.

V. disobey, violate, infringe; shirk; set at defiance etc. (*defy*) 715; set authority at naught, run riot, fly in the face of, bolt, take the law into one's own hands; kick over the traces.

turn –, run- restive; champ the bit; strike etc. (*resist*) 719; rise, – in arms; secede; mutiny, rebel.

Adj. disobedient; uncompl-ying, -iant; unsubmissive; unruly, ungovernable; insubordinate, impatient of control; rest-iff, -ive; refractory, contumacious; recusant etc. (*refuse*) 764; recalcitrant; resisting etc. 719; lawless, mutinous, seditious, insurgent, riotous, revolutionary.

disobeyed, unobeyed; unbidden.

743. Obedience.—N. obedience; observance etc. 772; compliance; submission etc. 725; subjection etc. 749; non-resistance; passiveness, passivity, resignation.

allegiance, loyalty, fealty, homage, deference, devotion, fidelity, constancy.

submiss-ness, -iveness; ductility etc. (*softness*) 324; obsequiousness etc. (*servility*) 886.

V. be -obedient etc. *adj.*; obey, bear obedience to; submit etc. 725; comply, answer the helm, come at one's call; do -one's bidding, – what one is told, – suit and service; attend to orders, serve - devotedly, –, loyally, – faithfully.

follow, – the lead of, – to the world's end; serve etc. 746; play second fiddle.

Adj. obedient; compl-ying, -iant; law-abiding, loyal, faithful, leal, devoted; at one's -call, – command, – orders, – beck and call; under - beck and call, – control.

restrainable; resigned, passive; submissive etc. 725; henpecked; pliant etc. (*soft*) 324.

unresist-ed, -ing.

Adv. obediently etc. *adj.*; in compliance with, in obedience to.

Phr. to hear is to obey; as – , if- you please; at your service.

744. Compulsion.—N. compulsion, coercion, coaction, constraint, eminent domain, duress, enforcement, press, conscription.

force; brute –, main –, physical- force; the sword, *ultima ratio*; club –, mob –, lynch- law; *argumentum baculinum*, *le droit du plus fort*, martial law.

restraint etc. 751; necessity etc. 601; *force majeure*; Hobson's choice; the spur of necessity.

V. compel, force, make, drive, coerce, constrain, enforce, necessitate, oblige.

force upon, press; cram –, thrust –, force-down the throat; say it must be done, make a point of, insist upon, take no denial; put down, dragoon.

extort, wring from; put –, turn- on the screw; drag into; bind, – over; pin –, tie- down; require, tax, put in force; commandeer; restrain etc. 751.

Adj. compelling etc. *v.*; coercive, coactive; inexorable etc. 739; compuls-ory, -atory; obligatory, stringent, peremptory, binding.

forcible, not to be trifled with; irresistible etc. 601; compelled etc. *v.*; fain to.

Adv. by -force etc. *n.*, – force of arms; on compulsion, perforce; *vi et armis*, under the lash; at the point of the -sword, – bayonet; forcibly; by a strong arm.

under protest, in spite of one's teeth; against one's will etc. 603; *nolens volens* etc. (*of necessity*) 601; by stress of -circumstances, – weather; under press of; *de rigueur*.

745. Master.—N. master, *padrone*; lord, – paramount; command-er, -ant; captain; chief, -tain; *sahib*, sirdar, sachem, sheik, head, senior, governor, *duce*, ruler, dictator; leader etc. (*director*) 694.

lord of the ascendant; cock of the -walk, – roost; grey mare; mistress.

potentate; liege, – lord; suzerain, sovereign, monarch, autocrat, despot, tyrant, oligarch, overlord.

crowned head, emperor, king, anointed king, majesty, *imperator*, protector, president, stadtholder, judge.

caesar, kaiser, czar, sultan, grand Turk, caliph, imaum, shah, padishah, sophi, mogul, great mogul, khan, cham; lama, tycoon, mikado, inca, cazique; domn; vaivode; wai-, way-wode; landamman; seyyid, cacique.

prince, duke etc. (*nobility*) 875; arch-duke, doge, elector; seignior; mar-, land-grave; rajah, emir, nizam, nawab, negus.

empress, queen, sultana, czarina, princess, infanta, duchess, margravine, begum, maharani.

regent, viceroy, exarch, palatine, khedive, hospodar, beglerbeg, three-tailed bashaw, pasha, pashaw, bashaw, bey, beg, dey, scherif, tetrarch, satrap, mandarin, subhadar, nabob, maharajah; burgrave; laird etc. (*proprietor*) 779; High Commissioner.

the -authorities, – powers that be, – government; staff, *état major*, aga, official, man in office, person in authority.

[Naval authorities] admiral, -ty, – of the fleet; rear-, vice-, port-admiral; senior-, naval officer, S.N.O., commodore, captain, commander, lieutenant-commander, lieutenant, sub-lieutenant, midshipman, warrant –, petty- officer, leading seaman; skipper, mate, master.

[Military authorities] marshal, field-marshal, *maréchal*; general, -issimo; commander-in-chief, *seraskier*, *hetman*; lieutenant–, major-general; commandant; colonel, lieutenant-colonel, major, captain, centurion, skipper, lieutenant, second-lieutenant, officer, staff-officer, *aide de camp*, brigadier, brigade-major, adjutant, *jemidar*, ensign, cornet, cadet, subaltern, warrant officer, quartermaster, noncommissioned officer, N.C.O.; sergeant, -major; top-sergeant, color sergeant; corporal, -major; lance-, acting-corporal; drum major; shavetail.

[Air authorities] air -marshal, – commodore; group captain, squadron leader, wing commander, flight lieutenant, flying –, pilot- officer.

[Civil authorities] judge etc. 967; mayor, -alty; prefect, chancellor, archon, provost, magistrate, syndic; alcalde, alcaid; burgomaster, *corregidor*, seneschal, alderman, warden, constable, portreeve; lord mayor, sheriff; officer etc. (*executive*) 965.

746. Servant.—N. subject, liegeman; servant, retainer, follower, henchman, servitor, domestic, menial, help, lady help, *employé, attaché*; official.

retinue, suite, *cortège*, staff, court.

attendant, squire, usher, page, buttons, donzel, footboy; dog robber; train-, cup-bearer; waiter, busboy, tapster, butler, livery servant, lackey, footman, flunkey, valet, *valet de chambre*; boots; scout, gyp; equerry, groom; jockey, hostler, ostler, tiger, orderly, messenger, cad, gillie, caddie; *wallah*; journeyman, herdsman, swineherd.

bailiff, castellan, seneschal, chamberlain, *major-domo*, groom of the chambers.

secretary; under −, assistant- secretary; clerk; clerical staff, stenographer, subsidiary; agent etc. 758; subaltern; under-ling, -strapper; man.

maid, -servant, waitress; handmaid; *confidente*, lady's maid, abigail, *soubrette*; nurse, *bonne, ayah*; nurse-, nursery-, house-, parlor-, waiting-, chamber-, kitchen-, scullery-, between −, laundry −, dairy-maid; *femme* −, *fille- de chambre*; *camarista*; *chef de cuisine, cordon bleu*, cook, scullion, Cinderella; maid −, servant- of all work, tweeny, general servant, girl, slavey; laundress, bed-maker, goodie, char-woman etc. (*worker*) 690.

serf, vassal, slave, negro, helot; bondsman, -woman; bondslave; *âme damnée, odalisque*, ryot, *adscriptus glebae*; vill-ain, -ein; bead-, bede-sman; sizar; pension-er, -ary; client; dependant, -ent; hanger on, stooge, satellite; parasite etc. (*servility*) 886; led captain; *protégé*, ward, hireling, mercenary, puppet, creature.

badge of slavery; bonds etc. 752.

V. serve; minister to, wait −, attend −, dance attendance −, pin oneself- upon; squire, tend, hang on the sleeve of, char, do for; fag; valet.

Adj. in the train of; in one's -pay, − employ; at one's call etc. (*obedient*) 743; in bonds.

747. Scepter. [Insignia of authority.]—N. scepter, regalia, rod of empire, sword of state, mace, *fasces*, wand; staff, − of office; *bâton*, truncheon; flag etc. (*insignia*) 550; ensign −, emblem −, badge −, insignia- of authority, rank marks, brassard, badge, sash; cocked −, brass- hat.

epaulette, aiguilette, crown, star, eagle, bar, double bar, pip, stripe, chevron, curl, ring, anchor, shoulder-strap, tab.

throne, chair, musnud, divan, dais, woolsack.

toga, pall, mantle, robes of state, ermine, purple.

crown, coronet, diadem, tiara, triple crown, miter, crozier, cardinal's hat etc.; cap of maintenance; decoration; title etc. 877; portfolio.

key, signet, seals, talisman; helm; reins etc. (*means of restraint*) 752.

748. Freedom.—N. freedom, liberty, independence; license etc. (*permission*) 760; facility etc. 705.

scope, range, latitude, play; free −, full- -play, − scope; free stage and no favor; swing, full swing, elbow-room, margin, rope, wide berth; Liberty Hall.

franchise, denization; free −, freed-, liveryman; denizen.

autonomy, self-government, homerule, self-determination, liberalism, free trade; non-interference etc. 706.

immunity, exemption; emancipation etc. (*liberation*) 750; en-, af-franchisement; rights, privileges.

free land, freehold; allodium; frankalmoigne, mortmain.

independent, free-lance, -thinker, -trader.

V. be -free etc. *adj.*; have -scope etc. *n.*, − the run of, − one's own way, − a will of one's own, − one's fling; do what one -likes, − wishes, − pleases, − chooses; go at large, feel at home, paddle one's own canoe; stand on one's -legs, − rights; shift for oneself.

take a liberty; make -free with, − oneself quite at home; use a freedom; take -leave, − French leave.

set free etc. (*liberate*) 750; give the reins to etc. (*permit*) 760; allow −, give- scope etc. *n.* to; give a horse his head.

make free of; give the -freedom of, − franchise; en-, af-franchise.

laisser -faire, − aller; live and let live; leave to oneself; leave −, let- alone; mind one's own business.

Adj. free, − as air; out of harness, independent, at large, loose, scot free; left -alone, − to oneself.

in full swing; uncaught, unconstrained, unbuttoned, unconfined, unrestrained, unchecked, unprevented, unhindered, unobstructed, unbound, uncontrolled, untrammeled.

unsubject, ungoverned, unenslaved, unenthralled, unchained, unshackled, unfettered, unreined, unbridled, uncurbed, unmuzzled, unimpeded.

unrestricted, unlimited, unconditional; absolute; discretionary etc. (*optional*) 600.

unassailed, unforced, uncompelled.

unbiassed, unprejudiced, uninfluenced, spontaneous.

free and easy; at −, at one's- ease; *dégagé*, quite at home; wanton, rampant, irrepressible, unvanquished.

exempt; freed etc. 750; freeborn; autonomous, freehold, allodial; *gratis* etc. 815.

unclaimed, going a begging.

Adv. freely etc. *adj.*; *ad libitum* etc. (*at will*) 600.

749. Subjection.—N. subjection; depend-ence, -ance, -ency; subordination; thrall, thraldom, enthralment, subjugation, bondage, serfdom; feudal--ism, -ity; vassalage, villenage; slavery, enslavement, involuntary servitude.

service; servi-tude, -torship; tendence, employ, tutelage, clientship; liability etc. 177; constraint etc. 751; oppression etc. (*severity*) 739; yoke etc. (*means of restraint*) submission etc. 725; obedience etc. 743.

V. be -subject etc. *adj.*; be −, lie- at the mercy of; depend −, lean −, hang- upon; fall -a prey to, − under; play second fiddle.

be a -mere machine, − puppet, − football; not dare to say one's soul is his own; drag a chain.

serve etc. 746; obey etc. 743; submit etc. 725.

break in, tame; subject, subjugate; master etc. 731; tread -down, − under foot; weigh down; drag at one's chariot wheels; reduce to -subjection, −

slavery; en-, in-, be-thral; enslave, lead captive; take into custody etc. (*restrain*) 751; rule etc. 737; drive into a corner, hold at the sword's point; keep under; hold in -bondage, - leading strings, - swaddling clothes.

Adj. subject, dependent, subordinate; feud-al, - atory; in subjection to, under control; in -leading strings, - harness; subjected, enslaved etc. *v*.; con-strained etc. 751; subservient, servile, fawning, slavish, obsequious, cringing; down-trodden; over-borne, -whelmed; under the lash, on the hip, led by the nose, henpecked; the -puppet, - sport, - plaything- of; under one's -orders, - command, - thumb; like dirt under one's feet; a slave to; at the mercy of; in the -power, - hands, - clutches- of; at the feet of; at one's beck and call etc. (*obedient*) 743; liable etc. 177; parasitical; stipendiary.

Adv. under.

750. Liberation.—N. liberation, disengagement, release, disenthrallment, enlargement, emancipation; af-, en-franchisement; manumission; discharge, dismissal.

deliverance etc. 672; redemption, extrication, acquittance, absolution; acquittal etc. 970; escape etc. 671.

V. liberate, free; set -free, - clear, - at liberty; render free, emancipate, release; en-, af-franchise; manumit; enlarge; dis-band, -charge, -miss, - enthral; let -go, - loose, - out, - slip; cast -, turn- adrift; deliver etc. 672; absolve etc. (*acquit*) 970; reprieve.

unfetter etc. 751; untie etc. 44; loose etc. (*disjoin*) 44; loosen, relax; un-bolt, -bar, -close, -cork, -clog, -hand, -bind, -latch, -chain, -harness; dis-engage, -entangle; clear, extricate, unloose.

gain -, obtain -, acquire- one's -liberty etc. 748; get -rid, - clear- of; deliver oneself from; shake off the yoke, slip the collar; break -loose, - prison; tear asunder one's bonds, cast off trammels; escape etc. 671.

Adj. at -liberty, - large, free, liberated etc. *v*.; out of harness etc. 748; adrift.

Int. unhand me! let me go!

751. Restraint.—N. restraint; hindrance etc. 706; coercion etc. (*compulsion*) 744; cohibition, constraint, repression; discipline, control, self-restraint etc. 604.

confinement; durance, duress; im-, prisonment; incarceration, coarctation, entombment, man-cipation, durance vile, thrall, -dom, limbo, cap-tivity; blockade; quarantine; detention.

arrest, -ation; custody, keep, care, charge, ward, restringency.

curb etc. (*means of restraint*) 752; *lettres de cachet*.

limitation, restriction, protection, monopoly; prohibition etc. 761; economic pressure.

prisoner etc. 754.

V. restrain, check; put -, lay- under restraint; en-, in-, be-thral; restrict; debar etc. (*hinder*) 706; constrain; coerce etc. (*compel*) 744; curb, control; hold -, keep- -back, - from, - in, - in check, - within bounds; hold in -leash, - leading strings; withhold.

keep under; repress, suppress; smother; pull in, rein in; hold, - fast; keep a tight hand on; prohibit etc. 761; in-, co-hibit.

enchain; fasten etc. (*join*) 43; fetter, shackle; en-, trammel; bridle, muzzle, gag, pinion, manacle, handcuff, tie one's hands, hobble, bind hand and foot; swathe, swaddle; pin -, peg- down; tether, picket; tie -, up, - down; secure; forge fetters.

confine; shut -, clap -, lock -, box -, mew -, bottle -, cork -, seal -, button- up; shut -, hem -, bolt -, wall -, rail- in; impound, pen, coop; enclose etc. (*circumscribe*) 229; cage; in-, en-cage; close the door upon, cloister; imprison, immure; incarcerate, entomb; clap -, lay- under hatches; put in -irons, - a strait waistcoat; throw -, cast- into prison; put into bilboes.

arrest; take -up, - charge of, - into custody; take -, make- -prisoner, - captive; captivate; lead -captive, - into captivity; send -, commit- to prison; commit; give in -charge, - custody; subjugate etc. 749.

Adj. re-, con-strained; imprisoned etc. *v*.; pent up; jammed in, wedged in; under -restraint, - lock and key, - hatches; serving -, doing- time; in swaddling clothes; on *parole*; in custody etc. (*prisoner*) 754; cohibitive; coactive etc. (*compulsory*) 744.

stiff, restringent, straitlaced, hide-bound.

ice-, wind-, weather-bound; 'cabined, cribbed, confined;' in Lob's pound, laid by the heels.

Adv. in captivity, under arrest, behind the bars, in -prison, - jail, - durance vile.

752. Prison. [Means of restraint.]—**N.** prison, -house; jail, gaol, cage, coop, den, death house, condemned -, cell; stronghold, fortress, keep, donjon, dungeon, *Bastille, oubliette*, bridewell, house of correction, hulks, tool-booth, panopticon, penitentiary, guard-room, clink, can, stir, tronk, jug, lock-up, hold; round -, watch -, station -, sponging-house; station; house of detention, black hole, pen, fold, pound; enclosure etc. 232; penal settlement; chain gang; debtors' prison; reform-atory; federal penitentiary, state prison; criminal lunatic asylum; bilboes, stocks, limbo, quod.

Dartmoor, Newgate, Fleet, Marshalsea; King's (*or* Queen's) Bench; Sing Sing, Dannemora.

bond; strap, bandage, splint, tourniquet; irons, pinion, gyve, fetter, shackle, trammel, manacle, handcuff, bracelets, darbies, strait waistcoat, strait-jacket.

yoke, collar, halter, harness; muzzle, gag, bit, brake, curb, snaffle, bridle, rein, -s; ribbons, lines, bearing-rein; martingale, leading string; tether, picket, band, guy, chain; cord etc. (*fastening*) 45.

bolt, bar, lock, padlock, rail, wall; paling, palisade; fence; barrier, barricade.

brake, drag etc. (*hindrance*) 706.

753. Keeper.—N. keeper, custodian, *custos*, ranger, warder, jailer, gaoler, turnkey, castellan, guard; watch, -dog, -man; Charley; sen-try, -tinel; watch and ward; *concierge*, coast-guard, *guarda costa*, gamekeeper.

escort, body guard, convoy.

protector, governor, duenna; guardian; gover-ness etc. (*teacher*) 540; nurse, *bonne, ayah, amah*.

754. Prisoner.—N. prisoner, captive, *détenu*, close prisoner.

jail-bird, ticket-of-leave man.

V. stand committed; be -imprisoned etc. 751.

Adj. imprisoned etc. 751; in -prison, − quod, − durance vile, − limbo, − custody, − charge, − chains; under -lock and key, − hatches; on *parole*; detained at his Majesty's pleasure.

755. Commission. [Vicarious authority.]—N. commission, delegation; con−, as-signment; procuration; deputation, legation, mission, embassy; agency, agentship; power of attorney, proxy; clerkship.

errand, charge, *brevet*, diploma, *exequatur*, permit etc. (*permission*) 760.

appointment, nomination, return; charter; ordination; installation, inauguration, investiture; accession, coronation, enthronement.

vicegerency; regency, regentship.

viceroy etc. 745; consignee etc. 758; deputy etc. 759.

V. commission, delegate, depute; consign, assign; charge; in−, en-trust; turn over to; commit, − to the hands of; authorize etc. (*permit*) 760.

put in commission, accredit, engage, hire, bespeak, appoint, name, nominate, return, ordain; install, induct, inaugurate, invest, crown; en-roll, -list.

employ, empower; give power of attorney to; set −, place- over; send out.

be commissioned, be accredited; represent, stand for; stand in the -stead, − place, − shoes- of.

Adj. commissioned etc. *v.*

Adv. *per procuratione.*

756. Abrogation.—N. abrogation, annulment, nullification; cancelling etc. *v.*; cancel; revo-cation, -kement; repeal, rescission, defeasance.

dismissal, *congé*, demission; depos-al, -ition; sack, dethronement; disestablish-, disendow-ment; deconsecration.

aboli-tion, -shment; dissolution.

counter-order, -mand; repudiation, retractation; recantation etc. (*tergiversation*) 607.

V. abrogate, annul, cancel; destroy etc. 162; abolish; revoke, repeal, rescind, reverse, retract, recall; over-rule, -ride; set aside; disannul, dissolve, quash, nullify; declare null and void; dis-establish, -endow; deconsecrate.

disclaim etc. (*deny*) 536; ignore, repudiate; recant etc. 607; divest oneself, break off.

counter-mand, -order; do away with; sweep −, brush- away; throw -overboard, − to the dogs; scatter to the winds, cast behind.

dismiss, discard; cast −, turn- -off, − out, − adrift, − out of doors, − aside, − away; send -off, − away, − about one's business; discharge, get rid of, fire out, fire etc. (*eject*) 297; jilt.

cashier; break; oust; set down, unseat, -saddle; un−, de−, disen-throne; depose, uncrown; unfrock, strike off the roll; dis-bar, -bench.

be -abrogated etc.; receive its quietus.

Adj. abrogated etc. *v.*; *functus officio.*

Int. get along with you! begone! go about your business! away with!

757. Resignation.—N. resignation, retirement, abdication, renunciation, abjuration, disclaimer, abandonment, relinquishment.

V. resign; give −, throw- up; lay down, throw up the cards, wash one's hands of, abjure, renounce, forego, disclaim, abandon, relinquish, retract, demit; deny etc. 536.

abrogate etc. 756; desert etc. (*relinquish*) 624; get rid of etc. 782.

abdicate; vacate, − one's seat; accept the stewardship of the Chiltern Hundreds; retire; tender −, send in −, hand in- one's resignation.

Adj. abdicant, renunciatory etc. *v.*

Phr. 'Othello's occupation's gone.'

758. Consignee.—N. consignee, trustee, nominee, committee.

delegate; commiss-ary, -ioner; emissary, envoy, commissionaire; messenger etc. 534.

diplomatist, diplomat, *corps diplomatique*, embassy; am−, em-bassador; representative, resident, consul, legate, nuncio, internuncio, *chargé d' affaires, attaché.*

vicegerent etc. (*deputy*) 759; plenipotentiary.

functionary, placeman, curator; treasurer etc. 801; agent, factor, bailiff, steward, clerk, secretary, attorney, solicitor, proctor, broker, underwriter, commission agent, auctioneer, one's man of business; factotum etc. (*director*) 694; caretaker.

negotiator, go between; middleman; under agent, *employé*; servant etc. 746.

salesman; commercial, − traveler; bagman, *commis-voyageur*, touter.

newspaper −, own −, war −, special-correspondent; reporter.

759. Deputy.—N. deputy, substitute, vice, proxy, *locum tenens*, delegate, representative, next friend, surrogate, secondary.

regent, vicegerent, vizier, minister, vicar; premier etc. (*director*) 694; chancellor, prefect, provost, warden, lieutenant, archon, consul, proconsul; viceroy etc. (*governor*) 745; commissioner etc. 758; plenipotentiary, *alter ego.*

team, eight, eleven; champion.

V. be -deputy etc. *n.*; stand −, appear −, hold a brief −, answer- for; represent; stand −, walk- in the shoes of; stand in the stead of.

substitute, ablegate, accredit; commission, empower, delegate etc. 755.

Adj. acting; vice, -regal; accredited to.

Adv. in behalf of, by proxy.

760. Permission.—N. permission, leave, allow-, suffer-ance; toler-ance, -ation; liberty, law, license, concession, grace; indulgence etc. (*lenity*) 740; favor, dispensation, exemption, release; connivance; vouchsafement.

authorization, warranty, accordance, admission.

permit, warrant, *brevet*, precept, sanction, authority, *firman*; pass, -port; furlough, license, *carte blanche*, ticket of leave; grant, charter, patent.

V. permit; give -permission etc. *n.*, − power;

let, allow, admit; suffer, bear with, tolerate, recognize; concede etc. 762; accord, vouchsafe, favor, humor, gratify, indulge, stretch a point; wink at, connive at; shut one's eyes to.

grant, empower, charter, enfranchise, privilege, confer a privilege, license, authorize, warrant; sanction; entrust etc. (*commission*) 755.

give -*carte blanche*; – the reins to, – scope to etc. (*freedom*) 748; leave -alone, – it to one, – the door open; open the -door to, – floodgates; give a loose to.

let off; absolve etc. (*acquit*) 970; release, exonerate, dispense with.

ask –, beg –, request- -leave, – permission.

Adj. permitting etc. *v.*; permissive, indulgent; permitted etc. *v.*; patent, chartered, permissible, allowable, lawful, legitimate, legal; legalized etc. (*law*) 963; licit; unforbid, -den; unconditional.

Adv. permissibly; by –, with –, on- -leave etc. *n.*; *speciali gratiá*; under favor of; *pace*; *ad libitum* etc. (*freely*) 748, (*at will*) 600; by all means etc. (*willingly*) 602; yes etc. (*assent*) 488.

761. Prohibition.—N. pro-, in-hibition; *veto*, disallowance; interdict, -ion; injunction; embargo, ban, *verboten*, taboo, proscription; *index expurgatorius*; restriction etc. (*restraint*) 751; hindrance etc. 706; forbidden fruit.

V. pro-, in-hibit; forbid, put one's *veto* upon, disallow; bar; debar etc. (*hinder*) 706, forefend.

keep -in, – within bounds; restrain etc. 751; cohibit, withhold, limit, circumscribe, clip the wings of, restrict, narrow; interdict, taboo; put –, place- under -an interdiction, – the ban; proscribe, censor; exclude, shut out; shut –, bolt –, show- the door; warn off; dash the cup from one's lips; forbid the banns.

Adj. prohibit-ive, -ory; interdictive; proscriptive; restrictive, exclusive; forbidding etc. *v.*

prohibited etc. *v.*; not -permitted etc. 760; unlicensed, contraband, under the ban of; illegal etc. 964; unauthorized, not to be thought of.

Adv. on no account etc. (*no*) 536.

Int. forbid it heaven! etc. (*deprecation*) 766. hands –, keep- off! hold! stop! avast!

Phr. that will never do.

762. Consent.—N. consent; assent etc. 488; acquiescence; approval etc. 931; compliance, agreement, concession; yield-ance, -ingness; accession, acknowledgment, acceptance, agnition.

settlement, ratification, confirmation, adjustment.

permit etc. (*permission*) 760; promise etc. 768.

V. consent; assent etc. 488; yield assent, admit, allow, concede, grant, yield; come -over, – round; give in to, acknowledge, agnize, give consent, comply with, acquiesce, agree to, fall in with, accede, accept, embrace an offer, close with, take at one's word, have no objection.

satisfy, meet one's wishes, settle, come to terms etc. 488; not -refuse etc. 764; turn a willing ear etc. (*willingness*) 602; jump at; deign, vouchsafe; promise etc. 768.

Adj. consenting etc. *v.*; agreeable, compliant; agreed etc. (*assent*) 488; unconditional.

Adv. yes etc. (*assent*) 488; by all means etc. (*willingly*) 602; if –, as- you please; be it so, so be it, well and good, of course.

763. Offer.—N. offer, proffer, presentation, tender, bid, overture; propos-al, -ition; motion, invitation; candidature; offering etc. (*gift*) 784.

V. offer, proffer, present, tender; bid; propose, move; make -a motion, – advances; start; invite, hold out, place- at one's disposal, – in one's way, put forward.

hawk about; offer for sale etc. 796; press etc. (*request*) 765; lay at one's feet.

offer –, present- oneself; volunteer, come forward, be a candidate; stand –, bid- for; seek; be at one's service; go a begging; bribe etc. (*give*) 784.

Adj. offer-ing, -ed etc. *v.*; in the market, for sale, to let, disengaged, on hire.

764. Refusal.—N. refusal, rejection; non-, incompliance; denial; declining etc. *v.*; declension; peremptory –, flat –, point blank- refusal; repulse, rebuff; discountenance.

recusancy, renunciation, abnegation, negation, protest, disclaimer; dissent etc. 489; revocation etc. 756.

V. refuse, reject, deny, decline; nill, negative; refuse –, withhold- one's assent; shake the head; close the -hand, – purse; grudge, begrudge, be slow to, hang fire.

be deaf to; turn -a deaf ear to, – one's back upon; set one's face against, discountenance, not hear of, have nothing to do with, wash one's hands of, stand aloof, forswear, set aside, cast behind one; not yield an inch etc. (*obstinacy*) 606.

resist, cross; not -grant etc. 762; repel, repulse; shut –, slam- the door in one's face; rebuff; send -back, – to the right about, – away with a flea in the ear; deny oneself, not be at home to; discard etc. (*repudiate*) 610; rescind etc. (*revoke*) 756; disclaim, protest; dissent etc. 489.

Adj. refusing etc. *v.*; rest-ive, -iff; recusant; uncomplying, noncompliant, unconsenting, uncomplaisant, protestant; not willing to hear of, deaf to.

refused etc. *v.*; ungranted, out of the question, not to be thought of, impossible.

Adv. no etc. 536; on no account, not for the world; no thank you.

Phr. *non possumus*; [ironically] your humble servant; *bien obligé*.

765. Request.—N. requ-est, -isition; claim etc. (*demand*) 741; petition, suit, prayer; begging letter, round-robin.

motion, overture, application, canvass, address, appeal, apostrophe; imprecation; rogation; proposal, proposition.

orison etc. (*worship*) 990; incantation etc. (*spell*) 993.

mendicancy; asking, panhandling, begging etc. *v.*; postulation, solicitation, invitation, entreaty, importunity, supplication, instance, impetration, imploration, obsecration, obtestation, invocation, interpellation.

V. request, ask; beg, crave, sue, pray, petition, solicit, invite, pop the question, make bold to ask; beg -leave, — a boon; apply to, call to, put to; call -upon, — for; make —, address —, prefer —, put up- a -request, — prayer, — petition; make - application, — a requisition; ask —, trouble- one for; claim etc. (*demand*) 741; offer up prayers etc. (*worship*) 990; whistle for.

beg hard, entreat, beseech, plead, supplicate, implore, apostrophize; conjure, adjure; obtest; cry to, kneel to, appeal to; invoke, evoke; impetrate, imprecate, ply, press, urge, beset, importune, dun, tax, clamor for; cry -aloud, — for help; fall on one's knees; throw oneself at the feet of; come down on one's marrow-bones.

beg from door to door, send the hat round, go a begging; mendicate, mump, cadge, panhandle, beg one's bread.

dance attendance on, besiege, knock at the door.

bespeak, canvass, tout, make interest, court; seek, bid for etc. (*offer*) 763; publish the banns.

Adj. requesting etc. *v.*; precatory; suppli-ant, -cant, -catory; invoc-, imprec-, rog-atory; postulant, mendicant.

importunate, clamorous, urgent; solicitous; cap in hand; on one's -knees, — bended knees, — marrow-bones.

Adv. prithee, do, please, pray; be so good as, be good enough; have the goodness, vouchsafe, will you, I pray thee, if you please.

Int. for -God's, — heaven's, — goodness', — mercy's- sake.

---

766. Deprecation. [Negative request.]—**N.** deprecation, expostulation; remonstrance; intercession, mediation.

V. deprecate, protest, expostulate, enter a protest, intercede for.

Adj. deprecatory, expostulatory, intercessory, mediatorial.

deprecated, protested.

un-, unbe-sought; unasked etc. (*see* ask etc. 765).

Int. cry you mercy! God forbid! forbid it Heaven! Heaven -forefend, — forbid! far be it from! hands off! etc. (*prohibition*) 761.

---

767. Petitioner.—**N.** petitioner, solicitor, applicant; suppli-ant, -cant; suitor, candidate, claimant, postulant, aspirant, competitor, bidder; place —, pot- hunter; prizer.

beggar, mendicant, mumper, sturdy beggar, cadger, panhandler.

canvasser, barker, touter etc. 768.

sycophant, parasite etc. 886.

---

768. Promise.—**N.** promise, undertaking, word, troth, plight, pledge, *parole*, word of honor, vow; oath etc. (*affirmation*) 535; profession, assurance, warranty, guarantee, insurance, obligation; contract etc. 769.

engagement, pre-engagement; affiance; betroth, -al, -ment; marriage -compact, — vow.

V. promise; give a promise etc. *n.*; undertake, engage; make —, form- an engagement; enter - into, — on- an engagement; bind —, tie —, pledge —, commit —, take upon- oneself; vow; swear etc. (*affirm*) 535; give —, pass —, pledge —, plight- one's -word, — honor, — credit, — troth; betroth, plight faith; take the vows.

assure, warrant, guarantee, vouch for, avouch, covenant etc. 769; attest etc. (*bear witness*) 467.

hold out an expectation; contract an obligation; become -bound to, — sponsor for; answer —, be answerable- for; secure; give security etc. 771; underwrite.

adjure, administer an oath, put to one's oath, swear a witness.

Adj. promising etc. *v.*; promissory; votive; under hand and seal; upon -oath, — affirmation.

promised etc. *v.*; affianced, pledged, bound; committed, compromised; in for it.

Adv. as one's head shall answer for; upon my honor.

Phr. in for a penny, in for a pound.

768a. Release from engagement.—**N.** release etc. (*liberation*) 750.

Adj. absolute; unconditional etc. (*free*) 748.

---

769. Compact.—**N.** compact, contract, agreement, bargain, deal, transaction; affidation; pact, -ion; bond, covenant, indenture.

stipulation, settlement, convention; compromise, *cartel*.

protocol, treaty, *concordat, Zollverein, Sonderbund*, charter, *Magna Charta*, Pragmatic Sanction.

negotiation etc. (*bargaining*) 794; diplomacy etc. (*mediation*) 724; negotiator etc. (*agent*) 758.

ratification, completion, signature, seal, sigil, signet.

V. contract, covenant, agree for, engage etc. (*promise*) 768.

treat, negotiate, stipulate, make terms; bargain etc. (*barter*) 794.

make —, strike- a bargain; come to -terms, — an understanding; compromise etc. 774; set at rest; close, — with; conclude, complete, settle; confirm, ratify, clench, subscribe, underwrite; en-, in-dorse; put the seal to; sign, seal etc. (*attest*) 467; indent.

take one at one's word, bargain by inch of candle.

Adj. contractual, agreed etc. *v.*; conventional; under hand and seal; signed, sealed and delivered.

Phr. *caveat emptor.*

---

770. Conditions.—**N.** conditions, terms; articles, — of agreement.

clauses, provisions; proviso etc. (*qualification*) 469; covenant, stipulation, obligation, *ultimatum, sine quâ non*; *casus foederis*.

V. make —, come to- -terms etc. (*contract*) 769; make it a condition, stipulate, insist upon, make a point of; bind, tie up.

Adj. conditional, provisional, guarded, fenced, hedged in.

Adv. conditionally etc. (*with qualification*) 469; provisionally, *pro re natâ*; on condition; with a reservation.

771. Security.—N. security; guaran-ty, -tee; gage, waranty, bond, tie, pledge, plight, mortgage, debenture, hypothecation, bill of sale, lien, pignus, pawn, pignoration; real security; bottomry; collateral, vadium.

stake, deposit, earnest, handsel, caution.

promissory note; bill, – of exchange; I.O.U.: personal security, covenant, specialty; *parole* etc. (*promise*) 768.

acceptance, indorsement, signature, execution, stamp, seal.

spon-sor, -sion, -sorship; surety, bail; mainpernor, hostage.

recognizance; deed –, covenant- of indemnity.

authentication, verfication, warrant, certificate, voucher, docket, doquet; record etc. 551; probate, attested copy.

receipt; ac-, quittance; discharge, release.

muniment, title-deed, instrument; deed, – poll; assurance, insurance, indenture; charter etc. (*compact*) 769; charter-poll; paper, parchment, settlement, will, testament, last will and testament, codicil.

V. give -security, – bail; – substantial bail; go bail; pawn, impawn, hock, spout, mortgage, hypothecate, impignorate.

guarantee, warrant, assure; accept, indorse, underwrite, insure.

execute, stamp; sign, seal etc. (*evidence*) 467.

let, set; grant –, take –, hold- a lease; hold in pledge; lend on security etc. 787.

Adj. secure, -ed; pledged etc. *v.*; in pawn, on deposit.

772. Observance.—N. observance, performance, compliance; obedience, etc. 743; fulfilment, satisfaction, discharge; acquit-tance, - tal.

adhesion, acknowledgment; fidelity etc. (*probity*) 939; exact etc. 494- observance.

V. observe, comply with, respect, acknowledge, abide by; cling to, adhere to, be faithful to, act up to; meet, fulfil; carry -out, – into execution; execute, perform, keep, satisfy, discharge; do one's office.

perform –, fulfill –, discharge –, acquit oneself of- an obligation; make good; make good –, keep- one's -word, – promise; redeem one's pledge; keep faith with, stand to one's engagement.

Adj. observant, faithful, true, loyal; honorable etc. 939; true as the -dial to the sun, – needle to the pole; punct-ual, -ilious; meticulous; literal etc. (*exact*) 494; as good as one's word.

Adv. faithfully etc. *adj.*

773. Non-observance.—N. non-observance etc. 772; evasion, inobservance, failure, omission, neglect, laches, laxity, informality.

infringement, infraction; violation, transgression.

retractation, repudiation, nullification; protest; forfeiture.

lawlessness; disobedience etc. 742; bad faith etc. 940.

V. fail, neglect, omit, elude, evade, give the go by to, cut, set aside, ignore; shut –, close- one's eyes to, avoid.

infringe, transgress, pirate, violate, break, trample under foot, do violence to, drive a coach and six through.

discard, protest, repudiate, fling to the winds, set at naught, nullify, declare null and void; cancel etc. (*wipe off*) 552.

retract, go back from, be off, forfeit, go from one's word, palter; stretch –, strain- a point.

Adj. violating etc. *v.*; lawless, transgressive; elusive, evasive; lax, easual; non-observant.

unfulfilled etc. (*see* fulfil etc. 772).

774. Compromise.—N. com-promise, - mutation, -position; middle term, *mezzo termine*; compensation etc. 30; adjustment, mutual concession.

V. com-promise, -mute, -pound; take the mean; split the difference, meet one half way, give and take; come to terms etc. (*contract*) 769; submit to –, abide by- arbitration; patch up, bridge over, fix up, arrange; adjust, – differences; agree; make -the best of, – a virtue of necessity; take the will for the deed.

775. Acquisition.—N. acquisition; gaining etc. *v.*; obtainment; procur-ation, -ement; purchase, descent, inheritance; gift etc. 784.

recovery, retrieval, revendication, replevin; redemption, salvage, trover; find, *trouvaille*, foundling.

gain, thrift; money-making, -grubbing; lucre, filthy lucre, loaves and fishes, the main chance, pelf; emolument etc. 973; wealth etc. 803.

profit, earnings, winnings, innings, clean-up, pickings, perquisite, net profit; income etc. (*receipt*) 810; pro-ceeds, -duce, -duct; out-come, - put; return, fruit, crop, harvest, tilth; second crop, aftermath; benefit etc. (*good*) 618.

sweepstakes, trick, prize, pool.

[Fraudulent acquisition] subreption; theft, stealing etc. 791.

V. acquire, get, gain, win, earn, obtain, procure, gather, annex; collect etc. 72; pick, – up; glean, take etc. 789.

find; come –, pitch –, light- upon; scrape -up, – together; get in, reap and carry, net, bag, sack, bring home, secure, come across, derive, draw, get in the harvest.

profit; make –, draw- profit; turn to -profit, – account; make -capital out of, – money by; obtain a return, reap the fruits of; reap –, gain- an advantage; turn -a penny, – an honest penny; make the pot boil, bring grist to the mill; make –, coin –, raise- money; raise -funds, – the wind; fill one's pocket etc. (*wealth*) 803.

treasure up etc. (*store*) 636; realize, clear; produce etc. 161; take etc. 789.

get back, recover, regain, retrieve, revendicate, replevy, redeem, come by one's own.

come -by, – in for; receive etc. 785; inherit;
step into, – a fortune, – the shoes of; succeed to.

get -hold of, – between one's finger and thumb,
– into one's hand, – at; take –, come into –,
enter into- possession.

be -profitable etc. *adj.*; pay, answer.

accrue etc. (*be received*) 785.

Adj. acquir-ing, -ed etc. *v.*; acquisitive; productive, profitable, advantageous, gainful,
remunerative, paying, lucrative.

776. Loss.—N. loss; de-, perdition; forfeiture,
lapse.

privation, bereavement; deprivation etc.
(*dispossession*) 789; riddance.

V. lose; incur –, experience –, meet with- a
loss; miss; mislay, let slip, allow to slip through the
fingers, squander; be without etc. (*exempt*) 777a;
forfeit.

get rid of etc. 782; waste etc. 638.

be lost, lapse.

Adj. losing etc. *v.*; not having etc. 777a.

shorn of, deprived of; denuded, bereaved, bereft,
minus, cut off; dispossessed etc. 789; rid of, quit of;
out of pocket.

lost etc. *v.*; long lost; irretrievable etc. (*hopeless*)
859; irredentist; off one's hands.

Int. farewell to! adieu to! good riddance!

777. Possession.—N. possession, seisin; ownership etc. 780; occupancy; hold, -ing; tenure,
tenancy, feodality, dependency; villenage; socage,
chivalry, knight service.

exclusive possession, impropriation, monopoly,
corner; retention etc. 781; pre-possession, -
occupancy; nine points of the law.

future possession, heritage, inheritance, heirship,
reversion, fee, seigniority, feud, fief.

bird in hand, *uti possidetis, chose* in possession.

V. possess, have, hold, occupy, enjoy; be -
possessed of etc. *adj.*; have -in hand etc. *adj.*; own
etc. 780; command.

inherit; come -to, – in for.

engross, monopolize, forestall, regrate, im-
propriate, have all to oneself, corner; have a firm
hold of etc. (*retain*) 781; get into one's hand etc.
(*acquire*) 775.

belong to, appertain to, pertain to; be -in one's
possession etc. *adj.*; vest in.

Adj. possessing etc. *v.*; worth; possessed of,
seized of, master of, in possession of; endowed –,
blest –, instinct –, fraught –, laden –, charged
–, instilled –, with.

possessed etc. *v.*; on hand, by one; in hand, in
store, in stock; in one's -hands, – grasp, –
possession; at one's -command, – disposal; one's
own etc. (*property*) 780.

unsold, unshared.

777a. Exemption.—N. exemption; exception,
immunity, privilege, release etc. 927a; absence etc.
187.

V. not -have etc. 777; be -without etc. *adj.*

Adj. exempt from, devoid of, without, unpossessed of, unblest with, immune from.

not -having etc. 777; unpossessed; untenanted
etc. (*vacant*) 187; without an owner.

unobtained, unacquired.

778. Participation. [Joint possession.]—**N.**
participation; co-, joint-tenancy; possession –,
tenancy- in common; joint –, common- stock; co-,
partnership; communion; community of -
possessions, – goods; communalism, communism,
socialism, collectivism; co-operation etc. 709;
profit sharing.

snacks, co-portion, picnic, hotchpotch; co-
heirship, -parceny, -parcenary; gavelkind.

participator, sharer; co-, partner; shareholder;
co-, joint-tenant; tenants in common; co-heir, -
parcener.

communist, socialist.

V. par-ticipate, -take; share, – in; come in for a
share; go -shares, – snacks, – halves; share and
share alike.

have –, possess –, be seized- -in common, –
as joint tenants etc. *n.*

join in; have a hand in etc. (*co-operate*) 709.

Adj. partaking etc. *v.*; communistic, socialistic,
co-operative, profit sharing.

Adv. share and share alike.

779. Possessor.—N. possessor, holder; occupant, -ier; tenant; person –, man- -in possession etc.
777; renter, lodger, lessee, under-lessee; zemindar,
ryot; tenant -on sufferance, – at will, – from year
to year, – for years, – for life.

owner; propriet-or, -ress, -ary; impropriator,
master, mistress, lord.

land-holder, -owner, -lord, -lady; lord -of the
manor, – paramount; heritor, laird, vavasor,
landed gentry, mesne lord.

cestui-que-trust, beneficiary, mortgagor.

grantee, feoffee, relessee, devisee; legat-ee, -ary.

trustee; holder etc.- of the legal estate; mortgagee.

right –, rightful- owner.

[Future possessor] heir, – apparent; –
presumptive; heiress; inherit-or, -ress, -rix; rever-
sioner, remainder-man.

780. Property.—N. property, possession, *suum
cuique, meum et tuum.*

owner-, proprietor, lord-ship; seignority; empire
etc. (*dominion*) 737.

interest, stake, estate, right, title, claim, demand,
holding; tenure etc. (*possession*) 777; vested –,
contingent –, beneficial –, equitable- interest;
use, trust, benefit; legal –, equitable- estate; seisin.

absolute interest, paramount estate, freehold; fee,
– simple, – tail; estate -in fee, – in tail, – tail;
estate in tail -male, – female, – general.

limitation, term, lease, settlement, strict settlement, particular estate; estate -for life, – for
years, – *pur autre vie*; remainder, reversion, ex-
pectancy, possibility.

dower, dowry, *dot*, jointure, marriage portion, appanage, inheritance, heritage, patrimony, alimony; legacy etc. (*gift*) 784.

assets, belongings, means, resources, circumstances; wealth etc. 803; money etc. 800; what one -is worth, – will cut up for; estate and effects.

landed –, real- -estate, – property; realty; land, -s; subdivision; plot, site; tenements; hereditaments; corporeal –, incorporeal- hereditaments; acres; ground etc. (*earth*) 342; acquest; messuage.

territory, state, kingdom, principality, realm, empire, protectorate, margravate, dependancy, colony, sphere of influence, mandate.

manor, honor, domain, demesne; farm, ranch, plantation, *hacienda*; allodium etc. (*free*) 748; fieff, feoff, feud, zemindary, dependency.

free-, copy-, lease-holds; chattels real; fixtures, plant, heirloom easement; folkland; right of - common, – user.

personal -property, – estate, – effects; personalty, chattels, goods, effects, movables; stock, – in trade; things, traps, rattle-traps, paraphernalia; equipage etc. 633.

parcels, appurtenances.

impedimenta; lug-, bag-gage; bag and baggage; pelf; cargo, lading.

rent-roll; income etc. (*receipts*) 810.

patent, copyright; *chose* in action; credit etc. 805; debt etc. 806.

V. possess etc. 777; be the -possessor etc. 779- of own; have for one's own, – very own; come in for, inherit; enfeoff.

savor of the realty.

be one's own -property etc. *n*.; belong to; ap-, pertain to.

Adj. one's own; landed, predial, manorial, allodial, seignorial; free-, copy-, lease-hold; feu-, feo-dal; hereditary, entailed, personal.

Adv. to one's -credit, – account; to the good.

to one and -his heirs for ever, – the heirs of his body, – his heirs and assigns, – his executors, administrators and assigns.

781. Retention.—N. retention; retaining etc. *v*.; keep, detention, custody; tenacity, firm hold, grasp, gripe, grip, iron grip.

fangs, teeth, claws, talons, nail, hook, tentacle, *tenaculum*; bond etc. (*vinculum*) 45.

clutches, tongs, forceps, pincers, nippers, pliers, tweezers, vise.

paw, hand, finger, wrist, fist, neaf, neif.

bird in hand; captive etc. 754.

V. retain, keep; hold, – fast, – tight, – one's own, – one's ground; clinch, clench, clutch, grasp, gripe, hug, have a firm hold of.

secure, withold, detain; hold – , keepback; keep close; husband etc. (*store*) 636; reserve; have – , keep- in stock etc. (*possess*) 777; enfail, tie up, settle.

Adj. retaining etc. *v*.; retentive, tenacious.

unforfeited, undeprived, undisposed, uncommunicated.

incommunicable, inalienable; in mortmain; in strict settlement.

Phr. *uti possidetis*.

782. Relinquishment.—N. relinquishment, abandonment etc. (*of a course*) 624; renunciation,

expropriation, dereliction; cession, surrender, dispensation; resignation etc. 757; riddance.

derelict etc. *adj.*; jetsam; waif, foundling, orphan.

v. relinquish, give up, surrender, yield, cede; let -go, – slip; spare, drop, resign, forego, renounce, abjure, abandon, expropriate, give away, dispose of, part with; lay -aside, – apart, – down, – on the shelf etc. (*disuse*) 678; set – , put- aside; make away with, cast behind; discard, cast off, dismiss; maroon.

give -notice to quit, – warning; supersede; be – , get- -rid of, – quit of; eject etc. 297.

rid –, disburden –, divest –, djspossess-oneself of; wash one's hands of; divorce, desert; disinherit, cut off.

cast –, throw –, pitch –, fling- -away, – aside, – overboard, – to the dogs; cast – , throw –, sweep- to the winds; put –, turn –, sweep-away; jettison.

quit one's hold.

Adj. relinquished etc. *v*.; cast off, derelict; unowned, unappropriated, unculled; left etc. (*residuary*) 40; divorced; disinherited.

Int. away with!

783. Transfer.—N. transfer, conveyance, assignment, alienation, abalienation; demise, limitation; conveyancing; transmission etc. (*transference*) 270; enfeoffment, bargain and sale, lease and release; exchange etc. (*interchange*) 148; barter etc. 794; substitution etc. 147.

succession, reversion; shifting -use, – trust; devolution.

V. transfer, convey, alien, -ate; assign; grant etc. (*confer*) 784; consign; make – , hand- over; pass, hand, transmit, negotiate; hand down; exchange etc. (*interchange*) 148.

change -hands, – from one to another; devolve, succeed; come into possession etc. (*acquire*) 775; take over.

abalienate; disinherit; dispossess etc. 789; substitute etc. 147.

Adj. alienable, negotiable, transferable, reversional.

Phr. estate coming into possession.

784. Giving.—N. giving etc. *v*.; bestowal, donation; present-ation, -ment; accordance; con-, cession; delivery, consignment, dispensation, communication, endowment; invest-ment, -iture; award.

almsgiving, charity, liberality, generosity; philanthropy etc. 910.

[Thing given] gift, donation, present, *cadeau*; fairing; free gift, boon, favor, benefaction, grant, offering, oblation, sacrifice, immolation.

grace, act of grace, *bonus, bonanza*.

allowance, contribution, subscription, subsidy, tribute, subvention.

bequest, legacy, devise, will, dotation, appanage; dowry; voluntary -settlement, – conveyance etc. 783; amortization.

alms, largess, bounty, dole, sportule, donative, help, oblation, offertory, Peter's pence, *honorarium*, gratuity, Maundy money, Christmas box, Easter offering, vail, tip, *douceur*, drink money, *pourboire, trinkgeld, backsheesh*; fee etc. (*recompense*) 973; consideration.

bribe, bait, ground-bait; peace-offering, handsel.

giver, grantor etc. *v.*; donor, feoffer, settlor; almoner; testator; investor, subscriber, contributor; fairy godmother; Santa Claus, benefactor etc. 816.

V. deliver, hand, pass, put into the hands of; hand −, make −, deliver −, pass −, turn- over.

present, give away, dispense, dispose of; give −, deal −, dole −, mete −, fork −, shell −, squeeze- out.

pay etc. 807; render, impart, communicate.

concede, cede, yield, part with, shed cast; spend etc. 809.

give, bestow, confer, grant, accord, award, assign.

entrust, consign, vest in.

make a present; allow, contribute, subscribe, donate, furnish its quota.

invest, endow, settle upon; bequesth, leave, devise.

furnish, supply, help; ad-, minister to; afford, spare; accommodate −, indulge −, favor- with; shower down upon; lavish, pour on, thrust upon; tip, bribe; tickle −, grease- the palm; offer etc. 763; sacrifice, immolate.

Adj. giving etc. *v.*; given etc. *v.*; allow-ed, -able; concessional; communicable; charitable, eleemosynary, sportulary, tributary; *gratis* etc. 815.

785. Receiving.—N. receiving etc. *v.*; acquisition etc. 775; reception etc. (*introduction*) 296; suscipiency, acceptance, admission.

re-, ac-cipient; assignee, devisee; lega-tee, -tary; grantee, feoffee, donee, relessee, lessee.

sportulary, stipendiary; beneficiary; pension-er, -ary; almsman.

income etc. (*receipt*) 810.

v. receive; take etc. 789; acquire etc. 775; admit.

take- in, catch, touch; pocket; put into one's pocket, − purse; accept; take off one's hands.

be received; come -in, − to hand; pass −, fall- into one's hand; go into one's pocket; fall to one's lot, − share; come −, fall- to one; accrue; have - given etc. 784 to one.

Adj. receiving etc. *v.*; re-, suscipient.

received etc. *v.*; given etc. 784; second-hand.

not given, unbestowed etc. (*see* give, bestow etc. 784).

786. Apportionment.—N. apportion-, allot-, consign-, assign-, appoint-ment; appropriation; dispensation, -tribution; allocation, division, deal; repartition; administration.

dividend, portion, contingent, share, allotment, lot, cut, split, measure, dose; dole, meed, pittance; *quantum*, ration; ratio, proportion, quota, *modicum*, mess, allowance.

V. apportion, divide; cut, split, divvy; distribute, administer, dispense; billet, allot, detail, cast, share, mete; portion −, parcel −, dole- out; deal, carve.

partition, assign, appropriate, appoint.

come in for one's share etc. (*participate*) 778.

Adj. apportioning etc. *v.*; respective.

Adv. respectively, each to each.

787. Lending.—N. lending etc. *v.*; loan, advance, accommodation, feneration; mortgage etc. (*security*) 771; investment.

mont de piété, pawnshop, hock shop, spout, my uncle's.

lender, pawnbroker, money lender, usurer, Jew, Shylock.

V. lend, advance, loan, accommodate with; lend on security; pawn etc. (*security*) 771.

intrust, invest; place −, put- out to interest; sink, risk.

let, demise, lease, set, under-, sub-let.

Adj. lending etc. *v.*; lent etc. *v.*; unborrowed etc. (*see* borrowed etc. 788).

Adv. in advance; on -loan, − security.

788. Borrowing.—N. borrowing, pledging, pawning.

borrowed plumes; plagiarism etc. (*thieving*) 791. replevin.

V. borrow, desume; pawn.

hire, rent, farm; take a -lease, − demise; take −, hire- by the -hour, − mile, − year etc.

raise −, take up- money; float bonds; raise the wind; fly a kite, borrow of Peter to pay Paul; run into debt etc. (*debt*) 806.

make use of, plagiarize, pirate.

replevy.

789. Taking.—N. taking etc. *v.*; reception etc. (*taking in*) 296; deglutition etc. (*taking food*) 298; appropriation, prehension, prensation; capture, caption; ap-, de-prehension; abreption, seizure; abduction, -lation; subtraction etc. (*subduction*) 38; abstraction, ademption.

dispossession; depriv-ation, -ement; bereavement; divestment; disherison; distraint, distress; sequestration, confiscation, attachment, execution; eviction etc. 297.

rapacity, extortion, vampirism, predacity, blood-sucking; theft etc. 791.

resumption; repris-e, -al; recovery etc. 775.

clutch, swoop, wrench; grip etc. (*retention*) 781; haul, take, catch; scramble.

taker, captor, capturer; vampire; extortioner.

V. take, catch, hook, nab, bag, sack, pocket, put into one's pocket, scrounge; receive; accept.

reap, crop, cull, pluck; gather etc. (*get*) 775; draw.

ap-, im-propriate; assume, possess oneself of; take possession of; commandeer; lay −, clap- one's hands on; help oneself to; make free with, dip one's hands into, lay under contribution; intercept; scramble for; deprive of.

take −, carry −, bear- -away, − off; abstract; hurry off −, run away- with; abduct; steal etc. 791; ravish; seize; pounce −, spring- upon; swoop -to, − down upon; take by -storm, − assault; snatch, reave.

snap up, nip up, whip up, catch up; kidnap, crimp, capture, lay violent hands on.

get −, lay −, take −, catch −, lay fast −, take firm- hold of; lay by the heels, take prisoner; fasten upon, grip, grapple, embrace, gripe, clasp, grab, clutch, collar, throttle, take by the throat, claw, clinch, clench, make sure of.

catch at, jump at, make a grab at, snap at, snatch at; reach, make a long arm, stretch forth one's hand.

take -from, − away from; deduct etc. 38; retrench etc. (*curtail*) 201; dispossess, ease one of, snatch from one's grasp; tear −, tear away −, wrench −, wrest −, wring- from; extort; deprive of, bereave; disinherit, cut off with a shilling.

oust etc. (*eject*) 297; divest; levy, distrain, confiscate; sequest-er, -rate, accroach; usurp; despoil, strip, fleece, shear, displume, impoverish, eat out of house and home; drain, − to the dregs; gut, dry, exhaust, swallow up; absorb etc. (*suck in*) 296; draw off; suck, − like a leech, − the blood of.

retake, resume; recover etc. 775.

Adj. taking etc. *v.*; privative, prehensile; predaceous, -al, -atory, -atorial; rap-acious, -torial; ravenous; parasitic; all-devouring, -engulfing.

bereft etc. 776.

Adv. at one fell swoop.

Phr. give an inch and take an ell.

790. Restitution.—N. restitution, return; ren-, red-dition; reinstatement, restoration; reinvestment, recuperation; repatriation; rehabilitation etc. (*reconstruction*) 660; reparation, atonement, indemnity, compensation, recompense.

release, replevin, redemption; recovery etc. (*getting back*) 775; remitter, reversion.

V. return, restore; recondition; give −, carry −, bring- back; render, − up; give up; let go, unclutch; dis-, re-gorge; regurgitate; recoup, reimburse, repay, indemnify, reinvest, remit, rehabilitate; repair etc. (*make good*) 660.

redeem, recover etc. (*get back*) 775; take back again; revest, revert.

Adj. restoring etc. *v.*; recuperative etc. 660; in full restitution, to compensate for.

Phr. *suum cuique*.

791. Stealing.—N. stealing etc. *v.*; theft, thievery, robbery, latrociny, direption; abstraction, appropriation; plagiar-y, -ism; rape, kidnapping, depredation; raid, hold up.

spoliation, plunder, pillage; sack, -age; rapine, *brigandage*; highway robbery, foray, *razzia*; black-mail; piracy, privateering, buccaneering; filibustering, -ism; burglary; house-breaking; cattle-stealing, -rustling, -lifting.

peculation, embezzlement; fraud etc. 545; larceny, petty larceny, pilfering, shop-lifting.

thievishness, rapacity, kleptomania, Alsatia; den of -Cacus; − thieves.

license to plunder, letters of marque.

V. steal, thieve, rob, purloin, pilfer, filch, lift, prig, bag, nim, crib, cabbage, palm; abstract; appropriate, plagiarize.

convey away, carry off, abduct, kidnap, shanghai, impress, crimp; make −, walk −, runoff with; run away with; spirit away; seize etc. (*lay violent hands on*) 789.

plunder, pillage, rifle, sack, loot, ransack, spoil, spoliate, despoil, strip, sweep, gut, forage, levy black-mail, pirate, pickeer, maraud, lift cattle, rustle, poach, smuggle, run.

stick −, hold- up.

swindle, peculate, embezzle; sponge, mulct, rook, bilk, pluck, pigeon, skin, fleece, diddle; defraud etc. 545; obtain under false pretences; live by one's wits

rob −, borrow of- Peter to Paul; set a thief to catch a thief.

disregard the distinction between *meum* and *tuum*.

Adj. thieving etc. *v.*; thievish, light-fingered; furacious, -tive; piratical; pred-aceous, -al, -atory, -atorial; raptorial etc. (*rapacious*) 789.

stolen etc. *v.*

Phr. *sic vos non vobis*.

792. Thief.—N. thief, robber, *homo trium literarum*, pilferer, rifler, filcher, plagiarist.

spoiler, depredator, pillager, marauder; harpy, shark, land-shark, falcon, moss-trooper, bushranger, Bedouin, brigand, freebooter, bandit, thug, dacoit, pirate, corsair, viking, Paul Jones; buccan-eer, -ier; piqu-, pick-eerer; rover, ranger, privateer, filibuster; rapparee, wrecker, picaroon; smuggler, poacher, plunderer; racketeer.

highwayman, Dick Turpin, Claude Duval, Macheath, knight of the road, footpad, sturdy beggar; abductor, kidnapper.

cut-, pick-purse; pick-pocket, light-fingered gentry; sharper; card-, skittle-sharper; crook; thimblerigger; rook, Greek, blackleg, leg, welsher, defaulter; Autolycus, Cacus, Barabbas, Jeremy Diddler, Robert Macaire, artful dodger, trickster; swell mob, *chevalier d'industrie*; shop-lifter.

swindler, peculator; forger, coiner, counterfeiter, shoful; fence, receiver of stolen goods, duffer; smasher.

burglar, housebreaker; cracks-, mags-man; Bill Sikes, Jack Sheppard, Jonathan Wild, Raffles, cat burglar.

793. Booty.—N. booty, spoil, plunder, price, loot, graft, swag, pickings, boodle; *spolia opima*, prey; blackmail; stolen goods.

Adj. looting etc. *n.*; manubial, spoliative.

794. Barter.—N. barter, exchange, scorse, truck system; interchange etc. 148.

a Roland for an Oliver; *quid pro quo*; commutation, -position.

trade, commerce, mercature, buying and selling, bargain and sale; traffic, business, nundination, custom, shopping; commercial enterprise, speculation, jobbing, stock-jobbing, *agiotage*, brokery, arbitrage.

dealing, transaction, negotiation, bargain.

free trade.

V. barter, exchange, truck, scorse, swop; interchange etc. 148; commutate etc. (*substitute*) 147; compound for.

trade, traffic, buy and sell, give and take, nundinate; carry on −, ply −, drive- a trade; be in -

business, − the city; keep a shop, deal in, employ one's capital in.

trade −, deal −, have dealings- with; transact −, do- business with; open −, keep- an account with.

bargain; drive −, make- a bargain; negotiate, bid for; dicker, haggle, higgle; chaffer, huckster, cheapen, beat down; stickle, − for; out-, under-bid; ask, charge; strike a bargain etc. (*contract*) 769.

speculate, give a sprat to catch a herring; buy in the cheapest and sell in the dearest market; rig the market.

Adj. commercial, mercantile, trading; inter-changeable, marketable, staple, in the market, for sale.

wholesale, retail.

Adv. across the counter; on 'change.

795. Purchase.—N. purchase, emption; buying, purchasing, shopping; pre-emption; refusal.

coemption, bribery; slave trade.

buyer, purchaser, *emptor*, vendee; patron, employer, client, customer, *clientèle*.

V. buy, purchase, invest in, procure; rent etc. (*hire*) 788; repurchase, buy in.

keep in one's pay, bribe, suborn; pay etc. 807; spend etc. 809.

make −, complete- a purchase; buy over the counter; pay cash for.

shop, market, go a shopping.

Adj. purchased etc. *v.*

Phr. *caveat emptor*.

796. Sale.—N. sale, vent, disposal; auction, roup, Dutch auction; custom etc. (*traffic*) 794.

vendi-bility, -bleness.

seller, salesman; peddler, smous; vender, vendor, consignor; merchant etc. 797; auctioneer.

V. sell, vend, dispose of, effect a sale; sell -over the counter, − by auction etc. *n.*; dispense, retail; deal in etc. 794; sell -off, − out; turn into money; realize; bring -to, − under- the hammer; put up to auction; auction, offer −, put up- for sale; hawk, peddle, bring to market; offer etc. 763; undersell; dump, unload.

let; mortgage etc. (*security*) 771.

Adj. under the hammer, in the market, for sale.

saleable, marketable, vendible, in demand, having a ready sale; unsaleable etc., unpurchased, unbought; on one's hands.

797. Merchant.—N. merchant, trader, dealer, monger, chandler, salesman; changer; regrater; shop-keeper, -man; trades-man, -people, -folk.

retailer; chapman, hawker, huckster, higgler; peddler, smous, pedlar, *colporteur*, cadger, Autolycus; sutler, *vivandière*, coster-man, -monger; market woman; cheap jack; caterer etc. 637; tallyman.

money-broker, -changer, -lender; stock-broker, -jobber; cambist, usurer, moneyer, banker.

jobber; broker etc. (*agent*) 758; buyer etc. 795; seller etc. 796.

concern; firm etc. (*partnership*) 712.

798. Merchandise.—N. merchandise, ware, commodity, effects, goods, article, stock, produce, staple commodity; stock in trade etc. (*store*) 636; cargo etc. (*contents*) 190.

799. Mart.—N. mart; market, -place, *forum*; fair, bazaar, staple; stock −, exchange; 'change, *bourse*, Wall Street, Rialto, hall, guildhall; toll-booth, custom-house; Tattersalls.

shop, stall, booth; wharf; office, chambers, counting-house, *bureau*; coun-, comp-ter.

ware-house, -room; *dépôt*, interposit, *entrepôt*, *emporium*, establishment; store etc. 636.

open market, market-overt.

800. Money.—N. money -matters, − market; finance; accounts etc. 811; funds, treasure; capital, stock; assets etc. (*property*) 780; wealth etc. 803; supplies, ways and means, wherewithal, sinews of war, almighty dollar, needful, cash.

sum, amount; balance, -sheet; sum total; proceeds etc. (*receipts*) 810.

currency, circulating medium, specie; coin, − of the realm; piece, hard cash, dollar, sterling coin; pounds, shillings and pence; L s. d.; guineas; pocket, breeches pocket, purse; money in hand; the best, ready, − money; filthy lucre, shekels, roll, jack, rhino, blunt, dust, bawbees, brass, dibs, dough, mopus, tin, salt, chink, oof, spondulics, pile, wads.

precious metals, gold, silver, copper, nickel; bullion, bar, ingot, nugget.

petty cash; pocket-, pin-money; small −, change; small coin, loose cash; doit, stiver, rap, mite, farthing, *sou*, penny, shilling, bob, tanner, tester, groat, guinea, ducat; *rouleau*; *wampum*; good −, round −, lump- sum; power −, mint −, tons- of money; plum, lac of rupees, millions, money-bags, miser's hoard, stocking, mine of wealth etc. 803.

[Science of coins] numismatics, chrysology.

paper-money; money −, postal −, Post Office-order; note, − of hand; bank −, treasury- note; Bradbury; promissory note; I.O.U., bond; bill, − of exchange; draft, check, order, warrant, *coupon*, debenture, exchequer bill, *assignat*, greenback, gold −, silver- certificate.

copper, nickel, dime, quarter, two bits, half a dollar, dollar, buck, simoleon, fiver, tenner, a twenty, a sawbuck, a century, a grand; eagle, double eagle.

gold standard, bimetallism, fiat money; rate of −, exchange; in-, de-flation.

remittance etc. (*payment*) 807; credit etc. 805; liability etc. 806; solvency etc. 803.

draw-er, -ee; oblig-or, -ee; moneyer, coiner, counterfeiter, forger.

false −, bad- money; base −, counterfeit- coin, flash note, slip, kite; Bank of Elegance.

argumentum ad crumenam.

V. amount to, come to, mount up to; touch the pocket; draw, − upon; endorse etc. (*security*) 771; issue, utter, circulate; discount etc. 813.

forge, counterfeit, coin, circulate −, pass- bad money.

Adj. monetary, pecuniary, crumenal, fiscal, financial, sumptuary, numismatical; sterling; solvent etc. 803.

801. Treasurer.—N. treasurer; bursar, -y; purser, purse-bearer; cash-keeper, banker; depositary; questor, receiver, steward, trustee, chartered –, accountant; Accountant-General, almoner, liquidator, paymaster, cashier, teller; cambist; money-changer etc. (*merchant*) 797.

financier, Chancellor of the Exchequer, minister of finance; Secretary of the Treasury, Director of the Budget, Controller of Currency.

802. Treasury.—N. treasury, bank, exchequer, almonry, fisc, hanaper, bursary; safe; strong-box, -hold, -room; coffer; chest etc. (*receptacle*) 191; depository etc. 636; till, -er; cash-box, -register, purse, pocketbook, wallet; money-bag, -belt, -box, *porte-monnaie*.

purse-strings; pocket, breeches pocket.

sinking fund; stocks; government –, public –, parliamentary- -stocks, – funds, – securities; bonds; gild-edged securities; Consols, Liberty bonds, government bonds, *crédit mobilier*.

803. Wealth.—N. wealth, riches, fortune, handsome fortune, opulence, affluence; good –, easy- circumstances; independence; competence etc. (*sufficiency*) 639; solvency, soundness, solidity.

provision, livelihood, maintenance; alimony, dowry; means, resources, substance; property etc. 780; command of money.

income etc. 810; capital, money; round sum etc. (*treasure*) 800; mint of money, mine of wealth, El Dorado, Pactolus, Golconda, Potosi, *bonanza*; philosopher's stone.

long –, full –, well lined –, heavy- purse; purse of Fortunatus.

pelf, Mammon, lucre, filthy lucre; loaves and fishes; fleshpots of Egypt.

rich –, moneyed –, warm- man; man of substance; capitalist, millionaire, Nabob, Croesus, Midas, Plutus, Dives, Timon of Athens; Timo-, Pluto-cracy; Danaë.

V. be -rich etc. *adj.*; roll –, wallow- in -wealth, – riches; have money to burn.

afford, well afford; command -money, – a sum; make both ends meet, hold one's head above water.

become -rich etc. *adj.*; fill one's -pocket etc. (*treasury*) 802; feather one's nest, clean up –, make- a fortune; make money etc. (*acquire*) 775.

enrich, imburse.

worship -Mammon, – the golden calf.

Adj. wealthy, rich, affluent, opulent, moneyed, monied, worth -a great deal, – much; well -to do, – off; warm; well –, provided for.

made of money; rich as Croesus; rolling in -riches, – wealth.

flush, – of -cash, – money, – tin; in -funds, – cash, – full feather; solvent, solid, sound, pecunious, out of debt, all straight; able to pay 20s in the L.

Phr. one's ship coming in.

804. Poverty.—N. poverty, indigence, penury, pauperism, destitution, want; need, -iness; lack,

necessity, privation, distress, difficulties, wolf at the door.

bad –, poor –, needy –, embarrassed –, reduced –, straitened- circumstances; slender –, narrow- means; straits; hand to mouth existence, *res angusta domi*, low water, impecuniosity.

beggary; mendi-cancy, -city; broken –, loss of-fortune; insolvency etc. (*non-payment*) 808.

empty -purse, – pocket; light purse; beggarly account of empty boxes.

poor man, pauper, mendicant, mumper, beggar, starveling; *pauvre diable*.

V. be -poor etc. *adj.*; want, lack, starve, live from hand to mouth, have seen better days, go down in the world, be on one's uppers, come upon the parish; go to -the dogs, – wrack and ruin; not have a -penny etc. (*money*) 800, – shot in one's locker; beg one's bread; *tirer le diable par la queue*; run into debt etc. (*debt*) 806.

render -poor etc. *adj.*; impoverish; reduce, – to poverty; pauperize, fleece, ruin, bring to the parish.

Adj. poor, indigent; poverty-striken; badly –, poorly –, ill- off; poor as -a rat, – a church mouse, – Job's turkey, – Job; fortune-, dower-, money-, penni-less; unportioned, unmoneyed; impecunious; broke, flat; out –, short- of -money, – cash; without –, not worth- a rap etc. (*money*) 800; *qui n'a pas le sou*, out of pocket, hard up; out at -elbows, – heels; seedy, bare-footed; beggar-ly, -ed; destitute; fleeced, strapped, stripped; bereft, bereaved; reduced.

in -want etc. *n.*; needy, necessitous, distressed, pinched, straitened; put to one's -shifts, – last shifts; unable to -keep the wolf from the door, – make both ends meet; embarrassed, under hatches; involved etc. (*in debt*) 806; insolvent etc. (*not paying*) 808.

Adv. in formâ pauperis.

Phr. *zonam perdidit*.

805. Credit.—N. credit, trust, tick, score, tally, account.

letter of credit, circular note; duplicate; mortgage, lien, debenture, paper credit, floating capital; draft; securities.

creditor, lender, lessor, mortgagee; dun; usurer.

V. keep –, run up- an account with; entrust, credit, accredit.

place to one's -credit, – account; give –, take-credit; fly a kite.

Adj. credit-ing, -ed; accredited.

Adv. on -credit etc. *n.*; to the -account, – credit- of.

806. Debt.—N. debt, obligation, liability, indebtment, debit, score.

arrears, deferred payment, deficit, default; insolvency etc. (*non-payment*) 808; bad debt.

interest; usance, usury; premium; floating -debt, – capital.

debtor, debitor; mortgagor; defaulter etc. 808; borrower.

V. be -in debt etc. *adj.*; owe; incur –, contract- a debt etc. *n.*; run up -a bill, – a score, – an account; go on tick, put on the cuff; borrow etc. 788; run –, get- into debt; outrun the constable.

answer –, go bail- for; back one's note.

Adj. indebted; liable, chargeable, answerable for.

in -debt, — embarrassed circumstances, — difficulties; incumbered, involved; involved —, plunged —, deep —, over head and ears- in debt; deeply involved; fast tied up; insolvent etc. (*not paying*) 808; *minus*, out of pocket.

unpaid; unrequieted, unrewarded; owing, due, in arrear, outstanding.

807. Payment.—N. pay-, defray-ment; discharge; ac-, quittance; settlement, clearance, liquidation, satisfaction, reckoning, arrangement.

acknowledgment, release; receipt, — in full, — in full of all demands; voucher.

repayment, reimbursement, retribution; pay etc. (*reward*) 973; money paid etc. (*expenditure*) 809.

ready money etc. (*cash*) 800; stake, remittance, instalment.

payer, liquidator etc. 801.

V. pay, defray, make payment; pay -down, — on the nail, — ready money, — at sight, — in advance; cash, honor a bill, acknowledge; redeem; pay in kind.

pay one's -way, — shot, — footing; pay -the piper, — sauce for all, — costs; do the needful; come across; shell —, fork- out; come down with, — the dust; tickle —, grease- the palm; expend etc. 809; put —, lay- down.

discharge, settle, quit, acquit oneself of; account —, reckon —, settle —, be even —, be quits- with; strike a balance; settle —, balance —, square- accounts with; quit scores; foot the bill; wipe —, clear- off old scores; satisfy; pay in full; satisfy —, pay in full of- all demands; clear, liquidate; pay -up, — old debts.

disgorge, make repayment; repay, refund, reimburse, retribute; make compensation etc. 30.

Adj. paying etc., paid etc. *v.*; owing nothing, out of debt, all straight, clear of -debt, — encumbrance; unowed, never indebted.

Adv. to the tune of; on the nail; money —, cash-down; cash on delivery.

808. Non-payment.—N. non-payment; default, defalcation; protest, repudiation; application of the sponge; whitewashing.

insolvency, bankruptcy, failure; overdraft, overdrawn account; insufficiency etc. 640; run upon a bank.

waste paper bonds; dishonored —, protested-bills; bogus cheque.

bankrupt, insolvent debtor, lame duck, man of straw, welsher, stag, defaulter, absconder, levanter.

V. non -pay etc. 807; fail, break, stop payment; become -insolvent, — bankrupt; be gazetted.

protest, dishonor, repudiate, nullify.

pay under protest; button up one's pockets, draw the purse strings; apply the sponge; pay over the left shoulder, get whitewashed; swindle etc. 791; run up bills, fly kites.

Adj. not paying; in debt etc. 806; behindhand, in arrear; beggared etc. (*poor*) 804; unable to make both ends meet; *minus*; worse than nothing.

insolvent, bankrupt, in the gazette, gazetted, ruined.

unpaid etc. (*outstanding*) 806; *gratis* etc. 815; unremunerated.

809. Expenditure.—N. expenditure, money going out; out-goings, -lay; expenses, disbursement; prime cost etc. (*price*) 812; circulation; run upon a bank.

[Money paid] payment etc. 807; pay etc. (*remuneration*) 973; bribe etc. 973; fee, footing, garnish; subsidy; tribute, Peter's pence; contingent, quota; donation etc. 784.

pay in advance, earnest, handsel, deposit, instalment.

investment; purchase etc. 795.

V. expend, spend; run —, get- through; pay, disburse; open —, loose —, untie- the purse strings; lay —, shell —, fork- out; bleed; make up a sum, invest, sink money.

fee etc. (*reward*) 973; pay one's way etc. (*pay*) 807; subscribe etc. (*give*) 784; subsidize, bribe.

Adj. expend-ing, -ed etc. *v.*; sumptuary, liberal etc. 816; openhanded, lavish etc. 818; extensive etc. 814.

810. Receipt—N. receipt, accountable —, conditional —, binding —, return- receipt; value received, money coming in; income, incomings, innings, revenue, return, proceeds; gross receipts, net profit; earnings etc. (*gain*) 775.

rent, — roll; rent-al, -age; rack-rent.

premium, *bonus*; sweepstakes, tontine, prize, drawing.

pension, annuity; jointure etc. (*property*) 780; alimony, pittance; emolument etc. (*remuneration*) 973.

V. receive etc. 785; take money; draw —, derive- from; get, be in receipt of, acquire etc. 775; take etc. 789.

bring in, yield, afford, pay, return; accrue etc. (*be received from*) 785.

Adj. receiv-ing, -ed etc. *v.*; profitable etc. (*gainful*) 775.

811. Accounts.—N. accounts, accompts; commercial —, monetary- arithmetic; statistics etc. (*numeration*) 85; money matters, finance, budget, bill, score, reckoning, account.

books, account book, ledger; day —, cash —, pass- book; journal; debtor and creditor —, cash —, petty cash —, running- account; account-current; balance, — sheet; *compte rendu*, account settled.

book-keeping, audit; double —, single- entry; reckoning etc. 85.

chartered —, certified public —, accountant; auditor, actuary, bookkeeper; financier etc. 801; accounting party.

V. keep accounts, enter, post, book, credit, debit, carry over; take stock; balance —, make up —, square —, settle —, wind up —, cast up —, add up —, tot up- accounts; make accounts square.

bring to book, audit, tax, surcharge and falsify.

falsify —, garble —, cook —, doctor- an account.

Adj. monetary etc. 800; account-able, -ing; statistical.

812. Price.—N. price, amount, cost, expense, prime cost, charge, figure, demand, damage, fare, hire; wages etc. (*remuneration*) 973.

dues, duty, toll, tax, impost, cess, sess, tallage, levy, capitation-, poll-, income-, sur-, sales-, super-tax; gabel, *gabelle*; gavel, *octroi*, custom, tariff, excise, assessment, taxation, benevolence, tithe, tenths, exactment, ransom, salvage; broker-, wharf-, lighter-, ton-, freight-age.

worth, rate, value, valuation, appraisement, money's worth, par value; penny etc. -worth; price current, market price, quotation; what it will -fetch etc. *v.*

bill etc. (*account*) 811; shot.

V. bear -, set -, fix- a price; appraise, assess, price, charge, demand, ask, require, exact, run up; distrain; run up a bill etc. (*debt*) 806; have one's price; liquidate.

amount to, come to, mount up to; stand one in.
fetch, sell for, cost, bring in, yield, afford.

Adj. priced etc. *v.*; to the tune of, *ad valorem*; mercenary, venal.

Phr. no penny, no paternoster; *point d'argent, point de Suisse*, no longer pipe, no longer dance, no song, no supper.

one may have it for.

813. Discount.—N.
discount, abatement, concession, reduction, depreciation, allowance, qualification, set off, drawback, poundage, *agio*, percentage; rebate, -ment; backwardation, contango; salvage; tare and tret.

V. discount, bate; a-, re-bate; deduct, reduce, mark down, take off, allow, give, make allowance, tax, depreciate.

Adj. discounting etc. *v.*

Adv. at a discount, below par.

814. Dearness.—N.
dearness etc. *adj.*; high -, famine -, fancy- price; overcharge; extravagance; exorbitance, extortion; heavy pull upon the purse; Pyrrhic victory.

V. be -dear etc. *adj.*; cost -much, - a pretty penny; rise in price, look up.

overcharge, bleed, fleece, skin, extort.

pay -too much, - through the nose, -, too dear for one's whistle.

Adj. dear; high, -priced; of great price, expensive, costly, precious, worth a Jew's eye, dear bought; unreasonable, extravagant, exorbitant, extortionate.

at a premium; not to be had, - for love or money; beyond -, above- price; priceless, of priceless value.

Adv. dear, -ly; at great -, heavy- cost; *à grands frais*.

Phr. prices looking up; *le jeu ne vaut pas la chandelle*.

815. Cheapness.—N.
cheapness, low price; depreciation; bargain; good penny etc.- worth, *bon marché*.

[Absence of charge] gratuity; free -quarters, - seats, - admission, - warren; pass, Annie Oakley; run of one's teeth; nominal price, peppercorn rent; labor of love.

drug in the market.

V. be -cheap etc. *adj.*; cost little; come down -, fall- in price.

buy for -a mere nothing, - an old song; have one's money's worth; cheapen, beat down.

Adj. cheap; low, - priced; moderate, reasonable; in-, un-expensive; well -, worth the money; *magnifique et pas cher*; good -, cheap- at the price; dirt -, dog- cheap; cheap, -as dirt, - and nasty; catchpenny.

reduced, marked down, half-price, depreciated, unsaleable.

gratuitous, *gratis*, free, for love, - nothing; cost-, expense-less; without charge, not charged, untaxed; scot -, shot -, rent- free; free of -cost, - expense; honorary, unbought, unpaid, complimentary.

Adv. for a mere song; at -cost price, - prime cost, - a reduction, - a bargain; on the cheap.

816. Liberality.—N.
liberality, generosity, munificence; bount-y, -eousness, -ifulness; hospitality; charity etc. (*beneficence*) 906.

benefactor, free giver, Lady Bountiful.

V. be -liberal etc. *adj.*; spend -, bleed- freely; shower down upon; open one's purse strings etc. (*disburse*) 809; spare no expense, give -with both hands, - *carte blanche*.

Adj. liberal, free, generous; charitable etc. (*beneficent*) 906; hospitable; bount-iful, -eous; handsome; unsparing, ungrudging; open-, free-, full-handed; open-, large-, free-hearted; munificent, princely, unstinting.

overpaid.

Adv. liberally, ungrudgingly, with open hand.

817. Economy.—N.
economy, frugality; thrift, -iness; prudence, care, husbandry, good housewifery, savingness, retrenchment.

savings; prevention of waste, save-all; cheese parings and candle ends; parsimony etc. 819.

V. be -economical etc. *adj.*; economize, save; retrench; cut- down expenses, - one's coat according to one's cloth, make both ends meet, keep within compass, meet one's expenses, pay one's way; keep one's head above water; husband etc. (*lay by*) 636; save -, invest- money; put out to interest; provide -, save- -for, - against- a rainy day; feather one's nest; look after the main chance.

Adj. economical, frugal, careful, thrifty, saving, chary, spare, sparing; parsimonious etc. 819.

underpaid.

Adv. sparingly etc. *adj.*; *ne quid nimis*.

818. Prodigality.—N.
prodi-gality, -gence; unthriftiness, waste, -fulness; profus-ion, -eness; extravagance; squandering etc. *v.*; lavishness; malversation.

prodigal; spend-, waste-thrift; losel, play-boy, spender, squanderer, locust.

V. be -prodigal etc. *adj.*; squander, lavish, sow broadcast; pour forth like water; pay through the nose etc. (*dear*) 814; spill, waste, dissipate, exhaust, drain, eat out of house and home, overdraw, outrun the constable; run -out, - through; misspend; throw -good money after bad, - the helve after the hatchet; burn the candle at both ends; make ducks and drakes of one's money;

squander one's substance, spend money like water; fool –, potter –, muddle –, fritter –, throw-away one's money; pour water into a sieve, kill the goose that lays the golden eggs; *manger son blé en herbe*.

Adj. prodigal, profuse, thriftless, unthrifty, im-provident, wasteful, losel, extravagant, lavish, dissipated, over liberal; full-handed etc. (*liberal*) 816.

penny wise and pound foolish.

Adv. with an unsparing hand; money burning one's pocket; recklessly profuse.

Int. hang the expense!

819. Parsimony.—N. parsimony, parcity; par-simoniousness, stinginess etc. *adj.*; stint; illiberality, avarice, tenacity, avidity, rapacity, extortion, venality, cupidity; selfishness etc. 943; *auri sacra fames*.

miser, niggard, churl, screw, tightwad, skinflint, crib, codger, muckworm, money-grubber, pinch-fist, scrimp, lickpenny, hunks, curmudgeon, *Harpagon*, Silas Marner, harpy, extortioner, Jew, usurer.

V. be -parsimonious etc. *adj.*; grudge, begrudge, stint, skimp, pinch, gripe, screw, dole out, hold back, withhold, starve, famish, live upon nothing, skin a flint.

drive a -bargain, – hard bargain; cheapen, beat down; stop one hole in a sieve; have an itching palm, grasp, grab.

Adj. parsimonious, penurious, stingy, miserly, mean, shabby, peddling, scrubby, pennywise, near, niggardly, frugal to excess; close; fast-, close-, strait-handed; close-, hard-, tight-fisted; tight, sparing, chary, grudging, griping etc. *v.*; illiberal, ungenerous, churlish, hidebound, sordid, mer-cenary, venal, covetous, usurious, avaricious, greedy, extortionate, rapacious.

Adv. with a sparing hand.

820. Affections.—N. affections, character, qualities, disposition, nature, spirit, tone; temper, -ament; *diathesis*, idiosyncrasy; cast –, habit –, frame- of -mind, – soul; predilection, turn; natural –, turn of mind; bent, bias, predisposition, proneness, proclivity; propen-sity, -sedness, -sion, -dency; vein, humor, mood, grain, mettle; sympathy etc. (*love*) 897.

soul, heart, breast, bosom, inner man; heart's -core, – strings, – blood; heart of hearts, *penetralia mentis*; secret and inmost recesses of the –, cockles of one's- heart; inmost -heart, – soul; back-bone.

passion, pervading spirit; ruling –, master-passion; *furore*; fulness of the heart, heyday of the blood, flesh and blood, flow of soul, force of character.

V. have –, possess- -affections etc. *n.*; be of a -character etc. *n.*; be -affected etc. *adj.*; breathe.

Adj. affected, characterized, formed, molded, cast; at-, tempered; framed; pre-, disposed; prone, inclined; having a -bias etc. *n.*; tinctured –, im-bued –, penetrated –, eaten up- with.

inborn, inbred, ingrained, in the grain, congenital, inherent, bred in the bone; deep-rooted, ineffaceable, inveterate; pathoscopic.

Adv. in one's -heart etc. *n.*; at heart; heart and soul etc. 821; in the -vein, – mood.

821. Feeling.—N. feeling; suffering etc. *v.*; en-durance, tolerance, sufferance, supportance, ex-perience, response; sympathy etc. (*love*) 897; im-pression, inspiration, affection, sensation, emotion, pathos, deep sense.

fire, warmth, glow, unction, *gusto*, vehemence; ferv-or, -ency; heartiness, cordiality; earnestness, eagerness; *empressement*, ardor, zeal, passion, en-thusiasm, *verve, furore*, fanaticism; excitation of feeling etc. 824; fulness of the heart etc. (*disposition*) 820; passion etc. (*state of ex-citability*) 825; ecstasy etc. (*pleasure*) 827.

blush, suffusion, flush; hectic; tingling, thrill, kick, turn, shock; agitation etc. (*irregular motion*) 315; quiver, heaving, flutter, flurry, fluster, twitter, tremor; throb, -bing; pulsation, palpitation, paint-ing; trepid-, perturb-ation; ruffle, hurry of spirits, pother, stew, ferment.

V. feel; receive an -impression etc. *n.*; be -impressed with etc. *adj.*; entertain –, harbor –, cherish- -feeling etc. *n.*

respond; catch the -flame, – infection; enter the spirit of.

bear, suffer, support, sustain, endure, brook, thole, aby; abide etc. (*be composed*) 826; ex-perience etc. (*meet with*) 151; taste, prove; labor –, smart- under; bear the brunt of, brave, stand.

swell, glow, warm, flush, blush, change color, mantle; turn -color, – pale, – red, – black in the face; blench, crimson, whiten, pale, tingle, thrill, heave, pant, throb, palpitate, go pit-a-pat, tremble, quiver, flutter, twitter; stagger, reel; shake etc. 315; be -agitated, – excited etc. 824; look -blue, – black; wince, draw a deep breath.

impress etc. (*excite the feelings*) 824.

Adj. feeling etc. *v.*; sentient; sensuous; sensor-ial, -y; emo-tive, -tional; of –, with- feeling etc. *n.*

warm, quick, lively, smart, strong, sharp, acute, cutting, piercing, incisive; keen, – as a' razor; trench-ant, pungent, racy, *piquant*, poignant, caustic.

impressive, deep, profound, indelible; deep-, home-, heart-felt; swelling, soul-stirring, deep-mouthed, heart-expanding, electric, thrilling, rap-turous, ecstatic.

earnest, wistful, eager, breathless; fer-vent, -vid; gushing, passionate, warmhearted, hearty, cordial, sincere, zealous, enthusiastic, glowing, ardent, burning, red-hot, fiery, flaming; boiling, – over.

pervading, penetrating, absorbing; rabid, raving feverish, fanatical, hysterical; impetuous etc. (*ex-citable*) 825; overmastering.

impressed –, moved –, touched –, affected –, penetrated –, seized –, imbued etc. 820- with; devoured by; wrought up etc. (*excited*) 824; struck all of a heap; rapt; in a -quiver etc. *n.*; enraptured etc. 829.

Adv. heart and soul, from the bottom of one's heart, *ab imo pectore, de profundis*, at heart, *con amore*, heartily, devoutly, over head and ears.

Phr. the heart -big, – full, – swelling, – beating, – pulsating, – throbbing, – thumping, – beating high, – melting, – overflowing, – bursting, – breaking.

822. Sensibility.—N. sensi-bility, -bleness, -tiveness; moral sensibility; impress-, affect-ibility; suscepti-bleness, -bility, -vity; mobility; viva-city, -ciousness; tender-, soft-ness; sentimental-ity, -ism.

excitability etc. 825; fastidiousness etc. 868; physical sensibility etc. 375.

sore -point, – place; where the shoe pinches.
V. be -sensible etc. *adj.*; have a -tender, –
warm, – sensitive- heart.

take to –, treasure up in the- heart; shrink.
'die of a rose in aromatic pain;' touch to the
quick.

Adj. sensi-ble, -tive; impressi-ble, -onable;
suscepti-ve, -ble; alive to, impassion-able, -ed;
gushing; warm-, tender-, soft-hearted; tender –, as
a chicken; soft, sentimental, romantic; enthusiastic,
highflying, spirited, mettlesome, vivacious, lively,
expressive, mobile, tremblingly alive; excitable etc.
825; over-sensitive, without skin, thin-skinned;
fastidious etc. 868.

Adv. sensibly etc. *adj.*; to the -quick, – inmost
core.

---

823. Insensibility.—N. insensi-bility, -bleness;
moral insensibility; inertness, *inertia, vis inertiae*;
impassi-bility, -bleness; inappetency, apathy,
phlegm, dulness, hebetude, supineness, lukewarmness, insusceptibility, unimpressibility.

cold -fit, – blood, – heart; cold-, cool-ness;
frigidity, *sang-froid*; stoicism, imperturbation etc.
(*inexcitability*) 826; *nonchalance*, unconcern, dry
eyes; *insouciance* etc. (*indifference*) 866;
recklessness etc. 863; callousness; heart of stone,
stock and stone, marble, deadness.

torp-or, -idity; obstupefaction, lethargy, coma,
trance; sleep etc. 683; suspended animation; stup-
or, -efaction; paralysis, palsy; numbness etc.
(*physical insensibility*) 376.

neutrality; quietism, vegetation.

V. be -insensible etc. *adj.*; have a rhinoceros
. hide; show -insensibility etc. *n.*; not -mind, – care,
– be affected by; have no desire for etc. 866; have
–, feel –, take- no interest in; *nil admirari*; not care
a -straw etc. (*unimportance*) 643 for; disregard etc.
(*neglect*) 460; set at naught etc. (*make light of*)
483; turn a deaf ear to etc. (*inattention*) 458;
vegetate.

render -insensible, – callous; blunt, obtund,
numb, benumb, paralyze, chloroform, deaden,
hebetate, stun, stupefy; brut-ify, -alize.

inure; harden, – the heart; steel, case-harden,
sear.

Adj. insensible, unconscious; impassi-ve, -ble;
blind to, deaf to, dead to; un-, in-susceptible; unim-
press-ionable, -ible; passion-, spirit-, heart-, soulless; unfeeling, unmoral.

apathetic; leuco-, phlegmatic; dull, frigid; cold, -
blooded, -hearted; unemotional; cold as charity;
flat, obtuse, inert, supine, sluggish, torpid; sleepy
etc. (*inactive*) 683; languid, half-hearted, tame;
numb, -ed; comatose; anesthetic etc. 376;
stupefied, chloroformed, palsy-stricken.

indifferent, lukewarm; Laodicean; careless, mindless, regardless; inattentive etc. 458; neglectful
etc. 460; disregarding.

unconcerned, *nonchalant, pococurante, insouciant, sans souci*; unambitious etc. 866.

un-affected, -ruffled, -impressed, -inspired, -
excited, -moved, -stirred, -touched, -shocked, -
struck; unblushing etc. (*shameless*) 885;
unanimated; vegetative.

callous, thick-skinned, pachydermatous, impervious, hard, -ened; inured, case-hardened;
steeled –, proof- against; imperturbable etc. (*inexcitable*) 826; unfelt.

Adv. insensibly etc. *adj.*; *aequo animo*; without
being -moved, – touched, – impressed; in cold
blood; with -dry eyes, – withers unwrung.

Phr. never mind; it is of no consequence etc.
(*unimportant*) 643; it cannot be helped; nothing
coming amiss; it is all -the same, – one- to.

---

824. Excitation.—N. excitation of feeling;
mental –, excitement; suscitation, galvanism,
stimulation, piquancy, provocation inspiration,
calling forth, infection; interest, animation,
agitation, perturbation; subjugation, fascination,
intoxication; en-, ravishment; entrancement, high
pressure.

unction, impressiveness etc. *adj.*; emotional appeal; melodrama; psychological moment, crisis;
sensationalism.

trail of temper, *casus belli*; irritation etc. (*anger*)
900; passion etc. (*state of excitability*) 825; thrill
etc. (*feeling*) 821; repression of feeling etc. 826.

V. excite, affect, touch, move, impress, strike, interest, intrigue, animate, inspire, impassion, smite,
infect; stir –, fire –, warm- the blood; set astir; a-,
wake; a-, waken; call forth; e-, pro-voke; raise up,
summon up, call up, wake up, blow up, get up,
light up; raise; get up steam, rouse, arouse, stir, fire,
kindle, enkindle, apply the torch, set on fire, inflame, illuminate.

stimulate; ex-, suscitate; inspirit; spirit up, stir up,
work up; infuse life into, five new life to; bring –,
introduce- new blood; `quicken; sharpen, whet;
work upon etc. (*incite*) 615; hurry on, give a fillip,
put on one's mettle.

fan the -fire, – flame; blow the coals, stir the
embers; fan, – into a flame; foster, heat, warm,
foment, raise to a fever heat; keep -up, – the pot
boiling; revive, rekindle; rake up, rip up.

stir –, play on –, come home to the feelings;
touch -a string, – a chord, – the soul, – the
heart; go to one's heart, penetrate, pierce, go
through one, touch to the quick, open the wound;
possess –, pervade –, penetrate –, imbrue –,
absorb –, affect –, disturb- the soul.

absorb, rivet the attention; sink into the -mind,
– heart; prey on the mind; intoxicate; over-whelm,
-power; *bouleverser*, upset, turn one's head.

fascinate; enrapture etc. (*give pleasure*) 829.

agitate, perturb, ruffle, fluster, flutter, shake,
disturb, faze, startle, shock, stagger; give one a -
shock, – turn; strike -dumb, – all of a heap; stun,
astound, electrify, galvanize, petrify.

irritate, sting; cut, – to the -heart, – quick; try
one's temper; fool to the top of one's bent, pique;
infuriate, madden, make one's blood boil; lash into
fury etc. (*wrath*) 900.

be -excited etc. *adj.*; flash up, flare up; catch the
infection; thrill etc. (*feel*) 821; mantle; work
oneself up; seethe, boil, simmer, foam, fume,
flame, rage, rave; run mad etc. (*passion*) 825.

Adj. excited etc. *v.*; wrought up, on the *qui vive*,
astir, sparkling; in a -quiver etc. 821, – fever, –
ferment, – blaze, – state of excitement; in
hysterics; black in the face, over-wrought; hot, red-
hot, flushed, feverish; all -of a twitter, – of a flutter, – of a dither, – in a pucker; with -quivering
lips, – tears in one's eyes.

flaming; boiling, – over; ebullient, seething;
foaming, – at the mouth; fuming, raging, carried
away by passion, wild, raving, frantic, mad, dis-

tracted, distraught, beside oneself, out of one's wits, amuck, ready to burst, *bouleversé*, demoniacal.

lost, *eperdu*, tempest-tossed; haggard; ready to sink.

stung to the quick, up, on one's high ropes.

exciting etc. *v.*; impressive, warm, glowing, fervid, swelling, imposing, spirit-stirring, thrilling; high-wrought; soul-stirring, -subduing; heart-swelling, -thrilling; agonizing etc. (*painful*) 830; telling, sensational, melodramatic, hysterical; overpowering, -whelming; more than flesh and blood can bear.

piquant etc. (*pungent*) 392; spicy, appetizing, provocative, *provaquant*, tantalizing.

Adv. till one is black in the face.

Phr. the heart -beating high, − going pit-a-pat, − leaping into one's mouth; the blood -being up, − boiling in one's veins; the eye -glistening, − 'in a fine frenzy rolling;' the head turned.

825. Excitability. [Excess of sensitiveness.]—**N.** excitability, impetuosity, vehemence; boisterousness etc. *adj.*; turbulence; impatience, intolerance, non-endurance; irritability etc. (*irascibility*) 901; itching etc. (*desire*) 865; wincing; disquiet, -ude; restlessness; fidge-ts, -tiness; agitation etc. (*irregular motion*) 315.

trepidation, perturbation, ruffle, hurry, -skurry, fuss, flurry; fluster, flutter; pother, stew, ferment; whirl; thrill etc. (*feeling*) 821; state −, fever- of excitement; transport.

passion, excitement, flush, heat; fever, -heat; fire, flame, fume, blood boiling; tumult; effervescence, ebullition; boiling, − over; whiff, gust, storm, tempest; scene, breaking out, burst, fit, paroxysm, explosion; out-break, -burst; agony.

violence etc. 173; fierceness etc. *adj.*; rage, fury, *furor, furore*, desperation, madness, distraction, raving, delirium, brain storm; frenzy, hysterics; intoxication; tearing −, raging- passion, towering rage; anger etc. 900.

fascination, infatuation, fanaticism; Quixot-ism, -ry; *tête montée*.

V. be -impatient etc. *adj.*; not be able to -bear etc. 826; bear ill, wince, chafe, champ the bit; be in a -stew etc. *n.*; be out of all patience, fidget, fuss, not have a wink of sleep; toss, − on one's pillow.

lose one's temper etc. 900; break −, burst −, fly- out; go −, fly- -off, − off the handle, − off at a tangent; explode; flare up, flame up, fire up, burst into a flame, take fire, fire, burn; boil, − over; foam, fume, rage, rave, rant, tear; go −, run- wild, − mad; go into hysterics; run -riot, − amuck; *battre la campagne, faire le diable à quatre*, play the deuce; raise -Cain, − the devil.

Adj. excitable, easily excited, in an excitable state; high strung, irritable etc. (*irascible*) 901; impatient, intolerant.

feverish, febrile, hysterical; delirious, mad, moody, maggoty-headed.

unquiet, mercurial, electric, galvanic, hasty, hurried, restless, fidgety, fussy; chafing etc. *v.*

startlish, mettlesome, high mettled, skittish.

vehement, demonstrative, violent, wild, furious, fierce, fiery, hot-headed, mad-cap.

over-zealous, enthusiastic, impassioned, fanatical; rabid etc. (*eager*) 865.

rampant, clamorous, uproarious, turbulent, tempestuous, tumultuary, boisterous.

impulsive, impetuous, passionate; uncontroll-ed, -able; ungovernable, irrepressible, stanchless, inextinguishable, burning, simmering, volcanic, ready to burst forth.

excit-ed, -ing etc. 824.

Int. pish! pshaw!

Phr. *noli me tangere*.

826. Inexcitability. [Absence of excitability, or of excitement.]—**N.** inexcit-, imperturb-, inirritability; even temper, tranquil mind, dispassion; tolerance, toleration, patience.

passiveness etc. (*physical inertness*) 172; hebetude, -ation; impassibility etc. (*insensibility*) 823; stupefaction.

coolness, calmness etc. *adj.*; composure, placidity, indisturbance, imperturbation, *sang-froid*, tranquility, serenity; quiet, -ude; peace of mind, mental calmness.

staidness etc. *adj.*; gravity, sobriety, Quakerism; philosophy, equanimity, stoicism, command of temper; self-possession, -control, -command, -restraint; presence of mind.

submission etc. 725; resignation; suffer-, support-, endur-, long-suffer-, forbear-ance; longanimity; fortitude; patience -of Job, − 'on a monument,' − 'sovereign o'er transmuted ill;' moderation; repression −, subjugation- of feeling; restraint etc. 751.

tranquilization etc. (*moderation*) 174.

V. be -composed etc. *adj.*

laisser -faire, − aller; take things -easily, − as they come; take it easy, run on, live and let live; take -easily, − cooly, − in good part; *aequam serva e mentem*.

bear, − well, − the brunt; go through, support, endure, brave, disregard.

tolerate, suffer, stand, bide; abide, aby; bear −, put up −, abide- with; acquiesce; submit etc. (*yield*) 725; submit with a good grace; resign −, reconcile- oneself to; brook, digest, eat, swallow, pocket, stomach; make -light of, − the best of, − a virtue of necessity; put a good face on, keep one's countenance; carry -on, − through; check etc. 751- oneself.

compose, appease etc. (*moderate*) 174; propitiate; repress etc. (*restrain*) 751; render insensible etc. 823; overcome −, allay −, repress- one's -excitability etc. 825; master one's feelings.

make -oneself, − one's mind- easy; set one's mind at -ease, − rest.

calm −, cool- down; thaw, grow cool.

be -borne, − endured; go down.

Adj. in-, un-excitable; imperturbable; unsusceptible etc. (*insensible*) 823; un-, dis-passionate; cold-blooded, inirritable; enduring etc. *v.*; stoical, Platonic, philosophic, staid, stayed; sober, − minded; grave; sober −, grave- as a judge; sedate, demure, cool-, level-headed; steady.

easy-going, peaceful, placid, calm; quiet, − as a mouse; tranquil, serene; cool, − as a cucumber, − custard; undemonstrative.

temperate etc. (*moderate*) 174; composed, collected; un-excited, -stirred, -ruffled, -disturbed, -perturbed, -impassioned; unoffended; unresisting.

meek, tolerant, patient, − as Job; submissive etc. 725; tame; content, resigned, chastened, subdued, lamblike; gentle, − as a lamb; *suaviter in modo*; mild, − as mother's milk; soft as pep-

permint; armed with patience, bearing with,
clement, forbearant, long-suffering.

Adv. 'like patience on a monument smiling at
grief;' *aequo animo,* in cold blood etc. 823; more
in sorrow than in anger.

Int. patience! and shuffle the cards.

827. Pleasure.—N. pleasure, gratification, enjoyment, fruition; ob-, de-lectation; relish, zest;
gusto etc. (*physical pleasure*) 377; satisfaction etc.
(*content*) 831; complacency.

well-being; good etc. 618; snugness, comfort,
ease; cushion etc. 215; *sans souci,* mind at ease.

joy, gladness, delight, glee, cheer, sunshine;
cheerfulness etc. 836.

treat, refreshment; frolic, fun, lark, gambol,
merry-making; amusement etc. 840; luxury etc.
377; hedonism.

mens sana in corpore sano.

happiness, felicity, bliss; beati-tude, -fication; enchantment, transport, rapture, ravishment, ecstasy;
summum bonum; paradise, elysium etc. (*heaven*)
981; third —, seventh- heaven; unalloyed -
happiness etc.

honeymoon; palmy —, halcyon- days; golden -
age, — time; *Saturnia regna,* Eden, Arcadia,
happy valley, Agapemone; Cockaigne.

V. be pleased etc. 829; feel —, experience-
pleasure etc. *n.*; joy; enjoy —, hug- oneself; be in -
clover etc. 377, — elysium etc. 981; tread on enchanted ground; fall —, go- into raptures.

feel at home, breathe freely, bask in the sunshine.

be -pleased etc. 829- with; receive —, derive-
pleasure etc. *n.*- from; take -pleasure etc. *n.*- in;
delight in, rejoice in, indulge in, luxuriate in; gloat
over etc. (*physical pleasure*) 377; enjoy, relish,
like; love etc. 897; take -to, — a fancy to; have a
liking for; enter into the spirit of.

take in good part.

treat oneself to, solace oneself with.

Adj. pleased etc. 829; not sorry; glad, -some;
pleased as Punch.

happy, blest, blessed, blissful, beatified; happy as
-a king, — the day is long; thrice happy, *ter
quaterque beatus;* enjoying etc. *v.*; joyful etc. (*in
spirits*) 836; hedonic.

in -a blissful state, — paradise etc. 981; — raptures, — ecstasies, — a transport of delight.

comfortable etc. (*physical pleasure*) 377; at
ease; content etc. 831; *sans souci,* in clover.

overjoyed, entranced, enchanted; enraptured;
en-, ravished; transported; fascinated, captivated.
with -a joyful face, — sparkling eyes.

pleasing etc. 829; ecstatic, beat-ic, -ific; painless,
unalloyed, without alloy, cloudless.

Adv. happily etc. *adj.*; with pleasure etc.
(*willingly*) 60; with -glee etc. *n.*

phr. one's heart leaping with joy.

828. Pain.—N. mental suffering, pain, dolor;
suffer-ing, -ance; ache, smart etc. (*physical pain*)
378; passion.

displeasure, dissatisfaction, discomfort, discomposure, disquiet; *malaise;* inquietude, uneasiness,
vexation of spirit; taking; discontent etc. 832.

dejection etc. 837; weariness etc. 841.

annoyance, irritation, worry, infliction,
visitation; plague, bore; bother, -ation; stew,
vexation, mortification, chagrin, *esclandre;*
mauvais quart d'heure.

care, anxiety, solicitude, trouble, trial, ordeal,
fiery ordeal, shock, blow, cark, dole, fret, burden,
load.

concern, grief, sorrow, distress, affliction, woe,
bitterness, gloom, heartache; heavy —, aching —,
bleeding —, broken- heart; heavy affliction,
gnawing grief; unhappiness, infelicity, misery,
tribulation, wretchedness, desolation; despair etc.
859; extremity, prostration, depth of misery.

nightmare, *ephialtes,* incubus.

anguish, agony; throe, tor-ture, -ment;
crucifixion, martyrdom; pang, twinge, stab; the
rack, the stake; purgatory etc. (*hell*) 982.

hell upon earth; iron age, reign of terror; slough
of despond etc. (*adversity*) 735; peck —, sea- of
troubles; ills that flesh is heir to etc. (*evil*) 619;
miseries of human life; unkindest cut of all.

sufferer, victim, prey, martyr, object of compassion, wretch, shorn lamb.

V. feel —, suffer —, experience —, undergo —,
bear —, endure- pain etc. *n.*; smart, ache etc.
(*physical pain*) 378; suffer, bleed, ail; be the victim
of; bear — take up- the cross.

labor under afflictions; quaff the bitter cup, have
a bad time of it; fall on evil days etc. (*adversity*)
735; go hard with, come to grief, pay a sacrifice to,
drain the cup of misery to the dregs, sup full of
horrors.

sit on thorns, be on pins and needles, wince, fret,
chafe, worry oneself, be in a taking, fret and fume,
take -on, — to heart.

grieve; mourn etc. (*lament*) 839; yearn, repine,
pine, droop, languish, sink; give way; despair etc.
859; break one's heart; weigh upon the heart etc.
(*inflict pain*) 830.

Adj. in —, in a state of —, full of- pain etc. *n.*;
suffering etc. *v.*; pained, afflicted, worried,
displeased etc. 830; aching, griped, sore etc.
(*physical pain*) 378; on the rack; in limbo; between hawk and buzzard.

un-comfortable, -easy; ill at ease; in a -taking, —
way; disturbed; discontented etc. 832; out of
humor etc. 901a; weary etc. 841.

heavy laden, stricken, crushed, a prey to, victimized, ill-used.

unfortunate etc. (*hapless*) 735; to be pitied,
doomed, devoted, accursed, undone, lost, stranded.

unhappy, infelicitous, poor, wretched, miserable,
woe-begone; cheerless etc. (*dejected*) 837;
careworn.

concerned, sorry; sorrow-ing, -ful; cut up,
chagrined, horrified, horror-stricken; in —,
plunged in —, a prey to- grief etc. *n.*; in tears etc.
(*lamenting*) 839; steeped to the lips in misery;
heart-stricken, -broken, -scalded; broken-hearted;
in despair etc. 859.

Phr. 'the iron entered into our soul;' *haeret
lateri lethalis arundo;'* one's heart bleeding.

829. Pleasurableness. [Capability of giving
pleasure; cause or source of pleasure.]—**N.**
pleasurable-, pleasant-, agreeable-ness etc. *adj.*;
pleasure giving, jocundity, delectability;
amusement etc. 840.

attraction etc. (*motive*) 615; attractiveness, -

ability; invitingness etc. *adj.*; charm, fascination, captivation, enchantment, witchery, seduction, winsomeness, winning ways, amenity, amiability, sweetness.

loveliness etc. (*beauty*) 845; sunny –, brightside; sweets etc. (*sugar*) 396; goodness etc. 648; manna in the wilderness, land flowing with milk and honey.

treat; regale etc. (*physical pleasure*) 377; dainty; tit-, tid-bit; nuts, *sauce piquante.*

V. cause –, produce –, create –, give –, afford –, procure –, offer –, present –, yield-pleasure etc. 827.

please, charm, delight; gladden etc. (*make cheerful*) 836; take, captivate, fascinate; enchant, entrance, enrapture, transport, bewitch; en–, ravish.

bless, beatify; satisfy; gratify –, desire etc. 865; slake, satiate, quench; indulge, humor, flatter, tickle; tickle the palate etc. (*savory*) 394; regale, refresh; enliven; treat; amuse etc. 840; take –, tickle –, hit- one's fancy; meet one's wishes; win –, gladden –, rejoice –, warm the cockles of- the heart; do one's heart good.

attract, allure etc. (*move*) 615; stimulate etc. (*excite*) 824; interest, intrigue.

make things pleasant, popularize, gild the pill, sweeten.

Adj. causing pleasure etc. *v.*; pleasure-giving; pleas-ing, -ant, -urable; agreeable, cushy; grat-eful, -ifying; leef, lief, acceptable; welcome, – as the roses in May; welcomed; favorite; to one's -taste, – mind, – liking, – heart's content; satisfactory etc. (*good*) 648.

refreshing; comfortable; cordial; genial; glad, – some; sweet, delectable, nice, dainty; delic-ate, -ious; dulcet; luscious etc. 396; palatable etc. 394; luxurious, voluptuous; sensual etc. 377.

attractive etc. 615; inviting, prepossessing, engaging; win-ning, -some; taking, fascinating, captivating, killing; seduc-ing, -tive; alluring, enticing; appetizing etc. (*exciting*) 824; cheering etc. 836; bewitching; interesting, absorbing, enchanting, entrancing, enravishing.

charming; delightful, felicitous, exquisite; lovely etc. (*beautiful*) 845; ravishing, rapturous; heartfelt; thrilling, ecstatic; beat-ic, -ific; seraphic; empyrean; elysian etc. (*heavenly*) 981.

palmy, halcyon, Saturnian.

Phr. *decies repetita placebit.*

830. Painfulness. [Capability of giving pain; cause or source of pain.]—**N.** painfulness etc. *adj.* ; trouble, care etc. (*pain*) 828; trial; af-, in-fliction; cross, blow, stroke, burden, load, curse; bitter -pill, –ʼ draught, – cup; waters of bitterness.

annoyance, grievance, nuisance, vexation, mortification, sickener; bore, bother, pother, hot water, sea of troubles, hornet's nest, plague, pest.

cancer, ulcer, sting, thorn; canker etc. (*bane*) 663; scorpion etc. (*evil-doer*) 913; dagger etc. (*arms*) 727; scourge etc. (*instrument of punishment*) 975; carking –, canker worm of- care.

mishap, misfortune etc. (*adversity*) 735; *désagrément, esclandre,* rub.

source of -irritation, – annoyance; wound, sore subject, skeleton in the closet; thorn in -the flesh, – one's side; where the shoe pinches, gall and wormwood.

sorry sight, heavy news, provocation; affront etc. 929; head and front of one's offending.

infestation, molestation; malignity etc. (*malevolence*) 907.

V. cause –, occasion –, give –, bring –, induce –, produce –, create –, inflict- pain etc. 828; pain, hurt, wound.

pinch, prick, gripe etc. (*physical pain*) 378; pierce, lancinate, cut.

hurt –, wound –, grate upon –, jar upon- the feelings; wring –, pierce –, lacerate –, break –, rend- the heart; make the heart bleed; tear –, rend- the heart-strings; draw tears from the eyes.

sadden; make -unhappy etc. 828; plunge into sorrow, grieve, fash, afflict, distress; cut -up, – to the heart.

displease, annoy, incommode, discommode, discompose, trouble, disquiet, disturb, thwart, cross, perplex, molest, tease, rag, tire, irk, vex, mortify, wherret, worry, plague, bother, pester, bore, pother, harass, harry, badger, heckle, bait, beset, infest, persecute, importune, be troublesome.

wring, harrow, torment, torture; put to the -rack, – question; break on the wheel, rack, scarify; cruci-ate, -fy; convulse, agonize; barb the dart; plant a -dagger in the breast, – thron in one's side.

irritate, provoke, sting, nettle, try the patience, pique, fret, rile, tweak the nose, chafe, gall; sting –, wound –, cut- to the quick; aggrieve, affront, enchafe, enrage, ruffle, sour the temper; give offence etc. (*resentment*) 900.

maltreat, bite, snap at, assail, bully; smite etc. (*punish*) 972.

sicken, disgust, revolt, nauseate, disenchant, repel, offend, shock, stink in the nostrils; go against –, turn- the stomach; make one sick, set the teeth on edge, go against the grain, grate on the ear; stick in one's -throat, – gizzard; rankle, gnaw, corrode, horrify, appal, freeze the blood; chill the spine; make the -flesh creep, – hair stand on end; make the blood -curdle, – run cold; make one shudder.

haunt, – the memory; weigh –, prey- on the -heart, – mind, – spirits; bring one's grey hairs with sorrow to the grave; add a nail to one's coffin.

Adj. causing pain, hurting etc. *v.*; hurtful etc. (*bad*) 649; painful; dolor-ific, -ous; unpleasant; un-, dis-pleasing; disagreeable, unpalatable, bitter, distasteful; uninviting; unwelcome; undesir-able, -ed; obnoxious; unacceptable, unpopular, thankless.

unsatisfactory, untoward, unlucky, uncomfortable.

distressing; afflict-ing, -ive; joy-, cheer-, comfort-less; dismal, disheartening; depress-ing, -ive; dreary, melancholy, grievous, piteous, woeful, rueful, mournful, deplorable, pitiable, lamentable; sad, affecting, touching, pathetic.

irritating, provoking, stinging, annoying, aggravating, mortifying, galling; unac-commodating, invidious, vexatious; trouble-, tire-, irk-, weari-some; plagu-ing, -y; awkward.

importunate; teas-, pester-, bother-, harass-, worry-, torment-, cark-ing.

in-toler-, -suffer-, -support-able; un-bear-, -endur-able; past bearing; not to be -borne, – endured; more than flesh and blood can bear; enough to -drive one mad, – provoke a saint, – make a parson swear, – try the patience of Job.

shocking, terrific, grim, appalling, crushing; dreadful, fearful, frightful; thrilling, tremendous, dire; heart-breaking, -rending, -wounding, -corroding, -sickening; harrowing, rending.

odious, hateful, execrable, repulsive, repellent; abhorrent; horri-d, -ble, -fic, -fying; offensive; nause-ous, -ating; disgust-, sicken-, revolt-ing; nasty; loath-some, -ful; fulsome; vile etc. (*bad*) 649; hideous etc. 846.

sharp, acute, sore, severe, grave, hard, harsh, cruel, biting, acrimonious, caustic; cutting, corroding, consuming, racking, excruciating, searching, searing, grinding, grating, agonizing; envenomed.

ruinous, disastrous, calamitous, tragical; desolating, withering; burdensome, onerous, oppressive; cumb-rous, -ersome.

Adv. painfully etc. *adj.*; with -pain etc. 828; deuced.

Int. *hinc illae lachrymae!* woe is me!

Phr. *surgit amari aliquid;* the place being too hot to hold one; the iron entering the soul.

831. Content.—N. content, -ment, -edness; complacency, satisfaction, entire satisfaction, ease, heart's ease, peace of mind; serenity etc. 826; cheerfulness etc. 836; ray of comfort; comfort etc. (*well-being*) 827.

re-, conciliation; resignation etc. (*patience*) 826. waiter on Providence.

V. be -content etc. *adj.*; rest -satisfied, — and be thankful; take the good the gods provide, let well alone, feel oneself at home, hug oneself, lay the flattering unction to one's soul.

take -up with, — in good part; assent etc. 488; be reconciled to, make one's peace with; get over it; take -heart, — comfort; put up with etc. (*bear*) 826.

render -content etc. *adj.*; set at ease, comfort; set one's -heart, — mind- at -ease, — rest; speak peace; conciliate, reconcile, win over, propitiate, disarm, beguile; content, satisfy; gratify etc. 829.

be -tolerated etc. 826; go down, — with; do.

Adj. content, -ed; satisfied etc. *v.*; at -ease, — one's ease, — home; with the mind at ease, *sans souci, sine curâ,* easy-going, not particular; conciliatory; unrepining, of good comfort; resigned etc. (*patient*) 826; cheerful etc. 836.

un-afflicted, -vexed, -molested, -plagued; serene etc. 826; at rest; snug, comfortable; in one's element.

satisfactory, satisfying, ample, sufficient, adequate, tolerable.

Adv. to one's heart's content; *à la bonne heure;* all for the best.

Int. amen etc. (*assent*) 488; very well, so much the better, well and good; it —, that- will do; it cannot be helped.

Phr. nothing comes amiss.

832. Discontent.—N. discontent, -ment; dissatisfaction; dissent etc. 489; labor unrest.

disappointment, mortification; cold comfort; regret etc. 833; repining, taking on etc. *v.*; inquietude, vexation of spirit, soreness; heart-burning, -grief; querulousness etc. (*lamentation*) 839; hypercriticism.

malcontent, grumbler, growler, croaker, *laudator temporis acti;* censurer, complainer,

faultfinder, murmurer, Adullamite, Diehard, Bitterender.

the Opposition, cave of Adullam, indignation meeting, 'winter of our discontent.'

V. be -discontented etc. *adj.*; quarrel with one's bread and butter; repine; regret etc. 833; wish one at the bottom of the Red Sea; take -on, — to heart; shrug the shoulders; make a wry —, pull a long-face; knit one's brows; look -blue, — black, — black as thunder, — blank, — glum.

take -in bad part, — ill; fret, chafe, make a piece of work; grumble, croak, grouse; lament etc. 839.

cause -discontent etc. *n.*; dissatisfy, disappoint, mortify, put out, disconcert; cut up; dishearten.

Adj. discontented; dissatisfied etc. *v.*; unsatisfied, ungratified; dissident; dissentient etc. 489; malcontent, exigent, exacting, hypercritical.

repining etc. *v.*; regretful etc. 833; down in the mouth etc. (*dejected*) 837.

in -high dudgeon, — a fume, — the sulks, — the dumps, — bad humor; glum, sulky; sour, — as a crab; soured, sore; out of -humor, — temper.

disappointing etc. *v.*; unsatisfactory.

Int. so much the worse!

Phr. that —, it- will never do.

833. Regret.—N. regret, repining; home sickness, nostalgia; *mal —, maladie- du pays;* lamentation etc. 839; contrition, compunction, penitence etc. 950.

bitterness, heart-burning.

laudator temporis acti etc. (*discontent*) 832.

V. regret, deplore; bewail etc. (*lament*) 839; repine, cast a longing lingering look behind; rue, — the day; repent etc. 950; *infandum renovare dolorem.*

prey —, weigh —, have a weight- on the mind; leave an aching void.

Adj. regretting etc. *v.*; regretful; home-sick.

regretted etc. *v.*; much to be regretted, regrettable; lamentable etc. (*bad*) 649.

Int. what a pity! hang it!

Phr. 'tis -pity, — too true.

834. Relief.—N. relief; deliverance; refreshment etc. 689; easement, softening, alleviation, mitigation, palliation etc. 174; soothing, lullaby; cradle song, *berceuse.*

solace, consolation, comfort, encouragement.

lenitive, restorative etc. (*remedy*) 662; poultice etc. *v.*; cushion etc. 215; crumb of comfort, balm in Gilead; aspirin.

V. relieve, ease, alleviate, mitigate, palliate, soothe, addulce; salve; soften, — down; foment, stupe, poultice; assuage, allay.

cheer, comfort, console; encourage, bear up, pat on the back, give comfort, set at ease; enliven, gladden —, cheer- the heart.

remedy; cure etc. (*restore*) 660; refresh; pour -balm into, — oil on.

smoothe the ruffled brow of care, temper the wind to the shorn lamb, lay the flattering unction to one's soul.

disburden etc. (*free*) 705; take off a load of care.

be relieved; breathe more freely, draw a long breath; take comfort; dry —, wipe- the -tears, — eyes.

Adj. relieving etc. *v.*; consolatory, soothing; assua-ging, -sive; bal-my, -samic; lenitive, palliative; anodyne etc. (*remedial*) 662; curative etc. 660.

835. Aggravation.—N. aggravation, heightening; exacerbation; exasperation; overestimation etc. 482; exaggeration etc. 549.

V. aggravate, render worse, heighten, embitter, sour; ex-, acerbate; exasperate, envenom; tease, provoke, enrage.

add fuel to the -fire, — flame; fan the flame etc. (*excite*) 824; go from bad to worse etc. (*deteriorate*) 659.

Adj. aggravated etc. *v.*; worse, unrelieved; aggravable; aggravating etc. *v.*

Adv. out of the frying pan into the fire, from bad to worse, worse and worse.

Int. so much the worse!

836. Cheerfulness.—N. cheerfulness etc. *adj.*; geniality, gaiety, *l'allegro*, cheer, good humor, spirits; high —, animal —, flow of- spirits; glee, high glee, light heart; sunshine of the -mind, — breast; *gaieté de coeur*, *bon naturel*.

liveliness etc. *adj.*; life, alacrity, vivacity, animation, *allégresse*; jocundity, joviality, jollity; levity; jocularity etc. (*wit*) 842.

mirth, merriment, hilarity, exhilaration; laughter etc. 838; merry-making etc. (*amusement*) 840; heyday, rejoicing etc. 838; marriage bells.

nepenthe, Euphrosyne.

optimism etc. (*hopefulness*) 858; self-complacency.

V. be -cheerful etc. *adj.*; have the mind at ease, smile, put a good face upon, keep up one's spirits; view -the bright side of the picture, — things *en couleur de rose*; *ridentem dicere verum*, cheer up, brighten up, light up, bear up; chirp, take heart, cast away care, drive dull care away, perk up.

rejoice etc. 838; carol, chirrup, lilt; frisk, rollick, give a loose to mirth.

cheer, enliven, elate, exhilarate, gladden, in-spirit, animate, raise the spirits, inspire; put in good humor; cheer —, rejoice- the heart; delight etc. (*give pleasure*) 829.

Adj. cheerful; happy etc. 827; cheer-y, -ly; of good cheer, smiling; blithe; in —, in good- spirits; in high -spirits, — feather; happy as -the day is long, — a king; gay, — as a lark; *allegro*; light, -some, -hearted; buoyant, *débonnaire*, bright, free and easy, airy; janty, jaunty, canty; spright-ly, -ful; spry; spirit-ed, -ful; lively, animated, breezy, vivacious; brisk, — as a bee; sparkling, sportive; full of -play, — spirit; all alive.

sunny, palmy; hopeful etc. 858.

merry, — as a -cricket, — grig, — marriage bell; joyful, joyous, jocund, jovial; jolly, — as a thrush, — as a sandboy; blithesome; glee-ful, -some; hilarious, rattling.

winsome, bonny, hearty, buxom.

play-ful, -some; *folâtre*, playful as a kitten, tricksy, frisky, frolicsome; gamesome; jocose, jocular, waggish; mirth-, laughter-loving; mirthful, rollicking.

elate, -d; exulting, jubilant, flushed; rejoicing etc. 838; cock-a-hoop.

cheering, inspiriting, exhilarating; cardiac, -al; pleasing etc. 829; flourishing, halcyon.

Adv. cheerfully etc. *adj.*

Int. never say die! come! cheer up! hurrah! etc. 838; 'hence loathed melancholy!' begone dull care! away with melancholy!

837. Dejection.—N. dejection; dejectedness etc. *adj.*; depression, prosternation; lowness —, depression- of spirits; weight —, oppression —, damp- on the spirits; low —, bad —, drooping —, depressed- spirits; heart sinking; heaviness —, failure- of heart.

heaviness etc. *adj.*; infestivity, gloom; weariness etc. 841; *taedium vitae*, disgust of life; *mal du pays* etc. (*regret*) 833.

melancholy; sadness etc. *adj.*; *il penseroso*, *melancholia*, dismals, mumps, mopes, lachrymals, dumps, blues, blue devils, doldrums, vapors, megrims, spleen, horrors, hypochondriasis, pessimism; despondency, slough of Despond; disconsolateness etc. *adj.*; hope deferred, blank despondency.

prostration, — of soul; broken heart; despair etc. 859; cave of -despair, — Trophonius.

demureness etc. *adj.*; gravity, solemnity; long —, grave- face.

hypochondriac, seek-sorrow, self-tormentor, *heautontimorumenos*, *malade imaginaire*, *médecin tant pis*; croaker, pessimist; mope, mopus.

[Cause of dejection] affliction etc. 830; sorry sight; *memento mori*; damper, wet blanket, Job's comforter; death's head, skeleton at the feast.

V. be -dejected etc. *adj.*; grieve; mourn etc. (*lament*) 839; take on, give way, lose heart, despond, droop, sink.

lower, look downcast, frown, pout; hang down the head; pull —, make- a long face; laugh on the wrong side of the mouth; grin a ghastly smile; look -blue, — like a drowned man; lay —, take- to heart.

mope, brood over; fret; sulk; pine, — away; yearn; repine etc. (*regret*) 833; despair etc. 859.

refrain from laughter, keep one's countenance; be —, look- grave etc. *adj.*; repress a smile, keep a straight face.

depress; dis-courage, -hearten; dis-pirit; damp, dull, deject, lower, sink, dash, knock down, un-man, prostrate, break one's heart; frown upon; cast a -gloom, — shade- on; sadden; damp —, dash —, wither- one's hopes; weigh —, lie heavy —, prey- on the -mind, — spirits; damp —, depress- the spirits.

Adj. cheer-, joy-, spirit-less; uncheer-ful, -y; unlively; unhappy etc. 828; melancholy, dismal, somber, dark, gloomy, adust, *trïste*, clouded, murky, lowering, frowning, lugubrious, Acheron-tic, funereal, mournful, lamentable, dreadful.

dreary, flat; dull, — as -a beetle, — ditchwater; depressing etc. *v.*

'melancholy as a gib cat;' oppressed with —; a prey to- melancholy; down-cast, -hearted; down -in the mouth, — on one's luck; heavy-hearted; in the -dumps, — suds, — sulks, — doldrums; in doleful dumps, in bad humor; sullen; mumpish, dumpish; mopish, moping; moody, glum; sulky etc. (*discontented*) 832; out of -sorts, — humor, — heart, — spirits; ill at ease, low-spirited, in low spirits, a cup

:oo low; weary etc. 841; dis-couraged, -heartened; -desponding; chop-, jaw-, crest-fallen.

sad, pensive, *penseroso*, tristful; dole-some, -ful; woebegone, lachrymose, in tears, melancholic, hypped, hypochondriacal, bilious, jaundiced, atrabilious, saturnine, splenetic; lackadaisical.

serious, sedate, staid, stayed; grave, – as -a judge, – an undertaker, – a mustard pot; sober, solemn, demure; grim; grim-faced, -visaged; rueful, wan, long-faced.

disconsolate; un-, in-consolable; forlorn, comfortless, desolate, *désolé*, sick at heart; soul-, heart-sick; *au désepoir*; in despair etc. 859; lost.

overcome; broken-, borne-, bowed-down; heart-stricken etc. (*mental suffering*) 828; cut up, dashed, sunk; unnerved, unmanned; down-fallen, -trodden; broken-hearted; care-worn.

Adv. with -a long face, – tears in one's eyes; sadly etc. *adj.*

Phr. the countenance falling; the heart -failing, – sinking within- one.

838. Rejoicing. [Expression of pleasure.]—**N.** rejoicing, exultation, triumph, jubilation, heyday, flush, revelling; merry-making etc. (*amusement*) 840; jubilee etc. (*celebration*) 883; *paean, Te Deum* etc. (*thanksgiving*) 990; congratulation etc. 896; applause etc. 971.

smile, simper, smirk, grin; broad –, sardonic-grin.

laughter, giggle, titter, crow, cheer, chuckle, snicker, snigger, shout; Homeric laughter, horse –, hearty- laugh; guffaw; burst –, fit –, shout –, roar –, peal- of laughter; cachinnation.

risibility; derision etc. 856.

Momus; Democritus the Abderite; rollicker; Laughter holding both his sides.

V. rejoice; thank –, bless- one's stars; congratulate –, hug- oneself; rub –, clap- one's hands; smack the lips, fling up one's cap; dance, skip, caleer; sing, carol, chirrup, chirp; hurrah; cry for –, leap with- joy; exult etc. (*boast*) 884; triumph; hold jubilee etc. (*celebrate*) 883; make merry etc. (*sport*) 840; sing a paean of joy.

smile, simper, smirk, grin; – like a Cheshire cat; mock, laugh in one's sleeve; laugh, – outright; giggle, titter, snigger, crow, smicker, chuckle, snicker, cackle; burst -out, – into a fit of laughter; shout, split, roar.

shake –, split –, hold both- one's sides; roar –, die- with laughter.

raise laughter etc. (*amuse*) 840.

Adj. rejoicing etc. *v.*; jubilant, exultant, triumphant; flushed, elated; laughing etc. *v.*; risible; ready to -burst, – split, – die with laughter; convulsed with laughter.

laughable etc. (*ludicrous*) 853.

Int. hip, hip, -hurrah! huzza! aha! hail! tolderolloll! tra-la la! Heaven be praised! *io triumphe! tant mieux!* so much the better.

Phr. the heart leaping with joy.

839. Lamentation. [Expression of pain.]—**N.** lament, -ation; wail, complaint, plaint, murmur, mutter, grumble, groan, moan, whine, whimper, sob, sigh, suspiration, heaving, deep sigh.

cry etc. (*vociferation*) 411; scream, howl, outcry, wail of woe, frown, scowl.

tear; weeping etc. *v.*; flood of tears, fit of crying, lachrymation, melting mood, weeping and gnashing of teeth.

plaintiveness etc. *adj.*; languishment; condolence etc. 915.

mourning, weeds, willow, cypress, crêpe, crape, deep mourning; sackcloth and ashes; knell etc. 363; dump, deathsong, dirge, coronach, keen, *nenia*, requiem, elegy, *epicedium*; threne; mon-, thren-ody; jeremiad; ululation.

mourner, professional mourner, keener; grumbler etc. (*discontent*) 832; Niobe; Heraclitus.

V. lament, mourn, deplore, grieve, weep over; be-wail, -moan; keen; condole with etc. 915; fret etc. (*suffer*) 828; wear –, go into –, put on- mourning; wear -the willow, – sackcloth and ashes; *infandum renovare dolorem* etc. (*regret*) 833; give sorrow words.

sigh; give –, heave –, fetch- a sigh; 'waft a sigh from Indus to the pole;' sigh 'like furnace;' wail.

cry, weep, sob, greet, blubber, pipe, snivel, bibber, whimper, pule; pipe one's eye; drop –, shed- -tears, – a tear; melt –, burst- into tears; *fondre en larmes*; cry -oneself blind, – one's eyes out.

scream etc. (*cry out*) 411; mew etc. (*animal sounds*) 412; groan, moan, whine, yammer; roar; roar –, bellow- like a bull; cry out lustily, rend the air, yell.

frown, scowl, make a wry face, grimace, gnash one's teeth, wring one's hands, tear one's hair, beat one's breast, roll on the ground, burst with grief.

complain, murmur, mutter, grumble, growl, clamor, make a fuss about, croak, grunt, maunder; deprecate etc. (*disapprove*) 932.

cry out before one is hurt, complain without cause.

Adj. lamenting etc. *v.*; in mourning, in sackcloth and ashes; crying, sorrowing, -ful etc. (*unhappy*) 828; mourn-, tear-ful; lachrymose; plaint-ive, -ful, quer-ulous, -imonious; in the melting mood.

in tears, with tears in one's eyes; with -moistened, – watery- eyes; bathed –, dissolved-in tears; 'like Niobe all tears.'

elagiac, epicedial, threnetic.

Adv. *de profundis; les larmes aux yeux.*

Int. heigh-ho! alas! alack! O dear! ah –, woe is-me! lackadaisy! well –, lack –, alack- a day! well-a-way! alas the day! *O tempora! O mores!* what a pity! *miserabile dictu!* O lud lud! too true!

Phr. tears -standing in, – starting from- the eyes; eyes -suffused, – swimming, – brimming –, over- flowing- with tears.

840. Amusement.—**N.** amuse-, entertain-ment; diver-sion, -tissement; reaction, relaxation, solace; pastime, *passetemps*, sport; labor of love; pleasure etc. 827.

fun, frolic, merriment, whoopee, jollity; jovial-ity, -ness; heyday; laughter etc. 838; jocos-ity, -eness; droll-, buffoon-, tomfool-ery; mummery, masquing, pleasantry; wit etc. 842; quip, quirk.

play; game, – at romps; gambol, romp, prank, antic, rig, lark, spree, skylarking, vagary, trick, monkey trick, *gambade, fredaine, escapade, échappée*, bout, *espièglerie*; practical joke etc. (*ridicule*) 856.

dance; round –, square –, solo –, step –, tap –, clog –, skirt –, sand –, folk –, morris-dance, *pas seul*, step, turn, *chassé*, cut, shuffle, double shuffle; hop, reel, rigadoon, saraband, hornpipe, bolero, fandango, pavan, tarantella, minuet, waltz, polka; galop, -ade; Schottische, *pas de quatre*, Boston, one-, two-step, rumba, tango, maxixe, fox-, turkey-trot, shimmy, ragtime, cakewalk, jazz, blues, Charleston; jig, breakdown, fling, strathspey; *allemande*; gavot, -te; mazurka, morisco; quadrille, lancers, country dance, *cotillon*, polonaise, Sir Roger de Coverley, Swedish dance; *ballet* etc. (*drama*) 599; ball; *bal*, — *masqué*, — *costumé*; masquerade, fancy dress ball; *thé dansant*; Terpsichore, choreography, Russian ballet, classical dancing; eurythmics; nautch dance, *danse du ventre*, cancan.

festivity, merry-making; party etc. (*social gathering*) 892; *fête*, festival, gala, *ridotto*; revel-s, -ry, -ling; carnival, brawl, saturnalia, high jinks; feast, banquet etc. (*food*) 298; regale, *symposium*, wassail; carous-e, -al; jollification, junket, wake-pic-nic, *fête champêtre*, garden party, gymkhana, regatta, track meet, field day, jamboree, treat.

round of pleasures, dissipation, a short life and a merry one, racketing, holiday making, high jinks.

rejoicing etc. 838; jubilee etc. (*celebration*) 883.

bonfire, fireworks, *feu-de-joie*, rocket, catherine wheel, roman candle etc.

holiday; gala —, red letter —, play- day; high days and holidays; high —, Bank- holiday; May —, Derby- day; Saint —, Easter —, Whit- Monday; King's birthday, Empire Day; *mi-carême*; Bairam; wayzgoose, bean feast, beano.

place of amusement, theater etc. 599; concert-, ball-, assembly-room; music-hall, cinema, movies, talkies, vaudeville; hippodrome, circus, rodeo; *casino*, *kursaal*; winter garden; park, pleasance, ar-bor; garden etc. 371; pleasure-, play-, cricket-, football-, polo-, croquet-, archery-, hunting-ground; golf links, race course, stadium, gridiron, bowl, speedway, racing track, ring; gymnasium, swimming pool; shooting gallery; tennis-, racket-court; bowling-green, -alley; croquet-lawn, rink, skating rink; roller-coaster, roundabout, carousel, merry-go-round; swing; *montagne russe*; switch-back, scenic railway etc.

game, — of -chance, — skill; athletic sports, gymnastics; fencing; archery, rifle-shooting; tour-nament, pugilism etc. (*contention*) 720; sporting etc. 622; horse-racing, the turf; aquatics etc. 267; skating, roller skating; ski-running, -joring, -jumping, bobsleighing, luging, tobogganing, winter sports; sliding; cricket, tennis, lawn —, table —, deck-tennis, rackets, fives, squash, ping pong, trap bat and ball, battledore and shuttlecock, bad-minton, *la grâce*; pall mall, tip-cat, croquet, golf, curling, hockey, basketball, soccer, football, Rugby, Association, *pallone*, polo; tent-pegging, tilting at the ring, quintain, greasy pole; quoits, *discus*; throwing the hammer, putting the -weight, — shot, tossing the caber; knurr and spell; leap-frog; hop, skip and jump; French and English, tug of war; blind man's buff, hunt the slipper, hide-and-seek, kiss in the ring; snapdragon; cross questions and crooked answers; jig-saw puzzle; rounders, base-ball, *la crosse* etc.; angling; swim-ming, diving, water-polo.

billiards, pool, pyramids, snooker, bagatelle; bowls, skittles, ninepins, kail, American bowls.

cards; bridge, auction, contract, whist, rubber;

round game, coon-can, loo, cribbage, *bésique*, pinocle, euchre, drole, *écarté*, skat, picquet, all-fours, quadrille, ombre, reverse, Pope Joan, com-mit; bo-, boa-ston; *vingt-et-un*; *quinze*, thirty-one, put-and-take, speculation, connections, brag, cassino, lottery, commerce, snip-snap-snorem, lift smoke, blind hookey, Polish bank, poker, banker; faro; Earl of Coventry, Napoleon, nap, patience, pairs; old maid, fright, beggar-my-neighbor; *bac-carat*, *chemin de fer*, *monté*, *roulette*.

chess, draughts, backgammon, dominoes, checkers, mah jong, merelles, nine men's morris, go-bang, solitaire; game of —, fox and-goose; lotto; etc.

morra; gambling etc. (*chance*) 621.

toy, plaything, bauble; doll etc. (*puppet*) 554; teetotum; knick-knack etc. (*trifle*) 643; magic lan-tern etc. (*show*) 448; peep-, puppet-, raree-, gallanty-show; marionettes, Punch and Judy; toy-shop; 'quips and cranks and wanton wiles, nods and becks and wreathed smiles.'

sportsman, gamester, gambler etc. 621; reveler, master of the -ceremonies, — revels; *arbiter elegantiarum*.

V. amuse, entertain, divert, enliven; tickle, — the fancy; titillate, raise a smile, put in good humor; cause —, create —, occasion —, raise —, excite —, produce —, convulse with- laughter; set the table in a roar, be the death of one.

recreate, solace, cheer, rejoice; please etc. 829; interest; treat, regale.

amuse oneself; game; play, — a game, — pranks, — tricks; sport, disport, toy, wanton, revel, junket, feast, carouse, banquet, make merry; drown care; drive dull care away; frolic, gambol, frisk, romp; caper; dance etc. (*leap*) 309; keep up the ball; run a rig, sow one's wild oats, have one's fling, paint the town red, take one's pleasure; see life; *desipere in loco*, play the fool.

make —, keep- holiday; go a Maying.

while away —, beguile- the time; kill time, dally.

Adj. amusing, entertaining, diverting etc. *v.*; recreative, lusory; pleasant etc. (*pleasing*) 829; laughable etc. (*ludicrous*) 853; witty etc. 842; fest-ive, -al; jovial, jolly, jocund, roguish, rompish; sporting; playful — as a kitten; sportive, ludibrious.

amused etc. *v.*; 'pleased with a feather, tickled with a straw.'

Adv. 'on the light fantastic toe,' at play, in sport.

Int. *vive la bagatelle! vogue la galère!*

Phr. *Deus nobis haec otia fecit; dum vivimus vivamus.*

841. Weariness.

—N. weariness, defatigation, boredom, *ennui*; lassitude etc. (*fatigue*) 688; drowsiness etc. 683.

disgust, nausea, loathing, sickness; satiety etc. 869; *taedium vitae* etc. (*dejection*) 837.

wearisome-, tedious-ness etc. *adj.*; dull work, tedium, monotony, twice told tale.

bore, button-hole, proser, wet blanket; heavy hours, 'the enemy' [time].

V. weary; tire etc. (*fatigue*) 688; bore; bore —, weary —, tire- -to death, — out of one's life, — out of all patience; set —, send- to sleep.

pall, sicken, nauseate, disgust.

harp on the same string; drag its -slow, — weary-length along.

never hear the last of; be -tired etc. *adj.* -of, − with; yawn; died with *ennui.*

Adj. wearying etc. *v.*; wearing; weari-, tire-, irksome; uninteresting, stupid, bald, devoid of interest, dry, monotonous, dull, arid, tedious, humdrum, mortal, flat; pros-y, -ing; slow; soporific, somniferous, dormitive.

disgusting etc. *v.*; unenjoyed.

weary; tired etc. *v.*; drowsy etc. *(sleepy)* 683; uninterested, flagging, used up, worn out, *blasé*, life-weary, weary of life; sick of.

Adv. wearily etc. *adj.*; *usque ad nauseam.*

Phr. time hanging heavily on one's hands; *toujours perdrix; crambe repetita.*

842. Wit.—**N.** wit, -tiness; attic -wit, − salt; atticism; salt, *esprit*, point, fancy, whim, humor, drollery, pleasantry.

farce, buffoonery, fooling, tomfoolery; harlequinade etc. 599; broad -farce, − humor; fun, *espièglerie; vis comica.*

jocularity; jocos-ity, -eness; facetiousness; waggery, -ishness; whimsicality; comicality etc. 853.

smartness, ready wit, banter, *badinage, persiflage*, retort, repartee, *quid pro quo*; ridicule etc. 856.

facetiae, quips and cranks; jest, joke, capital joke; standing -jest, − joke; conceit, quip, quirk, crank, quiddity, *concetto, plaisanterie*, brilliant idea; merry −, bright −, happy- thought; sally; flash, − of wit, − of merriment; scintillation; *mot*, − *pour rire*; witticism, smart saying, *bon mot, jeu d'esprit*, epigram; jest book; dry joke, *quodlibet*, cream of the jest.

word-play, *jeu de mots*; play -of, − upon-words; pun, -ning; *double entente* etc. *(ambiguity)* 520; quibble, verbal quibble; conundrum etc. *(riddle)* 533; anagram, acrostic, double acrostic, *nugae canorae*, trifling, idle conceit, *turlupinade.*

old joke, Joe Miller, chestnut, hoary-headed jest.

V. joke, jest, cut jokes; crack a joke; perpetrate a -joke, − pun; make -fun of, − merry with; set the table in a roar etc. *(amuse)* 840; scintillate.

retort, flash back; banter etc. *(ridicule)* 856; *ridentem dicere verum*; joke at one's expense.

Adj. witty, attic, salty; quick-, nimble-witted; keen, clever, smart, brilliant, pungent, jocular, jocose, funny, waggish, facetious, whimsical, humorous, gilbertian; playful etc. 840; merry and wise; pleasant, sprightly, *spirituel*, sparkling, epigrammatic, full of point, *ben trovato*; comic etc. 853.

Adv. in joke, in jest, in sport, in play.

843. Dullness.—**N.** dullness, heaviness, flatness; infestivity etc. 837; stupidity etc. 499; want of originality, dearth of ideas.

prose, matter of fact; heavy book, *conte à dormir debout*; platitude.

V. be -dull etc. *adj.*; prose, platitudinize, take *au sérieux*, be caught napping.

render -dull etc. *adj.*; damp, depress, throw cold water on, lay a wet blanket on; fall flat upon the ear; hang fire.

Adj. dull, − as ditch water; dry, insipid, jejune; unentertaining, uninteresting, unlively,

unimaginative; heavisome, heavy-gaited; dry as dust; pros-y, -ing, -aic; matter of fact, commonplace, banal, pointless; 'weary, flat, stale and unprofitable.'

stupid, slow, flat, sluggish, ponderous, humdrum, monotonous; melancholic etc. 837; stolid etc. 499; plodding.

Phr. *Davus sum non Oedipus.*

844. Humorist.—**N.** humorist, wag, wit, reparteeist, epigrammatist, gag man, punster; *bel esprit*, life of the party; wit-snapper, -cracker, -worm; joker, jester, jokesmith, Joe Miller, *drôle de corps, gaillard*, spark, *persiffleur*, banterer.

buffoon, *farceur*, merry-andrew, mime, tumbler, acrobat, mountebank, charlatan, posturemaster, harlequin, punch, *pulcinella*, scaramouch, clown; wearer of the -cap and bells, − motley; motley fool; pantaloon, gipsy; jack -pudding, − in the green, − a dandy; zany; mad-cap, pickle-herring, witling, caricaturist. *grimacier.*

845. Beauty.—**N.** beauty, the beautiful, *le beau ideal*, loveliness.

[Science of the perception of beauty] Callaesthetics.

form, elegance, grace, beauty unadorned; symmetry etc. 242; comeliness, fairness etc. *adj.*; pulchritude, polish, gloss; good -effect, − looks; *belle tournure*; bloom, brilliancy, radiance, splendor, gorgeousness, magnificence; sublimi-ty, -fication.

concinnity, delicacy, refinement; charm, *je ne sais quoi*, style, *chic*, swank.

Venus, − of Milo; Aphrodite, Hebe, the Graces, Peri, Houri, Cupid, Apollo, Hyperion, Adonis, Antinous, Narcissus; Helen of Troy.

peacock, butterfly; flower, flow'ret gay, rose, lily, asphodel; garden; flower of, pink of; *bijou*; jewel etc. *(ornament)* 847; work of art.

pleasurableness etc. 829.

beautifying; landscape gardening; decoration etc. 847; calisthenics.

V. be -beautiful etc. *adj.*; shine, beam, bloom; become one etc. *(accord)* 23; set off, grace, flatter one.

render -beautiful etc. *adj.*; beautify; polish, burnish; gild etc. *(decorate)* 847; set out.

'snatch a grace beyond the reach of art.'

Adj. beaut-iful, -eous; handsome; pretty; lovely, graceful, elegant; delicate, dainty, refined, exquisite; fair, personable, comely, seemly; bonny; good-looking; well-favored, -made, -formed, -proportioned; proper, shapely; symmetrical etc. *(regular)* 242; harmonious etc. *(color)* 428; sightly.

fit to be seen, passable, not amiss.

goodly, dapper, tight, jimp; gimp; janty, jaunty; natty, quaint, trim, tidy, neat, spruce, smart, tricksy.

bright, -eyed; rosy-, cherry-cheeked; rosy, ruddy; blooming, in full bloom.

brilliant, shining; beam-y, -ing; sparkling, swanky, splendid, resplendent, dazzling, glowing; glossy, sleek.

showy, specious; rich, gorgeous, superb, magnificent, grand, fine, sublime, imposing; majestic 873.

artistic, -al; aesthetic; pict-uresque, -orial; *fait à piendre*, paintable; well-composed, -grouped, -varied; curious.

enchanting etc. (*pleasure-giving*) 829; attractive etc. (*inviting*) 615; becoming etc. (*accordant*) 23; ornamental etc. 847.

undeformed, undefaced, unspotted; spotless etc. (*perfect*) 650.

846. Ugliness.—N. ugliness etc. *adj.*; deformity, inelegance; disfigurement etc. (*blemsih*) 848; want of symmetry, inconcinnity; distortion etc. 243; squalor etc. (*uncleanness*) 653.

forbidding countenance, vinegar aspect, hanging look, wry face, '*spretae injuria formae.*'

eyesore, object, figure, sight, fright, specter, scarecrow, hag, harridan, satyr, witch, toad, baboon, monster, Caliban, Aesop, '*monstrum horrendum informe ingens cui lumen ademptum.*'

V. be -ugly etc. *adj.*; look ill, grin horribly a ghastly smile, make faces.

render -ugly etc. *adj.*; deface; dis-, de-figure; deform, spoil, distort etc. 243; blemish etc. (*injure*) 659; soil etc. (*render unclean*) 653.

Adj. ugly, – as -sin, – a toad, – a scarecrow, – a dead monkey; plain, bald etc. 226; homely etc. (*unadorned*) 849; ordinary, unornamental, inartistic; unsightly, unseemly, uncomely, unshapely, unlovely; sightless, seemless; not fit to be seen; unbeaut-eous, -iful; beautiless; shapeless etc. (*amorphous*) 241; course; garish, over-decorated etc. 882.

mis-shapen, -proportioned; monstrous; gaunt etc. (*thin*) 203; dumpy etc. (*short*) 201; curtailed of its fair proportions; ill-made, -shaped, -proportioned; crooked etc. (*distorted*) 243; hard-featured, -visaged; ill-, hard-, evil-favored; ill-looking; unprepossessing.

graceless, inelegant; ungraceful, ungainly, uncouth; stiff, rugged, rough, gross, rude, awkward, clumsy, slouching, rickety; gawky; lump-ing, -ish; lumbering; hulk-y, -ing; unwieldy.

squalid, haggard; grim, -faced, -visaged; grisly, ghastly; ghost-, death-like; cadaverous, gruesome.

frightful, hideous, odious, uncanny, forbidding, repellant, repulsive; horri-d, -ble; shocking etc. (*painful*) 830.

foul etc. (*dirty*) 653; dingy etc. (*colorless*) 429; gaudy etc. (*color*) 428; disfigured etc. *v.*; discolored (*blemished*) etc. 848.

847. Ornament.—N. ornament, -ation, -al art; ornat-ture, -eness; adorn-ment, decoration, embellishment; architecture.

garnish, polish, varnish, French polish, gilding, japanning, lacquer, ormolu, enamel.

cosmetics, rouge, powder, lipstick, lip salve, mascara; manicure; nail polish; permanent –, Marcel –, finger-wave.

pattern, diaper, powdering, panelling, graining, pargeting, inlay, detail; texture etc. 329; richness; tracery, molding, beading, reeding, fillet, listel, strapwork, *coquillage*, flourish, *fleur-de-lis*, arabesque, fret, *anthemion*; egg and -tongue, –dart; *astragal*, zigzag, *acanthus, cartouche*; pilaster etc. (*projection*) 250; cyma, ogee.

em-, broidery, needlework; knitting, crochet, tatting, brocade, *brocatelle*, beads, bugles; galloon, lace, gimp, *guipure*, fringe, trapping, border, edging, insertion, *motif*, trimming; *passementerie*; drapery, hanging, tapestry, arras; millinery, ermine.

wreath, festoon, garland, lei, chaplet, flower, nosegay, *bouquet*, posy, 'daisies pied and violets blue.'

tassle, knot; shoulder-knot, *épaulette*, epaulet, aiglulet, *aiguilette*, frog; star, rosette, bow; feather, plume, *panache, aigrette*.

jewel, -ry, -lery; bijoutry; *bijou, -terie*; diadem, tiara; pendant, trinket, locket, necklace, armilla, bracelet, bangle, armlet, anklet, ear-, nose- ring, carcanet, chain, *châtelaine*, albert, brooch, torque.

gem, precious stone; diamond, brilliant, beryl, aquamarine, alexandrite, cat's eye, emerald, calcedony, chrysoprase, cornelian, jasper, bloodstone, agate, heliotrope; girasol, -e; onyx, plasma; sard, -onyx; garnet, lapis-lazuli, opal, peridot, chrysolite, sapphire, ruby; spinel, -le; balais; oriental –, topaz; turquois, -e; zircon, jacinth, hyacinth, carbuncle, amethyst; moonstone; pearl, coral.

finery, frippery, gewgaw, gimcrack, knick-knack, tinsel, spangle, sequin, *clinquant*, pinch-beck, paste; excess of ornament etc. (*vulgarity*) 851; gaud, pride, ostentation; frills and furbelows.

illustration, illumination, *vignette; fleuron*; head-, tail-piece; *cul-de-lampe*; flowers of rhetoric etc. 577; work of art, article of vertu, *bric-à-brac*, curio, *bibelot*.

V. ornament, embellish, enrich, decorate, adorn, beautify, adonize.

smarten, furbish, polish, gild, varnish, whitewash, enamel, japan, lacquer, paint, grain.

garnish, trim, dizen, bedizen, prink, prank; trick –, fig- out; deck, bedeck, dight, bedight, array; dress, – up, preen, spruce up, titivate; spangle, bespangle, powder; embroider, work; chase, tool, emboss, fret; emblazon, blazon, illuminate; illustrate.

become etc. (*accord with*) 23.

Adj. ornamented, beautified etc. *v.*; ornate, rich, gilt, begilt, tesselated, enamelled, inlaid; festooned; topiary.

smart, gay, tricksy, flowery, glittering; new-gilt, -spangled; fine, – as -a Mayday queen, –fivepence, – a carrot fresh scraped; pranked out, bedight, well-groomed.

in full dress etc. (*fashion*) 852; *en grande tenue*, – *toilette*; in best bib and tucker, in Sunday best, *endimanché*; dressed to advantage.

showy, flashy; gaudy etc. (*vulgar*) 851; garish; gorgeous.

ornamental, decorative; becoming etc. (*accordant*) 23.

848. Blemish.—N. blemish, disfigurement, deformity; defect etc. (*imperfection*) 651; flaw; injury etc. (*deterioration*) 659; spots on the sun; eyesore.

stain, blot, slur; spot, -tiness; speck, -le; blur, freckle, mole, *macula*, patch, blotch, birthmark, blain, maculation, tarnish, smudge, smear; dirt etc. 653; bruise, black eye, scar, wem; pustule; excrescence, pimple etc. (*protuberance*) 250.

V. disfigure etc. (*injure*) 659; speckle; render ugly etc. 846.

Adj. pitted, freckled, discolored, bloodshot, bruised, disfigured; stained etc. *n.*; imperfect etc. 651; injured etc. (*deteriorated*) 659.

849. Simplicity.—N. simplicity; plain-, homeli-ness; undress, nudity, nakedness, beauty unadorned, chastity, chasteness.

V. be -simple etc. *adj.*
render -simple etc. *adj.*; simplify, chasten, strip of ornament. -

Adj. simple, plain; home-ly, -spun; ordinary, household.

natural, unaffected; free from -affectation, - ornament; *simplex munditiis*; *sans façon, en déshabillé*, nude, naked.

chaste, inornate, severe.

un-adorned, -ornamented, -decked, -garnished, -arranged, -trimmed, -varnished.

bald, flat, dull, blank.

850. Taste. [Good taste.]—**N.** taste; good -, refined -, cultivated- taste; delicacy, refinement, fine feeling, gust, *gusto*, tact, *finesse*; nicety etc. (*discrimination*) 465; polish, elegance, grace.

virtu; dilettanteism, virtuosity; fine art; cul-ture, -ivation.

[Science of taste] esthetics.

man of -taste etc.; *connoisseur*, judge, critic, *conoscente, virtuoso, amateur, dilettante*, Aristarchus, Corinthian, *arbiter elegantarum*, stagirite, euphemist.

'caviar to the general.'

V. appreciate, judge, criticize, discriminate etc. 465.

Adj. in good taste; tasteful, tasty; unaffected, pure, chaste, classical, attic; cultivated, refined; dainty, esthetic, artistic; elegant etc. 578; euphemistic.

to one's -taste, - mind; after one's fancy; *comme il faut; tiré à quatre épingles.*

Adv. elegantly etc. *adj.*

Phr. *nihil tetigit quod non ornavit.*

851. Vulgarity. [Bad taste.]—**N.** vulgar-ity, -ism; barbar-, Vandal-, Gothic-ism; *mauvais goût*, bad taste; Babbittry; *gaucherie*, awkwardness, want of tact; ill-breeding etc. (*discourtesy*) 895; ungentlemanly behavior.

coarseness etc. *adj.*; indecorum, misbehavior.

low-, homeli-ness; low life, *mauvais ton*, rusticity; boorishness etc. *adj.*; brutality; rowdy-, ruffian-, blackguard-ism; ribaldry; slang etc. (*neology*) 563.

bad joke, *mauvaise plaisanterie.*

[Excell of ornament] gaudi-, tawdri-ness; false ornament; finery, frippery, trickery, tinsel, gewgaw, *clinquant.*

rough diamond, tomboy, hoyden, cub, unlicked cub; clown etc. (*commonalty*) 876; Hun, Goth, Vandal, Boeotian; vulgarian; snob, cad, bounder, gent; *parvenu* etc. 876; frump, dowdy; slattern etc. 653.

V. be -vulgar etc. *adj.*; misbehave; talk -, smell of the- shop.

Adj. in bad taste, vulgar, unrefined, gutter.
coarse, indecorus, ribald, gross; unseemly, un-

beseeming, unpresentable; *contra bonos mores*; ungraceful etc. (*ugly*) 846.

dowdy, slovenly etc. (*dirty*) 653; ungenteel, shabby genteel; low etc. (*plebeian*) 876;uncourtly; uncivil etc. (*discourteous*) 895; ill-bred, -mannered; underbred; ungentleman-ly, -like; unladylike, unfeminine; wild, - as an unbacked colt.

unkempt, uncombed, untamed, unlicked, unpolished, uncouth, plebeian; incondite; heavy, rude, awkward; home-ly, -spun, -bred; provincial, hick, countrified, rustic, uncultivated, freshwater; boorish, clownish; savage, brutish, blackguard, rowdy, snobbish; barbar-ous, -ic; Gothic, unclassical, doggerel, heathenish, tramontane, outlandish; Bohemian.

obsolete etc. (*antiquated*) 124; unfashionable, old-fashioned, out of date; new-fangled etc. (*unfamiliar*) 83; fantastic, odd etc. (*ridiculous*) 853.

particular; affected etc. 855; meretricious; extravagant, monstrous, horrid; shocking etc. (*painful*) 830.

gaudy, tawdry, bedizened, tricked out, gingerbread; obtrusive, flaunting, loud, flashy, garish, showy.

852. Fashion.—N. fashion, style, *ton, bon ton*, society; good -, polite- society; drawing room, civilized life, civilization, town, *beau monde*, high life, court; world; fashionable -, gay- world; Vanity Fair; show etc. (*ostentation*) 822.

manners, breeding etc. (*politeness*) 894; air, demeanor etc. (*appearance*) 448; *savoir faire*; gentlemanliness, gentility, decorum, propriety, *bienséance*; conventions -, dictates- of society; Mrs. Grundy; convention, -ality; punctilio; form, -ality; etiquette, point of etiquette; custom etc. 613; mode, vogue, style, go; rage etc. (*desire*) 865; prevailing taste, *dernier cri*, dress etc. 225.

man -, woman- of -fashion, - the world; height -, pink -, star -, glass -, leader- of fashion; *arbiter elegantiarum* etc. (*taste*) 850; upper ten thousand etc. (*nobility*) 875; *élite* etc. (*distinction*) 873.

V. be -fashionable etc. *adj.*, - the rage etc. *n.*; have a run, pass current.

follow -, conform to -, fall in with- the fashion etc. *n.*; go with the stream etc. (*conform*) 82; *savoir -vivre, - faire*; keep up appearances, behave oneself.

set the -, bring into- fashion; give a tone to -, cut a figure in- society, rub shoulders with nobility, keep one's carriage.

Adj. fashionable; in -fashion etc. *n.*; *à la mode, comme il faut*; admitted -, admissible- in -society etc. *n.*; presentable, decorous, punctilious, conventional etc. (*customary*) 613; genteel; well-bred, -mannered, -behaved, -spoken; gentleman-like, -ly; ladylike; civil, polite etc. (*courteous*) 894.

polished, refined, thoroughbred, courtly; *distingué*, aristocratic, unembarrassed, poised, *dégagé*; ja-, jau-nty; dashing, fast, showy, high toned, toney.

modish, stylish, in the latest style, *recherché*; new-fangled etc. (*unfamiliar*) 83.

in -court, - full, - evening- dress; *en grande tenue* etc. (*ornament*) 847.

Adv. fashionably etc. *adj.*; for fashion's sake.

853. Ridiculousness.—N. ridiculousness etc.
adj.; comical-, odd-ity etc. *adj.*; extravagance,
drollery.

farce, comedy; burlesque etc. (*ridicule*) 856;
buffoonery etc. (*fun*) 840; frippery; doggerel verses;
Irish bull, Hibernianism, Hibernicism; Spoonerism;
absurdity etc. 497; bombast etc. (*unmeaning*) 517;
anticlimax, bathos; monstrosity etc. (*unconformity*) 83; laughing stock etc. 857.

V. be -ridiculous etc. *adj.*; pass from the sublime
to the ridiculous; make one laugh; play the fool,
make a fool of oneself, commit an absurdity.

play a joke on, make a -fool of, − sucker of, −
monkey of.

Adj. ridiculous, ludicrous, comic, -al; droll,
funny, laughable, *pour rire*, grotesque, farcical,
odd; whimsical, − as a dancing bear; fanciful, fantastic, queer, rum, quizzical, waggish, quaint,
bizarre; eccentric etc. (*unconformable*) 83;
strange, outlandish, out of the way, *baroque*,
rocaille, rococo; awkward etc. (*ugly*) 846.

absurd, extravagant, *outré*, monstrous,
preposterous, bombastic, inflated, stilted,
burlesque, mock heroic.

drollish; serio-, tragic-comic; gimcrack, contemptible etc. (*unimportant*) 643; doggerel;
ironical etc. (*derisive*) 856; risible.

Phr. *'risum teneatis amici?' rideret Heraclitus.*

854. Fop.—N. fop, fine gentleman; swell;
dand-y, -iprat; exquisite, coxcomb, toff, beau,
macaroni, blade, blood, buck, man about town,
fast man; fribble, jemmy, spark, popinjay, puppy,
prig, *petit maître*; jacka-napes, -dandy; man
milliner; Jemmy Jessamy, carpet-knight, masher,
Dundreary, Johnnie, dude.

belle, fine lady, *coquette*, flirt.

855. Affectation.—N. affectation; affectedness
etc. *adj.*; acting a part etc. *v.*; pretence etc.
(*falsehood*) 544; (*ostentation*) 882; boasting etc.
884.

charlatanism, quakery, shallow profundity, humbug, pretension, airs, pedantry, purism,
precisianism, euphuism, prunes and prisms;
teratology etc. (*altiloquence*) 577.

mannerism, *simagrée*, grimace.

conceit, foppery, dandyism, man millinery, coxcombry, puppyism.

stiffness, formality, buckram; prudery,
demureness, coquetry, mock modesty, *minauderie*,
sentimentalism; *mauvaise honte*, false shame.

affector, performer, actor; pedant, pedagogue,
doctrinaire, purist, euphuist, mannerist; shoneen;
grimacier; lump of affectation, *précieuse ridicule*,
bas bleu, blue stocking, poetaster; prig, hypocrite;
charlatan etc. (*deceiver*) 548; *petit maître* etc.
(*fop*) 854; flatterer etc. 935; *coquette*, prude,
puritan; precisian, formalist.

V. affect, act a part, put on; give oneself airs etc.
(*arrogance*) 885; boast etc. 884; coquet; simper,
mince, attitudinize, strike a pose, pose; flirt a fan;
over-act, -do.

Adj. affected, full of affectation, pretentious,
pedantic, stilted, stagey, theatrical, big-sounding,
ad captandum, canting, insincere.

not natural, unnatural; self-conscious; *maniéré*;
artificial; over-wrought, -done, -acted; euphuistic
etc. 577.

stiff, starch, formal, prim, smug, demure, *tiré à-
quatre épingles*, quakerish, puritanical, prudish,
pragmatical, priggish, conceited, coxcomical, fop-
pish, dandified; fini-cal, -kin, -cky, mincing,
simpering, namby-pamby, sentimental,
languishing.

856. Ridicule.—N. ridicule, derision; sardonic
-smile, − grin; irrision; snigger; scoffing etc.
(*disrespect*) 929; mockery, quiz, banter, irony,
persiflage, raillery, chaff, *badinage*; quizzing etc.
v.

squib, satire, skit, quip, quib, grin.

parody, burlesque, travesty; farce etc. (*drama*)
599; caricature, take-off.

buffoonery etc. (*fun*) 840; practical joke, horse-
play.

V. ridicule, deride; laugh at, grin at, smile at;
snigger; laugh in one's sleeve; banter, rally, chaff,
joke, twit, quiz, poke fun at, jolly, roast, rag; fleer;
play −, play tricks- upon; fool, − to the top of
one's bent; show up.

satirize, parody, caricature, burlesque, travesty.

turn into ridicule; make merry with; make -fun,
− game, − a fool, − an April fool- of; rally; scoff
etc. (*disrespect*) 929.

raise a laugh etc. (*amuse*) 840; play the fool,
make a fool of oneself.

be ridiculous etc. 853.

Adj. deris-ory, -ive; mock; sarcastic, ironical,
quizzical, burlesque, Hudibrastic; scurrilous etc.
(*disrespectful*) 929.

Adv. in -ridicule etc. *n.*

857. Laughing-stock. [Object and cause of
ridicule.]—N. laughing-, jesting-, gazing-stock;
butt, game, fair game; April fool etc. (*dupe*) 547.

original, oddity; queer −, odd- fish; quiz, square
toes; old −, fogey *or* fogy..

monkey; buffoon etc. (*jester*) 844; pantomimist
etc. (*actor*) 599.

jest etc. (*wit*) 842.

858. Hope.—N. hope, -s; desire etc. 865; fervent hope, sanguine expectation, trust, confidence,
reliance; faith etc. (*belief*) 484; affiance, assurance;
secur-eness, -ity; reassurance.

good -omen, − auspices; promise; well-
grounded hopes; good −, bright- prospect; clear
sky.

as-, pre-sumption; anticipation etc. (*expectation*)
507.

hopefulness, buoyancy, optimism, enthusiasm,
heart of grace, aspiration; optimist, utop-ian, -ist;
Pollyanna.

castles in the air, *châteaux en Espagne*, hope
chest, *le pot au lait*, Utopia, millennium; day −,
golden- dream; dream of Alnaschar; airy hopes,
fool's paradise; *mirage* etc. (*fallacies of vision*)
443; fond hope.

beam −, ray −, gleam −, glimmer −, dawn
−, flash −, star- of hope; cheer; bit of blue sky,

silver lining of the cloud, bottom of Pandora's box, balm in Gilead.

anchor, sheet-anchor, main-stay; staff etc. (*support*) 215; heaven etc. 981.

V. hope, trust, confide, rely on, put one's trust in, lean upon; pin one's -hope, – faith- upon etc. (*believe*) 484.

feel –, entertain –, harbor –, indulge –, cherish –, feed –, foster –, nourish –, encourage –, cling to –, live in- hope etc. *n.*; see land; feel –, rest- -assured, – confident etc. *adj*.

presume; promise oneself; expect etc. (*look forward to*) 507.

hope for etc. (*desire*) 865; anticipate.

be -hopeful etc. *adj.*; look on the bright side of, view on the sunny side, make the best of it, hope for the best; put -a good, – a bold, – the best- face upon; keep one's spirits up; take heart, – of grace; be of good -heart, – cheer; flatter oneself, lay the flattering unction to one's soul.

catch at a straw, hope against hope, count one's chickens before they are hatched.

give –, inspire –, raise –, hold out- hope etc. *n.*; raise expectations; encourage, hearten, cheer, assure, reassure, buoy up, embolden; promise, bid fair, augur well, be in a fair way, look up, flatter, tell a flattering tale.

Adj. hoping etc. *v.*; in -hopes etc. *n.*; hopeful, confident; secure etc. (*certain*) 484; sanguine, in good heart, buoyed up, buoyant, elated, flushed, exultant, enthusiastic; utopian.

unsus-pecting, -picious; fearless, free –, exempt from- -fear, – suspicion, – distrust, – despair; undespairing, self-reliant.

probable, on the high road to; within sight of - shore, – land; promising, propitious; of –, full of- promise; of good omen; auspicious, *de bon augure*; reassuring; encouraging, cheering, inspiriting, looking up, bright, roseate, *couleur de rose*, rose-colored.

Adv. hopefully etc. *adj*.

Phr. *nil desperandum*; never say die, *dum spiro spero, latet scintillula forsan*, all is for the best, *spero meliora*; the wish being father to the thought; 'hope told a flattering tale;' *rusticus expectat dum defluat amnis*.

859. Hopelessness. [Absence, want, or loss of hope.] —**N.** hopelessness etc. *adj.*; despair, desperation; despondency etc. (*dejection*) 837; pessimism.

hope deferred, dashed hopes; vain expectation etc. (*disappointment*) 509.

airy hopes etc. 858; forlorn hope; bad -job, – business; *enfant perdu*; gloomy –, black spots in the- horizon; slough of Despond, cave of Despair.

Job's comforter; bird of -bad, – ill-omen.

V. despair; lose –, give up –, abandon –, relinquish- -all hope, – the hope of; give -up, – over; yield to despair; falter; despond etc. (*be dejected*) 837; *jeter le manche après la cognée*.

inspire –, drive to- despair etc. *n.*; disconcert; dash –, crush –, shatter –, destroy- one's hopes; hope against hope.

Adj. hopeless, desperate, despairing, in despair, *au désespoir*, forlorn; inconsolable etc. (*dejected*) 837; broken-hearted.

out of the question, not to be thought of; im-practicable etc. 471; past -hope, – cure, – mending, – recall; at one's last gasp etc. (*death*) 360; given -up, – over.

incurable, cureless, immedicable, remediless, beyond remedy; incorrigible; irre-parable, -mediable, -coverable, -versible, -trievable, -claimable, -deemable, -vocable; ruined, undone; immitigable.

unpromising, unpropitious; inauspicious, ill-omened, threatening, clouded over, lowering, ominous.

Phr. *'lasciate ogni speranza voi ch' entrate;'* its days are numbered; the worst come to the worst.

860. Fear.—**N.** fear, timidity, diffidence, want of confidence; apprehensive-, fearful-ness etc. *adj.*; solicitude, anxiety, care, apprehension, misgiving; mistrust etc. (*doubt*) 485; suspicion, qualm; hesitation etc. (*irresolution*) 605.

nervous-, restless-ness etc. *adj.*; in-, dis-quietude; flutter, trepidation, fear and trembling, perturbation, tremor, quivering, shaking, trembling, throbbing heart, palpitation, ague fit, cold sweat; abject fear etc. (*cowardice*) 862; mortal funk, heart-sinking, despondency; despair etc. 859.

fright; affright, -ment; alarm, pavor, dread, awe, terror, horror, dismay, consternation, panic, scare, stampede [of horses].

intimidation, terrorism, reign of terror.

[Object of fear] bug-bear, -aboo; scarecrow; hobgoblin etc. (*demon*) 980; daymare, nightmare, Gorgon, Medusa, mormo, ogre, Hurlothrumbo; raw head and bloody bones, fee faw fum, *bête noire, enfant terrible*.

alarmist etc. (*coward*) 862.

V. fear, stand in awe of; be -afraid etc. *adj.*; have -qualms etc. *n.*; apprehend, sit upon thorns, eye askance; distrust etc. (*disbelieve*) 485.

hesitate etc. (*be irresolute*) 605; falter, funk, cower, crouch; skulk etc. (*cowardice*) 862; let 'I dare not' wait upon 'I would;' take -fright, – alarm; start, wince, flinch, shy, shrink; fly etc. (*avoid*) 623.

tremble, shake; shiver, – in one's shoes; shudder, flutter; shake –, tremble- -like an aspen leaf, – all over; quake, quaver, quiver, quail; get the wind up.

grow –, turn- pale; blench, stand aghast; not dare to say one's soul is one's own.

inspire –, excite- -fear, – awe; raise apprehensions; give –, raise –, sound- an alarm; alarm, startle, scare, cry 'wolf,' disquiet, dismay; fright, -en; affright, terrify; astound; frighten from one's propriety; frighten out of one's -wits, – senses, – seven senses; awe; strike -all of a heap, – an awe into, – terror; harrow up the soul, appal, unman, petrify, horrify.

make one's -flesh creep, – hair stand on end, -- blood run cold, – teeth chatter; chill one's spine; take away –, stop- one's breath; make one -tremble etc.

haunt, obsess, beset; prey –, weigh- on the mind.

put in -fear, – bodily fear; terrorize, intimidate, cow, daunt, over-awe, abash, deter, discourage; browbeat, bully; threaten etc. 909.

Adj. fearing etc. *v.*; frightened etc. *v.*; in -fear, – a fright etc. *n.*; haunted with the -fear etc. *n.*- of.

afraid, fearful; tim-id, -orous; nervous, diffident, coy, faint-hearted, tremulous, shaky, afraid of one's shadow, apprehensive, restless, fidgety; more frightened than hurt.

aghast; awe-, horror-, terror-, panic- -struck, -stricken; frightened to death, white as a sheet; pale, – as -death, – ashes, – a ghost; breathless, in hysterics.

inspiring fear etc. *v.*; alarming; formidable, redoubtable; perilous etc. (*danger*) 665; portentous; fear-ful, -some; dread, -ful; fell; dire, -ful; shocking; terri-ble, -fic; tremendous; horri-d, -ble, -fic; ghastly; awful, awe-inspiring, eerie, weird; revolting etc. (*painful*) 830.

Adv. in terrorem.

Int. 'angels and ministers of grace defend us!'

Phr. *ante tubam trepidat; horresco referens,* one's heart failing one, *obstupui steteruntque comae et vox faucibus haesit.*

861. Courage. [Absence of fear.]—**N.** courage, bravery, valor; resolute-, bold-ness etc. *adj.*; spirit, daring, gallantry, intrepidity; contempt –, defiance- of danger; derring-do; audacity; rashness etc. 863; dash; defiance etc. 715; confidence, self-reliance.

man-liness, -hood; nerve, pluck, mettle, game; heart, – of grace; spunk, gameness, grit, face, virtue, hardihood, fortitude; firmness etc. (*stability*) 150; heart of oak; bottom, backbone etc. (*perseverance*) 604a.

resolution etc. (*determination*) 604; tenacity, bull-dog courage.

prowess, heroism, chivalry.

exploit, feat, achievement; heroic -deed, – act; bold stroke.

man, – of mettle; hero, demigod, paladin, heroine, Amazon, Hector, Joan of Arc; lion, tiger, panther, bulldog; game-, fighting-cock; bully, fire-eater etc. 863; dare-devil.

V. be -courageous etc. *adj.*; dare, venture, make bold; face –, front –, affront –, confront –, brave –, defy –, despise –, mock- danger; look in the face; look -full, – boldly, – danger- in the face; face; meet, – in front; brave, beard; defy etc. 715.

take –, muster –, summon up –, pluck up-courage; nerve oneself, take heart; take –, pluck up- heart of grace; hold up one's head, screw one's courage to the sticking place; come -to, – up to- the scratch; stand, – to one's guns, – fire, – against; bear up – against; hold out etc. (*persevere*) 604a.

put a bold face upon; show –, present- a bold front, face the music; envisage; show fight.

bell the cat, take the bull by the horns, beard the lion in his den, march up to the cannon's mouth, go through fire and water, run the gauntlet, go over the top.

give –, infuse –, inspire- courage; reassure, encourage, embolden, inspirit; cheer, hearten, nerve, put upon one's mettle, rally, raise a rallying cry; pat on the back, make a man of, keep in countenance.

Adj. courageous, brave; val-iant, -orous; gallant, intrepid; spirit-ed, -ful; high-spirited, -mettled; mettlesome, game, plucky; man-ly, -ful; resolute; stout, -hearted; iron-, lion-hearted; heart of oak; Penthesilean.

bold, – spirited; daring, audacious; fear-, daunt-, dread-, awe-less; un-daunted, -appalled, -dismayed, -awed, -blenched, -abashed, -alarmed, -flinching, -shrinking, -blenching; apprehensive; confident, self-reliant; bold as -a lion, – brass.

enterprising, adventurous; ventur-ous, -esome; dashing, chivalrous; soldierly etc. (*warlike*) 722; heroic.

fierce, savage; pugnacious etc. (*bellicose*) 720.

strong-minded, hardy, doughty; firm etc. (*stable*) 150; determined etc. (*resolved*) 604; dogged, indomitable etc. (*persevering*) 604a.

up to, – the scratch; upon one's mettle; reassured etc. *v.*; unfeared, undreaded.

Phr. one's blood being up.

862. Cowardice. [Excess of fear.]—**N.** cowardice, pusillanimity; cowardliness etc. *adj.*; timidity, effeminacy.

poltroonery, baseness; dastard-ness, -y; abject fear, funk; Dutch courage; fear etc. 860; white feather, faint heart.

coward, poltroon, dastard, sneak, recreant; shy –, dunghill- cock; coistril, milksop, white-liver, nidget, cur, craven, one that cannot say 'Boo' to a goose; Bob Acres, Jerry Sneak.

alarm-, terror-, pessim-ist; runagate etc. (*fugitive*) 623; shirker.

V. quail etc. (*fear*) 860; be -cowardly etc. *adj.*, – a coward etc. *n.*; funk; cower, skulk, sneak; flinch, shy, fight shy, slink, turn tail; run away etc. (*avoid*) 623; show the white feather, have cold feet, show a yellow streak.

Adj. coward, -ly; fearful, shy; tim-id, -orous; skittish; poor-spirited, spirit-less, soft, effeminate.

weak-minded; infirm of purpose etc. 605; weak-, faint-, chicken-, lily-, pigeon-hearted; yellow; white-, lily-, milk-livered; milksop, smock-faced; unable to say 'Boo' to a goose.

dastard, -ly; base, craven, sneaking, dunghill, recreant; unwar-, unsoldier-like.

'in face a lion but in heart a deer.'

unmanned; frightened etc. 860.

Int. *sauve qui peut!* devil take the hindmost!

Adv. in fear and trembling, in fear of one's life, in a blue funk.

Phr. *ante tubam trepidat*, one's courage oozing out.

863. Rashness.—N. rashness etc. *adj.*; temerity, want of caution, imprudence, indiscretion; over-confidence, presumption, audacity.

precipit-ancy, -ation; impetuosity; levity; foolhardi-hood, -ness; heed-, thought-lessness etc. (*inattention*) 458; carelessness etc. (*neglect*) 460; desperation; Quixotism, knight-errantry; fire-eating.

gam-ing, -bling; blind bargain, leap in the dark, fool's paradise; too many eggs in one basket.

desperado, rashling, mad-cap, dare-devil, Hotspur, fire-eater, bully, *bravo,* Hector, scapegrace, *enfant perdu;* Don Quixote, knight-errant, Icarus; adventurer; gam-bler, -ester; dynamitard.

V. be -rash etc. *adj.*; stick at nothing, play a desperate game; run into danger etc. 665; play with -fire, – edge tools.

carry too much sail, sail too near the wind, ride at single anchor, go out of one's depth.

take a leap in the dark, buy a pig in a poke.

donner tête baissée; knock one's head against a wall etc. (*be unskilful*) 699; rush on destruction; kick against the pricks, tempt Providence, go on a forlorn hope.

count one's chickens before they are hatched; reckon without one's host; catch at straws; trust to —, lean on- a broken reed.

Adj. rash, incautious, indiscreet, injudicious; imprudent, improvident, temerarious; uncalculating; heedless; careless etc. (*neglectful*) 460; without ballast, heels over head; giddy etc. (*inattentive*) 458; wanton, reckless, wild, madcap; desperate, devil-may-care.

hot-blooded, -headed, -brained; head-long, -strong; break-neck; fool-hardy; harebrained; precipitate, impulsive.

over-confident, -weening; ventur-esome, -ous; adventurous, Quixotic; fire-eating, cavalier; free-and-easy.

off one's guard etc. (*inexpectant*) 508.

Adv. post haste, *à corps perdu,* hand over head, *tête baissée,* head- foremost; happen what may.

Phr. neck or nothing, the devil being in one.

864. Caution.—N. caution; cautiousness etc. *adj.*; discretion, prudence, cautel, heed, circumspection, calculation, deliberation; safety first.

foresight etc. 510; vigilance etc. 459; warning etc. 668.

coolness etc. *adj.*; self-possession, -command; presence of mind, *sang froid;* well-regulated mind; worldly wisdom, Fabian policy.

V. be -cautious etc. *adj.*; take -care, — heed, — good care; have a care; mind, — what one is about; be on one's guard etc. (*keep watch*) 459; make assurance double sure; ca' canny.

bespeak etc. (*be early*) 132.

think twice, look before one leaps, keep one's weather eye open, count the cost, look to the main chance, cut one's coat according to one's cloth; feel one's -ground, — way; see how the land lies etc. (*foresight*) 510; wait to see how the cat jumps; bridle one's tongue; *reculer pour mieux sauter* etc. (*prepare*) 673; let well alone, let sleeping dogs lie, *ne pas réveiller le chat qui dort.*

keep out of -harm's way, — troubled waters; keep at a respectful distance, stand aloof; keep —, be- on the safe side.

husband one's resources etc. 636.

caution etc. (*warn*) 668.

Adj. cautious, wary, guarded; on one's guard etc. (*watchful*) 459; *cavendo tutus; in medio tutissimus.*

care-, heed-ful; cautelous, stealthy, chary, shy of, circumspect, prudent, canny, safe, non-committal, discreet, politic; sure-footed etc. (*skilful*) 698.

unenterprising, unadventurous, cool, steady, self-possessed; over-cautious.

suspicious, leery, vigilant.

Adv. cautiously, gingerly etc. *adj.*

Int. have a care! look out! *cave canem!*

Phr. *timeo Danaos; festina lente.*

865. Desire.—N. desire, wish, fancy, fantasy; want, need, exigency.

mind, inclination, leaning, bent, *animus,* partiality, *penchant,* predilection; propensity etc. 820; willingness etc. 602; liking, love, fondness, relish.

longing, hankering; solicitude, anxiety; yearning, coveting; aspiration, ambition, vaulting ambition; eagerness, zeal, ardor, *empressement,* breathless impatience, over-anxiety; solicitude, impetuosity etc. 825.

appet-ite, -ition, -ence, -ency; sharp appetite, keenness, hunger, stomach, twist; thirst, -iness; drouth, mouth-watering; itch, -ing; prurience, *cacoëthes,* cupidity, lust, concupiscence.

edge of -appetite, — hunger; torment of Tantalus; sweet —, lickerish- tooth; itching palm; longing —, wistful —, sheep's-eye.

avidity; greed, -iness; covetous-, ravenous-ness etc. *adj.*; grasping, craving, canine appetite, rapacity; voracity etc. (*gluttony*) 957.

passion, rage, *furore,* mania, *manie;* inextinguishable desire; dips-, klept-, mon-omania.

[Person desiring] desirer, lover, *amateur,* votary, devotee, aspirant, solicitant, candidate; cormorant etc. 957; sycophant.

[Object of desire] *desideratum;* want etc. (*requirement*) 630; 'consumation devoutly to be wished;' attraction, magnet, allurement, fancy, temptation, seduction, lure, fascination, *prestige,* height of one's ambition, idol; whim, -sey; maggot; hobby, -horse.

Fortunatus's cap, wishing cap, love potion.

V. desire; wish, — for; be -desirous etc. *adj.*; have a -longing etc. *n.*; hope etc. 858.

care for, affect, like, list; take to, cling to, take a fancy to; fancy; prefer etc. (*choose*) 609.

have -an eye, — a mind- to; find it in one's heart etc. (*be willing*) 602; have a fancy for, set one's eyes upon; cast a sheep's eye —, look sweet- upon; take into one's head, have a heart, be bent upon; set one's -cap at, — heart upon, — mind upon; covet.

want, miss, need, lack, desiderate, feel the want of; would fain -have, — do; would be glad of.

be -hungry etc. *adj.*; have a good appetite, play a good knife and fork; hunger —, thirst —, crave —, lust —, itch —, hanker —, run mad- after; raven —, die- for; burn to.

desiderate; sigh —, cry —, gape —, gasp —, pine —, pant —, languish —, yearn —, long —, be on thorns —, hope- for; aspire after; catch at, grasp at, jump at.

woo, court, solicit; fish —, spell —, whistle —, put up- for; ogle.

cause —, create —, raise —, excite —, provoke-desire; whet the appetite; appetize, titillate, allure, attract, take one's fancy, tempt; hold out -temptation, — allurement; tantalize, make one's mouth water, *faire venir l'eau à la bouche.*

gratify desire etc. (*give pleasure*) 829.

Adj. desirous; desiring etc. *v.*; orectic, appetitive; inclined etc. (*willing*) 602; partial to; fain, wishful, optative; anxious, wistful, curious; at a loss for, sedulous, solicitous.

craving, hungry, sharp-set, peckish, ravening, with an empty stomach, esurient, lickerish, thirsty, athirst, parched with thirst, pinched with hunger, famished, dry, drouthy; hungry as a -hunter, — hawk, — horse, — church mouse.

greedy, — as a hog; over-eager, voracious; ravenous, — as a wolf; open-mouthed, covetous, rapacious, grasping, extortionate, exacting, sordid, *alieni appetens*; insati-able, -ate; unquenchable, quenchless; omnivorous.

unsatisfied, unsated, unslaked.

eager, avid, keen; burning, fervent, ardent; agog; all agog; breathless; impatient etc. (*impetuous*) 825; bent −, intent −, set- -on, − upon; mad after, *enragé*, rabid, dying for, devoured by desire.

aspiring, ambitious, vaulting, sky-aspiring.

desirable; popular; desired etc. *v.*; in demand; pleasing etc. (*giving pleasure*) 829; appeti-zing, -ble; tantalizing.

Adv. wistfully etc. *adj.*; fain.

Int. would -that, − it were! O for! *esto perpetua!* if only!

Phr. the wish being the father to the thought; *sua cuique voluptas; hoc erat in votis*, the mouth watering, the fingers itching; *aut Caesar aut nullus.*

866. Indifference.—N. indifference, neutrality; coldness etc. *adj.*; unconcern, *insouciance, nonchalance*; want of -interest, − earnestness; anorexy, inappetency; apathy etc. (*insensibility*) 823; supineness etc. (*inactivity*) 683; disdain etc. 930; recklessness etc. 863; inattention etc. 458.

V. be -indifferent etc. *adj.*; stand neuter; take no interest in etc. (*insensibility*) 823; have no -desire etc. 865, − taste, − relish- for; not care for; care nothing -for, − about; not care a -straw etc. (*unimportance*) 643 -about, − for; not mind.

set at naught etc. (*make light of*) 483; spurn etc. (*disdain*) 930.

Adj. indifferent, cold, frigid, lukewarm; cool, − as a cucumber; unconcerned, *insouciant*, phlegmatic, *pococurante*, easy-going, devil-may-care, careless, listless, lackadaisical, feckless; half-hearted; un-ambitious, -aspiring, -desirous, - solicitous, -attracted.

un-attractive, -alluring, -desired, -desirable, -cared for, -wished, -valued, all one to.

insipid etc. 391; vain.

Adv. for aught one cares.

Int. never mind.

867. Dislike.—N. dis-like, -taste, -relish, -inclination, -placency.

reluctance; backwardness etc. (*unwillingness*) 603.

repugnance, disgust, queasiness, turn, nausea, loathing; avers-eness, -ation, -ion; abomination, antipathy, abhorrence, horror; mortal −, rooted- -antipathy, − horror; hatred, detestation; hate etc. 898; animosity etc. 900; hydrophobia.

sickener; gall and wormwood etc. (*unsavory*) 395; shuddering, cold sweat.

V. dis-, mis-like, -relish; mind, object to; have rather not, not care for; have −, conceive −, entertain −, take- -a dislike, − an aversion- to; have no -taste, − stomach- for.

shun, avoid etc. 623; eschew; withdraw −, shrink −, recoil- from; not be able to -bear, − abide, − endure; shrug the shoulders at, shudder at, turn up the nose at, look askance at; make a -mouth, − wry face, − grimace; make faces.

loathe, nauseate, abominate, detest, abhor; hate etc. 898; take amiss etc. 900; have enough of etc. (*be satiated*) 869.

cause −, excite- dislike; disincline, repel, sicken; make −, render- sick; turn one's stomach, nauseate, wamble, disgust, shock, stink in the nostrils; go against the -grain, − stomach; stick in the throat; make one's blood run cold etc. (*give pain*) 830; pall.

Adj. disliking etc. *v.*; averse to, loth, adverse; shy of, sick of, out of conceit with; disinclined; heart-, dog-sick; queasy.

disliked etc. *v.*; uncared for, unpopular; out of favor; repulsive, repugnant, repellent; abhorrent, insufferable, fulsome, nauseous; loath-some, -ful; offensive; disgusting etc. *v.*; disagreeable etc. (*painful*) 830; unsavory etc. 395.

Adv. *usque ad nauseam.*

Int. faugh! foh! ugh!

868. Fastidiousness.—N. fastidiousness etc. *adj.*; nicety, meticulosity, hypercriticism, difficulty in being pleased, *friandise*, epicurism, *omnia suspendens naso.*

discrimination, discernment, good taste, perspicacity.

epicure, gourmet.

[Excess of delicacy] prudery, prudishness, primness.

V. be -fastidious etc. *adj.*; split hairs, discriminate, have a sweet tooth.

mince the matter; turn up one's nose at etc. (*disdain*) 930; look a gift horse in the mouth, see spots on the sun.

Adj. fastidious, meticulous, exacting, nice, delicate, *délicat*, finical, finicky, difficult, dainty, lickerish, squeamish, thin-skinned; s-, queasy; hard −, difficult- to please; querulous, particular, over-particular, straitlaced, prudish, prim, scrupulous; censorious etc. 932; hypercritical, discriminating, discerning, perspicacious.

Phr. *noli me tangere.*

869. Satiety.—N. satiety, satisfaction, saturation, repletion, glut, surfeit; weariness etc. 841.

spoiled child; *enfant gâté*; too much of a good thing, *toujours perdrix*; *crambe repetita.*

V. sate, satiate, satisfy, saturate; cloy, quench, slake, pall, glut, gorge, surfeit; bore etc. (*weary*) 841; tire etc. (*fatigue*) 688; spoil.

have -enough of, − quite enough of, − one's fill, − too much of; be -satiated etc. *adj.*

Adj. satiated etc. *v.*; overgorged; *blasé*, used up, sick of, heart-sick.

Int. enough! hold! *eheu jam satis!*

870. Wonder.—N. wonder, marvel; astonish-, amaze-, wonder-, bewilder-ment; amazedness etc. *adj.*; admiration, awe; stup-or, -efaction; stound, fascination; sensation; surprise etc. (*inexpectation*) 508; cynosure.

note of admiration; thaumaturgy etc. (*sorcery*) 992.

V. wonder, marvel, admire; be -surprised etc. *adj.*; start; stare; open −, rub −, turn up- one's eyes; gloar; gape, open one's mouth, hold one's breath; look −, stand- -aghast, − agog; look blank etc. (*disappointment*) 509; *tomber des nues*; not believe one's -eyes, − ears, − senses.

not be able to account for etc. (*unintelligible*) 519; not know whether one stands on one's head or one's heels.

surprise, astonish, amaze, astound; dumbfound, -er; startle, dazzle; strike, − with -wonder, − awe; electrify; stun, stupefy, petrify, confound, bewilder, flabbergast; stagger, throw on one's beam ends, fascinate, turn the head, take away one's breath, strike dumb; make one's -hair stand on end, − tongue cleave to the roof of one's mouth; make one stare.

take by surprise etc. (*be unexpected*) 508.

be -wonderful etc. *adj.*; beggar −, baffle-description; stagger belief.

Adj. surprised etc. *v.*; aghast, all agog, breathless, agape; open-mouthed; awe-, thunder-, moon-, planet-struck; spell-bound; lost in -amazement, − wonder − astonishment; struck all of a heap, unable to believe one's senses, like a duck in thunder.

wonderful, wondrous; surprising etc. *v.*; unexpected etc. 508; unheard of; mysterious etc. (*inexplicable*) 519; miraculous; *foudroyant*.

in-describable, -expressible, -effable; un-utterable, -speakable.

monstrous, prodigious, stupendous, marvelous; in-conceivable, -credible; in-, un-imaginable; strange etc. (*uncommon*) 83; passing strange.

striking etc. *v.*; over-whelming; wonder-working.

Adv. wonderfully etc. *adj.*; fearfully; for a −, in the name of- wonder; strange to say; *mirabile -dictu*, − visu; to one's great surprise.

with -wonder etc. *n.*, − gaping mouth, − open eyes, − upturned eyes; eyes starting out of one's head.

Int. lo, − and behold! O! hey-day! halloo! what! indeed! really! surely! humph! hem! good -lack, − heavens, − gracious! − lord! by jove! gad so! well a day! dear me! only think! lack-a-daisy! my -stars, − goodness! gracious goodness! goodness gracious! mercy on us! heavens and earth! God bless me! bless -us, − my heart! odzookens! *O gemini!* adzooks! hoity-toity! strong! Heaven save −, bless-the mark! can such things be! zounds! 'sdeath! what -on earth, − in the world! who would have thought it! etc. (*inexpectation*) 508; fancy! did you ever? you don't say so! what do you say to that! how now! where am I? well I'm blowed! etc.

Phr. *vox faucibus haesit*; one's hair standing on end.

871. Expectance. [Absence of wonder.]—**N.** expectan-ce, -cy etc. (*expectation*) 507; calmness, composure, tranquillity, serenity, coolness, imperturbability etc. 826.

nine days' wonder.

V. expect etc. 507; not -be surprised, − wonder etc. 870; *nil admirari*, make nothing of.

Adj. expecting etc. *v.*; unamazed, astonished at nothing; *blasé* etc. (*weary*) 841; unimaginative, calm, serene, imperturbable etc. 826; expected etc. *v.*; foreseen.

common, ordinary etc. (*habitual*) 613.

Int. no wonder; of course; why not?

872. Prodigy.—**N.** prodigy, phenomenon; wonder, -ment; genius, marvel, miracle; freak, monster etc. (*unconformity*) 83; curiosity, lion, infant prodigy, sight, spectacle; *jeu* −, *coup- de théâtre*; gazing-stock; sign; portent etc. 512.

bursting of a -shell, − bomb; volcanic eruption, peal of thunder; thunder-clap, -bolt.

what no words can paint; wonders of the world; *annus mirabilis*; *dignus vindice nodus*.

873. Repute.—**N.** distinction, mark, name, figure; repute, reputation, character; good −, high-repute; note, notability, notoriety, *éclat*, 'the bubble reputation,' vogue, celebrity; fame, famousness; renown; populairty, *aura popularis*; esteem, approval, approbation etc. 931; credit, *succès d'estime*, *prestige*, talk of the town; name to conjure with.

glory, honor; luster etc. (*light*) 420; illustriouness etc. *adj.*

account, regard, respect; reputableness etc. *adj.*; respectability etc. (*probity*) 939; good -name, − report; fair name.

dignity; stateliness etc. *adj.*; solemnity, grandeur, splendor, nobility, majesty, sublimity.

rank, standing, brevet rank, precedence, *pas*, station, place, *status*; position, − in society; order, degree, *locus standi*, caste, condition.

greatness etc. *adj.*; eminence; height etc. 206; importance etc. 642; pre-, super-eminence; high mightiness, primacy; top of the -ladder, − tree.

elevation; ascent etc. 305; super-, ex-altation; dignification, aggrandizement.

dedication, consecration, enthronement, canonization, apotheosis, deification, celebration, enshrinement, glorification.

hero, man of mark, great card, celebrity, worthy, lion, *rara avis*, notability, somebody; man of rank etc. (*nobleman*) 875; pillar of the -state, − socïety, − church.

chief etc. (*master*) 745; first fiddle etc. (*proficient*) 700; scholar etc. 492; cynosure, mirror; flower, pink, pearl; paragon etc. (*perfection*) 650; choice and master spirits of the age; *élite*; star, sun, constellation, galaxy.

ornament, honor, feather in one's cap, halo, aureole, nimbus; halo −, blaze- of glory; blushing honors; laurels etc. (*trophy*) 733.

memory, posthumous fame, niche in the temple of fame; immor-tality, -tal name; *magni nominis umbra*.

V. be conscious of glory; be proud of etc. (*pride*) 878; exult etc. (*boast*) 884; be vain of etc. (*vanity*) 880.

be -distinguished etc. *adj.*; shine etc. (*light*) 420; shine forth, figure; make −, cut- a -figure, − dash, − splash.

rival, surpass; out-shine, -rival, -vie, -jump; emulate, vie with, eclipse; throw −, cast- into the shade; overshadow.

live, flourish, glitter, scintillate, flaunt; gain −, acquire- honor etc. *n.*; play first fiddle etc. (*be of importance*) 642; bear the -palm, − bell; lead the way; take -precedence, − the wall of; gain −, win-laurels, − spurs, − golden opinions etc. (*approbation*) 931; graduate, take one's degree, pass one's examination, win a -scholarship, − fellowship.

make -a, − some- -noise, − noise in the world; leave one's mark, exalt one's horn, star, have a run, be run after; enjoy popularity, come -into vogue, − to the front; raise one's head.

enthrone, signalize, immortalize, deify, exalt to the skies; hand one's name down to posterity.

consecrate; dedicate to, devote to; enshrine, inscribe, blazon, lionize, blow the trumpet, crown with laurel.

confer –, reflect- honor etc. *n.* on; shed a luster on; redound to one's honor, ennoble.

give –, do –, pay –, render- honor to; honor, accredit, pay regard to, dignify, glorify; sing praises to etc. (*approve*) 931; look up to; exalt, aggrandize, elevate, nobilitate.

Adj. distinguished, *distingué*, noted; of -note etc. *n.*; honored etc. *v.*; popular; fashionable etc. 852.

in good odor; in –, in high- favor; reput-, respect-, credit-able.

remarkable etc. (*important*) 642; notable, notorious; celebrated, renowned, in every one's mouth, talked of; fam-ous, -ed; far-famed; conspicuous, to the front; foremost; in the -front rank, – ascendant.

imperishable, deathless, immortal, never fading, *aere perennius*; time-honored.

illustrious, glorious, splendid, brilliant, radiant; bright etc. 420; full-blown; honorific.

eminent, prominent; high etc. 206; in the zenith; at the -head of, – top of the tree; peerless, of the first water; superior etc. 33; super-, pre-eminent.

great, dignified, proud, noble, honorable, worshipful, lordly, grand, stately, august, princely, imposing, solemn, transcendent, majestic, sacred, sublime, heaven-born, heroic, *sans peur et sans reproche*; sacrosanct.

Int. hail! all hail! *ave! viva! vive!* long life to! glory –, honor- be to!

Phr. one's name -being in every mouth, – living for ever; *sic itur ad astra, fama volat, aut Caesar aut nullus*; not to know him argues oneself unknown; none but himself could be his parallel, *palmam qui meruit ferat.*

874. Disrepute.—N. disrepute, discredit; ill-, bad- -repute, -name, -odor, -favor; disapprobation etc. 932; in-gloriousness, derogation; a-, debasement; abjectness etc. *adj.*; degradation, dedecoration; 'a long farewell to all one's greatness;' odium, obloquy, opprobrium, ignominy.

dishonor, disgrace; shame, humiliation; scandal, baseness, vileness; perfidy, turpitude etc. (*improbity*) 940; infamy.

tarnish, taint, defilement, pollution.

stain, blot, spot, blur, stigma, brand, reproach, imputation, slur.

crying –, burning- shame; *scandalum magnatum*, badge of infamy, blot in one's escutcheon; bend –, bar- sinister; champain, point champain; by- word of reproach; Ichabod.

argumentum ad verecundiam; sense of shame etc. 879.

V. be -inglorious etc. *adj.*; incur -disgrace etc. *n.*; have –, earn- a bad name; put –, wear- a halter round one's neck; disgrace –, expose- oneself.

play second fiddle; lose caste; pale one's ineffectual fire; recede into the shade; fall from one's high estate; keep in the background etc. (*modesty*) 881; be conscious of disgrace etc. (*humility*) 879; look -blue, – foolish, – like a fool; cut a -poor,

– sorry- figure; laugh on the wrong side of the mouth; make a sorry face, go away with a flea in one's ear, slink away.

cause -shame etc. *n.*; shame, disgrace, put to shame, dishonor; throw –, cast –, fling –, reflect- dishonor etc. *n.* upon; be a -reproach etc. *n.* to; derogate from.

tarnish, stain, blot, sully, taint; discredit, degrade, debase, defile; beggar; expel etc. (*punish*) 972.

impute shame to, brand, post, stigmatize, vilify, defame, slur, cast a slur upon, hold up to shame, send to Coventry; tread –, trample- under foot; show up, drag through the mire, heap dirt upon; reprehend etc. 932.

bring low, put down, snub; take down a peg. – lower, – or two.

obscure, eclipse, outshine, take the shine out of; throw –, cast- into the shade; overshadow; leave –, put- in the background; push into a corner, put one's nose out of joint; put out, – of countenance.

upset, throw off one's center; discompose, disconcert; put to the blush etc. (*humble*) 879.

Adj. disgraced etc. *v.*; blown upon; shorn of -its beams, – one' glory; overcome, down-trodden; loaded with -shame etc. *n.*; in -bad repute etc. *n.*; out of -repute, – favor, – fashion, – countenance; at a discount; under -a cloud, – an eclipse; unable to show one's face; in the -shade, – background; out at elbows, down in the world, down and out.

inglorious; nameless, renownless, obscure, unknown to fame; un-noticed, -noted, -honored, -glorified.

shameful; dis-graceful, -creditable, -reputable; despicable; questionable; unbecoming, unworthy; derogatory; degrading, humiliating, *infra dignitatem*, dedecorous; scandalous, infamous, too bad, unmentionable; ribald, opprobrious; arrant, shocking, outrageous, notorious, shady.

ignominious, scrubby, dirty, abject, vile, beggarly, pitiful, low, mean, shabby; base etc. (*dishonorable*) 940.

Adv. to one's shame be it spoken.

Int. fie! shame! for shame! *proh pudor! O tempora! O mores!* ough! *sic transit gloria mundi!*

875. Nobility.—N. nobility, rank, condition, distinction, optimacy, blood, *pur sang*, birth, high descent, order; quality, gentility; blue blood of Castile; *ancien régime.*

high life, *haut monde*; upper -classes, – ten thousand; *élite*, aristocracy, great folks; fashionable world etc. (*fashion*) 852; salariat.

peer, -age; house of -lords, – peers; lords, – temporal and spiritual; *noblesse*; baronage, knightage; noble, -man; lord, -ling; grandee, *magnifico, hidalgo*; don, -ship; aristocrat, swell, three-tailed bashaw; gentleman, squire, squireen, patrician, laureate.

gentry, gentlefolk; squirarchy, better sort, *magnates, primates, optimates.*

king etc. (*master*) 745; prince, crown prince, *Dauphin*; duke; marquis, -ate; earl, viscount, baron, thane, banneret; baronet, -cy; knight, -hood; count, armiger, laird; sig-, seig-nior; esquire, boyar, margrave, vavasor, sheik, emir, ameer, scherif, *pasha*, effendi, sahib.

queen etc. 745; princess, begum, duchess, marchioness; countess etc.; lady, dame.

personage —, man- of -distinction, — mark, — rank; nota-bles, -bilities; celebrity, big-wig, magnate, great man, star; *magni nominis umbra*; 'every inch a king;' grand Panjandrum

V. be -noble etc. *adj.*

Adj. noble, exalted; of -rank etc. *n.*; princely, titled, patrician, aristocratic; high-, well-born; of gentle blood; genteel, *comme il faut*, gentlemanlike, courtly etc. (*fashionable*) 852; highly respectable.

Adv. in high quarters.

876. Commonalty.—N. commonalty, democracy; obscruity; low -condition, — life, — society, — company; *bourgeoisie*; mass of -the people, — society; Brown, Jones, and Robinson; Tom, Dick, and Harry; lower —, humbler- -classes, — orders; vulgar —, common- herd; rank and file, *hoc genus omne*; the -many, — general, — crowd, — people, — populace, — multitude, — million, — masses, — mobility, — peasantry; king Mob; proletariat, *fruges consumere nati*, great unwashed; man in the street

mob; rabble, — rout; chaff, rout, horde, *canaille*; scum —, *residuum* —; dregs- of -the people, — society; swinish multitude, *faex populi*; *profanum* —, *ignobile- vulgus*; vermin, riff-raff, tag-rag and bobtail; small fry.

commoner, one of the people, democrat, plebeian, republican, proletary, *prolétaire, roturier*, Mr. Snooks, *bourgeois, épicier*, Philistine, cockney; *grisette, demi-monde*.

peasant, count_ryman, boor, carle, churl; vill-ain, -ein; serf, kern, tyke, tike, chuff, ryot, fellah; longshoreman; swain, clown, hind; clod, -hopper; fishnail, yokel, hick, rube, cider squeezer, bog-trotter, bumpkin; ploughman, -boy; rustic, chawbacon, tiller of the soil; hewers of wood and drawers of water, groundling; gaffer, loon; put, cub, Tony Lumpkin, looby, lout, under-ling; *gamin*, guttersnipe, street arab, mudlark; rough, rowdy, ruffian, roughneck; pot-wallopper, slubberdegullion; vulgar —, low- fellow; cad, curmudgeon.

upstart, *parvenu, nouveau-riche*, skipjack; nobody, — one knows; *hesterni quirites, pessoribus orti; bourgeois gentilhomme, novus homo*, snob, gent, mushroom, no one knows who, adventurer; man of straw.

beggar, panhandler, gaberlunzie, muckworm, mudlark, *sans-culotte*, raff, tatterdemalion, caitiff, ragamuffin, Pariah, outcast of society, tramp, weary Willie, bum, vagabond, *chiffonaier*, rag-picker, Cinderella, cinderwench, scrub, jade; boots, gossoon.

Goth, Vandal, Hottentot, savage, barbarian, Yahoo; unlicked cub, rough diamond.

barbar-ousness, -ism; Boeotia.

V. be -ignoble etc. *adj.*, — nobody etc. *n.*

Adj. ignoble, common, mean, low, base, vile, sorry, scrubby, beggarly, below par; no great shakes etc. (*unimportant*) 643; home-ly, -spun; vulgar, low-minded; snobbish, *parvenu*.

plebeian, proletarian; of -low, — mean- -parentage, — origin, extraction; low-, base-, earth-born, low bred; mushroom, dunghill, risen from the ranks; unknown to fame, obscure, untitled.

rustic, uncivilized; lout-, boor-, clown-, churl-, brut-, raff-ish; rude, unlicked, unpolished.

barbar-ous, -ian, -ic, -esque; cockney, born within sound of Bow bells.

underling, menial, servile, subaltern.

Adv. below the salt.

877. Title.—N. title, honor; knighthood etc. (*nobility*) 875.

royal —, serene- highness, excellency, grace; lordship, worship, Rt. Hon., rever-ence, -end; esquire, sir; madam, *madame*; master, mistress, Mr., Mrs., *signor, señor, Mein Herr, mynheer*; your —, his- honor; handle to one's name.

decoration, laurel, palm, wreath, garland, bays, medal, ribbon, riband, blue ribbon, *cordon*, cross, crown, coronet, star, garter; feather, — in one's cap; chevron, epaulet, *épaulette*, colors, cockade; livery; order, arms, armorial bearings, shield, scutcheon, crest, reward etc. 973.

878. Pride.—N. dignity, self-respect, *mens sibi conscia recti*.

pride; haughtiness etc. *adj.*; high notions, *hauteur*; vainglory, crest; arrogance etc. (*assumption*) 885; pomposity etc. 882.

proud man, highflier; fine -gentleman, — lady, *grande dame*.

V. be -proud etc. *adj.*; put a good face on; look one in the face; stalk abroad, perk oneself up; presume, swagger, strut; rear —, lift up —, hold up- one's head; hold one's head high, look big, take the wall, 'bear like the Turk no rival near the throne,' carry with a high hand; ride the —, mount on one's- high horse; set one's back up, bridle, toss the head; give oneself airs etc. (*assume*) 885; boast etc. 884.

pride oneself on; glory in, take pride in; pique —, plume —, hug- oneself; stand upon, be proud of; put a good face on; not -hide one's light under a bushel, — put one's talent in a napkin; not think small beer of oneself etc. (*vanity*) 880.

Adj. dignified; stately; proud, -crested; lordly, baronial; lofty-minded; high-souled, -minded, -mettled, -handed, -plumed, -flown, -toned.

haughty, paughty, insolent, lofty, high, mighty, swollen, puffed up, flushed, blown; vain-glorious; purse-proud, fine; proud as -a peacock, Lucifer; bloated with pride.

supercilious, disdainful, bumptious, magisterial, imperious; high-handed, — and mighty; overweening, consequential; arrogant etc. 885; unblushing etc. 880.

stiff, -necked; starch; perked —, stuck- up; in buckram, straitlaced; prim etc. (*affected*) 855.

on one's -high horses, — tight ropes, — high ropes; on stilts; *en grand seigneur*.

Adv. with head erect, with one's nose in the air.

Phr. *odi profanum vulgus et arceo.*

879. Humility.—N. hum-ility, -bleness; meek-, low-ness; lowli-ness, -hood; abasement, self-abasement, -effacement; submission etc. 725; resignation.

condescension; affability etc. (*courtesy*) 894.

modesty etc. 881; verecundity, blush, suffusion, confusion; sense of -shame, — disgrace; humiliation, mortification; let —, set- down.

V. be -humble etc. *adj*.; deign, vouchsafe, condescend; humble\ — , demean- oneself; stoop, — to conquer; carry coals; submit etc. 725; submit with a good grace etc. (*brook*) 826; yield the palm.

lower one's -tone, — note; sing small, draw in one's horns, sober down; hide one's -face, — diminished head; not dare to show one's face, take shame to oneself, not have a word to say for oneself; feel —, be conscious of- -shame, — disgrace; drink the cup of humiliation to the dregs; eat -humble pie, — one's words, — dirt; be humiliated, receive a snub.

blush -for, — up to the eyes; redden, change color; color up; hang one's head, look foolish, feel small.

render humble; humble, humiliate; let —, set —, take —, tread —, frown- down; snub, abash, abase, make one sing small, teach one -his distance, — his place; take down a peg, — lower; throw —, cast- into the shade etc. 874; stare —, put- out of countenance; put to the blush; confuse, ashame, mortify, disgrace, crush; send away with a flea in one's ear.

get a set down.

Adj. humble, lowly, meek; modest etc. 881; humble-, sober-minded; unoffended; submissive etc. 725; servile etc. 886.

condescending; affable etc. (*courteous*) 894.

humbled etc. *v*.; bowed down, resigned; abashed, ashamed, dashed; out of countenance; down in the mouth; down on one's -knees, — marrow-bones; humbled in the dust, brow-beaten; chap-, crest-fallen; dumbfoundered, flabbergasted, struck all of a heap.

shorn of one's glory etc. (*disrepute*) 874.

Adv. with -downcast eyes, — bated breath, — bended knee; on all fours, on one's feet.

under correction, with due deference.

Phr. I am your -obedient, — very humble- servant; my service to you.

880. Vanity.—**N.** vanity; conceit, -edness; self-conceit, -complacency, -confidence, -sufficiency, -esteem, -love, -approbation, -praise, -glorification, -laudation, -gratulation, -applause, -admiration; *amour-propre*; selfishness etc. 943.

airs, pretensions, mannerism; egotism; prigg-ism, -ishness; coxcombery, gaudery, vainglory, elation; pride etc. 878; ostentation etc. 882; assurance etc. 885.

vox et praeterea nihil; *cheval de bataille*.

ego-ist, -tist; peacock, coxcomb etc. 854; Sir Oracle etc. 887.

V. be -vain etc. *adj*., — vain of; pique oneself etc. (*pride*) 878; lay the flattering unction to one's soul.

have -too high, — an overweening- opinion of -oneself, — one's talents; blind oneself as to one's own merit; not think -small beer, — *vin ordinaire*- of oneself; put oneself forward; fish for compliments; give oneself airs etc. (*assume*) 885; boast etc. 884.

render -vain etc. *adj*.; inspire with -vanity etc. *n*.; inflate, puff up, turn up, turn one's head.

Adj. vain, — as a peacock; conceited, assured, overweening, pert, forward, perky; vain-glorious, high-flown; ostentatious etc. 882; puffed up, inflated, flushed.

self-satisfied, -confident, -sufficient, -flattering, -admiring, -applauding, -glorious, -opinionated; *entêté* etc. (*wrong-headed*) 481; wise in one's own conceit, pragmatical, overwise, pretentious, priggish; egotistic, -al; *soi-disant* etc. (*boastful*) 884; arrogant etc. 885.

un-abashed, -blushing; un-constrained, -ceremonious; free and easy.

Adv. vainly etc. *adj*.

Phr. how we apples swim!

881. Modesty.—**N.** modesty; humility etc. 879; diffidence, timidity; retiring disposition, unobtrusiveness, bashfulness etc. *adj*.; *mauvaise honte*; blush, -ing; verecundity; self-knowledge.

reserve, constraint; demureness etc. *adj*.; blushing honors.

V. be -modest etc. *adj*.; retire, reserve oneself; give way to; draw in one's horns etc. 879; hide one's face.

keep -private, — in the background, — one's distance; pursue the noiseless tenor of one's way, 'do good by stealth and blush to find it fame,' hide one's light under a bushel, cast a sheep's eye.

Adj. modest, diffident; humble etc. 879; timid, timorous, bashful; shy, nervous, skittish, coy, sheepish, shamefaced, blushing, over-modest.

unpreten-ding, -tious; un-obtrusive, -assuming, -ostentatious, -boastful, -aspiring; poor in spirit.

out of countenance etc. (*humbled*) 879.

reserved, constrained, demure.

Adv. humbly etc. *adj*.; quietly, privately; without -ceremony, — beat of the drum; *sans façon*.

882. Ostentation.—**N.** ostentation, display, show, flourish, parade, *étalage*, pomp, array, state, solemnity; dash, splash, glitter, strut, swank, side, swagger, pomposity; preten-se, -sions; showing off; fuss.

magnificence, splendor; *coup d'oeil*; grand doings.

coup de théâter; stage -effect, — trick; clap-trap; *mise en scène*; *tour de force*; chic.

demonstration, flying colors; tomfoolery; flourish of trumpets etc. (*celebration*) 883; pageant, -ry; spectacle, exhibition, procession; turn —, set- out; grand function; *fête*, gala, field-day, review, march past, promenade, insubstantial pageant.

dress; court —, full —, evening —, ball —, fancy- dress; tailoring, millinery, man-millinery, frippery; foppery, equipage.

ceremon-y, -ial; ritual; form, -ality; etiquette; punct-o, -ilio, -ilious-ness; starched-, stateli-ness.

mummery, solemn mockery, mouth honor.

attitudinarian; fop etc. 854.

V. be -ostentatious etc. *adj*.; come —, put oneself- forward; attract attention, star it.

make —, cut- a -figure, — dash, — splash; strut, blow one's own trumpet; figure, — away; make a show, — display; glitter.

show -off, — one's paces; parade, march past;

display, exhibit, put forward, hold up; trot –,
hang- out; sport, brandish, blazon forth; dangle, –
before the eyes.

cry up etc. (*praise*) 931; *prôner*, flaunt, emblazon, prink, set off, mount, have framed and
glazed.

put a good, – smiling- face upon; clean the outside of the platter etc. (*disguise*) 544.

Adj. ostentatious, showy, dashing, pretentious,
ja-, jau-nty; grand, pompous, palatial; high
sounding; turgid etc. (*big-sounding*) 577; garish,
gorgeous; gaudy, – as a -peacock, – butterfly, –
tulip; flaunting, flashing, flaming, glittering; gay
etc. (*ornate*) 847; colorful.

splendid, magnificent, sumptuous.

theatrical, dramatic, spectacular, scenic,
ceremonial, ritual, -istic.

solemn, stately, majestic, formal, 'stiff,
ceremonious, punctilious, starch-ed, -y.

en grande tenue, in best bib and tucker, in Sunday best, *endimanché*.

Adv. with -flourish of trumpet, – beat of drum,
– flying colors, – a brass band.

ad captandum vulgus.

883. Celebration.—N. celebration, solemnization, jubilee, diamond jubilee, commemoration, ovation, paean, triumph, jubilation.

triumphal arch, bonfire, salute; salvo, – of artillery; *feu de joie*, flourish of trumpets, *fanfare*,
colors flying, illuminations, fireworks.

inauguration, installation, presentation; *début*,
coming out, birthday anniversary, bi-, ter-, centenary; silver –, golden –, diamond- wedding, -
day; coronation; Lord Mayor's show; harvest
home, red letter day, festival; trophy etc. 733; *Te
Deum* etc. (*thanksgiving*) 990; fête etc. 882;
holiday etc. 840.

V. celebrate, keep, signalize, do honor to, commemorate, solemnize, hallow, mark with a red letter, hold high festival, maffick.

pledge, drink to, toast, hob and nob.

inaugurate, install, instate, induct, chair.

rejoice etc. 838; kill the fatted calf, hold jubilee,
roast an ox, fire a salute.

Adj. celebrating etc. *v.*; commemorative,
celebrated, immortal.

Adv. in -honor, – commemoration, –
celebration of.

Int. hail! all hail! *io -paean, – triumphe!* 'see the
conquering hero comes!'

884. Boasting.—N. boasting etc. *v.*; boast,
vaunt, crake; preten-ce, -sions; puff, -ery; flourish,
fanfaronnade; gasconade; bluff, swank, brag, -
gardism; bravado, bunkum, Buncombe; high-
falutin; jact-itation, -ancy; bounce, rant, bluster;
venditation, vaporing, rodomontade, bombast, fine
talking, tall talk, magniloquence, teratology,
heroics; jingoism, Chauvinism; exaggeration etc.
549; gas, hot air.

vanity etc. 880; *vox et praeterea nihil*; much cry
and little wool, *brutum fulmen*.

exultation; glorification; flourish of trumpets;
triumph etc. 883.

boaster; bragg-art, -adocio; hot air merchant;

Gascon, *fanfaron*, pretender, fourflusher, *soi-
disant*; windbag, blowhard, bluffer; chauvinist;
blusterer etc. 887; charlatan, jack-pudding, trumpeter; puppy etc. (*fop*) 854.

V. boast, make a boast of, brag, vaunt, puff,
show off, flourish, crake, crack, trumpet, strut,
swagger, vapor, bluff; draw the long bow.

exult, crow over, neigh, chuckle, triumph; glory,
gloat, jubilate; throw up one's cap; talk big, *se faire
valoir*, *faire claquer son fouet*, take merit to
oneself, make a merit of, sing *Io triumphe*, holloa
before one is out of the wood.

Adj. boasting etc. *v.*; magniloquent, flaming,
Thrasonic, stilted, gasconading, braggart, boastful,
pretentious, *soi-disant*; vain-glorious etc. (*conceited*) 880.

elate, -d; jubilant, triumphant, exultant; in high
feather; flushed, – with victory; cock-a-hoop; on
stilts.

vaunted etc. *v.*

Adv. vauntingly etc. *adj.*; with a brass band.

Phr. 'let the galled jade wince.'

885. Insolence. [Undue assumption of
superiority.]**—N.** insolence; haughtiness etc. *adj.*;
arrogance, airs; overbearance, brashness, bump-
tiousness, contumely, disdain; domineering etc. *v.*;
tyranny etc. 739.

impertinence; cheek, nerve, sauce; sauciness etc.
adj.; flippancy, dicacity, petulance; procacity,
bluster; swagger, -ing etc. *v.*; bounce; terrorism;
jingoism, chauvinism.

as-, pre-sumption; beggar on horseback; usurpation.

impudence, assurance, audacity, self-assertion,
hardihood, front, face, brass; shamelessness etc.
adj.; effrontery, hardened front, face of brass.

assumption of infallibility.

malapert, saucebox etc. (*blusterer*) 887.

V. be -insolent etc. *adj.*; bluster, vapor, swagger,
swell, give oneself airs; snap one's fingers, kick up a
dust; swear etc. (*affirm*) 535; rap out oaths; roister.

arrogate; as-, pre-sume; make -bold, – free; take
a liberty, give an inch and take an ell.

domineer, bully, dictate, hector; lord it over,
bulldoze; *traiter de haut, regarder de haut en bas*;
exact; snub, huff, beard, fly in the face of; put to
the blush; bear –, beat- down; browbeat, intimidate; trample –, tread- -down, – under foot;
dragoon, ride roughshod over; terrorize.

out-face, -look, -stare, -brazen, -brave; stare out
of countenance; brazen out; lay down the law;
teach one's grandmother to suck eggs; assume a
lofty bearing; talk –, look- big; put on big looks,
act the *grand seigneur*; mount –, ride- the high
horse; toss the head, carry with a high hand.

tempt Providence, want snuffing.

Adj. insolent, haughty, arrogant, imperious,
magisterial, dictatorial, arbitrary; high-handed,
high and mighty; contumelious, supercilious, over-
bearing, intolerant, domineering; overweening,
high-flown.

flippant, pert, cavalier, saucy, forward, impertinent, fresh, malapert.

precocious, assuming, would-be, bumptious.

bluff; brazen-, browed-faced, shameless, aweless,
unblushing, unabashed; bold-, bare-faced; dead –,
lost- to shame.

impudent, audacious, presumptuous, free and easy, devil-may-care, rollicking; janty, jaunty; roistering, blustering, hectoring, swaggering, vaporing; thrasonic, fire-eating, 'full of sound and fury.'

Adv. insolently, with a high hand; *ex cathedrâ*.
Phr. one's bark being worse than his bite.

886. Servility.—N. servility; slavery etc. (*subjection*) 749; obsequiousness etc. *adj.*; subserviency; abasement; pros-tration, -ternation; genuflexion etc. (*worship*) 990; fawning etc. *v.*; tuft-hunting, time-serving, flunkeyism; sycophancy etc. (*flattery*) 933; humility etc. 879.

sycophant, parasite, yes-man; toad, -y, -eater; tuft-hunter; snob, flunkey, lap-dog, spaniel, lick-spittle, smell-feast, *Graeculus esuriens*, hanger on, stooge, *cavaliere servente*, led captain, carpet knight; time-server, fortune-hunter, Vicar of Bray, Sir Pertinax Mac Sycophant, pick-thank; flatterer etc. 935; doer of dirty work; *âme damnée*, tool; reptile; slave etc. (*servant*) 746; courtier; sponge, jackal; truckler.

V. cringe, bow, stoop, kneel, bend the knee; fall on one's knees, prostrate oneself; worship etc. 990.

sneak, crawl, crouch, cower, truckle to, grovel, fawn, toady, lick the feet of, kiss the hem of one's garment.

pay court to; feed −, fatten −, batten- on; dance attendance on, pin oneself upon, hang on the sleeve of, *avaler des couleuvres*, keep time to, fetch and carry, do the dirty work of.

go with the stream, follow the crowd, worship the rising sun, hold with the hare and run with the hounds.

Adj. servile, obsequious; supple, − as a glove; soapy, oily, pliant, cringing, fawning, slavish, groveling, sniveling, mealy-mouthed; beggarly, sycophantic, parasitical; abject, prostrate, down on one's marrow-bones; base, mean, sneaking; crouching etc. *v.*

Adv. hat −, cap- in hand.

887. Blusterer.—N. bluster-, swagger-, vapor-, roister-, brawl-er; brazen-face; *fanfaron*; braggart etc. (*boaster*) 884; bully, terrorist, rough, rough-neck; hooligan, hoodlum, larrikin, ruffian; Mohock, -hawk; drawcansir, swashbuckler, Captain Boabdil, Sir Lucius O'Trigger, Thraso, Pistol, Parolles, Bombastes Furioso, Hector, Chrononhotonthologos; jingo; desperado, dare-devil, fire-eater; fury etc. (*violent person*) 173; rowdy.

puppy etc. (*fop*) 854; prig; Sir Oracle, dogmatist, *doctrinaire*, stump orator, jack-in-office; saucebox, malapert, jackanapes, minx; bantam-cock.

888. Friendship.—N. friendship, amity; friendliness etc. *adj.*; brotherhood, fraternity, sodality, confraternity, sorosis, sisterhood; harmony etc. (*concord*) 714; peace etc. 721.

firm −, staunch −, intimate −, familiar −, bosom −, cordial −, tried −, devoted −, lasting −, fast −, sincere −, warm −, ardent- friendship. cordiality, fraternization, *entente cordiale*, good

understanding, *rapprochement*, sympathy, fellow-feeling, response, welcomeness; *camaraderie*.

affection etc. (*love*) 897; favoritism; goodwill etc. (*benovolence*) 906; partiality.

acquaintance, familiarity, intimacy, intercourse, fellowship, knowledge of; introduction.

V. be -friendly etc. *adj.*, − friends etc. 890; − acquainted with etc. *adj.*; know; have the ear of; keep- company with etc. (*sociality*) 892; hold communication −, have dealings −, sympathize- with; have a leaning to; bear good will etc. (*benevolence*) 906; love etc. 897; make much of; befriend etc. (*aid*) 707; introduce to.

set one's horses together; hold out −, extend the right hand of -friendship, − fellowship; become -friendly etc. *adj.*; make -friends etc. 890 with; break the ice, be introduced to; make −, pick −, scrape- acquaintance with; get into favor, gain the friendship of.

shake hands with, fraternize, embrace; receive with open arms, throw oneself into the arms of; meet half way, take in good part.

Adj. friendly, amic-able, -al; well affected, unhostile, neighborly, brotherly, fraternal, sisterly, sympathetic, harmonious, hearty, cordial, warm-hearted, devoted.

friends −, well −, at home −, hand in hand-with; on -good, − friendly, − amicable, − cordial, − familiar, − intimate- -terms, − footing; on -speaking, − visiting- terms; in one's good -graces, − books.

acquainted, familiar, intimate, thick, hand and glove, hail fellow well met, free and easy; welcome.

Adv. amicably etc. *adj.*; with open arms; *sans cérémonie*; arm in arm.

889. Enmity.—N. enmity, hostility; un-friendliness etc. *adj.*; discord etc. 713.

alienation, estrangement; dislike etc. 867; hate etc. 898; antagonism.

heartburning; animosity etc. 900; malevolence etc. 907.

V. be -inimical etc. *adj.*; keep −, hold- at arm's length; be at loggerheads; bear malice etc. 907; fall out; take umbrage etc. 900; harden the heart, alienate, estrange.

Adj. inimical, unfriendly, hostile; at -enmity, − variance, − swords points, − daggers drawn, − open war with; up in arms against; in bad odor with.

on bad −, not on speaking- terms; cool; cold, -hearted; estranged, alienated, disaffected, irreconcilable.

890. Friend.—N. friend, − of one's bosom, intimate acquaintance, neighbor, well-wisher; *alter ego*; best −, bosom −, fast- friend; *amicus usque ad aras*; *fidus Achates*; *persona grata*.

favorer, *fautor*, patron, backer, Maecenas; tutelary saint, good genius, advocate, partisan, sympathizer; ally; friend in need etc. (*auxiliary*) 711.

associate, compeer, comrade, mate, companion, *confrère*, *camarade*, *confidante*, colleague; old −, crony; side-kick; chum, buddy, bunkie, roommate, pal; play-fellow, -mate; classmate, schoolfellow; bed-fellow, -mate; maid of honor.

compatriot; fellow –, countryman, – towns-man.

shop-, ship-, mess-mate; fellow –, boon –, pot-companion; co-partner.

Arcades ambo, Pylades and Orestes, Castor and Pollux, Nisus and Euryalus, Damon and Pythias, *par nobile fratrum*.

host, Amphitryon, Boniface; guest, visitor, frequenter, *habitué*; *protégé*.

891. Enemy.—N. enemy; antagonist, foeman; open –, bitter- enemy; opponent etc. 710; back friend.

public enemy, enemy to society, traitor, anar-chist etc. 743.

Phr. every hand being against one.

892. Sociality.—N. soci-ality, -ability, -ableness etc. *adj.*; social intercourse; consociation; inter-course, -community; consort-, companion-, fellow-, comrade-ship; clubbism; *esprit de corps*.

conviviality; good -fellowship, – company, *camaraderie*; joviality, jollity, *savoir -vivre*, festivity, festive board, merry-making; loving cup; hospitality, heartiness; cheer.

welcome, -ness; greeting; hearty –, warm –, welcome- reception; urbanity etc. (*courtesy*) 894; intimacy, familiarity.

good –, jolly- fellow, good mixer, Rotarian; *bon enfant*.

social –, family- circle; circle of acquaintance, *coterie*, society, company.

social -gathering, – *réunion*; assembly etc. (*assemblage*) 72; party, entertainment, reception, *levée*, at home, *conversazione*, *soirée*, *matinée*, evening –, morning –, afternoon –, garden –, dinner –, tea –, cocktail- party; symposium, sing-song; kettle-, drum; *partie carrée*, dish of tea, *ridotto*, rout, housewarming; ball, prom, hop, dance, *thé dansant*; festival etc. (*amusement*) 840; wedding breakfast; 'the feast of reason and the flow of soul.'

visit, -ing; round of visits; call, morning call; in-terview etc. (*interlocution*) 588; assignation; tryst, -ing place; appointment.

club etc. (*association*) 712.

V. be -sociable etc. *adj.*; know; be -acquainted etc. *adj.*; associate –, sort –, keep company –, walk hand in hand -with; eat off the same trencher, club together, consort, bear one company, join; make acquaintance with etc. (*friendship*) 888; make advances, fraternize, embrace; in-tercommunicate.

be –, feel –, make oneself- at home with; make free with; crack a bottle with; take pot luck with, receive hospitality, live at free quarters.

visit, pay a visit; interchange -visits, – cards; call -at, – upon; leave a card; drop in, look in; look one up, beat up one's quarters.

entertain; give a -party etc. *n.*; be at home, see one's friends, hang out, keep open house, do the honors; receive, – with open arms; welcome; give a warm reception etc. *n.* to; kill the fatted calf.

Adj. sociable, companionable, clubbable, clubby, conversable, cosy, cosey, chatty, con-versational; homiletical.

convivial; fest-ive, -al; jovial, jolly, hospitable. welcome, – as the roses in May; *fêté*, en-tertained.

free and easy, hail fellow well met, familiar, on visiting terms, acquainted.

social, neighborly; international, cosmopolitan, gregarious.

Adv. *en famille*, in the family circle; *sans -façon*, – *cérémonie*, arm in arm.

893. Seclusion. Exclusion.—N. seclusion, privacy; retirement; concealment; reclusion, recess; snugness etc. *adj.*; delitescence; rustication, *rus in urbe*; solitude; solitariness etc. (*singleness*) 87; isolation; loneliness etc. *adj.*; estrangement from the world, anchoritism, voluntary exile; aloofness.

cell, hermitage; convent etc. 1000; *sanctum sanctorum*; study, library, den; hide-out.

depopulation, desertion, desolation; wilderness etc. (*unproductive*) 169; howling wilderness; rot-ten borough, Old Sarum.

exclusion, excommunication, banishment, exile, ostracism, proscription; cut, – direct; dead cut.

inhospit-ality, -ableness etc. *adj.*; un-, dis-sociability; domesticity, Darby and Joan.

recluse, hermit, eremite, cenobite; anchor-et, -ite; Simon Stylites; Troglodyte, Timon of Athens, Santon, *solitaire*, ruralist, disciple of Zim-mermann, closet cynic, Diogenes; outcast, Pariah, castaway, outsider, pilgarlic; wastrel, foundling, or-phan.

V. be –, live- secluded etc. *adj.*; keep –, stand –, hold oneself- -aloof, – in the background; keep snug; shut oneself up; deny –, seclude-oneself; creep into a corner, rusticate, *aller planter ses choux*; retire, – from the world; hermetize, take the veil; abandon etc. 624.

cut, – dead; refuse to -associate with, – acknowledge; look cool –, turn one's back –, shut the door- upon; repel, blackball, ex-communicate, exclude, exile, expatriate; banish, outlaw, maroon, ostracize, proscribe, cut off from, send to Coventry, keep at arm's length, draw a cor-don round; boycott, blockade, lay an embargo on, isolate.

depopulate; dis-, un-people.

Adj. secluded, sequestered, retired, delitescent, private, bye; out of the -world, -way; in a back-water; 'the world forgetting by the world forgot.'

snug, domestic, stay-at-home.

unsociable; un-, dis-social; inhospitable, cynical, inconversable, unclubbable, *sauvage*, eremitic.

solitary; lone-ly, -some; isolated, single.

excluded, estranged; unfrequented; uninhabit-able, -ed; tenantless; un-tenanted, -occupied; aban-doned; deserted, – in one's utmost need; un-friended; kith-, friend-, home-less; lorn, forlorn, desolate.

un-visited, -introduced, -invited, -welcome; un-der a cloud, left to shift for oneself, derelict, out-cast, outside the gates.

banished etc. *v.*; under an embargo.

Phr. *noli me tangere*.

894. Courtesy.—N. courtesy; respect etc. 928; good -manners, – behavior, – breeding; manners; politeness etc. *adj.*; *bienséance*, urbanity, comity, gentility; gentle –, breeding; polish, presence, cultivation, culture; civili-ty, -zation; amenity, suavity; good -temper, – humor; amiability, easy temper, complacency, soft tongue, mansuetude; condescension etc. (*humility*) 879; affability, complaisance, *prévenance*, amiability, gallantry, chivalry; pink of -politeness, – courtesy.

compliment; fair –, soft –, sweet- words; honeyed phrases, flattering remarks. ceremonial; salutation, reception, presentation, introduction, *accueil*, greeting, recognition; welcome, *abord*, respects, *devoir*, regards, remembrances; kind -regards, – remembrances; love, best love, duty; deference.

obeisance etc. (*reverence*) 928; bow, courtesy, curtsy, scrape, *salaam, kow-tow*, bowing and scraping; kneeling; genuflexion etc. (*worship*) 990; obsequiousness etc. 886; capping, shaking hands etc. *v.*; grip of the hand, embrace, hug, squeeze, *accolade*, loving cup, *vin d'honneur*, pledge; love token etc. (*endearment*) 902; kiss, buss, salute.

mark of recognition, not; 'nods and becks and wreathed smiles;' valediction etc. 293; condolence etc. 915.

V. be -courteous etc. *adj.*; show -courtesy etc. *n.*

mind one's P's and Q's, behave oneself, be all things to all men, conciliate, speak one fair, take in good part; make –, do- the amiable; look as if butter would not melt in one's mouth; mend one's manners.

receive, do the honors, usher, greet, hail, bid welcome; welcome, – with open arms; shake hands; hold out –, press –, squeeze- the hand; bid God speed; speed the parting guest; cheer, serenade.

salute; embrace etc. (*endearment*) 902; kiss, – hands; drink to, pledge, hob and nob; move to, nod to; smile upon.

uncover, cap; touch –, take off- the hat; doff the cap; pull the forelock; present arms; make way for; bow; make one's bow; scrape, curtsy, courtesy; bob a -curtsy, – courtesy; kneel; bow –, bend- the knee; salaam, *kowtow*.

visit, wait upon, present oneself, pay one's respects, pay a visit etc. (*sociability*) 892; dance attendance on etc. (*servility*) 886; pay attentions to; do homage to etc. (*respect*) 928.

prostrate oneself etc. (*worship*) 990.

give –, send- one's duty etc. *n.*, to.

render -polite etc. *adj.*; polish, civilize, humanize.

Adj. courteous, polite, civil, mannerly, urbane; well-behaved, -mannered, -bred, -brought up, gently bred, of gentle -breeding, – manners, good-mannered, polished, civilized, cultivated; refined etc. (*taste*) 850; gentlemanlike etc. (*fashion*) 852; gallant, chivalrous, on one's good behavior.

fine –, fair –, soft- spoken; honey-mouthed, -tongued; oily, unctuous, bland, suave; obliging, conciliatory, complaisant, complacent; obsequious etc. 886.

ingratiating, winning; gentle, mild; good-humored, cordial, gracious, amiable, tactful, addressful, affable, genial, friendly, familiar; neighborly.

Adv. courteously etc. *adj.*; with a good grace; with -open, – outstretched- arms; *à bras ouverts; suaviter in modo*, in good humor.

Int. hail! welcome! well met! *ave!* all hail! good -day, – morning etc., – morrow! God speed! *pax vobiscum!* may your shadow never be less! *chin-chin!*

895. Discourtesy.—N. discourtesy; ill-breeding; ill –, bad –, ungainly- manners; insuavity; grouchiness; un-courteousness etc. *adj.*, tactlessness; rusticity, inurbanity; illiberality, incivility, displacency.

disrespect etc. 929; procacity, impudence; barbar-ism, -ity; misbehavior, brutality, blackguard--ism, conduct unbecoming a gentleman, *grossièreté, brusquerie*; vulgarity etc. 851.

churlishness etc. *adj.*; spinosity, perversity; moroseness etc. (*sullenness*) 901*a*.

bad-, ill-temper; sternness etc. *adj.*; austerity, moodishness, captiousness etc. 901; cynicism; tartness etc. *adj.*; acrimony, acerbity, virulence, asperity.

scowl, black looks, frown; short answer, rebuff; hard words, contumely; unparliamentary language, personality.

bear, bruin, brute, grouch, blackguard, beast; unlicked cub; frump, cross-patch; saucebox etc. 887.

V. be -rude etc. *adj.*; insult etc. 929; treat with discourtesy; take a name in vain; make -bold, – free- with; take a liberty; stare out of countenance, ogle, point at, put to the blush.

cut; turn -one's back upon, – on one's heel; give the cold shoulder; keep at -a distance, – arm's length; look -cool, – coldly, – black- upon; show the door to, send away with a flea in the ear.

lose one's temper etc. (*resentment*) 900; sulk etc. 901*a*; frown, scowl, glower, pout; snap, snarl, growl.

render -rude etc. *adj.*; brut-alize, -ify.

Adj. dis-, un-courteous; uncourtly; ill-bred, -mannered, -behaved, -conditioned; unbred; un-manner-ly, -ed; im-, un-polite; un-polished, -civilized, -genteel; ungentleman-like, -ly; unladylike; blackguard; vulgar etc. 851; dedecorous; foul-mouthed, -spoken; abusive.

un-civil, -gracious, -ceremonious; cool; pert, forward, obtrusive, impudent, rude, saucy, precocious; insolent etc. 885.

repulsive; un-complaisant, -accommodating, -neighborly, -gallant; inaffable; un-gentle, -gainly; rough, rugged, bluff, blunt, gruff; churl-ish, boor-, bear-ish; brutal, *brusque*; stern, harsh, austere; cavalier.

tart, sour, crabbed, sharp, short, trenchant, sarcastic, crusty, biting, caustic, virulent, bitter, acrimonious, venomous, contumelious; snarling etc., *v.*; surly, – as a bear; perverse; grim, sullen etc. 901*a*; peevish etc. (*irascible*) 901.

Adv. discourteously etc. *adj.*; with -discourtesy etc. *n.*, – a bad grace.

896. Congratulations.—N. con-, gratulation; felicitation; salute etc. 894; condolence etc. 915; compliments of the season; good –, best- wishes.

V. con-, gratulate; felicitate, compliment; give –, wish one- joy; tender –, offer- one's congratulations; wish -many happy returns of the day, – a merry Christmas and a happy new year.

congratulate oneself etc. (*rejoice*) 838.

Adj. con-, gratulatory.

897. Love.—N. love; fondness etc. *adj.*; liking; inclination etc. (*desire*) 865; regard, dilection, admiration, fancy.

affection, sympathy, fellow-felling; tenderness etc. *adj.*; heart, brotherly love; benevolence etc. 906; attachment.

yearning, tender passion, *affaire de coeur*, *amour*, gallantry, inamorato, flame, devotion, fervor, enthusiasm, transport of love, rapture, enchantment, infatuation, adoration, idolatry.

narcissism, Oedipus complex, Electra complex.

Cupid, Venus, Eros; myrtle; true lover's knot; love -token, — suit, — affair, — tale, — story; the old story, plighted love; courtship etc. 902; *amourette*.

maternal love.

attractiveness, charm; popularity; favorite etc. 899.

lover, suitor, follower, admirer, adorer, wooer, amoret, beau, sweetheart, inamorato, swain, young man, flame, love, truelove; leman, Lothario, gallant, paramor, *amoroso*, *cavaliere servente*, captive, *cicisbeo*; *caro sposo*, Don Juan, sheik, ladies' man, squire of dames, Knave of Hearts.

inamorata, lady-love, idol, darling, duck, Dulcinea, angel, goddess, *cara sposa*; mistress.

betrothed, affianced, *fiancée*.

flirt, *coquette*; amorette; pair of turtle doves; abode of love, *agapemone*.

V. love, like, affect, fancy, care for, take an interest in, be partial to, sympathize with; be -in love etc. *adj.*- with; have —, entertain —, harbor —, cherish- a -love etc. *n.* for; regard, revere; take to, bear love to, be wedded to; set one's affections on; make much of, feast one's eyes on; hold dear, prize, treasure; hug, cling to, cherish, pet, caress etc. 902.

burn; adore, idolize, love to distraction, *aimer eperdument*; dote -on, — upon.

take a fancy to, fall for, be stuck on, look sweet upon; become -enamored etc. *adj.*; fall in love with, lose one's heart; desire etc. 865.

excite love; win —, gain —, secure —, engage- the -love, — affections, — heart; take the fancy of; have a place in —, wind round- the heart; attract, attach, endear, charm, fascinate, captivate, bewitch, seduce, enamor, enrapture, turn the head.

get into favor; ingratiate —, insinuate —, worm- oneself; propitiate, curry favor with, pay one's court to, make a date with, *faire l'aimable*, set one's cap at, flirt, coquet.

Adv. loving etc. *v.*; fond of; taken —, struck- with; smitten, bitten; attached to, wedded to; enamored; charmed etc. *v.*; in love; lovesick; over head and ears in love.

affectionate, tender, sweet upon, sympathetic, loving, fond, amorous, amatory; erotic, uxurious, ardent, passionate, rapturous, devoted, motherly.

loved etc. *v.*; beloved; well —, dearly- beloved; dear, precious, darling, pet, little; favorite, popular.

congenial; to —, after- one's -mind, — taste, — fancy, — own heart.

in one's good -graces etc. (*friendly*) 888; dear as the apple of one's eye, nearest to one's heart.

lovable, adorable; lovely, sweet; attractive, seductive, winning; charming, engaging, interesting, enchanting, captivating, fascinating, intriguing, bewitching; amiable, like an angel, angelic, seraphic.

898. Hate.—N. hate, hatred, vials of hate; Hymn of Hate.

dis-affection, -favor; alienation, estrangement, coolness; enmity etc. 889; animosity etc. 900.

umbrage, pique, grudge; dudgeon, spleen; bitterness, — of feeling; ill —, bad- blood; acrimony; malice etc. 907; implacability etc. (*revenge*) 919.

repugnance etc. (*dislike*) 867; odium, unpopularity; loathing, detestation, antipathy; object of -hatred, — execration; abomination, aversion, *bête noire*; enemy etc. 891; bitter pill; source of annoyance etc. 830.

V. hate, detest, abominate, abhor, loathe; recoil —, shudder- at; shrink from, view with horror, hold in abomination, revolt against, execrate; scowl etc. 895; disrelish etc. (*dislike*) 867.

owe a grudge; bear -spleen, — a grudge, — malice etc. (*malevolence*) 907; conceive an aversion to.

excite —, provoke- hatred etc. *n.*; be -hateful etc. *adj.*; stink in the nostrils; estrange, alienate, repel, set against, sow dissension, set by the ears, envenom, incense, irritate, rile, ruffle, vex; horrify etc. 830.

Adj. hating etc. *v.*; abhorrent; averse from etc. (*disliking*) 867; set against.

bitter etc. (*acrimonious*) 895; implacable etc. (*revengeful*) 919.

un-loved, -beloved, -lamented, -deplored, -mourned, -cared for, -endured, -valued; disliked etc. 867.

crossed in love, forsaken, rejected, love-lorn, jilted.

obnoxious, hateful, odious, abominable, repulsive, offensive, shocking; disgusting etc. (*disagreeable*) 830.

invidious, spiteful; malicious etc. 907.

insulting, irritating, provoking.

[Mutual hate] at -daggers drawn, — swords points; not on speaking terms etc. (*enmity*) 889.

Phr. no love lost between.

899. Favorite.—N. favorite, pet, cosset, minion, idol, jewel, spoiled child, *enfant gâté*; led captain; crony; fondling; apple of one's eye, man after one's own heart; *persona grata*.

love, dear, darling, duck, honey, jewel; mopsey, moppet; sweetheart etc. (*love*) 897.

general —, universal- favorite; idol of the people; matinée idol, movie —, radio- star.

900. Resentment.—N. resentment, displeasure, animosity, anger, wrath, indignation; vexation, exasperation, bitter resentment, wrathful indignation.

pique, umbrage, huff, miff, soreness, dudgeon, acerbity, virulence, bitterness, acrimony, asperity, spleen, gall; heart-burning, -swelling; rankling.

ill —, bad- -humor, — temper; irascibility etc. 901; ill blood etc. (*hate*) 898; revenge etc. 919.

excitement, irritation; warmth, bile, choler, ire, fume, pucker, dander, ferment, ebullition; towering -passion, — rage, *acharnement*, angry mood, taking, pet, tiff, passion, fit, tantrums.

burst, explosion, paroxysm, storm, rage, fury, desperation; violence etc. 173; fire and fury; vials of wrath; gnashing of teeth, hot blood, high words.

scowl etc. 895; sulks etc. 901a.

[Cause of umbrage] affront, provocation, offence; indignity etc. (insult) 929; grudge, crow to pluck, sore subject; red rag to a bull; casus belli.

Furies, Erinys, Eumenides, Alecto, Megaera, Tisiphone.

buffet, slap in the face, box on the ear, rap on the knuckles.

V. resent; take -amiss, – ill, – to heart, – offence, – umbrage, – huff, – exception; take in - ill part, – bad part, – dudgeon; ne pas entendre raillerie; breathe revenge, cut up rough.

fly –, fall –, get- into a -rage, – passion; bridle –, bristle –, froth –, fire –, flare- up; open –, pour out- the vials of one's wrath.

pout, knit the brow, frown, scowl, lower, snarl, growl, gnarl, gnash, snap; redden, color; look - black, – black as thunder, – daggers; bite one's thumb; show –, grind- one's teeth; champ the bit.

chafe, mantle, fume, kindle, fly out, take fire; boil, – over; boil with -indignation, – rage; rage, storm, foam; vent one's -rage, – spleen; lose one's temper, stand on one's hind legs, stamp the foot, kick up a row, fly off the handle, cut up rough; stamp –, quiver –, swell –, foam- with rage; burst with anger; raise Cain, breathe fire and fury.

have a fling at; bear malice etc. (revenge) 919.

cause –, raise- anger; affront, offend; give - offence, – umbrage; anger; hurt the feelings; insult, discompose, fret, ruffle, nettle, heckle, huff, pique; excite etc. 824; irritate, stir the blood, stir up bile; sting, – to the quick; rile, provoke, chafe, wound, incense, inflame, enrage, aggravate, add fuel to the flame, fan into a flame, widen the breach, envenom, embitter, exasperate, infuriate, kindle wrath; stick in one's gizzard; rankle etc. 919.

put out of humor; put one's -monkey, – backup; set –, get- one's back up; raise one's -gorge, – dander, – choler; work up into a passion; make - one's blood boil, – the ears tingle; throw into a ferment, madden, drive one mad; lash into -fury, – madness; fool to the top of one's bent; set by the ears.

bring a hornet's nest about one's ears.

Adj. angry, wrath, irate; ire-, wrath-ful; cross etc. (irascible) 901; sulky etc. 901a; bitter, virulent; acrimonious etc. (discourteous) etc. 895; violent etc. 173.

warm, burning; boiling, – over; fuming, raging; foaming, – at the mouth; convulsed with rage.

offended etc. v.; waxy, acharné, wrought, worked up; indignant, hurt, sore, peeved; set against.

fierce, wild, rageful, furious, mad with rage, fiery, infuriate, rabid, savage; relentless etc. 919.

flushed with -anger, – rage; in a -huff, – stew, – fume, – pucker, – passion, – rage, – fury; on one's high ropes, up in arms; in high dudgeon.

Adv. angrily etc. adj.; in the height of passion; in the heat of -passion, – the moment.

Phr. one's -blood, – back, – monkey- being up; fervens difficili bile jecur; the gorge rising, eyes flashing fire; the blood -rising, – boiling; haeret lateri lethalis arundo.

901. Irascibility.—N. irascibility, temper; crossness etc. adj.; susceptibility, procacity,

petulance, irritability, tartness, acerbity, protervity; pugnacity etc. (contentiousness) 720.

excitability etc. 825; bad –, fiery –, crooked –, irritable etc. adj.- temper; genus irritabile, hot blood.

ill humor etc. (sullenness) 901a; asperity etc., churlishness etc. (discourtesy) 895.

huff etc. (resentment) 900; a word and·a blow.

Sir Fretful Plagiary; brabbler, Tartar; shrew, vixen, virago, termagant, dragon, scold, Xanthippe; porcupine; spit-fire; fire-eater etc. (blusterer) 887; fury etc. (violent person) 173.

V. be -irascible etc. adj.; have a -temper etc. n., – devil in one; fire up etc. (be angry) 900.

Adj. irascible; bad-, ill-tempered; irritable, susceptible; excitable etc. 825; thin-skinned etc. (sensitive) 822; fretful, fidgety; on the fret.

hasty, over-hasty, quick, warm, hot, testy, touchy, techy, tetchy; like -touchwood, – tinder; huffy; pet-tish, -ulant; waspish, snapp-y, -ish, peppery, fiery, passionate, choleric, shrewish, 'sudden and quick in quarrel.'

querulous, captious, mood-y, -ish; quarrelsome, contentious, disputatious; pugnacious etc. (bellicose) 720; cantankerous, exceptious; restive etc. (perverse) 901a; churlish etc. (discourteous) 895.

cross, – as -crabs, – two sticks, – a cat, – a dog, – the tongs; like a bear with a sore head; fractious, peevish, acariâtre.

in a bad temper; sulky etc. 901a; angry etc. 900. resent-ful, -ive; vindictive etc. 919.

Int. pish!

901a. Sullenness.—N. sullenness etc. adj.; morosity, spleen; churlishness etc. (discourtesy) 895; irascibility etc. 901.

moodiness etc. adj.; perversity; obstinacy etc. 606; torvity, spinosity; crabbedness etc. adj.

ill –, bad- -temper, – humor; sulks, dudgeon, mumps, doleful dumps, doldrums, fit of the sulks, bouderie, black looks, scowl; huff etc. (resentment) 900.

V. be -sullen etc. adj.; sulk; frown, scowl, lower, glower, grouse, grouch, crab, gloam, pout, have a hang-dog look, glout.

Adj. sullen, sulky; ill-tempered, -humored, - affected, -disposed; in -an ill, – a bad, – a shocking- -temper, – humor; out of -temper, – humor; knaggy, torvous, crusty, crabbed; sore as a boil; surly etc. (discourteous) 895.

moody; spleen-ish, -ly; splenetic, cankered.

cross, -grained; perverse, wayward, humorsome; restive; cantankerous, refractory, intractable, exceptious, sinistrous, deaf to reason, unaccommodating, rusty, crust, froward.

dogged etc. (stubborn) 606.

grumpy, glum, grim, grum, morose, frumpish; in the -sulks etc. n.; out of sorts; scowl-, glower-, growl-ing.

peevish etc. (irascible) 901.

902. Endearment. [Expression of affection or love.]**—N.** endearment, caress; blandish-, blandiment; épanchement, fondling, billing and cooing, dalliance.

embrace, salute, kiss, buss, smack, osculation,

deosculation; amorous glances; ogle, side glance, sheep's eyes.

courtship, wooing, suit, addresses, the soft impeachment; love-making; an affair; serenading; caterwauling.

flirting etc. v.; flirtation, gallantry; coquetry, spooning.

ture lover's knot, plighted love, engagement, bethrothal; love -tale, − token, − letter; billet-doux, valentine.

honeymoon; Strephon and Chloe, 'Arry and 'Arriet.

V. caress, fondle, pet, dandle, nurse; pat, − on the -head, − cheek; chuck under the chin, smile upon, coax, wheedle, cosset, coddle, cocker; make -of, − much of, pamper; cherish, foster, kill with kindness.

clasp, hug, cuddle; fold −, strain- in one's arms; nestle, nuzzle, neck, embrace, kiss, buss, smack, blow a kiss; salute etc. (courtesy) 894.

bill and coo, spoon, toy, dally, flirt, coquet; galli-, gala-vant; philander; make love; pay one's -court, − addresses, − attentions- to; serenade; court, woo; set one's cap at; be −, look- sweet upon; ogle, cast sheep's eyes upon; faire les yeux doux.

fall in love with, win the affections etc. (love) 897; die for.

propose; make −, have- an offer; pop the question; plight one's -troth, − faith; become - engaged, − betrothed.

Adj. caressing etc. v.; 'sighing like furnace;' love-sick, spoony.

carressed etc. v.

903. Marriage.—N. marriage, matrimony, wedlock, union, intermarriage, vinculum matrimonii, nuptial tie, knot.

married state, coverture, bed, cohabitation.

match; betrothment etc. (promise) 768; wedding, nuptials, Hymen, bridal; e-, spousals; leading to the altar etc. v.; nuptial benediction, epithalamium,

torch −, temple- of Hymen; hymeneal altar; honeymoon.

bride, bridegroom; brides-maid; -man.

best −, grooms-man, page, usher.

married -man, − woman, − couple; neogamist, Benedick, partner, spouse, mate, yokemate; husband, man, consort, baron; old −, good- man; wife of one's bosom; help-meet, -mate, rib, better half, grey mare, old woman, good wife; feme, − coverte; squaw, lady; matron, -age, -hood; man and wife; wedded pair, Darby and Joan.

affinity, soul-mate.

mono-, bi-, di-, deutero-, tri-, poly-gamy; mormonism; poly-andry; Turk, Bluebeard.

unlawful −, left-handed −, companionate −, morganatic −, ill-assorted- marriage; mésalliance; mariage de convenance; an affair.

match-maker, marriage broker, matrimonial agent.

V. marry, wive, take to oneself a wife; be - married, − spliced; go −, pair- off; wed, espouse, lead to the hymeneal altar, take 'for better, for worse,' give one's hand to, bestow one's hand upon; remarry; intermarry.

marry, join, handfast; couple etc. (unite) 43; tie

the nuptial knot; give -away, − in marriage; affy, affiance; betroth etc. (promise) 768; publish −, bid- the banns; be asked in church.

Adj. married etc. v.; one, − bone and one flesh. marriageable, nubile.

engaged, betrothed, affianced.

matrimonial, marital, conjugal, connubial, wedded; nuptial, hymeneal, spousal, bridal.

Phr. the gray mare the better horse.

904. Celibacy.—N. celibacy, singleness, single blessedness; bachelor-hood, -ship; miso-gamy, - gyny.

virginity, pueelage; maiden-hood, -head.

unmarried man, bachelor, agamist, old bachelor; misò-gamist, -gynist; celibate.

unmarried woman, spinster; maid, -en; virgin, feme sole, old maid; bachelor girl; nun etc.

V. live single; keep bachelor hall.

Adj. un-married, -wedded; wife-, spouse-less; single, virgin, celibate.

905. Divorce.—N. divorce, -ment; separation; judicial separation, separate maintenance; separatio a -mensâ et thoro, − vinculo matrimonii.

widowhood, viduage, viduity, weeds.

widow, -er; relict; dowager; divorcée; cuckold.

V. live -separately, − apart; separate, divorce, disespouse, put away; wear the horns.

906. Benevolence.—N. benevolence, Christian charity; God's -love, − grace; good-will; philanthropy etc. 910; unselfishness etc. 942.

good -nature, − feeling, − wishes; kind-, kindliness etc. adj.; lovingkindness, benignity, brotherly love, charity, humanity, fellow-feeling, sympathy; goodness −, warmth- of heart; bon-homie; kindheartedness; amiability, milk of human kindness, tenderness; love etc. 897; friendship etc. 888.

toleration, consideration, generosity; mercy etc. (pity) 914.

charitableness etc. adj.; bounty, alms-giving; good works, beneficence, the luxury of doing good.

acts of kindness, a good turn; good −, kind- - offices, − treatment.

good Samaritan, sympathizer, well-wisher, philanthropist, bon enfant; altruist.

V. be -benevolent etc. adj.; have one's heart in the right place, bear good will; wish -well, − God speed; view −, regard- with an eye of favor; take in good part; take −, feel- an interest in; be −, feel- interested- in; sympathize with, feel for; fraternize etc. (be friendly) 888.

enter into the feelings of others, do as you would be done by, meet halfway.

treat well; give comfort, smooth the bed of death; do -good, − a good turn; benefit etc. (goodness) 648; render a service, be of use; aid etc. 707.

Adj. benevolent; kind, -ly; well-meaning; amiable; obliging, accommodating, indulgent, considerate, gracious, complacent, good-humored.

warm-, soft-, kind-, tender-, large-, broad-hearted; merciful etc. 914; philanthropic etc. 910; charitable, beneficent, humane, benign, benignant; bount-eous, -iful etc. 816.

good-, well-natured; spleenless; sympath-izing, -etic; complaisant etc. (*courteous*) 894; kindly, well-meant, -intentioned.

fatherly, motherly, brotherly, sisterly; pat-, mat-, frat-ernal; friendly etc. 888.

Adv. with -a good intention, – the best intentions.

Int. God speed! much good may it do!

907. Malevolence.—N. malevolence; bad intent, -ion; un-, dis-kindness; ill -nature, – will, – blood; bad blood; enmity etc. 889; hate etc. 898; malignity; malice, – aforethought, – prepense; maliciousness etc. *adj.*; spite, despite; resentment etc. 900.

uncharitableness etc. *adj.*; incompassionateness etc. 914a; gall, venom, rancor, rankling, virulence, mordacity, acerbity; churlishness etc. (*discourtesy*) 895.

hardness of heart, heart of stone, obduracy; cruelty; cruelness etc. *adj.*; brutality, savagery; ferity, -ocity; barbarity, inhumanity, immanity, truculence, ruffianism; evil eye, cloven -foot, – hoof; Inquisition; torture.

ill –, bad- turn; affront etc. (*disrespect*) 929; outrage, atrocity; ill usage; intolerance, bigotry, persecution; tender mercies [ironical]; 'unkindest cut of all.'

V. be -malevolent etc. *adj.*; bear –, harbor- -spleen, – a grudge, – malice; betray –, show- the cloven foot.

hurt etc. (*physical pain*) 378; annoy etc. 830; injure, harm, wrong; do -harm, – an ill office- to; outrage; disoblige, malign, plant a thorn in the breast.

molest, worry, harass, haunt, harry, bait, tease, throw stones at; play the devil with; hunt down, dragoon, hound; persecute, oppress, grind; maltreat; ill-treat, -use.

wreak one's malice on, do one's worst, break a butterfly on the wheel; dip –, imbrue- one's hands in blood; have no mercy etc. 914a.

Adj. male- volent, unbene-volent; unbenign; ill-disposed, -intentioned, -natured, -conditioned, -contrived; evil-minded, -disposed.

malicious; malign, -ant; rancorous; de-, spiteful; mordacious, caustic, bitter, envenomed, acrimonious, virulent; un-amiable, -charitable; maleficent, venomous, grinding, galling.

harsh, disobliging; un-kind, -friendly, -gracious; treacherous; inofficious; invidious; uncandid; churlish etc. (*uncourteous*) 895; surly, sullen etc. 901a.

cold, -blooded, -hearted; hard-, flint-, marble-, stony-hearted; hard of heart, unnatural; ruthless etc. (*unmerciful*) 914a; relentless etc. (*revengeful*) 919.

cruel; brut-al, -ish; savage; – as a -bear, – tiger; ferine, feral, ferocious; inhuman; barbarous, fell, untamed, tameless, truculent, incendiary; blood-thirsty etc. (*murderous*) 361; atrocious.

fiend-ish, -like; demoniacal; diabolic, -al; devilish, infernal, hellish, Satanic.

Adv. malevolently etc. *adj.*; with -bad intent etc. *n.*

908. Malediction.—N. malediction, malison, curse, imprecation, denunciation, execration,

anathema, ban, proscription, excommunication, commination, thunders of the Vatican, fulmination, *maranatha*, aspersion, vilification, vituperation, scurrility.

abuse; foul –, bad –, strong –, unparliamentary- language, Limehouse; Billingsgate, sauce, evil speaking; cursing etc. *v.*; profane swearing, oath.

threat etc. 909; more bark than bite; invective etc. (*disapprobation*) 932.

V. curse, accurse, imprecate, damn, swear at; slang; curse with bell, book and candle; invoke –, call down- curses on the head of; devote to destruction.

execrate, beshrew, scold; anathematize etc. (*censure*) 932; hold up to execration, denounce, proscribe, excommunicate, fulminate, thunder against; threaten etc. 909; curse up hill and down dale.

curse and swear; swear, – like a trooper; fall a cursing, rap out an oath, damn, cuss.

Adj. curs-ing, -ed etc. *v.*; maledictory.

Int. woe to! beshrew! *ruat coelum!* ill –, woe-betide! confusion seize! damn! confound! blast! curse! devil take! hang! out with! a plague –, out-upon! aroynt! *honi soit!*

Phr. *delenda est Carthago.*

909. Threat.—N. threat, menace; defiance etc. 715; abuse, minacity, intimidation; fulmination; commination etc. (*curse*) 908; gathering clouds etc. (*warning*) 668.

V. threat, -en; menace; snarl, growl, gnarl, mutter, bark, bully.

defy etc. 715; intimidate etc. 860; keep –, hold up –, hold out- *in terrorem*; shake –, double –, clinch- the fist at; thunder, talk big, fulminate, use big words, bluster, look daggers.

Adj. threatening, menacing; mina-tory, -cious; comminatory, abusive; *in terrorem*; ominous etc. (*predicting*) 511; defiant etc. 715; under the ban.

Int. *vae victis!* at your peril! do your worst!

910. Philanthropy.—N. philanthropy; altruism, humanit-y, -arianism; universal benevolence; *deliciae humani generis*; cosmopolitanism, utilitarianism, the greatest happiness of the greatest number, social science, sociology.

common weal, public welfare, socialism, communism.

patriotism, civism, nationality, love of country, *amor patriae*, public spirit.

chivalry, knight errantry; generosity etc. 942.

philanthropist, altruist etc. 906; utilitarian, Benthamite, socialist, communist, cosmopolite, citizen of the world, *amicus humani generis*; knight errant; patriot.

Adj. philanthropic, altruistic, humanitarian, utilitarian, cosmopolitan; public-spirited, patriotic; humane, large-hearted etc. (*benevolent*) 906; chival-ric, -rous, generous etc. 942.

Adv. pro -bono publico, – aris et focis.

Phr. 'humani nihil a me alienum puto.'

911. Misanthropy.—N. misanthropy, incivism; egotism etc. (*selfishness*)· 943; moroseness etc. 901a; cynicism; defeatism.

misanthrope, misanthropist, egotist, cynic, man-hater, Timon, Diogenes.

woman-hater, misogynist.

Adj. misanthropic, antisocial, unpatriotic; egotistical etc. (*selfish*) 943; morose etc. 901*a*.

912. Benefactor.—**N.** benefactor, savior, good genius, tutelary saint, patron, guardian angel, fairy godmother, good Samaritan; *pater patriae*; salt of the earth etc. (*good man*) 948; auxiliary etc. 711.

913. Evil-doer. [*Maleficent being.*]—**N.** evil--doer, – worker; wrong doer etc. 949; mischief maker, marplot; oppressor, tyrant; firebrand, incendiary, pyromaniac, anarchist, destroyer, Hun, *Boche*, Vandal, iconoclast; communist; terrorist, *apache*, gunman, gangster, racketeer.

savage, brute, ruffian, barbarian, semi-barbarian, caitiff, desperado; Mo-hock, -hawk; bludgeon man, bully, rough, hooligan, larrikin, dangerous classes, ugly customer; thief etc. 792.

cockatrice, scorpion, hornet; viper, adder; snake, – in the grass; serpent, cobra, asp, rattlesnake, anaconda; canker-, wire-worm; locust, Colorado beetle; torpedo; bane etc. 663.

cannibal; Anthropophag-us, -ist; bloodsucker, vampire, ogre, ghoul, gorilla; vulture; gyr-, ger-falcon.

wild beast, tiger, hyaena, butcher, hangman; cutthroat etc. (*killer*) 361; blood-, sleuth-, hell-hound.

hag, hellhag, beldam, Jezebel.

monster; fiend etc. (*demon*) 980; homicidal maniac, devil incarnate, demon in human shape; Frankenstein's monster.

harpy, siren, vampire; Furies, Eumenides etc. 900.

Attila, scourge of the human race.

Phr. *foenum habet in cornu.*

914. Pity.—**N.** pity, compassion, commiseration; bowels, – of compassion; condolence etc. 915; sympathy, fellow-feeling, tenderness, yearning, forbearance, humanity, mercy, clemency, exorability; leniency etc. (*lenity*) 740; charity, ruth, long-suffering.

melting mood; *argumentum ad misericordiam*; quarter, grace, *locus poenitentiae*.

sympathizer, champion, partisan.

V. pity; have –, show –, take- pity etc. *n.*; commiserate, compassionate; condole etc. 915; sympathize; feel –, be sorry –, yearn- for; weep, melt, thaw, enter into the feelings of.

forbear, relent, relax, give quarter, wipe the tears, *parcere subjectis*, give a *coup de grâce*, put out of one's misery; be cruel to be kind.

raise –, excite- pity etc. *n.*; touch, soften; melt, – the heart; appeal to one's better feelings; propitiate, disarm.

ask for -mercy etc. *n.*; supplicate etc. (*request*) 765; cry for quarter, beg one's life, kneel; deprecate.

Adj. pitying etc. *v.*; pitiful, compassionate, sympathetic, touched.

merciful, clement, ruthful; humane; humanitarian etc. (*philanthropic*) 910; tender, –

hearted, – as a chicken; soft, – hearted; unhardened; lenient etc. 740; exorable, forbearing; melting etc. *v.*; weak.

Int. for pity's sake! mercy! have –, cry you-mercy! God help you! poor -thing, – dear, –fellow! woe betide! *quis talia fando temperet a lachrymis!*

Phr. one's heart bleeding for; *haud ignara mali miseris succurrere disco.*

914a. Pitilessness.—**N.** pitilessness etc. *adj.*; inclemency; inexorability, hardness of heart; inflexibility; severity etc. 739; malevolence etc. 907.

V. have no –, shut the gates of- mercy etc. 914; give no quarter.

Adj. piti-, merci-, ruth-, bowel-less; unpitying, unmerciful, inclement; in-, un-compassionate; inexorable, inflexible; harsh etc. 739; cruel etc. 907; unrelenting etc. 919.

915. Condolence.—**N.** condolence; lamentation etc. 839; sympathy, consolation.

V. condole with, console, sympathize etc. 914; share one's misery; feel for; express –, testify- pity; afford –, supply- consolation; lament etc. 839- with; send one's condolences.

916. Gratitude.—**N.** gratitude, thankfulness, gratefulness, feeling of obligation.

acknowledgement, recognition, thanksgiving, giving thanks.

thanks, praise, benediction; paean; *Te Deum* etc. (*worship*) 990; grace, – before, – after-meat; thank-offering.

requital.

V. be -grateful etc. *adj.*; thank; give –, render –, return –, offer –, tender- thanks etc. *n.*; acknowledge, requite.

feel –, be –, lie- under an obligation; *savoir gré*; not look a gift horse in the mouth; never forget, overflow with gratitude; thank –, bless-one's stars; fall on one's knees.

Adj. grateful, thankful, obliged, beholden, indebted to, under obligation.

Int. thanks! many thanks! gramercy! much obliged! thank you! thank Heaven! Heaven be praised!

917. Ingratitude.—**N.** ingratitude, thanklessness, oblivion of benefits; unthankfulness.

'benefits forgot;' thankless -task, – office.

V. be -ungrateful etc. *adj.*; forget benefits; look a gift horse in the mouth.

Adj. un-grateful, -mindful, -thankful; thankless, ingrate, wanting in gratitude, insensible of benefits.

forgotten; un-acknowledged, -thanked, -requited, -rewarded; ill-requited.

Int. thank you for nothing! *'et tu Brute!'*

918. Forgiveness.—**N.** forgiveness, pardon, condonation, grace, remission, absolution, amnesty, oblivion; indulgence; reprieve.

conciliation; reconciliation etc. (*pacification*) 723; propitiation.

excuse, exoneration, quittance, release, indemnity; bill –, act –, covenant –, deed- of indemnity; exculpation etc. (*acquittal*) 970.

longanimity, placability, forbearance; *amantium irae*; *locus poenitentiae*.

V. forgive, – and forget; pardon, condone, think no more of, let bygones be bygones, shake hands; forget an injury, bury the hatchet; clean the slate.

excuse, pass over, overlook; wink at etc. (*neglect*) 460; bear with; allow –, make allowances- for; let one down easily, not be too hard upon, pocket the affront; blot out one's transgression.

let off, remit, absolve, give absolution, reprieve; acquit etc. 970.

beg –, ask –, implore- pardon etc. *n.*; conciliate, propitiate, placate; make up a quarrel etc. (*pacify*) 723; let the wound heal.

Adj. forgiving, placable, conciliatory.

forgiven etc. *v.*; un-resented, -avenged, revenged.

Adv. cry you mercy.

Phr. *veniam petimusque damusque vicissim*; more in sorrow than in anger.

919. Revenge.—**N.** revenge, -ment; vengeance; avenge-ment, -ance; sweet revenge, *vendetta*, death-feud, eye for an eye, blood for blood, a Roland for an Oliver; retaliation etc. 718; day of reckoning.

rancor, vindictiveness, implacability; malevolence etc. 907; ruthlessness etc. 914*a*.

avenger, vindicator, Nemesis, Eumenides.

V. re-, a-venge; take –, have one's- revenge; breathe -revenge, – vengeance; wreak one's -vengeance, – anger; give no quarter.

have -accounts to settle, – a crow to pluck, – a rod in pickle; pay off old scores.

keep the wound green; harbor -revenge, – vindictive feeling; bear malice; rankle, – in the breast; have at one's mercy.

Adj. revenge-, venge-ful; vindictive, rancorous; pitiless etc. 914*a*; ruthless, rigorous, avenging, retaliative.

unforgiving, unrelenting; inexorable, stonyhearted, implacable; relent-, remorse-less.

aeternum servans sub pectore vulnus; rankling, immitigable.

Phr. *manet -cicatrix,– altâ mente repostum*. revenge is sweet.

920. Jealousy.—**N.** jealous-y, -ness; jaundiced eye, heartburning; green-eyed monster; yellows; Juno.

V. be -jealous etc. *adj.*; view with -jealousy, – a jealous eye.

Adj. jealous; – as a Barbary pigeon; jaundiced, yellow-eyed, horn-mad.

921. Envy.—**N.** envy; enviousness etc. *adj.*; rivalry; *jalousie de métier*.

V. envy, covet, lust after, crave, burst with envy, regard with envious eyes.

Adj. envious, invidious, covetous; *alieni appetens*.

922. Right.—**N.** right; what -ought to, – should- be; fitness etc. *adj.*; *summum jus*.

justice, equity; equitableness etc. *adj.*; propriety; fair play, impartiality, measure for measure, give and take, *lex talionis*, square deal.

Astraea, Nemesis, Themis.

scales of justice, even-handed justice, retributive justice, *suum cuique*; clear stage –, fair field- and no favor; Queensberry rules.

morals etc. (*duty*) 926; law etc. 963; honor etc. (*probity*) 939; virtue etc. 944.

V. be -right etc. *adj.*; stand to reason.

see -justice done, – one righted, – fair play; do justice to; recompense etc. (*reward*) 973; hold the scales even, give and take; serve one right, put the saddle on the right horse; give -every one, – the devil- his due; *audire alteram partem*.

deserve etc. (*be entitled to*) 924.

Adj. right, good; just, reasonable; fit etc. 924; equ-al, -able, -itable; evenhanded, fair, – and square.

legitimate, justifiable, rightful; as it -should, – ought to- be; lawful etc. (*permitted*) 760, (*legal*) 963.

deserved etc. 924.

Adv. rightly etc. *adj.*; in -justice, – equity, – reason.

without -distinction of, – regard to, – respect to- persons; upon even terms.

Int. all right!

923. Wrong.—**N.** wrong; what -ought not to, – should not- be; *malum in se*; unreasonableness, grievance; shame.

injustice; unfairness etc. *adj.*; iniquity, foul play, partiality, leaning; favor, -itism; nepotism, party spirit, partisanship; undueness etc. 925; unlawfulness etc. 964.

robbing Peter to pay Paul etc. *v.*; the wolf and the lamb; vice etc. 945.

a custom more honored in the breach than the observance.

V. be -wrong etc. *adj.*; cry to heaven for vengeance.

do -wrong etc. *n.*; be -inequitable etc. *adj.*; favor, lean towards; encroach; impose upon; reap where one has not sown; give an inch and take an ell; rob Peter to pay Paul.

Adj. wrong, -ful; bad, too bad; unjust, -fair; in-, un-equitable; unequal, partial, one-sided.

objectionable; un-reasonable, -allowable, -warrantable, -justifiable; not cricket, not playing the game; improper, unfit; unjustified etc. 925; illegal etc. 964; iniquitous, criminal; immoral etc. 945; injurious etc. 649.

in the wrong, – box.

Adv. wrongly etc. *adj.*

Phr. it will not do; this is too bad.

924. Dueness.—**N.** due, -ness; right, privilege, prerogative, prescription, title, claim, pretension, demand, birthright.

immunity, license, liberty, franchise; vested -
interest, − right; licitness.

sanction, authority, warranty, charter; warrant
etc. (*permission*) 760; constitution etc. (*law*) 963;
tenure; bond etc. (*security*) 771.

deserts, merits, dues.

claimant, appellant; plaintiff etc. 938.

V. be -due etc. *adj.* to, − the due etc. *n.* of; have
-right, − title, − claim- to; be entitled to; have a
claim upon; belong to etc. (*property*) 780.

deserve, merit, be worthy of, richly deserve.

demand, claim; call upon −, come upon −, appeal to- for; re-vendicate, -claim; exact; insist -on,
− upon; challenge; take one's stand, make a point
of, require, lay claim to, assert, assume, arrogate,
make good; substantiate; vindicate a -claim, −
right; make out a case.

give −, confer- a right; sanction, entitle;
authorize etc. 760; sanctify, legalize, ordain,
prescribe, allot.

give every one his due etc. 922; pay one's dues;
have one's -due, − rights; stand upon one's rights.

use a right, assert, enforce, put in force; lay under contribution.

Adj. having a right to etc. *v.*; entitled to;
claiming; deserving, meriting, worthy of.

privileged, allowed, sanctioned, warranted,
authorized; ordained, prescribed, constitutional,
chartered, enfranchised.

prescriptive, presumptive; absolute; indefeasible;
un-, in-alienable.

imprescriptible, inviolable, unimpeachable, un-
challenged; sacrosanct.

due to, merited, deserved, condign, richly deserved, *emeritus*.

allowable etc. (*permitted*) 760; lawful, licit,
legitimate, legal; legalized etc. (*law*) 963.

square, unexceptionable, right; equitable etc.
922; due, *en règle*; fit, -ting; correct, proper, meet,
befitting, becoming, seemly; decorous; creditable,
up to the mark, right as a trivet; just −, quite- the
thing; *selon les règles*.

Adv. duly, *ex officio*, *de jure*; by -right, −
divine right; as is -fitting, − proper, − fitting and
proper; *jure divino*, *Dei gratiâ*, in the name of.

Phr. *civis Romanus sum*.

925. Undueness. [Absence of right.]—**N.** undueness etc. *adj.*; *malum prohibitum*; impropriety;
illegality etc. 964.

falseness etc. *adj.*; emptiness −, invalidity- of
title; illegitimacy.

loss of right, disfranchisement, forfeiture.

usurpation, assumption, tort, violation, breach,
encroachment, presumption, seizure, stretch, exaction, imposition, lion's share.

usurper, pretender, Carlist; imposter.

V. be -undue etc. *adj.*; not be -due etc. 924.

infringe, encroach, trench on; exact; arrogate, −
to oneself; give an inch and take an ell; stretch −,
strain- a point; usurp, violate, do violence to; sail
under false colors.

dis-franchise, -entitle, -qualify; invalidate.

relax etc. (*be lax*) 738; misbehave etc. (*vice*)
945; misbecome.

Adj. undue; unlawful etc. (*illegal*) 964; unconstitutional, *ultra vires*; illicit; un-authorized, -
warranted, -allowed, -sanctioned, -justified; un-,
dis-entitled, -qualified; un-privileged, -chartered.

illegitimate, bastard, spurious, false; usurped,
tortious.

un-deserved, -merited, -earned; unfulfilled.

forfeited, disfranchised.

improper; un-meet, -fit, -befitting, -seemly; un-,
mis-becoming; seemless; *contra bonos mores*; not
the thing, out of the question, not to be thought of;
preposterous, pretentious, would- be.

926. Duty.—N. duty, what ought to be done,
moral obligation, accountableness, liability, *onus*,
responsibility; bounden −, imperative- duty; call,
− of duty.

allegiance, fealty, tie; engagement etc. (*promise*)
768; part; function, calling etc. (*business*) 625.

morality, morals, decalogue; case of conscience;
conscientiousness etc. (*probity*) 939; conscience,
inward monitor, still small voice within, sense of
duty, tender conscience.

dueness etc. 924; propriety, fitness, seemliness,
amenableness, decorum; the -thing, − proper
thing; the -right, − proper- thing to do.

[Science of morals] eth-ics, -ology; deon-, aretology; moral −, ethical-philosophy; casuistry,
polity.

observance, fulfilment, discharge, performance,
acquittal, satisfaction, redemption; good behavior.

V. be -the duty of, − incumbent etc. *adj.* on, −
responsible etc. *adj.*; behoove, become, befit,
beseem; belong −, pertain- to; fall to one's lot;
devolve on; lie -upon, − on one's head, − at one's
door; rest -with, − on the shoulders of.

take upon oneself etc. (*promise*) 768.

be −, become- -bound to, − sponsor for; be
responsible for; incur a -responsibility etc. *n.*; be
−, stand −, lie- under an obligation; have to answer for, owe it to oneself.

impose a -duty etc. *n.*; enjoin, require, exact;
bind, − over; saddle with, prescribe, assign, call
upon, look to, oblige.

enter upon −, perform −, observe −, fulfil −,
discharge −, adhere to −, acquit oneself of −,
satisfy- -a duty, − an obligation; act one's part,
redeem one's pledge, do justice to, be at one's post;
do duty; do one's duty etc. (*be virtuous*) 944.

be on one's good behavior, mind one's P's and
Q's.

Adj. obligatory, binding; imperative, peremptory; stringent etc. (*severe*) 739; behooving etc. *v.*;
incumbent −, chargeable- on; under obligation;
obliged −, bound −, tied- by; saddled with.

due −, beholden −, bound −, indebted- to;
tied down; compromised etc. (*promised*) 768; in
duty bound.

amenable, liable, accountable, responsible, answerable.

right, meet etc. (*due*) 924; moral, ethical,
casuistical, conscientious, ethological.

Adv. with a safe conscience, as in duty bound,
on one's own responsibility, at one's own risk, *suo
periculo*; *in foro conscientiae*; *quamdiu se bene
gesserit*; at one's post, on duty.

Phr. *dura lex sed lex*.

927. Dereliction of Duty.—N. dere; liction of
duty; fault etc. (*guilt*) 947- sin etc. (*vice*) 945; non-
observance, -performance, -co-operation; neglect,
carelessness, laziness, incompetence, eye-service,

relaxation, infraction, violation, transgression, failure, evasion, indolence; dead letter.

slacker, loafer, striker, non-co-operator.

V. violate; break, − through; infringe; set - aside, − at naught; trample -on, − under foot; slight, neglect, evade, renounce, forswear, repudiate; wash one's hands of; escape, transgress, fail.

call to account etc. (*disapprobation*) 932.

927a. Exemption.—N. exemption, freedom, irresponsibility, immunity, liberty, license, release, exoneration, excuse, dispensation, absolution, franchise, renunciation, discharge; exculpation etc. 970; *aegrotat*.

V. be -exempt etc. *adj.*

exempt, release, acquit, discharge, quit-claim, remise, remit; free, set at liberty, let off, pass over, spare, excuse, dispense with, give dispensation, license; stretch a point; absolve etc. (*forgive*) 918; exonerate etc. (*exculpate*) 970; save the necessity.

Adj. exempt, free, immune, at liberty, scot free; released etc. *v.*; unbound, unencumbered; irresponsible, unaccountable, not answerable; excusable.

928. Respect.—N. respect, regard, consideration; courtesy etc. 894; attention, deference, reverence, honor, esteem, estimation, veneration, admiration; approbation etc. 931.

homage, fealty, obeisance, genuflexion, kneeling, prostration; obsequiousness etc. 886; salaam, *kowtow*, bow, presenting arms, salute.

respects, regards, duty, *devoirs*, *égards*.

devotion etc. (*piety*) 987.

V. respect, regard; revere, -nce; hold in reverence, honor, venerate, hallow; esteem etc. (*approve of*) 931; think much of; entertain −, bear- respect for; have a high opinion of; look up to, defer to; pay -attention, − respect etc. *n.* - to; do −, render- honor to; do the honors, hail; show courtesy etc. 894; salute, present arms; do − , pay-homage; pay tribute to; kneel to, bow to, bend the knee to; fall down before, prostrate oneself, kiss the hem of one's garment; worship etc. 990.

keep one's distance, make room, observe due decorum, stand upon ceremony.

command −, inspire- respect; awe, impose, overawe, dazzle.

Adj. respecting etc. *v.*; respectful, deferential, decorous, reverential, obsequious, ceremonious, bare-headed, cap in hand, on one's knees; prostrate etc. (*servile*) 886.

respected etc. *v.*; in high -esteem, − estimation; time-honored, venerable, *emeritus*.

Adv. in deference to; with -all, − due, − the highest- respect; with submission.

saving your -grace, − presence; *salva sit reverentia*; *pace tanti nominis*.

Int. hail! all hail! *esto perpetua!* may your shadow never be less!

929. Disrespect.—N. dis-respect, -esteem, -estimation, -favor, -repute; low estimation; disparagement etc. (*dispraise*) 932; (*detraction*) 934.

irreverence; slight, neglect; *spretae injuria formae*; superciliousness etc. (*contempt*) 930.

vilipendency, contumely, affront, dishonor, insult, indignity, outrage, discourtesy etc. 895; practical joking; scurrility, scoffing, sibilation; ir-, derision; mockery; irony etc. (*ridicule*) 856; sarcasm.

hiss, hoot, gibe, flout, jeer, scoff, gleek, taunt, sneer, quip, fling, wipe, slap in the face.

V. hold in disrespect etc. (*despise*) 930; misprize, disregard, slight, undervalue, depreciate, trifle with, set at naught, pass by, push aside, overlook, turn one's back upon, laugh in one's sleeve; be -disrespectful etc. *adj.*, − discourteous etc. 895; treat with -disrespect etc. *n.*; set down, browbeat.

dishonor, desecrate; insult, affront, outrage.

speak slightingly of; disparage etc. (*dispraise*) 932; vilipend, call names; throw −, fling- dirt; drag through the mud, point at, indulge in personalities; make -mouths, − faces; bite the thumb; take −, pluck- by the beard; toss in a blanket, tar and feather.

have −, hold- in derision; deride, scoff, sneer, laugh at, snigger, ridicule, gibe, mock, jeer, taunt, twit, niggle, gleek, gird, flout, fleer; roast, turn into ridicule; guy, burlesque etc. 856; laugh to scorn etc. (*contempt*) 930; smoke; fool; make -game, − a fool, − an April fool- of; play a practical joke; rag; lead one a dance, run the rig upon, have a fling at, scout, hiss, hoot, mob.

Adj. disrespectful; aweless, irreverent; disparaging etc. 934; insulting etc. *v.*; supercilious etc. (*scornful*) 930; rude, derisive, contemptuous, sarcastic; scurri-le, -lous; contumelious.

un-respected, -worshipped, -envied, -saluted; un-dis-regarded.

Adv. disrespectfully etc. *adj.*

930. Contempt.—N. contempt, disdain, scorn, sovereign contempt; despi-sal, -ciency; vilipendency, contumely; slight, sneer, spurn, by-word.

contemptuousness etc. *adj.*; scornful eye; smile of contempt; derision etc. (*disrespect*) 929.

[State of being despised] despisedness.

V. despise, contemn, scorn, disdain, feel contempt for, view with a scornful eye; disregard, slight, not mind; pass by etc. (*neglect*) 460.

look down upon; hold -cheap, − in contempt, − in disrespect; think -nothing, − small beer- of; make light of; underestimate etc. 483; esteem -slightly, − of small or no account; take no account of, care nothing for; set no store by; not care a -straw etc. (*unimportance*) 643; set at naught, laugh in one's sleeve, snap one's fingers at, shrug one's shoulders, turn up one's nose at, pooh-pooh, damn with faint praise; sneeze −, whistle −, sneer- at; curl up one's lip, toss the head, *traiter de haut*; laugh at etc. (*be disrespectful*) 929.

point the finger of −, hold up to −, laugh to-scorn; scout, hoot, flout, hiss, scoff at.

turn -one's back, − a cold shoulder- upon; tread −, trample -upon, − under foot; spurn, kick; fling to the winds etc. (*repudiate*) 610; send away with a flea in the ear.

Adj. contemptuous; disdain-, scorn-ful; withering, contumelious, supercilious, cynical, haughty, bumptious, cavalier; derisive.

contemptible, despicable; pitiable; pitiful etc. (*unimportant*) 643; despised etc. *v.*; downtrodden; unenvied.

Adv. contemptuously etc. *adj.*

Int. a fig for etc. (*unimportant*) 643; bah! never mind! away with! hang it! fiddle-de-dee!

931. Approbation.—N. approbation; approval, -ement; sanction, advocacy; nod of approbation; esteem, estimation, good opinion, golden opinions, admiration; love etc. 897; appreciation, regard, account, popularity, *kudos*, credit; repute etc. 873.

commendation, praise; laud, -ation; good word; meed −, tribute- of praise; encomium; eulog-y, -ium; *éloge*, panegyric; homage, hero worship; benediction, blessing, benison.

applause, plaudit, clap; clapping, − of hands; accl-aim, -amation; cheer; paean, hosannah; shout −, peal −, chorus −, thunders- of -applause etc. Kentish fire; Prytaneum; blurb.

V. approve; think -good, − much of, − well of, − highly of; esteem, value, prize; set great store -by, − on.

do justice to, appreciate; honor, hold in esteem, look up to, admire; like etc. 897; be in favor of, wish God speed; hail, − with satisfaction.

stand −, stick- up for; uphold, hold up, countenance, sanction; clap −, pat- on the back; keep in countenance, endorse, give credit, recommend; mark with a white -mark, − stone.

commend, praise; be-, laud; compliment, pay a tribute, bepraise; clap, − the hands; applaud, cheer, acclaim, acclamate, encore; panegyrize, eulogize, cry up, *prôner*, puff; extol, − to the skies; magnify, glorify, exalt, boost, swell, make much of; flatter etc. 933; bless, give a blessing to; have −, say- a good word for; speak -well, − highly, − in high terms- of; sing −, sound −, chaunt −, resound- the praises of; sing praises to; cheer −, applaud- to the -echo, − very echo.

redound to the -honor, − praise, − credit- of; do credit to; deserve -praise etc. *n.*; recommend itself; pass muster.

be -praised etc.; receive honorable mention; be in -favor, − high favor- with; ring with the praises of, win golden opinions, gain credit, find favor with, stand well in the opinion of; *laudari a laudato viro.*

Adj. approving etc. *v.*; in favor of; lost in admiration.

commendatory, complimentary, benedictory, laudatory, panegyrical, eulogistic, encomiastic, acclamatory, lavish of praise, uncritical.

approved, praised etc. *v.*; un-censured, - impeached; popular, in good odor; in high esteem etc. (*respected*) 928; in −, in high- favor.

deserving −, worthy of- praise etc. *n.*; praiseworthy, commendable, of estimation; good etc. 648; meritorious, estimable, creditable, plausible, unimpeachable; beyond all praise.

Adv. commendably, with credit, to admiration; well etc. 681; with three times three.

Int. hear, hear! well done! *brav-o! -a! -i! bravissimo! euge! macte virtute!* so far so good, that's right, quite right; *optime!* one cheer more; may your shadow never be less! *esto perpetua!* long life to! *viva! enviva!* God speed! *valete et plaudite! encore! bis!*

Phr. *probatum est.*

932. Disapprobation.—N. disappro-bation, -val; improbation; dis-esteem, -valuation, -placency; odium; dislike etc. 867; dissent etc. 489.

dis-praise, -commendation; blame, censure, obloquy; detraction etc. 934; disparagement, depreciation; denunciation; condemnation etc. 971; ostracism; boycott; black-list, -ball; *index - expurgatorius, − librorum prohibitorum.*

animadversion, reflection, stricture, objection, exception, criticism; sardonic -grin, − laugh; sarcasm, insinuation, innuendo; bad −, poor −, left-handed- compliment.

satire; sneer etc. (*contempt*) 930; taunt etc. (*disrespect*) 929; cavil, carping, censoriousness; hypercriticism etc. (*fastidiousness*) 868.

reprehension, remonstrance, expostulation, reproof, reprobation, admonition, increpation, reproach; rebuke, reprimand, castigation, jobation, lecture, curtain lecture, blow up, wigging, dressing, − down; rating, scolding, trimming; correction, set down, rap on the knuckles, *coup de bec*, rebuff; slap, − on the face; home thrust; hit, frown, scowl, black look.

diatribe; jeremiad; *tirade*, philippic.

clamor, outcry, hue and cry; hiss, -ing; sibilation, cat-call; execration etc. 908.

chiding, upbraiding etc. *v.*; exprobration, abuse, vituperation, invective, objurgation, contumely, personal remarks; hard −, cutting −, bitter-words.

evil-speaking; bad language etc. 908; personality.

V. disapprove; dislike etc. 867; lament etc. 839; object to, take exception to; be scandalized at, think ill of; view with -disfavor, − dark eyes, − jaundiced eyes; *nil admirari*, disvalue, improbate.

frown upon, look grave; bend −, knit- the brows; shake the head at, shrug the shoulders; turn up the nose etc. (*contempt*) 930; look -askance, − black upon; look with an evil eye; make a wry -face, − mouth- at; set one's face against.

dis-praise, -commend, -parage; deprecate, speak ill of, not speak well of, slate, condemn etc. (*find guilty*) 971.

blame; lay −, cast- blame upon; censure, *fronder*, reproach, pass censure on, reprobate, impugn. remonstrate, expostulate, recriminate.

reprehend, chide, admonish; bring −, call- -to account, − over the coals, − to order; take to task, reprove, lecture, bring to book; read a -lesson, − lecture- to; rebuke, correct.

reprimand, chastise, castigate, lash, blow up, trounce, trim, *laver la tête*, overhaul; give it one, − finely; gibbet.

accuse etc. 938; impeach, denounce; hold up to -reprobation, − execration; expose, brand, gibbet, stigmatize; show −, pull −, take- up; cry 'shame' upon; be outspoken; raise a hue and cry against.

execrate etc. 908; exprobrate, speak daggers, vituperate; abuse, −, like a pickpocket; scold, rate, objurage, upbraid, fall foul of; jaw; rail, − at, − in good set terms; bark at; anathematize, call names; call by -hard, − ugly- names; a-, re-vile; vili-fy, -pend; bespatter; backbite; clapperclaw; rave −, thunder −, fulminate- against; load with reproaches; lash with the tongue.

exclaim, − protest, − inveigh −, declaim −, cry out −, raise one's voice- against.

decry; cry −, run −, frown- down; clamor, hiss,

hoot, mob, ostracize; draw up –, sing- a round robin; black-ball, -list.

animadvert –, reflect- upon; glance at; cast -reflection, – reproach, – a slur- upon; insinuate, damn with faint praise; 'hint a fault and hesitate dislike;' not to be able to say much for.

scoff at, point at; twit, taunt etc. (*disrespect*) 929; sneer at etc. (*despise*) 230; satirize, lampoon; defame etc. (*detract*) 934; depreciate, find fault with, criticize, cut up; pull –, pick- to pieces; take exception; cavil; peck –, nibble –, carp- at; be -censorious etc. *adj.*; pick -holes, – a hole, – a hole in one's coat; make a fuss about.

take –, set- down; snub, snap one up, give a rap on the knuckles; throw a stone -at, – in one's garden; have a -fling, – snap- at; have words with, pluck a crow with; give one a -wipe, – lick with the rough side of the tongue.

incur blame, excite disapprobation, scandalize, shock, revolt; get a bad name, forfeit one's good opinion, be under a cloud, come under the ferule, bring a hornet's nest about one's ears.

take blame, stand corrected; have to answer for.

Adj. disapproving etc. *v.*; scandalized.

disparaging, condemnatory, damnatory, denunciatory, reproachful, abusive, objurgatory, clamorous, vituperative; defamatory etc. 934.

satirical, sarcastic, sardonic, cynical, dry, sharp, cutting, biting, severe, virulent, withering, trenchant, hard upon; censorious, critical, captious, carping, hypercritical; fastidious etc. 868; sparing of –, grudging- praise.

disapproved, chid etc. *v.*; in bad odor, blown upon, unapproved; unblest; at a discount, exploded; weighed in the balance and found wanting.

blameworthy, reprehensible etc. (*guilt*) 947; to –, worthy of- blame, answerable, uncommendable, exceptionable, not to be thought of, bad etc. 649; vicious etc. 945.

un-lamented, -bewailed, -pitied.

Adv. with a wry face; reproachfully etc. *adj.*

Int. it is too bad! it -won't, – will never- do! marry come up! Oh! come! 'sdeath!

forbid it Heaven! God –, Heaven- forbid! out –, fie- upon it! away with! tut! *O tempora! O mores!* shame! fie, – for shame! out on you! tell it not in Gath!

933. Flattery.—N. flattery, adulation, gloze; bland-ishment, -iloquence; cajolery; fawning, wheedling etc. *v.*; captation, coquetry, sycophancy, obsequiousness, flunkeyism, toad-eating, tufthunting; snobbishness.

incense, honeyed words, flummery; bun-kum, -combe; blarney, *placebo*, butter; soft -soap, – sawder; rose water.

voice of the charmer, mouth honor; lip-homage; euphemism; unctuousness etc. *adj.*

V. flatter, praise to the skies, puff; wheedle, cajole, glaver, coax; fawn, –, upon; humor, gloze, soothe, pet, coquet, slaver, butter; be-spatter, -slubber, -plaster, -slaver; lay it on thick, overpraise; earwig, cog, collogue; truckle –, pander *or* pandar –, pay court- to; court; creep into the good graces of; curry favor with, hang on the sleeve of; fool to the top of one's bent; lick the dust.

lay the flattering unction to one's soul, gild the pill, make things pleasant.

overestimate etc. 482; exaggerate etc. 549.

Adj. flattering etc. *v.*; adulatory; mealy-, honey-mouthed; honeyed; smooth, – tongued; soapy, oily, unctuous, blandiloquent, specious; fine-, fair-spoken; plausible, servile, sycophantic, fulsome; courtier-ly, -like.

Adv. *ad captandum.*

934. Detraction.—N. detraction, disparagement, depreciation, vilification, obloquy, scurrility, scandal, defamation, aspersion, traducement, slander, calumny, obtrectation, evil-speaking, backbiting, *scandalum magnatum*.

personality, libel, squib, lampoon, skit, pasquinade; *chronique scandaleuse.*

sarcasm, cynicism; criticism (*disapprobation*) 932; invective etc. 932; envenomed tongue; *spretae injuria formae.*

detractor etc. 936.

V. detract, derogate, decry, depreciate, disparage; run –, cry- down; minimize, make light of; belittle, sneer at etc. (*contemn*) 930; criticize, pull to pieces, pick a hole in one's coat, asperse, cast aspersions, blow upon, bespatter, blacken; vilify, -pend; avile; give a dog a bad name, brand, malign, backbite, libel, lampoon, traduce, slander, defame, calumniate, bear false witness against; speak ill of behind one's back.

'damn with faint praise, assent with civil leer; and without sneering, others teach to sneer.'

fling dirt etc. (*disrespect*) 929; anathematize etc. 932; dip the pen in gall, view in a bad light.

Adj. detracting etc. *v.*; defamatory, detractory, derogatory; disparaging, libellous; scurril-e, -ous; abusive; foul-spoken, -tongued, -mouthed; slanderous; calumni-ous, -atory; sar-castic, -donic; satirical, cynical.

935. Flatterer.—N. flatterer, adulator; eulogist, -phemist; optimist, encomiast, *laudator*, whitewasher, booster.

toad-y, -eater; sycophant, courtier, pickthank, Sir Pertinax MacSycophant; *flâneur, prôneur*; puffer, touter, *claqueur*; claw-back, ear-wig, doer of dirty work; parasite, hanger on etc. (*servility*) 886.

936. Detractor.—N. detractor, reprover; censor, -urer; cynic, critic, caviller, carper, word-catcher.

defamer, backbiter, slanderer, knocker, Sir Benjamin Backbite, lampooner, satirist, traducer, libeller, calumniator, dearest foe, dawplucker, Thersites; Zoilus; good-natured –, candid- friend [satirically]; reviler, vituperator, castigator; shrew etc. 901.

disapprover, *laudator temporis acti.*

937. Vindication.—N. vindication, justification, warrant; exoneration, exculpation; acquittal etc. 970; whitewashing.

extenuation; pallia-tion, -tive; softening, mitigation.

reply, defense; recrimination etc. 938.

apology, gloss, varnish; plea etc. 617; salvo; ex-

cuse, extenuating circumstances; allowance, – to
be made; *locus poenitentiae.*

apologist, vindicator, justifier; defendant etc.
938.

justifiable charge, true bill.

V. justify, warrant; be an -excuse etc. *n.*- for;
lend a color, furnish a handle; vindicate; ex-, disculpate; acquit etc. 970; clear, set right, exonerate,
whitewash.

extenuate, palliate, excuse, soften, apologize,
varnish, white-, gloze; put a -gloss, – good face-
upon; mince; gloss over, bolster up, help a lame
dog over a stile.

advocate, defend, plead one's cause; stand –,
stick –, speak- up for; contend –, speak- for; bear
out, keep in countenance, support; plead etc. 617;
say in defense; plead ignorance; confess and avoid,
propugn, put in a good word for.

take the will for the deed, make allowance for,
do justice to; give -one, – the Devil- his due.

make good; prove -the truth of, – one's case; be
justified by the event.

Adj. vindicat-ed, -ing etc. *v.*; vindicat-ive, -ory;
palliative; exculpatory; apologetic.

excusable, defensible, pardonable; veni-al, -able;
specious, plausible, justifiable.

Phr. *'honi soit qui mal y pense.'*

938. Accusation.—N. accusation, charge, imputation, slur, inculpation, exprobration, delation;
crimination; in-, ac-, re-crimination; *tu quoque*
argument; invective etc. 932.

de-nunciation, -nouncement; libel, challenge,
citation, arraignment; im-, ap-peachment; indictment, bill of indictment, true bill; lawsuit etc.
969; condemnation etc. 971.

gravamen of a charge, head and front of one's
offending, *argumentum ad hominem*; scandal etc.
(*detraction*) 934; *scandalum magnatum.*

accuser, prosecutor, plaintiff, complainant,
petitioner; relator, informer; appellant.

accused, defendant, prisoner, panel, co-, respondent; litigant.

V. accuse, charge, tax, impute, twit, taunt with,
reproach.

brand with reproach; stigmatize, slur; cast a -
stone at, – slur on; incriminate; inculpate, implicate; call to account etc. (*censure*) 932; take to-
blame, – task; put in the black book.

inform against, indict, denounce, arraign; im-,
ap-peach; have up, show up, pull up, challenge,
cite, lodge a complaint; prosecute, bring an action
against etc. 969.

charge –, saddle- with; lay to one's -door, –
charge; lay the blame on, bring home to; cast –,
throw- in one's teeth; cast the first stone at.

have –, keep- a rod in pickle for; have a crow to
pluck with.

trump up a charge.

Adj. accusing etc. *v.*; accusat-ory, -ive; im-
putative, denunciatory; re-, criminatory.

accused etc. *v.*; suspected; under -suspicion, – a
cloud, – *surveillance*; in -custody, – detention;
in the -lock up, – watch house, – house of detention.

accusable, imputable; in-defensible, -excusable;
un-pardonable, -justifiable; vicious etc. 945.

Int. look at home; *tu quoque* etc. (*retaliation*)
718.

939. Probity.—N. probity, integrity, rectitude;
uprightness etc. *adj.*; honesty, faith; honor; good
faith, *bona fides*; purity, clean hands.

fairness etc. *adj.*; fair play, justice, equity, impartiality, principle; grace.

constancy; faithfulness etc. *adj.*; fidelity, loyalty;
incorrupt-ion, -ibility.

trustworthiness etc. *adj.*; truth, candor,
singleness of heart; veracity etc. 543; tender conscience etc. (*sense of duty*) 926.

punctil-iousness, -io; delicacy, nicety; scrupulosity, -ousness etc. *adj.*; scruple; point, – of honor;
punctuality.

dignity etc. (*repute*) 873; respectability, -bleness
etc. *adj.*; gentleman; man of -honor, – his word;
fidus Achates, preux chevalier; galantuomo;
truepenny, trump, brick; true Briton, white man,
sportsman.

court of honor, a fair field and no favor;
argumentum ad verecundiam.

V. be -honorable etc. *adj.*; deal -honorably, –
squarely, – impartially, – fairly; speak the truth
etc. (*veracity*) 543; tell the truth and shame the
devil, *vitam impendere vero*; show a proper spirit,
make a point of; do one's duty etc. 944; play the
game.

redeem one's pledge etc. 926; keep –, be as
good as- one's -promise, – word; keep faith with,
not fail.

give and take, *audire alteram partem*, give the
devil his due, put the saddle on the right horse.

redound to one's honor.

Adj. upright; honest, – as daylight; veracious
etc. 543; virtuous etc. 944; honorable; fair, right,
just, equitable, impartial, even-handed, square; fair
–, open- and aboveboard.

constant, – as the northern star; faithful, loyal,
staunch; true, – blue, – to one's colors, – to the
core, – as the needle to the pole; true-hearted,
trust-y, -worthy; as good as one's word, to be
depended on, incorruptible.

manly, straightforward etc. (*ingenuous*) 703;
frank, candid, open-hearted.

conscientious, tender-conscienced, right-minded;
high-principled, -minded; scrupulous, religious,
strict; nice, punctilious, correct, punctual; respect-,
reput-able; gentlemanlike.

inviol-able, -ate; un-violated, -broken, -betrayed;
un-bought, -bribed.

innocent etc. 946; pure; stainless; un-stained, -
tarnished, -sullied, -tainted, -perjured; uncorrupt, -
ed; unde-filed, -praved, -bauched; *integer vitae
scelerisque purus; justus et non fraus propositi.*

chivalrous, jealous of honor, *sans peur et sans
reproche*; high-spirited.

supra-mundane, unworldly, overscrupulous.

Adv. honorably etc. *adj.*; *bona fide*; on the
square, in good faith, honor bright, *foro conscientiae*, with clean hands; by fair means.

940. Improbity.—N. improbity; dishon-esty,
-our; deviation from rectitude; disgrace etc.
(*disrepute*) 874; fraud etc. (*deception*) 545; lying
etc. 544; bad –, Punic- faith; *mala –, Punica,
fides*; infidelity; faithlessness etc. *adj.*; Judas kiss,
betrayal; scrap of paper.

breach of -promise, – trust, – faith; prodition,
disloyalty, divided allegiance, treason, high

treason; apostacy etc. (*tergiversation*) 607; non-observance etc. 773.

shabbiness etc. *adj.*; villainy; baseness etc. *adj.*; abjection, debasement, turpitude, moral turpitude, laxity, trimming, shuffling.

perfidy; perfidiousness etc. *adj.*; treachery, double-dealing; unfairness etc. *adj.*; knavery, roguery, rascality, foul-play; jobb-ing, -ery; Tammany, graft; venality, nepotism; corruption, job, shuffle, fishy transaction, barratry; sharp practice, heads I win, tails you lose; mouth-honor etc. (*flattery*) 933.

V. be -dishonest etc. *adj.*; play false; break one's -word, − faith, − promise; jilt, betray, forswear; shuffle etc. (*lie*) 544; live by one's wits, sail near the wind; play with marked cards.

disgrace −, dishonor −, demean −, degrade-oneself; derogate, stoop, grovel, sneak, lose caste; sell oneself, go over to the enemy; seal one's infamy.

Adj. dishon-est, -orable; un-conscientious, -scrupulous; fraudulent etc. 545; knavish; disgraceful etc. (*disreputable*) 874; wicked etc. 945.

false-hearted, disingenuous; unfair, one-sided; double, -tongued, -faced; time-serving, crooked, tortuous, insidious, Machiavellian, dark, slippery; questionable; fishy; perfidious, treacherous, perjured.

infamous, arrant, foul, base, vile, low, ignominious, blackguard;

contemptible, abject, mean, shabby, little, paltry, dirty, scurvy, scabby, sneaking, groveling, scrubby, rascally, pettifogging; beneath one; not cricket.

low-minded, -thoughted; base-minded.

undignified, indign; unbe-coming, -seeming, fitting; de-rogatory, -grading; *infra dignitatem*; ungentleman-ly, -like; un-knightly, -chivalric, -manly, -handsome; recreant, inglorious.

corrupt, venal; debased, mongrel.

faithless, of bad faith, false, unfaithful, disloyal; untrustworthy; trust-, troth-less; lost to shame, dead to honor.

Adv. dishonestly etc. *adj.*; *malâ fide*, like a thief in the night, by crooked paths; by foul means.

Int. *O tempora! O mores!*

941. Knave.—**N.** knave, rogue, villain; Seapin, rascal; Lazarillo de Tormes; bad man etc. 949; blackguard etc. 949.

traitor, betrayer, arch-traitor, conspirator, stool pigeon, Judas, Catiline; reptile, serpent, snake in the grass, wolf in sheep's clothing, sneak, Jerry Sneak, tell-tale, squealer, mischief-maker, trimmer; renegade etc. (*tergiversation*) 607; truant, recreant; sycophant etc. (*servility*) 886.

942. Disinterestedness.—**N.** disinterestedness etc. *adj.*; generosity; liberal-ity, -ism; altruism; benevolence etc. 906; elevation, loftiness of purpose, exaltation, magnanimity; chival-ry, -rous spirit; heroism, sublimity.

self-denial, -abnegation, -effacement, -sacrifice, -immolation, -control etc. (*resolution*) 604; stoicism, devotion, martyrdom, *suttee*.

labor of love.

V. be -disinterested etc. *adj.*; make a sacrifice, lay one's head on the block; put oneself in the place of others, do as one would be done by, do unto others as we would men should do unto us.

Adj. disinterested; unselfish; self-denying, -sacrificing, -devoted; generous.

handsome, liberal, noble; noble-, high-minded; princely-, great, high, elevated, lofty, exalted, spirited, stoical, magnanimous; great-, large-hearted, chivalrous, heroic, sublime.

un-bought, -bribed; uncorrupted etc. (*upright*) 939.

943. Selfishness.—**N.** selfishness etc. *adj.*; self-love, -indulgence, -worship, -interest; ego-tism, -ism; egocentrism, narcissism; *amour propre* etc. (*vanity*) 880; nepotism.

worldliness etc. *adj.*; world wisdom.

illiberality; meanness etc. *adj.*

time-server; tuft-, fortune-hunter; self-seeker; jobber, worldling; egotist, egoist, monopolist, nepotist, profiteer; temporizer, trimmer; dog in the manger, charity that begins at home.

V. be -selfish etc. *adj.*; please −, indulge −, coddle- oneself; consult one's own -wishes, − pleasure; look after one's own interest; feather one's nest; take care of number one, have an eye to the main chance, know on which side one's bread is buttered; give an inch and take an ell; wangle.

Adj. selfish; self-seeking, -indulgent, -interested; wrapt up −, centered- in self; egotistic, -al; egoistical; egocentric.

illiberal, mean, ungenerous, narrowminded; mercenary, venal; covetous etc. 819.

unspiritual; earthly, -minded; mundane; worldly, -minded, -wise; time-serving.

interested; *alieni appetens sui profusus*.

Adv. ungenerously etc. *adj.*; to gain some private ends; from selfish −, interested- motives.

Phr. *après nous le déluge.*

944. Virtue.—**N.** virtue; virtuousness etc. *adj.*; morality; moral rectitude; integrity etc. (*probity*) 939; nobleness etc. 873.

morals; ethics etc. (*duty*) 926; cardinal virtues.

merit, worth, desert, excellence, credit; self-control etc. (*resolution*) 604; self-denial etc. (*temperance*) 953.

well-doing; good -actions, − behavior; discharge −, fulfilment −, performance- of duty; well spent life; innocence etc. 946.

V. be -virtuous etc. *adj.*; practice -virtue etc. *n.*; do −, fulfil −, perform −, discharge- one's duty; redeem one's pledge etc. 926; act well, − one's part; fight the good fight; acquit oneself well; command −, master- one's passions; keep -straight, − in the right path.

set -an, − a good- example; be on one's -good, − best- behavior.

Adj. virtuous, good; innocent etc. 946; meritorious, deserving, worthy, desertful, correct; dut-iful, -eous; moral; right, -eous, -minded; well-intentioned, creditable, laudable, commendable, praiseworthy; above −, beyond- all praise; excellent, admirable; sterling, pure, noble.

exemplary; match-, peer-less; saint-ly, -like; heaven-born, angelic, seraphic, godlike.

Adv. virtuously etc. *adj.*; *e merito.*

945. Vice.—N. vice; evil-doing, – courses; wrong doing; wickedness, viciousness etc. *adj.*; iniquity, peccability, demerit; sin, Adam; old – offending- Adam.

immorality, impropriety, indecorum, scandal; laxity, looseness of morals; want of -principle, – ballast; obliquity, backsliding, infamy, demoralization, pravity, depravity, pollution; hardness of heart; brutality etc. (*malevolence*) 907; corruption etc. (*debasement*) 659; knavery etc. (*improbity*) 940; profligacy; lust etc. 961; flagrancy, atrocity; cannibalism.

infirmity; weakness etc. *adj.*; weakness of the flesh, frailty, imperfection; error; weak side; foible; fail-ing, -ure; crying –, besetting- sin; defect, deficiency, shortcoming; cloven foot.

lowest dregs of vice, sink of iniquity, Alsatian den; *gusto picaresco*.

fault, crime; criminality etc. (*guilt*) 947.

sinner etc. 949.

V. be -vicious etc. *adj.*; sin, commit sin, do amiss, err, transgress; misdemean –, forget –, misconduct- oneself; mis-do, -behave; fall, lapse, slip, trip, offend, trespass; deviate from the -line of duty, – path of virtue etc. 944; take a wrong course, go astray; hug a -sin, – fault; sow one's wild oats.

render -vicious etc. *adj.*; demoralize, brutalize; corrupt etc. (*degrade*) 659.

Adj.* vicious; sinful; sinning etc. *v.*; wicked, iniquitous, bad, immoral, unrighteous, wrong, criminal; naughty, incorrect; undut-eous, -iful.

unprincipled, lawless, disorderly, *contra bonos mores*, indecorous, unseemly, improper; dissolute, profligate, scampish; unworthy; worth-, desert-less; disgraceful, recreant; reprehensible, blameworthy, uncommendable; dis-creditable, -reputable.

base, sinister, scurvy, foul, gross, vile, black, grave, facinorous, felonious, nefarious, shameful, scandalous, infamous, villainous, of a deep dye, heinous; flag-rant, -itious; atrocious, incarnate, accursed.

Mephistophelian, satanic, diabolic, hellish, infernal, stygian, fiend-ish, -like, hell-born, demoniacal, devilish.

mis-created, -begotten; demoralized, corrupt, depraved.

evil-minded, -disposed; ill-conditioned; malevolent etc. 907; heart-, grace-, shame-, virtueless; abandoned, lost to virtue; unconscionable; sunk –, lost –, deep –, steeped- in iniquity.

incorrigible, irreclaimable, obdurate, reprobate, past praying for; culpable, reprehensible etc. (*guilty*) 947.

unjustifiable; in-defensible, -excusable; inexpiable, unpardonable, irremissible.

weak, frail, lax, infirm, imperfect, indiscreet; demoralizing, degrading.

Adv. wrong; sinfully etc. *adj.*; without excuse.

Int. *O tempora! O mores!*

*Most of these adjectives are applicable both to the act and to the agent.

946. Innocence.—N. innocence; guiltlessness etc. *adj.*; incorruption, impeccability.

clean hands, clear conscience, *mens sibi conscia recti*.

innocent, new born babe, lamb, dove.

V. be -innocent etc. *adj.*; *nil conscire sibi nullâ pallescere culpâ*.

acquit etc. 970; exculpate etc. (*vindicate*) 937.

Adj. innocent, not guilty, unguilty; guilt-, fault-, sin-, stain-, blood-, spot-less; clear, immaculate; *rectus in curiâ*; un-spotted, -blemished, -erring; undefiled etc. 939; unhardened, Saturnian; Arcadian etc. (*artless*) 703.

in-, un-culpable; unblam-ed, -able; blameless, inerrable, above suspicion; irrepr-oachable, -ovable, -ehensible; un-exceptionable, -objectionable, -impeachable; salvable; venial etc. 937.

harmless; in-offensive, -noxious, -nocuous; dove-, lamb-like; pure, harmless as doves; innocent as -a lamb, – the babe unborn; more sinned against than sinning.

virtuous etc. 944; un-reproved, -impeached, -reproached.

Adv. innocently etc. *adj.*; with clean hands; with a -clear, – safe- conscience.

947. Guilt.—N. guilt, -iness; culpability; crimin-ality, -ousness; deviation from rectitude etc. (*improbity*) 940; sinfulness etc. (*vice*) 945; peccability.

mis-conduct, -behavior, -doing, -deed; malpractice, fault, sin, error, transgression; dereliction, delinquency; indiscretion, lapse, slip, trip, *faux pas, peccadillo*; flaw, blot, omission; fail-ing, -ure.

offence, trespass; mis-demeanor, -feasance, -prision, tort; mal-efaction, -feasance, -versation; crime, felony.

enormity, atrocity, outrage; deadly –, mortal –, unpardonable- sin; died without a name. *corpus delicti*.

Adj. guilty, to blame, culpable, peccable, in fault, censurable, reprehensible, blameworthy, uncommendable, illaudable; weighed in the balance and found wanting; exceptionable, objectionable.

Adv. *in flagrante delicto*; red-handed, in the very act.

948. Good Man.—N. good man, worthy. good woman, goddess, *madonna*, virgin.

model, paragon etc. (*perfection*) 650; good example; hero, demigod, seraph, angel; innocent etc. 946; saint etc. (*piety*) 987; benefactor etc. 912; philanthropist etc. 910; Aristides.

brick, trump, rough diamond, ugly duckling. salt of the earth; one in ten thousand; one of the best.

Phr. *si sic omnes!*

949. Bad Man.—N. bad man, wrongdoer, worker of iniquity; evil-doer etc. 913; sinner; the -wicked etc. 945; bad example.

rascal, scoundrel, villain, miscreant, caitiff; wretch, reptile, viper, serpent, cockatrice, basilisk, urchin; tiger, monster; devil etc. (*demon*) 980; devil incarnate; demon in human shape, Nana Sahib; hell-hound, -cat; rake-hell.

bad woman, jade, Jezebel, adultress, etc. 962; scamp, scapegrace, rip, runagate, ne'er-do-well, reprobate, *roué*, rake; limb; one who has sold himself to the devil, fallen angel, *âme damnée*, *vaurien, mauvais sujet*, loose fish, sad, dog; lost —, black-sheep; castaway, recreant, defaulter; prodigal etc. 818; libertine etc. 962.

rough, rowdy, ugly customer, ruffian, hoodlum, bully; Jonathan Wild; hangman; incendiary; thief etc. 792; murderer etc. 361.

culprit, delinquent, criminal, melefactor, misdemeanant; felon; convict, jail-bird, ticket-of-leave man; outlaw.

blackguard, *polisson*, loafer, sneak; raps-, rascallion; cullion, mean wretch, varlet, kern, *âme-de-boue, drôle*; cur, dog, hound, whelp, mongrel; lown, loon, runnion, outcast, vagabond; rogue etc. (*knave*) 941; scum of the earth, riff-raff; *Arcades ambo.*

Int. sirrah!

950. Penitence.—N. penitence, contrition, compunction, repentance, remorse; regret etc. 833.

self-reproach, -reproof, -accusation, -condemnation, -humiliation; stings —, pangs —, qualms —, prickings —, twinge —, twitch —, touch —, voice- of conscience; compunctious visitings of nature.

acknowledgment, confession etc. (*disclosure*) 529; apology etc. 952; recantation etc. 607; penance etc. 952; resipiscence.

awakened conscience, deathbed repentance, *locus poenitentiae*, stool of repentance, cutty stool.

penitent, Magdalen, prodigal son, returned prodigal, a sadder and wiser man.

V. repent, be sorry for; be -penitent etc. *adj.*; rue; regret etc. 833; think better of; recant etc. 607; knock under etc. (*submit*) 725; plead guilty; sing *miserere, — de profundis*; cry *peccavi*; own oneself in the wrong; acknowledge, confess etc. (*disclose*) 529; humble oneself; beg pardon etc. (*apologize*) 952; turn over a new leaf, put on the new man, turn from sin; reclaim; repent in sackcloth and ashes etc. (*do penance*) 952; learn by experience.

Adj. penitent; repenting etc. *v.*; repentant, contrite; conscience-smitten, -stricken; self-accusing, -convicted.

penitenti-ai, -ary; chastened, reclaimed; not hardened; un-hardened.

Adv. meâ culpâ.

Phr. *peccavi*; *erubuit*; *salva res est*; *vous l'avez voulu, Georges Dandin.*

951. Impenitence.—N. impenitence, irrepentance, recusance.

hardness of heart, seared conscience, induration, obduracy.

V. be -impenitent etc. *adj.*; steel —, harden- the heart; die -game, — and make no sign.

Adj. impenitent uncontrite, obdurate; hard, -ened; seared, recusant; unrepentant; relent-, remorse-, grace-, shrift-less.

lost, incorrigible, irreclaimable.

unre-claimed, -formed; unrepented, unatoned.

952. Atonement.—N. atonement, reparation; compromise, composition; compensation etc. 30; quittance, quits; indemni-ty, -fication; expiation,

redemption, reclamation, conciliation, propitiation.

amends, apology, *amende honorable*, satisfaction; peace —, sin —, burnt- offering; scapegoat, sacrifice.

penance, fasting, maceration, sackcloth and ashes, white sheet, shrift, flagellation, lustration; purga-tion, -tory.

V. atone, — for; expiate; propitiate; make -amends, — good; reclaim, redeem, repair, ransom, absolve, purge, shrive, do penance, stand in a white sheet, repent in sackcloth and ashes.

set one's house in order, wipe off old scores, make matters up; pay the -forfeit, — penalty.

apologize, beg pardon, express regret, *faire amende honorable*, give satisfaction; come —, fall-down on one's -knees, — marrow bones.

Adj. propitiatory, expiatory; sacrific, -ial, -atory; piacul-ar, -ous.

953. Temperance.—N. temperance, moderation, sobriety, soberness.

forbearance, abnegation; self-denial, -restraint, -control etc. (*resolution*) 604.

frugality; vegetarianism, teetotalism, total abstinence, prohibition; abst-inence, -emiousness, asceticism etc. 955; system of -Pythagoras, — Cornaro; Pythagorism, Stoicism.

vegetarian; Pythagorean, gymnosophist; teetotaler etc. 958; abstainer.

V. be -temperate etc. *adj.*; abstain, forbear, refrain, deny oneself, spare; know when one has had enough; take the pledge; look not upon the wine when it is red.

Adj. temperate, moderate, sober, frugal, sparing; abst-emious, -inent; within compass; measured etc. (*sufficient*) 639.

Pythagorean; vegetarian; teetotal, pussy-foot.

954. Intemperance.—N. intemperance; sensuality, animalism, carnality; pleasure; effeminacy, silkiness; luxur-y, -iousness; lap of -pleasure, — luxury.

indulgence; high-, free- living, in-abstinence, self-indulgence; voluptuousness etc. *adj.*; epicurism, -eanism; sybaritism.

dissipation; licentiousness etc. *adj.*; debauchery; crapulence.

revel-s, -ry; debauch, carousal, jollification, drinking bout, wassail, Saturnalia, orgies; excess, too much; intoxication etc. 959.

Circean cup; drug habit etc. 663.

V. be -intemperate etc. *adj.*; indulge, exceed; live -well, — high, — on the fat of the land; give a loose to -indulgence etc. *n.*; dine not wisely but too well; wallow in -voluptuousness etc. *n.*; plunge into dissipation.

revel, rake, live hard, run riot, sow one's wild oats; slake one's -appetite, — thirst; swill; pamper.

Adj. intemperate, inabstinent, intoxicated etc. 958; sensual, self-indulgent; voluptuous, luxurious, licentious, wild, dissolute, rakish, fast, debauched.

brutish, crapulous, swinish, piggish, hoggish, bestial.

Paphian, Epicurean, Sybaritical; bred —, nursed- in the lap of luxury; indulged, pampered, full-fed.

954a. Sensualist.—N. Sybarite, voluptuary, Sardanapalus, man of pleasure, carpet knight; epicure, -an; *gourm-et, -and;* gormandizer, gutling, glutton, pig, hog; votary –, swine- of Epicurus; sensualist; Heliogabalus; free –, hard- liver; libertine etc. 962; hedonist.

955. Asceticism.—N. asceticism, puritanism, sabbatarianism; cynicism, austerity; total abstinence.

mortification, maceration, sackcloth and ashes, flagellation; penance etc. 952; fasting etc. 956; martyrdom.

ascetic; anchor-et, -ite; martyr; *Heautontimorumenos;* hermit etc. (*recluse*) 893; puritan, sabbatarian, cynic.

Adj. ascetic, austere, puritanical; cynical; over-religious.

956. Fasting.—N. fasting; exrophagy; famishment, starvation; banting.

fast, *jour maigre;* fast –, banyan-day; Lent, quadragesima; Rama-dan, -zan; spare –, meagerdiet; lenten -diet, – entertainment; *soupe maigre,* short -rations, – commons; Barmecide feast; hunger strike.

V. fast, starve, clem, famish, perish with hunger; dine with Duke Humphrey; make two bites of a cherry.

Adj. lenten, quadragesimal; unfed; starved etc. *v.;* half-starved; fasting etc. *v.;* hungry etc. 865.

957. Gluttony.—N. gluttony; greed; greediness etc. *adj.;* voracity.

epicurism; good –, high- living; edacity, gulosity, crapulence; gutt-, guzz-ling; over-indulgence.

good cheer, blow out; feast etc. (*food*) 298; gastronomy.

epicure, *bon vivant, gourmand;* glutton, cormorant, hog, belly-god, Apicius, gastronome, gormandizer.

V. gormandize, gorge; over-gorge, -eat- oneself; engorge, eat one's fill, cram, stuff, stodge, glut, satiate; gutt-le, guzz-le; bolt, devour, gobble up; gulp etc. (*swallow food*) 298; raven, eat out of house and home.

have the stomach of an ostrich; play a good knife and fork etc. (*appetite*) 865.

Adj. gluttonous, greedy; gormandizing etc. *v.;* edacious, omnivorous, crapulent, swinish, voracious, devouring.

pampered; over-fed, -gorged.

958. Sobriety.—N. sobriety; teetotalism, temperance etc. 953.

water-drinker; teetotal-er, -ist; abstainer, Good Templar, Rechabite, band of hope; prohibitionist, pussyfoot.

V. take the pledge.

Adj. sober, – as a judge; dry, on the water wagon.

959. Drunkenness.—N. drunkenness etc. *adj.;* intemperance; drinking etc. *v.;* inebri-ety, -ation; ebri-ety, -osity; befuddlement; insobriety; intoxication; temulency, bibacity, wine-bibbing; com-, potation; deep potations, bacchanals, *bacchanalia,* libations.

oino-, dipso-mania; *delirium tremens,* d.t., alcohol, -ism.

drink; alcoholic drinks, alcohol, booze; gin, blue ruin, grog, brandy, port wine; punch, -bowl; cup, rosy wine, flowing bowl; drop, – too much; dram; beer, wine, spirits etc. (*beverage*) 298; cocktail, nip, peg; stirrup cup.

drunkard, sot, toper, tippler, bibber, wine-bibber; hard –, gin –, dram- drinker; soak, soaker, sponge, tun; love-, toss-pot; thirsty soul, reveller, carouser; Bacchanal, -ian; Bacch-al, -ante; devotee to Bacchus, dipsomaniac.

V. get –, be- drunk etc. *adj.;* see double; take a -drop, – glass- too much; drink, tipple, tope, booze, bouse, guzzle, swill, soak, sot, lush, bib, swig, carouse; sacrifice at the shrine of Bacchus; take to drinking; drink -hard, – deep, – like a fish; have one's swill, drain the cup, splice the main brace, take a hair of the dog that bit you.

liquor, – up; wet one's whistle, take a whet; lift one's elbow; crack a –, pass the- bottle; toss of etc. (*drink up*) 298; go to the -ale, – public house.

make one-drunk etc. *adj.;* inebriate, fuddle, fuzzle, get into one's head.

Adj. drunk, tipsy; intoxicated; inebri-ous, -ate, -ated; in one's cups; in a state of -intoxication etc. *n.;* temulent, -ive; fuddled, mellow, cut, boosy, fou, fresh, merry, elevatèd, squiffy; plastered, befuddled, sozzled; flush, -ed; flustered, disguised, groggy, beery; topheavy; potvaliant, glorious; potulent; over-come, -taken; whittled, screwed, tight, primed, oiled, corned, raddled, sewed up, lushy, nappy, muddled, muzzy, bosky, obfuscated, maudlin; crapulous, dead –, blind- drunk.

inter pocula; in –, the worse for- liquor, having had a drop too much, half seas over, three sheets in the wind; under the table, blind to the world, one over the eight.

drunk as -a piper, – a fiddler, – a lord, – Chloe, – an owl, – David's sow, – a wheelbarrow.

drunken, bibacious, bibulous, sottish; given –, addicted- to -drink, – the bottle; toping etc. *v.;* wet.

Phr. *nunc est bibendum.*

960. Purity.—N. purity; decency, decorum, delicacy; continence, chastity, honesty, virtue, modesty, shame; pudicity, *pucelage,* virginity.

vestal, virgin, Joseph, Hippolytus; Lucretia, Diana; prude.

Adj. pure, undefiled, modest, delicate, decent, decorous; *virginibus puerisque;* chaste, continent, virtuous, honest, Platonic.

961. Impurity.—N. impurity; uncleanness etc. (*filth*) 653; immodesty; grossness etc. *adj.;* indelicacy, indecency; impudicity; obscenity, ribaldry, smut, bawdry, *double entendre, équivoque;* Aretinism; pornography.

concupiscence, lust, carnality, flesh, salacity; pruriency, lechery, lasciviency, lubricity, lewdness.

incontinence, intrigue, *faux pas*; *amour, -ette*; gallantry; dabauchery, libertinism, *libertinage*, fornication; *liaison*; wenching, venery, dissipation.

seduction; defloration, defilement, abuse, violation, rape; incest.

social evil, harlotry, stupration, whoredom, concubinage, cuckoldom, adultery, advoutry, *crim. con.*; free love.

seraglio, harem, zenana; brothel, bagnio, stew, bawdy-house, *lupanar*, house of ill fame, *bordel*, kip.

V. be -impure etc. *adj.*; intrigue; debauch, defile, assault, attack, seduce; prostitute; abuse, violate, deflower; commit -adultery etc. *n.*

Adj. impure; unclean etc. (*dirty*) 653; not to be mentioned to ears polite; immodest, shameless; indecorous, -delicate, -decent; loose, suggestive, *risqué*, coarse, gross, broad, free, equivocal, smutty, fulsome, ribald, obscene, bawdy, pornographic.

concupiscent, prurient, lickerish, rampant, lustful; carnal, -minded; lewd, lascivious, lecherous, libidinous, erotic, ruttish, salacious; Paphian; voluptuous; incestuous.

· unchaste, -light, wanton, licentious, adulterous, debauched, dissolute; of -loose character, − easy virtue; frail, gay, riggish, incontinent, meretricious, rakish, gallant, dissipated; no better than she should be; on the -town, − streets, − *pavé*, − loose.

adulterous, incestuous, bestial.

962. Libertine.—N. libertine; voluptuary etc. 954a; rake, debauchee, loose fish, rip, rake-hell, fast man; *intrigant*, gallant, seducer, fornicator, lecher, satyr, goat, whoremonger, *paillard*, adulterer, gay deceiver, Lothario, Don Juan, Bluebeard.

adulteress, advoutress, courtesan, prostitute, strumpet, tart, hustler, chippy, broad, harlot, whore, punk, *fille de joie*; woman, − of the town; street-walker, Cyprian, miss, piece; frail sisterhood, fallen woman; demirep, wench, trollop, trull, baggage, hussy, drab, bitch, jade, skit, rig, quean, mopsy, slut, minx, harridan; woman -of easy virtue etc. (*unchaste*) 961; wanton, fornicatress; Jezebel, Messalina, Delilah, Thaïs, Phryne, Aspasia, Lais, *lorette, cocotte, petite dame, grisette*; *demimonde*; white slave.

concubine, mistress, fancy woman, kept woman, doxy, *chère amie, bona roba*.

pimp; pand-er, -ar; bawd, *conciliatrix*, procuress, mackerel, wittol.

963. Legality.—N. legality; legitima-cy, -teness, legitimization.

legislature; law, code, *corpus juris*, constitution, pandect, charter, act, enactment, statute, rule; canon etc. (*precept*) 697; ordinance, institution, regulation; by-, bye-law, rescript; decree etc. (*order*) 741; *ordonnance*; standing order; *plébiscite* etc. (*choice*) 609.

legal process; form, -ula, -ality; rite; arm of the law; *habeas corpus*.

[Science of law] jurisprudence, nomology; legislation, codification.

equity, common law; *lex* −, *lex nonscripta*, unwritten law; law of nations, international law, *jus gentium*; *jus civile*; civil −, criminal −, canon −, statute −, ecclesiastical- law; *lex mercatoria*.

constitutional-ism, -ity; justice etc. 922.

V. legalize, legitimize; enact, ordain; decree etc. (*order*) 741; pass a law; legislate; codify, formulate; authorize.

Adj. legal, legitimate; according to law; vested, constitutional, chartered, legalized; lawful etc. (*permitted*) 760; statut-able, -ory; legislat-orial, -ive.

Adv. legally etc. *adj.*; in the eye of the law; *de jure.*

964. Illegality. [Absence or violation of law.]**—N.** lawlessness; breach −, violation- of law; disobedience etc. 742; unconformity etc. 83.

arbitrariness etc. *adj.*; antinomy, violence, brute force, despotism, outlawry.

mob −, lynch −, club −, Lydford −, martial −, drumhead- law; *coup d'état*; *le droit du plus fort*; *argumentum baculinum*.

illegality, informality, unlawfulness, illegitimacy, bar sinister.

trover and conversion; smuggling, boot-legging, rum-running, poaching; simony.

speakeasy, speakie, blind pig.

V. offend against −, violate- the law; set the law at defiance, ride rough-shod over, drive a coach and six through a statute; make the law a dead letter, take the law into one's own hands.

smuggle, run, poach.

Adj. illegal; prohibited etc. 761; not allowed, unlawful, illegitimate, illicit, contraband, actionable.

unchartered, unconstitutional; unwarrant-ed, -able; unauthorized; informal, unofficial; in-, extra-judicial.

lawless, arbitrary; despotic, -al; summary, irresponsible; un-answerable, -accountable.

null and void; a dead letter.

Adv. illegally etc. *adj.*; with a high hand, in violation of law.

965. Jurisdiction. [Executive.]**—N.** jurisdiction, judicature, administration of justice, soc; executive, commission of the peace; magistracy etc. (*authority*) 737.

judge etc. 967; tribunal etc. 966; municipality, corporation, bailiwick, shrievalty; lord lieutenant; lord −, mayor, city manager, alderman etc. 745; sheriff, bailie, shrieve, chief −, constable; police, − force; constabulary, bumbledom.

officer; proctor, high −, commissioner; bailiff, tipstaff, bum-bailiff, catchpoll, beadle; police-man, -constable, -sergeant; *sbirro, alguazil, gendarme*, kavass, *lictor*, macebearer, *huissier*, bedel.

press-gang; exciseman, gauger, custom-house officer, *douanier.*

coroner, edile, aedile, portreeve, paritor; *posse comitatus.*

V. judge, sit in judgment.

Adj. executive, administrative, municipal;

inquisitorial, causidical; judic-atory, -iary, -ial; juridical.

Adv. *coram judice.*

966. Tribunal.—N. tribunal, court, board, bench, judicatory, curia; court of -justice, — law, — arbitration; inquisition; guild.

justice —, judgment —, mercy- seat; woolsack; bar, — of justice; dock; forum, hustings, *bureau*, drum-head; jury-, witness-box.

senate-house, town-hall, theater; House of - Lords, — Commons.

assize, eyre; ward-, burgh-mote; superior courts of Westminister; court of -record, — oyer and ter- miner, — assize, — appeal — error; High court of -Judicature, — Appeal; Judicial Committee of the Privy Council; Star-Chamber; Court of -Chancery, — King's *or* Queen's Bench, — Exchequer, — Common Pleas, — Probate, — Arches, — Ad- miralty, — Criminal Appeal; Lords Justices' —, Rolls —, Vice Chancellor's —, Stannary —, Divorce —, Palatine —, ecclesiastical —, county —, police- court; sessions; quarter —, petty- sessions; court -leet, — baron, — of pie poudre, — of common council; board of green cloth.

court-martial; drum-head court-martial; *durbar*, divan; Areopagus; *rota.*

Adj. judicial etc. 965; appellate; curial.

967. Judge.—N. judge; justi-ce, -ciar, -ciary; chancellor; justice —, judge- of assize; recorder, common serjeant; puisne —, assistant —, county court- judge; conservator —, justice- of the peace, J.P.; court etc. (*tribunal*) 966; grand —, petty —, coroner's- jury; panel, juror, juryman; twelve men in a box; magistrate, police magistrate, stipendiary, the great unpaid, beak; his -worship, — honor, — lordship; deemster, moderator.

Lord -Chancellor, — Justice; Master of the Rolls, Vice-Chancellor; Lord Chief -Justice, — Baron; Mr. Justice; Baron, — of the Exchequer.

jurat, assessor; arbi-ter, -trator; umpire; refer-ee, -endary; revising barrister; domesman; censor etc. (*critic*) 480; official —, receiver.

archon, tribune, praetor, *ephor*, syndic, *podestà*, mullah, ulema, mufti, cadi, kadi; Rhadamanthus. litigant etc. (*accusation*) 938.

V. adjudge etc. (*determine*) 480; try a -case, — prisoner.

Adj. judicial etc. 965.

Phr. 'a Daniel come to judgment.'

968. Lawyer.—N. lawyer, jurist, legist, civilian, pundit, publicist, jurisconsult, legal adviser, ad- vocate; barrister, — at law; counsel, -lor; King's *or* Queen's counsel; K.C.; Q.C.; silk gown, leader; junior; — counsel; stuff gown, serjeant-at-law; bencher, tubman; judge etc. 967.

bar, legal profession, gentleman of the long robe; junior —, outer —, inner- bar; Inns of Court; equity draftsman, conveyancer, pleader, special pleader.

solicitor, attorney, proctor; notary, — public; scrivener, cursitor; writer, — to the signet; S.S.C.; limb of the law; pettifogger.

V. practice -at, — within- the bar; plead; call —, to called- -to, — within- the bar; take silk.

Adj. learned in the law; at the bar; forensic.

969. Lawsuit.—N. lawsuit, suit, action, cause, petition; litigation; dispute etc. 713.

citation, arraignment, prosecution, im- peachment; accusation etc. 938; presentment, true bill, indictment.

apprehension, arrest; committal; imprisonment etc. (*restraint*) 751.

writ, summons, subpoena, *latitat*, *nisi prius*; *habeas corpus.*

pleadings; declaration, bill, claim; *procès- verbal*, bill of right, information, *corpus delicti*; affidavit, state of facts; answer, replication, plea, demurrer, rebutter, rejoinder; surre-butter, - joinder.

suitor, party to a suit; litigant etc. 938; libellant.

hearing, trial; verdict etc. (*judgment*) 480; ap- peal, — motion; writ of error; *certiorari.*

case, decision, precedent, ruling; decided case, reports.

V. go to —, appeal to the- law; bring to -justice, — trial, — the bar; put on trial, pull up; accuse etc. 938; prefer —, file- a claim etc. *n.*; take the law of, inform against.

serve with a writ, cite, apprehend, arraign, sue, prosecute, bring an action against, indict, impeach, attach, distrain, commit; arrest; summon, -s; give in charge etc. (*restrain*) 751.

empanel a jury, implead, join issue; close the pleadings; set down for hearing.

try, hear a cause; sit in judgment; adjudicate etc. 480.

Adj. litigious etc. (*quarrelsome*) 713; *qui tam*; *coram* —, sub- *judice.*

Adv. *pendente lite.*

Phr. *adhuc sub judice lis est.*

970. Acquittal.—N. acquit-tal, -ment; clearance, exculpation, exoneration; discharge etc. (*release*) 750; *quietus*, absolution, compurgation, reprieve, respite; pardon etc. (*forgiveness*) 918.

[Exemption from punishment] impunity, im- munity.

V. acquit, exculpate, exonerate, clear; absolve, whitewash, assoil, discharge, release; liberate etc. 750.

reprieve, respite; pardon etc. (*forgive*) 918; let off, — scot free.

Adj. acquitted etc. *v.*; un-condemned, - punished, -chastised; recommended to mercy.

971. Condemnation.—N. condemnation, con- viction, proscription, damnation; death warrant; penalty etc. 974.

attain-der, -ture, -tment.

V. condemn, convict, cast, bring home to, find guilty, damn, doom, sign the death warrant, sen- tence, pass sentence on, attaint, confiscate, proscribe, sequestrate; non-suit.

disapprove etc. 932; accuse etc. 938.

stand condemned.

Adj. condem-, dam-natory; condemned etc. *v.*; non-suited etc. (*failure*) 732; self-convicted.

Phr. *mutato nomine de te fabula narratur.*

972. Punishment.—N. punishment, punition; chast-isement, -ening; correction, castigation.

discipline, infliction, trial; judgment; penalty etc. 974; retribution; thunderbolt, Nemesis; requital etc. (*reward*) 973; penology; retributive justice.

lash, scaffold etc. (*instrument of punishment*) 975; imprisonment etc. (*restraint*) 751; chain gang; transportation, banishment, expulsion, deportation, exile, involuntary exile, ostracism; penal servitude, hard labor; galleys etc. 975; beating etc. *v.*; flagellation, fustigation, gantlet, *strappado*, *estrapade*, *bastinado*, *argumentum baculinum*, stick law, rap on the knuckles, box on the ear; blow etc. (*impulse*) 276; stripe, cuff, kick, buffet, pummel; slap, – in the face; wipe, douse; *coup de grâce*; torture, rack; picket, -ing; *dragon-nade*; capital punishment, extreme penalty; execution; hanging etc. *v.*; de-capitation, -collation; *garrot-te*, *-to*; electrocution, lethal chamber; crucifixion, impalement; martyrdom, *auto-da-fé*; *noyade*; *hara-kiri*, happy despatch.

V. punish; chast-ise, -en; castigate, correct, in-flict punishment, administer correction, deal retributive justice.

visit upon, pay; pay –, serve- out; settle with, get even with, get one's own back; do for; make short work of, give a lesson to, strafe, serve one right, make an example of; have a rod in pickle for; give it one.

strike etc. 276; deal a blow to, administer the lash, smite; slap, – the face; smack, cuff, box the ears, spank, thwack, thump, beat, lay on, swinge, buffet; thresh, thrash, pummel, drub, leather, trounce, baste, belabor; lace, – one's jacket; dress, give a -dressing, – down; trim, warm, wipe, tund, cob, bang, strap, comb, lash, lick, larrup, whallop, whop, flog, scourge, whip, birch, cane, give the stick, switch, flagellate, horsewhip, *bastinado*, towel, rub down with an oaken towel, rib roast, dust one's jacket, fustigate, pitch into, lay about one, beat black and blue; beat to a -mummy, – jelly; give a black eye; hit on the head; sandbag.

tar and feather; pelt, stone, lapidate; mast-head, keelhaul.

execute; bring to the -block, – gallows; behead; de-capitate, -collate; guillotine; hang, turn off, gib-bet, bowstring, hang, draw and quarter; shoot; decimate; burn; electrocute; break on the wheel, crucify; em-, im-pale; flay; lynch; put to death.

torture; put -on, – to- the rack; picket.

banish, exile; trans-, de-port; expel, ostracize; rusticate; drum out; dismiss, -bar, -bench; strike off the roll, unfrock; post.

suffer, – for, – punishment; be -flogged, – hanged etc.; come to the gallows, dance upon nothing, die in one's shoes, be rightly served.

Adj. punishing etc. *v.*; penal; puni-tory, -tive; in-flictive, castigatory; punished etc. *v.*

Int. *à la lanterne!*

973. Reward.—N. reward, recompense, remuneration, prize, meed, guerdon, reguerdon; indemni-ty, -fication, price; quittance; com-pensation; reparation, *ersatz*, assythment, redress; retribution, reckoning, acknowledgment, requital, amends, sop; atonement; consideration, return, *quid pro quo*; salvage, perquisite; vail etc. (*donation*) 784; *douceur*, bribe, bait, baksheesh,

tip; hush-, smart-money; black-mail; carcelage; *solatium*.

allowance, salary, stipend, wages, pay, -ment; emolument; tribute; batta, shot, scot; premium, fee, *honorarium*; hire.

crown etc. (*decoration of honor*) 877.

V. re-ward, -compense, -pay, -quite; re-, munerate; compensate; fee, tip, bribe; pay one's footing etc. (*pay*) 807; make amends, indemnify, atone; satisfy, acknowledge.

get for one's pains, reap the fruits of.

Adj. remunerat-ive, -ory; munerary, com-pensatory, retributive, reparatory.

974. Penalty.—N. penalty; retribution etc. (*punishment*) 972; pain, pains and penalties; *peine forte et dure*; penance etc. (*atonement*) 952; the devil to pay.

fine, mulct, amercement; forfeit, -ure; escheat, damages, deodand, sequestration, confiscation, *premunire*.

V. penalize, fine, mulct, amerce, sconce, con-fiscate; sequest-rate, -er; escheat; estreat, forfeit.

975. Scourge. [Instrument of punish-ment.]—**N.** scourge, rod, cane, stick; ra-, rat-tan; birch, – rod; rod in pickle; switch, ferule, cudgel, truncheon; rubber hose.

whip, lash, strap, thong, cowhide, knout; cat, – o'-nine-tails, *sjambok*, quirt; rope's end.

pillory, stocks, whipping-post; cuck-, duck-ing stool; brank; triangle, wooden horse, maiden, thumbscrew, boot, rack, wheel, iron heel; tread-mill, crank, galleys.

scaffold; block, axe, *guillotine*; stake; cross; gallows, gibbet, Tyburn tree; drop, noose, rope, halter, bowstring; electric chair, lethal chamber.

house of correction etc. (*prison*) 752.

gaol-, jail-er; executioner; hang-, heads-man; Jack Ketch; lyncher.

976. Deity.—N. Deity, Divinity; God-head, -ship; Omnipotence, Providence.

[Quality of being divine] divin-eness, -ity.

God, Lord, Jehovah, *Deus*; The -Almighty, – Supreme Being, – First Cause; *Ens Entium*; Author –, Creator- of all things; Author of our being; The -Infinite, – Eternal; The All-powerfull, -wise, -merciful, -holy; The Omni-potent, -scient.

[Attributes and perfections] infinite -power, – wisdom, – goodness, – justice, – truth, – love, – mercy; omni-potence, -science, -presence; unity, immutability, holiness, glory, majesty, sovereignty, infinity, eternity.

The -Trinity, – Holy Trinity, – Trinity in Unity, – Triune God; Three in One and One in Three.

God the Father; The -Maker, – Creator, – Preserver.

[Functions] creation, preservation, divine government; The-ocracy, -archy; providence; ways –, dealings –, dispensations –, visitations- of Providence.

God the Son, Jesus, Christ; The -Messiah, – Anointed, – Savior, – Redeemer, – Mediator,

– Intercessor, – Advocate, – Judge; The Son of -
God, – Man, – David; The Only Begotten; The
Lamb of God, The Word; Em-, Im-manuel; The -
King of Kings and Lord of Lords, – King of
Glory, – Prince of Peace, – Good Shepherd, –
Way, – Truth, – Life, – Bread of Life, – Light
of the World; The -Lord our, – Sun of-
Righteousness.

The -Incarnation, – Hypostatic Union, –
Word made Flesh.

[Functions] salvation, redemption, atonement,
propitiation, mediation, intercession, judgment.

God the Holy Ghost, The Holy Spirit, Paraclete;
The -Comforter, – Consoler, – Spirit of Truth,
– Dove.

[Functions] inspiration, unction, regeneration,
sanctification, consolation.

eon, aeon, special providence, *Deus ex
machinâ*; *Avatar*.

V. create, uphold, preserve, govern etc.

atone, redeem, save, propitiate, mediate etc.

predestinate, elect, call, ordain, bless, justify,
sanctify, glorify etc.

Adj. almighty, holy, hallowed, sacred, divine,
heavenly, celestial; messianic; sacrosanct; all-
powerful, -wise, -seeing, -knowing; omnipotent,
omniscient; supreme.

super-human, -natural; ghostly, spiritual, hyper-
physical, unearthly; the-istic, -ocratic, deistic;
anointed.

Adv. *jure divino*, by divine right; *Deo volente*,
D.V.

977. Angel. [Beneficent spirits.]—**N.** angel,
archangel; heavenly host, choir invisible, host of
heaven, sons of God; Michael, Gabriel etc.; seraph,
-im; cherub, -im; ministering spirit, morning star;
saint, *Madonna*; Our Lady, the Blessed Virgin, the
Virgin Mary.

Adj. angelic, seraphic, cherubic.

978. Satan. [Maleficent spirits.]—**N.** Satan, the
Devil, Lucifer, Ahrimanes, Belial; Sammael,
Zamiel, Beelzebub, the Prince of the Devils;
Mephistopheles, his satanic majesty.

the tempter; the evil -one, – spirit; the -author
of evil, – wicked one, – old Serpent; the Prince
of -darkness, – this world, – the power of the air;
the -foul, – arch- fiend; the devil incarnate; the -
common enemy, – angel of the bottomless pit;
Abaddon, Apollyon, Mammon.

fallen agnels, unclean spirits, devils; the -rulers,
– powers- of darkness; inhabitants of Pàn-
demonium; demon etc. 980.

diabolism; devil-ism, -ship, -dom, -ry, -worship;
diablerie; satanism, manicheism; the cloven foot;
black magic etc. 992.

Adj. satanic, diabolic, devilish, infernal, hell-
born.

979. Jupiter.—**N.** god, -dess; heathen gods and
goddesses; Pantheon; Jupiter, Jove, Zeus, Apollo,
Mars, Mercury, Neptune, Vulcan, Bacchus, Pluto,
Saturn, Cupid, Eros, Pan; Juno, Ceres, Proserpina,
Dina, Minerva, Pallas, Athenae, Venus, Aphrodite,
Vesta; The Fates etc. 601.

Allah, Brahma, Vishnu, Siva, Shiva, Krishna,
Juggernaut, Buddha; Ra, Isis, Osiris; Belus, Bel,
Baal, Asteroth etc.; Thor, Odin; Mumbo Jumbo;
good –, tutelary- genius; demiurge, familiar, –
spirit; Sibyl; fairy, fay; sylph, -id; Ariel, peri,
nymph, nereid, dryad, oread, sea-maid, Banshee,
Benshie, Ormuzd; Oberon, Titania, Mab,
hamadryad, naiad, mermaid, kelpie, Ondine, nix,
nixie, sprite; denizens of the air; pixy etc. (*bad
spirit*) 980.

mythology; heathen –, fairy- mythology; Lemprière, folklore.

Adj. fairy-, sylph-like; sylphic.

980. Demon.—**N.** demon, -ry, -ism, -ology; evil
genius, fiend, familiar, – spirit, devil; bad –, un-
clean- spirit; cacodemon, incubus, Frankenstein's
monster, succubus and succuba, Titan, Shedim,
Mephistopheles, Asmodeus, Moloch, Belial,
Ahriman, fury, The Furies etc. 900; harpy; Friar
Rush.

vampire, ghoul; af-, ef-freet; afrite; ogre, -ss;
gnome, gin, djinn, imp, deev, *lamia*; bo-gie, -gle;
nis, kobold, flibbertigibbet, fairy, brownie, pixy,
elf, dwarf, urchin, Puck, Robin Goodfellow; lepre-,
cluri-chaune; troll, dwerger, sprite, oaf, changeling,
bad fairy, nixe, pigwidgeon, Will-o'-the-wisp; Erl
King.

[Supernatural appearance] ghost, specter, apparition, genie, spirit, shade, shadow, vision, phantom etc. 443; materialization (*spiritualism*) 992;
hob-, goblin; wraith, spook, werwolf, boggart, banshee, *loup-garou*, *lemures*; evil eye.

nisse, necks; mer-man, -maid, -folk; siren,
Lorelei; satyr, faun.

Adj. supernatural, weird, uncanny, unearthly,
spectral; ghost-ly, -like; elf-in, -like; fiend-ish, -like;
impish, demoniacal; haunted.

981. Heaven.—**N.** heaven; kingdom of -
heaven, – God; heavenly kingdom; throne –,
presence- of God; inheritance of the saints in light.

Paradise, Eden, abode of the blessed; Holy City,
New Jerusalem; celestial bliss, glory.

[Mythological -heaven] Olympus; [–
paradise] Elysium, Elysian fields, Arcadia, bowers
of bliss, garden of the Hesperides, Islands of the
Blessed; happy hunting-ground; third –, seventh-
heaven; Valhalla (Scandinavian); Nirvana (Buddhist).

future state, eternity, eternal life, life after death,
eternal home, resurrection, translation;
resuscitation etc. 660; apotheosis, deification.

Adj. heavenly, celestial, supernal, unearthly,
from on high, paradisiacal, beatific, elysian, Olym-
pian, Arcadian.

982. Hell.—**N.** hell, bottomless pit, place of
torment; habitation of fallen angels; Pandemonium, Abaddon, Domdaniel.

hell fire; everlasting -fire, – torment; lake of fire
and brimstone; fire that is never quenched, worm
that never dies.

purgatory, limbo, gehenna, abyss.

[Mythological hell] Tartarus, Hades, Avernus,
Styx, Stygian creek, pit of Acheron, Cocytus,

Phlegethon, Lethe; infernal regions, *inferno*, shades below, realms of Pluto.
· Pluto, Rhadamanthus, Erebus, Charon, Cerberus; Tophet.
Adj. hellish, infernal, stygian.

983. Theology. [Religious Knowledge.]—**N.** Theology (natural and revealed); Theo-gony, -sophy; Divinity; Hagio-logy, -graphy; Caucasian mystery; monotheism; religion; religious -persuasion, — sect, — denomination; cult; creed etc. (*belief*) 484; articles —, declaration —, profession —, confession- of faith.
theolog-ue, -ian; divine, schoolman, canonist, monotheist.
Adj. theological, religious; canonical; denominational; sectarian etc. 984.

983a. Orthodoxy.—N. orthodoxy; strictness, soundness, religious truth, true faith; truth etc. 494.
Christian-ity, -ism; Catholic-ism, -ity; 'the faith once delivered to the saints;' hyperorthodoxy etc. 984; iconoclasm.
the Holy —, the Orthodox- Church; Catholic —, Universal —, Apostolic —, Established- Church; temple of the Holy Ghost; Church —, body —, members —, disciples —, followers- of Christ; Christian, — community; true believer; canonist etc. (*theologian*) 983; Christendom, collective body of Christians, the Church Militant.
canons etc. (*belief*) 484; thirty-nine articles; Apostles' —, Nicene —, Athanasian- Creed; Church Catechism; textuary.
Adj. orthodox, sound, literal, strict, faithful, catholic, schismless, Christian, evangelical, scriptural, divine, monotheistic; true etc. 494.

984. Heterodoxy. [Sectarianism.]—**N.** heterodoxy; error etc. 495; false doctrine, heresy, schism; schismantic-ism, -alness; recusancy, backsliding, apostasy; atheism etc. (*irreligion*) 989.
bigotry etc. (*obstinacy*) 606; fanaticism, iconoclasm; hyperorthodoxy, precisianism, bibliolatry, hagiolatry, sabbatarianism, puritanism; idolatry etc. 991; superstition etc. (*credulity*) 486; dissent etc. 489.
sectar-ism, -ianism; nonconformity; secularism; syncretism, religious sects; the clash of creeds.
protestant-, advent-, Arian-, Erastian-, Calvin-, quaker-, method-, anabapt-, Pusey-, tractarian-, ritual-, Origen-, Sabellian-, Socinian-, De-, The-, mon-, material-, positiv-, latitudinairan-ism etc.
High —, Low —, Broad —, Free- Church; ultramontanism; monasticism; pap-ism, -istry; papacy; Anglican-, Catholic-, Roman-ism; popery, Scarlet Lady, Church of Rome, Greek Church; Christian Science, The Church of Christ Scientist.
pagan-, heathen-, ethic-ism; mythology; animism; poly-, di-, tri-, pan-theism; dualism; heathendom.
Juda-, Gentil-, Mahometan-, Islam-, Turc-, Brahmin-, Hindoo-, Buddh-, Lama-, Confucian-, Shinto-, Sabian-, Gnostic- Soofee-, Hylothe-, Mormon-ism.
Theosophy; Spiritualism, Occultism.

heretic, antichrist; pagan, heathen; pai-, pay-nim; *giaour*; gentile; pan-, poly-theist; idolator; misbeliever, apostate, backslider.
bigot etc. (*obstinacy*) 606; fanatic, dervish, abdal, iconoclast.
latitudinarian, limitarian, Deist, Theist, Unitarian; positivist, materialist; agnostic, sceptic etc. 989.
schismatic; sectar-y, -ian, -ist; seceder, separatist, recusant, dissenter; non-conformist, -juror; Huguenot, Protestant; orthodox dissenter, Congregationalist, Independent; Episcopalian, Presbyterian; Lutheran, Calvinist, Quaker, Methodist, Weslayan; Ana-, Baptist; Dunker; Mormon, Latter-day Saint, Irvingite, Sandemanian, Glassite, Erastian; Sub-, Supra-lapsarian; Gentoo, Antinomian, Swedenborgian, Adventist, Plymouth Brother; Theosophist etc.
Catholic, Roman Catholic, Romanist, papist, ultramontane; Old Catholic, tractarian, Anglican, Puseyite, ritualist; Puritan.
Jew, Hebrew, Rabbist; Mahometan, Mohammedan, Mussulman, Moslem, Islamite, Osmanli; Brahm-in, -an; Parsee, Sofi, Soofee; Buddhist; Zoroastrian, Magi, Gymnosophist, fire-worshipper, Sabian, Gnostic, Sadducee, Rosicrucian etc.
Adj. heterodox, heretical; un-orthodox, -scriptural, -canonical; antiscriptural, apocryphal; un-, anti-christian; schismatic, recusant, iconoclastic; sectarian; dis-senting, -sident; secular etc. (*lay*) 997.
pagan; heathen, -ish; ethnic, -al; gentile, painim; pan-, poly-theistic; agnostic, sceptic.
Judaical, Mohammedan, Moslem, Brahminical, Buddhist etc. *n.*; Romish, Protestant etc. *n.*
bigoted etc. (*prejudiced*) 481; (*obstinate*) 606; superstitious etc. (*credulous*) 486; fanatical; idolatrous etc. 991; visionary etc. (*imaginative*) 515.

985. Revelation.—N. revelation, inspiration, *afflatus*.
Word, — of God; Scripture; the -Scriptures, — Bible, — Book of Books; Holy -Writ, — Scriptures; inspired writings, Gospel.
Old Testament, Septuagint, Vulgate, Pentateuch; Octateuch; the -Law, — Jewish Law, — Prophets; major —, minor- Prophets; Hagio-grapha, -logy; Hierographa; Apocrypha.
New Testament; Gospels, Evangelists, Acts, Epistles, Apocalypse, Revelations.
Talmud; Mishna, Masorah.
prophet etc. (*seer*) 513; evangelist, apostle, disciple, saint; the —, the Apostolical- fathers; Holy Men of old, inspired -writers, — penmen.
Adj. scriptural, biblical, sacred, prophetic; evangel-ical, -istic; apostolic, -al; inspired, theopneustic, apocalyptic, ecclesiastical, canonical, textuary.

986. Pseudo-Revelation.—N. the -Koran, — Alcoran; Ly-king, Shaster, Vedas, Zendavesta, Vedidad, Purana, Edda; Go-, Gau-tama; Book of Mormon.
[False prophets and religious founders] Buddha, Zoroaster, Zerdhusht, Confucius, Mahomet.
[Idols] golden calf etc. 991; Baal, Moloch, Dagon.

987. Piety.—N. piety, religion, theism, faith; religiousness, holiness etc. *adj.*; saintship; religionism; sanctimony etc. (*assumed piety*) 988; reverence etc. (*respect*) 928; humility, veneration, devotion; prostration etc. (*worship*) 990; grace, unction, edification; sancti-ty, -tude; consecration.

spiritual existence, odor of sanctity, beauty of holiness.

theopathy, beatification, adoption, regeneration, conversion, justification, sanctification, salvation, inspiration, bread of life; Body and Blood of Christ.

believer, convert, theist, Christian, devotee, pietist; the -good, — righteous, — just, — believing, — elect; Saint, *Madonna*.

the children of -God, — the kingdom, — light.

V. be -pious etc. *adj.*; have -faith etc. *n.*; believe, receive Christ; revere etc. 928; worship etc. 950; be -converted etc.

convert, edify, sanctify, hallow, keep holy, beatify, regenerate, inspire, consecrate, enshrine.

Adj. pious, religious, devout, devoted, reverent, godly, heavenly minded, humble; pure, — in heart; holy, spiritual, pietistic; saint-ly, -like; seraphic, sacred, solemn.

believing, faithful, Christian, Catholic.

elected, adopted, justified, sanctified, regenerated, inspired, consecrated, converted, unearthly, not of the earth.

988. Impiety.—N. impiety; sin etc. 945; irreverence; profan-eness etc. *adj.*, -ity, -ation; blasphemy, desecration, sacrilege; scoffing etc. *v.*

[Assumed piety] hypocrisy etc. (*falsehood*) 544; pietism, cant, pious fraud; lip-devotion, -service, -reverence; mis-devotion, formalism, austerity; sanctimon-y, -iousness etc. *adj.*; pharisaism, precisianism; sabbat-ism, -arianism; *odium theologicum*; sacerdotalism; bigotry etc. (*obstinacy*) 606, (*prejudice*) 481.

hardening, backsliding, declension, perversion, reprobation apostasy, recusancy.

sinner etc. 949; scoffer, blasphemer; sacrilegist; worldling; hypocrite etc. (*dissembler*) 548; Scribes and Pharisees; Tartufe, Maw-worm.

bigot; saint [ironically]; Pharisee, sabbatarian, formalist, methodist, puritan, pietist, precisian, religionist, devotee, ranter, fanatic, wowser.

the -wicked, — evil, — unjust, — reprobate; son of -men, — Belial, — the wicked one; children of darkness.

V. be -impious etc. *adj.*; profane, desecrate, blaspheme, revile, scoff; swear etc. (*malediction*) 908; commit sacrilege.

snuffle; turn up the whites of the eyes; idolize.

Adj. impious; irreligious etc. 989; desecrating etc. *v.*; profane, irreverent, sacrilegious, blasphemous.

un-hallowed, -sanctified, -regenerate; hardened, perverted, reprobate.

hypocritical etc. (*false*) 544; canting, pietistical, sanctimonious, unctuous, pharisaical, over-righteous, righteous over much.

bigoted, fanatical etc. 481 and 606; priest-ridden.

Adv. under the -mask, — cloak, — pretence, — form, — guise- of religion.

989. Irreligion.—N. irreligion, indevotion; ungodliness etc. *adj.*; laxity, quietism, apathy, indifference, passivity.

scepticism, doubt; un-, dis-belief; incredul-ity, -ousness etc. *adj.*; want of -faith, — belief; pyrrhonism; doubt etc. 485; agnosticism.

atheism, deism; hylotheism; materialism; positivism; nihilism.

infidelity, freethinking, antichristianity, rationalism.

atheist, anti-christian, sceptic, unbeliever, deist, infidel, pyrrhonist; *giaour*, heathen, alien, gentile, Nazarene; *esprit fort*, freethinker, latitudinarian, rationalist; materialist, positivist, nihilist, agnostic.

V. be -irreligious etc. *adj.*; disbelieve, lack faith; doubt, question etc. 485.

dechristianize; serve Mammon, love darkness better than light.

Adj. irreligious; in-, un-devout; devout-, god-, grace-less; un-godly, -holy, -sanctified, -hallowed; atheistic, without God.

sceptical, free-thinking, un-believing, -converted; incredulous, faithless, lacking faith; deistical; un-, anti-christian.

worldly, mundane, earthly, carnal, unspiritual; worldly etc.- minded.

Adv. irreligiously etc. *adj.*

990. Worship.—N. worship, adoration, devotion, aspiration, latria, homage, service, humiliation; kneeling, genuflexion, prostration.

prayer, invocation, supplication, rogation, intercession, orison, holy breathing; petition etc. (*request*) 765; collect, litany, Lord's prayer, paternoster, *Ave Maria*, rosary; bead-roll; latria, dulia, hyperdulia, vigils; revival; cult.

thanksgiving; giving —, returning- thanks; grace, praise, glorification, benediction, doxology, hosanna; h-, allelujah; *Te Deum*, *non nobis Domine*, *nunc dimittis*; paean.

psalm, -ody; hymn, plainsong, chant, chaunt, response, anthem, motet; antiphon, -y.

oblation, sacrifice, incense, libation; burnt —, votive —, thank-offering; offertory, collection.

discipline; self-discipline, -examination, -denial; fasting.

divine service, office, duty; morning prayer; mass, matins, evensong, vespers, compline; holy day etc. (*rites*) 998.

worshipper, congregation, communicant, celebrant.

V. worship, lift up the heart, aspire; revere etc. 928; adore, do service, pay homage; humble oneself, kneel; bow —, bend- the knee; fall -down, — on one's knees; prostrate oneself, bow down and worship, recite the rosary.

pray, invoke, supplicate; put —, offer- up -prayers, — petitions; beseech etc. (*ask*) 765; say one's prayers, tell one's beads.

return —, give- thanks; say grace, bless, praise, laud, glorify, magnify, sing praises; give benediction, lead the choir, intone, chant, sing.

propitiate, offer sacrifice, fast, deny oneself; vow, offer vows, give alms.

work out one's salvation; go to church; attend -service, — mass; communicate etc. (*rite*) 998.

Adj. worshipping etc. *v.*; devout, devotional, reverent, pure, solemn; fervid etc. (*heartfelt*) 821.

Int. h-, allelujah! hosanna! glory be to God! O Lord! pray God that! God -grant, - bless, - save, - forbid! *sursum corda.*

991. Idolatry.—N. idol-atry, -ism; demon-ism, -olatry; idol -, demon -, devil -, fire- worship; zoolatry, fetishism, Mari-, Bibli-, ecclesi-, heli-olatry.

deification, apotheosis, canonization; hero worship.

sacrifices, hecatomb, holocaust; human sacrifices, immolation, mactation, infanticide, self-immolation, *suttee.*

idol, golden calf, graven image, fetish, *avatar,* Juggernaut, joss, *lares et penates;* Baal etc. 986. idolator etc. *n.*

V. worship -idols, - pictures, - relics; put on a pedestal, bow down to, prostrate oneself before, make sacrifice to; deify, canonize, idolize.

Adj. idolatrous.

992. Sorcery.—N. sorcery; superstition; occult -art, - sciences; black -, magic; the black art, necromancy, theurgy, thaumaturgy; demon-ology, -omy, -ship; *diablerie,* bedevilment; witch-craft, -ery; glamor; fetis-hism, -ism; ghost dance; hoodoo, voodoo; Shamanism [Esquimaux], vampirism; conjuration; bewitchery, exorcism, enchantment, incantation, obsession, possession, mysticism, second sight, mesmerism, animal magnetism; od -, odylic- force; electro-biology, *clairvoyance';* spiritualism, spirit-rapping, table-turning; thought reading, telepathy, thought transference, automatic writing, *planchette,* ouija board; crystal gazing; spirit manifestation, materialization, astral body, ectoplasm etc.

divination etc. (*prediction*) 511; sortilege, ordeal, *sortes Virgiliance';* hocus-pocus etc. (*deception*) 545; oracle etc. 513.

V. practice -sorcery etc. *n.;* cast a -horoscope, - nativity; conjure, exorcise, charm, enchant; bewitch, -devil; overlook, look on with the evil eye; entrance, mesmerize, magnetize; fascinate etc. (*influence*) 615; taboo; wave a wand; rub the -ring, - lamp; cast a spell; call up spirits, - from the vasty deep; raise spirits from the dead; raise -, lay-ghosts; command genii.

Adj. magic, -al; mystic, weird, cabalistic, talismanic, phylacteric, incantatory; charmed etc. *v.*

993. Spell.—N. spell, charm, incantation, exorcism, weird, cabala, exsufflation, cantrap, runes, abracadabra, hocus-pocus, open *sesame,* counter-charm, Ephesian letters, bell, book and candle, Mumbo-jumbo, evil-eye, fee-faw-fum.

talisman, amulet, periapt, telesm, phylactery, philter, wish-bone, merry-thought, mascot, scarab, swastika; fetish; *agnus Dei.*

wand, caduceus, rod, divining rod, lamp of Aladdin, magic carpet, seven-league boots; magic ring; wishing -, Fortunatus's- cap.

994. Sorcerer.—N. sorcerer, magician; thaumat-, the-urgist; conjuror, necromancer, seer,

wizard, witch; fairy etc. 980; *lamia,* hag, warlock, charmer, exorcist, voodoo, mage, diviner, dowser; cunning | -, , medicine- | man, witch doctor; Shaman, figure-flinger, ecstatica, medium, *clairvoyant,* mesmerist, hypnotist; *deus ex machinâ;* astrologer; soothsayer etc. 513.

Katerfelto, Cagliostro, Merlin, Comus, Mesmer, Rosicrucian; Hecate, Circe, Lilith, siren, weird sisters; witch of Endor.

995. Churchdom.—N. church, -dom; ministry, apostleship, priesthood, prelacy, hierarchy, church government, christendom, pale of the church.

clerical-, sacerdotal-, episcopalian-, ultramontan-ism; Theocracy; ecclesiolog-y, -ist; priestcraft, *odium theologicum.*

monach-ism, -y; monasticism, monkhood.

[Ecclesiastical offices and dignities] pontificate, primacy, archbishopric, archiepiscopacy; prelacy; bishop-ric, -dom; episcop-ate, -acy; see, diocese; deanery, stall; canon-ry, -icate; prebend, -aryship; benefice, incumbency, glebe, advowson, living, cure, - of souls; rectorship; vicar-iate, -ship; pastor-ate, -ship; deacon-ry, -ship; -curacy; chaplain, -cy, -ship; cardinal-ate, -ship; abbacy, presbytery.

holy orders, ordination, institution, consecration, induction, reading in, preferment, translation, presentation.

popedom, papacy; the -Vatican, - apostolic see, - see of Rome; religious sects etc. 984.

council etc. 696; conclave, college of cardinals, convocation, synod, consistory, chapter, vestry, presbytery; sanhedrim, *congé d'élire;* ecclesiastical courts, consistorial court, court of Arches.

V. call, ordain, induct, prefer, translate, consecrate, present, elect, bestow.

take -orders, - the veil, - vows.

Adj. ecclesi-astical, -ological; clerical, sacerdotal, priestly, prelatical, pastoral, ministerial, capitular, theocratic; hierarchical, archiepiscopal; episcopal, -ian; canonical; mon-astic, -achal; monkish; abbati-al, -cal; pontifical, papal, apostolic; untramontane, priest-ridden.

996. Clergy.—N. clergy, clericals, ministry, priesthood, presbytery, the cloth, the pulpit.

clergyman, divine, ecclesiastic, churchman, priest, presbyter, hierophant, pastor, shepherd, minister, clerk in holy orders; father, - in Christ; *padre, abbé, curé;* patriarch; reverend; black coat; confessor; sky pilot.

dignitaries of the church; ecclesi-, hier-arch; eminence, reverence, elder, primate, metropolitan, archimandrite, archbishop, bishop, prelate, diocesan, suffragan, dean, subdean, archdeacon, prebendary, canon, rural dean, rector, parson, vicar, perpetual curate, residentiary, beneficiary, incumbent, chaplain, curate, - in charge; deacon, -ess; preacher; lay reader, lecturer; capitular; missionary, propagandist, Jesuit, revivalist, field preacher.

churchwarden, sidesman; clerk, precentor, choir; almoner, *suisse,* verger, beadle, sexton, sacristan; acol-yth, -othyst, -yte; thurifer; chorister, choir boy.

[Roman Catholic priesthood] Pope, *Papa,* Holy

Father, pontiff, high priest, cardinal; ancient −, flamen; confessor, penitentiary; spiritual director.

cenobite, conventual, abbot, prior, monk, friar, lay brother, beadsman, mendicant, pilgrim, palmer; canon-regular, -secular; Jesuit, Franciscan, Friars minor, Minorites; Observant, Capuchin, Dominican, Carmelite; Augustinian; Gilbertine; Austin-, Black-, White-, Grey-, Crossed-, Crutched- Friars; Bonhomme, Carthusian, Benedictine, Cistercian, Trappist, Cluniac, Premonstratensian, Maturine; Templar, Hospitaller.

abb-, prior-, canon-ess; mother superior; *religieuse*, nun, sister, *beguine*, novice, postulant.

[Under the Jewish dispensation] prophet, priest, high priest, Levite; Rabbi, -n; scribe.

[Mohammedan etc.] mullah, ulema, imauam, sheik; so-fi, -phi; mufti, hadji, muezzin, dervish; fakir, -quir; brahmin, gooroo, druid, bonze, santon, abdal, Lama, talapoin, caloyer etc.

V. take orders etc. 995.

Adj. the −, the very −, the Right- Reverend; ordained, in orders, called to the ministry.

997. Laity.—N. laity, flock, fold, congregation, assembly, brethren, people.

temporality, secularization.

layman, civilian; parishioner, catechumen; secularist.

V. secularize.

Adj. secular, lay, laical, civil, temporal, profane.

998. Rite.—N. rite; ceremon-y, -ial; ordinance, observance, function, duty; form, -ulary; solemnity, sacrament; incantation etc. (*spell*) 993; service, psalmody etc. (*worship*) 990; liturgies.

ministration; preach-ing, -ment; predication, sermon, homily, exhortation, lecture, discourse, pastoral.

baptism, christening, chrism; immersion; baptismal regeneration; font; circumcision.

confirmation; imposition −, laying on- of hands; churching, purification, ordination etc. (*churchdom*) 995; excommunication.

Eucharist, Lord's supper, communion; the −, the holy- sacrament; celebration, high celebration; *missa cantata*; offertory; introit; consecration; con-, tran-substantiation; real presence; elements, bread and wine; mass; high −, low −, dry- mass.

matrimony etc. 903; burial etc. 363; visitation of the sick.

seven sacraments, impanation, extreme unction, last rites, *viaticum*, invocation of saints, canonization, transfiguration, auricular confession; fasting; maceration, flagellation, sackcloth and ashes; penance etc. (*atonement*) 952; absolution; telling of beads, reciting the rosary, processional; thurification, incense, holy water, aspersion.

relics, rosary, beads, reliquary, host, cross, rood, crucifix, pax, pix, pyx, *agnus Dei*, censer, thurible, patera, urceole; chalice, patten, Holy Grail, sangrail; seven-branch candle stick, monstrance, sacring bell.

ritual, rubric, canon, ordinal; liturgy, prayer-book, book of common prayer, pietas, euchology,

litany, lectionary; missal, breviary, mass-book, bead-roll.

psalter; psalm −, hymn- book; hymn-al, -ology; psalmody.

ritual-, ceremonial-ism; sabbat-ism, -arianism; ritualist, sabbatarian.

holyday, feast, fast; Sabbath, Passover, Pentecost; Advent, Christmas, Noel, Epiphany, Lent, Shrove Tuesday, Ash Wednesday, Maundy Thursday; Passion −, Holy- week; Good Friday, Easter, Ascension Day, Whitsuntide; Trinity Sunday, Corpus Christi; All-Saints' −, − Souls'- Day; Candle-, Lam-, Martin-, Michael-mas; hogmanay; Ramadan, -zan; Bairam etc. etc.

V. perform service, do duty, minister, officiate, baptize, dip, sprinkle; confirm, lay hands on; give −, administer −, take −, receive −, attend −, partake of- the -sacrament, − communion; communicate; celebrate mass; administer −, receive-extreme unction; anele, shrive, absolve, confess; do penance; genuflect; cross oneself, make the sign of the cross.

excommunicate, ban with bell, book and candle.

preach, sermonize, predicate, lecture.

Adj. ritual, -istic; ceremonial, liturgic; baptismal, eucharistical; paschal.

999. Canonicals.—N. canonicals, vestments; robe, gown, Geneva gown, frock, pallium, surplice, cassock, dalmatic, scapulary, cope, scarf, tunicle, chasuble, alb, *alba*, stole; fan-oh, -nel; tonsure, cowl, hood; calo-te, -tte; bands; capouch, amice, orarium, ephod; apron, lawn sleeves, pontificals, pall; miter, tiara, triple crown; shovel −, cardinal's- hat; biretta; crosier; pastoral staff; costume etc. 225.

1000. Temple.—N. place of worship; house of -God, − prayer.

temple, cathedral, minister, church, kirk, chapel, meeting-house, bethel, tabernacle, conventicle, *basilica*, fane, holy place, chantry, oratory.

synagogue; mosque; marabout; pantheon; pagoda; joss-house; dagobah, tope; kiosk.

parsonage, rectory, vicarage, manse, deanery, glebe, church house; Vatican; bishop's palace; Lambeth.

altar, shrine, sanctuary, Holy of Holies, *sanctum sanctorum*, sacrarium, -isty; communion −, holy −, Lord's- table; table of the Lord; pyx; baptistery, font; piscina, stoup; aumbry; sedile; reredos; rood-loft, − screen; jube.

chancel, quire, choir, nave, aisle, transept, lady chapel, vestry, crypt, cloisters, porch; triforum, clerestory, churchyard, *golgotha*, calvary, Easter sepulcher; stall, pew, sitting; pulpit, ambo, lectern, reading-desk, confessional, prothesis, credence, baldachin, *baldacchino*; jesse, apse, belfry; chapter-house; presbytery.

monastery, priory, abbey, friary, convent, nunnery, cloister.

Adj. claustral, cloistered; monast-ic, -erial; conventual.

INDEX

The numbers refer to the headings under which the words or phrases occur. When the same word or phrase may be used in various senses, the several headings under which it, or its synonyms, will be found, according to those meanings, are indicated by the words printed in Italics. These words in Italics are not intended to explain the meaning of the word or phrase to which they are annexed, but only to assist in the required reference.

When the word given in the Index is itself the title or heading of a category, the number of reference is printed in blacker type, thus: **abode 189.**

abundanti cautelâ,
ex – 664
abuse *deceive* 545
ill-treat 649
misuse 679
malediction 908
threat 909
upbraid 932
violate 961
– of language 563
– of terms 523
abusive 895, 934
abut *near* 197 *touch*
199, 215
abutment 717
aby *remain* 141
endure 821, 826
abysmal *deep* 208
abyss *space* 180
depth 208
interval 198
danger 667
hell 982
A.C. 106
academic
teaching 537, 542
theory 514
academical
style 578
academicals
225 robes
academician 492
Royal – 559
academy 542
acanthus 847
a capite ad calcem
52
acariâtre 901
acarpous 169
acatalectic 597
acaudal 38
accede 488, 725, 762
accelerate
early 132
stimulate 173
velocity 274
hasten 684
accension 384
accent *sound* 402
tone of voice 580
rhythm 597
accentuate 642
accentuated 580
accept *assent* 488
consent 762
receive 785
take 789
acceptable 646, 829
acceptance 771
acceptation 522
acception 522
access 286
easy of – 705
means of – 627
accessible 470, 705
accession
adjunct 39
increase 35
addition 37
- to office 737, 755
consent 762
accessory
extrinsic 6
additive 37
adjunct 39
accompanying 88
aid 707
auxiliary 711

acciaccatura 413
accidence 567
accident *event* 151
chance 156
disaster 619
misfortune 735
fatal – 361
accidental
extrinsic 6
fortuitous 156
undesigned 621
accidents,
trust to the chap-
ter of – 621
accipient 785
acclamation
assent 488
approbation 931
acclimatize 370, 613
acclivity 217
accloy 641
accolade 894
accommodate
suit 23
adjust 27
aid 707
reconcile 723
give 784
lend 787
– oneself to 82
accommodation
space 180
accommodating
kind 906
accompaniment
adjunct 39
coexistence 88
musical 415
accompany
add 37
coexist 88
concur 120
music 416
accompli, fait – 729
accomplice 711
accomplish
execute 161
complete 729
succeed 731
accomplishment
490, 698
accompts 811
accord
uniform 16
agree 23
music 413
assent 488
concord 714
grant 760
give 784
of one's own – 602
according
– as *qualification*
469
– to *evidence* 467
– to circumstances
8
– to law 963
– to rule
conformably 82
– rumor 527
accordingly
logically 476
accordion 417
accost 586
accoucheur 631, 662
accouchment 161
account *list* 86

adjudge 480
description 594
credit 805
money – 811
fame 873
approbation 931
call to – 932
find one's – in
useful 644
success 731
make no – of 483,
930
not – for 519
on – of *motive* 615
behalf 707
on no – 536
send to one's – 361
take into – 457,
469
small – 643
to one's – 780
turn to –
improve 658
use 677
success 731
gain 775
– as *deem* 484
– book 551
– for 155, 522
– with 794, 807
accountable
liable 177
debit 811
duty 926
accountant 301, 811
certified public –
811
accounts 811
accouple 43
accoutered
armed 717
accouterment
dress 225
appliance 633
equipment 673
accoy 174
accredit
commission 755,
759
money 805
honor 873
accredited 484, 613
– to 755, 759
accretion 35, 46
accrimination 938
accroach 789
accrue *add* 37
result 154
acquire 775
be received 785,
810
accubation 213
accueil 894
accultural 35
accumbent 213
accumulate
collect 72
store 636
redundance 641
accurate 494
– knowledge 490
accurse 908
accursed
disastrous 649
undone 828
vicious 945
accusation 938
accuse

disapprove 932
charge 938
lawsuit 969
accustom 613
ace *small* 32
unit 87
within an – 197
aceldama *kill* 361
arena 728
acephalous 59
acerbate 659, 835
acerbity
acrimony 395
sourness 397
rudeness 895
spleen 900, 901
malevolence 907
acervate 72
acetous 397
acetylene 388
acharné 900
Achates, fidus –
890, 939
ache *physical* 378
mental 828
Acheron
pit of – 982
Acherontic
moribund 360
gloomy 837
achievable 470
achieve *end* 67
produce 161
do 680
accomplish 729
achievement 551,
861
Achilles, heel of –
vulnerable 665
achromatism 429
acicular 253
acid 397
acid test 463
acknowledge
answer 462
assent 488
disclose 529
avow 535
consent 762
observe 772
pay 807
thank 916
repent 950
reward 973
acknowledged
custom 613
acknowledged
acme 210
– of perfection 650
Acology 662
acolyte 996
acomous 226
aconite 663
acoustic 418
– organs 418
acoustics 402
acquaint
– oneself with 539
– with 527
acquaintance
knowledge 490
information 527
friend 890
make – with 888
acquiesce
assent 488
willing 488
consent 762
tolerate 826

acquire
develop 161
get 775
receive 785
– a habit 613
– learning 539
acquirement
knowledge 490
learning 539
talent 698
receipt 810
acquisition
knowledge 490
gain 775
acquit
liberate 750
exempt 927a
vindicate 937
innocent 946
absolve 970
acquit oneself
behave 692
– of a debt 807
– of a duty 926
– of an obligation
772
acquittal 506, 970
acquittance 771
acres *space* 180
land 342
property 780
Acres, Bob 862
acrid 392, 395
acridity 171
acrimony
physical 171
caustic 830
discourtesy 895
hatred 898
anger 900
malevolence 907
acroamatism 490
acrobat
strength 159
actor 599
proficient 700
mountebank 844
Acropolis 210
across 219, 708
acrostic 533, 561,
842
act *imitate* 19
physical 170
- of a play 599
personate 599
voluntary 680
statute 697
in the – 680, 947
– a part *feign* 544
– one's part 625,
926
– upon
physical 170
mental 615
take steps 680
– up to 772
– well one's part
944
– without author-
ity 738
acting *deputy* 759
actinic 420
actinometer 445
action *physical* 170
voluntary 680
battle 720
law 969
line of – 692

put in – 677
suit the – to the
  word 550
thick of the – 682
activate 171
actionable 964
active *physical* 171
  voluntary 682
  – *service* 722
  – *thought* 457
activity 682
actor
  impostor 548
  player 599
  agent 690
  affectation 855
Acts *record* 551
  Apostolic 985
actual *existing* 1
  present 118
  real 494
actuary 85, 811
actuate 176, 615
actum est 729
acu tetigisti, rem
  465, 494
acuity 253
aculeated 253
acumen 498
acuminated 253
acupuncture 260
acustics 402
acute *energetic* 171
  physically violent
    173
  pointed 253
  physically sensible
    375
  musical tone 410
  perspicacious 498
  cunning 702
  strong feeling 821
  morally painful
    830
  – *angle* 244
  – *ear* 418
  – *note* 410
acutely 31
acuteness 465
ad
  – *eundem* 27
  – *hominem* 79
  – *infinitum* 105
  – *instar* 82
  – *interim* 106
  – *lib* 705
  – *rem* 23
A.D. 106
adage 496
adagio *music* 415
  slow 275
Adam *sin* 945
  – 's *apple* 250
adamant 159, 323
adapt 23, 27
  – *oneself to* 82
adaptable
  conformable 82
  useful 644
add *increase* 35
  join 37
  numerically 85
  – *up* 811
addendum 39
adder 913
addict *habit* 613
adding machine 85
additament 39

addition
  extrinsical 6
  increase 35
  adjunction **37**
  thing added 39
  arithmetical 85
addle *barren* 169
  incomplete 730
  abortive 732
  – *the wits*, 475, 503
addlehead 501
addleheaded 499
address
  residence 189
  direction 550
  speech 582
  speak to 586
  skill 698
  request 765
  – *oneself to* 673
addresses
  courtship 902
addressful 894
adduce
  bring to 288
  evidence 467
addulce 834
ademption 789
adenoid 250
adenology 329
adept 700
adequate *power* 157
  sufficient 639
  for a purpose 644
adhere *stick* 46
  – *to* 604a, 613
  – *to an obligation*
    772
  – *to a duty* 926
adherent
  follower 711
adhesive, 46, 327,
  352
adhibit 677
adhortation 695
adieu *departure* 293
  loss 776
adipocere 356
adipose 355
adit *orifice* 260
  conduit 350
  passage 627
adjacent 197
adjection 37
adjective 39
adjoin 197, 199
adjourn 133
adjudge 480
adjudicate 480
adjunct
  thing added **39**
  accompaniment 88
  aid 707
  auxiliary 711
adjuration 535, 536
adjure 765, 768
adjust *adapt* 23
  equalize 27
  order 58
  prepare 673
  settle 723, 762
  – *differences* 774
adjutage 260, 350
adjutant
  auxiliary 711
  military 745
adjuvant *helping*
  707

auxiliary 711
admeasurement
  466
adminicle 467
administer
  utilize 677
  conduct 693
  exercise authority
    737
  distribute 786
  – *correction* 972
  – *oath* 768
  – *sacrament* 998
  – *to aid* 707
  give 784
administration of
  justice 965
administrative 737,
  965
administrator 694
admirable 648, 744
admiral 745
Admiralty, court of
  – 966
admirari, nil – 871,
  932
admiration
  wonder 870
  love 897
  respect 928
  approval 931
admired disorder 59
admirer 897
admissible
  relevant 23
  receivable 296
  tolerable 651
  – *in society* 852
admit
  composition 54
  include 76
  let in 296
  assent 488
  acknowledge 529
  permit 760
  concede 762
  accept 785
  – *exceptions* 469
  – *of* 470
admitted
  customary 613
  – *maxim &c.* 496
admixture 41
admonish
  warn 668
  advise 695
  reprove 932
ado *activity* 682
  exertion 686
  difficulty 704
  make much –
    about 542
  much – *about*
    nothing
  overestimate 482
  unimportant 643
  unskilful 699
adolescence **131**
Adonis 845
adonize 847
adopt
  naturalize 184
  choose 609
  – *a cause aid* 707
  – *a course* 692
  – *an opinion* 484
adoption
  religious 987

adore 897, 990
adorn 847
adown 207
adrift *unrelated* 10
  disjoined 44
  dispersed 73
  uncertain 475
  unapt 699
  free 750
  go – *deviate* 279
  turn – *disperse* 73
  liberate 750
  dismiss 756
adroit 698
adscititious
  extrinsic 6
  added 37
  redundant 641
adscriptus glebae
  746
adulation 933
adulator 935
adult 131
adulterate *mix* 41
  deteriorate 659
adulterated 545
adulterer 962
adultery 961
adumbrate
  darkness 421
  allegorize 521
  represent 554
adumbration
  semblance 21
  allusion 526
aduncity 244, 245
adust
  color 433
  gloomy 837
adustion 384
advance *increase* 35
  course 109
  progress 282
  assert 535
  improve 658
  aid 707
  succeed 731
  lend 787
  in – *precedence* 62
  front 234
  precession 280
  in – *of* 33
  in – *of one's age*
    498
  – *against* 716
  – *of learning &c.*
    490
advanced 282
  – *in life* 128
  – *guard* 234
  – *student* 541
  – *work* 717
advances, make –
  offer 763
  social 892
advantage
  superiority 33
  influence 175
  good 618
  expedience 646
  mechanical – 633
  dressed to – 847
  find one's – *in* 644
  gain an – 775
  set off to – 658

take – *of* 677, 698
  – *over success* 731
advantageous
  beneficial 648
  profitable 775
advene 37
advent
  futurity 121
  event 151
  approach 286
  arrival 292
Advent 998
adventism 984
adventitious 6, 156
adventive 156
adventure *event* 151
  chance 156
  pursuit 622
  danger 665
  trial 675
  the great – 360
adventurer
  traveler 268
  deceiver 548
  experimenter 463
  gambler 621
  rash 863
  ignoble 876
adventures 594
adventurous
  undertaking 676
  bold 861
  rash 863
adversaria 551
adversary 710
adverse
  contrary 14
  opposed 708
  unprosperous 735
  disliking 867
  – *party* 710
adversity 735
advert 457
advertise 531
advice *notice* 527
  news 532
  counsel 695
advisable 646
advise *predict* 511
  inform 527
  counsel 695
  – *with one's pillow*
    451
advised *predeter-*
  mined 611
  intended 620
  better – 658
adviser 540, 695
advocacy 931
advocate
  prompt 615
  recommend 695
  aid 707
  auxiliary 711
  friend 890
  vindicate 937
  counsellor 968
Advocate, the – 976
advocation 617
advoutress 962
advoutry 961
advowson 995
adynamic 160
adytum *room* 191
  prediction 511
  secret place 530
adze 253
adzooks 870

aidless 160
aigrette 847
aiguille 253
aiguillette 747, 847
aigulet 847
ail 655, 828
aileron 267, 273
ailment 655
aim 278, 620, 675
 - a blow at 716
aimable 894
 faire l' — 897
aimer éperdument
 897
aimless *without*
 motive 615a
 chance 621
air *unsubstantial* 4
 broach 66
 lightness 320
 gas 334
 atmospheric **338**
 wind 349
 tune 415
 appearance 448
 refresh 689
 demeanor 692
 fashionable 852
 beat the — 645
 fill the — 404
 fine — *salubrity* 656
 fish in the — 645
 fowls of the — 366
 in the — 527
 rend the — 404
 take — 531
air-balloon 273
air base 728
air-commodore 745
aircraft 273, 726
air-drawn 515
airdrome 273
air-force 726
air-gun 727
airing 266
air-mail 273
airman 269
airmanship 698
air-marshal 745
air-passage 351
air-pipe **351**
airport 273, 292,
 728
air-pump 349
air-raid 716
airs *affectation* 855
 pride 878
 vanity 880
 arrogance 885
air-shaft 351
air service 267
airship 273, 726
air-tight 261
airways 267
airworthy 273, 664
airy [*see air*]
 windy 349
 unimportant 643
 gay 836
 - hopes 858, 859
 give to — nothing
  a local habita-
  tion &c. 515
aisle *passage* 260
 way 627
 in a church 1000
ait 346
ajar *open* 260

discordant 713
ajee 217
ajutage 260, 350
akimbo *angular* 244
 stand — 715
akin *related* 9
 *consanguineous*11
 similar 17
al fresco 220
alabaster *white* 430
alack! 839
alacrity *willing* 602
 active 682
 cheerful 836
Aladdin's lamp 993
alar 267
alarm *warning* 668
 notice of danger
  669
 fear 860
 cause for — 665
 give an — *indicate*
  550
alarmist 862
alarum 114, 550, 669
alas! 839
alate 267
alb 999
albeit 30
albert
 chain 847
albification 430
albinescence 430
albinism 430
albino 443
album 593, 596
albumen
 semi-liquid 352
 protein 357
Alcaic 597
alcaid 745
alcalde 745
alcazar 189
alchemy 144
alcohol 995
Alcoran 986
alcove 191, 252
Aldebaran 423
alderman 745
ale 298
alea, jacta est—601
aleatory 665
Alecto 173
alectromancy 511
alehouse 189
 go to the — 959
alembic
 conversion 144
 vessel 191
 furnace 386
 laboratory 691
alentours 197
alert *watchful* 457,
 459
 active 682
alerte 669
aleuromancy 511
Alexandrine
 ornate style 577
 verse 597
alexandrite 848
alexipharmic 662
alexiteric 662
algebra 85
algid 383
algology 369
algorithm 85
alguazil 965

alias
 otherwise 18
 pseudonym 565
alibi 187
alien *irrelevant* 10
 foreign 57
 transfer 783
 gentile 989
alienable 783
alienate
 transfer 783
 estrange 44, 889
 set against 898
alienation
 mental — 503
alieni appetens
 grasping 865
 envious 921
 selfish 943
alienism 54
align 278
alight *stop* 265
 arrive 292
 descend 306
 on fire 382
alike 17
 share and share —
  778
aliment *food* 298
alimentary 662
 - canal 350
alimentation
 aid 707
alimony
 property 780
 provision 803
 income 810
aliquot 51, 84
aliter visum, diis —
 601
alive
 living 359
 intelligent 498
 active 682
 cheerful 836
 be — with 102
 keep — *continue*
  143
 keep the memory
  — 505
 look — 684
 - to *attention* 457
 cognizant 490
 informed 527
 able 698
 sensible 822
alkahest 335
all *whole* 50
 complete 52
 generality 78
 - absorbing 642
 in - ages 112
 - aboard 495
 - agog 865
 - in all 50
 - along 106
 - along of 154
 - but 32
 - colors 440
 - considered 451,
  480
 - day long 110
 - devouring 190
 in - directions 278
 - engrossing 190
 at - events *com-
  pensation* 30
 qualification 469

true 494
 resolve 604
 - fours *easy* 705
 cards 840
 - in good time 152
 - hail! *welcome* 292
 honor to 873
 celebration 883
 courtesy 894
 - hands *everybody*
  78
 on - hands 488
 - of a dither 824
 - of a heap 72
 - knowing 976
 - manner of *differ-
  ence* 15
 multiform 81
 with - one's might
  686
 - at once 113
 - one 27, 866
 - out 52
 - over *end* 67
 universal 78
 destruction 162
 space 180
 at - points 52
 - in one's power
  686
 - powerful
  mighty 159
 God 976
 in - quarters 180
 with - respect 928
 in - respects 52,
  494
 - right! 922
 - Saints' day 998
 - searching 461
 - seeing 976
 on - sides 227
 - sorts *diverse* 16a
 mixed 41
 multiform 81
 - talk 4
 - things to all
  men 894
 - the time 106
 at - times 136
 - together 50
 - ways 243, 279
 - wise 976
 - the world and
  his wife 78
 - of - work
  useful 644
 maid - 746
Allah 979
allay
 moderate 174
 pacify 723
 relieve 834
 - excitability 826
allective 615
allege *evidence* 467
 assert 535
 plea 617
allegiance 743, 926
allegory 464, 521,
 594
allegro *music* 415
 cheerful 836
allelujah 990
allemande 840
all-embracing 76
alleviate 174, 834
alley *court* 189

passage 26
 way 627
alliance *relation* 9
 kindred 11
 *physical co-opera-
  tion* 178
 *voluntary co-oper-
  ation* 709
 party 712
 union 714
allied to *like* 17
alligation 43
allign 278
alliteration
 similarity 17
 style in writing
  577
 poetry 597
allocation 60, 786
allocution **586**
allodium *free* 748
 property 780
allopathy 662
alloquy 586
allot *arrange* 60
 distribute 786
 due 924
allow *assent* 488
 admit 529
 permit 760
 consent 762
 give 784
 - to have one's
  own way 740
allowable 760, 924
allowance
 qualification 469
 gift 784
 allotment 786
 discount 813
 salary 973
 with grains of -
  485
 make - for *forgive*
  918
 vindicate 937
alloy *mixture* 41
 combination 48
 debase 659
allude *hint* 514
 mean 516
 refer to 521
 latent 526
 inform 527
allure *move* 615
 create desire 865
alluring 829
allusive
 relative 9
alluvial *level* 213
 land 342
 plain 344
alluvium
 deposit 40
 land 342
 soil 653
ally *combine* 48
 auxiliary 711
 friend 891
alma mater 542
almanac
 list 86
 chronometry 114
 record 551
almighty 157
Almighty, the — 976
almoner
 treasurer 801

giver 784
 church officer 996
almonry 802
almost nearly 32
 not quite 651
 - all 50
 - immediately 132
alms gift 784
 benevolence 906
 worship 990
almshouse 189, 666
almsman 785
Alnaschar's dream
 . 515, 858
aloes 395
aloft 206
alogy 497
alone single 87
 unaided 706
 let - not use 678
 not restrain 748
along 200
 get - progress 282
 go - depart 293
 go - with concur
 178
 assent 488
 co-operate 709
 - of caused by 154
 - with added 37
 together 88
 by means of 631
alongside near 197
 parallel 216
 laterally 236
aloof distant 196
 high 206
 secluded 893
 stand - inaction
 681
 refuse 764
 cautious 864
alopecia 226
aloud 404
 think - 589
 naiveté 703
Alp 206
alpenstock 215
Alpha 66
 - and Omega 50
alphabet
 beginning 66
 letters 561
alphabetarian 541
alphabeticize 60
alphitomancy 511
alpine high 206
Alpine Club 268, 305
already
 antecedently 116
 even now 118
 past time 122
Alsatia 791, 945
also 37
altar 903, 1000
alter 140
 - the case 468
 - one's course 279
alter ego similar 17
 auxiliary 711
 deputy 759
 friend 890
alterable 149
alteram partem,
 audire–468, 922
alterative
 substitute 634
 remedy 662

altercation 713
altered worn 688
 - for the worse 659
alternate
 reciprocal 12
 sequence 63
 discontinuous 70
 periodic 138
 changeable 149
 oscillate 314
alternative
 substitute 147
 choice 609
 plan 626
although
 compensation 30
 counteraction 179
 unless 469
altiloquence 577
altimetry
 height 206
 angle 244
 measurement 466
altitude height 206
 - and azimuth 466
alto 410, 416
 - part 415
alto-rilievo 250, 557
altogether 50, 51
 nude 226
altruism 910, 942
altruist 906
alum 397
alumnus 541
alveolus 252
always
 uniformly 16
 generally 78
 during 106
 perpetually 112
 habitually 613
a.m. 114, 125
amability 829, 894
amah 753
amain 173, 684
amalgam, -ate 41,
 48
amalgamation 709
Amalthea's horn
 639
amantium iræ 918
amanuensis 553,
 590
amaranthine 112
amari aliquid
 bad 649
 imperfect 651
 painful 830
amaritude 395
amass whole 50
 collect 72
 store 636
amateur volunteer
 602
 layman 699
 taste 850
 votary 865
amatory 897
amaurosis 442
amaze 870
amazingly 31
Amazon
 woman 374
 warrior 726
 courage 861
ambages
 convolutions 248
 circumlocution

573
 circuit 629
ambagious 573
ambassador
 messenger 534
 representative 758
 recall of -s 713
amber 356a
 - color 436
ambidexter
 right and left 238
 fickle 607
 clever 698
ambient 227
ambigu 41
ambiguas spargere
 voces
 uncertain 475
 misteach 538
 false 544
 cunning 702
ambiguous
 uncertain 475
 unintelligible 519
 equivocal 520
 obscure 571
ambiloquy 520
ambit 230
ambition 620, 865
ambivalence 605,
 708
amble 266
ambo school 542
 pulpit 1000
ambo, Arcades -
 alike 17
 friends 890
 bad men 949
ambrosia 298
ambrosial 394, 490
ambulance
 vehicle 272
 hospital 662
ambulation 266
ambuscade 530
ambush 530, 667
 lie in - 528
âme - de boue 949
 - damnée
 catspaw 711
 servant 746
 servile 886
 bad man 949
 - qui vive 101, 187
ameer 875
ameliorate 658
amen assent 488
 submission 725
 content 831
amenable 177, 602,
 926
 not - to reason 608
amend 658
amendatory 20
amende honorable
 952
amends
 compensation 50
 atonement 952
 reward 973
amenity 829, 894
amentia 503
amerce 974
American organ 417
Americanism 563
amethyst
 purple 437
 jewel 847

amiable
 courteous 894
 loving 897
 kind 906
amicable 707, 888
amice 999
amicus – curiæ 527
 - humani generis
 910
 - usque ad aras
 890
amidships 68
amidst 41, 228
amiss 619
 come - disagree 24
 mistime 135
 inexpedient 647
 do - 945
 nothing comes -
 823
 take - 867, 900
amity concord 714
 peace 721
 friendship 888
ammunition 635,
 727
amnesia 506
amnesty 506, 723,
 918
amnis, rusticus ex-
 pectat dum de-
 fluat - hope 858
amœbæan 63
amok 503
among 41, 228
amor patriæ 910
amore, con – 602,
 821
amoroso 599
amorous 897
 - glances 902
amorphous 83, 241
amorphism 241
amortization 784
amotion 270
amount
 quantity 25
 degree 26
 sum of money 800
 price 812
 gross – 50
 - to 27, 85
amour 897, 961
 - propre 880
ampere 466
amphibian 366
amphibious 83
amphibology 520
Amphictyonic
 council 696
amphigouri 497
amphitheatre
 prospect 441
 school 542
 theater 599
 arena 728
Amphitryon 890
amphora 191
ample much 31
 spacious 180
 large 192
 broad 202
 copious 639
amplify
 expand 194
 exaggerate 549
 diffuse style 573
amplitude

quantity 25
 degree 26
 size 192
 breadth 202
 enough 639
ampoulé 191
ampulla 191
amputate 38
amuck 824
 run - 503
amulet 247, 993
amusare la bocca,
 per - 394
amuse 829, 840
amusement 840
 place of - 840
amussim, ad - 494
amylaceous 352
an if 514
ana 594
Anabaptist 984
anabasis 35
anachronism
 false time 115
 inopportune 135
 error 495
anacoluthon 70
anaconda 913
anacreontic 597
anaglyph 554, 557
anagoge 521, 526
anagram
 double sense 520
 secret 533
 letter 561
 .wit 842
analecta 596
analeptic 662
analgesia 376
analogy 9, 17
analogous 12
analysis
 decomposition 49
 arrangement 60
 algebra 85
 inquiry 461
 experiment 463
 reasoning 476
 grammar 567
 compendium 596
analyst 461, 463
anamorphosis
 distortion 243
 optical 443
 misrepresentation
 555
anapest 597
anaphylaxis 375
anarchist
 destroyer 165
 disobedient 742
 evil-doer 913
anarchy 59, 738
anastatic printing
 558
anastomosis 43, 219
anastrophe 218
anathema 908
anathematize 908
 censure 932
 detract 934
anatomize dissect 44
 investigate 461
anatomy
 dissection 44
 leanness 203
 texture 329
anatomy

science 357
comparative – 368
anatriptic 331
ancestral
  bygone 122
  old 124
  aged 128
ancestry 166
anchor
  connection 45
  stop 265
  safeguard 666
  badge 747
  hope 858
  at – *fixed* 150
  stationed 184
  safe 664
  cast – *settle* 184
  arrive 292
  have an – to wind-
    ward 664
  sheet – *means* 632
anchorage
  location 184
  roadstead 189
  refuge 866
anchored 150
anchorite 893, 955
ancien régime 875
ancient *old* 124
  flag 550
  – *times* 122
ancientness 122
ancillary 707
and 37, 88
andante 415
andiron 386
androgynous 83
anecdote 594
anele 998
anemia 160
anemography 349
ἀνεμώλια βάζειν 497
anemometer
  wind 349
  measure 466
anent 9
aneroid 338
anesthesia 376,
  381, 683
anew *again* 104
  newly 123
anfractuosity 248
angel
  object of love 897
  good person 948
  supernatural
    being 977
  fallen –
    bad man 949
    devil 978
  guardian –
    safety 664
    auxiliary 711
    benefactor 912
  – of Death 362
  – 's visits 137
angelic 944
angels and minis-
  ters of grace de-
  fend us! 860
angelus 550
anger 900
  more in sorrow
    than in – 826,
    918
angiology 329
angle 244

try 463
  at an – 217
Anglicanism 984
angling 622, 840
anguille au genou,
  rompre l' – 158,
  471
anguilliform 205,
  248
anguis in herbâ 667
anguish
  physical 378
  moral 828
angular 244
  – *velocity* 264
angularity 244
angusta domi, res
  – 804
angustation 203
anhelation 688
anhydrate 340
anhydrous 340
aniline dyes 437
anility 128, 499
animadvert
  consider 451
  attend to 457
  reprehend 932
animal 366
  female – 374
  – cries 412
  – economy 359
  – gratification 377
  – life 364
  – physiology 368
  – spirits 836
  – and vegetable
    kingdom 357
animalcule 193, 366
animalism
  sensuality 954
animality 364
animate
  induce 615
  excite 824
  enliven 836
animation
  life 359
  animality 364
  activity 682
  vivacity 836
  suspended – 823
animism 984
animo, ex – 602
  quo – 620
animosity
  dislike 867
  enmity 889
  hatred 898
  anger 900
animus
  willingness 602
  intention 620
  desire 865
ankle 244
  – deep 208, 209
anklet 847
ankylosis 150
annalist 114, 553
annals
  chronology 114
  record 551
  account 594
anneal 673
annex
  addition 37
  adjunct 39
  junction 43

acquire 775
Annie Oakley 815
annihilate 2, 162
anniversary 138
anno 106
Anno Domini
  era 106
  old age 124
annotation 522, 550
annotator 524
  scholar 492
  interpreter 524
  editor 595
annotto 434
announce
  predict 511
  inform 527
  publish 531
  assert 535
announcer 527
annoy
  molest 649, 907
  disquiet 830
annoyance 828
  source of – 830
annual *periodic* 138
  plant 367
  book 593
annuity 810
annul 162, 750
annular 247
annunciate 527
annus magnus 108
anodyne
  lenitive 174
  remedial 662
  relief 834
anoint *coat* 223
  lubricate 332
  oil 355
anointed
  deity 976
  king 745
anomaly 59, 83
  disorder 59
  irregularity 83
anon 132
anonymous 565
anopsia 442
anorexy 866
another
  different 15
  repetition 104
  – story 468, 526
  go upon – tack 607
  – time 119
answer
  to an inquiry 462
  confute 479
  solution 522
  succeed 731
  pecuniary profit
    775
  pleadings 969
  require an – 461
  – for *deputy* 759
  promise 768
  go bail 806
  I'll – for it 535
  – the helm 745
  – the purpose 731
  – to correspond 9
  – one's turn 644
answerable
  agreement 23
  liable 177
  bail 806
  duty 926

censurable 932
ant 690
Antaeus 159, 192
antagonism
  difference 14
  physical 179
  voluntary 708
  enmity 889
antagonist 710, 891
antagonistic 24
antarctic 237
antecedence 62, 116
antecedent 64
antechamber 191
ante Christum 106
antedate 115
antediluvian 124
antelope 274
antemundane 124
antenna 379
anteposition 62
anterior
  in order 62
  in time 116
  in place 234
  – to *reason* 477
anteroom 191
antevert 706
anthem 990
anthemion 847
anthology
  book 533
  collection 596
  poem 597
anthracite 388
anthropoid 372
anthropology
  zoology 368
  mankind 372
anthropomancy 511
anthropophagi 913
anthroposcopy 511
anthroposophy 372
antic 840
anti-aircraft gun
  564, 727
antichambre,
  faire – 133
antichristian 984,
  989
antichronism 115
anticipate
  anachronism 115
  priority 116
  future 121
  early 132
  expect 507
  foresee 510
  prepare 673
  hope 858
  in – 116
anticlimax
  decrease 36
  bathos 497, 853
anticlinal 217
anticyclone 265
antidote 662
antigropelos 225
antilogarithm 84
antilogy 477
antimony 663
Antinomian 984
antinomy 964
Antinous 845
antiparallel 217
antipathy 867, 898
antiphon *music* 415
  answer 462

worship 990
antiphrasis 563
antipodes
  difference 14
  distance 196
  contraposition
    237
antipoison 660
antiquary
  past times 122
  scholar 492
  historian 553
antiquas vias,
  stare super –
  613, 670
antiquated 128
antique 124
antiquity 122
antiscriptural 984
antiseptic 652, 662
antisocial 911
antistrophe 597
antithesis
  contrast 14
  difference 15
  opposite 237
  style 574, 577
antitoxin 662
antitype 22
antler 253
antonomasia
  metaphor 521
  nomenclature 564
antonym 14
antrum 252
anvil *support* 215
  on the –
  intended 620
  in hand 625
  preparing 673
anxiety *pain* 828
  fear 860
  desire 865
anxious expectation
  507
any *some* 25
  part 51
  no choice 609a
  at – *price* 604a
  at – *rate*
  certain 474
  true 494
  at all hazards 604
anybody 78
anyhow 460, 627
anything one
  knows, for – 491
aorist 109, 119
aorta 350
apace *early* 132
  swift 274
apache 913
apart 44, 87
  set – 636
  wide – 196
apartment 191
  –s 189
  –s to let
  imbecile 499
apathetic 275
apathy
  indifference 465
  insensibility 823
  irreligion 989
ape *imitate* 19
Apelles 559
aperçu 596
aperture 260

arctic *northern* 237
  cold 383
arctics 225
arcuation 245
ardent *fiery* 382
  eager 682
  feeling 821
  loving 897
  — expectation 507
  — imagination 515
ardet, proximus —
  665, 667
ardor *vigor* 574
  activity 821
  feeling 821
  desire 865
arduous 704
area 181, 182
arefaction 340
arena *space* 180
  region 181
  field of view 441
  field of battle 728
arenaceous 330
areola 247
areolar 219
areometer 321
Areopagus 966
arête 253
aretinism 961
aretology 926
Argand lamp 423
argent 430
argillaceous 324
argosy 273
argot 563
argonaut 269
argue *evidence* 467
  reason 476
  indicate 550
  dissectation 595
argument *disagree-
  ment* 24
  topic 454
  discussion 476
  meaning 516
  have the best of
   an — 478
argumentum
  — baculinum
   compel 744
   lawless 964
   punish 972
  — ad crumenam
   800
  — ad hominem
   reasoning 476
   accuse 938
  — ad verecundiam
   939
Argus-eyed 441, 459
argute 498
aria 415
arianism 984
arid 340
  unproductive 169
  uninteresting 841
Ariel *courier* 268
  swift 274
  messenger 534
  spirit 979
arietation 276
arietta 415
aright *well* 618
Ariman [*see* Ahri-
  manes]
ariolation 511
arioso 415

aris et focis, pro —
  defence 717
  philanthropy 910
arise *exist* 1
  begin 66
  happen 151
  mount 305
  appear 446
  — from 154
Aristarchus 850
Aristides
  good man 948
aristocracy
  power 737
  fashion 852
  nobility 875
ἄριστον μέτρον 628
Arithmancy 511
arithmetic 85
ark *abode* 189
  asylum 666
arm *part* 51
  power 157
  instrument 633
  provide 637
  prepare 673
  war 722
  weapon 727
  make a long — 200
  — chair 215
  — in arm
   together 88
   friends 888
   sociable 892
  — of the law 963
  — of the sea 343
armada 726
Armageddon 720,
  722
armament 673, 727
armed 717
  — at all points 673
  — force 726
  — guard 664
armet 717
armful 25
armiger 875
armigerent 726
armigerous 722
armilla 247, 847
armillary sphere
  466
armipotent 157
armistice
  cessation 142
  respite 672
  pacification 723
armless 158
armlet *ring* 247
  gulf 343
armored
  — car 726
  — cruiser 726
  — train 726
armorial bearings
  550, 877
armory *store* 636
  workshop 691
arm's length
  at — 196
  keep at —

repel 289
  defence 717
  enmity 889
  seclusion 893
  discourtesy 895
arms 727 [*see* arm]
  heraldry 550
  war 722
  honors 877
  clash of — 720
  deeds of — 720
  with folded — 681
  in — *infant* 129
  throw oneself into
   the — of 666, 880
  under — 722
  up in — *active* 682
  discord 713
  resistance 719
  resentment 900
  enmity 889
Armstrong gun 727
army *collection* 72
  multitude 102
  troops 726
aroma 400
around 227
  lie — 220
arouse *move* 615
  excite 824
  — oneself 682
aroynt *begone* 297
  malediction 908
arquebusade 662
arquebuse 727
arraign 938, 969
arrange
  set in order 60
  plan 626
  compromise 774
  — with creditors
   807
  — itself 58
arrange — matters
  pacify 723
  — music 413, 416
  — in a series 69
  — under 76
arrangement 23, 60
  [*see* arrange]
  order 58
  temporary — 111
arrant *identical* 31
  manifest 525
  notorious 531
  bad 649
  disreputable 874
  base 940
arras 847
array *order* 58, 60
  series 69
  assemblage 72
  multitude 102
  dress 225
  prepare 673
  adorn 847
  ostentation 882
  battle — 722
arrear, in — 53, 808
arrears *debt* 806
arrectis auribus
  hear 418
  expect 507
arrest *stop* 142
  restrain 751
  in law 969
  — the attention 457
arrière-pensée

after-thought 65
  mental reservation
   528
  motive 615
  set purpose 620
arrival 292
arrive *happen* 151
  reach 292
  complete 729
  — at a conclusion
   480
  — at the truth 480a
arrogant *severe* 739
  proud 878
  insolent 885
arrogate 885, 924
  — to oneself
   undue 925
arrondissement 181
arrosion 331
arrow *swift* 274
  missile 284
  arms 727
  broad — 550
arrow-head
  form 253
  writing 590
'Arry and 'Arriet
  902
ars celare artem
  698
arsenal *store* 636
  workshop 661
arsenic 663
arson 384
art *representation*
  554
  business 625
  skill 698
  cunning 702
  fine — 850
  work of — 845, 847
  — gallery 556
artery 350, 627
artes, hae tibi
  erunt — 627
artesian well 343
artful 544, 702
  — dodge 545, 702
article *thing* 3
  part 51
  matter 316
  chapter 593
  review 595
  goods 798
articled clerk 541
articles
  thirty-nine — 983a
  — of agreement
   770
  — of faith 484, 983
articulate 366
articulation
  junction 43
  speech 580
articulo, in —
  transient 111
  dying 360
artifice 626, 702
artificer 690
artificial
  fictitious 545
  cunning 702
  affected 855
  — language 579
artillery
  explosion 404
  arms 727

artilleryman 726
artisan 690
artist *painter* &c.
  559
  contriver 626
  agent 690
artiste *music* 416
  drama 599
artistic *skilful* 698
  beautiful 845
  taste 850
  — language 578
artlessness **703**
aruspex 513
aruspicy 511
arundo, haeret
  lateri lethalis —
  828
as *motive* 615
  — broad as long 27
  — can be 52
  — good as 27
  — if *similar* 17
  suppose 514
  — little as may be
   32
  — it may be
  circumstance 8
  event 151
  chance 156
  — much again 90
  — soon as 120
  — they say 496, 532
  — things are 7
  — things go 151,
   613
  — to 9
  — usual 82
  — it were 17, 521
  — you were 141,
   283
  — well as 37
  — the world wags
   151
ascend *be great* 31
  increase 35
  rise 305
  improve 658
ascendancy
  power 157
  influence 175
  success 731
ascendant
  lord of the — 745
  in the —
  influence 175
  important 642
  success 731
  authority 737
  repute 873
  one's star in the —
  prosperity 734
ascension
  [*see* ascend]
  calefaction 384
  — Day 998
ascent
  [*see* ascend]
  gradient 217
  rise **305**
  glory 873
ascertain *fix* 150
  determine 480
ascertained 474,
  490
ascertainment 480a
asceticism **955**
ascititious

intrinsic 6
additional 37
supplementary 52
ascribe 155
aseptic 652
ash 384
  – colored 432
  – blond 430
ashen 429
  Ash Wednesday
    998
ashamed 879
ashes *corpse* 362
  dirt 653
  lay in – 162
  pale as – 429, 860
  rise from one's –
    660
ashore 342
  go – *arrive* 292
ashy 429
Asian mystery 533
aside *laterally* 236
  whisper 405
  private 528
  say – 589
  set &c. – *displace*
    185
  neglect 460
  negative 536
  reject 610
  disuse 678
  abrogate 756
  discard 782
  step – 279
asinine *ass* 271
  fool 499
ask *inquire* 461
  request 765
  for sale 794
  price 812
  – leave 760
askance 217
  eye – *fear* 860
  look – *vision* 441,
    443
  dissent 489
  dislike 867
  disapproval 932
askari 726
asked in church 903
askew 217, 243
aslant 217
asleep 683
aslope 217
Asmodeus 980
asomatous 317
asp *animal* 366
  evil-doer 913
Aspasia 962
aspect *feature* 5
  state 7
  situation 183
  appearance 448
aspen leaf
  shake like an –
    315, 860
asperity
  roughness 256
  discourtesy 895
  anger 900
  irascibility 901
asperse 934
aspersion
  malediction 908
  rite 998
asphalt
  smooth 255

resin 356a
  material 635
asphodel 845
aspic 352
asphyxia 360
asphyxiate 361
aspirant 767, 865
aspirate 580
aspirator 349
aspire *rise* 305
  hope 858
  desire 865
  worship 990
aspirin 834
asportation 270
asquint 217
ass *beast of burden*
  271
  fool 501
  make an – of
    delude 545
  – between two
    bundles of
    hay 605
  –'s bridge 519
  – in lion's skin
    cheat 548
  bungler 701
assafetida 401
assagai 727
assail 716, 830
assailant 710, 726
assassin, –ate 361
assault 716, 961
  take by – 789
assay 463
asseguay 727
assemblage 72
assembly
  council 696
  society 892
  religious 997
assembly hall 588
assembly room 189
assent *belief* 484
  agree 488
  willing 602
  consent 762
  content 831
assert 535, 924
assess *measure* 466
  determine 480
  tax 812
assessor
  judge 967
assets 780, 800
asseverate 535
assiduity 110
assiduous 682
assign
  commission 755
  transfer 270, 783
  give 784
  allot 786
  – as cause 155
  – a duty 926
  – places 60
assignat 800
assignation 892
  place of – 74
assignee *donee* 785
assimilate
  uniform 16
  resemble 17
  imitate 19
  agree 23
  transmute 144
assist 707

– at 186
assistant 711
assister *be present*
  186
assize *measure* 466
  tribunal 966
  justice of – 967
associate *mix* 41
  unite 43
  collect 72
  accompany 88
  colleague 690
  auxiliary 711
  friend 890
  – with 892
association
  [*see* associate]
  relation 9
  combination 48
  co-operation 709
  partnership 712
  – of ideas
    intellect 450
    thought 451
    intuition 477
    hint 514
  – football 840
assoil *acquit* 970
assonance
  music 413
  poetry 597
assort *arrange* 60
assortment 72, 75
assuage 174, 834
assuetude 613
assume *believe* 484
  suppose 514
  falsehood 544
  take 789
  insolent 885
  right 924
  – authority 737
  – a character 554
  – command 741
  – a form 144
  – the offensive 716
assumed name 565
assumption
  [*see* assume]
  severity 739
  hope 858
  usurpation 925
assurance
  speculation 156
  certainty 474
  belief 484
  assertion 535
  promise 768
  security 771
  hope 858
  vanity 880
  insolence 885
  make – double
    sure *safe* 664
  caution 864
assuredly
  assent 488
assythment 973
astatic 320
asterisk 550
astern 235
  put the engines –
    275
  fall – 283
asteroid 318
Asteroth 979
asthenia 160
astigmatism 443

astir 682
  set – 824
astonish 870
astonished
  – at nothing 871
astonishing
  great 31
astound *excite* 824
  fear 860
  surprise 870
astra, sic itur ad –
  360, 873
astraddle 215
Astraea 922
astragal 847
astral 318
  – body 717, 992
  – influence 601
  – plane 317
astray 475, 495
  go – *deviate* 279
  sin 945
astriction 43
astride 215
astringent 195
astrolabe 466
astrologer 994
astrology 511
astromancy 511
astronomy 318
astute 498, 702
asunder 44, 196
  as poles – 237
asylum *hospital* 663
  retreat 666
  defence 717
asymptote 290
at, be – 620
  up and – them!
    716
ataghan 727
atavism 144, 163
ataxia 158
atelier 556, 691
athanasia 112
Athanasian creed
  983a
athanor 386
atheism 989
atheist 487
Athenae 979
Athens, owls to –
  641
athirst 865
athlete *strong* 159
  gladiator 726
athletic *strong* 159
  strenuous 686
  – sports
    contest 720
    games 840
athwart
  oblique 217
  crossing 219
  opposing 708
Atkins, Tommy 726
Atlantis 515
Atlas *arrangement*
  60
  list 86
  strength 159
  support 215
  maps 554
atmosphere
  circumambience
    227
  air 338
  painting 556

atmospheric blue
  438
atoll 346
atom *small* 32, 193
atomic energy 157
atomics 316
atomizer 336
atoms
  crush to – 162
atomy 193
atonement
  restitution 790
  expiation 952
  amends 973
  religious 976
atony 160
atrabilious 837
atramentous 431
atrium 191
atrocity
  malevolence 907
  vice 945
  guilt 947
atrophy
  shrinking 195
  disease 655
  decay 659
atropos 601
attach *join* 43
  love 897
  legal 969
  – importance to
    642
attaché
  employé 746
  diplomatic 758
  – case 191
attack *singing* 580
  disease 655
  assault 716
  debauch 961
attaghan 727
attain *arrive* 292
  succeed 731
  – majority 131
attainable 470
attainder
  taint 651
  at law 971
attainment
  knowledge 490
  learning 539
  skill 698
attar 400
attempter 41, 174
attempered 820
attempt 675
  vain – 732
  – impossibilities
    471
attend
  accompany 88
  be present 186
  follow 281
  apply the mind
    457
  medically 662
  aid 707
  serve 746
  – to business 625
  – to orders 743
attendance on
  dance – 886
attendant
  [*see* attend]
attention 457
  care 459
  respect 928

attract – 882
call to – 457
call – to 550
give – 418
pay –s to 894
pay one's –s to 902

attenuate
  decrease 36
  weaken 158
  reduce 195
  rarefy 322
attenuated 203
attest
  bear testimony 467
  affirm 535
  adjure 768
attested copy 771
attic *simple* 42
  garret 191
  summit 210
  style 578
  wit 842
  taste 850
Attila 913
attire 225
attitude
  circumstance 8
  situation 183
  posture 240
attitudinarian 882
attitudinize 855
attollent 307
attorney
  consignee 758
  at law 968
  power of – 755
attract
  bring towards 288
  induce 615
  allure 865
  excite love 897
  – the attention 457
  visible 446
attraction
  [see attract]
  natural power 157
  bring towards 288
attractive
  [see attract]
  pleasing 829
  beautiful 845
attrahent 288
attribute
  speciality 79
  accompaniment 88
  power 157
  –s of the Deity 976
  – to 155
attribution 155
attrite 330
attrition 330, 331
attroupement 72
attune *music* 415
  prepare 673
attuned to
  habit 613
attunement 23
auburn 433
A.U.C. 106
auction 796, 840
auctioneer 758, 796
auctorial 599
audacity
  courage 861

rashness 863
  insolence 885
audible 402
  become – 418
  scarcely – 405
Auroral 236
audience
  hearing 418
  conversation 588
  before an – 599
audire alteram partem
  counter-evidence 468
  right 922
  justice 939
audit
  numeration 85
  examination 461
  accounts 811
auditive 418
auditor
  hearer 418
  accountant 811
auditorium 189, 588
auditory
  sound 402
  hearing 418
  theater 599
  – *apparatus* 418
au fait 698
au fond 5
auf wiedersehen 293
Augean
  – *stable* 653
  – *task* 704
auger 262
aught 51
  for – one cares
  unimportant 643
  indifferent 866
  for – one knows
  ignorance 491
  conjecture 514
augment
  increase 35
  thing added 39
  expand 194
augur 513
  – *well* 858
augurate 511
augury 512
august 873
Augustinian 996
auk 366
auld lang syne 122
aulic council 696
aumbry 1000
aunt 11
aura *wind* 349
  sensation 380
aurea mediocritas 628
aureate 436
aureola 420
aureole 420, 873
aureolin 436
auribus, arrectis – 418
auricular *hearing* 418
  clandestine 528
  – *confession* 998
auri sacra fames 819
aurist 662
aurora
  dawn 125

light 420, 423
  twilight 422
  – *australes* 423
  – *borealis* 423
ausculation 418
auspice *omen* 512
auspices
  influence 175
  prediction 511
  protection 664
  direction 693
  aid 707
  under the – of 693, 737
auspicious
  opportune 134
  prosperous 734
  hopeful 858
austerity
  harsh taste 395
  severe 739
  discourteous 895
  ascetic 955
  pietism 988
austral 237
austromancy 511
authentic 467
  certain 474
  true 494
authentication
  evidence 467
  security 771
author 164, 593
  projector 626
  dramatic – 599
  – of our being 976
  – of evil 978
  – 's proof 591
authoritative 474, 741
authority
  testimony 467
  sage 500
  informant 527
  power 737
  permission 760
  right 924
  ensign of – 747
  person in – 745
  do upon one's own – 600
authorized *due* 924
  legalized 963
authorship
  production 161
  style 569
  writing 590
autobiography 594
autocar 272
autochthonous 188
autocracy 737, 739
autocrat 745
autocratic 600, 737
auto-da-fe 384, 972
autograph 550, 590
Autolycus *thief* 792
  pedlar 797
automaniac 504
automatic 601, 633
  – *pistol* 727
  – *writing* 992
automaton 554, 601
automobile 272
automobilist 268
automotive 266
autonomasia 521
autonomy 737, 748

autopsy
  post-mortem 363
  vision 441
autoptical 446, 535
autotype 558
autumn 126
auxiliary 711
  additional 34
  helpful 707
  – *forces* 726
avail *benefit* 618
  useful 644
  succeed 731
  of no – 645
  – oneself of 677
avalanche *fall* 306
  snow 383
  redundance 641
avaler les couleuvres 725, 886
avant-courier 64, 673
avant-propos 64
avarice 819
avast! *stop* 142, 265
  desist 624
  forbid 761
avatar *change* 140
  deity 976
  idol 991
avaunt! 297, 449
ave! *honor* 873
  courtesy 894
Ave maria 990
avenge 919
avenue
  plantation 371
  way 627
aver 535
average *mean* 29, 628
  médiocre 651
  – *circumstances* 736
  take an – 466
Averni, facilis descensus – 217, 665
Avernus 982
averruncate 297, 301
aversion *unwillingness* 603
  dislike 867
  hate 898
avert 706
  – the eyes 442
aviary 370
aviation 267
aviator 269
avidity *avarice* 819
  desire 865
airette 273
avile 932, 934
avion 273
aviso 532
avocation 625
avoidance 623
avoidless 474, 601
avoirdupois 319
avolation 623, 671
avouch 535, 768
avow *assent* 488
  disclose 529
  assert 535
avulsion 44, 301
avuncular 11
await *future* 121

be kept waiting 133
  impend 152
  expect 507
awake *attentive* 457
  careful 459
  intelligent 498
  active 682
  – to life immortal 360
awaken *inform* 527
  excite 824
  – the attention 457
  – the memory 505
award *adjudge* 480
  give 784
aware 490
away 187, 196
  break – 623
  fly – 293
  move – 287
  take – from 789
  get &c. – 671
  throw &c. –
  eject 297
  reject 610
  waste 638
  relinquish 782
  – *from unrelated* 10
  – *with!* 930, 932
  do – *with undo* 681
  abrogate 756
awe *fear* 860
  wonder 870
  respect 928
aweless *fearless* 861
  insolent 885
  disrespectful 329
awful 31, 860
  – *silence* 403
awhile 111
awkward
  inelegant 579
  inexpedient 647
  unskilful 699
  difficult 704
  painful 830
  ugly 846
  vulgar 851
  ridiculous 853
  – *squad* 701
awl 262
awn 253
awning 223, 424
awry *oblique* 217
  distorted 243
  evil 619
axe *edge tool* 253
  impulse 276
  weapon 727
  for beheading 975
  have an – to grind 702
Axinomancy 511
axiom 496
axiomatic 474
axis *support* 215
  center 222
  rotation 312
axle 312
  wheel and – 633
axle load 466
axletree 215
ay 488
ayah 746, 753
aye *ever* 112
  yes 488
azimuth

all for the –
  good 618
  prosper 734
  content 831
  hope 858
bad is the – 649
do one's –
  care 459
  try 675
  activity 682
  exertion 686
have the – of it 731
make the – of it
  over-estimate 482
  use 677
  submit 725
  compromise 774
  take easily 826
  hope 858
the – 800
to the – of one's
  belief 484
– bib and tucker
  prepared 673
  ornament 847
  ostentation 882
– friends 890
– intentions 906
– man 903
– part 31, 50
– seller 731
make the – of
  one's time 684
bestead 644
bestial 954, 961
bestir oneself
  activity 682
  haste 684
  exertion 686
bestow 784
– one's hand 903
– thought 451
bestraddle 215
bestrew 73
bestride 206, 215
bet 621
betake oneself to
  journey 266
  business 625
  use 677
bête, pas si – 498
bête noire *bane* 663
  fear 860
  hate 898
bethel 1000
bethink 451, 505
bethral 749, 751
betide 151
betimes 132
betoken
  evidence 467
  predict 511
  indicate 550
betray *disclose* 529
  deceive 545
  dishonor 940
– itself *visible* 446
betrayer 941
betrim 673
betroth 768, 903
betrothed 897
better *good* 648
  improve 658
appeal to one's –
  feelings 914
get – *health* 654
  improve 658
  refreshment 689

restoration 660
get the – of, 479,
  702, 731
think – of 658, 950
seen – days
  deteriorate 659
  adversity 735
  poor 804
– half 903
only – than noth-
  ing 651
– sort 875
for – for worse
  choice 609
  marriage 903
between 228
– cup and lip 111
far – 198
lie – 228
– the lines 526
vibrate – two ex-
  tremes 149
– ourselves 528
– two fires 665
– maid 746
betwixt 228
bevel 217
– gearing 653
bever 298
beverage 298
bévue 732
bevy 72, 102
bewail *regret* 833
  lament 839
beware 665, 668
bewilder
  put out 458
  uncertainty 475
  astonish 870
bewitch
  fascinate 615
  please 829
  excite love 897
  exorcise 992
bey 745
beyond *superior* 33
  distance 196
  go – 303
– compare 31, 33
– control 471
– one's depth 208,
  519
– expression 31
– one's grasp 471
– hope 731, 534
– the mark 303,
  641
– measure 641
– possibility 471
– praise
  perfect 650
  approbation 931
  virtue 944
– price 814
– question 474, 494
– reason 471
– remedy 859
– seas 57
bezel 217
bhang 663
bias *influence* 175
  tendency 176
  slope 217
  prepossession 481
  disposition 820
bib *pinafore* 225
  drink 959
bibber *weep* 839

tope 959
bibble-babble 584
bibelot 847
bibendum, nunc
  est – 959
Bible 895
– oath 535
biblioclasm 162
bibliography 593
bibliolatry
  learning 490
  heterodoxy 984
  idolatry 991
bibliomancy 511
bibliomania 490
bibliomaniac 492
bibliophile 492
bibliopole 593
bibliotheca 593
bibulous 298, 959
bicameral 90
bicapital 90
bice 435, 438
bicentenary 98,
  138, 883
bicker *flutter* 315
  quarrel 713
bicolor 440
biconjugate 91
bicuspid 91
bicycle 272
bid *order* 741
  offer 763
– the banns 903
– defiance 715
– fair *tend* 176
  probable 472
  promise 511
  hope 858
– a long farewell
  624
– for *intend* 620
  offer 763
  request 765
  bargain 794
bidder 767
bide *wait* 133
  remain 141
  take coolly 806
– one's time 133
  watch 507
  inactive 681
bidet 271
biennial
  periodic 138
  plant 367
bienséance 852, 894
bier 363
bifacial 90
bifarious 90
bifid 91
bifold 90
biform 90
bifurcate 91, 244
big *in degree* 31
  in size 192
  wide 194
look – *defy* 715
  proud 878
  insolent 885
talk – 885, 909
– sounding
  loud 404
  words 577
  affected 855
– swollen 194
– with $\frac{1}{2}1$
– with the fate of

511
bigamy 903
biggin 191
bight 343
bigot *positive* 474
  prejudice 481
  obstinate 606
  heterodox 984
  impious 988
bigotry 907
bigwig *scholar* 492
  sage 500
  nobility 875
bijou *goodness* 648
  beauty 845
  ornament 847
bilander 273
bilateral 90, 236
bilbao 727
bilboes 752
  put into – 751
bile 900
bilge *base* 211
  convex 250
  yawn 260
– water 653
bilious 837
bilingual 560
bilk
  disappoint 509
  cheat 545
  steal 791
bill *list* 86
  hatchet 253
  placard 531
  ticket 550
  paper 593
  plan 626
  weapon 727
  money order 800
  money account
  811
  charge 812
  in law, 969
true – 969
– and coo 902
– of exchange 771
– of fare *food* 298
  plan 626
– of indictment
  938
–s of mortality 360
– of sale 771
billet *locate* 184
  ticket 550
  apportion 786
billet *epistle* 592
– doux 902
billfold 191
billhook 253
billiard – ball 249
– room 191
– table *flat* 213
billiards 840
Billingsgate 563,
  908
billion 98
billow *sea* 348
  river 341
billy-cock 225
billy-goat 373
bimetallism 800
bin 191
binary 89
bind *connect* 43
  cover 223
  compel 744
  condition 770

obligation 926
– hand and foot
  751
– oneself 768
– over 744
– up wounds 660
binding 681, 744
bine 367
binnacle 693
binocular 445
binomial 89
biogenesis 161
biograph 448
biography 594
biology 357, 359
bioscope 448
biota 357
biparous 89
bipartite 44, 91
biplane 273
biplicity 89
biquadrate 96
birch *flog* 972
– rod 975
bird 366
  kill two –s with
  one stone 682
–'s eye view 441,
  448
–s of a feather 17
the – has flown
  187, 671
– in hand 777, 781
– of ill omen
  omen 512
  warning 668
  hopeless 859
– of passage 268
– of prey 739
a little – told me
  527
birdcage 370
birdlime *glue* 45
  trap 545
biretta 999
birth *beginning* 66
  production 161
  paternity 166
  nobility 875
– place 153
– right 924
birthday 138, 883
– suit 226
birthmark 848
bis *repeat* 104
  approval 931
biscuits, s'embar-
  quer sans – 674
bise 349
bisection 68, **91**
bishop *punch* 298
  clergy 996
–'s palace 1000
–'s purple 437
bishopric 995
bisque 33
bissextile 138
bister 433
bistoury 253
bisulcate 259
bit
  small quantity 32
  part 51
  interval 106
  curb 752
just a – 26
– by bit
  by degrees 26

unexpected 508
disappointment 509
evil 619
action 680
get wind 688
failure 732
prosper 734
pain 828, 830
come to –s 720, 722
deal a – at 716
deal a – to 972
death – 360, 361
– for blow 718
– one's brains out 361
– the coals 824
– down 162
– the fire 384
– the gaff 529
– hole 351
– the horn 416
– hot and cold lie 544
irresolute 605
tergiversation 607
caprice 608
– a kiss 902
– off disperse 73
– out food 298
darken 421
gorge 957
– over past 122
– pipe 349, 727
– the trumpet 873
– one's own trumpet 882
– up destroy 162
eruption 173
inflate 194
wind 349
excite 824
objurgate 932, 934
blower 349
blowhard 884
blown [see blow]
fatigued 688
proud 878
storm – over 664, 721
– upon 874, 932
blow-out 406
blowzy swollen 194
red 434
blubber fat 356
cry 839
Blucher boot 225
bludgeon 727
– man 726, 913
blue sky 338
color 438
learned 490
bit of – hope 858
look –
disappointed 509
feeling 821
discontent 832
disrepute – 874
out of the – 508
swear till all's – 535
true – 543, 939
– book 86, 551
– blood 875
– devils 837
– jacket 269
– light 550, 669

– pencil 174, 596
– moon 110
– Peter 293, 550
– and red 437
– ribbon 733, 877
– ruin 959
– stocking
scholar 492
affectation 855
– and yellow 435
Bluebeard
marriage 903
libertine 962
blueness 438
blues 837, 840
bluff violent 173
high cliff 206
blunt 254
deceive 545
boasting 884
insolent 885
discourteous 895
blunder error 495
absurdity 497
awkward 699
failure 732
– upon 156
blunderbuss 727
blunderhead 701
blunderheaded 499
blunt weaken 160
inert 172
– moderate v. 174
obtuse 254
benumb 376
damp v. 616
plain-spoken 703
cash 800
deaden 823
discourteous 895
– tool 645
– witted 499
bluntness 254
blur
imperfect vision 443
dirt 653
blemish 848
stigma 874
blurb 931
blurred
invisible 447
blurt out 529, 582
blush flush 382
redden 434
feel 821
humbled 879
modest 881
at first – see 441
appear 448
manifest 525
put to the –
humble 897
browbeat 885
discourtesy 895
blushing honors 873, 881
bluster violent 173
defiant 715
boasting 884
insolent 885
threaten 909
blusterer 887
blustering [see bluster]
windy 349
Bo to a goose, not say – 862.

boa 225
boanerges 540
boar 366, 373
board layer 204
support 215
food 298
hard 323
council 696
attack 716
tribunal 966
festive – 892
go by the – 158, 162
go on – 293
on – 186, 273
preside at the – 693
– of trade 621
– school 542
boarding-house 189
boarder 188
boards 599, 728
boast 884
not much to – of 651
boasting 884
boaston 840
boat 273
in the same – 88
– race 720
boating 267
boatman 269
boatswain 269
bob depress 308
leap 309
oscillate 314
agitate 315
money 800
– a curtsy 894
– for fish 463
Bobadil, Captain – 887
bobbed
hair 53
bobbin 312
bobbing fuel 388
bobbish 654
bobby police 664
bobsleigh 272
bobsleighing 840
bobtailed 53
bocage 367
bocca, per amusare la – 394
Boche 913
boddice 225
bode 511
bodega 189
bodily
substantially 3
wholly 50
material 316
– enjoyment 377
– fear 860
– pain 378
bodkin
go between 228
perforator 262
body substance 3
whole 50
assemblage 72
frame 215
matter 316
party 712
in a – together 88
– and blood of Christ 987
– clothes 225

– color 556
– of doctrine 490
– forth 554
– guard 717, 753
– of knowledge 490
– politic
mankind 372
authority 737
keep – and soul together 654
– of water 438
Boeotian rustic 371
stupid 499
fool 501
vulgar 851
ignoble 876
Boer 371
bog 345, 653
– trotter 876
boggart 980
boggle hesitate 605
awkward 699
difficulty 704
bogie 980
truck 272
bogle 980
bogus 545
Bohemian
unconventional 83
nomad 268
ungenteel 851
boil violence 173
effervesce 315
bubble 353
heat 382, 384
ulceration 655
excitement 824, 825
anger 900
– down 195
boiler 386
boisterous
violent 173
hasty 684
excitable 825
bold prominent 250
unreserved 525
vigorous 574
brave 861
make – with 895
show a – front 715, 861
– faced 885
– push essay 675
– relief visible 446
– stroke plan 626
success 731
bole 50
bolero 840
bollard 45
bolshevik 144, 146
bolshevist 737, 742
bolster support 215
repair 658
aid 707
'– up vindicate 937
bolt sift 42
fasten 43
fastening 45
close 261
move rapidly 274
propel 284
run away 623
escape 671
hindrance 706
shaft 727
disobey 742

shackle 752
thunder – 872
– the door 761
– food 298, 957
– in 751
– upright 212
bolthead 191
bolus mouthful 298
remedy 662
bomb 404, 727
– proof 664, 717
– vessel 726
bombard 716
bombardier 726
bombardon 417
bombast
unmeaning 517
magniloquence 577
ridiculous 853
boasting 884
exaggeration 549
Bombastes Furioso 887
bomber
aeroplane 726
bombilation 404
bon de – augure 858
– enfant social 892
kindly 906
– gré mal gré 601
– marché 815
– mot 842
– naturel 836
– ton 852
– vivant 957
– voyage 293
bona – fides
veracity 543
probity 939
– roba 962
bonanza 641, 784
wealth 803
bonbon 396
bond relation 9
tie 45
compact 769
security 771
money 800
right 924
– of union 9, 45
government – 802
Liberty – 802
bondage 749
bonded together 712
bonds [see bond]
fetters 752
funds 802
in – service 746
tear asunder one's – 750
– of harmony 714
bondsman 746
bone strength 159
dense 321
hard 323
bred in the – 5
feel it in one's – 510
– of contention 713, 720
one – and one flesh 903
– to pick difficulty 704
discord 713

refresh 689
bracelet circle 247
 handcuff 752
 ornament 847
bracer 392
braces 45
brachial 633
Brachygraphy 590
bracing 656
bracken 367
bracket tie 43, 45
 couple 89
 support 215
brackish 392
brad 45
bradawl 262
Bradbury 800
Bradshaw 266
brae 206
brag cards 840
 boast 884
braggart 884
Braggadocio 884
Brahma 979
Brahmin 984, 996
braid tie 43
 ligature 45
 net 219
 variegate 440
brain kill 361
 intellect 450
 skill 498
 blow one's –s out 361
 coinage of the – 515
 suck one's –s 461
 rack one's –s 451, 515
brainless 499
brainpan 450
brainsick 458
brain-storm 503, 825
brainwork 451
brainy 498
brake carriage 272
 copse 367
 hindrance 706
 curb 752
 apply the – 275
brakeman 268
bramble thorn 253
 bane 663
bran 330
brancard 272
branch member 51
 class 75
 posterity 167
 fork 244
 tree 367
 – off 91, 291
 – out ramify 91
 diffuse style 573
branching
 symmetry 242
brand burn 384
 fuel 388
 torch 423
 mark 550
 sword 727
 disrepute 874
 censure 932
 stigmatize 934
 – of discord 713
 – new 123
 – with reproach 938

brandish
 oscillate 314
 flourish 315
 display 882
brandy 959
brangle 713
brangler 710
brank 975
bras
 les – croisés 681
 à – ouverts 894
brashness 885
brass alloy 41
 money 800
 insolence 885
 bold as – 861
 – band 417, 882
 with a – 884
 – colored 439
 – hat 745
 – farthing 643
brassard 550, 747
brat 129
brattice 224, 228
bravado 884
brave confront 234
 healthy 654
 defy 715
 warrior 726
 bear 821, 826
 courage 861
 – a thousand years 110
bravo
 assassin 361
 desperado 863
 applause 931
bravura 415
brawl cry 411
 discord 713
 revel 840
brawler
 disputant 710
 rioter 742
 blusterer 887
brawny 159, 192
bray grind 330
 cry 412
Bray, Vicar of – 607, 886
braze 43
brazen 525, 885
 – browed 885
 – faced 885
brazier 386
breach crack 44
 gap 198
 quarrel 713
 violation 925
 custom honored in the – 614
 – of faith 940
 – of law 83, 964
 – of the peace 713
bread 298
 beg – 765
 selfish 943
 quarrel with – and butter 699
 – of idleness 683
 – of life Christ 976
 piety 987
 – upon the waters 638
 – and wine 998
breadbasket 191

breadth 202
 chiaroscuro 420
break
 fracture 44
 discontinuity 70
 change 140
 gap 198
 carriage 272
 crumble 328
 disclose 529
 cashier 756
 violate 773, 927
 bankrupt 808
 – away 623
 – bread 298
 – bulk 297
 – camp 293
 – of day morning 125
 twilight 422
 – down destroy 162
 fall short 304
 decay 659
 fail 732
 dance 840
 – one's fetters 614
 – forth 295
 – ground 66
 – a habit 614
 – the heart pain 828, 830
 dejection 837
 – the ice 888
 – in ingress 294
 domesticate 370
 teach 537
 tame 749
 – in upon derange 61
 inopportune 135
 hinder 706
 – a lance 716, 722
 – a law 83
 – loose 671, 750
 – one's neck powerless 158
 die 360
 – the neck of task 676
 success 731
 – the news 529
 – no bones 648
 – of 660
 – off cease 142
 relinquish 624
 abrogate 756
 – out begin 66
 violent 173
 disease 655
 excited 825
 – the peace 173, 720
 – Priscian's head 568
 – prison 750
 – the ranks 61
 – short 328
 – silence 582
 – the teeth 579
 – the thread 70
 – through the clouds visible 446
 disclose 529
 – through a custom 614
 – up disjoin 44

 decompose 49
 end 67
 revolution 146
 destroy 162
 – up of the system, 360, 665
 – on the wheel
 physical pain 378
 mental pain 830
 punishment 972
 – with 713
 – with the past 146
 – word deceive 525
 improbity 940
breaker
 of horses 268
 reef 346
 wave 348
breakers 348, 667
 surrounded by – 704
 – ahead 665
breakfast 298
breakneck
 precipice 217
 rash 863
breakwater
 refuge 666
 obstruction 706
breast interior 221
 confront 234
 convex 250
 mind 450
 oppose 708
 soul 820
 at the – 129
 in the – of 620
 – the current 719
 – high 206
breastplate 717
breastwork 717
breath instant 113
 breeze 349
 life 359
 animality 364
 faint sound 405
 with bated – 581
 hold – quiet 265
 expect 507
 wonder 870
 not a – of air 265, 382
 out of – 688
 in the same – 120
 shortness of – 688
 take – 265, 689
 take away one's –
 unexpected 508
 fear 860
 wonder 870
breathe exist 1
 blow 349
 live 359
 faint sound 405
 evince 467
 mean 516
 inform 527
 disclose 529
 utter 580
 speak 582
 refresh 689
 – freely 827, 834
 – one's last 360
 not – a word 528
breathing time 687, 723
breathless

 voiceless 581
 out of breath 688
 feeling 821
 fear 860
 eager 865
 wonder 870
 – attention 457
 – expectation 507
 – impatience 865
 – speed 684
bred in the bone 820
breech 235
 – loader 727
breeches 225
 wear the – 737
 – buoy 666
 – maker 225
 – pocket
 money 800, 802
breed kind 75
 multiply 161
 progeny 167
 animals 370
 rear 537
breeding 161, 852, 894
breeze wind 349
 discord 713
breezy 836
brethren 997
breve 413
brevet
 warrant 741
 commission 755
 permit 760
 – rank 873
breviary 998
brevier 591
brevity 201, 572
brew 41, 673
brewing
 impending 152
 storm – 665
bribe equivalent 30
 tempt 615
 offer 763
 gift 784
 buy 795
 expenditure 809
 reward 973
bric-à-brac 847
brick hard 323
 pottery 384
 material 635
 trump 939, 948
 make -s without straw 471
 – color 434
brickbat 727
bricklayer 690
bride 903
bridewell 752
bridge 45, 627
 – over join 43
 facilitate 705
 make peace 723
 compromise 774
 cards 840
bridle restrain 751
 rein 752
 – road 627
 – one's tongue 585, 864
 – up 900
brief time 111
 space 201
 concise 572
 compendium 596

circumfluent
  lie round 227
  move round 311
circumforaneous
  traveling 266
  circuition 311
circumfuse 73
circumgyration 312
circumjacence **227**
circumlocution 573
circumnavigate
  navigation 267
  circuition 311
circumrotation 312
circumscribe
  surround 229
  limit 233, 761
circumscription **229**
circumspection
  attention 457
  care 459
  caution 459
circumstance
  phase 8
  event 151
circumstances
  property 780
  bad – 804
  depend on – 475
  good – 803
  under the – 8
circumstantial 8
  – *account* 594
  – *evidence* 467
  probability 472
circumstantiality
  459
circumstantiate 467
circumvallation
  enclosure 229,
    232
  defence 717
  line of – 233
circumvent
  environ 227
  move round 311
  cheat 545
  cunning 702
  hinder 706
  defeat 731
circumvest 225
circumvolution
  winding 248
  rotation 312
circus
  buildings 189
  drama 599
  arena 728
  amusement 840
cirrus 353
cistern
  receptacle 191
  store 636
Cistercian 996
cit 188
citadel 717
citation 467, 733
cite
  quote as example
    82
  as evidence 467
  summon 741
  accuse 938
  arraign 969
cithern 417
citizen 188
  – of the world 910
citriculture 371

citrine 436
city 189
  in the – 794
city manager 965
civet 400
civic 372
civil *courteous* 894
  laity 997
  – authorities 745
  – crown 733
  – law 963
  – war 722
civilian *lawyer* 968
  layman 997
civilization
  improvement 658
  fashion 852
  courtesy 894
civilized *life* 852
civism 910
clack *clatter* 407
  animal cry 412
  talkative 584 /
clad 225
claim *requisition*
    630
  demand 741
  property 780
  right 924
  lawsuit 969
  – the attention
    457
claimant
  petitioner 767
  right 924
clair-obscur 420
clairvoyance 992
clairvoyant 513, 994
clamant 411
clamber 305
clammy 352
clamor *cry* 411
  wail 839
  – against 932
  – for 765
clamorous
  [*see clamor*]
  loud 404
  excitable 825
clamp *fasten* 43
  fastening 45
clan *race* 11
  class 75
  family 166
  party 712
clandestine 528
clangor 404
clank 410
clannishness 481
clanship 709
clap *explosion* 406
  applaud 931
  thunder –
  prodigy 872
  – the hands
  rejoice 838
  – on 31
  – on the shoulder
    615
  – together 43
  – up *imprison* 751
clapperclaw
  contention 720
  censure 932
claptrap
  pretence 546
  display 882
claquer 935

faire – son fouet
    884
clarence 272
claret color 434
clarify 652
clarinet 417
clarion *music* 417
  war 722
clarity 518
clash *disagree* 24
  cross 179
  concussion 276
  sound 406
  oppose 708
  discord 713
  – of arms 720
clasp *fasten* 43
  fastening 45
  stick 46
  come close 197
  belt 230
  embrace 902
class *arrange* 60
  category **75**
  learners 541
  party 712
  – *prejudice* 481
  – room 542
classic *old* 124
  symmetry 242
classical
  elegant writing
    578
  taste 850
  – art 556
  – dancing 840
  – education 537
  – music 415
classicist 492
classics 560
classify 60
classmate 890
clatter 404, 407
claudication
  slowness 275
  failure 732
clause *part* 51
  passage 593
  condition 770
clausis, januis –
    528
clearheaded 498
clear-obscure 420
cleat 45
cleavage
  cutting 44
  structure 329
cleave *sunder* 44
  adhere 46
  bisect 91
cleaver 253
cledge 342
clef 413
cleft *divided* 44
  bisected 91
  chink 198
  in a – stick
  difficulty 704
clem 956
clement
  lenient 740
  long-suffering
    826
  compassionate
    914
clench *compact* 769
  retain 781
  take 789
clepe 564

– out *empty* 297
– shaven 226
– sweep
  revolution 146
  destruction 162
clean-up 775
clear *simple* 42
  sound 413
  light 420
  transparent 425
  visible 446
  certain 474
  intelligible 518
  manifest 525
  easy 705
  liberate 750
  profit 775
  vindicate 937
  innocent 946
  acquit 975
  all – 664, 705
  coast – 664
  get – off 671
  keep – of 623
  make – 529
  – for action
  prepare 673
  – articulation 580
  – conscience 946
  – the course 302
  – cut 518
  – the ground
  facilitate 705
  – of distant 196
  – off *pay* 807
  – out *empty* 297
  clean 652
  – sighted
  vision 441
  shrewd 498
  – sky *hope* 858
  – stage
  occasion 134
  easy 705
  right 922
  – thinking 498
  – the throat 297
  – up *light* 420
  intelligible 518
  interpret 522
clearheaded 498
clear-obscure 420
cleat 45
cleavage
  cutting 44
  structure 329
cleave *sunder* 44
  adhere 46
  bisect 91
cleaver 253
cledge 342
clef 413
cleft *divided* 44
  bisected 91
  chink 198
  in a – stick
  difficulty 704
clem 956
clement
  lenient 740
  long-suffering
    826
  compassionate
    914
clench *compact* 769
  retain 781
  take 789
clepe 564

clepsydra 114
clerestory 191, 1000
clergy 996
clerical 995, 996
  – error 495
  – staff 746
clerk *scholar* 492
  recorder 553
  writer 590
  helper 711
  servant 746
  agent 758
  clergy 996
  articled – 541
  – in holy orders
    995
  – of works 694
clerkship
  commission 755
cleromancy 511
clever
  intelligent 498
  skilful 698
  smart 842
  too – by half 702
clew *ball* 249
  interpretation 522
  indication 550
  seek a – 461
click 406
client
  dependant 746
  customer 795
clientship
  subjection 749
cliff *height* 206
  vertical 212
  steep 217
  land 342
climacteric 128
climate *region* 181
  weather 338
  fine – 656
climatology 338
climax
  supremacy 33
  summit 210
  culmination 729
climb 305
  – on the band-
    wagon 731
clime 181
clinal 217
clinch *fasten* 43
  close 261
  certify 474
  pun 563
  complete 729
  clutch 781
  snatch 789
  – an argument 47
  – the fist at 909
clincher 479
cling *adhere* 46
  – to *near* 197
  willing 602
  persevere 604a
  habit 613
  observe 772
  desire 865
  love 897
  – to *hope* 858
  – to one another
    709
clinic 662
clink
  resonance 408
  stridor 410

clay *soft* 324
  earth 342
  corpse 362
  material 635
  – pipe 392
clay-cold 383
claymore 727
clean
  entirely 52
  perfect 650
  unstained 652
  – bill of health 654
  – breast
  disclose 529
  – forgotten 506
  – hand
  proficient 700
  with – hands
  honesty 939
  innocence 946

claw *hook* 781
  grasp 789
  – back 935

physical − 316
conditional 8
conditions **770**
condolence 914, **915**
condone 917
condottiere
  traveller 268
  fighter 726
conduce
  contribute 153
  tend 176
  concur 178
  avail 644
conducive 631
conduct
  transfer 270
  music 416
  procedure **692**
  lead 693
  safe −
    passport 631
    safety 664
  − a *funeral* 363
  − an *inquiry* 461
  − to 278
conduction 264
conductor 269
  conveyer 271
  director 694
  lightning − 666
conduit **350**
conduplicate 89
condyle 250
cone *round* 249
  pointed 253
confabulation 588
confection 396
  confectionary 396
confectioner 637
confederacy
  co-operation 709
  party 712
confederate 711
confer *advise* 695
  give 784
  − *benefit* 648
  − *power* 157
  − *privilege* 760
  − *right* 924
  − with 588
conference [*see*
  confer]
  council 696
confess *assent* 488
  avow 529
  penitence 950,
  998
  − and avoid 937
confession [*see*
  confess]
  auricular − 998
  − of *faith* 983
confessional 1000
confessions
  biography 594
confessor 996
confidant 711
confidante
  servant 746
  friend 890
confidence
  trust 484
  hope 858
  courage 861
  in − 528
  − *trick* 545
confident 535
configuration 240

confine
  region 182
  circumscribe 229
  limit 231, 233
  imprison 751
confined
  narrow judgment
  481
  ill 655
confinement
  childbed 161
confines of
  on the − 197
confirm
  corroborate 467
  assent 488
  consent 762
  compact 769
  rite 998
confirmed 150
  − *habit* 613
confiscate *take* 789
  condemn 971
  penalty 974
confiture 396
conflagration 382,
  384
conflexure 245
conflict
  opposition 708
  discord 713
  contention 720
conflicting
  contrary 14
  counteracting 179
  − *evidence* 468
confluence
  junction 43
  convergence 290
  river 348
conflux
  assemblage 72
  convergence 290
conform *assent* 488
  − to *rule* 494
conformable 23,
  178
conformation 54,
  240
conformity **82**, 178
confound
  disorder 61
  destroy 162
  not discriminate
  465a
  perplex 475
  defeat 731
  astonish 870
  curse 908
confounded
  great 31
  bad 649
confraternity
  party 712
  friendship 888
confrère
  colleague 711
  friend 890
confrication 331
confront *face* 234
  compare 464
  oppose 708
  resist 719
  − *danger* 861
  − *witnesses* 467
confucianism 984
Confucius 986
confuse *derange* 61

perplex 458
  obscure 519
  not discriminate
  465a
  abash 879
confused *disorder*
  59
  invisible 447
  uncertain 475
  style 571
confusion
  [*see* confuse]
  − *seize* 908
  − of *tongues* 560,
  563
  − of *vision* 443
  − *worse-con-*
  founded 59
confutation **479**
congé 293, 756
  − d'élire 995
congeal *dense* 321
  cold 385
congeneric
  similar 17
  included 76
congenial
  related 9
  agreeing 23
  concord 714
  love 897
congenital 5, 820
congeries 72
congestion 641
conglaciation 385
conglobation 72
conglomerate
  cohere 46
  assemblage 72
  council 696
  dense 321
conglutinate 46
congratulate 896
  − oneself 838
congratulation **896**
congregation
  assemblage 72
  worshippers 990
  laity 997
Congregationalist
  984
congress
  assembly 72
  convergence 290
  conference 588
  council 698
Congressional
  Medal 733
Congressional
  Record 551
congreve *fuel* 388
  − *rocket* 727
congruous
  agreeing 23
  (*expedient* 646)
conical *round* 249
  pointed 253
conjecture 475, 514
conjoin 43
conjoint 48
conjointly 37
conjugal 903
conjugate
  words 562
  grammar 567
  − in all its tenses
  &c. 104
conjugation

junction 43
  pair 89
  phase 144
  grammar 567
conjunction 43
  in − with 37
conjuncture
  contingency **8**
  occasion 134
conjure *deceive* 545
  entreat 765
  sorcery 992
  name to − with
  873
  − up *recall* 505
  − up a *vision* 505
conjuror
  deceiver 548
  sorcerer 994
connaître les des-
  sous des cartes
  490
connate
  intrinsic 5
  kindred 11
  cause 153
connatural
  uniform 16
  similar 17
connect *relate* 9
  link 43
connection
  [*see* connect]
  kin 11
  in − with 9
connections
  cards 840
connective 45
conned, well − 490
connive
  overlook 460
  co-operate 709
  allow 760
connoisseur
  critic 480
  scholar 492
  taste 850
connotate 550
connote 516, 550
  imply 526
connubial 903
connuted 9
conoscente 850
conquer 731
conquered
  (*failure* 732)
conquering hero
  comes 883
conqueror 731
consanguinity 11
consciarecti, mens-
  pride 878
  innocence 946
conscience
  knowledge 490
  moral sense 926
  in all − *great* 31
  affirmation 535
  awakened − 950
  qualms of − 603
  clear − 946
  stricken − 950
  tender − 926
  honor 939
conscientious 926
  scrupulous 939
  − *objector* 489
conscious

intuitive 450
  knowledge 490
  − of *disgrace* 874
  − of *glory* 873
conscript 726
conscription 744
consecrate *use* 677
  dedicate 873
  sanctify 987
  holy orders 995
consecration
  rite 998
consectory 478
  − *reasoning* 476
consecution 63
consecutive
  following 63
  continuous 69
  − *fifth* 414
consecutively
  slowly 275
consensus 488
  − of *opinion* 23
consent *assent* 488
  compliance **762**
  with one − 178
consentaneous
  agreeing 23
  (*expedient* 646)
consequence
  event 151
  effect 154
  importance 642
  in − 478
  of no − 643
  take the −s 154
consequent 63
consequential
  deducible 478
  arrogant 878
consequently
  reasoning 476
  effect 154
conservation
  permanence 141
  storage 636
  preservation 670
conservatism 141,
  670
conservative 141,
  712
  − *policy* 681
conservatoire 542
conservator
  of the peace 967
conservatory
  receptacle 191
  floriculture 371
  furnace 386
  store 636
conserve 396, 636
consider *think* 451
  attend to 457
  examine 461
  adjudge 480
  believe 484
considerable
  in degree 31
  in size 192
  important 642
considerate
  careful 459
  judicious 498
  benevolent 906
consideration
  purchase money
  147
  thought 451

contrition
  abrasion 331
  regret 833
  penitence 950
contrivance 633
contrive
  produce 161
  plan 626
  – to succeed in 731
contriving
  cunning 702
control
  power 157
  influence 175
  regulate 693
  authority 737
  restrain 751
  board of – 696
  under –
  obedience 743
  subjection 749
controller of
  currency 801
controls 273, 693
controversial
  discussion 476
  discordant 713
controversialist
  476, 726
controversy
  disagreement 24
  discussion 476
  debate 588
  contention 720
controvert
  deny 536
controvertible
  uncertain 475
  debatable 476
  untrue 495
contumacy
  obstinacy 606
  disobedience 742
contumely
  arrogance 885
  rudeness 895
  disrespect 929
  scorn 930
  reproach 932
contund 330
contuse 330
conundrum pun
  520
  riddle 533
  wit 842
convalescence 654,
  660
convection 270
convenance
  mariage de – 903
convene 72
conveniences 632
convenient 646, 705
convent 1000
conventicle
  assembly 72
  council 696
  chapel 1000
convention
  agreement 23
  assembly 72
  rule 80
  council 696
  precept 697
  treaty of peace
  723
  compact 769

–s of society 852
conventional 82,
  613
conventual 996,
  1000
convergence 290
convergent 286
conversable
  talk 588
  sociable 892
conversant
  know 490
  skilful 698
conversation 588
conversational
  loquacious 584
  interlocution 588
  sociable 892
conversazione 588,
  892
converse
  reverse 14
  talk 588
conversely 468
conversion 144
  trover and – 964
convert
  change to 140, 144
  opinion 484
  tergiversation 607
  religion 987
  – to use 677
convertible 13, 27
  – terms 522
convexity 250
convey
  transfer 270
  mean 516
  assign 783
  – away 791
  – the knowledge
  of 527
conveyance
  [see convey]
  vehicle 272
conveyancer 968
conveyancing 783
convict
  convince 484
  condemned 949
  condemn 971
convicted, self –
  950
conviction
  confutation 479
  belief 484
  prove guilty 971
convince
  belief 484
  confute 479
  teach 537
convivial 892
convocate 72
convocation
  council 696
  church 995
convoke 72
convolution
  coil 248
  rotation 312
convoy
  accompany 88
  transfer 270
  guard 664
  escort 753
convulse
  derange 61

violent 173
  agitate 315
  bodily pain 378
  mental pain 830
convulsed with
  – laughter 838
  – rage 900
convulsion
  [see convulse]
  disorder 59
  revolution 146
  in –s 325
coo 412
cook heat 384
  falsify 544
  improve 658
  prepare 673
  servant 746
  too many –s 699
  – accounts 811
cool moderate 174
  cold 383
  refrigerate 385
  grey 432
  dissuade 616
  cautious 864
  indifferent 866
  unamazed 871
  unfriendly 889
  discourteous 895
  look – upon
  unsocial 893
  take –ly 826
  – down 826
  – one's heels
  kept waiting 133
  inaction 681
cooler 387
coolheaded
  judicious 498
  unexcitable 826
coolie
  bearer 271
  military 726
coolness
  insensibility 823
  estrangement 898
coon-can 840
coop abode 189
  restrain 751
  prison 752
co-operation
  physical 178
  voluntary 709
  participation 778
co-operator 690, 711
co-optation 609
co-ordinate
  equal 27
  arrange 60
  measure 466
cootie 653
cop 664
copal 356a
coparcener 778
copartner
  accompanying 88
  participator 778
  associate 890
copartnership
  co-operation 709
  party 712
cope equal 27
  oppose 708
  contend 720
  canonicals 999
copia verborum

diffuse 573
  loquacious 584
coping stone
  top 210
  completion 729
copious
  diffuse style 573
  abundant 639
coportion 778
copper money 800
  policeman 664
copper-colored
  433, 439
copper-plate
  engraving 558
  writing 590
coppice 367
coprolite 653
copse 367
copula 45
copulation 43
copy
  imitate 19
  facsimile 21
  prototype 22
  news 532
  record 551
  represent 554
  write 590
  for the press 591
  plan 626
  – book 22
copyhold 780
copyist
  imitator 19
  artist 559
  writer 590
copyright 780
coquet lie 544
  change the mind
  607
  affected 855
  endearment 902
  flattery 933
  – with
  irresolute 605
coquette
  affected 854, 855
  flirt 897
coquillage 847
coracle 273
coral 847
  – reef 667
coram judice
  jurisdiction 965
  lawsuit 969
cor Anglais 417
corbeille 191
corbel 215
cord tie 45
  filament 205
cordage 45
cordated 245
cordial
  pleasure 377
  dram 392
  willing 602
  remedy 662
  feeling 821
  grateful 829
  friendly 888
  courteous 894
cordiform 245
cordite 727
cordon
  inclosure 232
  circularity 247

decoration 877
  – bleu 733, 746
  – sanitaire
  safety 664
  preservation 670
corduroy 259
cordwainer
  shoemaker 225
  artificer 690
core gist 5
  source 153
  center 222
  gist 642
  true to the – 939
coriaceous 327
Corinthian 850
co-rival
  [see corrival]
cork plug 263
  lightness 320
  – jacket 666
  – up close 261
  restrain 751
corking pin 45
corkscrew
  spiral 248
  perforator 262
  circuition 311
cormorant
  desire 865
  gluttony 957
corn
  projection 250
Cornaro 953
cornea 441
corned 959
cornelian 847
corneous 323
corner place 182
  receptacle 191
  angle 244
  monopoly 777
  – creep into a –
  893
  in a dark – 528
  drive into a – 706
  push into a – 874
  rub off –s 82
  – turn a – 311
  turn the – 658
  – stone
  support 215
  importance 642
  defence 717
cornet music 417
  officer 745
cornice 210
corniculate 253
cornification 323
Cornish hug 545
corno 417
cornopean 417
cornucopia 639
cornute
  projecting 250
  sharp 253
corollary
  adjunct 39
  deduction 480
corona 247
coronach 839
coronation
  enthronement 755
  celebration 883
coroner 363, 965
  –'s jury 967
coronet hoop 247

insignia 747
title 877
corporal
  corporeal 316
  officer 745
corporate 43
  – *body* 712
corporation
  bulk 192
  convex 250
  association 712
  jurisdiction 965
corporeal 3, 316,
  364
  – *hereditaments*
    780
corporeity 316
corps *assemblage* 72
  troops 726
  à – *perdu*
  haste 684
  rash 863
  – *de reserve* 636
corpse 362
corpulence 192
corpus 316
  – *Christi* 998
  – *delicti*
  guilt 947
  lawsuit 969
  – *juris*
  precept 697
  law 963
corpuscle
  small 32
  little 193
corradiation
  focus 74
  convergence 290
corral 232, 370
correct
  orderly 58
  true 494
  inform 527
  disclose 529
  improve 658
  repair 660
  due 924
  censure 932
  honorable 939
  virtuous 944
  punish 972
  – *ear* 416, 418
  – *memory* 505
  – *reasoning* 476
  – *style*
  grammatical 567
  elegant 578
correction
  [*see* correct]
  house of – 752
  under – 879
corrective 662
corregidor 745
correlation
  relation 9
  reciprocity **12**
correspondence
  correlation 12
  similarity 17
  agreement 23
  writing **592**
  – *course* 537
correspondent
  messenger 534
  journalist 593
  consignee 758
corresponding

similar 17
agreeing 23
corridor *region* 181
  place 191
  passage 627
  – *train* 272
corrigendum 495
corrigible 658
corrival 726
corrivalry 720
corrivation 348
corroborant 662
corroboration
  evidence 467
  assent 488
corrode *burn* 384
  erode 659
  afflict 830
corrosive
  [*see* corrode]
  acrid 171
  destructive 649
  – *sublimate* 663
corrugate
  derange 61
  constrict 195
  roughen 256
  rumple 258
  furrow 259
corruption
  decomposition 49
  neology 563
  foulness 653
  disease 655
  deterioration 659
  improbity 940
  vice 945
corrupting
  noxious 649
corsage 225
corsair 273, 792
corse 362
corselet 225
corset 225
corso 728
cortège
  adjunct 39
  continuity 69
  accompaniment
    88
  journey 266
  suite 746
cortes 696
cortex
  cortical 223
coruscate 420
corvette 273, 726
corybantic 503
coryphée 599
Corypheus
  teacher 540
  director 694
coscinomancy 511
cosey 892
cosignificative 522
cosine 217
cosmetic
  remedy 662
  ornament 847
cosmic 318
cosmogony &c. 318
cosmopolitan
  abode 189
  mankind 372
  philanthropic 910
  sociality 892
cosmorama 448
cosmos 60, 318

Cossack 726
cosset
  darling 899
  caress 902
cost 812
  pay –s 807
  to one's –
  evil 619
  badness 649
  – *what it may* 604
  – *price* 815
costermonger 797
costless 815
costly 814
costive
  taciturn 585
costume 225
  theatrical – 599
costumé 225
  bal – 840
costumier 225
  theatrical 599
cosy *snug* 377
  sociable 892
cot *abode* 189
  bed 215
cote 189
cotenancy 778
coterie *class* 75
  junto 712
  society 892
coterminous 120
cothurnus 599
cotillon 840
cottage 189
  – *piano* 417
cottager 188
cotter 188
cotton 205
  – *seed oil* 356
couch *lie* 213
  bed 215
  stoop 308
  lurk 528
  – *one's lance* 720
  – *in terms* 566
couchant 213
couci-couci 651
cough 349
  churchyard – 655
couleur de rose
  good 648
  prosperity 734
  view en – 836
coulisses 599
coulter 253
council
  senate **696**
  church 995
  hold a – 695
  – *of education* 542
  – *school* 542
councillor 696
counsel
  advice 695
  lawyer 968
  keep one's own –
    528
  take – *think* 451
  inquire 461
  be advised 695
count *clause* 51
  item 79
  compute 85
  estimate 480
  lord 875
  – *one's chickens*
    before they are

hatched 858,
  863
  – *the cost* 864
  – *upon*
  believe 484
  expect 507
  to be –ed *on one's*
  fingers 103
countenance
  face 234
  appearance 448
  favor 707
  approve 931
  keep in –
  conform 82
  induce 615
  encourage 861
  vindicate 937
  keep one's –
  brook 826
  not laugh 837
  out of –
  abashed 879
  put out of – 874
  stare out of – 885
  – *falling*
  disappointment
    509
  dejection 837
counter *contrary* 14
  number 84
  table 215
  stern 235
  token 550
  shop-board 799
  over the –
  barter 794
  buy 795
  sell 796
  run – 179
  – *to* 708
counteract
  compensate 30
  physically 179
  hinder 706
  voluntarily 708
counteraction 14,
  179
counterbalance 30
counterblast
  counteract 179
  retaliate 718
countercharge 462
counterchange
  correlation 12
  interchange 148
countercharm 993
countercheck
  mark 550
  hindrance 706
counterclaim 30
counter-evidence
  468
counterfeit
  imitate 19
  copy 21
  simulate 544
  sham 545
  coinage 792
counterfoil 550
countermand 756
countermarch 266,
  283
countermark 550
countermine
  plan 626
  oppose 708
countermotion 283

counterorder 756
counterpane 223
counterpart
  match 17
  copy 21
  reverse 237
counterplot
  plan 626
  oppose 708
  retaliate 718
counterpoint 415
counterpoise
  compensate 30
  weight 319
  hinder 706
counter-poison 662
counterpole 14
counter-project 718
counter-protest 468
counter-revolution
  146
counterscarp 717
countersign
  evidence 467
  assent 488
  mark 550
counterstroke 718
countervail
  outweigh 28
  compensate 30
  evidence 468
counterwork 708
countess 875
counting-house 799
countless 105
countrified 189
  vulgar 851
country
  region 181
  abode 189
  rural 371
  authority 737
  love of – 910
country-dance 840
countryman
  commonalty 876
  friend 890
county 181
  – *seat* 189
  – *town* 189
  – *school* 542
  – *council* 696
  – *court* 966
coup
  instantaneous 113
  action 680
  – *de bec*
  attack 716
  censure 932
  – *d'épée dans*
  l'eau 645
  – *d'essai* 675
  – *d'état*
  revolution 146
  plan 626
  action 680
  lawless 964
  – *de grâce*
  end 67
  death-blow 361
  completion 729
  punishment 972
  – *de main*
  violence 173
  action 680
  attack 716
  – *de maître*
  excellent 648

skilful 698
success 731
– d'oeil
sight 441
appearance 448
display 882
– de plume 590
– de soleil
hot 384
mad 503
à – sûr 474
– de théâtre
appearance 448
display 882
coupé 272
couple
unite 43
two 89
–d with
added 37
accompanied 88
coupler 45
couplet 89, 597
coupling 45
coupon 800
courage 861
moral – 604
– oozing out 862
courant, au – 490
coureur, avant –
673
courier
traveler 268
guide 524
messenger 534
course *order* 58
continuity 69
time 106, 109
layer 204
motion 264
locomotion 266,
267
direction 278
dinner 298
river 348
pursuit 622
way 627
conduct 692
arena 728
bend one's – 266
in due – 134
hold a – 278
in the – of
during 106
keep one's –
progress 282
persevere 604a
let things take
their –
continue 143
inaction 681
follow as of – 478
mark out a – 626
of –
conformity 82
effect 154
certain 474
assent 488
necessity 601
willingly 602
custom 613
consent 762
expect 871
race – 840
run its –
end 67
complete 729
take a – 622

take its – 151
– of action 692
– of business 625
– of events 151
– of inquiry 461
– of preparation
673
– runs smooth 734
– of study 537
– of things 151
– of time 121
courser
horse 271
swift 274
coursing
kill 361
pursue 622
court *close* 181, 182
house 189
hall 191
flatness 213
invite 615
pursue 622
council 696
retinue 746
solicit 765
gentility 852
wish 865
woo 902
flatter 933
tribunal 966
bring into – 467
friend at – 526,
711
pay – to
servile 886
love 897, 902
flatter 933
put out of – 731
– card 840
– of honor 939
courteous 894
courtesan 962
courtesy
stoop 308, 314
submit 725
politeness 894
show –
respect 928
courtier
servile 886
flatterer 935
–like 933
courtly 852
courtship 902
courtyard 182
cousin 11
coûte-que-coûte
certainly 474
necessary 601
resolution 604
cove *cell* 191
hollow 252
bay 343
covenant
compact 769
condition 770
security 771
covenanter 488
Coventry
Earl of –
cards 840
send to –
eject 297
disrepute 874
seclusion 893
cover
compensate 30

include 76
superpose, lid 223
dress 225
stopper 263
meal 298
conceal 528
retreat 530
report 531
keep clean 652
keep safe 664
preserve 670
under –
hidden 528
pretence 545
safe 664
with dust 653
covercle 223
covering 223
coverlet 223
Coverley, Sir Roger
de – 840
covert *abode* 189
invisible 447
latent 526
refuge 666
feme –e 903
– way 627
coverture 903
covet *desire* 865
envy 921
covetous
miserly 819
covey
assemblage 72
multitude 102
cow
animal 366
female 374
intimidate 860
coward 862
cowardice 862
cowboy 370
cower *stoop* 308
fear 860
cowardice 862
servile 886
cowherd 370
cowhide 223, 975
cowhouse 189
cowkeeper 370
cowl *sacerdotal* 999
dress 225
cowled 999
cowl-staff 215
co-worker 690
coxcomb 854
coxcombry
affectation 855
vanity 880
coxswain 269
coy *timid* 860
modest 881
cozen 545
crab *sourness* 397
–like motion
deviation 279
regression 283
grouch 901a
crabbed *sour* 397
unintelligible 519
obscure style 571
difficult 704
uncivil 895
sulky 901a
crack *split* 44
discontinuity 70
instantaneous 113
fissure 198

furrow 259
brittle 328
sound 406
excellent 648
injure 659
skilful 698
boast 884
– a bottle
food 298
social 892
drunken 959
– of doom
end 67
future 121
destruction 162
– one's invention
515
– a joke 842
– shot 700
crackbrained 503
cracked
unmusical 410
fanatical 481
mad 503
faulty 651
– bell 408a
– voice 581
cracker 406
crackle 406
cracksman 792
crack-up 162
cradle
beginning 66
infancy 127
origin 153
placing 184
bed 215
training 673
aid 707
in the – 129
– song 415
craft *shipping* 273
business 625
skill 698
cunning 702
craftiness 498
craftsman 690
craftsmanship 680
crag *pointed* 253
hard 323
land 342
craggy
rough 256
craig *height* 206
crake 884
cram *crowd* 72
stuff 194
choke 261
teach 537
learn 539
gorge 957
– down the throat
induce belief 484
compel 744
crambe repetita
weariness 841
satiety 869
crambo 597
crammed 52
– to overflowing
641
crammer *lie* 546
teacher 537
cramp
fastening 45
paralyze 158
weaken 160
little 193

compress 195
spasm 378
hinder 706
cramped *style* 579
cran 191
cranch
[see craunch]
crane *angle* 244
elevate 307
instrument 633
– neck 245
craniology &c. 450
cranium 450
crank
fanatic 504
instrument 633
wit 842
treadmill 975
crankle *fold* 258
crankling
rough 256
cranky *weak* 160
ill health 655
cranny 198
crape
crinkle 248
mourning 839
crapulence
intemperance 95
gluttony 957
drunken 959
crash
destruction 162
collision 276
gain entrance 29
sound 406
crasis *nature* 5
coherence 48
composition 54
crass 31
– ignorance 491
crassitude
breadth 202
thickness 352
crate
receptacle 191
vehicle 272
crater *deep* 208
hollow 252
craunch
shatter 44
chew 298
pulverize 330
cravat 225
crave *ask* 765
desire 865
envy 921
craven *submit* 725
cowardly 862
craw 191
crawfish 607
crawl *time* 109
creep 275
back down 283,
606
servile 886
– with 102
crawling 102
crayons 556
craze 481
crazy *weak* 160
mad 503
creachy 160
creak 410
cream
emulsion 352
oil 356
important part

physical pain 378
mental pain 830
crucible
  dish 191
  conversion 144
  furnace 386
  experiment 463
  laboratory 691
  put into the – 163
crucifix 219, 998
crucifixion 828
cruciform 219
crucify
  physical torture 378
  mental agony 830
  execution 972
crucis, experimentum – 463
crude *color* 428
  - *style* 579
  unprepared 674
cruel
  painful 830
  inhuman 907
  – to be kind 914
cruelly *much* 31
cruet 191
cruise
  vessel 191
  navigation 267
cruiser 726
cruising 267
crumb *small* 32
  powder 330
  – of comfort 834
crumble
  decrease 36
  weak 160
  destruction 162
  brittle 328
  pulverize 330
  spoil 659
  – into dust
  decompose 49
  – under one's feet 735
crumbling
  [see crumble]
  dangerous 665
crumenal 800
crump
  distorted 243
  curved 245
crumple
  ruffle 256
  fold 258
  – up *destroy* 162
  crush 195
crunch
  shatter 44
  chew 298
  pulverize 330
crupper 235
crusade 722
crush *crowd* 72
  destroy 162
  compress 195
  pulverize 330
  humble 879
  – under an iron heel 739
  – one's hopes
  disappoint 509
  hopeless 859
crushed 828
crushing 830
crust 223

crustacean 366
crusty 895, 901*a*
crutch
  support 215
  angle 244
  -ed Friars 996
crux 219, 704
  – *criticorum* 533
cry *human* **411**
  animal 412
  publish 531, 532
  call 550
  voice 580
  vogue 613
  weep 839
  far – to 196
  full – *loud* 404
  raise a – 550
  – aloud
  implore 765
  – out against
  dissuade 616
  censure 932
  – down 932, 934
  – for 865
  – before hurt 839
  – for joy 838
  – you mercy
  deprecate 766
  pity 914
  forgive 918
  – shame 932
  – to beseech 765
  – up 931
  – for vengeance 923
  – wolf *false* 544
  alarm 669
  – and little wool
  overrate 482
  boast 884
  disappoint 509
crying [see cry]
  urgent 630
  weary 841
  – evil 619
  – shame 874
  – sin 945
crypt *cell* 191
  grave 363
  ambush 530
  altar 1000
cryptic 475, 528
cryptography
  hidden 528
  writing 590
crystal *hard* 323
  transparent 425
  snow – 383
  – gazer 513
  – gazing 511, 992
  – oil 356
  clear as – 519
crystalline
  dense 321
  hard 323
  transparent 425
crystallization 321, 323
csako 225, 717
cub *young* 129
  vulgar 851
  clown 876
  unlicked – 241
cubby-hole 191
cube
  three dimensions 92, 93

  form 244
cubicle 191
cubist 556
cubit 200
cucking stool 975
cuckold 905
cuckoldom 961
cuckoo
  imitation 19
  repetition 104
  sound 407
  cry 412
cuddle 196, 902
cudgel *beat* 276
  weapon 727
  punish 975
  take up the –s
  aid 707
  attack 716
  contention 720
  – one's brains
  think 451
  imagine 515
cue *hint* 527
  watchword 550
  plea 617
  rôle 625
  take one's – from 695
  in proper – 698
cuff *sleeve* 225
  blow 276
  punishment 972
cui bono 644, 645
cuique voluptas
  sui – 865
cuirass 717
cuirassier 726
cuisine 298
  batterie de – 957
culbute
  inversion 218
  fall 306
cul-de-lampe
  engraving 558
  ornament 847
cul-de-sac
  concave 252
  closed 261
  difficulty 704
culinary 298
  – art 673
cull *dupe* 547
  choose 609
  take 789
cullender 260
cullibility 486
cullion 949
cully *deceive* 545, 547
culm 388
culminate
  maximum 33
  height 206
  top 210
  complete 729
culpability *vice* 945
  guilt 947
culprit 949
cult 983
cultivate *till* 365, 371
  sharpen 375
  improve 658
  prepare 673
  aid 707
cultivated
  courteous 894

  – taste 850
cultivator 371
culture
  knowledge 490
  improvement 658
  taste 850
  politeness 894
culverin 727
culvert 350
cum multis aliis 37, 102
cumber *load* 319
  obstruct 706
cumbersome
  incommodious 647
  disagreeable 830
cummerbund 225
cumulative 72
  increasing 35
  assembled 72
  – evidence 467
  – vote 609
cumulus 353
cunctando restituit
  rem 681
cunctation 133
cuneiform 244
  – character 590
cunning
  prepense 611
  sagacious 698
  artful **702**
  – fellow 700
  – man 994
cup *vessel* 191
  hollow 252
  beverage 298
  remedy 662
  trophy 733
  tipple 959
  between – and lip 111
  in one's –s 959
  – that cheers &c. 298
  – of humiliation 879
  dash the – from one's lips 509
  – too low 837
cupbearer 746
cupboard 191
cupellation 384
Cupid *beauty* 845
  love 897
  gods 979
cupidity
  avarice 819
  desire 865
cupola *height* 206
  roof 223
  dome 250
cup-tossing 621
cur *dog* 366
  coward 862
  sneak 949
curable 658, 660, 662
curacy 995
curare 663
curate 996
curative 660
curator 694, 758
curb *moderate* 174
  slacken 275
  dissuade 616
  restrain 751

  shackle 752
  curb exchange 621
curbstone 233
curd *density* 321
  pulp 354
  (*cohere* 46)
curdle *condense* 321
  (*cohere* 46)
  make the blood – 830
curdled 352
cure *reinstate* 660
  remedy 662
  preserve 670
  benefice 995
curé 996
cureless 859
curfew 126
curia 966
curio 847
curiosa felicitas 698
curiosity
  unconformity 83
  inquiring **455**
  phenomenon 872
curious
  exceptional 83
  inquisitive 455
  true 494
  beautiful 845
  desirous 865
curiously *very* 31
curl *bend* 245
  convolution 248
  hair 256
  cockle up 258
  badge 747
  – up one's lip 930
curling *game* 840
curmudgeon
  miser 819
  plebeian 876
currency
  publicity 531
  money 800
current *existing* 1
  usual 78
  present 118
  happening 151
  flow 264
  of water 348
  of air 349
  rife 531, 532
  language 560
  habit 613
  danger 667
  account – 811
  against the – 708
  go with the – 82
  pass –
  believed 484
  fashion 852
  stem the – 708
  – belief 488
  – of events 151
  – of ideas 451
  – of time 109
currente calamo 590
curricle 272
curriculum 537
curry *food* 298
  rub 331
  condiment 392, 393
  – favour with
  love 897
  flatter 933

curry-comb 370
curse *bane* 663
  adversity 735
  painful 830
  malediction 908
cursed *bad* 649
cursitor 968
cursive 590
cursory
  transient 111
  inattentive 458
  hasty 684
  take a – view of
    457
  neglect 460
curst 901a
curt *short* 201
  concise 572
  taciturn 585
curtail *retrench* 38
  shorten 201
  –ed of its fair pro-
    portions
  distorted 243
  ugly 846
curtain 223
  shade 424
  hide 528, 530
  theatre 599
  fortification 717
  behind the –
    invisible 447
    inquiry 461
    knowledge 490
  close the – 528
  raise the – 529
  rising of the – 448
  – lecture 932
  – raiser 66, 599
curtsy
  stoop 308, 314
  submit 725
  polite 894
curule 696
curvature 245
curvet *leap* 309
  turn 311
  oscillate 314
  agitate 315
curvilinear 245
  – motion 311
cushion *pillow* 215
  soft 324
  relief 834
cushy 829
cusp *angle* 244
  sharp 253
cuspidor 191
cuss 908
custard 298
custodes? quis cus-
  todiet – 459
custodian 753
custody *safe* 664
  captive 751
  retention 781
  in – *prisoner* 754
  accused 938
  take into – 751
custom *old* 124
  habit 613
  barter 794
  sale 796
  tax 812
  fashion 852
  – honored in
    breach 614
customary

[*see custom*]
  regular 80
customer 795
custom-house 799
  – officer 965
custos 753
  – rotulorum 553
cut *divide* 44
  bit 51
  discontinuity 70
  interval 198
  curtail 201
  layer 204
  form 240
  notch 257
  blow 276
  eject 297
  reap 371
  physical pain 378
  cold 385
  neglect 460
  carve 557
  engraving 558
  road 627
  attack 716
  portion 786
  affect 824
  mental pain 830
  dance step 840
  decline acquaint-
    ance 893
  discourtesy 895
  tipsy 959
  – short 628
  unkindest – of all
    pain 828
  malevolence 907
  – across 302
  – adrift 44
  – along 274
  have a – at 716
  – away 274
  – a whetstone with
    a razor
    sophistry 477
  waste 638
  misuse 679
  – both ways 468
  – capers 309
  – according to
    cloth
    economy 817
    caution 864
  – and come again
    repeat 104
    enough 639
  – dead 893
  – direct 893
  – down *destroy* 162
    shorten 201
    fell 308
    kill 361
  – down expenses
    817
  – and dried
    arranged 60
    prepared 673
  – a figure
    appearance 448
    fashion 852
    repute 873
    display 882
  – the first turf 66
  – the ground from
    under one
    confute 479
    hinder 706
  – to the heart 824,

830
  – ice with
    influence 175
  – of one's jib 448
  – jokes 842
  – the knot 705
  – off *subduct* 38
    disjoin 44
    kill 361
    impede 706
    bereft 776
    secluded 893
  – off with a shil-
    ling 789
  – open 260
  – out *surpass* 33
    stop 142
    substitute 147
    plan 626
  – out for 698
  – out work
    prepare 673
    direct 693
  – to pieces
    destroy 162
    kill 361
  – a poor figure 874
  – to the quick 830
  – up root and
    branch 162
  – up rough 900
  – and run 274
  depart 293
  escape 623
  – short *stop* 142
  destroy 162
  shorten 201
  silence 581
  – one's stick
    depart 283
    avoid 623
  – one's own throat
    699
  – and thrust 716
  – in two 91
  – up *divide* 44
    destroy 162
    pained 828
    give pain 830
    discontented 832
    dejected 837
    censure 932
  what one will – up
    for 780
  – one's way
    through 302
cutaneous 223
cute 698
cuticle 223
cutlass 727
cutlery 253
cut-purse 792
cutter 273
cut-throat
  killer 361
  evil-doer 913
cutting *sharp* 253
  cold 383
  path 627
  affecting 821
  painful 830
  reproachful 932
cuttings
  excerpta 596
  selections 609
cutty stool 950
cwt. 98, 319
cyanogen 438

cyanide of potas-
  sium *poison* 663
cycle *time* 106
  period 138
  circle 247
  ride 266
  vehicle 272
  – car 272
cyclist 268
cycloid 247
cyclometer 200
cyclone
  rotation 312
  wind 349
Cyclopean
  strong 159
  huge 192
cyclopedia
  knowledge 490
  book 593
Cyclops
  monster 83
  mighty 159
  huge 192
  dupe 547
cygne
  chant du – 360
  – noir 650
cylindric 249
cyma 847
cymbal 417
cymbalo 417
cymophanous 440
cynic
  misanthrope 911
  detractor 936
  ascetic 955
  closet – 893
cynical
  contemptuous 930
  censorious 932
  detracting 934
cynicism
  discourtesy 895
  contempt 930
cynosure *sign* 550
  direction 693
  wonder 870
  repute 873
Cynthia of the
  minute 149
cypher [*see cipher*]
cypress
  interment 363
  mourning 839
Cyprian 962
cyst 191
czar 745

D

da capo 104
dab *small* 32
  paint 223
  slap 276
  clever 700
dabble *water* 337
  dirty 653
  meddle 682
  fribble 683
dabbled *wet* 339
dabbler 493
dachshund 366
dacoit 792
dactyl 597
dactylogram 467
dactyliomancy 511

dactylonomy
  numeration 85
  symbol 550
dad 166
daddy 166
dado 211
daedal
  variegated 440
daedalion
  convoluted 248
  artistic 698
daft 503
dagger 727
  look –s *anger* 900
  threat 909
  air drawn – 515
  plant – in breast
    give pain 830
  speak –s 932
  at –s drawn
    opposed 708
    discord 713
    enmity 889
    hate 898
daggle *hang* 214
  dirty 653
dagobah 1000
Dagon 986
daguerreotype
  represent 554
  paint 556
dahabeah 273
Dail Eireann 696
daily
  frequent 136
  periodic 138
  – occurrence
    normal 82
    habitual 613
  – paper 531
dainty *food* 298
  savory 394
  pleasing 829
  delicate 845
  tasty 850
  fastidious 868
dairy 191, 370
  – maid 946
dais *support* 215
  throne 747
daisy
  fresh as a – 654
  – pied 847
dale 252
dally *delay* 133
  irresolute 605
  inactive 683
  amuse 840
  fondle 902
dalmatic 999
Daltonism 443
dam *parent* 166
  close 261
  pond 343
  obstruct 706
damage *evil* 619
  injure, spoil 659
  price 812
damages 974
damascene 440
damask 434
dame
  woman 374
  teacher 540
  lady 875
damn
  malediction 908
  condemn 971

– with faint praise 932, 934
damnable 649
damnatory
  disapprove 932
  condemn 971
damnify
  damage 649
  spoil 659
damnosa hereditas 663
Damocles
  sword of – 667
Damon and Pythias 890
damozel 129
damp
  moderate 174
  moist 339
  cold 385
  sound 405
  dissuade 616
  hinder 706
  depress 837
  dull 843
  – the sound 408a
damper 387
damsel
  youth 129
  female 374
Dan to Beersheba 52, 180
Danaë 803
Danaos, timeo –
  doubt 485
  caution 864
dance
  jump 309
  oscillate 314
  agitate 315
  rejoice 838
  sport 840
  sociality 892
  lead the – 175
  lead one a –
  run away 623
  circuit 629
  difficult 704
  practical joke 929
  St. Vitus' – 315
  – attendance
  waiting 133
  follow 281
  servant 746
  petition 765
  servility 886
  – the back step 283
  – upon nothing 972
  – the war dance 715
dance-band 417
dance-music 415
dander 900
Dandie Dinmont 366
dandiprat 193
dandle 902
dandruff 653
dandy
  ship 273
  fop 854
dandyism 855
danger 665
  in – *liable* 177
  source of – 667
  – past 664

– signal 669
dangerous
  [*see* danger]
  – classes 913
  – illness 655
  – person 667
dangle *hang* 214
  swing 314
  display 882
dangler 281
Daniel *sage* 500
  judge 967
dank 339
Dannemora 752
danseuse 599
dapper
  little 193
  elegant 845
dapple 433
dappled 440
darbies
  handcuffs 752
Darby and Joan
  secluded 893
  married 903
dare *defy* 715
  face danger 861
  – not 860
  – say *probable* 472
  believe 484
  suppose 514
dare-devil
  courage 861
  rash 863
  bluster 887
daring 861
  unreserved 525
  – imagination 515
dark
  obscure 421
  dim 422
  black 431
  blind 442
  invisible 447
  unintelligible 519
  latent 526
  joyless 837
  insidious 940
  in the –
  ignorant 491
  leap in the –
  experiment 463
  chance 621
  rash 863
  keep – *hide* 528
  – ages 491
  – cloud 735
  view with – eyes 932
  – lantern 423
darkly
  see through a glass – 443
darkness [*see* dark] 421
  children of – 988
  love – better than light 989
  powers of – 978
darky 431
darling *beloved* 897
  favorite 899
darn 660
dart *swift* 274
  propel 284
  missile 727
  – to and fro 684
Dartmoor 752

Darwinism 357
dash
  small quantity 32
  mix 41
  swift 276
  fling 284
  mark 550
  courage 861
  cut a – *repute* 873
  display 882
  – at *resolution* 604
  attack 716
  – board 666
  – cup from lips 761
  – down 308
  – hopes
  disappoint 509
  fail 732
  dejected 837
  despair 859
  – on 274
  – off *paint* 556
  write 590
  active 682
  haste 684
  – of the pen 590
dashed [*see* dash]
  humbled 879
dashing
  fashionable 852
  brave 861
  ostentatious 882
dastard 862
data *evidence* 467
  reasoning 476
  supposition 514
date *time* 106
  chronology 114
datum 673
daub *cover* 223
  paint 428
  misrepresent 555
  dirt 653
daughter 167
daunt 860
dauntless 861
Dauphin 875
davenport 191, 215
davit 214
Davus sum non Oedipus
  unintelligent 499
  artless 703
  dull 843
Davy Jones' locker 310
dawdle *tardy* 133
  slow 275
  inactive 683
dawk 534
dawn
  precursor 64
  begin 66
  priority 116
  morning 125
  light 420
  dim 422
  glimpse 490
dawplucker 936
day
  period 108
  present time 118
  light 410
  all – 110
  clear as –
  certain 474
  intelligible 518
  manifest 525

close of – 126
decline of – 126
denizens of the – 366
good old –'s 122
have had its – 124
one fine – 119
open as – 703
order of the – 613
red letter – 642
see the light of – 446
– after day
  diuturnal 110
  frequent 136
– by day
  repeatedly 104
  time 106
  periodic 138
– after the fair 135
–s gone by 122
– of judgment 121
happy as the – is long 827, 836
– and night
  frequent 136
labor – and night 686
–s numbered
  transient 111
  death 360
– one's own 731
– of rest 686
– star 423
– after to-morrow 121
– before yesterday 122
–s of week 138
all in –'s work 625
daybed 215
daybook *record* 551
  accounts 811
daybreak
  morning 125
  dim 422
day-dream
  fancy 515
  hope 858
day-laborer 690
daylight 125, 420
  see – *intelligible* 518
  – saving 114
daymare 859
daze 420
dazed 376
dazzle
  light 420
  blind 422, 443
  put out 458
  astonish 870
  awe 928
dazzling
  [*see* dazzle]
  beautiful 845
de: – die in diem *time* 106
  periodic 138
  – facto 1
  – fond en comble 52
  – novo 104
  – omnibus rebus 81
  – profundis 821
deacon 996

deaconry 995
dead *complete* 52
  inert 172
  colorless 429
  lifeless 360
  insensible 376
  – against
  contrary 14
  oppose 708
  more – than alive 688
  – asleep 683
  – beat
  powerless 158
  – certainty 474
  – color 556
  – cut 893
  – drunk 959
  – failure 732
  – flat 213
  – heat 27
  – languages 560
  – letter
  impotent 158
  unmeaning 517
  useless 645
  laxity 738
  exempt 927
  illegal 964
  – level 16
  – lift *exertion* 686
  difficulty 704, 706
  – lock *cease* 142
  stoppage 265
  – march 363, 415
  – of night
  midnight 126
  dark 421
  – reckoning
  numeration 85
  measurement 466
  – secret 533
  – set against 708
  – set at
  attack 716
  – shot 700
  – silence 403
  – sound 408a
  – stop 142
  – to 823
  – wall
  hindrance 706
  defence 717
  – weight 706
  – water 343
deaden
  weaken 158
  moderate 174
  sound 405
  mute 408a
  benumb 823
dead-house 363
deadlock 142, 704
deadly *killing* 361
  pernicious 649
  unhealthy 657
  – sin 947
  – weapon 727
deads 645
deaf 419
  inattentive 458
  – to advice 606
  – and dumb 581
  turn – ear to
  neglect 460
  unbelief 487
  refuse 764
  – to reason 901a

censure 932
detract 934
defamer 936
defatigation 841
default
  incomplete 53
  shortcoming 304
  neglect 460
  insufficiency 640
  debt 806
  non-payment 808
in – of 187
judgment by – 725
defaulter *thief* 792
  non-payer 808
  rogue 949
defeasance 756
defeat
  confute 479
  succeed 731
  failure 732
– one's hope 509
defeatism 911
defecate 652
defecation 299
defect
  decrement 40a
  incomplete 53
  imperfect 651
  failing 945
defection
  relinquishment 624
  disobedience 742
defective
  incomplete 53
  insufficient 640
  imperfect 651
defence
  plea 462
  resist 717
  vindication 937
first line of – 726
defenceless
  impotent 158
  weak 160
  exposed 665
defendant 938
defensible *safe* 664
  excusable 937
defensive alliance 712
defer 133
– to *assent* 488
  submit 725
  respect 928
deference
  obedience 743
  humility 879
  courtesy 894
  respect 928
defiance 715, 909
  threat 909
in – opposition 708
set at – disobey 742
– of danger 861
deficiency
  [see deficient]
  vice 945
deficient
  inferior 34
  incomplete 53
  shortcoming 304
  insufficient 640
  imperfect 651
deficit
  incompleteness 53
  debt 806

defigure 846
defile
  interval 198
  march 266
  dirt 653
  spoil 659
  shame 874
  impure 961
define
  specify 79
  limit 233
  explain 522
  name 564
definite
  [see define]
  visible 446
  certain 474
  exact 494
  intelligible 518
  manifest 525
  perspicuous 570
definition
  interpretation 521
definitive *final* 67
  affirmative 535
  decided 604
deflagration 384
deflate 195
deflation
  currency 800
deflect
  curve 245
  deviate 279
deflower
  spoil 659
  violate 961
defluxion
  egress 295
  flowing 348
defœdation 653, 659
deform 241
deformity
  distortion 243
  ugliness 846
  blemish 848
defraud *cheat* 545
  swindle 791
defray 807
deft *suitable* 23
  clever 698
defunct 360, 362
defy 715
  disobey 742
  threaten 909
– danger 861
dégagé *free* 748
  fashion 852
degenerate 659
  deterioration 659
  shame 874
  dishonor 940
degradation
  deterioration 659
  shame 874
  dishonor 940
degree 26
  term 71
  honor 873
by –s 26
by slow –s 275
degustation 390
dehiscence 260
dehort
  dissuade 616
  advise 695
dehydrate 340
Dei gratiâ 924
deification 873, 981
deify

hono
  idolatry 991
deign
  condescend 762
  consent 879
Deism
  heterodoxy 984
  irreligion 989
Deity 976
  tutelary – 664
dejection
  excretion 299
  melancholy 837
déjeûner 298
délabrement 162
delaceration 659
delation 938
delator 527
delay 133
dele 552
delectable
  savory 394
  agreeable 829
delectation 827
delectus 562
delegate
  transfer 270
  commission 755
  consignee 758
  deputy 759
delenda est Carthago
  destroy 162
  curse 908
delete 162
deleterious
  pernicious 649
  unwholesome 657
deletion 552
deletory
  destructive 162
deliberate
  slow 275
  think 451
  attentive 457
  leisure 685
  advise 695
  cautious 864
deliberately
  [see deliberate]
  late 133
  with premeditation 611
delicacy *weak* 160
  slender 203
  dainty 298
  brittleness 328
  texture 329
  savory 394
  color 428
  exact 494
  scruple 603
  ill health 655
  difficult 704
  pleasing 829
  beauty 845
  taste 850
  fastidious 868
  honor 939
  pure 960
  delicate ear 418
délice 377
delicious *taste* 394
  pleasing 829
delicti, corpus –
  guilt 947
  lawsuit 969
delicto, in

flagrante – 947
delight
  pleasure 827
  pleasing 829
Delilah 962
delimit 233
delineate
  outline 230
  represent 554
  describe 594
delineator 559
delineavit 556
delinquency 304, 947
delinquent 949
deliquation 335
deliquesce 36
deliquescence 335
deliquium
  paralysis 158
  fatigue 688
delirant reges plectuntur Achivi 739
delirium
  raving 503
  passion 825
– tremens 503, 959
delitescence
  invisible 447
  latency 526
  seclusion 893
deliver
  transfer 270
  utter 580, 582
  birth 662
  rescue 672
  liberate 750
  give 784
  relieve 834
– as one's act and deed 467
– the goods 729
– judgment 480
– a speech 582
deliverance 672
delivery
  [see deliver]
  bring forth 161
  cash on – 807
dell 252
Delphic oracle
  prophetic 513
  equivocal 520
  latent 526
delta 342
delude *error* 495
  deceive 545
deluge *crowd* 72
  water 337
  flood 348
  redundance 641
delusion
  [see delude]
  insane 503
  self – credulous 486
delve *dig* 252
  till 371
– into inquire 461
demagogue
  director 694
  malcontent 710
  rebel 742
demagogy 737
demand
  inquire 461

order 741
ask 765
price 812
claim 924
in – require 630
desire 865
saleable 796
demarcation 233
dematerialize 317
demean oneself
  conduct 692
  humble 879
  dishonor 940
demeanor
  air 448
  conduct 692
  fashion 852
demency 503
dementia 503
demerit 945
demesne
  abode 189
  property 780
demi- 91
demigod *hero* 861
  angel 948
demigration 266
demijohn 191
demi-jour 422
demi-lune 717
demi-monde
  plebeian 876
  licentious 962
démenti 536
demirep 962
demise *death* 360
  transfer 783
  lease 787
demisemiquaver 413
demission 756
demit 757
demiurge
  deity 979
demivolt 309
demobilize 73
democracy *rule* 737
  commonalty 876
Democrats
  party 712
Democritus 838
demoiselle 129
demolish 479
demon *violent* 173
  bane 663
  devil 980
– in human shape 913, 949
– worship 991
demoniacal
  malevolent 907
  furious 824
  wicked 945
demonology
  demons 980
  sorcery 992
demonstration
  number 85
  proof 478
  manifest 525
  ostentation 882
  ocular – 441, 446
demonstrative
  manifest 525
  indicative 550
  vehement 825
demonstrator 524
demoralize

unnerve 158
spoil 659
vicious 945
Demosthenes 582
demotic 590
demulcent
  mild 174
  soothing 662
demur
  disbelieve 485
  dissent 489
  unwilling 603
  hesitate 605
  without – 602
demure
  grave 826
  sad 837
  affected 855
  modest 881
demurrage 132
demurrer 969
den *abode* 189
  study 191, 893
  sty 653
  prison 752
  – of thieves 791
denary 98
denaturalize
  corrupt 659
denaturalized
  abnormal 83
dendriform 242, 367
dendrology 369
denial
  negation 536
  refusal 764
  self- 953
denigrate 431
denization 748
denizen
  inhabitant 188
  freeman 748
  –s of the air 979
  –s of the day 366
Denmark, rotten in
  the state of –
  526
denomination
  class 75
  name 564
  sect 712
  religious – 983
denominational
  dissent 489
  theological 983
  – education 537
denominator 84
denote
  specify 79
  mean 516
  indicate 550
dénouement
  end 67
  result 154
  disclosure 529
  completion 729
denounce
  curse 908
  disapprove 932
  accuse 938
dense
  crowded 72
  ignorant 493
density 321
dent 252, 257
dental 561
denticulated 253,
  257

dentifrice 652
dentistry 662
denude 226
denuded *loss* 776
  – of
    insufficient 640
denunciation
  [*see* denounce]
deny *dissent* 489
  negative 556
  refuse 764
  – oneself
    avoid 623
    seclude 893
    temperate 953
    ascetic 990
Deo volente 470,
  976
deobstruct 705
deodand 974
deodorize 399
  clean 652
deontology 926
deoppilation 705
deorganization 61
deosculation 902
depart 293
  – from
    deviate 15, 279
    relinquish 624
  – this life 360
departed
  non-existent 2
department
  class 75
  region 181
  business 625
departure 293
  new – 66
  point of – 293
depend *hang* 214
  contingent 475
  – upon
    be the effect of 154
    evidence 467
    trust 484
  – on circumstan-
    ces 475
depended on, to
  be –
    certain 474
    reliable 484
    honorable 939
dependency 777,
  780
dependent
  effect 154
  liable 177
  hanging 214
  puppet 711
  servant 746
  subject 749
deperdition 776
dephlegmation 340
depict 554, 556
  describe 594
depilation 226
depilatory 662
depletion 638, 640
deplorable *bad* 649
  disastrous 735
  painful 830
deplore *regret* 833
  complain 839
  remorse 950
deploy 194
depone 535
deponent 467

depopulate
  eject 297
  desert 893
deportation
  removal 270
  emigration 297
  expulsion 972
deportment 692
depose
  evidence 467
  declare 535
  dethrone 738, 756
deposit *place* 184
  precipitate 321
  store 636
  security 771
  payment 809
depositary 801
deposition
  [*see* depose,
  deposit]
  record 551
depository 636
depôt *terminal* 292
  store 636
  shop 799
  – ship 726
deprave *spoil* 659
depraved *bad* 649
  vicious 945
deprecation 766
  pity 914
  disapprove 932
depreciation
  decrease 36
  underestimate 483
  discount 813
  cheap 815
  disrespect 929
  censure 932
  detraction 934
  accusation 938
depredation 791
depredator 792
deprehension 789
depression
  lowness 207
  depth 208
  concavity 252
  lowering 308
  dejection 837
  dulness 843
depressing
  painful 830
deprive *subduct* 38
  take 798
  – of life 361
  – of power 158
  – of property 789
  – of strength 160
  deprived of 776
depth *physical* 208
  mental 498
  out of one's – 304
  310
  – bomb 727
  – of misery 828
  – of thought 451
  – of winter 383
depurate *clean* 652
  improve 658
depuratory 662
deputation 755
depute 755
deputies, chamber
  of – 696
deputy 759
dequantitate 36

derangement 61
  mental – 503
Derby-day 720
derelict *land* 342
  danger 667
  relinquish 782
  outcast 893
dereliction
  relinquishment
    624, 782
  guilt 947
  – of duty 927
deride
  ridicule 856
  disrespect 929
  contempt 930
derivation
  origin 153, 154,
    155
  verbal 562
derive
  attribute 155
  deduce 480
  acquire 775
  income 810
dermal 223
dermatology 223
dernier
  – cri 850
  – ressort 601
dérobée, à la – 528
derogate
  underrate 483
  disparage 934
  dishonor 940
  – from 874
derogatory
  shame 874
  dishonor 940
derrick 307, 633
derring-do 861
dervish 996
désagrément 830
descant *music* 415
  diffuseness 573
  loquacity 584
  dissert 595
descend *slope* 217
  go down 306
  – to particulars
    special 79
    describe 594
descendant 167
descensus Averni,
  facilis – 665
descent *lineage* 166
  fall 306
  inheritance 775
description
  kind 75
  name 564
  narration 594
descriptive music
  415
descry 441
desecrate
  misuse 679
  disrespect 929
  profane 988
desert
  unproductive 169
  empty 187
  plain 344
  run away 623
  relinquish 624,
    782
  merit 944
  waste sweetness

on – air 638
deserted
  outcast 893
deserter 144, 607,
  623
desertless 945
deserts 924
deserve
  be entitled to 924
  merit 944
  – notice 642
  – belief 484
désespoir, au –
  dejected 837
  hopeless 859
déshabillé, en –
  not dressed 226
  unprepared 674
  homely 849
desiccate 340
desiccator 340
desiderate *need* 630
  desire 865
desideratum
  inquiry 461
  requirement 630
desire 865
design
  prototype 22
  form 240
  delineation 554
  painting 556
  intention 620
  plan 626
designate
  specify 79
  call 564
designation 75
designed
  aforethought 611
designer 164, 559
designing
  cunning 702
designless 621
désillusioner 529
desinence *end* 67
  discontinuance
    142
desipience 499
desipere in loco 840
desirable 646
desire 865
  will 600
  have no – for 866
desist
  discontinue 142
  relinquish 624
  inaction 681
desk *box* 191
  support 215
  school 542
  pulpit 1000
désobligeant 272
désoeuvré 681
desolate *alone* 87
  ravage 162
  afflicted 828
  dejected 837
  secluded 893
desolating
  painful 830
désorienté 475
despair *grief* 828,
  859
despatch *eject* 297
  kill 361
  news 532
  epistle 592

expedition 682
haste 684
conduct 692
complete 729
command 741
happy – 972
– *case* 191
– *food* 298
– *rider* 534
desperado
rash 863
blusterer 887
evil-doer 913
desperate *great* 31
violent 173
impossible 471
resolved 604
difficult 704
excitable 825
hopeless 859
rash 863
anger 900
despicable
trifling 643
shameful 874
contemptible 930
despise 930
– *danger* 861
despite 30, 907
in – 708
despoil *injure* 659
take 789
rob 791
despond 837, 860
despot 745
despotism
authority 737
severity 739
arbitrary 964
despumate 652
desquamation 226
dessert 298
dessous des cartes
cause 153
latent 526
secret 533
connaître le – 490
dessus dessous
sens – 218
destination *end* 67
arrival 292
intention 620
destiny *chance* **152**
fate 601
fight against – 606
destitute
insufficient 640
poor 804
refuge for – 666
destrier 726
destroy
demolish 162
injure 659
– *hopes* 859
– *life* 361
destroyed
[*see destroy*]
inexistent 2
failure 732
destroyer **165**
warship 726
evil-doer 913
destructive
bad 649
destructor 383
desuetude **614**
disuse 678
desultory

disordered 59
fitful 70
multiform 81
irregular in time 139
changeable 149
deviating 279
agitated 315
desume 788
detach 44
detached
irrelated 10
loose 47
detachment
part 51
army 726
detail *describe* 594
special portions 79
allot 786
ornament 847
attention to – 457, 459
in – 51
details
minutiæ 32
unimportant 643
detain 781
detect 480a
detective 527, 664
detention 133, 751, 781
house of – 752
in house of – 938
détenu 754
deter *dissuade* 616
alarm 860
deterge *clean* 652
detergent
remedy 662
deterioration **659**
determinate
special 79
exact 474
conclusive 480
intended 620
determine *end* 67
define 79
cause 153
direction 278
satisfy 462
make sure 474
judge 480
discover 480a
resolve 604
determined
resolute 604
determinism 601
deterration 529
detersion 652
detersive 662
detest *dislike* 867
hate 898
detestable 649
dethronement
anarchy 738
abrogation 756
detonate
explode 173
sound 406
detortion *form* 243
meaning 523
détour *curve* 245
circuit 629
detract *subduct* 38
underrate 483
defame 934
slander 938

detraction 934
detractor 936
detrain 292
detriment
evil 619
deterioration 659
detrimental 649
detrition 330
detritus
fragments 51
deposit 270
powder 330
detrude
cast out 297
cut down 308
detruncate 38
deuce *two* 89
devil 978
play the – 825
– is in him 608
deuced *great* 31
painful 830
deus 976
– *ex machinâ*
aid 707
auxiliary 711
deity 976
sorcerer 994
deuterogamy 903
devastate
destroy 162
havoc 659
develop
increase 35
produce 161
expand 194
evolve 313
development 144, 154
devexity
bending 217
curvature 245
deviate *vary* 20a
change 140
turn 279
diverge 291
circuit 629
– *from* 15
– *from rectitude* 940
– *from virtue* 945
deviation 279
device *motto* 550
expedient 626
artifice 702
devil
seasoned food 392
evil-doer 913
bad man 949
Satan 978
demon 980
fight like –s 722
have a – 503
machinations of the – 619
play the – with
injure 659
malevolent 907
printer's – 591
raise the – 828
– *may care*
rash 863
indifferent 866
insolent 885
give the – his due
right 922
vindicate 937
fair 939

– in one
headstrong 863
temper 901
– to pay
disorder 59
violence 173
evil 619
failure 732
penalty 974
– *take* 908
– take the hindmost
run away 623
haste 684
cowardice 862
–'s *tattoo* 407
devilish *great* 31
bad 649
malevolent 907
devious *curved* 245
deviating 279
circuitous 311
devisable 270
devise *imagine* 515
plan 626
bequeath 784
devised by the enemy 546
devisee *possess* 779
receive 785
deviser 164
devitalize 158
devoid *absent* 187
empty 640
not having 777a
devoir *courtesy* 894
respect 928
devolve 783
– *on* 926
devote *destine* 601
employ 677
consecrate 873
– *to destruction* 908
– the mind to 457
– *oneself to* 604
devoted
habit 613
ill-fated 735
obedient 743
undone 828
friendship 888
love 897
devotee
zealot 682
aspirant 865
pious 987
fanatic 988
devotion [*see devotee, devoted*]
love 897
piety 987
worship 990
self – 942
devour
destroy 162
eat 298
gluttony 957
devoured by
feeling 821
devouring element 382
devout 987, 990
devoutless 989
devoutly 821
dew 339
shake as –drops from lion's .

mane 483
dewy eve 126
dexterous 238, 698
dextrality **238**
dey 745
dhow 273
diable:
avoir le – au corps 503
– à quatre
disorder 59
violence 173
loud 404
excitement 825
tirer le – par la queue 804
diablerie 978, 992
diabolic
bad 649
malevolent 907
wicked 945
Satanic 978
Diacoustics 402
diacritical 550
diadem 747, 847
diaeresis 49
diagnosis 465, 655
diagnostic
special 79
experiment 463
indication 550
(*intrinsic* 5)
diagonal 217
diagram 554
dial 114
as the – to the sun
veracious 543
faithful 772
dialect 563
dialectic
argument 476
language 560
dialogism 586
dialogue 588
diameter 202
diametrically opposite
contrariety 14
contraposition 237
diamond
lozenge 244
type 591
goodness 648
ornament 847
rough – 703
– cut diamond
cunning 702
retaliation 718
– *jubilee* 883
– *wedding* 883
Diana *moon* 318
chaste 960
goddess 979
diapason 413
diaper 847
diaphanous 425
diaphonics 402
diaphoresis 299
diaphragm 68, 228
diaporesis 475
diarchy 737
diarrhea 299
diary 114, 551
diastole 194
diatessaron 413
diathermancy 384
diathesis

nature 5
state 7
temperament 820
diatonic 413
diatribe 932
dibble
  perforator 262
  till 371
dibs *money* 800
dicacity 885
dice 156, 621
  on the – 470
dicer 621
  false as –'s oaths
    546
dichotomy
  bisect 91
  angle 244
dichroism 440
dichromatic 443
dickens 978
dicker 794
dicky 215, 225
dictaphone 553
dictate
  write 590
  enjoin 615
  advise 695
  authority 737
  command 741
dictator 694, 745
  –'s of society 852
dictatorial
  dogmatic 481
  wilful 600
  insolent 885
dictatorship 737,
  739
diction 569
dictionary
  list 86
  words 562
  book 593
dictum
  judgment 480
  maxim 496
  affirmation 535
  command 741
didactic 537
didder 383
diddle 545, 791
Diddler, Jeremy –
  792
diduction 44
die *mould* 22
  expire 360
  engraving 558
  hazard of the –
    621
  never say – 604a
  not willingly let –
    670
  – away
    vanish 4
    decrease 36
    cease 142
  the – is cast 601
  – with ennui 841
  – for *desire* 865
    endearment 902
  – game 951
  – hard
    obstinate 606
    resist 719
  – in harness 143,
    604a
  – in the last ditch
    604a

– with laughter
  838
– from the mem-
  ory 536
– and make no
  sign 951
– out 2, 4
– of a rose in aro-
  matic pain 822
– in one's shoes
  972
– a violent death
  361
– hard 710, 832
dies non *never* 107
  rest 687
diet *food* 298
  council 696
  spare – 956
dietetics 662
differ 15
  discord 713
  agree to – 489
  beg to – 439
  – in opinion 489
  – toto coelo
    contrary 14
    dissimilar 18
    dissent 489
difference 15
  [see *differ*]
  numerical 84
  perception of –
    465
  split the – 774
  – engine 85
different 15
  multiform 81
  – time 119
differentia 15
differential 15, 84
  – calculus 85
differentiate 79, 465
differentiation
  calculation 85
  discrimination
    465
difficult 704
  – to please 868
difficulties
  poverty 804
  in – 806
difficulty 704
  question 461
diffide 485
diffident 860, 881
diffluent 348
diffraction 470
  – grating 445
diffuse *mix* 41
  disperse 73
  publish 531
  style 573
diffuseness 104, 573
dig *deepen* 208
  excavate 252
  till 371
  – out 461
  – the foundations
    673
  – up 455, 480a
digamy 903
digest *arrange* 60
  boil 384
  think 451
  compendium 596
  plan 626
  prepare 673

brook 826
diggings 189
dight *dress* 225
  ornament 847
digit 84
digitate 44
digitated 253
digladiation 720
dignify 873
dignitary
  clergy 996
dignity
  glory 873
  pride 878
  honour 939
dignus vindice
  nodus
  unintelligible 519
  difficulty 704
  prodigy 872
digress
  deviate 279
  style 573
digression
  circuit 629
dihedral 89
  – angle 244
diis alitur visum
  disappointment
    509
  necessity 601
dijudication 480
dike *gap* 198
  fence 232
  furrow 259
  gulf 343
  conduit 350
  defence 717
dilaceration 44
dilapidation 659
dilate
  increase 35
  swell 194
  widen 202
  rarefy 322
  expatiate 573
dilatory
  slow 275
  inactive 683
dilection 89
dilemma
  uncertain 475
  logic 476
  choice 609
  difficulty 704
dilettante 492, 850
dilettantism
  knowledge 490
diligence
  coach 272
diligent
  active 682
  – thought 457
dilly-dally
  irresolution 605
  inactivity 683
dilucidation 522
diluent 335
dilute *weaken* 160
  water 337
diluvian 124
dim *dark* 421
  faint 422
  invisible 447
  unintelligible 519
dime 800
dimension 192
dimidiate 91

diminish
  lessen 36
  contract 195
  – the number 103
diminutive 32, 193
diminuendo
  decreasingly 36
  music 415
dimness 422
dimple 252, 257
dimsightedness 443
  unwise 499
din 404
  – in the ear
    repeat 104
    drum 407
    loquacity 584
dine 298
  – with Duke
    Humphrey 87
ding 408
ding-dong
  repeat 104
  chime 407
dining-car 272
dining-room 191
dingle 252
dingy *boat* 273
  dark 421, 422
  colorless 429
  black 431
  gray 432
dinner 298
  – jacket 225
  – party 892
dint *power* 157
  concavity 252
  blow 276
  by – of
    instrumentality
    631
dio, sub – 220, 338
diocesan 996
diocese 181, 995
Diogenes
  recluse 893
  cynic 911
dioptrics 420
diorama *view* 448
  painting 556
diorism 465
dip *slope* 217
  concavity 252
  ladle 270
  direction 278
  insert 300
  descent 306
  plunge 310
  water 337
  candle 423
  baptize 998
  – one's hands into
    take 789
  – into
    glance at 457
    inquire 461
    learn 539
diphthong 561
diploma
  evidence 467
  commission 755
diplomacy
  artfulness 702
  mediation 724
  negotiation 769
diplomatist

messenger 534
  expert 700
  consignee 758
dipper 191
dipsomania
  insanity 503
  desire 865
  drunkenness 959
dipsomaniac 504
diptych 86, 551
dire *hateful* 649
  disastrous 735
  grievous 830
  fearful 860
direct
  straight 246
  teach 537
  artless 703
  command 741
  – attention to 457
  – one's course
    motion 278
    pursuit 622
  – the eyes to 441
direction
  [see *direct*]
  tendency 278
  indication 550
  management 693
  precept 697
directly *soon* 132
director
  teacher 540
  theater 599
  manager 694
  master 745
  – of the budget
    801
directorship 737
directory *list* 86
  council 696
diremption 44
direption 791
dirge
  funeral 363
  song 415
  lament 839
dirigible balloon
  273, 726
dirk 727
dirt 653
  throw –
    defame 874
    disrespect 929
  – cheap 815
  like – under one's
    feet 749
dirty *dim* 222
  opaque 426
  unclean 653
  disreputable 874
  dishonorable 940
  – end of stick 699
  – sky 353
  – weather 349
  do – work
    servile 886
    flatterer 935
diruption 162
disability
  impotence 158
disable 158
  weaken 160
disabuse 527, 529
disaccord 713
disadvantage
  evil 619
  inexpedience 647

at a – 34
lie under a – 651
disadvantageous 647, 649
disaffection
　dissent 489
　enmity 889
　hate 898
disaffirm 536
disagreeable 830, 867
disagreement
　difference 15
　incongruity 24
　dissent 489
　discord 713
disallow 761
disannul 756
disappearance 449
disappointment
　balk 509
　fail 732
　discontent 832
disapprobation 706, 932
disapprover 936
disarm disable 158
　weaken 160
　reconcile 831
　propitiate 914
disarrange 61
disarray
　disorder 59
　undress 226
disaster evil 619
　failure 732
　adversity 735
　calamity 830
disastrous bad 649
disavow 536
disband
　separate 44
　disperse 73
　liberate 750
disbar
　abrogate 756
　punish 972
disbarment 55
disbelief 485, 487
　religious 989
disbench 756, 972
disbowel 297
disbranch 44
disburden
　facilitate 705
　– one's mind 529
　– oneself of 782
disburse 809
disc 220, 234
discard eject 297
　relinquish 624
　disuse 678
　abrogate 756
　refuse 764
　repudiate 773
　surrender 782
　– from one's thoughts 458
discarded 495
disceptation 476
discern see 441
　know 490
discernible 446
discernment 498, 868
discerption 44
discharge
　violence 173

propel 284
emit 297
excrete 299
sound 406
acquit oneself 692
complete 729
liberate 750
abrogate 756
pay 807
exempt 927a
acquit 970
– a duty 926, 944
– a function
business 625
utility 644
– itself egress 295
river 348
– from the memory 506
– from the mind 458
– an obligation 772
discind 44
disciple pupil 541
　votary 711
　Christian 985
disciplinarian
　master 540
　martinet 739
discipline
　order 58
　teaching 537
　training 673
　restraint 751
　punishment 972
　religious 990
disclaim deny 536
　repudiate 756
　abjure 757
　refuse 764
disclosure 480a, 529
discoid layer 204
　frontal 220
　flat 251
discoloration 429
discolored
　shabby 659
　ugly 846
　blemish 848
discomfit 731
discomfiture 732
discomfort
　physical 378
　mental 828
discommend 932
discommode
　hinder 706
　annoy 830
discommodious 645, 647
discompose
　derange 61
　put out 458
　hinder 706
　pain 830
　disconcert 874
　anger 900
discomposure 828
disconcert
　derange 61
　distract 458
　disappoint 509
　hinder 706
　discontent 832
　confuse 879
disconcerted
　hopeless 859

disconformity 83
discongruity 24
disconnected
　style 575
disconnection
　irrelation 19
　disjunction 44
　discontinuity 70
disconsolate 837
discontent 832
discontinuance
　cessation 142
　relinquishment 624
discontinuity 70
discord
　difference 15
　disagreement 24
　of sound 414
　of color 428
　dissension 713
discount
　decrease 36
　decrement 40a
　money 813
　at a –
　disrepute 874
　disapproved 932
discountenance
　disfavor 706
　refuse 764
discourage
　dissuade 616
　sadden 837
　frighten 860
discourse
　teach 537
　speech 582
　talk 588
　dissert 595
　sermon 998
discourtesy 895
discous 202
discover
　perceive 441
　solve 462
　find 480a
　disclose 529
　– itself
　be seen 446
discovery 480a
discredit
　disbelief 485
　dishonor 874
discreditable
　vicious 945
discreet careful 459
　cautious 864
discrepancy 15
discrepant 24, 713
discrete
　separate 44, 70
　single 87
discretion will 600
　choice 609
　skill 698
　caution 864
　surrender at – 725
　use – 609
　years of – 131
discrétion à – 600
discrimination
　difference 15
　nice perception 465
　wisdom 498
　taste 850
　fastidiousness 868

disculpate 937
discumbency 213
discursion 266
discursive
　moving 264
　migratory 266
　wandering 279
　argumentative 476
　diffuse style 573
　conversable 588
　disserting 595
discus 840
discuss eat 298
　reflect 451
　inquire 461
　reason 476
　dissert 595
discussion
　[see discuss]
　open to – 475
　under – 461
disdain
　indifference 866
　fastidious 868
　arrogance 885
　pride 878
　contempt 930
disease 655
　occupational – 655
　–d mind 503
disembark 292
disembarrass 705
disembody
　decompose 49
　disperse 73
　spiritualize 317
disembogue
　emit 295
　eject 297
　flow out 348
disembowel 297, 301
disembroil 60
disenable 158
disenchant
　discover 480a
　dissuade 616
　displease 830
disencumber 705
disendow 756
disengage
　detach 44
　facilitate 705
　liberate 750
disengaged
　to let 763
disentangle
　separate 44
　arrange 60
　unroll 313
　decipher 522
　facilitate 705
　liberate 750
disenthral 750
disenthrone 756
disentitle 925
disespouse 905
disestablish
　displace 185
　abrogate 756
disesteem 929, 932
disfavor
　oppose 708
　hate 898
　disrespect 929
　view with – 932
disfigure
　deface 241

injure 659
deform 846
blemish 848
disfranchise 925
disgorge emit 297
　flow out 348
　restore 790
　pay 807
disgrace
　shame 874
　dishonor 940
　sense of – 879
disgraceful
　vice 945
disgruntle 509
disguise
　unlikeness 18
　conceal 528
　mask 530
　falsify 544
　untruth 546
disguised in drink 959
disgust taste 395
　offensive 830
　weary 841
　dislike 867
　hatred 898
　– of life 837
dish destroy 162
　plate 191
　food 298
　– of tea 892
dishabille
　undress 225
　unprepared 674
dishearten
　dissuade 616
　pain 830
　discontent 832
　deject 837
dished 252, 732
disherison 789
dishevel
　loose 47
　untidy 59
　disorder 61
　disperse 73
　intermix 219
dishonest false 544
　base 940
dishonour
　disrepute 874
　disrespect 929
　baseness 940
　– bills 808
dish-water 653
disillusion 509
disincline
　dissuade 616
　dislike 867
disinclined 603
disinfect
　purify 652
　restore 660
disinfectant 662
disingenuous
　false 544
　dishonorable 940
disinherit
　relinquish 782
　transfer 783
　deprive 789
disintegrate
　separate 44
　decompose 49
　pulverize 330
disinter exhume 363

discover 480a
disinterested **942**
disjecta membra
  separate 44
  disorder 59
  dispersed 73
  – *poetae* 597
disjoin 44
disjointed
  disorder 59
  powerless 158
  style 575
disjunction **44**
disjunctive 70
diskindness 907
dislike **867**
  reluctance 603
  hate 898
dislocate
  separate 44
  put out of joint 61
dislocated
  disorder 59
dislodge
  displace 185
  eject 297
disloyal 940
dismal
  depressing 830
  dejected 837
dismantle
  destroy 162
  divest 226
  render useless 645
  injure 659
  disuse 678
dismask 529
dismast
  render useless 645
  injure 659
  disuse 678
dismay 860
dismember
  separate 44
  disperse 73
dismiss
  send away 289
  discharge 297
  discard 678
  liberate 750
  abrogate 756
  relinquish 782
  punish 972
  – from the mind
    452, 458
dismount
  arrive 292
  descend 306
  render useless 645
disnest 185
disobedience **742**
  non-observance
    773
disoblige 907
disorder
  confusion **59**
  derange 61
  turbulent 173
  disease 655
  –ed intellect 503
disorderly
  unprincipled 945
disorganize
  derange 61
  destroy 162
  spoil 659
disorganized 59
disown 536

dispair 44
disparage
  underrate 483
  disrespect 929
  dispraise 932
  detract 934
disparity
  different 15
  dissimilar 18
  disagreeing 24
  unequal 28
  isolated 44
dispart 44
dispassionate 826
  – *opinion* 484
dispatch
  [*see* despatch]
dispel *scatter* 73
dispensable
  useless 645
dispensary 662
dispensation
  [*see* dispense]
  command 741
  licence 760
  relinquishment
    782
  exemption 927a
  –s of Providence
    976
dispense
  disperse 73
  give 784
  apportion 786
  retail 796
  – with
  disuse 678
  permit 760
  exempt 927a
  cannot be –d with
    630
dispeople
  eject 297
  expatriate 893
disperse
  separate 44
  scatter 73
  diverge 291
  waste 638
dispersion **73**
  – of light 420
  chromatic – 428
dispirit
  discourage 616
  sadden 837
displacement
  derange 61
  remove **185**
  transfer 270
displacency
  dislike 867
  incivility 895
  disapprobation
    932
displant 185
display *appear* 448
  show 525
  parade 882
displease 830
displeasure 828
  anger 900
displosion 173
displume 789
disport 840
disposal

[*see* dispose]
  at one's – 763, 777
dispose
  arrange 60
  tend 176
  induce 615
  – of *use* 677
  complete 729
  relinquish 782
  give 784
  sell 796
disposed 620
disposition
  nature 5
  order 58
  arrangement 60
  inclination 602
  mind 820
dispossess
  transfer 783
  take away 789
  – oneself of 782
dispraise 932
dispread 73
disprize 483
disproof
  counter-evidence
    468
  confutation 479
disproportion
  irrelation 10
  disagreement 24
disprove 479
disputable 475, 485
disputant 710, 726
disputatious 901
dispute
  discuss 476
  doubt 485
  deny 536
  discord 713
  in – 461
disqualification
  incapacitate 158
  useless 645
  unprepared 674
  unskilful 699
  disentitle 925
disquiet
  changeable 149
  agitation 315
  excitement 825
  uneasiness 828
  give pain 830
disquietude
  apprehension 860
disquisition 539,
    595
disregard
  overlook 458
  neglect 460
  make light of 483
  insensible to 823,
    826
  disrespect **929**
  contempt 930
  – of time 115
disrelish 867, 898
disreputable 874
  vicious 945
disrepute **874**, 929
disrespect **929**
  despise 930
disrobe 226
disruption
  disjunction 44
  destruction 162
  discord 713

dissatisfaction
  disappointment
    509
  sorrow 828
  discontent 832
dissect
  anatomize 44, 49
  investigate 461
dissemblance 18
dissemble 544
dissembler 548
disseminate
  scatter 73
  pervade 186
  publish 531
  teach 537
dissension 713
  sow – 898
dissent
  disagree **489**
  refuse 764
  heterodoxy 984
dissentient 15
dissentious 24
dissertation **595**
disservice
  disadvantage 619
  useless 645
disserviceable 649
dissever 44
dissidence
  disagreement 24
  dissent 489
  discord 713
  discontent 832
  heterodoxy 984
dissilience 173
dissimilarity **18**
dissimulate 544
dissipate *scatter* 73
  destroy 162
  pleasure 377
  prodigality 818
  amusement 840
  intemperance 954
  dissolute 961
dissocial 893
dissociate 44
dissociation
  irrelation 10
  separation 44
dissolute 961
  profligate 945
  intemperate 954
dissolution
  [*see* dissolve]
  decomposition 49
  destruction 162
  death 360
dissolve *vanish* 2, 4
  liquefy 335
  disappear 449
  abrogate 756
dissolving views
    448, 449
dissonance
  disagreement 24
  unmusical 414
  discord 713
dissuasion **616**
dissyllable 561
distaff
  – side 374
distain *dirty* 653
  ugly 846
distal 196
distance **196**
  overtake 282

go beyond 303
defeat 731
angular – 244
keep at a –
  discourtesy 895
keep one's –
  avoid 623
  modest 881
  respect 928
teach one his – 879
  – of time
  long time 110
  past 122
distaste 867
distasteful 830
distemper 299, 428
  color 428
  painting 556
  disease 655
distend 194
distended 192
distich 89, 597
distil *come out* 295
  extract 301
  evaporate 336
  drop 348
distinct
  disjoined 44
  audible 402
  visible 446
  intelligible 518
  manifest 525
  express 535
  articulate 580
distinction
  difference 15
  discrimination
    465
  style 578
  fame 873
  rank 875
  – without a differ-
    ence 27
distinctive 15
  – *feature* 79
distinctness 15
distingué 852, 873
distinguish
  perceive 441
  discriminate 465
  – by the name of
    564
distinguishable 15
distinguished
  superior 33
  repute 873
Distinguished
  Service Cross
    733
distortion
  obliquity 217
  twist **243**
  of vision 443
  misinterpret 523
  falsehood 544
  misrepresent 555
  ugly 846
distract 458
distracted
  confused 475
  insane 503
  excited 824
distraction
  passion 825
  love to – 897
distrain *take* 789
  appraise 812
  attach 969

distrait 458
distraught 824
distress
 distraint 789
 poverty 804
 affliction 828
 cause pain 830
signal of – 669
distressingly
 excessively 31
distribute
 arrange 60
 disperse 44, 73
 allot 786
district 181
 – council 696
distrust
 disbelief 485
 fear 860
distrustful 487
disturb
 derange 61
 change 140
 agitate 315
 excite 824
 distress 828, 830
disturbance 59
disunion
 discord 24
 separation 44
 disorder 59
 discord 713
disuse
 desuetude 614
 relinquish 624
 unemploy **678**
disused
 old 124
disvalue 932
ditch
 inclosure 232
 trench 259
 water 343
 conduit 350
 defence 717
to the last – 606
ditch-water 653
ditheism 984
dither 315
dithyramb
 music 415
 poetry 597
dithyrambic 503
ditto 13, 104
say – to 488
ditty 415
 – box 191
diurnal 138
diuturnity **110**
diva 416
divagate 279, 629
divan *sofa* 215
 council 696
 throne 747
 tribunal 966
divaricate *differ* 15
 bifurcate 91
 diverge 291
dive *swim* 267
 fly 267
 plunge 306, 310
 – into *inquire* 461
divellicate 44
diver 208
divergence
 difference 15
 variation 20a
 disagreement 24

deviation 279
separation 291
divers *different* 15
 multiform 81
 many 102
 – *coloured* 440
diverse 15
diversify
 very 20a
 change 140
diversion
 change 140
 deviation 279
 pleasure 377
 amusement 840
diversity
 difference 15
 irregular 16a
 dissimilar 18
 multiform 81
 – of *opinion* 489
divert *turn* 279
 deceive 545
 amuse 840
 – the *mind* 452,
 458
divertissement
 diversion 377
 drama 599
 amusement 840
Dives 803
divest *denude* 226
 take 789
 – oneself of
 abrogate 756
 relinquish 782
divestment **226**
divide *differ* 15
 separate 44
 part 51
 arrange 60
 arithmetic 85
 bisect 91
 vote 609
 apportion 786
dividend *part* 51
 number 84
 portion 786
divina particula
 aurae 450
divination
 prediction 511
 sorcery 992
divine *predict* 511
 guess 514
 perfect 650
 of God 976, 983,
 983a
 clergyman 996
divine afflatus 515
 – *right*
 authority 737
 due 924
 – *service* 990
diving 840
diving-bell 208
divining-rod 550,
 993
Divinity *God* 976
 theology 983
divisible
 number 84
division
 [*see* divide]
 part 51
 class 75
 arithmetic 85
 discord 713

military 726
divisor 84
divorce
 separation 44
 relinquish 782
 matrimonial **905**
Divorce Court 966
divulge 529
divulsion 44
divvy 786
dixi 535
dizen 847
dizzard 501
dizzy
 dimsighted 443
 confused 458
 vertigo 503
 – *height* 206
 – *round* 312
djerrid 727
djinn 980
do *fare* 7
 suit 23
 produce 161
 cheat 545
 act 680
 complete 729
 succeed 731
 I beg 765
all one can – 686
plenty to – 682
thing to – 625
 – away with
 destroy 162
 eject 297
 abrogate 756
 – battle 722
 – one's bidding
 743
 – business 625
 – to death 361
 – as done by 906,
 942
 – for *destroy* 162
 kill 361
 conquer 731
 serve 746
 punish 972
 – good 906
 – harm 907
 – honor 873
 – into
 translate 522
 – justice to 595
 – like 19
 – little 683
 – no harm 648
 – nothing 681
 – nothing but 136
 – one's office 772
 – as others do 82
 – over 223
 – as one pleases
 748
 – a service
 useful 644
 aid 707
 – up 660
have to – with
 680, 692
 – without 678
 – the work 686
 – wrong 923
docere, pisces na-
 tare – 641
docile *domesticated*
 370
 learning 539

willing 602
docimastic 463
dock *diminish* 36
 cut off 38
 port 189
 shorten 201
 edge 231
 store 636
 tribunal 966
docked
 incomplete 53
docker 690
docket
 list 86
 evidence 467
 note 550
 record 551
 security 771
dockyard 691
doctor
 learned man 492
 restore 660
 remedy 662
 after death the –
 135
 – accounts 811
 when –s disagree
 475
doctrinaire
 positive 474
 pedant 492
 affectation 855
 blusterer 887
doctrinal 537
doctrinarian 514
doctrine *tenet* 484
 knowledge 490
document 551
documentary
 evidence 467
dodder 315
doddering 128
dodecahedron 244
dodge *change* 140
 shift 264
 deviate 279
 oscillate 314
 pursue 461
 avoid 623
 stratagem 702
dodger, *artful* – 792
dodo 366
 extinct as the –
 122
doe *swift* 274
 deer 366
 female 374
doer
 originator 164
 agent 690
doff 226
 – the *cap* 894
dog *follow* 281
 animal 366
 male 373
 pursue 622
 wretch 949
cast to the –s
 destroy 162
 reject 610
 disuse 678
 abrogate 756
 relinquish 782
fire – 386
go to the –s
 destruction 162
 fail 732
 adversity 735

poverty 804
sea – 269
watch –
 safety 664
 warning 668
 keeper 753
hair of – that bit
 you 959
let sleeping –s lie
 141
 – in manger 706,
 943
 –tired 686
 –s of war 722
dog-cart 272
dog-cheap 815
dog-days 382
doge 745
dogged
 obstinate 606
 valour 861
 sullen 901a
dogger 273
doggerel
 verse 597
 ridiculous 851,
 853
dog-hole 189
dog-Latin 563
dogma *tenet* 484
 theology 983
dogmatic
 certain 474
 positive 481
 assertion 535
 obstinate 606
dogmatist 887
dog's ear 258
dog robber 746
dog-sick 867
dog-star 423
dog-trot 275
dog-weary 688
doily 852
doing
 up and – 682
 what one is – 625
doings
 events 151
 actions 680
 conduct 692
doit *trifle* 643
 coin 800
dolce far niente 681
doldrums
 dejection 837
 sulks 901a
dole
 small quantity 32
 scant 640
 give 784
 allot 786
 parsimony 819
 grief 828
doleful 837
 – *dumps* 901a
doll *small* 193
 image 554
dollar 800
dolman 225
dolmen 363, 551
dolor
 physical 378
 moral 828
dolorem, infandum
 renovare – 833
dolorous 830
dolphin 341

- the cup of
  misery 828
- into 348
- pipe 249
- of resources 640
drake *male* 373
  fire - 423
dram *drink* 298
  pungent 392
  stimulus 615
- *drinking* 959
drama 599
dramatic 599
  ostentation 882
- *author* 599
- *critic* 599
- *poetry* 597
dramatis personæ
  mankind 372
  play 599
  agents 690
  party 712
drapery 225, 847
drast 645
drastic 171
draught
  [*see also* draft]
  depth 208
  traction 285
  drink 298
  stream of air 349
  delineation 554,
    556
  plan 626
  physic 662
  troops 726
- *off* 73
draughts
  game 840
draughtsman
  artist 559
draw *equality* 27
  compose 54
  pull 285
  delineate 554, 556
- *aside* 279
- *off the attention*
  458
- *back*
  deduction 40a
  regret 283
  avoid 623
- *breath*
  refresh 689
  feeling 821
  relief 834
- *a cheque* 800
- *a curtain* 424
- *down* 153
- *forth* 677
- *from* 810
- *on futurity* 132
- *in one's horns*
  tergiversation 607
  humility 879
- *in* 195
- *an inference* 480
- *the line* 465
- *lots* 621
- *near time* 121
  approach 286
- *off eject* 297
  hinder 706
  take 789
- *on time* 121
  event 151
  induce 615
- *out*

protract 110
  late 133
  prolong 200
  extract 301
  discover 480a
  exhibit 525
  diffuse style 573
- *over induce* 615
- *a parallel* 9
- *the pen through*
  552
- *a picture* 594
- *profit* 775
- *and quarter* 972
- *the sword*
  attack 716
  war 722
- *the teeth of* 158
- *together*
  assemble 72
  co-operate 709
- *towards* 288
- *up order* 58
  stop 265
  write 590
- *up a statement*
  594
- *upon money* 800
- *the veil* 528
drawback *evil* 619
  imperfection 651
  hindrance 706
  discount 813
drawbar 45
drawbridge
  way 627
  escape 671
  raise the - 666
drawcansir 887
drawee 800
drawer
  receptacle 191
  artist 559
- *of water* 690
drawers
  dress 225
drawhead 45
drawing
  delineation 554,
    556
  prize 810
drawing-room
  assembly 72
  room 191
  fashion 852
drawl *prolong* 200
  creep 275
  in speech 583
  sluggish 683
drawn *equated* 27
- *battle*
- *irresistibly* 601
  pacification 723
  incomplete 730
dray 272
- *horse* 271
drayman 268
dread 860
dreadful *great* 31
  bad 649
  dire 830
  depressing 837
  fearful 860
dreadless 861
dreadnought
  warship 726
dream
  unsubstantial 4

error 495
  fancy 515
  sleep 683
  golden - 858
- *of think* 451
  intend 620
- *on other things*
  458
dreamer
  madman 504
  imaginative 515
dreamy
  unsubstantial 4
  inattentive 458
  sleepy 683
dreary
  monotonous 16
  solitary 87
  melancholy 830,
    837
dredge *collect* 72
  extract 301
  raise 307
dregs
  remainder 40
  refuse 645
  dirt 653
- *of the people* 876
- *of vice* 945
drench *drink* 298
  water 337
  redundance 641
- *with physic* 662
drencher 248
drenching rain 348
dress
  uniformity 16
  agree 23
  equalize 27
  clothes 225
  prepare 673
  ornament 847
  ostentation 882
  full - 852
- *circle* 599
- *the ground* 371
- *up falsehood* 544
  represent 554
- *wounds* 662
- *to advantage*
  847
dress-coat 225
dresser
  sideboard 215
  surgeon 662
dressing 932, 972
- *room* 191, 599
dressing-gown 225
dressmaker 225
dribble 295, 348
driblet 25, 32
drift
  accumulate 72
  distance 196
  motion 264
  flying 267
  float 267
  transfer 270
  direction 278
  deviation 279
  approach 286
  wind 349
  meaning 516
  intention 620
  snow - 383
drifter 273
drifting 605
driftless 621

drill *fabric* 219
  bore 260
  auger 262
  teach 537
  prepare 673
- *hall* 191
drink
  swallow 296
  liquor 298
  tipple 959
- *one's fill*
  enough 639
- *in imbibe* 296,
    298
- *in learning* 539
- *to celebrate* 883
  courtesy 894
drinking-bout 954
drink-money 784
drip 295, 348
dripping *wet* 330
  fat 356
drive *airing* 266
  impel 276
  propel 284
  break in 370
  urge 615
  haste 684
  direct 693
  attack 716
  compel 744
- *at mean* 516
  intend 620
- *a bargain*
  barter 794
  parsimony 819
- *care away* 836
- *a coach and six*
  through 83
- *into a corner*
  difficult 704
  hinder 706
  defeat 731
  subjection 749
- *to despair* 859
- *matters to an*
  extremity 604
- *from repel* 289
- *one hard* 716
- *home* 729
- *in* 300
- *to the last* 133
- *out* 297
- *trade*
  business 625
  barter 794
drivel *slobber* 297
  imbecile 499
  mad 503
  rubbish 517
driveler 501, 584
driver 268
  director 694
driving rain 348
drizzle 348
droil 683
droit du plus fort
  744
drôle *cards* 840
drole 949
- *de corps* 844
drollery
  amusement 840
  wit 842
  ridiculous 853
dromedary 271
drone *slow* 275
  sound 407, 412,

413
  inactive 683
drool 297
droop
  weak 160
  hang 214
  sink 306
  disease 655
  decline 659
  flag 688
  sorrow 828
  dejection 837
drop *small quantity*
  32
  discontinue 142
  powerless 158
  bring forth 161
  spherule 249
  emerge 295
  fall 306
  trickle 348
  relinquish 624
  discard 782
  gallows 975
  let - 308
  ready to -
  fatigue 688
- *asleep* 683
- *astern* 283
- *from the couds*
  508
- *dead* 360
- *by drop*
  by degrees 26
  in parts 51
- *in the bucket* 32
- *in upon* 674
- *into a good*
  thing 734
- *into the grave*
  360
- *a hint* 527
- *all idea of* 624
- *in arrive* 292
  immerse 300
  sociality 892
- *the mask* 529
- *off decrease* 36
  die 360
  sleep 683
- *in the ocean*
  trifling 643
- *the subject* 458
- *too much* 959
dropping fire 70
drop-scene 599
dropsical 194, 641
droshki 272
dross
  remainder 40
  slag 384
  trash 643, 645
  dirt 653
drought
  dryness 340
  insufficiency 640
drouth *desire* 865
drove
  assemblage 72
  multitude 102
drover 370
drown
  affusion 337
  kill 361
  ruin 731, 732
- *care* 840
- *the voice* 581
drowsy *slow* 275

sleepy 683
weary 841

drub
defeat 731, 732
punish 972

drudge *labour* 686
worker 682, 690

drug
render insensible 376
superfluity 641
trash 643
remedy 662
bane 663
– *in the market* 815

drugget
cover 223
clean 652
preserve 670

druggist 662

druid 996

drum
repeat 104
cylinder 249
sound 407
music 417
party 892
beat of –
signal 550
alarm 669
war 722
command 741
parade 882
ear – 418
muffled –
funeral 363
non-resonance 408a
– *and fife band* 417
– *fire* 407
– *out* 972

drum-head 964, 966

drum-major 745

drummer 416

drunken 959
reel like a – *man* 315

drunkenness 959

dry *arid* 340
style 575, 576, 579
hoarse 581
scanty 640
preserve 670
exhaust 789
tedious 841
dull 842
thirsty 865
cynical 932
teetotal 958
run – 640
with – *eyes* 823
– *dock* 189
– *joke* 842
– *land* 342
– *the tears* 834
– *up* 340, 638

dryad 979

dry-as-dust
antiquarian 122
dull 843

dryness 340

dry-nurse
teach 537
teacher 540
aid 707

dry-point 558

dry-rot
dirt 653
decay 659
bane 663

dualism 984

duality 89

duarchy 737

dub 564

dubious 475

ducat 800

duce 745

duchess 745, 875

duchy 181

duck *stoop* 308
plunge 310
water 337
darling 897, 899
play –*s and drakes*
recoil 277
prodigality 818
–*'s egg*
zero 101
– *in thunder* 870

ducking-stool 975

duckling 127

duck-pond 370

duct 350

ductile
elastic 323
flexible 324
trimming 607
easy 705
docile 743

dud 158, 727

dude 854

duds 225

dudgeon
dagger 727
discontent 832
churlishness 895
hate 898
anger 900
sullenness 901a

due
expedient 646
owing 806
proper 924, 926
give his – *to*
right 922
vindication 937
fair 939
in – *course* 109
occasion 134
– *respect* 928
– *sense of* 498
– *time*
soon 132
– *to*
cause and effect 154, 155
give – *weight* 465

duel 720

duelist 726

dueness 924

duenna
teacher 540
guardian 664
keeper 753

dues 812

duet 415

duff 298

duffer
bungler 701
smuggler 792

dug 250

dug-out
old man 130

boat 273
defence 717

duke *ruler* 745
noble 875

dulce domum 189

dulcet
sweet 396
sound 405
melodious 413
agreeable 829

dulcify 174, 396

dulcimer 417

Dulcinea 897

dulcorate 396

dulia 990

dull *weak* 160
inert 172
moderate 174
blunt 254
insensible 376, 381
sound 405
dim 422
colorless 429
ignorant 493
stolid 499
style 575
inactive 683
unapt 699
callous 823
dejected 837
weary 841
prosing 843
simple 849
– *of hearing* 419
– *sight* 443

dullard 501

dullness 843

duly 924

duma 696

dumb 581
– *animal* 366
– *show* 550
– *waiter* 307
strike –
ignorant 493
astonish 870
humble 879

dumbfounder
disappoint 509
silence 581
astonish 870
humble 879

dummy
substitute 147
impotent 158
speechless 581
inactive 683

dump *music* 415
store 636
undersell 796

dumpling 298

dumps
discontent 832
dejection 837
sulk 901a

dumpy *little* 193
short 201
thick 202

dun *dim* 422
colorless 429
grey 432
importune 765
creditor 805

dunce
ignoramus 493
fool 501

dunderhead 501

dune 206

dung 653

dungeon 752

dunghill
dirt 653
cowardly 862
baseborn 876
– *cock* 366

Dunker 984

dunt 716

duo 415

duodecimal 99

duodecimo
little 193
book 593

duodenary 98

duodenum 98

duologue
interlocution 588
drama 599

dupe
credulous 486
deceive 545
deceived **547**

duplex 90, 189

duplicate
imitate 19
copy 21
double 90
tally 550
record 551
redundant 641
pawn 805

duplication
imitation 19
doubling **90**
repetition 104

duplicature
fold 258

duplicity
duality 89
falsehood 544

dura lex sed lex 926

durable
long time 110
stable 150

durance 141, 751
in – 754

duration 106
contingent – **108a**
infinite – 112

durbar
conference 588
council 696
tribunal 966

duress
compulsion 744
restraint 751

during 106
– *pleasure &c.* 108a

durity 323

dusk
evening 126
half-light 422

dusky
dark 421
black 431

dust *levity* 320
powder 330
corpse 362
trash 643
dirt 653
money 800
come to –
die 360
come down with the – 807

humbled in the – 879
kick up a – 885
level with the – 162
lick the –
submit 725
fail 732
make to bite the – 731
turn to –
deorganized 358
die 360
– *in the balance* 643
throw – *in the eyes*
blind 442
deceive 545
plead 617
– *one's jacket* 972

duster 652

dust-bin, dust-hole 191, 645
fit for the –
useless 645
dirty 653
spoilt 659

dustman
cleaner 652

dust-storm 330

dusty
powder 330
dirt 653

Dutch
double – 519
high – 519
– *auction* 796
– *courage* 862

Dutchman, flying 515

dutiful 944

duty
business 625
work 686
tax 812
courtesy 894
obligation **926**
respect 928
worship 990
rite 998
do one's –
virtue 944
on – 680, 682

duumvirate 737

Duval, Claude – 792

D.V. 470, 976

dwarf
lessen 36
small 193
elf 980

dwell
reside 186
abide 265
– *upon*
descant 573

dweller 188

dwelling 184, 189

dwindle *lessen* 36
shrink 195

dyad 89

dye 428

dying 360

dyke [*see* dike]

dynamic energy 157

dynamics 276

dynamitard 863
dynamite 727
dynamo 153
dynasty 737
dysentery 299
dyspepsia 655
dysphony 581

E

each 79
- to each 786
- other 12
- in his turn 148
eager
willing 602
active 682
ardent 821
desirous 865
- expectation 507
eagle
standard 550
money 800
- boat 726
- eye *sight* 441
intelligence 498
- winged *swift* 274
insignia 747
eagre 348
ean 161
ear 418
corn 154
come to one's -s
527
din in the -
loud 404
drum 407
all - 418
have the - of
belief 484
friendship 888
lend an -
hear 418
attend 457
meet the - 418
nice - 418
no - 419
offend the - 410
pick up the -s
attention 457
expectation 507
put about one's -s
308
quick - 418
reach one's -s 527
ring in the - 408
set by the -s
discord 713
hate 898
resentment 900
split the -s 404
together by the -s
discord 713
contention 720
up to one's -s
redundance 641
active 680, 682
willing - 602
word in the - 586
- for music 416,
418
in at one - out at
the other
inattention 458
forget 506
not for -s polite
961

make the -s tingle
anger 900
- ache 378
ear-drum 418
earl 875
earless 419
earliness **132**
early 132
get up - 682
earmark 550
earn 775
earnest *willing* 602
determined 604
emphatic 642
pledge 771
pay in advance
809
eager 821
in -
affirmation 535
veracious 543
strenuous 682
ear-piercing 410
ear-ring 847
ear-shot 197
out of - 405
ear-splitting 404
earth *ground* 211
world 318
land 342
corpse 362
what on -
inquiry 461
wonder 870
- closet 653
earthenware
baked 384
sculpture 557
earthling 372
earthly 318
end of one's -
career 360
of no - use 645
earthly-minded
943, 989
earthquake 146,
173
earthwork 717
earwig *flatter* 933,
935
ear-witness 467
ease *bodily* 377
style 578
leisure 685
facility 705
mental 827
content 831
at one's -
prosperous 734
mind at -
cheerful 836
set at - *relief* 834
take one's - 687
- off *deviate* 297
- one of take 789
easel *support* 215
painting 556
- picture 556
easement
property 780
relief 834
easily
[*see easy*]
let one down - 918
- accomplished
705
- deceived 486
- persuaded 602

East 236, 278
Easter *period* 138
rite 998
- Monday
holiday 840
- offering
gift 784
- sepulcher 1000
easy *gentle* 275
style 578
facile 705
make oneself -
about 484
take it -
inactive 683
inexcitable 826
- ascent 217
- of belief 472
- chair
support 215
repose 687
- circumstances
803
- going
willing 602
irresolute 605
lenient 740
inexcitable 826
contented 831
indifferent 866
- sail
moderate 174
slow 275
- temper 894
- terms 705
- to understand
518
- virtue 961
eat *food* 298
tolerate 826
- dirt 725, 879
- one's fill
enough 639
gorge 957
- heartily 298
- one's words 879
- out of house and
home *take* 789
prodigal 818
gluttony 957
- of the same
trencher 892
- one's words 607
eatables 298
eaten up with 820
eau, battre l' - 645
faire venir l' - à la
bouche 865
mettre de l' - dans
son vin 174
eaves 250
eavesdropper 455,
527
eavesdropping 418,
532
ébauche 626
ebb *decrease* 36
contract 195
regress 283
recede 287
waste 638
spoil 659
low - 36
low 207
depression 308
insufficient 640
- and flow 314
- of life 360

ebb-tide *low* 207
dry 340
ebony 431
ebriety 959
ebullient
violent 173
hot 382
excited 824
ebullition
energy 171
violence 173
agitation 315
heating 384
excitation 825
anger 900
écarté 840
ecce
- iterum Crispinus
104
- signum 550
eccentric 220
irregular 83
foolish 499
crazed 503, 504
capricious 608
ecchymosis 299
ecclesiastic
church 995
clergy 996
ecclesiastical
canonical 985
- court 966
- law 963
ecclesiolatry 991
écervelé 458
échafaudage 673
échappée 840
échapper belle 671
échelon 279
echo *imitate* 19
copy 21
repeat 104
reflection 277
resonance 408
answer 462
assent 488
applaud to the -
931
awake -es 404
éclaircissement 522
éclat 873
eclectic 609
eclipse *surpass* 33
disappearance
449
hide 528
outshine 873, 874
partial - *dim* 422
total - *dark* 421
under an -
invisible 447
out of repute 874
ecliptic 318
eclogue 597
economic pressure
751
economy
order 58
conduct 692
frugality **817**
animal - 359
écorcher les oreilles
410
ecphorize 615
écru 433
ecstasis 683
ecstasy
frenzy 515

transport 821
rapture 827
ecstatic 829
ecstatica 994
ectoplasm 992
ectype 21
ecumenical 78
edacity 957
Edda 986
eddy
whirlpool 348
current 312
danger 667
edematous 194, 324
Eden 827
edge *energy* 171
height 206
brink **231**
sidle 279
advantage 731
cutting - 253
on - 256, 507
take the - off 174
- of hunger 865
- in 228
- one's way 282
edge-tools 253
play with - 863
edgewise 217
edging
obliquity 217
border 231
ornament 847
edible 298
edict 741
edification
building 161
teaching 537
learning 539
piety 987
edifice 161
edifying *good* 648
edile 965
edit
publication 531
condense 596
revise 658
edition, new - 658
editor 593
educate 537
educated 490
self - 490
education
teaching 537
knowledge 490
man of - 492
higher - 490
educational 537,
542
educe *extract* 301
discover 480a
educt 40
eduction 40a
edulcorate 396, 652
eel 248
wriggle like an -
315
eerie 860
efface
delete 162
disappear 449
obliterate 552
- from the
memory 506
effect
consequence **154**
product 161
impression 375

complete 729
carry into – 692
with crushing –
  162
in – 5
take – 731
to that – 516
effective
  capable 157
  useful 644
effectuation 729
expedient 646
effects 780, 798
effectual 731
effectually 52
effectuate 729
effeminate
  weak 160
  womenlike 374
  timorous 862
  sensual 954
effeminize 158
effendi 875
effervesce
  energy 171
  violence 173
  agitate 315
  bubble 353
  excited 825
effervescent 338
effete *old* 128
  weak 160
  useless 645
  spoiled 659
efficacious
  [*see* efficient]
efficient
  power 157
  agency 170
  utility 644
  skill 698
effigy 21, 554
effleurer *skim* 267,
  460
efflorescence 330
effluxion of time
  109
effluence *egress* 295
  flow 348
effluvium 334, 398
efflux 295
efformation 240
effort 686
effreet 980
effrontery 885
effulgence 420
effuse
  pour out 295, 297
  excrete 299
  speech 582
  loquacity 584
effusion of blood
  361
effusive 573
eft 366
eftsoons 117
egad 535
égards 928
egesta 299
egestion 297
egg *beginning* 66
  cause 153
  food 298
walk among –s
  704
too many –s in
  one basket
  unskilful 699

(*imprudent* 863)
– and dart
  ornament 847
– on 615
egg-shaped 247,
  249
ego *intrinsic* 5
  speciality 79
  immaterial 317
non – 6
egocentrism 943
egotism
  vanity 880
  cynicism 911
  selfishness 943
egregious
  exceptional 83
  absurd 497
  exaggerated 549
  important 642
egregiously 31, 33
egress 295
Egyptian darkness
  421
eheu! fugaces
  labuntur anni
  111
eiderdown 223
eidouranion 318
Eiffel tower 206
eight *number* 98
  boat 273
  representative 759
eisteddfod 72, 416
eighty 98
either *choice* 609
  happy with – 605
ejaculate
  propel 284
  utter 580
ejection 185, 297
ejecta 299
ejector 349
eke *also* 37
  – out *complete* 52
  spin out 110
ekka 272
El Dorado 803
elaborate
  improve 658
  prepare 673
  laborious 686
  work out 729
elaine 356
élan 276
elapse 109, 122
elastic fluid 334
elasticity
  power 157
  strength 159
  energy 171
  spring 325
elate *cheer* 836
  rejoice 838
  hope 858
  vain 880
  boast 884
elbow *angle* 244
  projection 250
  push 276
at one's –
  near 197
  advice 695
lift one's –
  drink 959
out at –s
  undress 226
  poor 804

disrepute 874
– one's way
  progress 282
  pursuit 622
  active 682
elbow-chair 215
elbow-grease 331
elbow-room 180,
  748
elder *older* 124
  aged 128
  veteran 130
  clergy 996
elect *choose* 609
  good 648
  predestinate 976
  pious 987
  clergy 996
election
  numerical 84
  necessity 601
electioneering 609
elector 745
electorate 737
Electra complex
  897
electric
  swift 274
  sensation 821
  excitable 825
  car 272
– blue 438
– chair 974
– light 423
– piano 417
electrician 599, 690
electricity 157, 388
electrify
  unexpected 508
  excite 824
  astonish 870
electro-biology 992
electrocution 972
electrolier 274, 423
electrolyze 49
electro-magnetism
  157
electromobile 272
electron 32
electronics 157
electroplate 223
electrotype 21, 591
electuary 662
eleemosynary 784
elegance
  in style 578
  beauty 845
  taste 859
Bank of – 800
elegy *interment* 363
  poetry 597
  lament 839
element
  component 56
  beginning 66
  cause 153
  matter 316
in one's –
  facility 705
  content 831
devouring – 382
out of its – 195
elementary 42
– education 537
– school 542
elements
  Eucharist 998
elench 477

elephant
  large 192
  carrier 271
  white – *bane* 663
elevated
  tipsy 959
elevation
  height 206
  vertical 212
  raising 307
  plan 554
– of style 574
  improvement 658
  glory 873
– of mind 942
angular – 244
élève 541
eleven 98
  representative 759
eleventh hour
  evening 126
  late 133
  opportune 134
elf *infant* 129
  little 193
  imp 980
elicit *cause* 153
  draw out 301
  discover 480a
  manifest 525
eligible 646
Elijah's mantle 63
eliminant 299
eliminate
  subduct 38
  simplify 42
  exclude 55
  weed 103
  extract 301
  reject 610
elision 44, 201
élite *best* 648
  distinguished 873
  aristocratic 875
elixation 384
elixir 662
– of life 471
elk 223
ell 200
take an –
  take 789
  insolence 885
  wrong 923
  undue 925
  selfish 943
ellipse 247
ellipsis *shorten* 201
  style 572
ellipsoid 247, 249
elocation 185, 270
elocution 582
éloge 931
elongation 196, 200
elopement 623, 671
eloquence 572, 582
else 37
elsewhere 187
elucidate 522
elude
  sophistry 477
  avoid 623
  escape 671
  succeed 731
  palter 773
elusive 545
elusory 546
elutriate 652
elysian 829, 981

Elysium 827, 981
elytron 223
Elzevir edition 193
emaciation 195,
  203, 640
emanate 151
  go out of 295
  excrete 299
– from 544
emanation 398
emancipate
  facilitate 705
  free 748, 750
emasculate
  impotent 158
embalm
  interment 363
  perfume 400
  preserve 670
– in the memory
  505
embankment
  esplanade 189
  refuge 666
  fence 717
embar 229
embargo
  stoppage 265
  prohibition 761
  exclusion 893
embark
  transfer 270
  depart 293
– in *begin* 66
  engage in 676
embarquer sans
  biscuits, s' – 674
embarras de
– *choix* 609
embarrass 641,
  704, 706
embarrassed 804,
  806
embarrassing 475
embase 659
embassy
  errand 532
  commission 755
  consignee 758
embattled
  arranged 60
  leagued 712
  war array 722
embed
  locate 184
  base 215
  enclose 221
  insert 300
embellish 847
embers 384
embezzle 791
embitter
  deteriorate 659
  aggravate 835
  acerbate 900
emblazon
  color 428
  ornament 847
  display 882
emblem 550, 747
embody
  join 43
  combine 48
  form a whole 50
  compose 54
embolden
  hope 858
  encourage 861

embolism 228, 261, 300
embonpoint 192
embosomed
  lodged 184
  interjacent 228
  circumscribed 229
emboss *convex* 250
  ornament 847
embouchure 260
embowel 297
embrace
  cohere 46
  compose 54
  include 76
  enclose 227
  choose 609
  take 789
  friendship 888
  sociality 892
  courtesy 894
  endearment 902
  – an offer 760
embrangle 61
embranglement 713
embrasure 257, 260
embrocation 662
embroider
  variegate 440
  lie 544
  ornament 847
embroidery
  adjunct 39
  exaggeration 549
embroil *derange* 61
  discord 713
embroilment 59
embrown 433
embryo
  beginning 66
  cause 153
  in – *destined* 152
  preparing 673
embryology 357
embryonic 193, 674
embus 293
embusqué 603
emendation 658
emerald *green* 435
  jewel 847
emerge 295, 446
emergency
  circumstance 8
  event 151
  difficulty 704
emeritus 500, 928
emersion 295, 446
emery
  sharpener 253
  – paper
  smooth 255
emetic *remedy* 662
émeute 742
emication 420
emigrant 57, 268
emigrate 266, 295
emigré 268, 295
eminence
  height 206
  fame 873
  church dignitary 996
eminent domain 744
eminently 33
emir 745, 875
emissary
  messenger 534

consignee 758
emission 297
emit *eject* 297
  publish 531
  voice 580
  – *vapour* 336
Emmanuel 976
emmet 193
emollient 662
emolument
  acquisition 775
  receipt 810
  remuneration 973
emotion 821
  -al *appeal* 824
  -al *drama* 599
empale 260, 972
empanel 86, 969
empathy 515
emperor 745
emphasis 580
emphatic 535, 642
emphatically 31
empierce
  perforate 260
  insert 300
empire 737, 789
  – day 840
empiric 548
empirical 463, 675
empiricism 463
emplane 293
employ
  business 625
  use 677
  servitude 749
  commission 755
  in one's – 746
  – one's capital in 794
  – oneself 680
  – one's time in 625
employé
  servant 746
  agent 758
employer 795
empoison 659
emporium 799
empower
  power 157
  commission 755
  accredit 759
  permit 760
empress 745
empressement
  activity 682
  emotion 821
  desire 865
emprise 676
emption 795
emptor 795
  caveat – 769
empty *clear* 185
  vacant 187
  deflate 195
  drain 297
  ignorant 491
  waste 638
  deficient 640
  useless 645
  beggarly account of – boxes
  poverty 804
  – one's glass 298
  – purse 804
  – sound 517
  – stomach 865

– title *name* 564
  undue 925
  – words 546
empty-handed 640
empty-headed 4, 491
empurple 437
empyrean *sky* 318
  blissful 829
empyreuma 41
empyrosis 384
emulate *imitate* 19
  goodness 648
  rival 708
  compete 720
  glory 873
emulsion 352
emunctory 350
en – bloc 50
  – masse 50
  – passant
  parenthetical 10
  transient 111
  à propos 134
  – rapport 9
  – règle *order* 58
  conformity 82
  – route
  journey 266
  progress 282
enable 157
enact *drama* 599
  action 680
  conduct 692
  complete 729
  order 741
  law 963
enallage 521
enamel *coating* 223
  painting 556
  ornament 847
enameller 559
enamor 897
encage 751
encamp 184, 189
encampment 184
encaustic 556
enceinte
  with child 161
  region 181
  inclosure 232
enchafe 830
enchain 751
enchant *please* 829
enchanted 827
enchanting 845, 897
enchantment
  sorcery 992
enchase 43, 259
enchiridion 593
enchorial 188
encincture 229
encircle 76, 227, 311
enclave *close* 181
  boundary 233
enclose 227, 229
enclosure
  region 181
  envelope 232
  fence 752
encomiast 935
encomium 931
encompass 227, 233
  -ed with difficulties 704
encore 104, 931

encounter
  undergo 151
  clash 276
  meet 292
  withstand 708
  contest 720
  – danger 665
  – risk 621
encourage
  animate 615
  aid 707
  comfort 834
  hope 858
  embolden 861
encroach
  transcursion 303
  do wrong 923
  infringe 925
encumber 704, 706
encumbrance
  clear of – 807
encyclical 531
encyclopedia 490, 593
  walking – 700
encyclopedical
  general 78
  – *knowledge* 490
encysted 229
end
  termination 67
  effect 154
  object 620
  at an – 142
  come to its – 729
  one's journey's – 292
  on – 212
  put an – to
  destroy 162
  kill 361
  begin at the wrong – 699
  – one's days 360
  –s of the earth 196
  – to end *space* 180
  touching 199
  length 200
  – of life 360
  – in smoke 732
  – of one's tether
  sophistry 477
  ignorant 491
  insufficient 640
  difficult 704
endamage 649
endanger 665
endear 897
endearment 902
endeavor
  pursue 622
  attempt 675
  use one's best – 686
  – after 620
endemic
  special 79
  interior 221
  disease 657
endimanché 847, 882
endless
  multitudinous 102
  infinite 105
  perpetual 112
endlessly 16
endlong 200

endocrine 221
endogenous 367
endorse
  evidence 467
  assent 488
  compact 769
  – a bill 800
  approve 931
endorsement 550
endosmose 302
endow
  confer power 157
endowed with
  possessed of 777
endowment
  intrinsic 5
  power 157
  talent 698
  gift 784
endrogynous 83
endue 157
endure *time* 106
  last 110
  persist 143
  continue 141
  undergo 151
  feel 821
  submit to 826
  unable to – 867
  – for ever 112
  – pain 828
enduring
  indelible 505
endwise 212
enemy *time* 841
  foe 891
  the common – 978
  thing devised by the – 546
  – to society 891
energumen 504
energy *power* 157
  strength 159
  physical 171
  resolution 604
  activity 682
enervate 158, 160
enfant, bon – 906
  – gâté
  prosperity 734
  satiety 869
  favorite 899
  – perdu
  hopeless 859
  reckless 863
  – terrible
  curiosity 455
  artless 703
  object of fear 860
enfeeble 160
enfeoff 780, 783
Enfield rifle 727
enfilade
  lengthwise 200
  pierce 260
  pass through 302
enfold 229
enforce *urge* 615
  advise 695
  compel 744
  require 924
enfranchise
  free 748
  liberate 750
  permit 760
enfranchised 924
engage
  bespeak 132

etiology *causes* 155, 359
  knowledge 490
  disease 655
etiquette
  custom 613
  fashion 832
  ceremony 882
étoile, à la belle –
  out of doors 220
  in the air 338
Eton jacket 225
étourderie
  inattention 458
  unskilfulness 699
etymological 560
etymology 562
etymon *origin* 153
  verbal 562
Eucharist 998
euchology 998
euchre 840
eudiometer
  air 338
  salubrity 656
euge! 931
eugenics 658
eulogist 935
eulogize 482
eulogy 931
Eumenides *fury* 900
  evil-doers 913
  revenge 919
eunuch 158
eupepsia 654
euphemism
  metaphor 521
  style 577, 578
  flattery 933
euphemist
  man of taste 850
  flatterer 935
euphony 413, 578
Euphrosyne 836
euphuism
  metaphor 521
  elegant style 577
  affected style 579
  affectation 855
Eurasian 41
eureka! 462, 480a
Euripus 343
Eurus 349
eurythmics 537, 840
eurythmy 242
Euterpe 416
euthanasia 360
euthenics 658
evacuate
  quit 293
  excrete 295
  emit 297
evacuation 299
evade *sophistry* 477
  avoid 623
  not observe 773
  exempt 927
evagation 279
evanescent
  small 32
  transient 111
  little 193
  disappearing 449
evangelical 983a, 985
Evangelists 985

evanid 160
evaporable 334
evaporate
  unsubstantial 4
  transient 111
  vaporize 336
evaporation 340
evasion
  sophistry 477
  concealment 528
  falsehood 544
  untruth 546
  avoidance 623
  escape 671
  cunning 702
  non-observance 773
  dereliction 927
eve 126
  on the – of
  transient 111
  prior 116
  future 121
evection 61
even
  uniform 16
  equal 27
  still more 33
  regular 138
  level 213
  straight 246
  flat 251
  smooth 255
  although 469
  in spite of 708
  – course 628
  – now 118
  – so
  for all that 30
  yes 488
  – temper 826
  – terms 922
  – tenor
  uniform 16
  order 58
  continuity 58
  pursue the –
  tenor
  continue 143
  avoid 623
  business 625
  be – with
  retaliate 718
  pay 807
  get – with 972
even-handed 922, 939
evening 126
  shades of – 422
  – classes 537
  – star 423
evenness 16
evensong 126, 990
event 151
  bout 720
  in the – of
  circumstance 8
  expectation 507
  supposition 514
  justified by the – 937
eventful 151
  remarkable 642
  stirring 682
eventide 126
eventual 121
eventuality 151
eventually

effect 154
ever 16, 112
  did you – ? 870
  – and anon 136
  – changing 149
  – recurring 104
ever so 31
  – little 32
  – long 110
  – many 102
evergreen
  continuous 69
  lasting 110
  always 112
  fresh 123
everlasting 112
  – life 152
  – fire 982
evermore 112
eversion 218
evert 140
every 78
  – hand against one 891
  – day
  conformity 82
  frequent 136
  habit 613
  – description 81
  – inch 50
  in – mouth
  assent 488
  news 532
  repute 873
  – other 138
  in – quarter 180
  in – respect 494
  on – side 227
  at – turn 186
  – whit 52
everybody 78
everyone 78
  – his due 922
  – in his turn 148
everywhere 180, 186
evict 297
evidence 467
  disclose 529
  ocular – 446
évidence, en – 446
evident
  concrete 3
  visible 446
  certain 474
  manifest 525
evidently 516
evil *harm* 619
  badness 649
  impious 988
  – day
  prepare for – 673
  adversity 735
  – eye *vision* 441
  malevolence 907
  disapprobation 932
  demon 980
  sorcery 992
  spell 993
  – favored 846
  – fortune 735
  – genius 980
  – hour 135
  – one 978
  – plight 735
  through – report &c. 604a

  – star 649
evil-doer **913**
evil-doing 945
evil-minded 907, 945
evil-speaking
  malediction 908
  censure 932
  detraction 934
evince *show* 467
  prove 478
  disclose 529
eviscerate 297, 301
eviscerated 4
evoke *cause* 153
  call upon 765
  excite 824
evolution
  numerical 85
  production 161
  motion 264
  extraction 301
  circuition 311
  turning out **313**
  organization 357
  training 673
  action 680
  military –s 722
evolve
  discover 480a
  evolved from 154
  [*and see* evolution]
evulgate 531
evulsion 301
evviva! 931
ewe 366, 374
  – lamb 366
ewer 191
ex
  – animo 602
  – cathedra 542
  – officio 494, 924
  – parte 467
  – pede Herculem 82
  – post facto 122, 133
  – tempore
  instant 113
  occasion 134
exacerbate
  increase 35
  exasperate 173
  aggravate 659, 835
exact *similar* 17
  special 79
  true 494
  style 572
  require 741
  tax 812
  insolence 885
  claim 924, 926
  – meaning 516
  – memory 505
  – observance 772
  – truth 494
exacting
  severe 739
  discontented 832
  grasping 865
  fastidious 868
exaction
  [*see* exact]
  undue 925
exactly
  just so 488

exaggeration
  increase 35
  expand 194
  overestimate 482
  magnify **549**
  misrepresent 555
exalt
  increase 35
  elevate 307
  extol 931
  – one's horn 873
exalté 504
exalted *high* 206
  repute 873
  noble 875
  magnanimous 942
examination
  [*see* examine]
  evidence 467
  undergo – 461
examine 457, 461
example
  pattern 22
  instance 82
  bad – 949
  good – 948
  make an – of 974
  set a good – 944
exanimate
  dead 360
  supine 360
exarch 745
exasperate
  exacerbate 173
  aggravate 835
  enrage 900
excavate 252
excecation 442
exceed *surpass* 33
  remain 40
  transgress 303
  intemperance 954
excel *surpass* 33
  – in *skilful* 698
excellence 648, 944
excellence, par – 642
excellency 877
excelsior 305
except *subduct* 38
  exclude 55
  reject 610
exception
  unconformity 83
  qualification 469
  exemption 777a
  disapproval 932
  take –
  qualify 469
  resent 900
exceptionable
  bad 649
  guilty 947
exceptional
  original 20
  extraneous 57
  unconformable 83
  in an – degree 31
exceptious 901, 901a
exceptis
  excipiendis 469
excern 297
excerpt 609
excerpta *parts* 51
  compendium 596

irresolute 605
easy 705
facile princeps 33
facilis descensus
  Averni
sloping 217
danger 665
facilitate 705
facility *skill* 698
easy **705**
facing *covering* 223
facinorous 945
façon de parler 521, 549
fac-simile 21, 554
fact *existence* 1
event 151
certainty 474
truth 494
in — 535
faction 712, 713
factious 24
factitious 545, 546
factor
numerical 84
director 694
consignee 758
factory 691
factotum
agent 690
manager 694
employé 758
facts *evidence* 467
summary of — 594
at variance with — 471
facula 420
faculties 450
in possession of one's — 502
faculty
power 157
profession 625
skill 698
facundity 582
fad 481, 608
faddle 683
fade *vanish* 4
transient 111
become old 124
droop 160
grow dim 422
lose color 429
disappear 449
spoil 659
— from the memory 506
fade 391
fadge 23
faex populi 876
fag *cigarette* 392
labor 686
fatigue 688
drudge 690, 746
— end
remainder 40
end 67
faggot 72, 388
fagots et fagots 15, 465
faïence 557
fail *droop* 160
shortcoming 304
be confuted 479
illness 655
not succeed 732

not observe 773
not pay 808
dereliction 927
failing [see **fail**]
• *incomplete* 53
insufficient 640
vice 945
guilt 947
— heart 837
— luck 735
— memory 506
⌐ sight 443
— strength 160
failure **732**
heart — 360
fain *willing* 602
compulsive 744
wish 865
fainéant 683
faint
small in degree 32
impotent 158
weak 160
sound 405
dim 422
color 429
swoon 688
— heart *fear* 860
cowardice 862
damn with —
praise 930, 932, 934
faintness **405**
fair *in degree* 31
pale 429
white 430
wise 498
important 643
good 648
moderate 651
mart 799
beautiful 845
just 922
honorable 939
— chance 472
— copy *copy* 21
writing 590
— field
occasion 134
— game 857
by — means 631, 940
— name 873
— play 922, 923
— question 461
— sex 374
in a — way
tending 176
probable 472
convalescent 658
prosperous 734
hopeful 858
— weather 734
— weather sailor 701
— wind 705
— words 894
fairing 784
fairly
intrinsically 5
get on — 736
— well 643
fair-spoken
courtesy 894
flattery 933
fairy *fanciful* 515
fay 979

imp 980
— godmother 711, 784, 912
— tale 545, 594
fairy-land 515
fait: au —
knowledge 490
skilful 698
— accompli
certain 474
complete 729
faith *belief* 484
hope 858
honor 939
piety 987
declaration of — 983
bad — 544
i' — 535
keep — with
observe 772
plight —
promise 768
love 902
true —
orthodox 983a
want of —
incredulity 487
irreligious 989
— healing 662
faithful [see **faith**]
like 17
copy 21
exact 494
obedient 743
— memory 505
— to 772
faithless *false* 544
dishonorable 940
sceptical 989
fake 544, 545
fakir 996
falcate 244, 245
falchion 727
falciform
[see **falcate**]
falcon 792
falconet 727
faldstool 215
fall *autumn* 126
happen 151
perish 162
slope 217
regression 283
descend 306
die 360
fail 732
adversity 73
vice 945
let — *lower* 308
inform 527
water — 348
— asleep 683
— astern 235, 283
— away 105
— back *return* 283
recede 287
relapse 661
— back upon 677, 717
have to — back upon 637
— a cursing 908
— of the curtain 67
— into a custom 82
— of day 125
— dead 360

— into decay 659
— down 990
— down before 928
— upon the ear 418
— flat on the ear 843
— at one's feet 725
— foul of *blow* 276
hinder 706
oppose 708
discord 713
— attack 716
contention 720
censure 932
— for 897
— to the ground
be confuted 479
fail 732
— into a habit 613
— from one's high estate
adversity 735
disrepute 874
— in order 58
continuity 69
— into
conversion 144
river 348
— in with *agree* 23
conform 82
converge 2
discover 480a
concord 714
consent 762
— on one's knees
submit 725
servile 886
gratitude 916
worship 990
— of the leaf 126
— from the lips 582
— in love with 897
— to one's lot
event 151
chance 156
receive 785
duty 926
— under one's notice 457
— into oblivion 506
— off *decrease* 36
deteriorate 659
— off again 661
— out *happen* 151
quarrel 713
enmity 889
— into a passion 900
— to pieces
disjunction 44
destruction 162
brittle 328
— a prey to 732, 749
— in price 815
— into raptures 827
— back *inferior* 32
contract 195
shortcoming 304
— of snow 383
— through *fail* 734
— to *eat* 298
take in hand 676
do battle 722
— into a trap 547

— under
inclusion 76
subjection 749
— upon
discover 480a
unexpected 508
devise 626
attack 716
— in the way of 186
— to work 686
fallacy *sophistry* 477
error 495
show the — of 497
fallen angel 949, 978
fallible 475, 477
falling-out 24
falling star 318, 423
fallow
unproductive 169
yellow 436
unready 674
inactive 681
false *imitation* 10
sophistry 477
error 495
untrue 544, 546
spurious 925
dishonorable 940
— alarm 669
— coloring
misinterpretation 523
• *falsehood* 544
— construction 523, 544
— doctrine 984
— expectation 509
— hearted 940
— impression 495
— light *vision* 443
— money 800
— ornament 851
— plea *untruth* 546 .
plea 617
— position 704
— pretences 791
— prophet
disappoint 509
pseudo-revelation 986
— reasoning 477
— scent 495, 538
— shame 855
— statement 546
— step 732
— teaching 538
— witness
deceiver 548
detraction 934
falsehood **544**, 546
falsetto *squeak* 410
want of voice 581
falsify *error* 495
falsehood 544, 546
— accounts 811
— one's hope 509
falter *slow* 275
stammer 583
hesitate 605
slip 732
hopeless 859
fear 860
faltering accents 605

fame *greatness* 31
  news 532
  renown 873
familiar
  known 490
  habitual 613
  sociable 892
  affable 894
  – *spirit* 979, 980
  on – terms 888
familiarize
  teach 537
  habit 613
famille, en – 892
family
  kin 11
  class 75
  ancestors 166
  posterity 167
  party 712
  in the bosom of
    one's – 221
  happy – 714
  – circle 892
  – jars 713
  – likeness 17
  – tie 11
  in the – way 161
famine 640
  – price 814
famine-stricken
  640
famish
  stingy 819
  fasting 956
famished
  insufficient 640
  hungry 865
famous 873
famously 31
fan *blow* 349
  cool 385
  refresh 689
  stimulate 824
  flirt a – 855
  – the embers 505
  – the flame
    violence 173
    heat 384
    aid 707
    excite 824
  – into a flame
    anger 900
  –shaped 194
fanatic
  madman 504
  imaginative 515
  zealot 682
  religious – 988
fanatical
  misjudging 481
  insane 503
  emotional 821
  excitable 825
  heterodox 984
  over-righteous 988
fanaticism 606
fanciful
  imaginative 515
  capricious 608
  ridiculous 853
fancy *think* 451
  idea 453
  believe 484
  suppose 514
  imagine 515
  caprice 608

choice 609
  pugilism 726
  wit 842
  desire 865
  wonder 870
  love 897
  after one's – 850
  indulge one's –
    609
  take a – to
    delight in 827
    desire 865
  take one's –
    please 829
  – dog 366
  – dress 840
  – price 814
  – woman 962
fandango 840
fandi, mollia tem-
  pora – 588
fane 1000
fanfare *loudness*
  404
  celebration 883
fanfaron 887
fanfaronnade 884
fangs *venom* 663
  rule 737
  retention 781
fan-light 260
fan-like 202
fannel 999
fanon 999
fantasia 415
fantastic *odd* 83
  absurd 497
  imaginative 515
  capricious 608
  unfashionable 851
  ridiculous 853
fantasy
  imagination 515
  desire 865
fantoccini 554, 599
faquir 996
far – *away* 196
  – be it from
    unwilling 603
    deprecation 766
  – *between*
    disjunction 44
    few 103
    interval 198
  – from it
    unlike 18
    shortcoming 304
    no 536
  – from the truth
    546
  – and near 180
  – off 196
  – and wide 31,
    180, 196
farce
  absurdity 497
  untruth 546
  drama 599
  wit 842
  ridiculous 853
  mere –
    unimportant 643
    useless 645
farceur
  actor 599
  humorist 844
fardel

bundle 72
  hindrance 706
fare *state* 7
  food 298
  price 812
  bill of –
    list 86
farewell
  departure 293
  relinquishment
    624
  loss 776
  – to greatness 874
far-famed 873
far-fetched 10
far-flung 73
far-gone
  much 31
  insane 503
  spoiled 654
farinaceous 330
farm *till* 371
  property 780
  rent 788
  farmer 188, 342,
    371
  afternoon – 683
farm-house 189
Farmer-Labor 712
faro 840
farrago 59
farrier 370
farrow
  produce 161
  litter 167
  multitude 102
far-sighted 442, 510
farther 196
  [*and see* **further**]
farthing
  quarter 97
  worthless 643
  coin 800
  – candle 422
farthingale 225
fasces 747
fascia 205, 247
fascicule 51
fasciculated 72
fascinate
  influence 615
  excite 824
  please 829
  astonish 870
  love 897
  conjure 992
fascinated
  pleased 827
fascination [*see*
  fascinate]
  infatuation 825
  desire 870
fascine 72
Fascisti 712
fas et nefas, per –
  604a, 631
fash 830
fashion
  state 7
  form 240
  custom 613
  method 627
  ton 852
  after a –
    middling 32
  after this – 617
  follow the – 82

be in the – 488
  man of – 852
  set the –
    influence 175
    authority 737
  for –'s sake 852
fast *joined* 43
  steadfast 150
  rapid 274
  fashionable 852
  intemperate 954
  not eat 956
  worship 990
  rite 998
  stick – 704
  – asleep 683
  – by 197
  – day 956
  – friend 890
  – and loose
    sophistry 477
    falsehood 544
    irresolute 605
    tergiversation 607
    caprice 608
  – man *fop* 854
    libertine 962
fasten *join* 43
  hang 214
  restrain 751
  – on the mind 451
  – a quarrel upon
    713
  – upon 789
fastening 45
fast-handed 819
fastidious
  censorious 932
fastidiousness 868
fasting
  insufficiency 640
  worship 990
  penance 952
  abstinence 956
fastness
  asylum 666
  defence 717
fat *corpulent* 192
  expansion 194
  unctuous 355
  oleaginous 356
  kill the –ted calf
    celebration 883
    sociality 892
  – in the fire
    disorder 59
    violence 173
  – of the land
    pleasure 377
    enough 639
    prosperity 734
    intemperance 95
fata – Morgana
  occasion 134
  ignis fatuus 423
  – obstant 601
fatal 361
  – disease 655
fatalism 601
fatality 601
fate *end* 67
  necessity 601
  chance 621
  be one's – 156
  sure as – 474
Fates 601, 979
fat-head 501

father *eldest* 128
  paternity 166
  priest 996
  Apostolical –s 985
  gathered to one's
    –s 360
  heavy – 599
  – upon 155
Father, God the –
  976
fatherland 189
fatherless 158
fatherly 906
fathom
  length 200
  investigate 461
  solve 462
  measure 466
  discover 480a
  knowledge 490
fathomless 208
fatidical 511
fatigation 688
fatigue 688
fatras 643
fatten
  expand 194
  improve 658
  prosperous 734
  – on *parasite* 886
  – upon
    feed 298
fatuity 4, 499
fatuous 517
faubourg 227
fauces 231
faucet 252
faugh! 867
fault
  break 70
  error 495
  imperfection 651
  failure 732
  vice 945
  guilt 947
  at –
    uncertain 475
    ignorant 491
    unskilful 699
  find – with 932
faultless 650, 946
faulty 495, 651
faun 980
fauna 366
faut: comme il –
  taste 850
  fashion 852
  il s'en – bien 489
  tant s'en – 536
faute 732
  – de mieux
    substitution 147
    necessity 601
fauteuil 215
fautor 890
faux pas
  error 568
  failure 732
  misconduct 947
  intrigue 961
favor
  resemble 16
  badge 550
  letter 592
  aid 707
  indulgence 740

permit 760
gift 784
partiality 923
appearances in –
of 472
get into –
friendship 888
love 897
in – *repute* 873
approbation 931
in – of
approve 931
under – of 760
view with – 906
– with 784
favorable
occasion 134
willing 602
good 648
aid 707
– *prospect* 472
– to 709
take a – turn
improve 658
prosperity 734
favorably
well 618
favorer 890
favorite
pleasing 829
beloved 897, **899**
favoritism
friendship 888
wrong 923
fawn *color* 433
cringe 749, 886
flatter 993
fay 979
fealty
obedience 743
duty 926
respect 928
fear **860**
fearful
painful 830
timid 862
fearfully 31, 870
fearless *hope* 858
courage 861
fearsome 860
feasible 470, 705
feast *period* 138
repast 298
pleasure 377
revel 840
rite 998
– one's eyes 897
feast of reason
conversation 588
– and flow of soul
sociality 892
feat *action* 680
courage 861
– of arms 720
– of strength 159
feather
class 75
tuft 256
light 320
trifle 643
ornament 847
decoration 877
in full –
prepared 673
prosperous 734
rich 803
hear a – drop 403

in high –
health 654
cheerful 884
pleased with a –
840
– in one's cap
honor 873
decoration 877
– one's nest
prepare 673
prosperity 734
wealth 803
economy 817
selfish 943
– the oar 698
– in the scale 643
feather-bed 324
feathered tribes
366
feathery 256
featly 682
feature
character 5
component 56
form 240
appearance 448
press 531
lineament 550
– in 56
features
face 234
febrifuge 662
febrile 382, 825
fecal 653
feces 299, 653
fecit 556
feckless 866
feculence 653
fecund 168
fecundate 161
federal council 696
– penitentiary 752
federalism 737
federation 48, 709,
712
fee *possession* 777
property 780
pay 809
reward 973
feeble *weak* 160
illogical 477
feeble-minded 497,
605
feebleness
style **575**
feed *eat* 298
supply 637
– the flame 707
fee-faw-fum
bugbear 860
spell 993
feel *sense* 375
touch 379
emotion 821
– for *try* 463
benevolence 906
pity 914
condole with 915
– the pulse 461
– the want of 865
– one's way
essay 675
caution 864
feeler 379
inquiry 461
experiment 463
feeling 698, **821**

feet *low* 207
walkers 266
at one's –
near 197
subjection 749
humility 879
fall at one's –
submit 725
fall on one's –
prosper 734
lick the – of
servile 886
light upon one's
safe 664
spring to one's –
307
throw oneself at
the – of
entreat 765
feign 544, 546
feigned 545
feint 545
felicitas, curiosa –
698
felicitate 896
felicitous
agreeing 23
– *style* 578
skilful 698
successful 731
pleasant 829
felicity 827
feline *cat* 366
stealthy 528
cunning 702
fell *destroy* 162
mountain 206
lay flat 21
skin 223
lay low 308
moor 344
dire 860
malevolent 907
fellah 876
felloe 231
fellow *similar* 17
equal 27
companion 88
dual 89
man 373
scholar 492, 541
fellow-commoner
541
fellow-companion
890
fellow-countryman
890
fellow-creature 372
fellow-feeling
friendship 888
love 897
benevolence 906
pity 914
fellowship
partnership 712
distinction 873
friendship 888
companionship
890
good – 892
fellow-student 541
fellow-worker 690
felly 231
felo-de-se 361
felon 949
felonious 945
felony 947

felt *texture* 219
heart– 821
felucca 273
female 374
feme coverte 903
feme sole 904
femininity
weakness 160
woman 374
feminine 374
feminism 374
femme de chambre
746
fen 345
fence *enclose* 232
evade 544
defence 717
fight 720
prison 752
thief 792
– round 229
– with a question
528
fenced 770
fenceless 665
fencible 726
fencing 840
feneration 787
fend 717
fender 717
Fenian 710, 742
fenum habet in
cornu 668, 913
feodal 780
feodality 737, 777
feoff *property* 780
feoffee 779, 785
feoffer 784
ferae naturae 366
feral 907
ferine 907
ferment
disorder 59
energy 171
violence 173
agitation 315
lightness 320
effervesce 353
emotion 821
excitement 824,
825
anger 900
fermentation,
acetous – 397
fern 367
ferocity 173, 907
Ferrara
sword 727
ferret out 461, 480a
ferro-concrete 635
ferrule 223
ferry 270, 627
ferry-boat 273
ferry-man 269
fertile 161, 168
– *imagination* 515
ferule 975
come under the –
932
fervent *hot* 382
desirous 865
– *hope* 858
fervid *hot* 382
heartfelt 821
excited 824
fervour *heat* 382
animation 821
love 897

festal *eating* 298
social 892
fester 653, 655
festina lente 864
festival
music 416
celebration 883
festivity 840, 892
festoon 245, 847
fetch *bring* 270
arrive 292
evasion 545
sell for 812
– one a blow
strike 276
attack 716
– and carry
servile 886
– a sigh 839
fête 840, 882
fêté 892
fetishism 992
fetid 401
fetish 991, 993
fetter 751, 752
fettle 673
state 5
prepare 673
in fine – 159, 654
fetus 129, 153
feu
– d'enfer 716
– de joie
amusement 840
celebration 883
feud *discord* 713
possess 777
property 780
death – 919
feudal 737, 780
feudatory 749
feuilleton 593
fever *heat* 382
disease 655
excitement 825
feverish *hurry* 684
animated 821
excited 824
few
a – 100
– and far between
70
– words
concise 572
taciturn 585
compendium 596
fewness **103**
fey 360
fez 225
fiancée 897
fiasco 732
fiat 741
– money 800
fib *falsehood* 544,
546
thump 720
fiber *link* 45
filament 205
moral – 60
fickle 149, 605
fictile 240
fiction *untruth* 546
work of – 594
fictitious 515, 546
fiddle 416, 417
fiddle-de-dee
absurd 497

unimportant 643
contempt 930

fiddlefaddle
unmeaning 517
trifle 643
dawdle 683

fiddler 416
fiddlestick 417
– end 643

fidelity
veracity 543
obedience 743
observance 772
honor 939

fidget *changes* 149
activity 682
hurry 684
excitability 825

fidgety
irresolute 605
fearful 860
irascible 901

fiducial 156
fiduciary 484
fidus Achates
auxiliary 711
associate 743
friend 890

fie *disreputable* 874
– upon it
censure 932

fief 777
field *opportunity* 134
scope 180
region 181
plain 344
agriculture 371
business 625
arena 728
property 780
the – *hunting* 622
beasts of the – 366
playing –s 728
the potter's – 361
take the – 722
– artillery 726
the – of blood 361
– of inquiry
topic 454
inquiry 461
– of view
vista 441
idea 453

field-day
contention 720
amusement 840
display 882

field-glass 445
field-marshal 745
field-piece 727
field-preacher 996
field-work 717
fiend 913, 980
fiend-like
malevolent 907
wicked 945
fiend 980

fierce *violent* 173
passion 825
daring 861
angry 900

fiery *violent* 173
hot 382
strong feeling 821
excitable 825
angry 900
irascible 901

– cross 550, 722
– furnace 386
– imagination 515
– ordeal 828

fife 417
fifer 416
fifth 98, 99
fifty 98
fig
unimportance 643
in the name of the prophet –s! 497
– out 847

fight
contention 720
warfare 722
show –
defence 717
courage 861
– one's battles again 594
– against destiny 606
– the good fight 944
– it out 722
– shy *avoid* 603, 623
coward 862
– one's way
pursue 622
active 682
exertion 686

fighter 726
fighting-cock 726, 861
fighting-man 726
figment 515
figurante 599
figurate number 84
figuration 240
figurative
metaphorical 521
representing 554
– *style* 577

figure
number 84
form 240
appearance 448
metaphor 521
indicate 550
represent 554
price 812
ugly 846
cut a –
repute 873
display 882
poor – 874
– to oneself 515
– of speech 521
– out 522
exaggeration 549

figure-flinger 994
figure-head 4, 550, 554, 643
figurine 554
figuriste 559
filaceous 205
filament 205
filamentous 256
filch 791
filcher 762
file *subduct* 38
arrange 60
row 69
assemblage 72
list 86
reduce 195

smooth 255
pulverize 330
record 551
store 636
soldiers 726
– a claim &c. 969
– off *march* 266
diverge 291

file-fire 716
filial 167
filiation
consanguinity 11
attribution 155
posterity 167

filibuster 133, 706, 792
filibustering 791
filiform 205
filigree 219
filings 330
fill *complete* 52
occupy 186
contents 190
stuff 224
provision 637
eat one's – 957
have one's –
enough 639
satiety 869
– the bill 229
– an office
business 625
government 737
– out
expand 194
– ed to overflowing 641
– one's pocket 803
– time 106
– up *compensate* 30
compose 54
close 261
restore 660
– up the time
inaction 681

fille
– de chambre 746
– de joie 962

filled
– to overflowing 641

filler 532
fillet *band* 45
filament 205
circle 247
insignia 550
ornament 847

fillibeg 225
filling 224
fillip
impulse 276
propulsion 284
stimulus 615
excite 824

filly 271
film *layer* 204
opaque 426
semitransparent 427
– over the eyes
dim sight 443
cinema 448
ignorant 491

filmy *texture* 329
filter *percolate* 295
clean 652
filth 653

–y lucre 800

filtrate 652
fimbriated 256
fin 267
final *ending* 67
conclusive 474
completing 729
court of – *appeal* 474
– cause 620
– stroke 729
– touch 729

finale *end* 67
completion 729
finality 67, 729
finally
for good 141
on the whole 476

finance 800, 811
minister of – 801
financier 801
finch 366
find
eventuality 151
adjudge 480
discover 480a
acquire 775
– one's account in 644
– the cause of 522
– a clue to 480a
– to one's cost 509
– credence 484
– it in one's heart 602
– in *provide* 637
– the key of 522
– the meaning 522
– means 632
– oneself *be* 1
present 186
– out 480a
– vent 671
– one's way 731
– one's way into 294

finding
judgment 480
fine *small* 32
large 192
thin 203
rare 322
not raining 340
exact 494
good 648
beautiful 845
adorned 847
proud 878
mulct 974
in – *end* 67
after all 476
– air 656
– arts 554
– feather 159, 654
– feeling 850
– frenzy 515
– gentleman
fop 854
proud 878
– grain 329
– lady 854, 878
one – morning 106
some – morning 119
– powder 330
– talking
overrate 482

boast 884
– writing 577
– time of it 734
– voice 580

fine-draw 660
fine-fingered 698
fine-spoken 894, 933
fine-spun *thin* 203
sophistry 477
fine-toned 413
finem, respicere – 510
finery 847, 851
finesse *tact* 698
artifice 702
taste 850
finger *touch* 379
hold 781
lay the – on
point out 457
discover 480a
lift a – 680
not lift a – 681
point the – at 457
turn round one's little – 737
– 's breadth 203
at one's –s' end
near 197
know 490
remember 505
– on the lips
aphony 581
taciturnity 585
– in the pie
cause 153
interfere 228
act 680
active 682
co-operate 709

fingerling 193
finger-post 550
finger-print 467
finger-stall 223
fingle-fangle 643
finical
trifling 643
affected 855
fastidious 868
finicky 855, 868
finikin 643
finis 67
– coronat opus 729
finish *lend* 67
symmetry 242
complete 729
skill 698
finished
absolute 31
perfect 650
skilled 698
finishing
– stroke 361
– touch 729
finite 32
fiord 343
fire *energy* 171
heat 382
make hot 384
stoke 388
vigor 574
discharge 756
enthusiasm 821
excite 824, 825
catch – 384

hell – 982
on – 382
open – *begin* 66
play with – 863
signal – 550
take –
  excitable 825
  angry 900
between two –s
  665
under – 665, 722
  – at 716
  – the blood 824
  – and fury 900
  – the first shot 716
  – of genius 498
  – off 284
  – a salute 883
  – and sword 162
  – up *excite* 825
  anger 900
  – a volley 716
go through – and
  water
  resolution 604
  perseverance 604*a*
  courage 861
fire-alarm 669
fire-annihilator 385
fire-arms 727
fire-ball *fuel* 388
  arms 727
fire-balloon 273
fire-barrel 388
fire-bell 669
fire-boat 726
fire-brand
  fuel 388
  instigator 615
  dangerous man
    667
  incendiary 913
fire-brigade 385
fire-curtain 599
fire-drake 423
fire-eater
  fighter 726
  blusterer 887
fire-eating
  rashness 863
  insolence 885
fire-engine 348
fire-escape 671
fire-extinguisher
  385
fire-fly 423
fireless cooker 386
fire-light 422
firelock 727
fireman *stoker* 268
  extinguisher 385
fire-place 386
fire-proof 385, 644
fireside 189
firewood 388
firework
  fire 382
  luminary 423
  celebration 883
  amusement 840
fire-worship 991
fire-worshipper 984
firing *fuel* 388
  explosion 406
firkin 191
firm
  junction 43

stable 150
hard 323
resolute 604
partnership 712
merchant 797
brave 861
stand – 719
  – as a rock 604
  – belief 484
  – hold 781
firmament 318
firman 741, 760
first 66
  – blush
  morning 125
  leading 280
  vision 441
  appearance 448
  manifest 525
  – blow 716
  – cause 976
  – that comes 609*a*
  – fiddle
  importance 642
  proficient 700
  authority 737
  – come first
    served 609*a*
  – and foremost 66
  – impression 66
  – and last 87
  – line 234
come back to –
  love 607
  – move 66
  – opportunity 132
at – sight 448
  – stage 66
  – stone
  preparation 673
  attack 716
on the – summons
  741
of the – water
  best 648
  repute 873
first-born 124, 128
first-fruits·154
first-hand 20, 467
firstlings 128, 154
first-rate
  important 642
  excellent 648
  man-of-war 726
firth 343
fisc 802
fiscal 800
fish *food* 298
  sport 361, 622
  animal 366
food for –es 362
other – to fry
  ill-timed 135
  busy 682
queer – 857
  – in the air 645
  – for compliments
    880
  – for *seek* 4
  experiment 463
  desire 865
  – hatchery 370
  – out *inquire* 461
  discover 480*a*
  – in troubled
    waters
  difficult 704

discord 713
  – up *raise* 307
find 480*a*
  – out of water
disagree 24
unconformable 83
displaced 185
bungler 701
fisherman 361
fishery 370
fishing *kill* 361
  pursue 622
fishing-boat 273
fishpond 343, 370
fish-trail 267
fishy transaction
  940
fisk 266, 274
fissile 328
fission 44
fissure 44
  chink 198
fist
  handwriting 590
  grip 781
shake the –
  defy 515
  threat 909
fisticuffs 720
fistula 260
fit *state* 7
  agreeing 23
  equal 27
  paroxysm 173
  agitation 315
  caprice 608
  expedient 646
  healthy 654
  disease 655
  excitement 825
  anger 900
  right 922
  due 924
  duty 926
  in –s 315
think – 600
  – of abstraction
    458
  – of crying 839
  – for 698
  – out *dress* 225
  prepare 673
  – to be seen 845
  by –s and starts
  irregular 59
  discontinuous 70
  agitated 315
  capricious 608
  haste 684
fitful
  irregular 139
  changeable 149
  capricious 608
fittings 633
five 98
  division by – 99
  – act play 599
  – and twenty 98
Five Year Plan 626
fiver 800
fives *game* 840
fix *join* 43
  arrange 60
  establish 150
  place 184
  immovable 265
  solidify 321

resolve 604
difficulty 704
  – the eyes upon
    441
  – the foundations
    673
  – the memory 505
  – the time 114
  – the thoughts
    457
  – up 774 ·
  – upon *discover*
    480*a*
fixed *intrinsic* 5
  permanent 141
  stable 150
  quiescent 265
  habitual 613
  – idea 481
  – opinion 484
  – periods 138
fixity 141
fixity of purpose
  141
fixture
  appointment 741
  property 780
fizgig 423
fizz 409
fizzle 353
  – out 304
flabelliform 194
flabbergast 870,
  879
flabby 324
flabbiness 324
flaccid *weak* 160
  soft 324
  empty 640
flag *weak* 160
  flat stone 204
  floor 211
  smoothness 255
  slow 275
  leaf 367
  sign 550
  path 627
  infirm 655
  inactive 683
  tired 688
  weary 841
lower one's – 725
red – *alarm* 669
yellow –
  warning 668
  alarm 669
  – man 668
  – ship 726
  – of truce 723
flag-bearer 534
flagellation
  penance 952
  asceticism 955
  flogging 972
  rite 998
flagelliform 205
flageolet 417
flagitious 945
flagon 191
flagrant
  great 31
  manifest 525
  notorious 531
  atrocious 945
flagrante
  – bello 722

  – delicto
  sure enough 474
  act 680
  guilt 947
flagration 384
flagstaff *tall* 206
  signal 550
flail 276
flair 450, 698
flake 204
  snow – 383
  – white 430
flam 544
flambé 732
flambeau 423
flamboyant 577
flame *fire* 382
  light 420
  luminary 423
  passion 824, 825
  love 897
catch the –
  emotion 821
consign to the –s
  384
add fuel to the –
  173
in –s 382
  – up 825
  –colored
  red 434
  orange 439
flame-projector 527
flamen 996
flaming *violent* 173
  feeling 821
  excited 824
  ostentatious 882
  boasting 884
flâneur 935
flange *support* 215
  rim 231
  projection 250
flank *side* 236
  protect 664
flannel 384
flap *adjunct* 39
  hanging 214
  move to and fro
    315
  – the memory 505
flapdoodle 517
flapper *girl* 129
flapping *loose* 47
flare *violent* 173
  glare 420
  light 423
  – up
  excited 824, 825
  angry 900
flaring *color* 428
flash *instant* 113
  violent 173
  fire 382
  light 420
  eyes – fire 900
  – lamp 550
  – light 423
  – across the mem-
    ory 505
  – on the mind
  thought 451
  disclose 529
  impulse 612
  – note 800
  – in the pan
  unsubstantial 4
  transientness 111

impotent 158
　unproductive 169
　failure 732
　– tongue 563
　– up *excited* 824
　– upon
　unexpected 508
　– of wit 842
flashing
　ostentatious 882
flashy
　gaudy color 428
　style 577
　ornament 847
　vulgar 851
flask 191
flat *inert* 172
　abode 189
　story 191
　low 207
　horizontal 213
　vapid 391
　low tone 408
　musical note 413
　positive 535
　dupe 547
　back-scene 599
　shoal 667
　bungler 701
　poor 804
　insensible 823
　dejected 837
　weary 841
　dull 843
　simple 849
　fall – 732
　– contradiction
　　536
　– iron 255
　– refusal 764
flatfoot 664
flatness **251**
flatter *deceive* 545
　cunning 702
　please 829
　grace 845
　encourage 858
　approbation 931
　adulation 933
　– oneself
　probable 472
　hope 858
　– the palate 394
flatterer **935**
flattering
　– remarks 894
　– tale
　hope 858
　– unction to one's
　　soul
　content 831
　vain 880
　flattery 933
flattery 544, **933**
flatulent
　gaseous 334
　air 338
　wind 349
　- *style* 573, 575
flatus 334, 349
flaunt 873, 882
flaunting *vulgar* 85
　gaudy 428
　unreserved 525
flautist 416
Flavian amphi-
　theater 728

flavor 390
flavoring 393
flavous 436
flaw *break* 70
　crack 198
　error 495
　imperfection 651
　blemish 848
　fault 947
　– in an argument
　　477
flaxen 436
flay *divest* 226
　punish 972
flea *jumper* 309
　dirt 653
　– in one's ear
　repel 289
　eject 297
　refuse 764
　disrepute 874
　abashed 879
　discourteous 895
　contempt 930
flea-bite 643
flea-bitten 440
fleck 32
flecked 440
flection 279
fled *escaped* 671
fledge 673
fledgling 123
flee *avoid* 623
fleece *tegument* 223
　strip 789
　rob 791
　impoverish 804
　surcharge 814
fleet *ridicule* 856
　insult 929
fleet *ships* 273
　swift 274
　navy 726
Fleet *prison* 752
fleeting 4, 111
flesh *bulk* 192
　animal 364
　mankind 372
　carnal 961
　gain – 194
　ills that – is heir
　　to *evil* 619
　disease 655
　in the – 359
　one – 903
　way of all – 360
　weakness of the –
　　945
　– and blood
　substance 3
　materiality 316
　animality 364
　affections 820
　make the – creep
　pain 830
　fear 860
flesh-color 434
flesh-pots 298
　– of Egypt 734,
　　803
fleshly 316
fleur-de-lis 847
fleuron 847
flexible 324, 705
flexion
　curvature 245
　fold 258

deviation 279
flexuous 248
flexure 245, 258
flibbertigibbet 980
flicker
　changing 149
　waver 314
　flutter 315
　light 420
　dim 422
flickering 139
flier 621
flies *theatre* 599
flight *flock* 102
　volitation 267
　swiftness 274
　departure 293
　avoidance 623
　escape 671
　– lieutenant 745
　put to –
　propel 284
　repel 717
　vanquish 731
　– of fancy 515
　– of stairs 305,
　　627
　– of time 109
flighty *inattentive*
　　458
　mad 503
　fanciful 515
flim-flam 544, 608
flimsy *unsubstan-
　tial* 4
　weak 160
　rarity 322
　soft 324
　sophistical 477
　trifling 643
flinch *swerve* 607
　avoid 623
　fear 860
　cowardice 862
fling *propel* 284
　jig 840
　jeer 929
　have one's –
　active 682
　laxity 738
　freedom 748
　amusement 840
　– aside 782
　have a – at
　attack 716
　resent 900
　disrespect 929
　censure 932
　– away *reject* 610
　waste 638
　relinquish 782
　– down 308
　– to the winds
　destroy 162
　not observe 773
flint *hard* 323
flint-hearted 907
flintlock 727
flip *beverage* 298
flippant *fluent* 584
　pert 885
flipper *paddle* 267
flirt *propel* 284
　coquet 607, 854
　love 897
　endearment 902
　– a fan 855

flit *elapse* 109
　changeable 149
　move 264
　travel 266
　swift 274
　depart 293
　run away 623
flitter
　small part 32
　changeable 149
　flutter 315
flitting 111
float *establish* 150
　navigate 267
　boat 273
　buoy up 305
　lightness 320
　before the –s
　on the stage 599
　– on the air 405
　– before the eyes
　　446
　– bonds 788
　– in the mind
　thought 451
　imagination 515
floater 683
floating
　[*see* float]
　rumoured 532
　– battery 726
　– capital 805
　– debt 806
　– dock 189
flocculent
　woolly 256
　soft 324
　pulverulent 330
flock
　assemblage 72
　multitude 102
　laity 997
　–s and herds 366
　– together 72
floe *ice* 383
flog 972
　hasten 684
flood *much* 31
　crowd 102
　river 348
　abundance 639
　redundance 641
　prosperity 734
　stem the – 708
　– of light 420
　– of tears 839
flood-gate
　limit 233
　egress 295
　conduit 350
　open the –s
　eject 297
　permit 760
flood-light 423,
　　599
flood-mark 466
flood-tide
　increase 35
　complete 52
　height 206
　advance 282
　water 337
floor *level* 204
　base 211
　horizontal 213
　support 215
　overthrow 731

ground – 191
flop 315
Flora 369
floral 367
florescence 154
floriculture 371
florid *color* 428
　red 434
　- *style* 577
　health 654
florist 371
floss 256
flotilla 273, 726
flotsam and jetsam
　　73
flounce
　trimming 231
　jump 309
　agitation 315
flounder
　change 149
　toss 315
　uncertain 475
　bungle 699
　difficulty 704
　fail 732
flour 330
flourish
　brandish 314, 315
　exaggerate 549
　language 577
　speech 582
　prosper 618
　healthy 654
　prosperous 734
　ornament 847
　repute 873
　display 882
　boast 884
　– of trumpets
　loud 404
　cheerfulness 836
　publish 531
　ostentation 882
　celebrate 883
　boast 884
flout 929, 936
flow *course* 109
　hang 214
　motion 264
　stream 348
　murmur 405
　abundance 639
　– from
　result 154
　– of ideas 451
　– in 294
　– into *river* 348
　– out 295
　– over 641
　– of soul
　conversation 588
　affections 820
　cheerful 836
　social 892
　– with the tide
　　705
　– of time 109
　– of words 582,
　　584
flower *essence* 5
　produce 161
　vegetable 367
　prosper 734
　beauty 845
　ornament 847
　repute 873

fortunes of
  narrative 594
forty 98
– winks 683
forum 799
  school 542
  tribunal 966
forward *early* 132
  transmit 270
  advance 282
  willing 602
  improve 658
  active 682
  help 707
  vain 880
  insolent 885
  uncourteous 895
bend – 234
come –
  in sight 446
  offer 763
  display 882
look – to 507
move – 282
press – *haste* 684
put – *aid* 507
  offer 763
put oneself – 880
set – 676
  – in *knowledge* 490
foss 348
fosse
  inclosure 232
  ditch 259
  defence 717
fossil
  ancient 124
  hard 323
  organic 357
  dry bones 362
foster *aid* 707
  excite 824
  caress 902
  – a *belief* 484
fou 959
foudroyant 870
foul
  collide 276
  bad 649
  dirty 653
  unhealthy 657
  ugly 846
  base 940
  vicious 945
fall – of
  oppose 708
  quarrel 713
  attack 716
  fight 720
  censure 932
run – of
  impede 706
  – fiend 978
  – means 940
  – language
    malediction 908
  – odor 401
  – play *evil* 619
  cunning 702
  wrong 923
  improbity 940
foul-mouthed 895
foul-spoken 934
found 153, 215
foundation
  beginning 66
  stability 150

base 211
  support 215
lay the –s 673
  sandy – 667
shake to its –s 315
founded
  well – 472
  – on *base* 211
  evidence 467
founder
  originator 164
  sink 310
  fail 732
  religious –s 986
foundery 691
founding 22
foundling
  trover 775
  derelict 782
  outcast 893
fount *type* 591
fountain
  source 153
  river 348
  store 636
  – head 210
  – pen 590
four 95
on all –s 13, 23
  horizontal 213
  easy 705
  prosperous 734
  humble 879
  – in hand 272
  – score &c. 98
  – square 244
  – times 96
from the – winds
  278
fourflusher 884
fourfold 96
four-oar 273
four-poster 215
fourth 96, 97
  musical 413
  – estate 531
four-wheeler 272
fowl 366
fowling-piece 727
fox *animal* 366
  cunning 702
  – chase 622
fox-trot 840
foxy *color* 433, 434
  cunning 720
foyer 191, 599
fracas
  disorder 59
  noise 404
  discord 713
  contention 720
fraction *part* 51
  numerical 84
  less than one 100a
fractious 901
fracture
  disjunction 44
  discontinuity 70
  fissure 198
fragile 160, 328
fragment
  small 32, 193
  part 51, 100a
fragrance 400
fragrant *weed* 392
frail *weak* 160
  brittle 328

feeble 575
  irresolute 605
  imperfect 651
  failing 945
  impure 961
  – sisterhood 962
frais, à grands –
  481
frame
  condition 7
  make 161
  support 215
  border 231
  form 240
  substance 316
  structure 329
  contrive 626
cucumber – 371
have –d and
  glazed 822
– of mind
  inclination 602
  disposition 820
frame-up 626
framework
  support 215
  structure 329
franchise
  voting 609
  freedom 748
  right 924
  exemption 927a
Franciscan 996
franc-tireur 726
frangible 160, 328
frank *open* 525
  sincere 543
  artless 703
  honorable 939
frankalmoigne 748
Frankenstein 913,
  980
frankincense 400
frantic
  violent 173
  delirious 503
  excited 824
fraternal
  brother 11
  concord 714
  friendly 888
fraternity
  [see fraternal]
  party 712
fraternize
  co-operate 48, 709
  agree 714
  sympathize 888
  associate 892
fratricide 361
Frau 374
fraud
  falsehood 544
  deception 545
  pretender 548
  dishonor 940
  pious – 988
fraught *full* 52
  pregnant 161
  possessing 777
  – with danger 665
fray *rub* 331
  battle 720
in the thick of
  the – 722
frayed 659
frazzle

beaten to a – 732
freak 608, 872
  – of Nature 83
freckle 848
freckled 440
fredaine 840
free
  detached 44, 47
  unconditional 52
  liberate 672
  unobstructed 705
  at liberty 748, 750
  gratis 815
  liberal 816
  insolent 885
  exempt 927a
  impure 961
  – balloon 273
  – and easy
    cheerful 836
    adventurous 863
    vain 880
    insolent 885
    friendly 888
    sociable 892
  – fight 720
  – from
    simple 42
    never – from 613
  – gift 784
  – from imperfec-
    tion 650
  – lance 726
  – land 748
  – liver 954a
  – love 961
make – of 748
  – play 170, 748
  – quarters
    cheap 815
    hospitality 892
  – space 180
  – stage 748
  – trade
    commerce 794
  – translation 522
  – will 600
make – with
  frank 703
  take 789
  sociable 892
  uncourteous 895
freebooter 792
freeborn 748
freedman 748
freedom 748
free-handed 816
freehold 780
freely
  willingly 602
freeman 748
freemasonry
  unintelligible 519
  secret 528
  sign 550
  co-operation 709
  party 712
free-spoken 703
freethinker 989
freeze
  benumb 381
  cold 385
  – the blood 830
freezing 38.
  – mixture 387
freight *lade* 184
  cargo 190

transfer 270
freightage 812
freighter 273
freight train 272
French
  peddler's – 563
  – and English 840
  – horn 417
  – leave *avoid* 623
freedom 748
  – polish 847
frenetic 503
frenzy
  madness 503
  imagination 515
  excitement 825
frequency 136
frequent
  in number 104
  in time 136
  in space 186
  habitual 613
  visit 892
fresco *cold* 383
  painting 556
al |–
  out of doors 220
  in the air 338
fresh *additional* 37
  new 123
  flood 348
  cold 383
  color 428
  remembered 505
  unaccustomed 614
  good 648
  healthy 654
  impertinent 885
  tipsy 959
  – breeze 349
  – color 434
  – news 532
freshen 658, 689
freshet 348
freshman 541
freshwater 851
freshwater sailor
  701
fret *suffer* 378
  grieve 828
  gall 830
  discontent 832
  sad 837
  ornament 847
  irritate 900
  – and fume 828
fretful 901
fret-work 219
friable 328, 330
friandise 868
friar 996
  –'s lantern 423
  – Rush 980
  Black –s 996
friary 1000
fribble
  slur over 460
  trifle 643
  dawdle 683
  fop 854
fricassee 298
frication 331
friction *force* 157
  obstacle 179
  rubbing 331
on – wheels 705
friend 711, **890**

comic 853
fur *covering* 223
  hair 256
  warm 384
  dirt 653
furacious 791
furbelow 231
furbish
  improve 658
  prepare 673
  adorn 847
furcated 244
furcation 91
furcular 244
furfur 653
furfuraceous 330
Furies *anger* 900
  evil-doers 913
  demons 980
furious *violent* 173
  haste 684
  passion 825
  anger 900
furiously 31
furl 312
furlong 200
furlough 760
furnace 386
  workshop 691
  like a – *hot* 382
  sighing like –
    lament 839
  in love 902
furnish
  provide 637
  prepare 673
  give 784
  – *aid* 707
  – a handle 617
  – its quota 784
furniture 633
  – *van* 272
furor
  insanity 503
  passion 825
furore
  emotion 820, 821
  passion 825
  desire 865
furrow **259**
further
  added 37
  distant 196
  aid 707
  go – and fare
    worse
    worse 659
    bungle 699
  not let it go – 528
furthermore 37
furtive
  clandestine 528
  stealing 791
furuncle 250
fury *violence* 173
  excitation 825
  anger 900
  demon 980
furze 367
fuscous 433
fuse *join* 43
  combine 48
  heat 382, 384
  torch 388
fuselage 215
fusel oil 356
fusiform 244, 253

fusil 727
fusileer 726
fusillade 361, 716
fusion *union* 48
  heat 384
  co-operation 709
fuss *agitation* 315
  activity 682
  haste 684
  difficulty 704
  excitement 825
  ostentation 882
  kick up a – 173
  make a – *about*
    importance 642
  lament 839
  disapprove 932
fussy *crotchety* 481
  bustling 682
  excitable 825
fustian
  absurd 497
  unmeaning 517
  - *style* 577, 579
fustigate 972
fusty 124, 401, 653
futhorc 590
futile 497, 645
future 121
  eye to the – 510
  – *possession* 777
  – *state*
    destiny 152
    heaven 981
futurity **121**
fuzzle 959
fuzzy 447

G

gab 284
  gift of the – 582
gabardine 225
gabble 517, 583
gabelle 812
gaberlunzie 876
gabion 717
gable *side* 236
  – *end* 67
Gabriel 977
Gaby 501
gad
  about 266, 268
gadget 626
gad-so 870
gaff 727
gaffer *old* 130
  man 373
  clown 876
gag
  closure 261
  render mute 403,
    581
  dramatic 599
  muzzle 551
  imprison 752
gage *measure* 466
  security 771
  throw down the –
    715
gaggle 412
gag-man 844
gaieté de cœur 836
gaiety
  [*see gay*] 836
gaillard 844

gain
  increase 35
  advantage 618
  skilful 698
  acquisition 775
  – the confidence
    of 484
  – *credit* 931
  – one's ends 731
  – *ground*
    progress 282
    improve 658
  – *head* 175
  – *laurels* 873
  – *learning* 539
  – *over* 615
  – a point 731
  – private ends 943
  – the start
    priority 116
    early 132
  – strength 35
  – *time*
    protract 110
    early 132
    late 133
  – *upon*
    approach 286
    pass 303
    become a habit
      613
  – a victory 731
gainful *useful* 644
gainless 646
gainsay 536
gait 264, 627
gaiter 225
gala 840, 882
galactic circle 318
galantuomo 939
galavant 902
galaxy
  assemblage 72
  multitude 102
  stars 318
  luminary 423
  glory 873
gale 349
Galen 662
galenicals 662
galimatias 497
galipot 191
galopade 840
galore 639
gall *hurt* 378
  bitter 395
  annoy 830
  anger 900
  malevolence 907
  dip the pen in –
    934
gallant *brave* 861
  courteous 894
  love 897
  licentious 961,
    962
gallantry
  dalliance 902
gallanty-show 448,
  840
galled jade wince,
  let the – 884
galleon 273
gallery *room* 191
  passage 260
  auditory 599
  museum 636

picture – 556
galley *ship* 273
  punishment 972,
    975
  work like a – *slave*
    686
  – *proof* 591
galliass 273
Gallicism 563
galligaskin 225
gallimaufry 41
galliot 273
gallipot 191
gallivant 902
galloon 847
gallop
  pass away 111
  ride 266
  scamper 274
galloping consump-
  tion 655
galloway 271
gallows 361, 975
  come to the – 972
galoche 225
galore 102
galvanic
  excitable 825
galvanism 157
galvanize 824
gamache 225
Gamaliel
  brought up at the
    feet of – 492
gambade *leap* 309
  prank 840
gamble 156
gambado
  gaiter 225
  leap 309
gambit 66
gambling
  chance 621
  rashness 863
gambling-house
  621
gamboge 436
gambol 309, 827,
  840
game *lame* 160
  food 298
  animal 366
  savory 394
  resolute 604
  persevering 604a
  aim 620
  gamble 612
  pursuit 622
  tactics 692
  amusement 840
  laughing-stock
    857
  brave 861
  make – *of*
    deceive 545
    ridicule 856
    disrespect 929
  play the – 709, 939
  – in one's hands
    easy 705
    succeed 731
    command 737
  – to the last 604a
  – at which two
    can play 718
  – up 732
game-cock 726, 861

game-keeper 370,
  753
gameness 861
gamesome 836
gamester
  chance 621
  play 840
  rash 863
gamin 876
gaming-house 621
gammer *old* 130
  woman 374
gammon 544, 545
gamey 392
gamut 413
gander 373
gang
  assemblage 72
  go 264
  party 712
  – *agley* 732
ganger 690
gangrene 655
gangster 361, 913
gangway 260, 627
gantlet 972
  run the –
    resolution 604
    dare 861
gaol 752
  – *delivery* 672
gaoler 753, 975
gap 70, 198, 252
  stand in the – 717
gape *open* 260
  curiosity 455
  wonder 870
  – *for desire* 865
gaping [*see gape*]
  expectant 507
gar 161
garage 191
garb 225
  under the – of 545
garbage 653
garble
  take from 38
  exclude 55
  erroneous 495
  misinterpret 523
  falsify 544
  – *accounts* 811
garbled
  incomplete 53
garden *grounds* 189
  horticulture 371
  beautiful 845
  botanic – 371
  zoological – 370
  – *party* 840
gardener 371
gardens *street* 189
Gargantua 192
gargle 337
gargoyle 350
garish
  light 420
  color 428
  ugly 846
  ornament 847
  vulgar 851
  display 882
garland
  circle 247
  sign 550
  trophy 733
  ornament 847

- ready 673
- rid of 672
- a sight of 441, 490
- through
  end 67
  transact 692
  complete 729
  expend 809
- to
  extend to 196
  arrive 292
- together 72
- into trouble 732
- the wind up 860
- up *produce* 161
  ascend 305
  raise 307
  learn 539
  fabricate 544
  prepare 673
  rise early 682
  foment 824
- into the way of 613
get-away 671
gewgaw
  trifle 643
  ornament 847
  vulgar 851
geyser 382, 386
ghastly
  pale 429
  hideous 846
  frightful 860
ghaut 203
ghetto 189
ghost *shade* 362
  fallacy of vision 443
  soul 450
  writer 593
  apparition 980
give up the – 360
  needs no – to tell us 525
  pale as a –
  colorless 429
  fear 860
- dance 992
ghost-like
  ugly 846
ghostly
  intellectual 450
  supernatural 976, 980
Ghost, Holy – 976
ghoul 913, 980
ghyll 348
giant
  large 192
  tall 206
- refreshed
  strong 159
  refreshed 689
-'s strides
  distance 196
  swift 294
giaour 984, 989
gibber 583
gibberish 517, 563
gibbet
  brand 932
  execute 972
  gallows 975
gibble-gabble 584
gibbous 249, 250

gib-cat *male* 373
gibe 929
giblets 298
gibus 225
giddy
  inattentive 458
  vertiginous 503
  irresolute 605
  capricious 608
  bungling 699
giddy-head 501
giddy-paced 315
gift *power* 157
  talent 698
  given 784
- of the gab 582
  look a – horse in the mouth
  fastidious 868
  ungrateful 917
gifted 698
gig 272, 273
gigantic
  strong 159
  large 192
  tall 206
giggle 838
giglamps 445
Gilbertian 842
Gilbertine 996
gild *coat* 223
  color 439
  ornament 847
- refined gold 641
- the pill
  deceive 545
  tempt 615
  please 829
  flatter 933
Gilead, balm in – 834, 858
Giles's Greek, St. – 563
gill 348
gillie 746
gilt 436, 847
- edged 648
gimbals 312
gimcrack
  weak 160
  brittle 328
  trifling 643
  ornament 847
  ridiculous 853
gimlet 262
gimp
  clean 652
  pretty 845
  decoration 847
gin *trap* 545
  instrument 633
  intoxicating 959
  demon 980
gin mill 189
gin palace 189
gingerbread
  weak 160
  vulgar 851
gingerly 174, 459, 864
gingle 408
gipsy
  wanderer 268
  wag 933
- lingo 563
giraffe 206
girandole 423

girasol 847
gird *bind* 43
  strengthen 159
  surround 227
  jeer 929
- up one's loins
  brace 159
  prepare 673
girder 45, 215
girdle *bond* 45
  encircle 227
  circumference 230
  circle 247
  put a – round the earth 311
girl 129, 374
girlhood 127
girt 45
girth
  bond 45
  circumference 230
gisarm 727
gist *essence* 5
  meaning 516
  important 642
git, ci – 363
gittern 417
give *yield* 324
  melt 382
  bestow 784
  discount 813
- away 782, 784
  in marriage 903
- back 790
- birth to 161
- with both hands 816
- in charge
  restrain 751
- chase 622
- consent 762
- one credit for 484
- in custody 751
- expression to 566
- forth 531
- the go by 623
- a horse his head 748
- in *submit* 725
- into *consent* 762
- light 420
- the mind to 457
- notice
  inform 527
  warn 668
- it one
  censure 932
  punish 972
- out *emit* 297
  publish 531
  bestow 784
- over *cease* 142
  relinquish 624
  lose hope 859
- place to *substitute* 147
  avoid 623
- play to the imagination 515
- points to 27
- quarter 740
- rise to 153
- one the slip 671
- security 771
- and take

reciprocate 12
  compensation 30
  interchange 148
  retaliation 718
  compromise 774
  barter 794
  equity 922
  honour 939
- tongue 531
- a turn to 140
- one to understand 527
- up
  not understand 519
  unwilling 603
  reject 610
  relinquish 624
  submit 725
  resign 757
  surrender 782
  restore 790
  hopeless 859
- up the ghost 360
- way weak 160
giț, ci – 363
  brittle 328
  submit 725
  pine 828
  despond 837
  modest 881
given [see give]
  circumstances 8
  supposition 514
  received 785
- over dying 360
- time 134
- to 613
giving 784
gizzard 191
  stick in one's – 900
glabrous 225
glacial 383
glaciate 385
glacier 383
glacis 217, 717
glad 827, 829
  give the – eye 441
  would be – of 865
- tidings 532
gladden 834, 836
glade hollow 252
  opening 260
  shade 424
gladiator 726
gladiatorial 361, 713, 720
gladsome 827, 829
Gladstone bag 191
glair 352
glaive 727
glamor 992
glance look 441
  sign 550
  see at a – 498
- at
  take notice of 457
  allude to 527
  censure 932
- off deviate 279
  diverge 291
gland 221
glare light 420
  stare 441
  imperfect vision 443
  visible 446

glaring
  [see glare]
  great 31
  color 428
  visible 446
  manifest 525
glass vessel 191
  smooth 255
  brittle 328
  transparent 425
  lens 445
  musical –es 47
  see through a – darkly 491
- of fashion 852
  live in a – house
  brittle 328
  visible 446
  danger 665
- too much 959
glass-coach 272
glasshouse 191, 371
Glassite 984
glassy [see glass]
  shining 420
  colorless 429
glaucous 435
glave 727
glaver 933
glaze 255
gleam small 32
  light 420
glean 609, 775
gleanings 636
glebe land 342
  ecclesiastical 995
  church 1000
glee music 415
  satisfaction 827
  merriment 836
gleek 929
glen 252
glengarry 225
glib voluble 584
  facile 705
glide lapse 109
  move 264
  travel 266
  fly 267
- into
  conversion 144
glider 273
glimmer
  light 420
  dim 422
  visible 446
  slight knowledge 490, 491
glimpse 441, 490
glint 420
glissade 306
glisten 420
glitter
  shine 420
  appear 446
  illustrious 882
glittering
  ornament 847
  display 882
gloam 901a
gloaming 126, 422
gloar look 441
  wonder 970
gloat 884
- on look 441
- over 441
  pleasure 377

grandfather 130,
166
grandiloquent 577
grandiose 577
grandmother 166
  simple 501
  teach – 538
grandsire 130, 166
grange 189
granite 323
granivorous 298
grano salis, cum
469, 485
grant *admit* 529
  permit 760
  consent 762
  confer 784
  God – 990
  – a lease 771
granted 488
  take for –
  believe 484
  suppose 514
grantee
  possessor 779
  receiver 785
granular 330
granulate 330
granule 32
grapes, sour –
  unattainable 471
  falsehood 544
  excuse 617
grape-shot
  attack 716
  arms 727
graph 554
graphic
  intelligible 518
  painting 556
  descriptive 594
graphite 332
graphito 556
graphology 590
graphometer 244
graphotype 558
grapnel 666
grapple
  fasten 43
  clutch 789
  – with
  - a question 461
  - difficulties 704
  oppose 708
  resist 719
  contention 720
grappling-iron
  fastening 45
  safety 666
grasp
  comprehend 518
  power 737
  retain 781
  seize 789
  in one's – 737
  possess 777
  tight – *severe* 739
  – at 865
  – of intellect 498
grasping
  miserly 819
  covetous 865
grass 344, 367
  let the – grow
    under one's feet
  neglect 460
  inactive 683

not let the – &c.
  active 682
grasshopper 309
grass-plat 371
grate *rub* 330
  physical pain 378
  stove 386
  – on the ear
  harsh sound 410
  – on the feelings
  830
grated
  barred 219
grateful
  physically pleas-
  ant 377
  agreeable 829
  thankful 916
grater 260, 330
gratification
  animal – 377
  moral – 827
gratify 829
  permit 760
  please 829
grating [*see* grate]
  lattice 219
  harsh 713
gratis 815
gratitude **916**
gratuitous
  inconsequent 477
  supposititious
  514
  voluntary 602
  payless 815
gratuity
  gift 784
  gratis 815
gratulate 896
gravaman 642
  – of a charge 938
grave *great* 31
  engrave 259, 558
  tomb 363
  important 642
  composed 826
  distressing 830
  sad 837
  heinous 945
  beyond the – 360
  look –
  disapprove 932
  rise from the – 660
  silent as the – 403
  sink into the – 360
  on this side of the
    – 359
  – in the memory
  505
  – note 408
  – trap 599
gravel
  earth 342
  material 635
  puzzle 704
graveolent 398
graven image 991
graver 558
graving dock 189
gravitate
  descend 306
  weigh 319
  – towards 176
gravity *force* 157
  weight **319**
  vigor 574

importance 642
sedateness 826
seriousness 827
center of – 222
specific –
  weight 319
  density 321
gravy 333
  – boat 191
gray **432** [and *see*
  grey]
graze *touch* 199
  browse 298
  rub 331
  brush 379
grazier 370
gré, savoir – 916
grease
  lubricate 332
  oil 356
  – the palm
  tempt 615
  give 784
  pay 807
greasy 355
great *much* 31
  big 192
  glorious 873
  magnanimous
  942
  (*important* 642)
  – bear 318
  – circle sailing 628
  – coat 225
  – doings
  importance 642
  bustle 682
  – folks 875
  – gun 626
  – hearted 942
  – Mogul 745
  – number 102
  – primer 591
  – quantity 31
greater 33
  – number 102
  – part 31
  nearly all 50
greatest 33
greatness **31**
greave 225
greed
  desire 865
  gluttony 957
greedy
  avaricious 819
green
  new 123
  young 127
  lawn 344
  grass 367
  unripe 397
  color 435
  credulous 486
  novice 491
  unused 614
  healthy 654
  immature 674
  unskilled 699
  board of – cloth
  966
  – memory 505
  – old age 128
greenback 800
green-eyed mon-
  ster 920
greenhorn

novice 493
dupe 547
bungler 701
greenhouse
  receptacle 191
  horticulture 371
greenness **435**
green-room 599
greensward 344
Greenwich time
  114
greenwood 367
Greek
  unintelligible 519
  sharper 792
  St. Giles's – 563
  – Church 984
  – Kalends 107
greet *weep* 839
  hail 894
greeting
  sociality 892
  –'s! 292
gregarious 892
grenade 727
grenadier
  tall 206
  soldier 726
grey 432
  – beard 130
  – friar 996
  – hairs 128
  bring – hairs to
    the grave
  adversity 735
  harass 830
  – mare
  ruler 737
  master 745
  wife 903
  – matter
  brain 498
  –hound
  swift 274
  animal 366
  ocean –hound 273
gridelin 437
gridiron
  flatness 213
  crossing 219
  stove 386
  stage 599
  stadium 840
grief 828
  come to – 735
grievance
  evil 619
  painful 830
  wrong 923
grieve *mourn* 828
  pain 830
  dejected 837
  complain 839
grievous 649, 830
grievously 31
griffin 83, 366, 493
griffo 41
griffonage 590
grig *merry* 836
grill 382, 384, 461
  – room 189
grille 219
grim
  resolved 604
  painful 830
  doleful 837
  ugly 846

discourteous 895
sullen 901a
–visaged war 722
grimace 243, 839,
  855
grimacier
  actor 599
  humorist 844
  affected 855
grimalkin 366
grimy 652
grin *laugh* 838
  ridicule 856
  – and abide 725
  – a ghastly smile
  dejected 837
  ugly 846
grind
  reduce 195
  sharpen 253
  pulverize 330
  pain 378
  learn 539
  oppress 907
  – the organ 416
  – one's teeth 900
grinder
  teacher 330
  noise 404
grinding 739, 830
grindstone 253, 330
grip
  indication 550
  power 737
  retention 781
  clutch 789
  – of the hand 894
gripe [*see* grip]
  pain 378
  parsimony 819
grisaille
  grey 432
  painting 556
grisette
  woman 374
  commonalty 876
  libertine 962
grisly 846
grist
  materials 635
  provision 637
  – to the mill
  useful 644
  acquire 775
gristle 321, 327
grit
  strength 159
  powder 330
  stamina 604a
  courage 861
  – in the oil
  hindrance 706
gritty 323
grizzled
  grey 432
  variegated 440
groan 411, 839
groat 800
grocer 637
grocery 396
grog 298, 959
groin 244
groom 370, 746
  – well
  – of the chambers
  746
  –'s man 903

groove
furrow 259
habit 613
in a – 16
move in a – 82
put in a – for 673

grope
feel 379
experiment 463
try 675
in the dark 442,
704

gross
great 31
whole 50
number 98
ugly 846
vulgar 851
vicious 945
impure 961
– credulity 486
– receipts 810

grosshead 501
grossheaded 499
grossièreté 895
grot [see grotto]
grotesque
odd 83
distorted 243
– *style* 579
ridiculous 853

grotto
alcove 191
hollow 252

grouch 895, 901a
ground
cause 153
region 181
base 211
lay down 213
support 215
coating 223
land 342
plain 344
evidence 467
teach 537
motive 615
plea 617
above – 359
down to the – 52
dress the – 371
fall to the – 732
get over the – 274
go over the – 302
level with the –
162
maintain one's –
persevere 604a
play– 840
prepare the – 673
stand one's –
defend 717
resist 719
– bait 784
– cut from under
one 732
– floor
chamber 191
low 207
base 211
– on
attribute 155
– plan 554
– of quarrel 713
– sliding from
under one 665
– swell

agitation 315
waves 348
grounded
stranded 732
well– 490
– on *basis* 211
evidence 467
groundless
unsubstantial 4
illogical 477
erroneous 495
groundling 876
grounds
dregs 653
groundwork
precursor 64
cause 153
basis 211
support 215
preparation 673
group
marshal 60
cluster 72
– *captain* 745
grouping 60
grouse 852, 901a
grout 45
grove
street 189
glade 252
wood 367
grovel
below 207
move slowly 275
cringe 886
base 940
grow
increase 35
become 144
expand 194
– from
effect 154
– into 144
– less 195
– taller 206
– together 46
– up 194
– upon one 613
grower 164
growl *cry* 412
complain 839
discourtesy 895
anger 900
threat 909
growler *cab* 272
discontented 832
sulky 901a
grown up 131
growth [see grow]
development 161
– in size 194
tumor 250
vegetation 367
groyne 706
grub
small animal 193
food 298
– up
eradicate 301
discover 480a
Grub-street writer
593
grudge
unwilling 603
refuse 764
stingy 819
hate 898

anger 900
bear a – 907
owe a – 898
grudging 603
– *praise* 932
gruel 298
gruesome 846
gruff
harsh sound 410
discourteous 895
grum
harsh sound 410
morose 901a
grumble
cry 411
complain 832,
839
grume 321, 354
grumous 321, 354
grumpy 901a
Grundy, Mrs. 852
grunt 412
complain 839
guano 653
guarantee 768, 771
guard
traveling 268
safety 664
defence 717
soldier 726
sentry 753
advanced – 668
mount –
care 459
safety 664
off one's –
inexpectant 508
throw off one's –
cunning 702
on one's –
careful 459
cautious 864
rear – 668
– against
prepare 673
defence 717
– ship 664, 726
guarda costa 753
guarded
conditions 770
guardian
safety 664
defence 717
keeper 753
– angel
helper 711
benefactor 912
guardless 665
guard-room 752
gubernation 693
gubernatorial 737
gudgeon 547
guerdon 973
guernsey 225
guerre:
nom de – 565
– à outrance &c.
722
guerilla 726
– *warfare* 720
guess 514
guesswork 514
guest 890
paying – 188
guet:
mot de – 550
–à-pens 545

guffaw 838
guggle
gush 348
bubble 353
resound 408
cry 412
guide
pattern 22
courier 524
teach 537
teacher 540
indicate 550
direct 693
director 694
advise 695
guide-book 527
guided by, be – 82
guideless 665
guide-post 550
guiding star 693
guild 712, 966
guildhall 799
guile
deceit 544, 545
cunning 702
guileless 543, 703
guillotine 972, 975
guilt 947
guiltless 946
guilty:
find – 971
plead – 950
guindé 579
guinea 800
guipure 847
guisard 599
guise
state 7
dress 225
appearance 448
plea 617
mode 627
conduct 692
guiser 599
guitar 417
gulch 198
gules 434
gulf
interval 198
deep 208
lake 343
gull 545, 547
gullible 486
gullet *throat* 260
rivulet 348
gully *gorge* 198
hollow 252
opening 260
conduit 350
gulosity 957
gulp *swallow* 296
take food 298
– down
credulity 486
submit 725
gum *fastening* 45
fasten 46
resin 356a
– elastic 325
– tree 367
gumbo 298
gummy 352
gumption 498
gun *report* 406
weapon 727
great – 626
blow great –s 349

sure as a – 474
gunboat 726
gunfire 404
gunman 361
gunner 776
gunnery
warfare 722
cannon 727
gunlayer 284
gunpowder
warfare 722
ammunition 727
not invent – 499
sit on barrel of –
501
gunroom 193
gun-shot 197
gunwale 232
gurge 312, 348
gurgle
flow 348
bubble 353
faint sound 405
resonance 408
gurgoyle 350
gush
flow out 295
flood 348
exaggeration 482
talk 584
gushing
emotional 821
impressible 822
gusset 43
gust *wind* 349
physical taste 390
passion 825
moral taste 850
gustation 390
gustful 394
gustless 391
gusto [see gust]
physical pleasure
377
emotion 821
gut *destroy* 162
opening 260
strait 343
eviscerate 297
sack 789
steal 791
gutling 954a
guts *inside* 221
guttapercha 325
gutter *groove* 259
conduit 350
vulgarity 851
guttersnipe 876
guttle 957
guttural
letter 561
inarticulate 583
guy
fastening 45, 752
fellow 373
disrespect 929
grotesque 853
guzzle
gluttony 957
drunkenness 959
gybe [see jibe]
gymkhana 720, 840
gymnasium 191
school 542
arena 728, 840
gymnast 159
gymnastics

training 537
exercise 686
contention 720
sport 840
gymnosophist
  abstainer 953
  sectarian 984
gynander 83
gynarchy 727
gynecaeum 374
gynecology 662
gyniatrics 374
gynics 374
gyp 545, 746
gyre 311
gyrate 312
gyrfalcon 913
gyromancy 511
gyrostat 312
gysart 599
gyve 752

H

habeas corpus 963, 969
haberdasher 225
habergeon 717
habiliment 225
habilitation 698
habit
  essence 5
  coat 225
  custom **613**
  want of – 614
  –s of business 682
  – of mind 820
habitant 188
habitat 189
habitation 189
habit-maker 225
habitual
  unvariable 16
  orderly 58
  ordinary 82
  customary 613
habituate 537, 613
habitude
  stale 7
  habit 613
habitué 613
hacienda 189, 780
hack cut 44
  shorten 201
  horse 271
  writer 594
  worker 690
literary – 593
hackle 44
hackney-coach 272
hackneyed
  known 490
  trite 496
  habitual 613
Hades 982
Hadji
  traveler 268
  priest 996
hae tibi erunt artes 627
haeret lateri lethalis arundo
  displeasure 828
  anger 900
haft 633

hag age 128
  ugly 846
  wretch 913
  witch 994
haggard
  insane 503
  tired 688
  wild 824
  ugly 846
haggis 298
haggle cut 44
  chaffer 794
Hagiographa 985
Hagiolatry 984
Hagiology 983, 985
haguebut 727
ha-ha trench 198, 719
haik 225
hail welcome 292
  ice 383
  call 586
  rejoicing 838
  honor to 873
  celebration 883
  courtesy 894
  salute 928
  approve 931
  –fellow well met
  friendship 888
  sociality 892
hailstone 383
hair small 32
  filament 205
  roughness 256
  to a – 494
  –'s breadth
  near 197
  narrow 203
  –breadth escape
  danger 665
  escape 671
  –s on the head
  multitude 102
  make one's –
  stand on end
  distressing 830
  fear 860
  wonder 870
hairless 226
hairy rough 256
halberd 727
halberdier 726
halcyon calm 174
  peace 721
  prosperous 734
  joyful 827, 829
hale 654
half 91
  – the battle
  important 642
  success 731
  – distance 68
  – a dozen six 98
  several 102
  see with – an eye
  intelligent 498
  intelligible 518
  manifest 525
  – a gale 349
  – and half
  equal 27
  mixed 41
  incomplete 53
  – a hundred 98
  – light 422
  – measures

incomplete 53
  vacillating 605
  mid-course 628
  – moon 245
  – price 815
  – rations 640
  – scholar 493
  – seas over 959
  – sight 443
  – speed
  moderate 174
  slow 275
  – truth 546
half-blind 443
half-blood
  mixture 41
  unconformity 83
  imperfect 651
half-frozen 352
half-hearted
  irresolute 605
  insensible 823
  indifferent 866
half-learned 491
half-melted 352
halfpenny
  trifle 643
half-starved
  insufficient 640
  fasting 956
half-way
  small 32
  middle 68
  between 228
  go – irresolute 605
  mid-course 628
  meet –
  willing 602
  compromise 774
half-witted 499, 501
hall chamber 189
  receptacle 191
  mart 799
  music – 599
  – of audience 588
  – mark 550
hallelujah 990
halliard 45
halloo cry 411
  look here! 457
  call 586
  wonder 870
hallow
  celebrate 883
  respect 928
hallowed 976
hallucination
  error 495
  insanity 503
halo light 420
  glory 873
Halomancy 511
halser 45
halt cease 142
  weak 160
  rest 265
  go slowly 275
  lame 655
  fail 732
  at the – 265
halter rope 45
  restraint 752
  punishment 975
  wear a – 874
  with a – round
  one's neck 665
halting

style 579
  – place 292
halve [see half]
halves
  do by –
  neglect 460
  not complete 730
  not do by – 729
  go – 778
ham house 189
hamadryad 979
hammam 386, 652
hamlet 189
hammer
  repeat 104
  knock 276
  stammer 583
  under the –
  auction 796
  between the – and
  the anvil 665
  – at think 451
  work 686
  – out form 240
  prepare 673
  complete 729
hammock 215
hamper basket 191
  obstruct 706
hamstring 158, 659
hanaper 802
hand
  measure of
  length 200
  side 236
  transfer 270
  man 372
  organ of touch 379
  indicator 550
  writing 590
  medium 631
  agent 690
  grasp 781
  transfer 783
  at – future 121
  destined 152
  near 197
  useful 644
  bad – 590
  bird in – 781
  come to – 292, 785
  fold one's –s 681
  give one's – to
  marry 903
  good –
  writing 590
  skill 698
  proficiency 700
  helping – 707, 711
  hold in – 737
  hold out the – 894
  hold up the –
  vote 609
  in –
  incomplete 53
  business 625
  preparing 673
  not finished 730
  possessed 777
  money 800
  in the –s of
  authority 737
  subjection 749
  lay –s on
  discover 480a
  use 677

take 789
rite 998
much on one's –s 682
on one's –s
  business 625
  redundant 641
  not finished 730
  for sale 796
on the other – 468
no – in 623
poor – 701
put into one's –s 784
put one's – to 676
ready to one's – 673
shake –s 918
stretch forth one's – 680
take by the – 707
take in –
  teach 537
  undertake 676
time hanging on one's –s
  inaction 681
  leisure 685
  weary 841
try one's – 675
turn one's – 675
turn one's – to 625
under one's
  in writing 590
  promise 768
  compact 769
  – back 683
  – cart 272
  – of death 360
  – down
  record 551
  transfer 783
  have one's –s full 682
  – gallop 274
  – glass 445
  – and glove 709, 888
  – in hand
  joined 43
  accompanying 88
  same time 120
  concur 178
  co-operate 709
  party 712
  concord 714
  friend 888
  social 892
  – to hand
  touching 199
  transfer 270
  fight 720, 722
  – over head
  inattention 458
  neglect 460
  reckless 863
  have a – in
  cause 153
  act 680
  co-operate 709
  have one's – in
  skill 698
  keep one's – in 613
  live from – to mouth
  insufficient 640

unprepared 674
poor 804
–s off! *avoid* 623
leave alone 681
prohibition 761
– over
transfer 783
give 784
win –s down 731
with the –s in the
pockets 681
hand-bag 191
hand-barrow 272
handbook
travel 266
information 527
book 593
handcuff 751, 752
handfast 903
handful
quantity 25
small 32
few 103
handicap
equalize 27
inferiority 34
encumber 706
race 720
handicraft 625, 680
handicraftsman 690
effect 154
doing 680
handkerchief
clothes 225
cleaner 652
handle
feel, touch 379
name 565
dissert 595
plea 617
instrument 633
use 677
manage 693
furnish a – 937
make a – of 677
– a case 693
– to one's name
name 564
honor 877
handmaid
instrumentality
631
auxiliary 711
servant 746
handpost 550
handsel
begin 66
security 771
gift 784
pay 809
handsome
liberal 816
beautiful 845
disinterested 942
– *fortune* 803
handspike 633
handstaff 727
handwriting
signature 550
autograph 590
– on the wall
warning 668
handy
near 197
useful 644, 646
ready 673
dexterous 698

hang
pendency 214
kill 361
curse 908
execute 972
– about 133, 197
– back 133, 623
– in the balance
133
– in doubt 485
– fire *late* 133
cease 142
unproductive 169
inert 172
slow 275
reluctance 603
inactive 683
not finish 730
fail 732
refuse 764
dullness 843
– on hand 641
– down the head
837
– over the head
152
– it! *regret* 833
contempt 930
– out a light 420
– upon the lips of
418
– on
accompany 88
– out
display 882
entertain 892
– over
destiny 152
height 206
project 250
– out a signal 550
– on the sleeve of
servant 746
servility 886
flattery 933
– in suspense 605
– by a thread 665
– together
joined 43
cohere 46
concur 178
co-operate 709
– upon
effect 154
dependency 749
hangar 191, 273
hang-dog look 901a
hanged if, I'll be –
489
hanger
weapon 727
suspender 45, 214
pothooks and –s
590
– on
accompaniment
88
servant 746
servile 886
hanging [see hang]
elevated 307
ornament 847
– look 846
hangman
evil-doer 913
bad man 949
executioner 97ö

hank *tie* 45
hanker 865
hanky-panky 545
Hansard 551
hansom 272
hap 156
haphazard
chance 156, 621
hapless
unfortunate 735
(*miserable* 828)
(*hopeless* 859)
haply
possibly 470
(*by chance* 156)
happen 151
– as it may
chance 621
– what may
certain 474
reckless 863
happening 151
happiness
[see *happy*]
the greatest – of
the greatest
number 910
happy *fit* 23
opportune 134
style 578
glad 827
cheerful 836
– despatch 972
– go lucky 674
– hunting grounds
981
– returns of the
day 896
– thought 842
– valley
imagination 515
delight 827
harangue 582
hara-kiri 972
harass
fatigue 688
vex 830
worry 907
harbinger
precursor 64
omen 512
informant 527
harbor
abode 189
haven 292
refuge 666
cherish 821
natural – 343
– a design 620
in – 664
– an idea 451
– revenge 919
harborless 665
hard *strong* 159
dense 323
*physically insen-
sible* 376
sour 397
difficult 704
severe 739
*morally insen-
sible* 823
grievous 830
impenitent 951
blow – 349
go –
difficult 704

failure 732
adversity 735
pain 828
hit – 276
look – at 441
not be too – upon
918
strike –
energy 171
impulse 276
try – 675
work – 686
– at it 682
– bargain 819
– of belief 487
– to believe 485
– by 197
– case 735
– cash 800
– earned 704
– and fast rule 80
– fought 704
– frost 383
– of hearing 419
– heart
malevolent 907
vicious 945
impenitent 951
– hit 732
– knocks 720
– life 735
– lines
adversity 735
severity 739
– liver 954a
– lot 735
– master 739
– measure 739
– names 932
– necessity 601
– nut to crack 704
– to please 868
– pressed
haste 684
difficulty 704
hindrance 706
– put to it 704
– set 704
– tack 298
– task 703
– time 704
– up 704, 804
– upon
attack 715
severe 739
censure 932
– winter 383
– words
obscure 571
rude 895
censure 932
– work 686
– at work 682
harden [see *hard*]
strengthen 159
accustom 613
– the heart
insensible 823
enmity 889
impenitence 951
hardened
impious 988
– front
insolent 885
hardening
habit 613
hard-featured 846

hard-fisted 819
hard-headed 498,
739
hardihood 861, 885
hardly
scarcely 32
deal – with 739
– any *few* 103
– anything
small 32
unimportant 643
– ever 137
hard-mouthed 606
hardness 323
– of heart 914a
hardship 735
hardy
strong 159
healthy 654
brave 861
hare 274
hold with the –
and run with
the hounds
fickle 607
servile 886
hare-brained 458,
863
harem 961
hariolation 511
hark 418, 457
– back 283
harl 205
harlequin
changeable 149
nimble 274
motley 440
pantomimic 599
humorist 844
harlequinade 599
harlot 962
harlotry 961
harm
evil 619
badness 649
malevolence 907
harmless
impotent 158
good 648
perfect 650
salubrious 656
safe 664
innocent 946
bear – 717
harmonica 417
harmonics 413
harmonist 413
harmonize 178, 416
harmonium 417
harmony
agreement 23
order 58
music 413
color 428
concord 714
peace 721
friendship 888
harness
fasten 43
fastening 45
accouterment 225
yoke 370
instrument 633
restraint 752
in –
prepared 673

in action 680
active 682
subjection 749
– up 293

harp
repeat 104
musical instrument 417
weary 841
Harpagon 819
harper 416
harpist 416
harpoon 727
harpsichord 417
harpy
relentless 739
thief 792
miser 819
evil-doer 913
demon 980
harquebuss 727
harridan 846, 962
harrier 366
harrow
agriculture 371
– up the soul 860
harrowing 830
harry *pain* 830
attack 716
persecute 907
Harry, old – 978
harsh
acrid 171
sound 410
style 579
discordant 713
severe 739
disagreeable 830
morose 895
malevolent 907
– voice 581
hart 366, 373
hartal 142, 489
harum-scarum 59, 458
haruspice 513
Haruspicy 511
harvest
effect 154
profit 618
store 636
acquisition 775
get in the –
complete 729
succeed 731
– home
celebration 883
– time
autumn 126
exertion 686
has been 122
hash *mix* 41
cut 44
confusion 59
food 298
make a – 699
hashish 863
hasp 43, 45
hassock 215
hastate 253
haste
velocity 274
activity 682
hurry **684**
hasten
promote 707
hasty

transient 113
hurried 684
impatient 825
irritable 901
– pudding 298
hat 225
cardinal's – 999
send round the –
765
shovel – 999
– in hand 886
hatch
produce 161
gate 232
opening 260
chickens 370
fabricate 544
shading 556
plan 626
prepare 673
– a plot 626
hatches, under –
restraint 751
prisoner 754
poor 804
hatchet
cutting 253
bury the – 918
dig up the – 722
throw the helve
after the – 818
hatchet-faced 203
hatchment
funeral 363
arms 550
record 551
hatchway 260
hate 867, **898**
hateful 649, 830
hath been, the
time – 122
hatrack 215
hatter 225
mad as a – 503
hatti-sheriff 741
hatred [*see* hate]
object of – 898
hauberk 717
haud passibus
æquis 28, 275
haugh 344
haughty
proud 878
insolent 885
contemptuous 930
haul *drag* 285
catch of fish &c.
789
– down one's flag
725
– in 10
haunch 236
haunt *focus* 74
presence 186
abode 189
alarm 860
persecute 907
– the memory
remember 505
trouble 830
haunted 980
haut
traiter de –
insolence 885
contempt 930
hautboy 417
haut-goût 392

haut-monde 875
hauteur 878
have *confute* 479
ken 49
possess 777
– the advantage
28, 33
– at 716
– no choice 609a
– done! 142
– to do with 9
– no end 112
– other fish to fry
135
– it
discover 480a
believe 484
– one to know 527
– some knowledge
of 490
– nothing to do
with 10
– for one's own
780
– rather 609
– one's rights 924
– the start 116
– in store 152, 637
– to 620
– up 638
– it your own way
submission 725
haven 292, 666
haversack 191
havoc
destruction 162
cry – *war* 722
play – *spoil* 659
haw 583
hawk *spit* 297
stammer 583
eye of a – 498
– about
publish 531
offer 763
sell 796
– at 716
between – and
buzzard 315,
828
know a – from a
handsaw 465,
698
hawker 796
hawk-eyed 441
hawking *chase* 622
hawser 45
hay while the sun
shines, make –
134
haycock 72
hazard
chance 156, 621
danger 665
at all – s 604
– a conjecture 514
– a proposition
477
haze *mist* 353
uncertainty 475
in a –
hidden 528
hazel 433
hazy *opaque* 426
he 373
head *precedence* 62
beginning 66

class 75
summit 210
coiffure 225
lead 280
froth 353
person 372
intellect 450
topic 454
wisdom 498
picture 556
nomenclature 564
chapter 593
direct 693
director 694
master 745
at the – of
direction 693
authority 737
repute 873
bow the – 308
bring to a – 729
come into one's –
451
come to a – 729
drive into one's –
505
gain – 175
get into one's –
thought 451
learn 505
belief 484
intoxicate 959
give a horse his –
748
hang one's – 879
have in one's – 490
from – to heels 52,
200
hit on the – 912
knock on the –
361
knock one's –
against
impulse 276
unskilful 699
fail 732
lie on one's – 926
lift up one's – 878
make – against
oppose 708
resistance 719
success 731
never entered
into one's – 458
have no – 506
on one's – 218
off one's – 503
can't get out of
one's – 505
over – and ears
deep 641
debt 806
love 897
put into one's –
supposition 514
information 527
put out of one's –
458
run in the – 505
not know whether
one stands on –
or heels
uncertain 475
wonder 870
take into one's –
thought 451
caprice 608

intention 620
turn the – 824
trouble one's –
about 457
as one's – shall
answer for 768
with – erect 878
from – to foot 200
– and front
important 642
– and front of
one's offending
provocation 830
charge 938
– over heels
inversion 218
rotation 312
– light 423
– line 591
– and shoulders
irrelevant 10
complete 52
haste 684
make neither – nor
tail of 519
hold one's – up
307
– above water
safe 664
prosperous 743
wealth 803
with a – on 353
headache 378
head-dress 225
header 310
head-foremost
violent 173
rash 863
head-gear 225
heading *prefix* 64
beginning 66
indication 550
title 564
headland
height 206
projection 250
headlong
hurry 684
rush 863
rush –
violence 173
headman 694
headmost
front 234
precession 280
head-piece
summit 210
intellect 450
helmet 717
ornament 847
head-quarters
focus 74
abode 189
authority 737
head-race 350
head-stone 363
heads
compendium 596
– or tails 156, 621
lay – together
advice 695
co-operate 709
– I win tails you
lose
unfair 940
headship 737
headsman 975

helicopter 273
Heliogabalus 954a
heliograph
 signal 550
 picture 556
heliography 550
 light 420
 painting 556
Helios 423
heliotrope 847
heliotype 558
helix 248
hell abyss 208
 gaming-house 62
 gehenna 982
 — upon earth
  misfortune 735
  pain 828
 — broke loose 59
hell-born 945, 978
hellebore 663
hell-hound 913, 949
hellish
 malevolent 907
 vicious 945
 hell 982
helluo librorum 492
helm handle 633
 scepter 747
 (authority 737)
 answer the — 743
 at the — 693
 obey the — 705
 take the — 693
helmet 225, 717
helminthology 368
helmsman 269, 694
helot 746
help benefit 618
 utility 644
 remedy 662
 aid 707
 servant 746
 give 784
 it can't be —ed
  submission 725
 never mind 823
 content 831
 God — you 914
 so — me God 535
 — oneself to 789
helper 711
helpless 158, 665
helpmate
 auxiliary 711
 wife 903
helter-skelter 59,
 684
helve
 throw the — after
  the hatchet 818
hem edge 231
 fold 258
 indeed! 870
 kiss the — of one's
  garment 886
 — in enclose 220
 restrain 751
hemi- 91
hemisphere 181
hemispheric 250
hemlock 663
hemorrhage 299
hemp 205
hen 366, 374
 female 374
 — with one chicken

busy 682
henbane 663
hence
 arising from 155
 departure 293
 deduction 476
 — loathed mel-
  ancholy 836
henceforth 121
henchman 746
hencoop 370
hendiadis 91
henna 433
henpecked 743, 749
heptagon 244
heptarchy 98
Heraclitus 839
 rideret — 853
herald
 precursor 64
 precession 280
 predict 511
 forerunner 512
 proclaim 531
 messenger 534
heraldry 550
herb 367
herbage 365
herbal 369
herbivorous 298
herborize 369
herculean
 strong 159
 exertion 686
 difficult 704
Herculem, ex pede
 — 550
Hercules 159, 215
 pillars of — 233,
  550
herd 72, 102
herdsman 746
here
 situation 183
 presence 186
 arrival 292
 come —! 286
 — below 318
 — goes 676
 — and there
  dispersed 73
 few 103
 place 182, 183
 — there and
  everywhere
  diversity 16a
 space 180
 omnipresence 186
 — to-day and gone
  to-morrow 111
hereabouts 183,
 197
hereafter 121, 152
hereby 631
hereditament 780
hereditary
 intrinsic 5
 derivative 154,
  167
heredity 167
herein 221
heresy 495, 984
heretic 984
heretofore 122
hereupon 106
herewith 88, 632
heritage

futurity 121
 possession 777
 property 780
heritor 779
hermaphrodite 83
 — brig 273
hermeneutics 522
Hermes 534, 582
hermetically 261
hermit 893, 955
hermitage
 house 189
 cell 191
 seclusion 893
hero brave 861
 glory 873
 good man 948
 — worship 931, 991
Herod, out-Herod
 — 549
heroic [see hero]
 magnanimous
  942
 mock — 853
heroics 884
heroin 663
heroine 861
herpetology 368
Herr 373
herring
 pungent 392
 — pond 341
 draw a — across
  the trail 545
 trail of a red —
  615, 706
herring-gutted 203
hesitate
 uncertain 475
 sceptical 485
 stammer 583
 reluctant 603
 irresolute 605
 fearful 860
Hesperian 236
Hesperides, garden
 of the — 981
Hesperus 423
Hessian boot 225
hest 741
hesterni quirites
 876
heterarchy 737
heteroclite 83
heterodoxy 489,
 984
heterogeneous
 unrelated 10
 different 15
 mixed 41
 multiform 81
 exceptional 83
heterogeneity 15,
 16a
heteromorphism
 16a
hetman 745
hew cut 44
 shorten 201
 fashion 240
 — down 308
hewers of wood
 workers 690
 commonalty 876
hexagon 98, 244
hexahedron 244
hexameter 98, 597

hey! 586
heyday
 exultation 838
 festivity 840
 wonder 870
 — of the blood 820
 — of youth 127
hiation 260
hiatus 198
hibernal 383
hibernate 683
Hibernicism 497,
 563
hic:
 — jacet 363
 — labor hoc opus
  704
hick 701, 851, 876
hiccup 349
hid under a bushel
 460
hidalgo 875
hidden 528
 — meaning 526
hide skin 223
 conceal 528
 — diminished head
  inferior 34
 decrease 36
 humility 879
 — one's face
  modesty 881
 — and seek
  deception 545
 avoid 623
 game 840
hide-bound 751,
 819
hideous 846
hide-out 893
hiding-place
 abode 189
 ambush 530
 refuge 666
hie 264, 274
 — to 266
hiemal 126
hierarch 996
hierarchy 995
hieratic 590
hieroglyphic
 representation
  554
 letter 561
 writing 590
hierographa 985
hieromancy 511
hierophant 996
hieroscopy 511
higgle 794
higgledy piggledy
 59
higgler 797
high much 31
 lofty 206
 fetid 401
 treble 410
 foul 653
 noted 873
 proud 878
 from on — 981
 on — 206
 think —ly of 931
 — art 556
 — celebration 998
 — color
  color 428

red 434
 exaggerate 549
 — commissioner
  745
 — days and holi-
  days 840
 in a — degree 31
 — descent 875
 — and dry
 stable 150
 safe 664
 in — esteem 928
 in — feather
 strong 159
 health 654
 cheerful 836
 boasting 884
 — glee 836
 — hand
 violent 173
 resolved 604
 authority 737
 severe 739
 pride 878
 insolence 885
 lawless 964
 — jinks 840
 ride the — horse
  878
 — hat 225
 — life fashion 852
 rank 875
 — living
 intemperance 954
 gluttony 957
 — mass 998
 — mightiness 873
 — and mighty
 pride 878
 insolence 885
 — note 410
 — notions 878
 — places 210
 — pressure
 energy 171
 excitation of
  feeling 824
 — price 814
 — priest 996
 in — quarters 875
 — relief 448
 — repute 873
 —ly respectable
  875
 on the — road to
 way 627
 hope 858
 on one's — ropes
 excitation 824
 pride 878
 anger 900
 — seas 341
 in — spirits 836
 — tide wave 348
 prosperity 734
 — time late 133
 occasion 134
 — in tone
 while 430
 — treason
 disobedience 742
 dishonor 940
 — words
 quarrel 713
 anger 900
high-ball 298
high-born 875

holiness *God* 976
  piety 987
holloa 411
  – before one is out
    of the wood 884
hollow
  unsubstantial 4
  completely 52
  incomplete 53
  depth 208
  concavity 252
  channel 350
  - *sound* 408
  specious 477
  false 544
  voiceless 581
  beat – 731
  – truce 723
holm 346
holocaust
  kill 361
  sacrifice 991
  (*destruction* 162)
holograph 590
holster 191
holt 367
holus bolus 684
Holy *of God* 976
  pious 987
  keep – 987
  – breathing 990
  – Church 983*a*
  – City 981
  – day 998
  – Ghost 976
  temple of the –
    Ghost 983*a*
  – men of old 985
  – orders 995
  – place 1000
  – Scriptures 985
  – Spirit 976
  – water 998
  – week 998
holystone 652
homage
  submission 725
  fealty 743
  reverence 928
  approbation 931
  worship 990
home *focus* 74
  habitation 189
  near 197
  interior 221
  arrival 292
  refuge 666
  at – *party* 72
  present 186
  within 221
  at ease 705
  social gathering
    892
  be at –
  - *to visitors* 892
  feel at –
    freedom 748
    pleasure 827
    content 831
  look at –
    accusation 938
  make oneself at –
    free 748
    sociable 892
  not be at – 764
  stay at – 265
  at – in

knowledge 490
  skill 698
  at – with
    friendship 888
  bring – to
    evidence 467
    belief 484
    accuse 938
    condemn 971
  come – 292
  eternal – 98
  from – 187
  get – 292
  go – 283
  go from – 293
  long – 363
  strike –
    energy 171
    attack 716
  – stroke 170
  – thrust
    attack 716
    censure 932
home-bred 851
home-felt 821, 824
home-rule 737, 748
homeless
  unhoused 185
  banished 893
homely
  language 576
  unadorned 849
  common 851, 876
homeopathic
  small 32
  little 193
Homeopathy 662
Homeric
  – laughter 838
home-sick 833
home-spun
  texture 329
home-stall 189
homestead 189
homeward bound
  292
homicidal maniac
  913
homicide 361
homiletical 892
homily
  teaching 537
  advice 595
  sermon 998
hominem, argu-
  mentum ad –
  938
homogeneity
  relation 9
  identity 13
  uniformity 16
  simplicity 42
homogenesis 161
homologous 23
homology
  relation 9
  uniformity 16
  equality 27
  concord 714
homonym
  equivocal 520
  vocal sound 580
homophony 413
homunculus 193
Hon. 817
hone 253
honest

veracious 543
  honorable 939
  pure 960
  – meaning 516
  turn an – penny
    775
  – truth 494
honey
  sweet 396
  favorite 899
  milk and – 734
honeycomb
  concave 252
  opening 260
  deterioration 659
honeyed
  – phrases 894
  – words
    allurement 615
    flattery 933
honeymoon
  pleasure 827
  endearment 902
  marriage 903
honey-mouthed
  894, 933
honeysuckle 396
honorarium 784,973
honorary 815
honor
  demesne 780
  glory 873
  title 877
  respect 928
  approbation 931
  probity 939
  affair of – 720
  do – to 883
  do the –s
    sociality 892
    courtesy 894
    respect 928
  his – *judge* 967
  in – of 883
  man of – 939
  upon my – 535,
    768
  word of – 768
  – be to 873
  – a bill 807
  – in the breach
    923
  – bright
    veracity 543
    probity 939
honte, mauvaise –
  881
hood 225, 999
hooded 223
hoodlum 887
hoodoo 649
hoodwink
  ignore 491
  blind 442
  hide 528
  deceive 545
hoof 211
  cloven – 907
hook *fasten* 43
  fastening 45
  hang 214
  curve 245
  deceive 545
  retain 781
  take 789
  by – or by crook
    631

hookah 392
hooker *ship* 273
hookey, blind – 840
hooks, go off the
  360
hooligan 887, 913
hoop *circle* 247
  cry 411
hoot *cry* 411, 412
  deride 929
  contempt 930
  censure 932
hop *leap* 309
  dance 840, 892
  – off 293
  – skip and jump
    leap 309
    agitation 315
    haste 684
    game 840
  – the twig 360
hope **858**
  band of – 958
  beyond – 658, 734
  dash one's –s 837
  excite – 511
  foster – 858
  well-grounded –
    472
  – against hope 859
  – for the best 858
  – deferred
    dejection 837
    lamentation 859
  – for *expect* 507
    desire 865
hope chest 858
hopeful *infant* 129
  probable 472
  hope 858
hopelessness 471,
  859
Hop-o'-my-thumb
  193
hopper 191
horary 108
horde
  assemblage 72
  party 712
  commonalty 876
horizon
  distance 196
  view 441
  expectation 507
  appear on the –
    525
  gloomy – 859
horizontality **213**
horn
  receptacle 191
  sharp 253
  music 417
  draw in one's –s
    recant 607
    submit 725
    humility 879
  exalt one's – 873
  wear the –s 905
  –s of a dilemma
    reasoning 476
    difficulty 704
  – in 294
  – mad 920
  – of plenty 639
hornbook 542
hornet
  evil-doer 913

–'s nest
  pitfall 667
  difficulty 704
  adversity 735
  painful 830
  resentment 900
  censure 932
hornpipe 840
hornwork 717
horny 323
Horny, old – 978
horology 114
horoscope 511, 992
horresco referens
  860
horrible *great* 31
  noxious 649
  dire 830
  ugly 846
  fearful 860
horrid [see horrible]
  vulgar 851
horrida bella 722
horrific [see
  horrible]
horrified 828, 860
horrify 830, 860
horripilation 383
horrisonous 410
horror 860, 867
  view with – 898
horrors 837
  sup full of – 828
horror-stricken 828
hors de combat
  impotent 158
  useless 645
  tired out 688
  put – 731
hors-d'oeuvre 298
horse *hang on* 214
  stand 215
  carrier 271
  animal 366
  male 373
  cavalry 726
  ride the high –
    885
  put the –s to 673
  put up one's –s at
    184
  put up one's –s
    together
    concord 714
    friendship 888
  take – 266
  to – 293
  war – 726
  work like a – 686
  – artillery 726
  – of another color
    15
  – doctor 370
  – and foot 726
  – laugh 838
  – marine 701
  like a – in a mill
    613
  – racing
    pastime 840
    contention 720
  – soldier 726
  – track 627
horseback 266
horse-cloth 225
horseman 268
horsemanship

riding 266	**Hotchkiss gun** 727	– built on sand 160	*noise* 404	humation 363
skill 698	hotchpotch	turn – out of window 713	*discord* 713	humble *meek* 879
horseplay 856	*mixture* 41		huckster 794, 797	*modest* 881
horse power 466	*confusion* 59	housebreaker 792	huddle	*pious* 987
horse-shoe 245	*participation* 778	housebreaking 791	*disorder* 59	–r *classes* 876
horse-whip 972	hotel 189	house-dog 366	*derange* 61	– oneself
hortation 615, 695	hot-headed 684, 825	household	*collect* 72	*submit* 725
hortative 537		*inhabitants* 188	*hug* 197	*meek* 879
horticulture 371	hothouse	*abode* 189	– on 225	*penitent* 950
hortus siccus 369	*conservatory* 371, 636	– *gods* 189	**Hudibrastic** 856	*worship* 990
hosanna 931, 990	*furnace* 386	– *stuff* 635	– *verse* 597	eat – *pie* 725, 879
hose	*workshop* 691	– *troops* 726	hue 428	your – *servant*
stockings 225	hot-press 255	– *words*	– *and cry cry* 411	*dissent* 489
pipe 348, 350	**Hotspur** 863	*known* 490	*proclaim* 531	*refusal* 764
extinguisher 385	**Hottentot** 876	*language* 560	*pursuit* 622	humbug
hosier 225	hough 659	*plain* 576, 849	*alarm* 669	*falsehood* 544
hospice 189, 662	hound *animal* 366	householder 188	raise a – *and cry* 932	*deception* 545
hospitable 816, 892	*hunt* 622	housekeeper 637, 694	hueless 429	*deceiver* 548
hospital 189, 662	*persecute* 907	housekeeping 692	huff 885, 900	*trifle* 643
in – 655	*wretch* 949	houseless 185	huffy 901	*affectation* 855
hospitality	hold with the hare but run with the –s 607	housemaid 746	hug *cohere* 46	humdrum 841, 843
[see hospitable]		house-organ 531	*border on* 197	humectate 337, 339
hospodar 745	– on 615	**Houses of Parliament** 191, 696	*retain* 781	humid 339
host *collection* 72	houppelande 225	house-top 210	*courtesy* 894	humiliate 308
multitude 102	hour *period* 108	proclaim from – 531	*love* 897	humiliation
army 726	*point of time* 113	house-room 180	*endearment* 902	*adversity* 735
friend 890	*present time* 118	house-warming 892	– a *belief* 606	*disrepute* 874
rite 998	improve the shining – 682	housewife 682	– oneself	*sense of shame* 879
reckon without one's –	one's – is come	housewifery 692, 817	*pleasure* 827	*worship* 990
error 495	*occasion* 134	housing	*content* 831	self – 950
unskilful 699	*death* 360	*lodging* 189	*rejoicing* 838	humility 879, 987
rash 863	– *after hour* 110	*covering* 223	*pride* 878	humming-top 417
– of heaven 977	hour-glass	*horse-cloth* 225	– the shore	hummock 206, 250
– in himself 175	*chronometer* 114	hovel 189	*navigation* 267	humorist 844
hostage 771	*contraction* 195	hoveller 269	*approach* 286	humor *essence* 5
hostel 189	*narrow* 203	hover *high* 206	– a *sin* 945	*tendency* 176
hostelry 189	**Houri** 845	*rove* 266	huge 31, 192	*liquid* 333
hostile	hourly *time* 106	*soar* 267	hugger-mugger 528	*disposition* 602
disagreeing 24	*frequent* 136	*ascend* 305	**Huguenot** 984	*caprice* 608
opposed 708	*periodical* 138	*irresolute* 605	huis clos, à – 528	*aid* 707
enmity 889	house *family* 166	– *about*	huissier 965	*indulge* 760
in – *array* 708	*locate* 184	*move* 264	huke 225	*affections* 820
– *meeting* 720	*abode* 189	– *over*	hulk *body* 50	*please* 829
hostilities 722	*theater* 599	*near* 197	*ship* 273	*wit* 842
hostility 889	*make safe* 664	how *way* 627	hulks 752	*flatter* 933
hostler 746	*council* 696	*means* 632	hulky *big* 192	(*fun* 840)
hot *violent* 173	*firm* 712	– comes it?	*unwieldy* 647	in the – 602
warm 382	before the – 454	*attribution* 155	*ugly* 846	out of – 901*a*
pungent 392	keep – 184	*inquiry* 461	hull 50	peccant –
red 434	eat out of – and home	– now 870	hullabaloo 404, 411	*unclean* 853
orange 439	*prodigal* 818	howbeit 30	hullo! 292	*disease* 655
excited 824	*gluttony* 957	however	hum	humorous 842
irascible 901	turn out of – and home 297	*degree* 26	*faint sound* 405	humorsome
make – 384	– of cards 160	*notwithstanding* 30	*continued sound* 407	*capricious* 608
– air 482, 884	– of correction	*except* 83	*animal sound* 412	*sulky* 901*a*
– bath 386	*prison* 752	howitzer 727	*sing* 416	hump 250
– blood *rash* 863	*punishment* 975	howker 273	*deceive* 545, 546	hump-backed 243
angry 900	– of death 363	howl	– and haw	humph! 870
irascible 901	– of detention 752	*wind* 349	*stammer* 583	Humphrey, dine with Duke – 956
blow – and cold	– divided against itself 713	*human cry* 411	*irresolute* 605	Humpty-dumpty 193
inconsistent 477	bring the – about	*animal cry* 412	busy – of men 682	Hun 165, 851, 913
falsehood 544	one's ears 699	*lamentation* 839	human 372	hunch 250, 612
tergiversation 607	– of Commons 696, 966	howler 495	– *race* 372	hunch-backed 243
caprice 608	– of God 1000	howling wilderness 169, 893	– *sacrifices* 991	hundred
in – *haste* 684	– of Lords 696, 875, 966	hoy 273	humane	*number* 98
in – *pursuit* 622	set one's – in order 952	hoyden *girl* 129	*benevolent* 906	*many* 102
– *water*	– of peers 696, 875	*rude* 851	*philanthropic* 910	*region* 181
difficulty 704	– of prayer 1000	hub 222	*merciful* 914	the same a – *years hence* 460
quarrel 713		hubble-bubble 392	humanitarian 372, 910	hundredth 99
painful 830		hubbub *stir* 315	humanities 560	hundredweight 319
– water bottle 386			humanize 894	hunger 865
hot air merchant 884			humano capiti cervicem jungere equinam 24	hunger-strike 956
hot-bed *cause* 153				hunks 819
centre 222				
workshop 691				

465a
indispensable 630
indispose
dissuade 616
indisposed
unwilling 603
sick 655
indisputable 474
indissoluble,
indissolvable
joined 43
whole 50
stable 150
dense 321
indistinct 447
indistinction 465a
indistinguishable
identical 13
invisible 447
indisturbance 265, 826
indite 590
individual
whole 50
special 79
unity 87
person 372
indivisible *whole* 50
dense 321
indocility 158, 606
indoctrinate 537
indolence 683, 927
indomitable
strong 159
determined 604
persevering 604a
resisting 719
courage 861
indoor 221
indorse 769, 771
indorsement 550, 551
indraught 343, 348
indubitable 474
induce *cause* 153
power 157
produce 161
motive 615
induct 883
induction
inquiry 461
reasoning 476
drama 599
appointment 755
- *of a priest* 995
indulge *lenity* 740
allow 760
please 829
intemperance 954
gluttony 959
- *one's fancy* 609
- *in* 827
- *oneself* 943
- *in reverie*
inattention 458
fancy 515
- *with give* 784
indulgence
[*see* indulge]
absolution 918
indulgent *kind* 906
induration
hardening 323
impenitence 951
Indus to the pole,
from – 180
industry 625, 682

hive of – 691
indweller 188
indwelling 5
inebriety 959
inedible 395
ineffable *great* 31
inexpressible 521
wonderful 870
ineffaceable 820
ineffectual
incapable 158
useless 645
failing 732
- *attempt* 732
pale its – *fire* 422
inefficacious
incapable 158
useless 645
failing 732
inefficient 158
inelastic *soft* 324
- *fluid* 333
inelasticity 326
inelegance 579, 846
ineluctable 474
inept 24, 158, 645
inequality 28
inequitable 923
ineradicable
intrinsic 5
stable 150
inerrable 946
inertia 172
inertness
physical 172
inactive 683
moral 823
inestimable 648
inevitable 474, 601
inexact
erroneous 495
feeble 575
inexcitability 826
inexcusable
accusable 938
vicious 45
inexecution 730
inexhaustible 105, 639
inexistence 2
inexorable
unavoidable 601
resolved 604
stern 739
compelling 744
pitiless 914a
revengeful 919
inexpectation 508
inexpedience 647
inexpensive 815
inexperience 491, 699
inexpert 699
inexpiable 945
inexplicable 519
inexpressible
great 31
unmeaning 517
unintelligible 519
wonderful 870
inexpressibles 225
inexpression
latency 526
inexpensive 517
inexpugnable 664
inextension 180a
littleness 193

immateriality 317
inextinguishable
stable 150
strong 159
excitable 825
- *desire* 865
inextricable
coherent 46
disorder 59
impossible 471
infallibility 474
assumption of – 885
infamy *shame* 874
dishonor 940
vice 945
infancy 66, 127
infandum renovare
dolorem 505, 833
infant 129
fool 501
- *prodigy* 872
Infanta 745
infanticide 361, 991
infantine 129
foolish 499
infantry 726
infarction 261
infatuation
misjudgment 481
credulity 486
folly 499
insanity 503
obstinacy 606
passion 825
love 897
infeasible 471
infect *mix with* 41
contaminate 659
excite 824
infectâ, re –
shortcoming 304
non-completion 730
failure 732
infection
transference 270
disease 655
infectious 270, 657
infecund 169
infelicity
inexpertness 699
misery 828
infelicitous 24
infer 472
inference 476, 480
by – 467
inferential
demonstrative 478
latent 526
inferiority
in degree 34
in size 195
imperfection 651
personal – 34
infernal *bad* 649
malevolent 907
wicked 945
satanic 978
- *machine* 727
- *regions* 982
infertility 169
infest 830
infestivity 837, 843
infibulation 43
infidel 487, 989

infidelity
dishonor 940
irreligion 989
infiltrate *mix* 41
intervene 228
interpenetrate 294
moisten 337, 339
teach 537
infiltration
passage 302
Infinite, the – 976
infinite 105
- *goodness* 976
infinitely *great* 31
infinitesimal
small 32
little 193
- *calculus* 85
infinity 105
infirm *weak* 160
disease 655
vicious 945
- *of purpose* 605
infirmary 662
infirmity
[*see* infirm]
infix 537
inflame
render violent 173
burn 384
excite 824
anger 900
inflamed 382
inflammable 384, 388
inflammation
heating 384
disease 655
inflate *increase* 35
expand 194
blow 349
inflated
overestimation 482
style 573, 577
ridiculous 853
vain 880
inflation
[*see* inflate]
rarefaction 322
currency 800
inflect 245
inflexible *hard* 323
resolved 604
obstinate 606
stern 739
inexorable 914a
inflexion
change 140
curvature 245
grammar 567
inflict *act upon* 680
severity 739
- *evil* 649
- *pain*
bodily pain 378
mental pain 830
- *punishment* 972
infliction
adversity 735
mental pain 828, 830
punishment 972
influence 153
change 140
physical – 175
inducement 615

instrumentality 631
authority 737
absence of – **175a**
sphere of – 780
make one's – *felt* 631
influx 294
infold 232
inform 527
- *against*
accuse 938
go to law 969
informal 83, 964
informality 773
informant 527
information
knowledge 490
communication **527**
learning 539
lawsuit 969
pick up – 539
informer 532
informity 241
infra dignitatem 874, 940
infraction
trespass 303
disobedience 742
non-observance 773
exemption 927
- *of usage &c.*
unconformity 83
desuetude 614
infrangible
combined 46
dense 321
infra-red rays 420
infrequency **137**
infrigidation 385
infringe
transgress 303
disobey 742
not observe 773
undueness 925
dereliction 927
- *a law &c.* 83
infundibular 252, 269
infuriate
violent 173
excite 824
anger 900
infuscate 431
infuse *mix* 41
insert 300
teach 537
- *courage* 861
- *life into* 824
- *new blood* 658
infusible 321
infusion [*see* infuse]
liquefaction 335
infusoria 193
ingannation 545
ingathering 72
ingemination 90
ingenerate 5
ingenious 515, 698
ingenite 5
ingenium, per-
fervidum – 682
ingénu *artless* 703
ingénue *actress* 599
ingenuity 698

inebriation 959
intra, ab – 221
intractable
  obstinate 606
  difficult 704
  sullen 901a
intramural 221
intransient 110
intransigeance 604
intransitive 110
intransmutable
  110, 150
intrap 545
intraregarding 221
intrench 717
  – on 303
intrepid 861
intricate
  confused 59
  convoluted 248
  difficult 704
intrigant
  meddlesome 682
  cunning 702
  libertine 962
intrigue fascinate
  615, 897
  plot 626
  activity 682
  cunning 702
  excite 824
  interest 829
  licentiousness 961
intrinsic 5
  – evidence 467
  – habit 613
  – truth 494
intrinsicality 5
introception 296
introduce lead 62
  interpose 228
  precede 280
  insert 300
  – new blood 140
  – new conditions
    469
  – to 888
introduction
  [see introduce]
  preface 64
  reception 296
  drama 599
  friendship 888
  courtesy 894
introductory
  precursor 64
  beginning 66
  priority 116
introgression 294
introit 998
intromission 228
intromit
  discontinue 142
  receive 296
introspection 441,
  457
introspective 451
introvert 218
intrude
  interfere 24
  inopportune 135
  intervene 228
  enter 294
  encroach 303
intruder 57
intrusiveness 682
intrust 755, 787

intuition mind 450
  unreasoning 477
  knowledge 490
intumescence 194,
  250
intwine 43, 243
inunction 223
inundate
  effusion 337
  flow 348
  redundance 641
inunderstanding
  452
inurbanity 895
inure 613, 673
inured
  insensible 823
inusitation 614
inutility 645
invade ingress 294
  encroach 303
  attack 716
invalid
  powerless 158
  illogical 477
  diseased 655
  undue 925
invalidate
  disable 158
  weaken 160
  confute 479
invaluable 648
invariable
  intrinsic 5
  uniform 16
  conformable 82
  stable 150
invasion
  ingress 294
  attack 716
invective 932
inveigh 932
inveigle 545, 615
invent
  discover 480a
  imagine 515
  lie 544
  devise 626
invented
  untrue 546
invention 480a
inventive
  skilful 698
inventor 164
inventory 86
inverse 14, 218
inversion
  derangement 61
  change 140
  of position 218
  contraposition
    237
  reversion 145
  language 577
invertebrate 158
invest
  empower 157
  clothe 225
  besiege 227, 716
  commission 755
  give 784
  lend 787
  expend 809
  – in locate 184
  purchase 795
  – money 817
  – with ascribe 155

investigate 461
investment 225
  – trust 712
  make –s 673
inveterate old 124
  established 150
  inborn 820
  – belief 484
  – habit 613
invidious
  painful 830
  hatred 898
  spite 907
  envy 921
invigorate
  strengthen 159
invigorating
  healthy 656
invincible 159
inviolable
  secret 528
  right 924
  honor 939
inviolate
  permanent 141
  secret 528
  honorable 939
invious closed 261
  pathless 704
invisibility 447
invisible small 193
  not to be seen 447
  concealed 526
  – ink 528
  become – 4
invitâ Minervâ 603,
  704
invite induce 615
  offer 763
  ask 765
  – the attention
    457
inviting
  [see invite]
  pleasing 829
invoice 86
invoke address 586
  implore 765
  pray 990
  – curses 908
  – saints 998
involucrum 223
involuntary
  necessary 601
  unwilling 603
  – servitude 749
involution [see
  involve]
  algebra 85
involve include 54
  derange 61
  wrap 225
  evince 467
  mean 516
  latency 526
involved
  disorder 59
  convoluted 248
  obscure style 571
  in debt 806
involvement 704
invulnerable 664
inward intrinsic 5
  inside 221
  – bound 294
  – monitor 926
inweave 219

inwrap 225
inwrought 5
io triumphe! 838,
  883
Ionic 597
iota 32
I. O. U. 771, 800
ipse dixit 474, 535
ipsissima verba 494
ipso facto 1
irae
  amantium — 918
  tantaene animis
    coelestibus —900
irascibility 901
irate 900
ire 900
iridescent 440
Iris 268, 534
iris 440, 441
Irish Bull 353
Irishism 497
irk 688, 830
irksome
  tiresome 688
  difficult 704
  painful 830
  weary 841
iron strength 159
  smooth 255
  hard 323
  resolution 604
  rule with a rod of
    – 739
  – age adversity 735
  pain 828
  – cross 733
  – gray 432
  – grip 159
  – gripe 781
  – heel 739
  – necessity 601
  – rule 739
  – entering into the
    soul 828, 830
  – sway 739
  – will 604
iron-bound coast
  land 342
  danger 667
iron-clad
  covering 223
  defence 717
  man of war 726
iron-handed 739
iron-hearted 861
iron-mold 434
irons 752
  fire – 386
  put in – 751
  – in the fire
    business 625
    redundance 641
    active 682
    unskilful 699
irony
  figure of speech
    521
  untruth 546
  ridicule 856
irradiate 420
irrational
  number 84
  illogical 477
  silly 499
irreclaimable
  hopeless 859

vicious 945
  impenitent 951
irreconcilable
  unrelated 10
  discordant 24
  unwilling 603
  opponent 710
  enmity 889
irrecoverable
  past 122
  hopeless 859
irredeemable 859
irredentist 776
irreducible
  discordant 24
  out of order 59
  unchangeable 150
irrefragable 478
irrefutable 474, 478
irregular
  diverse 16a
  out of order 59
  multiform 81
  against rule 83
  – in recurrence
    139
  distorted 243
  combatant 726
irregularity 139
irrelation 10
irrelevant
  unrelated 10
  unaccordant 24
  sophistical 477
  unimportant 643
irreligion 989
irremediable
  bad 649
  hopeless 859
  (spoiled 659)
irremissible 945
irremovable 150
irreparable
  hopeless 859
irrepentance 951
irreprehensible 946
irrepressible
  violent 173
  free 748
  excitable 825
irreproachable 946
irreprovable 946
irresistible
  strong 159
  demonstration
    478
  necessary 601
irresoluble 150
irresolution 605
irresolvable 87
irresolvedly 605
irrespective 10
irresponsible
  irresolute 605
  exempt 927a
  arbitrary 964
irretrievable
  stable 150
  lost 776
  hopeless 859
irrevealable 528
irreverence 929,
  988
irreversible
  stable 150
  hopeless 859
irrevocable

John Doe and
   Richard Roe 4
Johnny 894
John's 653
Johnsonian 577
joie, feu de – 883
join *connect* 43
  assemble 72
  contiguous 199
  arrive 292
  party 712
  sociality 892
  marry 903
  – *battle* 722
  – in the chorus 488
  – forces, hands,
    709
  – in 778
  – issue *discuss* 476
  deny 536
  quarrel 713
  contend 720
  lawsuit 969
  – the majority 360
  – up
  enlist 723
  – with 709
joint *junction* 43
  part 51
  accompanying 88
  concurrent 178
  meat 298
  – concern 721
joint-stock 709, 778
joint-tenancy 778
jointure 780
joist 215
joke *absurdity* 497
  trifle 643
  wit 842
  ridicule 856
  in – 842
  mere – 643
  no – *existing* 1
  important 642
  practical –
  deception 545
  ridicule 856
  disrespect 929
  take a – 498
joker 844
jokesmith 844
joking apart 535,
  604
jole 236
jollification
  amusement 840
  intemperance 954
jollity 840, 892
jolly *plump* 192
  marine 269
  gay 836
  ridicule 856
  – boat 273
  – fellow 892
jolt 276, 315
jolthead 501
Jonah 649
Jones
  Davy –' locker 360
  Paul – 792
jorum 191
Joseph 960
  –'s coat 440
joss 991
  – house 1000
jostle *rush* 276

jog 315
  clash 713
jot 32, 643
jotting 550, 551
jounce 315
journal *annals* 114
  newspaper 531
  record 551
  magazine 593
  narrative 594
  accounts 811
journalist
  messenger 534
  recorder 553
  author 593
journey 266
journeyman
  artisan 690
  servant 746
joust 720
Jove 979
  by – 870
  sub –
    out of doors 220
    air 338
jovial *gay* 836
  amusement 840
  social 892
jowl 236
joy 827
  give one – 896
joyful 836
joyless *painful* 830
  sad 837
joy stick 693
J.P. 967
Juan, Don – 962
jube 1000
jubeo, sic volo sic –
  741
jubilant *gay* 836
  rejoicing 838
  boastful 884
jubilee 138, 883
jubilitate 884
Judaeus Apella,
  credat –
  disbelief 485
  absurdity 497
Judaism 984
Judas *deceiver* 548
  knave 941
  – kiss
  hypocrisy 544
  base 940
judge *decide* 480
  master 745
  taste 850
  magistrate 967
Judge *deity* 976
Judgment
  Day of – 67
judgment
  intellect 450
  discrimination
    465
  decision 480
  wisdom 498
  sentence 972
judgment-seat 966
judicata, res –
  certain 474
  judgment 480
judication 480
judicatory 965, 966
judicature 965
Judicature, High

Court of – 966
judice: coram –
  jurisdiction 965
  lawsuit 969
  me – 481
  sub – *inquiry* 461
  lawsuit 969
judicial 965
  – Astrology 511
  – murder 361
  – separation 905
judicious 498
jug 191, 752
juggernaut
  kill 361
  god 979
  idolatry 991
juggle *deceive* 545
  cunning 702
juggler 548, 599
jugulate 361
juice 333
juiceless 340
juicy 339
jujitsu 718
jujube 396
julep 396
jumble *mixture* 41
  confusion 59
  derange 61
  indiscriminate
    465a
jument 271
jump
  sudden change
    146
  leap 309
  neglect 460
  at one – 113
  – about 315
  – at *willing* 602
  pursue 622
  hasten 684
  consent 762
  seize 789
  desire 865
  – to a conclusion
  misjudge 481
  credulous 486
  – over 460
  – up 307, 309
jumper 225
junction 43
juncture
  circumstance 8
  junction 43
  period 134
jungle *disorder* 59
  vegetation 367
junior 127, 541
  – counsel 968
junk 273
junket *dish* 298
  merry-making
    840
Juno 920, 979
junta 696
junto 712
jupe 225
Jupiter 979
jurare in verba ma-
  gistri 481, 486
jurat 967
jure: de – *due* 924
  legal 963
  – divino *due* 924
  God 976

juridical 965
jurisconsult 968
jurisdiction 965
  authority 737
Jurisprudence 963
jurist 480, 968
jury 967
  empanel a – 969
  – box 966
  – mast
  substitute 147
  refuge 666
jus: summum –
  922
  – civile
  – gentium 963
  – nocendi 737
  – et norma
    loquendi 567
jussive 741
just *accurate* 494
  right 922
  equitable 939
  pious 987
  – as *similar* 17
  same time 120
  – do 639
  – now 118
  – out 123
  – reasoning 476
  – so 488
  – then 113
  – the thing
  agreement 23
  exact 494
  – in time 134
juste milieu
  middle 68
  moderation 174
  mid-course 628
justice
  right 922
  honor 939
  magistrate 967
  administration of
    – 965
  bring to – 969
  court of – 966
  do – to *eat* 298
  duty 926
  praise 931
  vindicate 937
  not do – to 483
  retributive – 922,
    972
  – seat 966
justifiable 922, 937
justification
  vindication 937
  religious 987
justle *push* 276
  contend 720
jut out 250
jute 205
jutty 250
juvenile 127
  – lead 599
juxtaposition 199
j'y suis j'y reste
  141

K

kadi 967
kail 840
kaiser 745

kaleidoscope 149,
  445
καλόν, τὸ – 845
kangaroo 309
κατ' ἐξοχήν
  greatness 31
  superiority 33
  importance 642
Katerfelto 994
kavass 965
K.C. 968
keck 297
kedge *navigate* 267
  anchor 666
keek 527
keel 211
  – upwards 21
keelhaul 972
keen *energetic* 171
  sharp 253
  sensible 375
  cold 383
  intelligent 498
  poignant 821
  lament 839
  witty 842
  eager 865
  – blast 349
keener 839
keen-eyed 441
keep *do often* 136
  persist 141
  continue 143
  food 298
  store 636
  provision 637
  refuge 666
  preserve 670
  citadel 717
  custody 751
  prison 752
  observe 772
  retain 781
  celebrate 883
  – alive 359, 670
  – aloof 196, 623
  – accounts 811
  – an account with
    805
  – apart 44
  – at it 143
  – away 187
  – back *late* 133
  conceal 528
  dissuade 616
  not use 678
  restrain 751
  retain 781
  – the ball rolling
    143
  – one's bed 655
  – body and soul
    together *life* 359
  health 654
  – within bounds
    304
  – close 781
  – company 88
  – one in counte-
    nance
  conformity 82
  induce 615
  aid 707
  encourage 861
  – one's counte-
    nance
  unexcitable 826

sad 837
- one's course 282
- an eye upon 459
- the field 722
- firm 150
- on foot
  continuance 143
  support 215
  preparation 673
- from *conceal* 528
  refrain 623
  not do 681
  restrain 751
- going
  continue 143
  move 264
- one's ground 141
- one's hand in 613
- one's head above
  water 731, 817
- hold 150
- holy 987
- house 184
- in ignorance 528
- in *restrain* 751
  prohibit 761
- on one's legs 654
- a good look out
  for 507
- in mind 505
- moving 682
- off *avoid* 623
  hinder 706
  defend 717
  resist 719
  prohibition 761
- on *do often* 136
  continue 143
  persevere 604a
- to oneself 528
- in order 693
- out
  - *of the way* 187
  - *of harm's way*
   864
- pace with 27,
  120
- the peace 714
- posted 527
- the pot boiling
  143
- one's promise
  772
- quiet 265
- a secret 528
- a shop 625
- in sight 459
- silence 585
- straight 944
- in suspense
  uncertainty 475
  irresolution 605
- in the thoughts
  505
- time
  punctual 132
  music 416
- to 604a
- together 709
- under
  authority 737
  subjection 749
  restraint 751
- up [*see below*]
- in view
  attend to 457
  remember 505

expect 507
- waiting 133
- watch 459
- one's word 939
keep up
  continue 143
  preserve 670
  stimulate 824
- appearances 852
- the ball 682, 840
- a correspond-
  ence 592
- the memory of
  505
- one's spirits 836
- with 274
keeper 370, **753**
keeping
  congruity 23
  in – 82
  safe – *safety* 664
  preservation 670
keepsake 505
keg 191
kelpie 979
kelson 211
kempt 652
ken 441, 490
  beyond mortal –
  360
kennel
  assemblage 72
  hovel 189
  ditch 259
  conduit 350
Kentish fire 931
képi 225
kérb-stone 233
kerchief 225
  wave a – 550
kern *quern* 330
  low fellow 876
  varlet 949
kernel *heart* 5
  cause 153
  central 222
  important 642
kerosene 356
ketch
  ship 273
Ketch, Jack – 975
kettle *vessel* 191
  caldron 386
  - drum *music* 417
  tea–party 892
  - of fish
   disorder 59
   difficulty 704
key *cause* 153
  opener 260
  music 413
  color 428
  interpretation 522
  indication 550
  instrument 631,
   633
  *emblem of au-
  thority* 747
  deliver the –s of
  the city 725
key-hole 260
key-note *model* 22
  rule 80
  music 413
key-stone
  support 215
  motive 615

importance 642
  completion 729
khaki 225, 433
khan *inn* 189
  governor 745
khedive 745
kibitka 272
kibitzer 682
kick *impulse* 276
  recoil 277
  assault 716
  thrill 821
  spurn 930
  punish 972
- against
  oppose 708
  resist 719
- against the
  pricks
  useless 645
  rash 863
  unequal 28
  superior 33
- up a dust
  active 682
  discord 713
  insolent 885
- a row 900
- one's heels
  kept waiting 133
  nothing to do 681
- off 62
- up a row
  violent 173
  discord 713
- over the traces
  742
kicking, alive and –
  359
kickshaw *food* 298
  trifle 643
kid *child* 129
  progeny 167
  leather 223
  not to be handled
  with – gloves
  dirty 653
  difficult 704
kidnap
  deceive 545
  take 789
  steal 791
kidney *class* 75
kilderkin 191
Kilkenny cats 713
kill 361
- or cure 662
- the fatted calf
  883
- the goose with
  golden eggs 699
- with kindness
  902
- the slain 641
- time 106
  inactivity 683
  amusement 840.
- two birds with
  one stone 682
killing 361
  delightful 829
kill-joy 706
kiln 386
kilowatt 466
kilt 225
kimbo 244
kimono 225

kin 75
kind *class* 75
  benevolent 906
- regards 894
kinder-garten 542
kindle *cause* 153
  produce 161
  quicken 171
  inflame 173
  set fire to 384
  excite 824
  incense 900
kindling wood 388
kindred 9, 11
kine 366
kinematics 264
kinetic energy 157
king 745
  every inch a –
  authority 737
  rank 875
  –maker 694
King –'s Bench
  752, 966
  –'s birthday 268
  –'s counsel 968
  - Death 360
  –'s English 560
  –'s evidence 529
  –'s highway 627
  –'s ransom 648
- of Kings 976
kingcraft 693
kingdom
  region 181
  property 780
- of heaven 981
kingly 737
king-post 215
kink 248, 378, 608
kiosk 189, 1000
kip 961
kirk 1000
kirtle 225
kismet 601
kiss *touch* 199
  courtesy 894
  endearment 902
- the book 535
- the hem of one's
  garment 928
- in the ring 840
- the rod 725
kit *class* 75
  equipment 191
  fiddle 417
  –bag 191
kitcat 556
kitchen 191, 691
- maid 746
- range 386
kitchener 386
kitchenette 691
kite *fly* 273
  bill 800
  fly a – *credit* 805
  insolvency 808
- balloon 273, 726
kith 11
kithless 87
kitten *animal* 366
  young 129
  bring forth 161
  playful as a – 836,
  840
kleptomania
  insanity 502

stealing 791
  desire 865
kleptomaniac 504
knack 698
  get into the – 613
knacker 361
knag 706
knaggy 901a
knap 206
knapsack 191
knave 548, **941**
- of hearts 897
knavery
  deception 545
  cunning 702
  improbity 940
  vice 945
knead *mix* 41
  mold 240
  soften 324
  stroke 379
knee *angle* 244
  bend the –
  stoop 30
  submission 725
  down on one's –s
  humble 879
  on one's –s
  beg 765
  respect 928
  atone 952
  on the –s of the
  gods 121, 152
knee-deep 208, 209
kneel *stoop* 308
  submit 725
  beg 765
  servility 886
  courtesy 894
  ask mercy 914
  respect 928
  worship 990
knell 363
  strike the death –
  361
knickerbockers 225
knicknack 643, 847
knife 253
  play a good – and
  fork *eat* 298
  appetite 865
  war to the – 708
knight 875
- errant
  madman 504
  defender 717
  rash 863
  philanthropist
  910
  –'s move 279
- service 777
- of the road 792
- Templar 71
knit 43
  well – 159
- the brow
  discontent 832
  anger 900
  disapprobation
  932
knitting 847
knob *pendency* 214
  ball 249
  protuberance 250
knock *blow* 276
  sound 406
  hard –s 720

landscape
 prospect 448
 – gardening
 agriculture 71
 beauty 845
 – – painting 556
 – painter 559
land-shark 792
land-slip 306
landsman 342
Landsturm 726
land-surveying 466
Landwehr 726
lane 189, 260, 627
langrel 727
lang-syne 122
language 560
 command of – 582
 strong –
 vigor 574
 malediction 908
languid *weak* 160
 inert 172
 slow 275
 – style 575
 inactive 683
 torpid 823
languish
 decrease 36
 ill 655
 inactive 683
 repine 828
 – for 865
languishing
 weak 160
 affected 855
languishment
 lament 839
languor
 [see languid]
lank 200
lanky 203, 206
lantern
 window 260
 lamp 423
 magic – 448
 – of Diogenes 461
 – jaws 203
lanterne, à la – 972
lanuginous 256
lanyard 45
Laodicean 823
lap *abode* 189
 support 215
 interior 221
 wrap 225
 encompass 227, 229
 drink 298
 – of luxury
 pleasure 377
 inactivity 683
 voluptuousness 954
lap-dog *animal* 366
 servile 886
lapel 39
lapidary 559
lapidate *kill* 361
 attack 716
 punish 972
lapidescence 323
lapis lazuli
 blue 438
 jewel 847
lappet 39, 214
lapse *course* 109

past 122
 conversion 144
 fall 306
 degeneracy 659
 relapse 661
 loss 776
 vice 945
 guilt 947
 – of memory 506
 – of time 109
lapsus calami 495
lapsus linguae
 mistake 495
 solecism 568
 stammering 583
Laputa, college of – 538
larboard 239
larceny 791
lard 356
lardaceous 355
larder 636
 contents of the – 298
lares et penates
 home 189
 idols 991
large
 quantity 31
 size 192
 at – *diffuse* 573
 free 748
 become – 194
 – number 102
 – type 642
large-hearted
 liberal 816
 benevolent 906
 disinterested 942
larger 194
largest 784
largest portion 192
larghetto 275, 415
largiloquent 573
largo 275, 415
lariat 45, 247
lark *ascent* 305
 pleasure 827
 spree 840
 with the – 125
larmes:
 fondre en – 839
 – aux yeux 839
larmoyante,
 comédie – 599
larrikin 887, 913
larrup 972
larum 404, 669
larva 129
larynx 351
lascar 269
lasciate ogni speranza 859
lascivious 961
lash *tie together* 43
 violence 173
 incite 615
 censure 932
 punish 972
 scourge 975
 under the – *compelled* 744
 subject 749
 – into fury 909
 – with the tongue 931
 – the waves 645

lass *girl* 129
lassitude 680, 841
lasso 45, 247
last *model* 22
 – in order 67
 endure 106
 durable 110
 – in time 122
 continue 141
 at – 133
 breathe one's – 360
 game to the – 604a
 never hear the – of 104
 – but one &c. 67
 die in the – ditch 604a
 – for ever 112
 at the – extremity 665
 – finish 729
 – gasp 360
 go to one's – home 360
 on – legs *weak* 160
 dying 360
 spoiled 659
 adversity 735
 – resort 666
 – rites 998
 – shift 601
 – sleep 360
 – stage 67
 – straw 153
 – stroke 729
 – touch 729
 – word
 affirmation 535
 obstinacy 606
 – year &c. 122
latch 43, 45
latchet 45
latch-key 631
late *past* 122
 new 123
 tardy 133
 dead 360
 too – 135
lately 122, 123
latency 526
lateness 133
latent 172, 526
 – organism 153
later 117
laterality 236
lateritious 434
latest 118
latet anguis in herbâ 66
lath 205
 thin as a – 203
lathe
 region 181
 machine 633
lather 332, 353
Latin
 au bout de son – 704
 perdre son – 704
 thieves' – 503
latitancy 528
latitat 969
latitude *extent* 180
 region 181
 breadth 202

measurement 466
 freedom 748
 – and longitude situation 183
latitudinarian 984, 989
latration 412
latria 990
latrines 653
latrociny 791
latter *sequent* 63
 past 122
Latter-day Saint 984
latterly 123
lattice *crossing* 219
 opening 260
laud 931, 990
laudable 944
laudanum 174
laudari a laudato viro 931
laudator 935
 – temporis acti
 past 122
 habit 613
 discontent 832
 detractor 936
laudatory 931
laugh 838
 make one – 853
 raise a – 840
 – at *ridicule* 856
 sneer 929
 (undervalue 483)
 – to scorn *defy* 715
 despise 930
 – in one's sleeve
 latent 526
 ridicule 856
 disrespect 929
 contempt 930
 – on the wrong side of one's mouth
 disappointed 509
 dejected 837
 in disrepute 874
laughable 853
laughing:
 no – matter 642
 – gas 376
laughing-stock 857
laughter-loving 836
launch *begin* 66
 boat 273
 propel 284
 – forth 676
 – into 676
 – into eternity 360, 361
 – out 573
 – out against 716
laundress 652, 746
laundry *room* 191
 heat 386
 clean 652
 – maid 746
 – man 652
laureate 875
 poet – 597
laurel *trophy* 733
 glory 873
 decoration 877
 repose on one's –s 265
lava *excretion* 299

semiliquid 352
lavatory 652
lave *water* 337
 clean 652
lavender *colour* 437
laver la tête 932
lavish *profuse* 641
 give 784
 squander 818
 – of praise 931
law *regularity* 80
 statue 697
 permission 760
 legality 963
 court of – 966
 give the – 737
 go to – 969
 Jewish – 985
 lay down the –
 certainty 474
 affirm 535
 command 741
 learned in the – 968
 set the – at defiance 964
 take the – into one's own hands 722, 742
 – of the Medes and Persians 80, 148
 take the – of 969
law-abiding 743
lawful
 permitted 760
 due 924
 legal 963
lawgiver 694
lawless 59
 irregular 83
 mutinous 742
 non-observant 773
 vicious 945
 arbitrary 964
lawn *plain* 344
 grass 367
 agriculture 371
 – sleeves 999
 – tennis 840
lawsuit 969
lawyer 968
lax *incoherent* 47
 soft 324
 error 495
 – style 575
 remiss 738
 non-observance 773
 dishonorable 940
 licentious 945
 irreligious 989
laxity 738
lay *moderate* 174
 place 184
 ley 344
 music 415
 poetry 597
 bet 621
 secular 997
 – about one
 active 682
 exertion 686
 attack 716
 contend 720
 punish 972
 – one's account for

thief 792
best – foremost
  686
fast as –s will
  carry 274
have a – to stand
  on 470
keep on one's –s
  654
last –s *spoiled* 659
  fatigue 688
light on one's –s
  734
make a – 894
not a – to stand on
  illogical 477
  confuted 479
  failure 732
off one's –s
  propulsion 284
on one's –s
  upright 212
  elevation 307
  speaking 582
  in health 654
  active 682
  free 748
set on one's –s 660
  – *bail* 623
legacy 270, 780, 784
legal *permitted* 760
  legitimate 924
  relating to law
  963
– adviser 968
– estate 780
legality 963
legate 534
legatee 779, 785
legation 755
legato 415
legend 551, 594
legendary
  imaginary 515
legerdemain 146,
  545
légèreté 605
leggings 225
leghorn hat 225
legible 518
– hand 590
legion
  multitude 102
  army 726
legionary 726
legislation 693, 963
legislative assem-
  bly 696
legislator 694
legislature 693, 696
legist 968
legitimate *true* 494
  permitted 760
  right 922
  due 924
  legal 963
legume 367
lei 847
leisure 685
  at one's – *late* 133
leisurely 275
leman 897
lemma 476
lemon *color* 436
Lemprière 979
lemures 980
lend 787

– aid 707
– countenance 707
– a hand 680
– oneself to
  assent 488
co-operate* 709
– on security 789
– wings to 707
lender *creditor* 805
lending 787
length 200
go all –s
  resolution 604
  activity 682
  exertion 686
at – *in time* 133
full – *portrait* 556
go great –s 549
– and breadth of
  50
– and breadth of
  the land
  space 180
  publication 531
– of time 110
lengthen 35, 200
– out
  diuturnity 110
  late 133
lengthwise 200
lengthy *long* 200
  diffuse 573
lenient
  moderate 174
  mild 740
  compassionate
  914
lenify 174
lenitive
  moderating 174
  remedy 662
  relieving 834
lenity 740
lens 445
Lent 956, 998
lenten 956
lenticular 245, 250
lentor *slowness* 275
  spissitude 352
  inactivity 683
lentous 352
leonem, ex ungue –
  550
leonine verses 597
leopard
  variegated 440
  –'s spots
  unchanging 150
leprechaune 980
leprosy 655
lerret 273
lèse-majesté 742
less *inferior* 34
  subduction 38
  – than no time
  113
lessee
  possessor 779
  receiver 785
lessen
  – in quantity or
  degree 36
  – in size 195
  – an evil 658
lesson *teaching* 537
  warning 668
give a – to

punish 972
read a – to
  censure 932
say one's –
  memory 505
lest 623
let *hindrance* 706
  permit 760
  lease 771
  lend 787
  sell 796
apartments to –
  fool 499
to – 763
– alone *besides* 37
  permanence 141
  quiescence 265
  avoid 623
  disuse 678
  inaction 681
  not complete 730
  free 748
– be
  permanence 141
  continuance 143
  inaction 681
– blood 297
– 'I dare not' wait
  upon 'I would'
  605
– down
  depress 308
  humble 879
– down easily
  forgive 918
– fall *drop* 308
  inform 527
  speak 582
– fly *violence* 173
  propel 284
– fly at 716
– go *neglect* 460
  liberate 750
  relinquish 782
  restitution 790
– in *interpose* 228
  admit 296
  trick 545
– into *inform* 490
  disclose 529
– one know 527
– off *violent* 173
  propel 284
  permit 760
  exempt 927a
  acquit 970
– out *disperse* 73
  lengthen 200
  eject 297
  disclose 529
  liberate 750
– out at 716
– pass 460
– slip
  miss an oppor-
  tunity 135
  neglect 460
  not complete 730
  lose 776
  relinquish 782
– the matter stand
  over 133
– things take their
  course 143
– well alone

content 831
caution 864
lethal 361
– chamber 975
lethalis arundo,
  haeret lateri –
  900
lethargy 683, 823
Lethe 982
waters of – 506
lethiferous 361
letter *mark* 550
  character 561
  epistle 592
to the – 494
– card 524
– of credit 805
– of the law 494
– writer 592
letter-bag 534
letter-carrier 534
lettered 490
letterpress 591
letters
  knowledge 490
  language 560
  description 594
in large – 642
man of – 492
– of marque 791
lettres de cachet
  751
leucophlegmatic
  823
leucorrhea 299
Levant *east* 236
levant *abscond* 623
levanter *wind* 349
  defaulter 808
levée *assemblage* 72
  sociality 892
– en masse 719
level *uniform* 16
  equal 27
  destroy 162
  horizontal 213
  instrument 213,
  217
  flat 251
  smooth 255
  lower 308
– at *direct* 278
  intend 620
  attack 716
– best 686
– headed 826
– off 27
– with the ground
  207
lever *cause* 153
  instrument 633
– de rideau 599
leverage 175
leviathan 192
levigate 255, 330
levitate 320
Levite 996
levity *lightness* 320
  irresolution 605
  trifle 643
  jocularity 836
  rashness 863
levy *muster* 72
  military 726
  distrain 789
  demand 812
lewd 961

Lewis gun 727
lex – mercatoria
  963
– scripta 697
– scripta et non-
  scripta 963
– talionis
  retaliation 718
  right 922
lexicography 562
lexicology 562
lexicon 86, 562
ley 344
liability 177
  debt 806
  duty 926
liaison 961
liar 548
libation
  potation 298
  drunkenness 959
  worship 990
libel 934, 938
libelant 989
libeller 936
liberal *ample* 639
  – *party* 712
  generous 816
  disinterested 942
  over – 818
– education
  knowledge 490
  teaching 537
liberalism
  freedom 748
liberality
  giving 784
  generosity 816
liberate 672
liberation 750
liberavi animam
  meam 703
libertinage 961
libertine 962
libertinism 961
liberty *freedom* 748
  permission 760
  right 924
  exemption 927a
gain one's – 750
set at – *free* 750
  exempt 927a
take a –
  arrogate 739
  make free 748
  insolence 885
  discourtesy 895
libidinous 961
libitum, ad –
  at will 600
  enough 639
  freely 748
librarian 593, 694
library *room* 191,
  593
  books 593
  storehouse 636
librate 314
libretto 593, 599
licence *laxity* 738
  permission 760
  right 924
  exemption 927a
– to plunder 791
licentiate 492
licentious *lax* 738
  dissolute 954

debauched 961
lichgate 363
lichen 367
licit 760, 924
lick *lap* 298
  conquer 731
  punish 972
  – the dust 933
  – into shape 240
lickerish
  savory 394
  desirous 865
  fastidious 868
  licentious 961
lickpenny 819
lickspittle 886
lictor 965
lid 223
lie *situation* 183
  presence 186
  recline 213
  falsehood 544
  untruth 546
give the– to 536
white – 617
– abed 683
– in ambush 528
– by 681
– at one's door 926
– down *flat* 213
  rest 687
  fallow 674
– hid 528
– in *be* 1
  give birth 161
– low 528
– under a necessity 601
– in a nutshell 32
– on 215
– over *defer* 133
  destiny 152
– in one's power 157
– at the root of 153
– still 265
– to
  quiescence 265
  inaction 681
– under 177
– in wait for
  expect 507
  inaction 681
lief *pleasant* 829
  as – *willing* 602
  choice 609
liege 745
liegeman 746
lien 771, 805
lienteria 653
lieu 182
  in – of 147
lieutenant 745, 759
lord – 965
life *essence* 5
  events 151
  vitality 359
  biography 594
  activity 682
  conduct 692
  cheerful 836
animal – 364
battle of – 682
come to – 660
infuse into

excite 824
put – into 359
recall to – 660
see – 840
support – 359
take away – 361
tenant for – 779
– to come 152
– after death 981
– or death
  need 630
  important 642
  contention 720
– and spirit 682
Life, the 976
life-blood 5, 359
life-boat 273, 666
life-giving 168
lifeguards 726
lifeless 172, 360
lifelike 17
lifelong 110
life-preserver 666, 727
life-size 192
lifetime 108
life-weary 841
lift *raise* 307
  aid 707
  steal 791
– cattle 791
– up the eyes 441
– a finger 680
– hand against 716
– one's head 734
– up the heart 990
– the mask 529
– the voice
  shout 411
  speak 582
lift-smoke 840
ligament 45
ligation 43
ligature 45
light *state* 7
  small 32
  window 260
  velocity 274
  arrive 292
  descend 306
  levity 320
  kindle 384
  watch 388
  luminosity 420
  luminary 423
  – in colour 429
  white 430
  aspect 448
  knowledge 490
  interpretation 522
  unimportant 643
  easy 705
  gay 836
  loose 961
blue – *signal* 550
bring to –
  discover 480a
  manifest 525
  disclose 529
children of – 987
come to – 529
false – 443
foot –s 599
half – 422
make – of
  underrate 483

easy 705
  inexcitable 826
  despise 930
in one's own – 699
obstruct the – 426
side – 490
see the – *life* 359
  publication 531
transmit – 425
throw – upon 522
a – breaks in upon one 529
– under a bushel
  hide 528
  not hide 878
  modesty 881
– comedy 599
– cruiser 726
– fantastic toe 309
– upon one's feet 664
– heart 836
– of heel 274
– horse 726
– infantry 726
– purse 804
– and shade 420
– of truth 543
– up *illumine* 420
  excite 824
  cheer 836
– upon *chance* 156
  arrive at 292
  discover 480a
  acquire 775
Light of the World 976
lighten
  make light 320
  illume 420
  facilitate 705
lighter *boat* 273
lighterage 812
lighterman 269
light-fingered 791, 792
light-footed 274, 682
light-headed 503
lighthouse 550
lightless 421
light-minded 605
lightning
  velocity 274
  flash 420
  spark 423
like greased – 113
lightsome
  luminous 420
  irresolute 605
  cheerful 836
ligneous 367
lignite 388
lignography 558
ligulate 205
like *similar* 17
  relish 394
  enjoy 377, 827
  wish 865
  love 897
do what one –s 748
look – 448
we shall not look upon his – again 33
– master like man 19

– a pin in paper 58
likely 472
  think – 507
likeness 21, 554
  bad – 555
likewise 37
liking 865, 897
  have a – for 827
  to one's – 829
lilac *color* 437
Liliputian 193
Lillith 994
lilt 416, 836
lily *white* 430
  beauty 845
  paint the – 641
lily-livered 862
limæ labor
  improve 658
  toil 686
limature 330, 331
limb *member* 51
  instrument 633
  scamp 949
  – of the law 968
limber 272, 324
limbo *prison* 751, 752
  pain 828
  purgatory 982
lime *entrap* 545
  – light 423, 531, 599
Limehouse 908
limine, in – 66
limit *complete* 52
  end 67
  circumscribe 229
  boundary **233**
  qualify 469
  restrain 751
  prohibit 761
limitarian 984
limitation [*see* limit]
  estate 780, 783
limited
  – in quantity 32
  – in size 393
  to a – extent
  imperfect 651
limitless 105
limitrophe 197
limn 556
limner 559
limousine 272
limp *weak* 160
  slow 275
  supple 324
  fail 732
limpid 425
lin 343, 348
lincture 662
line *fastening* 45
  continuous 69
  ancestors 166
  descendants 167
  length 200
  no breadth 203
  string 205
  lining 224
  outline 230
  straight 246
  of steamers 273
  direction 278
  music 413
  appearance 448

measure 466
mark 550
writing 590
verse 597
vocation 625
army and navy 726
boundary – 233
draw the – 465
drop a – to 526
in a –
  continuous 69
  straight 246
in a – with 278
read between the –s 522
sounding – 208
straight – 246
troops of the – 726
– of action 692
– of battle 69
– of battle ship 726
– engraving 558
– of march 278
– of road 627
lineage *kindred* 11
  series 69
  ancestry 166
  posterity 167
lineament
  outline 230
  feature 240
  appearance 448
  mark 550
linear
  continuity 69
  pedigree 166
  length 200
linen 225
liner 273
lines
  fortification 717
hard –
  adversity 735
  severity 739
  reins 752
linger *protract* 110
  delay 133
  loiter 275
lingerie 225
lingo 560, 563
lingua franca 563
linguaceous 584
lingual 560, 582
linguist 492
linguistics 560
liniment 356, 662
lining **224**
link *relation* 9
  connect 43
  connecting – 45
  part 51
  term 71
  crossing 219
  torch 423
golf –s 840
missing – 53, 729
linked together
  party 712
linoleum 223
linotype 591
linseed oil 356
linsey-wolsey 41
linstock 388
lint 223
lintel 215

lion
  courage 861
  prodigy 872
  repute 873
  come in like a –
    183
  as dewdrops from
    the –'s mane
    483
  in the –'s den 665
  – lies down with
    the lamb 721
  put one's head in
    the –'s mouth
    665
  – in the path 706
  –'s share *more* 33
  chief part 50
  too much 641
  undue 925
lioness 374
lion-hearted 861
lionize 455, 873
lip *beginning* 66
  edge 231
  side 236
  prominence 250
  between cup and
    – 111
  finger on the –s
    silent 581
    speechless 585
  hang on the –s of
    418
  open one's –s
    speak 582
  seal the –s 585
  smack the –
    taste 390
    savory 394
  – homage
    flattery 933
  – service
    falsehood 544
    hypocrisy 988
  – wisdom 499
lip salve 847
lipstick 847
lipothymy 688
lippitude 443
liquefaction 335,
  384
liquescence 335
liqueur 298, 396
liquid
  fluid 333
  sound 405
  letter 561
liquidate 807, 812
liquidator 801
liquor *potable* 298
  fluid 333
  in – 959
  – up 959
liquorice 396
liquorish [*see*
  lickerish]
lisp 583
lissom 324
list *catalogue* **86**
  strip 205
  leaning 217
  fringe 231
  hear 418
  record 551
  will 600
  choose 609

arena 728
desire 865
  enter the –s
  attack 716
  contend 720
listed 440
listel 847
listen 418
  – in 455
  – to 457
  be –ed to 175
  – to reason 498
listless
  inattentive 458
  inactive 683
  indifferent 866
litany 990, 998
lite, pendente – 969
literae scriptae 590
literal
  imitated 19
  exact 494
  manifest 525
  letter 561
  word 562
  orthodox 983a
  – meaning 516
  – translation 522
literarum
  homo multarum –
    492
  homo trium – 792
literary 560
  – hack 593
  – man 492
  – power 569
literati 492
literatim [*see*
  literal]
literature 490, 560
lithe 324
lithic 323
lithograph 558
lithology 358
lithomancy 511
lithotint 558
litigant
  litigious 713
  combatant 726
  accusation 938
litigation
  quarrel 713
  contention 730
  lawsuit 969
litigious 713
litter *disorder* 59
  derange 61
  multitude 102
  brood 167
  support 215
  vehicle 272
  useless 645
littéraire, la
  morgue – 569
littérateur 492, 593
little
  – *in degree* 32
  – *in size* 193
  darling 897
  mean 940
  cost – 815
  do – 683
  make – of 483
  signify – 643
  think – of 458
  – did one think
    508

– by little
  degree 26
  slowly 275
  – Mary 191
  – one 129
  to – purpose
    useless 645
    failure 732
littleness 193
littoral 342
liturgy 978
live *exist* 1
  continue 141
  energetic 171
  dwell 186
  life 359
  repute 873
  – to fight again
    110
  – from hand to
    mouth 674
  – hard 954
  – in hope 858
  – and let live
    inaction 681
    freedom 748
    inexcitability 826
  – in the memory
    505
  – upon nothing
    819
  – on 298
  – separately 905
  – by one's wits
    545
livelihood 803
livelong 110
lively *keen* 375
  – *style* 574
  active 682
  acute 821
  sensitive 822
  sprightly 836
  – *imagination* 515
  – *pace* 274
liver 83; hard –
    954a
  white – 862
liver-colored 433
livery *suit* 225
  color 428
  badge 550
  decoration 877
  – servant 746
liveryman 748
live wire 171
livid *dark* 431
  grey 432
  purple 437
living *life* 359
  business 625
  benefice 995
  good – 957
  – beings 357
  –room 191
  – soul 372
  – thing 366
livraison 593
livret 593
lixiviate 335, 652
lixivium 335
llama 271
lo! 457, 870
load *quantity* 31
  fill 52
  lade 184

cargo 190
  weight 319
  store 636
  redundance 641
  hindrance 706
  adversity 735
  anxiety 828
  oppress 830
  prime and – 673
  take off a – of care
    834
  – the memory 505
  – with 706
  – with reproaches
    932
loads 102
loadstar [*see* lode-
  star]
loaf *mass* 192
  do nothing 681
  dawdle 683
loafer
  stroller 268
  inactive 683
  neglect 927
  bad man 949
loam 342
loan 787
loathe 867, 898
loathing
  [*see* loathe]
  weariness 841
  hate 898
loathsome
  unsavory 395
  painful 830
  dislike 867
loaves and fishes
  prosperity 734
  acquisition 775
  wealth 803
Lob's pound, in –
  751
lobby 191, 615, 627
lobbying 615
lobe 51
local
  – habitation 184,
    189
  – board 966
locale 183
locality 182, 183
localize 184
location 184
loch 343
loci, genius – 664
lock *fasten* 43
  fastening 45
  tuft 256
  canal 350
  hindrance 706
  prison 752
  dead – 265
  in the –up 938
  under – and key
    safe 664
    restraint 751
    prisoner 754
  – hospital 662
  –out 55, 719
  – the stable door
    too late 135
    useless 645
    unskilful 699
  –, stock and
    barrel 50
  – up *hide* 528

imprison 751
locker 191
locket 847
lock-up *prison* 752
loco, in –
  agreeing 23
  situation 183
  expedience 646
locofoco 388
locomotion 264
  – by air 267
  – by land 266
  – by water 267
locomotive 266, 271
locular 191
locum tenens
  substitute 147
  inhabitant 188
  deputy 759
locus:
  – *poenitentiae* 937
  – *standi*
    support 215
    plea 617
    social rank 873
locust *prodigal* 818
  evil-doer 913
  swarm like –s 102
locution 582
lode 636
lodestar
  attraction 288
  indication 550
  direction 693
lodestone 288, 615
lodge *place* 184
  presence 186
  dwelling 189
  – a complaint 938
lodgement 184
lodger
  inhabitant 188
  possessor 779
lodging 189
loft 191, 210
lofty *high* 206
  – *style* 574
  proud 878
  insolent 885
  magnanimous
    942
log *velocity* 274
  fuel 388
  record 551
  heave the – 466
  sleep like a – 683
logarithm 84
loggerhead 501
  at –s *discord* 713
  contention 720
  enmity 889
loggia 191
logic 476
  – of facts 467
logician 476
logical acuteness
  570
logography 590
logogryph 533
logolept 562
logomachy
  discussion 476
  words 588
  dispute 720
logometer 85
logometric 84
log-rolling 709

love *desire* 865
  courtesy 894
  affection **897**
  favorite 899
  abode of – 897
  labor of –
    willing 602
  inexpensive 815
  amusement 840
  disinterested 942
  God's – 906
  make – 902
  no – lost 713
  – affair 897
  – of country 910
  – lock 256
  not for – or money
    640, 814
love-knot *token* 550
love-lorn 898
lovely 845, 897
love-making 902
love-pot 959
love-potion 865
lover [*see* love]
love-sick 897, 902
love-story 897, 902
love-token 897, 902
loving-cup 892, 894
loving-kindness
    906
low *small* 32
  - *not high* 207
  - *sound* 405
  moo 412
  vulgar 851
  disreputable 874
  common 876
  base 940
  bring – 308
  - *condition* 876
  - *comedy* 599
  at a – ebb
    small 32
    inferior 34
    depressed 308
    waste 638
    deteriorated 659
  - *fellow* 876
  - *life* 851
  - *note* 408
  - *origin* 876
  - *price* 815
  - *spirits* 837
  - *tide* 207
  - *tone black* 431
    mutter 581
  - *water low* 207
    dry 340
    insufficient 640
    poor 804
low-born 876
low-brow 491
low-lands 207
low-minded 876,
    940
lower *inferior* 34
  decrease 36
  overhang 214
  depress 308
  dark 421
  dim 422
  predict 511
  sad 837
  irate 900
  sulky 901a
  - one's flag 725

– one's note 879
– orders 876
lowering 668, 859
lowly 879
lown 501, 949
lowness [*see* low]
  207
  humility 879
loy 272
loyal *obedient* 743
  observant 772
  honourable 939
lozenge 244, 662
L. s. d. 800
lubbard [*see* lubber]
lubber 683, 701
lubberly 192, 699
lubricant 332
lubrication 255, **332**
lubricity
  slippery 255
  unctuous 355
  impure 961
lucent 420
lucid
  luminous 420
  transparent 425
  intelligible 518
  - *style* 570
  - *interval* 502
lucidus ordo 58
lucifer 388
Lucifer 423, 978
lucimeter 445
luck *chance* 156, 621
  prosperity 734
  good – 858
luckless 735
lucky 134, 731
lucrative 775
lucre 775, 803
Lucretia 960
luctation 720
lucubration 451
luculent 420
lucus a non lucendo
    18, 565
lud! O – 839
ludibrious 840
ludicrous 853
luff 267
lug *pull* 285
  ear 418
luge 272
luggage 270, 780
  - *van* 272
lugger 273
lugubrious 837
lukewarm
  temperate 382
  irresolute 605
  torpid 823
  indifferent 866
lull *cessation* 142
  mitigate 174
  silence 403
  - to sleep 265
lullaby
  moderate 174
  song 415
  verses 597
  inactivity 683
  relief 834
lumbago 378
lumbar 235
lumbar *disorder* 59
  slow 275

store 636
useless 645
hindrance 706
lumbering 647, 846
lumber-room 191
lumbriciform 249
luminary *star* 318
  light **423**
  sage 500
luminescence 420
luminous *light* 420
  intelligible 518
  – *paint* 423
lump *whole* 50
  chief part 51
  amass 72
  mass 192
  projection 250
  weight 319
  density 321
  in the – 50
  – of affectation
    855
  – *sum* 800
  – *together join* 43
    combine 48
    assemble 72
lumpish [*see* lump]
  inactive 683
  ugly 846
Luna 318
lunacy 503
lunar 318
  – *caustic* 384
lunatic 503, 504
luncheon 298
lune avec les dents,
  prendre la –
    158, 471
lunette 717
lunge 276, 716
lungs *wind* 349
  loudness 404
  shout 411
  voice 580
luniform &c. 245
lupanar 961
lurch *incline* 217
  sink 306
  oscillation 314
  failure 732
  leave in the –
    outstrip 303
    deceive 545
    relinquish 624
  left in the –
    defeated 732
lure *attraction* 288,
    865
  deceive 545
  entice 615
lurid *dark* 421
  dim 422
  red 434
lurk *unseen* 447
  latent 526
  hidden 528
lurking-place 530
luscious 394, 829
lush *vegetation* 365
  drunkenness 959
lushy 959
lusk 683
lusory 840
lust 865, 961
  – *after* 921
luster

brightness 420
chandelier 423
glory 873
lustily 404, 686
  cry out – 839
lustless 158
lustration 652, 952
lustrum 108
lusty 159, 192
lusus naturæ 80
lute *cement* 45, 46
  guitar 417
luteous 436
Lutheran 984
luxation 44
luxuriant 168, 639
luxuriate in 377,
    827
luxurious
  pleasant 377
  delightful 829
  intemperate 954
luxury
  physical – 377
  redundance 641
  enjoyment 827
  sensuality 954
lycanthropy 503
Lyceum 542
Lydford law 964
Lydian measure
    415
lyddite 727
lying
  decumbent 213
  deceptive 544
  faithless 986
Ly-king 986
lymph *fluid* 333
  water 337
  transparent 425
lymphatic 337
lynch 972
  – *law* 964
lyncher 975
lynching 361
lynx-eyed 441, 498
lyre 417
lyric 415
  – *poetry* 597
lyrist 597

M

Mab 979
macadamize 255,
    635
Macaire, Robert –
    792
macaroni 854
macaronic
  absurdity 497
  neology 563
  verses 597
Macchiavel [*see*
  Machiavelism]
mace
  weapon 727
  scepter 747
mace-bearer 965
maceration
  saturation 337
  atonement 952
  asceticism 955
  rite 998

Macheath 792
Machiavelism
  falsehood 544
  cunning 702
  dishonesty 940
machicolation 257,
    717
machination
  trick 545
  plan 626
  cunning 702
  –s of the devil 619
machinator 626
machine 633
  like a – 698
  – gun 407, 727
  be a mere – 749
machinist
  theatrical - 599
  workman 690
macilent 203
mackerel
  mottled 440
  procuress 962
  – *sky* 349, 353
mackintosh 225
macrobiotic 110
macrocosm 318
macrography 441
macrology 577
mac Sycophant,
  Sir Pertinax –
    886, 935
mactation 991
macte virtute 931
macula 848
maculate
  unclean 653
maculation 440, 848
mad *insane* 503
  excited 824
  drive one – 900
  go – 825
  – *after* 865
  – with rage 900
madam 374
mad-brained 503
madcap
  violent 173
  lunatic 504
  excitable 825
  buffoon 844
  rash 863
madder *color* 434
made
  – to one's hand
    673
  – *man* 734
  – to order 673
madefaction 339
madman **504**
Madonna
  good 948
  angel 977
  pious 987
madrigal *music* 415
  verses 597
Mæcenas 492, 890
Maelstrom
  whirl 312
  water 348
  pitfall 667
maestro 415
maffick 883
magazine
  periodical 53
  record 551

book 593
store 636
– rifle 727
Magdalen 950, 962
mage 994
magenta 434
maggot *little* 193
fancy 515
caprice 608
desire 865
maggoty
capricious 608
unclean 653
– headed
silly 499
excitable 825
Magi *sage* 500
sect 984
magic 175, 992
– lantern
instrument 445
show 448
magician 548, 994
magilp 356a
magisterial 878, 885
magistery 30
magistracy 737, 965
magistrate 745, 967
magistrature 737
magistri, jurare in verba – 481
nullius – 487
magma 41
Magna Charta 769
magna pars fui, quorum – 690
magnanimity 942
magnate 875
magnet *attract* 288
desire 865
magnetism
power 157
influence 175
attraction 288
motive 615
animal – 992
magnetize
influence 175
motive 615
conjure 992
magni nominis umbra
wreck 659
repute 873
rank 875
magnificent
large 192
fine 845
grand 882
magnifico 875
magnifier 445
magnifique et pas cher 815
magnify
increase 35
enlarge 194
over-rate 482
exaggerate 549
approve 931
praise 990
magniloquent 577, 884
magnitude 25, 31, 192
magno conatu magnas nugas

638, 643
Magnus Apollo 500
magpie 584
magsman 792
maharajah 745
maharani 745
– mah jong 840
mahl-stick [*see* maulstick]
mahogany
color 433
Mahomet 986
Mahometan 984
maid *girl* 129
servant 631, 746
spinster 374, 904
– of all work 690
– of honor 890
maiden *first* 66
girl 129
punishment 975
– speech 66
maidenhood 904
maidenly 374
maigre 956
mail *post* 270, 534
armor 717
– coach 272, 534
– steamer 273
– van 272, 534
maim 158, 659
main *tunnel* 260
ocean 341
conduct 350
principal 642
coup de – 680
in the –
intrinsically 5
greatly 31
on the whole 50
principally 642
with might and – 686
plough the – 267
main-chance 156
good 618
important 642
profit 775
look to the –
foresight 510
skill 698
economy 817
caution 864
selfish 943
main-force
strength 159
violence 173
compulsion 744
mainland 342
mainpernor 771
main-part 31, 50
main-spring 153, 633
mainstay
support 215
refuge 666
hope 858
maintain
permanence 141
continue 143
sustain 170
support 215
assert 535
preserve 670
– one's course
persevere 604a
– the even tenor of

one's way 623
– one's ground 717
maintenance
[*see* maintain]
assistance 707
wealth 803
maintien 692
maison de santé 662
maisonette 189
maître: coup de –
goodness 648
skill 698
l'œil e – 459
majesté, lèse– 742
majestic 873, 882
majesty *king* 745
rank 873
deity 976
major *greater* 33
officer 745
–domo
director 694
retainer 746
–general 745
– key 413
– part *great* 31
all 50
majority
superiority 33
multitude 102
age 131
join the – 360
majusculae 561
make
constitute 54, 56
render 144
produce 161
form 240
arrive at 292
complete 729
compel 744
– acquainted with 527, 539
– after 622
– its appearance 446
– away with 162, 361
– believe 544, 545, 546
– the best of 725
– bold to differ 489
– a date with 897
– choice of 609
– fast 43
– a fool of 853
– for 278
– one's fortune 734
– fun of 842, 856
– a fuss 642, 682
– good
compensation 30
complete 52, 729
establish 150
evidence 467
demonstrate 478
provide 637
restore 660
– one's escape 671
– one's word 772
– a go of 731
– haste 684
– hay while the sun shines 134
– interest 765
– known 527

– the land 292
– light of 483, 705, 934
– oneself master of 539
– money 775
– a monkey of 853
– much of 549, 642
– no doubt 484
– no secret of 525
– no sign 526, 528
– nothing of
unintelligible 519
not wonder 871
– of 902
– off 623, 671
– off with 791
– out *see* 441
evidence 467
demonstrate 478
discover 480a
know 490
intelligible 518
interpret 522
due 924
– over 658, 783, 784
– peace 723, 724
– a piece of work 832
– things pleasant 702
– a present 784
– public 531
– a push 682
– ready 673
– a requisition 741, 765
– a speech 582
– a sucker of 853
– sure 150, 673
– terms 769
– time 110
– tracks 293
– towards 278
– up [*see below*]
– use of 677
– way 282
– one's way 302, 734
– way for 147, 623
– a wry face 867
make up
complete 52
compose 54
– accounts 811
– for 30
– matters 952
– one's mind
judgment 480
belief 484
resolve 604
– a quarrel 723
– a sum 809
– to approach 286
address 586
maker *artificer* 690
Maker, the – 976
makeshift 147, 617
make-weight
inequality 28
compensation 30
completeness 52
making of, be the –
utility 644
goodness 648
aid 707

mal du pays 833
mala fides 940
malachite 435
malacology 368
malade imaginaire 837
maladie du pays 833
maladministration 699
maladroit 699
malady 655
malaise 378, 828
malapert 885, 887
Malaprop, Mrs. – 565
malapropism 495
mal à propos 24, 135
malaria 657, 663
malconformation 243
malcontent 710, 832
male 159, 373
– animal 373
malediction 908
malefaction 947
malefactor 949
malefic 649
maleficent 907
– being 913
malevolence 907
malfeasance 647
malformed 241
malformation 243
malgré 179
– soi 603
malice *hate* 898
spite 907
bear – *revenge* 919
– aforethought 907
– prepense 907
malign *bad* 649
malevolent 907
detract 934
malignant 649, 907
malignity
violence 173
malinger 544, 655
malison 908
malkin 653
mall *walk* 189
club 276
malleable 324
mallet 276
malnutrition 655
mal-odor 401
malpractice 947
malt liquor 298
maltreat
injure 649
aggrieve 830
molest 907
malum
– prohibitum 925
– in se 923
malversation 818, 947
Mameluke 726
mamelon 250
mamma 166
mammal 366
mammiform 250
mammilla 250
Mammon 803, 978

serve – 989
mammoth 192
man adult 131
  mankind 372
  male 373
  prepare 673
  workman 690
  servant 746
  courage 861
  husband 903
make a – of 648, 861
Son of – 976
straight – 599
to a – 488
  –at-arms 726
one's – of business 758
  –'s estate 131
  – in office 745
  – in the street 876
  –of-war 273, 726
  –of-war's man 269
  – at the wheel 694
  – and wife 903
manacle 751, 752
manage 693
  – to succeed 731
manageable 705
management
  conduct 692
  skill 698
manager
  stage - 599
  director 694
managery 693
manche après la cognée, jeter le – 859
mancible 637
mancipation 751
mandamus 741
mandarin 745
mandate 630, 741
mandible 298
mandolin 417
mandragora 174
mandrel 312
manduction 298
mane 256
man-eater 361
manége 266, 370
manes 362
manet: – altámente repostum 505
  – cicatrix 919
maneuver 680, 702
manful strong 159
  resolute 604
  brave 861
manger 191
manger:
  cela se laisse –.394
  – son blé en herbe 818
mangle
  separate 44
  smooth 255
  injure 659
mangled 53
mangy 655
man-hater 911
manhood 131, 861
mania insanity 503
  desire 865
maniac 504
manibus pedibus–

que 686
manic 503
manic-depressive 503
manicure 847
manicheism 978
manichord 417
manie 865
maniéré 855
manifest
  list 86
  visible 446
  obvious 525
  disclose 529
manifestation 525
manifesto 531
manifold 81, 102
manikin dwarf 193
  image 554
maniple 103
manipulate
  handle 379
  use 677
  conduct 692
manipulator 621
mankind 372
manly
  adolescent 131
  strong 159
  male 373
  brave 861
  honest 939
manna food 396
  – in the wilderness aid 707
  pleasing 829
manner kind 75
  style 569
  way 627
  conduct 692
  in a – 32
  by all – of means 536
  by no – of means 602
  to the – born 5
mannered 579
mannerism
  special 79
  unconformity 83
  affectation 855
  vanity 880
mannerly 894
manners 852, 894
manor 780
  lord of the – 779
  – house 189
manorial 780
Mansard roof 223
manse 1000
mansion 189
manslaughter 361
mansuetude 894
mantelpiece 215
mantilla 225
mantle spread 194
  dress 225
  foam 353
  shade 424
  redden 434
  robes 747
  flush 821, 824
  anger 900
mantlet cloak 225
  defence 717
Mantology 511
manual guide 527

schoolbook 542
book 593
advice 695
– labor 686
manubial 793
manufactory 691
manufacture 161, 680
manufacturer 690
manumission 750
manure
  agriculture 371
  dirt 653
  aid 707
manuscript 22, 590
many 102
  the – 876
  for – a day 110
  – irons in the fire 682
  – men many minds 489
  – times
  repeated 104
  frequent 136
many-colored 440
many-sided 81, 236
many-tóngued 532
map 234, 527, 554
  – out 626
mar 659, 706
marabou 83
marabout 1000
maranatha 908
marasmus
  shrinking 195
  atrophy 655
  deterioration 659
maraud 791
marauder 792
marble ball 249
  hard 323
  sculpture 557
  tablet 590
  insensible 823
marble 440
marble-hearted 907
march region 181
  journey 266
  progression 282
  music 415
  dead – 363
  forced – 684
  on the – 264
  steal a –
  advance 280
  go beyond 303
  deceive 545
  active 682
  cunning 702
  – against 716
  – of events 151
  – of intellect
  knowledge 490
  improvement 658
  – off 293
  – on a point 278
  – past 882
  – of time 109
  – with 199
March, Ides of – 601
marches 233
marchioness 875
marcid 203
marconigram 523
marcor 203
mare horse 271

female 374
  –'s nest 497, 546
  –'s tail wind 349
  cloud 353
marechal 745
margarine 356
margin space 180
  edge 231
  redundance 641
  latitude 748
margravate 780
margrave 745, 875
marimba 417
marine fleet 273
  sailor 269
  oceanic 341
  soldier 726
  tell it to the –s 489, 497
  – painter 559
  – painting 556
mariner 269
Mariolatry 991
marionnette
  representation 554
  drama 599
  amusement 840
marish 345
marital 903
maritime 267, 341
mark degree 26
  term 71
  take cognizance of 450
  attend to 457
  indication 550
  record 551
  writing 590
  object 620
  importance 642
  repute 873
  beyond the – 303
  leave one's – 873
  man of – 873, 875
  near the – 197
  overshoot the – 699
  put a – upon 457
  save the – 870
  up to the –
  enough 639
  good 648
  skill 698
  due 924
  wide of the – 196, 495
  within the – 304
  – down 813
  – off 551
  – out choose 609
  plan 626
  command 741
  – of recognition 894
  – with a red letter 883
  – time
  chronometry 114
  halt 265
  wait 507
  – with a white stone 931
marked [see mark]
  great 31
  affirmed 535
  well– 446

in a – degree 31
play with – cards 545
  – down 815
marker 550
market buy 795
  mart 799
  bring to – 796
  buy in the cheapest &c. – 794
  in the –
  offered 763
  barter 794
  sale 796
  rig the – 794
  – garden 371
  – overt
  manifest 525
  mart 799
  – place street 189
  mart 799
  – price 812
  – woman 797
marketable 794, 796
marksman 700
marksmanship 698
marl 342
marmalade 396
marmot 683
maroon
  color 433, 434
  abandon 782, 893
marplot
  bungler 701
  obstacle 706
  malicious 913
marque, letters of – 791
marquee 223
marquetry 440
marquis 875
marriage 903
  companionate – 903
  ill-assorted – 904
  – bells 836
  – portion 780
marriageable 131, 903
marrow essence 5
  interior 221
  central 222
  chill to the – 385
marrow-bones, on one's –
  submit 725
  beg 765
  humble 879
  servile 886
  atonement 952
marrowless 158
marry combine 48
  assertion 535
  wed 903
  – come up
  defiance 715
  anger 900
  censure 932
Mars 722, 979
  – orange 439
marsh 345
marshal
  arrange 60
  messenger 534
  auxiliary 711
  officer 745

Marshalsea 752
marsupial 191, 366
mart 799
Marte, suo —
  exertion 686
  skill 698
martello tower 717
martial 722
  court— 966
  – law 737, 739
  compulsory 744
  illegal 964
  – music 415
martinet 739
martingale 752
Martinmas 998
martyr
  bodily pain 378
  mental pain 828
  'ascetic 955
  – to disease 655
martyrdom
  killing 361
  agony 378, 828
  unselfish 942
  punishment 972
marvel 870, 872
  – whether 514
marvelous 31, 870
  deal in the – 549
Masaniello 742
mascara 847
mascot 993
masculine 159, 373
mash mix 41
  disorder 59
  soft 324
  semiliquid 253
  pulpify 354
masher 854
mask dress 225
  shade 424
  concealment 528
  ambush 530
  deceit 545
  shield 717
  put on the – 544
mason 690
Masorah 985
masque 599
masqué, bal – 840
masquerade
  dress 225
  concealment 528
  disguise 530
  frolic 840
mass quantity 25
  much 31
  whole 50
  heap 72
  size 192
  gravity 319
  density 321
  worship 990
  rite 998
  attend – 990
  in the – 50
  – book 998
  – of society 876
massacre 361
massage 33, 379, 662
masse, en – 712
masses, the – 876
massive large 31
  huge 192
  heavy 319

dense 321
mast 206
master
  boy 129
  influence 175
  man 373
  know 490
  understand 518
  learn 539
  teacher 540
  director 694
  proficient 698, 700
  succeed, conquer 731
  ruler 745
  possession 777
  possessor 779
  title 877
  eye of the – 693
  hard – 739
  past – 700
  – of Arts 492
  – one's feelings 826
  – hand 700
  – key open 260
  instrument 631
  – mariner 269
  – mind sage 500
  proficient 700
  – passion 820
  – one's passions 944
  – of the position 731
  – of the revels 840
  – of the Rolls 553, 967
  – of self 604
  – of the situation 731, 737
  – spirit of the age 500, 873
  – of one's time 685
masterdom 737
masterpiece
  good 648
  perfect 650
  skill 698
master-stroke 626, 731
mastery 731, 737
  get the – over 175
masthead
  punish 972
mastic viscid 352
  resin 356a
masticate 298
mastiff 366
mat support 215
  woven 219
  misty 427
  cover 652
matador 361
match coincide 13
  similar 17
  copy 19
  equal 27
  fuel 388
  contest 720
  marriage 903
matchless
  supreme 33
  excellent 648
  virtuous 944
matchlock 727

mate similar 17
  equal 27
  duplicate 89
  mariner 269
  auxiliary 711
  master 745
  friend 890
  wife 903
  check— 732
maté 298
mater alma – 542
  –familias 166
materia medica 662
material
  substance 316
  stuff 635
  important 642
  – for thought 454
  – point 32
materialism
  matter 316
  heterodoxy 984
  irreligion 989
materiality 316
materialize 446
materials 635
matériel 633
maternal
  parental 166
  benevolent 906
  – love 897
maternity 166
mathematical
  precise 494
  – point 193
mathematics 25
mathesis 25
matin 125
matinée 892
matins 990
matrass 191
matriarch 11, 166
matriarchate 737
matriculate 86
matriculation 539
matrilinear 11, 166
matrimony
  mixture 41
  wedlock 903
matrix mold 22
  workshop 691
matron 374, 903
matronly 128, 131
matross 726
matter substance 3
  material world 316
  topic 454
  meaning 516
  type 591
  business 625
  importance 642
  pus 653
  no – 460
  what – 643
  what's the – 455, 461
  – of course
  conformity 82
  certain 474
  habitual 613
  – in dispute 461
  – of fact event 151
  certainty 474
  truth 494
  language 576
  artless 703

dull 843
  – in hand 454, 625
  – of indifference 866
  – nothing 643
mattock 253
mattress 215
mature old 124
  adolescent 131
  conversion 144
  scheme 626
  perfect 650
  improve 658
  prepare 673
  complete 729
  – thought 451
maturely considered 611
maturine 996
maturity [see mature]
  bring to – 729
  matutinal 125
matzoon 298
maudlin
  inactive 683
  drunk 959
mauger 30
maukin 562
maul hammer 276
  hurt 649
maulstick 215
maund basket 191
  mumble 583
maunder
  diffuse style 573
  mumble 583
  talk 584
  lament 839
maundy
  – money 784
  – Thursday 988
Mauser rifle 727
mausoleum 363
mauvais
  – goût 851
  – quart d'heure 828
  – sujet 949
  – ton 851
mauvaise:
  .– honte
  affectation 855
  modesty 881
  – plaisanterie 851
mauve 437
maw 191
mawkish 391
Mawworm
  deceiver 548
  sham piety 988
maxim 80, 496
Maxim gun 727
maximal 33
maximalist 742
maximum 33, 210
maxixe 840
may be 470
  as it – 156
May-day 138, 840
May-fly 111
mayhap 470
mayor 745, 965
maypole 206
mayonnaise 298
May-queen 847
mazard 298

maze
  disorder 59
  convolution 248
  enigma 533
  difficulty 704
  in a –
  uncertain 475
mazed 503
mazurka 840
me 317
me judice 484
meâ culpâ 950
mead plain 344
  sweet 396
meadow plain 344
  grass 367
  – land 371
meager small 32
  incomplete 53
  thin 203
  - style 575
  scanty 640
  poor 643
  – diet 956
meal repast 298
  powder 330
mealy-mouthed
  falsehood 544
  servile 886
  flattering 933
mean average 29
  small 32
  middle 68, 228
  signify 516
  intend 620
  contemptible 643
  stingy 819
  shabby 874
  ignoble 876
  sneaking 886
  base 940
  selfish 943
  golden – 174
  take the – 774
  – nothing 517
  – parentage 876
  – time 114
  – wretch 949
meander
  convolution 248
  deviate 279
  circuition 311
  river 348
  – around Robin Hood's barn 279
meandering
  diffuse 573
meanest capacity 499
  intelligible to the – 518
meaning 516
meaningless 517
means
  appliances 632
  property 780
  wealth 803
  by all – 602
  by any – 632
  by no – 536
  – of access 627
meantime 106
meanwhile 106
measurable 466
  within – distance 470
measure extent 25

degree 26
  moderation 174
  music 413
  compute 466
  verse 597
  proceeding 626
  action 680
  apportion 786
angular – 244
full – 629
out of – 641
without – 641
– of inclination
  217
measured
  moderate 174
  sufficient 639
  temperate 953
measureless 105
measurement 25,
  466
measures
have no – with 713
take – *plan* 626
  prepare 673
  conduct 692
– of length 200
meat 298
broken – 645
one man's – is
  another man's
  poison 15
mechanic 690
mechanical 601,
  633
– warfare 722
– powers 633
mechanician 690
mechanism 633
medal
  record 551
  sculpture 557
  palm 733
  decoration 877
– of Honor 733
medalist 700
medallion 557
meddle 682
médecin tant pis
  837
médecine expec-
  tante 133, 662
Medes and Per-
  sians, law of the
  – 80, 141
mediaeval 124
mediaevalism 122
medial 29, 68
median 228
mediant 413
medias res, in – 68
plunge – 300, 576
mediation—*instru-*
  mentality 631
  intercession **724**
  deprecation 766
  Christ 976
mediator 711
Mediator
  Saviour 976
medical 662
medicament 662
medicaster 548
medicate
  compound 41
  heal 660
medicine 662

– man 994
medico 662
mediety 68
mediis rebus, in –
  682
medio tutissimus,
  in – 864
mediocritas,
  aurea – 628
mediocrity
  average 29
  smallness 32
  imperfect 651
  – *of fortune* **736**
meditate *think* 451
  purpose 620
mediterranean 68,
  228
medium *mean* 29
  middle 68
  atmosphere 227
  intermediary 228
  color 428
  oracle 513
  impostor 548
  instrument 631
  seer 994
  transparent – 425
medley 41, 59
  music 415
  chance – 156
medullary 324
Medusa 860
meed
  apportion 786
  reward 973
  – *of praise* 931
meek 826, 879
meerschaum 392
meet *agreement* 23
  assemble 72
  touch 199
  converge 290
  arrive 292
  expedient 646
  fulfil 772
  proper 924
make both ends –
  wealth 803
  economy 817
unable to make
  both ends –
  poverty 804
  not pay 808
– with attention
  457
– one's death 360
– the ear 418
– one at every
  turn
  present 186
  redundant 641
– one's expenses
  817
– the eye 446
– in front 861
– half way
  willing 602
  concord 714
  pacification 723
  mediation 724
  compromise 774
  friendship 888
  benevolence 906
– hand to hand
  720
– one's wishes

consent 762
  pleasurable 829
– with *event* 151
  find 480a
meeting [*see* meet]
  junction 43
  hostile – 720
  place of – 74
meeting-house
  hall 189
  chapel 1000
megacosm 318
Megaera 173, 900
megalomania 482,
  504
megaphone 404,
  418
megascope 445
megatherium 124
megrims *fits* 315
  melancholy 837
mehari 271
Mein Herr 877
meister-singer 597
melancholia
  insanity 503
  dejection 837
melancholy 830,
  837
away with – 836
mélange 41
mêlée *disorder* 59
  contention 720
melinite 727
meliora, spero –
  858
meliorate 658
meliorism 658
melius inquiren-
  dum, ad – 658
melliferous
  sweet 396
mellifluous
  music 413
  – *language* 578
mellow
  old 128
  grow into 144
  soft 324
  sound 413
  color 428
  improve 658
  prepare 673
  tipsy 959
melodeon 417
melodious 413
melodist 416
melodrama 599,
  824
melody **413**
Melpomene 599
melt *convert* 144
  liquefy 335
  fuse 384
  pity 914
– in the air 405
– away
  cease to exist 2
  unsubstantial 4
  decrease 36
  disappear 111,
  449
  waste 638
– the heart 914
– into one 48
– into tears 839
melting-pot 691

member *part* 51
  component 56
  councillor 696
membrane 204
même, quand – 708
memento 505
  – *mori* 363, 837
meminisse juvabit
  505
memoir 594, 595
memorabilia
  reminiscences 505
  important 642
memorable 642
memorandum
  memory 505
  record 551
  plan 626
  – book 505, 551
  compendium 596
memorial
  record 551
memorialist 553
memorialize 505
memorials 594
memoriam, in –
  363, 505
memory **505**
  fame 873
  failing – 506
  short – 506
  in the – of man
  122
– runneth not to
  the contrary
  124
mem-sahib 374
menace 909
ménage 692
menagerie
  collection 72
  animals 370
  store 636
mend 658, 660
– one's manners
  894
mendacity 544
mendicancy 765,
  804
mendicant
  beggar 767
  poor 804
  monk 996
menhir 363
menial 746, 876
meniscus 245, 445
mens sana 502
  – in corpore sano
  827
mens sibi conscia
  recti 878
mensâ et thoro,
  separatio a –
  905
menses 299
menstrual 138
menstruum 335
mensuration 466
mental 450
  – calm 826
  – excitement 824
  – pabulum 454
  – philosophy 450
  – reservation 528
  – suffering 828
menteur à triple
  étage 548

menticulture 658
mention 527
above –ed 104
not worth –ing 643
mentis gratissimus
  error 481
mentor *sage* 500
  teacher 540
  adviser 695
menu 86, 298
Mephistopheles
  980
Mephistophelian
  945
mephitic 401, 657
mephitis 663
meracious 392
mercantile 794
mercatoria, lex –
  963
mercature 794
mercenary
  soldier 726
  servant 746
  price 812
  parsimonious 819
  selfish 943
mercer 225
merchandise **798**
merchant 797
merchantman 273
merciful 914
merciless 914a
mercurial
  changeable 149
  mobile 264
  quick 274
  excitable 825
Mercury 979
  traveler 268
  quick 274
  messenger 534
mercy *lenity* 740
  pity 914
at the – of
  liable 177
  subject 749
cry you – 766
have at one's –
  919
have no – 914a
  – on us! 870
for –'s sake 765
– seat 966
mere *simple* 32
  lake 343
  trifling 643
  – nothing
  small 32
  trifle 643
buy for a – noth-
  ing 815
– pretext 617
– words 477
– wreck 659
merelles 840
meretricious
  false 495
  vulgar 851
  licentious 961
merfolk 980
merge *combine* 48
  include 76
  insert 300
  plunge 337
  – in 56
  – into *become* 144

merged 228
meridian
  region 181
  room 125
  summit 210
  light 420
  – of life 131
merit
  goodness 648
  due 924
  virtue 944
  make a – of 884
  – *notice* 642
merito, e – 944
meritorious 931
Merlin 994
mermaid 341
  monster 83
  mythology 979, 980
merman 341
mero motu, ex – 600
merriment
  cheerful 836
  amusement 840
merry *cheerful* 836
  drunk 959
  make – *sport* 840
  make – with *wit* 842
  ridicule 856
  wish a – Christmas &c. 896
  – and wise 842
merry-andrew 844
merry-go-round 312, 840
merry-making 827, 840, 892
merry-thought 842
mersion 337
meruit ferat, pal- mam qui – 873
merveille, à – 731
mesa 344
mésalliance 24, 903
meseems 484
mesh 198, 219
meshes *trap* 545
  difficulty 704
  – of sophistry 477
meshwork 219
mesial
  middle 68
mesmerism 992
mesmerist 994
mesne lord 779
mess *mixture* 41
  disorder 59
  barracks 191
  meal 298
  difficulty 704
  portion 786
  make a – *unskilful* 699
  fail 732
message
  intelligence 532
  command 741
Messalina 962
messenger 271
  envoy 534
  servant 746
  – *balloon* 463
Messiah 976
messianic 976

messmate 890
messuage 189
messy 59
metabolism 140
metacenter 222
metachronism 115
metage 466
metagenesis 140
metagrammatism 561
metal 635
  Brittania – 545
metallic *sound* 410
metalepsis 521
metallurgy 358
metamorphosis 140
metaphor
  comparison 464
  figure **521**
  (*analogy* 17)
metaphrase 522
metaphrast 524
metaphrastic 516
metaphysics 450
metastasis, meta- thesis
  change 140
  inversion 218
  displacement 270
mete *measure* 466
  distribute 786
  – out *give* 784
metempsychosis 140
meteor 318, 423
meteoric 173, 420
meteorology 338
meteoromancy 466
meter 466
meter
  length 200
  poetry 597
metheglin 396
methinks 484
method *order* 58
  way **627**
  want of – 59
methodical 60
Methodist 984
methodist
  journalist 988
methodize 60
Methuselah 130
  old as – 12
  since the days of – 124
meticulous 772
métier 625
métis 83
metonymy 521
metoposcopy
  front 234
  appearance 44
  interpret 522
metrical
  measured 466
  verse 597
metrology 466
  moderation 174
  mid-course 628
metropolis 189
metropolitan
  archbishop 996
mettle *spirit* 820
  courage 861

man of – 861
on one's –
  resolved 604
put on one's –
  excite 824
  encourage 861
mettlesome
  energetic 171
  sensitive 822
  excitable 825
  brave 861
mettre de l'eau dans son vin 160
meum et tuum 780
  disregard distinc- tion between – 791
mew *moult* 226
  cry 412
  – up 751
mewed up 229
mewl 412
mews 189
mezzanine floor 191, 599
mezzo rilievo
  convex 250
  sculpture 557
mezzo termine
  middle 68
  mid-course 628
  compromise 774
Mezzofanti 492
mezzosoprano 416
mezzotint 420, 558
miasm 663
mica 425
micaceous 204
mi-carême 840
Micawber 860
Michael 977
Michaelmas 998
Micomicon 515
microbe 163, 193
microcosm 193
micrography 193, 441
micrometer 193
micro-organism 193
microphone 418
microscope 193, 445
microscopic 32, 193
mid 68
Midas 803
mid-course **628**
mid-day 125
midden 653
middle - *in degree* 29
  - *in order* **68**
  - *in space* 222, 228
  – classes 736
  – *constriction* 203
  – course 29, 628
  – man *director* 694
    agent 758
  – point 29
  – term 68
    compromise 774
middlemost 222
middling 29, 32, 68, 651
middy 225, 269
midge 193
midget 193

midland 342
midnight *night* 126
  dark 421
  – oil 539, 689
mid-progress 282
midriff 68, 228
midshipman 269, 745
midships 68
midst – *in order* 68
  central 222
  interjacent 228
  in the – of
    mixed with 41
    doing 680
midsummer **125**
  – day 138
midway 68
midwife
  instrument 631
  remedy 662
  auxiliary 711
midwifery 161, 662
mien 448, 692
miff 900
might *power* 157
  violence 173
  energy 686
mightily 31
mighty *much* 31
  strong 159
  large 192
  haughty 878
migraine 378
migrate 266, 295
mikado 745
milch cow
  productive 168
  animal 366
  store 636
mild *moderate* 174
  warm 382
  insipid 391
  lenient 740
  calm 826
  courteous 894
mildew 653, 663
mildewed
  spoiled 659
mile 200
milestone 550
  whistle jigs to a – 645
milieu, juste – 174, 628
militant 722
  church – 983*a*
military
  warfare 722
  soldiers 726
  – authorities 745
  – band 417
  – power 737
  – time 132
  – train 726
militate against 708
militia 726
milk *moderate* 174
  semiliquid 352
  cows &c. 370
  white 430
  mild 740
  – a he-goat into a sieve 471
  flow with – and honey *plenty* 639

prosperity 734
  pleasant 829
  – of human kind- ness 906
  – the ram 645
  – and water
    weak 160
    insipid 391
    unimportant 643
    imperfect 651
milk-livered 862
milksop
  incapable 158
  fool 501
  coward 862
milky [see milk]
  semitransparent 427
  whiteness 430
  – way 318
mill 330
  notch 257
  machine 633
  workshop 691
  fight 720
  like a horse in a – 312
millennium
  number 98
  period 108
  futurity 121
  utopia 515
  hope 858
millesimal 99
millet seed 193
milliard 98
milliner 225
  man – 854
millinery *dress* 225
  ornament 847
  display 882
  man – 855
million 98
  multitude 102
  people 372
  populace 876
  for the –
    intelligible 518
    easy 705
  –s *money* 800
millionaire 803
mill-pond *level* 213
  pond 343
  store 636
mime 19, 599, 844
mimeograph 19
mimeotype 19
mimic 19
mimodrama 599
minacity 909
minaret 206
minatory 668
minauderie 855
mince *cut up* 44
  slow 275
  food 298
  stammer 583
  affected 855
  extenuate 937
  – the matter 868
  not – the matter
    affirm 525
    artless 703
  – the truth 544
mincemeat of
  make – 162
mincing 855

– steps 275
mind *intellect* 450
attend to 457
take care 459
believe 484
remember 505
will 600
willing 602
purpose 620
warning 668
desire 865
dislike 867
bear in – 451, 457
bit of one's – 527
food for the – 454
give the – to 457
have a – 602, 865
in the –
thought 451
topic 454
willing 602
make up one's –
484, 604
never – neglect 460
unimportant 643
not – 866
out of – 506
set one's – upon
604
speak one's – 582,
703
to one's – taste 850
love 897
willing – 602
– one's book 539
– one's business
456, 457
– at ease 827
make one's – easy
826
–'s eye 515
– what one is
about 864
minded 602, 620
mindful 457, 505
mindless
inattentive 458
imbecile 499
forgetful 506
insensible 823
mine
sap 162
hollow 252
open 260
snare 545
store 636
abundance 639
damage 659
attack 716
defence 717
explosive 727
dig a – plan 626
prepare 673
spring a –
unexpected 508
attack 716
– of information
700
–layer 726
–sweeper 726
–thrower 727
– of wealth 803
miner 252
sapper and – 726
mineral 358
– oil 356
mineralogy 358

Minerva 979
– invita 603, 709
– press 577, 594
mingle 41
miniature *small* 193
portrait 556
– painter 559
Minié rifle 727
minikin 193
minim *small* 32
music 413
minimize 36, 483,
934
minimum *small* 32
inferior 34
minion 899
type 591
minister *instru-
mentality* 631
remedy 662
director 694
aid 707
deputy 759
give 784
clergy 996
rites 998
– to 746
ministerial
clerical 995
ministering spirit
977
ministration
direction 693
aid 707
rite 998
ministry
direction 693
aid 707
church 995
clergy 996
miniver 223
minnesinger 597
minnow 193
minor *inferior* 34
infant 129
– key 413
Minorites 996
minority *few* 103
youth 127
Minos 694
minotaur 83
minster 1000
minstrel 416, 597
minstrelsy 415
mint *mold* 22
workshop 691
wealth 803
– of money 800
minuend 38
minuet 415, 840
minus *less* 34
subtracted 38
absent 187
deficient 304
loss 776
in debt 806
non-payment 808
minusculae 561
minute
– in degree 32
– of time 108
instant 113
– in size 193
record 551
compendium 596
to the – 132
– account 594

– attention 457
minuteness
care 459
minutiae 32, 79, 643
minx 887, 962
mirabile
– dictu &c. 870
mirabilis, annus –
872
miracle 83, 872
– play 599
miraculous 870
mirage 443
mire 653
mirror *imitate* 19
reflector 445
perfection 650
glory 873
hold up the – 525
hold the – up to
nature 554
magic – 443
mirth 836
misacceptation 235
misadventure 735
misadvised 699
misanthropy 911
misapply
misinterpret 523
misuse 679
mismanage 699
misapprehend 495,
523
misappropriate 679
misarrange 61
misbecome 925
misbegotten 243,
945
misbehave 851, 945
misbehavior 895,
947
misbelief 485
misbeliever 487,
984
miscalculate
misjudge 481
err 495
miscall 565
miscarry 732
miscegenation 41
miscellany
mixture 41
collection 72
generality 78
compendium 596
mischance 619, 735
mischief 619
do – 649
make – 649
mischief-maker
913, 941
miscible 41
miscite 544
miscompute 481,
495
misconceive 495,
523
misconduct 699,
947
– oneself 945
misconjecture 481
misconstrue 523
miscorrect 538
miscount 495
miscreance 485
miscreant 949

miscreated 945
misdate 115
misdeed 947
misdemean 945
misdemeanant 949
misdemeanor 947
misdevotion 988
misdirect 538, 699
misdo 945
misdoing 947
misdoubt 485, 523
mise en scène
appearance 448
drama 599
display 882
misemploy 679
miser 819
–'s hoard 800
miserabile dictu 839
miserable *small* 32
contemptible 943
unhappy 828
miserably *very* 31
miserere 215
sing – 950
misericordiam,
argumentum ad
– 914
miseries of human
life 828
miseris succurrere
disco 914
miserly 819
misery 828
put out of one's –
914
misestimate
misjudge 481
misfeasance 699,
947
misfit 24
misfortune
adversity 735
unhappiness 830
misgiving 485, 860
misgovern 699
misguide 495, 538
misguided 699
mishap *evil* 619
failure 732
misfortune 735
painful 830
Mishna 985
misinform 538
misinformed 491
misinstruct 538
misintelligence 538
misinterpretation
523
misjoined 24
misjudgment
sophistry 477
misjudge **481**
misinterpretation
523
mislay *derange* 61
lose 776
mislead *error* 495
misteach 538
deceive 545
mislike 867
mismanage 699
mismatch 15, 24
misname 565
misnomer **565**
misogamist 904,
911

misogyny 904
mispersuasion 538
misplace
derange 61
misplaced
intrusive 24
unconformable 83
displaced 185
misprint 495
misprision
concealment 528
guilt 947
– of treason 742
misprize 483, 929
mispronounce 583
misproportioned
243, 846
misquote 544
misreckon 481, 495
misrelish 867
misreport 495, 544
misrepresent
misinterpret 523
misteach 538
lie 544
misrepresentation
555
untruth 544, 546
misrule
misconduct 699
laxity 738
Lord of – 701
miss *girl* 19
neglect 460
error 495
unintelligible 519
fail 732
lose 776
want 865
courtesan 962
– one's aim 732
– fire 732
– stays 304
– one's way
uncertain 475
unskilful 699
missa cantata 998
missal 998
missay 563, 583
missend 699
misshapen 243, 846
missile 727
missing
non-existent 2
absent 187
disappear 449
– link 53, 83, 729
mission 625, 755
missionary 540, 996
missive 592
misspell 523
misspend 818
misstate 495, 544
misstatement 495,
546
mist 353, 424
in a – 528
seen through a –
519
–s of error 495
– before the eyes
443
mistake *error* 495
misconstrue 523
mismanage 699
failure 732
never was a

greater – 536
misteaching **538**
mister 373
misterm 565
misthink 481
mistime 135
mistral 349
mistranslate 523
mistress *lady* 374
  master 745
  possessor 779
  title 877
  love 897
  concubine 962
mistrust 485
misty [*see* mist]
  semi-transparent 427
misunderstand
  misinterpret 523
misunderstanding 495, 713
misuse **679**
mite *bit* 32
  small 193
  insufficiency 649
  money 800
  little – 129
miter *junction* 43
  angle 244
  crown 747, 999
Mithridate 662
mitigate *abate* 174
  improve 658
  relieve 834
mitigation
  [*see* mitigate]
  extenuation 937
mitraille 727
mitrailleur 727
mitten 225
mittimus 741
mix 41
  – oneself up with
  meddle 682
  co-operate 709
  – with 720
mixen 653
mixture **41**
  mere – 59
mix-up 59
mizzen 235
mizzle 348
mnemonics 505
Mnemosyne 505
moa 366
moan 405
  cry 411
  lament 839
moat *enclosure* 232
  ditch 259
  canal 350
  defence 717
mob *crowd* 72
  multitude 102
  vulgar 876
  hustle 929
  scold 932
  king – 876
  – cap 225
  – law
  authority 737
  illegality 964
mobile
  inconstant 149
  movable 264
  sensitive 822

mobility, the – 876
mobilize
  assemblage 72
  render movable 264
  – troops 722
mobocracy 737
mobster 361
moccasin 225
mock *imitate* 17, 19
  repeat 104
  erroneous 495
  deceptive 545
  chuckle 838
  ridicule 856
  disrespect 929
  – danger 861
  – modesty 855
  – sun 423
mockery
  [*see* mock]
  unsubstantial 4
  solemn – 882
  – delusion and
  snare
  sophistry 477
  deception 545
mocking-bird 19
modal 6, 7, 8
mode *state* 7
  music 413
  habit 613
  method 627
  fashion 852
  – of expression 569
mode, à la – 852
model *copy* 21
  prototype 22
  rule 80
  form 240
  representation 554
  sculpture 557
  perfection 650
  good man 948
  new – 658
  – after 19
  – condition 80
moderate
  average 29
  small 32
  allay **174**
  slow 275
  sufficient 639
  cheap 815
  temperate 953
  – circumstances
  mediocrity 736
moderately
  imperfect 651
moderation [*see*
  moderate] **174**
  mid-course 628
  inexcitability 826
moderato *music* 415
moderator 174
  lamp 423
  director 694
  mediator 724
  judge 967
modern 123
  music 415
  art 556
modest *small* 32
modesty

humility **881**
  purity 960
  mock – 855
modicum *little* 32
  allotment 786
modification
  difference 15
  variation 20a
  change 140
  qualification 469
modish 852
modulation
  variation 20a
  change 140
  music 413
module 22
modulus 84
modus: – operandi
  method 627
  conduct 692
  – in rebus 174
  – vivendi 723
mogul 745
Mohammedan 984
Mohawk
  swaggerer 887
  evil-doer 913
moiety 51, 91
moil *active* 682, 686
  exertion 686
moisture *wet* 337
  humid **339**
mokes 219
molar 330
molasses 396
mole *mound* 206
mold *condition* 7
  matrix 22
  convert 144
  form 240
  structure 329
  earth 342
  vegetation 367
  model 554
  carve 557
  decay 653
  turn to account 677
molded 820
  – on 19
molder 653, 659
molding 847
moldy 653, 659
  prominence 250
  color 432
  refuge 666
  defence 717
  spot 848
molecular 32
molecule 193
molehill *little* 193
  low 207
  trifling 643
molest *trouble* 830
molestation
  damage 649
  malevolence 907
mollia tempora 134
  – fandi 588
mollify *allay* 174
  soften 324
mollusk 366
mollycoddle 158
Molly Maguire 548
Moloch
  slaughter 361
  demon 980

heathen deity 986
molten 384
moment
  – *of time* 113
  importance 642
  for the – 111
  lose not a – 684
  not have a – 682
  on the spur of the
  – 612
momentous 152
momentum 276
Momus 838
monachism 995
monad 193
monarch 745
monarchy 737
monastery 1000
monastic 995
monasticism 984
monetary 800
  – arithmetic 11
money **800**
  wealth 803
  bad – 800
  command of – 803
  for one's – 609
  made of – 803
  make – 775
  raise – 788
  save – 817
  throw away one's
  – 818
  – to burn 641, 803
  – burning one's
  pocket 818
  – coming in 810
  – down 807
  – going out 809
  – market 800
  – matters 811
  – paid 809
  –'s worth
  useful 644
  price 812
  cheap 815
money-bag 800, 802
money-belt 800
money-broker 797
money-changer 797, 801
moneyed 803
moneyer 797
money-grubbing 775
moneyless 804
monger 797
mongrel
  mixture 41
  anomalous 83
  dog 366
  base 949
moniker 565
moniliform 249
monism 984
monition 527, 668
  information 527
  warning 668
monitor *hear* 418
  oracle 513
  pupil-teacher 540
  director 694
  adviser 695
  war-ship 726
  inward – 926
monitory

prediction 511
  dissuasion 616
  warning 668
monk 996
monkey
  imitative 19
  support 215
  catapult 276
  ridiculous 857
  play the – 499
  –jacket 225
  – trick
  absurdity 497
  sport 840
  – up 900
monkhood 995
monkish Latin 563
monochord 417
monochrome 429, 556
monocracy 737
monoculous 443
monode 445
monodrame 599
monody 597, 839
monogamist 904
monogamy 903
monogram
  sign 550
  cipher 533
  diagram 554
  letter 561
monograph
  publication 531
  writing 590
  book 593
  description 594
monolith 551
monolithic 983a
monologue
  soliloquy 589
  drama 599
monomachy 720
monomania 503
  obstinacy 606
  fanaticism 825
monomaniac 504
monomark 550
monoplane 273
monopolist 943
monopoly
  restraint 751
  possession 777
monostich 572
monosyllable 561
monotheism 983
monotonous
  uniform 16
  equal 27
  repetition 104
  permanent 141
  – *style* 575
  weary 841
  dull 843
monotype 591
monsoon 349
monsieur 370
monster
  exception 83
  large 192
  ugly 846
  prodigy 872
  evil-doer 913
  ruffian 949
monstrance 998
monstrosity
  [*see* monster]

forth – 509
not a – a – stirring 265
mouse-colored 432
mousehole 260
mouser 366
mousetrap 545
mousseux 353
moustache 256
mouth *entrance* 66
  receptacle 191
  brink 231
  opening 260
  eat 298
  estuary 343
  enunciate 580
  drawl 583
  deep –ed
  resonant 408
  bark 412
  down in the – 879
  make –s 929
  open one's – 582
  stop one's – 581
  word of – 582
  – honor
  falsehood 544
  show 882
  flattery 933
  pass from – to
  mouth 531
  – wash 652
  – watering 865
mouthful
  quantity 25
  small 32
  food 298
mouthpiece
  speaker 524
  information 527
  speech 582
mouthy *style* 577
moutonné 250
moutons, revenons
à nos – 660
movable 264, 270
movables 780
move *begin* 66
  motion 264
  propose 514
  induce 615
  undertake 676
  act 680
  offer 763
  excite 824
  get a – on 684
  good – 626
  on the – 293
  – forward 282
  – from 287
  – in a groove 82
  – heaven and
    earth 686
  – off 293
  – on *progress* 282
  activity 682
  – out of 295
  – quickly 274
  – slowly 275
  – to 894
moveless 265
movement
  motion 264
  music 415
  action 680
  activity 682

moved with 821
mover 164
movies 448, 599, 840
movie star 899
moving
  keep – 682
  self – 266
  – pictures 448
mow *shorten* 201
  smooth 255
  agriculture 371
  store 636
  – down
  destroy 162
moxa 384
M.P. 696
Mr. 373, 877
Mrs. 374
MS. 22, 590
much 31
make – of
  importance 642
  friends 888
  love 897
  endearment 902
  approval 931
  not say – for 932
  think – of 928, 931
  – ado *exertion* 686
  difficulty 704
  – ado about noth-
    ing
  over-estimate 482
  exaggerate 549
  unimportant 643
  unskilful 699
  – cry and little
    wool 884
  – the same
  identity 13
  similarity 17
  equality 27
  – speaking 584
mucid 352, 653
mucilage 352
muck 653
  run a – *kill* 361
  attack 716
  excitement 825
muckle 31
muckworm 819, 876
mucor 653
mucosity 352
mucronate 253
muculent 352
mud *marsh* 345
  semiliquid 352
  dirt 653
  clear as – 519
  stick in the – 704
  – guard 666
muddle *disorder* 59
  derange 61
  inattention 458
  absurd 497
  difficulty 704
  failure 732
  – one's brains 475
muddled 959
muddle-headed 499
muddy *moist* 339
  dim 422
  opaque 426
  color 429
  stupid 499

mudlark *dirty* 653
  commonalty 876
muezzin 550, 996
muff *incapable* 158
  dress 225
  bungle 699
  bungler 701
muffettee 225
muffle *wrap* 225
  silent 403
  deaden 408a
  conceal 528
  voiceless 581
  stammer 583
muffled *faint* 405
  latent 526
  – drums
  funeral 363
  non-resonance 408a
muffler 225, 384
mufti *undress* 225
  judge 967
  priest 996
mug *cup* 191
  face 234, 448
  pottery 384
  dupe 547
mug-house 189
muggy *moist* 339
  dim 422
  opaque 426
mugient 412
mugwump 607
mulatto
  mixture 41
  exception 83
mulct *steal* 791
  fine 974
mule *mongrel* 83
  beast of burden 271
  obstinate 606
muleteer 694
muliebrity 374
mull
  prominence 250
  sweeten 396
mullah 967, 996
muller 330
mullion 215
mullioned 219
multifarious
  irrelevant 10
  diverse 16a
  multiform 81
multiferous 102
multifid
  divided 51
multifold 81
multiformity 81
multigenerous 81
multilateral 236, 244
multilocular 191
multiloquence 582, 584
multinomial 102
multiparous 168
multipartite 44
multiple 84, 102
multiplex 81
multiplicand 84
multiplicate 81
multiplication
  increase 35
  arithmetic 85

multitude 102
  reproduction 163
  productiveness 168
multiplicator 84
multiplicity 102
multiplier 84
multiply 35
multipotent 157
multisonous 404
multitude 72, **102**
  the – 876
multum in parvo 596
multure 330
mum 581, 585
  –'s the word 403
mumble *chew* 298
  mutter 583
Mumbo Jumbo 979, 993
mummer 599
mummery
  absurdity 497
  imposture 545
  masquerade 840
  parade 882
mummify 363
mummy *dry* 340
  corpse 362
  beat to a – 972
mump *mutter* 583
  beg 765
mumper 767, 804
mumpish *sad* 837
mumps 837, 901a
munch 298
Munchausen 549
mundane
  world 318
  selfish 943
  irreligious 989
mundation 652
mundivagant 266
munerary 973
munerate 973
municipal 965
municipality 737
munificent 816
muniment
  evidence 465
  record 551
  defence 717
  security 771
munition
  materials 635
  defence 717
mural 717
murder 361
  – the King's Eng-
    lish
  solecism 568
  stammering 583
  the – is out 529
murderer 361
muricated 253
murky *dark* 421
  opaque 426
  black 431
  gloomy 837
murmur *purl* 348
  sound 405
  voice 580
  complain 839
murmurer 832
murrain 655
Murray *travel* 266

Lindley – 542
murrey 434
murrion 717
mus, nascitur ridi-
  culus – 509, 643
muscadine 400
muscle 159
muscular 159
muse 451
  [*and see* musing]
Muse *poetry* 597
  historic – 594
  unlettered – 579
musette 417
Muses, the – 416
museum
  collection 72
  store 636
mush 354
mushroom
  new 123
  fungus 367
  upstart 734
  low-born 876
  spring up like –s
    163
  – *anchor* 666
music **415**
  face the – 861
  set to – 416
  – of the spheres
  order 58
  universe 318
musical 413, 415, 416
  – comedy 599
  – ear
  musician 416
  hearing 418
  – instruments **417**
  – note 413
  – voice 580
music-hall 599, 840
musician **416**
musing 451
  – on other things
    458
musk 400
musket 727
  shoulder a – 722
musketeer 726
musketry 727
muslin
  semi-transparent 427
musnud
  support 215
  council 696
  scepter 747
muss 59
Mussulman 984
must *necessity* 601
  mucor 653
  compulsion 744
  it – follow 478
  I – say 535
mustachio 256
mustard 392, 393
  after meat – 135
  – gas 663, 727
mustard-seed 193
muster 72, 85
  pass – 639
  not pass – 651
  – courage 861
muster-roll 86
musty 401, 653

ihil – ad rem 10
  – tetigit quod non
    ornavit 850
ihilism 989
ihilist 165
ihility 2, 4
il 2, 4
  – admirari
    insensible 823
    no wonder 871
    disapproval 932
  – conscire sibi
    nullâ pallescere
    culpâ 946
  – desperandum
    858
ill unwilling 604
  refuse 764
iim 791
iimble 274, 682
iimble-witted 498,
    842
iimbus
    cloud 353
    halo 420
    glory 873
iimiety 641
iimis, ne quid –
    817
iimium ne crede
    colori 485
n'importe 643
Nimrod 361, 622
nincompoop 501
nine 98
  tuneful –
    music 416
    poetry 597
  – days' wonder
    transient 111
    unimportant 643
    no wonder 871
  – lives 359
  – men's morris 840
  – points of the
    law 777
ninefold 98
ninepins 840
ninety 98
ninny 501
Niobe 839
nip cut 44
    destroy 162
    shorten 201
    dram 298
    freeze 385
    pungent 392
    drink 959
  – in the bud
    check 201
    kill 361
    hinder 706
  – up 789
nipperkin 191
nippers 781
nipple 250
Nirwana 981
nis 980
nisi prius 741, 969
Nisus and Euryalus
    890
nisus formativus
    161
nitency 420
niter 392
nitor in adversum
    708

nitrous oxide 376
nit-wit 499, 501
niveous cold 383
    white 430
nixe demon 980
nixie fairy 979
nizam 745
nizy 501
N or M 78
no zero 101
    dissent 489
    negation 536
    refusal 764
  unable to say –
    605
  on – account 761
  have – business
    there 83
  – chicken 128, 131
  – choice 601, 609a
  – conjuror 501,
    701
  – consequence 643
  in – degree 32
  at – great distance
    197
  – doubt 474, 488
  have – end 112
  – end of great 31
    multitude 102
    length 200
  – fear 473
  – go 304, 732
  at – hand 32
  matter of – import
    4
  with – interval
    199
  – one knows who
    876
  – less 639
  – longer 122
  – love lost be-
    tween them 898
  – man's land 187,
    778
  – matter
    neglect 460
    unimportant 643
  and – mistake 474
  – more
    inexistent 2
    past 122
    dead 360
  – more than 32
  have – notion of
    489
  – object 643
  – one 4, 187
  – other 13, 87
  to – purpose
    shortcoming 304
    useless 645
    failure 732
  give – quarter 361
  – scholar 493
  make – scruple of
    602
  – great shakes
    small 32
    trifling 643
    imperfect 651
  – sooner said than
    done 113, 132
  – stranger to 490
  – such thing
    non-existent 2

unsubstantial 4
  contrary 14
  dissimilar 18
  – surrender 606,
    717
  – thank you 764
  at – time 107
  – wonder 871
Noah's ark 41, 72
nob 210
nobilitate 873
nobility 875
noble great 31
    important 642
    rank 873
    peer 875
    disinterested 942
    virtuous 944
noblesse 875
nobody
    unsubstantial 4
    zero 101
    absence 187
    low-born 876
  – knows
    ignorance 491
  – knows where
    distance 196
  – present 187
  – would think 508
noctambulation 266
noctivagant
    travel 266
    dark 421
noctograph 421
noctuary 421, 551
nocturnal
    night 126
    dark 421
    black 431
nocturne 415
nocuous 649
nod wag 314
    assent 488
    signal 550
    sleep 683
    command 741
    bow 894
  – of approbation
    931
  – of assent 488
nodding to its fall
    162, 306
noddle 210, 450
noddy 501
node 250
nodosity 250, 256
nodular 256
nodule 250
nodular 256
nodus, dignus vin-
    dice – 704
Noel 998
noggin 191
noise 402, 404
  – abroad 531
  make a – in the
    world 873
noiseless 403
noisome
    fetid 401
    bad 649
    unhealthy 657
nolens volens 601
noli me tangere

defiance 715
  excitable 825
  fastidious 868
nolition 603
nolle prosequi 624
nolumus leges
    Angliae mutari
    permanence 141
    continuance 143
    preservation 670
nom de: – guerre
    565
  – plume 565
nomad 268
nomadic 266
Nomancy 511
nomenclature 564
nominal
    unsubstantial 4
    word 562
    name 564
  – price 815
nomination 564,
    755
nominee 758
nominis umbra 4
Nomology 963
non:
  – compos mentis
    503
  – constat 477
  – deficit alter 100
  – est in ventus 187
  – haec in foedera
    536, 610
  – nobis Domine
    990
  – obstante 707
  – placet 489
  – possumus
    impossible 471
    obstinate 606
    refusal 764
  – nostrum tantas
    componere lites
    471, 713
  lex – scripta 963
  – semper erit
    aestas 111
  – sequitur 477
  – sum qualis eram
    140, 160
non-addition 38
non-admission 55
nonage 127
nonagenarian 98
non-appearance
    447
non-assemblage 73
non-attendance 187
nonce 118
  for the – 118, 134
nonchalance
    neglect 460
    insensibility 823
    indifference 866
non-coincidence 14
non-cohesive 47
non-com. 726
non-commissioned
    officer 745
non-committal 528,
    864
non-completion 730
non-compliance
    742, 764
nonconformity

difference 15
  exception 83
  dissent 489
    sectarianism 984
non-content 489
non-cooperation
    489, 927
nondescript 83
none 101
  – else 87
  – to spare 640
  – such
    superior 33
    exceptional 83
    very good 648
  – in the world 4
  – the worse 660
non-endurance 825
nonentity
    inexistence 2
    unsubstantial 4
    unimportant 643
non esse 2
non-essential 6,
    643
non-existence 2
non-expectance 508
non-extension 180a
non-fulfilment 730,
    732
  – of one's hopes
    509
non-imitation 20
non-interference
    inaction 681
    freedom 748
nonius 466
non-juror 489, 984
non-naturals 657
nonny 501
non-observance
    inattention 458
    desuetude 614
    infraction 773
    dereliction 927
nonpareil 648
    type 591
non-payment 808
non-performance
    non-completion
    730
    dereliction 927
non-plus
    uncertain 475
    difficulty 704
    conquer 731
non-preparation
    674
non-prevalence 614
non-residence 187
non-resistance 725,
    743
non-resonance
    408a
nonsense
    absurdity 497
    unmeaning 517
    trash 643
    talk – folly 499
non-subsistence 2
non-success 732
nonsuch [see none]
nonsuit defeat 731
    fail 732
    condemn 971
nonum prematur in
    annum 133

non-uniformity 16a
noodle 501
nook *place* 182
  receptacle 191
  corner 244
noology 450
noon *mid-day* 125
noon-day *light* 420
  clear as –
    intelligible 518
    manifest 525
nooscopic 450
noose *ligature* 45
  loop 247
  snare 545
  gallows 975
norma loquendi 567
normal
  intrinsic 5
  mean 29
  regular 82
  perpendicular 212
  – condition
  rule 80
normality 80, 502
Normand, répon-
  dre en – 544
Norns 601
North 278
  – and South 237
Northern 237
  – light 423
  – star
  constant 939
North-west
  passage 311
nose *prominence*
  250
  smell 398
  with one's – in
    the air 878
  lead by the – 615,
    737
  led by the – 749
  not see beyond
    one's –
    misjudge 481
    folly 499
    unskilful 699
  speak through
    the – 583
  thrust one's – in
    interjacence 228
    busy 682
  under one's –
    present 186
    near 197
    manifest 525
    defy 715
  put one's – out of
    joint *defeat* 731
    disrepute 874
  – ring 847
nose-dive 306
nosegay 400, 847
nosey 455
Nosology 655
nostalgia 833
nostril 351
  breath of one's –s
    359
  stink in the –s 401
nostrum 626, 662
not *negation* 536
  what is – 546
  what ought – 923
  – at all 32

– allowed 964
– amiss 618, 651,
  845
– any 101
– bad 651
– bargain for 508
– a bit 536
– to be borne 830
– a Chinaman's
  chance 471
– come up to 34
– cricket 923
– to be despised
  642
it will – do 923
– of the earth 987
– expect 508
– fail 939
– far from 197
– a few 102
– fit to be seen 846
– following 477
– grant 764
– guilty 946
– to be had 471,
  640
– having 187, 777a
– hardened 950
– hear of 764
– included 55
– know what to
  make of 519
– a leg to stand
  on 158
– likely 473
– a little 31
– matter 643
– to mention 585
– mind 823, 930
– often 137
– on your life 489
– one 101
– a particle 4
– particular 831
– pay 808
– a pin to choose
  27
– playing the
  game 923
– within previous
  experience 137
– to be put down
  604
– quite 32
– reach 304
– right 503
– sorry 827
– a soul 101
– on speaking
  terms 889
– the thing 925
– to be thought of
  incogitancy 452
  impossible 471
  refusal 764
  hopeless 859
  undue 925
  disapprobation
    932
  – trouble oneself
    about 460
  – understand 519
  – vote 609a
  – wonder 871
  – for the world
    603, 764
  – worth

trifling 643
useless 645
nota bene 457
notabilia 642
notabilities 875
notable
  manifest 525
  important 642
  active 682
  distinguished 873
notables 875
notably 31
notary 553, 968
notation 85
notch 198, **257**, 550
note *cry* 412
  music 413
  take cognizance
    450
  remark 457
  explanation 522
  sign 550
  record 551
  printing 591
  epistle 592
  minute 596
  money 800
  fame 873
  change one's – 607
  make a – of 551
  of – 873
  take – of 457
  – of admiration
    870
  – of alarm 669
  – of preparation
    673
note-book
  memorandum 505
  record 551
  compendium 569
  writing 590
noted 490, 873
noteworthy
  great 31
  exceptional 83
  important 642
nothing *nihility* 4
  zero 101
  trifle 643
  come to – 304, 732
  do – 681
  for – 815
  go for – 643
  good for – 646
  make – of
    under-estimate
      483
    fail 732
  take – by 732
  think of – 930
  worse than – 808
  – comes amiss 831
  – to do 681
  – to do with 764
  – doing 681
  – to go upon 471
  – in it 4
  – of the kind 18,
    536
  – loth 602
  – on 226
  – more to be said
    478
  – to signify 643
nothingness 2
notice *intellect* 450

observe 457
review 480
information 527
warning 668
bring into – 525
deserve – 642
give –
  manifest 525
  inform 527
  indicate 550
  short – 111
  take – of 450
  this is to give –
    457
  worthy of – 642
  – is hereby given
  publication 531
  – to quit 782
noticeable 31
notification 527
notion *idea* 453
notional 515
notoriety 531, 873
notorious
  known 490
  public 531
  famous 873
  infamous 874
notturno 415
notwithstanding 30
nought
  [*see* naught]
noun 564
nourish 707
nourishment
  food 298
nous 498
nous avons changé
  tout cela 140
nouveau riche 123,
  734, 876
Nova Zembla 383
novation 609
novel
  dissimilar 18
  new 123
  unknown 491
  tale 594
novelette 594
novelist 594
novice
  ignoramus 493
  learner 541
  bungler 701
  religious 996
novitiate 539, 673
novocaine 376, 381
novus homo 57,
  876
now 118
  – and then 136
  – or never 134
noways 32
nowhere 187
nowise 32, 536
noxious 649, 657
noyade 361, 972
noyerait dans une
  goutte d'eau, il
  se – 699
nozzle
  projection 250
  opening 260
  air-pipe 351
nuance 15, 465
nubibus, in – 2, 515
nubiferous 353, 426

nubile 131, 903
nucleus *middle* 68
  cause 153
  centre 222
  kernel 642
nuda veritas 494
nude 226, 849
nudge 550
nudity 226
nugacity 499, 645
nugae canorae 517,
  842
nugas, magno co-
  natu magnas –
  643
nugatory 158
  unimportant 643
nuggar 273
nugget *mass* 192
  money 800
nuisance 619, 830
null 4
  – and void
    inexistence 2
    powerless 158
    unproductive 169
    illegal 964
  declare – and void
    abrogation 756
    non-observance
      773
nulla dies sine
  lineâ 682
nullah 198
nullâ pallescere
  culpâ, nil con-
  scire sibi – 946
nulli secundus 33
nullibiety 187
nullify *inexistence* 2
  compensate 30
  destroy 162
  abrogate 756
  not observe 773
  not pay 808
nullity 2, 4
nullius jurare in
  verba magistri
  487
numb
  *physically insen-
    sible* 376, 381
  morally insensible
    823
  –skull 493
number
  part 51
  abstract – **84**
  count 85
  plural 100
  – of a magazine
    &c. 593
  – among 76
  take care of – one
    943
  – of times 104
numbered: days –
  kill 361
  necessity 601
  hopeless 859
  – with the dead
    360
numberless 105
numbers *many* 102
  verse 597
numbness 375, **381**
numerable 85

...meral 84, 85
...meration **85**
...merator 84
...merical 85
...merose
  many 102
...merous 102
...mismatics 800
...umps 501
...umskull 501
...un 996
...unc dimittis 990
...uncio 534, 758
...uncupation
  naming 564
...uncupatory
  informing 527
...unindation 794
...unnery 1000
...uptials 903
...rse *remedy* 662
  preserve 670
  help 707
  servant 746
  custodian 753
  fondle 902
  put to – 537
...urseling 129
...ursery *infancy* 127
  nest 153
  room 191
  garden 371
  school 542
  workshop 691
  – *rhymes* 597
  – *tale* 546, 594
...ursing home 493
...urture *feed* 298
  educate 537
  prepare 673
  aid 707
  – a belief 484
  – an idea 451
...ut
  – to crack
  fanatic 504
  riddle 533
  difficulty 704
  – oil 365
...ut-brown 433
nutmeg 393
nutmeg-grater 330
nuts 618, 829
nutshell *small* 32
  lie in a – 572
  little 193
  compendium 596
nutation 314
nutriment 298
nutrition 707
nutritious *food* 298
  healthy 656
  remedy 662
nutty 499
nuzzle 902
nyctalopy 443
nymph *girl* 129
  woman 374
  mythology 979
  sea – 341
nystagmus 443

O

O! *wonder* 870
  discontent 932

– for *desire* 865
oaf *fool* 501
  bungler 701
  changeling 980
oak *strong* 159
  heart of –
  hard 323
  brave 861
oakum 205
oar *paddle* 267
  oarsman 269
  instrument 633
  laboring – 686
  lie upon one's –s 681
  ply the –
  navigate 267
  exert 686
  pull an – 680
  put in an – 228, 682
  rest on one's –
  cease 142
  quiescence 265
  repose 687
  stroke – 693
oarsman 269
oasis *separate* 44
  exceptional 83
  land 342
oast-house 386
oath
  assertion 535
  bad language 908
  on – 543
  rap out –s 885
  upon – 768
oatmeal 298
obbligato 88, 415
obduction 223
obdurate
  obstinate 606
  severe 739
  malevolent 907
  graceless 945
  impenitent 951
obedience 743
obeisance *bow* 308
  submission 725
  courtesy 894
  reverence 928
obelisk 206, 551
Oberon 979
obese 194
obesity 192
obey 743
  be subject to 749
  – a call 615
  – the helm 705
  – rules 82
obfuscate 421, 426
obfuscated
  drunk 959
obit 360, 363
  post – 360, 363
obiter dictum
  irrelevant 10
  occasion 134
  interjacent 228
obituary 360, 594
object *thing* 3
  matter 316
  take exception 469
  intention 620
  ugly 846
  disapprove 932
  be an –

important 642
– to *dislike* 867
– *lesson* 82
objection 706, 932
  no – 762
objectionable
  inexpedient 647
  wrong 923, 947
objective
  extrinsic 6
  material 316
objector
  conscientious – 710
objurgate 932
oblate 201
  – spheroid 249
oblation *gift* 784
  religious - 990
oblectation 827
obligation
  necessity 601
  promise 768
  conditions 770
  debt 806
  confer an – 648
  feeling of – 916
  under an – 916, 926
oblige *benefit* 707
  compel 744
  duty 926
oblige, bien –
  refusal 764
obliged
  necessity 601
  grateful 916
  duty 926
obligee 800
obliging
  helping 707
  courteous 894
  kind 906
obliquation 279
obliquity
  slope **217**
  vice 945
  – of judgment 481
  – of vision 443
obliteration **552**
  – of the past 506
oblivion **506**
  nothingness 2
  pardon 506
  forgiveness 918
  redeem from – 505
  – of benefits 917
  – of time 115
oblivious 506
oblong 200
  – spheroid 249
obloquy
  disrepute 874
  disapprobation 932
  detraction 934
obmutescence 581, 585
obnoxious
  pernicious 649
  unpleasing 830
  hateful 898
  – to *liable* 177
obnubilated 422
oboe 417
obreption 528
obscene 653, 961

obscurantist 421, 519, 710
obscure *dark* 421
  dim 422
  unseen 447
  uncertain 475
  unintelligible 519
  eclipse 874
  ignoble 876
obscurity *style* **571**
obscurum per obscurius 519
obsecration 765
obsequies 363
obsequious
  subject 749
  servile 886
  courteous 894
  respectful 928
  flattery 932
observance *rule* 82
  attention 457
  habit 613
  practice 692
  fulfilment **772**
  duty 926
  rite 998
observant
  friar 996
observation
  intellect 450
  idea 453
  attention 457
  assertion 535
  – car 272
observatory 318
observe [see *observance, observation*]
  remark 535
  – a duty 926
  – rules 82
observer 444
obsess 860, 992
obsession 716
obsidional 716
obsolete *old* 124
  words 563
  effete 645
obstacle 179, 706
obstant, Fata – 601
obstetrician 631
obstetrics 161, 662
obstinacy **606**
  prejudice 481
obstipation 261
obstreperous 173, 404
obstruct *close* 261
  hinder 706
  – the passage of light 426
  – the view 424
obstructive
  opponent 710
obstruent 706
obstupefaction 823
obstupui steteruntque comæ 860
obtain *exist* 1
  prevail 78
  get 775
  – under false pretences 791
obtainable 470
obtenebration 421
obtestation 765

obtrectation 934
obtrude
  interfere 228
  insert 300
  meddle 682
obtruncate 201
obtrusion 228, 706
obtrusive
  interfering 228
  vulgar 851
  rude 895
obtund *mitigate* 174
  blunt 254
  deaden 376
  paralyze 823
obturate 261
obturator 263
obtuse *blunt* 253
  insensible 376
  imbecile 499
  dull 823
  – angle 244
obtuseness 456a
obumbrate 421
obverse 234
obviate 706
obvious *visible* 446
  evident 474
  clear 518
  manifest 525
ocarina 417
occasion
  juncture 8
  opportunity **134**
  cause 153
  befit the – 646
  have – for 630
  on the present – 118
  on the spur of – 612
occasional 475
occasionally 136
occidental 236, 560
occiput 235
occision 361
occlusion 261
  unintelligible 919
  latent 526
  hidden 528
  – art 992
occultism 984
occultation 449, 528
occupancy 186, 777
occupant 188, 779
occupation
  business 625
  in the – of 188
  – road 627
occupied 682
  – by 188
  – with 457, 625
occupier 188, 779
occupy 186, 777
  – the chair 693
  – oneself with 457, 625
  – the mind 451, 457
  – a post 737
  – time 106
occur 1, 151
  – to the mind 451
  – in a place 186
occurrence 151
  of daily – 613
occursion 276

ocean 341
plough the – 267
oceanography 341
ocher 433, 439
yellow – 436
ochlocracy 737
o'clock 114
know what's –
698
octagon 244
octahedron 244
Octateuch 895
octave
eight 98
music 413
period 108
octavo 593
octet 98
octifid 99
octodecimo 593
octogenarian 98,
130
octoroon 41
octroi 812
octuple 98
ocular 441
– demonstration
see 441
visible 446
– inspection 441
oculis subjecta
fidelibus 446
oculist 662
od force 992
odalisque 746
odd remaining 40
exception 83
single 87
insane 503
vulgar 851
ridiculous 853
– fellows 712
– fish 857
oddity 857
oddments 51
odds inequality 28
superiority 33
chance 156
discord 713
at – 24, 713
long – 704
what's the – 643
– against one 665
the – are 472
– and ends
remainder 40
mixture 41
part 51
useless 645
ode 597
odi profanum
vulgus 878
Odin 979
odious
disagreeable 830
ugly 846
hateful 898
odium disgrace 874
hatred 898
blame 932
odium theologicum
481, 988
church 995
odograph 200
odometer 200
odontoid 250, 253
odor 398

in bad – 932
– of sanctity 897
odylic force 992
odzookens 870
Oedipus 462, 524
– complex 897
Davus sum non –
703
oeil de maitre 459
o'er [see over]
oeuvre 161
of: – all things 33
– course 82, 154
– late 123
– one mind 23
– no effect 169
– old 122
– a piece
uniform 16
similar 17
agreeing 23
off 196
be – 623
keep – 623
make – with 791
move – 287
sheer – 287
stand – 287
start – 293
– one's balance
605
throw – one's
center 874
– one's guard 260,
508
– one's hands 776
take – one's hands
785
– one's head 503
– one's legs 284,
309
– one's mind 452
– and on
periodical 138
changeable 149
irresolute 605
throw – the scent
uncertain 475
avoid 623
– side 238
– with you 297
offal 653
offence attack 716
anger 900
guilt 947
offend 830, 945
– against the law
964
offensive
unsavory 395
fetid 401
foul 653
aggressive 716
displeasing 830
distasteful 867
obnoxious 898
– and defensive
alliance 712
– to ears polite 579
offer proposal 763
– the alternative
609
– a choice 609
– of marriage 902
– oneself 763
– up prayers 990
– sacrifice 990

– for sale 796
offering gift 784
burnt – 990
sin – 952
offertory gift 784
worship 990
rite 998
off-hand soon 132
inattentive 458
careless 460
spontaneous 612
office doing 170
room 191
business 625
mart 799
worship 900
do one's – 772
good –s 724, 906
hold – 693
kind –s 906
do an ill – 907
man in – 694
officer director 694
commander 745
constable 965
offices
kitchen &c. 191
official certain 474
true 494
business 625
man in office 694
authoritative 737
master 745
servant 746
officialism 739
officiate
business 625
act 680
conduct 692
religious 998
officio ex –
officer 694
authority 737
duly 924
officinal 613
officious 682
offing 196, 341
offscourings 645,
653
offset
compensation 30
offspring 167
offshoot adjunct 39
part 51
effect 154
offspring 167
offspring effect 154
posterity 167
ofuscate 121, 426
often repeated 104
frequent 136
most – 613
– to be met with
136
ogee 847
Ogham 590
ogive 215
ogle look 441
desire 865
rude 895
endearment 902
ogpu 696
ogre bugbear 860
evil-doer 913
demon 980
oil lubricate 332
grease 355, 356

pour – on
relieve 834
– on the troubled
waters 174, 714
– lamp 423
– stove 386
oiled drunk 959
oilcloth 223
oilskin 386
oil-painting 556
oily smooth 255
greasy 355
servile 886
courteous 894
flattery 933
oinomania 959
ointment
grease 356
remedy 662
O.K. 58
old 124
of – 122
– age 128
die of – age 729
– bachelor 904
– clothes 225
– fashioned 851
– fogey 501, 857
– joke 842
– maid cards 840
spinster 904
– man veteran 130
husband 903
– man of the sea
706
– Nick 978
– school 124
obstinate 606
habit 613
pay off – scores
718
– song
repetition 104
trifle 643
cheap 815
– stager
veteran 130
actor 599
proficient 700
– story
repetition 104
stale news 532
love 897
– times 122
one's – way 613
– woman fool 501
wife 903
Oldbuck 122
olden 124
older 128
oldest inhabitant
not in memory of
– 137
old-fashioned 124,
851
oldness 124
oleagine 356
oleaginous 355
oleomargarine 356
oleum addere
camino 35, 173
olfactory 398
olid 401
oligarch 745
oligarchy 737
olio 41
olive-branch

infant 129
offspring 167
pacification 723
olive-green 435
olla podrida 41
Olympiad 720
Olympus 981
omber|840
ombres chinoises
448
omega end 67
omelet 298
omen 512
ominate 511
ominous
predicting 511
indicating 550
danger 665
hopeless 859
omission
incomplete 53
exclusion 55
neglect 460
failure 732
non-observance
773
guilt 947
omitted 2, 187
omne tulit
punctum 731
omnibus 272
omnifarious 81
omnific 168
omniform 81
omnigenous 81
omnipotence 157,
976
omnipresence 186,
976
omniscience 490,
976
omnium gatherum
mixture 41
confusion 59
assemblage 72
omnivorous
eating 298
desire 865
gluttony 957
omphalos 68
on forwards 282
– account of 155
– all accounts 52
– that account 155
– approval 463
– an average 29
– the brink of 32
– the cards 152
– foot duration 106
event 151
doing 170
– the fire 730
– all fours 13, 23
– the other hand
30
– one's head 218
– the increase 35
– a large scale 31
– these lines 627
– the move 264
– the nail 118
– no account 32
– no occasion 107
– a par 27
– the part of 9
– the point of 111
– the present oc-

casion 118
- trial 463
- the whole 50
on dit 532, 588
once *past* 119, 122
seldom 137
at - 113, 132
- for all *final* 67
infrequency 137
tell one - 527
determine - 604
choose 609
- in a blue moon 137
- more 90, 104
- over 457
- upon a time
time 106
different time 119
formerly 122
- in a way 137
Ondine 979
one *identical* 13
whole 50
unity 87
somebody 372
married 903 -
all - to 823
at - with *agree* 23
concur 178
concord 714
make - of 186
neither - nor the other 610
of - *accord* 488
- and all
whole 50
general 78
unanimous 488
from - to another
transfer 783
- thing with another 476
- of the best 948
- bone and one flesh 903
- consent 178, 488
- of these days 121
- fell swoop 113, 173
- fine morning 106
- and a half 87
- horse 643
- idea 481
- jump 113
- leg in the grave 160
as - man 488, 709
- mind 178, 488
- by one
separately 44
respectively 79
unity 87
both the - and the other 89
the - or the other 609
- over the eight 959
- and the same 13
on - side 217, 236
- step 840
- in ten thousand 648, 948
- at a time 87
- or two 100
with - voice 488

- in a way 83
- way or another 627
at - with
agree 23
concur 178
concord 174
one-eyed 443
oneirocritic 524
oneiromancy 511
oneness 13
onerous *bad* 649
difficult 704
burdensome 706
troublesome 830
oneself 13
have all to - 777
kill - 361
take merit to - 884
take upon -
will 600
undertake 676
talk to - 589
true to - 604a
be - again 660
one-sided
misjudging 481
wrong 923
dishonorable 940
onion 393
onlooker 444
only *small* 32
simple 42
single 87
imperfect 651
if - 865
- think 870
- yesterday 123
only-begotten 87
onomancy 511
onomatopoeia 560, 564
onset *beginning* 66
attack 716
onslaught 716
ontology 1
onus *burden* 706
duty 926
- probandi
uncertainty 475
doubt 485
onward 282
onychomancy 511
onyx 847
oof 800
ooze *emerge* 295
flow 348
semiliquid 352
- out
disclosure 529
opacity **426**
opal 847
opalescent 427, 440
opaque 426
open *begin* 66
expand 194
unclose 260
manifest 525
reveal 529
frank 543
artless 703
break - 173
lay - 226
lay oneself - to 177
leave the matter - 705

pry - 173
throw - 296
- and above board 703, 939
- air 220, 338
- arms *willing* 602
friendship 888
social 892
courtesy 894
- the ball 62, 66
- a case 476
- country 344
in - court 525, 531
- a discussion 476
- to discussion 475
- the door to
cause 153
facilitate 705
permit 760
with - doors 531
- enemy 891
- eyes *see* 441
attention 457
discovery 480a
expectation 507
inform 527
undeceive 529
teach 537
predetermination 611
wonder 870
- fire 716
- house 892
- into
conversion 144
river 348
- the lips 529
- the lock 480a
- market 799
- one's mind 529
- order 194
- one's purse-strings 809
- question 461, 475
- rupture 713
- sesame 631, 993
- the sluices 297
- space 180
- to suspicion 485
- to *liable* 177
facile 705
- the trenches 716
- up *begin* 66
disclose 529
- to the view 446
- war 722, 889
- warfare 722
- the wound 824
opening
beginning 66
opportunity 134
space 180
gap 198
aperture **260**
open-handed 809, 816
open-hearted
veracious 543
artless 703
liberal 703
honorable 939
open-mouthed
cry 411
expectation 507
speak 582
loquacious 584

desire 865
wonder 870
opera *music* 415
poetry 597
drama 599
- glass 445
- hat 225
- house 599
opéra bouffe 599
operculum 261
operae pretium est 646
operandi, modus 627, 692
operate *cause* 153
produce 161
act 170
work 680
- upon *motive* 615
operation
[see operate]
arithmetical - 85
in - 680
put in - 677
surgical - 662
operative
acting 170
workman 690
operator
surgeon 662
doer 690
operculated 261
operculum 223
operetta 415
operose 686, 704
ophicleide 417
ophiology 368
ophiomancy 511
ophthalmia 443
ophthalmic 441
opiate 174
opine 484
opiniative 481
opiniator 606
opinion 484
give an - 480
have too high an - of oneself 880
popular - 488
system of -s 484
wedded to an - 606
opinionate 481, 606
opinionated 474
self- 880
opiniâtre 481
opinionist 474, 606
opitulation 707
opium *soothe* 174
deaden sense 376
bane 663
opium-eater 683
oppidan 188
oppilation 706
opponent **710**, 891
opportune
well-timed 134
expedient 646
opportunism 605, 646
opportunity 134
lose an - 135
oppose *contrary* 14
counteract 179
evidence 468
clash 708
opposite 14

- scale 30
- side 237
opposition
[see oppose] **708**
the - 710
oppositionist 710
oppress *molest* 649
severe 739
malevolence 907
oppressed with melancholy 837
oppressive *hot* 382
painful 830
oppressor 739, 913
opprobrium 874
oppugnation 708, 719
optative 865
optical 441
- instruments **445**
- lantern 448
optician 445
optics *light* 420, 445
optics *sight* 441
optimacy 875
optimates 875
optime! 931
optimism 482, 858
optimist 858
flatterer 935
option 609
optional 600
optometer 443
optometry 445
opulence 803
opuscule 593
or *yellow* 436
orange 439
alternative 609
oracle 500, **513**
Oracle, Sir -
positive 474
vanity 880
blusterer 887
oracular
answering 462
ambiguous 475
wise 498
prediction 511
oral *information* 527
voice 580
speech 582
- communication 588
- evidence 467
orange *round* 249
colour **439**
orangery 371
orarium 999
oration 582
funeral - 363
orator 582
oratoric 415
oratory
speaking 582
place of prayer 1000
orb *region* 181
circle 247
luminary 423
eye 441
sphere of action 625
- of day *sun* 318
luminary 423
- of night 318

orbicular 247
orbit *circle* 247
 heavens 318
 path 627
orchard 371
orchestra
 music 415
 musicians 416
 instruments 417
 theater 599
orchestral 415
orchestrate 60, 413, 416
orchestration 413
orchestrelle 417
ordain
 command 741
 commission 755
 due 924
 legal 963
 God 976
 church 995
ordained *due* 924
 clergy 996
ordeal
 experiment 463
 trouble 828
 sorcery 992
 – of battle 722
order
 regularity 58
 arrangement 60
 class 75
 record 551
 requisition 630
 direct 693
 command 741
 money 800
 rank 873
 quality 875
 decoration 877
 law 963
 at one's – 743
 call to – 932
 in – 620
 keep in – 693
 money – 800
 out of – 651
 put in – 60
 recur in regular – 138
 set in – 60
 set one's house in – 673
 standing – 613
 in working – 673
 – of the day
  conformity 82
  events 151
  habit 613
  plan 626
  command 741
 pass to the – of the day 624
orderless 59
orderly
 regular 58, 80
 arrange 60
 conformable 82
 servant 746
 – of succession 63
 – of things 80
orders, holy – 995
 in – 996
ordinal 998
ordinance
 command 741

law 963
 rite 998
ordinary *usual* 82
 meal 298
 habitual 613
 imperfect 651
 ugly 846
 simple 849
 in – *store* 636
 lie in – 681
 – condition
  rule 80
 – course of things 613
ordinate 466
ordination
 measurement 466
 command 741
 commission 755
 church 995
 rite 998
ordnance 727
ordonnance 963
ordure 653
ore 635
ore rotundo 577
oread 979
orectic 865
organ *music* 417
 voice 580
 instrument 633
 internal –s 221
 – point 413
organic *state* 7
 structural 329
 protoplastic 357
 – change 146
 – chemistry 357
 – remains 357
  dead 329
organism 329
organist 416
organization 60
 production 161
 structure 329
 animated nature 357
organize
 arrange 60
 produce 161
 plan 626
organized hypocrisy 544
organology 329
orgasm 173
orgies 954
oriel *recess* 191
 corner 244
 window 260
 chapel 1000
Orient 236, 420
orifice
 beginning 66
 opening 260
oriflamme 550
Origenism 984
origin 66, 153
 derive its – 154
original
 dissimilar 18
 not imitated 20
 model 22
 initial 66
 individual 79
 exceptional 83
 cause 153
 invented 515

unaccustomed 614
 laughing-stock 857
 return to – *state* 660
originality 600
 want of – 843
originate *begin* 66
 cause 153
 invent 515
 – in 154
originator 164
originative 168
Orion's belt 318
orismology 562, 564
orison *request* 765
 worship 990
orlop deck 211
ormolu
 sham 545
 ornament 847
Ormuzd 979
ornament
 in writing 577
 adornment 847
 glory 873
 excess of – 851
ornamental art 847
 painting 556
ornate
 – *writing* 577
 ornamental 847
ornavit, nihil tetigit quod non – 850
orniscopy 511
ornithology 368
ornithomancy 511
orotundity 577
orphan 893
Orpheus 416
orpiment 436
orrery 318
orthodox
 conformable 82
 – *religion* 983a
 – dissenter 984
orthodoxy 983a
orthoepy 562, 580
orthogonal 212
orthography 561
orthology 494
orthometry 466, 597
orthopaedy 662
orthopraxy 662
orts *remnants* 40
 useless 645
 (*trifles* 643)
oryctology
 minerals 358
 organic remains 368
oscillation
 change 149
 motion 314
 center of – 222
oscitancy
 opening 260
 sleepy 683
osculation
 contact 199
 endearment 902
Osiris 979
Osmanli 984
osmose 302
Ossa on Pelion 72, 319

osseous 323
ossify 323
ossuary 363
ostensible
 appearance 448
 probable 472
 manifest 525
 plea 617
ostentation 882
osteology 329
ostiary
 doorkeeper 263
 mouth 260
 estuary 343
ostler 370, 746
ostracize *exclude* 55
 eject 297
 banish 893
 censure 932
 punish 972
ostrich, stomach of an – 957
Othello's occupation's gone 757
other 15, 37
 do unto –s as we would men should do unto us 942
 enter into the feelings of –s 906
 every – 138
 put oneself in the place of –s 942
 the – day 123
 – extreme 14
 – side of the shield 468
 – than 18
 – things to do 683
 – time 119
 just the – way 14
 in – words 522
 otherwise 18
otia fecit, Deus nobis haec – 840
otiose 683
otium cum dignitate 685
ottar, otto 400
ottoman 215
oubliette
 ambush 530
 prison 752
ough! 874
ought:
 – to be 922, 926
oui-dire 532
oui-ja board 992
ounce *weight* 319
ourselves 372
oust *eject* 297
 dismiss 756
 deprive 789
out *exterior* 220
 in error 495
 come – 446
 go – *egress* 295
 cool 385
 play – 729
 send – 297
 time – of joint 735
 waters – 337
 – at elbows 874
 – at heels 804
 – of [*see below*]

– and out 52
 – in one's reckoning 495
 – upon it
  malediction 908
  censure 932
 – with it
  disclose 529
  obliterate 552
out of *motive* 615
  insufficient 640
 get well – 671
 – breath 688
 – cash 804
 – character 24
 – whole cloth 544
 – the common 83
 – conceit with 867
 – countenance
  disrepute 874
  humbled 879
 – danger 664
 – date
  anachronism 115
  old 124
  ill-timed 135
  unfashionable 851
 – one's depth
  deep 208
  shortcoming 340
  difficult 704
  rash 863
 – doors 220, 338
 turn – doors 297
 – employ 681
 – favor 867
 – focus 447
 – gear
  disorder 59
  powerless 158
  unprepared 674
 – hand *soon* 132
  completed 729
 – harness 748
 – health 655
 – hearing 196, 419
 – humour
  discontent 832
  anger 900
 – a job 681
 – joint
  disorder 59
  impotent 158
  evil 619
 – luck 735
 – one's mind 503
 – order
  disorder 59
  unconformity 83
  imperfect 651
  patience 825
 – the perpendicular 217
 – place
  disorder 59
  unconformable 83
  displaced 185
  inexpedient 647
 – pocket *loss* 776
  poverty 804
  debt 806
 – one's power 471
 – print 552
 – all proportion 31
 – the question
  impossible 471
  dissent 489

overmatch
unequal 28
superior 33
strength 159
conquer 731
over-measure 641
overmuch 641
over-night 122
– bag 191
over-officious 682
overpaid 816
overpass
exceed 33
transgress 303
overpersuade 615
overplay 855
overplus 40, 641
overpoise 179
overpower
subdue 731
emotion 824
overpowering
strong 159
overpraise
over-rate 482
exaggerate 549
flatter 933
overprize 482
overrate 482
overreach *pass* 303
deceive 545
baffle 731
overreckon 482
over-refinement
477
over-religious 955
override
superior 33
influence 175
pass 303
hinder 706
defeat 731
authority 737
severity 739
abrogate 756
over-righteous 988
overrule 737, 756
overruling
important 642
overrun
presence 186
spread 194
redundance 641
despoil 659
over-running
printing 591
over-scrupulous
939
overseas 57
oversee 693
overseer 694
over-sensitive 822
overset *invert* 218
level 308
subvert 731
overshadow
darken 421
repute 873
disrepute 874
overshoes 225
overshoot the mark
go beyond 303
exaggerate 549
overdo 682
clumsy 699
oversight
inattention 458

error 495
superintendence
693
failure 732
overskip 303
oversleep 683
overspent 688
overspread
disperse 73
be present 186
cover 233
overstate 549
overstep 303
overstock 641
overstrain
extol 482
fatigue 688
oversupply 641
overt 525
– *act* 680
overtake 292
overtaken
tipsy 959
overtask
overtax }679, 688
overthrow
undo 145
destroy 162
level 308
confute 479
vanquish 731
overthrown
vanquished 732
overthwart 708
overtired 688
overtone 413
overtop 31, 33, 206
overture
precursor 64
music 415
peace 723
offer 763
request 765
overturn
destroy 162
invert 218
level 308
confute 479
overvalue 482
overweening
excess 641
rash 863
pride 878
conceit 880
insolence 885
overweigh
exceed 33
influence 175
overrate 482
overwhelm
ruin 162
redundant 641
affect 824
overwhelmed
defeated 732
subjection 749
overwhelming
strong 159
wonderful 870
over-wise 880
overwork 679, 688
overwrought
exaggerated 549
emotion 824
affectation 855
over-zealous 825
oviform 249

ovo, in – 153
ovoid 247, 249
ovule 247
owe 806
– it to oneself 926
owing *debt* 806
– to *effect* 154
attribution 155
owl *fool* 501
–'s light 422
–s to Athens 641
own *assent* 488
divulge 529
possess 777
property 780
come by one's –
775
condemned out of
one's – mouth
479
consult one's –
pleasure 943
hold one's – 737
know one's –
mind 604
not know one's –
interest 699
not know one's –
mind 605
will of one's – 604
of one's – accord
600, 602
pay in one's –
coin 718
look with one's –
eyes 459
– flesh and blood
11
throw a stone in
one's – garden
699
take the law into
one's – hands
722, 964
out of one's –
head 600
after one's –
heart 897
look after one's –
interest 943
stand in one's –
light 699
act on one's –
responsibility
738
at one's – risk 926
have one's – way
will 600
easy 705
succeed 731
authority 737
freedom 748
– oneself in the
wrong 950
owner *possessor* 779
without an – 777a
ownership
property 780
ox 366, 373
hot enough to
roast an – 382
oxidation 659
oxymoron 24
oyer and terminer,
court of – 966
oyez! *hear* 418
O yes 531

Oyez! *hear* 418
publication 531

P

P:
mind one's –'s
and Q's
care 459
polite 894
duty 926
pabulum 298, 316
mental – 454
pace *walk* 264
journey 266
measure 466
permission 760
keep – with
concur 178
velocity 274
put through one's
–s 525
show one's –s
ostentation 882
– *tanti nominis*
928
– up and down 266
pachydermatous
376, 823
pacific 172, 721
pacification 723
pacificism 721
pacify 174
pack *arrange* 60
assemblage 72
locate 184
squeeze 195
prepare 673
burden 706
send –ing 297
– of nonsense 643
– off *depart* 293
eject 297
– up 229
package
assemblage 72
location 184
packer 673
packet
assemblage 72
ship 273
pack-horse 271
pack-saddle 215
pack-thread 205
pact 23, 769
Pactolus 803
pad *thicken* 194
line 224
horse 271
soft 324
expatiate 577
tablet 590
padding *lining* 224
stopper 263
soft 324
words 573
paddle *walk* 260
row 267
oar 633
– one's own canoe
conduct 692
free 748
– steamer 273
paddock 232
padishah 745
padlock 45, 752

put a – on one's
lips 585
padre 996
padrone 745
paean
rejoicing 838
celebration 883
gratitude 916
approbation 931
worship 990
paganism 984
page
numeration 85
printing 591
book 393
attendant 746
wedding 903
– *proof* 591
pageant 448, 882
paginate 85
pagoda 206, 1000
pah 717
pail 191
paillard 962
paillasse 215
pain *physical* - **378**
moral - **828**
penalty 974
painfulness **830**
painfully *very* 31
painim 984
painless 827
pains 686
get for one's – 973
take – 686
– and penalties
974
painstaking
active 682
laborious 686
paint *coat* 223
color 428
deceive 545
delineate 556
ornament 847
– the lily 641
paintable 845
painter *rope* 45
artist 559
painting **556**
pair *similar* 17
combine 48
couple 89
– off *average* 29
marry 903
pair-oar 273
pairs *cards* 840
pal 711, 890
palace 189
bishop's – 1000
floating – 273
Paladin 717, 726
hero 861
palaestra
school 542
arena 728
palais de vérité 703
palanquin 272
palatable 394, 829
palatal *letter* 561
palate 390
tickle the – 394
palatial *palace* 189
ostentatious 882
palatinate 181
palatine 745
Palatine Court 966

palaver
  unmeaning 517
  speech 582
  loquacity 584
  colloquy 588
  council 696
pale *stake* 45
  region 181
  inclosure 232
  limit 233
  dim 422
  colourless 429
  emotion 821
  frightened 860
turn –
  lose color 429
  emotion 821
  fear 860
  – of the church
    995
  – its ineffectual
    fire
    dim 422
    out of repute 874
pale-faced 429
paleocrystic 124
paleography
  past 122
  philology 560
paleology *past* 122
  language 160
paleontology 368
paleozoic 124
palestric 686, 720
paletot 225
palette 556
palfrey 271
palimpsest 147, 528
palindrone
  inversion 218
  neology 563
paling 232, 752
palingenesia 163
palingenesis 660
palinode 597
palinody 607
palisade
  wall 212
  defence 717
  prison 752
pall *covering* 223
  mantle 225
  funeral 363
  disgust 395
  insignia 747
  weary 841
  dislike 867
  satiety 869
  canonicals 999
palladium
  safety 664
Pallas 979
pall-bearer 363
pallet *support* 215
  painter's – 556
palliament 225
palliate
  moderate 174
  mind 658
  relieve 834
  extenuate 937
palliative 174
  remedy 662
pallid 429
pallium 999
pall-mall 840
pallone 840

pallor 429
palm
  measure of length
    200
  trophy 733
  steal 791
  laurel 877
  bear the – 873
  grease the –
    induce 615
    give 784
  itching – 865
  win the – 731
  – off, – upon 545
  – tree 367
palmated 257
palmer
  traveller 268
  clergy 996
palmist 513
palmistry 511
palmy
  prosperous 734
  pleasant 829
  – days
    prosperous 734
    pleasure 827
palpable
  material 316
  tactile 379
  obvious 446
  manifest 525
  – obscure 421
palpation 379
palpitate
  tremble 315
  color 440
  emotion 821
  fear 860
palsy
  impotence 158
  *physical insensi-
    bility* 376
  disease 655
  *mental insensi-
    bility* 823
palter
  falsehood 544
  shift 605
  elude 773
paltry *small* 32
  unimportant 643
  mean 940
paludal 345
pampas 344
pamper 902, 954,
  957
pamphlet 531, 593
pamphleteer 595
Pan 979
pan 191
panacea 662
panache 256, 847
panama *hat* 225
panary 636
pancake 298
pandar [*see* pander]
Pandean pipes 417
pandect
  knowledge 490
  dissertation 595
  compendium 596
  code 963
pandemonium 59,
  404, 982
  inhabitants of –
    978

pandemic 657
pander *pimp* 962
  – to *instrument*
    631
  help 707
  flatter 933
pandiculation
  expansion 194
  opening 260
  sleepy 683
Pandoor 726
Pandora's box 619
  bottom of 858
paned 440
panegyric 931
panegyrize 482
panel *list* 86
  layer 204
  partition 228
  accused 938
  jury 967
  sliding – 545
panelling 847
pang 378, 828
Pangloss 492
panguid 355
panhandle 765, 767,
  876
panic 860
panier 225
Panjandrum 875
pannel 213
pannikin 191
pannier 191
panoply 717, 727
panopticon 752
panorama 448, 556
panoramic 78, 446
  – view 441
pansophy 490
pant *heat* 382
  fatigue 688
  emotion 821
  – for 865
pantaloon
  old man 130
  pantomimist 599
  buffoon 844
pantaloons 225
pantechnicon 272,
  636
pantheism 984
Pantheon 979, 1000
panther 861
pantile 223, 350
pantologist 492, 700
pantology 490
pantomime 550, 599
pantry 191, 636
pants 225
panurgy 698
pap 250, 354
papa *father* 166
Papa *pope* 996
papacy 984, 995
papal 995
paper *cover* 223
  white 430
  writing 590
  book 593
  security 771
  exist only on – 4
  – credit 805
  – money 800
  – pellet 643
  – war 476, 720
Paphian 954, 961

papilla 250
papistry 984
papoose 129
pappous 256
papula 250
papulose 250
papyrus 590
par 27
  above – 648
  below – *low* 207
  imperfect 651
  – excellence 33
  – nobile fratrum
    alike 17
    friends 890
  de – le roi 737
  – parenthèse 134
  – pari refero 718
  – value 812
parable
  metaphor 521
  teaching 537
  description 594
parabola *curve* 245
parabolic
  metaphorical 521
paracentesis 297
parachronism 115
parachute
  balloon 273
  means of safety
    666
  – light 423
Paraclete 976
parade *procession*
  69, 266
  walk 189
  ostentation 882
paradigm 22, 567
Paradise *bliss* 827
  heaven 981
  in – 827
parados 717
paradox
  absurdity 497
  obscurity 519
  difficulty 704
paradoxical 475,
  519
paraffin 356
paragon
  perfect 650
  glory 873
  good man 948
paragram
  ambiguous 520
  neology 563
paragraph *part* 51
  phrase 566
  article 593
paraleipsis 460
parallax 196
parallel
  similarity 17
  imitate 19
  harmonious 178
  – *position* 216
  symmetry 242
  draw a – 464
  none but himself
    can be his – 873
  run – 178
parallelism 216
  agreement 23
parallelogram 244
parallelopiped 244
paralogism 477

paralogize 477
paralysis
  impotence 158
  *physical insensi-
    bility* 376
  *moral insensi-
    bility* 823
paralyze 158, 376,
  823
paramount
  supreme 33
  important 642
  authority 737
  lord – *master* 745
  possessor 779
  – *estate* 780
paramour 897
paranoia 503, 504
parapet 717
paraph 550
paraphernalia
  machinery 633
  belonging 780
paraphrase
  imitation 19
  copy 21
  synonym 522
  phrase 566
paraphrast 524
paraphrastic 19,
  522
parasite *auxiliary*
  711
  servile 886
  flatterer 935
parasitic
  subjection 749
  grasping 789
  servile 886
parasol *covering* 223
  shade 424
paratus:
  in utrumque –
    resolved 604
    ready 673
  semper – 673
parboil 384
parbuckle 633
Parcae 601
parcel *part* 51
  group 72
  part and – 56
  – out *arrange* 60
  allot 786
parcels
  property 780
parcere subjectis
  740, 914
parch *dry* 340
  heat 382
  bake 384
parched with thirst
  865
parchment
  writing 590
  security 771
parcity 819
pardi 535
pardon 506, 918
  beg – 952
  – me 489
pardonable 937
pare *cut* 38
  reduce 195
  peel 204
  divest 226

pedagogic 537
pedagogue
  scholar 492
  teacher 540
  pedantic 855
pedagogy 537
pedal 633
  – note 408
  – point 416
pedant *scholar* 492
pedantic
  half-learned 491
  - *style* 577
  affected 855
pedantry 481
peddle *meddle* 683
  hawk 796
peddler 796, 797
peddling
  trifling 643
  miserly 819
pederero 727
pedestal 215
  place on a – 307,
  931
pedestrian 268
pedicel 215
pedicle 215
pedigree 69, 166
pediment 210, 215
pedlar 797
  –'s French 563
pedometer 200
peduncle 215
peek 441
peel *layer* 204
  skin 223
  uncover 226
  – off *separate* 44
peeler 664
peel-house 717
peep 441
  – behind the cur-
  tain 461
  – of day 125
  – into the future
  510
  – out 446, 529
peep-hole 260
peep-show 448, 840
peer *equal* 27
  pry 441
  inquire 461
  lord 875
  – out 446
peerless *supreme* 33
  first rate 648
  glorious 873
  virtuous 944
peeved 900
peevish 895, 901
peg *grade* 71
  hang 214
  project 250
  drink 298, 959
  come down a –
  306
  let down a – 308
  not stir a – 265,
  681
  – away 682
  – to hang on 617
  – on *journey* 266
  – out *die* 360
Pegasus 271
pegomancy 511
pegs *legs* 266

peignoir 225
peindre, fait à –
  845
peine forte et dure
  974
pejorative 483
pelagic 341
pelerine 225
pelf *gain* 775
  property 780
  money 803
pelisse 225
Pelion, Ossa on –
  72, 319
pellet 249, 727
  paper – 643
pellicle 204, 223
pell-mell 59
pellucid 425
pelote 249
pelt *skin* 223
  dress 225
  throw 276
  attack 716
  punish 972
peltry 223
pemmican 298
pen *inclosure* 232
  write 590
  writer 593
  restrain 751
  imprison 752
  ready – 569
  slip of– 495, 568
  stroke of the –
  write 590
  authority 737
  command 741
  – in hand 590
  – and ink 590
  – name 565
  draw the –
  through 552
penal 972
  – servitude 972
penance 952, 974
  do – 998
penates, lares et –
  189, 991
penchant
  willing 602
  desire 865
  love 897
pencil *bundle* 72
  - *of light* 420
  write 590
pencil-drawing 556
pencraft 590
pendant *match* 17
  flag 550
  ornament 847
pendency *time* 106
  hanging **214**
pendente lite 106
  uncertain 475
  lawsuit 969
pendule 114
pendulous 214, 314
pendulum 114, 214
  motion of a – 314
Penelope, work of –
  645, 730
penetralia 221
  – mentis 450, **820**

penetrate
  ingress 294
  passage 302
  sagacity 498
  – the soul 824
penetrated with
  484, 821
penetrating
  sagacious 498
  feeling 821
  – glance 441
penfold 232
peninsula 342
penitence **950**
penitentiary 752,
  996
pen-knife 253
penman 590
  inspired – 985
penmanship 590
pennant 550
pennate 267
penniless 804
pennon 550
penny 800
  not have a – 804
  cost a pretty – 814
  turn a – 775
  no – no paternos-
  ter 812
  in for a – in for a
  pound 768
  – dreadful 594
  – trumpet 410
  – whistle 410
penny-a-liner 534,
  593
penny-a-lining 573
pennyweight 319
penny-wise 819
  – and pound fool-
  ish *caprice* 608
  waste 638
  prodigal 818
pennyworth 812
penology 972
penscript 590
pensée, arrière –
  528
penseroso 837
pensile 214
pension *income* 810
pensioner
  student 541
  servant 746
  receiver 785
pensive 451, 837
penstock 350
pent up 751
  – in one's mem-
  ory 505
pentagon 98, 244
pentahedron 244
pentameter 98, 597
Pentateuch 98, 985
Pentecost 998
Penthesilean 861
penthouse 189, 191
pentile 223
penultimate 67
penumbra 421
penurious 819
penury 804
peon 726
people
  kinsfolk 11
  multitude 102

  inhabit 186
  mankind 372
  commonalty 876
  laity 997
pep 171
  – up 171
pepastic 662
pepper *pungent* 392
  condiment 393
  attack 716
  – and salt 432,
  440
peppercorn 643
  – rent 815
peppery
  irascible 901
peptic 662
per 631
  – contra
  contrariety 14
  counter-evidence
  468
  opposition 708
  – procuratio 755
  – saltum 70, 113
  – se 87
peradventure 470
peragrate 266
perambulate 266
perambulator
  measure of length
  200
  vehicle 272
perceivable 446
perceive
  be sensible of 375
  see 441
  know 490
percentage 84, 813
perceptible 446
perception 453, 490
perceptive 375
perch *location* 184
  abide 186
  habitation 189
  length 200
  height 206
  support 215
  – up 307
perchance 156, 470
percipience 450
percolate 295, 348
percolator 191
percursory 458
percussion 276
  center of – 222
percussive 277
perdition
  destruction 162
  ruin 732
  loss 776
perdre son Latin
  704
perdrix, toujours –
  841
perdu 528
  enfant – 859, 863
perdurable 110
perdy 535
peregrination 266
peregrinator 268
peremptory
  assertion 535
  firm 604
  authoritative 737
  rigorous 739
  compulsory 744

  duty 926
  – denial 536
  – refusal 764
perennial
  continuous 69
  diuturnal 110
  - *plants* 367
perennius, aere –
  873
pererration 266
perfect
  great 31
  entire 52
  excellent 650
  complete 729
perfection **650**
  bring to – 729
perfervidum in-
  genium 682
perfidy 874, 940
perflate 349
perforate 260
perforator **262**
perforce 601, 744
perform
  produce 161
  do 170
  - *music* 416
  action 680
  achieve 729
  fulfil 772
  – a circuit 629
  – a duty 926
  – the duties of 625
  – a function 644
  – an obligation
  772
  – a part 599, 680
  – a service 998
performable 470
performance
  [see perform]
  effect 154
performer
  musician 416
  stage-player 599
  agent 690
  affectation 855
perfume 400
perfunctory 53, 460
pergola 191
perhaps 470, 514
peri 845, 979
periapt 993
pericranium 450
periculous 665
peridot 847
perihelion 197
peril 665
  at your – 909
  take heed at
  one's – 668
perilepsis 476
perimeter 230
period *end* 67
  point 79
  - *of time* 106, **108**
  recurrence 138
  at fixed –s 138
  well rounded –s
  577, 578
periodical
  recurring 138
  book 593
periodicity **138**
peripatetic 266, 268
periphery 230

speech 582
- spelling 561
phonics 402
phonograph 417, 418
phonography
  sound 402
  letter 361
  writing 590
phonology 562
Phosphor 423
phosphorescence 420, 423
phosphorus 423
photo-engraving 558
photograph *like* 17
photographer 559
photography 445
  light 420
  representation 554
photogravure 558
photolysis 49
photometer 445
photosphere 318
photostat 553
phrase *part* 51
  music 413
  language **566**
phrasemonger 577
phraseology 569
phrenetic 503
phrenitis 503
phrenology 450
phrenotypics 505
Phryne 962
phthisozoics 361
phylacteric
  sorcery 992
phylactery
  maxim 496
  spell 993
physic
  cure 660
  remedy 662
physical 316
- education
  material 316
  teaching 537
- force
  strength 159
  compulsion 744
- nature 3
- pleasure **377**
- pain **378**
- science 316
physician
  remedy 662
  advice 695
Physics 316
physiognomy
  face 234
  appearance 448
  interpret 522
Physiology
  organization 357
  life 359
  Vegetable - 369
physique
  strength 159
  animality 364
phytivorous 298
Phytology 369
pi 591
piacere, al - 600
piacular 952

pianino 417
pianissimo 415
pianist 416
piano *gentle* 174
  music 415
- organ 417
- player 417
pianoforte 417
pianola 417
piazza 189, 191
pibroch *music* 415
  war 722
pica 591
picaresco, gusto - 945
picaroon 792
piccolo 410, 417
pick *axe* 253
  eat 298
  select 609
  best 648
  clean 652
  gain 775
- a-back 215
- the brains of 461
- holes
  censure 932, 934
- the lock 480a
- me up 662
- out *extract* 301
  select 609
- to pieces
  separate 44
  destroy 162
  find fault 932
- a quarrel 713
- one's steps 459
- up *learn* 539
  get better 658
  gain 775
- one's way 675
pickaninny 129
pickaxe 253
picked 648
- men 700
pickeer 791
pickeerer 792
pickelhaube
  armor 717
picket *join* 43
  locate 184
  fence 229
  guard 668
  defence 717
  soldiers 726
  restrain 751
  imprison 752
  torture 972
- boat 273
pickings 775, 793
pickle *condition* 7
  macerate 337
  pungent 392
  condiment 393
  preserve 670
  difficulty 704
  have a rod in - 673
pickle-herring 844
pickpocket 792
  abuse like a - 932
pickthank *busy* 682
  servile 886
  flatterer 937
picnic *food* 298
  participation 778
  amusement 840
picquet 840

pictorial
  painting 556
  beauty 845
picture
  appearance 448
  representation 554
  painting 556
  description 594
- to oneself 515
picture-gallery 556
picture-theater 599
picturesque
  painting 556
  beauty 845
piddle *dawdle* 683
piddling *trivial* 643
pidgin English 563
pie *food* 298
  sweet 396
  printing 591
piebald 440
piece *adjunct* 59
  bit 31
  painting 556
  drama 599
  cannon 727
  coin 800
  courtesan 962
  fall to -s 162
  go to -s 162
  in -s 330
  of a - 42
  pull to -s 162
  give a - of advice 695
- of good fortune 618
- of music 415
- of news 532
- out 52
- together 43
- of work 713
  make a - of work about 642
pièce
- justificative 467
- de résistance 298
piecemeal 51
pied *variegated* 440
pied de la lettre, au - 494
pie-poudre, court of - 966
pier 189, 666
pierce
  perforate 260
  bodily pain 378
  chill 385
  hurt 649
  wound 659
  affect 824
  mental pain 830
- the head 410
- the heart 830
piercer 262
piercing *cold* 383
  loud 404
  shrill 410
  intelligent 498
  feeling 821
- eye 441
- pain 378
pier-glass 445
Pierian spring 597
pierre fendre, à - 383

Pierrot 599
pietas 998
piété, mont de - 787
pietism 988
pietist 987, 988
piety 987
pig *animal* 366
  sensual 954a
- in a poke
  uncertain 475
  chance 621
  rash 863
- together 72
pigeon
  dupe 547
  steal 791
  gorge de - 440
pigeon-hearted 862
pigeon-hole 191, 260
piggin 191
piggish 954
pig-headed 499, 606
pigment 428
pigmy 193
pignoration 771
pignus 771
pig-sticking 361
pigsty 653
pigtail 214
pigwidgeon 193, 980
pike *hill* 206
  sharp 253
  highway 627
  weapon 727
pikeman 726
pikestaff *tall* 206
  plain 525
pilaster
  support 215
  projection 250
  ornament 847
pile *stake* 45
  heap 72
  edifice 161
  post 215
  velvet 256
  money 800
  funeral - 363
- up 549, 641
pile-driver 276
pilfer *steal* 791
pilferer 792
pilgarlic
  outcast 893
pilgrim 268, 996
pilgrimage 266, 676
pill *sphere* 249
  medicine 662
  bitter - 735
pillage 659, 791
pillager 792
pillar *stable* 150
  lofty 206
  support 215
  monument 551
  tablet 590
-s of Hercules 550
- of the state &c. 873
  from - to post
  transfer 270
  agitation 315
  irresolute 505
  circuit 629

pillion 215
pillory 975
pillow
  support 215
  soft 324
  consult one's -
  temporize 133
  reflect 451
pilot *mariner* 269
  inform 527
  guide 693
  director 694
pilot-balloon 463
pilot-boat 273
pilot-officer 745
pilous 256
pimp 962
pimple 250, 848
pin *fasten* 43
  fastening 45
  locate 184
  sharp 253
  axis 312
  trifle 643
  might hear a - drop 403
  point of a - 193
  not a - to choose 27, 609a
- down 744, 751
- one's faith upon 484
- oneself upon 746, 886
pinafore 225
pince-nez 445
pincers 781
pinch *emergency* 8
  contract 195
  pain 378
  chill 385
  need 630
  difficulty 704
  adversity 735
  grudge 819
  hurt morally 830
  at a - 630, 704
  jack at a - 711
  where the shoe -s 830
- of snuff 643
pinchbeck 545, 847
pinched [see pinch]
  thin 203
  poor 804
- with hunger 865
pinching 383, 819
Pindaric 597
ping-pong 840
pine *disease* 655
  dejection 837
  suffer in mind 828
- away 837
- for 865
pinery 371
pinguid 355
pin-hole 260
pinion *fasten* 43
  wing 267
  instrument 633
  restrain 751
  fetter 752
pink *notch* 257
  pierce 260
  thrust 276

punctilio 939
at the – of 197
come to the –
 special 79
 attention 457
 reasoning 476
 plain language
 576
culminating – 210
disputed – 713
from all –s 180
full of – 574
give –s to 27
go straight to
 the – 278
in – *relative* 9
 agreeing 23
 conformable 82
knotty – 704
make a – of
 resolution 604
 contention 720
 compulsion 744
 conditions 770
 due 924
 honor 939
nice – 697
on the – of 111,
 121
to the – 572, 642
 – an antithesis 578
 – at *direction* 278
 direct attention
 457
 intend 620
 discourtesy 895
 disrespect 929
 censure 932
– of attack 716
at the – of the
 bayonet 173
– of the compass
 278
– of convergence
 74
– of death 360
– in dispute 461
– of etiquette 852
in – of fact 1
– the finger of
 scorn 930
– of honor 939
– of land 250
– a moral 537
– out 155, 457,
 527
– to – race 720
at the – of the
 sword
 violence 173
 severity 739
 compulsion 744
– to *attribute* 155
 direction 278
 probable 472
 predict 511
 mean 516
– of view 441, 448
point d'appui 215
point-blank
 direct 278
 plain language
 576
 refusal 764
point-champain 874
pointed
 great 31

sharp 253
 affirmation 535
 marked 550
 concise 572
 language 574
pointedly
 intention 620
pointer *dog* 366
 indicator 550
pointless 843
poise 27, 319, 852
 mental – 498
poison 659, 663
 – *gas* 722, 727
poisoned 655
 commend the –
 chalice 544
poisonous 657, 665
poke
 pocket 191
pig in a –
 uncertain 475
 chance 621
 dawdle 683
 rash 863
 – at 276, 716
 – the fire 384
 – fun at 856
 – one's nose in
 682
 – out *project* 250
poker 386
 cards 840
polacca 273
polacre 273
polar 270
 cold 383
 – co-ordinates 466
polarization 420
polariscope 445
polarity
 duality 89
 counteraction 179
 contraposition
 237
pole *measure of*
 length 200
 tall 206
 summit 210
 axis 222
 punt 267
 rotation 312
 greasy – 840
 opposite –s 237
from – to pole 180
pole-axe 727
polecat 401
pole-star 550, 693
polemic
 discussion 476
 discord 713
 contention 720
 combatant 726
polemoscope 445
police 965
 – court 966
 – magistrate 967
policeman 664, 965
policy 626, 692
polish *smooth* 255
 rub 331
 furbish 658
 beauty 845
 ornament 847
 taste 850
 politeness 894
 – off *finish* 729

Polish bank 840
polished
 – *language* 578
 fashionable 852
 polite 894
polisson 949
polite 894
 offensive to ears –
 579
 – *literature* 560
 – *society* 852
politic *wise* 498
 cunning 702
 cautious 864
 body –
 mankind 372
 government 737
political economy
 692
politician
 director 694
 proficient 700
politics 702
polity *conduct* 692
 authority 737
 duty 926
polka 840
poll 85, 609
 – tax 812
pollard 193, 201
 tree 367
Poll-parrot 584
pollute *soil* 653
 corrupt 659
 disgrace 874
pollution
 disease 655
 vice 945
Pollyanna 858
polo 840
polonaise 840
poltroon 862
polyandry 903
polychord 417
polychromatic 428,
 440
polychrome 440,
 556
polygamy 903
polygastric 191
polyglot 522, 560
polygon
 buildings 189
 figure 244
polygraphy 590
polylogy 573
polymorphic 81
polyphonism 580
polypus 250
polyscope 445
polysyllable 561
polytheism 984
pomade 356
pomatum 356
pommel
 support 215
 round 249
 beat 972
Pomona 369
pomp 882
pom-pom 727
pomposity 882
pompous
 language 577
poncho 225
pond 343, 636
 fish – 370

ponder 451
ponderable 316,
 319
ponderation 319,
 480
ponderous 319
 – *style* 574, 579
 dull 843
pondus fumo, dare
 – 481
poniard 727
pons asinorum 519,
 704
pontifical 995
pontificals 999
pontificate 995
pontiff 996
pontoon
 vehicle 272
 boat 273
 way 627
pony 271
poodle 366
pooh, pooh!
 unimportance 643
 contempt 930
pool *lake* 343
 combination 709
 prize 775
 billiards 840
poop 235
poor *weak* 160
 – *reasoning* 477
 – *style* 575
 insufficient 640
 trifling 643
 indigent 804
 unhappy 828
 cut a – figure 874
 – hand 701
 – head 499
 – house 189
 – man 804
 – in spirit 881
 – stick 501
 – thing 914
poorly 160, 655
 – off 804
poor-spirited 862
pop *noise* 406
 unexpected 508
 – at 716
 – in *ingress* 294
 insertion 300
 – off *die* 360
 – a question 461
 – the question
 request 765
 endearment 902
 – upon *arrive* 292
 discover 480a
Pope
 infallibility 474
 priest 996
Popedom 995
Pope Joan 840
Popery 984
pop-gun *trifle* 643
popinjay 854
poplar *tall* 206
poppy *sedative* 174
populace 876
popular
 in demand 865
 celebrated 873
 favorite 897
 approved 931

– *opinion* 488
popularis, aura –
 873
popularize
 render intelligible
 518
 facilitate 705
 make pleasant
 829
populate 184
population 188, 372
populi, vox –
 publication 531
 election 609
 authority 737
populous
 crowded 72
 multitude 102
 presence 186
porcelain
 baked 384
 sculpture 557
porch *entrance* 66
 lobby 191
 mouth 231
 opening 260
 church 1000
porcupine 253, 901
pore *opening* 260
 egress 295
 conduit 350
 – over *look* 441
 apply the mind
 457
 learn 539
porism 461, 480
pornographic 961
porous 260
porpoise 192
porridge 298
porringer 191
port *abode* 189
 sinistral 239
 gait 264
 arrival 292
 carriage 448
 harbor 666
 in – 664
 make – 666
 – admiral 745
 – fire 388
 – wine 959
portable *small* 193
 transferable 270
 light 320
portage 270
portal *entrance* 66
 mouth 231
 opening 260
portative 193, 270
portcullis 706, 717
 let down the – 666
porte-monnaie 802
portend 511
portent 512
portentous
 prophetic 511
 fearful 860
porter *janitor* 263
 carrier 271, 690
porterage 270
portfolio *case* 191
 book 593
 magazine 636
 direction 693
 insignia 747
porthole 260

portico 66, 191
portion 51, 786
– out 786
portly 192
portmanteau 191
– word 116
portrait 554
portrait painting 556
portrait painter 559
portraiture 554, 556
portray 19, 554
portreeve 745, 965
posada 189
pose *situation* 183
form 240
puzzle 475
difficulty 704
affectation 855
– as 554
strike a – 855
posited 184
position
circumstances 8
term 71
situation 183
proposition 514
assertion 535
– in society 873
positive *real* 1
great 31
strict 82
certain 474
narrow-minded 481
belief 484
unequivocal 518
assertion 535
obstinate 606
absolute 739
Philosophie – 316
– color 428
– degree 31
– fact 474
– quantity 84
positivism 984, 989
posnet 191
posology 662
posse 72, 712
in – 470
– *comitatûs*
collection 72
army 726
authority 737
jurisdiction 965
possess 777
– knowledge 490
– the mind 484
– oneself of 789
– the soul 824
– a state 7
possessed with a devil 503
possession 777, 780
sorcery 992
come into – 775, 783
in one's – 777
person in – 779
put one in – of 527
remain in – of the field 731
possessor 779
posset 298
possibility
chance 156
liability 177

may be 470
property 780
– upon a possibility 475
possidetis, uti –
possession 777
retention 781
post *fastening* 45
situation 183
location 184
support 215
transmit 270
swift 274
publish 531
mail 534
beacon 550
record 551
employment 625
accounts 811
stigmatize 874
punish 972
at one's –
persist 604a
prepared 673
on duty 926
sign – 550
stand like a – 265
– hoc ergo propter hoc 477
drive from – to pillar 704
postal order 800
postboy 268
post-card 592
postcenal 117
post-chaise 272
postcibal 117
post-date 115
post-diluvial 117
postfix 37
postprandial 117
post-war 116
poster 531
posterior
in order 63
in time 117
in space 235
posteriority 117
posterity 121, 167
hand down to – 551, 873
postern *portal* 66
back 235
opening 260
post-existence 152
post-graduate 492
– student 541
post-haste
swift 274
haste 864
rash 863
post-horse 271
posthumous 117, 133
– fame 873
postilion 268, 694
postliminious 117, 133
postman 534
post-meridiem 126
post-mortem 360, 363
postnate 117
post-obit 360, 363
post-office 534
– order 800
– red 434

postpone 133
postscript 39, 65
postulant
asking 765
petitioner 767
nun 996
postulate 496
reasoning 476
supposition 514
postulation
supposition 514
request 765
posture
circumstance 8
situation 183
form 240
posture-master 599, 844
posy *motto* 550
poem 597
flowers 847
pot *much* 31
mug 191
heat 384
saucepan 386
preserve 670
death in the – 657
go to – 162, 732
keep the – boiling 143, 682
make the – boil 775
le – au lait
imagination 515
hope 858
potable 298
potage 298
potager 191
potation 298, 959
pot-bellied 194
pot-companion 890
potency 157
potent 157, 159
potentate 745
potential
inexistent 2
potentiality 157, 470
pother *disorder* 59
feeling 821
excitement 825
annoyance 830
pot-herbs 393
pot-hooks 590
pot-house 189
pot-hunter 767
potion
beverage 298
medicine 662
cordial 992
pot-luck *eating* 298
chance 621
non-preparation 674
take – with 892
Potosi 803
pot-pourri
mixture 41
fragrance 400
music 415
pottage 298
pottering 682, 683
pottery *baked* 384
art 557
pottle 191
potulent 298, 959
power
much 31, 102

potwalloper 876
pouch 191
poudre:
qui n'a pas inventé la – 501, 701
jeter de la – aux yeux 442
poultice *pulp* 354
remedy 662
relief 834
poultry 298, 366
pounce upon
unexpected 508
attack 716
seize 789
pound *inclose* 232
weight 319
bruise 330
imprison 752
– together 41
poundage 813
pounds, shillings, and pence 800
pour *emerge* 295
stream 348
sufficient 639
it never rains but it –s 641
– out blood like water 361
– a broadside into 716
– forth *eject* 297
speak 582
loquacity 584
– forth like water 818
– in *converge* 290
ingress 294
sufficiency 639
– on *lavish* 784
– with rain 348
– water into a sieve 638, 818
– out 295, 297
pourboire 784
pourparler
interlocution 588
advice 695
council 696
pout *project* 250
sad 837
discourteous 895
irate 900
sulky 901a
poverty
insufficiency 640
unimportance 643
indigence 804
– of intellect 499
powder 330
cosmetics 847
food for – 726
gun– 727
smell – 722
keep one's – dry 673
– and shot 727
waste – 638
not worth – 645
powdered
variegated 440
powdering
ornament 847
power

numerical 84
efficacy 157
loud 404
– *of style* 574
authority 737
do all in one's – 686
give – 760
in the – of
authority 737
subjection 749
literary – 569
– of attorney 755
– behind the throne 694
– of money 800
powerful 159, 171
– voice 580
powerless 158, 160
powers that be 745
pow-wow 588, 696
pox 655
praam 273
practicable 470, 644
practical
acting 170
expedient 646
executive 692
– joke
absurdity 497
deception 545
ridicule 856
disrespect 929
– knowledge 698
practically
intrinsically 5
practice (nouns)
arithmetic 85
training 537
habit 613
conduct 692
in – prepared 673
skilled 698
put in – *use* 677
action 680
conduct 692
complete 729
out of – 699
– of medicine 662
practice (verbs)
train 537
use 677
act 680
– at the bar 968
– on one's credulity 545
– upon
experiment 463
deceive 545
practiced
skilled 698
– eye 700
– hand 700
practitioner
medical - 662
doer 690
praecognita 467
praenomen 564
practor 967
Pragmatic Sanction 769
pragmatical 855, 880
pragmatism 677
prahu 273
prairie *space* 180
plain 344

vegetation 367
praise *thanks* 916
  commendation
  931
  worship 990
praiseworthy 931,
  944
prame 273
prance 266, 315
prandial 298
prank *caprice* 608
  amusement 840
  adorn 847
prate 584
prattle 582, 584
pravity 945
praxis
  grammar 567
  action 680
Praxiteles 559
pray 765, 990
prayer 765, 990
  house of – 1000
prayer-book 998
preach *teach* 537
  speak 582
  predication 998
  – to the winds 645
  – to the wise 538
preacher
  teacher 540
  priest 996
preachment 998
preadamite 124,
  130
preamble 64
preapprehension
  481
prebend 995
prebendary 996
precarious
  transient 111
  uncertain 475
  dangerous 665
precatory 765
precaution
  care 459
  expedient 626
  safety 664
  preparation 673
precede
  superior 33
  – *in or* ler 62
  – *in time* 116
  – *in motion* 280
precedence 873
precedent
  [*see* precede]
  prototype 22
  precursor 64
  habit 613
  legal decision 969
  follow –s 82
precentor 694, 996
precept *adage* 496
  maxim 697
  order 641
  permit 760
preceptor 540
precession 62, 280
précieuse ridicule
  855
precinct *region* 181
  place 182
  environs 227
  boundary 233
precious *great* 31

excellent 648
  valuable 814
  beloved 897
  – metals 800
  – stone 648, 847
precipice
  vertical 212
  slope 217
  dangerous 667
  on the verge of
  a – 665
precipitancy 684,
  863
precipitate
  early 132
  sink 308
  consolidate 321
  refuse 653
  haste 684
  rash 863
  – oneself 306
precipitous 217
précis 596
precise *exact* 494
preciosity 578
precisely
  literally 19
  assent 488
precisianism
  affectation 855
  heterodoxy 984
  over-religious 988
preclude 55, 706
precocious
  early 132
  immature 674
  pert 885
  rude 895
precognition
  forethought 490
  knowledge 510
preconceived idea
  481
preconception 481
preconcert 611, 626
preconsideration 673
precursor
  – *in order* 62, **64**
  – *in time* 116
  predict 511
predatory 789, 791
predecessor 64
predeliberation
  510, 611
predella 215
predesigned 611
predestination
  fate 152
  necessity 601
  predetermination
  611
  Deity 976
predetermination
  611
predial
  land 342
  agriculture 371
  manorial 780
predicament 8, 75
predicate
  affirm 535
  preach 998
prediction **511**
predilection
  bias 481
  affection 820
  desire 865

predispose 615, 673
predisposed
  willing 602
predisposition 176,
  820
predominant 175,
  737
predominate 33
pre-eminent 33, 873
pre-emption 795
preen 847
pre-engage 132
pre-engagement
  768
pre-establish 626
pre-examine 461
pre-exist 1, 116
preface 62, 64
prefect 745, 759
prefecture 737
prefer *choose* 609
  – a claim 969
  – a petition 765
preference 62
preferment
  improvement 658
  ecclesiastical –
  995
prefigure 511
prefix 62, 64
  letter 561
pre-glacial 124
pregnable 158
pregnant
  producing 161
  productive 168
  predicting 511
  – *style* 572
  important 642
  – with meaning
  516
prehensile 789
prehension 789
pre-historic 124
pre-instruct 537
prejudge 481
prejudicate 481
prejudice
  misjudge 481
  evil 619
  detriment 659
prejudicial 481, 649
prelacy 995
prelate 996
prelation 609
prelection 537, 582
prelector 540
preliminaries:
  settle – 673
  – of peace 723
preliminary 62, 64
prelude 62, 64
  beginning 66
  music 415
premature 132, 674
premeditate 611,
  620
prémices 154
premier 694, 759
  – pas 66
premiership 693
premise *prefix* 62
  precede 116
  announce 511
premises
  precursor 64
  prior 116

ground 182
  evidence 467
  logic 476
premium
  debt 805
  receipt 810
  reward 783
  at a – 814
premonish 668
premonitory 511,
  668
Premonstratensian
  996
premonstration
  appearance 448
  prediction 511
  manifestation 525
premunire 742, 974
prendre la balle au
  bond 134 ·
prenotion
  misjudgment 481
  foresight 510
prensation 789
prentice 541
prenticeship 539
preoccupancy
  possession 777
preoccupation
  inattention 458
preoption 609
preordain 152, 601
preparation **673**
  music 413
  instruction 537
  in – 730
  in course of – 626
preparatory
  preceding 62
prepare the way
  facilitate 705
prepared *expectant*
  507
  ready 698
preparing
  destined 152
prepense
  spontaneous 600
  predetermined
  611
  intended 620
  malice – 907
prepollence 157
πρέπον, τό – 850,
  926
preponderance
  superiority 33
  influence 175
  dominance 737
prepossessed
  obstinate 606
prepossessing 829
prepossession
  prejudice 481
  possession 777
preposterous
  great 31
  absurd 497
  exaggerated 549
  ridiculous 853
  undue 925
prepotency 157
pre-Raphaelite 122,
  124, 556
pre-require 630
pre-resolve 611
prerogative 737,924

presage 511, 512
presbyopia 443
presbyter 996
Presbyterian 984
presbytery 995,
  996, 1000
prescience 510
prescious 511
prescribe *direct* 693
  advice 695
  order 741
  entitle 924
  enjoin 926
prescript 697, 741
prescription
  remedy 662
prescriptive *old* 124
  unchanged 141
  habitual 613
  due 924
presence
  in space **186**
  appearance 448
  breeding 894
  in the – of
  near 197
  real – 998
  saving one's – 928
  – of God 981
  – of mind 826,
  864
presence-chamber
  191
present
  – *in time* 118
  – *in space* 186
  offer 763
  give 784
  church prefer-
  ment 995
  at – 118
  these –s 590, 592
  – arms 894, 928
  – a bold front 861
  – a front 719
  – itself *event* 151
  visible 446
  thought 451
  – oneself
  presence 186
  offer 763 ·
  courtesy 894
  – to the mind
  457, 505
  – time **118**
  instant 113
  – to the view 448
presentable 852
presentation 883,
  894
presentiment
  instinct 477
  prejudgment 481
  foresight 510
presently 132
presentment
  information 527
  law proceeding
  969
preservation
  continuance 141
  conservation **670**
  Divine attributes
  976
preserve *sweets* 396
preserver 664
preshow 511

preside 693, 737
presidency 737
president 694, 745
press *crowd* 72
  closet 191
  weight 319
  public - 531
  printing 591
  book 593
  move 615
  compel 744
  offer 763
  solicit 765
go to - 591
under - of 744
writer for the -
  593
- of business 682
- one hard 716
- in 300
- on *course* 109
  progression 282
  haste 684
- into the service
  677, 707
- out 301
press-agent 599
pressed: hard - 704
- for time 684
press-gang 965
pressing *need* 630
  urgent 642
pressure *power* 157
  influence 175
  weight 319
  urgency 642
  exertion 686
  adversity 735
center of — 222
high - 824
work under - 684
Prester John 515
prestidigitation 545
prestidigitator 548
prestige *bias* 481
  authority 737
  fascination 865
  fame 873
prestigiation 545
prestissimo 415
presto
  instantly 113
  music 415
prestriction 442
presumable 472
presume
  misjudge 481
  believe 484
  suppose 514
  hope 858
  pride 878
presumption
  [see presume]
  probability 472
  expectation 507
  rashness 863
  arrogance 885
  unlawfulness 925
presumptive
  probable 472
  supposed 514
  due 924
heir - 779
- evidence
  evidence 467
  probability 472
presumptuous 885

presuppose
  misjudge 481
  suppose 514
presurmise 510,
  514
pretence
  imitation 19
  falsehood 544
  untruth 546
  excuse 617
  ostentation 882
  boast 884
pretend *assert* 535
  simulate 544, 546
pretended 545
pretender
  deceiver 548
  braggart 884
  unentitled 925
pretending 544
pretension
  ornament 577
  affectation 855
  due 924
pretentious
  affected 855
  vain 880
  ostentatious 882
  boasting 884
  undue 925
preterite 121
preterition 122
preterlapsed 122
pretermit 460
preternatural 83
preterperfect 122
pretext 546, 617
pretty
  much 31
  imperfectly 651
  beautiful 845
- fellow 501
- good 651
- kettle of fish,
  pass &c. 59, 704
- well *much* 31
  little 32
  trifling 643
preux chevalier 939
prevail *exist* 1
  superior 33
  general 78
  influence 175
  habit 613
  succeed 731
- upon 615
prevailing 78
- taste 852
prevalence
  [see prevail]
prevaricate 544
prévenance 894
prevenient 62, 132
prevention
  prejudice 481
  hindrance 706
- of waste 817
preventive 55
preventorium 656
previous 116
move the -
  question 624
not within -
  experience 137
prevision 510
pre-war 116
prewarn 668

prey *food* 298
  quarry 620
  booty 793
  victim 732, 828
fall a - to
  be defeated 732
  subjection 749
- to grief 828
- to melancholy
  837
- on the mind
  excite 824
  regret 833
  fear 860
- on the spirits
  837
price
  consideration 147
  value 648
  money 812
  reward 973
at any - 604a
beyond - 814
cheap at the - 815
of great -
  good 648
  dear 814
have one's - 812
price-current 812
priceless
  valueless 645
  dear 814
prick *sharp* 253
  hole 260
  sting 378
  sensation of touch
  380
  incite 615
  mental suffering
  830
kick against the -s
  useless 645
  resistance 719
- up one's ears
  hear 418
  curiosity 455
  attention 457
  expect 507
prickle 253, 380
pride
  ornament 847
  loftiness **878**
take a - in 878
prie-dieu 211
priest 996
priestcraft 995
priesthood 995, 996
priest-ridden 988,
  995
prig *steal* 791
  puppy 854
  affected 855
  blusterer 887
priggish 855, 880
prim *affected* 855
  fastidious 868
  proud 878
prima: - donna
  actress 599
  important 642
  proficient 700
- facie *sight* 441
  appearance 448
  probable 472
- meaning 516
  manifest 525
primacy

  superiority 33
  celebrity 873
  church 995
primary
  original 20
  cause 153
  important 642
- color 428
- education 537
primarily 66
primate 996
primates 875
prime
  primeval 124
  early 132
  teach 537
  important 642
  excellent 648
  prepare 673
in one's - 131
in the - of man-
  hood 159
- cost *price* 812
  cheap 815
- of life *youth* 127
  adolescence 131
- and load 673
- minister 694
- of the morning
  125
- mover 153
- number 84
prime constituent 1
primed
  skilled 698
  tipsy 959
primer 542
primeval 124 .
- forest 367
primigenous 124
primitive 124, 153
- colour 428
primogenial 66
primogeniture
  old 124
  age 128
  posterity 167
primordial 20, 124,
  153
primordinate 124
primrose-colored
  436
primum:
- mobile 153, 615
primus inter pares
  33
prince
  perfection 650
  master 745
  nobility 875
- of darkness 978
princely
  authoritative 737
  liberal 816
  famous 873
  noble 875
  generous 942
princeps
  facile - 33
princess 745, 875
principal
  important 642
  director 694
- part 31, 50
principality 181,
  780
principally 33

principia 66, 496
principiis obstare
  673
principle
  intrinsic 5
  rule 80
  cause 153
  element 316
  idea 453
  reasoning 476
  tenet 484
  maxim 496
  motive 615
  probity 939
on - 615
want of - 945
principled, high-
  939
prink 847, 882
print *copy* 21
  mark 550
  engraving 558
  letter-press 591
out of - 552
printer 591
printing 531, **591**
- telegraph 553
prior
- *in order* 62
- *in time* 116
  clergy 996
priori reasoning,
  a - 476
priority 116, 234
priory 1000
Priscian's head,
  break - 568
prism
  angularity 244
  optical 445
see through a -
  443
prismatic
  color 428
  variegated 440
prison **752**
  cast into - 751
  in - 754
prisoner **754**, 938
  take - 751, 789
prison-house
  secrets of the -
  529, 533
pristine 20, 122
prithee 765
prittle-prattle 588
private *special* 79
  hidden 528
  secluded 893
to gain some -
  ends 943
in - 528
keep - 881
talk to in - 586,
  588
- road 627
- soldier 726
privateer 726, 792
privateering 791
privately 881
privation 776, 804
privative 789
privilege
  freedom 748
  permission 760
  exemption 777a
  due 924

russic acid 663
ry look 441
  curiosity 455
  inquire 461
  - into the future 510
'rytaneum 931
salm 415, 990
salm-book 998
salmody 415, 998
salter 998
saltery 417
sephomancy 511
seudo 17, 545
seudoblepsis 443
seudonym 565
seudo-revelation **986**
seudoscope 445
shaw
  trifling 643
  excitement 825
sychiatry 662
sychical 450
sycho-analysis 662
sychological moment 824
Psychology 450
Psychomancy 511
sycho-therapy 662
tisan 662
tomaine poisoning 663
tyalism 229
puberty 127
pubescent 131
ublic, general - 372
make - 531
- enemy 891
- good 644
- opinion 488
- press 531
- school 542
- spirit 910
- welfare 910
publican 637
publication **531**
  production 161
  book 593
public-house 189
go to the - 959
publicist 593, 595, 968
publicity 531
publicly rumored 532
publico, pro bono - 644, 910
publish 531
- the banns 765
publisher 593
puce 433, 437
pucelage *youth* 127
  celibacy 904
  purity 960
Puck 980
play - 699
pucker *fold* 258
  anger 900
in a - 824
pudder
  disorder 59
pudding *food* 298
  soft 324
  pulpy 354

sweets 396
in - time 132
Pudding, Jack - **599**
puddle 343
pudicity 960
pudor, proh - 874
puerile *boyish* 129
  foolish 499
  feeble 575
  trifling 643
puerperal 161
puff *inflate* 194
  wind 349
  tartlet 396
  exaggerate 482
  advertisement 531
  pant 688
  boast 884
  praise 931
  flatter 933
- of smoke 330
- out 194
- up *vanity* 880
puffed up
  exaggerated 482
  pride 878
puffer 935
puffery 884
puffy 194
pug *short* 201
  dog 366
  pugilist 726
pugh! 643
pugilism 720
pugilist 726
pugilistic 720
pugnacity 720, 901
puisné
  posterior 117
  young 127
puissant 157, 159
puke 297
pukka 494
pulchritude 845
pulcinella 599, 844
pule *cry* 411, 412
  weep 839
pull *superiority* 33
  influence 175
  row 267
  draw 285
  printing 591
a long and a strong - 709
strong - 636
- the check string 142
- different ways 713
- down 162, 308
- about one's ears 308
- in 751
- an oar 680
- out 301
- to pieces
  separate 44
  destroy 162
  censure 932
  detract 934
- upon the purse 814
- by the sleeve 505
- the strings 631

- through 660, 707
- together 709
- towards 288
- up *stop* 142
  rest 265
root out 301
reprimand 932
accuse 969
- the wires 693
pulled down 160, 688
pullet 129
pulley 633
Pullman car 272
pullulate
  produce 161
  multiply 168
  grow 194
pulmonary 349
pulmotor 349
pulp 354
pulpiness **354**
pulpit *rostrum* 542
  church 1000
  the - 996
pulsate
  periodic 138
  oscillate 314
  agitate 315
pulsation
  feeling 821
pulse [see pulsate]
  vegetable 367
feel the -
  inquire 461
  test 463
pulsion 276
pultaceous 354
pulverize 330
  destroy 162
  dust 358
pulverulence **330**
pulvil 400
pummel
  [see pommel]
pump *shoe* 225
  water supply 348
  inquire 461
- up 349
pump-room
  house 189
  remedy 662
pun *similarity* 17
  absurdity 497
  ambiguity 520
  wit 842
punce 276
punch *mold* 22
  perforate 260
  perforator 262
  nag 271
  strike 276
  beverage 298
  engrave 558
  vigour 574
Punch *buffoon* 844
- and Judy 599, 840
punchbowl
  vessel 191
  hollow 252
  tippling 959
puncheon
  vessel 191
  perforator 262
punchinello 599

punctated 440
punctilio 852
punctilious
  exact 494
  observant 772
  ostentation 882
  scrupulous 939
puncto 882
punctual *early* 132
  periodical 138
  exact 494
  observance 772
  scrupulous 939
punctuation 567
puncture 260
pundit
  learned man 492, 500
  lawyer 968
pungency **392**
  physical energy 171
  taste 392
pungent *taste* 392
  odor 398
  vigor 574
  feeling 821
  wit 842
Punica fides 940
punishment **972**
punition 972
punk 962
punkah 349
punnet 191
punster 844
punt 267, 273
punter 621
puny 193
pup *infant* 129
  give birth 161
  dog 366
pupil 541
- of the eye 441
pupilage *youth* 127
  learning 539
pupillari, in statu - 541
puppet *little* 193
  dupe 547
  effigy 554
  auxiliary 711
  tool 746
make a - of 737
be the - of 749
puppet-show 599, 840
puppy *dog* 366
  fop 854
  braggart 884
  blusterer 887
puppyism 855
pur: - sang 875
Purana 986
purblind 443, 481
purchase
  support 215
  acquisition 775
  buy **795**
purchase-money 147
purchaser 795
purdah 374, 531
pure *simple* 42
  true 494
  truthful 543
- *style* 576, 578
  clean 652

  artless 703
- *taste* 850
  honorable 939
  virtuous 944
  innocent 946
  chaste 960
  devout 987, 990
- accent 580
- colour 428
- and simple 42
purée 298
purely 31, 32
purgation
  cleansing 652
  atonement 952
purgative 652
purgatory
  suffering 828
  atonement 952
  hell 982
purge *cast out* 297
  clean 652
  atone 952
purification 998
purify 652, 658
puris naturalibus, in - 226
purist *style* 578
  affected 855
  Pharisee 988
Puritan 984, 988
puritanical
  strict 739
  affected 855
  ascetic 955
purity 960
  [see pure]
purl *drink* 298
  stream 348
  faint sound 405
  music 416
purlieus 197, 227
purloin 791
purple
  violet **437**
  insignia 747
- and fine linen 377
purport 516, 600
purpose 620
at cross -s 523
infirm of - 605
to little or no - 645
on - 620
serve a - 644
to some - 731
tenacity of - 604a
purposeless 621
purpure 437
purr 412
purse 800, 802
  long - 803
put into one's - 785
- up 195
purse-bearer 801
purse-proud 878
purser 801
purse strings:
  draw the - 808
  open the - 809
pursuant to 620
pursue *continue* 143
  follow 281
  aim 622
- a course 680

radically 31
radication 613
radio 532
radio-active 171
316
radio-activity 420
radio-graph 421,
554
radiogram
wireless 532
X-ray 554
radiometer 420, 445
radiomicrometer
389
radiophone 418
radio star 899
radiotelegraph 534
radiotelephone 534
radium 423
radius 200, 202
radix 153
radoter 499
radoteur 501
raff 653, 876
raffle 156
Raffles
thief 792
raft 273
rafter 215
rag 32
tease 830, 856,
929
ragamuffin 876
rage *violence* 173
influence 175
excitement 824,
825
fashion 852
desire 865
wrath 900
the battle –s 722
ragged 226
ragoût 41, 298
rag-picker 876
rags *clothes* 225
useless 645
do to – 384
tear to – 162
worn to – 659
ragtime 415, 473
raid 716, 791
rail *inclosure* 232
prison 752
– at 932
– in
circumscribe 229
restrain 751
railing 232
raillerie, ne pas en-
tendre – 900
raillery 856
railway 627
– speed 274
– station 292
raiment 225
rain *stream* 348
sufficient 639
– or shine 474,
604
rainbow 440
raincoat 225
rainless 340
rains but it pours,
never – 641
rainy day 735
provide against
a – 673, 817

rainy season 348
raise *increase* 35
produce 161
erect 212
elevate 307
excite 824
– alarm 860
– anger 900
– one's banner
722
– a cry 531
– a dust 682
– expectations 858
– the finger 550
– funds 775
– one's head
improve 658
refresh 689
prosperity 734
repute 873
– ghosts 992
– hope 511
– a hue and cry
against 932
– a laugh 840
– the mask 529
– money 788
– a question 461,
485
– a report 531
– a siege 723
– the spirits 836
– spirits from the
dead 992
– a storm 173
– troops 722
– up 212, 824
– the voice 441
– one's voice 535,
932
– the wind 775,
778
raised *convex* 250
raison:
– d'être 620
– de plus 467
raj 737
rajah 745
rajpoot 726
rake *drag* 285
gardening 371
clean 652
profligate 949
intemperance 954
libertine 962
– out 301
– up *collect* 72
extract 301
recall 505
excite 824
– up evidence 467
rake-hell 949, 962
raking-fire 716
rakish
intemperate 954
licentious 961
rallentando 415
rally *arrange* 60
improve 658
restore 660
ridicule 856
encourage 861
– round *order* 58
co-operate 709
rallying: – cry 550,
861
– point 74

ram *impulse* 276
sheep 366
male 373
man-of-war 726
milk the – 645
– down 261, 321
– in 300
Ramadan 956, 993
ramage 367
ramble *stroll* 266
wander 279
folly 499
delirium 503
digress 573
rambler 269
rambling 139
ramification *part* 51
bisection 91
posterity 167
filament 205
symmetry 242
divergence 291
rammer 263, 276
ramose 242
ramp *slope* 217
climb 305
leap 309
rampage 173
rampant
violent 173
prevalent 175
vertical 212
raised 307
free 748
vehement 825
licentious 961
rampart 717
ramrod 263
ramshackle 665
ranch 780
rancid 401, 653
rancor 907, 919
randan 273
random *casual* 156
carriage 272
uncertain 475
aimless 621
talk at –
sophistry 477
exaggerate 549
loquacity 584
- *experiment* 463
chance 621
range *extent* 26
collocate 60
series 69
term 71
class 75
space 180
distance 196
roam 266
direction 278
stove 386
freedom 748
out– 196
long – 196
within – 197
–finder 200
– itself 58
– under, – with 76
ranger
director 694
keeper 753
thief 792
rank *have place* 1
degree 26
thorough 31

collocate 60
row 69
term 71
vegetation 365
fetid 401
estimate 480
bad 649
soldiers 726
glory 873
nobility 875
man of – 875
– and file
continuity 69
soldiers 726
commonalty 876
– marks 745
rankle *unclean* 653
corrupt 659
painful 830
animosity 900
malevolence 907
revenge 919
ranks
fill up the – 660
risen from the –
876
ransack *seek* 461
deliver 672
plunder 791
price 812
atonement 952
– one's brains
451, 515
ransom 672
rant
unmeaning 517
exaggeration 549
diffuse style 573
turgescence 577
speech 582
acting 599
excitement 825
boasting 884
ranter *talker* 584
false piety 988
rantipole 458
rap *blow* 276
sound 406
trifle 643
money 800
not worth a – 804
– on the knuckles
angry 900
censure 932
punish 972
– out *affirm* 535
voice 580
speak 582
– out oaths 885,
908
rapacity
taking 789
stealing 791
avarice 819
greed 865
rape 791, 961
– oil 356
rapid 274
– slope 217
– strides
progress 282
velocity 274
– succession 136
rapids 348
rapier 727
rapine 791
rapparee 792

rappel 722
rapping, spirit –
992
rapport 9
rapports, sous tous
les – 494
rapprochement
714, 888
rapscallion 949
rapt *attention* 457
inattention 458
emotion 821
– in thought 451
raptorial 789, 791
rapture 827, 897
rapturous 827
rara avis
exceptional 83
good 648
famous 873
rare *exceptional* 83
few 103
infrequent 137
light 322
excellent 648
raree show 448, 840
rarefaction 194, 322
rari nantes 103
rarity 322
rasa, tabula – 552
rascal 941, 949
rascality 940
rase *obliterate* 552
rash
skin disease 655
reckless 863
rasher 204
rashness 863
rasp 330, 331
rasper *difficult* 704
rasure 552
rat *recant* 607
smell a –
discover 480a
doubt 485
rataplan 407
rat-a-tat 407
ratchet 253
rate *degree* 26
motion 264
measure 466
estimation 480
price, tax 812
abuse 932
at a great – 274
rath *early* 132
fort 717
rather 32, 643
have – 609
– good 651
have – not 867
ratification
confirm 467
affirm 488
consent 762
compact 769
ratio *relation* 9
degree 26
proportion 84
apportionment
786
ratiocination 476
ration *quantity* 25
food 298
provisions 637
allotment 786
short –s 956

remainder 40
  corpse 362
  vestige 551
  organic – 357
remand *defer* 133
  order 741
remanet 40
remark *observe* 457
  affirmation 535
  worthy of – 642
remarkable
  great 31
  exceptional 83
  important 642
remarry 903
Rembrandtesque
  160
remediable, remedial 660, 662
remediless 859
remedy 660, **662**
remembrance 505
remembrances 894
rememoration 505
remigration
  regression 283
  arrival 292
  egress 295
remind 505
  that –s me 134
reminiscence 505
remise 927a
remiss
  neglectful 460
  reluctant 603
  idle 683
  lax 738
remission
  cessation 142
  moderation 174
  laxity 738
  forgiveness 918
  exemption 927a
remit
  [*see* remission]
  – one's efforts 681
remittance 807
remittent
  periodic 138
remitter 790
remnant 40
remodel
  convert 144
  revolutionize 146
  improve 658
remonstrance 615,
  766, 932
remora *cohere* 46
  hindrance 706
remorse 950
remorseless 919
remote 10, 196
  – age 122
  – cause 153
  – future 121
remotest idea, not
  have – 491
remotion 270
remount 147
remove *subduct* 38
  term 71
  displace 185
  transfer 270
  recede 287
  depart 293
  dinner 298
  extract 301

  school 541
  – the mask 529
removedness
  distance 196
remugient 412
remunerate 973
remunerative 644,
  775
renaissance 660
renascence 660
renascent 163
rencounter
  contact 199
  meeting 292
  fight 720
rend 44
  – the air 404, 411,
    839
  – the heart-strings
    830
render *convert* 144
  interpret 522
  give 784
  restore 790
  – an account
  inform 527
  describe 594
  – *horsdecombat* 645
  – a service 644
rendering
  covering 223
rendezvous 72, 74
rendition
  interpretation 522
  restore 790
renegade
  convert 144
  turncoat 607
  fugitive 623
  apostate 941
renew *twice* 90
  repeat 104
  reproduce 163
  recollect 505
  improve 658
  restore 660
  – one's strength
    689
reniform 245
renitence
  counteraction 179
  hardness 323
  elasticity 325
  unwillingness 603
  resistance 719
renitency
  light 420
renounce
  recant 607
  relinquish 624
  resign 757
  abnegate 764
  – *property* 782
  repudiate 927
renovare dolorem,
  infandum – 833
renovate 160, 660
renovated *new* 123
renown 873
renownless 874
rent *tear* 44
  fissure 198
  hire 788
  purchase 795
rental 810
renter 188, 779
rent-free 815

rent-roll 780, 810
rents *houses* 189
renunciation
  [*see* renounce]
  exemption 927a
reorganize
  order 60
  convert 144
  improve 658
  restore 660
repair
  mend 658
  make good 660
  refresh 689
  out of – 659
  – to 266
reparation
  [*see* repair]
  compensation 30
  restitution 790
  atonement 952
  reward 973
repartee 462, 842
reparteeist 844
repartition 786
repass, pass and –
  314
repast 298
repatriation 790
repay 790, 807, 973
repeal 756
repeat *imitate* 19
  duplication 90
  iterate 104
  – *reproduce* 163
  affirm 535
  – by rote 505
repeated 104, 136
repeater
  watch 114
  fire-arm 727
repel *repulse* 289
  deter 616
  defend 717
  resist 719
  refuse 764
  give pain 830
  disincline 867
  banish 893
  excite hate 898
repent 950
repercussion 277
répertoire 399
repertory 636
repetend
  arithmetical 84
  iteration 104
repetition 19, **104**
repine
  pain 828
  discontent 832
  regret 833
  sad 837
replace
  substitute 147
  locate 184
  restore 660
replenish 52, 637
repletion
  filling 639
  redundance 641
  satiety 869
replevin
  recovery 775
  borrow 788
  restore 790
replica 21

replication
  answer 462
  law pleadings 969
reply 462, 937
répondre en
  Normand 544
report *noise* 406
  judgment 480
  inform 527
  publish 531
  news 532
  rumor 532
  record 551
  statement 594
  good – 873
  through evil re-
    port and good –
    604a
  – *progress* 527
reporter
  informant 527
  messenger 534
  recorder 553
  journalist 593,
    758
reports *law* 969
repose
  quiescence 265
  leisure 685
  rest **687**
  – confidence in
    484
  – on *support* 215
  evidence 467
  – on one's laurels
    142
reposit 184
repository 636
repostum, manet
  alta mente –
  919
repoussé 250
reprehend 932
reprehensible 945,
  947
represent *similar* 17
  imitate 19
  exhibit 525
  intimate 527
  declare 535
  denote 550
  delineate 554
  commission 755
  deputy 759
  – to oneself 515
representation
  [*see* represent]
  copy 21
  portrait **554**
  drama 599
representative
  typical 79
  commissioner 758
  deputy 759
  – *government* 737
  – of the people 696
  – of the press
  messenger 534
  writer 593
repress 751
  – one's feelings
    826
  – a smile 837
reprieve
  respite 133, 970
  deliverance 672
  release 750
  pardon 918

reprimand 932
reprint
  copy 21
  repetition 104
  reproduce 183
reprisal
  retaliation 718
  resumption 789
reprise 40a
reproach
  disgrace 874
  blame 932
  accusation 938
reprobate
  disapproved 932
  vicious 945
  bad man 949
  sinner 988
reprobation 932,
  988
reproduce
  imitate 19
  repeat 104
  renovate 163
reproduction [*see*
  reproduce] 21,
  163
reproductive 163
reproof 932
reprover 936
reptile
  animal 366
  servile 886
  knave 941
  miscreant 949
republic
  country 181
  people 372
  government 737
  – of letters 560
republican
  party 712
  government 737
  commonalty 876
republicanism 737
repudiate
  exclude 55
  deny 489
  reject 610
  abrogate 756
  violate 773
  not pay 808
  evade 927
repugn 719
repugnance
  incongruity 24
  resistance 719
  dislike 867
  hate 898
repulse *recoil* 277
  repel 289
  resist 719
  failure 732
  refusal 764
repulsion 157, **289**
repulsive
  [*see* repulse]
  unsavory 395
  painful 830
  ugly 846
  disliked 867
  discourteous 895
  hateful 898
repurchase 795
reputable 873, 939
reputation 873
repute **873**

request **765**
in – 630
– permission 760
requiem 839
requies, nec mora
 nec – 682
requiescat in pace
 363, 723
require
 need 630
 insufficient 640
 exact 741
 compel 744
 price 812
 due 924
 duty 926
 – *explanation* 519
requirement **630**
requisite 630
requisition 741, 765
 put in – *use* 677
 order 741
requital
 retaliation 918
 gratitude 916
 punishment 972
 reward 973
reredos 1000
res ipsa loquitur
 525
rescind *cut off* 44
 abrogate 756
 refuse 746
rescission 44, 756
rescript *answer* 462
 transcript 590
 letter 592
 order 741, 963
rescriptive 761
rescue *preserve* 670
 deliver 672
 aid 707
research 461
 – *student* 541
reseat 660
resection 44
reseda 435
resemblance 17, 21
resent 900
resentful 901
resentment **900**
reservation
 location 184
 concealment 528
 mental – 477, 528
 equivocation 520
 untruth 546
 with a – 38, 770
reservatory 191,
 636
reserve
 concealment 528
 silence 585
 choose 609
 store 636
 disuse 678
 retain 781
 shyness 881
 in – *destined* 152
 prepared 673
 – *forces* 726
 – *oneself* 881
reservoir 636
re-shape 140
resiance 189
resiant 186
reside 1, 186

residence 189
resident
 consignee 758
 present 186
 inhabitant 188
residentiary 186,
 188
 clergy 996
residue 40
residuum
 remainder 40
 dregs 653
 commonalty 876
resign 757, 782
 – one's being 364
 – one's breath 360
 – oneself 725, 826
resignation [*see*
 resign]
 submission 725
 obedience 743
 abdication 757
 renunciation 782
 endurance 826
 humility 879
resile 277
resilience
 regression 283
 elasticity 325
resin **356a**
resipiscence 950
resist *oppose* 179
 withstand 719
 disobey 742
 refuse 764
resistance 719
résistance, pièce de
 – 298
resister
 passive – 710
resisting
 tenacious 327
resistless 159, 601
resolute 604, 861
resolution
 decomposition 49
 conversion 144
 music 413
 topic 454
 investigation 461
 mental energy **604**
 intention 620
 scheme 626
 courage 861
resolvable into 27,
 144
resolve *change* 140
 liquefy 335
 investigate 461
 discover 480a
 interpret 522
 determine 604
 predetermine 611
 intend 620
 – into elements 49
 – into *convert* 144
resonance 402, **408**
resorb 296
resort *assemble* 72
 focus 74
 dwelling 189
 converge 290
 last – 601
 – to *be present* 186
 travel 266
 employ 677
resound *loud* 404

ring 408
 – *praises* 931
resourceful 698
resources
 means 632
 property 780
 wealth 803
respect *relation* 9
 observe 772
 fame 873
 salutation 894
 deference **928**
 have – to 9
 in no – 536
 with – to 9
respectability
 mediocrity 736
 repute 873
 probity 939
respectable
 unimportant 643
respectful 928
 – *distance* 623,
 864
respective 79, 786
respectless 458
respects 894, 928
resperse 73
respicere finem 510
respire *breathe* 349
 live 359
 refresh 689
respite
 intermission 106
 defer 133
 pause 142
 deliver 672
 repose 687
 reprieve 970
resplendent
 luminous 420
 splendid 845
respond *accord* 23
 answer 462
 feel 821
respondent 462
 accused 938
response
 answer 462, **587**
 concord 714
 feeling 821
 friendship 888
 worship 990
responsible 177,
 926
responsibility
 upon one's own –
 600
responsive 375
rest *remainder* 40
 pause 141
 cessation 142
 support 215
 quiescence 265
 death 360
 silence 403
 music 413
 inaction 681
 repose 687
 at – *repose* 687
 content 831
 home of – 189
 set at –
 answer 462
 ascertain 474
 complete 729
 compact 769

set one's mind at –
 calm 826
set the question
 at – 478, 480
 – assured 484, 858
 – on *support* 215
 – on one's oars
 142, 687
 – satisfied 831
 – and be thankful
 681, 687
 – upon
 evidence 467
 confide 484
 – with *duty* 926
restaurant 189
 – *car* 272
restaurateur 637
restful 265
resting place
 support 215
 quiet 265
 arrival 292
restitution **790**, 660
restive *averse* 603
 obstinate 606
 disobedient 742
 refusal 764
 perverse 901a
restless
 changeable 149
 moving 264
 agitated 315
 active 682
 excited 825
 fearful 860
restoration **660**
restorative
 salubrious 656
 remedial 662
 relieving 834
restore *reinstate*
 660
 refresh 689
 return 790
 – *equilibrium* 27
 – *harmony* 723
 – to *health* 654
restrain 616, 706,
 751
restrainable 743
restrained 751
restraint 578, **751**
 self – 826, 953
restrict *hinder* 706
 restrain 751
 prohibit 761
restringency 751
result *remainder* 40
 follow 117
 effect 154
 conclusion 480
 completion 729
resultant 48, 154
resume *begin* 66
 repeat 104
 change 140
 restore 660
 take 789
résumé 596
resupination 213
resurgence 163, 660
resurrection
 reproduction 163
 restoration 660
 heaven 981

resuscitate
 reproduce 163
 reinstate 660
retable 215
retail *distribute* 73
 inform 527
 barter 794
 sell 796
retailer 797
retain *stand* 150
 keep 781
 – the memory of
 505
 – one's reason 502
retainer 746
retake 789
retaliation **718**, 919
retard *later* 133
 slower 275
 hinder 706
retch 297
retection 529
retention **781**
retentive 781
 – *memory* 505
reticence 528
reticle 219
reticulation 219,
 248
reticule 191
retiform 219
retina 441
retinue *followers* 65
 series 69
 servants 746
retire *move back* 283
 recede 287
 resign 757
 modest 881
 seclusion 893
 – into the shade
 inferior 34
 decrease 36
 – from sight
 disappear 449
 hide 528
retiring
 concave 252
 – *color* 438
retold 104
retort
 receptacle 191
 vaporizer 336
 boiler 386
 answer 462
 confutation 479
 – *retaliation* 718
 wit 842
retouch *restore* 660
retoucher 559
retrace 505
 – one's steps 607
retract
 recant 607
 annul 756
 abjure 757
 violate 773
retreat
 resort 74
 withdraw 187
 abode 189
 regression 283
 recede 287
 ambush 530
 refuge 666
 escape 671
 give way 725

riggish 961
right *dextral* 238
   straight 246
   true 494
   property 780
   just **922**
   privilege 924
   duty 926
   honor 939
   virtuous 944
   bill of – 969
   by – 924
   have a – to 924
   set – *inform* 527
    disclose 529
   that's – 931
   – about
    [*see below*]
   – ahead 234
   – angle 212
   – ascension 466
   – away 133
   step in the – direction 644
   – hand [*see below*]
   – itself 660
   – and left 180, 227, 236
   – line 246
   – man in the right place 23
   in one's – mind 498, 502
   hit the – nail on the head 480a, 698
   – owner 779
   keep the – path 944
   in the – place 646
   – thing to do 926
   – as a trivet 650
   – word in the right place 578
right about: to the – 283
   go to the – 311, 607
   send to the –
    eject 297
    reject 610
    refuse 764
   turn to the – 218, 279
right hand
   power 157
   dextrality 238
   help 711
   not let the – know what the left is doing 528
   – of friendship 888
righteous 944
   the – 987
   – overmuch 988
Righteousness:
   Lord our – 976
   Sun of – 976
rightful 922
   – owner 779
rightly served, be – 972
right-minded 939, 944
rights 748
   put to – 660
   set to – 60

stand on one's – 748
rigid *regular* 82
   hard 323
   exact 494
   severe 739
rigmarole 517, 573
rigor 383
   – mortis 360
rigorous *exact* 494
   severe 739
   revengeful 919
rigor 494, 739
Rigsdag 696
rigueur
   de – 744
rile *annoy* 830
   hate 898
   anger 900
rilievo *convex* 250
   sculpture 557
rill 348
rim 231
rime *chink* 198
   frost 383
rimer 262
rimple 258
rind 223
ring
   fastening 45
   pendency 214
   circle 247
   loud 404
   resonance 408
   test 463
   combination 709
   clique 712
   arena 728, 840
   badge 747
   rub the – 992
   have the true – 494
   – the changes
    repeat 104
    change 140
   changeable 149
   – in the ear 408
   in a – fence 229, 232
   – with the praises of 931
   – the tocsin 669
   – up 527
ringleader
   director 694
   mutineer 742
ringlet 247, 256
rink 840
rinse 652
rinsings 653
riot *confusion* 59
   derangement 61
   violence 173
   discord 713
   resist 719
   mutiny 742
   run – *activity* 682
    excitement 825
    intemperance 954
   – in *pleasure* 742
rioter 742
riotous 173
rip 949, 962
   – open 260
   – up *tear* 44
   recall the past 505
   excile 824

Rip van Winkle 130
riparian 342
ripe 673
   – *age old* 128
ripen *perfect* 650
   improve 658
   prepare 673
   complete 729
   – into 144
rippet 713
riposte 462
ripple *ruffle* 256
   shake 315
   water 348
   murmur 405
ripuarian 342
rire, pour – 853
rise *grow* 35
   begin 66
   slope 217
   progress 282
   ascend 305
   stir 682
   revolt 742
   – again 660
   – in arms 722
   – from 154
   – to the occasion 612
   – in price 814
   – up *elevation* 307
   – in the world 734
risible 838, 853
rising [*see rise*]
   – of the curtain 66, 448
   – generation 127, 167
   – ground
    height 206
    slope 217
   worship the – sun 886
risk *chance* 621
   danger 665
   invest 787
   at any – 604
risqué 961
rissole 298
risùm teneatis amici? 853
rite 963, **998**
   funeral – 363
ritornello 64, 104
ritual
   ostentation 882
   rite 998
ritualism 984
rival
   emulate 648
   oppose 708
   opponent 710
   compete 720
   combatant 726
   outshine 873
rivalry *envy* 921
rive 44
rivel 258
river **348**
rivet 43, 45
   – the attention 457, 824
   – the eyes upon 441
   – in the memory 505

– the yoke 739
riveted *firm* 150
rivulet 348
rixation 713
Ro 560
road *street* 189
   direction 278
   way 627
   on the –
    transference 270
    progression 282
    approach 286
   on the high – to 278
   – to ruin
    destruction 162
    danger 665
    adversity 735
road-book 266
roads *lake* 343
roadstead 154
   abode 189
   refuge 666
roadster 271
roadway 627
roam 266
roan *horse* 271
   color 433
roar *violence* 173
   wind 349
   sound 404, 407
   bellow 411, 412
   laugh 838
   weep 839
roaring *great* 31
   – trade 731, 734
roast *heat* 384
   ridicule 856
   rib – 972
   – and boiled 298
   – an ox 883
rob 354, 791
robber 792
robbery 791
robe 225, 999
   robes – of state 747
Robin Goodfellow 980
Robinson
   say Jack – 132
Robot 554
robust *strong* 159, 654
roc 83
rocaille 853
rock *firm* 150
   oscillate 314
   hard 323
   land 342
   safety 664
   danger 667
   build on a – 150
   founded on a – 664
   split upon a – 732
   – ahead 665
   –bound coast 342
   – oil 356
rocket *rapid* 274
   rise 305
   light 423
   ship 273
   signal 550
   arms 727
   fireworks 840
   go up like a – and come down like

the stick 732
rocking-chair 215
rococo 124, 853
rod *support* 215
   measure 466
   scourge 975
   divining 993
   kiss the – 725
   sounding – 208
   – of empire 747
   – in pickle
    prepared 673
    accusation 938
    punishment 972
    scourge 975
rodeo 720, 840
rodomontade
   exaggeration 482
   unmeaning 517
   boast 884
roe 366, 374
Roentgen rays 420
rogation
   request 765
   worship 990
rogue *cheat* 548
   knave 941
   scamp 949
   –'s march 297
roguery 940
roguish
   playful 840
Roi le veut, le – 741
roister 885
roisterer 887
Roland for an Oliver
   retaliation 716
   revenge 719
   barter 794
rôle *drama* 599
   business 625
   plan 626
   conduct 692
roll *list* 86
   fillet 205
   convolution 248
   rotundity 249
   make smooth 255
   move 264
   fly 267
   rotate 312
   rock 314
   flow 384
   sound **407**
   record 551
   money 800
   strike off the – 756, 972
   – along 312
   – in the dust 731
   – on the ground 839
   – of honour 86
   – in 639, 641
   – on 109
   – into one 43
   – in riches 803
   – up 312
   – up in 225
   – in wealth 803
roll-call 85
roller *fillet* 45
   round 249
   clothing 255
   rotate 312

rutilant 420
ruttish 961
ryot *servant* 746
 possessor 779
 commonalty 876

S

sabaoth 726
sabbatarian
 ascetic 955
 sectarian 984
 false piety 988
 ritualistic 998
Sabbath *rest* 687
 rite 998
sabbatism 988
Sabellianism 984
saber 361, 727
Sabianism 984
sable 223, 431
sabot 225
sabotage 162, 742
sabreur *slayer* 361
 soldier 726
sabulous 330
sac 191
 – de nuit 225
sacatra 83
saccharine 396
saccular 191
sacerdotal 995
sacerdotalism 988
sachel 191
sachem 745
sachet 400
sack *bag* 191
 discharge 297, 756
 gain 775
 take 789
 plunder 791
 give the – to 297
sackbut 297
sackcloth and ashes
 lament 839
 atonement 952
 ascetic 955
 rite 998
sacrament 998
sacrarium 1000
sacred
 dignified 873
 holy 976
 revelation 985
 piety 987
sacrifice
 destroy 162
 gift 784
 atonement 952
 worship 990
 idolatry 991
 at any – 604
 fall a – 828
 make a – 942
 make the supreme
  – 361
 self – 942
sacrificed 732
sacrilege 988
sacring bell 550, 998
sacristan 996
sacristy 1000
sacrosanct

honorable 873
inviolable 924
holy 976
sad *great* 31
 grey 432
 bad 649
 painful 830
 dejected 837
 – disappointment 509
 – dog 949
 – times 735
 – work 699
sadden 830, 837
sadder and wiser man 950
saddle 215
 in the – 673
 – on 37, 43
 – on the right horse
  discovery 480a
  skill 698
  right 922
  fair 939
 – with *add* 37
  attribute 155
  quarter on 184
  clog 706
  impose a duty 926
  accuse 938
 – on the wrong horse 495, 699
 – up 293
saddle-bags 191
Sadducee 984
sadness, in – 535
safe *cupboard* 191
 hiding place 530
 secure 664
 treasury 802
 cautious 864
 – conduct 631
 – conscience 926, 946
 – deposit 636
 – keeping 670
 – and sound 654
 on the – side 864
safety 664
 – bicycle 272
 – curtain 599
 – first 665, 864
 – match 388
 – valve 666
saffron *color* 436
sag 214, 217, 245
saga 594
sagacious 498, 510
sage 498, 500
 – maxim 496
saggar 386
sagittal 253
sagittary 83
sagum 225
Sahara 169
sahib 373, 745, 875
saick 273
said *preceding* 62
 repeated 104
 prior 116
 it is – 532
 thou hast – 488
 more easily – than done 704
sail *navigate* 267

ship 273
set out 293
 easy – 174
 full – 274
 press of – 274
 shorten – 275
 take in – 174
 take the wind out of one's –s 706
 too much – 863
 under – 267
 – before the wind 734
 – near the wind 698
 – too near the wind 863
sailing: plain – 705
 – vessel 273
sailor 269
 fair weather – 701
saint *angel* 977
 revelation 985
 piety 987
 false piety 988
 tutelary – 664
Saint Monday 840
saintly 944, 987
sais quoi, je ne – 563
sake:
 for the – of 615, 707
 for goodness' – 765
salaam
 bow 308
 submit 725
 courtesy 894
 respect 928
salacity 961
salad 41
 – oil 356
salade 717
salamander 386
salariat 875
salary 973
sale 796
 bill of – 771
 for – *offer* 763
 barter 794
saleable 796
salebrosity 256
salesman 797
salient
 projecting 250
 sharp 253
 manifest 525
 important 642
 – angle 244
 – points 642
saline 392
saliva 299, 332
salivate 297
salle-à-manger 191
sallet 717
sallow
 colorless 429
 yellow 436
sally *issue* 293
 attack 716
 wit 842
sally-port 295, 717
salmagundi 41
salmi 298
salmon-colored 434
saloon 189, 191

salt *sailor* 269
 pungent 392
 condiment 393
 importance 642
 preserve 670
 money 800
 wit 842
 below the – 876
 worth one's – 644
 – of the earth 648, 948
 – water 341
saltation 309
saltatory 315
saltinbanco 548
saltpeter 392, 727
saltum, per – 315
salubrity 656
salutary 656
salutatory 582
salute
 allocution 586
 celebration 883
 courtesy 894
 kiss 902
 respect 928
salutiferous
 [*see* salutary]
salva:
 – res est 664
 – sit reverentia 928
salvable 946
salvage
 acquisition 775
 tax 812
 discount 813
 reward 973
salvation
 preservation 670
 deliverance 672
 religious 976
 piety 987
 work out one's – 990
salve *unguent* 356
 remedy 662
 relieve 834
salver 191
salvo *exception* 83
 explosion 406
 qualification 469
 plea 617
 attack 716
 excuse 937
 – of artillery
  celebration 883
Samaritan, good – 906, 912
same 13
 all the – to 823
 in the – boat 709
 in the – breath 113, 120
 go over the – ground 104
 of the – mind 488
 on the – tack 709
 adds up to the – thing 27
 at the – time 30, 120
sameness 16
samiel 349
samisen 417
Sammael 978
samovar 191

sampan 273
sample 82, 463
Samson 159
sana, mens – 502
 – in corpore sano 827
sanation 660
sanative 662
sanatorium 662
sanctification 976
sanctify 926, 987
sanctimony 988
sanction
 permission 760
 dueness 924
 approbation 931
sanctitude 987
sanctity 987
sanctuary 666, 1000
sanctum 191
 – sanctorum
  abode 189
  privacy 893
  temple 1000
sand *powder* 330
 –bag 727
 built upon – 665
 –dance 840
 sow the – 645
sandal 225
sand-blind 442
Sandemanian 984
sand-paper 255
sands *danger* 667
 – on the seashore
  multitude 102
sand-storm 330
sandwich-wise 228
sandy *yellow* 436
sane 502
sangar 717
sang-froid
 insensibility 823
 inexcitability 826
 presence of mind 864
sangrail 998
sanguinary 361
sanguine *red* 434
 hopeful 858
 – expectation 507, 858
 – imagination 515
sanhedrim 696, 995
sanies 333
sanitaire, cordon – 670
sanitarian 656
sanitarium 656, 662
sanitary 656
sanity *mental* 502
 bodily – 654
sans 187
 – cérémonie 888, 892
 – façon
  simple 849
  modest 881
  social 892
 – pareil 33
 – peur et sans reproche
  perfect 650
  heroic 873
  honorable 939
 – souci
  insensible 823

at – 341
  uncertain 475
  erroneous 495
go to – 293
on the high –s 41
heavy – 315
the seven –s 341
  – of doubt 475
  – of troubles
  difficulty 704
  adversity 735
seaboard 342
seafarer 269
seafaring 267, 273
sea-fight 720
sea-girt 346
sea-going 267, 341
sea-green 435
seal
  matrix 22
  close 261
  evidence 467
  mark 550
  resolve 604
  complete 729
  compact 769
  security 771
break the – 529
under – 769
  – the doom of 162
  – one's infamy 940
  – the lips 585
  – of secrecy 528
  – up *restrain* 751
sealed:
  one's fate is – 601
  hermetically – 261
  – book
  ignorance 491
  unintelligible 519
  secret 533
sealing-wax 747
seals *insignia* 747
sealskin 223
seam 43
sea-maid 979
sea-man 269
seamanship 692, 698
sea-mark 550
seamless 50
seamstress 225, 690
seamy side 651
séance 525, 696
sea-piece 556
seaplane 273, 736
sea-port 666
sear *dry* 340
  burn 384
  deaden 823
  – and yellow leaf 128, 659
search *inquire* 461
searching
  severe 739
  painful 830
searchless 519
searchlight 423, 726
seared conscience 951
searing 830
seascape 556
sea-serpent 83
seaside 342
season *mix* 41

time 106
pungent 392
accustom 613
preserve 670
prepare 673
seasonable 23, 134
seasoning 393
seasons 138
seat *place* 183
locate 184
abode 189
support 215
posterior 235
parliament 693
country – 189
judgment – 966
– of government 737
– of war 728
seated, firmly – 150
seaway 180
seaweed 367
seaworthy 273, 604
sebaceous 355
secant 219
secede *dissent* 489
relinquish 624
disobey 742
seceder
heterodox 984
secern 297
seclusion **893**
second
duplication 90
- *of time* 108
instant 113
- *in music* 413, 415
abet 707
play or sing a – 416
– best 651, 732
– childhood 128, 499
– crop 168, 775
– edition 104
play – fiddle
obey 743
subject 749
disrepute 874
– nature 613
– to none 33
one's – self 17
– rate 659
– sight
foresight 510
sorcery 992
– thoughts
sequel 65
thought 451
improvement 658
– youth 660
secondary
inferior 34
following 63
imperfect 651
deputy 759
– education 537
– evidence 467
– school 542
seconder 711
second-hand
imitation 19
old 124
deteriorated 659
received 785
secondly 90

second-rate 651
secret *key* 522
latent 526
hidden 528
riddle **533**
in the – 490
keep a – 585
– motive 615
– passage 627, 671
– place 530
– writing 590
secrétaire 191
secretary
recorder 553
writer 590
director 694
auxiliary 711
servant 746
consignee 758
– of state 694
– of the treasury 801
secrete *excrete* 297
conceal 528
secretion 299
secretive 528
sect 75
religious – 983, 984
sectarian
dissent 489
ally 711
heterodox 984
sectary 489
section *division* 44
part 51
class 75
chapter 593
troops 726
sector *part* 51
circle 247
secula seculorum, in – 112
secular
centenary 98
periodic 138
laity 997
– education 537
secularism 984
secundum artem 82, 698
secure *fasten* 43
bespeak 132
belief 484
safe 664
restrain 751
engage 768
gain 775
confident 858
– an object 731
securities 802–805
security *safety* 664
pledge **771**
hope 858
lend on – 787
Sedan
disaster 162
sedan chair 272
sedate
thoughtful 451
calm 826
grave 837
sedative 174, 662
sedentary 265
sedge 367
sedile 1000
sediment *dregs* 653

sedimentary 40
sedition 742
seduce *entice* 615
love 897
debauch 961
seducer 962
seduction 829, 865
sedulous 682, 865
see *view* 441
look 457
believe 484
know 490
bishopric 995
we shall – 507
– after 459
– daylight 480a
– double 959
– fit 600, 602
– at a glance 498
– justice done 922
– life 840
– the light
born 359
published 531
– service 722
– sights 455
– through 480a, 498
– to *attention* 457
care 459
direction 693
– one's way
foresight 510
intelligible 518
skill 698
easy 705
seed *small* 32
cause 153
posterity 167
grain 330
run to – *age* 128
lose health 659
sow the – 673
seedling 129
seed-plot 168, 371
seed-time of life 127
seedy *weak* 160
disease 655
deteriorated 659
exhausted 688
needy 804
seeing that 8, 476
seek *inquire* 461
pursue 622
offer 763
request 765
– safety 664
seek-sorrow 837
seel 217
seem 448
as it –s good to 600
seeming 488
seemingly 472
seemless 846, 925
seemliness 926
seemly
expedient 646
handsome 845
due 924
seep 295
seer *veteran* 130
madman 504
oracle 513
sorcerer 994
see-saw 12, 314

seethe *wet* 339
hot 382
make hot 384
excitement 824
seething caldron 386
segar 392
segment 44, 51
segnitude 683
s'égosiller 411
segregate
not related 10
separate 44
exclude 55
segregated
incoherent 47
seigneur, grand –
pride 878
insolence 885
seignior 745, 875
seigniority
authority 737
possession 777
property 780
seigniory 737
seine net 232
seisin 777, 780
seismic 314
seismograph 553
seismometer 276, 314
seize 789, 791
– an opportunity 134
seized with
disease 655
feeling 821
seizure 925
sejunction 44
seldom 137
select *choose* 609
good 648
self 13, 79
–abasement 879
–accusing 950
–admiration 880
–applause 880
–appointed task 602
–assertion 885
–called 565
–command 604, 864
–communing 451
–complacency 836, 880
–confidence 880
–conquest 604
–conscious 855
–consultation 451
–contained 52
–control 604
–conviction
belief 484
penitent 950
condemned 971
–counsel 451
–deceit *error* 495
–deception 486
–defence 717
–delusion 486
–denial
disinterested 942
temperance 953
penance 990
–discipline 990
–effacement 879,

942
—esteem 880
—evident 474, 525
—examination 990
—existing 1
—government 748
—help 698
—immolation 991
—indulgence
  selfishness 943
  intemperance 954
—interest 943
—knowledge 881
—love 943
—luminous 423
—mastery 604
—opinioned 481
—possession
  sanity 502
  resolution 604
  inexcitability 826
  caution 864
—praise 880
—preservation 717
—reliance
  resolution 604
  hope 858
  courage 861
—reproach 950
—respect 878
—restraint 953
—sacrifice 942
—satisfied 880
—seeking 943
—styled 565
—sufficient 880
—taught 490
—tormentor 837
—will 606
selfishness 943
self-same 13
sell convince 484
  absurdity 497
  deception 545
  untruth 546
  sale 796
  — for 812
  — one's life dearly
  719, 722
  — off 796
  — oneself 940
  — out 796
seller 796
selon les règles 82
selvedge 231
semaphore 550
semblance
  similarity 17
  imitation 19
  copy 21
  probability 472
  wear the — of
  appearance 448
semeiology 522
semeiotics 550
semester 108
semi- 91
semi-barbarian 913
semibreve 413
semicircle 247
semicircular 245
semicolon 142
semi-diaphanous
  427
semi-fluid 352
semi-liquidity 352
semi-lunar 245

seminal 153
seminary 542
semination 673
semi-opaque 427
semi-pellucid 427
semiquaver 413
semitone 413
semi-transparency
  427
sempervirent 110
sempiternal 112
sempstress 225, 690
senary 98
senate 696
senate-house 966
senator 695, 696
senatorship 693
senatus consultum
  741
send 270, 284
  — adrift 597
  — away
  repel 289
  eject 297
  refuse 764
  — for 741
  — forth 284, 531
  — a letter to 592
  — off 284
  — out eject 297
  — packing 289
  commission 755
  — word 527
senescence 128
seneschal
  director 694
  master 745
  servant 746
seneschalship 737
senile 128
senility 158, 659
senior age 128
  student 541
  master 745
sēniores priores 62,
  380
seniority 124, 128
sennight 108
señor 373, 877
señora 374
sensation
  physical sensi-
  bility 375
  emotion 821
  wonder 870
sensational 574,
  824
sensation drama
  599
sensations of touch
  380
sense 498, 516
  deep — 821
  horse — 498
  in no — 565
  accept in a par-
  ticular — 522
  — of duty 926
senseless
  insensible 376
  absurd 497
  foolish 499
  unmeaning 517
senses
  external - 375
  intellect 450
  sanity 502

sensibility **375, 822**
sensible
  material 316
  wise 498
sensitive 375, 822
sensorial 821
sensorium 450
sensual 377, 954
sensualist 954a
sensuous
  sensibility 375
  pleasure 377
  feeling 821
sentence
  decision 480
  maxim 496
  affirmation 535
  phrase 566
  condemnation 971
sententious 572,
  574
sentient 375, 821
sentiment 453
sentimental
  sensitive 822
  affected 855
sentinel }
sentry } 263
  guardian 664
  watch 668
  keeper 753
separate disjoin 44
  exclude 55
  bisect 91
  diverge 291
  divorce 905
  — the chaff from
  the wheat
  discriminate 465
  select 609
  — into elements 49
  — maintenance 905
separation 49
separatist 489, 984
sepia 433
seposition 44, 55
sepoy 726
sept kin 11
  class 75
  clan 166
Septentrional 237
septett 415
septic 655, 657
septicemia 655
septuagenarian 98
Septuagint 985
septum 228
sepulcher 363
  whited — 545
sepulchral
  interment 363
  resonance 408
  stridor 410
  hoarse 581
sepulture 363
sequacious 63
sequacity soft 324
  tenacity 327
sequel 65, 117
sequela 65, 154
sequence
  - in order **63**
  - in time 117
  motion **281**
  logical — 476
sequent 63
sequester 789, 974

sequestered 893
sequestrate
  seize 789
  condemn 971
  confiscate 974
sequin 847
serac 383
seraglio 961
seraph 948, 977
seraphic
  blissful 829
  virtuous 944
  pious 987
seraphina 417
seraskier 745
sere and yellow
  leaf 128
serein 339, 348
serenade music 415
  compliment 894
  endearment 902
serene
  pellucid 425
  calm 826
  content 831
  imperturbable 871
  — highness 877
serf slave 746
  clown 876
serfdom 749
sergeant 745
serial
  continuous 69
  periodic 183
  book 593
seriatim
  in order 58
  continuously 69
  each to each 79
  slowly 275
series 69, 84
sérieux, take au —
  843
serio-comic 853
serious great 31
  resolved 604
  important 642
  dejected 837
seriously 535
serjeant:
  common — 967
  -at-law 968
sermon lesson 537
  speech 582
  dissertation 595
  pastoral 998
  funeral — 363
sermonizer 584
seroon 72
serosity 333, 337
serpent
  tortuous 248
  snake 366
  hiss 409
  wind instrument
  417
  wise 498
  deceiver 548
  cunning 702
  evil-doer 913
  knave 941
  demon 949
  the old — 978
  great sea — 515
serpentine 248
serrated 244, 257
serried 72, 321

serum 333, 337
servant instrumen-
  tality 631
  help 711
  retainer 746
  — of all work 690
serve benefit 618
  business 625
  utility 644
  aid 707
  warfare 722
  obey 743
  servant 746
  — an apprentice-
  ship 539
  — faithfully 743
  — loyally 743
  — notice 527
  — out 972
  — one right
  retaliation 718
  right 922
  punish 972
  — as a substitute
  147
  — one's turn 644
  — with a writ 969
service good 618
  utility 644
  use 677
  warfare 722
  servitude 749
  worship 990
  rite 998
  hold — 363
  at one's — 763
  press into the —
  677
  render a — 644,
  906
serviceable 644, 648
serviette 652
servile 749, 876, **836**
servitor 746
servitorship 749
servitude 749
  penal — 972
sesame, open — 260
  watchword 550
  spell 993
sesqui- 87
sesquipedalia verba
  577
sesquipedalian 200
sess 812
sessile 46
session council 696
sessions law 966
sestet 597
set
  condition 7
  join 43
  coherence 46
  group 72
  class 75
  firm 150
  tendency 176
  place 184
  form 240
  sharpen 253
  direction 278
  go down 306
  dense 321
  stage 599
  habit 613
  prepare 673
  gang 712

impose 741
lease 771, 787
make a dead – at 716
– about 66, 676
– abroach 73
– one's affections on 897
– afloat 153, 531
– against
  oppose 708
  quarrel 713
  hate 898
  angry 900
– against one another 464
– agoing
  impulse 276
  propulsion 284
  aid 717
– apart
  separate 44
  exclude 55
  select 609
– aside
  displace 185
  disregard 458
  neglect 460
  negative 536
  reject 610
  disuse 678
  annul 756
  refuse 764
  not observe 773
  relinquish 782
  dereliction 927
– one's back up 878
– before
  inform 527
  choice 609
– before oneself 620
– by 636
– one's cap at 897, 902
– on a cast 621
– down [*see below*]
– by the ears 898
– at ease 831
– an example
  model 22
  motive 615
– the eyes on 441
– one's face against
  oppose 708
  refuse 764
  disapprove 932
– the fashion
  influence 175
  authority 737
  fashion 852
– fast 704
– on fire
  ignite 384
  excite 824
– on foot 66
– foot on 294
– forth *show* 525
  assert 535
  describe 594
– forward 293
– free 750
– going
  [*see* – agoing]
– one's hand to

467
– one's heart upon 604, 865
– at hazard 665
– in *begin* 66
  rain 348
– on its legs 150
– on one's legs 159, 669
– in motion 264, 677
– to music 416
– at naught
  make light of 483
  reject 610
  oppose 708
  defy 715
  disobey 742
  not observe 773
  dereliction 927
– no store by 483, 930
– off
  compensation 30
  depart 293
  improve 658
  discount 813
  adorn 845
  display 882
– on 615
– in order 60
– out *arrange* 60
  begin 66
  depart 293
  decorate 845
  display 882
– over 755
– phrase 566
– a price 85, 812
– purpose 620
– at rest *end* 67
  answer 462
  adjudge 480
  complete 729
  compact 769
– right
  inform 527
  disclose 529
  teach 537
  reinstate 660
  vindicate 937
– to rights 60
– sail 293
– the seal on 729
– one's seal to 467
– store by 642
– straight 246, 723
– the table in a roar 840
– one's teeth 604
– terms
  manifest 525
  phrase 566
  style 574
– a trap for 545
– to 720, 722
– in towards 286
– up
  printing 54
  originate 153
  strengthen 159
  produce 161
  upright 212
  raise 307
  successful 731
  prosperous 734
– up shop 676

– upon
  resolved 604
  attack 716
  desirous 865
– too high a value upon 482
– watch 459
– one's wits to work *think* 451
  imagine 515
  plan 626
– to work
  undertake 676
  impose 741
set-back 735
set down
  record 551
  unseat 756
  humiliate 879
  slight 929
  censure 932
give one a –
  confute 479
– as 484
– for 484
– a cause for hearing 969
– to 155
– in writing 551
setaceous 256
seton 662
setose 256
settee 215
setter 366
settle *regulate* 60
  establish 150
  be located 184
  bench 215
  come to rest 265
  subside 306
  kill 361
  decide 480
  choose 609
  vanquish 731
  consent 762
  compact 769
  pay 807
– accounts 807, 811
– down 133
  stability 150
  moderate 174
  locate oneself 184
– into 144
– matters 723
– preliminaries 673
– property 781
– the question 478
– to sleep 683
– upon *give* 784
– with 807, 992
settled [*see* settle]
  characteristic 5
  ended 67
account – 811
– opinion 484
– purpose 620
settlement [*see* settle]
  location 184
  colony 188
  dregs 653
  compact 769
  deed 771
  property 780
strict – 781

settler 188
settlor 784
seven 98
–league boots 274, 992
wake the – sleepers 404
seventy 98
sever 38, 44
several *special* 79
  plural 100
  many 102
– times 104
severalize 465
severally 44, 79
severalty 44
severance 38
severe
  energetic 171
  symmetry 242
  exact 494
  - *style* 576
  harsh 739
  painful 830
  simple 849
  critical 932
severely *very* 31
severity **739**
sew 43
sewage 299, 653
sewed up
  drunk 959
sewer 350, 653
sewerage 652, 653
sewer-gas 663
sewing-silk 205
sex *kind* 75
  women 374
fair – 374
sexagenarian 98, 130
sexagenary 99
sextant 217, 244, 247
sextet 98
sextodecimo 593
sexton 363, 996
sextuple 98
seyyid 745
sforzando 415
shabbiness 34
shabby *trifling* 643
  deteriorated 659
  stingy 819
  mean 874
  disgraceful 940
shabby-genteel 851
shack 189
shackle
  fastening 45
  hinder 706
  restrain 751
  fetter 752
shade *degree* 26
  small quantity 32
  manes 362
  darkness 421
  shadow **424**
  color 428
  conceal 528
  screen 530
  paint 556
  ghost 980
eye – 443
in the – 528, 874
shadow of a – 32, 422

throw into the – *surpass* 303
  conceal 528
  glory 873
throw all else into the – 642
thrown into the – 34, 874
under the – of 664
without a – of doubt 474
shades:
– below 982
– of death 360
– of difference 15
– of evening 422
shading 421
– off 26
shadow
  unsubstantial 4
  copy 21
  small 32
  accompaniment 88
  thin 203
  be behind 235
  sequence 281
  dark 421
  shade 424
  pursue 461, 622
  dream 515
  demon 980
fight with a – 699
follow as a – 281
partial – 422
without a – of turning 141
worn to a –
  thin 203
  worse for wear 659
– of coming events 511
– forth *dim* 422
  predict 511
  metaphor 521
  represent 554
may your – never be less
  courtesy 894
  respect 928
  approbation 931
take the – for the substance
  credulous 486
  mistake 495
  unskilful 699
under the – of one's wing 664
shadowy 4, 447
shady 874
shaft *deep* 208
  frame 215
  pit 260
  missile 284
  axis 312
  air-pipe 351
  handle 633
  weapon 727
shaggy 256
shagreen 223
shah 745
shake *totter* 149
  weak 160
  vibrate 314
  agitation 315
  shiver 383

trill 407
music 416
dissuade 616
injure 659
impress 821
excited 824
fear 860
– one's faith 485
– hands
pacification 723
friendship 888
courtesy 894
forgive 918
– the head
dissent 489
deny 536
refuse 764
disapprove 932
– off 297
– off the yoke 759
– to pieces 162
– one's sides 838
– up 315
shakedown bed 215
shakes, no great –
643, 651
shako 225, 717
shaky weak 160
in danger 665
fearful 860
shallop 273
shallow
not deep 32, 209
ignorant 491
ignoramus 493
foolish 499
trifling 643
– pretext 617
– profundity 855
shallow-brain 501
shallowness 209
shallow-pated 499
shallows
danger 667
sham imitation 19
falsehood 544
deception 545,
546
– fight 720
shaman 994
shamanism 992
shamble 275, 315
shambles 361
shame
disrepute 874
wrong 923
censure 932
chastity 960
cry – upon 932
false – 855
for – 874
sense of – 879
– the devil 939
to one's – be it
spoken 874
shamefaced 881
shameful
disgraceful 874
profligate 945
shameless
bold 525
impudent 885
profligate 945
indecent 961
shampoo 652
shandredhan 272
shanghai 791

shank support 215
instrument 633
Shanks's mare 266
shanty 189
shape 240, 448
– one's course
direction 278
pursuit 622
conduct 692
– out a course 626
shapeless 241, 846
shapely 242, 845
shard 51
share
part 51
participate 778
allotted portion
786
– and share alike
778
shareholder 778
shark 792
sharp
energetic 171
violent 173
acute 253
sensible 375
pungent 392
– sound 410
musical tone 413
intelligent 498
active 682
clever 698
cunning 702
feeling 821
painful 830
rude 895
censorious 932
look – 459, 682
– appetite 865
– contest 720
– ear 418
– eye 441
– fellow 682, 700
– frost 383
– look-out 459,
507
– pain 378
– practice
cunning 702
severity 739
improbity 940
– set 865
sharpen
[see sharp]
excite 824
– one's tools 673
– one's wits 537
sharpener 253
sharper 792
sharpness 253
sharpshooter 726
sharpshooting 716
Shaster 986
shatter disjoin 44
disperse 73
render powerless
158
destroy 162
shatter-brained 503
shattered 160, 688
shave reduce 195
shorten 201
layer 204
smooth 255
grate 330
lie 546

close – 671
shaved 226
shaving small 32
layer 204
filament 205
shave-tail 726, 745
shawl 225
shawm 417
shay 272
she 374
sheaf 72
shear reduce 195
shorten 201
sheep 370
take 789
shears 253
sheath 191, 223
sheathe 225
moderate 174
– the sword 723
sheathing 223
sheave 633
shed scatter 73
building 189
divest 226
emit 297
give 784
– blood 361
– light upon 420
– a luster on 873
– tears 839
Shedim 980
sheen 420
sheep 366
sheep-dog 366
sheep-fold 232
sheepish 881
sheep's eye, cast a –
desire 865
modest 881
endearment 902
sheer simple 42
complete 52
deviate 279
– off avoid 623
sheet layer 204
covering 223
paper 593
come down in –s
rain 348
white – 952
winding – 363
– of fire 382
– of water 343
sheet-anchor
safety 664, 666
hope 858
sheet-lightning 423
sheik ruler 745, 875
lover 897
priest 996
shelf 215, 667
on the –
powerless 158
disused 678
inaction 681
shell cover 223
coffin 363
bombard 716
bomb 727
–burst 404
–shock 655
– out 784, 807,
809
shellac 356a
shellback 269
shell-fish 366

shelter 664, 666
– oneself under
plea of 617
sheltie 271
shelve defer 133
locate 184
slope 217
neglect 460
disuse 678
shelving beach 217
shend 659
shepherd tender of
sheep 370
director 694
pastor 996
Shepherd, the Good
– 976
shepherd's dog 366
Sheppard, Jack –
792
shere 32
sheriff 745, 965
Shetland pony 271
shew [see show].
shibboleth 550
shield
heraldry 550
safety 664
buckler 666
defend 717
scutcheon 877
look only at one
side of the – 481
reverse of the –
235, 468
under the – of 664
shift change 140
convert 144
substitute 147
changeable 149
chemise 225
move 264
transfer 270
deviate 279
prevaricate 546
plea 617
cunning 702
last – 601
make a – with
147, 677
put to one's –s
704, 804
– one's ground
607
– off defer 133
– for oneself 692,
748
left to – for one-
self 893
– one's quarters
264
– the scene 140
– to and fro 149
shifting [see shift]
transient 111
– sands 149
– trust or use 783
shiftless 674, 699
shillelagh 727
shilling 800
cut off with a –
789
– shocker 594
shilly-shally 605
shimmer 420
shimmy
dance 840

shindy 720
shine light 420
beauty 845
glory 873
take the – out of
874
– in conversation
588
– forth 873
– upon
illumine 420
aid 707
shingle 330
shingled
hair 53
shingles 223
shining [see shine]
– light sage 500
Shintoism 984
shiny 420
ship lade 190
transfer 270
vessel 273
take – 267, 293
one's – coming in
803
– of the line 726
shipboard, on – 273
ship-load 31, 190
shipman 269
shipmate 890
shipment
contents 190
transfer 270
shippen 189
shipping 273
shipshape order 58
conformity 82
skill 698
shipwreck
destruction 162
vanquish 731
failure 732
shire 181
shirk 603, 623, 742
shirker 862
shirt 225
Shiva 979
shive 22, 204
shiver
small piece 32
divide 44
destroy 162
filament 205
shake 315
brittle 328
cold 383
fear 860
go to –s 162
– in one's shoes
860
shivery brittle 328
powdery 330
shoal
assemblage 72
multitude 102
shallow 209
shoals danger 667
surrounded by –
difficulty 704
shoat 366
shock sheaf 72
violence 173
concussion 276
agitation 315
unexpected 508
disease 655

approve 931
worship 990
– in the shrouds
349
– small 879
singe 382, 384
singer 416
single *unmixed* 42
unit 87
secluded 893
unmarried 904
ride at – *anchor*
863
– *combat* 720
– *entry*
– *file* 69
– *out* 609
single-handed
one 87
easy 705
unassisted 706
single-minded 703
singleness
[*see* single]
– of heart 703, 939
– of purpose 604a,
703
single-stick 720
singlet 225
Sing Sing 752
sing-song 414, 892
singular *special* 79
exceptional 83
one 87
singularly *very* 31
sinister *left* 239
bad 649
vicious 945
bar –
imperfect 651
disrepute 874
sinistrality 239
sinistromanual 239
sinistrous
left-handed 239
sullen 901a
sink *disappear* 4
destroy 162
descend 306
lower 308
submerge 310
neglect 460
conceal 528
cloaca 653
fatigue 688
vanquish 731
fail 732
adversity 735
invest 787
pain 828
depressed 837
– back 661
– of corruption
653
– into the grave
360
– of iniquity 945
– in the mind
thought 451
memory 505
excite 824
– money 809
– into oblivion 506
– or swim
certainty 474
perseverance 604a
sinking

heart – 837
– fünd 802
sinless 946
sinned against than
sinning, more –
946
sinner 949
Sinn Fein 742
sin-offering 952
sinuous 243, 248
sinus 252
sip *small* 32
drink 298
siphon 350
sippet 298
sir *man* 373
title 877
– Oracle 887
sirdar 745
sire 166
siren
sea-nymph 341
loud sound 404
musician 416
seducing 615
warning 668
alarm 669
evil-doer 913
demon 980
sorcerer 994
song of the –s 615
– strains 415
sirene *musical
instrument* 417
siriasis 503
sirius 423
sirocco *wind* 349
heat 382
sirrah! 949
sister *kin* 11
likeness 17
nurse 662
nun 996
sisterhood
party 712
frail – 962
sisterly 906
sisters:
weird – 994
– three 601
sistrum 417
Sisyphus, task of –
useless 645
difficult 704
sit 308
– down *settle* 184
lie 213
stoop 308
– in judgment
adjudge 480
jurisdiction 965
lawsuit 969
– on 215
– on thorns
annoyance 828
fear 860
site 183, 780
sith 476
sitting [*see* sit]
incubation 673
convocation 696
– up *late* 133
work 686
sitting-room 191
situ, in – 183, 265
situation
circumstances 8

place **183**
location 184
business 625
out of a – 185
Siva 979
six 98
– of one and half-
a-dozen of the
other 27
sixes and sevens,
at – 59, 713
sixty 98
sizar 746
size *degree* 26
magnitude 31
glue 45
arrange 60
dimensions **192**
viscid 352
– up 480
sizzle 409
sjambok 975
skat 840
skate
locomotion 266
vehicle 272
skating 840
skean 727
skedaddle 623
skeel 191
skein 219
tangled – 59
skeleton
remains 40
essential part 30
thin 203
support 215
corpse 362
plan 626
reduced to a – 659
– in the closet
649, 830
– at the feast 836
skelter 276
skepticism
doubt 485
incredulity 487
irreligion 989
sketch
form 240
represent 554
paint 556
describe 594
plan 626
sketcher 559
sketchy
incomplete 53
feeble 575
unfinished 730
skew 217
–bald 440
skewer 45
ski 266, 272
–running 840
–joring 840
–jumping 840
skiagraphy 421,
554, 556
skid *support* 215
hindrance 706
skies:
exalt to the – 873
praise to the – 933
skiff 273
skill **698**
acquisition of –
539

game of – 840
skillet 191
skilly 293
skim *move* 266
navigate 267
rapid 274
neglect 460
summarize 596
skimp 460, 819
skimpy 640
skin *outside* 220
tegument 223
peel 226
swindle 791
fleece 814
wet to the – 339
with a whole – 670
without – 822
mere – and bone
203
– a flint 471, 819
– over 660
skin-deep
shallow 32, 209
external 220
skinned: thick– 376
thin– 375
skinny 203, 223
skip *jump* 309
neglect 460
rejoice 838
skipjack
prosperous 734
low-born 876
skipper
sea captain 269
captain 745
skippingly 70
skips, by – 70
skirmish 720
skirmisher 726
skirt
appendix 39
pendent 214
dress 225
surrounding 227
edge 231
side 236
– dance 840
skirting 231
skirts of:
hang upon the –
sequence 281
on the –
near 197
skit *ridicule* 856
detraction 934
prostitute 962
skittish
capricious 608
excitable 825
timid 862
bashful 881
skittle sharper 792
skittles 840
skiver 253
skulk 528, 862
skull 450
skull-cap 225
skunk 401
skurry 684
sky *summit* 210
world 318
air 338
necessity 601
sky-aspiring 865
sky-blue 438

sky-lark 305
sky-larking 840
sky-light 260
sky-line 196
sky-pilot 996
sky-rocket 305
sky-scraper 206,
210
slab *layer* 204
support 215
flat 251
viscous 352
record 551
slabber *slaver* 297
unclean 653
slack *loose* 47
weak 160
inert 172
slow 275
cool 385
fuel 388
neglectful 460
unwilling 603
insufficient 640
inactive 683
lax 738
slacken
loosen 47
moderate 174
repose 687
hinder 706
one's pace 275
slacker 460, 603,
623, 927
slag *embers* 384
inutility 641
dirt 653
slake *quench* 174
gratify 829
satiate 869
– one's appetite
intemperance 954
slam 276, 406
– the door in
one's face
oppose 708
refuse 764
slammerkin 653
slander 934
slanderer 936
slang 560, 563, 908
slant 217
slap *instantly* 113
strike 276
censure 932
punish 972
– in the face
opposition 708
attack 716
anger 900
disrespect 929
disapprobation
932
– the forehead 461
slap-dash 684
slash 44, 308
slashing *style* 574
slate
writing tablet 590
election 609
disparage 932
clean the – 918
– loose *mad* 503
slate-colored 432
slates *roof* 223
slattern
disorder 59

smooth *uniform* 16
calm 174
flattery 213, 251
not rough 255
easy 705
– the bed of death 707, 906
– down 174
– over 174
– the ruffled brow of care 834
– sailing 705
– water *easy* 705
– the way 705
smooth-bore 727
smoothly, go on – *prosperous* 734
smoothness **255**
smooth-tongued 544, 933
smother
repress 174
kill 361
stifle sound 581
restrain 751
smoulder *inert* 172
burn 382
latent 526
smous 796, 797
smudge 431, 653, 848
smug *affected* 855
smuggle
introduce 228
steal 791
illegal 964
smuggler 792
smut
dirt 653
impurity 961
smutch 431
snack
small quantity 32
food 298
snacks, go – 778
snaffle 752
snag *projection* 250
sharp 253
danger 667
hindrance 706
snail *slow* 275
snake *undulation* 248
serpent 366
hissing 406
miscreant 913
scotch the – 640
– in the grass hidden 528
deceiver 548
bad 649
source of danger 667
evil-doer 913
knave 941
snake-like convoluted 248
snap break 44
eat 298
brittle 328
noise **406**
rude 895
– at seize 789
bite 830
censure 932
– of the fingers trifle 643

– one's fingers at *defy* 715
insolence 885
despise 930
– the thread 70
– up seize 789
– one up
censure 932
–shot 554
snap-dragon 840
snappish 901
snare *deception* 545
snarl *growl* 412
rude 895
angry 900
threaten 909
snatch
small quantity 32
seize 789
– at pursue 622
seize 789
– a grace beyond the reach of art 845
– from one's grasp 789
– from the jaws of death 662, 672
– from under one's nose 702
– a verdict 545, 702
snatches, by – 70
sneak hide 528
coward 862
servile 886
base 940
knave 941
bad man 949
– off, – out of 623
sneer *disparage* 929
contempt 930
blame 932
sneeze blow 349
snuffle 409
– at despise 930
sneezed at, not to be – 642
snick 32, 51
snicker 838
sniff blow 349
odor 398
discovery 480a
sniffle 349
snigger *laugh* 838
ridicule 856
disrespect 929
sniggle 545
snip
small quantity 32
cut 44
short 201
tailor 225
sniping 716
snippet 32
snip-snap 713
snip-snap-snorem 840
snivel *weep* 839
sniveling
servile 886
snob *vulgar* 851
plebeian 876
servile 886
snobbishness
flattery 933
snood

headdress 225
circle 247
snooker 840
Snooks, Mr. – 876
snooze 683
snozzle 250
snore 411, 683
snort 411, 412
snout 250
snow *ship* 273
ice 383
white 430
snow-ball 72
snow-blindness 443
snow-drift 72
snow-shoe 272
snow-storm 383
snub *short* 201
hinder 706
cast a slur 874
humiliate 879
bluster 885
censure 932
snub-nosed 243
snuff blow 349
pungent 392
odor 398
up to – 698, 702
go out like the – of a candle 360
– out 162, 421
– up 296, 398
snuff-color 433
snuffing, want – pert 885
snuffle blow 349
hiss 409
stammer 583
hypocrisy 988
snuffy 653
snug *closed* 261
comfortable 377
safe 664
prepared 673
content 831
secluded 893
keep – 528, 893
make all – 673
snuggery 189
snugness 827
so *similar* 17
very 31
therefore 476
method 627
– be it 488, 762
– far so good 618
– let it be 681
– much the better 831, 838
– much the worse 832, 835
– to speak 17, 521
soak *immerse* 300
water 337
moist 339
drunkenness 959
– up 340
So-and-so, Mr. – neology 563
soap *lubricate* 332
oil 356
cleanser 652
soapy *unctuous* 355
servile 886
flattery 933
soar *great* 31
height 206

fly 267
rise 305
sob 839
sober *moderate* 174
wise 498
sane 502
style 576
grave 837
temperate 953
abstinent 958
– down 174, 502
humility 879
in – sadness
affirmation 535
– senses 502
– truth fact 494
sober-minded 502
calm 826
humble 879
sobriety **958**
sobriquet 565
sob sister 534
so-called 545, 565
soc *jurisdiction* 965
socage 777
soccer 840
sociable
carriage 272
sociality 892
social *mankind* 372
sociable 892
– circle 892
– evil 961
– gathering 892
– science 910
socialism
government 737
participation 778
philanthropy 910
socialist 712
sociality **892**
society
mankind 372
party 712
fashion 852
sociality 892
position in – 873
Socinianism 984
sociology 712
sock *hosiery* 225
drama 599
socket 191, 252
socle 215
Socratic method 461
sod 344
beneath the – 363
sodality 712, 888
sodden 339, 384
sofa 215
Sofi 984, 996
soft *stop!* 142
weak 160
moderate 174
smooth 255
not hard 324
moist 339
marsh 345
silence! 403
– sound 405
dulcet 413
credulous 486
silly 499
lenient 740
tender 822
timid 862
own to the – im-

peachment 529
– music 415
– pedal 405
– sawder 617, 933
– soap 356, 933
– tongue, – words 894
soften [*see* soft]
moderate 174
relieve 834
pity 914
palliate 937
softening of the brain 158
softer sex 374
soft-hearted 914
softling 160
softness **324**
persuasibility 615
soft-spoken 894
soggy 339
soho
attention 457
parley 586
hunting 622
soi-disant
asserting 535
pretender 548
misnomer 565
vain 880
boastful 884
soil *region* 18
land 342
dirt 653
deface 846
till the – 371, 673
soirée 892
sojourn 186, 189
sojourner 188
soke 181
solace *relief* 834
recreation 840
– oneself with pleasure 827
solar 318
– system 318
– time 114
solatium 973
sold to the devil 949
soldan [*see* sultan]
solder *join* 43
cement 45
cohere 46
soldier 726
soldier-like 722, 861
sole *alone* 87
base 211
support 215
feme – 904
solecism **568**
soleil, coup de – hot 384
mad 503
solemn
affirmation 535
important 642
grave 837
glorious 873
ostentatious 882
religious 987
worship 990
– mockery 882
– silence 403
solemnity *rite* 998
solemnization 883
sol-fa 416

solfeggio 415
solicit *induce* 615
  request 765
  desire 865
  – the attention
    457
solicitor *agent* 758
  petitioner 767
  lawyer 968
solicitous 865
solicitude *care* 459
  pain 828
  anxiety 860
  desire 865
solid *complete* 52
  dense 321
  certain 474
  learned 490
  exact 494
  wise 498
  persevering 604a
  solvent 803
  – angle 244
solidarity
  party 712
solidify 321
soliloquy **589**
solitaire *game* 840
  hermit 893
solitary }
solitude } *alone*
  } 87
  secluded 893
solmization 416
solo 87, 415
  – dance 840
Solomon } *wise*
Solon } 498
  sage 500
solstice 125, 126
soluble *fluid* 333
  liquefy 335
solus 87
solution
  liquefaction 335
  answer 462
  explanation 522
  – of continuity 70
solve *liquefy* 335
  discover 480a
  unriddle 522
solvent
  liquefier 335
  monied 803
somatics 316
somber *dark* 421
  black 431
  grey 432
  sad 837
sombrero 225
some *indefinite*
  quantity 25
  small quantity 32
  more than one
    100
–body *person* 372
  important or dis-
    tinguished 642
in – degree
  degree 26
  small 32
at – *other time* 119
in – place 182
  – ten or a dozen
    102
  – time ago 122
  – time or other
    119

somehow or other
  cause 155
  instrument 631
somersault 218
something *thing* 3
  small degree 32
  matter 316
  – else 15
  – like 17
  – or other 475
sometimes 136
somewhat
  a little 32
  a trifle 643
somewhere 182
  – about 32
somnambulism
  walking 266
  trance 515
somnambulist
  walker 268
  dreamer 515
somniferous
  sleepy 683
  weary 841
somnolence 683
son 167
Son, God the – 976
sonant 402
  letter 561
sonata 415
Sonderband 769
song *music* 415
  poem 597
  death – 360, 839
  love– 597
  for a mere – 815
  no – no supper 812
  old – 643
songster 416
soniferous 402
sonnet 597
sonneteer 597
sonority 712
sonorous *sound* 402
  loud 404
  language 577
sons of:
  – Belial 988
  – God 977
Soofeeism 984
soon *transient* 111
  future 121
  early 132
  too – for 135
sooner: – or later
  another time 119
  future 121
  – said than done
    704
soot 431, 653
sooth 511
  in good – 543
soothe
  allay 174
  relieve 834
  flatter 933
soothing
  faint sound 405
  – syrup 174
soothsay 511
soothsayer 513, 994
soothsaying 511
sop
  small quantity 32
  food 298
  fool 501
  inducement 615

  reward 973
  – to Cerberus 458
  – in the pan 615
soph 492, 541
Sophi 745, 996
sophism 477, 497
sophist *scholar* 492
  dissembler 548
sophister 492
  student 541
sophistical 477
sophisticate *mix* 41
  debase 659
sophisticated
  spurious 545
sophistry **477**
sophomore 541
soporific 683, 841
soporous 683
soprano 410, 416
sorbet 298
sorcerer **994**
sorcery **992**
sordes 653
sordet 417
sordid *stingy* 819
  covetous 865
sordine 417
sore
  bodily pain 378
  disease 655
  mental suffering
    828, 830
  discontent 832
  anger 900
  – as a boil 901a
  – place 822
  – subject 830, 900
sorely *very* 31
s'orienter 278
sorites 476
sorority 712
sorrel 433, 434
sorrow 828
  give – words 839
  grieved 828
  mean 876
  make a – face 874
  cut a – figure 874
  be – for 750, 914
  in a – plight 732
  – sight 830, 837
sort *degree* 26
  arrange 60
  kind 75
  – with
  sociality 892
sortable }
sortance }
  agreement 23
sortes
  chance 156, 621
  – Virgilianae
  sorcery 992
sortie 716
sortilege
  prediction 511
  sorcery 992
sortilegy 621
sortition 621
sorts, out of –
  ill-health 655
  sulky 901a
S.O.S. 669, 707
so-so *small* 32
  trifling 643

  imperfect 651
sostenuto 415
sot *fool* 501
  drunkard 959
sot à triple étage
  501
sotto voce
  faint sound 405
  conceal 528
  voiceless 581
sou *money* 800
  qui n'a pas le –
    804
soubrette 599, 746
sough *conduit* 350
  noise 405
  cloaca 653
soul *essence* 5
  person 372
  intellect 450
  genius 498
  affections 820
  cure of –s 995
  flow of – 588
  not a – 187
  not dare to say
    one's – is his
    own *subjection*
    749
  fear 860
  – of wit 572
  have one's whole
    – in his work
    686
soulless 683, 823
soul-mate 905
soul-sick 837
soul-stirring 821,
  824
sound *great* 31
  conformable 82
  stable 150
  strong 159
  fathom 208
  bay 343
  noise **402**
  investigate 461
  measure 466
  true 494
  wise 498
  sane 502
  good 648
  perfect 650
  healthy 654
  solvent 803
  orthodox 983a
  catch a – 418
  safe and – 654,
    670
  – the alarm
  indication 550
  warning 668
  alarm 669
  fear 860
  – asleep 683
  full of – and fury
  unmeaning 517
  insolent 885
  – the horn 416
  – of limb 654
  – locator 726
  – mind 502
  – the praises of
    931
  – the note of prep-
    aration 673
  – reasoning 476

  – a retreat 283
  – sleep 683
  – a trumpet
  publish 531
  alarm 669
  – of wind 654
sounding: big –
    577
  – brass 517
sounding-board 417
soundings 208
soundless
  unfathomable 208
  silent 403
soup 298, 352
soupçon 32, 41
soupled 298
sour *acid* 397
  discontented 832
  embitter 835
  uncivil 895
  sulky 901
  – grapes
  impossible 471
  excuse 617
  – the temper 830
source *beginning* 66
  cause 153
sourdet 417
sourdine 417
  à la – *noiseless* 405
  concealed 528
sourdough 463
soured 832
sourness **397**
sous tous les
  rapports 52
souse 310, 337
South *direction* 278
  North and –
  opposite 237
Southern
  antipodes 237
  – Cross 318
souvenir 505
sovereign
  superior 33
  all-powerful 159
  authorities 737
  ruler 745
  – contempt 930
  – remedy 662
Soviet 696, 702
sow *scatter* 73
  pig 366
  agriculture 371
  female 374
  get the wrong –
    by the ear
  misjudgment 481
  error 495
  mismanage 699
  fail 732
  – broadcast 818
  – dissension 713,
    898
  – the sand 645
  – the seed
  prepare 673
  – the seeds of
  cause 153
  teach 537
  – one's wild oats
  improve 658
  amusement 840
  vice 945
  intemperance 954

retract one's – 283
take – *plan* 626
  prepare 673
  conduct 692
tread in the – of
  281
stercoraceous 653
stereography 591
stereometry 466
stereopticon 445
stereoscope 445
stereoscopic 446
stereotype *copy* 21
  mark 550
  engraving 558
  printing 591
stereotyped
  uniform 16
  stable 150
  habit 613
sterile 169, 645, 732
sterilize 652
sterling *true* 494,
  944
– *coin* 800
stern *rear* 235
  severe 739
  discourteous 895
– *necessity* 601,
  603
– *truth* 494
sternmost 235
sternutation
  sneeze 349
  sound 409
sternway 267
stertorous 402, 580
stet 150
– pro ratione vo-
  luntas 600
stethoscope 418
stevedore 271, 613,
  690
stew *food* 298
  heat 382
  cook 384
  difficulty 704
  emotion 821
  excitement 825
  annoyance 828
  bagnio 961
  in a – *angry* 900
steward 637
  director 694
  agent 758
  treasurer 801
stewardship 692,
  693
stewpan 386
stichomancy 511
stick *adhere* 46
  cease 142
  staff 215
  stab 260
  remain quiet 265
  fool 501
  bungler 701
  weapon 727
  scourge 975
  dirty end of the –
    699
  give the – to 972
  – at *doubt* 485
  averse 603
  – *fast firm* 150
  difficulty 704
  – in one's gizzard

830, 900
– in 300
– *law* 972
– in the mud
  304, 732
– at nothing
  resolve 604
  active 682
  rash 863
– out 250
– to 143, 604a
– in the throat
  hoarse 581
  not say 585
  dislike 867
– up 212, 307, 791
– up for *aid* 707
  applaud 931
  vindicate 937
stickle 603, 616
– for 720, 794
stickler 606
  severity 739
sticky
  cohering 46
  viscid 352
stiff *rigid* 323
  style 579
  severe 739
  coactive 751
  ugly 846
  affected 855
  haughty 878
  pompous 882
  – *breeze* 349
stiffen 323
stiff-necked 606
stiffness
  stability 150
stifle *kill* 361
  silence 403
  conceal 528
stifled
  faint sound 405
stifling *hot* 382
stigmatize 874
  censure 932
  accuse 938
stile *way* 627
  hindrance 706
  help a lame dog
    over a – 707
stiletto 262, 727
still
  on the other hand
    30
  moderate 174
  not moving 265
  vaporization 336
  furnace 386
  silent 403
  – less 467
  – *life matter* 316
  painting 556
  – more
  superior 33
  evidence 467
  – small voice 405
  in – water 714
still-born 360, 732
stillroom 636
stillicidium 348
stilted
  elevated 307
  – *style* 577
  ridiculous 853
  affected 855

boasting 884
stilts *support* 215
  on – *high* 206
  elevated 307
  hyperbolical 549
  proud 878
  boasting 884
stimulant 662
stimulate
  energy 171
  violence 173
  incite 615
  excite 824
stimulating
  suggestive 514
stimulus 615
sting *pain* 378
  tingle 380
  poison 663
  excite 824
  mental suffering
    830
  anger 900
stinging
  pungent 392
stingo 298
stingy 819
stink 401
– in the nostrils
  unpleasant 830
  dislike 867
  hate 898
stink-bomb 727
stink-pot 401
stint *degree* 26
  limit 233
  scanty 640
  begrudge 819
stintless 639
stipend *salary* 973
stipendiary
  subject 749
  receiving 785
  magistrate 967
stipple
  variegate 440
  painting 556
  engraving 558
stipulate 769, 770
– for 720
stipule 51
stir *energy* 171
  move 264
  agitation 315
  excite 375
  activity 682
  jail 752
  emotion 824
  make a – 642, 682
  – about 682
  – the blood 824,
    900
  – up dissension
    713
  – the embers 163,
    824
  – the feelings 824
  – the fire 384
  – a question 461,
    476
  – one's stumps
    266, 682
  – up *mix* 41
  violent 173
  excite 824
stirps *kin* 11
  source 153

paternity 166
stirring *events* 151
  important 642
  active 682
  – *news* 532
stirrup
  support 215
  with a foot in the
    – 293
stirrup-cup 293, 959
stitch *junction* 43
  pain 378
  work 680
  – in time 132
  – of work 686
stive 384
stiver 800
stoat 401
stoccado 717
stock *kinship* 11
  quantity 25
  origin 153
  paternity 166
  collar 225
  soup 298
  fool 501
  habitual 613
  materials 635
  store 636
  property 780
  merchandise 798
  money 800
  in – 777
  laughing – 857
  lay in a – 637
  take – *inspect* 457
  accounts 811
  – *exchange* 799
  – *still* 265
  – in trade
  means 632
  store 636
  property 780
  merchandise 798
  – with 637
stockade 717
stocked, well – 639
stock exchange 621
stock-farm 370
stocking 225
  hoard 800
stock-jobbing 794
stock operator 621
stocks *prison* 752
  funds 802
  punishment 975
  on the –
  business 625
  preparation 673
  incomplete 730
  – and stones 316,
    823
stocky 201
stodge 957
stoicism
  insensibility 823
  inexcitability 826
  disinterested 942
  temperance 953
stoke 388
stoker 268
stole 999
stolen: – away 671
  – goods 793
stolid 499, 843
stomach *pouch* 191
  taste 390

brook 826
  desire 865
  not have the – to
    603
  turn the – 830
  – of an ostrich 957
stomacher 225
stone *heavy* 319
  dense 321
  hard 323
  kill 361
  lithography 558
  material 635
  attack 716
  weapon 727
  punish 972
  corner – 642
  go down like a –
    310
  cast the first – at
    938
  heart of – 823, 907
  key– 642
  musical –s 417
  no – unturned
    461, 686
  philosopher's –
    662
  precious – 648
  stepping – 627
  throw a – at
  attack 716
  censure 932
  accuse 938
  throw –s at 907
  tomb– 363
  mark with a
    white – 642
  throw a – in one's
    own garden 699
  – dead 360
  – of Sisyphus 645
stone-blind 442
stone-colored 432
stone-deaf 419
stone's throw 197
stoneware 384
stony 323
stony-hearted 907,
  919
stooge 711, 746, 886
stook 72
stool 215
  between two –s
    704
  – of repentance
    950
  – pigeon 527, 548
stoop *slope* 217
  lower 308
  humble 879
  servile 886
  dishonorable 940
  – to conquer 702
stop *end* 67
  cease 142
  close 261
  rest 265
  silent 403
  danger 665
  inaction 681
  hinder 706
  prohibit 761
  put a – to 142
  – the breath 361
  – the ears 419
  – a flow 348

– a gap 660
– the mouth 479, 581
– payment 808
– press news 532
– short 142, 265
– short of 304
– the sound 408a
– up 261
– the way 706
stopcock 263
stopgap
  substitute 147
  stopper 263
stoppage
  cessation 142
  hindrance 706
stopper 263
stopping place 292
store store 184
  stock 636
  shop 799
  in – destiny 152
  preparing 673
  lay in a – 637
  set – by 642, 931
  set no – 483
  – of knowledge 490
  – in the memory 505
store-house 636
store-keeper 636
store-ship 273, 726
storied 594
storm crowd 72
  convulsion 146
  violence 173
  agitation 315
  wind 349
  danger 667
  attack 716
  passion 825
  anger 900
  ride the – 267
  take by –
  conquer 731
  seize 789
  – brewing 665
  – in a teacup
  overrate 482
  exaggerate 549
  unimportance 643
storthing 696
story rooms 191
  layer 204
  news 532
  lie 546
  history 594
  the old – 897
  as the – goes 532
story-teller 548, 594
stot 366
stound 870
stoup cup 191
  altar 1000
stour 59
stout strong 159
  large 192
  drink 298
stout-hearted 861
stove fireplace 386
  – in 252
stow locate 184
  pack close 195
  store 636
stowage 180, 184

stowaway 528, 673
strabism 443
straddle 266, 607
Stradivarius 417
strafe 972
straggle 266, 279
straggler 268
straggling 44, 59
straight
  vertical 212
  rectilinear 246
  direction 278
  all – rich 803
  solvent 807
  – course 628
  – descent 167
  – face 837
  – sailing 705
straighten 246
  – up 60
straightforward 278
  truthful 543
  artless 703
  honorable 939
straightness 246
straight shot 278
straightway 132
strain race 11
  weaken 160
  operation 170
  violence 173
  percolate 295
  transgress 303
  sound 402
  melody 415
  overrate 482
  exaggerate 549
  style 569
  poetry 597
  voice 580
  clean 652
  effort 686
  fatigue 688
  – in the arms 902
  – one's eyes 441, 507
  – at a gnat and swallow a camel 608
  – one's invention 515
  – the meaning 523
  – every nerve 686
  – a point
  go beyond 303
  exaggerate 549
  not observe 773
  undue 925
  – the throat 411
strait
  interval 198
  water 343
  difficulty 704
straitened
  poor 804
strait-handed 819
strait-jacket 752
strait-laced
  severe 739
  restraint 751
  fastidious 868
  haughty 878
strait-waistcoat 751, 752
strake 205
stramash 720
strand thread 205

shore 231, 342
stranded
  stuck fast 150
  in difficulty 704
  failure 732
  pain 828
strange
  unrelated 10
  exceptional 83
  ridiculous 853
  wonderful 870
  – bedfellows 713
  – to say 870
strangely much 31
stranger 57
  a – to 491
strangle
  render powerless 158
  contract 195
  kill 361
strap fasten 43
  fastening 45
  restraint 752
  punish 972
  instrument of punishment 975
strappado 972
strapping
  mighty 31
  strong 159
  pace 272
  big 192
strapwork 847
stratagem
  deception 545
  plan 626
  artifice 702
strategic plan 626
  artifice 702
strategist
  planner 626
  director 694
  proficient 700
strategy 692, 722
strath 252
strathspey 840
stratification 204, 329
stratocracy 737
stratosphere 338
stratum 204
stratus 353
straw scatter 73
  light 320
  unimportant 643
  care not a – 866, 930
  catch at –s
  overrate 482
  credulous 486
  misuse 679
  unskilful 699
  hope 858
  rash 863
  the eyes drawing –s 683
  in the – 161
  man of –
  unsubstantial 4
  cheat 525
  insolvent 808
  low person 876
  not worth a – 643, 645
  – to show the wind 463

straw-colored 436
straw-hat 225
stray dispersion 73
  exceptional 83
  random 156
  wanderer 268
  deviate 279
streak intrinsicality 5
  long 200
  narrow 203
  furrow 259
  light 420
  stripe 440
  mark 550
streaked 219, 440
stream assemble 72
  move 264
  – of fluid 347
  – of water 348
  – of air 349
  – of light 420
  abundance 639
  against the – 708
  with the –
  conformity 82
  progression 282
  assent 488
  facility 705
  concord 714
  fashion 852
  servility 886
  – of events 151
  – of time 109
streamer flag 550
streaming 47, 73
streamlet 348
street 189, 627
  man in the – 876
streets:
  in the open – 525
  on the – 961
street-walker 962
strength
  quantity 25
  degree 26
  greatness 31
  vigor 159
  energy 171
  tenacity 327
  animality 364
  put all one's –
  into 686
  lose – 655
  tower of – 717
  – of mind 604
strengthen 35
strengthless 160
strenuous
  persevering 604a
  active 682
  exertion 686
Strephon and Chloe 902
stress emphasis 580
  requirement 630
  importance 642
  strain 686
  difficulty 704
  by – of 601
  lay – on 476
  – of circumstances
  compulsion 744
  – of weather 349
stretch expanse 180
  expand 194
  extend 200

exaggerate 549
exertion 686
encroach 925
at a – 69
mind on the – 451
on the – 686
upon the – 457
  – away to 196
  – forth one's hand 680, 789
  – of the imagination 515, 549
  – the meaning 523
  – a point 83, 303
  exaggerate 549
  severity 739
  permit 760
  not observe 773
  undue 925
  exempt 927a
  – to distance 196
  length 200
stretcher 215, 272
strew 73
stria, striated 259, 440
stricken pain 828
  terror– 860
  be – by 655
  – in years 128
strict
  in conformity 82
  exact 494
  severe 739
  conscientious 939
  orthodox 983a
  – inquiry 461
  – interpretation 522
  – search 461
  – settlement 780
strictly speaking
  literally 19
  exact 494
  interpreted 522
stricture
  constriction 203
  hindrance 706
  censure 932
stride distance 196
  motion 264
  walk 266
strident 410
strides: make – 282
  rapid – 274
stridor 410
strife 713, 720
strigil 652
strike operate 170
  hit 276
  resist 719
  disobey 742
  impress 824
  beat 972
  – at 716
  – a balance
  equalize 27
  mean 29
  pay 807
  – a bargain 769, 794
  – a blow act 680
  excitement 824
  wonder 870
  humble 879
  – the eye 457

- the first blow 716
- one's flag 725
- hard 171
- all of a heap 824, 860
- home 171
- in with
  imitate 19
  assent 488
  cooperate 709
- the iron while it is hot 134
- a light 384, 420
- the lyre 416
- the mind 457
- out something new 146, 515
- off exclude 55
- one 451
- out exclude 55
  destroy 162
  invent 515
  obliterate 552
  scheme 626
- off the roll 756, 972
- at the root of 162
- root 150
- sail 275
- tents 293
- terror 860
- up 416
- with wonder 870
striker 927
striking 525
- likeness 554
strikingly
  greatly 31
string tie 43
  ligature 45
  continuity 69
  filament 205
  musical note 413
- together 60, 69
stringed instruments 417
stringent
  energetic 171
  authoritative 737
  strict 739
  compulsory 744
strings: music 417
  leading - 541
  pull the - 175, 693
  two - to one's bow 632
stringy 205, 327
strip adjunct 39
  narrow 203
  filament 205
  divest 226
  take 780
  rob 791
stripe length 200
  variegation 440
  mark 550
  badge 747
  blow 972
stripling 129
stripped poor 804
strive endeavour 675
  exert 686
  contend 720
- against 720

stroke impulse 276
  touch 379
  mark 550
  evil 619
  expedient 626
  disease 655
  action 680
  success 731
  painful 830
at a - 113
good - 626
- of death 360
- of the pen
  writing 590
  command 741
- of policy 626
- of time 113
- of word 686
- the wrong way 256
stroll 266
strolling player 599
strong great 31
  powerful 159
  energetic 171
  tough 327
  taste 390
  pungent 392
  fetid 401
  healthy 654
  feeling 821
  wonderful! 870
  smell - of 398
- accent 580
- argument 476
by a - arm 744
- box 802
with a - hand
  resolution 604
  exertion 686
  severity 739
- language 574
- pull 686
- point 476
strong-headed 498
stronghold
  refuge 666
  defence 717
  prison 752
strong-minded 498, 861
strong-scented 398
strong-willed 604
strop 253
strophe 597
strow 73
struck [see stricken, strike]
  awe- 860
- down 732
- all of a heap
  emotion 821
  wonder 870
  humbled 879
- with love 897
structural state 7
structure
  production 161
  form 240
  texture 329
  organization 357
struggle exert 686
  difficulty 704
  contend 720
strum 416, 517
strumpet 962
strung

highly - 825
strut walk 266
  pride 878
  parade 882
  boast 884
- and fret one's hour upon a stage 359, 599
strychnine 663
stub 40, 550
stubbed 201
stubble remains 40
  useless 645
stubborn
  strong 159
  hard 323
  obstinate 606
  resistance 719
stubby 201
stucco 45, 223
stuck [see stick]
- fast 150, 704
  be - on 897
stuck-up 878
stud hanging-peg 214
  knob 250
  horses 271
studded many 102
  spiked 253
  variegated 440
student 541
stud-farm 370
studied
  predetermined 611
studio room 191
  painting 556
  workshop 691
studious
  thoughtful 451
  docile 539
  intending 620
study copy 21
  room 191
  thought 451
  attention 457
  research 461
  learning 539
  painting 556
  intention 620
  retreat 893
brown - 515
stuff substance 3
  contents 190
  expand 194
  line 224
  matter 316
  texture 329
  absurdity 497
  unmeaning 517
  material 635
  trifle 643
  overeat 957
such - as dreams are made of 515
- gown 968
- in 300
- the memory with 505
- and nonsense
  unsubstantial 4
  absurdity 497
  unmeaning 517
- up close 261
  hoax 545
stuffed

redundancy 641
stuffing contents 190
  lining 224
  stopper 263
stuffy 321, 382
stultified 732
stultify oneself 699
stultiloquy 497
stumble fall 306
  flounder 315
  error 495
  unskilful 699
  failure 732
- on chance 156
  discover 480a
stumbling-block
  difficulty 704
  hindrance 706
stump
  remainder 40
  trunk 51
  walk 266
  drawing 556
  speak 582
stir your -s
  active 682
  worn to the - 659
- along slow 275
stump orator 582, 887
stumpy short 201
stun physically
  insensible 376
  loud 404
  deafen 419
  unexpected 508
  morally insensible 823
  affect 824
  astonish 870
stung [see sting]
- to the quick 824
stunt shorten 201
  performance 680
stunted 193, 195
  insufficient 640
stupe 834
stupefaction 826
stupefy
- physically 376
- morally 823
  astonish 870
stupendous
  great 31
  large 192
  wonderful 870
stupid
  unsubstantial 4
  misjudging 481
  credulous 486
  unintelligent 499
  tiresome 841
  dull 843
stupor
  insensibility 823
  wonder 870
stupration 961
sturdy strong 159
  persevering 604a
- beggar 767, 792
stutter 583
sty house 189
  enclosure 232
  dirt 653
Stygian dark 421
  diabolic 945
  infernal 982

cross the - ferry die 360
- shore
  death 360
style state 7
  time 114
  painting 556
  graver 558
  name 564
  diction 569
  writing 590
  beauty 845
  fashion 852
stylet
  awl 262
  dagger 727
stylist 578
Stylites, Simon - 893
stylographic pen 590
stylography 590
stylus 590
styptic 397
Styx 982
suasible 602
suasion 615
suave mari magno 664
suaviter in modo 826, 894
suavity 894
sub 34
- spe rati 475
subacid 397
subaction 330
subahdar 745
subalpine 206
subaltern
  inferior 34
  soldier 726
  officer 745
  servant 746
  plebeian 876
subaqueous 208
subastral 318
subaudition 527
subcommittee 696
subconscious 317
subcontrary 237
subcutaneous 221
subdean 996
subdichotomy 91
subdititious 147
subdivide 44
subdivision
  part 51
  class 75
  military 726
  realty 780
subdolous 702
subdominant 413
subdual 731
subduction 38
subdue calm 174
  succeed 731
subdued
  morally 826
sub-editor 593
subitaneous 113
subito 113
subjacent 207
subject dominate 175
  liable 177
  topic 454
  meaning 516

servant 746
enthral 749
– of dispute 713
– to examination 461
– of inquiry 461
– of thought 454
– to 469, 475
subjection **749**
subjective
intrinsic 5
immaterial 317
intellectual 450
subjoin 37
subjugate 731, 749
subjugation 732, 824
subjunctive 37
sublapsarian 984
sublation 38
sublevation 307
sub-lieutenant 745
sublimate
elevate 307
lighten 320
vaporize 336
sublime *high* 206
language 574
beauty 845
glory 873
magnanimous 942
from the – to the ridiculous 853
subliminal 317
sublineation 550
sublunary 318
submarine
deep 208
ship 272
warship 726
– chaser 726
– warfare 722
submedian 413
submerge
destroy 162
immerse 300
plunge 310
steep 337
submersible 273, 726
submersion 208
subministration 707
submission **725**
obedience 743
submissive
tractable 705
enduring 826
humble 879
submit to arbitration 774
submonish 695
submultiple 84
subordinate
inferior 34
unimportant 643
subject 749
subordination 58
suborn 615, 795
subpoena 741, 969
subreption
falsehood 544
acquisition 775
subrogation 147
subscribe
assent 488

aid 707
agree to 769
give 784
subscript 39, 65
subscription
gift 784
subsequent
– *in order* 63
– *in time* 117
subserviency
servility 886
subservient
instrumental 631
aid 707
subject 749
subside 36, 306
subsidiary *aid* 707
servant 746
subsidy
assistance 707
gift 784
pay 809
subsist *exist* 1
continue 141
live 359
subsistence 298
subsoil 221, 342
substance
existence 1
thing 3
quantity 25
inside 221
matter 316
texture 329
important part 642
wealth 803
in – 596
man of – 803
substantial
existing 1
hypostatic 3
material 316
dense 321
true 494
– *meaning* 516
substantiality **3**
substantially
intrinsically 5
– true 494
substantiate 467, 924
substantive 1, 3
substitute
inferior 34
change 147
means **634**
deputy 759
substitution **147**
substratum
substance 3
layer 204
base 211
support 215
interior 221
materiality 316
substructure 211
subsultory 315
subsume 54
subtend 237
subterfuge 617
sophistry 477
lie 546
cunning 702
subterranean 208
subtile *light* 320
rare 322

– *texture* 329
subtilize *rarefy* 322
sophistry 477
subtle *slight* 32
light 320
cunning 702
– *point* 704
– *reasoning* 476
subtlety 477, 498
subtraction
subduction 38
arithmetic 85
taking 789
subtrahend 38, 84
suburb *town* 189
near 197
environs 227
subvention
. *support* 215
aid 707
gift 784
subversion 146
subvert *destroy* 162
invert 218
depress 308
subway 627
– *train* 272
succedaneum 147
succeed *follow* 63
posterior 117
success 731
transfer 783
– to *acquire* 775
succès d'estime 873
success **731**
succession
sequence 63
continuity 69
repetition 104
posteriority 117
transfer 783
in quick – 136
in regular – 138
– of ideas 451
– of time 109
successless 732
successor 65, 117
succinct 572
succor 707
succubus 980
succulent
nutritive 298
juicy 333
semiliquid 352
succumb
fatigue 688
yield 725
fail 732
succussion 315
such: – as 17
– being the case 8
– like 17
– a one 372
suchwise 8
suck
draw off 297
drink 298
take 789
– in 296
– the blood of 789
sucker 260, 547
suckle 707
suckling *infant* 129
suction *force* 157
reception 296
sudary 652
sudation 299.

sudatory 386
sudden
transient 111
instantaneous 113
soon 132
unexpected 508
– *burst* 508
– *death* 360
– and quick in quarrel 901
– *thought* 612
sudorific 382
suds *froth* 353
in the – 704, 837
sue *demand* 765
go to law 969
suet 356
suffer *physical pain* 378
disease 655
allow 760
feel 821
endure 826
moral pain 828
– for 972
– *punishment* 972
sufferance, tenant on – 779
suffice 639
sufficiency **639**
suffix *adjunct* 39
sequence 63
sequel 65
letter 561
suffiation 349
suffocate *kill* 361
excess 641
suffocating 382, 401
suffocation 361
suffragan 996
suffrage 609
suffragette 742
suffusion
mixture 41
feeling 821
blush 879
sugar 396
sugar-loaf 253
suggest *suppose* 514
inform 527
influence 615
advise 695
– *itself* 451, 515
– a *question* 461
suggestio falsi 546
suggestion 626, 695
suggestive
reminder 505
significant 516
descriptive 594
bawdy 961
sui generis 83
suicidal 162
suicide *killing* 361
suisse *beadle* 996
Suisse, point d'argent point de – 812
suit *accord* 23
series 69
class 75
clothes 225
expedient 646
petition 765
courtship 902
follow – 19
law– 969

love– 897
– the action to the word 550
– the occasion 646
do – and service 743
suit case 191
suitable 23, 646
– *season* 134
suite *sequel* 65
series 69
escort 88
retinue 746
– of rooms 189, 191
suitor
petitioner 767
lover 897
lawsuit 969
sulcated 259
sulky *carriage* 272
obstinate 606
discontented 832
dejected 837
sullen 901a
sullen
obstinate 606
gloomy 837
discourteous 895
sulky 901a
sullenness 901a
sully 653, 874
sulphur 388
– colored 436
sultan 745
sultry 382
sum *number* 84
money 800
– and substance *meaning* 516
synopsis 596
important part 642
– total 800
– up *reckon* 85
description 594
compendium 596
sumless 105
summation 37, 85
summary
transient 111
early 132
short 201
concise 572
compendious 596
illegal 964
– of facts 594
summer *season* 125
support 215
heat 382
Indian – 125
St. Luke's – 125
St. Martin's – 125
– lightning 423
– time 114
summer-house 191
summerset 218
summit *top* **210**
summon 741, 969
– up 505, 824
– up courage 861
summum:
– bonum 618, 827
– jus 922
sump *base* 211
pool 343
slough 345
store 636

velocity 274
messenger 534
signal 550
– boy 534
by – *haste* 684
telegraphone 553
telegraphy
  publication 531
teleology 620
telemeter 200
telepathy 992
telephone 418
  inform 527
  messenger 534
telescope 445
– word 572
telescopic 196
telesis 658
telesm 993
television 532
tell *count* 85
  influence 175
  evidence 467
  inform 527
  speak 582
  describe 594
  succeed 731
let me – you 535
who can – 475
– one's beads 990, 998
– the cause of 522
– fortunes 511
– how 155
– a lie 544
– a piece of one's mind 529
– of 467
– off 85
– one plainly 527
– its own tale 518
– tales
  disclose 529
– the truth 543
teller *treasurer* 801
– of tales 594
telling 175
  graphic 518
  important 642
  exciting 824
with – effect 171, 175
telltale *news* 532
  indicator 550
  knave 941
telluric 318
telum imbelle 158
temerity 863
temper *nature* 5
  state 7
  moderate 174
  elasticity 323
  pliability 324
  modify 469
  prepare 673
  affections 820
  irascibility 901
command of – 826
lose one's – 900
out of – 901a
trial of – 824
– the wind to the shorn lamb 834
tempera 556
témperament
  nature 5
  tendency 176

musical 413
  affections 820
temperance 174, 953
temperate
  [*see* temperance]
  mild 826
temperature 382
  increase of – 384
  réduction of – 385
tempest
  violence 173
  agitation 315
  wind 349
  excitement 825
tempestivity 134
tempest-tossed 824
tempestuous 59
Templar 996
  Good – 958
temple *house* 189
  side 236
  church 1000
  – of the Holy Ghost 983a
templet 22
tempora:
  O –! O mores!
  lament 839
  disreputable 874
  disapprobation 932
  improbity 940
  vice 945
  – mutantur 140
temporal
  transient 111
  laical 997
  lords – and spiritual 875
temporality 997
temporary 111
temporize
  protract 110
  defer 133
  cunning 702
temporizer 943
tempt *entice* 615
  attempt 675
  desire 865
  – fortune 621, 675
  – Providence 863, 885
tempter 615
  Satan 978
  voice of the – 615
temulency 959
ten 98
  – to one 472
  – thousand 98
tenable 664
tenacity
  coherence 46
  toughness 327
  memory 505
  resolution 604
  obstinacy 606
  retention 781
  avarice 819
  courage 861
  – of life 357
  – of purpose 604a
tenaculum 781
tenancy 777
tenant
  present 186
  occupier 188

possessor 779
tenantless
  absence 187
  seclusion 893
tenax propositi 204, 939
tend *conduce* 176
  – animals 370
  aid 707
  serve 631, 746
  – towards 278
tendence 749
tendency 176
tender *slight* 32
  ship 273
  soft 324
  painful 378
  color 428
  war vessel 726
  offer 763
  susceptible 822
  affectionate 897
  compassionate 914
  – age 127
  – conscience 926
  – heart *susceptible* 822
  kind 906
  compassionate 914
  – mercies [ironical]
  badness 649
  severity 739
  cruelty 907
  – passion 897
  – one's resignation 757
  – to 707
tenderfoot 57, 541
tendon 45
tendril *fastening* 45
  offshoot 51
  infant 129
  filament 205
  convoluted 248
  plant 367
tenebrious 421
tenebrosity 421
tenement 189, 780
  – of clay 362
tenet *belief* 484
tenner 800
tennis 840
  – ground 213
tenor *course* 7
  degree 26
  direction 278
  high note 410
  singer 416
  violin 417
  meaning 516
pursue the noise-less – of one's way 881
tense *hard* 323
tensile 325
tension 159, 200
tensure 200
tent *abode* 189
  covering 223
  pitch one's –
  locate 184
  arrive 292
tentacle 781
tentative 463, 675
tente d'abri 223

tented field 722
tenter-hook 214
  on –s 507
tenth 99
tenths
  tithe 812
tent-pegging 840
tents, O Israel, to your – 722
tenue, en grande – 847, 882
tenuity
  smallness 32
  thinness 203
  rarity 322
tenuous
  shadowy 4
tenure
  possession 777
  property 780
  due 924
tepee 189
tepefaction 384
Tephramancy 511
tepid 382
tepidarium 386
ter quaterque beatus 827
teratology
  unconformity 83
  distortion 243
  altiloquence 577
  boasting 884
tercentenary 98, 138, 883
terceron 41
terebration 260
teres atque rotundus 249
  in seipso – 650
tergiversation 283, 607
term *end* 67
  place in series 71
  period of time 106
  limit 233
  word 562
  name 564
  lease 780
termagant 901
terminal 67, 253, 292
terminate 67, 292
  limit 233
termination 154
termine, mezzo – 628
terminology 562
terminus *end* 67
  limit 233
  arrival 292
termless 105
terms [*see* term]
  circumstances 8
  reasoning 476
  pacification 723
  conditions 770
bring to – 723
come to –
  assent 488
  pacify 723
  submit 725
  consent 762
  compact 769
couch in – 566
on friendly – 888
in no measured –

574
ternary 93
ternion 92
Terpsichore 416, 840
terra: – cotta
  baked 384
  sculpture 557
  – firma
  support 215
  land 342
  safety 664
  – incognita 491
terrace *houses* 189
  level 213
terrain 181
terraqueous 318
terre verte 435
tèrrene 318, 342
terrine 191
terrestrial 318
terrible 860
terribly *greatly* 31
terrier *list* 86
  auger 262
  dog 366
terrific 31, 830, 860
terrify 860
territorial *land* 342
  soldier 726
territory 181, 780
terror 860
  King of –s 360
  reign of – 739, 828
terrorem, in – 860, 909
terrorism 860
  insolence 885
terrorist
  coward 862
  blusterer 887
  evil-doer 913
terse 572
tertian *periodic* 138
tertiary *three* 92
tertium quid
  dissimilar 18
  mixture 41
  combination 48
  unconformable 83
tesselated 440, 847
tesserae
  mosaic 440
  counters 550
test 463
testa, voce di – 410
testament 771
Testament 985
tester *bedstead* 215
  sixpence 800
testify 467, 550
testimonial 551
testimony 467
testy 901
tetanus 315
tetchy 901
tête: – baissée 863
  – exaltée 503
  – montée 503, 825
  –à-tête *two* 89
  near 197
  confer 588
tether *fasten* 43
  locate 184
  restrain 751
  means of restraint 752

life hangs by a –
360
worn to a – 659
– one's way 266,
302
threadbare 226, 659
threadpaper 203
threat 909
threaten
future 121
destiny 152
danger 665
threatening
warning 668
unhopeful 859
three 93
– in one and one
in – 976
sisters – 601
go through – hun-
dred and sixty
degrees 311
– sheets in the
wind 959
– times three
number 98
approbation 931
threefold 93
three-score 98
– years and ten
128
three-tailed
bashaw
master 745
nobility 875
threne 938
threnody 839
thresh 972
– out 461
threshold
beginning 66
edge 231
at the – *near* 197
– of an inquiry 461
thrice 93
– happy 827
– told tale 573
thrid 302
thrift
prosperity 734
gain 775
economy 817
thriftless 818
thrill
physical pain 378
touch 380
feeling 821
excitation 824
thrilling
pleasing 829
painful 830
thrive 734
throat *opening* 260
pipe 350, 351
cut the – 361
force down the –
739
stick in one's –
581, 585
take by the – 789
throb 315, 821
throbbing: – heart
860
– pain 378
throe
revolution 146
violence 173

agitation 315
physical pain 378
agony 828
birth– 161
throne *abode* 189
seat 215
emblem of au-
thority 747
ascend the – 737
occupy the – 737
power behind
the – 526
– of God 981
throng 72
throttle
render powerless
158
close 261
kill 361
seize 789
– down 275
through
owing to 154
riâ 278
by means of 631
get – 729
go – one 824
wet – 339
– thick and thin
complete 52
violence 173
perseverance 604a
throughout 50, 52
– the world 180
throw *impel* 276
propel 284
exertion 686
– oneself into the
arms of 664
– away *reject* 610
waste 638
relinquish 782
– back 144
– cold water on
616
– of the dice 156
– doubt upon 485
– down 162, 308
– oneself at the
feet of 725
– good money
after bad 818
– in 228
– off [*see below*]
– open 260, 296
– out [*see below*]
– over *destroy* 162
– overboard
exclude 55
destroy 162
eject 297
abrogate 756
– on paper 590
– away the scab-
bard 722
– into the shade
superior 33
lessen 36
surpass 303
important 642
– a tub to catch a
whale 545
– up [*see below*]
– a veil over 528
throw off 297
– all disguise 529
– one's guard 508

– the mask 529
– the scent
misdirect 538
avoid 623
throw out 284, 297
eject 297
– a feeler 379
– of gear
disjoin 44
derange 61
– a hint 527
– a suggestion 514
throwing stick 727
thrown out 704
throw up *eject* 297
resign 757
– one's cap 884
– the game 624
thrum 416
thrush 416
thrust *push* 276
attack 716
– in *insert* 300
(*interpose*) 228
– one's nose in 682
– out 55
– down one's
throat 744
– upon 784
thud 406, 408a
thug *murderer* 361
thief 792
thumb *touch* 379
bite the – 929
one's fingers all –s
699
rule of –
experiment 463
unreasoning 477
essay 675
twiddle one's –
681
under one's –
authority 737
subjection 749
– over 539
– screw 975
Thumb, Tom – 539
thump
beat 276
thud 406
non-resonance
408a
punish 972
thumping *great* 31
big 192
thunder
violence 173
noise 404
prodigy 872
threaten 909
look black as –
832, 900
– against 908, 932
– of applause 931
– forth 531
– at the top of
one's voice 411
–s of the Vatican
908
thunderbolt
weapon 727
prodigy 872
thunder-clap 508,
872
thundering *great* 31
big 192

thunderstorm 173
thunderstruck 870
thurible 400, 998
thurifer 996
thuriferous 400
thurification
fragrance 400
rite 998
thus *circumstance* 8
therefore 476
– far *little* 32
limit 233
thwack 276, 972
thwart
across 219
harm 649
obstruct 706
oppose 708
cross 830
thwarted 732
tiara *insignia* 747
ornament 847
canonicals 999
Tib's eve 107
tick *graze* 199, 379
oscillation 314
sound 407
mark 550
credit 805
go on – 806
– off *record* 551
ticker 553
ticket 86, 550, 609
ticket of leave 760
– man 754, 949
tickle *touch* 380
please 829
amuse 840
– the fancy 829,
840
– the ivories 416
– the palate 394
– the palm 784,
807
ticklish
uncertain 475
dangerous 665
difficult 704
tidal wave 348, 667
tid-bit 648, 829
tide *ocean* 341
wave 348
abundance 639
prosperity 734
against the – 708
drift with the –
705
go with the – 82
high &c. – 348
stem the – 708
swim with the –
734
turn of the – 210
– of events 151
– over *time* 106
defer 133
safe 664
inaction 681
succeed 731
– of time 109
tidings 532
tidy *orderly* 58
arrange 60
good 648
clean 652
pretty 845
– up 60

tie *relation* 9
equality 27
fasten 43
fastening 45
neckcloth 225
security 771
obligation 926
nuptial – 903
ride and – 266
–s of blood 11
– down
hinder 706
compel 744
restrain 751
– the hands 158,
751
– oneself 768
– up *restrain* 751
condition 770
entail 771
tie-beam 45
tied up
busy 135
in debt 806
tier *continuity* 69
layer 204
tierce 92
– and carte 716
tiff 713, 900
tiffin 298
tiger *violent* 173
servant 746
courage 861
savage 907
evil-doer 913
bad man 949
tight *fast* 43
closed 261
smart 845
drunk 959
– grasp 739
– hand 739
– rope dancing 698
keep a – hand on
751
on one's – ropes
878
tighten 43, 195
tight-fisted 819
tights 225
tightwad 819
tigress 374
tike 876
tilbury 272
tile *roof* 223
hat 225
– loose *insane* 503
till *up to the time*
106
coffer 191
cultivate 371
treasury 802
– doomsday 112
– now 122
– the soil 673
tiller
instrument 633
money-box 802
– of the soil
agriculture 371
clown 876
tilt *slope* 217
cover 223
propel 284
fall 306
contention 720
full – *direct* 278

trousers 225
trousseau 225
trouvaille 775
trouvère 597
trover 775, 964
trow *think* 451
  believe 484
  know 490
trowel 191
troy-weight 319
truant *absent* 187
  runaway 623
  idle 682
  apostate 941
truce *cessation* 142
  deliverance 672
  peace 721
  pacification 723
  flag of – 724
trucidation 361
truck *summit* 210
  vehicle 272
  barter 794
truck driver 268
truck farm 371
truckle to
  submit 725
  servile 886
  flatter 933
truckle-bed 215
truck-load 31
truckman 268
truculent 907
trudge 266, 275
truditur dies die
  109
true *real* 1
  straight 246
  assent 488
  accurate 494
  veracious 543
  faithful 772
  honorable 939
  orthodox 983a
  – bill
    vindicate 937
    accuse 938
    lawsuit 969
  see in its –
    colors 480a
  – meaning 516
  – to nature 17
  – to oneself 604a
  – saying 496
  – to scale 494
true-hearted 543,
  939
true-love 897
true-lover's knot
  897, 902
true-penny 939
truism *axiom* 496
  unmeaning 517
trull 962
truly *very* 31
  assent 488
  really 494
  indeed 535
trump *perfect* 650
  honorable 939
  good man 948
  turn up –s 731
  – card *device* 626
    success 731
  – up *falsehood* 544
    accuse 938
trumped up 468,

545, 546
trumpery 517, 643
trumpet *music* 417
  war cry 722
  boast 884
  flourish of –s
    ostentation 882
    celebration 883
    boasting 884
  ear– 418
  penny –
    skill 410
  sound of –
    alarm 669
  speaking – 418
  – blast 404
  – call 550, 741
  – forth 531
trumpeter
  musician 416
  messenger 534
  boaster 884
trumpet-toned 410
trumpet-tongued
  404, 531
truncate 201, 241
truncated 53
truncheon
  weapon 727
  staff of office 747
  instrument of
    punishment 975
trundle 284, 312
trunk *whole* 50
  origin 153
  paternity 166
  box 191
trunk-hose 225
trunnion
  support 215
  projection 250
truss *tie* 43
  pack, packet 72
  support 215
trust
  belief 484
  combination 709
  property 780
  credit 805
  hope 858
  – to a broken reed
    699
  – to the chapter of
    accidents 621
trustee
  consignee 758
  possessor 779
  treasurer 801
trustful 484
trustless 940
trustworthy
  certain 474
  belief 484
  - *memory* 505
  veracious 543
  honorable 939
truth
  exactness 494
  veracity 543
  probity 939
  arrive at the –
    480a
  in – *certainly* 474
  love of – 543
  of a – 535, 543
  prove the – of 937
  religious – 983a

  speak the – 529,
    543
  in very – 543
Truth, Spirit of –
  976
truthless 544
trutination 319
try *experiment* 463
  adjudge 480
  endeavor 675
  use 677
  lawsuit 969
  – a case 967
  – a cause 480
  – conclusions
    discuss 476
    quarrel 713
    contend 720
  – one's hand 675
  – one's luck 621
  – one 704
  – out 463
  – the patience 830
  – a prisoner 967
  – one's temper 824
  – one's utmost 686
trying 688, 704
tryst 892
trysting-place 74
tsar [*see* czar]
tu quoque 718
  – *argument*
    counter-evidence
    468
    confutation 479
    accuse 938
tub 191
  – thumper 582
  – to a whale 545,
    617
tuba 417
tubam trepidat,
  ante – 860, 862
tubby 202
tube 260
  test – 144
tubercle 250
tuberculous 655
tuberosity 250
tubman 968
tubular 260
tubulated 260
tubule 260
tuck *fold* 258
  dagger 727
  – in *locate* 184
  eat 298
  insert 300
tucker 225
tuft *collection* 72
  rough 256
tufted 256
tuft-hunter 836,
  943
tuft-hunting 886,
  933
tug *ship* 273
  pull 285
  effort 686
  – of war 720, 722
  athletic sport 840
tuition 537
tulip *variegated* 440
  gaudy 882
tumble *derange* 61
  destruction 162
  fall 306

  agitate 315
  fail 732
  rough and – 59
  – down 665
tumbler *athlete* 159
  glass 191
  actor 599
  buffoon 844
tumbrel 272
tumefaction 194
tumid
  expanded 194
  - *style* 577
tumor
  expansion 194
  prominence 250
tumult *disorder* 59
  agitation 315
  revolt 742
  emotion 825
tumultuous 59, 173
tumulus 363
tun *receptacle* 191
  large 192
  drunkard 959
tunable 413
tund 972
tundra 344
tune 402, 415
  in – 413
  out of –
    unmusical 414
    imperfect 651
    deteriorated 659
  put in –
    prepare 673
    concord 714
  to the – of
    quantity 25
    payment 807
    price 812
  – up 416
tuneful *music* 413
  poetry 597
  – nine 416, 597
tuneless 414
tunic 225
tunicle 999
tuning-fork 417
tunnage 192
tunnel *concave* 252
  opening 260
  passage 627
tup 366, 373
turb 225
turbary 267
turbid 426, 653
turbinated 248, 312
turbine 153
turbulence
  violence 173
  agitation 315
  excitation 825
turbulent 59
Turcism 984
tureen 191
turf *lawn* 344
  grass 367
  fuel 388
  gambling 621
  races 720
  race-course 728
  amusement 840
turgid
  expanded 194
  - *style* 577
  redundant 641

  ostentatious 882
Turk
  polygamist 903
  grand – 745
  'bear like the – no
    rival near the
    throne' 878
turkey-trot 840
Turkish bath 386,
  652
turlupinade 842
turmoil
  confusion 59
  violence 173
  agitation 315
turn *state* 7
  crisis 134
  period of time 138
  change 140
  tendency 176
  form 240
  curve 245
  blunt 254
  stroll 266
  deviate 279
  circuition 311
  rotate 312
  aptitude 698
  affections 820
  emotion 821
  dance 840
  nausea 867
  by –s 138, 148
  come in its – 138
  each in its – 148
  meet one at
    every – 641
  take a favorable
    – 658
  give one a –
    aid 707
    excite 824
  do a good – 648,
    906
  ill – 907
  in – 58, 138
  one's luck –s 735
  serve one's – 644
  to a – 494
  take a wrong – 732
  – about 148
  – to account 677,
    775
  – adrift 73, 297
  – aside *change* 140
    deviate 279
    hinder 706
  – one's attention
    from 458
  – away *eject* 297
    not look 442
    avoid 623
    dismiss 756
    relinquish 782
  – back 145, 283
  – one's back upon
    oppose 708
    refuse 764
    disrespect 929
    contempt 930
  – the brain 503
  – of the cards 156
  – color 821
  – a corner
    go round 311
    succeed 731
  – the corner 140,
    658

illogical 477
unconquerable
  strong 159
  persevering 604a
  – will 604
unconquered 719
unconscientious
  940
unconscionable
  excessive 31
  unprincipled 945
unconscious
  ignorant 491
  insensible 823
unconsenting 603,
  764
unconsidered 452
unconsolable 837
unconsolidated 47
unconsonant 24
unconspicuous 447
unconstitutional
  925, 964
unconstrained 748,
  880
unconsumed 40
uncontested 474
uncontradicted 488
uncontrite 951
uncontrollable
  violent 173
  necessity 601
  emotion 825
uncontrolled
  free 748
  excitability 825
uncontroverted 488
unconventional 83,
  614
unconversant 491,
  699
unconverted
  dissenting 489
  irreligious 989
unconvinced 489
uncooked 674
uncopied 20
uncork 750
uncorrupted 939
uncounted 475
uncouple 44
uncourteous 895
uncourtly 851, 895
uncouth
  – *style* 579
  ugly 846
  vulgar 851
uncover
  denude 226
  open 260
  disclose 529
  bow 894
uncreated 2
uncritical 931
uncropped 50
uncrown 756
unction
  emotion 821, 824
  divine functions
    976
  piety 987
  extreme – 998
  lay the flattering
    – to one's soul
    834, 858
unctuous *oily* 355,
  894

flattering 933
hypocritical 988
unctuousness 355
unculled
  unused 678
  relinquished 782
unculpable 946
uncultivated
  vulgar 85
  ignorant 491
  unprepared 674
uncurbed 748
uncurl 246
uncustomary 83
uncut 50
undamaged (648)
undamped 340
undated
  without date 115
  waving 248
undaunted 861
undazzled 498
undebauched 939
undeceive 527, 529
undeceived 490
undecided
  inquiring 461
  uncertain 475
  irresolute 605
  leave – 609a
undecipherable 519
undecked 849
undecomposed 42
undefaced 845
undefended 725
undefiled
  honest 939
  innocent 946
  chaste 960
undefinable
  uncertain 475
  unmeaning 517
  unintelligible 519
undefined
  invisible 447
  uncertain 475
undeformed 845
undemolished 50
undemonstrable
  485
undemonstrated
  475
undemonstrative
  826
undeniable 474, 478
undeplored 898
undepraved 939
undeprived 781
under *less* 34
  below 207
  subject to 749
  range – 76
  – advisement 454
  – age 127
  – agent 758
  – arrest 751
  – breath 405
  – the conditions 8
  – one's control 743
  – cover
    covered 223
    hidden 528
    safe 664
  – the domination
    of 737
  – one's eyes 446
  – foot [see below]

– full strength 651
– the head of 9
– lock and key 664
– the mark 34
– press of 744
– protest 489, 744
– restraint 751
– the rule of 737
– seal 467
– subjection 749
– the sun 1
– way 282
underbid 794
underbreath 405
underbred 851
underclothing 225
undercurrent
  cause 153
  stream 348, 349
  latent 526
  opposing 708
underestimation
  483
underfed 640
underfoot 207
  tread – 739
undergo 151
  – a change 144
  – pain 828
undergraduate 541
underground
  low 207
  deep 208
  latent 526
  hidden 528
underhand 526, 528
  – dealing 528
underhung 250
underived 20
underlessee 779
underlet 787
underlie 207, 526
underline
  mark 550
  emphatic 642
underling
  servant 746
  clown 876
undermine
  weaken 158
  burrow 252
  damage 659
  stratagem 702
  hinder 706
undermost 211
underneath 207
undernourished
  640
underpaid 817
underpin 215
underplot 626
underprop 215
underrate 483
underreckon 483
undersell 796
underset 215
undershot 250
undersign 467
undersized 193
understand
  know 490
  intelligible 518
  latent 526
  be informed 527
  give one to – 572
  – by 516, 522
  – one another

709, 714
understanding
  agreement 23
  intellect 450
  intelligence 498
  come to an – 488
  intelligible 518
  agree 714
  pacification 723
  compact 769
  good – 714, 888
  by a mutual – 526
  with the – 469
understate 489
understood
  meaning 516
  implied 526
  customary 613
understrapper 746
understudy 134
undertake
  endeavor 676
  promise 768
undertaker 363
undertaking 625,
  676
undertone 405
undertow 348
undervalue 483
underwood 367
underwrite
  promise 768
  compact 769
  insurance 771
underwriter 758
undescribed 83
undeserved 925
undeserving of be-
  lief 485
undesigned 621
undesigning 703
undesirable 647,
  830
undesired 830, 866
undesirous 866
undespairing 858
undestroyed
  existing 1
  whole 50
  persisting 141
undetermined
  chance 156
  inquiry 461
  uncertain 475
  unintelligible 519
  irresolute 605
undeveloped 526
undeviating
  uniform 16
  unchanged 150
  straight 246
  direct 278
  persevering 604a
undevout 989
undigested 674
undignified 940
undiminished 31,
  35, 50
undirected 279, 621
undiscernible 447,
  519
undiscerning
  blind 442
  inattentive 458
undisciplined 608
undisclosed 526,
  528

undiscoverable 519
undiscovered 526
undiscriminating
  465a
undisguised
  true 494
  manifest 525
  sincere 543
undismayed 861
undisposed of 678,
  781
undisputed 474
undissembling 543
undissolved
  entire 50
  dense 321
undistinguishable
  465a
undistinguished
  465a
undistorted 246,
  494
undistracted 457
undisturbed
  quiescent 265
  repose 685
  unexcited 826
undivided 50, 52
undo *untie* 44
  reverse 145
  destroy 162
  neutralize 179
  not do 681
undoing *ruin* 735
undone *failure* 732
  adversity 735
  pained 828
  hopeless 859
undoubted 474
undubitably 488
undraped 226
undreaded 861
undreamt of 452
undress *clothes* 225
  nude 226
  simple 849
undressed 226, 674
undried 339
undrilled 674
undrooping 604a
undueness 925
undulate 248, 314
unduly 32
undutiful 945
undying 112, 150
une aile, ne battre
  que d' – 683
unearned 925
unearth *eject* 297
  disinter 363
  inquire 461
  discover 480a
unearthly
  immaterial 317
  Deity 976
  demon 980
  heavenly 981
  pious 987
uneasy 828
uneatable 395
unedifying 538
uneducated 491,
  674
unembarrassed
  705, 852
unembodied 317
unemotional 823

unemployed 678, 681
unencumbered 705, 927a
unendeared 898
unending 112
unendowed 158
 — with reason 450a
unendurable 830
unenjoyed 841
unenlightened 491, 499
unenslaved 748
unenterprising 864
unentertaining 843
unenthralled 748
unentitled 925
unenvied 929, 930
unequal 28, 139
 inequitable 923
 — to 640
unequalled 33
unequipped 674
unequitable 923
unequivocal
 great 31
 sure 474
 clear 518
unerring
 certain 474
 tone 494
 innocent 946
unessayed 678
unessential 643
unestablished 185
uneven diverse 16a
 unequal 28
 irregular 139
 rough 256
uneventful 643
unexact 495
unexaggerated 494
unexamined 460
unexampled 83
unexceptionable
 good 648
 legitimate 924
 innocent 946
unexcitable 826
unexcited 823, 826
unexciting 174
unexecuted 730
unexempt 177
unexercised 674, 678
unexerted 172
unexhausted 159, 639
unexpanded 195, 203
unexpected
 exceptional 83
 inexpectation 508
unexpensive 815
unexplained
 not known 491
 unintelligible 519
 latent 626
unexplored
 neglected 460
 ignorant 491
 unseen 526
unexposed 526
unexpressed 536
unexpressive 517
unextended 317

unextinguished 173, 382
unfaded 428
unfading 112
unfailing 141
unfair false 544
 unjust 923
 dishonorable 940
unfaithful 940
unfaltering 604a
unfamiliar 83
unfashionable 83, 851
unfashioned 241, 674
unfasten 44
unfathomable
 infinite 105
 deep 208
 mysterious 519
unfavorable
 out of season 135
 hindrance 706
 obstructive 708
 — chance 473
unfeared 861
unfeasible 471
unfed 640, 956
unfeeling 376, 823
unfeigned 543
unfelt 823
unfeminine
 manly 373
 vulgar 851
unfertile 169
unfetter 750
unfettered 748
unfinished 53, 730
unfit
 inappropriate 24
 impotence 158
 inexpedient 647
 unskilful 699
 wrong 923
 undue 925
unfitted
 not prepared 674
unfix 44
unfixed 149
unflagging 604a
unflammable 385
unflattering 494, 703
unfledged
 young 127, 129
 unprepared 674
unflinching
 firm 604
 persevering 604a
 brave 861
unfold
 straighten 246
 evolve 313
 interpret 522
 manifest 525
 disclose 529
 — a tale 594
unforbidden 760
unforced 602, 748
unforeseen 508
unforfeited 781
unforgettable 505
unforgiving 919
unforgotten 505
unformed 241, 674
unfortified
 pure 42

powerless 158
unfortunate
 ill-timed 135
 failure 732
 adversity 735
 unhappy 828
 — woman 962
unfounded 546
unfrequent 137
unfrequented 893
unfriended
 powerless 158
 secluded 893
unfriendly
 opposed 708
 hostile 889
 malevolent 907
unfrock 756, 972
unfrozen 382
unfruitful 169
unfulfilled 713, 925
unfurl
 unfold 313
 — a flag 525, 550
unfurnished 640, 674
ungainly 846, 895
ungallant 895
ungarnished 849
ungathered 678
ungenerous 819, 943
ungenial 657
ungenteel 851, 895
ungentle 173, 895
ungentlemanly
 vulgar 851
 rude 895
 dishonorable 940
ungifted 499
unglorified 874
unglue 47
ungodly 989
ungovernable
 violent 173
 disobedient 742
 passionate 825
ungoverned 748
ungraceful
 — language 579
 ugly 846
 vulgar 851
ungracious 895, 907
ungrammatical 568
ungranted 764
ungrateful 917
ungratified 832
ungrounded
 unsubstantial 4
 erroneous 495
ungrudging 816
unguarded
 neglected 460
 spontaneous 612
 unprepared 674
 in an — moment
 unexpectedly 508
unguem, ad — 494, 650
unguent 356
unguibus et rostro 686
unguided
 ignorant 491
 impulsive 612
 unskilled 699
unguilty 946

unhabitable 187
unhabituated 614
unhackneyed 614
unhallowed 988, 989
unhand 750
unhandseled 123
unhandsome 940
unhandy 699
unhappy
 adversity 735
 pain 828
 dejected 837
 make — 830
unharbored 185
unhardened
 tender 914
 innocent 946
 penitent 950
unharmonious 24, 414
unharness 750
unhatched 674
unhazarded 664
unhealthy 655, 657
unheard of
 exceptional 83
 improbable 473
 ignorant 491
 wonderful 870
unheated 383
unheed, -ed 460
unheeding 458
unhesitating
 belief 484
 resolved 604
unhewn 241, 674
unhindered 748
unhinge 61, 158
unhinged
 impotent 158
 insane 503
 failure 732
unhitch 44
unholy 989
unhonored 874
unhook (44)
unhoped 508
unhorsed 732
unhostile 888
unhouse 297
unhoused 185
unhurt 670
unicorn
 monster 83
 carriage 272
unideal existing 1
 no thought 452
 true 494
unification 48, 87
uniform
 homogeneous 16
 simple 42
 orderly 58
 regular 80
 dress 225
 symmetry 242
 livery 550
uniformity 16
unilluminated 421
unimaginable 471, 473
 wonderful 870
unimaginative 576, 843, 868
unimagined 1, 494
unimitated 20

unimpaired 670
unimpassioned 826
unimpeachable
 certain 474
 true 494
 due 924
 approved 931
 innocent 946
unimpeached 931, 946
unimpeded 705, 748
unimportance 643
unimpressed 838
unimpressible 823
unimproved 659
unincreased 36
unincumbered
 easy 705
 exempt 927a
uninduced 616
uninfected 652
uninfectious 656
uninflammable 385
uninfluenced
 obstinate 606
 unactuated 616
 free 768
uninfluential 172, 175a
uninformed 491
uningenuous 544
uninhabit, -able, -ed 187, 893
uninitiated 491, 699
uninjured
 perfect 650
 healthy 654
 preserved 670
uninjurious 656
uninquisitive 456
uninspired 823
uninstructed 491
unintellectual 452, 499
unintelligent 499
unintelligibility 519
unintelligible 519
 — style 571
 render — 538
unintentional
 necessary 601
 undesigned 621
uninterested 456, 841, 843
unintermitting
 unbroken 69
 durable 110
 continuing 143
 persevering 604a
uninterrupted
 continuous 69
 perpetual 112
 unremitting 893
unintroduced 893
uninured 614
uninvented 526
uninvestigated 491
uninvited 893
uninviting 830
union
 agreement 23
 junction 43
 combination 48
 concurrence 178
 workhouse 189
 party 712
 concord 714

marriage 903
unionist 712
union-jack 550
union-pipes 417
unique
  dissimilar 18
  original 20
  exceptional 83
  alone 87
unirritating 174
unison
  agreement 23
  melody 413
  concord 714
unit 51, 87
Unitarian 984
unite *join* 43
  combine 48
  assemble 72
  concur 178
  converge 290
  party 712
  – one's efforts 709
  – in pairs 89
  – with 709
united 46, 714
unity *identity* 14
  uniformity 16
  whole 50
  complete 52
  single **87**
  concord 714
  – of time 120
Unity, Trinity in – 976
universal 78
  – Church 983*a*
  – favourite 899
universality 52
universe 318
university 542
  – education 537
  – extension 537
  go to the – 539
unjust *wrong* 923
  impious 988
unjustifiable
  wrong 923
  inexcusable 938
  wicked 945
unjustified 923
  undue 925
unkempt
  unclean 753
  vulgar 851
unkennel *eject* 297
  disclose 529
unkind 907
  –est cut of all 828
unknightly 940
unknit (44)
unknowable 519
unknowing 491
unknown
  ignorant 491
  latent 526
  – to fame
  inglorious 874
  low-born 876
  – quantities 491
unlabored
  – *style* 578
  unprepared 674
unlace (44)
unlade 297
unladylike
  vulgar 851

rude 895
unlamented
  hated 898
  disapproved 932
unlatch 44, 750
unlawful
  undue 925
  illegal 964
unlearn 506
unlearned 491
unleavened 674
unless
  circumstances 8
  except 83
  qualification 469
unlettered 491
  – Muse 579
unlicensed 761
unlicked
  unprepared 674
  vulgar 851
  clownish 876
  – cub
  youngster 129
  shapeless 241
  unmannerly 895
unlike 18
unlikely 473
unlikeness 15
unlimber 323
unlimited
  great 31
  infinite 105
  free 748
  – *space* 180
unliquefied 321
unlively 837, 843
unload
  displaced 185
  eject 297
  disencumber 705
unlock *unfasten* 44
  discover 480*a*
unlooked for 508
unloose
  unfasten 44
  liberate 750
unloved 898
unlovely 846
unlucky
  inopportune 135
  bad 649
  unfortunate 735
  in pain 830
unmade 2
unmaimed 654
unmake 145
unman
  mutilate 38
  render powerless 158
  madden 837
  frighten 860
unmanly
  effeminate 374
  dishonorable 940
unmanageable
  unwieldy 647
  perverse 704
unmanned
  dejected 837
  cowardly 862
unmannered 895
unmannerly 895
unmarked 460
unmarred 654, 670
unmarried 904

unmask 529
unmatched
  different 15
  dissimilar 18
  unparalleled 20
unmeaningness **517**
unmeant 517
unmeasured
  infinite 105
  undistinguished 465*a*
  abundant 639
unmeditated 612
unmeet 925
unmellowed 674
unmelodious 414
unmelted 321
unmentionable 874
  –s 225
unmentioned 526
unmerciful 914*a*
unmerited 925
unmethodical 59
unmindful
  inattentive 458
  neglectful 460
  ungrateful 917
unmingled 42
unmissed 460
unmistakable
  certain 474
  intelligible 518
  manifest 525
unmitigable 173
unmitigated
  great 31
  complete 52
  violent 173
unmixed 42
unmolested 664, 831
unmoneyed 804
unmoral 823
unmourned 898
unmoved
  quiescent 265
  obstinate 606
  insensible 823
unmusical 424
  – *voice* 581
unmuzzled 748
unnamed 565
unnatural
  exceptional 83
  affected 855
  spiteful 907
unnecessary
  redundant 641
  useless 645
  inexpedient 647
unneeded 645
unneighborly 895
unnerved
  powerless 158
  weak 160
  dejected 837
unnoted } 460
unnoticed }
unnumbered 105
unnurtured 674
uno saltu 113
unobeyed 742
unobjectionable
  good 648
  pretty good 651
  innocent 946
unobnoxious 648

unobscured 420
unobservant 458
unobserved 460
unobstructed 705, 749
unobtainable 471
unobtained 777*a*
unobtrusive 881
unoccupied
  vacant 187
  unthinking 452
  doing nothing 681
  inactive 683
  untenanted 893
unoffended
  enduring 826
  humble 879
unofficial 964
unoften 137
unopened 261
unopposed 709
unorganized 674
  – *matter* 358
unornamental 846
unornamented
  – *style* 576
  simple 849
unorthodox 984
unostentatious 881
unowed 807
unowned 782
unpacific 713, 722
unpacified 713
unpack
  unfasten 44
  take out 297
unpaid *debt* 806
  honorary 815
  the great –
  magistracy 967
  – worker 602
unpalatable 395, 830
unparagoned
  supreme 33
  best 648
  perfect 650
unparalleled
  unimitated 20
  supreme 33
  exceptional 83
unpardonable 938, 945
unparliamentary
  language 895, 908
unpassable 261
unpassionate 826
unpatriotic 911
unpeaceful 720, 722
unpeople
  emigration 297
  banishment 893
unperceived
  neglected 460
  unknown 491
unperformed 730
unperjured 543, 939
unperplexed 498
unpersuadable 606
unpersuaded 616
unperturbed 826
unphilosophical 499
unpierced 261
unpin (44)
unpitied 932

unpitying 914*a*
unplaced 185
unplagued 831
unpleasant 830
unpleasing 830
unpoetical 598, 703
unpolished
  rough 256
  inelegant 579
  unprepared 674
  vulgar 851, 876
  rude 895
unpolite 895
unpolluted
  good 648
  perfect 650
unpopular 830, 867
unpopularity 898
unportioned 804
unpossessed 777*a*
unpractical 699
unprecedented 83, 137
unprejudiced 498, 748
unpremeditated
  impulsive 612
  undesigned 621
  unprepared 674
unprepared 508, 674
unprepossessed 498
unprepossessing 846
unpresentable 851
unpretending 881
unprevented 748
unprincipled 945
unprivileged 925
unprized 483
unproclaimed 526
unproduced 2
unproductive 645
unproductiveness 169
unproficiency 699
unprofitable
  unproductive 169
  useless 645
  inexpedient 647
  bad 649
unprolific 169
unpromising 859
unprompted 612
unpronounceable 519
unpronounced 526
unpropitious
  ill-timed 135
  opposed 708
  hopeless 859
unproportioned 24
unprosperous 735
unprotected 665
unproved 477
unprovided
  scanty 640
  unprepared 674
unprovoked (616)
unpublished 526
unpunctual
  tardy 133
  untimely 135
  irregular 139
unpunished 970
unpurchased 796
unpurified 653

utilize 677
utmost 33
  do one's – 686
  – height 210
  in one's –need 735
  deserted in one's – need 893
Utopia 515, 858
utricle 191
utter extreme 31
  distribute 73
  disclose 529
  publish 531
  speak 580, 582
  money 800
utterly 52
uttermost 31
  to the – parts of the earth 180, 196
uxorious 897

V

va sans dire, cela 474, 525
vacant void 4
  absent 187
  thoughtless 452
  unmeaning 517
  scanty 640
  – hour 685
  – mind folly 499
vacate displace 185
  absent 187
  depart 293
  resign 757
vacation 687
vaccine 366
vache 191
vacillate
  changeable 149
  undulate 314
  waver 605
vacuity 187
vacuous
  unsubstantial 4
  absent 187
vacuum 187
  – cleaner 653
vade mecum 527, 542
vadium 771
væ victis! war 722
  threat 909
vagabond
  wanderer 268
  low person 876
  rogue 949
vagabondage 266
vagary
  absurdity 497
  imagination 515
  whim 608
  antic 840
vagrant
  changeable 149
  roving 266
  traveler 268
  deviating 279
vague
  unsubstantial 4
  uncertain 475

unreasoning 477
unmeaning 517
obscure 519
  - language 571
  – suggestion 514
vail panel 228
  donation 784
  reward 973
vain unreal 2
  unprofitable 645
  unvalued 866
  conceited 880
  in – failure 732
  labor in –
  come short 304
  useless 645
  fail 732
  take a name in – 895
  – attempt 732
  use – efforts 645
  – expectation 509
vainglorious
  haughty 878
  vain 880
  boasting 884
vaivode 745
valance 231
vale 252
  – of years 128
valeat quantum 467
valediction 293, 894
valedictory 293
valentine 902
valet 631, 746
valet
  – de chambre 746
  – de place 524, 527
valetudinarian 655, 656
Valhalla 981
valiant 861
valid confirmed 150
  powerful 157
  strong 159
  true 494
  sufficient 639
  – reasoning 476
valise 191
valley 252
  – of the shadow of death 360
vallum 717
valoir, se faire – 884
valor 861
valorem, ad – 812
valuable 644, 648
value color 423
  measure 466
  estimate 480
  importance 642
  utility 644
  goodness 648
  price 812
  approbation 931
  of priceless – 814
  set a – upon 482
  – received 810
valueless 645
valve stop 263
  conduit 350
  safety – safety 664
  refuge 666
  escape 671
vamp change 140

music 463
  - up improve 658
  restore 660
  prepare 673
vampire 913, 980
vampirism 789, 992
van beginning 66
  front 234
  wagon 272
  in the – 234
  precession 280
van-courier 64
Vandal
  destroyer 165
  vulgar 851
  commonalty 876
  evil-doer 913
vandalism 851
vandyke 257
Vandyke brown 433
vane wind 349
  indication 550
vanguard 234
vanish
  unsubstantial 4
  transient 111
  disappear 449
vanishing 32, 193
vanity useless 645
  conceit 880
  – bag 191
Vanity Fair 852
vanquish 731
vantage ground
  superiority 33
  power 157
  influence 175
  height 206
vapid insipid 391
  - style 575
vaporization 336
vaporous
  imaginary 515
  opaque 426
vapor gas 334
  bubbles 353
  fancy 515
  boast 884
  insolence 885
  – bath 386, 652
vaporer 887
vapors
  dejection 837
variable 149, 605
variance
  difference 15
  disagreement 24
  discord 713
  at – enmity 889
  at – with 489
variant 15
variation
  difference 15
  diverseness 20a
  number 84
  chance 140
  music 415
varied 15
variegated 16a, 440
variegation 440
variety
  difference 15
  class 75
  multiformity 81
  exception 83
  entertainment 599
variform 81

various 15, 102
  - places 182
  – times 119
varlet 949
varnish
  overlay 223
  resin 356a
  sophistry 477
  falsehood 544
  painting 556
  decorate 847
  excuse 937
vary differ 15
  dissimilar 18
  variation 20a
  change 140
  fluctuate 149
vascular cells 191
  holes 260
  pipes 350
vase 191
vassal 746
vassalage 749
vast great 31
  spacious 180
  large 192
  – learning 490
vasty deep 341
vat 191
Vatican 995, 1000
  thunders of the – 908
vaticination 511
vatum, genus irri-tabile – 597
vaudeville 599, 840
vault
  cellar 191
  curve 245
  leap 309
  tomb 363
  store 636
  – of heaven 318
vaulted 245, 252
vaulting 33, 865
vaunt 884
vaurien 949
vavasour
  possessor 779
  nobleman 875
V.C. 733
vection 270
Vedas 986
vedette 668
Vedidad 986
veer
  change 140
  deviate 279
  go back 283
  change intention 607
vegetability 365
vegetable 367
  – kingdom 367
  – life 386
  – oil 356
  – physiology 369
vegetarian 298, 953
vegetate 365
  exist 1
  grow 194
  stagnate 265
  inactive 681, 683
  insensible 823
vegetation 365
vehemence
  violence 173

feeling 821
  emotion 825
vehement
  - language 574
vehicle
  carriage 272
  instrument 631
veil covering 225
  shade 424
  concealment 526, 527
  conceal 528
  ambush 530
  behind the – 360
  draw aside the – 529
  take the – 893, 995
veiled
  uncertain 475
  invisible 447
  concealed 528
vein temper 5
  tendency 176
  thin 203
  thread 205
  channel 350
  humor 602
  mine 636
  affections 820
  in the – 602
  not in the – 603
veined 440
veld 344
velis et remis 274
velitation 720
velleity 600
vellicate 315
vellicating 392
vellum 590
veloce music 415
velocipede 272
velocity 264, 274
  angular – 244
veluti in speculum 17
velvet 255, 256
  pleasure 377
  on – easy 705
venal price 812
  stingy 819
  dishonest 940
  selfish 943
venation 622
vend 796
vendee 795
vender 796
vendetta 919
vendible 796
venditation 884
vendor 796
veneer 204, 223
venenation 659
venerable old 124
  aged 128
  sage 500
  respected 928
veneration
  respect 928
  piety 987
venereal disease 655
venery killing 361
  hunting 622
  impurity 961
venesection
  ejection 297

remedy 662
Venetian blinds 351
vengeance 919
  cry to heaven for - 923
  with a - 31, 173
vengeful 919
veni vidi vici 731
venial 937
veniam petimusque damusque vicissim 918
venienti occurrere morbo 673
venison 394
venom 663, 907
venomous *bad* 649
  poisonous 657
  rude 895
  maleficent 907
vent *opening* 260
  egress 295
  air-pipe 351
  disclose 529
  escape 671
  sale 796
  find - *egress* 295
  passage 302
  publish 531
  escape 671
  give - to 297, 529
  - one's rage 900
  - one's spleen 900
venter 191
ventiduct 351
ventilate
  begin 66
  air 338
  wind 349
  discuss 595
  - a question 461, 476
ventilator 349, 351
ventosity 349
vent-peg
  stopper 263
  safety 666
  escape 671
ventre
  - à terre 274
  danse du - 840
ventricle 191
ventriloquism 580
venture
  chance 621
  danger 665
  try 675
  courage 861
  I'll - to say 535
venturesome
  undertaking 677
  brave 861
  rash 863
venue 74, 183
Venus *woman* 374
  planet 423
  beauty 845
  love 897
  goddess 919
veracity 543
verandah 191
verbal 562
  - intercourse 582, 588
  - quibble 497, 842
verbatim

imitation 19
  exact 494
  words 562
verbiage
  unmeaning 517
  words 562
  diffuse 573
verbis:
  totidem - 494
  - ad verbera 720
verborum, copia -
  diffuse 573
  eloquence 582
  loquacious 584
verbosity
  words 562
  diffuse 573
  loquacity 584
verboten 761
verbum sapienti 527
verdant 367, 435
verd-antique 435
verdict
  opinion 480
  lawsuit 969
  snatch a - 545, 702
verdigris 435
verditer 435
verdure 367, 435
verecundiam, argumentum ad - 874, 939
verecundity 879, 881
veredical 543
Verein 712
verge
  tendency 176
  near 197
  edge 231
  limit 233
  direction 278
verger 996
veriest 31
verification 463, 771
verify 463
  evidence 467
  demonstrate 478
  find out 480a
verily *truly* 494
verisimilitude 472
veritable 494
veritas, nuda - 494
vérité, palais de - 703
verity 494
verjuice 397
vermicular
  convoluted 248
  worm 366
vermiform 248
vermilion 434
vermin
  animal 366
  unclean 653
  base 876
vernacular
  native 188
  internal 221
  language 560
  habitual 613
vernal 123, 125
vernier
  minuteness 193

- scale 466
vero, vitam impendere - 535, 939
verrons, nous - 507
versatile 149
verse *division* 51
  poetry 597
versed in 490
versicolor 440
versify 597
version *change* 140
  special 79
  interpretation 522
versus 278, 708
vert 435
vertebral 222
vertebrate 366
vertex 210
verticality **212**
verticity 312
vertigo
  rotation 312
  delirium 503
verve
  imagination 515
  vigorous language 574
  energy 682
  feeling 821
very 31
  - best 648
  - image 554
  - many 102
  - minute 113
  - much 31
  - picture 17
  - small 32
  - thing
  - identity 13
  - agreement 23
  - exact 494
  - true 488
  - well 831
Véry light 423
vesicle *cell* 191
  covering 223
  globe 249
vesicular 191, 260
vespers 126, 990
vespertine 126
vessel
  receptacle 191
  tube 260
  ship 273
vest *place* 184
  dress 225
  - in *belong to* 777
  give 784
Vesta 979
vesta *match* 388
vestal 960
vested *fixed* 150
  legal 963
  - in *located* 184
  - interest
  given 780
  due 924
vestibule 66, 191
vestige 551
vestigia:
  veteris - flammæ 505, 613
  - nulla retrorsum 282, 604a
vestment 225, 999
vestry *council* 696
  churchdom 995

church 1000
vesture 225
vesuvian
  match 388
veteran *old* **130**
  adept 700
  warrior 726
veterinary art 370
veteris vestigia flammae 505, 613
veto 761
vetturino 694
vex 830, 898
vexata quaestio 704, 713
vexation 828, 830
  - of spirit 828
  discontent 832
  resentment 900
vexatious 830
vexed question 704, 713
vi et armis
  violence 173
  exertion 686
  compulsion 744
viâ 278, 627
viable 359
via lactea 318
viaduct 627
vial 191
vials:
  - of hate 898
  - of wrath 900
viands 298
viaticum
  provision 637
  rite 998
vibrate 314
  - between two extremes 149
vibrato 415
vibratory 149
vibroscope 314
vicar *deputy* 759
  clergyman 996
  - of Bray 607, 886
vicarage 1000
vicariate 995
vicarious 147
vicarship 995
vice *deputy* 759
  holder 781
  wickedness **945**
vice versâ
  reciprocal 12
  contrary 14
  interchange 148
vice-admiral 745
Vice-Chancellor 967
  -'s Court 966
vicegerency 755
vicegerent 758, 759
vice-president 694
vice-regal 759
viceroy
  governor 745
  deputy 759
vicesimal 98
vicinage 197
vicinism 145
vicinity 197, 227
vicious 173, 945
  render - 659
  - reasoning 477

vicissitude 149
Vickers gun 727
victim *dupe* 547
  defeated 732
  sufferer 828
victimize *kill* 361
  deceive 545
  injure 649
  baffle 731
victis, væ - 722, 909
victor 731
victoria
  carriage 272
Victoria Cross 733
victory 731
victual *provide* 637
victuals 298
videlicet 79, 522
viduage 905
viduity 905
vie *good* 648
  - with 720
vielle 417
view
  sight 441
  appearance 448
  attend to 457
  opinion 484
  landscape painting 556
  intention 620
  bring into - 525
  come into - 446
  commanding - 441
  in - *visible* 446
  intended 420
  expected 507
  keep in - 457
  on - 448
  present to the - 448
  with a - to 620
  - as 484
  - in a new light 658
viewer 444
viewless 447
view-point 441
vigesimal 98
vigil *care* 459
vigilance *care* 459
  wisdom 498
  activity 682
  caution 864
vigils *worship* 990
vignette 558, 594, 847
vigor *strength* 159
  energy 171
  style **574**
  resolution 604
  health 654
  activity 682
viking 792
vile *valueless* 643
  bad 649
  painful 830
  disgraceful 874
  plebeian 876
  dishonorable 940
  vicious 945
vilify *shame* 874
  malediction 908
  censure 932
  detract 934
vilipend
  disrespect 929

cuique – 865
voluptuary 954a,
  962
voluptuous
  pleasure 377
  delightful 829
  intemperate 954
  impure 961
volutation 312
volute 248
vomit 297
vomitory 260, 295
voodoo 992, 994
voracious *desire* 865
  glutton 957
vortex *rotation* 312
  agitation 315
  river 348
  danger 667
vorticist 556
votary
  auxiliary 711
  devotee 865
vote 535, 609
  – for 488
voting machine 553
votis, hoc erat in –
  865
votive 768
  – *offering* 990
vouch *assert* 535
  – for 467
voucher
  evidence 467
  indication 550
  security 771
  payment 807
vouchsafe
  permit 760
  consent 762
  ask 765
  condescend 879
vow *affirmation* 535
  promise 768
  worship 990
  – take –s 995
vowel 561
vox:
  – *faucibus hæsit*
  voiceless 581
  fear 860
  wonder 870
  – *populi*
  assent 488
  publication 531
  choice 609
  – *et praeterea nihil*
  unsubstantial 4
  powerless 158
  unmeaning 517
  vain 880
  boasting 884
voyage 267
voyager 268
vraisemblance 472
vue d'oeil, à – 132,
  446
Vulcan 690, 979
vulgar *inelegant* 579
  low born 876
  – *tongue* 560
vulgarian 851
vulgarity
  want of refinement
  851
Vulgate 985
vulgus, ignobile –

876
vulnerable 665
vulnerary 662
vulnus:
  æternum servans
  sub pectore –
  919
  immedicabile –
  619
vulpine 702
vulture 739, 913

W

wabble *slow* 275
  oscillate 314
wad 263
wadding *lining* 224
  stopper 263
  soft 324
waddle 275
wade 267
  – *in blood* 361
  – *through*
  learn 539
  exertion 686
waddle 314
wafer *cement* 45
  thin 203
  lamina 204
waft *transfer* 270
  blow 349
wafted, be – 267
wag *oscillate* 314
  agitate 315
  joker 844
  – *on journey* 266
  progression 282
wage *war* 722
wager 621
  – *of battle* 722
  – *of law* 467
wages 973
waggery *wit* 842
waggish 836, 853
waggle 314, 315
wagon 272
wagoner 268
wagonette 272
wagon-load 31
waif 618, 782
waifs and estrays
  73, 268
wail 412, 839
wain 272
wainscot 211, 224
waist 203
waistcoat 225
  put in a strait –
  751
wait 133, 681
  lie in – for 530
  – for 507
  – *impatiently* 133
  – *on accompany* 88
  aid 707
  – *to see how the*
  wind blows 607
  – *upon serve* 746
  call on 894
waiter *servant* 746
  – *on Providence*
  neglect 460
  inactive 683
  content 831

waiting 507
  be kept – 133
waiting-maid 746
waitress 746
waits 416
waive *defer* 133
  not choose 609a
  not use 678
waiwode 745
wake *sequel* 65
  rear 235
  funeral 363
  trace 551
  excite 824
  amusement 840
  in the – *of* 281
  enough to – *the*
  dead 404
  – *the thoughts*
  457
  – *up* 824
wakeful
  careful 459
  active 682
Walhalla 981
walk *region* 181
  lane 189
  move 266
  business 625
  way 627
  conduct 692
  arena 728
  – *one's chalks*
  293, 623
  – *the earth* 359
  – *of life* 625
  –*ed off one's legs*
  688
  – *off with* 791
  – *over the course*
  705, 731
  – *in the shoes of*
  19
walker 268
walking gentleman
  599
wall *vertical* 212
  parietes 224
  inclosure 232
  refuge 666
  obstacle 706
  defence 717
  prison 752
  driven to the –
  704
  go to the –
  destruction 162
  die 360
  fail 732
  pushed to the –
  601
  take the – 873,
  878
  wooden –s 726
  –*eyed* 442
  – *in* 229, 751
wallah 746
wallet 191
wallop 315
wallow *low* 207
  plunge 310
  rotate 312
  – *in* 377, 641
  – *in the mire* 653
  – *in riches* 803
  – *in voluptuous-*
  ness 954

wallsend 388
Wall-street 799
  – *slang* 563
waltz 415, 840
wamble
  vacillate 149
  oscillate 314
  dislike 867
wampum 800
wan 429, 837
wand *scepter* 747
  magic 993
  wave a – 992
wander *move* 264
  journey 266
  deviate 279
  delirium 503
  the attention –s
  458
wanderer 268
wandering
  exceptional 83
  – *Jew* 268
wane
  decrease 36
  age 128
  contract 195
  decay 659
  one's star on the –
  735
  wax and – 140
wangle 943
want
  inferiority 34
  shortcoming 304
  requirement 630
  insufficiency 640
  poverty 804
  desire 865
wanted 187
wanting
  incomplete 53
  absent 187
  imbecile 499
  found –
  imperfect 651
  disapproval 932
  guilt 947
wantless 639
wanton
  unconformable 83
  capricious 608
  unrestrained 748
  amusement 840
  rash 863
  impure 961
wapentake 181
war 722
  at – 24, 720
  at – *with* 708, 722
  declare – 713
  man of – 727
  seat of – 728
  – *correspondent*
  534, 593
  – *of words* 588,
  720
warble 416
war-cry *alarm* 669
  defiance 715
  war 722
ward *part* 51
  parish 181
  safety 664
  asylum 666
  dependent 746
  restraint 751

watch *and* – 459,
  753
  – *off* 706, 717
war-dance 715
warden
  guardian 664
  master 745
  deputy 759
warder
  perforator 262
  porter 263
  guardian 664
  keeper 753
wardmote 966
wardrobe 191, 225
ward-room 191
war-drum 417
wardship 664
ware
  warning 668
  merchandise 798
warehouse 636, 799
warfare **722**
  discord 713
war-horse 726
warlike 722
warlock 994
warm
  violent 173
  hot 382
  make hot 384
  red 434
  orange 439
  wealthy 803
  ardent 821
  excited 824
  angry 900
  irascible 901
  flog 972
  – *bath* 386
  – *the blood* 824
  – *the cockles of*
  the heart 829
  – *imagination* 515
  – *man* 803
  – *reception*
  repel 717
  welcome 892
  – *up* 658, 660
  – *work* 686
warm-hearted
  feeling 821
  sensibility 822
  friendship 888
  benevolence 906
warming 384
warming-pan
  locum tenens 147
  heater 386
  preparation 673
warmth
  vigorous language
  574
warn *dissuade* 616
  caution 668
  – *off* 761
warning *omen* 512
  dissuasion 616
  caution **668**
  give – *dismiss* 678
  relinquish 782
  – *voice alarm* 666
warp *change* 140
  tend 176
  contract 195
  distort 243
  navigate 267

deviate 279
prejudice 481
deteriorate 659
– and weft 329
war-paint 673
war-path 72
on the – 716
warped 651
warped notion 495
warrant
evidence 467
protest 535
order 741
permit 760
promise 768
security 771
money order 800
justify 937
death – die 360
kill 361
condemn 971
I'll – you 535
– officer 745
warranted 924
warranty
permission 760
promise 768
security 771
sanction 924
warren 168
free – 815
warrior 726
warship 726
wart 250
wary 864
wash *cover* 223
water 337
marsh 345
color 428
paint 556
cleanse 652
– down 298
– one's hands of
relinquish 624
depute 757
refuse 764
part with 782
dereliction 927
– out
discolor 429
obliterate 552
deteriorate 659
– up 659
washer 247
washerwoman 652
washhouse 386, 652
washy *weak* 160
unmeaning 517
feeble style 575
wasp *narrow* 203
bring a –'s nest
about one's
ears 735
waspish 173, 901
wassail
beverage 298
feast 840
drunkenness 954
wastage 40a
waste *decrease* 36
decrement 40a
destroy 162
unproductive 169
space 180
contract 195
plain 344
consumption **638**

useless 645
spoiled 659
misuse 679
loss 776
prodigality 818
run to – 641, 659
watery – 341
– away 655
– time 683
wasted 160, 659
wasteful 818
waste-paper 158,
645
– basket 191, 645
– bonds 808
waste-pipe 350
waster 460
waste-thrift 818
wasting, wide – 649
wastrel 268, 893
Wat Tyler 742
watch *clock* 114
observe 441
attend to 457
take care of 459
expect 507
guardian 664
warning 668
keeper 753
death – *death* 360
warning 668
on the – 459, 507
– for 507
– out for 668
– over 664
– and pray 673
– and ward 459,
753
watch-dog 664, 753
watchet 438
watch-fire 550
watchful 459
watch-glass 191
watch-house 752
in the – 938
watchman -
guardian 664
sentinel 668
keeper 753
watch-tower
view 441
signal 550
warning 668
watchword
sign 550
military 722
water **337**
transparent 425
keep one's head
above – 664
back – 283
cast one's bread
upon the –s 638
throw cold – on
174
depth of – 208
of the first – 648
great –s 341
hold – 478, 494
land covered with
– 343
pour forth like –
818
make one's
mouth – 507
running – 348
walk the –s 267

pour – into a sieve
638
– bearer, carrier
348
water-color 556
watercourse 350
water-cure 662
water-dog 361
water-drinker 958
watered
variegated 440
waterfall 348
water-glass 556
water-gruel 160
watering
– cart 348
– place 189
– pot 348
waterless 340
water-logged
powerless 158
danger 665
hindrance 706
waterman 269
water-pipe 350
water-polo 840
waterproof
dress 225
dry 340
protection 664
waters
– of bitterness 830
– of oblivion 506
watershed 210
water-spaniel 366
waterspout 348
water-tight 261, 340
waterworks 350
watery *wet* 337
moist 339
– eyes 839
– grave 360
wattle 219
wave *sinuous* 248
oscillate 314
hair 847
– *of water* 348
[*and see* waive]
brain – 498
– a banner 550
– a wand 992
waver
changeable 149
doubt 485
irresolute 605
waverer 605
waves 341
buffet the –
navigate 267
difficult 704
oppose 708
lash the – 645
plough the – 267
wax *increase* 35
become 144
expand 194
soft 324
lubrication 332
viscid 352
substance 356
close as – 528
– and wane 140
– candle 423
waxwork 554
waxy *unctuous* 355
irate 900
way *degree* 26

space 180
habit 613
road 627
in a bad – 655
by – of 278, 627
by the –
in transitu 270
accidental 621
fall in the – of 186
fight one's – 622,
722
find its – 302
gather – 267
get into the – of
613
go one's – 293
go your – 297
let it have its –
681
it must have its –
601
have one's own –
748
in a – 828, 900
in the – *near* 197
in the – of 706,
708
make – 302
make one's –
journey 266
progression 282
passage 302
prosperity 734
make – for
substitution 147
opening 260
turn aside 279
avoid 623
facilitate 705
courtesy 894
on the – 282
place in one's –
763
put in the – of
470, 537
see one's – 490
show the – 693
under – *move* 264
sail 267
progression 282
depart 293
wing one's – 267
– in 294
long – off 196
have – on 267
– out 295
– of speaking 521
– of thinking 484
not know which –
to turn 475
Way, the – 976
wayfarer 268
wayfaring 266
waylay 545, 702
wayless 261
ways 692
in all manner of –
278
– and means 632,
800
wayward
changeable 149
obstinate 606
capricious 608
sullen 901a
waywode 745
wayworn 266, 688

wayzgoose 840
weak *feeble* 160
water 337
insipid 391
illogical 477
foolish 499
– *style* 575
irresolute 605
trifling 643
lax 738
compassionate
914
vicious 945
– point 477, 651
expose one's –
point 479
– side 499, 945
weaken
decrease 36, 37
enfeeble 160
refute 468
weaker vessel 374
weak-headed 499
weak-hearted 862
weak-kneed 725
weakness 160
– of the flesh 945
weal 618
common – 644
weald 367
wealth 780, **803**
wean 484, 614
– from 616
– one's thoughts
from 506
weanling 129
weapon 727
weaponless 158
wear *decrease* 36
clothes 225
deflect 279
use 677
– away *cease* 142
deteriorate 659
– the breeches 737
– off 142, 614
– on 109
– out 659, 688
– and tear
decrease 36
waste 638
injury 659
exertion 686
weariness 841
wearing 841
– apparel 225
wearisome
laborious 686
fatiguing 688
painful 830
weary *fatigue* 688
painful 828
sad 837
ennuyant 841
– flat, stale, and
unprofitable 843
– waste 344
– Willie 876
weasand 260, 351
weasel asleep,
catch a – 471, 682
weather 338
keep one's – eye
open 864
rough – 173, 349
– the storm
stability 150

– in sheep's cloth-
ing 548, 941
woman 131, **374**
– of the town 962
woman-hater 911
womanhood 131,
374
womanish 160
womanly
 adolescent 131
 feminine 374
womb *cause* 153
 interior 221
– of time 121, 152
wonder
 exception 83
 astonishment **870**
 prodigy 872
do –s 682, 731
for a – 870
nine days' – 643
not – 507
– whether
 uncertain 475
 ignorant 491
 suppose 514
–s of the world 872
wonderfully 31
wonder-working
 870
wondrous 870
wont *habitual* 613
won't do, it – 932
woo 865, 902
wood *trees* 367
 material 635
not out of the –
 665, 704
take to the –s 166
woodcut 558
woodcutter 371
wooded, well- 256
wooden 635
– horse 975
– spoon 493
– walls 717, 726
wood engraving 558
woodlands 367
wood-note 412
wood pavement 255
woody 367
wooer 897
woof
 warp and – 329
wool *flocculent* 256
 warm 238
 much cry and
 little – 482
woolgathering 458
woolly 255, 256
woolpack *cloud* 353
woolsack
 pillow 215
 authority 747
 tribunal 966
word *maxim* 496
 intelligence 532
 assertion 535
 vocable **562**
 phrase 566
 command 741
 promise 768
give the – 741
good as one's –
 veracious 543
 complete 729
 probity 939

in a – 572
keep one's – 939
man of his – 939
not a – to say 585,
 879
pass– 550
put in a – 582
take at one's –
 484, 762
upon my – 535
watch– 722
– and a blow
 hasty 684
 contentious 720
 irascible 901
– of command
 indication 550
 military 722
 command 741
– in the ear 527,
 586
– of honor 768
– it 566
– of mouth 582
– to the wise
 intelligible 518
 advice 695
– for word 19, 494
Word *Deity* 976
– of God 985
word-catcher 936
wordiness 573, 584
wording 569
wordless 581
word-play
 equivocal 520
 neology 563
 wit 842
words *quarrel* 713
 bandy – 588
 bitter – 932
 choice of – 569
 command of – 574
 express by – 566
 flow of – 582, 584
 mere – 477, 517
 no – can paint 872
 play of – 842
 put into – 566
 war of – 588, 720
 – that burn 574
 – painting 515
 – with 932
wordy 573
work
 product 154
 operation 170
 pass and repass
 302
 book 593
 business 625
 use 677
 action 680
 exertion 686
 ornament 847
at –
 in operation 170
 business 625
 doing 680
 active 682
 earth– 717
 field– 717
 hard – 686, 704
 piece of –
 importance 642
 discord 713
 stick to – 604a

stitch of – 686
stroke of – 686
– of art 845, 847
– a change 140
– a cure 662
– of fiction 594
– for 707
– hard 686, 704
– ill 732
– in 228
– out *conduct* 692
 complete 729
–room 191
– out one's salva-
tion 990
– against time 684
– up [*see below*]
– upon
 influence 175
 incite 615
 excite 824
– one's way
 progress 282
 ascent 305
 exertion 686
 succeed 731
– well 705, 731
– wonders 682, 731
work up
 prepare 673
 use 677
 excite 824
– into *form* 240
– into a passion
 900
workable 470
work-a-day 625,
 682
worker 690
workhouse 691
working *acting* 170
 active 682
– bee 690
– man 690
– order 673
– towards 176
workman 690
workmanlike 698
workmanship 161,
 680
works
 board of – 696
 good – 906
 – of the mind 451
workshop 691
workwoman 690
world *great* 31
 events 151
 space 180
 universe **318**
 mankind 372
 fashion 852
 all the – over 180
 citizen of the –
 910
 come into the –
 359
 for all the – 615
 give to the – 531
 knowledge of the –
 698
 man of the –
 proficient 700
 fashion 852
 not for the – 489,
 764
 organized – 357

Prince of this –
 978
rise in the – 734
throughout the –
 180
– to come 152
follow to the –'s
 end 743
– forgetting by the
 world forgot 893
as the – goes 613
– of good 618, 648
a – of 102
– and his wife 102
– without end 112
worldling 943, 988
worldly 943, 989
world-wide
 great 31
 universal 78
 space 180
world-wisdom
 skill 698
 caution 864
 selfishness 943
worm *small* 193
 spiral 248
 animal 366
 bane 663
– in 228
– oneself
 ingress 294
 love 897
– out 480a
– that never dies
 982
– one's way 275,
 302
worm-eaten 659
worms, food for –
 362
wormwood
 gall and – 395
worn *weak* 160
 damage 659
 fatigue 688
 well– *used* 677
– out 659, 841
worry
 vexation 828
 tease 830
 harass 907
worse 659, 835
– for wear 160
worship *title* 877
 servility 886
 religious **990**
 demon – 991
 idol – 991
 fire – 991
 his – 967
 place of – 1000
 – Mammon 803
 – the rising sun
 886
worshipful 873
worst *defeat* 731
 do one's – 659, 907
 do your – 715, 909
 have the – of it
 732
 make the – of 482
 worst come to the
 – *certain* 474
 bad 649
 hopeless 859
worsted 205

worth *value* 644
 goodness 648
 possession 777
 price 812
 virtue 944
 penny – 814
 what one is – 780
 – a great deal 803
 – the money 815
 – much 803
 – one's salt 644
 – while 646
worthless
 trifling 643
 useless 645
 profligate 945
worthy
 famous 873
 virtuous 944
 good 948
 – of 924
 – of belief 484
 – of blame 932
 – of notice 642
 – of remark 642
wot 490
would: – *fain* 865
 – that! 865
would-be *pert* 885
 usurping 925
wound *evil* 619
 injure 659
 pain 830
 anger 900
 keep the – green
 919
 – the feelings 830
 – up 704
woven fabrics 219
wowser 988
wrack 162
 go to – and ruin
 perish 162
 fail 732
 bankrupt 804
wraith 980
wrangle
 disagreement 24
 reason 476
 quarrel 713
 contend 720
wrangler
 reasoner 476
 scholar 492
 opponent 710
wrap 223, 225
wrapped in
 attention 457
 – clouds 528
 – self 943
 – thought 458
wrapper 223, 225
 inclosure 232
wraprascal 225
wrath 900
wreak *violent* 173
 harsh 739
 – one's anger 919
 – one's malice on
 907
wreath *woven* 219
 circle 247
 trophy 733
 ornament 847
 honor 877
wreathe *weave* 219
wreathy 248